UNIVERSITY OF MARY WASHINGTON

A CENTENNIAL HISTORY

1908–2008

UNIVERSITY OF MARY WASHINGTON

A CENTENNIAL HISTORY 1908–2008

William B. Crawley Jr.

UNIVERSITY OF MARY WASHINGTON | FREDERICKSBURG, VIRGINIA

University of Mary Washington
1301 College Avenue
Fredericksburg, Virginia 22401

First printing, 2008

Design and production by Chris Crochetière,
BW&A Books, Inc., Durham, North Carolina.

Unless otherwise noted, all photographs are from the
University of Mary Washington collection.

ISBN 978-0-615-21015-5

Library of Congress Control Number: 2008906688

For my students

and all Mary Washington alumni,

especially my favorite one, Terrie

CONTENTS

Preface ix

1. The First Half Century 1

2. The Simpson Era, 1955–1974 71

3. The Woodard Era, 1974–1982 175

4. The Anderson Era, 1983–2006 311

5. The Frawley Era, 2006–2007 787

Epilogue: The Centennial Year, 2007–2008 817

Appendix 1: Recipients of the Honorary Doctor of Humane Letters Degree 835

Appendix 2: Faculty Awards and Honors 836

Appendix 3: Members of the Board of Visitors 840

Notes 843

Index 859

About the Author 911

PREFACE

The spring of 1970 was a troubled time in America. Memories of the recent assassinations of Martin Luther King Jr. and Robert Kennedy, as well as the divisive presidential election that brought Richard Nixon to the White House, were still raw. The increasingly frustrating war in Vietnam was grinding on, evoking ever-more-militant protests, capped in May by the shooting deaths of four Kent State demonstrators by the Ohio National Guard.

Although I was certainly not unmindful of these larger issues, I had my own personal anxiety: wrapping up graduate school, I had no job—and the market for green historians was definitely bearish. Casting about for a teaching position, I applied at virtually every college in Virginia and the surrounding area and received the same response from all: rejection. That included Mary Washington College, whose department chairman, Joseph Vance, thanked me for my inquiry but politely explained that there were no openings at present. (For some reason, I kept the letter.)

But then fortune smiled. A last-minute resignation by one of the American history professors left the Mary Washington department in a bind for the rapidly approaching fall semester. In that predicament, Vance contacted my graduate mentor at the University of Virginia, Dean of the Graduate School Edward Younger (who had also been Vance's mentor), and my fate, happily, was sealed. The proffered job was not especially lucrative—$8,900 a year. But as it represented an increase of $8,900 over what I was then making, I accepted it with alacrity and with gratitude.

To an inexperienced twenty-five-year-old, the chance to teach at a first-rate school like Mary Washington seemed nothing less than providential. My impression of the College had always been particularly favorable. At that time, it was generally regarded as the premier public liberal arts college for women in Virginia—one with an educational philosophy much like that of my own undergraduate school, Hampden-Sydney College. In addition, my personal associations with Mary Washington College, though not extensive, were altogether positive. Several friends, as well as my closest cousin, had recently graduated from there, and they all loved the place. My own occasional forays onto the campus had confirmed their assessment. So, when I arrived to begin teaching in September 1970, I felt most fortunate. And I was.

That began what has been, as of this writing, a span of thirty-seven-plus years on the Mary Washington faculty, none of which I have regretted for a moment (with, to be honest, the exception of grading papers). During that time, I have also had the opportunity to serve in several capacities aside from teaching, one of which has been the position of institutional historian, to which I was appointed by the Board of Visitors in 1988. From that point onward, I have aimed toward the eventual writing of the school's history, sometimes engaged in desultory fashion, sometimes (as in the past several years) with greater intensity. It has been a challenging, but enjoyable, enterprise—one that has heightened my appreciation for, and attachment to, the institution.

The first question I had to resolve when I began the project was the basic one of where to begin. One possibility was simply to pick up the story where Edward Alvey, former dean of the College, left off in his *History of Mary Washington College, 1908–1972*. While that approach would have had the advantage of allowing me to focus exclusively on the more recent period, I felt that there would be some advantage in telling the whole story within the confines of a single book, especially at the time of the institution's centennial celebration. Yet it seemed redundant to rework those earlier years covered so exhaustively, and lovingly, by Alvey.

What I settled on was a compromise: to condense Alvey's lengthy narrative into a single chapter (covering roughly the first half century of the institution) and then concentrate my efforts on the period from the late 1960s to the 2007–8 centennial year. Accordingly, the first chapter of this book is based almost totally on Alvey's work; essentially it *is* his work, except for those instances, acknowledged in the notes, where I have added new material. For readers who desire more detailed information about the early years, Alvey's book remains an invaluable resource.

I trust that Dean Alvey (as I, and virtually everyone at Mary Washington, called him) would approve of this approach. Although his retirement coincided approximately with my arrival, we became friends during subsequent years. From our first meeting, he treated me with unfailing kindness—but then he treated everyone that way. It is a shame that the term "gentleman and scholar" has become a cliché, for that is precisely what he was.

All those who care about Mary Washington owe a great debt to Alvey for his meticulous history of the institution—I most of all. But his legacy exceeds even that singular achievement. Few persons ever made a greater impact on the character of Mary Washington College than he. As dean for over three decades, he earned respect for his fairness while winning friends with his genial manner. (Professor Emeritus George Van Sant recalled that as a young instructor he once had a conflict with Alvey that resulted in a summons to the dean's office. It was only after Van Sant left that he realized he had just received "the most graceful chewing out" of his life.)

Alvey's administrative skills—a combination of intellect, compassion, and tact—enabled him to play a crucial role in guiding the College through several potentially disruptive transitions, including the movement from a teachers college to a liberal arts college in the 1930s, the affiliation with the University of Virginia in the 1940s, and the racial integration of the student body in the 1960s. Moreover, he was able through both word and deed to inculcate within the very character of the College his own lofty ideals: constant intellectual curiosity, unbending personal integrity, genuine respect for others. He, more than anyone, was responsible for establishing the College's honor system, referring to it as "a way of life"—which, for him, it surely was. In recognition of his extraordinary service, the College bestowed on him during his retirement virtually every honor within the institution's power to grant, awarding him an honorary doctorate of humane letters in 1977, appointing him to the status of dean emeritus in 1984, and naming a residence hall for him in 1991.

Yet his accomplishments also went beyond the bounds of the campus. A man of exceptionally broad interests and talents, his involvement in various civic, social, and church organizations gained him recognition as one of the Fredericksburg area's most prominent and beloved citizens. When Ed Alvey died on July 11, 1999, at the age of ninety-seven, one of his former colleagues remarked, "Dean Alvey *was* Mary Washington College." Those who were privileged to know him can best appreciate the accuracy of that description.

Having decided where to begin my account, my next question was what to cover. I soon came to realize that even a topic as limited (in the larger scheme of things) as a single college nonetheless has many facets that deserve consideration. What I have tried to do is create a narrative that encompasses administrative developments, the academic program, and student activities while taking into account the likely interests of the book's prospective audience.

My suspicion is that most readers will probably be least interested in administrative operations. So am I. Accordingly, I have tried to limit such discussions to those that had significant long-term impact, paying scant attention to bureaucratic operations that, however important to the ongoing functioning of the institution at a given time, do not strike me as sufficiently compelling to include in this narrative.

I have found, somewhat to my surprise, that one of the most difficult parts of the story to convey is the academic program. It is odd that the essence of the institution's being—namely, the intellectual stimulation that takes place daily, hourly, in the classrooms and laboratories—almost defies capture on the printed page (or at least capture by me). I hope nevertheless that my descriptions of the academic departments—their programs and personnel—will revive pleasant memories for students whose minds were opened and whose horizons were expanded by the extraordinary Mary Washington faculty.

With regard to personnel, my guess is that, for most students, memories of their college days are often tied to relationships with individuals—their friends, of course, but also faculty members, coaches, and perhaps staff personnel. To have attempted to include all such persons, however, would have made an already long book even longer and would have, in any case, still been incomplete.

It will probably be evident that my main interest has been the students, and understandably so, given that the great majority of my career has been spent as a teacher. As such, I have come to appreciate and admire my students (most of them, anyway, most of the time). I have thus tried to give due consideration to their activities and, through focusing on their activities, have tried to place the narrative of the institution within a larger context of social and cultural developments beyond the campus. In so doing, I have constantly had to remind myself that the task at hand was a history of Mary Washington, not the entire United States.

A word of explanation concerning sources and documentation is in order. In the absence of secondary sources on the subject covered by this book (save, of course, Ed Alvey's work), I have perforce relied almost exclusively on primary materials. Foremost among them is the *Bullet*, the student newspaper that since the 1920s has provided a chronicle of campus events, usually on a weekly basis during the academic year. Though the paper has varied in quality, as is the nature of college newspapers, depending on the skill of its staff from year to year, it is nevertheless the basic record, for good or ill, of ongoing campus life. Simpson Library has virtually the complete run of the *Bullet* on microfilm. Other student publications of greater or lesser usefulness are the yearbook (*The Battlefield*) and various literary-artistic and political publications such as *Aubade* and *The Polemic*.

Several official institutional publications have also been useful, including the alumni magazine, the *President's Annual Message and Report of Gifts*, academic catalogs, and student handbooks. Other relevant sources include minutes of faculty meetings, institutional accreditation reports, and sundry administrative documents.

Among external sources, the Fredericksburg newspaper, the *Free Lance–Star*, has been the most helpful. An exceptionally fine newspaper overall, it has provided consistent and comprehensive coverage of events at Mary Washington. The *Richmond Times-Dispatch* has also often carried news stories and feature articles concerning major events at the institution.

In addition to these preexisting sources, my research has benefited from several investigations undertaken specifically for the project. These include questionnaires completed by alumni (whose cooperation is deeply appreciated) and taped interviews of alumni conducted over a period of years, mainly by historic preservation students under the direction of Professor Gary Stanton. Most helpful, too, were the numerous taped interviews with notable Mary Washington figures. I am grateful to those persons for allowing their memories to be mined, thus providing much useful information that did not appear in the written record. (All the resources just described are available in the Special Collections of Simpson Library.)

A fundamental question with which I wrestled was how to document such sources in the text. This was a familiar matter to me, as I have spent much of my teaching career instructing students—they would probably say hectoring them—on the necessity of proper techniques of documentation. Thus, when (if) they read this book, they will surely accuse me of hypocrisy, for I have not exactly applied my own lessons.

I hope that they, and others as well, will agree with my reason for taking a minimalist approach to citations: attempting to cite every source in the traditional manner of an academic study would have involved literally thousands of notes. This would have clogged the narrative unconscionably, in my opinion, for most readers—the majority of whom would have found that the practice tended to distract more than illuminate. For that reason, I have not employed citations for every item of information, the main exceptions being where new information has been added in the portion covered in Alvey's history or, in the rest of the book, where the reference provides significant additional information. (Note to my students: do not try this at home.)

One of the most satisfying tasks for any author is to acknowledge the contributions of others. In my case, this is a daunting challenge, as I am indebted to so many people for their help over so long a period.

First, in an overall sense, I appreciate the support through the years from close faculty friends including Otho Campbell, Carter Hudgins, and the late Joe Vance in history, and the late Dick Palmieri in geography. With specific regard to this book, I am grateful to the Mary Washington Board of Visitors for supporting me with leaves of absence to complete the work and especially to General Leonard Chapman, who insisted that such a volume be written. A highly respected former commandant of the Marine Corps, General Chapman provided the initial impetus for the book and followed its progress with great interest until the time of his death in January 2000.

I am also appreciative of the faculty and staff members who were constantly cooperative, responding graciously to my requests for information despite the intrusiveness on their busy schedules. These include, in particular, Executive Assistant to the President Ranny Corbin; Vice President for Planning, Assessment, and Institutional Research Roy Weinstock; and Vice President for University Relations Ron Singleton. I would also like to thank Margaret Mock, Neva Trenis, Teresa Mannix, and Marty Morrison for their help in securing photographs and Jerry Slezak and Tim Newman for graciously providing their technological expertise in reproducing those pictures. Director of Publications and Design Anna Barron Billingsley offered sage counsel, diplomatically delivered, as she shepherded the project through its final stages.

A large part of my research was conducted in Simpson Library, and I am indebted to the entire staff, starting with Roy Strohl, who expedited my use of all requisite library services. Carolyn Parsons gave generously of her time in the archives, cheerfully helping me to find sources that I requested and pointing out others that I might have missed. Donna Hudgins helped enormously by her promotion and direction of microfilming the *Bullet*, thereby making my research immeasurably more convenient and productive.

My secretarial assistance was exceptional, including over the course of the project the incomparable Vicki Campbell, along with Terry Luttrell, Lisa Patton, Pat Berry, and Betsy Chinn. In addition, I could not have asked for more capable or enthusiastic student aides, among them Allison Jennings, Maggie Lancaster, Sarah Miller, Katie Kelley, Melissa Rose, Juan Carlos Lopez, Marissa Allison, Anna Synnestvedt, Allyson Shull, and Elizabeth Weaver. A special debt is owed to Sarah Eckman and Megan McCrum, who so efficiently and with great dedication typed the bulk of the final manuscript. Both of them labored under difficult conditions: if working from written materials, my penmanship was a problem; if working from dictation, my accent was. I thank them for their indulgence and their good nature.

I would also like to acknowledge the research assistance rendered by a cadre of my best students: Lisa Baker, Rachael Deane, Joanna Duggan, Michele Heimiller, Lisa Hohl, Margaret Mazzola, Lauren McCreedy, Elizabeth McDowell, Emily Mushen (who was also an outstanding student aide), Christopher Rogers, Catherine Smith, and Richard Zinky. I should mention in particular the exceptional work of Noah Cincinnati, who has since gone on to pursue what I am confident will be an outstanding career as a historian. If the quality of the contributions of all these students is an indication—and I believe it is—it confirms my long-held conviction that Mary Washington students are indeed special.

Early in the project, the indefatigable Frances Armstrong provided valuable help with archival research, an undertaking that she approached with the skills of a longtime teacher and the devotion of a loyal alumna (class of 1936). Later, the manuscript profited from the perceptive suggestions of a number of readers, including Tracy Sutherland, Michael Hill, and Paulette Watson.

All along the way, my friend Elizabeth "Betty" Merrill was a constant source of sound editorial advice and, just as important, good humor. She also rendered a great service, not only to the writing of this book but to the historical record of the institution, through the numerous interviews—nearly a hundred—that she skillfully conducted. She was so good at it that one might be tempted to say she had missed her calling, except that in her actual calling, that of Latin teacher, she was similarly superb.

Then there was Mary Washington's reference and humanities librarian, Jack Bales, a long-suffering Cubs fan (a term he claims is redundant). He brought to the research the expertise of a world-class bibliographer and to the final manuscript the techniques of a prolific and proficient writer. His keen eye saved me from frequent stylistic errors; his quick wit rescued me from occasional tedium. I doubt that anyone ever had a better editor. I am confident that no one ever had a better friend.

As the book neared publication, it benefited immensely from the editorial and design work of Chris Crochetière of BW&A Books. I am grateful for her expertise, as well as for her patience and unflagging cheerfulness.

Finally, I thank my wife, Terrie, for her many and diverse contributions to this book. From a technical standpoint, she served as an astute proofreader. Though the writing of history is far removed from her profession as a dentist, she nonetheless discovered many an error (no doubt a testimony to her liberal education at Mary Washington) and, reflective of her spirit, made helpful suggestions for enlivening the text. Even more important were her constant support and encouragement throughout the project. The resulting book should thus be viewed, really, as evidence of our shared devotion to the institution we both cherish.

With the combined assistance of so many accomplished people, it would seem that the final product should be flawless. Of course, it will not be, since, after all, the author himself does play some role. For the errors that remain, of either commission or omission, I myself (having no recourse, alas) take responsibility.

One last note. Some years after Joe Vance hired me, he mentioned that Ed Younger had said to him at the outset, "Joe, I think Bill will be at Mary Washington for a long time." Evidently that comment was prescient, as I am now nearing my fourth decade, a span encompassing well over one-third of the institution's history. That lengthy tenure has allowed me to observe, and participate in, many of the events described in this book.

It is hard to believe that when I arrived, driving into town from Charlottesville on Route 3, then devoid of development west of the Sheraton Inn at the I-95 interchange, I was barely older than my students. In the interim, Fredericksburg has certainly changed, and so has Mary Washington in many ways. Surely I have changed, too, having reached the age of my students' parents—in some cases (can it be?) their grandparents.

Throughout this process I have come to realize the truth of the adage concerning the relationship between one's enjoyment of life and the passage of time. The time has flown. I've been having fun.

–1–
THE FIRST HALF CENTURY

THE FOUNDING

Generations of Mary Washington students began and ended their college careers singing praise to the school located "high on Marye's Hilltop" that was, in the words of the alma mater, "born in truth and honor."[1] A more accurate, if less poetic, description would have proclaimed a birth attended by controversy and political intrigue.

Virginia, like most southern states, gave little attention to public education until well after the Civil War; indeed, it was not until the early twentieth century that the commonwealth began to provide opportunities for the academic development of its children. With the growth of public schools naturally came the need to train more teachers for the elementary and secondary levels, a function that was being filled only partially by the State Normal School at Farmville (later Longwood College), which had been founded in 1884.

By the time the General Assembly convened in 1908, there was widespread support for the creation of another normal school. Inasmuch as such a facility was generally deemed both a civic adornment and an economic benefit, the prospect of attracting the new school precipitated spirited jockeying among various localities for the honor. It was, after all, a time in America when, according to one historian of higher education, "Every town wanted whatever was modern—a factory, a railroad, a canal, a daily newspaper, a cotton gin, a telegraph line. Every town also wanted to prove its cultural importance by having schools—the more advanced, the better . . . and colleges were best."[2]

And so, from the outset, Fredericksburg pursued the opportunity aggressively. A prime example of that effort was a petition to the General Assembly from the Fredericksburg City Council titled *The Action of the City of Fredericksburg in Relation to the Location of the Proposed State Female Normal School, with the Inducements and Reasons for Establishing the Same at Fredericksburg*. Several of the listed advantages revealed just how elemental were the concerns of that time, such as the availability of rail and steamboat transportation to the city. In addition, in the words of the pamphlet:

- Fredericksburg is free from the malaria of the lowlands and from the typhoid type of fever of higher latitudes. No city in Virginia has a better health record than Fredericksburg . . . [which] has never had an epidemic in its history.
- The water is equal in purity to any in the world.
- The food supply is equal to, and cheaper than, any other city in the State.

There was also, the document pointed out, another significant consideration: Fredericksburg was "the most historic city in Virginia. . . . Its Revolutionary history is familiar to every schoolboy and girl in this country. Its Civil War history, and that of the country adjacent, was more tragic and still more heroic."

The pamphlet went on, in its seventh and final point, to elaborate on the war's impact on the region—revealing in the process the persistence of wounds both physical and emotional. "Fredericksburg suffered more during the war in actual destruction of property and in the desolation of its homes, and in the tribulation of its people, than all the other cities and towns in the state," it declared, "and yet the General Assembly has never appropriated a dollar of the public money for the establishment of any State institution in her midst." The pamphlet concluded with a lament for the citizens of the region, whose "poverty now forbids them to compete on terms of equality with their richer neighbors for the favors which the State has to confer."[3]

Such arguments must have had some effect because as the time approached for the General Assembly to take action on the matter, Fredericksburg was clearly a front-runner, along with Harrisonburg. From a purely political standpoint, Harrisonburg appeared to have a significant advantage, owing to the clout of its veteran representative in the Senate, G. B. Keezell, who was serving as chair of the influential Senate Appropriations Committee. Such an assessment, however, did not take into sufficient account the ingenuity and tenacity of Fredericksburg's freshman member of the House of Delegates, thirty-two-year-old C. O'Conor Goolrick.

C. O'Conor Goolrick

Reflecting the influence of Keezell and Goolrick respectively, the Senate chose Harrisonburg, and the House chose Fredericksburg. With the session coming to an end, and facing a deadlock that would have doomed establishment of a college in either location, Governor Claude A. Swanson intervened to urge a compromise that would permit funds for a school in each locality to be included as amendments to the session's general appropriations act. Yet when the Senate bill was reported, it contained funds ($50,000) only for the college at Harrisonburg. Goolrick, however, held something of a parliamentary trump, in that, even though the House could not add anything (e.g., the Fredericksburg college) to the bill, it could delete the appropriations for Harrisonburg.

Caught in this dilemma, Goolrick and Keezell met privately and agreed on a compromise whereby both schools would be authorized. Though it seemed a sensible solution, especially since the commonwealth could certainly have used more schools anyway, the new proposal caused the threatened defections of partisans on both sides who claimed that the state could not afford two new colleges. Thus the matter hung in doubt until March 10, 1908, when the House approved the amended bill with the exact number of votes required for passage, touching off what the Fredericksburg newspaper described as "a scene of wild confusion, congratulations, and cheers" in the General Assembly. Having been subsequently approved by the Senate as well, the act simultaneously creating teacher-training institutions at both Harrisonburg and Fredericksburg was signed into law on March 14, 1908.

The role of O'Conor Goolrick in the affair was crucial. According to Edward Alvey, had it not been for the young delegate's "vigorous and influential work . . . the legislative conflict over the establishment of the school might never have been resolved . . . [and] certainly the solution would not have been the location . . . at Fredericksburg." As Goolrick himself wrote almost four decades after the event, "It was a fight that will be long remembered in Virginia legislative history." With good reason was Goolrick dubbed the "Father of Mary Washington College"—a title of which he was especially and justifiably proud.

Notwithstanding its controversial origins, the institution officially known as the Fredericksburg State Normal and Industrial School for Women began to take shape with surprising speed. Within two months of the enabling legislation, Governor Swanson appointed a board of trustees who, in May 1908, unanimously elected Edward Hutson Russell as the school's first president. Born in Petersburg in 1869, Russell was a graduate of Virginia Military Institute (VMI). Although he studied law at Richmond College, his entire career was spent in educa-

Edward Hutson Russell

tion, variously as a teacher, principal, superintendent, and school examiner. The extensiveness of his experience equipped him well for leadership of the fledgling school, designed as it was for the preparation of teachers.

But the task required more than knowledge in the field and executive ability. At a time when the success of the enterprise was by no measure assured, the presidency required a good deal of salesmanship as well—"boosterism," in the argot of the day. Here, too, Russell was well equipped; imposing in stature and commanding of voice, he was exceedingly energetic and utterly committed to promoting the school. In a pamphlet designed for distribution to prospective students (or their parents), Russell proclaimed that "it is not the mission of this school to make money, but to serve the State . . . [and] to educate for character, scholarship, and independence. . . . The faculty is composed of strong, skilled experts in their various departments. They are men and women of scholarship and Christian influence. . . . The grounds cover sixty acres of beautiful rolling land with delightful groves and valleys, [whose] scenery is perfectly beautiful and inspiring."[4]

There was no doubt that Russell was a promoter. Indeed, according to Alvey, his enthusiasm may even have been excessive, leading him occasionally to make "somewhat extravagant statements about the resources and facilities of the institution, . . . [but] his faith in the new school and his belief in its future were well justified, as the days to come were to prove."

One of the first tasks facing the leaders of the new normal school was, of course, the fundamental matter of selecting its location, an issue that produced sharp debate within the Board of Trustees. One faction advocated the purchase of a tract of land, then known as the Jones dairy farm, along Fall Hill Avenue; the other favored the heights west of the city (actually beyond the city limits in Spotsylvania County) then known as Rowe's Wood, after Captain Maurice B. Rowe, who owned a large parcel of land in that area.

Each faction could make a persuasive case. The proponents of the dairy farm tract emphasized that the site was convenient to the city, that its level terrain would minimize construction costs, and that it would include ample space for expansion. Advocates of the Rowe's Wood site acknowledged the validity of those arguments but asserted that such advantages were outweighed by two particularly attractive features of the location on the westerly bluffs, also known as Marye's Heights.

The first was the natural beauty of the area: a plateau crowned by a magnificent stand of trees, affording a panoramic vista of the city below. The only drawback, in terms of terrain, was that the area was—to a degree unimaginable to students of later years—rather remote from the city itself, unconnected by either streets or sidewalks. Making matters worse, the intervening area was generally swampy and bisected by a canal.

But if there were factors mitigating the aesthetic appeal of the heights, there was no denying its other essential advantage: its historical significance, dating from the earliest English settlement in America. As early as 1608, Captain John Smith, exploring along the Rappahannock River, encountered the Seacobeck Indian village that was located on the promontory. Over two centuries later, the heights were the scene of one of the Civil War's bloodiest battles, as the Confederate forces of General Robert E. Lee repulsed the attack of Union forces storming the heavily fortified hill.

With the champions of the two proposed sites at an impasse, it appeared for a time that construction of the school would be delayed. Just at that point, however, a coalition of prominent community leaders, headed by the redoubtable O'Conor Goolrick, intervened to persuade the board to choose the Marye's Heights location. Accordingly, in August 1909, the 45.4-acre tract was purchased by the school for the price of slightly over $8,500. It was a fortuitous decision—one that over time facilitated the development of the campus into one of the most beautiful in the commonwealth and, indeed, the nation. Moreover, in the words of Edward Alvey, "The historic ground was an appropriate place to erect an institution dedicated to the acquisition and dissemination of knowledge."

Groundbreaking ceremonies for the school's first building took place on December 14, 1909. The honor of throwing the first shovelful of earth went to Fredericksburg mayor H. Lewis Wallace, and the second to the institution's president-elect, Edward H. Russell. But the real "hero of the hour," as the local newspaper put it, was O'Conor Goolrick, and much of the ceremony consisted of encomiums to him for his crucial role in founding the school. Russell, having presented Goolrick with a massive sterling silver loving cup inscribed, "Well done, good and faithful servant," proclaimed that "but for Mr. Goolrick's tact, fearless pluck, and good diplomacy, we would not have the Normal [School] here."

Some eighteen months later, on July 4, 1911, the cornerstone of the first building was laid. The festive affair was very much a community celebration—to the extent that the local newspaper urged that residents contribute a dollar apiece toward defraying the expenses of the event. The rail and steamboat lines serving the city made additional provisions for services and offered special rates to accommodate those attending from afar.

Appropriately for Independence Day, the event began with a parade, nearly a mile long and complete with brass band, that proceeded from the downtown courthouse through the city to the hilltop site. There the large audience was treated to a program consisting of instrumental and choral music, as well as speeches by an assemblage of educational, political, and civic dignitaries, culminating in an address by Virginia governor William Hodges Mann.

Mann's participation was particularly appropriate, not only because of his official position but because the highlight of his pre-gubernatorial career had been his successful sponsorship of legislation to improve secondary education in Virginia. The last governor of the commonwealth to have served in the Civil War, Mann made a distinguished figure with his white beard and mustache. Resplendent in full dress uniform for the occasion, he delivered a passionate and flowery speech that, in both style and substance, recalled the rhetoric of an earlier day. It was his vision, he declared, that the nascent school would soon produce "teachers, who, strong in body, pure in heart, and vigorous in intellect, will go out with abounding youth and enthusiasm to carry abroad the teachings, standards, and ideals of this institution and impress [their students] with the best part of their character and life upon the youth of Virginia; teachers who will go throughout the length and breadth of the State sowing good seed, to blossom into an abundant harvest of beautiful lives, lives which will raise higher still the standard and ideals of this institution." "And so," concluded Edward Alvey, "on the day celebrated as the birthday of our independence, the cornerstone of a new college at Fredericksburg was laid with ceremony, music, oratory, and, most important, a deep sense of dedication."

Dedication was indeed needed to make the school ready in time for its projected opening in September 1911. Not least of the challenges was completion of the requisite physical facilities, the first two of which were an administration and classroom building and a dormitory. The former, known first simply as the Administration Building, was soon named Russell Hall in honor of the school's president (and subsequently renamed Monroe Hall in honor of President James Monroe). It was not fully completed when the session opened, but was serviceable. When finished soon thereafter, it housed not only the administrative offices but also the classrooms, library, and laboratories (such as they were). It also held the physical education facilities that included, in the basement, a small swimming pool and a basketball court—the latter of which remained the school's primary indoor arena for almost sixty years.

The College was rightly proud of the massive brick edifice, whose location dominated the ridge of Marye's Heights. The structure was aesthetically pleasing and, according to an early College catalog, an engineering triumph. "This building," boasted the catalog, "is heated and ventilated by the most perfect heating and ventilating system known." Though surely no deceit was intended, that statement must rank as one of the most misleading in the history of college publications (a genre in which a certain amount of exaggeration is almost expected), because over the decades that followed, the building's mechanized systems were a constant problem. Yet, mechanical difficulties notwithstanding, the institution's first building, with its spacious east and west porticoes adorned with massive Corinthian columns, came to be the architectural symbol of the campus, furnishing the stylistic standard that would be followed by the construction of many more similarly attractive buildings in the years ahead.

The first dormitory was constructed concurrently with, and approximately thirty yards northwest of, the administrative building. Although the dormitory was planned to accommodate two girls per room, the demand for housing soon necessitated placing three in each room, a practice that continued in the future and was tolerable owing to the capacious size of the rooms.

Known originally simply as "the Dormitory," the facility was later named Willard Hall in honor of temperance leader Frances Willard—a reflection of the political predominance of prohibitionists in Virginia at the time (and an irony for later student generations).

In addition to completing the physical facilities, the other pressing task was the procurement of faculty and staff, an endeavor to which President Russell devoted himself with characteristic energy. By the school's scheduled opening date, he had assembled a group of seventeen—five men and twelve women—who would constitute the school's first faculty. It was a cadre distinguished more by its enthusiasm than by its academic preparation: none held a degree beyond the master's level, including President Russell: only two had master's degrees, two had bachelor's degrees, two had engineering degrees, two had M.D. degrees, and the rest had no college degrees at all. Many were called on to teach subjects that were quite removed from their areas of expertise, slim even as that expertise may have been. And yet such was the state of education in that time and place that even such meager credentials could be regarded as not merely sufficient but superior. Indeed, in the opinion of Edward Alvey, the faculty in the aggregate "presented an impressive background of training and experience in comparison to the typical normal school faculty of the period."

Some of those faculty members were attracted by the intellectual challenge of the task, others by the allure of the new school's location. Among the latter was W. N. Hamlet, who was offered the position of head of math and science, as he put it, "at anything but a flattering salary." However, he explained, "Before declining, I decided to come and look over the ground. I came, I saw, and was conquered. For when I looked upon this beautiful hill, I saw in perspective what glorious things might be accomplished."[5]

As building construction and faculty assemblage proceeded apace in the spring and summer of 1911, so too did the effort to attract students. The school's first bulletin, which appeared that June, made clear that the institution's fundamental purpose was to prepare young women to teach in public schools. Beyond that, its professed aim was to provide the kind of education that would "not only make them superior teachers in the schoolroom, but leaders of thought in communities in which they make their homes." Moreover, because "it must be recognized that the greater part of the life of the graduates [will be] spent in the home circle rather than in the schoolroom, . . . the energies of the school will be focused upon the influences that contribute to the development and elevation of home life."

The requirements for admission were far from stringent. The initial bulletin specified only that applicants must be at least "fifteen years old, of good moral character, and must have a thorough knowledge of the subjects taught in the grammar grades of the public schools." That no high school diploma was required bore further testimony to the inadequacy of the state's public school system at the time.

Curricular options included a variety of courses in the industrial arts.

Completion of programs specializing in particular areas could lead (usually in two years) to diplomas in either the manual arts, the household arts, or the rural arts—the last of which comprised courses such as botany, zoology, horticulture, and entomology, as well as more practical subjects such as dairying and "school gardening."

The standard curriculum, one that was basic to normal schools of the era, was known as the Professional Course. Admission to the program was limited to applicants possessing a high school diploma or its equivalent. The two-year program consisted mainly of methods courses in education and, importantly, practice teaching in the local public schools—an undertaking that was facilitated by the fact that the head of the College's Department of Education, Hugh S. Bird, was also the superintendent of schools in Fredericksburg. Completion of the program entitled the graduate to the professional diploma and the normal professional certificate issued by the State Board of School Examiners.

One attractive feature of the new school was its modest cost. To maximize the potential for fulfilling the institution's primary purpose of preparing teachers for the state's public schools, tuition and fees were deliberately kept as low as possible. Indeed, no tuition at all was required from Virginia residents who agreed to teach at least four public school sessions upon graduation; all that was necessary to obtain the exemption was to submit a form approved by the superintendent of the applicant's school division. Tuition for Virginia residents who were not preparing to teach (there were few) or non-Virginia residents (fewer still) was a modest $15 per term. Other fees, including room and board ($67.50 per term), medical fees, gym uniforms, and textbooks were similarly minimal, meaning that the entire cost of one session came to approximately $144 for prospective Virginia teachers, and about $30 more for all others.

Another advantage prominently touted in the first catalog was the mundane, but critical, consideration of the school's accessibility. With the automobile still in its infancy and roads frequently impassable—even the major north–south artery that ran through Fredericksburg—it was fortunate that the College was accessible by both water and rail transportation. Located at the fall line of the Rappahannock River, Fredericksburg was served weekly, according to the catalog, by three "magnificent river boats" to and from Baltimore, as well as by a line from Norfolk. The availability of steamboat travel made the school particularly attractive to the "downriver" residents of communities such as Warsaw and Tappahannock, from which it was to draw a disproportionate number of students, especially during the early years. In addition, the city was served by no fewer than twenty-four north–south passenger trains a day and by daily east–west trains from Orange.

Actually, the more difficult part of the trip often came after the trains arrived in Fredericksburg. Professor Hamlet, an eyewitness to such endeavors, recalled "the old depot, the mud streets, and . . . the city street department of three or four men with scythes and hoes chopping weeds from the pavement or paths" along the way to the school. "With horror," he said, "I recall the perilous journey from Washington Avenue to the Hill when one had to arm oneself with boards to navigate the mud puddles and mosquito swamp holes of Cornell Street."

As for the facilities at the school itself, there had been doubt in some quarters that everything would be ready in time for the scheduled opening date of September 26, 1911. Yet the first day went smoothly, much to the relief of College officials and townsfolk alike. The occasion, according to the front-page story in the local newspaper, was "the most interesting educational scene this section of the State has ever witnessed." Among the noteworthy aspects of the opening, the paper found it "rather remarkable, but nonetheless gratifying that in starting the electric machinery, the boilers, the kitchen ranges, and all the plumbing, there was no accident of any sort."

This was not to say, however, that everything was in spruce condition. Neither Willard nor Monroe Hall was completed, and both were, according to Professor Hamlet, "surrounded by stables, mud, and flies." Only one classroom in Monroe was usable, and even it had "no door except movable boards which each teacher pulled down and replaced at each class period. Almost touching its only finished window was a mule stable and a constantly running concrete mixer ever ready to furnish flies and unutterable groans if one dared to attempt ventilation."

But in the euphoria of the moment, such inconveniences seemed negligible. As the *Free Lance–Star* reported with obvious pride, "The school is filled to its utmost capacity. Every room in the dormitory is taken. Some applicants could not be accommodated." The paper was particularly effusive in its assessment of the entering class, noting that "the student body consists of as bright, attractive, and earnest an aggregation of young women as can be found in the State. . . . They are jubilant over the prospect for a happy and successful session. They are contented and satisfied."

It was indeed a good augury for the future, marked by, in Alvey's words, "a spirit of contagious enthusiasm that made it all seem a great adventure."

THE RUSSELL ERA, 1908–19

The College's first decade, all under the stewardship of President Edward Russell, was characterized by gradual growth in enrollment and improvements to the physical plant, as well as some curricular revisions—though the emphasis clearly remained on teacher education.

A change in institutional governance occurred in 1914 when, by action of the General Assembly, the original board of trustees for the State Normal and Industrial School at Fredericksburg was abolished and the school was placed under the administrative supervision of a central "board of visitors for the State Normal schools for white women of Virginia," a corporation to be known as the Virginia Normal School Board. The same act also changed the names of the Fredericksburg school and the three other state female normal schools (at Harrisonburg, Radford, and Farmville), specifying that each be known thenceforth as the State Normal School at the respective locations of the institutions.

Although the "Industrial" part of the original name was thus deleted, courses in that area continued to be offered for several years. These included classes such as Home Mechanics, which involved instruction in the use of woodworking tools, soldering, and textile printing, as well as Advanced Wood and Cement Work, which taught the construction of "posts, blocks, sidewalks [and] troughs for feeding."

The latter skill may have been a useful adjunct to the agricultural component of the industrial arts curriculum. One area of campus, roughly between the later Chandler and Seacobeck Halls, was set aside for raising vegetables for the school table; another area was designated as a yard "for the scientific study of poultry"; and down the hill behind Willard Hall was a pigpen where leftovers from the dining hall provided nourishment for the swine.

"School gardening," an important element of the curriculum in those days, had both an academic and a utilitarian purpose, as students were expected not only to observe the botanical processes at work in the garden but also to assist in its cultivation. Yet, judging from a photograph in the 1916–17 catalog captioned "Working in the School Garden," it was problematic just how vigorously the students pursued this task. The picture showed about fifty girls, improbably attired, as Ed Alvey described them, "immaculately in long white skirts, high-button shoes, white middy blouses with large black ties, and white sailor hats, all with rakes and hoes, working almost shoulder to shoulder in a mass attack upon what appears to be bare, dry soil."

The industrial arts program, of which agricultural classes were a part, was discontinued in 1918, following the graduation of its last two students that spring. Even so, support for the "school gardening" idea remained, as indicated in the 1919 commencement address by the school president (by that time, A. B. Chandler Jr.), in which he listed as one of his priorities the development of a school farm, both as a laboratory and as a source of food for the students.

Concomitant with the gradual evolution of the curriculum came a slight expansion of the faculty during the Russell years. Perhaps the most significant addition, certainly in terms of length of service, was Roy Selden Cook, who was appointed in 1916 as assistant professor in science and mathematics and served the institution for the next thirty-three years, teaching mainly physics and chemistry.

The physical assets of the school during the period grew more rapidly than its human ones. A second dormitory, named Virginia Hall, was completed in time for the 1915–16 session. Besides more rooms for students, the building provided space for the library and for most administrative offices, including those of the president, dean, and business manager, all of which were moved from Russell (later Monroe) Hall.

About the same time, the president's home was completed. Located on the bluff of Marye's Heights somewhat to the south of Monroe Hall, the handsome white clapboard structure was first known, appropriately, as Ridge Crest. The building was destined to have a varied history. Until the purchase of Framar in 1946, it served intermittently as the president's home. (The second president, Chandler, chose to live in the house on College Avenue that he already owned.) After Framar became the president's official residence, the house was converted into a dormitory that, to make room for the construction of Randolph and Mason Halls in the mid-1950s, was moved slightly down the hill. By then known as Marye Hall, it continued as a student residence and served as the Spanish House for a number of years before eventually being converted to office space.

Among the most important physical improvements was the construction of a plank road, or boardwalk, from Washington Avenue, which then lay on the outskirts of Fredericksburg, through the marshy, often impassable, and virtually uninhabited area leading to campus. For many years this new passage served as the primary route by which students could shop, attend church, and socialize in the city. As President Russell proudly recalled years later, "We started with approximately forty-seven acres of woodlands and fields, no roads or driveways . . . [but] built a long and beautiful boardwalk from Washington Avenue to the Administration Building. We had boardwalks in every direction—enough to make Atlantic City green with envy."

The students' social life during the early years was limited by the lack of convenient transportation. Though trains and steamboats could provide a way to travel between home and school at the start and close of sessions and for holidays, the absence of automobiles (and reliable roads on which to drive them) meant that most social life ordinarily had to take place on or very near the campus.

Social behavior was also greatly influenced, of course, by the mores of the times, resulting in a campus lifestyle that later generations of students would have found restrictive beyond comprehension. Mandatory chapel services, for example, were held three times each week, where devotions were led by faculty members, local ministers, or Sunday inspirational speakers.

Religious influences were indeed strong. As one early promotional pamphlet for the school pointed out, "Fredericksburg is a progressive city of culture, refinement, and Christian influences. The Methodists, Catholics, Baptists, Presbyterians, and Episcopalians have flourishing churches, and the Disciples are organizing a church under the most favorable conditions. . . . Students are encouraged to respect the wishes of their parents in the matter of church attendance."[6]

In one of the earliest handbooks, a section called "Bits of Advice" provided insight into the social mind-set of the campus. Among the homilies were "Cultivate the habit of gentleness," "Make it a rule of your life to think kindly of others, no matter what they may think of you," and "Cheerfulness is contagious." Several admonitions revealed the religious orientation of the time and place. "Go to church as often as you can," read one. "It's a privilege after six days of studying." Another urged, "Don't forget your Bible; you will need it every day."[7]

The student handbook also addressed matters of student attire, noting in the 1918–19 edition that "there is no necessity for, and this school distinctly discourages, the wearing of either costly or gaudy clothing. Neat, simple, inexpensive dresses fully meet all requirements. Especially to be avoided is the appearance by students in public wearing extreme styles in dress. Simplicity and modesty should characterize the dress of all students." Seniors, furthermore, were "strongly advised" to have a commencement dress that was "simple in design, made of cotton material, such as organdy, batiste, etc., and whose material costs not exceed $10.00 in any case."

General discipline was based mainly on an appeal to the students' better instincts. "When young women come to us," explained President Russell in an early publication, "they are old enough to know what is right, and they usually do it. . . . Our theory of discipline is to give our students our confidence and have few rules, except that broad one to do their duty in accord with their conscientious conception of right."[8] Or as the school's 1911–12 bulletin put it, there were "few iron-clad rules," but instead "every student is expected to exhibit the demeanor of a gentlewoman and to show considerate regard for others. Such a disposition should be the desire and life habit of a well-poised and refined woman."

However, should any student interpret such genteel jargon as an invitation to license (a most unlikely scenario to be sure), the bulletin made it clear that there would be serious consequences, warning that "the management will not hesitate, in deserved cases, to administer admonition and reproof. Should the conduct of any of the students justify it or the general good of the school require it . . . students will be dismissed."

Though the catalog noted that "the Honor System will be maintained as fully as is practicable," the administering of disciplinary decisions actually fell to the president. It was not until a number of years later that a formal honor system was established, empowering students themselves to make such determinations relating to infractions of lying, stealing, and cheating.

The day-to-day supervision of student behavior was the responsibility of the Home Department and, in particular, the "head of the home"—the precursor to the position later known as dean of women and, even later, dean of students. The first to hold that job, Marion C. Forbes, was described as "a cultured Christian woman of long experience with such duties." It was she who, in Alvey's words, "made the dormitory a warm and friendly place in which to live, watched over the girls when they were sick, supervised their comings and goings, and listened to their problems." The result, President Russell observed, was a "happy spirit that prevails with all the Fredericksburg Normal girls."[9]

On the other hand, the head of the home also enforced dormitory regulations, which were numerous and rigid. The daily schedule was governed by the sounding of the bell—from the early summons to rise, through calls to meals and classes, to nightly study and quiet hours and, finally, lights-out. Repeated violations of dormitory rules, such as failure to retire at the appointed time, could lead to "campusing," whereby students were not only restricted to the College grounds but were forbidden to receive visitors.

Even under ordinary circumstances, visitation was strictly regulated and closely monitored. Only males whose names were on an approved calling list—an honor dependent on receipt of a written voucher—were permitted to visit students, and then only within the parlors or on the campus walkways. Men who transgressed were put on a "black list" prohibiting them from calling on students.

Though later generations of students fought strenuously, and successfully, against the concept of in loco parentis, students in the early years probably did not find the regulations so oppressive, as they were likely no more restrictive (and quite possibly less so) than the rules they had known at home. Parents expected the College to enforce decorous behavior, a situation that the daughters—while no doubt preferring (in the immutable fashion of all young people) greater laxity—apparently accepted with little or no overt complaint.

Within the constraints imposed by the school, and despite the relatively primitive state of technology, students in the early years nonetheless found numerous ways of disporting themselves. The school's first party was held on Saturday, October 7, 1911, hosted by President and Mrs. Russell and members of the faculty. After the "grand march" led by the Russells, the evening's entertainment included piano and vocal selections, as well as a Virginia reel danced by twenty girls in colonial costume. By account of the local newspaper, the students adjudged the event a great success, noting that "the girls were all heard declaring as they left the hall that it was the 'best' party."

Aside from the occasional celebrations of that sort, student diversions on a daily basis were usually mundane. As Ed Alvey put it:

> In a less complex era, the simpler pleasures provided welcome respite from the routine of class attendance and study. A walk in the woods, game of tennis, birthday party for a roommate, box of food from home, Sunday night chafing-dish party, church social—these pleasures brought relaxation, fostered friendships, and made the long months between holiday visits at home pass more quickly and more enjoyably. And they built up a store of memories of college days that, for alumnae of the period, [remained] vivid and heart-warming after the passage of many years.

From the outset, clubs and other campus organizations provided opportunities for extracurricular activities. Chief among them was the local chapter of the Young Women's Christian Association. Organized within a month of the school's opening, the "Y" quickly became (and for years remained) a strong influence on campus, not only by ministering to the spiritual concerns of students but by sponsoring various activities such as receptions, birthday parties, and an annual Christmas bazaar.

Some organizations had a more or less educational aspect, such as the glee club, the drama club, and the several literary societies. Others were regional clubs designed to bring together students from certain areas of the state—the Richmond Club, the Caroline Club, the Hanover Club, and (by far the largest) the Down the River Club for Northern Neck residents. Then there were the dozens of clubs that had no discernible purpose—among them the Mother Goose Club, the Red Head Club, and the Happy Dozen Club—other than providing camaraderie among like-minded souls.

There were also at least two local sororities in the early years, Pi Sigma and Phi, neither of which lasted past 1915. Another organization, Sphinx, while lacking the Greek-letter designation, seems to have been something of a secret society, but it too was short-lived.

All such groups were loosely structured, homegrown entities lacking any pretense at national affiliation or status. Indeed, as Alvey aptly observed, most "were simply groups of congenial souls who got together from time to time, elected members, and posed for a page in the annual." (The annual itself, known throughout its history as *The Battlefield*, began in 1913 as yet another outlet for student extracurricular interests.)

Of all the many student organizations at the young school, the most incongruous, albeit one of the largest, was the Rifle Club. Organized and vigorously promoted by a member of the original faculty, VMI graduate Gunyon M. Harrison, the club in 1914 boasted a membership of fifty-seven, a sizable portion of the school's entire enrollment, captained by a student with the improbable name of Sex Smith. Explaining the club's purpose in *The Battlefield*, one member, having noted that former president Theodore Roosevelt, in bemoaning the decline of American marksmanship, had said that "we should encourage rifle practice among schoolboys," asserted, "We think among schoolgirls also. There is no reason why a girl should not shoot as well as a boy."

Considerably handicapped by the lack of sufficient weapons for practice, membership in the club fluctuated, but in 1916 it had increased to sixty-eight, boosted perhaps by the looming possibility of American involvement in World War I, which was then raging in Europe. "Every good citizen of the United States should agree with President [Woodrow] Wilson's policy of 'Preparedness,'" declared a club statement, "and since all of us are expected to be future citizens, why not prepare us?"

That year turned out to be the high-water mark in club membership, at least in part because its animating force, Gunyon Harrison, joined the service and departed for Europe, where he attained the rank of captain. He never returned to the College, and the Rifle Club was soon defunct.

The early popularity of the Rifle Club was but one manifestation of students' interest in physical activity and competition. There were, for example, a Krokay Klub, several walking clubs, such as the Globe Trotters, and two

Tennis Club, 1913. The tennis court was located between the Administration Building (later Monroe Hall) and the Dormitory (later Willard Hall), the only two buildings on campus at the time.

softball teams. Tennis was quite popular, and matches were played on clay courts in front of Monroe and Willard Halls.

The sport that attracted the most participants, however, was basketball. The first games were played in the Monroe Hall gym against Fredericksburg High School. The first off-campus contest came during the 1914–15 session when the varsity club traveled to Richmond to play the YWCA team, which the Normal School defeated 14–9. By 1916 the varsity attracted sixty girls for the first practice, and the schedule included a trip to Washington.

An account in *The Battlefield* of that trip indicated vividly and rather poignantly just how much such events meant to that era's students, for whom the total experience far transcended the actual game itself. "We were all so happy," wrote one team member, "because [it was] the first time that many of us had been to Washington [and] we were all eager for the first view." Having taken an early train, the entourage spent most of the day sightseeing, and then, the account continued:

> The game—I've almost forgotten to mention it—and that's what we came for! Oh, yes, it was quite a hard game, between the Washington YWCA and our team, but because we always held the score at least two points ahead our hopes were never dimmed. And we had such an encouraging audience in the gallery, who spurred us on with their cheers. When the game was won with the score of 16 to 7 . . . we were

> truly happy. Our good time was continued at the YWCA, where we dined with the same girls with whom we had played. . . . When we returned to our dear old Normal we were given a hearty welcome, and then we knew how much our victory meant to those at home as well as to our team and coach.

Aside from the athletes who played on organized teams, virtually the whole student body participated in various contests culminating in an annual Field Day held each spring under the sponsorship of the Athletic Association. The event comprised competitions among representatives of each of the four classes in twelve events, including dashes, relays, broad and high jumps, and "throwing the ball," with a silver trophy going to the class amassing the highest point total.

The school held its first May Day in conjunction with the Field Day games in the spring of 1914. In the ensuing years, May Day, though still sponsored by the Athletic Association, came to eclipse the Field Day aspect of the celebration, becoming one of the school's most popular and venerable traditions, beloved by student participants and local spectators alike.

The first year and for a number thereafter, the event was held on the lawn in front of Monroe Hall, before being moved to the newly constructed amphitheater in 1923. The program generally followed a familiar script each year. It began with a processional led by the queen and her elegantly attired attendants, the senior Maypole dancers, and then the classes, in order, wearing their distinctive colors. After the singing of a May song, the queen was crowned, and the seniors performed the Maypole dance. Additional songs and dances might be included, as well as the presentation of awards for athletic achievement. A shepherds' dance and a garland dance completed the program, which concluded with the singing of the school song.

At Mary Washington, as at other women's colleges of the time (especially in the South), May Day was regarded by many as the highlight of the school year. No event was more eagerly anticipated than May Day, no title more coveted than "Queen of the May." Yet after decades of popularity, the event came into disfavor in the late 1960s, the victim of changing cultural ideals that made the celebration seem increasingly anachronistic, a frivolous exercise based on superficial—or, worse, sexist—attitudes. Accordingly, after 1968, the event was discontinued. To many alumnae, however, May Day remained a cherished memory of a frilly and fanciful adornment to a more innocent age.

Occupied as they were with classes and extracurricular diversions, students in the early years of the Normal School seem to have been only slightly interested in, or involved with, greater affairs beyond the campus. Nor was this insularity surprising, given the limitations of travel and communication at the time; even radio was not available until the 1920s. The culture of the time, moreover, before the advent of women's suffrage, offered few opportunities (and no encouragement) for female participation in public affairs.

Crowning of the May Queen, 1929

Even so, there were some occasions when students' interests stretched, either physically or intellectually, beyond the Hill, as, for example, when a group traveled to Washington on March 4, 1913, to attend the inauguration of Virginia-born president Woodrow Wilson. Some were also attracted to the growing women's suffrage movement, as evidenced by the debates on the subject held by the Woodrow Wilson Literary Society.

The paramount issue of the time, of course, was the Great War in Europe, and the controversy over American intervention. Though the war apparently did not affect enrollment at the Normal School, extracurricular activities did reflect the war's impact. One notable address on the subject was delivered by Douglas Southall Freeman, a historian and journalist from Richmond; other guest lecturers focused on topics such as firsthand experiences in France and the daily lives of the soldiers.

In the fall of 1918, just as the war was coming to an end, the country was struck by the worst influenza epidemic in its history—the so-called Spanish flu. The Fredericksburg area was hard hit, and the mayor ordered the closing of all places of public assembly, including churches and schools, as well as all places of amusement, a quarantine that lasted almost two months.

The epidemic did not spare the Normal School, striking shortly after students arrived in late September for the opening of the 1918–19 session. The siege did not last long, however, and according to the local newspaper, most cases were mild. "There are only 50 cases now under treatment," it reported in early October, noting that "there has not been a single death" among the students, though one faculty member, Virginia May Goolrick (first cousin of O'Conor Goolrick), did succumb to flu-related illness.

The hero of the hour at the school was a Fredericksburg physician, Dr. H. M. DeJarnette, a member of the Normal School Board, who attended to both students and faculty night and day during the epidemic. When he declined to present a bill for his services, the school voted to compensate him anyway, but DeJarnette refused on the grounds that it would, in his words, "establish a bad policy."

No sooner had the epidemic ebbed than the school experienced a different kind of problem, this one an administrative controversy that posed the most serious threat to the effective functioning of the school since its founding. For reasons not altogether clear, a number of faculty members resigned in early 1919—the result, according to Ed Alvey, of "a series of incidents, minor in themselves but the cumulative effect of which was to cause concern about the administration of the School." The board responded by appointing a special investigating committee, whose inquiry determined that the campus was beset with anxiety and low morale.

Partly as a consequence, President Russell tendered his resignation in May. In a terse, one-sentence message to the board, Russell announced: "For several years my health has been impaired and I feel impelled in justice to myself and the best interest of the School to herewith [resign]." Though his statement made no allusion to the controversy, the abruptness of his resignation and its immediate acceptance by the board gave the appearance that Russell left the school under something of a cloud, a conjecture augmented by the removal of his name from the administration building, which was subsequently re-christened Monroe Hall.

Yet there was evidence to the contrary. The local newspaper found Russell's explanation for resigning credible, noting that it was his strenuous efforts in getting the institution established that led his health to fail, and emphasizing that he "leaves the institution with the personal good wishes of the faculty and students." Moreover, though he soon moved to Washington, he was by no means a pariah at the College, returning to campus occasionally and, in 1949, delivering a memorable Founders Day speech. In 1965, nine years after Russell's death, the College named a beautiful new dormitory on Sunken Road in his honor.

In any event, the school's temporary turmoil soon dissipated. The board immediately designated Dean A. B. Chandler Jr., a member of the original faculty, as acting president. The next month, June 1919, he was appointed president.

In retrospect, the malaise of the end of Russell's presidency appeared an aberration, an unfortunate but transitory interlude that stood in contrast to the steady progress that had characterized the school's first decade. The environment on campus during the Russell years seems to have been a happy one. With a student body so small that everyone knew everyone else, and with lack of transportation largely confining the students to campus, a strong sense of camaraderie developed. There was no shortage of school spirit, and an atmosphere of good cheer prevailed.

This harmonious attitude resulted partly from the affection between the students and faculty, many of whom lived on or near campus and frequently invited the students to their homes for meals or picnics. The students also seemed especially to admire President Russell, as evidenced by a poetic tribute—stronger on sentiment than on scansion—that appeared in the 1914 edition of *The Battlefield*:

Mr. Russell is a great man;
  Mr. Russell is a pearl;
Mr. Russell rules our school,
  And is loved by every girl.

We even ask Mr. Russell
  If we may have a beau,
For everything is all right
  If Mr. Russell says so.

For later generations of students to whom college attendance was regarded as virtually a birthright, such expressions would seem surpassingly naive. But the young women who attended the Normal School recognized that, in the early twentieth century, this was not by any means an opportunity vouchsafed to all. Most were first-generation collegians, some quite likely the children of parents who could neither read nor write. To such young women, it was a godsend to be able not only to go to a college but to go to one that would equip them to teach others—this at a time when teaching was looked on as the ne plus ultra within the limited constellation of professions to which women might reasonably aspire.

And so they were genuinely grateful for the opportunity—and not ashamed, or too jaded, to say so.

THE CHANDLER ERA, 1919–28

Prospects for the future seemed bright in 1920 as the Normal School embarked on its second decade. On the national level, the Great War was over, and peace had been restored, presumably in perpetuity, inasmuch as President Wilson had touted the conflict as the war to end all wars. Women could now vote, courtesy of the Nineteenth Amendment, even if they—or anyone else (legally)—could not drink, courtesy of the Eighteenth. The economy was beginning to boom, bringing general prosperity that appeared permanent, though that prospect, like that of peace, was to prove evanescent.

On the campus as well, the outlook seemed propitious, as affairs soon returned to normal under the stewardship of the new president, A. B. Chandler Jr., whose training and experience equipped him well for the job. Having earned bachelor's and master's degrees from the University of Virginia, he briefly studied law at Washington and Lee University before joining his brother's law practice in Atlanta. After only a few years, he decided to pursue a career in the education field, which led him to several teaching and administrative positions in both private and public schools in Virginia, where he achieved considerable prominence in state educational circles. In 1911 he became a member of the Normal School's first faculty as a professor of Latin; within four years he was named dean.

Chandler's first priority as president was securing qualified faculty to replace those who had departed in the exodus near the end of Russell's tenure—not an easy task, given the low level of salaries at the time. When the school opened in 1911, faculty salaries ranged from $52 to $150 per month, and the salary of the president himself was only $250 per month. Faculty members were contractually obligated to eat their meals on campus, with the cost ($15 per month) covered by the school as a fringe benefit. Although Chandler requested an increase of 7 percent in the salary scale when he took office, the base was so low that the impact was minimal.

Algernon Bertrand Chandler Jr.

Despite such constraints, the school was able to attract a sufficient number of new faculty (ten), among them the school's first holder of a Ph.D. degree, Walter J. Young, who was hired to teach biology, geography, and education. Of all the early appointments made by President Chandler, the one that turned out to be unquestionably the most significant was that of Nina Gookin Bushnell, who came to the school in 1921 as dean of women and professor of Bible.

Born at a time when the Civil War had been over scarcely fifteen years, Mrs. Bushnell grew up in a South still redolent of the antebellum era. Though her professional career was spent mainly in the twentieth century, she remained largely a person of the nineteenth, and it was the social values of that earlier time that she endeavored to impart to her "girls," as she called them, at the Fredericksburg school.

A 1903 graduate of the University of Tennessee, Mrs. Bushnell did postgraduate work at Teachers College of Columbia University. At first she taught English and Latin in small high schools in North Carolina and Virginia, as well as at Winthrop College in South Carolina. (It was during that period, in 1911, that her husband, Charles, died of typhoid fever. She never remarried.) Her career before coming to State Teachers College also took her to Mississippi, South Carolina, and Missouri—in which places she held a variety of administrative as well as teaching positions. In addition, she spent time in France during World War I working for the YWCA. An athletic person of boundless energy, she especially enjoyed swimming, riding, and dancing.

At the College, Mrs. Bushnell's duties were extensive and varied. Among her specific responsibilities were room assignments, preparation and distribution of the handbook, and the supervision of all recreation and entertainment activities, notably May Day, an event that especially lent itself to her penchant for elegant celebration. Moreover, during those years when student rooms lacked telephones—there was not even a central switchboard for many years—all long-distance calls to the campus went to the phone in her Virginia Hall apartment.

Mrs. Bushnell's role, however, went far beyond the mere specifications of her "job description," if indeed she had one. For the three decades following her hiring, her duties and influence were so extensive that, to many students during that time, it seemed that Nina Bushnell *was* the College.

The academic program underwent several notable changes during the 1920s. One of the first resulted from a decision by the Virginia Normal School Board that, to eliminate duplication of effort, each of the state's four normal schools (at Farmville, Radford, Harrisonburg, and Fredericksburg) would offer teacher preparation only in certain assigned areas of specialization. The areas assigned to the Fredericksburg school were music, industrial arts, and commercial subjects, including standard business courses such as typing, shorthand, and bookkeeping.

In 1919 when the board first announced the policy, Edward Russell, then president, adamantly protested the action, asserting that a commercial program would have scant appeal at a normal school because business courses were also available in high schools and business colleges. As it turned out, he was both right and wrong. In the short term, he was wrong because, after implementation of the program in the 1920–21 session, the commercial program grew by 1940 to the point that its registration was over seven hundred, or about half the College's entire enrollment. In the longer run, however, he was prescient in that the College's increasing emphasis on the liberal arts and sciences spelled the demise, and eventual elimination, of practical business courses by the 1970s. In any event, the differentiation policy was rather quickly abandoned, as the governing body of the four state educational schools voted in 1924 to require that "all institutions be operated on the same basis."

Earlier in the same year, an even more significant development had occurred when the General Assembly enacted legislation changing the names of the normal schools to teachers colleges, whereupon, commencing with the 1924–25 academic session, the name of the institution officially became the State Teachers College at Fredericksburg. The change was made, according to the school's bulletin for that year, "in order that its name may conform to the character of the work done, that its students may enjoy the prestige due to the college name, and that the public school system of this State may reap the benefit of the services of teachers who are graduates of a standard teachers college."

Though the new nomenclature was to some extent cosmetic, it was accompanied by several substantive changes, including the introduction of a major in physical education. More important, in the long run, was the implementation of a bachelor of science degree in education that allowed students to major in particular subject areas, an initiative that foreshadowed the institution's movement away from teacher education and toward emphasis on the liberal arts and sciences. Meanwhile four-year courses for both high school and elementary teachers continued to be offered, as well as a two-year program leading to a professional certificate for elementary teachers until it was terminated in 1942.

Expansion of the academic program was accompanied by extension of physical facilities. One addition was a structure that would be much cherished by students over the years: the amphitheater (or "open-air theatre," as it was first called).[10] Completed in 1923, it was built into a natural slope in a grove of trees just below the main campus and could initially accommodate approximately eight hundred people, a capacity that was doubled some years later.

The dedication of the theater on May 11, 1923, was trumpeted on the front page of the *Daily Star* under the banner "Big Day at the Normal!" And a big day it was, with an afternoon program featuring addresses by President Chandler, founding patron and current state senator C. O'Conor Goolrick, and Virginia governor E. Lee Trinkle. The governor was widely known for his impassioned, flamboyant oratory, and he did not disappoint the gathering in the amphitheater. Having rhapsodized about "the beautiful sylvan scenes that

The open-air theater, better known as the amphitheater

surround them," he exhorted the school's future teachers to do nothing less than "banish ignorance from the grand old commonwealth"—a huge challenge, to be sure, but typical of the governor's rhetorical flights. The celebration concluded in the evening with a student production of Humperdinck's operetta *Hansel and Gretel.*

The amphitheater was an impressive venue, whose opening, reported the local newspaper, constituted "another step in the remarkable development of this splendid Virginia educational institution," adding that "the people of this section are very proud of this school and the work it is doing."

In subsequent years, the amphitheater served as the picturesque site for an array of events: senior class plays, professional performances, May Day programs, commencement exercises. But as the College eventually built other facilities that were more capacious and more convenient, the amphitheater was used less frequently, until by the end of the century it was rarely used at all. Yet for many alumni that wooded setting remained near the heart of the College in sentiment if no longer in reality.

Other construction in the 1920s involved more practical projects, driven either by enrollment growth or by expanding programs. Additional space for residential students was secured in 1923 through an unusual arrangement with a group of Fredericksburg businessmen who constructed a facility on Sunken Road, just below the existing campus, and leased it to the school for use as a dormitory. Named Betty Lewis Hall in honor of George Washington's sister, wife of the Revolutionary War patriot Fielding Lewis, the building provided accommodations for an additional 110 students. It functioned as a dormitory until 1930, when new rooming facilities rendered it unnecessary. Having been converted to apartments at that time, it was reconverted for dormitory use in 1937 and continued to be used as such until 1972, when once again new on-campus dormitory construction alleviated the need for Betty Lewis Hall, which was sold at auction.

From the early 1920s, it was evident to many, notably President Chandler, that the growing school needed additional recreational facilities as well as space for other student-related activities. Accordingly, he began to appeal for funds to construct a multipurpose facility (prominently including a swimming pool to replace the tiny one in the Monroe Hall basement) that would be called the Student-Alumnae Building. Despite continuing pleas to students, faculty, alumnae, and townsfolk, as well as to the state legislature, by 1927 the requisite funds had still not been secured.

At that point the school organized an all-out fund-raising blitz, aided by a professional agency, that made appeals especially to civic pride, emphasizing the economic advantages that a thriving college would provide for the community. The campaign succeeded in reaching its goal of $35,000, which, together with an $11,000 appropriation from the commonwealth, enabled work to begin on the structure, starting with the swimming pool.

As it happened, construction of the pool—and a commodious and beautiful one it was for its time—was as far as the project got at that point. In the absence of requested state funds to continue the work, the new pool was covered, creating an open-air roof garden that provided an enticing venue for campus social events for many years. Edward Alvey described the setting:

> At night, ornamental electrified lanterns were placed at intervals along the surrounding balustrade. From the dance floor the strains of soft music wafted across the campus. . . . A buffet for refreshments was set up at one end, where the diners could refresh themselves with cups of brightly colored cold punch and small cakes made by the home economics department. Occasionally, on warm summer evenings, the lights were dimmed so that dancers could enjoy the light of the moon and stars shining brightly above.

It turned out that the structure would not be completed for almost a quarter century, until it was incorporated into the capacious Ann Carter Lee Hall in the early 1950s. With the opening of the elegant Lee Hall Ballroom and the subsequent construction of additional locales for student social gatherings, the roof garden was gradually replaced as the site of most such activities, though it is doubtful that other venues surpassed its romantic ambience.

Another important construction project in the 1920s, albeit of more prosaic purpose, was prompted by the needs of the College's teacher-education program, which, despite the increasing tendency toward the liberal arts and sciences, was still central to the institution's mission. Of particular concern to President Chandler was the effectiveness of the supervised teaching, or student teaching, aspect of the program. From the founding of the institution, such training had usually involved some form of cooperative arrangement between the Normal School and the public schools of Fredericksburg and surrounding counties. Those arrangements sometimes proved bumpy, however, leading President Chandler to place high priority on establishing an on-campus facility wherein teacher training could be conducted under the direct control and supervision of the Normal School itself.

Despite Chandler's persistent advocacy from the outset of his administration, the project was slow to develop. Ultimately the General Assembly approved sufficient funding ($70,000) to permit the construction of the edifice variously called, at the time, the Campus Training School, College Heights High School, or generically the training school. The three-story brick structure, which opened for the fall 1928 session, contained classrooms for elementary, middle, and high school students, and pupils at all those levels were a common sight on campus until the school was discontinued in 1938.

The training school, with an athletic field behind it for high school students, was praised by the local paper as "the handsomest and most complete of all the college group," containing "every . . . needed modern facility both for the comfort and convenience of the teachers and students and for the program of education." Though the original plans for the inclusion of an auditorium and gymnasium were never implemented—Monroe Hall continued to house those facilities for many years—the building was reconfigured and enlarged when the training school was abolished; it subsequently served multiple purposes, primarily as an academic building housing a variety of departments over the years. Appropriately in 1938 it was renamed Chandler Hall in memory of the man whose tireless efforts had led to its construction.

Student life on campus in the 1920s was dictated by numerous rules and regulations that proscribed many activities and prescribed the rest. Hours for study, rest, and recreation were specified; conduct with dates, trips to town, and even walks around the campus were carefully regulated.

Vespers, conducted by the YWCA, were held each weekday evening at 6:30 following dinner. Every night except Saturday and Sunday, "study hour" began at 7:15 and lasted until 10:00, during which time students were required to be either in their rooms, in Monroe Hall, or in the library; no visitation was allowed. Following study hour, a "recreation period" from 10:00 to 10:30 allowed students to visit each other in their rooms before "quiet hour" began at 10:30. At that time each student was to be in her room when the lights-out bell rang; lights were not to be used again before 5:00 a.m.

Rules were relaxed somewhat on Saturday and Sunday nights, though not much. Students were permitted to visit each other in their rooms until 10:30, though dates were required to leave by 10:00 p.m. Lights were to be out at 10:45.

The number of evening trips to town was quite limited. Sophomores were allowed to go only one night a month, in groups of four, to movies or other approved entertainment. Juniors were allowed two night trips to town, in groups, and seniors could go once a week, but still in groups of three or more. Even then, the areas that students could legitimately visit were strictly limited.

According to Ed Alvey, "Riding in automobiles was regarded as an especially pernicious pastime, fraught with danger for the unsuspecting students." Accordingly, students were permitted to ride in cars only when accompanied by a faculty or family member, or in for-hire vehicles, or with "approved boys or men." Night riding was strictly forbidden, and violations of this rule could result in lengthy campusing or even suspension.

Students were required to eat all their meals in the dining hall, unless specific permission to be absent was granted by the dean of students, and were required to attend all meals except Saturday and Sunday breakfast. Dining rules were delineated in detail. Students were seated at tables of eight, each of which included representatives of each of the four classes, with a junior or senior in charge of the table. Meals were served family style, with student waitresses serving the tables. Proper dress was of course required, and no table could leave until dismissed by its hostess. At breakfast and lunch, the hostesses could dismiss their tables, but at dinner no one could leave until the dining room was dismissed as a whole by the dean of women—the signal for which was usually a slight nod of the head from Mrs. Bushnell.

Within such restrictive parameters, students in the 1920s still found a surprising number of avenues for entertainment. Because most students stayed on campus throughout the semester, leaving only for major holidays, the College actively strove to provide attractive diversions. On a more or less regular basis, such activities included parties sponsored by the YWCA and the student government, receptions sponsored by the city's churches, alumnae and YWCA bazaars, music recitals by both students and faculty, basketball games (both interclass and varsity), motion pictures, the senior class play, and an annual circus. The Field Day program continued to be a highlight of the school year, culminating in the crowning of the May queen.

The 1920s also witnessed the birth of a student activity known as Devil-Goat Day, which was destined to become an enduring campus tradition. The event developed spontaneously. Central to it was a new member of the faculty, Eileen Kramer Dodd, who joined the faculty in 1926 and was to have a lengthy and distinguished career at the College as a professor of education with specialization in psychology. During her first year, she was sponsor of the junior class. As she later recalled, "We decided to have a goat as our symbol. One morning at breakfast we all appeared in the dining hall wearing white skirts and white sweatshirts decorated with a felt green goat. Then the seniors decided to have a distinctive symbol, and they adopted a red devil as an emblem. So began the Devil-Goat rivalry that was to last for so many years."

Last it did. With alternating classes being designated as either Devils or Goats, spirited competitions occurred annually, culminating in Devil-Goat Day, featuring all manner of competitions between the two groups. Over the course of time, it became the College's oldest tradition, continuing into the twenty-first century, surpassing the May Day celebrations that ended in the late 1960s.

Beginning in the 1920s and continuing for several decades thereafter, the social highlights of the school year were the formal dances sponsored by the German Club, which was established by Dean Bushnell and President Chandler in 1922. The new organization, modeled on similar dance clubs popular at the time in Richmond and other Virginia cities, quickly supplanted the existing Virginia Reel Club—for the quite understandable reason that it permitted men at the dances, whereas the Virginia Reel did not.

The German Club was an exclusive organization whose membership was limited to sixty students chosen by secret ballot, with Dean Bushnell as the final arbiter of who would be admitted. Each club member was entitled to wear a distinctive pin, emblematic of the highest social honor that a student could achieve. The club's three formal dances each year—fall, midwinter, and spring—were elaborate events that involved months of detailed preparation. In addition to the sixty club members and their dates, a specified number of other students and their dates were allowed to attend. A German weekend included not only the dance itself from nine o'clock until midnight but a dinner before and supper following in the dining hall.

The events were, in Ed Alvey's depiction, "stately and sedate affairs," replete with engraved invitations, dance cards, and a carefully choreographed dance figure (members only) just before intermission. "The music itself," wrote Alvey, "was designed to encourage graceful and dignified dancing, with waltzes and fox trots predominating. There was no jitterbugging or other unseemly demonstrations of wild abandon to music or mood. A floor committee gently warned with a reproving but highly effective look at any couple whose dancing was inappropriate."

In the nation at large, it may have been the age of jazz, flappers, speakeasies, and bathtub gin, but on the campus of Fredericksburg State Teachers College, the Roaring Twenties barely whispered. Mrs. Bushnell saw to that.

On the eve of the opening of the fall 1928 session, the College and the community were stunned by the unexpected death of President Chandler. Returning from his office to his home on College Avenue, he suffered a stroke on September 20 and succumbed at the age of fifty-eight.

Chandler had been involved extensively in the cultural and civic activities of the Fredericksburg area, having served as president of the Rotary Club and the Chamber of Commerce, and eulogies reflected the esteem that he enjoyed in the community. "He had friends everywhere and few enemies," wrote the *Free Lance–Star*. "He kept himself from acrimony and did his work efficiently without offending others. . . . He led a useful life and one which will be of value to this and future generations." Much of his popularity, and his success, derived from his perpetually buoyant disposition—a characteristic described succinctly by the paper's comment that he was a man "who found life filled with things to smile at."

A campus memorial service in Monroe Hall allowed faculty and students to pay their respects for the leader whom they much admired. Students, all dressed in white, lined the way from the president's home to the auditorium, and as the procession passed, "swiftly the hand of every student was placed on her heart in final salute."

Chandler's long and productive service to the institution warranted such respect. As a member of the original faculty in 1911, he had taught until 1915 and then served as dean until 1919 and finally as president until 1928. During his presidency, significant improvements were made in crucial areas—breadth of the curriculum, quality of the faculty, expansion of physical facilities—and the College's enrollment more than doubled. Owing largely to Chandler's indefatigable efforts and energized by his boundless optimism, the institution made steady progress through a critical portion of its formative years. Though still in the early stages of its academic evolution, the College was thus well situated to survive in the subsequent years, even though the challenges of the Depression era loomed, as yet unsuspected, just beyond the horizon.

THE COMBS ERA, 1928–55

Like their contemporaries at similar institutions of the period—and quite in contrast to their Mary Washington successors in later decades—the young women of Fredericksburg State Teachers College in the 1920s appeared to take little interest in public affairs. Having achieved the vote only at the beginning of that decade, their slowness in embracing the political process that had been so long denied them was perhaps understandable. It would change.

Meanwhile an indication of growing political awareness on campus was evident in the unusual interest students showed in the presidential election of 1928 between Herbert Hoover and Alfred E. Smith. Weeks of student debate among partisans of the two men culminated in a straw vote taken before dinner on election night. After the votes were counted, reported the *Bullet*, "the dean of women withheld the returns from an excited and eager-to-know body of girls for fully five minutes. Finally, she announced that according to the student vote Hoover had won by a majority of twenty."

The debate did not end there. "Until the 10:30 bell rang," continued the article, "groups of girls could be seen standing about in the dormitories, and in the vicinity of a telephone to hear the returns as they came in. Many political battles were staged, the combatants hotly contesting for their candidate."[11]

The final results on the following morning indicated that the students' vote had accurately presaged the preference of the national electorate, though within a year many would rue Hoover's election.

Temporary interest in the election notwithstanding, the focus of attention for most students remained on more parochial events, especially the imminent arrival in the fall of 1928 of a new College president, Dr. Morgan Lafayette Combs, who was appointed by the Board of the State Teachers Colleges of Virginia on December 7 to succeed the late President Chandler. A native of southwestern Virginia, Combs received his bachelor's degree from the University of Richmond and master's from the University of Chicago, followed by a master's and doctorate in education from Harvard. His professional career included both teaching and administrative work at the local and state levels in Virginia.

Combs was also well connected politically. His kinsman E. R. "Ebbie" Combs was widely regarded as one of the most powerful figures in Virginia politics, perhaps second in influence only to the head of the dominant Democratic organization, Senator Harry F. Byrd. So impressive were Combs's credentials that the board considered no other candidate, naming him president of the State Teachers College at the age of thirty-five.

Members of the College community had their first opportunity to meet the new president and his wife at a reception held shortly before the Christmas break in 1928. Students and faculty alike were no doubt favorably impressed. Young for such a position, Combs not only possessed commendable academic and professional credentials but had personal characteristics that attracted attention; tall in stature and erect in bearing, he conveyed an image that was at the same time commanding and courtly.

Students in particular were taken with the whole Combs family, who, before finding suitable housing in town, lived for a while in a three-room suite in Willard Hall and took their meals in the College dining hall. According to the *Bullet*, "When Dr. Combs with his attractive wife and two handsome little boys, Bobbie and Morgan Jr., entered the dining hall for the first time, they were greeted with a roar of applause." The boys seem to have been regarded with special affection by the students, who called them "our pigmy co-eds" and joked that with the arrival of the Combs children, "the College boasts the youngest co-eds in the state."

Morgan Lafayette Combs

Certainly Combs could use all the

goodwill he could find, given the problems he would encounter. Not only was his administration soon forced to grapple with the difficulties of the Great Depression, but his assumption of office on January 3, 1929, coincided with the ravages of a statewide influenza epidemic. Some schools were forbidden by the State Health Department from reopening as scheduled after the Christmas recess. While the Teachers College at Fredericksburg was allowed to resume classes on time, stringent precautions were taken, including a personal screening of faculty and students by the assistant state health commissioner. Students who exhibited any suspicious respiratory symptoms were quarantined; no visitors were allowed on campus, nor were students permitted to go into town except in extraordinary circumstances and with explicit administrative permission.

It was a trying experience for the quarantined students, who were confined to the infirmary and barred from any contact with other students. The YWCA students took an active role in helping to improve the situation by running errands for them and by regularly delivering to the infirmary reading materials, notably including popular women's magazines such as *Ladies' Home Journal* and *Woman's Home Companion*. Within a few weeks the emergency subsided, and the school returned to normal, having fortunately suffered no serious illnesses from the epidemic.

Combs quickly recognized, however, that he faced a serious problem of an institutional nature, namely, the school's failure to achieve accreditation from the prestigious Southern Association of Colleges and Secondary Schools (SACS). The College's application had been rejected in 1927—a particularly hurtful blow, since the sister institutions at both Harrisonburg and Farmville had been approved at that time. Though the College had been a member in good standing with the American Association of Teachers Colleges, accreditation by SACS was a matter of considerable importance if the College was to move, as it was tentatively doing, toward a more liberal-arts-oriented curriculum. At the outset of his administration, Combs placed a high priority on rectifying this unfortunate and potentially catastrophic situation.

The rejection by SACS had come mainly because of two deficiencies at the College: inadequate faculty qualifications and insufficient salaries. Both were indeed problems. With regard to qualifications, for example, at the time Combs took office, only three faculty members held doctorates; several had only a bachelor's degree, and a few had no college degree at all.

Combs moved promptly to address this situation in two ways. First, he insisted that current faculty members with substandard preparation take leaves of absence to upgrade their credentials. A good many did so, and the contracts of those who did not were terminated. Second, he made possession of a doctoral degree a priority in new hirings whenever possible, a strategy that resulted in attracting eight additional holders of doctorates within four years, among them George Earlie Shankle and Charles George Gordon Moss, both of whom were to become prominent and much-beloved campus figures for many years.

Correcting the salary problem proved more difficult, especially after the onset of the Depression in October 1929. Having obtained modest increases for some faculty positions, the College reapplied for SACS accreditation, only to be rejected again in December 1929. Further increases the following year brought the annual salaries of full professors up to the $3,000 minimum standard established by SACS, and amid much rejoicing at the College, full accreditation was granted in December 1930.

As the College approached the twentieth anniversary of its opening, improvements were evident in many respects, but there was an increasing need for better facilities, notably for a more modern kitchen and dining hall to replace the Willard venue that had been used from the beginning. Rejecting the possibility of a modest structure that the economic conditions of the time might have suggested, President Combs proposed that a more imposing structure be built on the College Avenue side of campus in an area where formerly the school garden had been tended by agriculture students. Such a site presented an additional problem in the form of a ravine that lay between it and the main campus. No small thinker, Combs further proposed that an arched brick viaduct be constructed to enhance the beauty of the area while providing convenient access to the new building.

Funding, always a key consideration, was even more of a concern than usual, as Depression-era constraints had led to a state moratorium on any outlay for nonessential projects. Undeterred, Combs made his case in Richmond, where, in Ed Alvey's words, "he sought the assistance of his friends in state government." Friends he had—and good ones—foremost among them being "Ebbie" Combs, powerful head of the influential State Compensation Board.

In June 1930 Governor John Garland Pollard authorized the construction of the new kitchen and dining hall at a cost not to exceed $112,500. Unfortunately for the College, an unanticipated state revenue shortfall meant that the institution was forced eventually to assume approximately $40,000 of that amount itself, which it did by tapping its maintenance fund and economizing College operations over a two-year period. Meanwhile construction proceeded apace, and the new facility was ready for occupancy in the spring of 1931, providing not only modern cooking and dining facilities but also commodious quarters in the basement for the Home Economics Department.

A magnificent building it was. Named Seacobeck Hall, after the Indian village that once occupied the spot, it was reached by a series of terraced steps leading from the ravine bridge to a handsome pillared portico. The main entrance opened into the dome room, which served as a lobby leading to dining rooms on both sides. The dome room's central feature was an Italian marble fireplace; it was furnished with Chippendale mirrors and tables, lavish draperies, and elegant Persian rugs. From the time it opened and for many years thereafter, it served as an impressive venue for formal campus gatherings, such as annual spring receptions for friends and patrons of the school, including members of the State Board of Education.

Students were understandably thrilled with the new building. They were somewhat less enamored with the viaduct, which, though essential for transit from the main campus and unquestionably an aesthetic adornment, nonetheless presented significant drainage problems. According to the *Bullet*, during the first rain, "the lovely bridge was a bridge no more, but a pond-a-ducks—and not a human's passageway."[12] It was a situation that persisted for years, as generations of soggy-footed students could attest, even into the next century.

As it turned out, Seacobeck was only the first of many buildings that would be constructed during President Combs's tenure, despite the difficult economic environment during his first decade in office. Ironically, the funds provided by certain New Deal programs established in response to the Depression proved a boon to the physical expansion and beautification of the campus.

For example, in 1933 the College received a grant of $21,000 from the Civil Works Administration (CWA)—one of the first such awards in Virginia—that enabled the hiring of over one hundred workers to undertake various improvements on the grounds. When the CWA subsequently metamorphosed into the larger Works Progress Administration (WPA), the College continued to benefit from federal grants. The WPA employees, despite "boondoggle" accusations from New Deal critics, actually accomplished many salutary tasks, including the construction of walkways, the planting of trees and ornamental shrubs, and other landscaping jobs. Working in concert with regular College maintenance staff, they also constructed new tennis courts, an outdoor swimming pool, a field house, and two hockey fields located below and north of the central campus.

The creation of the Public Works Administration (PWA) presented the opportunity for the College to secure federal funds for much larger projects, with additional residential space at the top of the list. In November 1933 President Combs was part of a delegation, headed by Governor Pollard and Senator Byrd, that appeared before the PWA review board in support of the commonwealth's application for over $3 million for the state educational institutions. The result was a grant of $360,000 to Fredericksburg State Teachers College for the construction of dormitories—the largest amount awarded to any Virginia institution.

A portion of the money was used for an addition to Virginia Hall that completed the H shape of the building and provided space for fifty-four more students. The bulk of the funds went toward the construction of an impressive tri-unit of dormitories that would face north across an expanse of lawn toward Virginia Hall, creating from what had once been an athletic field an area soon to be known as Ball Circle. The plan, designed (as were several other campus buildings) by the Richmond architectural firm of J. Binford Walford, called for a central building distinguished by an imposing portico with massive columns, flanked on each side by smaller residence halls connected to it by curvilinear colonnades.

The main building, named Mary Ball Hall in honor of George Washington's mother, could house slightly over one hundred students. It possessed an elegance—indeed, grandeur—that would be unthinkable in the construction of later, purely functional, residence halls. On the first floor was a huge reception area with a circular stairway extending upward toward the amber-colored skylight three stories above; on either side were capacious parlors illuminated by crystal chandeliers and wall sconces.

The smaller units on either side were designed to house approximately fifty students each. One (on the right facing Ball) was named Custis Hall in honor of Mary Anne Randolph Custis Lee, the wife of Robert E. Lee; the other was named Madison Hall in honor of Dolly Payne Madison, the wife of James Madison. Together the new dormitory spaces made it possible to almost double the College's enrollment.

Though not of the magnitude of Seacobeck and Tri-Unit, other acquisitions during the period contributed in various ways to the growth of the physical plant. In 1930 the frame structure on College Avenue (just behind Tri-Unit) where President Chandler had lived was purchased from his widow and was subsequently named Anne Fairfax. Seven years later an adjacent frame structure, the longtime home of Professor and Mrs. W. N. Hamlet, a member of the College's original faculty, was purchased; it continued to be known as Hamlet House. Both structures over the years served variously as space for students, administrators, clinics, and special programs.

In 1932 the Athletic Association presented the College a gift in the form of a log cabin constructed on a promontory in a wooded area some distance from Willard Hall near the northern edge of campus. With its open fireplace and rustic appearance, the cabin became an attractive venue for groups of up to fifteen who could reserve it for special events.

In 1936, financed by donations from graduating classes and private individuals (most notably Mrs. A. B. Chandler), gates were constructed below Monroe Hall at the Sunken Road entrance to the College. The brick pillars and massive iron gates not only made an aesthetic addition but served the practical purpose of allowing the campus driveway to be closed at night to keep intruders out. Though the log cabin was razed in the late 1980s (amid considerable protest) to make way for a much-needed new residence hall, the gates remained as a stately and stern reminder of an era when there was a clear demarcation between the College and the world beyond its boundaries.

The physical growth of the College was accompanied in the 1930s by a commensurate increase in the faculty, as a number of persons arrived during that period who would be instrumental in the institution's development in the decades ahead. Foremost among these was Edward Alvey Jr., whose hiring in the summer of 1934 was a ramification of the so-called Alstetter affair, one of the more unseemly and mystifying incidents in the College's history.

Michael Louis Alstetter had come to Fredericksburg State Teachers College in 1929 to replace Bunyan Tyler as dean of instruction. For reasons not altogether clear, a serious rift developed between Alstetter and President Combs that apparently contributed to Combs's decision, approved by the College's governing board, to carry out an administrative reorganization that eliminated the position of dean of instruction and distributed the duties of that position among other personnel.

The abrupt removal of Alstetter's position—tantamount to his firing—produced considerable controversy both at the College and in the community. Within the faculty, partisan factions emerged, with some supporting Combs and others Alstetter. In the community, where both Alstetter and his wife had developed extensive ties through their civic and church affiliations, outrage was expressed over Alstetter's dismissal, with letters in the local paper calling for an explanation of the whole affair. Such explanation was not forthcoming, and Combs's motive, if there was an ulterior one beyond his stated claim that the reorganization was necessary to improve administrative efficiency, was never made public.

Whatever the case, the departure of Alstetter brought to Fredericksburg State Teachers College a young Richmonder, then an instructor in education at the University of Virginia, by the name of Edward Alvey. Appointed at the

Edward Alvey Jr.

rank of professor of education, Alvey was also named director of teacher training, a position that under the new administrative organization made him in effect the College's chief academic officer. Two years later, reflecting the actual scope of his responsibilities, Alvey's title was changed to dean of the college.

Thus began a career of unparalleled commitment to the institution. For thirty-three years, he served as dean, skillfully guiding the academic program as the College's curriculum evolved from a focus on teacher preparation to an emphasis on the liberal arts and sciences. Throughout that period Alvey was also usually a central figure in fundamental decisions affecting the direction of the College, relied on by President Combs and his successor, Grellet C. Simpson, as a constant repository of advice and sound judgment.

In addition to Alvey, the more influential new hires in the 1930s included Edgar E. Woodward as treasurer, Hobart C. Carter in mathematics, Almont Lindsey in history, E. Boyd Graves in education, and Ronald W. Faulkner in music and art. Though the extent and importance of Woodward's service as the chief fiscal steward of the institution in the three decades following his arrival in 1937 should not be minimized, no one played a larger role than Faulkner in shaping the College's public identity.

Faulkner's primary charge was to develop an academic program in instrumental music, which he did, but he went far beyond that to also create a concert orchestra, a dance orchestra, and a marching band. While the concerts were extremely successful, with the annual Christmas performances always drawing capacity crowds, it was the marching band that proved to be his most spectacular accomplishment.

In the days before high schools and colleges routinely had marching bands, the ensemble Faulkner created was a distinct novelty: an all-girl unit

All-Girl Marching Band, circa 1957

complete with majorettes and color guards. The band garnered attention not only for its musicianship but also for its colorful appearance: attired in white boots, blue jackets, and short—some prudes said too short—skirts, the young women created a sensation from their first performance.

The unit was much in demand for participation in parades in Richmond and Washington, as well as in Fredericksburg. The band often held the featured position in events such as the Apple Blossom Festival in Winchester and the Tobacco Festival in Richmond and was frequently invited to perform at halftime at college football games throughout the region, winning numerous prizes and awards in the process. Before the band's demise in the late 1950s—during a time before the institution had acquired substantial academic standing—there was a period when the predominant image of the College in the public mind was that of its all-girl marching band. Future generations of students might find that fact unimaginable, perhaps even somewhat unseemly, in light of the College's enhanced reputation for academic excellence. But thus it was.

Student behavior in the 1930s was on the whole decorous, chilled no doubt by the stern visage of Mrs. Bushnell looming ominously in the minds of potential culprits. There was on at least one occasion, however, a semblance of student protest.

The event that ignited the commotion was the announcement of new regulations developed by Joint Council (a body comprising three faculty and four students) governing visits to town. Existing rules were by no means lax, but the revisions further limited the areas within which students could travel and forbade them to ride with townspeople altogether. The new rules seemed to many students to be both unduly restrictive and unfairly promulgated.

Responses, including a threatened strike, were sufficiently disruptive to cause President Combs himself to intercede to quell several outbursts and to make an hour-long address to the student body. For their role in "leading the agitation against College authority," several students were campused, others were placed on probation, and one—the president of the highfalutin German Club, no less—was expelled. The turmoil dissipated within a few days, both sides admitting to rashness.

With tranquility restored to the campus, students generally occupied themselves with quotidian matters, seemingly unaffected and unconcerned with affairs beyond the campus, despite the ongoing economic depression and the pathbreaking federal programs designed to combat it. The students seemed to be mildly supportive of the New Deal, as Roosevelt won straw polls in 1936 and 1940, though with lesser percentages of the student vote than he received in the actual elections. But aside from periodic attention to national politics, it was for the most part "business as usual" at the College.

That routine, aside from purely academic tasks, included mandatory gatherings of the entire student body thrice weekly: for chapel on Tuesdays and Fridays between 12:30 and 1:00 p.m. and for convocation on Wednesday evenings from 7:00 to 8:00. Convocation was a more formal event to which seniors normally wore caps and gowns and marched in to occupy the front rows of the auditorium. Programs varied in content throughout the semester and included speeches by prominent figures, concerts, and drama presentations, always concluding with the singing of the alma mater.

Required attendance at these events may have been resented by some, but according to Dean Alvey, the overall response was "usually enthusiastic," though "there were times when inconsiderate speakers tried the fortitude of even the most patient." Whatever the students' attitude may have been, these mandatory meetings of the student body, from their inception in 1930 till their discontinuance in 1956, engendered a sense of unity that diminished in subsequent years as such gatherings became increasingly rare, finally disappearing by the 1980s.

Camaraderie was also boosted by various programs of weekend entertainment that, while not mandatory, were generally well attended because students were usually on campus. In fact, through the 1930s there were severe restrictions on the number of weekend absences students could have. In the 1920s, for example, only one cut per quarter, known as a "dance cut," was permitted; to receive approval for even that one absence, the student had to show Dean Bushnell the actual invitation. Even if there had been no administrative regulations, logistics would have meant minimal absences. In that environment, students appreciated the sundry diversions, often in the form of class or club "benefits" regularly held on Saturday evenings in the Monroe auditorium. For a number of years, beauty contests, too, enjoyed considerable popularity.

The early decades also witnessed the development of several traditions relating to the Christmas season—not surprising in light of the predominantly Christian backgrounds of the students. As the holidays approached, wrote Dean Alvey,

> excitement mounted, especially among students who had not seen home or family since early September. Room doors were elaborately decorated in each dormitory. Furthermore, scenes of the nativity, of Christmas in other lands, of carol singers serenading, and other imaginative representations were set up in the parlors of each residence hall. Competition was keen. A jury of faculty members evaluated each exhibition and awarded a prize for the best one. There were Christmas carols, programs of Christmas music, and a general breathlessness of excitement and anticipation as the days before the holiday grew fewer.

For a number of years, one popular element of the pre-holiday festivities was the doll show, sponsored by the YWCA. Freshmen were organized by upperclassmen to produce scenes typical of the Christmas season, including dolls in appropriate costumes. After prizes had been awarded for the best costumes, the dolls were given either to needy children in the area or to those institutionalized elsewhere in the state.

Another tradition was the annual "Peanut Week," held just before the Christmas holidays. Each student's name was inserted in a peanut shell and placed in a pile from which every student selected a peanut. The drawer of the name then gave her anonymous "peanut pal" a small gift each day for a week. Finally, at the annual Christmas dinner, a more substantial present was given, which also revealed the name of the secret donor. Until the student body became too large, these gifts were piled beneath the dining hall Christmas tree until they were distributed.

One of the most beloved spring traditions of this period (aside, of course, from the ever-popular May Day) was the "Daisy Chain" that became an integral part of commencement activities each year. The chain consisted of thousands of bunches of daisies, which, having been picked by the freshmen from abundant fields near the College, were tied around a manila rope so as to fashion a solid garland. This beautiful if burdensome chain was carried into the amphitheater on the shoulders of the two-year diploma graduates for Class Day ceremonies and subsequently transported to Virginia Hall to festoon the portico for the remainder of the graduation festivities. The colorful ritual came to an end in 1942 when the College ceased to award two-year diplomas.

Throughout the 1930s, an era when "big band" music predominated, formal dances sponsored by the German Club were the central feature of the student social calendar. Because the club had a limited membership that did not permit all students to participate in these galas, a movement developed to create another dance club. The result was the establishment in 1938 of the Cotillion Club, whose membership, like that of the German Club, was limited, selective, and chosen by secret ballots; its function, too, was similar—the sponsorship of seasonal formals each year.

Predictably, the two exclusive clubs became strong rivals, generating much debate among students as to which was superior and causing consternation among those receiving coveted bids to both as to which one to join. The two organizations dominated campus social life until the mid-1940s, when the College itself began to sponsor dances open to all students.

While the dance clubs swayed, several important developments occurred in the 1930s concerning the institution's metamorphosis into a liberal arts college.

For many years there had been some persons, especially women, who had urged that the commonwealth establish a liberal arts college for women commensurate with the facilities available to men at the University of Virginia. Tangible movement in that direction came in 1928 when the General Assembly established a commission to study the matter. The nine-person group consisted of two members of the State Senate, three members of the House of Delegates, and four Virginia citizens appointed by the governor; it was chaired by Judge Don P. Halsey of Lynchburg. The specific charge to the commission was to examine and report to the legislature on "the advisability of establishing a liberal arts college for undergraduate women at one of the state teachers colleges, or elsewhere."

If approved, the key question, of course, was where—a subject that produced spirited responses from those who made presentations before the commission. The position taken by the women speakers, led by Mrs. Beverly B. Munford, herself a member of the Board of Visitors of the University of Virginia, was that the only way to ensure the equality of such a school was to locate it in Charlottesville.

That idea was adamantly opposed by the rector of the University of Virginia's Board of Visitors, C. Harding Walker, by its president, Edwin A. Alderman, and by its alumni association—all of whom made it emphatically clear that they wanted no part of such a school in, or even near, the hallowed Jeffersonian grounds of the Charlottesville institution. Alderman, among others, did support the creation of a liberal arts college for women but urged that either a private women's school (naming Hollins or Sweetbriar as possibilities) or one of the existing teachers colleges (citing the ones at Harrisonburg or Fredericksburg in particular) be converted for that purpose. Such a college would be under the control of the University of Virginia and equivalent to it in requirements and standards.

There was no shortage of suitors for the proposed school, as envoys from each of the leading sites (Roanoke, Lynchburg, Harrisonburg, and Fredericksburg) made their pitch for their locales before the Halsey Commission. Fredericksburg sent a large and distinguished delegation headed by Mayor Jere M. H. Willis and including Judge Alvin T. Embrey and College president Morgan Combs, as well as former state senator C. O'Conor Goolrick.

It was Embrey who suggested that the proposed new women's college be named Mary Washington College, asserting that it would provide cachet somewhat in the manner of Thomas Jefferson's attachment to the University of Virginia—a bit of a stretch, inasmuch as Mary Washington, however an admirable figure she may have been, had obviously not (unlike Jefferson) had anything to do with the creation of the associated institution. Undeterred by such a consideration, Embrey declared that "the establishment of this University for Women at Fredericksburg under the name of Mary Washington College, in part as a memorial to the noble woman who lived and is buried in Fredericksburg would endow the institution with a charm and appeal to all womankind that could be secured in no other way."

When the Halsey commission delivered its report to the 1930 session of the General Assembly, it opposed having the college in Charlottesville, recommending instead that it be located either in Roanoke, Lynchburg, Harrisonburg, or Fredericksburg, though it did not specify which one. The deadlock unbroken, the legislative session adjourned, but not before extending the charge of the commission for another biennium. In the interim, Fredericksburg partisans lobbied assiduously for their site, including the publication of a twelve-page brochure titled "The Liberal Arts College for Women at Fredericksburg, Virginia," which extolled the many advantages of converting the State Teachers College into the proposed women's college.

Fredericksburg's efforts appeared to have paid off, as the Halsey commission did indeed finally recommend that the new (or at least newly converted) college be located there, a decision that was hailed with enthusiasm and gratification both in the city and at the College. The rejoicing, alas, proved premature.

The plan was given initial impetus when the University of Virginia's Board of Visitors formally endorsed it, as did the University of Virginia alumni association. However, as the proposal began to wend through the legislative process at the 1932 General Assembly, it attracted opposition, notably from women's organizations that continued to advocate the University of Virginia as the only viable location for the women's branch.

Eventually, having survived committee votes by narrow margins in both the House of Delegates and the Senate, the bill passed by substantial margins in the votes of the whole House (72–21) and Senate (30–9). It was all to no avail, though, as Governor John Garland Pollard vetoed the measure.

Pollard's veto was likely due not to personal opposition or the opposition of women's groups but rather to the condition of the economy. With the Depression having depleted the commonwealth's coffers to an alarming extent, he vetoed the bill, he said, because he did not believe it prudent to commit the funds (estimated to be about $250,000) that would be required to effect the conversion—funds, he asserted, that were more desperately needed by the elementary and secondary public schools. With that, the initial movement to transform Fredericksburg State Teachers College into a liberal arts institution ended. It proved to be merely a postponement.

During the first two decades of its existence, Fredericksburg State Teachers College had been primarily concerned, as its name indicated, with training teachers, and its curriculum had been heavily methodological, as opposed to academic, in content; graduates of the four-year program received the bachelor of science degree in education, along with the collegiate professional certificate. By the mid-1930s, a change was evident as more and more liberal arts courses were added. The College thus sought and received authorization from the State Board of Education in 1935 to offer, in addition, a bachelor of arts degree.

The new degree option placed primacy on academic courses, most of which were prescribed. They included, for example, eighteen hours per academic quarter in English, eighteen in history, eighteen in science, and twenty-seven in foreign language—eight of them in Latin or Greek—as well as nine each in social science, physical education and hygiene, mathematics, and philosophy or psychology. In addition to satisfying these general education requirements, students had to complete thirty-six quarter hours in a major field and twenty-seven in each of two minor fields. Majors and minors tended at this time to be in broad academic areas, such as science or social science; only later did more narrow specializations such as biology, chemistry, and physics appear.

Once the College had gone beyond granting only education degrees and had begun to confer B.A. degrees in academic subjects, a feeling quickly and quite reasonably developed that the institution's name should reflect the change—that is, that the "teachers college" designation was too narrow and, in fact, somewhat misleading, since the preparation of teachers was no longer its sole or even primary purpose. According to the catalog for 1938–39:

> The purpose of the college is to provide for the young women of today the opportunity for broad and liberal culture and for training in certain specialized fields of professional, vocational, and technical work, including teaching, business, home economics and dietetics, music, fine and industrial arts, and related fields, thus enabling the student to prepare herself thoroughly and harmoniously for her modern dual capacity of wage earner and home maker. The aim at all times shall be to effect a wise compromise between the demands of a modern, practical, and complex society on the one hand, and the claims of an exclusive and traditional culture on the other.

Immediately Mary Washington College became the foremost choice for the institution's new name, favored by all the College's constituent groups including, chiefly, the students, whose views were expressed in a front-page *Bullet* article titled "Mary Washington College—Reasons Why We Want Our Name Changed." Among those reasons were, first, "to honor Mary Washington, the mother of George, whose life was so closely identified with Fredericksburg where her home and tomb are located"; second, to be more indicative of the College's expanded mission beyond teacher preparation; third, to encourage donations from private sources; and fourth, to avoid confusion with the state's three other teachers colleges.

Such arguments proved persuasive when the 1938 General Assembly considered the matter. Early in that session, the state senator who represented the Fredericksburg area, S. Bernard Coleman, introduced a bill to change the institution's name to Mary Washington College. The primary objection voiced during subsequent committee hearings was that such action would give the Fredericksburg school an unfair advantage over the other teachers colleges. This seems to have been of particular concern to officials at STC-Harrisonburg, who successfully argued that the bill be amended to change the name of that school to Madison College. In its final version, the measure also permitted the teachers colleges at Farmville and Radford to change their names if they wished to. Thus amended, the bill was signed into law by Governor James H. Price on March 9, 1938.

According to Edward Alvey, "The new name met with ready and enthusiastic reception at the college, in the community, and among the alumnae." Such uniformity of support would appear ironic in light of controversies that arose a half century later concerning the appropriateness of the "Mary Washington" designation.

Though almost nothing is known about the historical Mary Washington, it is true that as George's mother she had close ties to Fredericksburg; it is also true that her name conveyed an unmistakable feminine image—qualities that in 1938 made her a quite reasonable choice for the name of a women's college in Fredericksburg. With the advent of coeducation in the 1970s, however, some would claim that the name was an impediment to student recruitment and should again be changed.

But for the nonce, controversy over the name lay in an unforeseen future, and in the spring of 1938 reaction to the new name was joyous. Plans were quickly made to have the diplomas for that year bear the new name, and President Combs proudly announced that the commencement ceremony would celebrate not only the institution's thirtieth anniversary but also the inauguration of a new name—Mary Washington College—the name under which in the years ahead the school would achieve increasing acclaim for excellence in the liberal arts and sciences.

Mary Washington College

With its new name proudly emblazoned on admissions materials for the first time, Mary Washington College attracted a record enrollment for the 1938–39 session. The 1,160 full-time students represented an increase of nearly 200 from the previous year.

Though the rise in enrollment indicated an increase in the College's prestige and attractiveness, it also created a housing problem on campus, as students far outnumbered the available dormitory spaces. The solution, for the time being, was to rescind the requirement that all students (save commuters) must live on campus, and instead permit them—even entering freshmen—to find accommodations in the city, mainly in approved homes along College Avenue or on the streets just below the gates on Sunken Road. During the peak period of this practice, which lasted until 1954, between 250 and 300 students lived off campus each year.

The arrangement had some positive aspects, among them the lasting friendships that were often forged between the landlords and the girls who lived in their homes. Overall, however, the liabilities outweighed the advantages. Major problems arose over the enforcement of regulations such as study hours and weekend permissions; facilities were sometimes too small, too noisy, or otherwise not conducive to studying; students occasionally abused their quarters; and perhaps worst of all, off-campus students felt left out of College activities—as, in fact, they were.

The College acted in two ways to address the problem of overcrowding. One was to lease additional residential space, including Cornell Hall, located several blocks below Sunken Road. Designed originally as an apartment building, Cornell was rearranged into suites for student occupancy and served as a dormitory from 1940 to 1959.

A more permanent solution involved building additional residential space on campus. In October 1938, with the aid of a PWA loan and grant, a contract was awarded for the construction of a new facility that would accommodate 116 students. Designed by the architect J. Binford Walford, the imposing three-story brick structure with its facade of stately columns was consistent with the existing campus architecture and further enhanced the beauty of the expanding built environment. Named Westmoreland Hall, it was first available for occupancy during the 1939–40 session.

The increasing enrollment created a need not only for more dormitory rooms but also for additional classroom and administrative space, as well as for a larger auditorium. Fortunately the PWA once again provided funds to help address these needs, and in late 1938 construction began on what was to be George Washington Hall. Upon its completion a year later, at a cost of approximately $350,000 (a sizable sum at the time), "GW" quickly became the focal and functional heart of the campus.

In appearance the new structure was commanding: each of the massive pillars constituting the portico was of Indiana marble and weighed 270 tons. On the first floor were administrative offices on each wing and a handsome auditorium in the middle with a seating capacity of 1,624 and a spacious stage across the front. Beneath were dressing rooms for stage productions and—one of the building's most distinctive features—a recreation room/ballroom that was mirrored on all four sides. Known as the Hall of Mirrors, it served for many years as the scene of gala affairs following the inaugural dance sponsored by the Cotillion Club in January 1940. (The last formal dance in the Monroe gymnasium, prior venue for such events, had taken place the previous December, sponsored by the German Club.)

The second floor housed mainly offices, and the third contained five large classrooms in addition to more offices and a broadcasting studio. Above the third floor was another of the structure's most notable features: a roof garden that covered the entire front part of the building. This, too, proved a popular venue for formal dances during the warm-weather months.

The grand edifice officially opened on January 11, 1940, with a concert by the National Symphony Orchestra. The performance was preceded by a formal dinner in Seacobeck for various dignitaries as well as the entire student body. It was, as the *Bullet* described it, "a really stupendous happening."

In April of that year, cornerstone-laying ceremonies took place, with C. O'Conor Goolrick introducing the principal speaker, Governor Price. While the stone was being placed, President Combs was asked to inspect it. As he peered around all sides, Governor Price quipped that he wondered if the president was looking for another appropriation. In light of the remarkable funding for construction that Combs had secured during the first decade of his tenure, the observation was apt.

As the College's physical plant expanded, so too did its academic program. It was a bit ironic that even as the emphasis on liberal arts increased, a major factor in the growth of the College was its Commerce Department. Under the leadership of Eileen Dodd, the department had gained a national reputation for its high standard of instruction and the quality of its equipment. By 1940 nearly half of the student body was enrolled in courses such as typewriting, shorthand, bookkeeping, and office practice. The College even sponsored annual statewide contests for high school commercial students, bringing them to campus to compete in various business subjects; many returned as students in the Commerce Department.

Simultaneously, the academic area was strengthened by the hiring of several new faculty who over the years would grace the College with their vibrant personalities, as well as enhance it with their erudition and intellect. Among the most prominent of this group were Emil Schnellock in art and Levin Houston III in music. Schnellock was reared in Brooklyn, where he was a childhood (and lifelong) friend of the playwright Arthur Miller. After years as a commercial artist—Campbell's Soup was one notable client—Schnellock came to Mary Washington in 1938 to teach art. His most lasting contribution to the College, however, was not in the classroom but in the murals he painted in Monroe and George Washington Halls. In 1960 the Emil Schnellock Award was established to recognize annually the College's outstanding student in painting.

The multitalented Levin Houston joined the faculty in 1939 and from then until his retirement in the 1970s was one of the College's and the town's most active and creative members. Though his primary role was as an instructor in music (piano, mainly), he was also acclaimed as a composer, performer, artist, and writer. He was especially active in College drama productions, playing leading roles for over twenty years.

As the 1930s neared an end, it was evident that Mary Washington College was prospering and that its future seemed bright. Yet at the same time—though the tranquility on the Hill made it easy to ignore such things—forces were at work in the larger world that would eventually affect the course of life at the College.

As the threat of war loomed increasingly in both Europe and Asia during the 1930s, most Mary Washington students tended to ignore it, their interests focused on more immediate matters, especially social and romantic ones. Representative of such concerns was a *Bullet* column titled "Headache Advisor," which fell essentially within the "advice to the lovelorn" genre. "I'm a junior and very much in love with a boy back home," read one letter. "He wants me to leave and marry him, but my parents have made sacrifices to keep me in school and I feel that perhaps I should finish as they wish, particularly as he hasn't got a job. Please help me. [Signed] Tormented."

The "Headache Advisor's" advice: "Stay in school at all costs. A young man with no visible means of support who asks a girl to leave school and marry him is NOT the answer to a Maiden's Prayer. If you MUST marry him, wait until you've graduated. You will need all your schooling to support him."[13]

Interest in parochial and personal matters, however, did not preclude a larger view, and in fact there was evidence in the 1930s that students were becoming less insular in their concerns. One indication was the prominence of the International Relations Club, which worked to promote international awareness through activities such as holding discussion groups and bringing lecturers to the College to speak about contemporary issues in foreign relations.

At the same time, though, the prevailing spirit on campus—like that throughout the United States—tended toward isolationism. The International Relations Club itself was instrumental in forming a Peace Council, comprising representatives from each club on campus, for the purpose of bringing "the ideals of peace to the attention of all the students." As the outbreak of war appeared more imminent, peace advocates stepped up their activities. The club sponsored a play with a pacifistic theme depicting the horrors of war and suggesting what students could do "to make peace supreme."

On December 5, 1941, the *Bullet* carried an editorial headlined "Are You An Isolationist?" Asserting that the term "isolationist" had an applicability beyond the basic issue of foreign intervention, the editorial criticized what it viewed as the complacency of current Mary Washington students. "We are isolationists," it said, "well-fed, well-housed, well-clothed, we seldom hoist ourselves from our own little puddle to take a keen, searching glance at conditions . . . outside our own community. Beyond a cursory glance at the morning paper on our way to the 8:30 [a.m. class], and perhaps at the evening paper, we wrap ourselves in the warm, snug blanket of our own well-being and continue to occupy ourselves with our own affairs."

Two days later, on Sunday, December 7, that attitude changed dramatically as the result of the Japanese attack on Pearl Harbor. On Monday, the student body, along with many faculty members, gathered in GW auditorium to listen to the radio as President Franklin D. Roosevelt delivered his "day of infamy" speech in which he officially announced the existence of a state of war with Japan. Thereafter, Mary Washington president Morgan Combs sent a telegram to Roosevelt on behalf of the College, declaring the institution's full support. "The faculty and student body of Mary Washington College," he wrote, "are deeply conscious of the great responsibility recent events have placed upon you. Along with millions of other loyal Americans, we desire to express our full accord with you and our complete faith in your leadership.

We wish also to offer you any service which this institution or any individual therein can render to you or to our country in this time of crisis, and we ask God's blessing upon you."[14]

The editorial in that week's issue of the *Bullet* expressed a far different attitude from the previous one. "Within an hour of Japan's bombing of U.S. possessions," it said, "Mary Washington girls were shocked from an everyday academic apathy into one of the most historic and momentous periods of their lives. . . . Japan's declaration of war woke up a lot of college students. . . . The foremost question in the minds of students is: 'Where do we come in? What part should we play?'"

President Combs addressed those very questions during the ensuing weeks, emphasizing the need to maintain high morale. "Don't be discontented because you cannot take up a rifle," he said. "Your place is just as important. . . . I don't want to see long and gloomy faces." To those who were considering leaving the school, he admonished that "the wisest thing a Mary Washington student can do is to stay in college and finish her course as soon as possible."[15]

Within that framework, students found many ways to support the war effort. One was participation in a national "student day of prayer," the announcement of which declared that "more than at any other time in our lives, we need such a day." On a more practical level, students engaged in a book drive for soldiers, wherein books were collected at Trinkle Library and forwarded to campaign headquarters in New York. "This is no laughing matter!" exhorted a *Bullet* editorial.

> We at Mary Washington are in an outstanding position to give all we can in this matter. In fact we must. For the duration we will be expected to sacrifice, to give, to cooperate to the nth degree. . . . Keeping the boys in service in good spirits is up to us here in civilian life. We must do our utmost to make their job our job. . . . Here is our chance! Right now! These boys do have recreation periods, scattered as they may be. During these recreation periods . . . it is only natural for them to want to relax. Usually they are out from towns or else they feel too tired to indulge in any type of physical recreation. . . . Thousands of books are needed to satisfy the wishes of these boys.[16]

Among the most enduring of Mary Washington's war efforts was the program to promote the sale of war savings stamps and bonds. As early as January 1942, the Student Government Association established a "victory booth" on the terrace of the swimming pool roof garden where students could purchase stamps at any time of day. As one of the first drives of its kind in the country, the program attracted wide publicity. One photograph of the booth, showing students lined up to purchase stamps, was distributed by the Associated Press and carried by newspapers across the nation. Later, similar photographs were featured on the front pages, along with laudatory articles in the *Virginia Journal of Education* and in a U.S. Treasury Department publication, "Colleges at War." The Treasury pamphlet praised the exceptional commitment of the Mary Washington students, noting that over 90 percent bought war stamps each week. Before the war ended, the program had generated thousands of dollars, earning the College the right to fly a special "schools-at-war" flag as a symbol of its patriotic contributions.

Faculty as well as students were heavily involved in the war. Like the students, they contributed financial support; at one point 100 percent of faculty and staff were enrolled in a systematic purchase of war bonds. Beyond that, many participated more directly by taking leaves of absence to enlist in the military. At least fifteen male and five female faculty did so, with several of the women becoming officers. The 1942 yearbook was dedicated to "Members of Our Faculty Who Have Entered the Service of Our Country."

The war affected life on campus in myriad ways. In 1942, for example, the Thanksgiving and Easter holidays were abolished, as they were at many schools, in accordance with President Roosevelt's request. The cancellation was probably moot for most students anyway, given the transportation difficulties of the time: gasoline was strictly rationed, and trains were crowded with the movement of troops.

On campus there was a pervasive fear of air raids, particularly during the early months of the war following the Pearl Harbor attack. In January 1942 the College established a twenty-four-hour plane-spotting station, operated by students working in pairs in two-hour duty shifts. The spotters were instructed to report all types of planes seen or heard. A huge air-raid alarm was installed that could be heard throughout the city in the event of an actual attack, and first-aid organizations were set up in every dormitory. There were practice alerts, both announced and surprise, when blackout regulations were rigidly enforced, with watchers stationed on the roof of George Washington Hall to search for any violative ray of light anywhere on campus. Such was the social atmosphere at the time—an amalgam of patriotism and fear, most likely—that there seems to have been minimal violation of the restrictive regulations, nor much resentment of them.

As it turned out, wartime exigencies led to the development of a campus entity that would quickly become one of the College's most visible—and to the public as well as the student body, one of its most popular—elements: the MWC Cavalry. The genesis of the idea came early in the war when President Combs called on each student organization to indicate to him how it might contribute to the national defense. At the suggestion of its adviser, Russell Walther, who had come to the College in 1940 to teach riding, the Hoof Prints Club decided to organize a cavalry troop among equestrian students. The premise was that a mounted troop could render important civil defense work in the event of an air raid or other emergency. Crisply attired in khaki uniforms, members of the cavalry were trained by Walther and volunteers of the local Virginia Protective Force not only in handling horses among crowds or in noisy and distracting situations but also in many phases of general police work.

(Above) Cavalry, unmounted, march past Trinkle Hall.

(Left) Cavalry member Nancy Mosher Weir '53 and "Sharp."

In the end, the unit was not called on for actual defense work, but during the war and thereafter it did provide useful crowd-control service from time to time on campus and in the city. Also among its peacetime duties was the raising and lowering of the campus flags each day. The outfit proved to be a constant source of interest to photographers and newspaper reporters, and pictures and articles about the cavalry appeared widely during the decade and a half of its existence. Interest in the cavalry declined by the mid-1950s, especially after Walther's departure in 1956, and the troop disbanded two years later.

The MWC Cavalry was not the only campus group to be spawned in response to the war. There was, for example, the Victory Chorus, founded in September 1942. For the next two years, this enthusiastic chorus of thirty young women presented a weekly radio program; gave numerous performances for College organizations, civic clubs, and local churches; and contributed their talents to many bond rallies and USO programs. Unlike the cavalry, the Victory Chorus did not outlive the war, disbanding at the end of the 1944 session.

Whether through buying war stamps, manning air-raid stations, giving blood (as scores of students did throughout the war), riding in the cavalry, or singing in the Victory Chorus, Mary Washington students devoted both their time and their talents to the war effort. In this they were encouraged not only by President Combs but by Dean Alvey, who organized many of their supportive activities, and perhaps most of all by Dean Bushnell.

In Mrs. Bushnell's constellation of values, patriotism seemed to rank only slightly below protocol—perhaps as a result of her experience in France during the Great War—and her devotion to country was particularly evident during World War II. At a time when television was nonexistent and radios were rare on campus, she delivered wartime news of the day before the evening meal, sometimes incorporating a prayer for "our boys" in her blessing. "She kept us aware of the sacrifices our fathers, brothers, and friends were making for us," recalled one 1946 graduate, "encouraging us to be supportive and hopeful."

Whatever their motivation, the young women of MWC displayed steady support for the war effort. Even in an era of pandemic patriotism, their dedication was exceptional. Few colleges—be they male, female, or coeducational—exceeded Mary Washington in commitment to the cause of victory.

Amid the wartime activities, the College was further disrupted by one of the most dramatic natural disasters ever to afflict the Fredericksburg area: the Great Flood of 1942. In mid-October, three days of rain in the city and the counties to the north and west had caused the Rappahannock River to rise significantly; then, on October 15, a cloudburst dropped an additional six inches within two hours. That deluge caused the usually placid river to rise an astounding forty-five feet above its normal level.

The results were catastrophic. The entire downtown portion of Caroline Street was flooded, inundating stores and necessitating the use of boats to rescue residents. The swirling waters even reached as far as Kenmore Avenue, a mere three blocks below the campus.

One of the first casualties was the city's electric plant, leaving the city and the College without power. Fires broke out in the huge petroleum storage tanks along the river, and the flooded roads made it impossible for firefighting equipment to reach them. The enormous force of the water caused spans of the U.S. Route 1 bridge at Falmouth to drop, and the city's other main bridge (leading to the Northern Neck) was so battered by the huge tree trunks swept along by the torrent that it too had to be closed. Even the railroad bridge was blocked temporarily as officials of the Richmond, Fredericksburg & Potomac railroad stationed loaded coal cars across the span to provide greater stability against the rushing waters. As a result, access to the city from the north was cut off.

The disaster directly endangered the Mary Washington students living in Cornell Hall, then a freshman dorm, located on Kenmore Avenue. Floodwaters rose completely above the basement rooms and lapped at the doors of first-floor rooms, wreaking untold damage on furniture and personal belongings. The residents were removed by the Fredericksburg rescue squad in boats and transported by ambulance to the Hill, where dormitory dwellers made room for the refugees.

There they found conditions that were drier, certainly, but still difficult. In the absence of electricity and water, food preparation was obviously a challenge. The greatest threat arose from the contamination of the city's water supply, necessitating the inoculation of all students for typhoid and the boiling of all drinking water.

Despite the hardships, the students proved not only resilient but resourceful. For example, when the *Bullet* could not be printed as it customarily was on downtown presses, its staff continued publication in mimeographed form, keeping students apprised of conditions both on and off campus. It also endeavored to put the situation in perspective, pointing out in its October 16 edition: "We on the hill are most fortunate with just no lights or running water facilities. There are those who have no beds, food, or clothing. There are also many in other parts of the world with even less than that, accompanied by the roar of guns."

Heeding that sentiment, many students volunteered their services in the community. Most visible was the work of the MWC Cavalry, which responded to an urgent request from Fredericksburg mayor W. Marshall King for help in patrolling the ravaged city. For several days, until adequate help arrived in the form of state police and military personnel, the cavalry rendered effective around-the-clock aid in directing traffic and protecting against looters. In addition, some two hundred students, organized and directed by Mrs. Bushnell, served in canteens set up throughout the city to feed and care for the homeless; still others assisted with administering typhoid shots.

Within a few weeks, life returned to more or less normal on campus, but the flood of '42 remained an indelible memory for those who witnessed it. Even against the backdrop of world war, for many students the flood was the most memorable event of their college years, as it touched them more personally and more tangibly than did reports from the far-off theaters of military engagement.

The mid-1940s were a time of momentous change at Mary Washington. Even in the social arena, where Mrs. Bushnell continued to exercise her velvet-gloved control, there were some changes. The College had long prohibited sororities, believing that exclusive social organizations weakened the harmonious spirit that it wished to encourage on campus. Yet over the years the German and Cotillion Clubs had become in operation ersatz sororities, fostering cliquishness through their practice of limited membership, sponsored nominations, and secret elections. Moreover, because the clubs sponsored the formal dances, nonmembers were often precluded from participating. To address this discriminatory situation, the student body itself, at the suggestion of the administration, voted to abolish the clubs and replace them with a College-sponsored series of dances that were open to all students. The plan was first implemented in 1948 and continued to the satisfaction of all parties.

Also in the 1940s, a new social tradition developed in the form of an annual Spanish fiesta held in the spring. The origin of the event was twofold. One element was the hiring of Louis J. Cabrera, a native of Puerto Rico, as a Spanish professor in 1943. About the same time, an appreciable number of Latin American students, often from the families of envoys to Washington, began to enroll at Mary Washington College, many of them attracted through Cabrera's contacts.

As adviser to the Spanish Club, Cabrera encouraged and directed the club in its sponsorship of the fiestas. Though the programs varied each year, they usually featured Spanish songs, dances, and plays, as well as, according to Edward Alvey, "a pseudo-bullfight, with a snorting bull propelled by two anonymous but energetic students in a highly imaginative replica of *el toro*." For a number of years, the spring fiesta enjoyed great popularity, providing an exotic cultural experience for a decidedly Waspish student body and serving as a precursor of the Multicultural Fair that was begun decades later.

Cabrera was but one of several professors who joined the faculty about the same time and who, like him, were to have substantial impact on the College. They included the English professor Reginald W. Whidden, who would eventually succeed Ed Alvey as dean of the faculty, and Hugo Iltis, a native of Czechoslovakia, who joined the faculty in 1940 as professor of biology. An expert on the work of the Austrian botanist Gregor Mendel, Iltis was largely

Cotillion Club officers surrounding the College seal in the Trinkle Hall rotunda, 1942

responsible for propagating Mendel's reputation as the father of modern genetics. Iltis assembled an unparalleled collection of Mendelian items in the College's world-recognized Mendel Museum, which he lovingly maintained until his sudden death in 1952.[17]

The museum was housed in the new E. Lee Trinkle Library, yet another of the many construction projects brought to fruition under President Combs's administration. From the time of the school's founding, the library had been located in Virginia Hall, where it remained through the 1930s, even as student enrollment burgeoned. Citing the hopeless inadequacy of the facility, Combs began in the late thirties to appeal for state appropriations for a new building and in 1939 invited Governor Price and his budget commission to the campus to view the situation themselves. At the suggestion of administrators, students dutifully packed the cramped Virginia library to the gunwales for the occasion. There, according to Dean Alvey's account, the visitors "saw students sitting on the floor among the rows of shelves, leaning against the walls and windowsills, and occupying every bit of available space at the tables, all reading intently." The ploy certainly demonstrated overcrowding but may have been a bit excessive; as Alvey recalled, "One visitor remarked, with a twinkle in his eye, that he had never seen so many students in a library in his four years of college."

More persuasive, most likely, was the influence exerted on Governor Price and the legislature by the popular former governor Trinkle, who, as a personal friend of President Combs and a consistent advocate of higher education, lobbied actively on behalf of the new facility. In any case, the 1940 General Assembly appropriated the requisite funds and construction began that fall. At a cost of $250,000, the building opened the following fall and was named E. Lee Trinkle Library, a fitting tribute to the enlightened politician whose support had been so crucial in making it possible. With a sizable addition in 1960, Trinkle remained the College library for half a century, until the expanding collection necessitated larger quarters in 1989.

Like the other campus buildings constructed in the period, the library was designed by J. Binford Walford of Richmond, and like them it was aesthetically impressive. The main entrance, graced by a handsome Grecian portico supported by massive columns, opened into a large rotunda surrounded by a railed balcony. Set in the center of the rotunda's terrazzo floor was a large bronze replica of the College seal. Rising above was a domed ceiling with a blue-glass circular window at the apex.

The capacious stacks provided space for 150,000 volumes; study carrels on each floor facilitated research by students and faculty; and two large reference rooms flanked the central rotunda where the circulation desk was situated. The second-floor reading rooms were especially impressive, furnished with an elegance—including solid walnut tables and custom-crafted Windsor chairs—that would have appeared extravagant in later years when increased costs (coupled perhaps with decreased tastes) dictated less-elaborate designs.

The browsing room was especially luxurious, replete with fireplace and wood paneling, illuminated by soft lights and reading lamps. Though it provided a hospitable environment for informal lectures by visiting luminaries such as William Faulkner, its cozy ambience may have been counterproductive for students, who frequently found the soothing atmosphere more conducive to snoozing than studying. Not without reason was it sometimes called the "drowsing room."

Pride in the beautiful new building was such that students and faculty immediately adopted the practice of scrupulously not stepping on the College seal on the rotunda floor. The forbearance began to decline in the 1960s and 1970s, a time when it, like so many other traditions, lost appeal to a newer generation of students (and faculty) who were less concerned with such historical niceties. By the end of the century, Trinkle had been converted to classrooms, and students routinely strode across the seal, blithely unaware of the totemic status it had held for earlier generations.

Mary Washington College of the University of Virginia

Of all the wartime developments at the College, by far the most significant was the administrative merger with the University of Virginia, an action that instantly vaulted the institution to unique prominence among women's colleges in the commonwealth.

The idea of establishing a state-supported liberal arts college for women was not new. In fact, had it not been for Governor Pollard's veto, Mary Washington College would have become just such a place in 1932. The concept survived, however, and Governor Colgate W. Darden Jr. resurrected it in 1943 with a proposal to consolidate Mary Washington with the University of Virginia as its college of arts and sciences for women.

To study the feasibility of that plan, as well as to examine certain other educational matters, Darden appointed a commission in the summer of 1943 with the charge of delivering recommendations for consideration by the General Assembly at its 1944 session. Known as the Commission on the Consolidation of Colleges, it was chaired by J. Sinclair Brown, former head of the State Board of Education, and included the ubiquitous C. O'Conor Goolrick of Fredericksburg. The governor incorporated the commission's findings in his recommendations to the General Assembly, and they were subsequently introduced as the McCue-Randolph Bill, after the delegates from Charlottesville who sponsored it. The bill had five main provisions:

1. That the college be known as Mary Washington College of the University of Virginia.
2. That supervision, management, and control pass from the State Board of Education to the Rector and Visitors of the University of Virginia and that "the college shall hereafter be affiliated with the University of Virginia as an integral part thereof."
3. That the board of visitors of the university be increased by the addition of four members.
4. That the president of the University of Virginia be the chancellor of Mary Washington College of the University of Virginia and its chief administrative officer, and that the title of the chief local administrative officer be that of president.
5. That Mary Washington be converted into a liberal arts college for women, "with the same standards of admission and graduation as obtained for male students in the College of Arts and Sciences . . . located at Charlottesville."

There was little opposition to the bill in the General Assembly. In the House only the delegates from Harrisonburg spoke against it, and the final vote was eighty-two to two; the Senate passed it unanimously. Governor Darden signed it on February 22, and it took effect ninety days thereafter, in mid-June 1944.

News of the bill's passage evoked enthusiastic responses both on the MWC campus and in the city of Fredericksburg. A special issue of the *Bullet* on February 28 hailed the event, glorying in the newfound relationship to the University. A full-page advertisement in that edition contained a congratulatory message signed by sixteen business firms in the Fredericksburg area.

Once the celebrating was over, the tedious task of implementation began, the plan for which was outlined in a University report concerning departmental structure and curricular revision. The document's recommendations—in effect, directives—specified that degree work no longer be offered in home economics, library science, or commerce courses such as stenography, typewriting, and office practice. Furthermore, the degree program in physical education should be abolished and the number of PE credits be limited. Finally, the Department of Education should be eliminated, and teacher-training courses were to be discontinued.

In addressing faculty concerns, the report urged hiring an additional nineteen instructors and raising salaries, which were described as "far too low." Although it found class size to be satisfactory, the report criticized the fifteen- to sixteen-hour teaching load, deeming it "heavy, particularly in the absence of student assistance."

The report's harshest criticism was directed at the minimal role being played by the faculty in conducting the affairs of the College, noting that "the faculty as a body seems to have practically no functions at all, other than ceremonial. . . . [It] is hardly a faculty in any democratic sense, but only a group of teachers of classes. It can hardly have any real corporate morale." It went on to recommend that the faculty be a legislative body with final authority, subject to approval by the Board of Visitors, on all matters pertaining to academic regulations. (This recommendation was to be the genesis of a vastly expanded role of the faculty in determining academic policy in the years ahead.)

The primary upshot of the report was the creation of a new set of degree requirements that became effective for entering freshmen in the fall of 1945. Both bachelor of arts and bachelor of science degrees were established, the only difference between the two being that the B.S. degree (available for biology and chemistry majors) required that a modern, rather than ancient, foreign language be taken and that math be taken instead of fine arts. Among the most significant developments was the establishment of a more substantial major requirement in lieu of the old practice of requiring one major and two minors.

The curriculum modification soon proved to have at least one downside, as the elimination of the technical courses in education made it impossible for graduates who wanted to teach to qualify for anything other than a temporary certificate. To address this situation, College officials urgently petitioned the University Board of Visitors to authorize the inclusion of sufficient education courses to permit the earning of a regular teaching certificate. The board acquiesced, with the result that prospective teachers could be fully certified to teach while simultaneously majoring in an academic subject. This policy, though reached in somewhat desultory fashion, proved not only workable and popular but, in the opinion of many, superior to the pedagogical preparation provided by more traditional teacher-education programs elsewhere. The practice continued at Mary Washington and was eventually copied by other schools.

In other curricular adjustments, the discontinued PE and home economics majors were restored within a few years. So despite a few understandable glitches along the way, the overall conversion proceeded apace, and by midcentury Mary Washington College of the University of Virginia was well on its way toward establishing a reputation for excellence as the sister of its Charlottesville male sibling.

The post–World War II era at Mary Washington was marked by a resumption of the war-interrupted expansion of physical facilities that had characterized the Combs presidency. The process included not only new construction but the acquisition of several preexisting properties near the campus.

In 1944 the College had purchased for $50,000 a brick residence located diagonally across from George Washington Hall that occupied a commanding site overlooking Fredericksburg. It was named Brent Hall in honor of Margaret Brent, a Catholic Englishwoman who came to America in 1638 to escape religious persecution. A shrewd businesswoman, she eventually acquired vast land holdings, including the site of what would become Fredericksburg. The structure served as the president's home from the time of its purchase until 1947; thereafter, it became a residence hall—reserved for a time as the French language house—before being eventually converted to administrative office space.

Two major properties were acquired in 1946: Framar and Brompton. Framar was purchased from Dr. and Mrs. Frank Reichel—the name of the residence being a combination of their given names, Frank and Marion. The purchase price of $125,000 included the handsome brick residence on William Street, a five-room guesthouse and garage, a swimming pool and picnic area, and a rose and boxwood garden as part of a seven-and-a-half-acre tract. The purchase was especially desirable because it made the campus a contiguous unit, extending east–west from Sunken Road to College Avenue and north–south from the U.S. Route 1 bypass to William Street. Framar served as the president's home for several years while Brompton was undergoing renovation. It was used subsequently as a residence hall, variously designated for special purposes such as the Spanish house or the leadership house.

Brompton, an imposing brick structure on the crest of Marye's Heights overlooking Sunken Road and the city of Fredericksburg, was acquired from the heirs of Maurice B. Rowe for the sum of $71,000. The estate included 171 acres of land, on which were also located two small frame houses and a barn, dairy, and garage.

Sometimes described as one of the most historic houses in America, Brompton had been situated in the midst of the Union attack on Fredericksburg in the Civil War battle that took place in December 1862. That encounter, a devastating defeat for Union forces, resulted in the loss of over 12,600 Northern soldiers, many of whom were buried in the cemetery proximal to the Brompton property—the third-largest national cemetery in the United States after Arlington and Gettysburg. Tradition has it that the legendary

Brompton

nurse Clara Barton attended soldiers under the huge Brompton oak, a landmark tree that was still standing in the twenty-first century.

For over two years after the College acquired the property, Brompton underwent extensive renovation. Part of the new interior decorations included damask wall coverings designed by the renowned Franco Scalamandre. President Combs oversaw much of the work personally and, upon its completion, became Brompton's first Mary Washington tenant. From that point onward, the house served as the official residence of the institution's president.

In 1947 the College made another important acquisition when it acquired Trench Hill, located directly across Hanover Street from Brompton. After thorough remodeling, it became a student residence, designated for academically talented students and later for the College's first male students; it eventually became the headquarters of the Alumni Association. In 2004 it was converted to an elegant inn as part of the Jepson Alumni Executive Center.

Shortly after the off-campus acquisitions, the College embarked on a remarkable building boom that would include within a five-year period beginning in 1950 an infirmary (Hugh Mercer Hall), a student activities building (Ann Carter Lee Hall), a fine arts center (duPont, Pollard, and Melchers Halls), and two dormitories (Mason and Randolph Halls). Never had the face of the campus changed so much, so quickly.

The academic program during the postwar years was augmented by the appointment of several notable faculty members including Julien Binford in art and Kurt F. Leidecker in philosophy. As an internationally recognized scholar of Buddhism, Leidecker was instrumental in developing a program in Asian studies.

The most colorful individual to join the faculty during that time was Matila Ghyka, a native of Romania who was, literally, a prince. His peripatetic career before arriving at Mary Washington included service in the French navy, Romanian diplomatic posts in Spain and Persia, graduate work at the University of Brussels, and a faculty position at the University of Southern California.

Prince Ghyka joined the Mary Washington faculty in 1947 to teach aesthetics and art history, specializing in Far Eastern art. Though he left in 1950, the three-year experience evidently made quite an impression on him, as is clear from his autobiography, *The World Mine Oyster*, published in 1961. In a remarkable and rather libidinous account, Ghyka offered an extraordinary description of the student body:

> There were only fifteen hundred students instead of the twelve thousand in my Californian University. My first contact with this virtual gynaeceum of virgins, made me feel rather like a eunuch in a harem—with, of course, an essential difference—but this feeling soon disappeared. Most of the girls were charming and delightfully natural, with all the distinction and manners of Southern young ladies in life as well as in magazine stories. Some were very pretty, often with the dreamy expression and the slim ankles one would attribute to the heroines of Edgar Allan Poe, and the pre-Raphaelite charm of the Ophelias and *Dames sans Merci* of Burne-Jones and Rossetti. Here were not the vitamin-loaded bodies and the concentrated sex appeal of the Californian girls, reminding one of ripening pomegranates or peaches. The eighteenth-century atmosphere peculiar to Virginia spun a web of elegant courteousness round teachers and students; a chaste, avuncular gallantry on the one side; a trusting coquetry on the other.

As to his teaching, the prince expressed pleasant surprise that "the girls in my class, a dozen or so of the most intelligent and ambitious . . . took to my rather abstruse discourses with unexpected gusto and competence," adding that "it must have been very different from anything they had ever heard before."

There was also an important administrative change in October 1947 when former governor Colgate Darden was elected to replace the retiring John Lloyd Newcomb as president of the University of Virginia. Though Morgan Combs remained as president of Mary Washington, under the new arrangement it was Darden who held ultimate administrative authority as chancellor of the College, a position he held until his retirement in 1959.

President Combs, right, with University of Virginia president Colgate Darden on the steps of Trinkle Library

As the key figure in promoting Mary Washington's merger with the University of Virginia during his governorship, and as the College's chancellor for many years, Darden was notably instrumental in the institution's evolution toward excellence. In recognition of his contributions, the College in 1960 established the Colgate W. Darden Award to be given annually to the graduating senior with the highest overall academic average—a fitting tribute to one of Virginia's most estimable political and educational leaders of the twentieth century.

In the academic area, the postwar years brought an expansion of opportunities for student engagement. One was the implementation of an honors program, begun in 1947. An overall average of B and an average of B+ in the major field were required for eligibility. Beyond that, individual departments established criteria appropriate for their own disciplines. Requirements—typically involving extensive original research—were usually so stringent that only a few students graduated with honors each year, even as the program continued in perpetuity.[18]

Another innovation, at the suggestion of Dean Alvey, was the introduction of interdepartmental majors in the 1949–50 session. The first to be adopted was in pre-medical sciences. With Professor William Castle as adviser, the program was designed to prepare students for schools of medicine, dentistry, or medical technology.

The second, directed by history professor Robert Hilldrup, was initially called American Ideals and Institutions. Incorporating courses in American art, literature, history, government, economics, and sociology, it became known as the American Studies major, functioning for a while as a separate department and later within the Department of History and American Studies.

The third interdepartmental major was called Early Humanities. Developed and directed for many years by Professor Laura Voelkel (later Sumner), it focused on courses in the art, philosophy, history, and literature of ancient Greece and Rome; either Greek or Latin was required, and both were recommended. The major was later retitled Classical Civilization.

During this period the College also began to develop cooperative programs with other institutions. The first of these, and the most popular for many years, was the one in nursing, started in 1949. It required four years of course work, including summer school. The first two years were offered at Mary Washington, with six-week summer sessions at the University of Virginia School of Nursing. The third and fourth years were taken at the University, and after successful completion, the student received a B.S. degree in nursing from the University of Virginia. The success of the nursing venture led to other programs of varying success and popularity, including elementary education, medical technology, physical therapy, and speech pathology.[19]

The midpoint of the twentieth century coincided, roughly, with a number of social changes at the College. Some traditions endured, of course, but others, like the formal reception held annually for incoming freshmen, were headed for extinction.

The reception had been one of the social highlights throughout the 1940s, for faculty as well as students. It was held on the first Saturday evening of the new session either on the roof garden of George Washington Hall or, in case of inclement weather, in the Hall of Mirrors. The receiving line comprised the entire faculty and administration. In his history of the College, Alvey in his distinctively genteel idiom provided a vivid description conveying not only the elements but the ambience of the occasion:

> Resplendent in full dress or tuxedo, with formal evening dress for the ladies, the assembled faculty presented a formidable appearance, especially to youthful freshmen as they emerged from the stairs leading to the roof garden. The line was headed by President and Mrs. Combs, with Dean and Mrs. Alvey next, then department heads, full professors, and so on down the line of academic hierarchy. There was no actual lining up in terms of rank or seniority; it was simply understood that the professors and their wives or husbands would be at the beginning of the line and the newly appointed instructors would stand at the far end.
>
> The president of the student government stood next to Dr. Combs and presented each student by name to the president of the College.

Names were passed along in formal introductions as the students progressed slowly down the long line. Every new student—and there were often between six and seven hundred—shook hands with every faculty member until the end of the line was reached. Introductions were usually followed by a polite, "So glad to have you" or "Where are you from?" Any further conversation usually was cut short by the piling up of students waiting to shake hands. . . .

A steady flow of students was ensured by setting exact times, such as the second floor of Willard on the stairs at 8:15, the third floor at 8:40, and so forth. The dean of women, in the background, saw that the line progressed evenly and without a break until the entire group of freshmen and transfer students had passed along. Students were told in advance to have an evening dress ready for this formal occasion. For some, it was their first long dress, and their apprehension was often apparent as they faced the prospect before them.

The vista that greeted new arrivals was pleasing and picturesque. Electric lanterns around the parapet gave a mellow illumination to the entire scene. . . . Candlelight and silverware gleamed on the white cloths of the buffet tables where bowls of bright red punch and plates of petits fours, ready to be served by students of the home economics department, also in evening dress, awaited the conquerors of the receiving line. . . .

Throughout the reception, the orchestra had been playing in the background. There was little dancing of students with each other until the receiving line disbanded and the male faculty members became available. Then wives surrendered their husbands to a waiting group of eager dancers. Young unmarried men of the faculty were particularly in demand as partners, and some could dance only a few steps until the next student cut in. It was a heady experience for both young and old, and their wives graciously stood in little groups on the sidelines to allow husbands to savor the rush to the fullest. Young single instructors, new to an all-girl college, found the entire procedure somewhat disturbing, but in a rather delightful way.

It was pleasant to watch as the sheen of silk evening gowns caught the flashes of reflected light from the lanterns, and white shirt fronts gleamed in sharp contrast to the rich colors of the dresses.

These dances always ended at midnight at the latest. By that time, all but the most ardent dancers had drifted away. It was customary to close with a medley of dreamy selections rather than "Home, Sweet Home," for the latter seemed a little too risky on a freshman's first Saturday night away at college. The usual sequence included "Goodnight, Sweet Heart," "I'll See You in My Dreams," and finally "Aloha-Oe" with its beautiful refrain, "Farewell to thee . . . until we meet again." The notes of the violin carried the melody in a way that seemed to stimulate soft humming as the dancers concluded their final turns.[20]

The event continued to be held until the mid-fifties, though by then the venue had been moved to the "Golden Horseshoe" between the brand-new Mason and Randolph dorms, and the receiving line had shrunk to the administrative officers only and their wives. The faculty were grouped by departments at various spots on the lawn, where upperclassmen acted as guides and introduced the new students to the faculty members of the department in which they planned to major. Colored lanterns, orchestra music, and tables of refreshments created a festive air, but the elegance of earlier years was missing. Though welcoming events of different kinds would be held regularly in the future, the formal receptions for freshmen came to an end in 1955.

Another change during the period was the adoption of a new alma mater. Throughout the 1930s and into the 1940s, the alma mater had been "Eager Voices Singing," composed by two members of the class of 1928, Sally B. Walker, who wrote the words, and Mildred P. Stewart (later head of the MWC Physical Education Department) the music. The tune was sung on both formal and informal occasions, including at the close of each weekly convocation.

During those years, song contests among the dormitories were held annually, including the composition of an alma mater. One notable effort was "High on Marye's Hilltop," written by Jeanne Crotty (lyrics) and Irene Taylor (music), both members of the class of 1947. Students liked the song and began to sing it on many occasions, leading eventually to a movement to make it the official alma mater. When copies of the sheet music sent to all alumnae chapters for consideration elicited strong approval, the Student Government Association recommended to the Alumnae Association that the song be made official. At its spring meeting in 1952, the Alumnae Association formally endorsed it, and beginning with that year's graduating class, "High on Marye's Hilltop" was used to close every commencement, as well as on other ceremonial occasions.

The most notable social change on campus in the postwar period—or at least the most visible—was the appearance of male students. Actually it was not the first time males had been enrolled; that had occurred in 1929, when a few men were enrolled in the summer session. The number increased slightly the next summer, with the understanding that they would be allowed to continue as students in the regular session that fall.

In his report to the State Board of Education in October 1930, President Combs noted that eighteen men, sixteen of whom were boarding students (housed in Betty Lewis Hall), had been admitted to the 1930–31 session and had paid their fees. The board was neither amused nor amenable and, while agreeing that the men could finish out the current semester, ordered that thereafter they must "make other arrangements." In the following spring, Combs pleaded for permission for the men to attend another year, this time with the provision that they were not to be housed on campus; again the board refused. Thus ended Combs's stealthy approach to coeducation.

Though interdicted from the regular session, men continued to attend

The original coeds: World War II veterans on the steps of Trinkle, 1948

summer school throughout the 1930s—never in large numbers—and a few were able to earn their degrees in that fashion. But, as Edward Alvey notes, "The number of men attending summer sessions began to diminish especially after 1938 when, incidentally, the name of the college was changed to Mary Washington." When in 1944 the College became the women's branch of the University of Virginia, admission of male students was discontinued altogether.

Such prohibition was short-lived, however, as a consequence of the Servicemen's Readjustment Act of 1944, commonly known as the GI Bill, which provided federal tuition payments for hundreds of World War II veterans. To accommodate this unanticipated glut of students, a number of women's colleges, Mary Washington included, opened their doors to the returning servicemen.

The largest contingent of veterans was in 1946–47, the session immediately after the war ended, when a total of forty-eight were enrolled. Many did not stay to complete their degrees, but a number did, including Robert H. Combs, the president's son, who earned his B.A. in 1948. The number of veterans dropped sharply after the first year, though the last one, a former Marine named Dennis Chauncey Moriarity, did not enter the College until 1953, receiving his B.A. in music in 1958. During his last two years, Moriarity was the only male student at MWC, a situation that attracted considerable journalistic interest, with newspapers in Washington and Richmond publishing feature stories about the "one man among 2,000 girls."

Though the veterans were not housed on campus, they were well received by the regular students, and many of them participated extensively in College activities, especially plays and benefits. For several years there was a Veterans Club and a veterans' representative on the Student Council, as well as a basketball team that played periodic games with other area squads. On the whole, the veterans' experience seems to have been a positive one for all concerned; in subsequent years, these alumni were wont to talk with great pride about having graduated from the "girls' school."

It was novel to have male students on campus, but it is debatable which would have been more striking to a returning student in the fall of 1950: the appearance of a few men or the disappearance of one woman—Nina Bushnell. Inconceivable as it may have been to students who saw her as the institution incarnate, and the chief avatar of its values, Mrs. Bushnell had in fact retired over the summer and moved from Fredericksburg.

Ever since her hiring in 1921, during decades when the principle of in loco parentis was the norm, Mrs. Bushnell had carried the concept to a higher power, determined not only to maintain decorum but to inculcate refinement. As one 1940 graduate put it, Mrs. Bushnell "felt that she had a sacred covenant with the parents who entrusted their daughters to her for four years. . . . If any girl was going to go astray [she] was determined that it would be through no lack of vigilance on her part!"[21]

Vigilant she was, and nowhere more so than in her screening of prospective "gentlemen callers." First the young man had to be on the "approved list," as attested by a guest card issued from her office. Then, upon arriving on campus, he had to pass muster personally with Mrs. Bushnell. "If she detected any whiff of tobacco or (heaven forbid) alcohol," recalled one student, "or if she was not thoroughly satisfied with his answers to her questions, she sent him packing."

Mealtime in Seacobeck, shared by all students, provided Mrs. Bushnell with numerous opportunities to impart lessons in etiquette. Lunches often turned didactic, as she typically held forth on arcane matters such as the proper method of eating soup, or peeling a banana, or removing a cherry pit from one's mouth. The latter topic was so recurrent that some students came to believe that the frequency of cherries on the menu was merely a pretext for Mrs. Bushnell's lesson on manners.

Nina Bushnell

The evening meal provided her with the opportunity to teach not only by precept but by example. Formally dressed herself, she expected all students to be appropriately attired and to be seated promptly by six o'clock, whereupon she would begin dinner with a brief blessing. ("Mrs. Bushnell doesn't exactly *pray to* God," commented one observer, "she *talks with* God.") Students were excused from their tables only after the dean had nodded her assent.

Heaven help any student who breached Mrs. Bushnell's finely honed sense of decorum. One 1942 graduate recalled an occasion when a student who, having slipped in the mud hurrying to Seacobeck from the playing fields, had the temerity to remove her shoes before entering the hall. It was not the kind of thing Mrs. Bushnell would overlook or let pass without reprimand. "I cannot understand how your fellow students can tolerate such an affront—bare feet and dirty clothes—from a Mary Washington girl," she scolded. And with the theatricality that she sometimes affected, announced, "As for me, I have lost my appetite," and summarily left the room with a flourish.

Displays of that kind, understandably, did not endear her to some students, one of whom observed that "infractions of behavior, no matter how minor, met with a poker face and a complete lack of sympathy." As Ed Alvey put it in his history of the College, Mrs. Bushnell did not always "relate to people in the modern sense of the word, nor did she try to make people feel comfortable."

After she left Mary Washington in 1950, having reached the state-mandated retirement age of seventy, Mrs. Bushnell worked for several more years as dean of women at Moravian College in Pennsylvania. In 1957 she retired to Florida, where she remained active in the League of Women Voters and as a Red Cross volunteer for a number of years before her death in 1970.

By the time of her retirement, Mrs. Bushnell had come to be regarded by some students as an anachronism, the imperious enforcer of Victorian mores whose time had long since passed. It was not without reason that many of her former charges referred to her tenure as her "reign." And if her approach had begun to seem dated in 1950, it would appear positively antediluvian a half-century later when, in an increasingly coarsened society, her ideals would strike most students as quaint to the point of absurdity, devalued if not utterly discredited. Yet for three decades she was to many students the very embodiment of Mary Washington College.

Her replacement as dean of students was Mary Ellen Stephenson, a popular assistant professor of Spanish who had previously been in charge of the Spanish house. Though Mrs. Bushnell had enjoyed the respect of most students (and the adoration of some), it is likely that the majority appreciated the appointment of a more youthful and open dean—one whom they deemed more pliable (who would not have been?) and responsive to their wishes.

At the outset, Dean Stephenson's actions seemed to justify those roseate hopes, as she announced plans to mingle more closely with students, to visit them in their dormitories, and to sit at various tables with them in the dining hall. More tangibly, she relaxed certain rules to give them more social freedom, a move that the students hailed enthusiastically.

As it turned out, Stephenson served as dean for only three years before returning to full-time teaching in Spanish; she was replaced as dean at the beginning of the 1953–54 session by Isabelle Lawrence Gonon, who had been counselor of women students at Michigan State University. The softening of the rules that Dean Stephenson had implemented was a decidedly relative one, far from libertine. Virtually all aspects of student life, including matters such as hours for lights-out and conditions for riding in cars, were prescribed in detail in page upon page of rules to be enforced by the Student Government Association and the dean of women's staff.

Students came to regard as particularly oppressive the regulations concerning their conduct and, perhaps most vexing of all, their dress. The 1953–54 College handbook, for example, declared under the heading of "Dress" that "jeans and other unconventional apparel are prohibited in the classrooms, studios, laboratories, . . . in the dining rooms, and on the campus; are looked upon with disfavor under any conditions; and are not in keeping with the standards and conditions of the college."

Moreover, students were exhorted not to complain about their plight. The first issue of the *Bullet* for that same year carried on its editorial page an article titled "A Statement of Policy" submitted by the "Faculty Committee on the Student Newspaper." The piece adjured the paper to report campus news accurately, but with discretion and good taste, in order that the image of the College not be sullied in print. "It is a doubtful practice," admonished the article, "for students to wash their soiled linen in public [and] to air their grievances in the columns of their college newspaper until every other means of rectifying just complaints, if there be any, have been exhausted."

The atmosphere of the times was not conducive to protesting the status quo. The Korean War was ending, McCarthyism beginning—neither of which appeared to have noticeably affected campus life; the civil rights movement lay a few years off. With the avuncular Dwight Eisenhower newly ensconced in the White House, the mood of the nation overall was one of complacency and conformity. In the dorms, the few students who had televisions watched benign shows such as *I Love Lucy* and *Your Hit Parade* or watched Edward R. Murrow deliver the news while puffing his ever-present cigarette. Radios were still a more common medium of entertainment for most students, with stars such as Perry Como and Patti Page delivering ditties like "How Much Is That Doggie in the Window?"—tunes that, unlike those of a decade later, were hardly likely to foment rebellious behavior.

Even in such placid times, however, and even on the normally tranquil campus of Mary Washington College, unrest could develop, as it did in the fall of 1953. During that semester, a number of incidents occurred that, though petty individually, had the cumulative effect of creating an unusual degree of tension between students and administrators, particularly those in charge of enforcing social regulations. It was within that atmosphere that a student uprising occurred whose ramifications were to lead indirectly to the demise of President Combs's administration.

The grievance that sparked the uprising, improbably enough, involved uniforms for student waitresses. Like most colleges, Mary Washington provided part-time employment to its students on the basis of financial need. About this time, approximately two hundred students held such jobs, with assignments in the library, residence halls, academic departments, and (mainly) in the dining hall, which employed about eighty in 1953. Within a student body of largely middle-class roots, such work bore much less stigma than it would have at snootier places; most Mary Washington students came from families where work was valued—and expected.

There was, however, a subtle, unarticulated hierarchy among campus jobs, one in which waitressing was viewed as the least desirable. Certainly it was the most demanding. Waitresses worked long hours, seven days a week, with only one weekend a month free. They ate either before or after their classmates. And the work itself was arduous, requiring (in the days before cafeteria service was instituted) heavy trays of food and dishes to be carried to each table. The postmeal cleanup and disposal of refuse prompted the waitresses' nickname of "slop girls." For this they earned the munificent sum of sixty-five cents an hour.

In November 1953 the administration, presumably in an effort to upgrade the dining service, summarily announced a plan that would require waitresses to wear caps and uniforms. Previously they had simply worn apron-smocks over their regular dress. Kept in closets near the dining room where students could don them quickly as they dashed in from class, the aprons hardly qualified as haute couture, but they were utilitarian and convenient.

The new uniforms presented much greater practical problems, since they would require changing clothes several times a day within a schedule that was often already tight. But it was not merely the logistics that the waitresses resented. Some complained that the mandated uniforms were demeaning; in addition, they were irritated by the very term "directive" as used in announcing the policy. It was evident that underlying the whole issue was a pervasive student hostility toward an administration that they increasingly viewed as unreasonably strict in its rules and unappealingly autocratic in its methods—an assessment that, in light of subsequent developments, appears to have had some validity.

In any case, a meeting called by the dining hall director to discuss the new dress regulations proved to be, in Dean Alvey's words, "antagonistic and disorderly," with some students expressing vehement opposition and others walking out. As a result several waitresses were notified that their student aide positions had been canceled owing to their lack of cooperation.

The pivotal incident occurred when one of the dormitory hostesses (housemothers), Hester Zella Jacobus, was summoned to President Combs's office, where, according to her account, she was accused of "siding with the students," whereupon she was told to "pack her trunk and leave at once," since she was "fired." Instead of leaving, Jacobus quickly contacted a member of the Board of Visitors, who instructed her to stay in her job until further notice while the matter was investigated.

The ensuing investigation was intense and prolonged as the Mary Washington committee of the board held hearings in both Charlottesville and

Fredericksburg. Over the course of several weeks, faculty, administrators, and students were called on to testify concerning the situation on campus; at one meeting, President Combs addressed the board for two hours. The climactic session came on February 12, 1954, when the committee, meeting in Fredericksburg, delivered its report to the full board. Combs, represented by two prominent local attorneys, Jere M. H. Willis and A. W. Garnett, was in attendance. At the conclusion of a five-hour session, the board released a carefully crafted resolution, unanimously adopted, that called for a thorough reorganization of Combs's position and a consequent diminution of his authority.

According to the new administrative structure, "supreme authority" was vested in the president of the University of Virginia, Colgate Darden. Combs's major responsibilities were split between Dean Alvey, who was placed in charge of student and faculty relations and curriculum, and Edgar Woodward, then bursar, who was assigned direct control over business affairs. Combs, while permitted to retain the title of president, was restricted to duties such as "construction and development, solicitation of funds, and related matters."

The new reorganization at the College generated front-page headlines across the state. It was, of course, particularly big news in Fredericksburg, where the *Free Lance–Star* carried an editorial titled "Brighter Days Ahead" that offered an optimistic outlook. "Though the final chapter may not yet have been written about the recent startling events," the paper presciently suggested, "our hope is that we can expect a period of relative quiet which will be a welcome respite after the difficult days through which the College has just passed."

For the moment, such hope seemed reasonable, particularly since Combs himself assented to the new arrangement, averring in a letter to the board that it had his "full approval and the implementation of it will have my full cooperation." With that, campus life returned before long to normal as the new administrative structure worked smoothly. The session ended with commencement exercises presided over by Combs, who counseled the graduates to "walk humbly" and, in an ironic touch, to refrain from bitterness. It was his twenty-fifth commencement as president—and would be his last.[22]

The 1954–55 session got off to an auspicious start, though students (and their parents) were probably none too happy to see a tuition increase, the first in many years. The general fees for all students were raised from $170 to $270, bringing the total charge for Virginia students to $757 for the academic year; out-of-state students paid $1,097. Among the bright spots was the opening of two new dormitories, Mason and Randolph, that together accommodated over four hundred additional students. For the first time in several years, no students had to live off-campus in private homes.

The faculty was augmented by the addition of new instructors, some of whom would play leading roles in coming years, either as teachers or as administrators. The group notably included Sidney Mitchell in English, Mary Jo Parrish in biology, Mildred Droste in physical education (later to be named dean of students), and Cornelia Oliver in art history, who was also assigned as a residence counselor in Willard Hall, then a freshman dorm.

Another faculty member, Associate Professor of English Charmenz Lenhart, drew considerable attention to the College that fall when she ran for Congress as a Republican against longtime Democratic incumbent Howard W. Smith, a stalwart of the reigning Byrd organization. Several aspects of her candidacy were noteworthy, one being the very novelty of a female candidate in Virginia of that period. (The *Free Lance–Star* described her as the "blonde, attractive Mary Washington professor.") There was also much controversy over whether, as a recent resident of the state, she was eligible to run. The issue was finally resolved by a circuit court judge in Richmond who ruled in her favor. The voters, alas for Lenhart, did not concur, as Congressman Smith prevailed by a margin of two to one in the November election.

The session appeared to proceed normally, but trouble was again developing in the president's office. Despite his avowed acceptance the previous spring, Combs was never really satisfied with the new administrative arrangement. He recognized it for what it was—a de facto demotion—and according to some close to the situation, his goal became "vindication." As a man whose pride seems to have been commensurate with—maybe greater than—his considerable achievements, he naturally resented not only the loss of control but also the tarnishing of his image. In addition to this—and perhaps partly because of it—his health began to fail.

Near the end of the fall semester, Combs's festering hostility exploded. In the course of a meeting on December 9 with the Mary Washington College committee of the board, he delivered a stunning letter charging that he had agreed to the previous spring's arrangements only "under duress." The whole affair, he asserted, had resulted from a conspiracy against him by five members of the faculty and staff, abetted by the chairman of the Mary Washington College committee himself.

Combs's deteriorating situation was made worse—immeasurably worse—by the concurrent appearance of a nine-page mimeographed screed luridly titled "The Whole Story at Mary Washington College," copies of which were sent to newspapers, public officials, and influential citizens. Termed "scurrilous" by the Board of Visitors, it constituted further attacks on those whom Combs viewed as his tormentors. Though the actual authorship of the document was never clearly determined, it became evident to many, including board members, that the president was aware of its circulation and sympathetic with the sentiments it expressed.

As far as the board was concerned, this was the last straw. Meeting on April 9, 1955, it issued a statement announcing, "It is clear to the Board that continued retention of Dr. Combs in any active capacity at Mary Washington would be against the best interests of the College. Accordingly, the Board has today adopted a resolution removing him from office, effective immediately."

So ended, ingloriously and tragically, the career of one of the most significant figures in the history of the institution. In a sympathetic editorial, the *Richmond News Leader* later suggested that "the mistakes of a few months should not be permitted to obscure the labor of a lifetime."[23]

The paper thus acknowledged what those closest to the president had known all along: by the time of his ouster, Combs was clearly not well, suffering from what turned out to be leukemia. Beyond that, though there is no tangible evidence of it, circumstances suggest that he may also have had other undiagnosed problems as well. It was difficult to imagine how someone of his demonstrated intellectual power and political acumen would have acted as imprudently as he did during his final year in office had he not been impaired in some way.

At the time of his termination, one final building project was under way: a science hall, for which Combs had persistently sought legislative appropriations. He did not live to see it completed, passing away in Richmond on October 25, 1955, at the age of sixty-four. His funeral was held at Brompton, and he was buried at Fredericksburg's Oak Hill Cemetery. The science building, completed in 1959, was named in his memory.

Morgan Combs served Mary Washington with consuming devotion for twenty-six years. During that time the institution improved by every conceivable measure as it developed from a small teachers college to a solid liberal arts college for women. He was fundamentally a builder who liked to see things grow—whether it was plants or buildings or faculty credentials or the institution's reputation—and he had the personality and the political connections to make such things happen.

His most enduring (and endearing) legacy was the campus itself, whose beauty, according to his contemporary Carroll Quenzel, owed much to Combs's "widely acknowledged flair for landscaping and the meticulous care he lavished on the minute details of construction." After his death, thousands paid unknowing homage through their appreciation, spoken or silent, for the magnificence of the surroundings. Many have been the students attracted to the College by the allure of its campus; many are the graduates whose memories are framed by visions of the environment that he labored so lovingly to create.

The magnitude of his accomplishments called to mind the tribute to the architect Sir Christopher Wren in St. Paul's Cathedral in London: *si monumentum queris, circumspice.* So it was with Morgan Combs: "If you seek his monument, look about you." He was, quite simply, the president who built the place.

–2–
THE SIMPSON ERA, 1955–1974

MARY WASHINGTON COLLEGE during the waning years of Morgan Combs's presidency was clearly in a precarious situation. Although Edward Alvey provided a sense of stability as dean, it was obvious that the institution's long-term health required vigorous and enlightened leadership from the president's office. Well aware of that fact, the Board of Visitors in May 1955 appointed a special committee, chaired by Henry McWane of Lynchburg, to recommend a new president. Among the members of the committee was the venerable C. O'Conor Goolrick, the College's original patron.

The committee solicited nominations from other members of the board, from the faculty and alumnae of Mary Washington College, from the faculty of the University of Virginia, and from the presidents of leading colleges around the country. The result was a list of 137 nominees for the committee's consideration—among them, according to an article in the *Free Lance–Star*, was Edward Alvey. However, the dean reportedly withdrew his name from consideration before the interview stage was reached in September.

Eventually the committee invited six finalists for interviews in Charlottesville. In September the rector of the board, Barron F. Black, announced the election of the institution's fourth president: Grellet Collins Simpson.

The forty-six-year-old Simpson possessed impressive (and appropriate) credentials to head a liberal arts college such as Mary Washington at that period in its history. A native of Norfolk, he earned his bachelor of arts degree from Randolph-Macon College in Ashland in 1930 and returned there a year later to teach English, which he continued to do while earning his master's (1936) and doctoral (1949) degrees in English at the University of Virginia. His career was interrupted by World War II, when he spent four years as a field supervisor for the American Red Cross in southern Italy.

Following that service he became increasingly engaged in administrative work, in addition to his teaching, at Randolph-Macon, serving variously as director of counseling and as the de facto dean of students. In 1952 he was appointed dean of the faculty, the position he held at the time of his selection for the presidency of Mary Washington.

A Chaucerian scholar, Simpson had accumulated numerous academic honors during his career, including election to Phi Beta Kappa, Omicron Delta Kappa, and the University of Virginia's Raven Society. Besides his academic credentials, Simpson could also claim a personal asset that would prove to be of incalculable value as president of Mary Washington: his wife, née Dorothy Cottrell of Richmond. The Simpsons, who had no children, were an especially close couple. According to Ed Alvey's history of the College, their marriage "seemed a partnership, whether the sphere of activity was social, academic, or recreational." Together they made Brompton a warm and welcoming place for faculty, staff, and students. The College became their family.

Simpson officially assumed his duties on February 1, 1956, by which time the title of his position had been changed from president to chancellor.[1] Within days of arriving on campus, Simpson met with the student body in a special convocation at which he delivered an address emphasizing individual freedom and personal responsibility. The students responded with a prolonged standing ovation and crowded around him afterward to greet him personally. A few days later, the *Bullet*, in its usual editorial space, carried a special message from the chancellor that portended an administration of friendliness and open communication. "I do hope," he wrote,

> that you will always feel perfectly free to come and see me both in the office and at home. Mrs. Simpson and I want to know you and want to feel that we are part of your college life. Likewise, when you are sincerely disturbed about aspects of college life which are of mutual concern to you and me that you will come and tell me. I will not always be able to do what you suggest. At times, it will be not only possible, but advisable. It is the little things in life that frequently bother us most. Please be frank and straight-forward with me. I will be equally frank with you. We must trust each other. I shall try to play the game fairly, and when I do not obey the rules or the spirit of the rules, I want to know.

Little could he or the students have then known how much and how quickly things would change in the coming years. Before his presidency was over, students would indeed be frank—even belligerent—in letting him know exactly how they felt. In that sense, he got more than he bargained for.

The inauguration of the new chancellor was marked by a three-day celebration, October 17–19, 1956. The affair began on Wednesday with the opening of a juried art exhibition, chaired by Professor Julien Binford, in the duPont galleries—the first of its kind at the College and the model for similar events held annually for many years thereafter.

The central event of the next day was a symposium, chaired by Assistant Dean of the College Reginald Whidden, titled "Woman, Catalyst of Modern Society." That event, which might have been presumed to be a sedate, scholarly affair, turned out to be explosive owing to the opposition of a Mary Washington alumna and her husband to the participation on the symposium panel by anthropologist Ashley Montagu, author of *The Natural Superiority of Women*. The source of their opposition apparently was not Montagu's views on gender but his endorsement of racial integration, including intermarriage. Having failed to block his participation through letters to the administration, the Board of Visitors, and even the governor, the couple announced their intention to harass the speaker during his presentation and during the subsequent discussion period. In the end, the audience's expression of collective disgust with the pair squelched the planned disruption, but not before (in Alvey's words) "the threat of a demonstration added zest and excitement to a scholarly discussion of the role of women."

That evening Chancellor and Mrs. Simpson hosted a formal dinner at Brompton for board members and distinguished guests, which was followed by the inaugural concert. The soloist was Herva Nelli, soprano of the Metropolitan Opera Company, whom Simpson and Alvey (chair of the inaugural committee) had personally chosen after a trip to New York. In his history of the College, Alvey, in his distinctive style, described the singer's inaugural performance. "When Miss Nelli strode forth imperiously onto the stage of George Washington Hall," he wrote, "a stunning blonde in a shimmering evening dress with deep décolletage, a surprised gasp escaped the audience. It was difficult to convince some of the inaugural party that she had been selected because of the reviews of the quality of her voice, rather than a visual encounter with the prima donna in New York."

The inauguration on Friday was "one of the most impressive and colorful ceremonies ever held at the college," according to Alvey (who had seen many of them during his long tenure). The event began with the procession of faculty, administrators, and visiting dignitaries into George Washington auditorium as the combined glee clubs of Mary Washington and Randolph-Macon Colleges sang Martin Luther's "Ein' Feste Burg." The featured speaker was Harlan H. Hatcher, president of the University of Michigan. Following his remarks, the oath of office was ad-

Grellet Collins Simpson

ministered to Simpson by Edward W. Hudgins, chief justice of the Virginia Supreme Court of Appeals. The packed audience responded with a standing ovation for the new chancellor.

Simpson's inaugural address foreshadowed what would become key characteristics of his administration. One was his commitment to the education of women. He touched on the matter lightly, saying at one point, "In truth, colleges for women are always more attractive than colleges for men—a fact which I fully realized thirty years ago as a student, and which I have rediscovered with happiness after an interval of approximately twenty-five years, during which I had the opportunity to assist in the education of young men [at Randolph-Macon]." But his commitment to the concept of all-female colleges was serious—and it was sustained, as subsequent events would prove.

Another theme that was clearly evident was his commitment to the literally "liberating" influence of the liberal arts. Noting that his address might well be titled "Lessons Learned from Literature," he urged a resurgence of what he called the comic spirit in life, so that "we may once again hear the 'tinkling of silver bells' and not merely the blaring of trumpets or the moan of the saxophone." He challenged students and faculty alike to engage in a shared commitment to learning that would enable the whole college community to "share with the poet Schiller his *Freude, Freude, Freude*."

The program concluded with the singing of the alma mater and a benediction by Theodore F. Adams, the widely respected minister of Richmond's First Baptist Church. The procession then filed out as the combined choirs sang Beethoven's "Hymn to Joy."

Though the ceremony was conducted with a solemnity appropriate to the occasion, there were also indications that the new chancellor's approach would be somewhat less stuffy than that of his predecessor. An illustrative moment came when a member of the platform party pointed out to Simpson just before the processional that his shirt collar was unbuttoned. The chancellor replied, "Yes, I know. I unbuttoned it."

Evening events began with a reception at Brompton, followed by an inaugural ball from nine to one o'clock in the Ann Carter Lee Hall Ballroom. Immediately thereafter, the festive day concluded with breakfast in Seacobeck.

Chancellor Simpson's administrative staff at the outset drew heavily from personnel already in place. Financial affairs were under the supervision of Edgar Woodward, who had held that responsibility since 1937 as either treasurer, bursar, or finally comptroller. He continued as the College's chief financial officer until his retirement in 1970, when he was succeeded by Edward V. Allison Jr., who had served as business manager since 1967.

Edward Alvey continued as dean of the College, quickly developing a close and enduring bond—both personal and professional—with Simpson, who appeared to regard Alvey as the embodiment of the history and virtues of Mary

Washington College.[2] Alvey served until his retirement in 1967, at which time he was replaced by professor of English and former associate dean Reginald W. Whidden. After three years, Whidden retired and was succeeded by English professor James H. Croushore, who also had served previously as associate dean of the College.

Carrol H. Quenzel, initially hired as head librarian in 1943, continued in that capacity under Simpson. Simultaneously serving as a professor in the History Department, Quenzel became a beloved campus legend whom students held in awe because of his uncanny ability to recognize and instantly recall the name of every student he had ever taught—and they were numerous. Seldom had the campus community been more saddened than by the news that the courtly "Dr. Q" had died in his sleep on June 3, 1968, the day after participating in that year's commencement exercises.

Quenzel was replaced as head librarian by English professor Daniel Woodward, a member of the faculty since 1957. When Woodward left Mary Washington in 1972 to become head of the Huntington Library at Stanford University, the College named its rare books room in his honor. He was succeeded as librarian by Mary Washington alumna Ruby York Weinbrecht '48, who had previous library experience in various capacities at Vassar College, Ball State University, Indiana State University, and the Library of Congress. In 1970–71 she had served as president of the MWC Alumnae Association.[3]

Beginning in 1957 the admissions office was headed by Michael Houston, who was also a member of the History Department. In 1967 he was appointed assistant to the chancellor (later changed to assistant chancellor), in which position he became a close and invaluable aide to Simpson. Succeeding him as director of admissions was A. R. "Ray" Merchent, formerly the registrar and chairman of the Education Department. From that position, Merchent would go on to hold a number of key posts, culminating with his appointment as the College's executive vice president.

For fourteen years beginning in 1956, student life was supervised by Margaret Hargrove, who, upon taking the job, insisted that the position's title be changed from dean of women to dean of students. During much of that period, she was ably assisted by Spanish professor Mary Ellen Stephenson, who had held the job for most of the time since the departure of Nina Bushnell.

Under Dean Hargrove's leadership, the Student Government Association was strengthened and the residence hall staff upgraded.[4] Also, for the first time, "mixed" dormitories were created—that is, dorms in which students from different classes were housed, replacing the traditional segregation of classes in specific residence halls. Throughout her tenure as dean, Hargrove continued to teach at least one class in Latin each session. When she retired in 1968, she was succeeded as dean by Mildred Droste, a member of the Physical Education Department.

The most notable staffing change on campus during the early Simpson years involved the creation of a more professional police force. Before that time, security (such as it was) was largely the responsibility of one man, Officer Clifton H. Reeves, together with several (often part-time) assistants. Reeves, known well throughout the student body as "Pat," gave yeoman service for a quarter century following his initial employment in 1939, but the College's expansion by the mid-1950s required more manpower.

A new era began in 1958 with the appointment of Medford D. Haynes as chief of the College security force. A former Fredericksburg city police officer, Haynes led the development of the force in both the number of officers employed and the scope of services provided. For the first time, the department began to be proactive in attempting to prevent crimes rather than in merely apprehending miscreants—an approach that was vastly extended over the years.

From the outset it was evident that Chancellor Simpson's main focus would be on improving the College's academic quality, a goal that he approached from several angles. A major initial concern was to increase the role of the faculty in its own governance. Toward that end, one of his first acts as chancellor was to appoint a special study committee "to investigate and suggest to the faculty a committee set-up through which the faculty would be able to work more efficiently and constructively for the total welfare of the college."

The report of that committee—jokingly referred to by some as the "committee on committees"—called for sweeping reforms that would vest much decision-making responsibility in the hands of the faculty. Specifically, it proposed a system of eighteen faculty committees, broadly divided into two groups—one dealing with academic policies and procedures, the other dealing with non-academic matters (e.g., admissions, catalog, May Day, student publications).

Implementation of the proposed plan in the fall of 1957 constituted a significant change in the way the College functioned, as faculty for the first time enjoyed genuine participation in policy development. It was a drastic change from the previous autocratic process—and a welcome one in the view of the faculty. Academic administration was further democratized in 1962 when the appointment of department chairs was placed on a term, rather than lifetime, basis and made largely dependent on the preference of each department's faculty. With minor revisions from time to time, it would remain the basic structure of faculty governance for decades. The next major organizational change would not occur until 2000, when a representative faculty senate format was instituted in lieu of monthly meetings of the general faculty.

Chancellor Simpson's desire to upgrade the quality of the faculty included encouragement of attendance at, and participation in, professional meetings. More importantly, he exhorted younger faculty members to use state funds that were available to help defray the costs of completing their Ph.D. programs. Between 1961 and 1970, thirty instructors took advantage of that opportunity, elevating the overall academic credentials of the faculty.

Progress with faculty salaries was far less evident. Because the College was overstaffed for the amount of funds allocated by the state, faculty members tended to be undercompensated, even by the meager standards of academe at the time. As late as the early 1970s, faculty were being hired for less than $10,000 per year, and the salaries of senior faculty were not much better. Yet such was the mind-set of the Mary Washington professoriat in those days that such penury did not seem so onerous. Indeed, in response to a modest salary increase for the 1959–60 session, the faculty unanimously passed a resolution declaring that "the faculty of Mary Washington College appreciate the continuing improvement in the salary scale, which mirrors the mutual confidence continuing among the faculty, the chancellor, and the other governing authorities." That complaisant attitude would not last.

Another academic area of concern to Simpson was the curriculum, especially after receiving reports of the 1962 reaccreditation self-study conducted for the Southern Association of Colleges and Secondary Schools and Mary Washington's own long-range planning committee, appointed by the chancellor in 1960. Perhaps the most substantive, and certainly the most controversial, recommendation of each of those reports was that majors in both physical education and home economics be discontinued as inconsistent with the purposes of a liberal arts college. The issue was debated for the better part of the decade before the faculty finally voted to eliminate the home economics major in 1968 and the physical education major in 1969. Under the new regulations, courses could continue to be taught in each discipline, but no major could be awarded. Moreover, courses in physical education, two of which had to be taken to meet general education requirements for graduation, would not receive graded credit but would instead be evaluated only on the basis of "satisfactory" or "unsatisfactory."

Even as those majors were being phased out, others were being added. A major in dance was established within the Physical Education Department; some years later it became a separate department before being conjoined to the Drama Department in an attempt (ultimately fruitless) to save it from elimination. Before the Simpson presidency ended, additional majors were established in a number of disciplines, including physics in 1959. In 1963 the faculty approved a joint major in geography and geology, but the student demand for courses in each area was such that in 1972 separate majors and departments were created, with Samuel T. Emory chairing geography and Samuel O. Bird heading geology. In 1964 a Department of Religion was established, chaired by Elizabeth A. Clark, and five years later the faculty voted to establish a major in that discipline.

Reconfigurations of existing departments created several new disciplinary arrangements. In 1964 the sudden death of Robert L. Hilldrup, longtime chair of the Department of History and Political Science, precipitated a realignment that resulted in separate departments of history, headed by Joseph C. Vance, and of political science and economics, headed by Henry W. Hewetson, who was succeeded in 1970 by Lewis P. Fickett Jr. Some years later political science and economics, both highly popular, were divided into individual departments. In 1967 the Art Department received approval to offer a distinct major in studio art in addition to its traditional major in art history.

Several new interdisciplinary majors were established during the Simpson years, expanding the concept inaugurated in the early 1950s with premed, American studies, and classical civilization programs. In 1959 the faculty approved a pre–foreign service major with philosophy professor Kurt F. Leidecker as adviser. Drawing on contacts with the Foreign Service and other diplomatic resources in Washington, the program proved to be immediately successful and continued to grow for many years under the astute direction of the program's advisers—first Lew Fickett and later Jack Kramer. Reflecting a growing national trend, several interdisciplinary majors were developed in the late sixties and early seventies, including Russian studies, with Joseph Bozicevic as adviser; Asian studies, under Kurt Leidecker's direction; and Latin American studies, headed by Mary Ellen Stephenson.

In addition, the curriculum was expanded with the development of a number of summer institutes and workshops in the early seventies, mainly owing to the initiative of Laura Sumner, who served as director of summer programs. Among the most successful—and one that had the longest run—was a course in marine biology first offered by William Pinschmidt and for many years thereafter by Anna Scott Hoye at her Cross Rip Camp near Deltaville, Virginia.

The College's oldest academic program, education, also experienced change, prompted in part by new certification requirements for teachers in Virginia. When implemented, the new plan, which mandated a significant increase in the supervised teaching component, was so successful that the College secured state approval for every area in which certification was requested; moreover, it enabled MWC graduates to become automatically eligible for certification in many other parts of the country through reciprocity agreements with thirty states.

A number of academic developments during the Simpson years launched trends that would flower in later decades. One example was the growth of interest in seminars and independent study projects. Volunteer noncredit seminars held in the residence halls, initiated by the students, were organized by philosophy professor George Van Sant shortly after he joined the faculty in 1958. Having participated as an undergraduate in the acclaimed Great Books Program at St. John's College, Van Sant envisioned a similar program at Mary Washington. In its first year, the seminar was housed in Trench Hill, where twenty-one students, representing all four classes, were selected from more than one hundred applicants to live and to engage in analysis of the great works of Western thought.

The success of the Trench Hill experiment led to its extension to Framar, where a series of similar seminars was conducted by another member of the Philosophy Department, Peter Coffin. As the movement continued to grow, Dean Reginald Whidden was named coordinator for the seminars. Eventually other residence halls followed the lead of Trench Hill and Framar, as seminars were offered in Ball, Bushnell, Betty Lewis, Marye, and Russell. Numerous faculty members volunteered to lead the dormitory seminars, which focused on topics ranging across modern art, religion, existentialism, communism, modern music, psychoanalysis, current drama, politics, and contemporary literature. So great was the interest in the volunteer study groups that in 1961 the College established liberal arts seminars for credit, after which the dormitory programs were phased out.

The liberal arts seminars reached the height of their popularity during the 1965–66 session. Enrollments, however, began to decline thereafter, mainly because many individual departments were beginning to offer, and sometimes require, their own discipline-specific independent study programs and senior seminars. Consequently, the broad liberal arts seminars were discontinued in 1970.

During the Simpson years, and in no small part because of the chancellor's persona, advocacy, and leadership, interest in foreign studies increased substantially. This trend was evident in many ways, including the success of the pre–foreign service major and the popularity of courses in history and political science dealing with the culture and politics of foreign countries. It was also sustained by the College's emphasis on the study of foreign languages as a graduation requirement, an outgrowth of which was the observance of Modern Foreign Language Week. In the 1960s that annual event featured exhibitions of art and culture from other countries, lectures by embassy staff members from Washington, and foreign-language films and plays.

Global awareness was also promoted by a number of special programs such as a 1966 "summer school in Spain" project. Organized by Dean Alvey, with courses taught by Spanish professor Josefa Rivas, the program (in Alvey's words) "sought to offer a new dimension to serious academic study of Spanish literature through the living culture of Spain—its people, places, language, architecture, music, and art." The experience, which involved a final exam on the lectures and field trips, as well as a comprehensive essay on some aspect of Spanish culture, carried three hours of academic credit. Though well received by the MWC students who participated (along with those from other colleges), the program was essentially subsumed after one year by the University of Virginia, which initiated a similar project.

Other examples of specific MWC events with an international focus included a 1967 symposium under the aegis of the Modern Foreign Language Department on the works of Benito Pérez Galdós and an Asian studies institute in the summer of 1971 directed by Kurt Leidecker in cooperation with the Virginia Asian Studies Consortium.

Of longer duration (and more ambitious) was an exchange program between the United States and India that began in 1963, whereby Mary Washington faculty spent a year teaching at an Indian college while Indian professors taught at MWC. The program, funded mainly by the U.S. State Department and the Danforth Foundation, was avidly promoted by Chancellor Simpson, who himself made several trips to India. Before the program ended in the early 1970s owing to lack of funding, five Mary Washington professors had participated.

Perhaps the clearest evidence that MWC students were expanding their horizons was the increased participation in junior-year-abroad programs sponsored by various schools in the 1960s. Interest grew to such an extent in later years that by the 1990s a special office was created to organize and facilitate overseas study. The broadened academic outlook of the Simpson presidency thus portended the rise of emphasis on globalism and multicultural studies at the College in the years ahead.

Beyond revising the curriculum and adding new programs, the College sought in various ways to improve students' overall academic experience. One was through refining the process of academic advising, an effort in which Reginald Whidden played a leading role. Following an extensive study of academic guidance programs at institutions similar to Mary Washington during the 1958–59 session, Whidden proposed, and the College adopted, a new system of advising. Under the revamped program, each new student was assigned to a faculty adviser, preferably in the student's proposed major field of study. The adviser, aided by a dossier including the student's high school record, test scores, and other pertinent data, then worked with the student to plan a course schedule for the semester. Subsequent group meetings of students with their adviser were scheduled at intervals throughout the session. Beginning in 1960, advisers were aided by the publication of a handbook that detailed information on degree requirements, major programs, teacher certification, and other data useful in devising schedules. Although participation by faculty members as advisers was voluntary, there was never any trouble in obtaining the seventy to eighty persons needed to accomplish the task each semester.

Students were required to declare a major by the end of the sophomore year. To assist in making decisions, a major-counseling night was held, usually in April. At that time, representatives of each department were available for conferences with interested students—and, it seems, for occasional arm-twisting as well. "Some departments served refreshments," wrote Dean Alvey, "and on one occasion, the mathematics department was accused of undue proselytizing when a large bowl of punch, surrounded by cookies, met the eager glance of prospective majors." In any event, once a major was declared, the student was assigned to a departmental adviser who was responsible for guiding the student's academic progress through to graduation.

The Whidden system continued in operation until 1971, when most of the pre-major advising was turned over to several assistant deans for counseling and to divisional advisers—a procedure that reduced the number of needed faculty advisers to approximately thirty. Some years later, the Whidden system, in essence, was reinstituted, to be followed by various alterations and innovations in search of the most effective method.

Devising an ideal advising system was a continual challenge, and students (as well as some faculty) never seemed quite satisfied with the process. The root of the problem lay in the fact that effective guidance depended not only on the quality of the advice being dispensed but also on the attitude and diligence of its recipient. Consequently few aspects of the academic program drew more frequent complaints than the advising system, no matter how it was structured and regardless of how earnestly the College tried to improve it. (Writing in the *Bullet*, one student wag defined a faculty adviser as a "professional leg-puller [who] tells you which classes to take and, later, why you can't get a job because of the classes you took.")

An important innovation in 1965 was the creation of a counseling center. Beginning as a testing facility in Hamlet House, it administered both individual and group tests such as the College Board and Graduate Record Exams. By the end of the decade, under the direction of Mary Annette "Toni" Kelly, a professor of psychology, its mission broadened to offer (free) a wide range of services to assist students with personal and emotional problems.

In addition to providing wider services for its students in the classroom and on campus, the College, beginning in the 1950s, devoted greater effort to meeting the postgraduation needs of its students. In an earlier day, most alumnae who pursued a professional career had gone into teaching, but with multiple job opportunities opening to women, career guidance became a more important aspect of college life. The first efforts in that direction were undertaken as a function of the dean's office, but as demand for such services increased, the College established a separate placement bureau. In 1955 an alumna, Isabel Gordon '42, was appointed as its full-time director.

Under Gordon's energetic leadership, the bureau greatly expanded its services by assisting students in developing résumés, which were kept on file in the office, and by arranging campus visits by prospective employers from diverse areas such as business and industrial corporations, government agencies, the armed forces, and retail stores, as well as public and private schools. Through such connections, many graduates were able to obtain their first jobs. In recognition of her accomplishments in developing the program, Gordon was elected president of the Virginia College Placement Association in 1967 and president of the Southern Placement Association in 1972.

Where the administration of President Morgan Combs had been characterized above all by campus construction, the hallmark of Grellet Simpson's was the elevation of academic standards. Yet under Simpson's stewardship, there also were significant improvements in College facilities.

Some involved the implementation of new technology, such as the installation of a switchboard telephone system in 1958. The new network of 135 phones and 165 extensions provided coverage (albeit sparse) for all campus offices and dormitories and required six employees working in shifts for its operation. Another technological innovation, much appreciated by staff and by students, was the introduction in 1965 of IBM equipment for tasks such as registering students, reporting grades, and updating student records.

Rising enrollment prompted the construction of new dormitories, four of which were built during the Simpson years at a cost of approximately $3 million. The first, completed in 1959, had a capacity of 144 students and was named for Nina Bushnell. Though flattered by the gesture, the former dean seemed uncertain that she wanted such recognition. According to Alvey, Bushnell "loved words and used them affectionately and at times extravagantly," as was evident in her response to Chancellor Simpson's request that the new dorm bear her name. "With profound humility," she wrote from retirement, "I have read your telegram and it is not understandable that so great [an] honor has been accorded me. I beg of the board of visitors [that] they will try to sense my profound gratitude but also to try to understand that I do not wish the publicity attendant on giving my name to the new dormitory though [it is] an honor anyone would covet. If I can but have a place in the hearts of the girls who knew me and shared in work and service and in rich comradeship I shall be content." Her demurrer notwithstanding, Bushnell Hall it became—the first time in the College's history that a dormitory had been named for a living person. It was also the first dorm to house students from all four classes in the same building.

In 1960 came Marshall Hall, a 144-bed facility located at the extreme southeast corner of campus at the intersection of William Street and Sunken Road. It was named in honor of Mary Willis Ambler Marshall, wife of the noted chief justice John Marshall. Five years later, Russell Hall opened. Located just down the hill from Bushnell and fronting Sunken Road, it provided space for 179 students and was named for the College's first president, Edward Hutson Russell. The building featured a brick terrace at the rear and a spacious oblong lobby with curving stairways at each end. Interior decorating was directed by an alumna, Camilla Moody Payne '29.

Construction of the last of the four dormitories involved demolition of a campus landmark, the city reservoir that had long dominated the terrain on the southern end of campus. In its place was constructed a quadrangle founded on its southern border by a new dormitory named for Thomas Jefferson. The building, which housed 195 students, had several innovative features including the campus's first dorm elevator, a cluster arrangement of rooms that included kitchenettes, and a number of single rooms for students who desired privacy. It opened at the beginning of the 1967 session.

Construction projects included not only residence halls but also academic facilities, the most substantial of which was a new science building. Located across from, and completed about the same time as, Bushnell, the new building was named in honor of the former president Morgan Combs. When it opened in 1959, Combs provided quarters for the Departments of Mathematics in the basement, Biology on the first floor, Physics and Biology on the second, and Chemistry on the third.

During the 1962–63 session, Trinkle Library was significantly enlarged at a cost of almost a half million dollars (about twice what the original construction had cost). Taking out the entire rear wall of the building (overlooking the amphitheater) made it possible to add stacks that expanded the library's capacity from 150,000 to 250,000 volumes. Other amenities, such as an air-conditioned rare-books room, were included in the project, which was completed at the beginning of the spring 1963 semester. It would be the last major structural change in library facilities until a new building was constructed a quarter century later.

Though not as prominent, other changes in physical facilities also took place. In the early 1970s, for example, the old building in the ravine behind Willard and Mercer that had long housed the maintenance department was replaced with a structure located on the far side of the Hanover Street golf course. The new $800,000 building was designed to house all maintenance units of the College, including the supply rooms and the carpentry, plumbing, and painting shops, as well as offices for all supervisory personnel. (Usually referred to at that time as the Buildings and Grounds Department, the operation was subsequently called the Physical Plant Department and, even later, Facilities Services.)

The last major building project of the Simpson years was a center for physical education activities. It was perhaps the most badly needed facility on campus, yet its construction became the most controversial. In April 1960, eight years before ground was actually broken, the Board of Visitors had passed a resolution naming the proposed edifice for C. O'Conor Goolrick, who was in effect the founding father of the College; only two months later, Goolrick died. In the six years that followed, the building did not progress from the drawing board, as the General Assembly thrice rejected requests for its funding. Finally, in 1966, the state appropriated $1,252,000 for the building that, when originally proposed in 1960, was estimated to cost only around $800,000. Augmented by a federal grant of approximately $443,000, the total outlay for the building came to $1,755,000, and construction began in the fall of 1967.[5]

Problems arose, however, when it was suggested that a planned multipurpose room be used as a rifle range—the brainchild of Board of Visitors member Richard Cross. The elderly Cross, whose interest in riflery dated to 1912, was a director of the National Rifle Association and had been involved in establishing rifle ranges and programs at several colleges, including the University of Virginia. In the fall of 1968, as Goolrick Hall moved toward completion, Cross announced his plan to give the College a number of .22 caliber target rifles, backstops, mats, and other paraphernalia with the hope of establishing intramural and intercollegiate competition, as well as a riflery club.

The temper of the times was not propitious for such a proposal, even at a school whose most popular organized extracurricular activity in its early years, ironically, had been the Rifle Club. Uninfluenced by (or more likely unaware of) that history, students immediately attacked Cross's idea. The *Bullet* opined that "at a time when many Americans are beginning to question the need for guns, and their consequences, Mary Washington College may be on the verge of a backward fall into the past"; the creation of a rifle range would thus be "a waste of money and an ideological outrage." Linda Gattis Shull '69 agreed, asserting in a letter to the paper that "the proposed rifle range would be an outright insult to our professed ideology. I seriously doubt that there are girls here who receive aesthetic exhilaration from the sight of a .22, or are thrilled at the sensation of the forefinger against a steel trigger."[6]

Chancellor Simpson himself was evidently not enamored with the plan, commenting that he was "not sure it is the best use of the money." At the same time, he responded diplomatically to Cross's offer. It was "not a moral issue," Simpson said. "I don't think Mr. Cross wants to give anything the girls don't want. It never occurred to him that people wouldn't want it." Ultimately the building opened in September 1969 sans rifle range—as well as, it might be noted, without certain other, and more important, amenities including air-conditioning, a casualty of construction costs that exceeded initial projections. But meanwhile the northernmost end of the campus provided gleaming quarters for physical education classes and the nascent athletic program: a main gymnasium and an auxiliary gym, a natatorium with seventy-foot swimming pool, several dance studios, a handball and racquetball court, exercise room, sundecks, classrooms, offices, and lounge.

The opening of the Goolrick facilities, important in themselves, also had the domino effect of making several other spaces on campus available for conversion to more profitable uses. In particular, the removal of the swimming pool, bowling alley, dance studios, and PE offices from Lee Hall allowed that building to be reconfigured to house the bookstore, student lounge, police office, and a branch bank. As for Goolrick Hall itself, after finally being retrofitted for air conditioning in 2000, it continued into the twenty-first century to serve as the primary locus of the MWC athletic program—intramural, intercollegiate, and recreational.

During Grellet Simpson's final dozen years as chancellor, Mary Washington changed significantly in some ways, minimally in others. Social life on campus remained much as it had been for decades, with students finding diversion mainly in weekend visits to or from males from other schools or by the campus presence of Marines from nearby Quantico.

Activities on campus were diminished in 1958 by the dissolution of the famed marching band. Opportunities for musical participation, however, were still available through the concert band that replaced the marching band or through the MWC Chorus, which expanded notably when, in that same year,

George E. Luntz was appointed chairman of the Music Department. Traditions such as Devil-Goat Day and Junior Ring Dance continued, as did activities such as dormitory competitions for the best Christmas decorations.

But if social life witnessed little change, the academic program was a different matter. Chancellor Simpson's leadership resulted in significant improvement. Qualifications of entering students increased steadily. For example, by 1967, the average combined SAT score of first-year students was 1,142, and 97 percent of the freshmen had been in the highest two-fifths of their graduating high school classes.

Another tangible measurement was the College's successful petition for a Phi Beta Kappa chapter. Efforts to secure a chapter began in 1964 when Chancellor Simpson called a meeting of the twenty-three faculty and staff members who were currently members of the fraternity. A steering committee was established that worked during the next several years with the national headquarters of the organization in an effort to secure recognition for a chapter at MWC, a process that involved an extensive site visit that included interviews with College officials, department chairs, selected faculty members, and student leaders.

On September 11, 1970, the College was formally notified of approval for the chapter, which was designated the Kappa of Virginia Chapter. An installation ceremony was held in the foyer of GW in February 1971, where the charter was officially presented to the College. In May of that year, the first students were inducted—twenty-two seniors and one junior—at a banquet in Seacobeck.

The securing of Phi Beta Kappa recognition was clear evidence of the College's rise in academic stature. By the end of the 1960s, Mary Washington was widely regarded in Virginia and beyond as the commonwealth's preeminent public college for women. Camaraderie among its students—a sense of being part of an elite cohort—was at its peak. Never had more graduates gone forth to careers of noteworthy accomplishment in business, government service, academia, and the legal and medical professions.

Yet even as it enjoyed its position of unprecedented prominence as a women's college, Mary Washington approached its end as a single-sex institution. Change loomed, vast and unexpected, as the College was about to be affected by larger social, cultural, and political currents whose ramifications on campus would forever alter the institution. In the years ahead, Mary Washington would not necessarily be a worse place; by many measurements, it might well have been considered, in fact, a better place.

But it would not be the *same* place.

FUNDAMENTAL CHANGES

By the time of its fiftieth anniversary, Mary Washington College had gone through several distinct incarnations: from normal and industrial school, to state teachers college, to independent liberal arts college, to the women's branch of the University of Virginia. Yet even at an institution where metamorphosis was ongoing, the extent and pervasiveness of change in the late 1960s and early 1970s were remarkable.

As with many institutions of higher learning, Mary Washington both reflected and contributed to pervasive social and cultural currents that swept across the United States during that period. At MWC these developments included the alteration of the structure and governance of the institution as well as significant changes in the composition and behavior of the student body. Indeed, by 1974, with the end of Grellet Simpson's lengthy term as head of the institution, the College had in many respects been transformed in ways unforeseen, and almost unimaginable, as recently as a decade earlier.

The three most fundamental changes involved the advent of male coeducation, the separation from the University of Virginia, and the coming of racial integration. Of those, the most visible, both on campus and to outside observers, was the arrival of male students.

It was not, of course, the first time that men had attended the College, but earlier instances had been on a limited and essentially ad hoc basis, most notably the male day students who were admitted under provisions of the postwar GI Bill. Those applications had dwindled, however, to the point that only five men enrolled in the freshman class of 1954–55, the final year in which such applications were accepted; the last graduated in 1958. This time, it would be different.

The possibility of coeducation at both the University of Virginia and Mary Washington had been bandied about in desultory fashion for several years, usually generating negative responses on both campuses. Opposition was especially strong in Charlottesville, where the admitting of women was widely viewed (inexplicably) as portending the death of the honor system and, even worse, as an indication of "creeping state-U-ism"—an inchoate but pernicious phenomenon that would presumably destroy the institution's distinctive character.

As early as 1929, a proposal to admit women to the University of Virginia elicited such vehement student opposition that the effort was abandoned. Attitudes had evidently not changed much with the passage of four decades, judging by the response to the suggestion of admitting women in the late 1960s. There was, for example, a widely reported discussion of the issue between debate teams from the University of Virginia and Princeton, covered by the *Washington Post* and MWC's *Bullet*, during which one participant expressed his opposition to coeducation by claiming facetiously (one assumes) that if women were admitted, "the man's work is going to be hampered by the presence of women in his classes, and the man's play is going to be hampered by the presence of education in his women."

While the *Post* noted that the teams "had great fun with the topic," the *Bullet* reporter was not so charitable. "The event," she wrote, "was more of a contest of ribald and, at times crude, wit than a sincere attempt to discuss a serious problem."

She was right, of course, but the debate, however frivolous, did reflect the predominant feeling of U.Va. students toward coeducation. A poll taken by the student newspaper, the *Cavalier Daily*, revealed "wholehearted" opposition to any such plan. The paper itself agreed editorially. "We look with horror," it declared, "upon the prospect of a large-scale female invasion other than for the purpose of a party weekend on these traditionally male grounds."

Dissent from such a view was scant. One of the few was a *Cavalier Daily* columnist who predicted that "the female pagan hordes will soon be bounding over the serpentine walls of Paradise, not merely for a weekend plunder raid on Mr. Jefferson's University, but for permanent residence. There is no good reason," he declared, "to impede the deluge of pulchritude." The coordinate college arrangement, he continued, was unacceptable "for the simple reason that it has not worked. Mary Washington College is, technically, our women's coordinate school, yet our friends in Fredericksburg are leading the clamor to get in."[7]

Regarding coeducation at Mary Washington, opposition on the Fredericksburg campus was not as adamant as at U.Va., but it was still predominant. A *Bullet* poll in 1967 revealed that 76 percent of the respondents preferred that MWC remain all female; only 16 percent favored admitting men.

Among those who did support coeducation at Mary Washington, a common rationale was that it would improve the academic environment. As one student put it, "Girls tend to slip into not studying to their full capacity unless they can be stimulated by outstanding male students." Others were not so sure. "You think you have trouble studying now," wrote one. "Imagine going to the library to study and sitting down next to a boy."

An important step toward coeducation came in the fall of 1967 when Chancellor Simpson appointed a ten-member faculty committee, known as the Committee on the Future of the College. It was charged with investigating and making recommendations concerning several key areas, among them the possibility of accepting male students and the ancillary question of the institution's subsequent relationship with the University of Virginia in the event that coeducation did occur.[8] Having held over twenty meetings, including consultation with College faculty and administrators both active and retired, and having solicited input from the Student Government Association, the Alumnae Association, and the State Council of Higher Education, the committee recommended that men be admitted on a nonresidential basis to both summer and regular sessions and, moreover, that plans be developed for the eventual enrollment of men on a residential basis as well.

Predictably, the prospect of coeducation became the "hot topic" on campus in the ensuing months among all elements of the College community. There was by no means unanimity of opinion; a *Bullet* poll early in 1969 revealed that approximately 60 percent of the student respondents were still opposed, while slightly over 50 percent of faculty were in favor.

But even among the students there was ambivalence. Assessing the climate in early 1969, the College newspaper concluded that "there is not a consensus of opinion to 'integrate,' nor is there a movement to build a high wall around our bastion of womanhood. In fact, Mary Wash girls seem fairly open-minded on the subject." While admitting that some perquisites of the all-female arrangement would be lost, the same article suggested that coeducation would also have advantages, especially in the non-curricular aspect: "Socially the pressure would not be so great to latch on to a permanent boyfriend just to have a date, nor would there be the weekend mass exodus. A more casual, friendly social atmosphere would be created."

Chancellor Simpson, for his part, approached the issue with his customary caution. He was not opposed in principle to coeducation and even stated publicly in May of 1967 that "it's something that ought to be investigated." At the same time, he felt that students should have an option concerning single-sex or coeducational colleges. Fundamentally he was skeptical about the necessity for coeducation—as might be expected, given his long tenure as head of an all-female institution. As he frankly confided some years after his retirement, "I would not have wished in other circumstances for the college to go coed. But it seemed inevitable."

His greatest concern seems to have been the potential social impact of having men on campus, particularly the possibility of coed residence halls, a practice that was then becoming more prevalent in colleges across the country. At the time, he commented that "coeducation means living together, not learning together, and I don't think we have to provide that." It was a view that he continued to maintain, claiming years later that "there are people who really believe in coed education—not coed living necessarily—but [with] coed education, one leads to the other. Once you start that, it goes the whole way."

He also adamantly rejected the prevalent notion that the presence of males would enhance the academic environment, scorning (privately) the view that "you had to have some boys in there to get the male point of view, and that's all poppycock. Girls have sense, too."[9]

The tentativeness of his position was manifested in a May 1969 interview with the *Bullet* in which he explained that he did not think it was "of any great significance whether the student body be made up of men and women, or [only] men or [only] women. I think the main question is the education of the person. So that I can, in all honesty, agree that for some people a coeducational institution is exactly right. And I would like to feel that diversity can be maintained, and should be maintained."

As the possibility increased that Mary Washington would become coeducational, either by its own choice or forced to do so by external fiat, students seemed to accept the pending change with equanimity, though not without some expressions of concern. One *Bullet* op-ed article, for example, having noted the unmistakable trend toward coeducation across the country, questioned whether MWC should be similarly "integrated." Claiming that coeducation would necessitate both curricular and physical changes—including "the removal of the nude or semi-nude female statues sprinkled abundantly over campus"—the columnist concluded, "There are obvious alterations that would have to be made, starting with the basics of our own spinning wheel seal and the 'God, home, and country' motto. Somehow it's hard to visualize an 'MWC Charlie' sprinting to Modern Marriage [class] with his spinning wheel seal notebook under his arm . . . [and] even more difficult to visualize the same 'MWC Charlie' with both the notebook and his leotard for Fundamentals of Movement."

Notwithstanding such concerns, be they trivial or substantive, it was clear by the fall of 1969 that coeducation was likely to be entailed upon MWC in consequence of a lawsuit in federal district court to force the admission of a female undergraduate student at the University of Virginia. As Chancellor Simpson himself later acknowledged, "Once girls were admitted to undergraduate classes at Charlottesville, there wasn't any sense in having a separate girl's college."

At the time, however, the chancellor did what he could to maintain the status quo. Summoned to testify in the pending lawsuit, he argued in his August 1969 deposition that men and women should have a choice in the type of college they attended, in terms of gender, noting that his own experience as student, faculty member, and dean at Randolph-Macon College convinced him that there were some advantages to single-sex arrangements. At Randolph-Macon, he said, "There were not all the women running around" to cause distractions. "I don't think [coeducation] is harmful," he concluded, "I just don't think it's necessarily beneficial."

At one point in the course of aggressive interrogation by the plaintiff's attorney, noted ACLU lawyer Philip Hirschkop, the discussion turned to social ramifications of single-sex education, specifically Hirschkop's allegation that Mary Washington students suffered from limited dating opportunities:

HIRSCHKOP: "Do you genuinely feel that the girls at Mary Washington have full opportunity to see boys on a daily basis as they would if they were going to a coed school?"

SIMPSON: "As much as it's necessary to see the boy, yes. . . ."

HIRSCHKOP: "Don't you feel that dating includes maybe having lunch with a man or even having breakfast or studying with him?"

SIMPSON: "Yes, she can have breakfast with him or lunch with him at a women's college."

HIRSCHKOP: "Are there enough men available in Fredericksburg that a woman can regularly see a man three or four afternoons a week?"

SIMPSON: "There is Quantico right there."

The exchange grew testy when Hirschkop bore down on a critical aspect of the suit—namely, the claim that relegating female applicants to Mary Washington College denied them access to superior educational opportunities available at U.Va. To Simpson, whose primary goal as chancellor had been to elevate the academic quality of the College, such an allegation was infuriating. Though admitting that the U.Va. library might be superior in terms of its special collections, Simpson took heated exception to Hirschkop's assertion of the University's overall academic superiority, a contention based largely on the fact that, according to the lawyer, MWC offered only twenty-nine courses in English as compared to over fifty offered at U.Va. "That doesn't necessarily mean what the comparison of the figures would indicate," Simpson replied. "The vast majority of institutions have far more courses in undergraduate school than there is absolutely any sense in having."

"Would your conclusion be that the University of Virginia has more than they need?" asked Hirschkop. "So does Mary Washington, probably," retorted Simpson.

In an ironic contretemps just a few weeks later, Hirschkop appeared on the Mary Washington campus, the guest of the Political Science Department, whose chair, Lewis P. Fickett Jr., had invited Hirschkop to speak on the general topic of civil liberties. Hirschkop, however, used the occasion to focus on issues in the pending suit, notably the College's presumed academic inferiority. Comparing the two institutions statistically, he asserted that faculty salaries overall at MWC were 35 percent lower than at the university and that U.Va. had almost twice as many undergraduate courses and thirteen more majors. Mary Washington—"Mary Monastery" in his snide terminology—was being subjected to repression, he claimed, warning that riots and student upheavals would result unless such grievances were redressed by administrators he assailed as "female racists."

Professor Fickett fired back, stoutly defending the academic integrity of the College—"we have nothing for which to apologize"—and blasting the guest, whom he felt had betrayed him. He had invited Hirschkop, he explained, because he "respected his reputation as a dedicated fighter for the rights of all kinds of minority interests," but his guest had "turned out to be a Leftist version of Senator Joseph McCarthy—a demagogue who distorted, quoted out of context, twisted, maligned and abused respected public officials. As a comedy show, it deserved a passing grade. As a serious presentation of the exceedingly complex issues involved, it was a disgraceful performance."[10]

However accurate the professor's assessment may have been, the fact was that, before the federal bench, arguments such as Hirschkop's carried the day. A three-judge panel of the U.S. District Court on September 30, 1969, issued a decision that was tantamount to outlawing gender discrimination in admissions policy at the University of Virginia, and by implication at Mary Washington as well. Accordingly, the following February, the Board of Visitors passed a resolution proclaiming that "the restrictions heretofore placed on the admission of men to Mary Washington College for the regular sessions be and they hereby are unconditionally removed, so that commencing with the regular academic session of 1970–71, there shall be no restrictions on the admission of male applicants . . . other than the same restrictions imposed upon female applicants."

With that, after more than six decades as a women's college, Mary Washington became coeducational. The change did not provoke any great outcry of opposition—it was, after all, the result of a legal mandate—but on the other hand, it was not accomplished as gracefully as it might have been, a situation that Chancellor Simpson later acknowledged with some regret. "I think we were dragged into it screaming and hollering in a way," he said. "I resented the way it was done, because I think free choice would have been so much healthier." It was a decision, he added, "which we would have made" anyway, in due course.[11]

It soon became apparent that establishing a policy of coeducation did not necessarily mean embracing it, and the administration's initial attitude was decidedly more one of acquiescence than enthusiasm. Nor was such an attitude surprising. After all, the onetime teachers' college had risen, especially under Simpson's stewardship, to a widely acknowledged level of excellence as a women's college of liberal studies (notwithstanding attorney Hirschkop's plaint to the contrary). Though such an assessment might have been disputed in some quarters—particularly in the environs of Harrisonburg, Farmville, and Radford—there was a widespread perception within the state that by the 1960s Mary Washington was the most prestigious of the commonwealth's four women's colleges. In that light, students and alumnae might well have wondered what was to be gained by admitting men. Might not the College's distinctiveness be undermined and its lofty status diminished?

To assuage such concerns, the chancellor made it clear from the outset that there would be no headlong rush to enroll men, and he repeatedly emphasized that academic standards would not be lowered to accomplish that purpose. The approach that resulted could hardly be considered aggressive. The year after the new policy was announced, admissions officer G. Forrest Dickinson told the *Bullet*, in words that accurately described the institutional position, that his staff would "make it known that Mary Washington is coed," but that "we won't actively seek men." Citing alumnae opposition as well as practical problems such as housing for males, he continued, "Right now we're just going along, . . . seeing if coeducation is just a fad."

Though not a "fad," coeducation developed slowly—some would say glacially—at Mary Washington. Even before the first men enrolled, the *Bullet* deplored the College's complacent approach and, while counseling against "football fraternities, and separate dorms," urged that an active effort be instigated to recruit males. If the College did so, the *Bullet* proclaimed, "Mary Washington (or the University of Virginia at Fredericksburg, or whatever) has the opportunity to become a top liberal arts institution, with equality for men and women."

In the first year, 1970–71, twenty-two male students enrolled, only one of whom—a transfer from Antioch College named Bruce Finke—resided on campus, in an apartment on the second floor of Hamlet House. Judging from a lengthy year-end *Bullet* interview with Finke, it appeared that his experience was not a particularly happy one. He found the academic program to be adequate; he was not bothered by being the only male student in his classes—even when called on, as he sometimes was, to "give the man's point of view"—nor did he feel he was given any special treatment academically.

The social situation was another matter altogether. While the impressions of a single student formed no adequate basis for generalization, his comments presaged problems that would arise during the early stages of coeducation. Within "a strictly female environment," he said, there was no "opportunity to go out with the boys." Visitation regulations and the absence of coed dorms he found annoying. Most of all he expressed frustration over a general lack of "community," a condition he attributed largely to the school's "suitcase college" mentality. "This is definitely a weekend-away-from-campus school," he said. "The first part of each week is spent discussing what happened last weekend; and along about Thursday you start talking about what you're going to do for the coming weekend. And when you find somebody on campus for the weekend, they are usually complaining about a paper they have to do, or they have so much work that they can't get away; or they complain about not being able to get away in some other fashion. When I was at Antioch, the people didn't go away that much. They were involved with things on campus."

In addressing what might need to be done to make coeducation more successful, Finke raised an issue that would prove a perennial bugaboo for years to come, asserting, "I think any aim at coeducation would have to start with changing the name." Oddly, his reasoning was related not to the potentially negative effect of the name on recruiting males but to its effect on their employment opportunities after graduation: "At first glance it may appear a little bit absurd, but in the outside world—in the world of 'reality'—where you go to school quite often makes as much difference as how well you did in school, and a name means a great deal. A man applying for a job saying he graduated from Mary Washington could conceivably raise some eyebrows."

Taking his own advice, Finke did not return to MWC, presumably transferring to an institution where his employment prospects would not be hampered by attendant feminine connotations. But the issue he raised would prove much more difficult to dispatch, destined to linger as perhaps the most divisive topic during the institution's next three decades.

In the second year of the coeducational era, male enrollment increased to forty-two, with four living on campus: two in Hamlet House and two in the garage apartment adjoining the Alumnae House. At commencement that year, 1972, the first male graduates received their diplomas. All four of them were Fredericksburg residents who had transferred into Mary Washington. As the first of them, Raymond C. Cote, walked across the stage, he was

Early male coeds included, left to right: Dwight Lyons '77, Rennie Archibald '76, and David Kitterman '76.

greeted with what the local newspaper called "thunderous applause from the 367 member senior class," as were the three males who followed. According to the paper, there were apparently many in the audience who had not known until that moment that men were attending Mary Washington.

As the number of male students gradually increased in the next few years, a variety of difficulties arose. One of the main problems involved housing. Beginning with the 1972–73 session, ten male students were housed in Trench Hill, which the *Bullet* called (not without reason) "perhaps the most unusual dorm on campus." Visitation hours in the male residence were the same as for most of the other dorms: 11 a.m. to midnight during the week and until 2 a.m. on weekends. According to a spokesman for the group, the rules were generally obeyed. "Of course the girls are out on time," he said, "because I like to run around nude."

The following year, with Trench Hill filled, seven male freshmen were housed in Willard, thereby making the College's oldest dorm its first coed one. The arrangement was far from open, however. The men were cordoned off into what was previously known as the "Psych Ward," the only student rooms on the first floor, and they were not allowed weekday visitation with the Willard women. Moreover, the men's use of the hall kitchens and laundry room was restricted, and they were required to shout "man on the hall!" before entering the basement, where the showers were located.

The situation improved the following year with the establishment of the first all-male residence hall on the campus itself. The move was particularly lauded by the male students, who occasionally complained that they felt alienated from the College community. According to one of them, "The male population has become an autonomically isolated segment of the campus environment." The new arrangement, they believed, would help unify the males on campus; as one of them put it, "It will be better with all the guys together, like a frat."

The question was which dorm should be designated for that purpose, since the one chosen would mean displacing the female students who had planned on being "squatters" in their current rooms. After much debate and consideration of various options, Dean of Students Mildred Droste selected Madison Hall to be the men's dorm, effective with the 1974–75 session, and so it remained for a number of years.

In addition to some squabbles over housing, coeducation led to other occasional, and usually minor, contentious episodes. There was, for example, one gender-based skirmish in the fall of 1974 that dominated campus attention for several weeks, creating a controversy that, while developing from a serious incident, came to acquire a rather farcical dimension. The brouhaha began with the report of two attempted rapes on campus, incidents bad enough in themselves, but magnified by occurring in close succession and on the normally tranquil College grounds.

In an ostensible effort to augment campus security, the male residents of Madison Hall announced their intention to patrol the campus on upcoming weekends to apprehend any intruders whose intentions seemed questionable and to eject such undesirables from campus—or worse. "All the guys are pretty uptight about this," said junior counselor Rennie Archibald. "We are going to kick ass this weekend. We are out for blood. . . . We don't want to come across as overprotective, but we find these incidents disgusting."

The men's vigilante effort, presumably undertaken with good (if naive) intentions, produced a furor of condemnation, including an admonition from College Chief of Security Medford Haynes. "Anyone who goes out and takes the law in their own hands . . . may wind up in jail themselves," he warned. "If the boys go out to bust someone's skull, they may get their own skull busted. . . . I'd hate to see more trouble caused by our own boys overdoing it."

The harshest criticism came from the *Bullet* and from the feminist contingent on campus. Among the feminists, religion professor Elizabeth Clark emphasized in a letter to the College paper the seriousness of rape but skewered the clumsy efforts of the Madison cohort. She was puzzled, she said, as to how she "should picture those Madison men: as male apes defending . . . their female preserve from intruding bands, or as Oriental potentates guarding their harem (and which of the men, I wondered, was going to make the ultimate sacrifice to become the ever-protecting eunuch)?"

To which the *Bullet* added its own editorial ridicule: "If the co-eds [i.e., men] were not so serious about their chosen right to protect, the affair would be funny. . . . [Their] sorry attempt makes a mockery of what even Andy Griffith's 'Mayberry RFD' [might] have done with such a story line." And so, the paper advised the men, "Go home to your dorm and keep off the streets—'us girls' can take care of ourselves."

In response, Archibald claimed that he had been misquoted and that the Madison posse never had any intention of inflicting general mayhem on innocuous campus visitors. "What was meant," he explained, "was that anyone attempting rape would get his ass kicked." The *Bullet*'s attack, he concluded, could not "be considered an editorial, but rather a poor example of exaggerated feminist mud-slinging."

The offer of protection by the Madison men was, in fact, appreciated by many students, even those who regarded the effort as benighted. One such student noted that the charge that the Madison men had made an unseemly claim of protective authority over women was as absurd as it would have been "to assume that the residents of Custis [all female] would volunteer to do the mending for the Madison residents." And yet, she continued, "the most unfortunate aspect of this affair is the *Bullet*'s attempt to create opposition between men and women on campus. . . . Now, when we are consciously forging ahead towards a new equality between men and women, we must learn to stop slinging arrows and work for a more livable mutual respect."

From a longer perspective, the whole episode was symptomatic of the malaise that affected the College during the early years of coeducation as both men and women tried to adjust to the changing culture of the institution. In truth, the course for coeducation had not been well charted, as even its implementers acknowledged; developments tended to unfold in ad hoc fashion. The resulting journey was not altogether unpleasant, but neither was it smooth. And the situation was exacerbated by its occurrence during a time when gender roles in the larger society were in flux, often producing tensions that had not existed (openly at least) in an earlier time.

Evidence, some of it anecdotal, suggests that the attitudes of the College's main constituent groups toward the advent of coeducation were varied: faculty were the most supportive, though opinion was clearly divided; students seemed generally in favor of maintaining the status quo, but not adamantly so; alumni (in this case, more accurately, alumnae) were the most vocally opposed. Yet the negative attitude of the graduates did not necessarily so much betray an anti-male bias as it revealed the depth of their devotion to an institution whose influence on them had been so powerful that they feared the loss of those special qualities they believed peculiar to an all-female environment and impossible to maintain otherwise.

By all odds, the younger male faculty members were the group who most appreciated the presence of other men on campus. There was frequent social interaction between the two groups, including such events as faculty-versus-student touch-football games on Ball Circle. These were spirited contests that the students, with the athletic hubris characteristic of the callow, always expected to win against their elders—which they did not.

Overall, most of the College's constituents eventually came to appreciate that in the matter of coeducation there were trade-offs to be considered. If the enrollment of men meant the lamentable loss of certain niceties afforded by an all-female environment, then something might be gained by the addition of a male perspective in the academic arena and by the creation of a campus culture that in its gender configuration more closely resembled that of the "real world" to be encountered after graduation.

In any case, coeducation became a fact of life at the College in the early 1970s. A number of years would pass, however, and a number of controversies would arise, before Mary Washington would become comfortably coed.

Hard on the heels of coeducation came another highly significant development at Mary Washington: separation from the University of Virginia. Though the College had risen in quality and in public esteem in the years since its 1944 affiliation with U.Va., by the mid-1960s some had begun to wonder whether the arrangement was still beneficial to Mary Washington. The issue became public in 1965 with the release of the report of the Higher Education Study Commission, a panel charged with analyzing the commonwealth's colleges and universities and making recommendations to the governor and General Assembly concerning possible changes. Regarding Mary Washington, the report asserted that the existing structure of governance involved "few advantages and some handicaps to Mary Washington" and went on to suggest that separation "at some time in the future . . . may be advisable."[12]

Yet support for independent status was by no means unanimous. The student newspaper was initially skeptical. Separation "would be of no benefit to the college," the *Bullet* claimed. It recognized some disadvantages inherent in the existing arrangement but advocated organizational restructuring rather than severance as the solution: "To lose our relationship with the University of Virginia, no matter how meager at present, would perhaps be cutting off our legs to spite our backbone."

Mary Washington's Committee on the Future of the College came to much the same conclusion. Its 1969 report acknowledged the "possible need for eventual severance of the connection" but still advocated that MWC remain within the university system, inasmuch as "not only Mary Washington, but the entire university and the State benefit from this present relationship."

Alumni were conflicted on the issue. On the one hand, some resented what seemed to them "second-class citizenship" under the coordinate affiliation. On the other hand, there were those who believed that the university connection gave Mary Washington a cachet that would be destroyed by separation; many were the alumni who took great pride that their diploma declared them to be graduates of Mary Washington College "of the University of Virginia." At a time when the commonwealth decreed that females could not be enrolled in the undergraduate program in Charlottesville, Mary

Washington was as close to "the University" as a woman could get. The result of such antipodal opinions was the recommendation from an Alumni Association study committee in 1967 that the College should either become a fully coordinate—that is, equal—part of the university or else separate from it.

The whole scenario changed abruptly in 1970 when both the University and the College became coeducational, thereby removing any real reason for having a women's branch of the institution. With that, the movement for separation quickened, given a further boost in July 1971 by the College's decennial reaccreditation Self-Study Report for the Southern Association of Colleges and Secondary Schools, which found that the institution had outgrown its "branch" status. "The College has reached a stage in development," said the report, "in which the advantages of full autonomy outweigh the disadvantages of severing the existing nominal affiliation."

Mary Washington's status within the University connection seems to have declined, especially in fiscal terms, with the passage of time. One person who, perhaps better than any other, understood the situation was Lewis M. Walker Jr., a prominent Petersburg businessman who served for a number of years on the Mary Washington Committee of the University's Board of Visitors. According to Walker, University President Colgate Darden had assured him that MWC would be fully the equivalent of the Charlottesville school, including status and faculty salaries, but, in Walker's words, "as time went on, this was not the case . . . [and] when there's such a great disparity in faculty salaries, there's room for bitching."[13]

The problem became more acute, in Walker's opinion, when Darden was replaced as University president by Edgar Shannon, whose interests lay elsewhere. "He just wanted to get rid of . . . Mary Washington," recalled Walker. "I think it disappointed [Darden]."

Separation might have come sooner except that Mary Washington served an important function in the University's scheme of things. As Walker put it, Mary Washington "saved Colgate's skin because it saved him from having to face the issue of coeducation at the University." Grellet Simpson agreed, commenting some years after his retirement that the two schools had initially been "brought together for ulterior purposes, . . . to keep girls out of Charlottesville."[14]

With the coming of mandated coeducation at the University, such a dodge was no longer needed. By then Simpson had become increasingly frustrated with the administrative arrangement. Though normally circumspect in speaking about the relationship, he sometimes complained about its restrictive nature, commenting on one occasion that "if we had been a free agent, we would have gone coeducation sooner." Increasingly inclined to favor separation, Simpson sought the advice of one whom he (and many other Virginians, both in education and in politics) greatly admired. "So finally," he recalled, "I asked Mr. Darden. I said, 'Shouldn't we separate?' He said, 'Yes, long ago.'"

Chancellor Simpson took the initiative and, after conferring with faculty and staff, asked the Board of Visitors to consider the matter of separation. In the whole process, Simpson appears to have been concerned that the College be perceived as acting independently, not as the passive recipient of decisions made in Charlottesville. "I made the move," he maintained. "I didn't get fired. They didn't drop us."

Acting on Simpson's request, the board requested the advice of the State Council of Higher Education, which, in January 1972, endorsed the concept of autonomy for Mary Washington. At its next meeting, in February, the University's Board of Visitors approved the concept and forwarded its recommendation to the General Assembly of Virginia. That body, which was then in session, promptly enacted legislation creating an independent Mary Washington College.

According to the legislation, the College would thenceforth be governed by its own board, to be known as the Rector and Visitors of Mary Washington College. The board, to be appointed by the governor, was to comprise twelve members, at least half of whom were to be graduates of the institution; no more than three could be nonresidents of Virginia. They were to serve four-year appointments and be eligible to serve only two terms. The body would be chaired by a rector whom the members themselves would elect.

The legislation also conveyed to the College's board control over two properties: Belmont, the estate of the artist Gari Melchers, located just across the Rappahannock River from Fredericksburg; and the James Monroe Law Office–Museum and Memorial Library, located in the city. (The latter delegation of authority, seemingly innocuous enough, was to prove a source of inordinate contention in the years ahead.)

When the College's independent status took effect on July 1, 1972, the title of the institution's chief administrative officer was changed from chancellor to president, so that Grellet Simpson became what he had been when first hired: President Simpson. On that same date, Governor Linwood Holton announced the appointments of the College's first independent governing board, consisting of seven alumnae and five males. Lewis M. Walker, who had retired earlier from the University's board and had chaired the board's Mary Washington Committee, was elected rector; Irene Lundy Brown of Newport News (MWC '39) was chosen as vice rector; and Katherine E. Hopper of Fairfax (MWC '30) was named secretary of the new governing body. The only black member appointed was Samuel Dewitt Proctor, professor of education at Rutgers University and former president of Virginia Union University in Richmond.[15]

Thus did the institution on Marye's Heights begin yet another incarnation, this time as a coeducational college enjoying (once again) independent status within the commonwealth's system of higher education.

Racial integration came slowly to Mary Washington College. Although the epochal *Brown* decision in May 1954 mandated an end to racial segregation in public schools—and, by extension, in colleges as well—it was not until almost exactly ten years later that the barrier to the admission of black students to Mary Washington was officially removed when the Board of Visitors formally approved a desegregation policy.

Even before the board's decree there had been some indications that integration was becoming a concern at the College. There was, for example, a campus panel in 1961 titled "What Is the Responsibility of College Faculties and Students in the Integration Crisis?" Two years later the College YWCA formed a race relations committee "to act as a forum for discussion, to stimulate thinking and an exchange of ideas on the problem," in the words of its chair, Martha Coates.[16]

By the time the board announced its new policy on black admissions, there had in fact already been several African Americans—or, in the usual parlance of the time, "Negroes"—who had attended Mary Washington. The first was Jacquelyn Pulliam, a teacher in Culpeper County who attended summer classes as a commuter student in 1962. The second was Gaye Todd, who had earlier graduated as valedictorian at Walker-Grant High School, then Fredericksburg's high school for blacks. Todd, who as Gaye Adegbalola would go on to gain wide recognition for excellence in teaching and for performance as a member of the acclaimed blues group Saffire, was currently a student at Boston University when she enrolled for transfer credits in French in the 1963 summer session. The first black residential student arrived on campus the following year when Kaye Estelle Savage of Richmond was accepted for admission. After two years she transferred to Howard University, from which she subsequently graduated.

Though the Mary Washington campus was far from a cauldron of social protest in the mid-1960s—selection of the May Queen and similar traditional campus events still tended to dominate the headlines of the *Bullet*—there was a small cadre of activists who became directly involved in the civil rights movement, which was then in its most crucial stage. One student, Erin Simms, took the fall 1964 semester off to work with the Student Nonviolent Coordinating Committee; three others spent their Christmas vacations that year working on biracial projects in Mississippi under the aegis of the Southern Student Organizing Committee, a predominantly white group that encouraged and coordinated student activism on campus. Closer to home, a contingent of twenty-six students led by Nan Grogan (who as Nan Grogan Orrock would eventually become a Georgia legislator) joined area residents in downtown Fredericksburg in March 1965 to protest recent incidents of police brutality against blacks in Selma, Alabama, as well as to express support for abolition of the poll tax and for passage of the Voting Rights Bill then pending in Congress. It was symptomatic of racial tensions at the time that Chancellor Simpson felt constrained to explain to the local media that the students' actions should not be construed as representing the views of the College at large, though he emphasized that "as individuals acting on their own time, they have a right to exercise their privilege as citizens."

To concerned students such as these, the slow pace of integration at the College was frustrating, and some of them set about on their own to address the situation. Noting that the College did not as a rule send representatives to "college day" events at predominantly black high schools, some members of the committee announced their intention to do this themselves. Chancellor Simpson responded that though he would not prohibit such activity, he believed a less-public approach would be better. The *Bullet*, in an editorial titled "Progress in Race Relations," endorsed Simpson's advice. "This committee can do excellent work," it suggested, "and accomplish much if it goes about its work tactfully and diplomatically. There is great potential in this group of girls devoted to human equality, but since we are in an area of racial tension, common sense should tell them that they must progress slowly and carefully."

Undeterred by that admonition, a number of students proceeded to visit local black high schools, extolling the virtues of Mary Washington. The results were negligible: only three black students were enrolled at the College in 1965–66 and two in 1966–67.

In April 1967 Henry Marsh, a black city councilman from Richmond (and later its mayor), delivered a campus speech titled "Why Mary Washington Is a White College." He cited a number of factors, some of them not directly the fault of the institution, but his remarks emphasized the need for active recruitment of black students. He was generally correct in asserting that the College had been lax in its efforts. The approach to integration had essentially been passive up to that time: if black students wished to come, fine; but little attempt was made to entice them. (It was much the same approach as that taken toward males.)

In the late 1960s, racial tensions rose across the country as the civil rights movement evolved from the benign leadership of Martin Luther King Jr. to the more confrontational tactics of Black Power advocates. Whereas many Americans had earlier been moved by the plaintive yet triumphant strains of "We Shall Overcome," increasing numbers now felt threatened by raucous taunts of "Burn, baby, burn."

The greater wariness about race relations was evident at Mary Washington, where a student poll in 1967 indicated that approximately half of the student body believed that the civil rights movement was "demanding too much, too soon." An extensive *Bullet* article on the subject the following year devoted several pages to the rise of Black Power, including a survey of students, faculty, and employees that "turned up a decidedly negative attitude toward the term." According to the article, most associated Black Power with "aggression calculated to put Negroes in political, economic, and social dominance. Black power means violence. It is a destructive force that angrily spurns equality and goes for . . . control." Within such an environment did the black experience at Mary Washington develop.

Integration at the College had increased very slowly since the first black student enrolled in 1962. By 1968 there were still only five African Americans living on campus. Keenly cognizant of their exceedingly minority status, the group naturally bonded, referring to themselves as the "Big Five" in half-joking analogy to the civil rights movement's so-called Big Four leaders: King, Roy Wilkins, Whitney Young, and James Farmer (who in his later years would become a revered member of the Mary Washington faculty).

Their experiences as racial pioneers were clearly mixed, as was evident in a lengthy 1968 *Bullet* article about them titled "The Negro on Campus." Contacts with black townsfolk, for example, were usually positive, with some local families inviting the women for meals after church on Sundays. And the faculty were generally supportive. One of the students, Claudith "Dottie" Holmes, later recalled in particular the kindness of English professor Don Glover and his wife, who would invite her into their home: "You could just drop in and have dinner. . . . I'll always remember. I sat right at the table with his children. You were always welcome." (For later generations of students to whom such behavior would seem unremarkable, it should be noted that in the Virginia of that time, such socializing between races was still viewed askance by many whites, and such actions still carried the chance of opprobrium and even ostracism within certain elements of the community.)

Accordingly the black students were confronted not so much by anger as by what they perceived as oversensitivity and forced friendliness—often epitomized by the sugary assurance that, as the bromide put it, "Some of my best friends are colored." Which, of course, involved another affront, albeit an unintended one. Many white students, having been reared in traditional southern homes, were habituated to say "colored," deeming it somehow more genteel than "Negro." It was a linguistic faux pas that rankled the black students, who made known their strong preference for "Negro" (though the appellation of choice would soon evolve to "black" to "Afro-American" to "African American").

For the most part, the early black students forbore such indignities, intuiting that difficulties were bound to arise during a time in which race relations were changing so rapidly and fundamentally, especially in the South. They also perceived that in many cases, problems arose not so much from inherent hostility but simply from whites' lack of knowledge about black culture and a consequent uneasiness in its presence. One of the "Big Five," Venus Jones—who in June 1968 would become the College's first black graduate and go on to a distinguished career in medicine—described the scenario succinctly. "Many girls," she observed, "feel embarrassed

Venus Jones '68

because of their utter ignorance about the Negro race. Some are embarrassed to mention the word 'Negro' in your presence. Some have never even held a conversation with a Negro," which she termed "an absurd situation in an institution of higher learning."[17]

The black students' overriding disappointment with life at the College lay in being viewed as curiosities on campus, lumped together as "the Negroes," rather than being viewed as individuals. It was a situation that could be changed, they surmised, only if the number of minority students increased—a circumstance that would necessitate an expansion of recruitment efforts.

Mary Washington's visibility at predominantly black secondary schools (an entity still prevalent in Virginia even a decade or more after *Brown*) was virtually nil. It was the practice of the College to send admissions representatives only to high schools that requested them, according to Director of Admissions Michael Houston, and owing to the College's history as an all-white school, almost no black schools did so, even as late as 1968. The situation began to change somewhat, though not appreciably, in 1970 with the appointment of the College's first African American admissions counselor, Diane-Louise Kenny. The following year, black enrollment grew to twenty-six, but attracting minority students remained a troublesome challenge for years to come.

Meanwhile the College's small contingent of blacks voiced a specific grievance during the spring of 1968. The issue was segregated housing. Noting that the three black freshmen that year had all been placed in the same dormitory room, one of them, Claudith Holmes, wryly commented that she was "sure a computer didn't do it."

She was right about that. In fact, the room-assignment system (if a "system" it could be called) was utterly unsophisticated. As the then-assistant dean of students, Mildred Droste, recalled years later: "We had cards with pictures on them and [history professor] Myra Irby came in and helped me with room assignments. . . . So, we would look at these pictures and try to match them up according to information that was on the card. She'd say, 'Well, this girl's a cutie. Maybe these two would go together.' And that was how we did room assignments."[18]

Eventually the issue became moot when, at the insistence of the NAACP, the practice of including photographs with student applications was abandoned. As for the spring 1968 controversy, it would arise again but in the short term was overshadowed by the news of the murder of Martin Luther King Jr. on April 4.

The Mary Washington community shared fully in the national sense of shock and subsequent mourning over the assassination of the civil rights movement's most powerful and respected leader. Anita Whitehead Scott, one of the College's black students, later recalled the day as the most transformative experience of her career at Mary Washington, especially the impromptu gathering of students on Ball Circle, holding hands and singing choruses of "We Shall Overcome." At a later memorial march in downtown Fredericksburg, many College personnel participated, including philosophy professor George Van Sant, who served as a marshal for the event. "We marched into St. George's Episcopal Church and filled it," he recalled. "Black and white, completely integrated. It was a beautiful service."

Because it occurred during spring break, few students participated in the march, but many were deeply moved by King's death. One of them, Claudith Holmes (who was emerging as a leader among the black students), wrote a poignant tribute in the College paper, mourning King's loss in highly personal terms and concluding with a challenge to the community: "Those people," she said, "who have never thought of the racial problem that exists in our country today must kindle a flame in their hearts and dedicate themselves to do something today to help solve the problem. . . . All of us can and must do something. This is not an impossible dream."

For its part, the faculty passed a resolution urging that the College "strive to become more relevant in the area of human rights and dignity lest we contribute to the growing polarization of white and black America." Specifically the resolution expressed a commitment to reevaluating the institution's policies regarding admissions, hiring practices, and curriculum.

Several subsequent developments offered hope that such a commitment was being fulfilled. For one thing, the College established the Martin Luther King Scholarship in the aftermath of the assassination, and the first such grant was awarded to Marsha Meekins of Richmond. Having applied for admission in late 1968, Meekins received the grant of $500 (to be available during her sophomore year), along with additional assistance, and enrolled as a freshman for the 1969–70 session.

For another, the College employed its first African American faculty member in 1968 when Johnny Johnson was hired as a part-time art instructor in the Education Department. The choice was a sound one, inasmuch as Johnson was already a widely admired veteran of the local public school system. He cannily used his position at Mary Washington to stimulate his students' sensitivity to racial issues. When white students would ask him for a tube of flesh-colored paint, he would give them a tube of black paint. "We'd laugh," he said, "and they'd get the message—flesh color for whom?"

Despite such advances, vestiges of a less-enlightened time remained. In the fall of 1968, for example, the practice of residential segregation persisted—remarkably, in light of the previous spring's avowals—prompting the feisty Holmes to vent her frustration. "It's very disappointing and disheartening," she said, "to think that you've come to an institution of higher learning and open-mindedness and find out that you've come to a place that's living twenty-five years in the past."

The College newspaper took up the issue with alacrity and, in a blistering editorial titled "Equal but Separate," demanded an immediate end to the practice. A few weeks later the paper again addressed the issue in the course of a long interview with Chancellor Simpson, asking him directly if "the placing together of Negro freshmen in the same room can be justified." Simpson, in his own estimation, held enlightened racial views (as indeed he did within the context of his time and place), having been one of the founders of the Virginia Council on Human Relations, a group formed to encourage a positive interracial attitude following the *Brown* decision. He thus prefaced his response to the question with an explanation of how he had earlier risked censure by being in the vanguard of racial justice in Virginia. As a specific example, he pointed out that when his inauguration was being planned, at the peak of the "massive resistance" movement, some urged that the presidents of the commonwealth's black colleges be excluded from the event. He told them, he recalled, "Either the Negro college presidents will be invited or there will be none [i.e., no inauguration]. . . . I thought that was fundamental and I took a stand on that, and they were invited. They came. . . . I was vilified, but . . . I won my point."

The reporter, apparently not appreciating Simpson's constitutional propensity for circumlocution—a habit that tended to become more acute if the subject was controversial—persisted. "Well," she asked pointedly, "do you think it was an accident that the three Negro freshmen were put in the same room last year?"

It was "a fair question," Simpson responded, "but a loaded question." (He might have added that it was also a question of such audacity that it would never have been asked by a student of an earlier generation.) At any rate, he eventually replied more forthrightly: "I was just thunderstruck when I saw it. . . . This is contrary to everything I believe in. I don't agree with what has happened. . . . It was a grave mistake, and I don't think it should happen again."

It did not. When eleven black students were accepted for the 1970 freshman class, Mildred Droste, who by then had replaced the retired Margaret Hargrove as dean of students, announced that they would be assigned indiscriminately to freshman dorms according to the order in which their applications were accepted.

But that practice, too, caused problems from another direction: white parents who objected to having their child room with an African American. "That was a no-no as far as some of our parents were concerned," Droste recalled.

> They did not want their daughter, under any conditions, living with a black student. One of the black students that we had was a wonderful person, Chris[tine] Hall. I'll remember her to my dying day. . . . I assigned a white girl to Chris Hall. The white girl's father called and said that he wanted her moved; otherwise he was going to take her out of school. So, I had to talk to Chris. I told her, "Chris, this is prejudice that has been going on for years and years. You understand that it is not my idea that you have to move? I have been given an ultimatum that I have to move you out of this room. Do you have any idea who you would like to room with?

Hall did find a willing roommate, and so that particular crisis was settled. But Droste also felt she should discuss the matter with the original roommate. "I remember," she said, "I asked the white girl, 'Your father is a dentist?' She said, 'Yes.' I said, 'Does he have two chairs, one for whites and one for blacks?' She said, 'Yes, he does.' So that was a key to me, right there. . . . [But] she was rather embarrassed about the way her father had acted. This was very traumatic. It was one of those things that I had to handle with kid gloves."

The *Bullet* scorned such an approach. "Though it is true that many white parents have objected to their daughter rooming with a black," it admonished, "it seems pointless to take such petty views into serious consideration. The only way prejudices can be overcome is by facing them, and the only way social barriers can be struck down is by refusing to recognize them."

Admirable as that stance may have been, it perhaps underestimated the weight of discriminatory tradition that bore heavily on administrators in that time and place, making it extremely difficult to effect progressive change, no matter how ardently desired by those in authority—in this case, Chancellor Simpson and Dean Droste, specifically. It was indeed a "kid-glove" problem whose remediation required not only goodwill but the tincture of time.

Even as the housing controversy died down, it was followed by reports of institutional racism regarding certain dining hall practices. Questions arose specifically as to why black employees—the majority of the kitchen employees were black—consistently ate as a group apart from the white workers, who routinely ate with the student waitresses in the regular dining areas. There were also rumors that some black workers and white waitresses had been fired because of interracial dating.

At the request of the Student Association Senate, its National, State, and Community Affairs Committee investigated the allegations, questioning among others the director of the dining hall, Pal Robison, and various employees, both students and non-students, white and black. The committee's detailed findings were published in a lengthy *Bullet* article in December 1969.

The investigation paid particular attention to the potentially most explosive of the accusations—the alleged firing because of interracial dating. The former black employee did maintain that such was the cause of his termination, not incompetence, as claimed by food service supervisors. The white student waitresses, on the other hand, averred that the dating relationship could not have been the cause, inasmuch as "no one could possibly have known that it existed." In fact, management did not know about it, and several other waitresses testified that the employee (who had already been fired and rehired several times) "had proved undependable and more interested in talking to people than in working."

The investigation ultimately concluded that it was "unlikely that institutional racism exists in the treatment of help in Seacobeck," noting that "lack of concrete test cases makes it impossible to objectively prove discrimination." It is doubtful, however, that the overall tenor of the report did much to allay the concerns of those who suspected the subtly insidious influence of racism at work.

Though moderate by the standards of behavior at some other colleges at the time, Mary Washington's black students did become somewhat more assertive in the early 1970s. The Afro-American Association began functioning in the fall of 1970 with Claudith Holmes as its president. While the organization was mainly for blacks, it was not exclusively so, and any white student who had "a genuine, sincere interest in belonging to the club" could join, provided the student was recommended by at least one black member.

The club served not only as the nexus for social and cultural relationships among black students but also as a conduit for sharing their concerns with the larger MWC community. In that regard the Afro-American Association in 1972 published several articles in the *Bullet* setting forth the general viewpoint of the black students and expressing some specific complaints. High on their agenda was the establishment of a black studies program, and they minced no words in demanding it: "Mary Washington College is behind the times. This college is slowly losing relevance. . . . We feel insulted by this school with its feeble excuses for courses in Black Studies. . . . Black people have been deprived of racial pride for too long. . . . White culture has been shoved down Black college students' throats in hopes that the regurgitation of [it] would prevent future riots and uprisings."

Other articles addressed specific concerns of the black students (who were all female at the time). One, titled "We Want Our Men Back," was a critique of interracial dating, deploring what it called white girls' "current fad to date Black men." Consistent with the "black is beautiful" attitude of the time, it asserted that whereas blacks had once been led to imitate white standards of beauty and fashion, the African American woman "is no longer ashamed of her kinky hair or her dark complexion. She is very proud of these features because they are the things that make her different from the white woman—the things that make her a beautiful woman in the eyes of her man."

In a subsequent article, "Black Woman's Needs," the club laid out an agenda. "It is a necessity," it proclaimed, "that I be referred to as being Black, because the words *Negro* and *colored* are degrading to my dignity. These words are offensive." It went on to demand that "at least one-third of the social activities be Black oriented—for example, concerts with soulful all-Black bands [and] movies with all-Black casts." Moreover, the manifesto insisted that greater efforts be made to ensure that African American males were welcome on campus, as "the Black woman is not meant to survive without her Black man." Finally, it asserted the need for the opportunity to be alone or to socialize just with fellow blacks—"to be in a private room with her other Black friends, where she can be intimate with her thoughts and aspirations, where she can just 'hang loose and find satisfaction.'"

The article was revelatory of the rapidly changing racial climate. Whereas only a few years earlier it was segregation that created controversy, now racial pride and solidarity drove a desire for separation. Even the terminology had evolved, as the very word "Negro" went from the appellation of choice to one of disdain.

In this unsettled atmosphere, a few awkward incidents occurred on campus. One involved a showing of the southern classic *Gone with the Wind* in a crowded GW auditorium. At the moment actress Hattie McDaniel appeared on the screen as the stereotypical Mammy, the contingent of black students, seated together at the front of the auditorium, rose en masse and ceremoniously strode up the aisle and out of the building. From the astonished reaction of the white audience, it was evident that many had no understanding of why the African Americans found the caricature demeaning, and among those who did, disdain for the demonstration seemed to outweigh sympathy for its cause.

As the number of black students at Mary Washington slowly increased, so too did their involvement in the life of the campus. One notable early example came in the fall of 1972 when the Afro-American Association sponsored a daylong program to benefit the Janice Collier Sickle Cell Anemia Fund that had been established in memory of the Mary Washington freshman who had died from the disease in the previous year. "We felt this was better than putting flowers on her grave to wilt every year," said a club spokesperson. "Janice was always exuberant. . . . [She] was very proud of her color. She was very intelligent and would have been an asset to the Black race if she'd lived."

The event, which included a carnival on Ball Circle and an auction of artworks by MWC instructor Johnny Johnson, was highlighted by an evening performance by the local black theater group, Harambee 360°, among whose members were several Mary Washington students. Commenting on the power of that performance, the *Bullet* asked, "Is there now any doubt that Black is Beautiful?"

From that beginning, other events celebrating the African American heritage evolved in the coming years. In February 1973 Black Culture Week sponsored a variety of activities, including, again, performances by Harambee 360°, a concert by a black gospel group, and a rousing speech by Washington, D.C., congressman Walter Fauntroy in which he urged rejection of the prevailing view of black history that perpetuates a "sense of shame [and] deepens our sense of nobodyness." That blacks survived slavery, he said, "is a miracle; that we should be ashamed is immoral."

One of the highlights of the week was a fashion show in GW auditorium which, as the hostesses for the evening announced at the outset, would feature some "bad rags." That it did—in several different categories, including date wear, formal wear, and dress wear. In introducing the dress-wear segment, emcee Sondra Powell explained that "the church has long been an important part of Black culture. Though it's hard for Mary Washington girls to go every week, they're dressed in style when they do." At the end, all the models assembled onstage and saluted the audience with the Black Power gesture of upraised fists.

The 1974 Black Culture Week included similar elements, with Curtis W.

Harris of Hopewell as the keynote speaker. Though the response of minority students both on campus and in the community was enthusiastic, the participation of white students was negligible—a situation that left the organizers of the Afro-American Association disappointed but not despondent. Most whites did not come, commented one member, "but that doesn't mean there wasn't a Black Culture Week. And that doesn't mean that the world's going to stop and that Blacks aren't still living. Because we *are* living, and we're not going to hang our heads either."

Nor should they have. The early efforts of the Afro-American Association paved the way for an increased focus on campus minorities—a trend that in the future culminated in the rise of the Multicultural Fair, which would become one of the College's most popular annual events. But for the trailblazing blacks, the task was not easy. As one of them, Anita Whitehead Scott, aptly recalled three decades later, "Students today have no understanding of the struggle people had to go through."

AN AGE OF ACTIVISM

Even as the College was grappling with issues of coeducation, independence, and race, changes of commensurate significance were taking place in the attitudes and behavior of its student body. In this process, Mary Washington was a microcosm of developments in the larger society.

Few periods in modern American history have been more turbulent than the late 1960s and early 1970s. It was a troubling time to many, especially as manifested in the behavior of young people. As the historian William Manchester has described it: "To . . . the aroused young ideologues, nothing seemed to be sacred: not the American flag, God, motherhood, knowledge, honor, modesty, chastity, or simple honesty. . . . It was almost [as if] the Boy Scout pledge . . . had become inverted: they strove to be untrustworthy, disloyal, unhelpful, hostile, discourteous, unkind, disobedient, cheerless, wasteful, craven, dirty, and irreverent."[19]

Nowhere was this unsettling scenario more evident than on college campuses, where young people were concentrated—and highly visible. Mary Washington was by no means immune to the tumult; moreover, because of the College's traditional image as a sedate bastion of feminine propriety (not to say primness), any manifestation of rebellion was magnified. The period of ferment produced unprecedented student activism on campus with regard to administrative and academic, as well as social, issues.

One intimate and perceptive observer of those developments was Mona Davis Albertine '71, who went on to become rector of the Board of Visitors. Having arrived on campus in 1967, and thus having lived through those turbulent times, she recalled later that it was as if she had attended two different schools. "When I got there," she said, "it was still like the '50s. It felt basically like a finishing school, with lots of emphasis on manners and dress. Everyone was very respectful of all the 'authority figures,' especially Chancellor Simpson. And the clothes were very 'preppy'—Villager sweaters, Bass Weejuns and all that. But before I left, students were marching on the chancellor's office, and the dress had turned to fatigues and army boots. . . . It was a wild time, I can tell you!"

Early in his administration, Chancellor Simpson had proved amenable to change, as evidenced in 1955–56 by his decisions—gladly received by the students—to relax the dress code, albeit minimally, to permit the wearing of shorts or slacks under narrowly defined conditions. In 1957 the long-standing practice of holding required convocations every Wednesday evening and "chapels" or other assemblies on Tuesday and Friday was eliminated. In the early 1960s, Religious Emphasis Week, sponsored for many years by the campus YWCA, was discontinued, owing largely to student apathy. In 1962–63 seniors were allowed to have cars on campus. The proscriptive "cut" system was abolished in 1964–65, replaced with a basically voluntary class attendance plan.

But to the student generation of the late sixties, such reforms did not go nearly far enough. Sometimes in alliance with faculty members, they began to demand a greater voice in curricular matters theretofore generally deemed to be beyond the legitimate purview of students.

One of the most popular innovations of the time, lauded by students and faculty alike, came in spring 1968 with the abolishing of Saturday classes and the establishing of a five-day academic week. The action followed study by a faculty committee in response to growing concern about the high incidence of absenteeism on Saturdays. The committee noted that many colleges had recently abandoned Saturday classes, and unanimously recommended that Mary Washington do likewise. When the faculty at its monthly meeting voted for the plan and Chancellor Simpson expressed his assent, the assembly erupted with "enthusiastic applause."

The main flaw in the new system was that it initially employed an irregular class schedule that proved somewhat cumbersome, so that a few years later it was replaced by a more workable agreement that basically established fifty-minute daytime periods on Mondays, Wednesdays, and Fridays; seventy-five-minute daytime periods on Tuesdays and Thursdays; and two seventy-five-minute evening periods, Monday through Thursday. Aside from occasional proposals for change—such as a failed boomlet during the 1968–69 session for converting to a 4-1-4 semester system—the basic academic framework, with periodic alterations, remained in place throughout the subsequent four decades.

Another 1968 initiative heartily welcomed by students was the "pass-fail" grading option. The purpose of the option, according to the faculty committee that recommended it, was to "permit students to choose courses they would like to take, but are afraid of." That is what it essentially accomplished, with certain stipulations incorporated to prevent serious dilution of the overall grading system—namely, that (1) only elective courses could be taken pass-fail; (2) only one such course could be taken per semester; and (3) those courses could not be averaged in determining the student's grade-point average.

Students rejoiced in the implementation of the pass-fail option, but it was not long before a movement began to abolish the traditional A–F grading scale and replace it with more generalized categories: H (honors), S (satisfactory), and U (unsatisfactory). Such a proposal was consonant with the times—an era in which any judgmental process was increasingly regarded as abhorrent. In that environment, even the benign distinctions embodied in assigning grades seemed to some (the young especially) to smack of discrimination that promoted elitism and even, in the more extreme view, provided a tool for the perpetuation of the existing "power structure." On a more mundane level, advocates of HSU claimed that it would encourage emphasis on "learning for learning's sake"; after all, grades were inherently subjective and hence not a valid appraisal of one's ability.

Discussion of the issue played a prominent part in an All-College Day in May 1970, an event designed to bring together all of the institution's constituent groups—students, faculty, and administrators—for informal, wide-ranging discussion of College concerns. Opponents of the HSU plan, including many faculty members, countered that adopting such a system would compromise the prospects of students after college, inasmuch as graduate schools and potential employers would expect traditional letter grades; in addition, some claimed, the less-rigorous system would diminish student incentive.

The most cogent rebuttal came from English professor Dan Dervin, who was invited by the *Bullet*, which supported HSU, to present the opposing viewpoint. The proposed plan was flawed from the standpoint of both professors and students, he wrote: instructors needed more, not fewer, gradations—the better to provide students with an accurate evaluation of their work; students needed this too, as they deserved "the clearest, most exacting feedback possible. . . . And instructors should discourage loose generalizations [e.g., HSU], rather than indulge them." To Dervin, it would be better to have no grades at all than to adopt HSU, and simply "turn the groves of academe into a hippie grazing pasture—groovy but not graded."

As it turned out, All-College Day came at a time when Vietnam War protests were escalating, a development that tended to divert attention from the controversy over grading. The issue, in fact, never became a prominent concern on campus thereafter, and the traditional A–F (along with the pass-fail system) remained unchanged for several decades, until it was modified by the addition of pluses and minuses in the fall of 1999.

Besides the addition of the pass-fail policy, student options were further expanded in May 1969 by faculty approval of a credit-by-examination plan. This arrangement allowed a student to apply to the department chair for examination in an appropriate course—one in which the student had never been enrolled. Upon passing the exam, the student would receive due credit for it with the grade of P. Failing the exam would result in an incomplete, which would become an F unless the student attended and passed the course, or an equivalent, in the next semester. Though this option remained for many years, in practice it was rarely used.

In June of the same year, Chancellor Simpson appointed a special committee whose work was to have significant impact on the academic program. Known as the Ad Hoc Committee on Degree Requirements and College Calendar, it was energetically chaired by philosophy professor George Van Sant, whose influence on College affairs was pervasive and profound. As a result of his committee's report, delivered in the spring of 1970, the faculty approved several fundamental changes. For one, the B.S. degree was eliminated, meaning that thenceforth only the B.A. degree would be awarded. The change was mostly a technicality, as the new degree requirements soon to be implemented made no distinction in requirements between the two programs.

A second change was revision of the College calendar. Whereas previously the first semester had carried over into January, the revised plan called for the fall semester to begin in August and end before Christmas, followed by a break of approximately a month, with the spring semester beginning in mid-January and running until early May.

The main change that resulted was a wholesale reconfiguration (and simplification) of degree requirements. Gone were the various course requirements, replaced by a system that in more general terms required the equivalent of one year's work in each of four areas—literature, humanities, social sciences, and natural science and mathematics—thereby allowing students much greater latitude when selecting courses.

Despite these changes, which on the whole significantly liberalized the old system, students began to push for additional reforms, two of which involved final exams. One had to do with whether final exams should be mandatory. In April 1970 the faculty had voted to make them optional at the discretion of the individual instructor, but a few years later a number of faculty members began to advocate reinstating mandatory exams. At the faculty's February 1973 meeting, the majority of those who voted supported (sixty-five to fifty-four) the move, but the body voted to table final action until March, since it had been approved by fewer than half of the total faculty.[20]

In the interim, students, who naturally favored the optional approach—only one student in a *Bullet* poll felt otherwise—immediately set about, exhorted by the Student Association, to lobby professors to support the student position. Their efforts were evidently efficacious, for when the question arose at the March meeting, the faculty adopted a procedure requiring that examination periods must be held, but the use of that time, either for an exam or for further instruction, was left to each professor's discretion. The solution was sufficiently Solomonic to last, essentially unchanged, into the next century.

The other major issue involved the self-scheduling of exams—that is, permitting students to take an exam in a given course at any time slot in which the instructor for that course was scheduled to give an exam. The idea was first put forward in 1968 by a candidate for SGA president. Though the proposal was subsequently taken under consideration by the faculty, two years passed without favorable action, leading the *Bullet* to complain in April 1970 that "the faculty seem to resist change in the academic realm at every turn except when they are sure to benefit directly. (Remember how fast the five-day week proposal was passed.)" When the faculty again failed to approve the procedure the following fall, the paper noted with heavy sarcasm, "In these times of unrest and upheaval, we should feel secure in knowing that there is at least one body on campus that remains steadfast in the face of change and disruption."

When the question came up yet again the next semester at the April faculty meeting, it elicited a barrage of opposition. Some faculty argued that combined with the recently approved five-day week and optional exams, self-scheduling would further erode academic standards; others, from a more practical standpoint, emphasized the inconvenience that it would entail on instructors. The most powerful argument of all seemed to be that self-scheduling would put too much strain on the honor system, since a student taking an exam on an early track would be sworn to not reveal its nature or contents before the end of the exam period, which might be many days later. It came as small surprise, then, that the faculty voted the proposal down by a margin of sixty-six to fifty-six.

The bigger surprise was that the faculty decided not to let the matter drop but to resurrect it at its next meeting, the following month. At that time, many of the same opposing arguments were reprised, but for reasons not altogether clear, the advocates of self-scheduling ultimately prevailed by a vote of eighty-one to fifty-six. Beginning in the fall of 1971, self-scheduling went into effect and remained until the faculty voted in 1989 to rescind the policy.

Beyond concerns specifically about exams, students also sought more control generally over the structure and content of the academic program. One of their primary goals was to be allowed representation at faculty meetings. In the first semester of the 1969–70 session, the Student Association formally petitioned the faculty to request that a student representative be permitted to attend meetings "solely to facilitate communication between students and faculty." After customarily tedious debate covering several meetings, the faculty in essence denied the request, pointing out that sufficient channels of communication already existed, such as the faculty's Committee on College Affairs, further noting that students already served regularly on various faculty committees. As something of a concession to students' demands, the faculty did agree to make minutes of each meeting available in the library's reserve room.

That sop did not mollify the students, who continued to press for more direct involvement. In the vanguard of the movement were American studies majors who in the spring of 1970 petitioned the administration for certain reforms, including the hiring of additional instructors and the right of students to have a voice in such personnel decisions. The request received strong editorial support from the *Bullet*, which commended the effort toward achieving "student power in the decision-making processes of the academic realm of the college." Though that particular request was denied by the administration, the faculty did vote to require all departments to "develop and implement policies of student participation in departmental affairs, including voting representation at departmental meetings," stipulating that student representatives were to be elected by the majors in their respective departments. Thus began the "department rep" position, an arrangement that became a permanent and generally beneficial aspect of academic life in the years ahead.

Students of this era may have been no more critical of the College than those of earlier times, but they were certainly more vociferous in expressing their complaints. "We are not moving forward," lamented one *Bullet* editorial. "We have our feet stuck in 50 years of history and our minds are still wearing hoop skirts. Students must realize that it is they who must foster change. No one is going to give us anything. . . . It is up to us to liberate Mary Washington. For, until Mary Washington ceases to prostitute herself to the town of Fredericksburg; to the Virginia legislators; to the administration; to our parents; etc., we cannot cease to be anything but academic and social bastards."

Acting from such sentiment, some students took the initiative in trying to address certain aspects of what they perceived to be the problem. One effort involved the creation of the "Free University" on campus. The idea was not peculiar to Mary Washington but was part of a national movement in the mid- to late sixties to create, in essence, a "countercollege" within the larger institution. The concept was that of a curriculum of "relevant" courses on an array of subjects, either academic (e.g., "American Military and Diplomatic Policy in Asia, 1945–1953") or more practical (e.g., photography, emergency automobile repair, self-defense), taught on a flexible schedule either by faculty, by laymen, or by students themselves. It was to be free-form, with no grades, and open to all without charge—in short, an entity that seemed perfectly attuned to the prevailing culture.

The Free University, which first went into operation in the 1967–68 session, was enthusiastically endorsed by the *Bullet* as "the answer to several needs: Its merits are obvious. The courses deal with the timeliest of topics: the new culture, dissent, and women's liberation, to name a few. Class format is unstructured and particularly conducive to a free and open exchange of knowledge. Lack of pressure about grading and quality points make these courses more experimental and stimulating."

Alas, it failed; the enterprise that seemed so promising in concept fizzled in practice. Even at the beginning, when hopes were highest, it attracted few students, and though it struggled through several more years, there was no appreciable increase in interest. When a *Bullet* columnist inquired in January 1974 why there was no longer a Free University, an answer appeared the following week in the form of a black-bordered open letter signed, "The Spirit of Free University Past": "I would like to acknowledge my disappearance. I died from a terminal case of non-interest. . . . My death was a peaceful one, and I personally regard it to be a most desirable state."

There were several reasons for the demise of the Free University. For one thing, changes in the "normal" academic program—introduction of new courses, relaxation of attendance requirements, establishment of the pass-fail option, reform of the examination policy—meant that the traditional system no longer seemed as restrictive as it once did. Then, too, there was a more fundamental problem that affected all such progress, at Mary Washington and elsewhere. As a *New York Times* article explained: "Free universities were largely exercises in dilettantism. . . . While the lack of requirements and direction may have at first looked like utopia, it eventually turned into lack of motivation and cohesion."[21] More simply put, students found better (or at least more alluring) things to do. By the early seventies, the Free University had disappeared.

Though efforts to create a parallel curriculum came to naught, students took other avenues to assert more control over their academic destinies. One such effort involved a student-run independently produced publication called *YET*, an acronym for *Youth Evaluate Teachers*. Its main purpose was to provide students with an analysis of each course and an evaluation of the instructor; an ancillary goal, according to one of the editors, was "to provide professors with a picture of themselves as students see them."

The first issue came out in 1968, selling for one dollar per copy. Over the next several years, the publication became somewhat more sophisticated, employing a volunteer staff of approximately twenty-five students who prepared, administered, and summarized course surveys and developed analyses that graded both the content of the course and the performance of the instructor. The reaction of faculty members was mixed; some welcomed the idea and offered their cooperation, while others deplored the possibility that such a practice might encourage classroom instruction to devolve into a popularity contest to curry students' favor.

In any case, *YET* was well-received by the student body, with six hundred copies of the 1969 edition being sold. The following year the price increased to $1.50 per copy, but according to that year's editor, Kathy Schroeder, "$1.50 is not a lot when it comes to picking courses, selecting professors, and planning next year in general."

As it turned out, the 1969–70 edition was the last to be published, not because of its lack of acceptance by the students but simply because the cost of production made it unfeasible. Though *YET* died, yet did it live—or at least the concept did—for students continued to publish informal evaluations of professors on an ad hoc basis, and within a few years, annual student evaluations of faculty would become formalized as a standard feature of the academic program.

Student protest went well beyond matters of academics, and the rebels were not subtle. The *Bullet* in December 1969 ridiculed the timidity of all elements of the College community in an editorial with the provocative title "We Are All Niggers Here"—words calculated to startle, but perhaps unwise in light of the College's racial composition. "From the Chancellor to the most lowly of freshmen," it said, "we are slaves under a system that most of us are too blind even to recognize. Those among us who recognize it are too impotent to change it."

Citing a long list of student complaints, including "poor teaching, bad reading lists, busy-work assignments, over-crowded classes, administrative in loco parentis, lack of meaningful student-teacher relationships, male chauvinism, [and] dictatorial classroom situations," the editorial called students "the biggest niggers of all" because "they do nothing . . . [and] fail to exert their enormous but unrecognized power." Faculty, too, were excoriated for submitting to "administrative intimidation" and for being "too frightened to press for higher salaries and better benefits." In short, the paper concluded, "neither students nor faculty have tried to overcome their subservient conditions or improve the inadequacies they bemoan. We deserve what we have, because we do nothing."

That docile situation was about to change drastically, beginning with an attack on the concept of in loco parentis, a practice whose strictures seemed more irksome in a time when behavioral constraints were weakening throughout American society in general. Even Chancellor Simpson himself questioned the wisdom of the concept. "I just don't believe institutions should ever take over people," he told the *Bullet* in 1969. "I would fight it wherever a college is acting in the role in place of a parent. . . . When you take over all the physical, mental, personal life of a student, you are presuming on the identity of that person. . . . That's not what colleges are for."

Nevertheless the College still had its share of regulations, none of which was more galling to students than the dress code. It was true that one of Simpson's earliest decisions as chancellor in 1955 had been to approve a slight modification in the dress code, but even so, students were still not permitted to wear Bermuda shorts, for example, when traversing the campus—a situation that meant an inordinate number of trench coats could be observed at almost any time, even during the warmest weather.

Because the dress code affected them on a daily basis, it became the focus of perennial student complaints. By the late sixties there was outright rebellion, mainly against the limitations on wearing slacks. Protesting that regulation, some fifty students in November 1967 appeared in classes and at meals wearing the forbidden attire. The issue went beyond the dress code itself, explained one of the protesters: "Dress is a stupid, asinine thing. We're concerned about the larger problem of enforced conformity, which we think this is."

Not all students agreed, and as was so often the case in these times, the protest itself provoked an opposing response. In this instance some students asserted that the image of the College would be diminished if the dress code was eliminated. "If everyone here started wearing slacks," said one, "think what type of student would be attracted to come here"—a comment that drew a derisive response from the protesters. "If Mary Washington's image depends on how people dress," one retorted, "then Mary Washington's image must not be very important."

The protesters drew a verbal reprimand from the Judicial Council, whose vice president sternly informed them that "a student government regulation has been blatantly violated. Judicial Council will not tolerate such disregard for the rules." The reprimand would go on the students' judicial records, she said, and warned that "more stringent action will be taken in the case of further violations."

Thus was launched a controversy of the teapot-tempest variety that roiled the campus for weeks. Despite years of student complaint about the strictness of the dress code, it became evident that there were some who, if letters to the *Bullet* were any indication, felt strongly about the maintenance of sartorial propriety. Typifying this point of view, one student expressed her chagrin in a fashion that Mrs. Bushnell would doubtless have admired:

> These girls who want to wear slacks and blue jeans anywhere would be very insulted if a young man did not treat them as ladies; yet they refuse to ACT like ladies. I have heard many people in Fredericksburg comment on how nice Mary Washington girls look. "You can always tell a Mary Washington girl," they say; "she's the one who's neat." In this day of protests against anything and everything, some people seem to have lost their self-pride and self-respect. . . . We are never too old to learn good taste; but if we do not learn self-discipline now, in another five years it WILL be too late. Self-discipline is not an easy thing to achieve; it takes years of hard work. . . . Some people here need to be taught BY RULES IF NECESSARY, that faded blue jeans, sloppy sweatshirts, and ragged tennis shoes are incorrect for all occasions except housecleaning and some types of painting. They will never be correct or attractive in classes, at meals, in the library, or downtown; and this is true both at college and at home. I do not want to live in a pig-pen, and I am sure that most of the students here feel the same way. For those students who do not like the Mary Washington traditions of ladylike dress and behavior, I can suggest several schools where they would feel right at home. All I ask is that they leave our school the way it is; if they do not like being in the minority, they should attend a school where they would be in the majority.

The *Bullet*'s own editorial position on the matter was somewhat surprising. Usually by this time in the vanguard of demands for change, the paper in the week before the protest had lambasted conformity on campus, inveighing specifically against the typical student's "conventional dress, her conservative attitudes toward campus issues, her apathy and-or ignorance regarding world and national issues, her lack of intellectual stimulation, and her avid desire to get away on weekends."

But the *Bullet* did not support the student protest. The problem lay not in the issue itself, as the paper made clear it favored a revision of the dress code, but in the method of promoting such change. Advocacy, it said, "when expressed through a flagrant flaunting of regulations, can be interpreted, in a broader sense, as a challenge to the entire democratic process of law and order." In that light, the paper proclaimed that "until these regulations have been changed, by the consent of the majority, we are bound to uphold them. To do otherwise would promote anarchy."

Then there were those who felt the entire controversy was overblown. Decrying the pettiness of the issue, one student suggested in the College paper that the activists against the dress code "expend their energy in a more useful way; for instance they might work peacefully to end discrimination against Negroes and other minority groups. It's sad that in this world of so such poverty and hunger and hatred they find the Mary Washington dress regulations most important."

A major step toward ending the dress code came during the winter of 1968. One factor was the persuasiveness of student leaders in their appeals to Chancellor Simpson to relax the regulations. At one point, Class President Pamela Tompkins Huggins and other class officers met with him and, as she recalled, "purposely wore 'very mini' miniskirts to make our point."

Fortuitously, the petitioners were aided by the winter elements. Soon after students returned from Christmas vacation, Simpson announced that, owing to the frigid temperatures, they would be permitted thenceforth to wear slacks to classes and to the dining hall. In Huggins's opinion, the chancellor "was looking for an excuse to do it [and] Mother Nature provided it."[22]

In any case, the decree elicited generally favorable responses from the students, sometimes expressed in the "it's about time" mode. "I was amazed to note, despite earlier predictions of doom," wrote one, "that the columns fronting academic buildings did not fall down, that masses of students did not pack their bags and leave, and that our scholastic accreditation was not suddenly withdrawn," adding that "perhaps the most incredible fact was that not one student was treated by the infirmary for shock, nervous prostration, or nausea."

The break with tradition did not go unnoticed in the local community among a citizenry accustomed to seeing Mary Washington students clad in dresses. Writing in the *Free Lance–Star*, columnist John Goolrick suggested that Chancellor Simpson would be hard-pressed to reverse the no-slacks policy once the cold wave ended. If Simpson's opposition hinged on the belief that wearing slacks was "unladylike," wrote Goolrick, "then it can also be said that smoking of pot and other asserted practices indulged in by at least a few young ladies of this new generation is not exactly in line with what Emily Post would recommend."

Goolrick then proceeded to suggest that the dress code might as well be permanently abolished. "Chancellor Simpson, I am afraid your cause is lost," he advised. "You have painted yourself into a corner and there is no graceful way out. Your sense of propriety rebels, perhaps, . . . but surely your intellect tells you that slacks . . . do cover more of the anatomy than minidresses and other such apparel."

The columnist had a point—two of them, in fact. First, his reference to minidresses was apt. That particular style was just then beginning to dominate campus fashions, with hemlines inching ever northward. He was also right about the difficulty of restoring the dress code. Acceding to that reality, Chancellor Simpson approved handbook regulations for the 1968–69 session that, with only minimal exceptions, essentially abolished the code. The abrupt change came as a shock to the local citizenry and also some faculty members. One of the keenest observers of campus affairs was philosophy professor George Van Sant. "The first few years after the dress code was dropped, people were really awful. . . . Of course, tattered jeans were very popular then, and some of the costumes were pretty skimpy, too, in those days. . . . They really got rid of the dress code with a vengeance."[23]

While some may have been aghast at the decline of standards of apparel, students were delighted with the demise of the dress code, as well as with the simultaneous relaxation of other social restrictions. Curfews, for example, were extended until 2:00 a.m. on Fridays and Saturdays, and male visitors were no longer required to carry guest cards when dating students on campus.

Trumpeting these and other changes in its first edition for 1968–69, the *Bullet* was little short of ecstatic. Such developments "seemed like distant dreams [last year], and we cannot adequately express our joy at their arrival," exulted the editorial. "Welcome to the new Mary Washington College."

The euphoria was short-lived. There seemed to be at work a principle—perhaps a function of human nature itself—whereby any extension of privilege instantly assumed, in the minds of students, the status of a natural right from which to demand even greater concessions still. So it was at Mary Washington in the fall of 1968.

The *Bullet* was in the forefront of the campus radical movement, if such it could be called. With Susan Wagner as its editor for 1968–69, the paper shocked many of the more conservative MWC students, as well as some local residents, by printing as the whole first page of its November 25, 1968, edition a "Wanted: Jesus" poster. Beneath a likeness of Jesus, it listed, in the usual "wanted poster" fashion, descriptors such as the following:

- Appearance: Typical "Hippie"—Beard, Long Hair, Sandals, Young—About 30 or Less
- Urges Love Not War—Love Of Everybody, Including Communists
- Is Given To Visions, Probably Hallucinatory: Turns People On
- This Man Is Dangerous. Warning: He Is Still At Large!

Inside, the bulk of the issue was devoted to articles that offered a reinterpretation of Christ's role in contemporary society, including lengthy exegeses of the term "Christian radicalism." Prominent was a piece in which religion professor Burton Cooper proclaimed that "a Christian in today's world must be a radical. . . . In light of Jesus' actions and teachings, a believer in his way is by definition a radical."

But it was the "Wanted: Jesus" front page, more than the paper's contents, that elicited the greatest criticism, mainly from those who viewed it as sacrilegious. The poster, it turned out, was not original but a reprint of one that appeared widely across the country at that time. In fact, Robert H. Shaw, pastor of Fredericksburg's Trinity Episcopal Church (and also a faculty member at Mary Washington), observed that the very poster had hung on the bulletin board of his own church for weeks and "there wasn't a single comment about it."

The tolerance exhibited by Shaw's parishioners was obviously not typical of the local community, whence came a barrage of criticism, the extent and vehemence of which had never been levied at any MWC publication—though opposition on the campus itself was negligible. For a time it was literally front-page news in Fredericksburg. The president of the local chapter of the Alumnae Association, for example, reported numerous calls from members and from parents of students expressing outrage, and noted that the chapter had earlier passed a resolution voicing concerns about behavior at the College, proclaiming that "good moral character among the students was as important as academic achievement"; she herself found the controversial issue to be "in poor taste."

One unnamed resident informed the local newspaper that copies of the issue's front page had been sent both to Governor Mills Godwin and to Senator Harry F. Byrd Jr., along with a request that officials investigate the administrative policies governing the *Bullet*. The same source indicated that there were others of like mind who were "thinking seriously about writing similar letters of protest of the kind of permissiveness which allows such disgraceful material to be published and circulated at one of our institutions of higher education."

The Washington, D.C., television station WTOP broadcast a story on the affair, including interviews with several students (notably *Bullet* editor Wagner) and an outspoken local critic of the publication. The television broadcast itself caused a further incident when the president of the local Chamber of Commerce publicly criticized the slant of the TV feature as portraying the city in a negative light—"living in the Dark Ages," as he put it.

Wagner came under attack in the form of anonymous threatening calls to the College to the extent that she was advised by administrative officials not to "go downtown alone or accept blind dates for several days." Throughout, she professed to be unalarmed. "It is nice to know the administration is concerned about me," she said, "but I don't think anybody would do anything."[24]

The controversy was not limited to the local community. Having been picked up by the Associated Press, the story generated over 130 responses to the *Bullet* office in the first week alone from all over the country, with letters from California actually outnumbering those from Virginia. Though acknowledging that a few of the respondents were "convinced that we were damned to Hell with no hope of salvation for such a blasphemous, irreverent piece of work," the *Bullet* reported that most of the comments were supportive, producing "a heartening effect on staff morale."

Editor Wagner did, in fact, have her defenders, prominent among them the editor of the *Free Lance–Star*, Charles Rowe, who published a letter from the editor in which he assured her that "much of the furor in town is being stirred up by a very small group of intolerant people, people apparently so insecure in their own beliefs that they are unwilling to permit the expression of any views with which they disagree. These are the people who are calling for investigation and censorship and the like. . . . Thank heaven most people are more tolerant than that."

While support for the *Bullet* might have been predictable from a fellow journalist, sympathy (of sorts) also came from a more surprising source, area ministers, a number of whom focused on the subject in subsequent sermons. Representative of their attitude, as expressed in numerous letters to the *Free Lance–Star*, was the position taken by J. Howard Cates, pastor of the Fredericksburg Baptist Church. In a lengthy statement, he was at pains to disavow some of the more questionable theological specifics of the *Bullet* presentation but was ultimately supportive of the paper's basic purpose: "I would commend the editors of the *Bullet* for making Jesus and His Way 'front-page' news. Too long we have ignored Him or hesitated to speak of His revolutionary teachings. . . . Too little and almost too late have we demonstrated in our lives the meaning of His love for ALL men, . . . letting Him transform our lives from within so that we might transform our society from without."

Whether or not the *Bullet* edition had the religious results that Cates hoped for is questionable; it did, however, have a pragmatic effect on campus: the *Bullet* staff, as well as other campus leaders, interpreted the message as a call to arms for demanding further reforms at the College. A stretch though it may have been, one columnist, having cited a number of issues of student concern, suggested that if "in your own way you are seeing wrong and trying to right it, . . . you are on your way to living out the idea of a Christian radical."

Within weeks a full-blown protest movement developed when approximately one hundred students gathered on Lee Hall terrace for a "Come and Think" rally that culminated in a procession to Chancellor Simpson's office in GW, where he was presented with a list of "challenges," as the petitioners termed it. "There are things that exist [at MWC] which are in total opposition to Christian ethics," declared Susan Wagner, one of the protest leaders. "I feel strongly that those of us who feel this situation is wrong can no longer tolerate it. We have a moral obligation to demand that these challenges be met and met soon." The Chancellor received the document stoically and promised to address the concerns promptly.[25]

There were essentially three challenges. The least significant, or most mundane, related to revisions in the judicial system (as opposed to the honor system). More substantive was the challenge—one concerning black students at the College, specifically the plea that "discrimination in the assignment of rooms will never again be practiced" and that a black recruitment program be established so that "the Negro citizens of the state should be proportionally represented in the student body."

A week later Simpson responded in a lengthy open letter that was thoughtful, direct, and on the whole gracious. He reiterated his earlier pledge that segregated housing would cease and offered an apology for previous practices. He promised also to "make every new and reasonable effort" to enhance black recruitment. "Such is my intent and purpose," he said, "both by personal conviction as well as by the responsibility which my office entails."

Concerning proportional representation, however, he demurred—strongly. "I cannot support this concept," he said, "or any such concept which basically is discriminating—intellectually, socially, geographically, religiously, or even personally." He would certainly not do so at the cost of lowered standards and stated that "in an academic institution . . . it would be unprofessional and unethical to admit any student who was unable to work effectively and constructively within the framework of its established program."

It was the third challenge that most perturbed the chancellor—namely, the expectation that he "stimulate the academic caliber" of the College, particularly by hiring and retaining better instructors. This was especially galling to Simpson, inasmuch as the main focus of his efforts all along had been to do just that. With barely concealed ire, he termed the students' accusations regarding academic caliber "undocumented, misinformed, and misleading" and stoutly defended the faculty as a "very eminent" and as comprising "scholars and teachers of unusual competence, sound training, and depth of learning."

Simpson was further annoyed by the confrontational manner in which the students' concerns were presented—"rather unnecessarily self-conscious procedures," he called them—and went on to deliver a somewhat plaintive discourse on the matter. Emphasizing that he was always willing to make himself available to students—a practice in which he took considerable pride—he insisted that he

> did not have to be challenged openly to be challenged privately—and I think it is a mistake for young people to make the assumption that fac-

ulty members and administrators are not willing and eager to listen to students. It may not always be possible to agree with the student view, or the faculty view, or the public view, but it would be inconceivable for me not to want to know the other points of view and to reckon with them. I would also plead that the students be equally willing to listen to points of view other than their own and be equally willing to be tolerant of others as they wish others to be tolerant of them.

Whether or not the students were satisfied with Simpson's responses, the controversy soon abated, which is not to say that the days of student protest were over—far from it. In fact, students were becoming even more aggressive in pursuit of what they deemed their rights, as evidenced by the approach of the 1969–70 SGA president, Kathi O'Neill, who exhorted her peers, "Don't grovel for change. Demand it!"

The most tangible product of such angst was something known as the Student Bill of Rights. Originally adapted by Mary Washington students from a statement devised by the Law Student Division of the American Bar Association, the bill was a long and (not surprisingly) tedious document covering in detail virtually every aspect of student life: judicial matters, freedom of expression, and administrative authority over the social and private conduct of students.

Almost a year in the making, the bill was finally presented to the student body in a November 1970 referendum. Urging support for the proposal, campus judicial chair Sue Cottingham acknowledged that some of the bill's provisions had already achieved de facto acceptance, but warned that "assurance from the present administration that our rights will not be abridged does not ensure that this will be the case in the future." For that reason, she said, the bill needed to be approved, lest "all of our complaining and frustration will be hollow—a stale joke that will give the administration a few chuckles in future years."

Student approval came easily—1,447 in favor, only 43 in opposition—but the response from the administration was chilly. For one thing, they appeared miffed at the lack of prior consultation, a fact that rendered the bill something of a fait accompli when it reached them. The document also contained, they pointed out, some items that could not legally be authorized by the College—on top of which, as Assistant Chancellor Michael Houston commented, "It's too darn long and tries to spell out too many things."

The situation left the student activists pessimistic. Noting that the bill was being threatened "both by compromise of content or total rejection," the *Bullet* raised the "ominous possibility that by the time the Bill is processed through the Chancellor's office and the board of visitors in Charlottesville, it may be dying of old age."

That, in effect, is what happened. The denouement was that the chancellor, after consulting with student leaders, appointed an ad hoc joint committee of faculty and students who produced a "Statement of Rights and

Responsibilities" incorporating many of the basic provisions of the earlier document. The revised version was subsequently endorsed by both faculty and students, thereby bringing closure to the movement—apparently to the general satisfaction of a student body whose interests by that time had been diverted by other issues, notably the Vietnam War.

It was at about the same time that smoking restrictions on students were lifted. During an era when smoking was still widely perceived as not only innocuous but actually glamorous in magazine ads and in Hollywood depictions, cigarette consumption was high. To many students, freed from parental observation, "lighting up" seemed a rather harmless, yet worldly, indulgence.

By the late sixties, they could do so even in the classrooms, with results that could be appalling. "People were not real careful sometimes," recalled Professor George Van Sant, who himself smoked continuously during his lectures. "Sometimes I'd have a class where the whole room would be full of smoke. By the end of the period, the floor was covered with butts. . . . When you look back on that, it is disgusting how we lived in those days."[26]

More health-conscious student generations in future years would no doubt have agreed. To them, the administrative endorsement of smoking appeared in retrospect to have been unconscionably wrongheaded, and when several decades later smoking was virtually banned in campus facilities, almost no one complained about the diminution of rights.

The period was also characterized by ongoing student demands for more liberal drinking rules—in essence, for the abandonment of all restrictions. By the fall of 1969, the administration had reached the point of acceding to student wishes, whereupon the issue became entangled in local politics.

Running for the Fredericksburg House of Delegates seat against liberal Democrat George Rawlings, the conservative Republican Benjamin Woodbridge, in the course of a public debate in George Washington Hall, launched into criticism of what he called "unwholesome activities" at the College, citing protests against the Vietnam War, the *Bullet*'s advocacy of legalizing marijuana, and (he claimed) one professor's defense of communism. When asked if he thought academic freedom should be eliminated, Woodbridge replied, "I think it is unwholesome when a professor can advocate a system so repugnant to our own."

A few days later he publicly called on the MWC administration not to yield on its prohibition against drinking on campus. Expressing his doubt that "parents who foot the bill for the education of their children favor the use of multi-million dollar dormitories as bottle clubs," he declared, "there is absolutely no excuse to turn our institutions of higher learning into barrooms."

Such rhetoric may have been effective politically—Woodbridge defeated Rawlings in the November election—but his position did not prevail on campus. In early December new rules went into effect that, with one minor exception, permitted students to drink alcohol in their rooms—the exception being that drinking was still prohibited in dorm rooms during the hours of Sunday afternoon open house, when men were permitted to visit.

The long-awaited date on which restrictions ended precipitated bibulous celebration, as Professor Van Sant vividly recalled:

> Word got around, and so the great day came, and we went through class with no problem, but it was a night that will forever, I think, be in the college's history. Both the 7-11 and the Giant sold out of beer. Literally, the 7-11 ran out of beer! . . . The beer consumption was great, particularly in Bushnell dormitory, which was sort of ironic. The trash chutes in Bushnell are in the hallways, and on any of the floors you can open the door and drop your trash down and it goes into a container in the basement. The two trash chutes in Bushnell filled up with beer cans all the way to the fifth floor. There were solid beer cans from basement to [top] floor, and I heard later that it took two or three dump-truck loads to haul the beer cans out of Bushnell dormitory alone the next day. I mean the college went on one mighty binge. It was unbelievable. We came back the next morning and it was one massive hangover. The students were just awful the next day. They were just terrible. There were quite a few beer cans around on the campus. It's the only time I have ever seen the campus look like that ever in thirty-some years. But, after that, no problems.[27]

Another major aspect of the student's assault on the concept of in loco parentis was the effort to secure more extensive visitation rights in the dormitories. In one March 1969 article on the subject, a front-page *Bullet* headline complained, "MWC Defies Evolution." An accompanying editorial, "Women Are Free Agents," noted the liberalized curfew and visitation regulations at other "top-flight women's colleges" such as Vassar and Smith, and proceeded with an invidious comparison: "Mary Washington is termed a women's college and we want to be treated as women, not girls. . . . The desire to be free of social regulations does not stem from a desire to 'run wild,' . . . [but to live] comparably to the 'world outside.' We don't want to live in a glorified Girl Scout camp and certainly don't feel we need this protection." Though the restrictions were relaxed somewhat, they were not totally removed during Simpson's presidency, and the demand for "24-hour visitation" would emerge as one of his successor's most vexatious problems.

Consistent with the temper of the times, several long-standing campus traditions—some frivolous, some serious—came under attack during this period. Among such developments, the one that was probably the most evident to outside observers was the demise of May Day, which had been a cherished feature of the institution almost from its founding.

The May Queen and her court, 1955

After all, no event at the College more palpably evoked the genteel finishing-school image than May Day. And that was just the problem. By the late sixties, the celebration had become, in the eyes of many, not just an anachronism but almost an embarrassment.

One student who was on campus during the period, Linda Gattis Shull '69, perceptively described the evolution of attitudes that occurred. "It was so hokey anyway," she recalled. "When we arrived as freshman and looked at the older yearbooks, we were 'smitten' by those girls. The whole thing had a southern-prep-school, white-dress, floral-wreath kind of aura, and we thought it was cool. [But] by 1968, with the war, divisive campus politics, and rabble-rousing *Bullet* editorials, our attention was obviously directed elsewhere. . . . May Court was trivial in comparison."

Chancellor Simpson himself later said essentially as much. "It was part of the anti-feminist point of view," he admitted, "and there is nothing more artificial than May Day. But it was pretty to look at . . . and it was top-flight entertainment, aside from all the prissy dancing around; so it was enjoyable. I kind of hated to see it go, but it had become even more artificial and pointless."

And so the last May Day program was held in 1968, whereupon it quickly vanished, unmourned by a student generation that had better, or at least more substantive, things to do. "My conclusion," Linda Shull perceptively commented years later, "is that it ended with a whimper, not a bang, due to the nature of the bigger bangs happening elsewhere."

Soon after the demise of May Day came an attack on yet another tradition—

one not as grandiose as the courtly spring ceremony, yet one that, unlike May Day, involved the participation of every student at one point: the custom of requiring freshmen to wear beanies for the first several weeks of the fall semester. The idea, in part, was to foster class spirit—the odd-numbered class years (Devils) wore red, the even-numbered ones (Goats) wore green—and the identities thus forged were deemed to be an integral element of campus life, as various activities were organized on the basis of Devils versus Goats. The custom was touted poetically in doggerel that appeared in a 1938 *Bullet*:

> Just after you've been entered
> here in the fall,
> You'll be heralded and welcomed
> by a tribal call.
>
> Either Devil or Goat as the case
> may be
> And expected to support it with
> loyalty. . . .
>
> The emblems of green Goats and
> Devils of red
> Are sported by students—
> even to bed.

Woe to the freshman discovered without the identifying attire by an upperclassman, for the miscreant might be compelled to carry out some subservient, usually inconsequential, chore such as doing laundry or carrying books. Most colleges at the time, male or female, condoned some degree of freshman hazing and, as such things went, Mary Washington's was rather tame. In fact, many a graduate over the years saved her beanie as a treasured memento of the nostalgic transition to college life.

But times had changed. To a more self-consciously sophisticated student generation, beanies just "weren't cool." Certainly from a fashion standpoint they had little to recommend them, and the damage they could do to meticulously coiffed tresses was deplorable. Consequently students sometimes met the letter of the code by folding their beanies and affixing them with bobby pins rather than wearing them in the conventional manner.

In any case, opposition to beanies was wrought not so much by their sartorial inelegance as by the social stigmatization that they presumably inflicted on the wearer. In a scathing piece in the first issue of the *Bullet* at the beginning of the fall 1970 semester, op-ed columnist Yuri McCarthy disparaged the caps as "badges of immaturity and inferiority" and went on to decry the "victimizing of girls" who were too gullible to resist the demeaning practice. "Let's cut the corn," she urged, "and not segregate the freshmen. . . . It's bad enough that they're crammed together in those ghettos known as freshman dorms" (another perennial target of dissidents' wrath). "Enforcing childish activities on freshmen can only end up making freshmen childish."

Beanies abound in the amphitheater as the class of 1955 welcomes the class of 1957.

A *Bullet* poll of new students some weeks later, after the beanie-wearing period was over, indicated that not all freshmen agreed with the *Bullet*'s stance. Of all the respondents, 41 percent indicated that it "added to" orientation, while 39.5 percent thought that it "did nothing for" the process; only 8.4 percent said that it "detracted from" it. In response to a similar query, a small majority indicated that they regarded being asked to wear a beanie as "a fairly reasonable demand"; only 7.6 percent found it humiliating.

On the basis of such less-than-definitive results, the *Bullet* proceeded to call for abolition of the beanies, claiming that their enforced wearing constituted "blatant repression of individual rights and preference." The next year the little circular chapeaus were nowhere to be seen—their disappearance, as with May Day, largely unlamented. Such were the times.

There was no clearer evidence of the unsettled campus environment than when, in the early 1970s, "the 'unthinkable' happened," as the *Bullet* put it: an actual assault on the honor system. Since its formal adoption in 1946, the honor system had undergone a number of changes, mostly minor ones relating to composition of the Honor Council. In 1953, for example, a separate office of Honor Council president was established, apart from the Student Government Association. In the 1960s, the council's membership was changed to comprise two elected representatives from each class (plus the president), instead of consisting of the presidents of each class.

Every entering student at the College was made aware from the outset of the institution's emphasis on honor. Much of orientation week each year was devoted to explanation of the system's operation and warnings of the dire consequences of its violation. The culminating event of the week was an honor convocation, attended by all faculty members in their academic regalia. It was an impressive sight for the wide-eyed freshmen; over the years, the tradition developed in which they stood and applauded without cessation as the entire faculty filed into GW auditorium. (A freshman once commented that he found the show of respect somewhat amusing, since, as he put it, "these are the same people that I'm going to blame for every grade of C or lower the rest of my college career.")

The convocation featured a speaker who delivered an inspiring message (in theory, at least) on the importance of honorable behavior and ended with the individual signing of pledge cards by the new students, who thus bound themselves to uphold the tenets of the honor system throughout their stay at Mary Washington. The cards were kept in the registrar's office, and no grades were given to any student whose card was not on file.

With the passage of time, the honor system grew increasingly venerable, eventually becoming the most sacrosanct of the College's traditions. Yet in early 1969, the *Bullet* noted that "just recently, in the last two years, the student body's Honor Code has become affected with apathy. . . . This situation is dangerous."

Before long, apathy turned to antipathy. Aside from the general influence exerted by a cultural environment in which rebellion against authority and skepticism toward convention were pervasive, specific aspects of the honor system offended an increasing number of students.

There was a growing feeling, for example, that the code was not uniformly applied and that it was fundamentally hypocritical. As one *Bullet* editorial pointed out, "Every student who received honor counseling freshman year remembers the admonitions against lying . . . juxtaposed with the admission that lies to boyfriends and parents were a social necessity." Many felt that social matters should be removed entirely from the purview of the system.

Most of all, critics complained that punishment was too draconian. In a time of moral relativism, the single-sanction penalty—that is, permanent dismissal from the College—appeared unacceptable to many. As the *Bullet* put it in May 1969, "Ours is a most strict code, with no leniency whatsoever for those found guilty," and suggested that "it is time to reexamine the entire system, perhaps to even do away with it for its hollowness and strict punishment."

Just such a reexamination took place the following year, with emphasis on eliminating the single-sanction penalty. By then it was apparent that the "chilling effect" of that provision was so great that the Honor Council had become reluctant to convict even obvious offenders out of concern about the effects of absolute dismissal.

The council accordingly proposed an amendment in February 1970 that would provide the option of waiving dismissal in the event of extenuating circumstances, or of dismissing the convicted student for a definite period, after which the person could reapply for admission. The Honor Council, read the amendment, "will impose any penalty according to the circumstances surrounding the individual cases."

In an editorial titled "An Overdue Revision," the *Bullet* supported the proposal. "The honor council, in effect, plays God with the lives of those brought before it," it said, adding that the proposed amendment "would help in eliminating the inhumanity of the present system." Eventual passage of the proposal, by creating a range of penalties that could be imposed, marked a break from the University of Virginia's honor code, on which Mary Washington's had been modeled; U.Va. continued to maintain absolute dismissal as its only sanction for convicted students.

The revision did not quell opposition to the system; in fact, a movement for its abolishment erupted just the next year. The effort was spearheaded by a sophomore day student named Jack Flynn, who announced in November 1971 that he was working on a plan "to do away with the whole thing," not just modify it. "I want to replace it with a simple two-sentence academic code," he explained, "saying something like 'plagiarism and cheating are not accepted here,' and [stating] what the consequences would be. This would be strictly academic; there would be nothing social about it."

Flynn's plan won predictable support from the College newspaper, which earlier that year had assailed the honor system as "a hangover from the past, a disposable relic," calling it "ludicrous because it is meaningless and because it is worn out." More surprising was the endorsement, of sorts, that came from none other than the president of the Honor Council herself, Beth Conrad, who commented that Flynn had "really good ideas, and maybe there's some value in what he has to say. There's no safety and security in the system the way it is now."

To effect the change, Flynn would have had to bring before the Honor Council a petition signed by 10 percent of the student body (about 230 students). The Council would then need to endorse the petition and put it before the student body; passage would require approval by a two-thirds vote.

It did not happen. A number of widely respected faculty members spoke out in support of the system, albeit usually with caveats concerning its social aspects: Lewis Fickett in political science, Roger Bourdon in history, Donald Glover in English, Samuel Emory in geography, and Cornelia Oliver (then serving as an Honor Council adviser) in art history.

A poll conducted by the Honor Council revealed no substantial opposition to the system, although response to some questions indicated concern in certain areas. Over half of the respondents believed the council should not have the power of absolute dismissal; only 53 percent believed the code should cover social as well as academic violations. On the larger question of whether they believed the system was working effectively, 75 percent responded in the affirmative. Most telling, perhaps, was that only 5 percent thought the system should be abolished. Eventually Jack Flynn abandoned his quest. "I got so little positive support from the students," he said, "it's just not worth my time."

But the honor system's troubles were not over. No sooner had Flynn's quixotic crusade subsided than the system faced a threat from an entirely different quarter—namely, a legal challenge brought by an aggrieved student named Brenda Page Bright.

In December 1971, Bright was dismissed from Mary Washington College by the Honor Council when found guilty of an on-campus theft from another student. Seeking a temporary restraining order that would allow her to be reinstated at the College, Bright filed suit in Richmond's federal district court, claiming that, first, the Board of Visitors had no right to delegate powers of dismissal to the Honor Council and, second, her Fourteenth Amendment due process rights had been violated because the verdict was not supported by evidence sufficient to meet an established level for determining guilt. Thus began months of judicial wrangling.

Initially District Court Judge Robert Merhige denied the request for the temporary restraining order on the grounds that more damage would be done to the campus community if she were reinstated than to Bright if she were not, but the fundamental issues raised in the suit remained, pending resolution in an upcoming trial. In the meantime, College counsel from the state attorney general's office suggested that the evidence on which Bright was convicted may not, in fact, have been sufficient, whereupon Bright was offered readmission to the College—an offer that she rejected by refusing to sign the requisite honor pledge. When the case eventually came to trial, District Court Judge Albert V. Bryan Jr. dismissed the suit against MWC on the grounds that no substantial federal question was involved.

But that did not end the affair. Bright proceeded to file an appeal requesting that the Fourth U.S. Circuit Court review Judge Bryan's decision. Before that matter could be resolved, Bright was once again offered readmission to Mary Washington, which she this time accepted, and returned in the fall of 1973; she graduated with a degree in political science in 1975, the first "permanently dismissed" student ever to do so.

An important consequence of the episode was that because of the potential legal implications of Bright's case for the viability of all student-run College judicial systems, efforts were made to refine certain provisions of the Mary Washington honor code. The most significant change was an amendment to provide for review of Honor Council decisions by the president of the College. Specifically, a convicted student was given the right to appeal for presidential review on three possible grounds: whether the evidence was sufficient to support the verdict, whether the accused had been afforded due process, or whether the penalty was too harsh for the offense committed. Though the change did not mandate automatic presidential review of all convictions, as some believed it should, it nonetheless marked a notable change from previous practice, wherein decisions of the council were final.

In an age of increased activism, Mary Washington students began to look beyond purely insular concerns such as the honor system to involve themselves to a far greater extent than ever before in a variety of extramural political and social issues. A *Bullet* column described the situation with perceptivity (as well as with several neologisms): "The sixties children grew into the most vocal group this century has heard thus far. Its members were hippied into flower power or radicated into the New Left or graduated into looking at their values. Most shared a new ethic that placed justice above civil order, social welfare above self-comfort, moral conviction above legality, and human life above institutions." With stunning speed, the blasé student attitudes of the past changed as disinterest turned dramatically to activism. The primary catalyst at Mary Washington, as on campuses across the country, was the Vietnam War.

At a college that lacked male students until the 1970s and did not have antiwar irritants such as ROTC units or government-military research contracts, concern about the war might have been expected to be less present than at larger coeducational research institutions. Yet there were several factors that led to unusual intensity of interest in the Vietnam conflict among Mary Washington students. For one thing, many students came from northern Virginia—an area that had extensive governmental ties, either political or military—and were thus reared in an environment of unusual sensitivity to issues of foreign involvement; a significant number came from families who either were in the military or were civil servants.

More important, again because of the College's location, there was the U.S. Marine Corps connection. Located only twenty miles from Quantico, Mary Washington's more than two thousand students were an alluring source of dates for the young officers being trained at the base. In the 1960s particularly, formal social events on campus were notable for the grandeur of the young men in their immaculate dress uniforms. On a weekly basis, it was the Marines who supplied many of the dates for Mary Washington girls, leading to relationships that often developed into engagements and ultimately marriage. The uniqueness of the Marine connection was indicated by the fact that even though Mary Washington students were prohibited from consuming alcohol within a fifty-mile radius of the campus, the student handbook granted a specific exemption for the Officers' Club at Quantico.

The scenario was well depicted some years later by a member of the class of 1968, Donna Sheehan Gladis, who eventually married a Marine. "There were still lots of girls who dated men at U.Va.," she recalled,

> and went back and forth on road trips to Charlottesville. On the weekends, Mary Washington kind of disappeared. They all went somewhere else. But the Marines were always around. At the beginning it

was kind of, "Oh, they're older, we can't go there, they've got short hair, et cetera." But these young men were from all over the country. They weren't local guys: they were from everywhere, and they were smart—they were all college graduates, all the ones that went through OCS—and more and more young women started dating Marines. . . . They were a special group of guys—just really top notch, very mature. . . . The Marines were more present on campus than, say, boys from other colleges [who] were in class, hopefully. So Marines were around all the time. And people were good friends with them, as well as dating them—just got to know them. Then they would leave and a whole other group would come in. It was just a real interesting time.[28]

But the Vietnam War cast a pall over this felicitous arrangement—sometimes in an all-too-literal sense. This was because, in a war in which the Marines played an extensive combat role, the young officers who were often in the forefront of battles were the very men who had trained at Quantico. As the war stretched on and the casualty lists mounted, the grim reality of it too often came home to Mary Washington in a personal way as word arrived that boyfriends or fiancés had been wounded, or worse. Indeed, one member of the class of 1968 later recalled that her most lasting memory of her years at the College was not the frivolity of May Days, or the joy of Ring Dance, or even the elation of graduation itself, but the piercing scream that echoed through the dorm when her suite mate, called to the hall phone, learned that her Marine fiancé had been killed in the 1968 Tet Offensive.

The president of the class of 1968, Pamela Tompkins Huggins, poignantly recalled, more than thirty years later, the trauma of those days:

Even girls who didn't date or become seriously involved with a Marine could not escape the very personal toll that time exacted from all of us. . . . It became an ever-present "cloud" on our minds and hearts. In those days, we didn't have cell phones or personal lines in the rooms, so we all shared hall phones. One of my most vivid memories of my senior year is sitting around gabbing in one of our rooms at night and upon hearing the phone ring down the hall, we would all sorta freeze and stare at each other. Calls at odd hours were rarely good news. I particularly remember one time after we had had several very bad-news calls, when the phone rang, one of the girls jumped up and said, "Let me answer it. I don't think anyone I really love is over there right now."[29]

So it was that the war to many Mary Washington students was not an abstraction. And when they began to protest against it, their actions often came not just from an ideological position but from anguished personal experience.

At Mary Washington, as on most American campuses, opposition to the war developed gradually. In the early stages, most MWC students supported the war, apparently accepting the prevailing notion that it was a necessary measure in defense of American ideals against the perils of communist encroachment. A student opinion poll conducted by the International Relations Club in late 1965 revealed that 90 percent of the respondents were opposed to American withdrawal from Vietnam (and 63 percent even advocated escalation of the war), though an almost equal number (89 percent) favored efforts to negotiate a settlement. Indicative of such attitudes was the work of students during the Christmas season of that year to "collect money in order to buy gifts for men in the armed forces fighting in Vietnam . . . [as tokens of] the true rigor of proud citizens in support of their nation."

Then there was the personal aspect. As one student recalled, "So many women were dating Marines that just about every dorm room had a map of Vietnam. We had luaus for the girls who were going to Hawaii to meet their boyfriends for R&R. . . . We weren't necessarily pro-war. But we were pro-Marines." Or as another remembered the era, "I wouldn't say we were 'hawks,' but most of us didn't relate to the hippy protesters or draft dodgers, as we were raised to be 'patriotic' and desperately wanted to believe that all of this loss was for a higher cause."[30]

Yet signs of increasing concern about the war began to appear. In early 1966 a faculty panel discussion of the issue drew a near-capacity crowd, including the majority of the student body as well as many faculty and townsfolk, to GW auditorium. The debate between three defenders of America's involvement and three opponents was broadcast by local radio station WFLS. According to the *Bullet*, there was "an air of expectancy" throughout the debate, not only because of the volatility of the issue itself but because students anticipated "a swash-buckling personality contest"—a reasonable expectation, given that the panelists included some of the faculty's more dynamic individuals, including Lewis Fickett and George Grayson from political science (both opposed to the war) and George Van Sant from philosophy (supportive of the war).

Student opposition, at least on a limited basis, emerged later that year when the president of the Student Government Association, Patricia Marilla, joined other student leaders from across the country in signing an open letter to President Lyndon Johnson on December 26, 1966, expressing concerns about the war. (The letter itself became the focus of campus controversy when student supporters of the war objected to the fact that Marilla's action may have indicated that she was speaking officially on behalf of the student body.) The following February, Marilla was one of forty student leaders invited by Secretary of State Dean Rusk to discuss the conflict, a meeting that left her disillusioned. "At no time," she lamented in the *Bullet*, "was the welfare of the Vietnamese people discussed."

Later that spring, faculty members joined in the dissent when twenty-seven of them signed a letter urging a reconsideration of "a war doggedly pursued at the expense of this nation's most precious resource: her brave young men." The petition, which was printed as a letter to the editor in the Richmond and Fredericksburg newspapers and as a paid advertisement in the *Washington*

Post, was described by one of its signers, history professor George Moulton, as "the patriotic and American thing to do. The time to exercise your freedom is in a time of crisis."

By the fall of 1967, opposition on campus was clearly growing. Approximately thirty Mary Washington students took part that October in a massive antiwar demonstration at the Pentagon, an involvement that profoundly affected the participants. One of them, Glenna Booth, described in the *Bullet* what she witnessed as some of the demonstrators rushed toward the Pentagon. "Police fought with their clubs and riot sticks," she wrote. "The military police seemed satisfied by merely holding their lines, but the federal marshals brutally beat the marchers with their clubs. On more than one occasion, marshals continued beating a demonstrator after he had fallen. . . . What was the reaction of the government? President Johnson went to church on Sunday. Do you suppose he prayed for peace?"

The first overt incidence of student protest at Mary Washington itself came in February 1968, when a small number of students, joined by three faculty members (Professors George Grayson, Morris Rossabi, and Glen Thomas) mounted a modest demonstration against campus recruiters from Dow Chemical, makers of the incendiary compound napalm being extensively used by American forces in Vietnam. Working from a card table set up in the foyer of Lee Hall, with protest songs by Bob Dylan and Joan Baez on a record player in the background, the protesters distributed information about napalm and tried to engage students in discussion of the issues. The group issued a statement asserting its belief that "the use of napalm by the U.S. is immoral; its use in the war is unnecessary; and Dow is responsible for this immoral act by manufacturing and selling napalm." Their efforts were supported by the *Bullet* in an editorial admonition to the company headlined "Make Saran Wrap, Not War."

Though the protesters had received administrative permission for their demonstration, and though they made no effort to actually disrupt the work of the Dow recruiter, the incident quickly spawned a counterprotest on the part of pro-war students (joined by several Marines). Such an action was necessary, said one proponent, lest the anti-Dow group "give the impression that the whole school is against the war, and it's just not that way." Another concurred, "If napalm will win the war faster, I don't see anything against using it. . . . Why don't they say anything about what the Viet Cong are doing to our boys?"

A more public, and much more controversial, antiwar episode occurred the following year in response to a scheduled appearance in May 1969 by the director of the Selective Service, General Lewis Hershey, at a Boy Scout banquet to be held at a junior high school in neighboring Stafford County. At that time Hershey was a primary focus of antiwar protests not only because he was in charge of the draft but because of his tendency toward blunt and often inflammatory defense of his agency's role. Anticipating a student confrontation with Hershey, the *Bullet* described the general as "a white-haired, bespectacled, surprisingly old man," and noted, with some hyperbole, that he had been "harassed more than any other military man in the history of the country, and ranks with controversial political leaders in the amount of abuse and ill will he has engendered." The paper went on to warn potential protesters that "if he is engaged in debate with college students, . . . let the students beware! This man knows his answers well, and the military mind and manner worries little over arguments of conscience."

As it turned out, the confrontation never took place, as the event's organizers canceled Hershey's visit, citing concern over possible damage to school property that might occur as a result of the protest—a scenario that the MWC protest leader called "absurd," pointing out that "we had no intention of harassing speakers at the dinner, nor of a loud protest, . . . [but] to quietly carry our signs around the cafeteria." The flap escalated when John H. Chichester, then a Democratic candidate for an area House of Delegates seat, publicly deplored the cancellation of the event, which he attributed to the work of "a group of extremists who choose to tear down the principles of this great country in lieu of using what talents they have to make it better." More than any incident to date involving Mary Washington College, the affair showed how increasingly divided the country was becoming over the Vietnam War.

By the fall of 1969, student opposition to the war nationwide resulted in a call for a Vietnam Moratorium that would include canceling all classes on Wednesday, October 15. In light of Virginia governor Mills Godwin's declaration that he would not countenance such disruptions at state-supported schools, the Mary Washington administration declined to cancel classes officially, but around campus there was considerable evidence of antiwar sentiment. A letter to the editor of the *Bullet*, for example, was signed by twenty-eight faculty members who endorsed the objectives of the moratorium and urged "the college community to observe the day in an appropriate manner."

The *Bullet* itself suggested what that "appropriate manner" might be. The moratorium, it counseled, should be "a very peaceful affair," advising, "We can all wear black armbands to class. Or, if black armbands have an unsavory connotation, there are neat little blue badges to display in place of fraternity pins. We don't have to picket or rally in the streets or face National Guard bayonets. We don't have to say anything. Our parents will never know. We can just appear en masse on Wednesday with our little blue badges. . . . We will all be a part of the grand coalition of students for peace, a faith-restoring example of participatory democracy in action."

Not all faculty members were favorably impressed with the moratorium idea, some viewing it cynically, as did biology professor Thomas Johnson, who asserted that the event was "going over big with many students for the precise reason that they would be delighted with any excuse not to attend classes." That proved to be a minority opinion, however, as the faculty passed a resolution commending the Student Government Association for "the manner in which they have chosen to respond to the movement for a student moratorium."

The response included, besides the wearing of badges and arm bands, a faculty panel discussion in the afternoon and a candlelight service that evening in Ball Circle, replete with poetry readings and songs for peace. Participation in the protest, even in so benign a fashion, meant that, according to the *Bullet*, "we can pat ourselves on the back, knowing that we have played a part in the movement to 'bring the boys home.'" The next month, a number of Mary Washington students participated in a huge antiwar demonstration in the nation's capital.

Such activism, though unprecedented at the College, was but a prelude to the antiwar tumult that swept the campus the following spring. The flash point occurred when President Richard Nixon, who had promised to reduce the number of American forces in Vietnam, suddenly on April 30, 1970, expanded U.S. involvement by ordering troops into neighboring Cambodia, belligerently declaring, "Only the power of the United States deters aggression. . . . It is not our power but our will and character that is being tested tonight. . . . We will not be humiliated."[31]

In frustration and despair over the apparent abnegation of the earlier presidential pledge, protests erupted on many campuses amid calls for a general student strike. The initial response at Mary Washington was a bit more restrained, though still assertive. Several student leaders signed a statement issued by the National Student Association calling for Nixon's impeachment. One of them, Mimi Hearne, explained her position at a press conference in Washington, saying, "I worked for Nixon in '68 and I supported him in November [i.e., at the time of the antiwar rally in Washington], but I now feel that he has overextended his power as President."

The *Bullet* likewise called for impeachment. Referring to Nixon's recent speech, it declared, "We have already been humiliated, and our humiliation grows each day we continue to kill in Southeast Asia. . . . A great responsibility challenges us. . . . Our futures are at stake and we must act now. We must say 'no' to Richard Nixon before it is too late to say anything."

As it turned out, on the very day that the editorial appeared—May 4, 1970—an event occurred that drastically escalated the antiwar movement, igniting protest of a far more incendiary nature: the killing of four Kent State University students by Ohio National Guardsmen. It is certain that Mary Washington College had never witnessed anything remotely like the May antiwar protest that followed. Events occurred so rapidly and on so many fronts that the *Bullet* resorted to printing mimeographed "special editions" in an effort to keep students apprised of developments.

The organization of the antiwar protest efforts began with two meetings of the student body on May 4—the first attended by an estimated 250 students and faculty in Lee Ballroom at 9:00 p.m., and the second, held in Ball Circle at 11:00 p.m., attended by approximately twice that many. Out of these meetings, a Strike Committee was formed, headed by Susan Randolph, with student coordinators assigned to handle various areas, including community relations, picketing, fund-raising, and legal matters.

As at many other colleges, there was a movement to have students in essence "shut down" the institution by boycotting classes. Urging the crowd in Ball Circle to consider such a tactic, Strike Chairman Randolph put the matter forcefully. "This is your chance," she exhorted them. "I'm not telling you to boycott classes—that's up to you. But . . . if we all sit in the dorms on our little fannies we won't accomplish a goddamn thing."

Though in the end there was no general strike, the normal campus routine was disrupted during the first weeks of May by an extraordinary variety of activities related to antiwar efforts: a memorial service for the Kent State students was held on Ball Circle; a number of professors devoted their classes to discussion of the Vietnam War; and several forums addressed the East Asian situation, notably including a panel of faculty members Raman Singh, Taketo Ohtani, and Key Sun Ryang titled "The Asian Viewpoint."

A number of prominent antiwar activists spoke on campus, among them Arthur Waskow, resident fellow at the Institute of Policy Studies and author of *From Race Riot to Sit-In*. Speaking to a capacity crowd in Lee Ballroom, Waskow declared, "We are now at a crossroads in human history. . . . This is going to be a turning point for the future of the world. We must turn back from the road of self-destruction." A bloodbath could be averted, he said, "if millions of us are together and [are] clear about what we want."

Addressing the same audience, religion professor Burton Cooper, one of the most outspoken faculty members on the war, sounded a similarly apocalyptic note. Asserting that the solution to the crisis was the creation of a society based on principles of human love, Cooper proclaimed, to a standing ovation, that "we had better start loving, or, to quote James Baldwin, there will be a 'fire next time.'"

A number of students traveled to Charlottesville to participate in antiwar activities at the University of Virginia, whose grounds were also seething with protest. A particular attraction was the appearance by two high-profile activists, William Kunstler, a longtime radical gadfly, and Jerry Rubin, who had gained notoriety as one of the Chicago Seven. To a tumultuous University Hall crowd estimated at seven thousand, Kunstler declared, "Every institution that can be shut down must be shut down. [Our] fists have to be clenched and in the air, and if we ever have the power to open them again, I hope it is in friendship and not around the trigger of a rifle."

Perhaps the most controversial incident involving the College during the chaotic period of protest was related to an event (or, more accurately, a nonevent) in Fredericksburg itself. It so happened that Mrs. Richard Nixon had been scheduled to visit the city—specifically historic Kenmore and the James

Monroe Museum and Memorial Library—on May 6. However, when word reached the White House that the First Lady might be confronted with antiwar demonstrators, the visit was abruptly canceled.

Local civic leaders were understandably disappointed. Mayor Josiah P. Rowe III called the cancellation "unfortunate and regrettable," pointing out that, in his view, "the right of students to express their views and concern about the war is clear and valid, but good manners should permit a social visit by the first lady without the intrusion of political issues." A spokesman for the Monroe Museum decried a demonstration that "was going to be disrespectful to quite an innocent lady," while the chairwoman of the Kenmore Board of Regents perceived the whole situation simply as "dreadful." A sizable number of students also deplored the episode, with some three hundred of them signing a letter to Mrs. Nixon expressing their dismay and offering an apology for the disruption of her planned visit.

Chancellor Simpson likewise lamented the turn of events, especially since he had been reassured by the protest planners, he said, that the demonstration would not be discourteous to Mrs. Nixon. "The girls had tried to make it a dignified protest," he explained, adding that he was confident they would have treated her with respect, even though they disagreed with her husband's policy.

Indeed, as Kathi O'Neill, one of the protest leaders, explained later, "We had planned . . . marching very peacefully, trying to demonstrate to [Mrs. Nixon] that we, as children of the 'silent majority' establishment—not radicals and not hippies—are interested in just letting her know that we disagree with this [the Cambodian incursion], and we were not trying to disrupt anything she'd be doing."

There was one person in particular, however, who did not buy such an innocuous explanation—Republican delegate Benjamin H. Woodbridge Jr., who represented the Fredericksburg area in the Virginia General Assembly and the previous year had publicly denounced the College for liberalizing its drinking policy. Now his vociferous denunciation of the students' behavior (and that of the faculty and administration as well) helped create a public furor. "The reputation of our city and our area," he proclaimed, "has been severely damaged by the vocal, immature, and shabby minority at Mary Washington College whose action forced the cancellation," adding that it was "the same noisy minority" that had caused the disruption of General Hershey's planned local appearance the previous year.

Angered as he apparently was by cancellation of Mrs. Nixon's visit, Delegate Woodbridge was further incensed a few days later by another event at the College: a concert in the amphitheater to raise funds to support a student antiwar protest march to Washington, scheduled for May 8–9. "I strongly object," he said, "to the use of colleges for the purpose of raising money to finance a protest which the vast majority of Virginia taxpayers who support the institution . . . are undoubtedly opposed to."

Accordingly, Woodbridge proceeded to write Governor Linwood Holton, urging him to appoint a commission to investigate all state-supported educational institutions with the purpose of making recommendations for changes that would "assure the taxpayers of Virginia that their money is not being squandered on educational facilities for those who come not to learn, but to undermine the very educational system which provides them sanctuary and a forum for their childish rantings."

Woodbridge's actions prompted a tart rejoinder from the chair of UMW's Religion Department, Elizabeth Clark, in the form of her own letter to the governor, made public in the local newspaper. Noting that the delegate's letter to Holton was "the second such attack Mr. Woodbridge has made upon our college community in this academic year," Clark asserted that Woodbridge "understands neither the meaning of academic freedom nor the constitutional rights of American citizens. . . . No one on campus expected him to agree personally with the views of the students, but we did expect him to realize that rights of peaceful assembly and freedom of speech and press must be granted even to students who disagree with him."

Unabashed by such criticism, Woodbridge persisted in his criticism of the College's students and administrators, noting that he was "very pleased and heartened" by the "overwhelmingly favorable" public response to his allegations. "I am convinced," he said, "the great mass of people are fed up to the teeth with the crude acts of a small minority."

Echoing as it did the general tone of the Nixon administration's appeal to the "great silent majority," there were those who perceived a political purpose in Woodbridge's position. But whether his stridency arose from genuine conviction or from partisan purposes, the whole exchange contributed to the creation of an unseemly, and uncharacteristic, tension between the College and the community.

Meanwhile, the peace movement on campus culminated with a student march to Washington to participate in a massive demonstration on the weekend following the Kent State incident. Aided by donations collected at the amphitheater concert, approximately eighty students left campus at eight o'clock on Friday morning to begin their trek up U.S. Route 1. As described by the local newspaper, the group departed with "bed rolls strapped to their backs, wearing what has come to be the regulation attire of the anti-war advocates—jeans, army fatigue jackets, hats or bandanas, and heavy walking shoes," and carrying with them items such as bug spray, suntan lotion, Band-Aids, and blister medication.

Declining offers of transportation along the way, most continued mainly on foot, arriving by evening at the Alexandria home of a movement sympathizer who invited the entourage to spend the night on her lawn. "We just fell on the ground when we got here," said one marcher. "We had lots of blisters, but . . . everyone came through fine." Neighbors treated the demonstrators cordially, bringing them food and allowing them to use bathrooms, telephones, and televisions in their homes.

Early the next morning, the polite protesters, having taken care to clean up all their litter, decamped for Memorial Bridge, where they were joined by other students and faculty, bringing the Mary Washington contingent to approximately 150. From there they walked in a group to the Ellipse, where they joined other demonstrators from colleges across the country. Most stayed until late afternoon before returning to Fredericksburg.

The Washington march was the last of the notable antiwar activities by MWC students. What remained were the mundane but thorny academic questions arising from inordinate absences and their effect on class participation, the completion of assignments, and preparation for final exams—issues that were especially critical, since the whole affair cropped up so near the end of the semester.

Student requests for relief from various requirements, given the unprecedented circumstances, occasioned not one but two faculty meetings devoted to the matter. In light of the passions on both sides of the Vietnam issue, the meetings produced spirited, sometimes acrimonious, debate. In the end, a compromise of sorts resulted in the passage of motions that bowed to students' interests by (1) extending the deadline both for changing elective courses to pass-fail and for dropping courses without penalty and (2) giving faculty greater latitude in assigning grades of "incomplete." Thus, without assenting to the more radical student proposals, the faculty did evince a degree of sympathy for the students' position and in doing so succeeded in mollifying the protesters (for the most part) while simultaneously salvaging the integrity of the academic program.

In retrospect, the period of antiwar protest appeared as a tableau of academe in a troubled time. While many students acted from a heartfelt desire to end a war they believed unjust and immoral, others (truth be told) acted from the mere impetuosity of youth, motivated by no compelling ideology. The establishment they attacked had never witnessed, and could not fathom, student behavior so aggressive, so confrontational, so . . . rude. For a while, the worst of each side was on display.

With the end of the semester, the celebration of commencement, and the coming of summer vacation, emotions cooled, and when classes resumed in the fall, student life on campus returned more or less to normal—but not quite. A residue of unrest remained, continuing, however subtly, to influence the ambience of the campus. From time to time, antiwar protests of varying types and sizes emerged, and the *Bullet* persisted in its policy of opposition. "Sooner or later, the United States is going to lose this war," the paper declared in April 1971. "There is no longer a question of victory. . . . There is no reason why American troops must continue to be killed and wounded while the nation continues to play a foolish and deadly waiting game."

Antiwar sentiment was also evident in a more subtle way in an effort to change the name of the College newspaper—an effort initiated by the *Bullet* staffers themselves. The underlying concern was that the name conveyed an overly militaristic image, though, as the paper itself admitted, it did embody an appropriate association with Fredericksburg's history; in addition, it was consistent in imagery with the yearbook, *The Battlefield*. (Martial allusions were also evident in the name of an earlier literary magazine, the *Epaulet*, and in the titles of *Bullet* columns such as "Shrapnel" and "Crossfire" that had been used periodically.) A student poll revealed no enthusiasm for the change, partly because of a desire to maintain tradition and partly because the proposed new name, "Fifth Season," had slight appeal. Opponents ridiculed it as sounding variously like the name of a "rock group," a "new kind of perfume," an "old ladies' tea club," or just plain "corny." The preponderant student attitude seemed to be indifference. In any case, the proposal was rather quickly cashiered, and the paper remained the *Bullet*.

As it turned out, the antiwar movement had crested with the demonstration in May 1970. But things would not quite be the same again, and though complex factors were at work—not just the antiwar protests—any effort thereafter to explain the evolution of the College could not ignore those turbulent spring weeks. May days of a very different kind, indeed, were they.

POLITICS: SEXUAL AND OTHERWISE

Though antiwar activities attracted the most attention at Mary Washington during the late sixties and early seventies, students were also drawn to other matters of national concern during that period, notably gender issues. Such was to be expected during a time when the feminist movement was at its peak and debate raged over abortion—*Roe v. Wade* being decided in 1973—and the proposed Equal Rights Amendment.

Interest in gender issues did not, of course, ignite instantly with the coming of the seventies. From the beginning of the modern feminist movement (usually traced to the publication of Betty Friedan's *The Feminine Mystique* in 1963), Mary Washington students—still all female at that time—had shown sporadic interest in women's rights, but there was also ample evidence of interest in more traditional social concerns of girls: boys. For example, in January 1963, the *Bullet* carried an article about a recent national survey of coeds' preference for boys' names (the winner was "William"). In terminology that would be deemed abominable by subsequent generations of female students, one respondent said, "No matter what his real name is, I'll call him 'Honey,'" and another professed, "I don't care what his name is as long as he calls me for a date." The article concluded with the observation that while there was interest in first names, "college girls are very much interested in their last names, too!"

As late as 1969, a *Bullet* column titled "The Social Merry-Go-Round" described the dating habits of MWC students. The pattern began the freshman year when girls typically joined the "road team," usually bound for any of the various male or coed schools within a hundred-mile radius. Once the "fraternity party syndrome" wore off, either Marines or graduate students became the preferred dates, though the former were to be approached with an awareness that "Marines have a common blasé attitude, and . . . too often shell out their 'bed-time' stories as if Mary Washington girls haven't heard them time and again."

But even as such advice was being proffered, there was evidence that newer attitudes were emerging. In a late-sixties article called "The 'Lady' Myth," one *Bullet* columnist lampooned the old scenario, ridiculing the earlier purpose of the College as an institution primarily designed to transform

> an entering freshman into a fine southern lady. Gone were all the nasty habits she had picked up during the eighteen years before she came to MWC. She emerged at graduation a refined lady, schooled in all the fine points of the genteel way of life. Alas, those days now belong to the ages! A girl entering Mary Washington College today can expect to graduate with all her former vices, as well as many new ones, intact. . . . No longer are the women of Mary Washington College expected to conduct themselves in a manner becoming their sex. . . . Who are we kidding? There is no place in the world today for women, or ladies, whose function is purely ornamental. Girls no longer come to college to be "finished," or if they do, they shouldn't.

By the advent of a new decade, interest in gender issues had burgeoned. For the first time, matters pertaining to sexuality became the subject of open and frank discussion, sometimes expressed with an explicitness that an earlier generation of students—and not that long ago—would have found salacious. The first issue of the *Bullet* in January 1970, for example, carried a full-page reprint of a *Ramparts* magazine essay, "Understanding Orgasm," that examined that phenomenon in graphic detail, drawing largely on the popular 1966 study by Masters and Johnson, *Human Sexual Response*.

Personalizing and bringing sexual concerns much closer to home, the same issue featured an extensive interview with one MWC student (anonymous) who discussed, in terms alternatively poignant and piquant, the experience of her own recent abortion. It was, on the one hand, she admitted, an emotional event; she recalled crying in the recovery room and "asking the nurse the most stupid question: whether she could tell if it was a girl or a boy." But there was little remorse. "As far as I'm concerned," she said, "a fetus isn't a human life. . . . I was almost six weeks pregnant, so what was it, almost an inch long? That's not a life. I'm sorry, that's not a life."

She agreed with her boyfriend (who was then serving in Vietnam) that abortion was the best course. "I didn't go crazy," she said, "I didn't have a nervous breakdown, and I'm very happy I had [the abortion]. . . . As long as you keep your sense of humor—it sounds impossible, but it really helps. . . . All I can say is that they should be legal and they should be cheaper. . . . I didn't even feel guilty about it. But now when I have my period, I just sit back and enjoy every little cramp!"

The apparent change in mores at the once-staid college did not go unnoticed by the public, attracting attention as far away as (of all places) the Southside Virginia town of South Boston, where the local paper pilloried the presumed libertines of MWC. Time was, it said, when the institution produced "prim, polite, and proper" ladies. "But no more. Mary Washington is now an avant garde institution where hippies flower, students march in Vietnam Moratorium demonstrations, and whisky is allowed to be consumed and kept by the girls in their dormitory rooms." Aghast at such behavior, the paper went on to urge the removal of the College's "morally corrupt" administration. "No amount of bellywash about student academic and personal freedom," it declared, "can erase the fact that Mary Washington is fast becoming a bordello and a haven for women of loose morals."[32]

Unaffected by such hectoring, the sexual revolution (such as it was) at Mary Washington continued apace. Later that same year, an entire issue of the *Bullet* was devoted to homosexuality. Among its contents was an extensive survey of MWC students concerning their attitudes on a wide range of issues related to homosexuality. Though two-thirds of them professed to have views on the subject that were either "very liberal" or "fairly liberal," some of the responses cast doubt on their avowed open-mindedness. Approximately 83 percent, for example, believed that "there should be laws prohibiting homosexual behavior between consenting persons"; 77 percent regarded homosexuals as "psychologically disturbed"; and 92 percent felt such persons could be "'cured' if they want to be." As one respondent put it, "True, they are human beings, but they are sick human beings. It is a mental disorder."

In terms of their own associations, almost 80 percent said they would not accept a homosexual roommate if they did not know her personally beforehand, whereas only 16 percent would object to having a homosexual on their hall, and a mere 5 percent would object to attending class with one—all of which prompted the *Bullet* to surmise that "the farther away the problem gets, the more liberal the opinions become."

Attitudes were somewhat more open on the question of how homosexuals should be treated overall, as 74 percent agreed that they "should be allowed to be themselves among the rest of society"—or, as one student put it, "I really don't give a damn as long as I'm not personally affronted." Indeed, according to the pollsters, one of the most common responses of interviewees was "I never thought about any of this before."

In addition to the survey, the paper included two other extraordinary articles on the subject. One was an exceedingly long and detailed interview with a homosexual student. Though candid on a panoply of issues regarding her sexual orientation, the student chose to remain anonymous, mainly because she did not want her parents to know. "I'm sure they would feel shocked and probably sick," she said. "My parents have sort of a harsh viewpoint about 'queers.'"[33]

In addition to a perceptive and highly articulate analysis of overall issues of homosexuality in contemporary American society, the student (who was having a lesbian affair at the time) addressed directly the question of what it was like to be a gay student at Mary Washington. "It's sometimes very difficult," she said, "because you're always under a strain and always worried that somebody is going to find out. . . . Right now I consider exposure dangerous . . . [because] if anyone found out it would get around really fast because things spread so fast here; within a week everyone on campus would know. I would probably be miserable if everyone found out, and I'm sure I would be treated like the school freak. It's probably almost as miserable, though, when people don't know, because you really can't be yourself."

The second article was a reprint from the *Black Panther* titled "A Letter from Huey to the Revolutionary Brothers and Sisters about the Women's Liberation and Gay Liberation Movements," written by Huey Newton, "Minister of Defense and Supreme Commander" of the Black Panther Party. The screed, accompanied by an almost page-length picture of Newton decked out in bandolier and hefting an automatic rifle, was an incendiary call for a revolutionary alliance of blacks with gay and feminist groups. "Homosexuals are not enemies of the people," he declared, though he admitted, "I have hang-ups myself about male homosexuality. Where, on the other hand," he graciously conceded, "I have no hang-ups about female homosexuality."

The efficacy (or even the relevance) of such an article in the *Bullet*, whose primary readership likely did not share its sentiments, was questionable—unless perhaps as a means of enhancing the paper's bona fides as an increasingly radical publication. In any case, its editorial stance heartily supported toleration in matters of sexual preference. "No matter how you get it all together," it concluded, "an orgasm is an orgasm."

(Mrs. Bushnell, it might be noted, had died earlier that year—perhaps mercifully, because assuredly the College, and the world, she had known had likewise passed on.)

If campus newspapers are reliable barometers of student interest—a somewhat dubious proposition—then Mary Washington students appear to have been nearly consumed by gender concerns in the early seventies. Following within a month of the *Bullet* edition on homosexuality came what was by all measures among the most memorable publications in its entire history (along with the earlier "Wanted: Jesus" issue).

The main focus was on feminist issues, as evidenced by articles such as "Whatever Happened to Women's Rights," a piece bemoaning the recent demise of the proposed Equal Rights Amendment, "deliberately killed by a group of male Senators who used as their explanation the fact that they were, after all, only trying to protect women from the rigors which equal rights might entail"; "The Pill," which pointed out that even though Mary Washington students could obtain birth control pills from a few local doctors, "the process is simpler at the free clinics in D.C. and Richmond, and much less expensive," and reminded them that "there is little bother in taking a pill every night"; and (presumably for those who failed to do so) "The Whens and

Hows of Abortion," an explanation, in grisly detail, of the various methods for terminating pregnancy—all still illegal in Virginia at that time.

In addition there was an advertisement for an abortion referral service and a news item, highlighted in a boxed format, concerning an "abortion information center" that had been established by a senior in her Jefferson Hall room. The article concluded with a plea that "contributions to an abortion loan fund for MWC students . . . are urgently requested from all sympathetic parties."

The portion of the paper, however, that was doubtless the most shocking to its readers was the reprint of an article from the *Village Voice* titled "Heavy Combat in the Erogenous Zone." The article not only explored in exhaustive detail the physics (and metaphysics) of sexual congress but did so in terminology that was neither euphemistic, nor polite, nor clinical, but simply raw; indeed, much of the article was devoted to an explication of the common word for sexual intercourse, a word that was then becoming a fashionable (if sometimes self-consciously overused) part of the liberal lexicon.

The article produced a barrage of complaints both to the paper itself and to Chancellor Simpson. The responses from parents, observed the chancellor, ranged from "being really shocked to being indignant." Typical of such reactions was that of one student's father, who complained to Simpson about the "unbelievable" language in the piece: "I have never used these words in front of my wife and certainly not my daughter or son. They are such as [are] found on a public restroom wall." It seemed to him to be symptomatic of what he termed the "almost fanatical hang-up with things sex-oriented" on the part of the *Bullet*.

There was another curious aspect to this particular edition of the paper. Though the issue was laden with feminist-oriented articles, it also contained, in astonishing juxtaposition, an interview with the reigning Miss U.S.A., Debbie Shelton, a native of Virginia. Visiting the campus as part of a national tour, Shelton responded to most questions with predictably bland (though generally not unintelligent) comments: the historical figure she would most like to be was the Virgin Mary; the contemporary American whom she most admired was "a toss-up between Martin Luther King and John Kennedy"; she did not feel exploited because "everybody wants to make lots of money with the least possible amount of work . . . [and] you're not exploited because you're exploiting them, too. They're not parading you like at some cattle show."

But when the subject turned to feminism, the gloves came off. "I think the women's liberation movement is silly, stupid, and ridiculous," she declared. "Every movement has good ideas—I think women should get equal pay too—but burning bras? . . . They're slobs, that's all they are. They haven't shaved their legs, and that's stupid. . . . They're so horrendous; they're the girls who can't make it looks-wise, so they're trying to find some way to stand out. . . . I'm talking about neatness and cleanliness, personal hygiene." Whereupon

Miss U.S.A. and her entourage entered a black Cadillac limousine and drove away, a hand flashing the peace sign out a window as they departed.

Remarkably, given the temper of the campus at that time, Shelton managed to escape without being physically assaulted. The strongest response—and a calm, conciliatory one at that—was a *Bullet* editorial, "Open Letter to Debbie," that chided her for rejecting "all supporters of the women's liberation movement as ranting, raving, unkempt revolutionaries" and urged her to join the "growing number of women who are earnestly trying to realize their potential as women."

The flap over the *Bullet* was simply one indication of campus behavior that led colleges to become the focus of increasing political interest in the commonwealth. It was about that same time that one state senator, Herbert Bateman of Newport News, was moved to introduce a resolution, passed by both houses of the General Assembly, designed to uphold "moral values at State-supported institutions." Apparently motivated by reports from the College of William and Mary, Bateman's resolution decried "regulations and policies which create, sanction, and condone co-educational dormitory units, wherein students of the opposite sex are known to frequently, if not regularly, co-habitate," and went on to declare it to be "contrary to the public policy of Virginia" for any institution to have regulations that were "inimical to the standards of morality, public decency and decorum which are indispensable for a stable, well-ordered society."[34]

More pertinent to MWC and the *Bullet*, there were also calls for withholding state funds from college publications deemed to be offensive. The problem for such critics, however, was that monies for publications, as well as for such things as movies and concerts, came not from the commonwealth's coffers but from students' compulsory annual activities fees ($27 at that time).

In an effort to address the situation, Fredericksburg delegate Benjamin Woodbridge, having already crossed swords with MWC students on previous issues, introduced a bill in the General Assembly that would deprive publications of support from such private fees, thereby making them dependent solely on the state budget for funding. The editor of the *Bullet*, Linda Cayton, promptly attacked the bill in an open letter to the members of the House of Delegates, claiming that "the implication of censorship which this bill carries is thinly veiled." Moreover, it was in her opinion the result of Woodbridge's vendetta against the MWC paper—"a one-man witch hunt . . . nothing more than McCarthyism." Though the whole effort turned out to be inconsequential in its actual effects, the affair was symptomatic of an era in which campus activities often provided fodder for those who sought to parlay the presumed decadence of college students into political advantage.

Rhetoric aside, the feminist movement wrought several initiatives on campus. One was the creation in April 1971 of the Student Center for Social Information Services, commonly known as SIS. Originally an independent organization operating outside the regular system of student governance, by 1974 it had been formalized under the supervision of the Student Association.

A major long-range goal of SIS was to create a contraception clinic on campus, an idea supported by 82 percent of student respondents, according to a *Bullet* poll. In the absence of such a facility, SIS acted mainly as an information service, compiling lists of doctors and agencies that would provide students with contraceptives, disseminating information on abortion, distributing handbooks on birth control, and making available copies of works such as *Our Bodies, Ourselves*. It also for a number of years periodically sponsored programs on the theme "Contraception, Abortion, and You"—events that usually attracted several hundred students to hear panel discussions, view films on contraception, and listen to presentations by representatives of Planned Parenthood.

At a time when most area gynecologists would not prescribe birth control pills or devices to students without parental consent (nor, of course, did the College itself), SIS attempted to aid students more directly by first establishing in 1972 a biweekly carpool service to a free clinic in Washington. Once the organization came under control of the Student Association, a referral service was set up to direct students to clinics in Washington and Richmond.

Within the range of issues relating to reproduction, abortion generated the most controversy—predictably so, in light of the national context at the time. The issue became especially heated on campus following the decision by the *Bullet* in 1971 to print advertisements for abortion referral services.

Biology professor Thomas Johnson was among those who publicly expressed opposition to the ads and, in a letter to the *Bullet*, suggested that to better understand the seriousness of abortion, students should see the "Life before Birth" exhibit on display in Combs Hall. In addition to photographs depicting the stages of human life from conception to birth, the exhibit contained specimens of human fetuses at the one-month, four-month, and five-month stages.

Besides creating campus controversy, the *Bullet* ads led to potential legal trouble for the publication. Noting that the practice violated Virginia Statute 18.1-63, Fredericksburg Commonwealth Attorney J. M. H. Willis Jr. met with the MWC Publications Board to advise that the ads cease, lest the paper (and possibly members of the board itself) risk prosecution for a misdemeanor, the penalty for which included a fine of up to $1,000 and a maximum of one year in jail. Clearly preferring not to press charges, Willis said that he would assume the editors were unaware of the putative violation, and would not pursue the matter if the ads were terminated. By a 6–5 vote, the editors agreed to stop publishing the ads and did discontinue them for some time.

But the issue resurfaced. The paper staunchly defended its publication of the materials, claiming no violation of the law was involved. As editor Robin Darling put it, "There can be no distinction drawn between encouragement of an action [which was what the law forbade] and dissemination of information." She admitted, moreover, that staff members were nonetheless aware of a possible accusation but went ahead anyway because they believed that the law itself was "unrespectable and illogical." Noting that Willis had said he preferred not to prosecute because he "didn't like to see Mary Washington girls in trouble," Darling retorted, "Well, we don't either. And that, in part, is why we printed the ad."

After a hiatus of some months, the paper, having received legal clearance, began running the ads again and continued to do so until early in 1973, when they were eliminated at the request of the National Planning Council on the grounds of insufficient response from the *Bullet* readership. Commenting on the termination, a *Bullet* staff member noted somewhat defensively that the abortion ads were "not removed for [their] unsuitability, but ironically, because of ours."

Though the specific matter of abortion ads thus came to an end, larger ramifications of abortion—medical, moral, and legal questions—persisted and became the focus of campus attention periodically in the coming years. At the time, however, interest shifted to other issues, notably including the establishment of a day care center on campus.

The whole matter of day care centers was a controversial one during this time. Feminists advocated their establishment as a means of freeing mothers from time-consuming constraints, enabling them to engage in productive careers outside the home. Conservatives, on the other hand, viewed child rearing by mothers as a necessity—for either religious, cultural, or economic reasons, or a combination thereof—and thus opposed the creation of such centers, especially at public expense.

An activist group of students at Mary Washington, however, led by Deborah Mandelker, boldly took the initiative and in late 1971 developed the concept of a student-run center on campus to provide day care for the children (up to age five) of College employees. At the outset, approximately fifty students, mainly from the Departments of Psychology, Sociology, and Education, formed the core staff. Their purpose, they emphasized, was not merely to provide a "baby-sitting service," but to make it a learning experience for the children, as well as a laboratory for applying the students' own academic interests.

Starting out in a lounge on the lower floor of Goolrick Hall, the center was initially equipped mainly through donations from various Fredericksburg merchants and schools and by MWC classes and clubs, all of which provided either monetary support or toys and other supplies. Such gifts were augmented by charging parents the nominal fee of one dollar per week for providing care from 8:00 a.m. to 5:00 p.m. Monday through Friday. The program continued to operate through the early seventies, moving in 1974 to better quarters in the Lee Hall "Owl's Nest." During a time when adversarial relationships seemed to predominate on campus, and when external observers were often critical, the day care center constituted an aberration of a more positive sort—an "unusual success story," the *Bullet* called it: "Unlike some organizations at MWC which continue only out of tradition, the center has a definite purpose. . . . [It] has the appealing quality of unselfishness. No one works [at] the center for the glory of it, for no room is afforded for reveling in self-importance. What is important there is not what one is, but what one has to give. . . . [The center] has done much to allay suspicions that MWC students are too self-centered and apathetic to care about anything but their own important individual selves."

Though the day care center flourished for a number of years as a student-run facility, it was destined not to be a permanent fixture on campus. Following the graduation of Deborah Mandelker in 1973 and her successor, Katherine O'Connell, in 1974, the enterprise gradually declined and eventually disappeared. In the years that followed, demands arose periodically for the reestablishment of such a facility to be funded by the College and staffed by professionals, but such pleas went unanswered by administrative officials who variously cited fiscal, legal, and logistical obstacles.[35]

Before the late 1960s, overt concern about politics had been minimal among Mary Washington students, mainly surfacing every four years with the coming of presidential elections. Ordinarily, activity was limited, and partisanship was balanced. As late as 1970, a *Bullet* poll revealed that only about 20 percent of the respondents acknowledged affiliation with, or loyalty to, any political party; among those who did, the split was almost exactly even between Democrats and Republicans. When the remaining, nonaffiliated respondents were asked if they even had a preference, the split was again almost identical: 28.9 percent favored Republicans, while 28.4 percent preferred Democrats.

Such a division was somewhat misleading, however, in that the political philosophy of the majority of students—to the extent that they had one—was more conservative than the partisan figures might indicate. This was because in mid-twentieth-century Virginia, whence most students hailed, the dominant political force, the Democratic "Byrd organization," was so conservative as to be tantamount to Republicanism. To be a Democrat in the commonwealth before the organization's demise in the late sixties was not to be left-wing by any means. In short, the politics of the student body tended to be conservative, a reflection of the generally middle-class backgrounds from which they came.

By the early 1970s, student interest had not only increased but moved somewhat leftward, at least temporarily. During a time of heightened awareness of social issues at the national level, a variety of concerns arose that from time to time piqued student interest, including drug legalization, the energy crisis, the plight of immigrant farmworkers, euthanasia, and public prayer. Those and other topical issues often sparked debate among students and faculty alike, resulting in the spirited exchange of ideas in classes, in public forums, and in the pages of the *Bullet*. But on a campus whose student body still

Susan J. Hanna

comprised mainly women, it was not surprising that feminist issues in general, and the proposed Equal Rights Amendment in particular, generated the most sustained interest.

The feminist movement at MWC was led by a cadre of energetic faculty members, each of whom possessed a dynamic, and distinctive, personality. English professor Susan J. Hanna, who was an acclaimed teacher (recipient of the 1985 Grellet Simpson Award for Excellence in Undergraduate Teaching), flouted convention both verbally with her boisterous pronouncements and visually with her characteristic army-fatigue-jacket attire. Psychology professor Alice Rabson—"Crazy Alice" to friend and foe alike—became a motorized icon as she putt-putted through campus in a purple VW Beetle plastered, almost literally covered, with stickers whose messages suggested that she had never met a liberal cause that she did not embrace. In 1972 she was named vice president for communications of the Professional Women's Caucus in Washington, D.C., and two years later was chosen to head the local chapter of the American Civil Liberties Union. Religion professor Elizabeth Clark was a teacher of exceptional erudition (also a Simpson Award honoree), whose commitment to women's issues was matched by her passion in their promotion. In 1974 she was elected president of the local chapter of the National Organization of Women.[36]

It was Clark who, in one typical exhortation to the MWC female population, issued the following advice via the *Bullet*:

> [There is] something I have long wanted to bring to the attention of you college women: do not imagine that the males you encounter on this campus or elsewhere are the possessors of "raised consciousness" simply because they espouse liberal social causes. Many men who would find it unthinkable to make derogatory comments about Jews or blacks seem totally unaware that their jokes and insinuations about the (supposed) irrationality, weakness, incompetence, and hysteria of women are offensive. It is highest time for all of us females to protest whenever we hear a man indulging in talk which is insulting and derogatory to women as a group. Pointing out a man's sexist attitudes probably won't do much for your popularity, but I can guarantee that it will do a lot for your feeling of self-respect.

In addition to the inspiration provided by feminist faculty, students were encouraged to pursue women's issues by guest speakers such as Flora Crater, the state coordinator of the Virginia Women's Political Caucus and (unsuccessful) candidate for lieutenant governor in 1973, who visited the campus on several occasions. Consciousness-raising groups were also formed, in the *Bullet*'s words, "to make women more aware of themselves and how they are affected by institutions, men, and other women. The idea is to create a sisterhood which is collectively supportive. These 'rap groups' are the basic unit of the Women's Movement." A number of courses with feminist perspectives were added to the curriculum, and occasional panel discussions of feminist issues were presented. One such was an April 1974 panel titled "Current Issues in Feminism," moderated by Elizabeth Clark, featuring presentations by faculty members from the Departments of Biology, Psychology, and Sociology, as well as Nathaniel Brown of the English Department, who discussed critical approaches to women in literature.

The most visible political manifestation of the feminist surge on campus involved efforts to secure ratification of the Equal Rights Amendment. The proposed constitutional amendment, which was passed by the House of Representatives in 1971, was sent to the states for ratification following its passage by the Senate in March 1972—whereupon a number of Mary Washington faculty and students began to work earnestly for its approval by the Virginia General Assembly.

The *Bullet* led the charge, declaring in an editorial that "women are still second-class citizens in America. This is a sad example of the American woman's ignorance of her own power and right in this country. . . . Women's rights are not trivial things. Women's rights are human rights and are very fragile. Women's rights need protection by laws."

Members of the American Civil Liberties Union at MWC urged their fellow students to lobby aggressively for the passage of the amendment when it first came before the General Assembly in January 1973: "Tell your mother, tell your sister, your neighbors, your friends, anyone you talk to that may be able to influence [a legislator]. . . . Do something! It is up to the mass of students [to] stick together, [so] we can make this college the college we really want to stay at because it affords us an equal education as well as treats us as equal human beings."

Despite such support, the legislature failed to take favorable action on the proposal at the 1973 session, leading its advocates at Mary Washington to redouble their efforts as the measure came before the General Assembly the following year. The campus paper urged students to participate in a letter-writing campaign in support of ERA and listed the addresses of a half-dozen organizations for whom students could work to promote its passage. Moreover, several students, along with Professors Clark and Rabson, attended a legislative hearing on the amendment in Richmond, at which Rabson, representing the Professional Women's Caucus, addressed the committee, urging endorsement.

Early in the ratification process, proponents of ERA were optimistic, as well they might have been, given that public opinion polls indicated preponderant popular support. Indeed, within the first year after its passage by

Congress, the amendment had garnered approval from the majority of the thirty-eight states necessary for its adoption. Small wonder that the *Bullet* could confidently declare, "The amendment will be passed. Sooner or later."

Such optimism proved to be ill-founded. At one point, the approval of only three more states was needed, but the requisite number was never achieved, despite the extension of the deadline for ratification from the original seven years to ten. Virginia was among the states that never approved it, though on one occasion it came within a single vote of doing so.

The defeat of ERA understandably dismayed campus feminists (though they were heartened by the pro-choice decision in *Roe v. Wade* around the same time). There were even suggestions that feminist efforts may inadvertently have produced negative results in some ways. A *Bullet* article in September 1974, written by Linda Cayton (who had been the paper's editor in 1970–71), pointed out that "the days of the coy, flirtatious sweet young thing are over. The well-scrubbed, all-American dimpled cheerleader no longer serves as the object of the standard American sexual fantasy." But, she went on to warn, there was a more sinister side to the new gender equation: "After all, the most popular feminist activity over the last few years, in the male view, has been the great bra burning. And liberated women tend to be more secure in, and open about, their sexuality. . . . Nowadays, all a man expects to do is exchange a greeting and a few key political words, and there she will be, assuming the basic gynecological examination position. . . . A liberated woman is necessarily a strong woman, and that means, to many men, an invulnerable woman, one who doesn't need emotional support, affection, time, or concern. Wham, bam, thank you ma'am. The all-American girl." Though a bit overwrought in its expression, the article was accurate in indicating a new dynamic emerging in gender relationships, at Mary Washington as elsewhere across the country.

By the mid-1970s, the feminist movement at the College had crested. Some battles had been won (legalization of abortion), others lost (ERA)—meaning that some of the most flammable issues were being contested less vigorously. In 1982 the polestar of the movement on campus, Elizabeth Clark, left the College to take a position in the religion department at Duke, significantly diminishing the charisma quotient of feminist leadership on campus. True, Alice Rabson remained actively engaged until her retirement in 1984, as did Susan Hanna until her untimely death in 1994; and others emerged as avatars of women's issues in the years ahead—faculty members like Christopher Kilmartin in psychology, Allyson Poska in history, and Mary Rigsby in English, among others. But the campus would not again be as energized on the issue of women's rights as it had been in the early seventies.

Political interest on campus during the period was not only driven by controversial issues but also spiked on a personal level by the emerging political career of one of the College's own faculty members, political science professor Lewis P. Fickett Jr. Widely admired as a teacher and long regarded as a leader within the faculty, Fickett had simultaneously established strong liberal credentials within the local Democratic party, being elected as its chairman in 1969 and 1971. In 1971 he sought one of the Fredericksburg area's two seats in the House of Delegates.

Lewis P. Fickett Jr.

The 1971 contest was particularly interesting in that one of Fickett's opponents was none other than the incumbent Republican and perennial MWC (or, more specifically, *Bullet*) nemesis, Benjamin Woodbridge. Not surprisingly, the two clashed repeatedly during the campaign. In one debate, for example, Woodbridge asserted that Fickett could not serve effectively because his teaching schedule would conflict with the General Assembly sessions—a claim that Fickett countered by charging that the incumbent had himself "set an all-time record for absenteeism."

On the eve of the election, the *Bullet* predictably endorsed Fickett, but with less enthusiasm than might have been expected. "While Lew Fickett is neither daring nor particularly progressive," it said, "the politics of Ben Woodbridge are abominable." Less reserved was the paper's support for the independent candidate for lieutenant governor, Henry Howell, whose daughter Mary was then a student at the College. A losing candidate in the previous gubernatorial campaign, Howell had subsequently emerged as the most successful liberal politician in recent Virginia history, irritating the commonwealth's establishment with his insistent "keep the big boys honest" rallying cry. "He is undoubtedly a valuable man to have around," said the *Bullet*. "It is his kind who have . . . put the Byrd Machine out of commission."[37] In the end Fickett lost, as Woodbridge and the other incumbent, Democrat Robert Gwathmey, were both reelected. (Howell, however, did win.)

The defeat did not mean the end of Fickett's career. Two years later, in 1973, he ran successfully for the same seat, Woodbridge having decided not to seek another term. Reelected three times, Fickett worked assiduously for progressive programs such as free textbooks for public schools and for reforms such as repeal of the sales tax on food and nonprescription drugs. In the process, he established himself as one of the legislature's most eloquent advocates of progressive policies until his defeat in 1981 by Republican Thomas Moncure.[38]

In terms of national politics, Mary Washington students during this era manifested greater interest than ever before, as evidenced by their involvement in the 1968 presidential election. Much like their peers across the country, a number of them, motivated mainly by their opposition to the Vietnam War, were initially attracted to the antiwar campaign of Eugene McCarthy, a senator from Minnesota. In February, eleven MWC students were among three busloads of students from the Washington area who traveled to New Hampshire to participate in a polling and pamphleteering effort on McCarthy's behalf in that state's primary election. It was indicative of concern about the public's increasingly negative view of current college students that none of the female volunteers who wore slacks (or any males with beards) were allowed to campaign door-to-door. "These unfortunates were carted off to Concord where they spent the weekend uneventfully licking envelopes," reported the *Bullet*, adding proudly that all MWC workers "were dressed properly and hence actively participated."

Fueled largely by student efforts such as these, the campaign succeeded far beyond expectations in New Hampshire, to the extent that McCarthy's showing vaulted him to the forefront of the race for the Democratic nomination. That status was short-lived, however, lasting only until Robert Kennedy announced his candidacy a few weeks later—whereupon much of McCarthy's support shifted to Kennedy. At MWC, supporters of the two candidates made common cause, bonding together to work toward the shared paramount goal of defeating the incumbent, Lyndon Johnson.

When the November election arrived, it involved none of these men: McCarthy's candidacy wilted in the course of the primary campaign; Johnson in late March renounced a bid for reelection; and Kennedy was murdered in June. In a campus poll regarding the two eventual nominees, students preferred Richard Nixon over Hubert Humphrey by a vote of 542 to 387, with right-wing independent candidate George Wallace receiving 37 votes—a result that presaged the outcome of the actual election (though Nixon's actual margin of victory in 1968 was much narrower).

In light of the antiwar hostility that developed during Nixon's first term, strong campus opposition to his reelection might have been expected. Indeed, his 1972 Democratic opponent, George McGovern, did attract considerable support among the College community. When the "Grassroots Grasshopper," a customized camper carrying a team of McGovern supporters—mainly celebrities and politicians—stopped in Fredericksburg in October as part of its southern tour, the bulk of the crowd that greeted the caravan in the Sheraton parking lot was composed of MWC students and faculty. There they cheered notables such as the feminist leader Gloria Steinem, who declared that "as women, we just can't stand four more years of Nixon," whom she pilloried for his anti-female views: "He has to have a memo written for him on how to talk to women, and that really amounts to how to talk *down* to women."

The *Bullet* likewise lambasted the incumbent and urged students to support McGovern—all to no avail, however, either on campus or beyond. In a student poll that attracted only a minimal response, Nixon won reelection overwhelmingly (205 to 99), a result replicated nationally in his landslide victory.

The continuing Republican affinity of the student body was in some ways surprising. Surely the policies of the Nixon administration were at times repugnant to many students, as evidenced most clearly by the antiwar protests. Then, too, the majority of the faculty, who might have influenced students, were inclined toward the Democratic Party—though not totally so, with Samuel Emory (geography), Laura Sumner (classics), and William "Bud" Clatanoff (economics) being stalwart, and vocal, Republicans. Yet the rightward bent of MWC students in the aggregate was such that only one Democrat—Lyndon Johnson against Barry Goldwater in 1964—had won a presidential preference poll on campus since the 1940s. The explanation seems to be that students basically reflected the views of their families, who in the late sixties and seventies were tending to become more politically cautious in the face of perceived threats posed by rapid social and cultural changes besetting them at every turn.

Support for Nixon began to diminish at Mary Washington, however, as details of the Watergate affair emerged following his reelection. By January 1974 a petition was circulated on campus calling on the chairman of the House Judiciary Committee to pursue impeachment proceedings against the president; it was signed by approximately one hundred persons, including several faculty members. The following month, the campus paper carried a prominent advertisement encouraging readers to attend an "impeachment lobby-in" to be held in Washington. The ad featured a picture of a scowling Nixon, accompanied with the warning caption "This man is armed, dangerous, and in office." Near the end of the semester, the *Bullet* took an unambiguous stand in an editorial headlined "Impeachment Now."

By the time classes resumed in the following fall, the Nixon adversaries had achieved their goal, not through impeachment but through the president's resignation in August. With his successor, Gerald Ford, having declared that "our national nightmare is over," political interest on campus (as in the nation) soon declined to a less feverish level.

LIFE AFTER CLASS

The early 1970s witnessed the inauguration of a number of extracurricular events, either educational or purely entertaining, some of which became permanent features of campus life. It was a good thing, too, for students were beginning to register increasing dissatisfaction with their non-academic opportunities. A 1970 *Bullet* poll, for example, revealed that only about 20 percent of the respondents were happy with available extracurricular activities, while 77 percent were dissatisfied with College social life in general. The result of such attitudes was that, according to the poll, almost three-quarters of those interviewed had at some point considered transferring from Mary Washington—termed by one of them "a small, backward, southern girls' school."

A certain amount of disgruntlement, of course, can be found on almost any campus at any given time, and the expression of such sentiments was not surprising in a poll that virtually invited complaint—all the more so in an era when protest was de rigueur. Yet the fact remained that the student body was experiencing an unusually high level of discontent as the institution moved uneasily into a new incarnation: no longer exclusively a women's college, it was not yet really coed, either; no longer part of U.Va., it had as yet acquired no distinctive identity of its own. And its social ambience continued to reflect in many ways the still-sleepy aura of Fredericksburg, a town more reminiscent of Richmond than of Washington, offering the College crowd few opportunities for revelry.

The paucity of venues for dining, drinking, and dancing was likely more vexing to this generation of students than to earlier ones, inasmuch as a larger proportion of them now came from more northerly and urbanized areas where entertainment opportunities were greater. In that light, Mary Washington seemed to be, in the words of one *Bullet* columnist, "a small college stuck in a small city whose potential for entertainment for anyone besides an American history buff is spectacularly minute. And the general conclusion reached by students who ask what there is to do in Fredericksburg . . . is that when you're bored in Fredericksburg you stay bored."

Such an assessment was perhaps too harsh but did contain some truth. On the one hand, for female students who liked to shop, there were a number of popular women's clothing stores: LaVogue, Sydney's, Carlton's, May's, Pappagallo's, Carley's, and Miller's. But dining was another matter, presenting something of a challenge when, as a *Bullet* writer put it, "the occasions arise that the Seacobeck fare somehow falls below one's culinary expectations and exceeds one's gastric tolerance." The family restaurants closest to campus—Hot Shoppes in the Fredericksburg Shopping Center and Howard Johnson's (later Hamway's) in Park & Shop—were undistinguished, in the manner typical of family restaurants. Downtown there were Goolrick's lunch counter and, somewhat more upscale, the Cellar Door, just off William Street, as well as the Kenmore Coffee Shop, genially presided over by the elderly Mr. Lakey, tie perpetually askew, described by the *Bullet* as "quite a good egg (not scrambled or hard-boiled, but sunny-side up!)." Then, for those times "when Mom and Dad, and Dad's wallet, come to visit their daughter in college," advised the *Bullet*, they should go to the Latchstring Restaurant on College Avenue, where "prices are high, but reasonable for their big dinners."

For those less interested in cuisine than in color (albeit of a questionable hue), there was the all-night Truck Stop just off Route 17 north. One *Bullet* columnist adjudged the fare a "catastrophe" and likened the aroma of the coffee to that emanating from the local FMC plant; moreover, it lampooned the waitresses as "450-pound Sherman tanks who have bought out People's drug store's supply of eye liner and hair spray" and described the atmosphere as a "redneck haven" dominated by a jukebox constantly playing "Thank God I'm a Country Boy." Then an observation: "Girls, if you are tired of the run-of-the-mill university boys or Quantico cuties, here at the Truck Stop you may find the man of your dreams, . . . those rugged he-man types who are so fashionably dressed in the latest 1950's greasy T-shirts with a pack of stale cigarettes rolled up in their sleeves. . . . [From them] you will receive your full share of ogles and glares, enough to last until the next MWC keg party."

Considerably more appealing were the two gustatory landmarks of the city: Allman's Bar-B-Q and Carl's Frozen Custard. Regarding Allman's, the *Bullet* offered some advice: "For all the Yankees at the college getting their first taste of Southern cooking and hating it, before you utter another nasty word about spoonbread and grits, go to Allman's on Route 1, across from (and a far cry from) McDonald's, and try a real sliced pork barbeque sandwich. . . . You will see what the South has that even Hoboken, New Jersey lacks."

As for Carl's, its popularity was attested over the years by the frequent block-long lines that began on the sidewalk and wound around the tiny building before reaching the single window where one could purchase the toothsome treat; offering only three flavors (vanilla, chocolate, and strawberry), Baskin-Robbins it was not. But so distinctive (some would say addictive) was the confection that Carl's achieved iconic status among MWC students. As one of them described it, "Cruising by Carl's on Princess Anne, there appeared to be a revival meeting of the campus community. Neither lack of transportation, cold of night, nor overdrawn checking accounts could dissuade these coeds from their destination! Students came by cars, trucks, motorcycles, bikes, jogging, and pulling wagons which contained roommates . . . [to procure] that thick, creamy, super keen, and groovy Carl's custard. . . . Carl's is the number one place to eat in Fredericksburg and your education at MWC will somehow be inadequate without many and frequent visits to this outstanding establishment."

Popular as both Allman's and Carl's were, barbeque and ice cream joints did not constitute the ideal venues for dating—and students in search of more amatory locations had little from which to choose. The *Bullet* in a 1969 column tried to be helpful: "DO take your blind date to the Coachman if he's a real loser. There you can't hear him so you don't have to listen to his trivia. Also there's the chance you can lose him on the jammed dance floor. DON'T try to peek down the stairs or through the double doors into the parlor at your date. He's inevitably peeking back. DO take an intelligent, interesting date to GW [the George Washington Inn]. Here you can talk, and get to know him. DO drag a rich date to Georgetown or Richmond. They both possess the inherent excitement of a city and a large selection of guys for future reference."

The situation improved appreciably in the early seventies with the opening of Bill "the Greek" Kertsos's My Brother's Place on William Street and Art Chiavaroli's bar, the eponymous Art's, located in the basement of the Latchstring. Both were within easy walking distance of the campus and for a number of years were convivial centers for socializing among students, younger faculty members, and "townies."

A wider range of on-campus activities became available to students in the late sixties and early seventies, including lectures by visiting luminaries in various fields. Visiting speakers were not a new phenomenon on campus, of course, as many notables had appeared over the years, frequently under the aegis of the University Center in Virginia. Prominent speakers included the Nobel Prize–winning novelist William Faulkner (1956) and the acclaimed British historian Arnold Toynbee (1958). But the practice reached a new high—or, in the view of some, a new low—with an appearance by Dick Gregory in early 1969.

Having gained acclaim earlier as perhaps the nation's most popular black comedian, Gregory had by that time turned his act to more serious subjects, especially using mordant humor to skewer whites on matters of race relations. He had even run for president in 1968—a quixotic attempt, to be sure, but one that provided a larger forum from which to deliver his provocative message. Following the election, he had whimsically declared himself "President in Exile."

It is safe to assume that GW auditorium, filled to overflowing for his presentation, had never witnessed anything quite like Gregory's performance that night, either in content or delivery. Indicting former president Lyndon Johnson as "the number one tyrant to walk the face of the earth since Julius Caesar," Gregory proceeded to inveigh against an assortment of ills that illustrated the "moral pollution" of America: "While we're in Southeast Asia trying to keep Communism from spreading, who's going to keep injustice from spreading here in America? . . . The only country in the world that has ever dropped an atomic bomb on people asks us [African Americans] to be nonviolent. . . . The Indians have been nonviolent for seventy-five years, and they are still on their reservations."

Gregory's performance was noteworthy not only for his opinions but also for his scatological expression of them—both of which were offensive to some of the more staid members of the audience. One faculty member recalled in particular observing the reactions of Dean of Students Margaret Hargrove. The lineal (and spiritual) heir of Nina Bushnell as the guardian of propriety at the College, the decorous Hargrove blanched at every vulgarism, occasionally wincing audibly; barely able to contain her contempt, she was not able to contain her revulsion. The students, quite to the contrary, loved it.

The College embarked on an ambitious plan in 1970 when the Alumnae Association announced the underwriting of a program to be known as the Distinguished Visitor in Residence. The concept was to bring to campus each year an eminent scholar or practitioner—selected by a committee comprising faculty, students, and alumnae—who would stay on campus for several days and during that time visit with students, in class and informally, as well as deliver a major public address. The program was inaugurated in the spring of 1970, and the visitors chosen during the first four years clearly reflected the prevailing cultural and intellectual currents of the time.

The first was Margaret Mead, who, then at the age of seventy, was probably the best-known anthropologist in the country. In a visit that lasted only about twenty-four hours, the energetic and outspoken Mead managed to meet informally and dine with students, visit Brompton, and deliver a public lecture titled "The Changing Male and Female Roles in the United States" to a capacity crowd in GW auditorium. She also sat for a lengthy interview with *Bullet* editors on a smorgasbord of subjects that took up four pages in the paper. Asked what she thought of Mary Washington College, she responded, "Do you mean the trees or the people?" before opining (presumably without intended condescension) that it was "quite a lively campus for a girls' college."

The choice of the second distinguished visitor, Saul Alinsky, struck some people as incongruous. Even the *Bullet* commented that "many students wondered why the MWC administration would welcome an avowed 'agitator,' a 'professional radical,' who had been banned from far more liberal communities than Fredericksburg." And, indeed, his message was provocative—but not incendiary. As the *Bullet* explained (in a story accompanied by a huge photograph of a smiling Alinsky flashing an obscene gesture at the camera), the controversial visitor actually "managed to bring many sectors of this campus together in a sense of community . . . [in which] for a little while, everyone knew that the others really cared."

There was a sad postscript to the visit. In one discussion group, someone asked Alinsky if he feared death. He replied that he did not because "when you are in the arena of conflict, you just don't have the time to grow older. . . . What I do fear is the possibility of outliving my life, of becoming useless and ineffective." His concern turned out to be unnecessary. Less than three months after his campus visit, he died suddenly at the age of sixty-three.

One of the most famous participants in the program's early years was the historian Arthur M. Schlesinger Jr., the distinguished visitor in residence for 1973. As the former special assistant to President Kennedy and author of the popular history of that administration, *A Thousand Days*, Schlesinger was sometimes referred to as Kennedy's "in-house intellectual." Given his political orientation, coupled with the hot topic of Watergate, he naturally spent much of his visit criticizing the Nixon administration, asserting on one occasion that the president's "peculiar combination of self-righteous condemnations of the permissive society on the one hand, with running the crookedest government we've seen in fifty years on the other, is going to provide material for satirists for many years to come."

The 1974 visitor was the acclaimed author Chaim Potok, whose most recent work was the best-selling novel *My Name is Asher Lev*. In the course of a weeklong stay on campus, Potok met with numerous classes in religion, philosophy, and literature and delivered a formal public presentation titled "Rebellion and Authority in Modern Literature." Asked near the end of his stay to characterize Mary Washington College as he had observed it, he commented (quite presciently): "I can see the college taking a very tentative, reluctant step away from its secure past, rather genteel and restricted, to a possibly unsecure future of wider horizons and more problems." And he offered a cautionary note for the times: "I think rebellion is basic to growing up," he said, "but too many are out to destroy everything. . . . It's absurd to think you can build a future on a totally annihilated past."

The success of the early visitors augured well for the future of the program, which for many years enlivened the campus with speakers of exceptional intellect and accomplishment until, in 1996, it was discontinued. By that time, however, its function had been assumed by other programs of similar purpose and import, such as the Distinguished Graduate in Residence (also sponsored by the Alumni Association) and the Fredericksburg Forum.

Aside from visiting speakers, entertainment opportunities in the late sixties and early seventies included campus performances by artists such as Mary Travers (the "Mary" of the folk trio Peter, Paul, and Mary) and the guitarist Charlie Byrd. One of the singers scheduled to perform, Jim Croce—he of the hit single, "Bad, Bad Leroy Brown"—was killed in a plane crash in September 1973, just weeks before he was scheduled to perform on campus; he was replaced by the folksinger Gordon Lightfoot.

As for homegrown entertainment, the Drama Department regularly offered productions that attracted enthusiastic audiences of students, faculty, and townsfolk to Klein Theatre, named in 1971 in honor of drama professor Albert R. Klein, who had died suddenly the previous year. Annual auctions sponsored by Chi Beta Phi, the science honorary, were popular with students and raised money to support science scholarships.

The sports program offered intercollegiate competition for women on a limited basis, but athletic opportunities for men in the early years of coeducation were virtually nil—with one interesting exception. In the late 1960s, a group of faculty and staff members cobbled together a basketball team that competed with similar clubs in the area—teams from the local public schools, the National Guard, Germanna Community College, Quantico Marine Base,

Dahlgren Naval Weapons Laboratory, and the like. With the arrival of male students on campus, the MWC club incorporated some younger talent as well, including 6' 6" Emmett Snead of Fredericksburg.

A motley outfit it was, but spirited—and not without ability. It had some height, too, in the persons of comptroller Edward Allison and faculty members Marshall Bowen, George Van Sant, Richard Hansen, and Sammy Merrill. All had actually been accomplished athletes in their day—the problem being that, in most cases, that day had not been recent.

The motivating force behind the club was Marsh Bowen. It was he who organized it, scheduled its games, and, if other sources of revenue proved insufficient, paid its expenses out of pocket. The club's nickname was the Dragons—appropriately chosen, according to Bowen, "because it stands for something worn and outdated, like most of the guys on the team."

They were not, to be sure, a major spectator attraction on campus, but they did serve as a forerunner to an impressive sports program that would develop later in the decade. As for the Dragons themselves, what they lacked in skill, they compensated for in camaraderie. It was, said Bowen, "a good way for the guys to get to know each other. We'll play a few games, then go out for a beer with the other team. It's a fun game."

Students themselves took the lead in creating the College's first homecoming, held in November 1972. The whole event was designed as a parody of the "big weekends" that female students traditionally attended at other universities. Playing on that idea, the theme of MWC's version was "Bring the Boys Home," an implicit invitation for dates to come to the Fredericksburg venue for a change.

The affair incorporated all the main elements of homecomings elsewhere, starting with a parade from the Monroe gates, through Campus Drive, and on to the Hanover Street golf course; it included a band from the local high school, a drill team of MWC girls, floats, and a convertible carrying the homecoming king. Sponsored by various dorms, the floats were decorated to represent social meccas for MWC students, such as U.Va., Randolph-Macon, Quantico, and the Naval Academy—as well as one devoted to "townies." Following the parade, there was a flag-football game between Devils and Goats, replete with cheerleaders and highlighted by the crowning of the homecoming king at halftime. The day's festivities concluded with a picnic dinner on the golf course and an evening bonfire.

Plans for the event prompted a rousing, if somewhat tongue-in-cheek, editorial in the *Bullet*. Noting that "school spirit at Mary Washington is practically non-existent," the paper went on to chide: "Do you want Fredericksburg to think you are all just a bunch of liberal, jaded do-nothings? It is your duty as students to promote enthusiasm for school functions. Do anything: organize pep rallies, try out for cheerleading, help decorate for the big dance, toilet-paper the dean's office, scribble 'MWC' and the date of your graduation on any available surface—anything! . . . You are all students at Mary Washington and you'd damn well better be proud of it!"

The event did, in fact, generate unaccustomed student spirit. The men on campus, all of whom then lived in Trench Hill, constituted the pool of candidates for homecoming king, and they good-naturedly cooperated with a two-page *Bullet* spread featuring their photos and qualifications, including age, hair and eye color, hobbies, and, in a bow to traditional female criteria, "measurements" (one of whose were listed at 54-54-54). In response to the query of why they were seeking the title, comments ran from "I didn't know I was a candidate" to "I ran because I'm queer" (presumably an attempt at humor) to a probably more truthful "I want the six-pack" (the grand prize for the winner).

The *Bullet*, too, had fun with the idea, running an article titled "A Socialite's Guide to Homecoming Fashions." Mary Wash girls, it began, would "no longer be deprived of the excitement of a homecoming celebration. From the moment you hear your name being called [in the dorm] and see your suitemate clutching the receiver of the phone, and hear her orgasmic whisper, 'It's a guy!', it's just one thrilling minute after another." As for the issue of attire, "The idea on fashion these days is originality: 'do your own thing!'"—but, just to be sure, "consult *Glamour* and *Seventeen* magazines."

In an era when students' seriousness of purpose, admirable though it was, sometimes verged on sanctimony, the homecoming celebration was a lighthearted aberration. It also proved to be the prototype of sorts for an event that, considerably modified in its particulars and more formalized in its structure, developed into an annual fall tradition by the 1990s.

Two other events that were to achieve permanence also originated in the early seventies. One was Parents Weekend, first held in April 1973; the following year it was switched to October, where it remained as an annual event. The first fall program included campus tours on which parents could meet faculty members, a reception in the Brompton Rose Garden, dance and fencing demonstrations in Goolrick, a synchronized swimming exhibition by the Terrapin Club, and a drama production, "The Prime of Miss Jean Brodie."

The College's first Career Day was also held in October 1973. Though the event was jointly sponsored by the Academic Advising Office, the Counseling Center, the Student Association, the Class of 1974, and Mortar Board, the main motivating and organizing force behind it was Isabel Gordon, director of the Placement Bureau. Whereas prospective employers had previously visited campus on an ad hoc basis, usually for evening interview sessions, this marked the first time that a large number of recruiters were assembled for a daylong program of interviews and career information sessions. Under Gordon's energetic initiative, the event included representatives from business and industry, government, retailing, publishing, and banking, as well as graduate schools. Career Day continued regularly on an annual basis thereafter, becoming more extensive as the years passed, providing students with valuable insights into postgraduation opportunities—something the College theretofore had not been conspicuously concerned about.

Throughout the period, especially after the demise of May Day, a major social event each spring was Junior Ring Dance. When it first started in the 1950s, it was largely modeled on the genteel dances of earlier times, with formal invitations, dance cards, elaborate decorations, expensive souvenirs, and well-known musical groups such as Fred Perry's Orchestra, the Billy Butterfield Orchestra, and the Chad Mitchell Trio. The weekend affairs typically began on Friday, when, as the *Bullet* said in announcing the 1957 event, "it is hoped that the girls and their dates may get together at one of the clubs in Fredericksburg." Saturday afternoons featured outdoor concerts on Westmoreland and Ball circles, followed by a banquet in Seacobeck.

The highlight of the evening was the Ring Dance itself, held on Saturday night in Lee Ballroom, where punch and cookies were served throughout the evening. The *Bullet*, in announcing the upcoming '57 event, provided a description of a typical Ring celebration (as well as an indication of campus ambience at the time): "The theme for the ring dance will be 'Southern Serenade.' This Southern atmosphere will be carried out by a backdrop of a plantation mansion and white trellises and flowers. The mood will be set by soft lights. Tables will be arranged along the sides of the dance floor for the couples. A grand march will lead the couples through the traditional 'ring figure' where the girls will receive their MWC rings from their escorts. Fol-

Ring Dance, 1963

lowing the dance, breakfast will be served from 12:00 to 2:00 in Seacobeck. Music will be played over the loudspeaker system."

The event underwent several changes during the 1960s. Before 1963 the format called for each couple to stand under a large model of the ring while the girl's escort placed the ring on her finger. In that year, however, the procedure was changed so that the couples formed a ring-shaped circle with only the president of the class and her date standing under the mock ring. At the appointed time, all the escorts would follow the example of the couple under the ring and bestow the rings simultaneously. "This simple ring ceremony," explained the *Bullet*, "will allow more time for dancing" inasmuch as the previous format had "proved to be too time-consuming." (The paper also noted that the dance would end at midnight, but that as a special concession, juniors would have "late permission until 2 o'clock.")

Another change in the ceremony was implemented in 1967, when in an effort to increase class unity and to emphasize the academic significance of the rings, a formal ring presentation ceremony was added to the schedule of events. In the first such ceremony, Dean Edward Alvey presented rings to 363 students at the ceremony held in George Washington Hall auditorium.

At the time of the first presentation ceremony, the juniors who had organized the event expressed their hope that it would become an annual affair. Their wish was granted, perhaps even beyond their expectations, as the ring celebration would continue for decades, becoming by the time of the institution's centennial year one of its most enduring and revered traditions.

But the ring event came only once a year and involved mainly the members of only one class. For the student body as a whole, on an informal, regular (almost weekly) basis, another form of socializing took hold in the early seventies: the keg party. These events, which quickly became enormously popular as campus drinking restrictions were relaxed, were usually held either in the basement of Seacobeck or in the Lee Ballroom, the floors of which were inevitably covered at evening's end with a sticky residue of beer.

Perhaps the most unusual manifestation of student exuberance during the period—one that (mercifully) did not become a tradition—occurred in the spring of 1974: the phenomenon known as "streaking." The activity, which involved shedding one's clothes and running naked through a public space, spread rapidly across the country as the weather grew warmer. There was even an Intercollegiate Streakers' Association, whose motto was "Study hard, but get a little behind in your work," and the *Bullet* carried several ads for streaker T-shirts. So popular was the fad that a novelty song by Ray Stevens, "The Streak," ended up as the third-best-selling Top 40 record in 1974:

> They call him "the streak."
> He likes to show off his physique.
> If there's an audience to be found,
> He'll be streaking around,
> Inviting public critique.[39]

The *Free Lance–Star* professed (flippantly) to see some benefit in the practice. "Streakers invariably are drawn from the ranks of the lithe and well-muscled," it observed. "Students toting a load of winter blubber balk at bare shenanigans in public. Aesthetically speaking, this is all to the good. But one must also consider the health benefits of streaking. . . . Few streakers, even in the most exhibitionist frame of mind, linger en route. They move briskly from one point of concealment to the next, and that is just what the doctor ordered for all-around muscle tone. . . . Streaking may yet turn out to be the biggest boon to student fitness since basketball was invented."

Mary Washington administrators did not share the paper's lighthearted view. Officials curtly counseled against streaking on campus, warning that participants would be summarily arrested. The *Bullet*, however, suggested that such admonitions might be to no avail, predicting that "with the advent of fair weather, the temptation to streak may be irresistible to devoted followers of this bizarre fad."

The prospect of a streak was eagerly anticipated on campus, especially by "townies" who, as rumors abounded that such an event was imminent, crowded campus drive nightly in the lascivious hope of gawking at unclad coeds bounding across Ball Circle. On the evening of March 17, their patience was rewarded when some ten people streaked—including males and females—much to the delight of an estimated crowd of more than four hundred.

Two of the daring dashers—both males and neither a student at Mary Washington—were apprehended by police, taken to local headquarters, and charged with indecent exposure, but not before a mob formed around the squad car shouting, "Let him go!" and "Streak on!" One of the nude female participants said afterward that they were aware of flashbulbs going off

Students streak across Ball Circle, spring 1974.

around them, but no one chased them, even though, she added, "we even started running from a place where a cop was hiding behind a bush!" The episode was reported in gleeful detail by the *Bullet*, along with photographs of the streakers (also printed in *The Battlefield*).

The episode had its tragicomic dimensions. In one of its more widely ridiculed aspects, the chief of campus security, Medford Haynes, broke his kneecap while chasing one of the streakers. It was an unfortunate coda to the career of the aging chief, an imposing and amiable figure who had served the College with decency and dedication since becoming head of security in 1958. Soon after his injury, he retired.

It was indicative of the fevered political environment at the time that so frivolous a fad could be invested, by some, with a serious purpose; but sure enough, it led to calls for a national "streak-in" against Nixon. Organizers of the event, employing the theme "The Emperor Wears No Clothes," called on students to streak in order to emphasize that (regarding Watergate) Nixon should "lay bare all the facts" and to convince him that "full disclosure can be fun." Despite reports of a few random sightings of bare flesh thereafter, including one in the library, the streaking fad at Mary Washington faded. Yet it stood as a graphic, if whimsical, example of how much the campus had changed in so short a time: from Villagers and Bass Weejuns to army fatigues and combat boots . . . and finally to au naturel.

A wild time it was—and then some.

THE END OF AN ERA

In October 1973 Grellet Simpson announced his decision to retire at the end of the 1973–74 academic year, by which time he would have reached the age of sixty-five and would have led the College for nineteen years—first as president, then as chancellor, then once again as president. His decision was based on various factors including health problems, but some observers believed that it was hastened by the sudden death of his valued associate Michael Houston at the opening of the 1973–74 session. Houston's unexpected death, apparently from heatstroke, stunned the College community (of which he was one of the most popular members) and dealt a severe blow to the president, who had enjoyed a close personal as well as professional relationship with his young protégé.

Simpson's tenure encompassed a period of unprecedented change in virtually every aspect of the institution, with such developments concentrated in the last half-dozen years of his administration. The frenzy of activity during those later years—racial integration, the coming of coeducation, separation from U.Va., assorted student protests—tended to obscure somewhat the overall accomplishments that occurred during his stewardship. Although his main emphasis, unlike that of his predecessor, Morgan Combs, was not on bricks and mortar, the construction of six major buildings (Combs, Bushnell, Russell, Marshall, Jefferson, and Goolrick) and a sizable addition to the library constituted no small achievement. Simpson also put his own personal imprint on the physical layout through his contributions to the design of the magnificent Brompton rose garden and orchard.

His impact on student life was also extensive. During his tenure, students gained increased power to govern themselves, and his approval of relaxed regulations regarding dress, alcohol, and visitation policy helped to bring the College more into line with typical social guidelines at institutions elsewhere.

It was true that such changes were sometimes more or less forced on him by the students, and he made no pretense of appreciating the tactics they employed; he was too much the product of his genteel Virginia heritage ever to find bullying admirable. Besides that, he later reflected, "The values were so murky and muddy and individually promulgated that it was pretty hard to deal with it and still be fair to the other people who wanted a saner and more placid, peaceful kind of life. That was certainly the hardest period we had because it evolved into personalities, and the student paper . . . said some very ugly things. But," he consoled himself, "they said it about everybody."[40]

Despite his aversion to confrontational tactics, Simpson retained his equanimity and, from the vantage of his retirement (and true to his iconoclastic penchant), even expressed grudging admiration. "I didn't like the methods the students used," he said, "but their basic concerns were essential. Someone needed to rock the academic world—and someone still does in some respects."

Accordingly, his responses at the time were consistently calm and reasonable, always considerate of other points of view, however inimical to his own. It was in large measure because students recognized his openness and fundamental sense of fairness that campus discord at Mary Washington, unpleasant though it was at times, never—even in the most heated episodes—descended into the disruptive viciousness that occurred contemporaneously on many other campuses.

It was in his influence on the academic program, however, that Simpson made his most significant and lasting contribution. Himself the product of a liberal education, he was utterly committed to infusing Mary Washington College with that same educational philosophy, and he preached it constantly in speech after speech, with eloquence and with passion, throughout his tenure.

Simpson was at heart a teacher. His presidency came during a time—a time soon to wane—when college heads often still came from teaching faculties, rather than from the ranks of professional administrators. "I don't have any patience with people who set out to be college presidents," he once said, "or go to school to be a college president. I don't understand that. It's beyond me." Reflecting in retirement on his own performance, he said, "I didn't have a stitch of training in being a college president," adding with a twinkle, "I somehow managed."

His success, in his estimation, was a testament to the efficacy of a liberal arts education. With that mind-set, his emphasis as president was always

President Simpson conferring degrees

on improving the quality of instruction, constantly challenging the faculty to pursue ever-higher standards, and giving them greater voice in charting appropriate policies to achieve those goals. In addition, he tailored the curriculum to make it more congruent with the liberal arts—for example, by eliminating majors in home economics and physical education—and hired new faculty who not only possessed outstanding qualifications on paper but also shared his educational philosophy. The result was a substantially stronger academic institution, as indicated by the credentials of its faculty, the quality of its students, and the elevation of its stature in academic circles—a stature attested by the establishment of a Phi Beta Kappa chapter at the College in 1971.

Despite such undeniable accomplishments, Simpson was not without his critics. Some, for example, condemned what they saw as a sluggish approach to coeducation—that he was not sufficiently aggressive in recruiting males. It was a charge to which Simpson pleaded (somewhat) guilty, cryptically commenting on one occasion, "Some people feel I haven't pushed it, but I also haven't not pushed it." One thing was beyond cavil: he did not push coeducation at the expense of academic standards. While admirable in its ideals, whether such an approach was advisable in practice was problematic.

Some also questioned his lack of enthusiasm for developing an athletic program, a criticism that appeared more pertinent following the admission of males. The truth was, the physical side of the students' experience simply did not interest Simpson. "I don't think you have to know how to swim to be educated," he once said, "so I would never have voted for requiring swimming or anything athletic for a degree. A degree is a totally different thing from muscles." Obviously, in that light, competitive sports held little attraction. "I myself would not favor intercollegiate programs in a small college," he said, "but that's just my own opinion." The sports boom thus awaited his successors.

The most valid criticism of Simpson's performance was that he did not pay enough attention to the College's fiscal health. Undeniably he was more interested in the academic aspects than in the fiduciary—an approach that he not only acknowledged but was proud of. "The last thing I was interested in," he declared, "was raising money."

It was unclear whether he failed to recognize the increasing need for funding as the years went by or whether he simply felt it to be beneath his dignity to search for it; certainly he did not think it was the president's job. Referring specifically to a subsequent director of development, Simpson once observed, "I'll go along with a Mickey Dowdy, who doesn't claim to do anything but raise money—[and] he's pretty damn good at it, too. That's his bailiwick, and he doesn't pretend anything else."

As for himself, Simpson had made it clear from the outset that such was not his métier. "I told the [search] committee," he said, "if you want a fundraiser, I'm not interested." True to his word, he never was interested, and in that regard, he failed to serve the College as well as he might have. For that reason, as well as the fact that his health had begun to decline, his decision to leave the College he had led for nearly two decades probably came at the right time, both for him and for the institution.

Immediately upon vacating Brompton, the Simpsons moved into Belmont, the College-administered estate of the artist Gari Melchers, located just across the Rappahannock River in Stafford County. They had lived there only a short while when an embarrassing flap arose regarding the appropriateness of such use of a state-owned property, and soon thereafter the Simpsons moved back into the city, purchasing a pleasant Dutch-style colonial on Fauquier Street.[41]

One of the attractions of the place was its ample space for gardening, wherein the former president could ply his avocation. The couple's main activity in their early years of retirement, however, was travel, as they visited England, France, North Africa, and the Soviet Union, as well as Grellet's first love, Italy. The trip to Italy was the most sentimental, for he had first visited there as a World War II volunteer with the Red Cross, reaching Naples via a troop ship filled with American GIs. Returning in the 1970s, he was moved by the opportunity to reconnect with that culture—the opera, the poetry, the art and architecture—that had so inspired him as a youth.

In retirement, Simpson had relatively little interaction with the College, seldom visiting the campus though he lived not too many blocks away. Part of this behavior was by design. "When you retire, you retire," he liked to say, "and it does no one any good to meddle." But it was also because he was skeptical of some of the new directions the institution was taking. On top of that, he was not personally close to his presidential successors, with whom his relationships were correct, but not warm—partly, no doubt, because he perceived them as basically managerial types, not up to his own scholarly standards. The result was not exactly bitterness, but neither did he exhibit any particular affection for the school on an ongoing basis.

Yet the few times he did return—usually for ceremonial occasions, sometimes in his honor—he seemed genuinely pleased to be there. One memorable event was an informal dedication of the new library in his honor in 1992. Another was the 1996 unveiling of the Phi Beta Kappa key between George Washington and Trinkle—appropriately, given his instrumental role in the establishment of the Kappa of Virginia chapter.

On such occasions, Simpson could bask in the adulation of those who recalled his estimable service to the College. "Any time he returns to campus," remarked Distinguished Professor of Religion David Cain, "something very special happens. There is a groundswell of appreciation and a standing ovation. Not perfunctory. Not nostalgic. Simply the felt recognition on the part of the faculty of . . . what this man did for the College. The passage of time has made so much clearer the magnitude of his achievement."

Apt as Cain's observation was, it should not have altogether discounted nostalgia, for surely there were faculty members who looked back to what they recalled as the College's halcyon period—a less structured and less stressful time when the prevailing atmosphere among faculty, administrators, and students was more familial. The institution in years to come may have improved by many tangible measurements but along the way lost—unintentionally but perhaps inevitably—some of the elements that had made it a special place. Simpson's contemporaries never ceased to revere him for that earlier time of grace for which, to them, he was the embodiment.

Although Simpson duly appreciated the visible honors bestowed on him after his retirement, the most fitting memorials to his service were several awards that bore his name and continued to keep his legacy alive in most appropriate ways. The first of these, established by an anonymous endowment in his honor, was the Grellet C. Simpson Award for Excellence in Undergraduate Teaching. First bestowed in 1971 (to modern language professor Carmen Rivera), the award was given each year thereafter to acknowledge an individual faculty member's distinguished teaching. Generally regarded as the highest faculty honor at the College, it was often awarded to those who were initially brought to the College by Simpson himself—including as late as 2008, when the award went to anthropology professor Margaret Huber.

While the Simpson Award reflected the former president's insistence on the primacy of effective teaching, a subsequent award was established to honor his own scholarly contributions as a medievalist. After his retirement, Simpson's dear friend and colleague, librarian Barbara Alden, endowed a chair in his honor dedicated to supporting the study of medieval English literature. Alden's generosity also resulted in the creation of the Grellet and Dorothy Simpson Series in Medieval Literature and the Simpson Summer Institute, which, under the dynamic direction of English professor Teresa Kennedy, was by the end of the century attracting favorable attention from scholars around the country.

Finally there was the Grellet C. Simpson International Scholarship, endowed by Simpson himself, to enable Mary Washington College students to study abroad. Growing out of his own lifelong attraction to foreign cultures, the highly competitive Simpson Scholarship became an important element in the College's emphasis on globalization as the century progressed.

Simpson's last years were marred by diabetes and heart ailments. Yet he remained unbowed by his infirmities, continuing to entertain visitors with his customary civility. As one guest described it, "Bell chimes, tingling from their perch on the eaves, greet neighbors and friends, who come frequently, and, when weather permits, Simpson often sits out on the porch to chat with acquaintances, joke with his visitors, and avidly watch for any new activity on the street." He also enjoyed listening to opera and reading modern novels, as well as, he confessed, perusing "the funny papers."

In 1995 Simpson suffered a crushing loss with the death of his wife of fifty-six years, the incomparable Dorothy, who passed away suddenly. A true team they had been: he, dedicated to developing the College's academic reputation; she, equally committed to promoting its social amenities. "As Dorothy always says," he once remarked, "your civilization begins to crack when you lose your manners, and I think she is right."

Together they did their part, and more, to ensure that civilization, at Mary Washington anyway, did not crack, as they happily hosted countless events at Brompton, entertaining students, faculty, staff, and townsfolk alike in grand (though never pretentious) style. Their annual Christmas party for Mary Washington employees became one of the College's most festive and enduring traditions, continuing in perpetuity as a social highlight of the year.

Dorothy and Grellet Simpson at Brompton

It was the opinion of one longtime faculty member that "Grellet's success was the result of a team presidency. . . . [Dorothy] brought out the underlying, even shy, sweetness in Grellet." Certainly her role as first lady—ever the gracious, but unaffected, hostess whose warm smile radiated genuine good cheer—earned her the devotion of the College community. Part of the charm was that she herself seemed to take such delight in it. "I enjoyed all of my part of it," she recalled in retirement. "I was very proud, of course, to be the president's wife—or the chancellor's wife—and to play whatever part seemed desirable at the time. And I loved Brompton, and I loved opening the doors to groups of any size, and enjoyed the preparation, and the event, and in fact grew from it in many cases."[42]

Few persons ever associated with Mary Washington College were as universally beloved as Dorothy Simpson. And with good reason.

The former president lived almost three years beyond his spouse's death and, according to intimates, handled the loss better than might have been expected, given the couple's closeness for so long. Yet, though he could summon affability in the presence of company, he became more forlorn. In 1997 he suffered a fall that resulted in a broken hip and shoulder, and never really recovered from the surgery to repair those injuries. Further debilitated by diabetes and kidney failure, he contracted pneumonia and died on December 24.

At his death, the local newspaper praised him for leading the College to a substantially higher academic level, noting also that his personality had made him well suited to steering the institution through a time of extraordinary social change. Moreover, it was he who was mainly responsible for "providing the administrative leadership that helped Mary Washington students and faculty members see the world beyond the tree-shaded campus on a hillside in a small Virginia town."

It was a measure of the man's complexity that he could be described by some as an "old-school gentleman" and by others, with equal accuracy, as "very much of a liberal arts thinker." Colleagues variously lionized him as "an inspiring academic leader," as "an understanding man, a man of compassion," and as a friendly and sincere person whom "people felt that they could trust."

Simpson himself would likely have rejected such encomiums. Though not completely the self-effacing type—like many who achieve such prominence, he had a sufficient amount of ego—he did remark on one occasion that, with regard to his presidency of the College, "my coming and going is really of no consequence."

He was wrong, of course, on many grounds. In truth, few people had a more pervasive, profound, and permanent influence on the development of Mary Washington College than Grellet Collins Simpson.

–3–
THE WOODARD ERA, 1974–1982

WITHOUT A DOUBT, Mary Washington College had improved in many ways during Grellet Simpson's tenure as president—most importantly in terms of its academic quality, with an attendant rise in prestige—but the College was not without its problems when he retired. The overarching concern was the question of establishing an identity as a coeducational institution apart from the University of Virginia after so many years as the women's branch of U.Va.. More specific matters that needed attention included physical facilities, faculty salaries, endowment, administrative structure, and curricular revision.

Central to resolving such problems was the acquisition of increased financial support from both public and private sources. No problem was more urgent, nor was any more distant from President Simpson's constellation of interests. Not only was he unconcerned about such matters, but he was essentially antagonistic toward them, contemptuously regarding monetary concerns as beneath the dignity of a college president, whose focus, he believed, should be squarely (almost exclusively) on academics.

What this meant was that, notwithstanding the undeniable contribution he had made toward enhancing the College's academic status, the institution that Simpson left to his successor was not in good fiscal condition—much worse, in fact, than was generally known. Accordingly, in searching for a new president, the Board of Visitors placed primacy on administrative expertise and fund-raising potential, especially in terms of working with the commonwealth's political and educational hierarchy.

In addition to the vagaries faced by any board in selecting a new president, the Mary Washington Board of Visitors in 1973 had several additional problems. One was the fundamental fact that its members were, by and large, new to the whole business of governing a college. Some of them had had analogous experiences, and the rector, Lewis Walker, along with Richard Cross, had served on the U.Va. board; but as a group, they were unaccustomed to the kind of decision making that the moment demanded. So the basic question was: how to go about it?

Lewis Walker took the leadership role, a status accorded him not only because of his position as rector but because his previous service on the U.Va. board invested him with a prestige unique among members of the fledgling Mary Washington board. Years later, in his typically colorful fashion, he described the selection process. The first thing he did was to contact his friend Weldon Cooper, a distinguished member of the U.Va. political science faculty. "They were going through the same thing [a presidential search]," Walker recalled. "I said, 'Weldon, you gotta tell me something. How are y'all proceeding on how to go about electing a president?' He said, 'Well, the board has just appropriated $50,000 as a search fund.' I thought, 'My God, we haven't got $50,000. We haven't got $5,000. . . . Hell, we didn't even have money enough to hire a secretary.'" In any case, the search was launched, and it yielded, as Walker remembered, a spate of applications: "Some were ridiculous, some funny, some tragic, I guess."[1]

Though the board members made it clear that it was they who would make the final selection, the faculty was allowed to participate via a committee (elected by the faculty themselves) whose involvement began once the field had been winnowed to approximately a dozen candidates. At that point, the faculty were invited to meet the remaining candidates and offer recommendations to the board. Walker admitted that he "wasn't looking forward to that particular arrangement," but it worked out better than he expected. The faculty "behaved very responsibly," he recalled, "and made some excellent points. We got along remarkably well."

Philosophy professor George Van Sant, a member of the committee, recalled that the faculty contingent, in fact, played a significant role in determining the outcome of the search. Once the field had been narrowed to three, it was clear that one candidate was the strong preference of the board's representatives (especially Walker); another was supported with equal vigor by the faculty, who (especially Van Sant) expressed vehement dislike for Walker's favorite. Thus at loggerheads, the committee turned to the third candidate, whom both sides regarded highly, as the compromise choice: Prince Briggs Woodard.[2] It was he whom the full board selected as the College's fifth president.

Prince Woodard was born and reared in the Southside Virginia town of Courtland, known in an earlier time as Jerusalem. He was not that small community's most famous figure; that distinction belonged to Nat Turner, the rebellious slave whose murderous rampage had shocked the state, and the entire South, in 1831.

Woodard received his B.A. degree from Virginia Military Institute, then served in the U.S. Army from 1943 to 1946 as a first lieutenant. He subsequently earned both a master's degree and a doctorate in educational administration from the University of Virginia. In 1973 he was awarded an honorary LL.D.

from West Virginia Wesleyan College. His professional career began as director of research and instruction for the Danville, Virginia, public school system. From there he moved to Pennsylvania, where he was an associate professor and graduate professor of educational administration at Temple University.

Prince Briggs Woodard

In 1964 Woodard returned to the commonwealth to become director of the State Council of Higher Education in Virginia (SCHEV) and served in that capacity for six years. During that time he streamlined and strengthened the agency, developing for the first time a comprehensive plan for higher education in Virginia, an accomplishment that won him plaudits from the state legislators. He was also instrumental in creating a major new state institution, Virginia Commonwealth University, which was achieved by combining two existing entities, Richmond Professional Institute and the Medical College of Virginia. Actions such as these were not without their critics but were typical of the bold and innovative "damn-the-torpedoes" style that would characterize his professional career.

In 1970 Woodard left SCHEV to become chancellor of the West Virginia Board of Regents, a job that gave him supervisory authority over all of that state's institutions of higher education. It was quite a challenge, as the majority of those schools were on academic probation from the North Central Accrediting Association when he arrived. Within four years, owing mainly to his initiatives, all had been fully accredited, a turnaround that further enhanced his reputation as an administrator of national stature.

It was not always smooth sailing, however. According to one Charleston journalist who covered West Virginia higher education, Woodard generally maintained good relations with the state legislature, but "some people felt that he . . . did not consult others enough in making . . . decisions. Some thought it was a dictator sort of thing."

That observation presaged the character of Woodard's Mary Washington career. In West Virginia, as previously at SCHEV, both his methods and his manner made him a controversial figure—the very embodiment of the type who, as was once said of the nineteenth-century politico James G. Blaine, "drives people wild, in pairs: one for, one against."

Woodard's success as an administrator was made possible by an amalgam of three main attributes. One was his considerable intellect, a quality sometimes obscured by his "no frills" demeanor and his occasional affectation of a self-deprecating "country boy" persona. But those who interpreted his lack of glitzy rhetoric as an absence of acumen misjudged the man—and at their peril, for his was a mind constitutionally predisposed to cut to the nub of every issue, undistracted by extraneous concerns.

A second characteristic was his audacious ability to move decisively, unimpeded by the tendency toward timidity and waffling often found in educational administrators. As William M. Anderson Jr., perhaps Woodard's closest protégé, put it: "He was not an individual who was scared of taking bold actions when he knew it was the right thing to do. He would always move to do the right thing for the organization and for the people the organization served."[3] Throughout Woodard's career, some may have questioned his judgment as to what those "right things" were, but assuredly no one doubted his determination in their implementation.

Then there was another trait, one that gave the other two greater potency: namely, his prodigious capacity for work—seemingly almost a craving for it; he was, indeed, the quintessential workaholic. He was capable of developing grand designs, but it was the details of any endeavor that captivated him; no aspect of a project was too minute to escape his scrutiny. Bill Anderson described Woodard as "one of the hardest workers—if not the hardest worker—I have ever known. He could work on detailed projects [for] hours and hours and hours on end. He was so precise, so meticulous in what he did."

Woodard also expected his associates to display comparable dedication. Anderson, who was on Woodard's staff in West Virginia, later recounted how the process worked: "I lived up in the same area of Charleston that he did, which was not a benefit at all to me, in that he gave me a ride to work, and we worked seven days a week from six in the morning to seven at night—and longer when we were on the road. I can remember other staff members who were my age—young—we'd be on the road looking forward to finally getting to a hotel to get some rest. As soon as we'd get there, he'd say, 'Why don't you all go ahead and check in, and we will meet in my room to start a meeting, and I'll get things ready for us.' . . . I just have never seen anything like it."

Constant exertion, combined with recurrent controversies, eventually took a toll on Woodard: while chancellor of the Regents, he suffered a heart attack that was no doubt induced, at least partly, by the stress of his job. Although he recovered sufficiently to return to work, the experience played a role in his seeking a position that would be (presumably) less stressful—hence his application for the presidency of Mary Washington.

It was not, however, merely the desire to escape the West Virginia job that drove his decision. The truth was that he did not want just *any* college presidency; it was Mary Washington's he wanted, and had wanted for a long time. Indeed, Bill Anderson later recalled that when he worked with Woodard at SCHEV—a vantage that provided insight into all the state institutions—Woodard had remarked that if he could have the presidency of any of them, it would be Mary Washington.

Woodard himself later confirmed that his special interest in MWC was genuine for two main reasons. The first was the College's tradition of academic excellence. The second was the school's size, which meant that, as he put it at the time, "the president can feel involved and really get to know the students and faculty . . . [and can] know the details from business to admissions." For someone whose attention to detail bordered on the obsessive, the College's small size must have been supremely attractive. (Money was certainly not the incentive, because his annual salary in West Virginia was $45,000, whereas the Mary Washington president was paid only $31,200 a year.)

But wanting the position and attaining it were not the same thing. There were several potential stumbling blocks in the way, despite his impressive credentials. For one thing, there had been some hostility between Woodard and Lewis Walker in the past, going back to the days when Woodard was at SCHEV and Walker was on the U.Va. Board of Visitors. By Walker's admission, the two had engaged in "some hot arguments" at that time.

Then, too, there were those avatars of the liberal arts who felt that Woodard's terminal degree—an Ed.D. rather than a Ph.D.—did not furnish appropriate credentials for leading an institution whose mission was grounded in the liberal arts. Chief among them was none other than Walker himself, who, as was his custom, expressed that view with candor and with color. "My only objection to Prince," he said, "was that he had a doctorate in education, which is a half-assed degree under the best of circumstances, even at U.Va."[4] (Woodard, naturally, did not see it that way, once describing himself as "a scholar in administration.")

More troublesome to the board was the matter of Woodard's health, in light of his heart attack the previous year. They were not unmindful of the issue, but according to Walker, they had "talked to his West Virginia doctor, who assured us he was in good shape and there was no reason for him not to lead a normal life." It was a prognosis that Bill Anderson later confirmed. "I know for a fact," he recalled, "that before he left West Virginia the doctors had given him a clean bill of health and told him to proceed with his career—that he should not be concerned with his heart problems . . . if he would continue to monitor his activities, especially avoiding stress. And cut back on his hours some." Therein would lie the problem.

But meanwhile fiscal exigencies trumped all other concerns, even academic ones. Other candidates may have "had better degrees," recalled Walker, but "Prince had one thing we needed more than anything else at that time: an entrée with the legislators. Grellet never really had this."

In that regard, Woodard did possess strong credentials—both tangible (his impressive work at SCHEV) and intangible (his political savvy) that seemed to bode well for success at the helm of a state college. Thus on February 9, 1974, when the Board of Visitors announced the selection of Mary Washington's president, it seemed that once again the College would be led by an individual who could provide precisely the kind of expertise that was most needed at the time.

The Woodard presidency began well enough. Despite skepticism about his academic credentials on the part of some liberal arts purists, the faculty as a whole did not seem predisposed against him. If they did not receive him with particular warmth, neither did they generally evince noticeable opposition. Overall they seemed to regard him with the kind of cautious optimism that often greets a new institutional leader.

For their part, the students were more effusive. In the first issue of the *Bullet* after his arrival, an editorial expressed hearty approval. "In all respects," it proclaimed, "from what has been seen so far of the new president, the college is lucky to have Prince Woodard." The executive chairman of the student association, Mary Mahon, agreed. "It may be hard for the students to get used to seeing the president walking around campus," she said, "but I think it's great. I think the Board has made a fabulous choice."

The amicable atmosphere did not last long. Student activism at Mary Washington, as on campuses elsewhere, had subsided as the Vietnam War wound down and the Watergate furor diminished—but it had not ceased altogether, as Woodard was about to find out.

The eye-opening episode occurred during the fall 1974 Career Day program. Recruiters from various employment sectors had been invited, including the federal government and, in particular, the Central Intelligence Agency. It was a time during which the CIA was in disrepute among many for its covert operations, most notably its perceived role in toppling the government of Chilean president Salvador Allende the previous year.

Two students, sophomore Stephen Galloway and freshman Kevin Flatt, were among those protesting the Career Day participation by the CIA by distributing leaflets outside the Lee Hall venue. To further dramatize the protest, they proceeded later in the day to approach the recruiter at his ballroom station with two bags of pig's blood—procured at a slaughterhouse, they said—one of which was lobbed in his direction, splattering his suit and recruitment materials. The students quickly fled the building, leaving onlookers stunned. Some who were attracted by the commotion assumed, terrified, that the recruiter had been shot when they first saw the bloody scene.

College authorities immediately made known their intention to prosecute the offenders. Vice President Ray Merchent, who termed his reaction one of "shock" and "disgust," asserted his support for the principle of dissent but condemned the blood throwing as "a totally unacceptable way of demonstration." Accordingly, the students were charged with assault, disturbing the peace, and profanity in public.

Student opinion toward the perpetrators initially seemed to be negative. The *Bullet* was especially jaundiced in its appraisal of what it called "a protest of the late-'60s variety." While not passing judgment on the validity of the cause, it suggested that the protest itself "was simply an indulgent one [in which] the accused protesters were trying to achieve a romantic character for their actions."

The two students rejected that charge, with Galloway specifically lamenting that "people are focusing on the act, not on the issue." Flatt was defiant, saying that he "did not regret the action" and declaring that (if he was convicted) "going to jail would be unjustified and politically repressive."

President Woodard, like Merchent, was outraged by the incident—a fully predictable response, given his background. Only a few days after the incident (and weeks before the November trial date), he summoned the two, accompanied by their attorneys, for a closed hearing, the result of which was their expulsion from the College. The action was taken in accordance with the College catalog's statement that the "administration reserves the right to request any student to withdraw whose conduct or general attitude is considered unsatisfactory, even though no specific charge is made." The behaviors cited as evidence of such conduct were a public embarrassment to the College, disrespect to an invited guest, destruction of private property (the recruiter's clothes), and disruption of a College function.

Similar to so many such incidents (e.g., Watergate), it was not so much the episode itself but the reaction that proved most significant. In this case, the administrative dismissal of the two students caused the most damaging, and lingering, impact. Students, most of whom were apparently unsympathetic to the perpetrators initially, began now to criticize the administration. A student government inquiry into the affair concluded that the expulsions were technically within the president's rights, but expressed the fear that, in his interpretation of the operative passage in the catalog, "a dangerous precedent may have been set."

Some faculty members, too, expressed concern over the procedure. Psychology professor Alice Rabson, for example, weighed in with her opinion that even though "the students acted unwisely and inappropriately," the administration's response was likewise misbegotten. "The rapidity and secrecy used in carrying out their sentences is reminiscent of the Star Chamber procedures used in England in the seventeenth century," she declared, and went on to opine that "their punishments were unjustly severe and that their hearing was premature."

No one was more upset with Woodard's actions than George Van Sant, who had so recently been instrumental in the president's hiring. In a sense, Van Sant would seem to have been an unlikely defender of the student demonstrators. Though active in local Democratic politics and generally sympathetic with liberal causes, he was also a former Marine who was inclined to prefer order and discipline. He had been one of the few faculty members who consistently, and very publicly, supported U.S. military involvement in Vietnam.

In this case, however, Van Sant was outraged by the treatment of Galloway and Flatt. His position derived in part from his personal relationship with the young Flatt, whom Van Sant had come to know and admire as a student in his

George M. Van Sant

class. Beyond that, he felt deeply that Woodard's handling of the situation was not only unjustified but well-nigh criminal. Furious, he confronted the president, creating a clash that led to a shouting match, culminating in Woodard's accusation, "You wouldn't talk to me that way if you didn't have tenure!"[5]

When the cases were actually heard in Fredericksburg General District Court in November, Kevin Flatt was convicted on charges of assault and battery, destroying public and personal property, and breach of the peace; a charge of profanity in public was dropped. He was fined $100 and sentenced to ten days in jail, suspended on condition of good behavior for a year. The case against Galloway was dropped because summonses to three key witnesses somehow failed to be delivered.

With that, the blood-throwing affair per se came to an end. But President Woodard's handling of it, in the minds of many students and some faculty, smacked of authoritarianism, leaving a residue of wariness on all sides that would make the resolution of subsequent problems more difficult whenever they occurred—as, predictably, they soon did.

The next to arise involved plans for the 1975 graduation ceremony, when Woodard announced in February that the commencement program would be held in the George Washington auditorium, rather than by tradition on Ball Circle. The reason for the change, as would be the case with numerous decisions during the Woodard presidency, was economic—in this instance, the desire to save the $1,700 for chair rental, plus a comparable amount for setting them up outdoors. Students (seniors especially) were chagrined, not only by the prospect of breaking a beautiful tradition but more tangibly by the fact that the 1,600 seats in GW would necessitate limiting each senior to having only three guests at the ceremony.

Following the vocal expression of dismay by the students, an amicable solution was devised whereby the seniors agreed to assume responsibility for setting up the chairs, with the institution bearing the rental fee. The agreement not only placated the students but actually set the precedent for what was to become an annual pre-graduation ritual for the senior class that endured for years to come. (In an ironic twist, rain on the date of the 1975 graduation forced the ceremony to be held in GW anyway—the last time such a change of venue was necessary for more than three decades.)

Students were also aroused by what they perceived as administrative jiggering of the academic program—moves that also raised the antennae of the faculty. Of particular concern was the decision to summarily terminate the home economics program, as well as indications of impending reductions in the number of faculty members. There were also incipient (and not completely unfounded) fears that the new president might have designs on broadening—opponents would say diluting—the College's focus on the liberal arts.

The accumulated angst resulted in student attacks on Woodard that were unprecedented in the history of the College. Earlier criticisms of the Simpson administration had been directed more at policy than personality. It was perhaps a reflection of the edginess of the times—an erosion of the standards of discourse, both public and private—that gave an unusually mean, ad hominem cast to the criticisms of Woodard.

Describing the situation in an early March 1975 editorial, the *Bullet* noted that "disturbing signs were evident on campus last week. It seemed that head-hunting, resignation, and impeachment fever had finally reached [the president's] office. . . . Rumors were flying . . . and the first consideration seemed to be 'to get' Mr. Woodard." And this even before his inauguration.

That event, set for April 11, became the focal point of student unrest. The primary protest effort was a movement led by seniors Angie Nash and Laraine Kelley to encourage their classmates to boycott the ceremony, in which they had been invited to participate as a group. Though they claimed it was "not singularly an attack against Woodard" so much as an attack against what they perceived as negative changes in overall institutional policy, personal animosity was still evident. "Mr. Woodard this year has touched every aspect of life [at] this College," said Nash, and not marching would tacitly emphasize opposition to one whom she described as "impossible to make an impact on and condescending in his attitude."

The *Bullet*, though it had already expressed its own concerns about the new president, sternly counseled against such action. "We as students," ran the editorial, "can be proud of this college, and senior attendance at the inauguration ceremonies is a good way to display this pride. The inauguration ceremonies will reflect on the entire college. Non-attendance or protest at the ceremonies would be only a cheap and lazy action. . . . In fact, some students seem only to have a general feeling of discontent without an actual pinpointing of their grievances. To protest with these feelings would be only spiteful. The inauguration should be a happy day for the college community."

In the end, the mass boycott did not materialize, and seniors who did not march likely did so for a variety of unrelated reasons. The most visible sign of protest was the appearance around campus of T-shirts emblazoned with the words "Dethrone the Prince." They were the work of student Don Mulcare, who had more than a hundred shirts printed and sold them all at cost ($2) within twenty-four hours. While not citing specifics, he said that his protest grew from opposition to the president's "decisions regarding academics, administrative, and residential concerns."

For his part, Woodard took the provocative T-shirts with overt good grace, facetiously commenting that he would have hoped Mulcare could turn a profit on their sale. In light of Woodard's nature, however, it is unlikely that he was genuinely amused.

In retrospect, the controversies leading up to the inauguration were harbingers of a discontent that was to persist throughout the Woodard years—sometimes vague and inchoate, sometimes overt and virulent—tainting, if not poisoning, the atmosphere of the institution as it moved through a difficult period of transition. It was a burden that Prince Woodard would unfortunately, and in many ways unnecessarily, have to bear.

The truth was that Woodard did not suffer fools gladly—and his definition of fools was broad. Whereas his directness was a virtue up to a point, it was perceived as rudeness by some, especially when it accompanied unwelcome decisions. Above all, he did not want to waste anyone's time, least of all his. People quickly found that the best time to catch him was early morning, when he could usually be found in his office by 7:00 a.m., often earlier. And woe betide anyone who arrived late to a meeting. The least to be expected upon arrival was a withering glance, which was a fortunate alternative to a verbal reprimand.

In short, Woodard approached life with the pace of a man who felt there was much to be done and not enough time to do it. As it turned out, he was right.

Despite prior threats of protest, the inauguration itself was not marred by any untoward incidents but was instead characterized by the pomp and pageantry normally attendant to such occasions, beginning with the colorful procession of representatives from numerous other institutions of higher learning as well as members of Mary Washington's own faculty and senior class. Platform guests included both the current governor of Virginia, Mills E. Godwin Jr., and former governor Albertis Harrison, by then a judge on the Virginia Supreme Court of Appeals, who administered the oath of office to the new president. There was distinctly an air of chumminess about the event, as Godwin, Harrison, and Woodard were all longtime acquaintances reared in the commonwealth's Southside, a region traditionally characterized as much by its political influence as by the tobacco, peanuts, and Smithfield ham that dominated its economy.

The governor in his remarks established a light tone at the outset when, in praising Woodard's qualifications for the presidency, he noted that "he is a graduate of VMI, which speaks well of his disciplined attitude. . . . His son attends VMI, which speaks well of his persuasiveness." The new president's "crowning recommendation," Godwin added, was that he came from Courtland, Virginia, which was near Godwin's own hometown.

Turning serious, the governor acknowledged that Woodard was coming to the presidency at a time when a "wave of change is washing over higher education across our country, rocking most severely some of the small liberal arts colleges." The current challenge to Mary Washington College was exacerbated by the "dual pressures of inflation and recession" that would necessitate an educational process "without undue frills and adornments" wherein the College might have to "reclassify as luxuries some of the things we now think of as necessities."

He extolled the virtues of Mary Washington's core philosophy: "I sense today that the pendulum is swinging back from the new math and new morality, and that as we search desperately for other answers, we will turn again to the liberal arts to find them." At the same time, however, he suggested that potential employers were looking for "liberal arts majors with some special skill, . . . for those properly grounded in business administration and certain other specialized fields."

The governor concluded with a personal admonition to Woodard, pointing out that success would require "a physical constitution of the toughest and most resilient variety [and] a sense of humor to relieve both the tensions and tempers in himself and others"—advice that Woodard largely failed to heed.

The new president's inaugural address began with the usual obligatory acknowledgments of various dignitaries who were in attendance. Those references were mostly perfunctory, with one exception—that being his heartfelt tribute to Dorothy Simpson, whom he saluted as "a lovely lady who, with graceful elegance and with a deep love of people served as an ambassador of happiness and charm for this college over the years."

The address itself displayed, both in its tenor and in its specifics, much that would characterize Woodard's administration. Roughly the first half of the speech constituted an overview of the development of higher education in Virginia and served to preface the statement of his agenda for Mary Washington. Having explained the need for increased state support, he acknowledged the College's duty to use such funds wisely. Toward that end, he proclaimed his

> wholehearted endorsement for the application of more sophisticated state-level and institutional planning and evaluation procedures. The state and higher educational institutions alike must be ever alert to insure that maximum return flows from each dollar spent. Bold attention and imaginative thought must be given to ways whereby the delivery system of higher education may become more effective and more efficient. Periodic analyses and comprehensive reviews by qualified professionals founded on accurate data are both desirable and welcomed by the higher education community.

Nothing could have demonstrated more starkly than that single paragraph the differences between Woodard and his predecessor, in terms of both style and substance; Grellet Simpson, the ultimate "un-bureaucrat," would have been constitutionally incapable of uttering it. As if to allay faculty concern that he might be overly bureaucratic, Woodard continued: "When, however, the primary purpose of so-called higher education efficiency or productivity studies conducted at either the state or institutional level is to reduce expenditures, irrespective of the negative impact on quality standards or program diversity, or to discredit, evoke controversy, or erode confidence, the future of higher education and, in turn, the state is adversely affected." In retrospect, the reference to the danger of administrative actions that might "evoke controversy or erode confidence" would prove ironic, as over the course of time, Woodard's detractors would claim that he did precisely that.

Other aspects of his inaugural address distanced Woodard even further from the central focus of the previous administration. On the one hand, he did duly emphasize his commitment to maintaining the institution as a "small, predominantly residential, liberal arts college committed to the pursuit of excellence," one that would "continue to be selective in the programs it provides, concentrating on those disciplines which it has the resources to offer exceedingly well." On the other hand, he made it clear that he envisioned innovations beyond the traditional curriculum—or, as he rather ambiguously expressed it, to "develop additional models for providing students with related experiences to further assist them in making significant contributions to a changing society . . . through pertinent exposure to the world of reality."

He went on to explicitly reject the ivory-tower concept of a college, noting that to many Americans that symbol—quoting the art historian Erwin Panofsky—"combines the stigma of egotistical self-isolation (on account of the tower) with that of snobbery (on account of the ivory) and dreamy inefficiency (on account of both)." Woodard made clear that such an approach would not prevail on his watch, declaring that detachment from worldly affairs "is of questionable validity in this age of social concern. For Mary Washington, such a posture would be totally unacceptable. . . . [The College] must develop and further cement the relationship of town and gown by constantly seeking new ways to be of service to the expanding community."

Without spelling out the details, Woodard was serving notice that his vision of the College's future role was an expanded one—one that Grellet Simpson (an ivory-towerist if ever there was one) must have found repugnant. But the fact was that in choosing a new president, the Board of Visitors had recognized that the College needed not so much a president who could enthrall with Chaucerian flourishes but one who could make hard decisions with steely resolve. In Prince Woodard, they had their man.

The Mary Washington College whose stewardship Woodard inherited was an institution in trouble, though its constituents, for the most part, did not know the nature or extent of its difficulties. Students could scarcely have been expected to see such problems, and faculty, who might have, were generally complacent, secure in the cocoon of academe, enjoying the perquisites of a clubby collegiality that tended to compensate for the lack of monetary reward. The administration, presided over by the gentlemanly Grellet Simpson, was not inclined by nature or by training to aggressively confront the issues before it, let alone prepare for the ones that lay ahead.

As Bill Anderson, who came to Mary Washington in 1976, saw it, the College at the outset of the Woodard administration had never yet effectively addressed the issues entailed on it by virtue of coeducation and separation from the University of Virginia. The College had instead "continued to proceed with blinders on, ignoring the reality of what it was faced with," he recalled. "It was just simply adrift in a sea of confusion, . . . having the currents of change direct the future of the institution. It had not done any planning or taken any deliberate action to restructure the institution or to change course."[6]

Challenges thus abounded for the new president, most of them related to finances. Though the College's gloomy fiscal picture had resulted in some measure from the lack of prudence and foresight on the part of the previous administration, it was also largely attributable to historic forces over which MWC had little control. During the years that it was part of the University of Virginia, Mary Washington's funding was determined by the U.Va. board. Such subsidiary status was not conducive to the generous procurement of funds.

Once independent, MWC had to fend for itself in the state legislature, a venue in which, for historical reasons, the College had little clout. As a women's college until 1970, in a place and time when males thoroughly dominated the commonwealth's politics, Mary Washington had no graduates in the General Assembly, nor, unlike most other state institutions, did it have many who were in position (by virtue of either money or status) to persuade members of the legislature.[7] The result was chronic underfunding, exacerbated by the fact that, for similar gender-based reasons, it did not have alumni with the financial resources to develop a significant endowment—though, in truth, the College to date had made little effort in that regard.

Whatever the cause, the resultant dearth of funds had begun by the early 1970s to have a detrimental effect on various aspects of the College's operation, most notably, in President Woodard's view and that of the Board of Visitors, faculty salaries. From the outset of his administration, Woodard proclaimed improvement of faculty compensation to be his highest priority, both to offset increases in the cost of living and to enable the College to compete in recruiting first-rate scholars. Doubtless, improvement was needed. With a scale that started at $9,100 for instructors and topped out at $17,700 for full professors, MWC faculty salaries were the lowest of any state-supported four-year institution in Virginia and only slightly higher than public school salaries in the area.

The basic problem was that the College was overstaffed with substantially more faculty members than were provided for according to state funding guidelines. Specifically, in the 1974–75 session, 141 faculty were employed, while the state provided (according to its formula) funding for only 126 positions.

This unbalanced situation had developed during the Simpson era, when departments were essentially permitted to hire however many instructors they claimed to need, irrespective of the instructional allocations by the state. The budgetary "pie" just had been sliced into more and smaller portions.

The good news from this arrangement was that the College's student–teacher ratio was extremely low (14:1) compared to the ratio on which funding was based (20:1). The bad news was that faculty salaries were also low, with the attendant negative impact on recruitment and, increasingly, faculty morale. "Lower salaries," Woodard affirmed, "are the premium we are paying to maintain smaller classes."

Mandated by the Board of Visitors to address the problem, Woodard had only two avenues open to him: to pry additional funds from the General Assembly and to reduce the number of faculty members. He tried both, but any increase in appropriations would have to await the next biennial budget. So for the short term, he focused on reducing the size of the faculty.

The first cuts came quickly in the fall of 1974, his first semester on the job, when he eliminated by executive fiat all courses in home economics. The decision, he insisted, should not be construed as an aspersion on the subject or its instructors but was simply a necessary response to "declining enrollment in home economics classes over the past five years and financial priorities in other areas of the college."

Whatever the case, the move meant the termination of two full-time faculty positions, held at the time by Ruby Harris and Mildred Jamison, who had been at the College since 1950 and 1952 respectively. He soon thereafter announced that several instructors in dance and art history who were scheduled to retire in the coming year would not be replaced.

Downsizing, not surprisingly, raised concerns across campus, both from students who feared for their academic programs and from faculty members who feared for their livelihoods. Expressing student alarm, the *Bullet* complained that "in the name of financing, class sizes are ballooning . . . [and] a particular area of study not producing its quota of majors is left sorely understaffed or simply done away with. . . . This college has not been in the past and cannot be in the future based on numbers. Financial problems are driving this college in the wrong direction for answers." The editorial went on to take up the cause of faculty members as well, urging that they "organize and unionize now, reviving the AAUP."[8]

Elimination of the home economics courses also raised eyebrows in the local community as well. "I think it's just dreadful," declared one resident, "that they're not going to learn to cook anymore." Harris scoffed at the notion that her courses amounted to nothing more than instructing future housewives in the fine art of using the kitchen range. "Cooking," she retorted, "that's not what we're doing anyway," and proceeded to point out that her International Cooking course was actually just another means of studying world cultures; a similar justification was offered for the courses taught by both her and Jamison in costuming and sewing. A number of students agreed.

Home economics was a popular major for many years before it was phased out in the 1970s.

One suggested that the home economics courses provided "something else to learn [from] besides books," and another claimed that they "make us culturally sophisticated." The instructors and their students thus concurred that the courses fell appropriately within the goals of a liberal arts education.

Galled by their abrupt and (they believed) unjustifiable termination, both Harris and Jamison filed suits against the College in the U.S. District Court in Richmond, naming as defendants President Woodard, Board of Visitors Rector Lewis Walker and other board members, and MWC Dean James Croushore. The plaintiffs were represented by Harris's two sons, both attorneys in Fredericksburg; the College was represented by lawyers from the state attorney general's office in Richmond.

Though the suits were filed separately and differed somewhat in their specific allegations and petitions for redress, their fundamental claims were similar—namely, that the professors' termination had resulted from sex discrimination and that they had been denied due process of law. Both women sought reinstatement to the faculty, with promotion to the rank of associate professor; back pay with interest to the date of discharge, plus full state benefits; and monetary damages from the defendants. The overall compensation sought amounted to approximately $200,000 for each.

Before the trial commenced in December 1977, the plaintiffs dropped their allegations of sex discrimination, so that the basic questions before the court revolved around the issue of tenure—a perennial source of controversy in higher education, and one amenable to an apparently endless variety of interpretations. According to convention, teachers holding the rank of professor or associate professor were generally deemed—by custom, not law—to possess tenure; as to those with lesser rank, such as assistant professor (which both Harris and Jamison held, despite their lengthy employment at the College), the matter was murkier.

The plaintiffs maintained that their repeated rehiring over the years amounted to de facto tenure, indicating every expectation of their continued employment. The College denied any such implicit guarantee and asserted further that, according to legal precedent, even tenured faculty could be dismissed whenever financial constraints demanded cutbacks, as was the case with Harris and Jamison.

The plaintiffs still emphasized that the College's lack of a formal grievance procedure through which they might initially have defended themselves constituted a denial of due process. To such an accusation, the College's attorneys maintained that even though no written grievance policy existed, by offering the two women the opportunity to discuss the matter with both President Woodard and the executive committee of the Board of Visitors, substantive due process had been provided.

The trial was an emotional one on both sides, with Harris at one point having to be excused from the witness stand because of an apparent flare-up of high blood pressure. In the end, Judge J. Calvitt Clarke ruled in favor of the College's position, noting in his opinion that, first, the plaintiff's claim of tenure was unsubstantiated and that, in any event, a federal court was not the proper venue for adjudicating a case dealing with what was essentially a state matter. He thus dismissed the case "without prejudice," implying some sympathy for the plaintiffs: "I have to rule on this case," he said, "with my head and not my heart."

The decision legitimized Woodard's reduction procedures. Within the first three years of his administration, he managed to eliminate thirteen full-time and five part-time faculty positions. "In these days of tight money," he explained, "institutions will only have courses they can well justify by enrollment."

Though he resolutely maintained that such reductions were the only way to escape the salary conundrum, it was nonetheless a painful experience for all concerned. In the words of one high-level administrator, "We had to get rid of faculty members, [and] poor Prince had the odious task of saying, 'Retire; we can't rehire, *et cetera*.' That was awful."[9]

Odious and awful it was, but apparently necessary; salaries did eventually rise to a more respectable level. But as was to prove true in much that Woodard did, what was helpful to the College as an institution was hurtful to him as its leader. In this case, it was a problem not of his own making that prompted a solution not of his own choice—the results of which put his administration under suspicious faculty scrutiny from its earliest days.

Faculty salaries were not the only problem initially confronting President Woodard; enrollment was another. Indeed, according to a study by Daniel Shaner and Associates of Chicago prepared for the Virginia General Assembly and completed just before Woodard's arrival, the College was suffering from a wide range of problems. The study, commonly known as the Shaner report, noted that "the appearance of Mary Washington College is pleasant," but beyond that found little that was praiseworthy, indicting the institution for, among other sins, an inefficient organizational structure, inadequate revenue from its auxiliary enterprises, an antiquated data system, lack of formal planning procedures, an unattractive (to potential students) curriculum, and insufficient enrollment in terms of available classroom space.

Mary Washington, it should be noted, was not alone in attracting the wrath of the report, as virtually every other state institution was cited for offenses ranging from unwarranted granting of tenure to excessive unpaid student loans. (The latter was not one of the problems at MWC, where the default rate was traditionally among the lowest in the state. In 1978, for example, the rate was a mere 3.2 percent, compared to a statewide rate of 18.8 percent.) The report contended that the state's public institutions, cumulatively, had wasted over $100 million through slipshod management and unnecessary construction.

The report itself had a curious history. After a summary of its contents was released upon its completion in 1974, it was allegedly locked away in the state archives at the direction of state senator Edward E. Willey, then chair of the Higher Education Study Commission, following pleas from college officials that the report's dissemination would damage the public image of higher education in Virginia. It was five years before Delegate Ray L. Garland, who had been a member of the by-then-defunct Study Commission, released the entire document—an action that Willey termed "crazy as hell."

In any case, the report, amid its extensive condemnations of various schools, had focused on some significant problems at Mary Washington specifically, the most immediately troublesome of which, perhaps, was declining enrollment. Woodard downplayed the danger, charging that the report's assertion that the College could accommodate 4,400 students—its enrollment at the time of the study was 1,950—was based on faulty methodology whose blanket formula failed to take into account the unique configurations of much of MWC's presumably usable classroom space.

The new president's defensiveness was understandable, but it was nonetheless true that in the five years before his coming, total enrollment had fallen by approximately two hundred students. The decline was not precipitous, nor was it extensive—but the trend was not good, and it had potentially dire consequences for two particular reasons: first, faculty funding, already meager, was tied directly to enrollment numbers, and second, declining applications would almost inevitably lead to a decrease in selectivity that would eventually erode the College's reputation for academic excellence. In snowball fashion, such diminution of status would impede recruitment of top-notch students in the years ahead.

A dangerous trend was clearly discernible in the number of freshman applicants. In 1969, the year before the advent of coeducation at both Mary Washington and the University of Virginia, there had been 1,886 applications for admission to MWC; by the time Woodard became president in 1974, the number had decreased by 500. The decline was qualitative as well as quantitative. The mean SAT score of applicants in 1969 was 1,122, and 75 percent of the applicants ranked in the top 20 percent of their high school classes. By 1974, the SAT average had fallen by over 100 points, and only 62 percent ranked in the top quintile of their graduating classes.

The fundamental reason for this development was not hard to divine: the now-coeducational U.Va. was luring many potential MWC students—and the best ones at that—to Charlottesville. The most obvious response to this drain of female applicants was for Mary Washington to compensate by attempting to attract comparable male students. But that approach was more easily perceived than accomplished—for many and complex reasons.

The underlying reason was that the College had really never actively embraced coeducation. Neither the students, the faculty, nor the administration before Woodard's arrival had indicated avidity for greater male enrollment. The *Bullet* at the outset of Woodard's administration claimed that the new president "favors the continuance of a predominantly female enrollment" and noted approvingly that his "own two daughters have attended women's colleges, giving Mr. Woodard an understanding of a college which has a female majority." (Such an interpretation may have resulted somewhat from wishful thinking, inasmuch as the same issue of the paper quoted Woodard as advocating increased male enrollment "because current male participation is tokenism.")

A *Bullet* poll, also in the fall of 1974, revealed that 51 percent of the one hundred students randomly surveyed favored a "substantial increase" in coeducation, 29 percent favored "only a slight increase," and 20 percent favored "no increase." Comments by respondents revealed a broad spectrum of attitudes, expressed with varying degrees of subtlety and introspection, including among the negative ones the following:

- Males are obnoxious.
- The way males have acted this year, I'm not keen on seeing [their enrollment] raised now.
- I don't think they add anything to the college.
- Males take the lead role too often. Females would take the subservient role in the classroom and also the student government offices.

Positive comments included the following:

- I enjoy coed classes. They add a sparkle of competition.
- When males begin coming we will have more extracurricular activities. Now there are too little sports to keep people here on weekends.
- I'm tired of seeing [just] girls.
- If you're going to have a few guys, you might as well have a lot.

The consensus was fairly well summarized in the comment of a respondent who said that increased enrollment of men was all right "as long as the standards aren't reduced and they don't take over."

For its part, the *Bullet* remained openly skeptical of the advantages of additional men on campus. At the beginning of the 1974–75 session, the paper warned against what it called "creeping coeducation," asserting that "in society's past it has been found that whatever men touch become[s] their own. If this were to happen at Mary Washington so quickly and subtly that no one noticed, all that Mary Washington has ever stood for could fall to ruins."

That apocalyptic admonition was to some extent a reflection of *Bullet* editor Joan McAllister, who asserted in an interview with the Fredericksburg *Free Lance–Star* that she was personally opposed to full coeducation and believed that most students shared her view. It was a position that she explained at some length in a November 4, 1974, editorial:

> There is still time to keep the college male enrollment at any level the students prefer. . . . The women's college as a concept has many possibilities, and it is unfortunate that some feel they must equate "the real world" with everything they consider. Yes, there are men in the real world. However, a women's college has its good points in being a place for women to concentrate on their studies and become sure of themselves. More importantly, a women's college lets women gain a respect for each other—without being in competition with each other over males at a co-ed college. Mary Washington is a small college. It cannot absorb many men without altering greatly its basic fabric, financially and physically. For example, while men may add to the social life, are women students here prepared to see college financing go into

expanded athletic facilities for men? . . . What future steps the college takes on coeducation should be determined by the students as well as the administration.

The McAllister/*Bullet* position was understandable in that the students then enrolled had all entered the College when it was either single-sex or coeducational only in the most minimal sense. They had voluntarily joined an academic society that they knew to be predominantly female, and they liked it that way. Unfortunately, such a stance was at odds both with the law and with the institution's need to recruit males to offset the declining number of female applicants.

Conrad Warlick was stunned. Brought in from U.Va. to head the admissions office near the end of the Simpson years, he was not prepared for the prevailing attitude of skepticism toward coeducation at Mary Washington. "It was only after I came that I realized that [situation]," he later recalled.

> I think the culture at Mary Washington, as I perceived it, was anti-coeducation—very strongly so. And I think it's because they had such a strong identity as a women's college. The faculty was very proud of the fact that this was a women's college. . . . There was no feeling at all among either the faculty or the student body to welcome men to Mary Washington College. They were happy being a women's college. Well, when U.Va. became co-ed, and Virginia Tech became co-ed, we had an awful lot of competition. And I will tell you, those first years were tough, tough, tough! . . . The attitude was, . . . "We will abide by the law, but we are basically a women's college, and that is what we really want to remain. And we will sort of grudgingly take a few men, and so be it!"[10]

It was a mind-set that Warlick was convinced had to be changed if, in light of increased competition for students, the College's applicant pool—and the institutional quality dependent on those applications—were to be salvaged. Accordingly, soon after Woodard's arrival, Warlick took his case directly to the new president. He later recalled the scenario this way:

> I went down to see him in his office, and said, "I would like to send out a recruitment letter to Virginia males who have qualifications to come to Mary Washington." And he said, "Absolutely! Why not?" So I remember sending a letter [to men] that said: "Dear student, you may be surprised in getting this letter from Mary Washington College." And I included a little brochure and sent it off. . . . It was the first time that we had ever recruited male students. And there were some people who were not too happy about that. They would have been perfectly happy—some members of the faculty and, Lord knows, some mem-

bers of the student body—to stay with the attitude, "If they come, talk to them; but we are not going to do anything to encourage them."

The effort to seek male applicants was accompanied by an attempt to give greater campus visibility to men who were already enrolled. Previously the few residential male students had been housed either in Hamlet House, in Willard's "Psych Ward," or, most recently, in Trench Hill. In Warlick's view, their placement in Trench Hill amounted to being "off the campus, out of sight, out of mind. If they are living in Trench Hill, you don't have to pay any attention to them. They are not on the campus; they are out in Siberia."

With the opening of the 1974–75 session came a dramatic change. From their "Siberian exile," the male students were assigned to Madison Hall, smack in the middle of campus. Though Warlick admitted that the relocation "was sort of 'in your face,'" he claimed that Madison "was not chosen for that reason. It was the right size residence hall to handle that many people. We could easily have taken the one on the other side of Tri-Unit [Custis], but Madison was chosen. So, that represented a real change in attitude."

If the housing of male students in the middle of campus was calculated to highlight their presence, the purpose was achieved. The *Bullet* even went so far as to assert that it was not until the debate over male housing—that is, Madison versus Custis—that "students first realized that coeducation was upon them."

Given the occasional antics of some of the Madison denizens, however, it is questionable whether their more prominent location was advantageous to the promotion of coeducation. Among their more boorish pastimes was the practice of rating the appearance of passing females on 1–10 scale and displaying the scores, à la the judging of skating competitions, on one-foot-square signs. Such behavior, which the young men themselves no doubt regarded as harmless (albeit blatantly sexist) fun, was just the kind of thing that gave credibility to the "all males are obnoxious" school of thought among some Mary Washington women.

NEW STRATEGIES

Despite periodic evidence of male mischief, the administration pushed onward in its effort to attract men. Contrary to widely held opinion, however, that attempt did not include lowering admissions standards for males. Indeed, one of the most pandemic campus canards of the era was that less-qualified male applicants were being accepted to the detriment of stronger female applicants. In reality, within a few years of the advent of coeducation, the qualifications of entering male students were actually by certain measures (e.g., SAT math scores) superior to those of the women.

Perhaps the most significant concession to pursuing potential male students was the establishment of an athletic program for men. The *Bullet* strongly endorsed such a move, commenting at the beginning of the 1975–76 session—five years after the advent of coeducation—that "little has been achieved in the area of sports which might help encourage men to attend Mary Washington College." It noted that while there was an extensive intercollegiate and intramural sports program for women, men had only one organized activity—Marsh Bowen's ragtag basketball squad—and little in the way of equipment, uniforms, or facilities. "In an age of equal opportunity," it continued,

> these practices hardly seem fair. Common sense indicates that in order to recruit more male students, and more importantly, give them equal satisfaction, choice, and treatment, a much more extensive sports program should be incorporated. . . . Money fairly distributed is a wise investment resulting in total student participation in all aspects of campus life. Like women's sports, an organized sports program for men is not only essential to their physical, psychological, and social well-being, but will also prove beneficial to Mary Washington in long-range terms.

A most significant step toward addressing that situation came in 1976 with the hiring of the College's first athletic director, Edward H. Hegmann, who during the next three decades would be the chief architect of the institution's physical education and intercollegiate sports programs. A native of Pittsburgh, Hegmann grew up in a middle-class family. His father was comptroller for Duquesne Light Company, his mother a PE teacher. His values remained rooted in the gritty work ethic of the (then) Steel City, even after he had earned his doctorate from Bucknell University. He served in the Army Corps of Engineers for two years, one of them in Vietnam. His career also included one year as a principal at a school for juvenile delinquents—an experience that, he later quipped, was "how I got prepared to deal with college students."

The background that actually provided the most relevant preparation for his MWC job was his work as athletic director and coach of the tennis, baseball, and soccer teams at a private secondary school in Cincinnati. Like Mary Washington, the Cincinnati school at the time of his employment had been going through a transition to coeducation, so the MWC challenge appealed to him.

On the other hand, the salary did not. As he recalled:

> When Dean [James] Croushore offered me the position, he preceded it with glowing words of praise for my background and what an [exceptional] candidate I was—and then actually offered me the position that would have been about a $12,000 cut in salary! When I balked at that, which was the first time I'd ever done that in my life, he made me wait a week before he called me back and said that if I was willing to do

> three weeks of on-campus consulting during the summer, that they could come up with an extra $500! . . . So I accepted the position and said, "I'll be down."[11]

It was clear to Hegmann from the outset why he was hired. "There's no doubt in my mind," he said years later, that President Woodard "wanted someone to come in here and build a program that would ultimately attract male student-athletes to Mary Washington College. He was serious about wanting this to become a coeducational institution. And he saw athletics as being a 'drawing card.'"

But Woodard was equally clear on how he wanted it done. As Hegmann explained:

> Basically, his charge to me was—he was big on giving charges—he said, "Mr. Hegmann, one thing I want you to keep in mind as you build this program is that we will build it equitably between men and women. I don't want you to think that I want you to build a big athletic program for men and not do the same for women." Of course, that was my philosophy anyway, so it wasn't really anything different than I expected to hear, but those definitely were my marching orders. . . . We did follow that kind of concept the whole way through as we developed the program. It was always meant to be on equal footing.

But to reach that equal footing meant that the main focus at first had to be on building the men's side of the program—an effort that, given the internal politics of the situation, had to be carried out, in Hegmann's description, "delicately." The initial approach was to add one women's sport whenever two were started for men. Thus in the first year after Hegmann's arrival, teams were established for men's tennis and men's soccer, while one was added for women's volleyball—a pattern that continued until by the end of the century there was virtual parity.

No matter how diplomatically Hegmann proceeded, it was not always smooth sailing. He quickly encountered problems when he became coach of the men's basketball team, one of the duties he assumed in addition to his positions as athletic director, instructor, and chair of the Department of Health and Physical Education. It did not help matters that the coach he replaced, Marsh Bowen, was a beloved, almost iconic, figure on campus—a jovial, fun-loving type who approached his coaching duties (as he approached virtually everything else, including his enormously popular geography classes) with the lightest of touches; his basketball players viewed him as a buddy as much as a mentor. Hegmann, by contrast, came across as a no-nonsense disciplinarian as he endeavored to elevate the competitive level of the team. Moreover, the players viewed it as something of a betrayal when Hegmann also became coach of the women's tennis team. The unhappy basketball experience ended for Hegmann in 1978 when Tom Davies was hired as the men's coach, leav-

Edward H. Hegmann

ing Hegmann to concentrate on what would become an extraordinarily successful career as women's tennis coach.

But Hegmann's challenges extended far beyond, and far deeper, than his difficulties with the basketball team. The basic problem lay in the fact that he—a young, handsome, ambitious man—had been brought in to run a sports program that had been run exclusively by women. And a formidable group those women were! Of the eight members of the department when Hegmann arrived, five had been at the college for twenty-five years or more, and two of them had served as dean of students: Mildred Droste and Juanita "Mickey" Clement.

It was a situation almost certain to produce discord—and it did, though not for reasons (overtly at least) related to gender. Hegmann viewed athletic participation very differently from the female coaches. In his view, most of the female coaches—the exceptions being Droste (golf and basketball) and Meg Kintzing (field hockey and lacrosse)—lacked sufficient competitive fire; certainly they lacked his.

The basic issue, as he put it, was that "athletics weren't being taken seriously. . . . The big problem was to try to get the coaches to stop coaching females and start coaching athletes." Such an approach was anathema to most of the women coaches, who tended to regard Hegmann as a brash interloper whose emphasis on winning was inappropriate to a genteel "girls' school"—which was understandable in light of their long experience at Mary Washington.

It was an attitude that appalled Hegmann. The very embodiment of the type A personality, he rejected the prevailing attitude he found among the coaching staff. As he explained it some years later: "At that time, if the teams screwed up and lost a game, they were told, 'Don't worry, you'll get 'em next time.' What they needed to be told was, 'You screwed up, and I don't want it to happen again.'"

Despite such philosophical differences, the College's athletic program grew steadily during the Woodard years, as Hegmann enjoyed the unwavering support of the president, who in many ways was his kindred spirit: a straight arrow, driven and direct. Although Woodard was not especially interested in sports himself, he believed strongly (in direct contrast to his predecessor, Grellet Simpson) that athletic activity—be it intercollegiate, intramural, or individual—should play an important role in the collegiate experience. For that reason, he exhorted Hegmann not only to proceed apace with developing a program for varsity athletes but also to design recreational opportunities for students in general, specifically instructing him to identify areas on campus that would be suitable for volleyball and other informal games.

The assignment proved to be an interesting one for the young athletic director. Woodard suggested that recreational sites be located near dormitories, the easier for students to use them. The areas, of course, had to be flat, which presented another problem, as Hegmann recalled:

> The undulating topography of our campus is such that there's just not that many flat spaces around of any size. And near a dormitory. [But] you didn't want to make them too close because they become noisy. So I identified some. Some were fairly far away, but one was, I thought, just perfect [but] it had these two mounds of earth. My vision was: you could just flatten those out. . . . [They were] behind Jefferson, between Jefferson and Route 3. I figured those were left over from the excavation to build the dormitory. I figured this would be absolutely perfect. It was up on a crest, and I wasn't sure about that, but I figured we'd put a fence around it and keep the balls from going down the hill and on to Route 3.

Although Hegmann was himself a history buff, he did not realize that the two mounds were actually the remnants of a Confederate cannon emplacement, nor could he, a native Yankee, likely have understood in any case the intensity with which a southerner of Woodard's age and historical sensibilities beheld such ground. To Woodard, the site was sacred, and he would have deemed its destruction nothing less than blasphemous.

Unaware, Hegmann proceeded jauntily to the president's office, armed with a campus map, to deliver his report. "So, I circled all these places," he later remembered,

> and I brought the map into his office. I was very excited, and I thought I'd fulfilled everything he'd wanted. He had these glasses . . . and he kind of looked up at me over the glasses and he's holding the map I had done, and he said, "Mr. Hegmann, I just want to let you know that it'll be a very cold day in you-know-where before we take a Confederate gun emplacement and make it into a recreation area." And I knew . . . I mean, he told me in no uncertain terms—he wasn't mean or angry or nasty about it—but I certainly got the message that that wasn't going to be a recreation area.

More than just amusing, the vignette actually revealed much about Prince Woodard, both his mind and his manner. It indicated his reverence for history and his consequent abhorrence of the possible destruction of its tangible manifestations. Moreover, his expression of that view, as quoted by Hegmann many years later, rang with verisimilitude. Given neither to familiarity nor to profanity, even its mildest forms, he doubtless did address Hegmann, though many years his junior, as "Mr."—and, in all probability, did indeed find it proper, and natural, to use a euphemism for "hell."

As for Hegmann's chosen spot, it never did become a recreation area. The mounds were still there decades later.

NEW ACADEMIC PROGRAMS

Prince Woodard made it clear all along that his concept of a liberal education was broader than that of many traditionalists. Shortly after taking office, he proclaimed his support for liberal arts education as being "most beneficial" because it "lets the student be flexible and a contributing citizen as times change." At the same time, however, he emphasized that his definition of that type of education was not a restrictive one, circumscribed by a set methodology or confined to a particular canon. "I do believe," he said, "that there is not a simple liberal arts education or a simple vocational education. There is a large area in between the two. I believe a student can gain from experiences other than just sitting in the classroom. I would like to see, at Mary Washington, . . . expansion of non-classroom oriented programs."

He later explained that "in addition to traditional and time-sanctioned expectations," students were "increasingly interested in acquiring skills and hands-on experience that would facilitate career exploration and successful entry into the job market." Such interests accorded well with his own pragmatic nature. He quickly set about "to determine how 'career preparation' might be most effectively woven into a liberal arts program."

A limited prototype for such an enterprise already existed at the College in the form of various off-campus individual student projects sponsored by certain departments, including Dramatic Arts, Economics, Political Science, and Geography. Drawing on those experiences, Woodard sought advice from area executives in business, industry, and government and consulted on campus with department chairs, the faculty's Curriculum Committee, and student representatives. Thus prepared, in April 1975, he appointed an ad hoc faculty committee to draft guidelines for an academic internship program, an innovation that the general faculty subsequently endorsed and the Board of Visitors approved in 1976.

The program enabled juniors and seniors to receive varying amounts of credit for academic-related work conducted with an off-campus host agency under the direction of a faculty adviser. The amount of credit awarded—usually three to six hours per semester, but no more than twelve—depended on the type of work done and the number of contact hours spent with the agency. Specific duties to be carried out and criteria for grading were determined by tripartite consultation among the student, the faculty adviser, and the host agency—the terms of which were then incorporated in a contract signed by all parties.

Some host agencies paid their interns, though most did not. But that was usually of no consequence to the students, whose main objective was simply to get experience beyond the classroom that would give them practical insight into careers that interested them and, ideally, would gain for them an advantage toward entering the job market. As one of the early participants in the program put it, internships provided "an excellent way to truly see how education can be applied. . . . They give exposure to the real world like nothing else can."

The program caught on immediately with a generation of students who tended to be more career-minded than those of an earlier day. Within the first four years of the program's operation, 335 students held internships provided by over 170 agencies and involving sponsorship by all but three of the College's academic departments. Initially directed by a faculty member who was assigned half-time for that purpose—the first being geography professor Samuel Emory—the rapid expansion soon necessitated a full-time administrator. With the hiring of Ronald Head as assistant dean in 1978, the program was subsequently coordinated by the Office of Career Services.

Aside from a few initial murmurs of discontent among faculty who disdained the program as too vocational for a liberal arts college, internships generally gained widespread acceptance, developing into an integral (and popular) part of the College's curriculum. Three decades after its creation, the program had placed over 5,800 students, involving the cooperation of over 4,500 host agencies, most of them located either in Fredericksburg or the Washington, D.C., area, but some as far afield as Spain and Nepal. In the process, countless students were launched on rewarding careers, and the internship program emerged as one of Prince Woodard's most enduring and positive legacies.

In addition to expanding the variety of educational opportunities for Mary Washington's traditional student population, one of Woodard's earliest objectives was to extend the reach of the College's services to the surrounding community. In fact, just such an effort was being encouraged at the time by the commonwealth.

In 1973 the General Assembly created a system of regional consortiums of state colleges and universities for the purpose of promoting opportunities for continuing adult education. The legislation mandated specifically that one senior institution in each consortium "be encouraged to develop non-traditional degree programs at the baccalaureate and master's levels which have minimum residency requirements and maximum transferability of credit from any accredited institution." As such an institution within the eleven-member Central Virginia Consortium, Mary Washington subsequently sought and received permission from the State Council of Higher Education to develop the nontraditional undergraduate degree program for its region.

The choice of Mary Washington for the assignment made sense for a number of reasons, notably because its reputation for high academic quality would prove attractive to potential students. The most compelling reason, however, was its location amid what had become, by 1970, the fastest-growing region in the state—a status it was projected to maintain through the end of the century (as it did). Accordingly, Woodard in the summer of 1976 appointed a committee to study the issue and design a program compatible with the College's mission and resources.

The result was the proposed creation of a nontraditional program that would lead to the awarding of a degree known as the bachelor of liberal studies (BLS). While retaining many of the essential requirements of the normal MWC bachelor's degree—one exception being the absence of a foreign-language requirement—the BLS incorporated some significant credit options, including, in addition to the acceptance of transfer credit from other institutions, the following:

1. challenge examinations by which command of course material could be demonstrated without actually taking the class;
2. procedures for validating courses taken through non-academic agencies, such as business, military, correspondence, and self-fulfillment courses; and
3. submission of a portfolio that could yield credit for learning acquired through life and work experiences.

Open to persons beyond traditional college-student age (defined as twenty-four or older), the BLS program had several other features with particular appeal to that group. For one thing, the residency requirement was minimal, stipulating that only thirty credit hours be taken at MWC. Also, there was no established timetable for degree completion, meaning that courses (including night classes) could be taken over an extended period of time convenient to students who might be constrained by work or family obligations.

The plan was approved by the faculty in October 1976, and by the Board of Visitors the following month. With subsequent endorsement by the State Council of Higher Education, the BLS program became operational at the beginning of the 1977–78 academic year, under the direction of Ray Merchent, vice president of the College, one of the institution's most respected administrators. Woodard touted the program as a milestone achievement whereby "adults with intellectual curiosity, self-discipline, and high motivation can pursue higher education according to individualized goals and time schedules."

There were ancillary academic benefits as well. Younger students and faculty soon realized that the older students contributed positively to the classroom academic environment both by the maturity of their general approach to learning and by the shared insights derived from their personal experiences, a situation that helped create an intellectual diversity often lacking theretofore in the classroom.

During the first two years of its operation, the program enrolled 111 students, with the first graduates (11 of them) receiving their BLS degrees at the

May 1979 commencement. From there the program grew steadily, producing 61 graduates in 1984, 97 in 1989, and 137 in 1995. Like the internship program, it stood as a testament to Woodard's expanded vision for the College and to his skill and energy in converting that vision into reality.

One of the cardinal tenets of Prince Woodard's philosophy of educational administration was the necessity for research, analysis, and planning. It must have been appalling to him to learn that among the Shaner report's specific criticisms of Mary Washington College was its lack of a formal mechanism for institutional planning. In any event, he addressed that problem by establishing in 1977 a College Planning and Priorities Advisory Council (C-PPAC), composed of administrators, faculty, and students, whose purpose was to advise the president on a broad range of issues from the standpoint of long-range goals and priority designations.

One of the first major issues addressed by C-PPAC was the possible revision of the College's curriculum—another area about which the Shaner report had expressed concern. The question, more specifically, was whether the College's offerings should be expanded to incorporate courses that might have greater appeal to prospective students who, studies indicated, were inclined to be more concerned than before about the marketability of a liberal arts degree. It was an issue that warranted serious consideration at a time when, as demographic analyses projected, the college-age population was due to decline, producing greater-than-ever competition for the better students. On the other hand, any suggestion of vocationally oriented courses was bound to raise the hackles of that segment of the faculty who were ever alert to any perceived dilution of the liberal arts curriculum.

Following months of study, C-PPAC endorsed six new major undergraduate programs for faculty consideration. Two of them, both of which drew heavily on existing courses, were proposed for introduction in the fall of 1979: performing arts and historic preservation. The former actually involved little more than a reconfiguration of two existing majors, dramatic arts and dance (both of which would continue separately), so as to permit students to concentrate on the performance aspect of the two fields.

The historic preservation major was developed under the aegis of the History Department, whose chair, William B. Crawley Jr., worked closely with advisers from prominent preservation organizations at the national, state, and local levels (e.g., the National Trust for Historic Preservation, the Association for the Preservation of Virginia Antiquities, and the Historic Fredericksburg Foundation) to devise a program that would be unique among undergraduate majors in Virginia and one of only a handful in the entire country. The curriculum included a core of new courses in historic preservation per se—a basic Principles of Preservation course, together with individual courses in the techniques of museum, archival, architectural, and archaeological preservation—augmented by appropriate courses drawn from related disciplines, notably history and art history. The potential for the major's success was enhanced by the location of the College in an area extraordinarily rich in historical resources, a circumstance that provided fertile ground for research and internship opportunities.

The other four proposed new majors were projected for implementation in the fall of 1980: environmental earth science, computer and information science, business administration, and public administration. The first amounted to an arrangement of existing courses in biology, chemistry, geology, geography, economics, political science, and sociology so as to provide its majors with the academic tools for dealing with real-world problems such as water pollution, acid rain, strip mining, and nuclear and chemical waste. Biology professor Michael Bass, who was mainly responsible for devising the curriculum, described it as "a true liberal arts major [that] cuts across the natural and social sciences."

Construction of the major involved something of a tug-of-war between Bass and Woodard. The president, reacting to SCHEV's desire to produce needed high school teachers, wanted a certification program in *earth* science; Bass believed that *environmental* science was more appropriate. "So I kept saying environmental science," recalled Bass. "Every time Dr. Woodard would bring it up, I said it needs to be an environmental science program. And he would get a little bit agitated, . . . and then finally, I think it was about the third time that I brought this up, he looked at me and said, 'All right, if you can put the two together, you can have your environmental science!' And I said, 'O.K. How about calling it environmental earth science?'"[12] And so environmental earth science became a major within a renamed Department of Biological Sciences.

The other three majors departed considerably further from the existing curriculum and necessitated the addition of a sizable number of new courses, a situation that drew the lion's share of faculty opposition. Proponents had to ensure that the programs' methodologies conformed, to the greatest possible extent, to the tenets of liberal learning. In addition, the advocates of the new majors emphasized that market surveys had indicated that such programs had strong appeal within the region. This was especially true among graduates of community college two-year programs, as well as employees of local businesses, industries, and government installations who wished to strengthen their professional qualifications through part-time study.

No matter how compelling the case made by each proposal, approval was by no means certain when they were presented to the general faculty. For one thing, there was opposition from some who, on philosophical grounds, questioned the appropriateness of at least some of the proposed new courses at a liberal arts institution. Moreover, passage was further imperiled by the fact that the vote on those proposals—generally, and correctly, viewed as Woodard's initiatives—came at a time when the president was coming under fire from a sizable portion of the faculty who, because of his perceived authoritarianism, were reflexively inclined to oppose anything he supported. Ultimately, however, all were approved by the faculty and subsequently endorsed by the State Council of Higher Education. Implementation began, as projected, during the 1979–80 and 1980–81 academic years.

The success of all the programs, save one, made Woodard seem prescient; public administration never really caught on and was soon phased out. The computer science program thrived, driven naturally by burgeoning technology throughout every aspect of American society. Business administration attracted many students (some of whom would otherwise have ignored Mary Washington) simply because that practical program seemed to answer their—or, perhaps more importantly, their parents'—concern about the employment prospects of traditional liberal arts graduates. Almost immediately business administration became the College's largest major.

The new major programs, though they involved to varying degrees elements of practicality that marked a departure from the pristine liberal arts approach, were all still within the College's undergraduate tradition. It was during this time, however, that Mary Washington embarked on expansion to the graduate level.

The idea of graduate study at MWC was not new. That possibility had been broached at least as early as 1968 in the report of the Simpson-appointed Committee on the Future of the College.[13] While emphasizing that it was not advocating "an indiscriminate, sprawling extension of the College's current functions," the committee recommended that the offering of graduate work in selected disciplines be considered. "Such courses," the committee suggested, "might answer the needs of graduate students in search of summer-session programs consistent with their educational interests and professional advancements; or, such courses might be distributed throughout the regular session of the college, perhaps being scheduled during evening and Saturday hours to the advantage of adults in the local community and surrounding areas. Projecting still farther into the future, it is conceivable that sequences of related courses could lead to a graduate degree."

The concept was further advanced with the institution's 1971 Self-Study Report, prepared as part of the requisite decennial application for reaccreditation from the Southern Association of Colleges and Schools. The premise of the expansion to graduate courses was, in the words of the report, "not to suggest that the College become multi-purpose but rather it should seek means for transmitting liberal learning more widely." Moreover, in words that anticipated Woodard's own views, the report urged that the College "come to recognize that professional and vocational preparation and liberal learning are not mutually exclusive," and concluded by "strongly recommending" that the College "undertake a carefully selected graduate program in areas where library resources and faculty competence guarantee the proper level of study.

Such a graduate program probably should not be directed toward a residential student body, but rather toward the commuting student."

The same approach was adumbrated in the 1974 State Council of Higher Education's publication, *The Virginian Plan for Higher Education*, which suggested that projected population growth in the Richmond–Washington urban corridor should "lead Mary Washington to propose curriculum additions to meet new and increased demands." Praising the high quality of existing liberal arts programs at the undergraduate level, the council noted that the development of advanced programs at MWC would "evolve naturally from its present strengths."

The introduction of graduate work was eagerly advocated by a wide spectrum of community leaders. For example, a public hearing sponsored by the Consortium for Continuing Higher Education, held on the MWC campus in late 1975, included pleas for such opportunities by representatives of the Naval Surface Weapons Center at Dahlgren, the Fredericksburg Education Association, and the local public schools.

Taking such evidence into account, C-PPAC, after extensive study of the issue during the 1977–78 session, unanimously recommended that the College proceed to request the necessary approvals for conferring master's degrees. The Board of Visitors, which had been considering such a plan since its inception as an independent body in 1972, concurred.

President Woodard announced the initiative to the faculty at the opening convocation in August 1978, noting that "this isn't some overnight idea. . . . The need is obvious." He went on to endorse the plan enthusiastically, projecting it as "a great asset for the College and the community—a breakthrough with [the potential for] quite an impact over the next ten to fifteen years."

The faculty greeted the announcement with a mixed, though generally not unfavorable, response. The veteran philosophy professor George Van Sant observed that he had the sense that "the overwhelming majority of the faculty [are] delighted with it." Some certainly were, including the chair of the Math Department, Al Lindsey, who hailed it as "a great opportunity."

Others were more cautious. Professor of English Nancy Mitchell, while noting that she personally was "very pleased" with the prospect of "expanding the directions" of the College and intuited that most of her colleagues felt the same way about the general concept of graduate studies, predicted that questions might arise subsequently when detailed plans were worked out concerning what exactly would be taught, by whom, and with what resources. Psychology professor J. Christopher Bill sounded a similar alarm, asserting that he "would have preferred to have seen a consensus of the faculty first . . . [because] we need to learn just what it is we have in mind before we go further with it."

Others no doubt shared such qualms but were ultimately constrained to support the plan either out of altruistic motives, such as the belief that a public institution has an obligation to serve the educational needs of citizens in its area, or personal considerations, such as the desire to teach more challenging (and thus more rewarding) courses at the graduate level. Then, too, from a practical standpoint the College could hardly afford to be unmindful of an additional pool of prospective students at a time when external agencies were increasingly inclined to raise management questions, including issues of enrollment and space allocations. Indeed, one of Woodard's specific justifications for the graduate program was that it would create more efficient use of existing buildings, since they could be used at times when not needed for undergraduate work. Summing the situation up, one faculty member succinctly concluded that whatever one's personal preferences might have been, "we had to go in that direction."

Once approved by the Board of Visitors, the graduate proposal required endorsement by the State Council of Higher Education. As part of that process, a five-member evaluation committee conducted an on-site review of the College's facilities in the fall of 1978 and, in the words of SCHEV director Gordon K. Davies, came away "generally very impressed by the College and all that was associated with it." The council accordingly approved the College's application, an action that led to unanimous approval by the General Assembly and by Governor John Dalton at the 1978 legislative session.

Once the general concept of graduate studies had been authorized, the question became how a specific program or programs should be structured. What emerged, first, was a program that would lead to the degree of master of liberal studies (MALS), which was scheduled to begin in the fall of 1980, with additional master's programs in business administration and public administration projected for implementation two years later.

The MALS program was intensely interdisciplinary, designed to take maximum advantage of existing faculty and library resources. It required thirty hours of academic work, which for part-time students was envisioned as typically taking three to five years to complete. If not unique, the program was certainly unusual; within Virginia at that time, only Hollins College offered the degree, and there it was chiefly a summer program.

Professor of English Donald E. Glover, a widely respected member of the faculty for two decades, was appointed director of graduate studies, assisted by a Graduate Council comprising nine other faculty from varied disciplines across the College.[14] Together they developed a degree program consisting of four basic elements.

The first, a six-hour course required of all MALS students, was the program's most innovative component. Ideas and Movements of the Western World was a team-taught course that focused on what Glover described as "the development and evolution of some of the basic ideas and movements which have given the Western World its great cultural heritage." Faculty chosen to teach the course during its first year came from diverse disciplines, and all were among the College's most highly regarded: Clavio Ascari (Italian), Elizabeth Clark (religion), William Kemp (English), Barbara Meyer (art history), George Van Sant (philosophy), and Lawrence Wishner (chemistry).

Having completed the required introductory courses, students could then choose six credit hours from a variety of colloquiums that again emphasized the interdisciplinary nature of the degree. Team-taught by three faculty members from different departments, the colloquiums had titles such as "Evolution: The Physical, Religious, and Economic Views" and "Aging: The Psychological, Biological, and Humanistic Implications."

The third element allowed students to choose fifteen hours in electives drawn from graduate-level courses in various departments. Finally, the capstone was a three-credit individual investigative or creative project carried out under the direction of a faculty member—analogous to the thesis requirement in more traditional master's programs.

On the eve of its implementation, MALS was not without it critics, both on campus and beyond. "The people at another school told us it couldn't be done," admitted Glover. At the College itself, there was skepticism about the merits of the program among those who felt that its interdisciplinary approach constituted no more than a watered-down version of the discipline-specific structures of traditional master's programs elsewhere. The situation prompted the *Free Lance–Star* to observe that "if it works—and there seems to be just enough uncertainty to make the experiment more interesting—the result will be a moving interdisciplinary experience."

For his part, Glover was optimistic, preferring to view the unusual MALS format as a benefit rather than a liability. He pointed out that liberal studies were catching on nationally as more and more adults were opting to return to the classroom for sundry reasons, be it career advancement or simply personal enrichment. For such persons, the MALS structure was ideally tailored, especially in light of its flexible hours and course sequencing. Moreover, as Glover somewhat puckishly put it, "It's here, it's cheap, and it's convenient."

From the outset, enrollment surpassed expectations. When more than fifty students signed up for the introductory course in the fall of 1980, a second section had to be added. A diverse lot they were, ranging in age from twenty-two to sixty-eight. There were more women than men; they lived from Fairfax to Richmond; seventeen were graduates of MWC; and five already held master's degrees from other institutions. The most common career was teaching, but their number also included engineers, business people, homemakers, and retirees—as well as at least one policeman, cab driver, editor, banker, doctor, and government intelligence worker.

What resulted, according to Glover, was "a unique chemistry" that developed from the blending of students from disparate backgrounds with professors from various academic disciplines. Faculty were energized by the experience, both because of interaction with students who were more mature and more diverse than the typical MWC undergraduates and because teaching the Great Ideas course forced them to go beyond their own sometimes narrow sphere of expertise to incorporate theories and methods from other areas.

The morale of the graduate cadre appeared particularly high. As Glover put it, "It's involved the faculty in doing things they haven't done before. . . . They've worked at bettering their credentials and seem to be publishing more." As a consequence, he continued, "it's raised faculty morale because they know there is someplace for them to go. . . . There is a new opportunity to excel and move up to graduate teaching."

The following year, MALS enrollment rose to eighty-nine students, including one seventy-eight-year-old. The first colloquium was introduced, "Language Acquisition," taught by instructors from biology, linguistics, and education. In addition, three electives were offered for the first time: "The Scope of Cervantes and His Work" (taught entirely in Spanish); "Philosophy, Philology, and Literature"; and "Historical Themes and Problems in Early Modern Europe."

At the 1983 commencement ceremony, the first graduates of the MALS program—five of them, all women, and all MWC alumni—received their degrees. Among them was Claudith "Dottie" Holmes, who in 1971 had been one of the first African Americans to graduate from Mary Washington. Thus did the MALS program get off to an auspicious start.

Simultaneously with the implementation of MALS, the College began to plan for a second graduate program, this one a master of business administration (MBA). As dean of graduate studies, Don Glover supervised the process, assisted primarily by Steven Czarsty, then chair of the Department of Economics, Business, and Public Affairs. Czarsty's expertise was essential, and his credentials were impressive; not only had he been instrumental in developing the undergraduate business curriculum at MWC, but he had previously taken an active role in establishing the master of business administration program at George Mason University.

Despite Czarsty's experience, establishing the College's MBA proved to be a formidable task. "It takes more time than you think it is going to," admitted Glover, "especially at an institution where . . . everything has always been undergraduate." It had also been—if not always, at least for the preceding several decades—focused almost exclusively on the liberal arts and sciences, making business administration, either graduate or undergraduate, appear to some to be out of place.

Not so, claimed Czarsty; it all depended on the educational theory that undergirded the business program. The structure of the MBA at Mary Washington, he insisted, would make it unique. "It's more than just business; it's also communications, and that's why the liberal arts philosophy at Mary Washington College is a natural to incorporate into our program," he explained. "A philosophy of this kind gets away from the technocratic MBA programs where you turn out robot-like graduates."

As finally devised, the MBA was similar to the MALS in that it consisted mainly of night courses, the better to serve a clientele consisting largely of adults with full-time day jobs. Since one of its key purposes was to assist liberal arts graduates who needed business skills for career advancement, it included introductory courses in economics and accounting as well as advanced courses such as managerial economics.

Like the MALS program, the MBA attracted a diverse enrollment, with students ranging from their twenties into their sixties; unlike the MALS students, a sizable majority were men. The largest single portion were employees of the federal government, but students also came from private businesses, the legal profession, the computer industry, and social welfare agencies.

From its modest beginnings in 1982, the program increased slightly in the several years that followed but ultimately withered to the point that it was discontinued late in the decade.[15]

President Woodard took considerable pride in the new programs created at his instigation, and though he avidly supported them all, it was evident that he had a personal favorite: historic preservation was his "pet." It was not just that he believed that its academic uniqueness, enhanced by being located amid an area of nearly unrivaled historical significance, would enable it to become the College's flagship program. More than that, his enthusiasm was the product of his childhood in Southside Virginia, an area where powerful images of the Old South—though not necessarily accurate or complete ones—lingered still. Like many a twentieth-century son of the Southside, he was nurtured by images of earlier times, developing an affinity for the past that was further burnished during his years as a history major at VMI.

Prince Woodard loved the commonwealth and all its glories, real or imagined. To him the program in historic preservation was not merely a means of attracting students to Mary Washington and of raising the College's visibility; it was fundamentally an effort to help sustain for posterity a heritage he never ceased to cherish. So enamored was he with the program that when the first preservation course was offered in the fall of 1979, he enrolled in it for credit—not just as an auditor but as a fee-paying, credit-seeking student who attended the classes, wrote the papers, delivered the oral reports, and took the examinations right along with the rest of the class.

He got an A.

FINANCES AND FACILITIES

Although the new majors were successfully launched, the fiscal difficulties that beset Mary Washington in the mid-1970s still affected virtually every aspect of the College. Relative to institutions of comparable academic quality, faculty salaries were too low; relative to other state institutions in Virginia, student tuition was too high. And on top of that, much of the College's physical plant was beginning to show signs of age and neglect.

President Woodard early in his administration had begun to address the salary issue by reducing the number of faculty positions—an approach that yielded some success but won him few friends. Moreover, it did not attack the root causes of the larger problem.

There were two fundamental reasons for the College's financial plight, the foremost being the low level of funding received from the commonwealth, the other being the lack of private endowment funds. Though a state institution, MWC in 1974–75 received only 49.7 percent of its revenues from the general fund, compared to the average of 66.4 percent received by its peer group institutions.[16] (All state schools were classified in peer groups according to the types of degrees offered. As a four-year undergraduate institution, MWC was grouped at that time with Madison, VMI, Clinch Valley, Norfolk State, Virginia State, Radford, Longwood, and George Mason.)

What this meant in actual dollar figures was that, in 1972–73, for example, Mary Washington received $799 per student from the state, while peer group schools received $956. Yet during that same period, MWC was actually spending almost the identical total amount on its students as its peers: $1,723 as opposed to $1,724 for the others. Mary Washington made up the difference by charging higher tuition.

A number of factors combined to create this discrepancy. One was the simple but unfortunate fact that, historically, some schools had worked more diligently in Richmond in pursuit of funds. Mary Washington's remaining aloof from the political fray may have appeared to be admirable, but the practical consequences were damaging over the course of time. There was also a more subtle psychological factor at work. Unlike MWC, some colleges at that time were in a growth mode, and legislators seemed more inclined to allocate funds for physical expansion than for enhancement of quality. Again, Mary Washington's more academic approach was laudable, but it was a hard sell in Richmond.

Whatever the causes, Woodard and the Board of Visitors early came to the conclusion that the situation had to change: the College could not continue to make up the revenue gap via tuition increases without the risk of losing students. Thus the decision was made to hold the line as long as possible on tuition and to make every effort to increase state appropriations.

In this endeavor, Woodard was well equipped by virtue of his Richmond contacts, both in the legislature and in the higher education establishment. No doubt influenced, at least in part, by his discussions with the State Council of Higher Education and the appropriate legislative committees, the General Assembly adopted the goal of providing 70 percent of the funding for each of the state's four-year colleges.

The resulting improvement was not immediate, nor was it complete, but it was significant. Within Woodard's first five years as president, the level of state funding for Mary Washington rose to 64 percent. That was the good news; the bad news was that the College remained the farthest of all state schools from the 70 percent benchmark. By 1977, for example, Clinch Valley College was funded at 77 percent of its budget. Nor was it just the small schools that benefited; both U.Va. and Virginia Tech received over 70 percent of their revenues from state coffers.

In addition, even though MWC's tuition and fees remained the same for five years beginning in 1974—$820 per year for Virginia residents, $1,665 for out-of-state students—they were still the second highest among the Commonwealth's fifteen state-supported four-year institutions; only William and Mary charged slightly more.[17]

Making matters even worse for Mary Washington was the almost total absence of private endowment funds that might have compensated to some extent for the state's stinginess. In the mid-1970s, a number of Virginia's private colleges had multi-million-dollar endowments, and the University of Virginia's was over $100 million; MWC's was virtually nil. In fact, only .3 percent of its total revenues came from private sources.

To a considerable extent, the problem was rooted in Mary Washington's history. During the years of its affiliation with the University of Virginia, essentially all fund-raising had been under the aegis of U.Va., with few dividends accruing to the women's branch. Then, when the separation occurred in 1972, the College did not share the largesse. As MWC administrator Conrad Warlick, a noted wit, put it, the situation was reminiscent of a divorce: "Mary Washington got back [its] maiden name, got the house, . . . [but] no alimony." He might have added, to carry the analogy further, that the union had been something of a shotgun wedding to begin with.

In any event, it was a doleful state of affairs that President Woodard endeavored to rectify. A crucial step in that direction occurred early in his administration with the chartering of the Mary Washington College Foundation in February 1975. The stated purposes of the nonprofit corporation were "to receive, hold, invest, administer, and distribute non-state funds and property of all kinds exclusively for the furtherance of the educational activities and objectives of Mary Washington College."

The governance of the foundation was in the hands of a thirty-member board of directors, with the rector of the Board of Visitors and the president and chief financial officer of the College serving as ex officio members. Irene Lundy Brown '39, a major supporter of the College who was then serving on the Board of Visitors, was chosen as the foundation's first president.

With the foundation in place, Woodard then created the administrative position of vice president for development and management information systems, a portion of whose responsibilities involved coordinating the goals of the College with the activities of the foundation. Though unforeseeable at the time by the president or anyone else, Woodard's choice for the post was serendipitous. The appointee was destined to become, over the course of the subsequent three decades, one of the most significant figures in the history of the institution: William M. Anderson Jr.

Anderson was thirty-four years old at the time of his appointment. Having earned his bachelor's degree in business from Virginia Commonwealth University and a master's degree in public administration from the West Virginia College of Graduate Studies, he was at the time completing work on a doctorate in educational administration from Virginia Tech while working for Woodard at the West Virginia board of regents. In that position, he was responsible for setting up the board's management information system. It was his success in that endeavor that led to his hiring at Mary Washington, where he was charged with implementing analogous technological capabilities for the College, as well as overseeing the nascent fund-raising operation.

In one of his first public statements after arriving on campus, Anderson asserted that "if we are going to pursue greatness as a small liberal arts college, it's going to take revenue in excess of what the state provides." Those words presaged what would become over the years a virtual mantra as he worked in ever-escalating positions of authority to bolster the College's fiscal assets.

Reflective of his own demeanor, he promised that fund-raising efforts would be energetic, but at the same time low-key. "We will let people know how they can go about leaving funds, gifts, securities, and property to the College," he said. "A lot of what we can do depends on the enthusiasm of the Mary Washington 'family.'" Before his tenure at the College ended, that faith would be amply rewarded.

In the meantime, it soon became apparent that the fund-raising effort required additional firepower, especially as Anderson found it necessary to devote an increasing amount of his time to the technology side of his two-pronged job. So in 1978 the position of director of development was created. It was filled first by George E. Ball, formerly associate director of development at Brown University, who was succeeded in 1982 by Charles Repp. Having begun his career at George Mason University as associate dean for student services, Repp, thirty-six, had gone on to become vice president for student affairs at the State University of New York. Most recently he had moved into the fund-raising field as dean of planning and development at the West Virginia School of Osteopathic Medicine.

Repp's work was clearly cut out for him. Since its establishment in 1975, the foundation had by 1982 amassed just over $150,000. The problem was not so much an unwillingness to give on the part of alumni—the rate of their participation was in fact quite respectable—but rather their financial inability to do so at a significant level. It was that situation to which Woodard alluded when he told the Board of Visitors in 1982 that Mary Washington was "perhaps the only school in Virginia . . . which does not have an alumnus serving as the president or chairman of the board of a corporation, large or small."

Repp addressed the issue more expansively. Noting that because through much of its history the College had been primarily concerned with training teachers, a traditionally low-paying profession, he said, "It's a hard project at Mary Washington because you don't have a great abundance of wealthy alumni who are able and willing to make gifts or ask others to do the same. This is something we have to face. It's not that it's good or bad, it just happens to be a fact of life." Even those who had married into wealth did not, as a rule, provide significant support because, as Repp explained, there was "a tendency for the husband to make the primary gift to his alma mater with the wife's school receiving a token gift. Unfortunately, we often wind up with the token."

Such obstacles notwithstanding, the effort made some progress by the early eighties. For example, the President's Club, established by the foundation to designate contributors of $1,000 or more, had no members as late as 1979; by 1982, the number had risen to twenty-two. An even greater harbinger of future success was the change in the institution's basic attitude toward the whole matter of fund-raising. Whereas it had once been regarded by the stewards of the College as somehow unseemly, the development process was now viewed, dignified or not, as necessary to fulfilling the institution's mission.

Symbolic of that change was the 1982 relocation of the development office from GW to larger and more impressive quarters in Trench Hill—a move that Repp found encouraging. "I think the future is bright," he said, "and I don't have any doubts that Mary Washington will continue to grow in the development area. I think we'll have to put more time and investment into it, and I think this building is a testament to that." He was right on all counts.

The College's endowment did eventually reach impressive levels, but it would take years to accomplish. Meanwhile, there were other pressing needs to be addressed, as by the mid-1970s the impact of chronic underfunding was beginning to be felt, not just in the academic program but in campus physical facilities as well.

There was not much need for new construction. Indeed, decreased demand for dormitory space had led in 1972 to the termination of the College's lease on the Betty Lewis Apartments, much to the dismay of local males who had grown fond of ogling the sunbathers on Betty Lewis "beach" as they cruised past on Sunken Road in the springtime. What was desperately needed was not so much new facilities—with one major exception—but repair and renovation of existing ones.

The one exception involved athletic facilities. Thanks to the completion of Goolrick Hall in 1969, the facilities for most indoor sports were adequate—and in the case of swimming, excellent—though competitors and spectators alike suffered in hot weather from the lack of air-conditioning.

Outdoors was a different matter. The venue for all such sports, save golf, was the elongated flat area parallel to Sunken Road below Goolrick and Mercer that included tennis courts (converted ice rinks) and playing fields for lacrosse and field hockey. Golf was played on the College's nine-hole course on the "other" (i.e., non-college) side of Hanover Street, a block south of the main campus.

Though such facilities may have been sufficient when there were only women's teams, and few of those, they were by no means adequate to support the expanded program of male and female intercollegiate sports that President Woodard and Athletic Director Ed Hegmann envisioned. In fact, a presidential promise to upgrade the athletic facilities, as Hegmann recalled, was part of the bargain to entice him to Mary Washington. "He told me," said Hegmann, "that if I took the position, they would sell the piece of property behind Trench Hill . . . to fund a tennis complex."

That is in fact what happened, and the construction of ten lighted tennis courts became the first elements of what was to evolve, under Hegmann's energetic and aggressive direction, into "The Battleground," a multipurpose outdoor athletic facility located on the site of the former Hanover Street golf course. By 1981 it also included a soccer field; a cross-country course; an eight-lane, 400-meter track; and a 10,000-square-foot athletic field. With the addition of other varsity teams and playing areas in subsequent years, The Battleground would become the finest Division III outdoor athletic complex in Virginia.

Aside from construction of the outdoor athletic complex, most of the capital-outlay projects of the 1970s involved repair of existing facilities. Such work did little to increase usable space or enhance beauty, but an aging infrastructure demanded that the electrical, steam, and water lines serving many buildings be replaced in order for the campus to remain functional.

A number of buildings were partially remodeled. Mercer Hall, then housing the infirmary (in the days before "wellness center" became the preferred designation), was renovated to accommodate the counseling center, headed by Mary Annette "Toni" Kelly. The auditorium of George Washington Hall was spruced up with new lighting and fresh paint—and, in 1980, was named Eileen Kramer Dodd Auditorium in honor of Professor Dodd, who had retired from the Psychology Department in 1970 after forty-four years on the faculty.

Several renovation projects were designed especially to appeal to students. One of the most innovative was the conversion of the former swimming pool below the Lee Hall terrace into what the *Bullet* hailed as a pub or "rathskeller-type" venue that would serve soft drinks, beer, and "munchies" and in general "provide an alternative to keg parties or driving into Georgetown for something to do." The room's decor featured a vinyl inlay of a pool table on the floor, and the serving area was constructed to resemble a pool ball rack—hence the double entendre in its rechristening as the "Pool Room."

Another popular venue on campus, the College Shop in Lee Hall (known variously as the C-Shop or C-Shoppe), underwent transformation of a largely cosmetic nature. Surprisingly, there was some student opposition, mainly on the grounds that the money could better be used in other ways, particularly, carped the *Bullet*, "at a time when a general belt-tightening is being called for." The project cost $15,000, which, though negligible in light of subsequent inflation, seemed prodigal in the context of the times. "What's the $15,000 question?" asked the paper. "How can that much money be spent in redecorating the C Shoppe. . . . Admittedly the C Shoppe's atmosphere is non-existent, . . . but who has so vehemently complained that a whopping $15,000 has been allotted to do what paint and new curtains could do?"

A vastly more substantial renovation project, the largest in the College's history to that time, involved Monroe Hall. The College's first building, Monroe had endured since 1911 as the institution's most powerful visual image—constituting, in President Woodard's words, "what the Wren Building is to William and Mary and the Rotunda is to the University of Virginia." Its value was not only symbolic but practical, housing six academic departments and providing 15 percent of the College's total instructional space.

But the grand old edifice was showing its age. The electrical wiring and the forced-air heating system were original to the building, the result being, said Woodard, that "it's like a blast furnace if you sit in front of one of the outlets, but if you happen to be sitting across the room, you might freeze." That was in winter; in summer, lacking air-conditioning, classrooms and offices sweltered in the Virginia heat and humidity. Then there were the restrooms, such as they were. Their location only in the basement required users on the upper two floors not only to go downstairs but to exit the building and reenter to reach the facilities.

Few would have denied that rehabilitation was needed. In fact, preliminary plans were approved by the state as early as 1968, but went unfunded, and by the time problems had reached a critical stage in the late seventies, the cost had reached $1.5 million. Fortunately, the requisite funds were incorporated as part of a $125 million bond referendum approved by Virginia voters in November 1977, and work commenced the following year.

Though completion of the project ran five months beyond the targeted date, the reopening for the 1980 session elicited general praise for the transformation that had been wrought. The mechanical systems were modernized, and many interior spaces were rearranged in a much more productive fashion, including conversion of the creaky second-floor auditorium into a capacious cartography lab and the outdated basketball court (site of the College's original swimming pool) into a two-hundred-seat tiered lecture hall. The renovation was noteworthy not only because of what it created but also for what it saved: namely, the elegant exterior and the first-floor Schnellock murals, the latter so meticulously crafted by the art professor and his students in the 1940s. But to students perhaps the most welcome change of all was that, as the *Bullet* elatedly put it, "You don't have to run around the outside of the building to get to the bathrooms anymore!"

Concurrently with the Monroe Hall project, a $1.72 million renovation was carried out on Willard Hall, the second of the College's two original buildings. As with Monroe, extensive upgrading of the entire infrastructure was required, along with some alterations to allow the dorm to meet new federal regulations regarding access for handicapped persons.

In contrast to the Monroe refurbishing, in which every effort was made to maintain the building's older ambience, the interior of the new Willard was designed to have a distinctly—critics would say excessively—modern appearance, using a color scheme that incorporated fire-engine red, bright orange, fuchsia, lavender, black, peacock blue, and white. Despite the complaints of some traditionalists, most of the remodeled dorm's first residents reacted favorably when they moved in at the start of the 1980 session. Certainly they liked the air-conditioning—Willard was the first dorm on campus to be so equipped. And a particular appeal was that, owing to the thick walls of the original structure, it was, as one student put it, "exceptionally quiet. . . . You can go wild on the outside and then come back here and sleep and study. . . . [It] seems almost soundproof."

With regard to the physical aspects of the College, one of President Woodard's paramount concerns was campus beautification. Though hampered by limited funds, he began several modest efforts, such as installing stone "Mary Washington College" markers at campus boundaries (the intersections of William Street with College Avenue and with Sunken Road, and the intersection of College Avenue with the Route 1 Bypass) and planting holly trees in the median strip of Campus Drive.

No aspect of his interest in the campus's appearance was as intense and persistent as his concern for maintaining its grassy areas, whose desecration by students' so-called pig paths he abhorred. The issue was not a new one. As early as 1964, the *Bullet* had inveighed against "campus cutting," a deplorable practice that, scolded the paper,

> has become a wanton rampage for some Mary Washington students. The tradition of using the sidewalks was well established as early as the 1920s. The abuse to the tradition, however, is not so relevant as the wanton destruction of property. Our campus is not only the property of the state, but is the property of each student who pays the college fees. . . . It is a waste of money to willfully destroy something for which we ourselves have paid. . . . If it is continued, some legislative action must be taken. In the meanwhile, each girl should stop and think before walking a foot beside the sidewalk instead of on it. Those who do use the sidewalks and who do have some pride in the appearance of their college can easily remind those who don't by simply vocalizing the name "campus cutter." Perhaps then the girl(s) approached will be appropriately embarrassed.

Apparently such peer pressure, if employed at all, was not efficacious, because by the time Woodard arrived ten years later, the problem remained—and he intended to fix it. Indeed, his repeated admonitions to stay off the grass, earnestly delivered to faculty and students alike, made him seem well-nigh obsessive about it. When words proved insufficient to rectify the problem, he employed more direct means, having brick sidewalks built in areas of heaviest traffic and low chains erected to dissuade shortcuts across particularly inviting areas, such as Ball Circle.

Some students clearly agreed with the president's concern, urging, through the *Bullet*, compliance with his campaign. One article, cast in the format of a plea from the grass itself, upbraided those who trampled the greensward: "You students of Mary Washington with your fancy sneakers, fancy heels, docksiders, Dr. Scholl's, saddle shoes, boots: I don't care what you wear on your feet. It still mashes down the grass, and pretty soon there will be another bare spot in the ground which will have to be bricked in." One student, a member of the newly organized Campus Conservation Committee, having noted that the area around the dining hall received particular abuse, raised a reasonable (if facetious) question in the *Bullet*: "If the food at Seacobeck is so bad, then what is the hurry to cut across the grass to get there?"

In a more serious vein, Associate Dean for Admissions Martin A. "Marty" Wilder Jr. offered a cogent observation. Writing to the *Bullet*, Wilder pointed out that "in surveys conducted annually with incoming MWC freshmen, students consistently cite the beauty of the campus as one of the major reasons why they chose to attend the college. One must then wonder why, upon matriculation to Mary Washington College, many of these same students begin to destroy, through abuse, the very beauty that drew them here."

The Ecology Club enlisted in the cause, working in various ways to save the grass, including sponsorship of a contest (with President Woodard as one of the judges) soliciting suggestions on how to combat the pig paths. There were a number of sincere and thoughtful responses, including the winning entry from geology professor King Stablein: "Pride in the campus, if it could be instilled, is a good motive. Try and get a campaign going designating MWC as the most beautiful campus on the East Coast."

Many of the suggestions, however, were far less serious, generated not so much by a real attempt to address the problem as by sophomoric humor. Student responses ranged from the fantastic to the simply crude:

- Put in monorails across grassy areas like they have in Seattle and amusement parks.
- Provide super pogo sticks so that people can bound over the grassy areas in a single bound.
- Make chalk drawings of people like when they get killed along the paths to scare people off.
- Have John Travolta giving out free kisses at various points only to those students who stay on the sidewalks.

- Paint pictures of President Woodard . . . all over the sidewalks so that people would prefer to walk there than on the grass.
- Implement the use of a slogan like, "Keep off the grass or I'll kick your ass."

The *Bullet* itself could not forbear periodic snipes at the president and his save-the-grass crusade. In one episode of a serial cartoon called "Alice in Wonderland," Alice is apprehended walking across the grass and brought before the ruler—a prince in the form of a playing-card jack.

> "Bow your head in the presence of the prince!" her captor tells her.
> "Some prince," she retorts. "Why, he's just a knave!"
> To which the prince replies, "Such insolence! Show respect, woman!"
> When told by the captor, "The prisoner is charged with walking on the grass, your princeship," the ruler commands, "A capital crime! Off with her head!"

In an April Fools' Day edition of the *Bullet*, one faux news story was titled "Exploding Signs Keep Students off Grass." The format was based on the old roadside advertisements for Burma-Shave, popular from the 1920s through the early 1960s, in which a rhyming slogan was posted on four successive billboards. "These days," said the *Bullet*, "Ball Circle contains a gloomier version of that lighthearted ad campaign":

> We don't mean
> To predict your doom
> But step past these signs
> And you'll go BOOM.

It is safe to assume that President Woodard did not find such mockeries funny. Protecting the campus lawns was to him a serious matter, as were most things relating to the College.

But there were some, even among those who agreed with his concern, who believed that he may have sometimes carried the effort too far. Marty Wilder, for example, later recalled his astonishment when, in the midst of a conference in the president's office, Woodard rushed to a window to order a hapless offender off the grass, adding, "Do you know how much grass seed cost?"

The price of seed was not really the main issue; it would not have been different had the seed been free. To the VMI graduate, it was a matter of principle—a matter of self-discipline. It was simply beyond his ken why people would make unsightly paths across beautiful grassy areas just to save a few steps when sidewalks were there for the obvious purpose of preventing such destruction.

On the whole, Woodard's crusade—and it was nothing less than that—did lead to greater awareness of the need for protecting the natural beauty of the campus. It was a theme that was to be promoted with continuing enthusiasm far beyond his own tenure, as the appearance of the campus eventually achieved the grandeur projected in Professor Stablein's contest proposal.

But for Woodard, there was a subtle price to be paid. Some faculty members felt it was beneath a president to be apparently preoccupied with such mundane matters when there were more pressing issues that, in their eyes, should have engaged his time—their own salaries, for instance. They did not realize that the man was constitutionally predisposed to addressing the details, as well as the larger dimensions, of an enterprise. It was simply his nature.

The unfortunate downside was that such an approach created in the minds of some a residue of negativism toward the president that would exacerbate the situation if more substantive problems arose. And they did.

COMMUNITY INVOLVEMENT

Throughout the first six decades, Mary Washington College remained generally removed from the affairs of the surrounding community. There were some connections, of course. Students in the education program were involved with the area schools, and periodically there were celebratory occasions to which local residents were invited. But there was no significant interaction on a regular basis with the public at large.

All of which is not to say that town-gown relationships were bad, but rather that they were sporadic and limited. In the College's earliest days, the community took great pride in being the site of one of the state's four normal schools. As time passed, the citizenry continued to appreciate and admire the young women—so well attired in the days before the demise of the dress code—as they strolled the city's streets (at least to the extent that restrictive regulations permitted such outings beyond the gates).

But all in all, the relationship was a distant one—literally, at first, and then as the town grew to surround the College, the distance became more psychological. The institution thus remained both in symbol and in reality the "College on the Hill," largely aloof from meaningful relationships with those who were its neighbors.

That situation changed dramatically with the arrival of Prince Woodard as president. In his inaugural address, he asserted his belief that Mary Washington College, as a state institution, had an obligation to use its resources "for the good of the surrounding community and the larger society" and pledged "to promote, with vigor, its [mission] . . . as a college in partnership with the community."

He wasted little time in implementing that philosophy. Within months after taking office, he secured the board's approval of a policy whereby "the physical facilities of the College may be made available to non-profit, nonsectarian, and non-political groups and organizations which serve the public welfare, provided that the college program is in no way adversely affected and payment is made in accordance with an established schedule of charges."

Not long thereafter, Goolrick Hall was opened to the area YMCA as a venue for Saturday morning classes in activities such as swimming and dancing, with a number of Mary Washington students serving as instructors. The College began the following year to offer a "community service program" that was advertised in the local newspaper as consisting of "fun courses for fitness or enlightenment." Meeting during afternoons and evenings, the non-credit courses were open to the public at a nominal charge of $15 and included instruction, usually by MWC faculty members, on diverse topics such as chess, individual exercise, social genetics, and Chinese history. The activities seemed, in the view of the Fredericksburg paper, to be part of an effort by which "MWC is trying to shed its image and come out of hiding."

Though that prospect was embraced by the community, support from students was lukewarm at best. "Who can argue," the *Bullet* asked, "with the hope of making this college a place less isolated from society and more socially concerned? However, . . . for Mary Washington, [that] can not be permitted to mean the opening up of the college to the community by all sorts of gimmicky attractions such as administrative plans for 'mini' and night courses geared for community adults. . . . To encourage even moderate community participation at the college is likely to quickly steer the college off course and away from the liberal arts tradition." Undeterred by such expressions of concern, the opening of the campus proceeded steadily, and within five years the College's facilities had been made available to outside groups on more than 250 occasions.

One of the most noteworthy examples of the College's expanding mission was its service, beginning in the summer of 1974, as the site of one of the commonwealth's three Governor's Schools for the Gifted. The state-funded program, conducted under the auspices of the Department of Education, was designed to bring together at each of the locations approximately 150 of the most talented high school juniors and seniors from across the state for a month of accelerated study.

The first director of the school at Mary Washington College was Katherine E. Hopper '30, a veteran educator in the Fairfax public school system. At the time she became director, she was a member of the College's Board of Visitors and subsequently became its rector. Operating out of Ball Hall, where all the students were housed, the genial and dynamic Hopper presided over her charges with motherly affection. Always upbeat, she guided them through an intensive program of academic and recreational activities that included, in addition to advanced classroom and laboratory work, presentations by eminent speakers, visits to nearby cultural centers, dormitory entertainment, and spirited athletic contests.

Hopper headed the program through 1977, when she was succeeded by English professor Carlton Lutterbie, who served as director for two years, after which it was directed from 1980 through 1982 by history professor William

B. Crawley Jr. In 1983, the program's final year at MWC, it was headed by Gardner and Alice Woodworth Campbell '80, both alumni of the Governor's School.[18]

As with other of the College's new departures, the Governor's School was viewed askance by some MWC students, mainly because they regarded it as an intrusion on their preserve and because of the favoritism that they felt the program received. A particular bone of contention arose over the perennial issue of grass maintenance. As one *Bullet* article put it, "If the Mary Washington College administration were really concerned with the care and feeding of the grass on the campus, why then would they erect a volleyball court on Ball Circle for the students of the Governor's School? Maybe if the administration had really cared, they would have used the crucial summer months to plant and seed those areas of the campus which are being worn thin. Does it make sense to construct a volleyball court for one faction of the students, and then ask another to stay off the grass?"

Such querulousness notwithstanding, the Governor's School during its ten-year stay at Mary Washington was, by consensus of all involved, an extraordinary success. The high school students who attended received the benefit of an accelerated program that, for most of them, would have been impossible at their own schools. For those from the commonwealth's westerly regions and its far-flung rural areas in particular, the opportunity to visit the political and cultural centers of the Washington area was a new and profound experience. There was also the incalculable worth of bonding with others of extreme talent and ability, especially when in many cases, such students theretofore had always shone as the brightest stars in their own provincial, sometimes dim, firmament.

The College, as well as the students, benefited. A number of Governor's School alumni, impressed by their stay on campus, chose to attend MWC. For faculty who participated, it was an opportunity to secure summer employment that, in some cases during those inflationary times, was of no small importance. Far more significant, however, were the intangible rewards of working for one lively month with a collection of the brightest young minds the commonwealth could produce.

In 1984 the administration decided not to apply to the state for selection as a Governor's School site the following year; it was no longer economically feasible for the College to underwrite the expenses incurred in support of the program. From a fiscal standpoint, the decision was sound, perhaps unavoidable. But to those who had been participants, students and faculty alike, it marked a melancholy end to what had been for a decade one of the College's happiest chapters.

Another opportunity for the College to expand its town-gown relationship came in 1976 with the observation of the nation's bicentennial. A bicentennial committee comprising students, faculty, and administrators and chaired by geography professor Sam Emory developed a diverse program of celebratory events of such appeal that the American Revolution Bicentennial Administration officially designated Mary Washington College as a "Bicentennial Campus."

Among the events scheduled throughout the year were several musical productions featuring early American music and an original play by drama professor Roger Kenvin based on the Revolutionary-era history of the Fredericksburg area. The event that drew perhaps the largest audience was a free public lecture series on various aspects of the American Revolution developed by history professor Roger Bourdon. Consisting of weekly evening lectures by faculty from the History Department and allied disciplines, the series attracted unexpectedly large numbers of townsfolk. So successful was it that the department perpetuated the concept for years thereafter, offering series on such topics as slavery, great discoveries, military commanders, and presidential elections.

While initiatives such as the history lecture series were primarily educational, other outreach efforts were designed more to provide opportunities for entertainment and cultural enrichment. It was a mission that Woodard avidly pursued. "Bringing music and drama to people outside the College," he once said, "was a public service that [MWC] was especially equipped to provide; and I felt it was our responsibility to do so—a public obligation that we should consciously fulfill."

One example of that effort was the Fredericksburg Summer Theater (FST), which used duPont Hall's Klein Theatre as the venue for its theatrical productions. The College's own plays had for years been open to the public, but the FST marked a departure in that it made a deliberate effort to involve not only MWC students and faculty but also local public school students and adults as performers and behind-the-curtains personnel. The high-quality productions provided exceptional entertainment opportunities for area residents while helping to sharpen the performing skills of local thespians.

The expansion of town-gown interaction was nowhere more evident than in the area of music. Both the Fredericksburg Singers in 1974 and the Fredericksburg Chamber Ensemble in 1977 were founded by MWC faculty members as community services. Composed of students, faculty, and local musicians, both thrived with the use of College facilities and with financial support from non-state discretionary funds allocated by the president of the College.

The most popular musical venture was the Mary Washington College–Community Symphony Orchestra. Though it was organized in 1971, before Woodard's arrival, it came into full flower through his support and encouragement. The animating creative force behind it, though—the man who made it work—was James E. Baker.

In 1965 Jim Baker joined the music faculty at Mary Washington, teaching a variety of performance courses, as well as orchestration and conducting. He was also responsible for directing a wind ensemble for a while, but when that group disintegrated during his sabbatical in 1969–70, he returned with his sights set on a more ambitious undertaking: creation of an orchestra that would incorporate performers besides just students. He broached the idea with President Simpson, who gave not only his assent but token funding. "He was very generous," Baker later joked. "He gave me a one-hundred dollar grant—which bought one piece of music, I think."

But it was a beginning. From there, Baker's enthusiasm took over as he wheedled faculty, students, and local acquaintances into joining the enterprise. "I was auditioning by phone," he recalled. "Nobody had to play anything. . . . [I'd just say] 'How long have you played? What sort of stuff have you been playing?' . . . And we advertised rehearsals [only] every other week so it wouldn't be a burden on anybody."

Though he had both academic training and high-school-level experience as a conductor, Baker's success at first was attributable more to his personality than to his technical expertise. An extrovert of consistently sunny disposition, he was a notorious teller of jokes—some ribald, some silly, and some actually funny. He was the very antithesis of the image of the temperamental artist; his style of direction, according to one veteran member of the orchestra, fell "somewhere between relaxed and more relaxed." The mellow maestro was he.

The laid-back approach was perfect for the task of recruiting performers and then melding the disparate crew—old and young, academics and townsfolk, seasoned and novice, talented and not-so—into a harmonious ensemble. But his easygoing appearance was deceptive, for no one worked harder than he, not just at preparing scores and directing rehearsals (which soon became weekly) but in handling the menial tasks that orchestra productions required. Without a manager to assist him, Baker himself assumed the mundane duties of ordering supplies, writing and printing programs, mailing materials, and even arranging chairs and stands in preparation for rehearsals.

The orchestra started modestly, with only thirty-five performers the first year, but within five years the number had doubled. The musicians included College personnel, area residents, and local high school students, as well as MWC students, who received one credit-hour for a semester's participation. As the orchestra grew in size, so too did it expand its repertoire, attempting pieces that offered increasing challenges. Audiences grew as well, forcing performance venues to move from Klein Theatre to Lee Hall Ballroom to Dodd Auditorium.

At the same time as the College–Community Orchestra was developing, the College embarked on an allied musical venture with the creation in 1976 of the Chatham Orchestra Institute, a two-week on-campus summer program for aspiring young musicians from ages twelve to nineteen. The goal was to increase the students' knowledge and skills in the historical, theoretical, and performance aspects of orchestral music. The busy schedule included sectional rehearsals, special interest sessions, performance evaluation, and full orchestral performances—the last being open to the public.

The institute thus served the dual purpose of educating its students and of providing entertainment for the community. It also had the ancillary, and not negligible, benefit of introducing talented young musicians to the MWC campus in the hope that the experience would entice them to apply for admission—as a few did each year. (One faculty member described it as the Music Department's "farm team.") "It helped," said Jim Baker, "when you have a department with low enrollment and you have a decline [as was true at MWC in the mid-1970s], those three or four students make a big difference." It was not only a quantitative improvement but a qualitative one too, as those students were sometimes among the department's most talented majors.

Alas, the institute did not last. The reason for its demise had little to do with the merit of the program itself, but rather with extraneous factors over which the College had no control. As Baker explained it, the tendency toward additional requirements in the high schools meant that more students had to go to summer school to take academic courses in order to have time for scheduling music courses during the regular year; ergo they had no time for summer experiences such as the Chatham Institute. After a ten-year run, it folded in 1986.

The College–Community Orchestra meanwhile thrived. A milestone occurred in 1976 when Dominion Bank, at the instigation of its president, Charles "Pete" Hearn, provided the funds to underwrite an additional performance besides the orchestra's usual annual complement of three. Thus was born the Pops Concert. From the first, community response was overwhelming, and the Pops became one of the entertainment highlights of the year for the Fredericksburg area, consistently drawing standing-room-only crowds to

James Baker conducting the College–Community Orchestra

Dodd Auditorium. Usually held in early December, the concert came to be regarded as the unofficial kickoff of the holiday season. It was eagerly awaited by local children (and, indeed, their parents as well), who never knew what ingenious delights the program might include, thanks to the fertile and whimsical imagination of maestro Baker. What they could count on was a rousing rendition of "Stars and Stripes Forever" at the end, followed by an encore of traditional Christmas carols guaranteed to put the crowd in a festive spirit.

The College–Community Symphony Orchestra was perhaps the most successful of all Prince Woodard's efforts toward building town-gown amity. Certainly it was the most fun.

By fortuitous circumstances, Mary Washington College possessed two unusual assets that accorded well with Woodard's twin commitment to public outreach and to historic preservation. In fact, MWC was unique among Virginia's institutions of higher education in having statutory responsibility for administering two of the state's historic properties: Belmont—the Gari Melchers Memorial Gallery (as it was then known)—and the James Monroe Museum and Memorial Library.

The situation clearly had the potential to significantly enhance the College's academic program in historic preservation, presenting valuable opportunities for research, internships, and hands-on museum experience. Unfortunately, both sites had problems that limited the realization of that potential and in the process caused (in varying degrees) anguish for Woodard himself.

Belmont had been the home, in his later life, of the artist Gari Melchers. Born Julius Garibaldi Melchers in Detroit in 1860, he was named by his German-born artist father for the Italian patriot Giuseppe Garibaldi. The multinational circumstances relating to his birth proved a harbinger of a peripatetic career.

Trained in art schools in Düsseldorf and Paris, Melchers became the leading American practitioner of naturalism, the branch of realism highly popular in late-nineteenth-century Europe. The apogee of his public acclaim came in 1889 when he and John Singer Sargent became the first two American painters to be awarded the grand prize at the Paris Universal Exposition.

During the later years of the century, Melchers traveled periodically to the United States but spent most of his time in Holland and also maintained a studio in Paris. His numerous depictions of Dutch peasant life, including two of his best-known works, *The Sermon* and *The Choirmaster*, exhibited such understanding of the character of that region that critics often mistook him for a native Dutchman.

When he visited the United States, he devoted most of his efforts to portrait painting—and did so with great financial (and, to a lesser degree, critical) success. Commissions from families like the Vanderbilts, Mellons, and Roosevelts earned him a lucrative income. Though later in his career he turned more to impressionism—earning not unfavorable comparisons to the better-known Mary Cassatt—it was always mainly portraiture that paid his bills.

In an effort to find respite from the exertions of his increasingly public career, Melchers and his wife, Corinne, in 1916 purchased the eighteenth-century Virginia estate known as Belmont, perched on a bluff overlooking the Rappahannock, just across the river from Fredericksburg. According to local lore, shortly after his arrival, Melchers, dressed in overalls, ambled into a nearby country store, where he was greeted by two local residents who inquired about his occupation. "I paint," Melchers replied. To which the locals shook their heads, and one of them somberly informed the newcomer, "Well, Mister, you won't get much work 'round here, 'cause we jist whitewash."

They, and the community at large, were soon to learn that Melchers was a painter of quite a different kind, one whose fame would frequently attract to Belmont luminaries from the worlds of art, literature, and finance, as well as political notables including Vice President Calvin Coolidge and former British prime minister David Lloyd George. They also came to know him because, living there during the last sixteen years of his life, Melchers painted many local scenes and often used local folks as his models.

Melchers died of a heart attack in 1932 at the age of seventy-two. Thereafter Corinne resumed on a limited basis the art career that she had put aside during their marriage. She also took an active role in charitable, artistic, and preservation efforts in the commonwealth, serving on the Virginia Art Commission and as a trustee of the Virginia Museum of Fine Arts, of which she was a founder.

Through these and similar activities during her twenty-three years of widowhood, Corinne Melchers's main focus was on perpetuating the legacy of her husband, whose reputation was threatening to slide into obscurity. With the assistance of her friend Thomas C. Colt, curator (and later director) of the Virginia Museum of Fine Arts (VMFA), she conceived the idea of a memorial based at Belmont under the trusteeship of the museum. In pursuit of that goal, in 1942 she deeded to the commonwealth the Belmont estate and its twenty-three-room mansion; an endowment of $115,000 for its maintenance; fifty of her husband's paintings, including *The Last Supper*, to be part of a permanent collection; and the authorization to sell the remainder of his works as necessary to supplement the original endowment. The General Assembly officially accepted the generous bequest and designated the Virginia Museum of Fine Arts to administer it.

By the time of Corinne Melchers's death in 1955, Tom Colt had been replaced as museum director by Leslie Cheek. The VMFA soon thereafter decided that it was impractical for the museum to administer the memorial from so far a distance as Richmond—at which point Mary Washington College agreed initially to oversee the shrine on a trial basis from November 1, 1957, to June 30, 1960. When that arrangement proved satisfactory to all parties, the General Assembly enacted legislation transferring the estate and the endowment to the University of Virginia to be administered by Mary Washington College as a memorial and art center. (When in 1972 MWC separated from U.Va., the legislation effecting the split also transferred the Belmont property and bequest to the control of the Mary Washington Board of Visitors.)

During the 1960s, the College made little use of Belmont, aside from periodic openings for Garden Week or for rare special events. Also, President Simpson permitted Mary Washington professors and their students to use the facility from time to time for research purposes and to organize occasional exhibitions. The basic reason for lack of activity at Belmont was financial: the College simply did not have sufficient resources to devote to the site—nor, in fact, was there much interest in doing so.

Meanwhile criticism developed concerning the College's stewardship of Belmont. Some questioned its collection management, especially its lending policy, while others criticized the property's uses (or lack thereof). The latter concern became a specific point of contention when in 1974 the Simpsons moved into Belmont as their retirement home (paying $150 per month rent). As one observer commented, "This was the last straw from many in the community . . . who demanded that the terms of the deed of gift be put into effect."

The Mary Washington Board of Visitors, only two years launched into the responsibilities of governing the College, was shaken by the unanticipated tumult over Belmont. The rector, Lewis Walker, was especially perturbed by the aspersions being cast on his old friend Grellet Simpson. "Most certainly," Walker said, "I did not anticipate the type of reaction that occurred as a result of Dr. Simpson's occupancy of [Belmont], and I most sincerely regret that the reaction at times appeared vindictive." But he saw a silver lining: "If, however, it did awaken the people of Fredericksburg to a potential use of the property, it may have served a useful purpose."

Caught in the conundrum, the board seemed uncertain as to which direction it should take regarding Belmont. Should it divest itself of the property (and the responsibility), or should it move toward greater use of the asset? Eventually—the Simpsons having moved out in the summer of 1974—the board chose the second alternative. Meeting in November, it voted to open the facility to the public on a regular, if limited, basis as soon as necessary repairs could be made. Though public criticism doubtless had some impact on the decision, that was not the sole factor, according to President Woodard, who cited his own personal interest in the venture. "It didn't result from pressure," he said.

Such an approach was consistent with Woodard's goals for the College. Though lacking Simpson's connoisseurship, Woodard had an affinity for history that nonetheless gave him an appreciation for Belmont's importance. Moreover, his entrepreneurial spirit (which Simpson lacked) enabled Woodard to foresee the property's potential as a key element in the historic preservation program that he envisioned at MWC.

And so, with Woodard's enthusiastic endorsement, Belmont began to

RON BLUNT

Belmont

emerge as a significant attraction. An important step in its evolution was the hiring of Richard S. Reid as the site's director in June 1975. Though his previous professional career had been spent mainly in the CIA, he was at the time of his hiring the assistant curator of the National Rifle Association Firearms Museum, and his formal education included training in drawing and design; he was also an amateur painter.

Reid approached his job zealously, and within a few months Belmont was ready for opening to the public. The long-anticipated event took place on October 19, 1975, when an overflow crowd of three hundred (admission price: seventy-five cents for adults, fifty cents for children) swarmed the home and studio, creating an unexpected traffic jam within the grounds. Opening remarks were delivered by Woodard and by Board of Visitors member Ralph M. Whitticar III of Fredericksburg, whose wife made the opening official by cutting a ribbon across the porch of the main house.

From that point onward, Belmont developed steadily, aided by an appraisal of the collection in 1976 by Sotheby Parke Bernet of New York (over $1.3 million) and the initiation of a conservation program. In 1977 the first holiday open house was held at Christmastime. By the end of the decade, annual attendance was approaching four thousand, and the authorized sale of various works had generated over $200,000 for the endowment. An education program had been developed including special exhibitions, a film series, lectures and demonstrations by Virginia artists, and tours designed for school groups. From the College's perspective, the greatest benefit was the internship opportunities that permitted students in art and preservation to gain practical experience preparing and hanging exhibits and cataloging the collection.

In the process, Corinne Melchers's dream of perpetuating her husband's legacy began to be fulfilled. Through Belmont, Gari Melchers's artistic reputation, which in the decades since his death had been far greater in Europe than in America, was once again brought to prominence in his native land.

Quarrels over Belmont, unseemly though they may have been, were mild compared to the disputes in which the College became embroiled over the operation of its other state-mandated property, the James Monroe Law Office–Museum and Memorial Library.[19]

The site was the brainchild of Laurence Gouverneur Hoes, a great-grandson of President James Monroe. Appalled at the dilapidated condition of what he claimed was Monroe's law office on Charles Street, Hoes, together with his mother, founded the Museum and Memorial Library in 1928. From that point onward for the rest of his life, particularly after retiring in 1950 from his Washington career in banking and finance, Hoes devoted himself to collecting books, furniture, documents, and other memorabilia of his illustrious kinsman for deposit in the memorial—a task at which he had considerable success.

There could be no doubt about one thing: Hoes was wholly dedicated to his Monroe mission. On one occasion in the 1960s when racial violence was wracking Washington and tensions ran high in Fredericksburg, Hoes, fearing damage to his beloved museum and library, spent a night camped on the floor of the place—revolver, hammer, and crowbar at the ready. On another occasion, in 1963, an entourage from the Soviet embassy unexpectedly stopped to visit the museum. Hoes proceeded to hand the startled consul a copy of the Monroe Doctrine, informing him that the principles contained therein were "very much alive," to which the consul retorted, "The document is completely dead." The contretemps, occurring so soon after the Cuban missile crisis, did little for diplomacy, but in the eyes of some Americans, it elevated Hoes to the status of a great patriot.

Long before his death in 1978, Hoes established the James Monroe Memorial Foundation and turned the property over to that body. In 1964 the property was deeded to the Commonwealth of Virginia to be managed by a Board of Regents appointed by the governor, with half coming from nominees of the foundation, half from nominees of the University of Virginia (of which Mary Washington was then a part). In addition, there were four ex officio members: the rector and president of the university, and the president and secretary of the foundation, who was also designated as secretary of the regents.

The statute accepting the bequest further stipulated that the Board of Visitors of the university had the right of approval of actions taken by the Board of Regents. When Mary Washington separated from the university in 1972, the responsibility for administering the shrine was transferred to the nascent MWC Board of Visitors.

It was, at best, a cumbersome structure of governance for a state-owned property, inasmuch as half of the regents came from the foundation, a private organization autonomous from the commonwealth. Still, such an arrangement might have worked, but only if both blocs had amiable members capable of compromising to achieve consensus. It turned out that nothing could have been further from the reality of it, as acrimony, not harmony, reigned.

From the beginning, the foundation opposed the transfer of authority to Mary Washington College. In a letter to Governor Linwood Holton, the incumbent at the time of the transfer, the chairman of the foundation's executive committee haughtily complained that "a girls' college is not qualified or suited to sponsor and promote the accomplishments and memory of the fifth President of the United States," adding that Mary Washington College and the museum had "nothing in common except for being located in Fredericksburg."

Given such an unpropitious start, it was not surprising that the setup never worked smoothly. As time passed, the cumulative effect of periodic flare-ups created within the Board of Regents a pervasive and poisonous atmosphere of distrust and discord between the representatives of the foundation and those of the College.

One of the earliest and most persistent disputes involved the role of the secretary of the Board of Regents. According to the foundation, that individual was to be the chief administrator of the museum's day-to-day operations, at an annual salary of $10,000. College officials claimed that such an arrangement was not sufficient to oversee the enterprise and proceeded to reduce the secretary's compensation to $50 per year, based on $25 per meeting of the Board of Regents. To run the museum on a daily basis, President Woodard hired Paulette S. Watson as its executive director, a move that was denounced by foundation president Helen Marie Taylor as an end run by Woodard, without the foundation's knowledge, in an attempt to secure the College's control.

While the issue of the secretary's position simmered, other disputes, ranging from the petty to the substantive, cropped up on a more or less regular basis over the years. One of the more heated came in early 1981 when College officials accused the foundation's representatives, led by its president, of removing two files allegedly containing (according to Taylor) foundation documents from the site without authorization.

That episode led to a flash point several months later at the June meeting of the Board of Regents. Taking advantage of the absence of two of the College's representatives—which gave the foundation a nine-to-seven majority—the regents voted to suspend the agenda, elect their own nominees as officers of the board (replacing the College's incumbents), and revise the bylaws to place final authority in the hands of the foundation's president, Helen Marie Taylor. For good measure, they also voted to abolish the position of executive director (Paulette Watson's job) and to vest those responsibilities in the foundation's secretary.

At its meeting the following month, the Mary Washington Board of Visitors responded by voting to declare the regents' actions null and void, thereby abrogating the new bylaws and removing the foundation-backed slate of officers. The action also restored Paulette Watson to her position as director, because, as Woodard noted, the regents had no power to fire a state employee anyway. Anticipating (correctly) that the affair might end up in court, the MWC board further authorized Woodard to seek legal counsel and to take "such action as deemed necessary to assert the College's statutory responsibility" for running the state-owned facility.

By this time, some observers had come to view the imbroglio as essentially a personal power struggle between Prince Woodard and Helen Marie Taylor. Both combatants denied it, of course. Such a claim was "just not true," said Woodard. "My only role has been and will continue to be that Mary Washington College carry out the responsibilities assigned to it by statute."

Taylor expressed similar purity of motive, asserting that she was merely trying to uphold the original intent of the bequest to the state from Hoes, who had been her friend. In that light, she viewed herself as more sinned against than sinning—and portrayed Woodard as the culprit. "He kicked us out," she said. "The poor old [MWC] Board of Visitors has been dragged into this by Woodard without knowing anything about it."

Such protestations of righteousness on both sides notwithstanding, it was true that the personalities involved did nothing to defuse the situation. Taylor was a wealthy conservative Republican from Orange County, Virginia, wife of the tobacco magnate Jacquelin Taylor. Bright, articulate, and volatile, she had a reputation for ardent—her opponents would say strident—support of causes in which she believed. Her combination of intellectual, financial, and political qualifications led President Ronald Reagan to appoint her as a member of the U.S. delegation to the United Nations in the mid-1980s.

Woodard shared many of the same characteristics (though not the wealth). In the heat of verbal battle, he might have been more restrained than she, but he was surely no less determined in defending what he deemed right. It was not without cause that an adjective frequently applied to him was "stubborn."

As the dispute moved ineluctably toward litigation, Taylor sought intervention by Republican governor John N. Dalton, requesting that the College be removed altogether from governance of the museum and that the Board of Regents be replaced by a nine-member body, all of whom would be nominated by the foundation. When that ploy failed, the affair moved in December 1981 to the Fredericksburg Circuit Court, presided over by Judge Richard H. C. Taylor of Hanover County, who was appointed in place of local judges who recused themselves.

In his ruling, Judge Taylor squarely upheld the contention of the College, cogently argued by Fredericksburg attorney Russell H. Roberts, that paramount authority for administering the museum resided in the MWC Board of Visitors. "It appears to me," Taylor announced from the bench, "that the ultimate authority . . . is in the Commonwealth acting through the College, and that gives the College the right of approval and veto" over actions of the Board of Regents (and hence the foundation).

The foundation appealed the decision to the state supreme court, but that body upheld the original verdict. Shortly thereafter the Mary Washington Board of Visitors cemented College control by passing a resolution requiring the Board of Regents to report all actions directly to the MWC Board of Visitors for approval. Thus did the protracted battle end in complete victory for the College's position and personal vindication for Woodard. Reaching that result, however, involved an investment of physical and emotional capital that Woodard, as it turned out, did not have to spare.

A far less controversial element of Mary Washington's expanded community involvement under President Woodard grew out of the historic preservation program. Shortly after the academic major in preservation had been approved, the College (with the instrumental support of the president) submitted a request to the State Council of Higher Education for a grant from the Governor's Fund for Excellence to be used over a two-year period for developing the program. (The purpose of the fund, according to its guidelines, was to "support activities which are demonstrably excellent, have the potential to become so in the immediate future or offer a unique or outstanding service to the Commonwealth.")

The successful application provided $33,200 for establishing the MWC Center for Historic Preservation, which began operation in 1980. The center had two broad purposes: to augment the academic program by developing the College's resources in historic preservation and to promote and assist preservation efforts in the local community and beyond.

The center began as a modest operation with a small staff, minimal financial resources, and cramped quarters. It was located in a small frame building (later named Cornell House) situated just off Sunken Road at the back gate of College Drive—a structure that in its previous inglorious incarnations had been variously a snack shop and a laundromat.

The Board of Visitors appointed as director of the center William B. Crawley Jr., who took the job in addition to his role as chair of the Department of

History and American Studies. Philip D. Spiess II was named associate director for the center's programs; having worked for the previous six years as research coordinator at the National Trust for Historic Preservation, Spiess was also responsible initially for teaching the core courses in the major. Richard Palmieri, besides his full-time work in the Department of Geography, was named curator of furniture and contributed considerable expertise on antiques as well as assistance in the center's administration. Holding the cadre together was the center's übersecretary, Louise Holz, an erudite and gracious lady whose consummate professional skills were matched by her personal charm. It was her expertise and energy that made the place hum, her good humor that made it happy.

Whatever the center may have lacked in tangible resources, it made up for in the ambition and enthusiasm of its staff. While simultaneously engaged in supporting the academic program, the center devoted much effort toward public outreach, a goal it pursued mainly by sponsoring conferences and lecture series. Within months of its founding, it offered a conference, "Old Dominions Regained: Town and County Preservation in Virginia," in July 1980 with the assistance of a grant from the Virginia Foundation for the Humanities and Public Policy.

The conference began with a candlelight wine-and-cheese reception at Belmont and ended with dinner on the lawn at Brompton. In between, the programs included presentations by notable preservationists and tours of local historic sites. The event attracted a substantial crowd, and the format—a mixture of social and academic elements—proved so popular that it served as a template for a number of annual conferences to follow, including "The Old House: Keeping It in Style" (1981) and "Furniture with a Southern Accent" (1982).

In addition to the yearly summer conferences, the center during its early years offered periodic workshops such as "To Make Old Houses Homes" (1981) and "Old Gardens Revised: Planting the Past Anew" (1982), sometimes in cooperation with other organizations such as, in the latter case, the Kenmore Association and the Garden Club of Virginia. It also sponsored a highly popular noncredit course every year on antique American furniture, taught by the endlessly entertaining Dick Palmieri.

Of all the public programs offered by the center in this period, the one that proved to have the greatest, and certainly the most lasting, appeal was called "Deck the Halls: Christmas with All the Trimmings," a one-day workshop led by the local floral designer Jan Williams, featuring instruction in creating historic holiday decorations. First offered in December 1981, the event was so popular that it was offered annually for decades thereafter, becoming, along with the College–Community Orchestra's pops concert, one of the most eagerly awaited traditions of the Fredericksburg Christmas season.

Overall, the Center for Historic Preservation was to become a key element in the College's burgeoning program in preservation. Combining both public outreach and concern for history, it was doubtless one of Prince Woodard's proudest achievements—and a fitting legacy both to his stewardship of the institution and to his love of the commonwealth.

STUDENT LIFE

Aside from the notable exception of the infamous "blood-throwing" protest against the CIA early in Prince Woodard's administration, campus activism at Mary Washington declined sharply in the 1970s. Compared to the frenetic upheavals of the later Simpson years, it was generally a tranquil time. And when student protests did occur, their foci were usually parochial. It was a trend that the *Bullet* recognized and perceptively diagnosed at the start of the 1976–77 session. "The issues that today's college journalists deal with," lamented an editorial,

> seem quite trivial when compared to the issues which concerned campus reporters six years ago. In 1970, students seemed much more involved with national affairs than we are. They held moratoriums for the soldiers in Vietnam, rallied against the Nixon administration's policies, and sat-in for Civil Rights. These students became disillusioned, however, when they realized that 10,000 youths marching on Washington did not change the government. . . . Whether due to disillusionment or the dying of a fad, the campus scene has become much quieter. The exuberance that students once showed when protesting or supporting national affairs has been replaced by a sincere concern for personal interests.

Along with the changes in behavior came changes in dress styles. Out were the dowdy duds of protest; in were the colorful threads of preppiness. A 1977 *Bullet* article titled "How to Be a Prep" noted that "the classic look" that was sweeping the country was nowhere more evident than at Mary Washington and proceeded to offer the following advice:

> If your hippie-freak days are over and insecurity has set in, now is the time to be like everybody else! Throw out your grubbies and head for Bloomie's, Talbot's, and Pappagallo's with the following list:
>
> 1. Tortoise shell headbands and combs
> 2. Hair ribbons (for your saucy ponytail)
> 3. Gold hoop earrings and diamond studs (gold-plated doesn't count)
> 4. Neck scarves (preferably silk or designer)
> 5. Gold chain necklaces (disregard anything under fourteen carats or eighteen inches; must be looped three times)
> 6. Grosgrain watchbands and belts (must have three stripes and an alligator)
> 7. Alligator shirts—especially preppie pink

Four preppies on the Mason portico, mid-1980s

8. Oxford shirts—light blue with monogrammed cuffs or collars
9. Rugby shirts (at least four with wide stripes)
10. Sweaters (monogrammed or circle design with collar tucked in)
11. Khaki skirts and pants (big butts need not apply!)
12. Wrap-around skirts (a must, especially if they are reversible or quilted)
13. Gym shorts (better still with UVa or William and Mary monograms)
14. Deck shoes—a must (throw out those extremely ratty and passé earth shoes)
15. Espadrilles (obviously)
16. Bermuda shorts and bags.

If you have five out of sixteen fashion musts, you are an amateur. Ten out of sixteen would give you a strong chance of landing a Sigma Nu wonder man. All sixteen? Congratulations! You are a genuine stereotype. "Polly Prep" would be proud of you!

So pandemic was the phenomenon that a popular book by Lisa "Bunny" Birnbach titled *The Official Preppy Handbook* (1981) was facetiously reviewed at some length in the *Bullet*. The book, said the paper, revealed everything about preppy behavior, including the proper way to hold a preppy wedding. "One MWC co-ed," it noted, "upon seeing this section, decided to cancel her reception at the Norfolk Elks Club in favor of a pink-and-white striped tent in her back yard." The reviewer, writing under the appropriate pseudonym of Morgan "Trip" Taylor III, concluded, "*The Preppy Handbook* is a definite must for all who often road-trip to UVa or Hampden-Sydney, or for those who aspire to do so."

Nothing was more emblematic of the preppy look than the Lacoste alligator, which prompted a 1978 *Bullet* article on the ubiquitous reptile. "Some French guy," it reported,

> who obviously does not know beans about the Everglades, . . . began producing inch replicas of alligators. Grey and olive being so boring, he made the little fellows royal blue, Kelly green, red, and other colors that would make Binney and Smith wish they had never marketed an assortment of 108 Crayola crayons. . . . Those little creatures were everywhere: on socks, on sweaters, on belts (they thrive on Grosgrain). . . . As an uninformed college student, I thought alligators belonged in swamps, not strategically placed on my roommates' shirts. (How did the Frenchman know that "Hey, Babe, I really like that alligator" would become a standard line at a fraternity party?)

But whether the prevailing mood on campus was one of protest or of preppiness, it was still true that throughout the 1970s, Mary Washington was largely a "suitcase college," as evidenced by the vacated parking lots when Friday evenings rolled around. In addition to road trips to other colleges for weekend dates, many students within easy driving distance went home to be with family and friends. Then there was the allure of Georgetown—notably Clyde's, and its Redskins-friendly atmosphere. With the rising popularity of disco music in the late seventies, many were also drawn to the fashionable bars of northern Virginia, such as Bachelors II and The Library.

Part of the weekly exodus was simply the result of inertia born of tradition. As one student put it, "The bad thing about everyone saying this is a suitcase college is that everyone . . . then starts acting like it is. Because they believe it—because it's the 'in' thing to say 'MWC is dead and let's get out'—they start living out the suitcase college syndrome." But, she added, "There are fun times here," and another agreed: "If you have friends here, you can make something to do—you can cause your own trouble."

A good example of just such an effort was a lark engineered in early 1977 by Moira McKeough involving *Glamour* magazine. As she recounted the situation to the *Bullet*, she was leafing through the magazine and was struck by how few of the women pictured were redheads. Whereupon she complained to the magazine, suggesting at the same time that MWC had an unusually large number of redheads (she among them) whose photographs in the publication would help to remediate that slight. In reply, the magazine pronounced it "a great idea" and arranged to photograph a large group of them that included, according to the *Bullet*, some whose tresses were "suspicious-looking," as well as Moira herself, "blushing to a shade that only redheads can."

With more students remaining on campus, life in the dormitories became a matter of increasing concern—especially the issue of visitation rules. Throughout the Woodard presidency, in fact, no student issue was more persistent; none was pursued more vigorously; nor, in the short run, was any less successful.

Of course, by the early seventies, visitation regulations had already changed starkly with the demise of the in loco parentis philosophy. And it was evident that the trend toward greater flexibility was likely to continue. Even Grellet Simpson, himself no fan of such a movement, admitted shortly before leaving the presidency that "colleges are going to have to face the fact that dormitories are like hotels. These are voting citizens now. If they rent a room, isn't it their room?" The answer was: not exactly—at least not at Mary Washington, where it was still impermissible, at the time Woodard arrived, for a student to have a guest overnight in his or her room.

Students who preferred unrestricted, twenty-four-hour visitation—and polls showed it was the majority—took comfort in their interpretation of some of President Woodard's early references to regulations in general. They were particularly encouraged by his comment to the alumni magazine that he thought the nationwide trend toward relaxing campus rules was "generally speaking . . . highly desirable because we have come into our colleges very mature young people, much more so than 20 or 30 years ago. Our society has become more sophisticated. Young people know and see many things, through television, for example, and travel. Students are much more worldly in their views than they were. Therefore, I think it makes sense that the rules and regulations under which they operate reflect this." Events in coming years would prove, however, that the students' optimistic interpretation of those words—insofar as visitation was concerned, at any rate—was not only premature but incorrect.

Actually, even if the president had favored open visitation personally (which he did not), he would have been otherwise constrained by the laws of the commonwealth, as then interpreted. There was, for example, the so-called Bateman Resolution, passed by the General Assembly during the 1971 high tide of student radicalism, which proclaimed: "Any policy which permits the visitation of students of the opposite sex in college dormitory bedrooms without proper regulations, control and supervision . . . is contrary to the public policy of the Commonwealth." The same idea was implicit in the state's criminal code forbidding cohabitation between unmarried persons. That provision, upheld in the 1973 case of *Everett v. Commonwealth*, was specifically designed to prohibit "conduct, which by its openness and notoriety, tends to affront the public conscience and debase the community morality."

Legal and moral considerations aside, there was a practical issue that Woodard had to take into account: given that state funding was critical, he was disinclined to raise the hackles of legislators who, for the most part, held conservative views on such matters. Especially at a time when College resources were meager, it was not prudent to rankle Richmond. Accordingly, when students petitioned the Board of Visitors in the spring of 1975 for all-night visitation, their plea was rejected.

The board did, however, grant some concessions, including the extension of visitation in upperclass dorms until 2:00 a.m. on Friday and Saturday nights and until midnight Sunday through Thursday; freshmen were permitted to have the same Friday and Saturday hours, but the midnight deadline only on Sundays.

At the same meeting, the board took the pathbreaking step of converting Westmoreland Hall to a coed dorm, effective beginning in fall 1975. With the male enrollment by then having surpassed the forty-seven-resident capacity of Madison Hall, it was decided to house the overflow of twenty men on the first floor of Westmoreland, with females occupying the top two floors.

The experiment in what was termed "sandwich-style" living seemed to work fine from the beginning, applauded by female and male students alike. Despite "a couple of slightly embarrassing incidents," said one female resident, the arrangement was useful because it helped integrate the males into campus life. It was "beneficial to all concerned," she explained, because it "brought students together in a natural setting, . . . so you run into each other constantly, and you get to know the guys as friends, not just as potential dates." Males liked it, too. As one of them put it, "It's a much better situation than being in an all-male dorm," where behavior tended to be "a little off-center, rowdy. Here, though, behavior is a lot more balanced, more natural, like living at home."

The experiment proved permanent, and coed dorms were at Mary Washington to stay. Two years later the first freshman coed dorm was established when six new male students were housed with freshman females in Willard. Once again, the concept appeared to work, according to a *Bullet* article titled "It's Nice to Have a Man in the House." The women responded favorably, as did the men, who, according to the article, "don't seem to lack anything—least of all ladies." That scenario was confirmed by one of the males, who several weeks into the semester commented, "The thing I like best about living with girls is they give you a lot of attention. . . . They'll do our laundry for us. I haven't done any laundry since I got here." The accommodating females had apparently not yet fully subscribed to the tenets of feminism. (But they were only freshmen.)

Meanwhile students turned up the volume of their demands for increased visitation privileges—or "rights," as they viewed them. They preferred to keep the discussion in the abstract, on matters of principle, and thus routinely denied that the expansion of opportunities for sexual encounters had anything to do with it. But that was a disingenuous claim that flew in the face of much of their own rhetoric and the temper of the times—to say nothing of common sense. It was, after all, a halcyon time for libertines, an era in which, because of antibiotics, the older venereal diseases (syphilis, gonorrhea) were becoming less fearsome, and the newer ones (herpes, AIDS) were just arriving. Moreover, the advent of the pill had made pregnancy less risky, and if prophylactic methods failed, abortion was now a legal, if drastic, option. As for the traditional restraints of religion and morality, there was every indication that those inhibiting influences were losing their potency.

Whatever their motivations, be they pure or prurient, students eagerly pressed for greater visitation opportunities. The most notable event in their crusade came in early November 1975 when a protest was held on Ball Circle to coincide with a Board of Visitors luncheon just across Campus Drive in Lee Hall. "It was shades of the sixties," reported the *Free Lance–Star*, with "350 chanting, sign-sprouting college students flocking together for a warm-weather demonstration against administration policies."

As protests went, it was a rather tame affair; students attempted to make their point without being unduly provocative, keeping a discreet distance from the board luncheon. The highlights were speeches by Student Association president Gwen Phillips and by Alan Schwalbe and David Kitterman, two of the more outspoken male advocates. Then there was the requisite chanting. As board members departed Lee Hall, they were serenaded with "Twenty-three for MWC, twenty-three for MWC!" (a reference to the extended hours being sought) and "We want an explanation, we want an explanation!" Such activities, reported the *Bullet*, "were interspersed with music, which added a pleasant touch to the afternoon."

The board members beheld the demonstration with equanimity if not enthusiasm. As one of them, Gwendolyn Amory Cumming '52, dryly noted, "Friday was a very beautiful day for a rally. However, the timing was a little bad; we had just finished eating our lunch." Another, Leah Fleet Waller '44, commented that the event "was a show of enthusiasm and it was boisterous. Yet it was not objectionable."

Neither was it efficacious. The board refused to alter its policy and, if anything, seemed to become more adamant, as was evident in a *Bullet* interview with Rector Lewis Walker the following spring. Having rejected the principle of in loco parentis—"We don't look at ourselves as being your parents by any manner or means"—Walker was drawn into the following discussion when asked if he favored extended visitation:

WALKER: Well, that's not within the rules of the college, so I would not be in favor of it.
BULLET: Would you favor changing the rules?
WALKER: I don't see any reason to change them.
BULLET: So you would not favor the creation of an experimental dorm [one plan proposed by SA] . . . just to see if it would work out?
WALKER: I don't think you need an experimental dormitory. . . .
BULLET: Could I ask you why you personally are not in favor of 23-hour visitation?
WALKER: You can ask, but I won't necessarily give you an answer. . . .

But students pushed the matter, as students will. In September 1978, the *Bullet* took the unusual step of directly approaching members of the board individually to solicit their opinions on the issue—with somewhat surprising results. Most categorically defended the status quo, along the lines of Katherine Hopper '30, who was by then rector. "We have a policy," she commented, "and I guess there's nothing more to say." Irene Lundy Brown '39, a member of the original board, was more expansive in expressing opposition. "I guess it's just the way I was reared," she said. "Anything you want to do, you can get done in the length of time already provided. The girls know the rules when they apply to come here, and I think those rules are sufficient."

But two visitors seemed to offer a glint of hope for change. Warner Dalhouse of Roanoke, whose own daughter was attending the College at the time, pronounced himself "very open-minded on the issue" and commented that "a valid poll of the students that shows strong support for 23-hour visitation would be a hard position for the Board to oppose." General John Castles concurred, calling the student poll "an excellent idea" and suggesting that "perhaps [the] poll should survey the parents as well."

Just such a student poll was, in fact, under way, sponsored by the "Student Lobby Research Committee." It was similar to an SA poll three years earlier on the same topic, and it reached the same unsurprising conclusion: a huge majority of respondents (more than 80 percent) favored having the option of living in a dorm with open visitation. The poll also posed questions concerning specific ramifications of such a policy, eliciting the following responses:

- 94 percent were willing to tolerate increased security precautions.
- 84 percent accepted the possibility of "sharing bathrooms with the opposite sex."
- 89 percent acknowledged that it might entail "occasionally making other sleeping arrangements."

Written comments accompanying the returned questionnaires revealed a range of opinions, pro and con. Some who were in favor of open visitation put it in practical terms: "It would legitimize a condition that already exists; then we could approach the problems directly and deal with them with our eyes open." Such problems included, in the words of another student, scenarios such as this: "If your friend comes for the weekend, he wouldn't have the hassle with the expense and inconvenience of finding a motel. Also, if he were too drunk after a party, it would be better than having him drive home under the influence."

Then there were those who believed the change was necessary to, as one said, "put this school into the twentieth century: this damn place is so protective, it's ridiculous. What are these poor, poor southern belles going to do when they're on their own and have their own apartments. There will be nobody to come down at 2:00 to say, 'Time's up, honey, now you'll have to leave.'"

But though most students supported the liberalization, all did not. Some of those who did not foresaw the rise of practical problems. As one of them put it, "It would result in all-night parties, roommate fights, decreased studying, increased violence, destruction of property, [and] loss of privacy." Others focused, sometimes quite colorfully, on the moral implications, for example:

- "Twenty-three hour visitation would lead to pregnancies and orgies. I can see no advantages: it's a disgusting breakdown of our moral standards."
- "If a poor, neurotic girl has to have her boyfriend around twenty-three hours a day, let them either go to a motel, get married, or make use of Ball Circle. It offers no advantages except for whores and their clients."
- "I wanna marry a virgin. . . . There won't be any left."

The student poll was but the first part of the student lobby's effort to drum up support. The second was a planned poll of parents on the issue, an approach that lobby members, citing the comments made by Dalhouse and Castles, claimed had been endorsed by members of the Board of Visitors. Woodard, however, short-circuited that attempt by forbidding the use of the College's computer center to generate the necessary list of parents' names and addresses. Such facilities, he pointed out, were for administrative purposes only, and in any case, the proposal by students would violate the Buckley Amendment.

Leaders of the visitation reform effort were furious, and the *Bullet* editorially agreed. "We have known for some time," it fumed, "that President Prince B. Woodard has a total lack of concern for how MWC students feel about the present college visitation policies, but it did come as a bit of a surprise to learn that Woodard doesn't care about how our parents feel about it either. . . . We condemn the attempts on the part of President Woodard to stymie that research."

The truth is that the polls would have made little difference anyway. As Woodard flatly declared in December 1978, during the midst of the controversy, "The Board of Visitors voted unanimously, and I have said many times that the visitation policy will not be changed, and results from polls will not make any difference."

If anything, the continued agitation of the issue seemed to make him more intransigent. The following spring, appearing before the Student Association Senate to report that the board had approved the SA's request for an additional hour of visitation (weekends only), he prefaced his announcement by warning, "Don't applaud yet, [because] you won't like what I am going to say next." What he proceeded to say was that "it doesn't matter who you elect for SA president next year, [the visitation policy] won't change," adding, "If there is anyone attending Mary Washington who will not be satisfied with the visitation policy next year, then he should not come back."

The perennial issue prompted a satirical blast from the College newspaper in its April 1, 1980, edition. It was something of a tradition for the paper to publish a humorous April Fools' issue, called at various times "The Bullsheet," or simply "The Bull," or, as in 1980, "The Bullshit." Under the headline "24-Hour Visitation Adopted," a faux news story reported that the move came as the result of "a petition signed by the fathers of 20 freshman girls and the decision was reached after only 30 minutes." Purported interviews with various board members revealed almost unanimous opinion. "I think it's a great idea," said one. "I'm surprised no one has thought of it before." Another, when asked if the board feared that such a policy might promote promiscuity, expressed unconcern, adding, "It wouldn't be much of a college if students couldn't get a little action on the weekends."

According to another, the board was still considering the addition of some restrictions, including "an amendment that would limit sexual acts to the missionary position and require a shower before and after," but admitted there might be some problems of enforcement. The dean of students remained wary, noting that "if students take this as a license for sex, we could have structural problems with the dorms at peak times, such as Saturday night after a keg party." Apparently the only dissenter on the board was a nonagenarian who cited morality as her grounds for opposition: "We're responsible for getting these girls through school with their virginity intact. If they want to play pass around with their 'sacred temples' like a bunch of shameless trollops then they can damn well do it at home. I don't want to see campus drive turned into another 14th Street."

It was a good thing students could get a laugh out of it, because one thing they were *not* going to get was open visitation—not on Prince Woodard's watch.

No doubt about it: social life on the MWC campus was changing in the 1970s. One of the main factors was the rise of female enrollment at the University of Virginia. The easier availability of dates in Charlottesville meant the decline of what had for years been a Mary Washington social tradition, albeit a dubious one: fraternity rolls.

As one senior recalled it in 1974, "The U.Va. guys would swarm by the carloads [sometimes via trucks as well] to the dorms, particularly the freshman ones. About thirty guys would enter, all laughing and asking for dates. Sometimes they had contacts, but mostly the corduroy, sweater, and Docksider-clad guys would [just] request a specific number of girls . . . and then they would go out, usually to the river or back to U.Va."

But by the mid-1970s, all that had changed. "On a typical night this year [1975]," observed the *Bullet*, "the freshman parlors are fairly quiet, . . . [indicating] that the traditional fraternity rolls have been replaced by predetermined individual dates . . . [who] head for the river, Art's, or a movie." It was not necessarily a change for the worse, in the eyes of some. As one senior said, "It is a healthier attitude. The girls realize that UVa fraternities are not the epitome of all that is good and holy."

One thing that compensated to some extent for the decline in intercollegiate dating was an increase in social activity on the MWC campus itself, especially in the dorms, where, even without open visitation, life was not dull. In fact, the residence halls became the main loci of student social life on a day-to-day basis. Over the course of time the upperclass halls acquired unique collective personalities, as described by the *Bullet* in 1977:

> BALL: The home of sophisticated girls, mostly seniors and lucky underclassmen . . . who act with a touch of class. Some noses are carried so high that . . . they are in danger of drowning in heavy rain.
>
> MARSHALL: Seldom heard from since it's tucked away under the rest of the campus. Rumors are that the inhabitants have quietly seceded from the rest of the college.
>
> RUSSELL AND JEFFERSON: Household words at UVa, U. of R., and Randy Mac. The ladies there are the darlings of the preps, and on most Friday and Saturday nights their dorm is the scene of more passes than a school of quarterbacks.
>
> VIRGINIA: Inhabited mostly by sophomores who get stuck with a low lottery number and others who like to be near the center of campus or who are too lazy to walk from Jefferson Square to Seacobeck.

Coed dorms proved especially popular. A Student Association poll of Westmoreland residents taken after one semester of the coed experiment revealed that all but one of the forty-six respondents advocated expanding the arrangement. "It's a perfectly natural situation," said one, "as most of us have grown up in coed houses."

Additional coed dorms were established, and to many, they offered attractive advantages. As a resident (female) of one such hall put it in a *Bullet* article, somewhat tongue-in-cheek, "I have reached the conclusion that living in a co-ed dorm is right up there with a six of Mick [Michelob beer]. . . . The skills one sex can provide for the other are not to be taken lightly: 'For God's sake, if you'll come up and kill the spider, I'll clean your entire hall!' . . . Co-ed dorm parties are—how shall I put it?—in the UVa vernacular, just dyno. In a matter of minutes—or if you're a slow sipper, a matter of hours—you've found that you have so many more friends in the dorm than before."

Outside the dorms, the staple of College-wide entertainment during the period was unquestionably the keg party. Such beer-driven fests originated shortly after drinking on campus was permitted, but they reached their heyday from the mid-seventies to mid-eighties. Originally held mainly in the ballroom of Ann Carter Lee Hall, the events were moved to the Pool Room to prevent damage to the ballroom's beautiful hardwood floor by the accumulated spillage of sudsy brew. That venue, however, proved inadequate, both because of its small size—its capacity was only six hundred—and, again, because of spilled beer. As Assistant Dean of Students Dorothy White told the *Bullet* in 1981, "After three or four parties in the pool room . . . twelve inches of beer had seeped through the floor to the crossbeam underneath it." Subsequently the venue was usually either Seacobeck basement or Goolrick Gymnasium, both of which had sufficient strength to withstand a four-hour kegger.

There were several reasons for the enormous popularity of keg parties during this period—aside from the natural, seemingly primal, affinity of college-age humans for malt (and its effects). One was simply a legal matter: the lowering of the minimum drinking age in Virginia to eighteen during this period meant that almost all students, even most freshmen, could legally imbibe. The second was demographic: there were increasing numbers of male students at MWC.

Then, too, it was a time when the vast majority of students still lived on campus—many did not have cars—and there was little to compete with the keg parties, either on campus or in the Fredericksburg environs. It was not exactly the "only game in town," but it was the most convenient—and the cheapest.

Finally there was the psychology of it: drinking was cool. It was not yet viewed with the caution of students in later years who—while certainly not teetotalers by any means—tended to be somewhat more concerned about the health risks posed by excessive use of alcohol (by which time College policy had also changed drastically). And so they drank, including—and sometimes especially—the freshmen.

Noting that "to a frosh, the prospect of a keg party thrills, chills, and altogether enhances the preceding week of labor," a *Bullet* column near the beginning of fall classes in 1977 issued a guide to the various types of males who might be encountered at such an event. In addition to MWC males, the categories included:

> TOWNIES: usually arrive in vintage '63 Chevy pick-up truck or something equally unidentifiable, jacked up, and ready to be junked [with] their ripe jeans and riper attitude [that] seem to repel rather than attract.
>
> FRAT GUYS: are often recognizable arriving in leering droves and (collectively) singing repulsive little ditties in order to attract attention. You also have your more refined, suave, and generally desirable frats, the members of which are often indiscernible from the [preppies].
>
> PREPPIES: khaki slacks (shorts when the weather permits), striped belt, color coordinated with a red or blue "izod" shirt, topsiders, impeccably swept-back short hair, post-braces perfection in their smile and a manner as expensively accurate as the heavy, gold digital watches on their wrists.

QUANTICO MARINES: usually decent fellows—sometimes, anyway. They . . . are hardly the type you could miss. Crew cuts, squeaky shoes, and mothballed civilian party clothes are easily distinguishable trademarks.

To MWC freshmen of that era, keg parties constituted something of a rite of passage, akin in some (not-so-lovely) ways to fraternity rushes at other schools. In a *Bullet* column in September 1978 titled "My First Keg Party, or Primitive Cultures 101," sophomore Laurie Shelor recalled her own eye-opening experience:

> It all began about a year ago, when I, a tender-hearted, barely legal soul, attended my first MWC keg party. Fun, fellows, and the Four Tops for only a dollar. Or perhaps misery, Marines, and music depending upon one's taste. . . . Anyhow, it smacked of adventure and . . . I marched, ponytail saucily bouncing, to that infamous building, ACL. My first impression was not particularly positive [as I went through the check-in procedure]. For the first time in my life I felt as if I'd been U.S. government inspected; little did I know the second time was to occur that same evening.

Mystified when the band leader announced, "This next one is for all you Wahoos," she thought, "Wahoos? My orientation guide mentioned nothing about Wahoos." Having espied a group of attractive young men who, she thought, might be able to define the term, she "debated the merits of tapping one on a Lacoste-clad shoulder" but thought better of it when she observed that the girl with whom he was talking "laughed appreciatively and snuggled up to him. All I could see was a tangle of monograms and grosgrain. I looked down at my feet and wondered how I could get back to the dorm in time to catch the second half of NBC Saturday night movies." Having decided to leave, she headed for the door, only to realize that she had suddenly been pinched. Stunned, and not a little annoyed, she turned to find a young man in "a pair of madras plaids and penny loafers enhanced by tan face and collegiately-styled hair. Regaining my composure, I brutally began my inquisition. 'Did you pinch me?' 'Yes,' he calmly replied. Honest. Well, they probably have a strict honor code at his school. . . . After studying me for a minute he said, 'Let's dance, this is an excellent tune.' To my disgust, I gave him my best smile (no braces) and said (throatily, I hoped), 'Okay.'"

The following year, Shelor, who would eventually become managing editor of the *Bullet*, offered another humorously perceptive analysis of the keg party experience. As the typical evening begins, she observed, "the fraternity brothers are surveying the Probables, Possibles, and Hopelesses in an effort to narrow down the quarry. . . . Of course, the point of this moment is to appear as if you don't want to dance. I was never sure why, but that's the suggested strategy."

The evening wears on, and

> those who have been in ACL since 8 P.M. are beginning to lower their standards. . . . Towards midnight, the lights come on; the Gestapo enters and those caught dancing when the buzzer goes off are shot on sight. Now comes the job of trying to mentally recall if your room is straight enough to admit visitors or if your visitor is straight enough to care. Fighting the mass of people, who make a race out of going down the steps, you find it is pouring, sleeting, the wind is blowing, and you, silly girl, neglected to wear a coat. Ah, gee, we are faced with the decision of whether to ditch your khaki-clad find and race for the dorm or risk pneumonia in an effort to get a date for Easters. As you might have guessed, . . . half of the campus has a chest cold Monday morning.

It was a scenario with which hundreds of MWC students of that era could identify—if not in its particulars, at least in its overall ambience. Most students, whether they regarded keg parties with delight, detachment, or disdain—too crowded, too hot; lines too long, beer too short—had one thing in common: they went.

Occasionally keggers had a theme, as in the case of the memorable TOGA '79 invitation-only party sponsored by the men of Hamlet House (the "Hamsters"). Drawing on the popularity of the movie *Animal House*, the party attracted a crowd characterized by, according to the *Bullet*, "bare arms, bare legs, bare shoulders, bare feet, and sheets barely covering the essentials." Moreover, "The people-to-beer ratio was one gallon to one per person (none was wasted), . . . [and] being scantily clad in a sheet seemed to break down the throng's inhibitions even more." The evening also featured the awarding of

Toga party

prizes in categories such as most stylish toga, most formal toga, and toga that best exemplified John Belushi, the boorish central character in the movie. The prize for the winners: six-packs of beer. (At the time there were actually "toga representatives" who traveled the college circuit encouraging such parties as a means of promoting the movie.)

Occasionally faculty members dared venture into the revelry. On this occasion two notables appeared: philosophy professor George Van Sant, attired in a "Fickett for Pro-Consul" toga, in support of Professor Lewis Fickett's current campaign for the House of Delegates, and English professor Susan Hanna, ever the feminist advocate, resplendent in a pink toga adorned with a "Cleopatra for Emperor-Person" button.

There were also popular activities that, although not actually called keg parties, revolved similarly around the consumption of beer, such as the semi-annual picnics sponsored jointly by the Departments of History and Political Science. The highlight of those events was a softball game between student-faculty teams from the two departments. In the early years, the games were utterly lighthearted, but as the male contingent on both sides increased, the rivalry became more intense. Even under the best of circumstances, however, the caliber of play was hardly stellar—the product of diminished skills on the part of the faculty (owing to age) and impaired skills on the part of the students (owing to the bibulous activities preceding the games).

Originally conceived as an event just for the majors and faculty of the two departments, the picnic soon began to attract many non-majors as well, drawn by the lure of off-campus camaraderie (St. Claire Brooks Park in Stafford County being the usual venue) and, of course, free beer. In time, it became one of the larger warm-weather attractions in both fall and spring semesters. It also demonstrated the extent to which beer was a social lubricant: in 1987, when the legal drinking age was raised to twenty-one, interest dropped precipitously, to the point that the event was soon discontinued.

There were also parties that involved only seniors, particularly 100th Night, held one hundred days before graduation, and a similar celebration held to coincide with the number of days before graduation that equaled the year of that year's graduating class (e.g., 75th Night for the class of '75). Both events, held variously at locations on and off campus, tended to be raucous celebrations eagerly anticipated by the soon-to-be graduates.

But of all the kegger-era social events, by far the largest—and the wildest—was Halloweens. The celebration of Halloween had a long history at Mary Washington, going back almost to the College's founding. As early as 1913, the school held something called "Witches' Dance," sponsored by the local YWCA, after which students sampled gingerbread and cider and had their fortunes read. In 1916 the celebration began with a special meal in the dining hall, where "witches appeared to serve the bounteous feast," followed by a program in the auditorium featuring ghost stories and "weird songs and fantastic dances; the evening ended with bonfires and marshmallow roasts."

Always held on or near October 30, such celebrations evolved over the years, becoming more elaborate (and much more beery), leading to the inauguration of the costume party known as Halloweens in 1977.[20]

The first Halloweens was held in the Lee Hall Ballroom, but the affair soon outgrew that venue and moved to Goolrick Gym; by 1981 even those quarters were cramped, as an estimated seventeen hundred people showed up. The event pretty much lived up to its self-proclaimed status—emblazoned on hundreds of T-shirts—as "Best Party in the County." Within a few years it even approached, in the view of some, the status of U.Va.'s Easters, which was at that time regarded as the gold standard of collegiate debauchery in the commonwealth.

There was music by bands such as Cold Duck and Casper and, naturally, beer in abundance, but the distinctive feature of the party was the extraordinary assemblage of revelers in all manner of masquerades: *Star Wars* characters, crayons, playing cards, vampires, Smurfs, belly dancers, gangsters, witches, *Playboy* bunnies, caricatures of College personnel, black Klansmen, pregnant nuns. Good costumes abounded; good taste did not.

For two decades, Halloweens was a memorable annual event for many a student—though sometimes the memories were bought at a considerable price. As one such victim (1982) described his experience in the *Bullet*:

> It's Saturday morning, October 30. Your mouth feels like the Russian army has camped on your tongue during the night. . . . There's nothing like waking up to see who the hell keeps knocking at your door only to find out that what you're hearing is your own brain banging against your skull. . . . You ooze out of bed and begin walking toward the bathroom. . . . When you reach the bathroom you find your head does not fit through the door. After finally getting in, you begin to pray to the porcelain altar. . . . Drinking heavily at Halloweens is kind of like electing the President of the United States: it's fun for a while, but later everyone feels like vomiting. . . . It's the day after Halloweens. Good morning.

Among the more interested observers who occasionally attended such events was President Woodard himself, usually viewing the antics from a discreet distance. Given his tendency to restrain frivolous impulses (assuming he had them), it is unlikely that he had any wish to participate in the merriment and mayhem. On the other hand, he did take interest in all aspects of the College, including the social life of its students. And so he attended, drawn no doubt more by duty than by desire.

It was one of the ironies of his presidency, in light of his personal rectitude and abstemiousness, that alcohol consumption on campus was probably greater during his tenure than at any other comparable period in the College's history. But such was the nature of campus behavior everywhere at the time.

Traditional celebrations such as Devil-Goat Day and Junior Ring Week continued on an annual basis, with Junior Ring Week undergoing a number of changes. The customary outdoor Saturday afternoon concert was moved indoors and scheduled on Friday evening, and the presentation ceremony was expanded to include the "tapping" of juniors into Mortar Board, the national honor society for scholarship, leadership, and service. In addition, the banquet and dance were combined into a dinner-dance that was held in the Sheraton Motor Inn to accommodate the growing number of participants.

One of the College's oldest yearly events, the Chi Beta Phi auction, also continued, attracting large crowds to the ACL ballroom, where students could bid on a wide array of items and events donated by faculty and staff. Much of the event's entertainment value lay in the banter provided throughout the evening by the auctioneers, who were usually drawn from the College's most exuberant personalities, including in the mid-seventies Jack Albertine (economics), Alexander Lindsey (math), William Pinschmidt (biology), Susan Hanna (English), George Van Sant (philosophy), and Ray Merchent (administration). Proceeds from the event were normally used to fund scholarships for deserving science majors but were also used during the seventies to help pay for a garden adjacent to Combs Hall established in memory of math professor Hobart Carter, who taught at the College from 1936 to 1973.

A newer tradition that grew in popularity during the period was the fall celebration originally known as Parents' Weekend but later renamed Family Weekend to connote a sense of inclusiveness. It was eagerly anticipated by many—especially by homesick freshmen and by upperclassmen who hoped a parental visit might yield pecuniary rewards—but for others there was a sizable downside, as amusingly described in a *Bullet* article titled "A Weekend on the Wagon": "Parents' Weekend is an enjoyable, refreshing experience—if you spend your free time watching Oral Roberts. . . . For those of us who lead a double life (i.e., what Mom doesn't know), Parents' Weekend could be a tragic snag in our social schedules. . . . I saw frantic fingers ripping Playgirl (boy) photos off the walls after debating whether or not they could pass for art. . . . Frenzied cries of 'Not in the drawer, stupid. That's the first place she'll look,' rebounded off the walls." Particularly at risk, according to the columnist, were "those who still let Mommy do their laundry when she comes to visit," necessitating "hurried searches for unexplainable items" and resulting in such conversations as "Well, actually, Dad, I've no idea what the stockings are doing in the closet. . . . The, um, slip in the drawer? Well, uh, my roommate's sister was here last weekend, oh, to help him with his . . . biology, and she probably left it."

The period also witnessed the development of several new extracurricular activities, among the most popular of which was Frisbee. The disc sport—with its emphasis on individual athleticism, its lack of regimentation, and its ambience of mellow sportsmanship—was in perfect accord with the countercultural tendencies of many college-age students at the time. Across the country, it achieved something of a cult status, especially among those with anti-establishment affinities.

At Mary Washington, the popularity of Frisbee was boosted by the achievements (and the enthusiasm) of economics professor John Pickerill and, even more perhaps, by the amazing skills of his Frisbee-catching dog, a sleek black Labrador retriever named Martha. "Dr. John," who was a disc competitor of national renown, and his canine companion regularly entertained students on Ball Circle with acrobatic demonstrations that led them to be featured frequently at football halftime shows and other sports events around the country. (The maverick owner of the Chicago White Sox, Bill Veeck, was once reported to have commented after seeing Martha perform, "If she could only throw, she'd be our center fielder.")

With Pickerill as its faculty adviser, a Mary Washington Frisbee Club was formed in the fall of 1976. It successfully applied to the International Frisbee Association to host the first Virginia state championship in 1977; the tournament involved events such as distance, accuracy, freestyle, and Frisbee golf. During the next few years, as the tournament was held annually on the College campus, Mary Washington became known as the "Frisbee capital" of the state, and several students (e.g., Hugh Lowry, Eric Wootten, Eric Olsen) won recognition for their exceptional performances.

There were some glitches along the way, however. Frisbee golf, for example, had the potential for damaging the terrain, a possibility that did not go unnoticed by the ever-vigilant President Woodard, who despaired of such a development. Accordingly, in 1979 an administrative directive placed limitations on the time and places that Frisbee golf could be played, noting that the game had "begun to pose problems for pedestrians, for automobiles driving through the campus, as well as damaging College property."

Negative administrative attitudes toward Frisbee playing provoked student hostility, as evidenced by a *Bullet* parody of the situation:

> Once upon a time there was a young boy named Prince. He was a likeable fellow, but for one reason or another he was never selected to play in pick-up football games on Ball Circle. Thirty years later, when he was elected President of a local college, he issued a new decree. It read: "Thou shalt not play on the grass." The students at this college were not about to give up playing on the grass, but they didn't want to disappoint their Prince either. After all, it isn't every college that can boast a Prince for a president. So the students decided that while the Prince was walking around the campus, they would restrain themselves, walking on the brick sidewalks only. But when the Prince went to bed in the evenings, the students would congregate on the grassy areas and drink beer and play Frisbee.

The disc devotees expressed even greater concern when it appeared that the state tournament might be withdrawn from MWC as a result of the restrictions on Frisbee golf. "I think it is a tradition the school should uphold," said Eric Wootten, "one which is more important than other traditions, such as Halloweens." Even though Frisbee's popularity gradually declined on campus (at least in terms of organized competitions) as the 1980s progressed, it remained the recreational activity of choice for some students well into the twenty-first century—indeed, outliving Halloweens.

Among the new campus activities that appeared during the 1970s, the most extraordinary (and inexplicable) was something called the Wo-Man Contest. The event was conceived in the fall of 1977 by the Afro-American Association, whose only male member, freshman Cedric Rucker, took the lead in the contest's development and promotion. Rucker, who would eventually return to MWC to become dean of students, recalled years later that the genesis of the idea had been the revulsion of the AAA's women over the sexism of the Miss America contest. "They were saying, 'Men never have to go through that sort of thing. What would it be like for men to have to [wear] swimsuits'" and compete against each other? To which Rucker proposed a solution: "Why don't we do something about that? Let's have a contest and see if we can get guys to go through this process."

It was certainly something new for Mary Washington, and even Rucker himself was not sanguine about the prospects for success. "Whoever thought we would get men to wear [women's] swimsuits," he recalled, "or come up with talent? . . . We didn't think that it would be successful, but it was."[21]

And how. The first contest drew a crowd of over four hundred to Dodd Auditorium, and the (literally) howling success of the inaugural event resulted in its annual return for a dozen or so years, during which it routinely attracted packed audiences to Dodd, emerging as an entertainment event rivaled only by Halloweens in popularity among the student body.

The format of the first contest, a lampoon of the real Miss America pageant, set the pattern for subsequent ones. The emcee was the irrepressible English professor Susan Hanna, whose feminist credentials as a prominent member of NOW would appear to have absolved the event of potential charges of sexism (which were nonetheless made with increasing frequency in later years). Her witty repartee with the contestants was a key element in the event's initial success.

There were twelve contestants, each of whom was introduced in his (her?) evening gown. The *Bullet* was impressed, complimenting "not only their stunning styles but also their superb make-up jobs and lovely nails," but added, "The only thing that detracted from these lovely beauties were their lack of shoes and hairy ankles." Next, according to the *Bullet*, "These males had to perform—in a talent show, that is." The acts ranged from the genuinely artful (singing and dancing), to the bizarre ("a sexually oriented reading on mathematics"), to the absurd (chugging a thirty-two-ounce bottle of Coke).

Then came the swimsuit competition, for which Ms. Hanna announced the "vital statistics" and zodiac signs of the contestants as they paraded before the judges to the appropriate accompaniment of "Brick House" by the Commodores. After five finalists were chosen, the contest concluded with each of them having to answer a customarily inane question extempore.

The first runner-up was Frank Shields, a freshman who wowed the crowd by dancing to "Turn the Beat Around" in his slip. The winner was Craig Howie, another freshman. The key to his victory was apparently his talent: miming the blues song "My Man." The *Bullet* reported that "sitting on top of a grand piano in a tuxedo top with shorts, to show off his nice legs, Craig captured the crowd with an emotional performance." His reward: a tiara and six long-stemmed American Beauty roses, presented by none other than President Woodard, who, being a good sport—and in a gesture that no doubt shocked the audience as well as the recipient—bestowed a (very) chaste kiss upon the newly crowned Wo-Man.

It was difficult to know who had more fun with the spoof, the audience or the contestants. One of the aspirants in the 1981 contest, John McCarthy, described in a self-mocking *Bullet* article how it felt to be a pageant participant:

> I'm willing to concede that what I did in front of upwards of eight hundred people may in fact be a violation of several statutes, but I don't care, because after all is said and done, and all subpoenas have been issued, I had a great time. . . . All told, fourteen males without even the most rudimentary sense of self-esteem became involved in this warped display. . . . [It was] a very impressive display of just how low a human male will stoop to get attention and be funny. . . . It's not that I mind dressing up in women's clothes . . . it's just that I found great trouble in trying to buy this stuff from various thrift shops in the area. Do you know how it feels . . . to buy a dress and have some old guy tell you that you'll look great in it? . . . By the way, does anyone need two yards of feather boa, a leopard-skin skirt, a black-and-orange Supremes' dress, or five-and-a-half-inch platform shoes?

The Wo-Man contest flourished for a number of years with only minor modifications. Various persons succeeded Sue Hanna as emcee, notably including geography professor Richard Palmieri, whose naturally bawdy and unbridled sense of humor equipped him well for the role.

Sponsorship of the event changed when the women of the Afro-American Association decided that involvement with it was inappropriate to the organization's mission. Despite Cedric Rucker's defense of the contest on the grounds that proceeds from it supported scholarships and many of the expenses of Black History Week, the organization ultimately declined sponsorship. So in 1980 that role was assumed by Hamlet House, whose president, not coincidentally, was Cedric Rucker. For more than a decade, Wo-Man continued and was still an annual event when Rucker, class of 1981, returned to Mary Washington in 1989 as associate dean of student activities.

The range of campus activities increased significantly during the late seventies and early eighties. One example was the establishment of a campus radio station. Actually, it was the *re*-establishment, as there had been an earlier station that was especially active in the 1940s and 1950s. Broadcasting first from a studio in the new George Washington Hall in 1939 and from even better facilities in duPont beginning in 1955, WMWC, staffed largely by members of the Mike Club, enjoyed wide popularity during the so-called golden age of radio. However, with the advent of television, WMWC went into decline, and by 1969 the station was defunct.[22]

In the 1970s, efforts were made to revive the station, and in November 1978, after six years of planning, the new WMWC (540 on the AM dial) went on the air. Hours of operation were limited at first, but within a few years the station was on the air with student deejays at the mike seven days a week, nineteen hours a day, ending its broadcast at 2:00 a.m. The station's ambitious plans called for radio dramas, educational segments, interviews with visiting scholars, as well as regular programming of weather, campus announcements, and news. In 1980 it carried its first live broadcast of a sports event: the women's basketball tournament, with former U.Va. hoopster Dan Bonner doing play-by-play and MWC student Duke Stableford providing commentary.

Given that the primary audience was college students, the core of the station's format was music. The station enjoyed modest success, particularly in the experience that it provided for the students involved in running it. But listenership disappointed those who had worked so hard for its creation. There were several reasons for this. One was that the effort to please constituencies of various musical tastes turned out to be counterproductive. As one *Bullet* critic put it, "With WMWC . . . it's potluck all the way. Listening to the station is like eating at Seacobeck: you never know what to expect."

More fundamentally, there were technical problems. Reception was limited and not always of the highest quality. Even more detrimental was the extensive competition from readily accessible commercial stations. In the end, the station never lived up to its initial, and probably unrealistic, promise.

Concurrent with the founding of the radio station was the establishment of the campus television station, AVC-TV, Channel 6. Unlike WMWC, which was funded by student fees, AVC-TV was operated as part of the College's audiovisual center (hence the call letters AVC-TV) and received state funding.

The AV center itself, located in the basement of Chandler Hall, was established in 1976, initially to service the College's technical equipment (such as it was) and to provide limited audiovisual aids. By 1979, however, it had developed to the point that it could provide audio, cinematic, graphic, photographic, and video support for College programs. Its responsibilities included operating a closed-circuit television channel to assist the instructional program, providing media internship opportunities for students, maintaining and operating audiovisual equipment in Dodd Auditorium and at other performance venues, and videotaping special events on campus.

Two years in the planning, the television station went into operation in 1978. While under the aegis of the AV Center—specifically, its director of programming, Mary Byrd '77—the station was mainly run by students, who received three credits for a semester's work. The most visible were the on-air anchorpersons, the first being Bonnie Berry '79, followed by Mary Russell '80 in 1979 and Jenifer Blair '82 (later to become a longtime member of the admissions staff) in 1980. Programming was not extensive, consisting mainly of a live news broadcast at 6:30 every Thursday evening, featuring campus events, followed by a "classic" movie such as *From Here to Eternity* or *The King and I*.

Though the station did provide a service to the College community, response to it, as with the radio station, was underwhelming—and for many of the same reasons. AVC-TV, for instance, was broadcast on a short wavelength that could be received only on the sets found in dorm parlors and rec rooms. In all, the greatest benefit of it was probably the experience afforded the student interns.

Having more activities available on campus did not deter students from engaging in that most ancient of collegiate traditions—complaining—nor did it preclude the periodic recrudescence of controversy.

Griping about food was always the most common of such complaints, affecting virtually all colleges (and institutions of every kind, for that matter). Even the *Bullet* prefaced a critical editorial in 1979 by admitting, "College students are not supposed to like their food. College students are not supposed to like much of anything except the proverbial 'sex, drugs, and rock'n'roll.' . . . As one ex-slop girl told this editor, complaining about food service is 'the nature of the beast.' So what's new?"

What was new was a change in the food service provider as the College shifted from its own institutional service to the corporate ARA. Judging from irate comments ensuing in the *Bullet*, the change was by no means an improvement. In student parlance, Seacobeck often became "Sickobeck" or "Seacobarf." As one editorial put it three years after the takeover by ARA, "Starch is certainly in abundance. Grease is everywhere. Something is definitely wrong. Just ask the scores of students who discover new intestinal revolts each fall." Not only that, there were complaints about dirty dishes, check-in hassles, and surly administrators.

Dissatisfaction reached the point that in October 1979 the *Bullet* called for a boycott of ARA—and suggested a specific means of collective student action. Merely not showing up en masse would be ineffective, the paper said, as ARA "would just save the food and use it later in the week." The protest needed to be more dramatic:

> Everyone comes to dinner, chooses a meal, and goes through the normal process of setting their tables and discarding their trays. At the appointed time, however, the diners walk out of Seacobeck, leaving the (cold) meal on their tables, untouched. Hygiene would dictate that this food could not be justifiably reused, and if it were, who would eat it? This is not as improbable as it seems, and as a matter of fact has been a technique used at many colleges, with excellent results. Any type of reasonably executed, but drastic, act might be a . . . sign that Mary Washington students are not all talk and no action.

As it turned out, the boycott never took place, and eventually complaints declined—at least to a more or less normal level—for two main reasons. First, the food service apparently did improve, particularly with the arrival of the affable and accommodating Gordon Inge as ARA director. Also, and perhaps equally important, other campus controversies arose that deflected attention from the woes of Seacobeck.

One of the most heated involved the case of the so-called Westmoreland Four. In late 1977, four male residents of Westmoreland Hall were accused by the dorm's student judicial representative of a number of disruptive acts, including egregious noise violations and destruction of College property (made worse by antisocial behavior such as "group retching," i.e., drunken communal vomiting). The question arose as to what body, or what person, should have jurisdiction in the matter. Consultation among several student leaders resulted in the recommendation that it be handled through an administrative hearing by President Woodard, rather than by Joint Council or Judicial Court. His decision resulted in expelling three of the accused from the dorm and allowing the fourth to stay, but under severe social sanctions.

There were several repercussions. For one, a recall petition was initiated against Student Association president Kathleen Mayer, citing several presumable offenses, including the allegation that because she was registered for only ten credit hours, she was not a full-time student and thus ineligible to hold office. It and the other allegations were all grounded mainly in anger over what was deemed her abdication of responsibility in permitting the Westmoreland Four matter to be adjudicated by the administration rather than by a student tribunal. The petition failed, and Mayer not only served out her term but, within a few years after her graduation, was named to the MWC Board of Visitors.

The fallout for President Woodard was worse, though not because of the verdict itself. "The judgment and punishment in the case [were] justifiable," opined the *Bullet*. "It is difficult to find fault with President Woodard's actions here. . . . There was no glaring and obvious injustice." On the other hand, there was strong criticism of his methods, including the absence of a transcript of the hearing and the lack of an appeal procedure. Accordingly, the editorial went on to assert, "The men were denied the due process of law guaranteed to them by the [MWC student] *Handbook* as well as by the Fourteenth Amendment to the U.S. Constitution."

Woodard staunchly denied that charge from the outset and abruptly dismissed it in a *Bullet* interview that included a curt exchange:

BULLET: I just would like to ask you a few questions about the trial. . . . The [four men] don't mind what questions we ask.
WOODARD: They might not mind, but [I do].
BULLET: Would you mind answering some of the questions?
WOODARD: That depends entirely on what the questions are. . . .
BULLET: There seems to be some discrepancy. . . .
WOODARD: I can tell you exactly how you can be 100 percent correct on that: look in the student *Handbook*, pages 28–30. Exactly the procedure set down there to be followed was followed.

The president was right, as he usually was; certainly he had the authority to evict the culprits from the dormitory. But as was also often the case, legal propriety did not equate to victory in the court of student opinion—not that he was unduly concerned about such matters. He believed in rules, and he believed in their enforcement. And when, as in this instance, their violation involved behavior that someone of his sensibilities must have found repugnant, he was not in the least inclined to be apologetic about his actions.

In any event, the affair contributed to the resurgence of a demand for a student "bill of rights," a proposal that had originally come up years earlier and had been approved by vote of the student body in April 1970, only to be rejected by President Simpson. Now, in the spring of 1978, the idea resurfaced as part of a document promulgated by an SA Constitutional Revision Committee—this time with the endorsement of the College president. It was greeted with glee by the *Bullet*, which heaped accolades on the committee that designed it: "The members of the committee exhibited a degree of courage and foresight not often seen on this campus. This Bill of Rights is an enormous gift to future generations of MWC students. It shall be a searchlight whose brilliance will continue to shine long after the Westmoreland Four and full-time student status controversies have faded from memory." The editorial went on to urge ratification, noting, "Eight years ago, the students ratified the bill and the administration vetoed it. Would it not be a slashing irony if this year it was the administration who embraced a Bill of Rights and the students who repudiated it?"

The students, of course, endorsed it overwhelmingly, whereupon the previously exuberant *Bullet* immediately found a cloud in the silver lining. The main problem, it pointed out, was that the bill was part of the Student Association's constitution and therefore applied only to actions of the student government, when "often it is the administration, rather than the SA, that encroaches on the rights of students, and here the Bill offers no protection." Nevertheless, it concluded, "Even with its limitations and ambiguities," the bill represented progress and was "certainly a tremendous improvement" in delineating (and presumably guarding) student rights.

It was not long before those putative rights were breached, in the view of some students, by another of President Woodard's decisions. Though the alleged offense occurred, as before, in Westmoreland Hall, this time it was more serious than the mere hooliganism of the Westmoreland Four; this time the issue was drugs.

Drugs were a subject of particular sensitivity to Woodard. According to his associate and confidant Bill Anderson, one of Woodard's greatest fears upon becoming president was that the College might become known as a haven for drug users. Just why that was such a preeminent concern is hard to say, as the institution had no reputation in that regard.

Which is not to say that use of illegal drugs, especially marijuana, was nonexistent at Mary Washington. As early as 1967, a *Bullet* survey, unscientific though it may have been, indicated that 5.6 percent of the respondents had used marijuana (16 percent of whom had done so while visiting U.Va.). The following year a freshman from New York became the first MWC student to be arrested for marijuana possession.

A similar "pot poll," taken only three years later, revealed that the number of students who had used some type of illegal drug had jumped dramatically—almost sixfold—to over 30 percent; among those who had not, another 20 percent indicated they would do so if given the chance. Over 60 percent advocated legalization of marijuana, up substantially from the 24 percent who had favored it in 1967. Indicative of the increased tolerance for marijuana use was the fact that only 6 percent said they would turn in a fellow student for doing so. "I am so enthusiastically convinced of the value of grass," said one, "that turning in an offender is one of the few school rules I refuse to abide by. . . . I feel sorry for the unfortunate being who is afraid to awaken himself to the completely unique experience [of] blowing weed."

Availability was apparently no problem. Over 50 percent of respondents indicated that they could, if they wished, easily obtain drugs—often from students at their old high schools. That situation seemed to be especially true for out-of-state students. "Southern schools are way behind," commented one student. "Too many things, such as smoking marijuana, which hardly means anything up North, are blown way out of proportion in the South."

The March 2, 1970, issue of the *Bullet* that announced the survey results also carried a lengthy interview with what the paper identified as "a student who has had extensive experience with the use of drugs." The attribution of "extensive experience" was evidently accurate, as the informant proceeded to describe in great detail the effects, both good and bad, of the various drugs that had been sampled.

The psychedelic drugs such as LSD and mescaline were attractive, said the user, especially mescaline: "It comes in a capsule and it's probably about the nicest hallucinogen around, if you get a nice, mild dose of it. . . . [You can] sit in your dorm and look at the blank walls and really just get ecstatic over the microscopic little designs that are going on—that are moving, constantly moving. Even the air is just filled with it."

Amphetamines (types of speed) were not so good: "I was getting DT's. I was seeing roaches out of the corner of my eye. I'd be studying late at night, . . . and I'd see these little roaches running by. . . . And I was getting really forgetful; . . . I couldn't remember days and weeks." Heroin was deemed beyond the pale, not from personal experience but because of a photograph the user had seen of "a 16-year-old heroin addict—a girl—and it was a full-length nude picture of her, and I'm not exaggerating, every inch of her body was covered with scabs—really gross, ugly scabs—everywhere. . . . I don't know how she got to some of the places where she had scabs."

Pot was another deal altogether. It was so much better than alcohol, for example:

> You never come back from a smoking date and retch, that's for sure. And pot kind of lulls you. With alcohol you sort of feel like you've had three Phenobarb tablets: you conk into bed and they could parade Ringling Brothers' Circus through your room and you wouldn't notice it. But falling asleep on marijuana is a really soothing thing; you kind of float in. It's a more personal thing when you get stoned on marijuana or on hash—it's not the sort of thing where you want to go out and put a lampshade on your head. . . . Listening to music is very enjoyable; your sensations are really heightened; and touching things, and people, are really heightened: so making it is really great on hash! . . . Eating is another good thing. Food tastes so fabulous when you're stoned, . . . [and] your sense of lighting—with a strobe light, it's just incredible.

The *Bullet*'s editorial position was somewhat ambivalent. On the one hand, it cautioned students to "not jump into the 'drug scene'" without understanding the effects of drugs, but at the same time it advocated toleration consistent with the prevailing "if it feels good, do it" attitude, proclaiming that "to punish a person for use of something which he has found to be personally satisfying is a denial of human rights"—a philosophy that would have validated virtually every form of (mis)behavior known to the species.

There was no doubt that marijuana use increased at Mary Washington during the seventies, both among students and some faculty members. Student interest in marijuana led to the founding of a campus chapter of the National Organization to Reform Marijuana Laws (NORML) in September 1976—the first college in Virginia to do so. The organizational meeting drew an SRO crowd to Lee Hall's Lounge A, despite the fact that, according to the *Bullet*, many students were deterred from attending out of fear of harassment by the police or College administrators—neither of which proved true.

The group's first president was the appropriately named Michael Mello, then a sophomore (who would go on to achieve prominence as an attorney, writer, and law professor). He noted that the chapter's founding in the nation's bicentennial year was an appropriate "reminder to our government [that] the self-evident truths proclaimed by our Founding Fathers [are] rendered meaningless by the arrest and prosecution of individuals for the private use of marijuana." Plans for NORML included the sponsorship of campus movies such as *Marijuana: The New Prohibition* and the infamous *Reefer Madness*. The organization's main effort, however, was directed toward lobbying the state legislature for reform of marijuana laws. "The biggest obstacle to pot law reform . . . is apathy," Mello declared. "So long as we continue to tolerate this prohibition, we will have it around our necks forever. But, when we let our opinions be known to our elected officials, these laws will change."

Meanwhile the most notable drug-related episode in the College's history erupted in the spring of 1979 with a raid on Madison Hall that resulted in the arrest of five students for possession of marijuana and drug paraphernalia—four at the time of the bust and another several days later. One student who was arrested told the *Bullet* that he "heard a knock on the door. I answered it and there were four cops; they showed me a search warrant and came into the room. Then they sat me down and read me my rights. At that point, a state policeman . . . searched my room. They didn't find any pot, only twelve seeds and a bong. Then they took me to the station and charged me with possession of marijuana and paraphernalia." President Woodard quickly suspended the first four from the College pending an administrative hearing.

The suspensions touched off a furor on campus that led to a protest rally in support of the four, an action described by the College paper as "uncharacteristic of the Somnolent Seventies in general and of MWC in particular." The protest organizers insisted that their grievance went beyond the specifics of the incident itself. "We are not protesting the present drug laws," said one. "We are not even really protesting these busts. Rather, we are protesting the fact that those guys have been suspended without first receiving a trial or hearing. . . .There comes a time when a statement of principle must be made." That theme was reiterated at the rally itself as one speaker asserted, "We are not a group of angry pot smokers. We are a group of concerned students."

The demonstration on Westmoreland Green, attended by over one hundred people, was covered by all campus media, the Fredericksburg newspaper, and the Richmond *Times-Dispatch*. Mike Mello, the former NORML president, began the rally by delineating the two legal problems he believed to be involved: first, that the suspensions amounted to violations of the innocent-until-proven-guilty concept; and second, that President Woodard's action before the students' court appearance was not only prejudiced but, according to Mello, constituted double jeopardy. The featured speaker, an Alexandria attorney and NORML volunteer, was more demagogic in his attack. "The administration only cares about raw, naked power," he declared. "They have it and you [students] are their slaves."

The protest also included a petition demanding the "immediate reversal of the unjustified suspension" of the four students. Woodard, however, was unmoved by either the rally or the petition, saying that such actions would have "absolutely no effect" on his decision. "The suspension will not be reversed," he informed the protesters, "even if you get every student on this campus to sign your petition."

As with the earlier eviction of students from Westmoreland on account of dormitory violations, it was clear that the president's actions were well within his rights. The only question was whether the price was too great in terms of student morale. A *Bullet* op-ed piece suggested as much, decrying "how aloof the administration is from student life and concerns." "I for one," claimed the writer, "feel like some kind of aboriginal native whose lifestyle is dictated by a colonial empire which makes no effort to understand the fine points of my culture."

The *Bullet* itself offered a doleful, albeit rather perceptive, analysis of the existing situation. "Prince Woodard has done much for MWC," it admitted, and proceeded to describe some of his accomplishments. But, it continued, "Woodard has a definite problem with public relations." The future, it suggested, did not look good, the way things were going. "How long," it asked, "can Woodard maintain his dictatorial reign over every aspect of the college arena? . . . Will MWC continue to draw students to an atmosphere of classical authoritarian regulation? . . . It would be terribly unfortunate for this college if the members of the community accepted Woodard's proposed solution to the problem—'If you don't like it, leave.' President Prince B. Woodard would suddenly find himself the leader of a very beautiful but very empty college."

Not all the campus controversies of the period pitted students against administration; there were periodic internecine ones among the students themselves, including the issue of fraternities—both those from elsewhere and those that were proposed at MWC.

Although U.Va. frat "rolls" declined as coeducation grew at Mary Washington, they did not disappear. Nor did they become any more refined. So much destruction was wreaked on College property in the fall of 1978 that Dean of Students Mickey Clement banned U.Va. fraternities from the campus, and the prohibition was renewed the following year by her successor, Suzanne Gordon. The *Bullet* expressed sympathy with that approach. In an October 1979 editorial, "In Defense of Feminism," the author waxed indignant over the "cavalier" implication "that I have nothing better to do on a weeknight than to dress up solely for the benefit of the frat, to be judged on my physical attributes in competition with my peers, and to get a cheap thrill from free alcohol and the abundance of men."

Notwithstanding the admonition printed in the College paper that students "who observe a group of U.Va. fraternity men on campus should immediately report this fact to the college police and . . . not attempt to forcibly remove [them]," an unseemly incident occurred in the fall of 1982. When one U.Va. group arrived on campus in a bus, MWC males lobbed a barrage of eggs, and a U.Va. student was allegedly dragged from his car and doused with paint.

The episode prompted the *Bullet* to launch a philippic, not against the U.Va. frats or the MWC vigilantes but against Mary Washington women who participated in the group escapades. The piece began by disavowing "egg-throwing at strangers" or "vandalism in general" but added, "We understand that not one individual, case of beer, or Izod was consequentially damaged—the only real casualty, in fact, was a little male U. Va. pride." The greater problem, however, lay elsewhere:

> MWC women, where is your pride? You set the women's movement back about two hundred years . . . [whenever you] clamber aboard a U-Haul to be carted away like choice heifers. . . . Female dignity isn't the only thing at stake here. There is a certain amount of personal risk involved. We have seen girls returning from a fraternity off-campus party—horizontally, laid out flat, oblivious to the abuse their bodies were taking as they were dragged up steps by huffing and panting roommates or friends. It is a common conception that U. Va. fraternity men are "utter gentlemen." Maybe so. But . . . let's face it, men are men and drunk girls are drunk girls.

That blast provoked a spate of rebuttals in the *Bullet* defending both the manners of the U.Va. frat boys and the virtue of the MWC girls who dated them. Typical was the response of senior Mary "Muffin" Wilkinson, who chided, "This was not the 'meat market' that everyone conjures up in their minds when they hear of a U.Va. frat coming down. The guys that planned the party were clean-cut, polite gentlemen who spent a lot of time and money in preparation for their trip. They rented a Trailways bus (not a U-Haul) and waited patiently for the girls to climb aboard. They did not cram us on the bus. . . . They did not deserve the treatment they received." Added another, "As for those few girls who supposedly do sacrifice their 'female dignity' and take 'personal risks,' I ask what business is it of the *Bullet*?"

Paradoxically, just at the time of the ruckus over the U.Va. fraternity visit, a movement was developing to establish a Greek system at Mary Washington. The issue had arisen occasionally before, and in 1980 it was promoted avidly by Westmoreland resident assistant Clark Little. Among the reasons for his advocacy were his beliefs that the existence of fraternities and sororities would make the College more appealing to potential applicants, especially males, and that the added social life would help to eradicate the "suitcase college" mentality. The *Bullet* editorialized against the plan, citing practical problems such as lack of on-campus housing for Greek organizations but emphasizing even more the potentially adverse social consequences:

> The establishment of fraternities and sororities would be impractical, unnecessary, and, in fact, divisive at Mary Washington. . . . Frats have not existed at Mary Washington as part of a distinctive tradition. Some may say that this tradition must go, along with the name that carries it, but we say that this should not be so. . . . Fraternities have the distinct possibility of being a destructive force rather than a unifying one. The cohesiveness that a fraternity offers is offset by exclusiveness— Is there a need to create any more exclusiveness than already exists?

Support for fraternities and sororities gained some momentum in 1982 and was the subject of a campus forum that spring. The *Bullet*, by then under its first male editor, Shannon McGurk, was less negative than it had been earlier, asking in an editorial headline, "Is the Greek System an Idea Whose Time Has Finally Come?" McGurk's own answer was, essentially, "maybe."

> Critics often point out that the Greek system simply extends from high school an opportunity for students to remain kids a little longer, with another excuse to drink and socialize, when already no excuse is really necessary. . . . Are we going to institutionalize and sanction "cliques" and divisiveness on a campus this small? It is true there is already snobbery and social exclusiveness, but at present the boundaries are informal and can be breached. The Greek system offers a formal institution for students to exclude other students from social functions. Whether or not our students will do this is debatable.

When put to a vote in a referendum the following year, the unambiguous response of the student body was no, as over 60 percent of the respondents expressed opposition to the establishment of fraternities and sororities. Thus was preserved intact—going back to the abolition in the 1940s of the German and Cotillion dance clubs—the College's tradition of opposition to exclusive social organizations. Support for a Greek system did not fade completely, however, and would re-emerge from time to time in the years ahead.

Although many student concerns in the 1970s focused on personal issues—the time was known, after all, as the "Me Decade" (and not without reason)—some campus issues reflected larger societal concerns, notably in the areas of gender and race. A prime example was the increased interest in matters relating to sexual orientation.

At Mary Washington during that time, as at colleges generally, heterosexuality was predominant, accompanied by a goodly amount of what some would later disparage as sexism. Such a tendency was evident in a 1980 *Bullet* questionnaire that asked, "In order of importance, name four things about a guy/girl that would made you rate him/her a 10"—the number being a reference to the popular movie featuring Bo Derek in the (presumably perfect) titular role. Although results revealed that among both men and women, "good personality" rated as the most desirable trait, there were indications that physical attributes were also of considerable importance. Among males, the perfect woman was described by one student, for example, as "this month's [*Playboy*] centerfold—although last month's came very close," and by another as "34-24-36. No, 38. No, 40-24-36."

Responses from women tended to dwell somewhat less on sex, but physical appearance and "traditional" behavior were clearly important, as indicated by suggestions from various female students that, to qualify as a 10, a male must:

- Look good in his Levi's.
- Be Bjorn Borg (or a twin brother).
- Not attack on the first date; maybe on the second instead.
- Think my long flannel nightgowns are just as sexy as my sheer lingerie.
- Not wear fingernail polish, bras, hose, more than one earring, or lipstick.
- Not be afraid to spend money on me, but not spend extravagantly. Although that wouldn't be altogether bad.

It was in the mid-1970s that homosexuality first became a topic of open discussion on campus. The specific stimulus was a September 1975 *Bullet* article, "Gay Student Speaks Out," attributed in the byline simply to "a MWC student," unnamed. The author described herself as a lesbian activist who had recently "come out" and had worked during the previous summer for various groups promoting "gay liberation." In so doing, she said, she had encountered "nothing short of total acceptance" in her own community, but upon entering MWC, she was "appalled by all the subtle hostilities, the indifference, and the utter ignorance most students on campus exhibited about gay people and their issue." The result, she said, was that "within three weeks, I was made aware of these 'vibrations' so strongly that I, like all other gays on campus, felt myself forced back into hiding. This return to 'the closet' has denied me on campus a personhood, my freedom, and my political expression."

What followed was a description of the student body that many must have found startling. "So many of you," she pointed out, "don't realize what an incredibly good possibility there is that one of your close friends is gay. Your best friend, your teammate, the kid you sit next to in econ, a fellow 'slopgirl,' your roommate, the good-looking fellow you turned to watch walk by, the girl you whistled at from your car, . . . are all possibilities—even your friend who goes 'road-tripping' every weekend and dates like crazy."

The article concluded with an admonition both poignant and pointed. Too many students, the author asserted, were complicit in perpetuating daily discrimination against homosexuals. "For instance," she wrote,

> you contribute to such injustices each time you tell a "fag" joke or let one pass by without contesting it. Did it ever occur to you how likely it is that one or more of those people you were "entertaining" bore the brunt of your joke? Sometimes I wonder how many times I have had to sit through "jokes" like that and control my natural urge to defend myself. . . . What we have on campus is a vicious circle that desperately needs to be broken. . . . It is your responsibility to make this college a place where not only you, but also your gay friends, can learn and grow in a healthy, accepting, supportive atmosphere. And it is up to you, my gay sisters and brothers, to demand your right . . . to freedoms you should never have been denied.

If the author anticipated a sympathetic response (which she probably did not), she was to be largely disappointed, judging from subsequent letters to the *Bullet*. The most hostile was one that addressed the anonymous lesbian directly. "You object to being labeled sick, perverted, disturbed, and not normal," it read, "but the homosexual is neither normal nor natural. . . . I believe there is a distinct, natural biological order in life, and the mutual attraction of two members of the opposite sex in the same species is in keeping with nature's design. It is a fact of life." The critic concluded with a challenge: "Be known as you are. . . . Where is your by-line? Why didn't you back up your statement . . . by putting your name on it?"

The original writer promptly responded with a lengthy missive devoted largely to an exegesis of the term "normal," including the observation that if her critic "defin[ed] people by what they do in bed, I doubt very seriously she would find many who fit her neat category of normality." But the most stunning part of the letter was her riposte to the condemnation of her anonymity. "My by-line," she declared, "is myself. What better backup is there than first-person experience? . . . My entire article was devoted to pointing out the hardships the unknown gay people on campus suffer and, worse, the incredible hardships an upfront gay person would have to experience. If this is not enough reason for not signing my article, I don't know what is." And then her signature: Ivy R. Martin.

It was a bold act and, especially on as generally conservative a campus as Mary Washington, a brave one. It did not effect an immediate sea change in attitudes, certainly, as for some years thereafter, according to the *Bullet*, students who "came out" were "subjected to harassment, ridicule, and ostracism." Indeed, said the paper, Martin herself, "who declared her sexuality in 1976, . . . was branded the 'campus queer' from that time until she graduated."

But her public avowal did lead to more open discussion of the issue, as pro-gay articles began to appear periodically in the *Bullet*. In late 1976, a Gay Student Union (GSU) was founded; it met covertly at first, but by 1979 it had achieved official club sanction by the Interclub Association. It served largely as a nexus for gay students on campus, publishing a newsletter and working to educate the student body on matters of homosexuality.

As part of that effort—and as an indication of how attitudes were evolving—the GSU held an open meeting in February 1980 to answer questions on the subject (e.g., the legality of gay sex) and to rebut various misconceptions (e.g., that homosexuals were prone to sexually molest children). "That gay sex is considered repugnant to many people," said club president Lisa Langenback, "is really rather interesting, since the acts themselves are not very much different from straight sex. . . . What it all boils down to is love. . . . What we all have to do is learn to love people as people."

Such admirable admonitions notwithstanding, homophobia on campus was not easily or quickly eradicated. But with general societal change over the years, tolerance of differing sexual orientations increased dramatically, and so it was at Mary Washington. The time would come when students would look back on this period and wonder why there was so much commotion over an issue that by then seemed, to many of them, to be of such small consequence.

Student radicalism in the late seventies was not what it had been a few years earlier, but neither was it extinct, as evidenced at Mary Washington by the fall 1977 appearance of an "underground" newspaper called *Prometheus*. The biweekly publication proclaimed in its first issue that its purpose was "to provide a forum for discussion of various topics of interest on campus," with the implicit promise of airing issues that the "official" newspaper, the *Bullet*, was too politic, or simply too timid, to address.

The *Bullet*, with its 2,800-copy circulation, was not much bothered by competition from the upstart *Prometheus* and its five hundred copies; in fact, there was significant overlap in the staffs of the two papers.[23] In that light, it was not surprising that the *Bullet* actually applauded its friendly rival for serving as a "watchdog for the *Bullet*, forcing [it] to be ever alert and poised lest the ragtag 'underground' press scoop the official MWC newspaper." *Prometheus* folded at the end of the 1977–78 session after seven months of publication, but during that time, as one of its chief writers noted, "It was a hell of an experience. And for a while it was even fun."

In actual operation, *Prometheus* was never quite as avant-garde as it purported to be. True, it did publish some articles on subjects that the *Bullet* had generally ignored, such as possible discrimination against day students and the (in)competence of dorm mothers; it also printed an eyewitness account of an honor trial. On the whole, however, its reputation as a radical paper may have rested less on its articles than on its advertisements for things such as drug paraphernalia and gay parties.

Perhaps the most sensitive issue tackled by *Prometheus* was student-faculty dating, which was the subject of a series of articles written by Ivy Martin—herself no stranger to controversy—beginning with a piece titled "Student-Faculty Affaires: No More Sweeping under the Rug." The most provocative installment was a lengthy interview with an anonymous female student who described in detail the vicissitudes of her (ultimately failed) romantic relationship with one of her professors.

The account, which alternated between poignancy and bathos, revealed the student's ambiguity on the desirability of such relationships. Asked if she would advocate a college policy against it, she replied, "If it would work, I would say that that would probably be a good policy, but I don't think it would stop anything. I think it would just create more injunctions. . . . You can't control their private lives." Having at one point professed to think "it's a bad idea," when later asked directly by Martin if she would date another professor, she replied, "That depends upon the situation. . . . Yeah, I guess I'd do it again if it was the right person [but] I might approach it differently, with a different frame of mind, at least."

The most startling part of the interview was the student's claim to know of twenty-eight such ongoing relationships at the time, a number that she determined by perusing the faculty roster. Of that number, eighteen of them (roughly 65 percent) involved faculty members who, she believed, were married.

Though the accuracy of her estimate was unverifiable, it was certainly true that student-faculty fraternization, both platonic and otherwise, was at its peak during that period, owing to several factors. For one thing, there was an unusually large number of young professors on campus as a result of President Simpson's effort to reinvigorate the faculty—many of them single males. And there was no sanction against such relationships, aside from the College handbook's admonition that professors who dated students must abide by the same rules as any of their other dates. (Such a policy, which amounted to implicit approval, was not difficult to abide by, since by that time there were few such rules anyway.)

Fundamentally there was simply a new cultural climate on campus, a manifestation of the broader relaxation of social strictures. In that milieu, behavior that would have struck previous generations as scandalous—and subsequent ones as inappropriate—seemed unremarkable to many at the time. To be sure, there were those who looked askance at such relationships, but disapproval was lessened during this period—a juncture between the time when the effect of feminism was to liberate young women from inhibitions, including those against socializing with professors, and a later time when that same philosophy tended to stigmatize such associations as inherently exploitative.

The relationships that occurred within this laissez-faire environment no doubt included some that were predatory—the "lay-for-an-A" syndrome—and resulted in emotional distress for the student victims. (In later years, College policy, without expressly forbidding student-faculty dating, would take a much more negative approach to it, warning professors against the serious dangers inherent therein.) On the other hand, a number of student-faculty relationships led to marriage, including some in which the former student, as spouse, continued to have a significant association with the institution.

Martha Van Zandt Fickett '63, Katherine Deneke Clatanoff '72, and Dawn Smith Bowen '86 became full-time faculty members; Patricia Bowles Tracy '73 became director of disability services; Theresa Young Crawley '77 became president of the Alumni Association and secretary of the Mary Washington Foundation; and Mona Davis Albertine '71 became rector of the Board of Visitors.[24]

Aside from student-faculty relationships, other issues related to gender periodically piqued student interest. For example, support for the Equal Rights Amendment, ratification of which was pending throughout the decade, never wavered, owing in large part to its effective advocacy by religion professor Elizabeth Clark and other persuasive feminist spokespersons. As the deadline for ratification neared, the *Bullet*, through the person of its male editor Shannon McGurk, offered a strong endorsement. "It should be remembered," he wrote, "that the ERA is not saying anything revolutionary, [nor] will it threaten anyone's rights. It simply states that sex should never be a deciding factor in determining legal rights for anyone. This should not even be open to debate. . . . Only three states stand between American women and the equality to which they are entitled, the equality to which they have been hitherto denied. Write your Congressman now. We cannot allow this amendment to go down in history as a mere attempt at freedom."

But a mere attempt it turned out to be, as the June 30, 1982, deadline passed without ratification by the requisite number of states. The proposed amendment, suggested the *Bullet*, was the "victim of a conservative shift in attitude throughout the nation. . . . To say this is discouraging is to state the feeling lightly; to the women who have spent this decade and the decades before working in the cause of equal rights, it is a constant source of anguish."

On campus, liberated attitudes occasionally produced conflicting feelings as the number of males in the student body gradually increased. On the one hand, most females seemed to favor that development, but some at the same time perceived an alarming trend: namely, in the words of the *Bullet*, "the disparity of having men hold major campus offices in disproportionate number to the male students that attend Mary Washington."

It was a state of affairs that the *Bullet* bemoaned, attributing it largely to the pusillanimity of female students. "Many women at MWC," admonished one editorial in 1979,

> are simply not aware that they do not possess equality and are being oppressed, and many do not care, or actually enjoy their current status. . . . Are the women on this campus really just afraid to challenge men, feeling that they are incompetent compared to a man, or do they feel that men will reject them for challenging male superiority? . . . Until people, especially women, on this campus care enough about

the lack of equality between men and women, not only at MWC, but throughout the world, the oppression will continue, and this society will become more stagnant (and frightening) than it is already.

For whatever reasons, the trend in campus elections continued, with major offices frequently being held by men, though by no means exclusively so.

Race was another area of concern on campus. Nationwide, the seventies were less racially tense than the turbulent previous decade, and that situation generally prevailed at Mary Washington as well. There were desultory calls for greater amity, and occasional expressions of student support for black causes, as when the *Bullet* heartily endorsed the establishment of Martin Luther King Jr.'s birthday as a national holiday. But the racial climate on campus during the period was, on the whole, not altogether a felicitous one, for whereas there were few overt instances of outright hostility, neither was there much evidence of camaraderie.

Black frustration was evident in a 1977 *Bullet* article titled "The Black Experience at MWC: What It's Really Like." In the piece, the president of the Afro-American Association, Sallie Washington (who would later serve for many years as a highly respected member of the College staff in various administrative capacities), set out several specific grievances shared by black students. High on the list were lack of curricular emphasis on black studies and what she regarded as minimal effort in recruiting minority students. These, however, were not matters within the control of students, but instead required administrative action.

Within the province of students, though, were other issues that Washington found disturbing. One was the lack of black-oriented entertainment on campus. Even movies, she said, were rejected if the subject was "touchy to whites," citing as an example *Mandingo*, a film that was both racy and interracial.

Most galling, perhaps, was the lack of white students' support for Black Culture Week. The celebration had been held annually since the early seventies, and the AAA put enormous effort into it. The week typically incorporated a variety of elements, such as addresses by prominent black politicians including Richmond mayor Henry Marsh, D.C. representative Walter Fauntroy, and Fredericksburg mayor Lawrence Davies (elected in 1977 as the city's first African American mayor), and educational presentations such as local historian Ruth Coder Fitzgerald's lecture on the history of African Americans in the Fredericksburg area. There were various forms of entertainment, including talent shows, gospel jamborees, and art exhibitions, as well as musical performances featuring local artists such as noted blues singer Gaye Adegbalola and, in 1980, the internationally renowned Ramsey Lewis Trio. The week typically concluded with a dance, the sophistication of which varied from the casual keg party, to a Valentine's dance, to a more formal Ebony Ball.

Yet no matter how appealing the program or how popular the events were among black students, one thing was consistent: white students, by and large, did not participate. It was a disheartening situation for the AAA members, who made conscientious efforts to ensure that their white peers knew they were included. "The total disinterest MWC white students have in Black Culture Week," wrote one *Bullet* editorialist, "do[es] not seem to indicate any real concern to bridge the gap between students of different races." So pessimistic was the 1977–78 AAA president, Marilyn Graves, that she somberly predicted that "the black population on this campus may become extinct."

That, of course, did not happen, but it was clear that in the area of racial matters at MWC, there was considerable room for improvement.

In the years immediately following Nixon's resignation in 1974 there were few national issues that stirred Mary Washington students. Not even the presidential election of 1976 generated much interest. In a poll conducted by the *Bullet* before the election, the Republican incumbent Gerald Ford narrowly defeated his Democratic challenger, Jimmy Carter, an outcome that proved to be the reverse of the actual election results. The remarkable part, however, was how few students bothered to participate, evidently deeming both candidates to be lackluster, with few crucial policy issues separating them—an attitude apparently shared by the general electorate, judging from the low voter turnout nationwide.

Though there were issues aplenty during the Carter years, they often involved matters somewhat tangential to students. One of the most serious problems, for example, was unemployment, but that was not of immediate concern to most students, save graduating seniors. On the other hand, the concurrent problem of inflation was of considerable concern to College students, many of whom had few disposable dollars. The *Bullet* in 1976 attempted to assist the cost-conscious by publishing a comparison of prices at local stores for what it described as "necessities," among them:

Item	*MWC Bookstore*	*Giant*	*People's*
Crest Toothpaste (3 oz.)	$0.72	$0.62	$0.69
Suave Shampoo (16 oz.)	0.89	0.89	1.39
Noxema (2.5 oz.)	0.65	1.15	0.91
Q-Tips (54 swabs)	0.43	0.43	0.69
Ban Roll-On (1.5 oz.)	1.20	1.19	1.17
Vaseline (1.75 oz.)	0.49	0.43	0.47
No-Doz (15 tablets)	0.79	1.19	0.77
Trojans (3, rolled)	—	—	0.85

Another major problem involved energy resources (notably petroleum shortages), but students, within the secure confines of the campus, were rarely inconvenienced directly, aside from being asked to turn thermostats down and conserve electricity in the dorms. Off campus they, like Americans everywhere, experienced occasional gas shortages, long lines at the pumps, and, for a brief while, odd/even-day rationing. But these were basically nuisances, not the kind of issues that impelled an earlier student generation to take up placards of protest.

Late in the Carter presidency, however, there occurred an international incident that once again provoked a campus rally over public policy—the first such protest in almost a decade. The November 29, 1979, demonstration on Ball Circle was in response to the taking of American hostages in Iran earlier that month by a mob under the influence of a radical Muslim cleric, the Ayatollah Khomeini. The mob was protesting the fact that the deposed Shah had been given asylum in the United States.

The rally, which was attended by townsfolk as well as students, commenced beneath the backdrop of a huge American flag adorning the front portico of Virginia Hall, as students chanted "Let our people go" and waved signs bearing demands such as "Unconditional Release Now." After a moment of silence and the playing of the "Star-Spangled Banner," the most dramatic moment occurred when rally leaders, mimicking the behavior of Iranian radicals against the United States, burned an Iranian flag to the accompaniment of loud cheering. (Actually, it was an Italian flag, but presumably close enough in appearance to convey the intended hostility.)

Though the prevailing tone of the demonstration was one of muscular patriotism, the views expressed by the various speakers—students, faculty, and administrators—ranged from pacifistic to bellicose. Among the pacifists was veteran antiwar activist Alice Rabson of the Psychology Department, who deplored the possible use of weapons "that will further jeopardize the lives of the people incarcerated in Iran." A similarly cautious approach was advocated by senior international affairs major Ford Hart (who would go on to a career in the State Department) in an impassioned plea for restraint. Burning the Iranian flag, he said, was "damn wrong. What are we like when we start burning flags? . . . Perhaps we might go to war, but by God, let's hope we don't have to. . . . If we don't watch ourselves, we will step into one. I'm not talking about just forty-nine lives, I'm talking about hundreds, perhaps thousands, of lives. I'm talking about you and me."

A decidedly more belligerent tone was sounded by Joe Freeman, one of the protest organizers. As students cheered the burning flag, he shouted, "Hear that, Iran? That's America talking!" and went on in his subsequent speech to proclaim, "I feel patriotic today. I hope you do, also. . . . The righteous wrath of America is more than any nation in the world can endure."

The tenth and final speaker was more temperate, urging that America not engage in a "bigoted, blind campaign of hate" against Iran, especially not against Iranian students in the United States, lest "they wonder where is the justice they came for." That reproof to the audience was welcomed in particular by Alireza Sezawarkeshavarz, an Iranian student who was then an MWC freshman. In a *Bullet* interview at the time of the protest rally, he made it clear that he opposed the taking of hostages but nonetheless preferred the Khomeini regime to that of its predecessor. "The Shah," he explained, "stole all our money. He tortured a lot of people . . . [and] killed 350,000 people. They were my brothers and sisters. Americans do not understand that in Iran we are all brothers and sisters." He also defended murders under Khomeini's rule because some were the Shah's henchmen and because others were potentially corrosive influences on society. For example, he noted, "Khomeini says that homosexuals make society bad, so he kills them."

The *Bullet* gave extensive coverage to the rally, including in its next issue not just one but three editorials on the subject, each advocating a different course of U.S. action, though all deplored the flag-burning incident. Editor-in-Chief Gary Webb took the hardest line. "The United States of America," he declared, "cannot allow itself to be pushed around by a crazed relic of the Middle Ages." He proposed that a deadline be set for release of the hostages and "if they are not released by that time, military action should be taken. It is not easy to call for such action, but neither is it easy to see our flag burned, our diplomats accused of spying, and our entire nation being held hostage."

News Editor Betsy Rohaly was more conciliatory. "Peaceful settlement is infinitely preferable to war," she wrote, "and we must avoid another international-scale war at all costs. . . . There are still diplomatic channels that must be used." Counseling against a military effort to rescue the hostages, she was coldly pragmatic: "Callous as it may seem, consider this: would you rather that fifty people die, or fifty thousand? I would hope that the lives of the fifty American hostages could be saved, . . . but if the only way to save those fifty Americans is to take the necessarily extensive military action that could free them, then I would rather sacrifice the few to save the many."

Business Manager Cynthia Nash took something of a middle ground between the two editors, proposing that there should be no military action "unless the United States has clear proof that a hostage has been killed by an Iranian captor." In that event, however, American retaliation would be imperative because if "no action is taken by the U.S., this will make America seem even more unstable, and may even invite more hostage situations to take place around the world."

Less than two months after the anti-Iranian rally, students' attention was again drawn to the Middle East when in January 1980 the Soviet Union invaded Afghanistan. President Carter's response to this Cold War aggression—to curtail arms limitation talks with the Soviets, embargo grain shipments to them, and boycott the 1980 Moscow Summer Olympics—was applauded by the *Bullet*. "We cannot allow our nation to be bullied by any group," stated an editorial, "including the fanatical Iranian government, . . . or the cold and calculating warriors in the Kremlin. . . . By taking peaceful, yet effective, steps against the Soviets, [Carter] has avoided both the potentially apocalyptic use of armed force and the embarrassing impotency of appeasement."

Meanwhile the hostage situation dragged on unresolved as winter turned into spring, then summer, then fall again. By that time, political interest at the College was focused mainly on the 1980 presidential campaign, an epochal contest between the increasingly unpopular incumbent and the conservative Republican challenger, Ronald Reagan. (There was also a third candidate, the independent John Anderson, a moderate Republican.)

Interest was spiked on campus throughout the fall by an ongoing battle of op-ed *Bullet* articles pitting Reagan devotee Vince DiBenedetto against Carter adherent Dan Steen. In the course of the series, the two students forcefully argued the merits of their respective candidates. DiBenedetto especially touted the economic benefits that would accrue from Reagan's proposed tax cuts, while Steen asserted that there was a "historic choice" to be made—either "giving our President the mandate he deserves or turning over the reins of government to a man who wants to set us back forty years."[25]

On campus, as at the national level, the Republicans got the better of it. In a mock election sponsored by Circle K one week before the national vote, Reagan received 50 percent, Carter 24 percent, and Anderson 19 percent. In the actual election, Reagan triumphed over Carter by a margin of approximately 51 to 41 percent.

Throughout the presidential campaign, the Iranian hostage conundrum proved exasperating to MWC students, as to the general American public, leading ultimately to an inchoate weariness well expressed in a November 1980 *Bullet* editorial, "The Forgotten Hostages." One year ago, it said,

> the main question everyone was concerned with was whether or not the U.S. would become involved in a war with Iran. Students talked in panic about family and friends being drafted, and wondered whether or not women would have to serve in the front lines. . . . Now, students are no longer concerned with that question. Many students feel the hostages will never be released; others feel that, even if they are, they will have suffered from brainwashing by the militants. . . . In any case no one speaks of war anymore. The burning of flags is over; . . . students no longer study maps of Canada; and the hostages are still not released. What now?

The answer to that question finally came in January 1981, when the captives were released on the last day of Carter's presidency, producing a sense of relief across the country. At Mary Washington, the Student Association initiated a drive to develop a letter of welcome to be signed by members of the College community and conveyed to the former hostages. "If we can apply to this gesture the same spirit and enthusiasm that existed at the Rally for Freedom held in November, 1979," said the *Bullet*, "we will have tremendous success."

The letter, addressed to "Our Fellow Americans, Recently Arrived from Iran," reflected the national mood at that moment: "The joy and thanksgiving which your safe return has brought to the nation as a whole, and to our campus in particular, has prompted us . . . to express to you our pride, affection, and congratulations. Throughout the late ordeal, your courage and perseverance have epitomized the best qualities of the American people and have earned you the respect and admiration of the Free World. . . . Welcome home."

Gratified as the public was by the hostages' safe return, the euphoria was more muted than might have been expected. At Mary Washington in particular, attention had by then been diverted by one of the most fearsome events in the College's history.

Every residential student at Mary Washington College had endured fire drills, those inconvenient but necessary exercises seemingly timed by fiendish design to cause maximum intrusion on study or slumber. No student, however, had ever had quite the experience as that of senior Eileen O'Connell on the morning of December 5, 1980.

O'Connell, a resident assistant living in Bushnell 412, was in her room when at about 6:30 a.m., she recalled, "Something was keeping me from sleeping. I could hear something in the next room like the sound of Christmas paper crinkling." But it was not paper crinkling; it was flames crackling—the igniting of the worst fire in Mary Washington's history.

It could scarcely have occurred at a worse time. Classes had ended for the semester the previous day, the consequence being that many students had stayed up late, either studying for upcoming exams or (more likely, perhaps) celebrating the end of classes. Whether the product of intellectual endeavor or beery indulgence, the residents of Bushnell were in a more torpid state than usual when the fire broke out. "There were quite a few parties last night," said O'Connell. "A few of the kids in the dorm had hangovers."

As for O'Connell herself, she "got up and noticed six inches of smoke up around the ceiling. I woke up my suitemates and pulled the fire alarm. Then we started getting people out of the building." Among them was the student in whose room the fire had started—the result, it was later determined, of carelessness with a cigarette. Alone because her two roommates were away, she awoke to find her room on fire. Unable to exit through the doorway to the hall, she managed to escape through an adjoining bathroom.

Meanwhile students were fleeing, clad only in bedclothes draped with blankets or robes, into the thirty-two-degree morning chill. Several male students stayed behind, armed with hall fire extinguishers, to try to do what they could to contain the blaze. Among them were junior David Hawkens and senior Mark Ingrao. According to Hawkens, "We got down on the floor when we opened the door because we knew the smoke and flames would be

THE FREE LANCE-STAR

Bushnell on fire, December 1980

bad. We looked in to make sure there was nobody left in there and then tried to get as much water down as we could."[26] It was all to little avail, however. Ingrao recalled that in less than a minute after the burning room was opened, the halls were filling with thick black smoke and the lights went out. "It was just a raging fire," he said.

> There were two beds on fire, the rug was on fire, the draperies were on fire [and] so we started pumping the extinguishers and trying to do what we could do. And we stayed in there for a couple of minutes and then something in the room exploded—whether it was a light bulb or a canister or whatever it was. And I said, "You know, guys, we're not doing any good here," because as we kept pumping the fire extinguishers, the fire kept coming closer and closer on the rug to us. We weren't making any headway. And I said, "I think we need to get out of here," so we went back the way we came, on our hands and knees, downstairs.

At that point the dorm fire marshal reported that there were people locked in a third-floor room who were not responding to evacuation efforts. Whereupon, Ingrao remembered, "I went in and broke through the bathroom door between the two suites to find two people sleeping—a girl and a guy, both of them naked—and I wasn't really sure what to do. . . . It wasn't easy to wake them both up, but I did wake up the guy and said, 'Help me get her dressed,' [but] after he dropped her a couple of times, I figured to heck with it. So I grabbed a blanket and I wrapped her up in the blanket and threw her over my shoulder and . . . [carried her outside]. He was just barely able to walk, so I walked him out, holding his arm, to the front parlor."

Under the circumstances, it was remarkable that the evacuation was as orderly and effective as it was. One reason for the successful outcome, according to the dorm's student fire marshal, was that there had been three fire drills that semester. In any case, by the time the Fredericksburg fire department arrived about ten minutes after the blaze was discovered, almost all of the approximately 135 occupants of the dorm that morning were already out. Soon thereafter, firemen completed a search of the building, despite dense smoke that greatly diminished visibility. All they found was a frightened kitten, which they rescued.

The first College administrator on the scene was Executive Vice President William Anderson, who tried to comfort the students shivering outside, organize them, and get them into neighboring Jefferson dorm, where the ARA food service soon arrived on the scene to provide coffee and breakfast. A few students, still wearing bathrobes and pajamas, decided to walk to Seacobeck for breakfast. Some students from other parts of campus who did not yet know about the fire assumed that the unusual attire was simply an exam week joke.

The fire department meanwhile had managed to extinguish the blaze, limiting actual fire damage mainly to the suite where it started, though that area was gutted. Damage from smoke and water was much more extensive, especially on the fourth floor. Later in the day, students on other floors were allowed to reenter their rooms, where they anxiously sought to determine the condition of their belongings—most especially, given the season, their class notes. "What a time for this to happen," said one. "All my books and notes were destroyed. How do you replace a whole semester of work?"

Even such concerns as those, however, were overshadowed by the relief that everyone had gotten out of the dorm—almost everyone, that is. It turned out that during the final inspection before allowing reentry, two firemen discovered still abed in her room near one end of the fifth floor a student, who, quite improbably, had managed to sleep safely through the whole thing.

With the semester nearly at an end, temporary quarters were found in other dorms through the exam period for the fourth-floor Bushnell residents, who were given the option of taking their exams as scheduled or deferring them without penalty until the spring semester. Residents of other floors were able to return to their rooms, thanks to the extraordinary efforts of

THE FREE LANCE-STAR

A resident inspects the charred remains of her Bushnell room.

the College's maintenance and custodial staffs. Even while the fire was being fought, maintenance personnel had constructed a sand barrier to contain the huge amount of water being sprayed into the fourth floor. And as soon as the building was released for reoccupancy, custodians went to work scrubbing the walls to remove soot and to dry the soggy floors.

Once the semester break began, heroic efforts were undertaken to get Bushnell ready for reopening on January 10. This involved overtime work not only by the College's physical plant employees but also by local contractor Franklin Powell, whose crew worked three shifts a day, seven days a week, throughout the period, taking only three days off during the holiday season. When opening day arrived, the dorm was ready, save for the two most damaged rooms, whose previous occupants were reassigned elsewhere. The cost of repairs was approximately $80,000.

There were some lingering consequences of the episode. One was a predictable increase in concern for fire safety. There was some criticism about the absence of an automatic sprinkler system in Bushnell, but at the time of its construction in 1959, such features were rare. (On the other hand, the building's sturdy cinder-block-wall construction was an important factor in limiting the spread of the fire.)

No one was more traumatized by the fire than President Woodard, aside from the Bushnell residents—and perhaps not even they. In the first issue of the *Bullet* after the second semester began, he addressed the College community regarding the matter in an open letter in which he displayed somewhat uncharacteristic emotion. "A major fire on a college campus," he wrote, "is something that is forever feared in the minds of college presidents." He expressed gratitude to those who had performed so admirably in the crisis, including the Fredericksburg fire department, College police, ARA food service, buildings and grounds employees, the Office of Student Housing, and the Health Center. The faculty he singled out for "generously [making] allowances during the exam period for those students whose books and notes were destroyed."

His greatest praise was reserved for the students, not just those in Bushnell for their orderly evacuation and for those who bravely fought the fire themselves, but for many others throughout the campus who "became aware of the needs of their friends in Bushnell and responded in force. Temporary lodging was offered, and clothes and personal items were loaned. Within a few hours, all of the displaced students had their basic needs met. Later . . . friends of those still displaced continued their support and provided more permanent living arrangements."

He concluded with a heartfelt expression of appreciation to "all who offered their help and for the quick thinking and actions of those directly involved." Although the fire itself was the signal event of the day, he said, "there were hundreds of other events that day, mostly in the form of extraordinary individual efforts on the part of students, college staff, and the public that linger uppermost in my mind. . . . The tragedy that struck Mary Washington College December 5 showed what truly dedicated people we have working and living in this college community."

Eventually, as the campus returned more or less to normal, some students were even able to find humor in the narrowly averted catastrophe. Soon after the spring semester began, the residents of Bushnell designed and had printed T-shirts that read, "I survived the Burning Bush, 12-05-80." Sale of the shirts was limited to only Bushnell students, who, when the shirts arrived, all wore them on the same day.

Mark Ingrao had a more personal memory. Later on the day of the fire, he entered the parlor of Jefferson. "As I walked in there," he recalled, "this young lady came up to me—this was the person that I had taken out. And she was conscious at this point, and she said, 'I have to tell you that I really appreciate what you did for me. I just don't know what to say.' I looked at her and—I just had to say it—I said, 'It was my pleasure.' . . . Unfortunately, she could never look me in the eye for the rest of the year."

Certainly it was a day never to be forgotten by any of the Bushnell residents, but especially by the residents of the room where the fire started. The one who was there at the time was admitted to the campus health center for smoke inhalation and released later the same day. Her two roommates returned only to find the charred remnants of their possessions. "Even though you don't have much when you're still in school," said one, "I guess you could say everything we had is gone. . . . But we're alive and that's what's really important."

Indeed so, for them and all the others in Bushnell—most particularly the somnolent student on the fifth floor. And the kitten.

As the 1970s progressed, an evolution occurred in the College's governing body as original members of the Board of Visitors retired or were not reappointed. Among the most surprising was the unexpected resignation in 1976 of Ralph M. "Tip" Whitticar, who was a member of the board's executive committee and a charter member of the MWC Foundation. The abruptness of his departure prompted speculation that it resulted from a disagreement between him and unspecified College officials. Whitticar denied such implications, claiming that it involved merely "a matter of personal priorities." Governor Mills Godwin named John G. Castles, a major general in the Virginia National Guard, to replace Whitticar.

Two years later, Lewis Walker, who had been rector of the board since its inception in 1972, was replaced by Katherine E. Hopper '30 of Fairfax. Her appointment was part of a new slate of board officers that included the election of Gwendolyn Cumming '52 as vice rector and Irene Lundy Brown '39 as secretary. It marked the first time that all three officers were women and also graduates of the College.

The 1978 board also included the youngest member in its history. During Republican John N. Dalton's successful gubernatorial campaign the previous year, he had pledged to appoint recent graduates to the board of the state colleges, and he fulfilled that pledge at Mary Washington by appointing twenty-four-year-old Sue Smith '76 (later Hane), who had received her degree in geography only two years earlier. Smith instantly endeared herself to students by declaring that she was "very open and responsive to student needs and desires" and gave substance to that statement by pledging to work for the inclusion of a student member on the Board of Visitors—an issue that was then foremost among the students' governance priorities. It would have to wait awhile.

In the normal course of affairs, students took little interest in the Board of Visitors, a group whose very name signified only an occasional presence on campus. A blatant exception to that blasé attitude occurred, however, in the fall of 1980 when Governor Dalton appointed the Fredericksburg attorney Benjamin H. Woodbridge to the board, a move that elicited an immediate outburst of opposition on campus. The reason lay in Woodbridge's actions a decade earlier, when, during the time of unusual student unrest, his salvos against college rebels in general—Mary Washington in particular and the *Bullet* most of all—had rendered him campus enemy number one. As a member of the House of Delegates, he had raised student hackles by sponsoring two bills—one to end nonvoluntary student support for campus newspapers (for which he was accused of censorship) and the other to expel any student or faculty member who disrupted activity on a state college campus. Though neither passed, local media, noting the irony of Woodbridge's appointment to the board, quickly brought the incident back to public attention.

His appointment led not only to predictable *Bullet* outcries but also to the sudden appearance on campus of an independent publication known as the *Mary Wash Free Times*, described in its masthead as "MWC's First Student-Controlled Newspaper." Judging from its thin and tendentious content, its minuscule circulation, and its brief life span, it appears that the main (perhaps sole) purpose of the screed was to vilify Woodbridge, whom it wildly described as an "infamous neo-fascist," among other unflattering phrases. "We as students," it declared, "can only despair at the prospect of another reactionary influence at Mary Wash. . . . Dark days seem to be just around the corner."

The *Bullet* was more temperate, providing a front-page forum for a lengthy interview with Woodbridge, who was, on the whole, cordial and conciliatory. He did not apologize for his earlier actions, describing them as "positions I took ten years ago when I was in the legislature, which I think are still valid positions given the conditions and situations that existed at that time." But times, he believed, had changed, and for the better. "I certainly like what I see," he remarked, "and I think that the students . . . at MWC seem to be more serious about their studies and seem to be more purposeful in their attitude about school" than they were in an earlier time.

As for his board appointment, what he mainly wanted, he said, was that students "at least wait and see what kind of person I am" before making judgments. What they saw, as it turned out, was a performance that gave no evidence of his earlier curmudgeonly behavior. Throughout his time on the board, including service on its executive committee, Woodbridge's supportive actions belied his anticipated role as the bête noire of the student body.

Though the appointment of Woodbridge had raised eyebrows at the College, other issues relating to the board proved to be of broader concern. One was the long-standing desire on the part of various groups—notably some students, faculty, and the media—for the meetings of the Board of Visitors to be open to the public, a situation that would require legislative approval. Governor Dalton had endorsed the idea in his campaign, but MWC Rector Katherine Hopper, essentially ambivalent about the change, was not enthusiastic.

Eventually, at its 1979 session, the General Assembly passed legislation requiring that all meetings be open. The vote in the Senate was extremely close—twenty to nineteen—with the crucial vote being cast by Fredericksburg's John H. Chichester, who had recently replaced the late Paul W. Manns, an opponent of the bill. From that point onward, all board meetings had to be open, with the stipulation that they could go into closed session to consider certain matters—specifically student discipline, acquisition of property, offers of private gifts, consideration of lawsuits, and personnel issues.

The legislation was welcomed by the *Bullet*, though its praise was suffused with a whiff of cynicism. "Open meetings will benefit all members of the MWC community," it editorialized. "As the veils of secrecy are ripped in half, and more institutional barriers are broken, Mary Washington may someday take on an almost democratic air."

To student activists, a matter of greater importance than open meetings was the inclusion of a student member on the board. The Student Association began to push the issue in 1977, but without success, owing in part to the intransigent opposition of the influential rector, Lewis Walker. Asked by the *Bullet* in 1978 if he would support such a move, Walker replied, "No. And here's why. . . . There is no continuity. Even a junior or a senior would have only a year or two of usefulness as far as the student body is concerned. . . . We don't think [it] would be a useful function either for the student or for the Board."

President Woodard was much of the same mind, though his reasoning was somewhat different. His opposition was based on the belief that boards should be composed of only persons of nonvested interests, which would clearly eliminate students. If students were granted a seat on the board, he claimed, faculty members would follow suit, as well as classified employees and other interested groups. Referring to his prior experience in West Virginia, he said, "I have worked with it both ways. [Vested representation] just doesn't work out."

The unsuccessful effort left students frustrated and searching for a means to force the issue. A *Bullet* editorial suggested various possibilities, including economic pressure—and even physical intimidation, which it ultimately rejected. "Ten years ago," said one editorial, "it might have been conceivable to use physical force to gain the objective of student power . . . [but] violence, as a means of gaining power, is out of the question for us, in this day and age." And so, the paper concluded, it was a "hopeless quest."

But that prediction turned out to be overly pessimistic, thanks largely to the efforts of energetic students across the commonwealth who organized a lobbying group known as the Virginia Student Association (VASA) to advocate the passage of legislation requiring student representation on boards. One of the group's most persuasive leaders was MWC's Dan Steen, who became president of the group in 1982. He pointed out that twenty-five states had already made provisions for such student input and that institutional governance would significantly benefit from the infusion of student views. Though the General Assembly voted down such a plan in 1981, Steen's efforts were rewarded the following year with the passage of a bill that did not require, but did permit, student representation on boards at the discretion of each college.

The question then became what the MWC board would do. To the pleasant surprise of student leaders, the board proved amenable to student representation, even before they could be importuned to do so. With board member Arabelle Arrington playing an instrumental role on their behalf, students were awarded, by a secret-ballot vote of eight to three, a seat on the board; Mary Washington thus joined Old Dominion as the only state schools with such an arrangement.

The board resolution specified that the student representative would be the president of the Student Association; he or she would be a nonvoting member and would be excluded from executive sessions but would otherwise be allowed to participate in all board deliberations. The arrangement, even if limited in some respects, was well received by the students. "Our representation," said Dan Steen, "proves that our Board of Visitors and our administration have sufficient trust in our student leadership—a relationship that has fully developed in the last few years."

The first student to serve as a member of the board was the SA president for 1982–83, Anne Thompson. Describing herself as "just thrilled to death" to have the opportunity, she reported that in her first meeting, "every member in some way welcomed me to the Board. They encouraged me to speak my mind. So, I'm not going to be hesitant." Thompson was an ideal person to blaze that trail. Her combination of enthusiasm, maturity, and graciousness facilitated easy rapport with the other members, setting an admirable precedent for future harmony between the other board members and the student representatives.[27]

Just as progress was made with student representation, so too did the enrollment situation improve during Woodard's administration. The enrollment decline was not only stanched but reversed to the point that between 1974 and 1978 the student population grew by 10 percent—the result of a 3 percent growth in full-time students and a doubling of part-time students.[28] The accomplishment was all the more remarkable because it occurred during a period when enrollments in Virginia and elsewhere had begun to level off or decline.

Success in admissions, of course, had to be judged not just by the number of students enrolled but also by their academic quality and their diversity (i.e., number of males and racial minorities). An important boon to recruitment of academically talented students was the 1973 establishment of a special fund for financial assistance known as the Regional Scholarship Program. The gift that created the program was kept anonymous for many years, but it was later revealed to have come from the estate of the General Motors magnate and local resident John Lee Pratt, via MWC board member Tip Whitticar, whose law firm administered Pratt's financial bequests.[29]

The program was structured to attract annually two students from each of Virginia's ten congressional districts, plus five from outside the state, for a total of twenty-five scholars each year. High schools in each district could nominate superior students who were then screened for scholarship awards by regional committees composed of Mary Washington alumni. Criteria for selection were outstanding academic achievement, promise of continued academic excellence, and potential for intellectual leadership—without regard to financial need. Each of the awards consisted of $1,000 and could automatically be renewed contingent on satisfactory performance, defined as a minimum grade-point average of 2.5 for the freshman year and 3.0 thereafter.

In the program's first five years, more than one thousand students applied for the 125 awards available during that time; of the students who were offered awards, 84 percent accepted. The vast majority of those who attended had ranked in the top 6 percent of their graduating classes, and their SAT scores averaged 1,147 (compared with an overall MWC average of just over 1,000).

The first two graduating classes that included Regional Scholars (1978 and 1979) clearly showed that the program was achieving its purpose of elevating the academic level of the student body. Of those original fifty scholars, ten were elected to Phi Beta Kappa, eight were chosen for Mortar Board, seven served on the Honor Council, and five were class officers. In addition, a 1979 Regional Scholar received the Darden Award as the senior with the highest academic average. The program continued to attract first-rate students to Mary Washington until some years later it was reconfigured and perpetuated in a somewhat altered format.

Efforts to enhance other aspects of enrollment were less successful. The number of male applicants during the period did increase, albeit not dramatically, and attempts to attract qualified minority applicants yielded disappointing returns. The shortfall in minority applicants was not for lack of effort, as least as President Woodard saw it. He explained in one formal report that the fundamental problem was an economic one:

> My colleagues and I have tried in numerous ways to increase the number of minority students that enroll at the college. Unfortunately for us, the quality of student admissible to Mary Washington is precisely the quality of student that many other institutions are able to go out and buy with a sizable pool of money. . . . It is a fact that we can and do offer every student who has financial need, aid to meet that need. But there are many institutions, including some state institutions in Virginia, that are going far above that at the present time. This is the kind of competition that Mary Washington faces.

True as Woodard's statement was, some black students felt that there was more to it than that—something more subtle and more sinister. As one of them explained it in a *Bullet* editorial, it also involved the fact that, to many potential black applicants, "the image which MWC boasts is not appealing (i.e., voluntary segregation in the dining hall, absence of blacks in the MWC sports programs, few black professors, and no promise of finding an identity). . . . The MWC image of a wealthy, white girl's finishing school apparently lingers on." So too, for many and varied reasons, did the problem of minority recruitment linger on for years to come.

In the 1970s, at the instigation of President Woodard, the College also began several initiatives not so much to attract students as to retain them once enrolled. Among the more innovative was the implementation in 1977 of a summer orientation program for entering freshmen designed to smooth their transition to college life. Incoming students were required to attend one of several daylong programs on campus, during which they were given the opportunity to meet the president, deans, and other college officials; mingle with future classmates and leaders of student organizations; tour the library, dining hall, and freshman residences; meet with a faculty adviser to select courses for the fall semester; and complete the registration process, which enabled them to commence classes immediately upon returning to campus at the start of the academic year. Parents, too, were encouraged to attend these orientation sessions and to participate in various activities arranged especially for them.

An innovation greatly appreciated by students came in the fall of 1978 with the implementation of a computerized system for class registration, reducing to about five minutes or less the previously tedious process of waiting interminably in long lines to reach crowded sign-up tables—often then only to find desired courses already filled. Vice President Anderson, who was responsible for developing the system, recalled years later the situation that existed. "The first time I observed registration it was just incredible. I mean it was so frustrating for the students, the faculty, everybody. It was just an awful process." But then "the word spread throughout campus that we were getting this new computer. . . . In the afternoon, about 4 o'clock, the truck came to deliver the machine—it was about the size of a refrigerator—[and] people congregated out on the side [of GW] to watch this box be unloaded."[30]

There was good reason for the excitement. The system, the heart of which was a Hewlett-Packard 3000 computer, was housed in the basement of GW in a computer center supervised by the director of institutional research, Dale Brown. Once in operation, the machine not only revolutionized the registration process but also facilitated various administrative functions such as assembling the vast quantities of data increasingly necessary for both internal purposes and for generating reports required by state and federal agencies. The HP 3000 proved durable, serving as the core of the institution's computer system into the twenty-first century.

Accompanying the technological innovations were a number of administrative changes that affected student life. Among these was the resignation in spring 1979 of Dean of Student Services Juanita Clement, who had held the post since replacing the popular Mildred Droste in 1975. Clement returned to a faculty position in the Department of Health and Physical Education, where she had taught before becoming dean.

Clement's tenure as dean was not an altogether happy one, either for the students, who tended to regard her administrative style as excessively heavy-handed, or for her, as she found the job extremely stressful. Her departure was greeted with glee by many students, reflecting the sentiment of one who commented in the *Bullet* that "her door may always be open, but her mind is closed." On the other hand, Steve Schlimgen, the SA president-elect at the time of her resignation, defended her before an open meeting of the student body, claiming that she "takes a lot of unnecessary grief. She's just doing her job and enforcing rules she didn't make." For his part, President Woodard praised the departing dean lavishly, describing her performance as "outstanding" and asserting that "no person could be more dedicated to Mary Washington College and to her job than Dean Clement has been."

To replace her, the College took the novel (for MWC) approach of hiring someone from outside the current faculty: Suzanne Gordon, the holder of a doctoral degree in the student affairs aspect of educational administration. Over the course of the next three years, Gordon worked productively to reorganize residential life and to develop a comprehensive program of student activities. In 1982, however, she resigned to take a similar position at the much larger University of Arkansas.

The search for her replacement was led by Vice President Anderson, who chaired a committee that comprised not only faculty and administrators but, in an unusual departure for the College, students as well. Evaluation of the 135 applicants for the position resulted in the in-house selection of Joanne G. Southworth, then an assistant professor of biology. Southworth, who held a bachelor's degree in biology and mathematics from Randolph-Macon Women's College and a Ph.D. in anatomy from the Medical College of Virginia, had taught at Mary Washington part-time since 1972 and full-time since 1977. The hiring of Southworth, a sprightly sylph of perpetually positive disposition, was warmly received by the students, many of whom already held her in high esteem because of her reputation as a teacher. "We were pleased with the choice," commented SA president Anne Thompson, "and I believe the students appreciated having the chance to participate in the whole process."

As a consequence of her career focus on teaching and research in biology, Southworth did not have the professional credentials in the area of student services that her predecessor, Gordon, possessed. She was, however, equipped with one quality of inestimable benefit for that particular job: she genuinely liked students. And it showed.

It was during the same period that the College employed its first full-time physician, an arrangement markedly superior to the previous reliance on local doctors to provide medical care on a part-time basis (though specialists were still available when needed). The first holder of the full-time position was one of the College's own, Ilma Meade "Pete" Overman '65. After Mary Washington, Overman earned her medical degree in 1970 from the Medical College of Virginia, whereupon she entered private practice in Fredericksburg and then worked in the area for the Health Department.

In 1977 she became the College physician, an appointment that was greeted favorably by the students, who were particularly gratified by some of the doctor's innovations, including the opportunity to schedule private appointments. Female students, according to the *Bullet*, especially appreciated the availability of pregnancy tests on campus (for only $1.50) instead of having to visit an off-campus facility for tests involving lab fees of ten to fifteen dollars. Overman would remain a much-appreciated fixture on campus for over three decades.

From a combination of such factors, the prevailing student attitude was undeniably becoming more upbeat. It was a trend that not even the College newspaper—normally negative, in the grand tradition of such publications—could deny, though sometimes admissions of felicity came almost grudgingly. "I realize that I am probably painting a rose-colored portrait of our college life," wrote one columnist in 1980, "[but] we do need to look around us from time to time and assess our good qualities." Among such qualities, she cited recent improvements ranging across academic, athletic, and residential areas, adding, "As much as I hate to admit it, I think there has [even] been terrific improvement in ARA, such as the salad bar, the sandwich bar, late continental breakfast, and Sunday morning brunch." That sentiment was echoed by another columnist who in 1982 declared, "Despite my constant urgings for change, . . . MWC has a lot going for it. I am proud to be a student here."

Another *Bullet* writer confessed that "despite consistent criticisms and barb-tipped jokes regarding various aspects of our esteemed campus, this editor feels that a statement should be made in defense of MWC." Its distinctiveness, she explained, lay in the harmony of relationships between faculty and students "in and out of the classroom" and, even more important, the amity that existed among students themselves. "For all the shortcomings and failings," she wrote, "Mary Washington College has one of the friendliest campuses in Virginia. . . . Any rivalry existing between dorms is friendly. . . . Close friends in dorms other than one's own is a common denominator shared by the majority of the campus. . . . Awed visitors remark at the atmosphere, almost wistfully, and have to agree that the aura of Mary Washington is one of genuine friendliness." The title of the editorial neatly summarized that viewpoint. Mary Washington, it read, was simply "A Nice Place."

ACADEMICS AND ACADEMICIANS

Late in the Woodard presidency, the academic program, which had already been broadened by the incorporation of new majors and new degrees, was further altered by significant revision of general education requirements. It was also a period that witnessed a decline in faculty morale and a rise in hostility toward the president.

In the fall of 1980, after two years of study, an ad hoc Committee on Degree Requirements in the fall of 1980 presented for faculty approval a proposal embodying significant revisions to an existing system that was, in the words of the *Bullet*, "both confused and confusing to students, and often to faculty." Accordingly, the committee, chaired by English professor Nancy Mitchell, sought first to clarify the requirements and second to ensure that the requirements incorporated sufficient curricular diversity. These goals, the committee asserted, would be "more readily obtained through the careful construction of general education requirements, firm constraints on what the major program can require, and a limitation of the number of hours a student may take in a single discipline."

The proposal set a limitation on the number of hours any major could require (forty) and restructured the general education requirements on the basis of inculcating certain sets of intellectual skills, rather than on mandating specific courses. There were five such areas:

Group A: Analyzing Aspects of the Physical and Biological Environment (6–8 credit hours chosen from courses in disciplines such as chemistry, biology and geology). This was necessary, the proposal argued, to ensure that even nonscientists "have at least a basic knowledge of the methodologies . . . and at least a rudimentary knowledge of some aspect of science."

Group B: Analyzing Aspects of Human Behavior (9–10 credits in at least two disciplines, selected from disciplines including political science, psychology, and sociology), the rationale being that "some knowledge of the social and individual behavior of humans is critical."

Group C: Reasoning with Pure Abstractions (3 credits from disciplines such as math, logic, and computer science).

Group D: Assessing Intellectual Frameworks (9 credits from at least two disciplines such as history and philosophy), the goal being "to help a person make responsible decisions while being aware of differing beliefs and the consequences of those beliefs."

Group E: Understanding the Creative Arts (9 credits from at least two disciplines, at least one of which must be literature). The purpose, said the committee, was to help students appreciate different aspects of the arts and "defend judgments in which emotions and sensibilities play a large role."

While thus revising the general education requirements, the proposal retained, unchanged, the foreign language and physical education requirements. In perhaps its most striking innovation, the proposal also called for the establishment of a writing-intensive requirement, mandating that one course so designated—from any of various disciplines, not exclusively English—be taken in each of a student's four years.

Despite a few concerns over what some regarded as the unwieldy titles of the general education categories and what others deemed the proposal's "anti-major" tenor, students generally supported the revisions. The SA Academic Affairs Committee, chaired by senior Mary Siegrist, endorsed it, saying that "the philosophical basis for the proposal is sound, if not impeccable. . . . Not only will the MWC degree be more 'sellable' to the contemporary job market and graduate schools, but it will facilitate the pursuit of a broad base of knowledge for knowledge's sake."

The *Bullet* concurred. In an editorial titled "Change Needed," it described the proposal as "well thought-out and carefully presented" and commended it for "ensuring that a student is well-rounded in the liberal arts and not overly concentrated in one specific field. This seems particularly important at a time when many colleges are emphasizing practical or career-oriented fields and many students are becoming increasingly specialized in their fields." Faculty passage of the proposal established the set of degree requirements that, beginning in the fall of 1981, would remain in effect, with only occasional tweaking, for decades to come.

Even as the new degree requirements were being implemented, another faculty committee was investigating another aspect of the academic program. Chaired by English professor Susan Hanna, the Ad Hoc Committee on Academic Regulations and Advising presented its report in the spring of 1982. The comprehensive proposal addressed several areas, including mid-semester progress reports and guidelines for probation and suspension, but the most controversial portion by far was the one that suggested a new class attendance policy. The gist of the original proposal, which would apply only to 100- and 200-level courses, was that students who missed 15 percent of the classes in such courses, for any reason, would have their grades automatically lowered.

Students immediately howled. "This is not high school, it is college," ran a typical complaint. "Now that we are here," protested another, "we are responsible for our own grades and attendance. No one should be forced."

It was not only the students who objected but many faculty as well, some simply because of the cumbersome and time-consuming need to take attendance each day. Others had more specific objections. Edward Hegmann, chair of the Department of Health and Physical Education, expressed concern about the proposal's impact on intercollegiate athletics, given that it did not recognize "excused" absences. "The aim of the regulations," he argued, "should be directed toward the students who sleep, watch TV, or take five-day weekends, not toward those students who participate in school-related activities, whether they be field trips or athletic events." Others raised the hoary bugaboo of "academic freedom." As psychology professor Alice Rabson put it, "I want to teach my class the way I want, and it should be up to the professor what rules to make."

The *Bullet*'s position on the issue was somewhat surprising. While expressing qualms about some features of the plan, it proffered an overall endorsement. "'Academic freedom,'" declared an editorial just before the faculty vote, "is a broad and vague term under which foolish ends are often served and practical ends are often lost. The proposals may mean that students will bow to a stricter discipline than in the past and may have more obligations than rights or freedoms. This," the paper added, "is not necessarily a bad turn of events."

It was just such practical ends that Hanna emphasized in advocating the proposal's passage. "This is not a school that merely provides information," she said. "The classroom is essential. By enforcing [an attendance] policy on the inexperienced student, we are providing every possible buttress against losing the student to poor grades as a result of excessive absences."

Such reasoning eventually prevailed, and the proposal won faculty approval, albeit with one substantial emendation: the punitive grade reduction for excessive absences was dropped, replaced by a policy of forced withdrawal. Specifically, students who missed the equivalent of six class hours were to receive a warning; if the absences continued to accrue to the level of nine hours, withdrawal from the course would be mandatory. The policy, as enacted, did not recognize "excused absences," but did include the right of student appeal to the instructor and, ultimately, the academic dean.

As was true of the revised degree requirements, the new attendance policy remained in force, virtually intact, for many years following its implementation at the outset of the 1982–83 academic year. Though not uniformly lauded, the regulations were accepted without undue student complaint. As one freshman at the time of their passage conceded, "They do seem like high school restrictions, but they will set a precedent by getting freshmen in the habit of regular attendance. The decision should be left to the person paying for the education, but if you're here, you should want to go to class. By cutting classes you are cheating yourself."

Prince Woodard's administration, scarred from the outset by the economy-driven reduction of faculty positions, continued for the remainder of his tenure to experience sporadic faculty unrest. One problem was the difficulty in attracting qualified minority faculty. Among the most insistent complaints of the College's African American students was the paucity of courses oriented toward black Americans and the near-total absence of black instructors to teach them.

Their concern was understandable. At the time there were few regular courses that dealt substantially with the black experience, notably an English course on black literature, taught by Raman Singh (an Indian); history of the American South, taught by Bill Crawley (a WASP); and the history of blacks in America, taught either by Crawley or by part-time adjunct instructor Lewis Suggs (African American) from Howard University. There were also occasional offerings bearing on black history, such as the 1977 public lecture series, sponsored by the History Department with the aid of a grant from the Virginia Foundation for the Humanities and Public Policy, titled "The Roots of Race Relations in America"—prompted by the recent popularity of the TV miniseries *Roots* (1977), based on Alex Haley's critically acclaimed genealogical novel of the same name. On the whole, however, the curriculum offered little in the way of black studies on a regular basis.

Although the lack of success raised in the minds of some critics doubts about the College's efforts to recruit black faculty, it was evident that failure in that quest was not attributable to absence of desire. In June 1978 the College officially instituted a policy known as the "Affirmative Action Plan for Equal Employment Opportunity," the purpose of which was "to guarantee that recruitment, employment, and promotion of faculty members and classified personnel are based on the merit of each individual without regard to race, color, religion, disability, national origin, political affiliation, marital status, sex, or age (except where age or sex is a bona fide occupational qualification)." That commitment was further confirmed in the same year when the Board of Visitors gave formal assent to the affirmative action objectives delineated by Governor Dalton in the 1978 revision of *The Virginia Plan for Equal Opportunity in State-Supported Institutions of Higher Education*.

But pledges, however genuine, did not readily translate into personnel, owing to several stumbling blocks. For one thing, according to Dean of the Faculty James Croushore, there were many qualified black academics who were simply not interested in teaching at a small liberal arts college located in a (relatively, at that time) rural area.

A far greater problem, however, involved basic economics. In a situation analogous to the problems in attracting black students, the recruitment of minority faculty largely boiled down to the fact that they could usually "get a better deal" at other institutions. The problem perplexed President Woodard, who in a 1979 report termed it "one of my most difficult challenges" and explained that "in a number of instances when we have invited minority candidates to visit the college and the question of salary has arisen, the answer has been, 'I'm sorry, but I have an offer of three to seven thousand dollars more elsewhere.' . . . [But] despite the frustrations and disappointments in its recent efforts to attract more minority students and faculty members, Mary Washington College, as long as I am its president, will not waver in its aggressive recruitment of minority persons." Yet the problem was destined to become chronic, good intentions notwithstanding.

In the mid-seventies and early eighties, a number of developments significantly affected the faculty in terms of both the faculty's internal procedures and its relationship to the administration—with consequences that were not always good.

A positive step came in 1975 when the Board of Visitors recognized the Faculty General Cooperative Committee (FGCC) as an official liaison between the faculty and the institution's governing body. A policy was established whereby the FGCC would meet twice annually with the executive committee of the board to "react to Board suggestions, answer Board inquiries, and apprise the Board of faculty opinion concerning matters of mutual concern, such as academic and social policies, directions and goals of the College, and matters of faculty welfare."

In the same year, the faculty formalized a procedure for handling student complaints by creating a grievance board with a ratio of two faculty members to one student. The panel's function was to review complaints related to matters such as classroom performance and attendance; grading practices, tests, papers, and assignments; and instructors' failure to keep office hours. The operative understanding was that the grievance board would be the last resort, used only if disputes could not be resolved within the department through the mediation of the chair and student representatives. Greeted approvingly by the students at its establishment, the grievance board over time was employed rather infrequently, serving mainly as a source of reassurance to students who appreciated the option of an appeal if treated (they felt) unjustly.

While students were thus comforted, faculty faced a new source of discontent. Following Woodard's initial faculty cuts, more conflict erupted in 1977 with the promulgation of a new tenure policy. The purpose of tenure, read that policy, "is to protect academic freedom. It provides a measure of job security to faculty members who have served the college faithfully and with professional excellence. . . . [It] is the assurance of a continuing full-time teaching position at Mary Washington College unless the faculty member is removed for cause, resigns, or retires, or, when due to bona fide financial exigency or the discontinuance or reduction of an academic program or department, his or her position becomes unnecessary."

The statement itself did not contain anything particularly novel or remarkable. The problem, in the minds of some faculty, was that it was accompanied by the requirement of an annual performance evaluation of each faculty member and department chair—which was indeed something new at Mary Washington. The board assigned the responsibility for determining the content and structure of the evaluations to the faculty and administration. In response to this mandate, the faculty's Instruction and Academic Affairs Committee devoted months of study to the issue, including open hearings, before eventually devising a system that set forth both the criteria for evaluation and the mechanism for implementation. Protracted faculty debate before passage of the plan suggested (presciently) that the issue would be capable of producing considerable mischief in the future.

With minor adjustments along the way, the process that ultimately evolved called for each department chair to evaluate each of his or her faculty members annually on the basis of three criteria: teaching effectiveness, professional activity, and service to the department, College, or community. Given the College's traditional primacy on teaching, the first of the criteria was deemed to be equivalent in importance to the other two combined.

The rub, of course, lay in determining what constituted so elusive and inherently subjective a quality as "teaching effectiveness." Aside from personal observations (often scarce) and anecdotal reports (often unreliable), chairs had little evidence to go on—except for student evaluations, which presented their own set of problems.

A far cry from the ad hoc student-generated faculty evaluations of earlier years (*Youth Evaluate Teachers* in the late sixties, for example), the process of rating professors had by this time become structured—and mandatory—much to the chagrin of some faculty. There was exhaustive faculty debate over the design of evaluation forms, what questions to ask, and how to pose them. At a more fundamental level than the matter of questionnaire design was the contention by some faculty that students were incompetent to judge whether or not a faculty member was effective; others, on the contrary, asked who could be a better judge of pedagogical prowess than its recipients.

Even those who favored student evaluations recognized the potential for abuse that the practice entailed. Students, for example, might use the evaluation as an opportunity to retaliate for a bad grade or some other perceived slight; conversely students might reward professors whom they liked for reasons unrelated to the quality of instruction and might even be more generous toward those whose standards were less rigorous. One of the main criticisms of the system, in fact, was that it might encourage faculty to pander to students in hopes of receiving a more favorable evaluation. There was clearly a host of concerns, but student evaluations were destined to remain, nonetheless, as a (presumably) necessary evil within the evaluation process.

Sometimes new faculty procedures that seemed beneficial at their inception turned out to be in some ways counterproductive. Such was the case with the creation of elected committees to make recommendations to the academic dean regarding promotion and tenure. Because it was rare that such recommendations were not followed, they were tantamount to final decisions. The theory was that if the procedure was more democratic (that is, with more power in the hands of the faculty), the outcomes would be, if not more just, at least more palatable, than previously when they were determined more autocratically (that is, by the dean in concert with department chairs).

In actual operation, however, the new procedure had a considerable downside in that it could force faculty members into the awkward position of having to make decisions bearing directly on the welfare of their peers. The potential for dissension was obvious.

An even more serious source of possible friction lay in the adoption of a merit pay plan. In July 1977 the Board of Visitors, endorsing "the propriety for, and the equity in, rewarding outstanding performance and achievement by faculty members," established the policy of including merit increases as part of future compensation plans, as long as the requisite resources were available after funding cost-of-living increases for all faculty. Following the principles of a merit plan developed by the Faculty General Cooperative Committee, the board approved a plan for the 1978–79 academic year whereby ten faculty members were to be awarded two merit units ($500 per unit) and thirty others one merit unit, which became part of their base salaries.

As with the creation of tenure and promotion committees, the merit pay plan seemed attractive in some ways but also harbored divisive potential. To wage earners in much of the non-academic world, the concept of evaluation and contingent rewards was commonplace. But among academics, it was a novel and, to many, an uncongenial practice. Mary Washington faculty salaries had theretofore been based on a "step" plan in which increases, when awarded, were on an across-the-board basis, with no consideration given to distinctions in the quality of performance. To a faculty habituated to that system, the new "competitive" plan seemed the antithesis of any notions of collegiality and a threat to the previous harmony produced by economic equity (albeit equity at a rather low level).

Once in operation, the merit plan, though stoutly defended by some, generally served to confirm the fears of skeptics. When coupled (as it was) with the performance evaluation system, the plan did indeed generate discontent, as faculty who were denied merit increases tended to become resentful. Even those who benefited from the largesse had to wonder if the rewarding of some was not bought at too high a price in the diminished morale of those who did not. Whatever the case, merit pay had arrived to stay, and with frequent efforts at refinement of one kind or another, the plan remained an integral part of the faculty compensation plan.

With various unpopular policies already having caused widespread deterioration of faculty morale, President Woodard in early 1979 embarked on an effort that would create the gravest crisis of his tenure: the merger of a number of academic departments. The plan, which he had been contemplating for at least two years, called for the consolidation of several smaller departments to reduce the total number from twenty-one to fifteen. The purpose, he explained, was threefold: to facilitate greater interdisciplinary planning and program development, to improve administrative efficiency in the academic area, and to create more time for department chairs to conduct their administrative chores. The latter, he said, was necessary because in some of the smaller departments the chairs could not actually take a reduced course load—the standard practice to provide time for administrative tasks—because of the harm to the departmental course offerings that would result.

The validity of such reasoning mattered little. To some members of the faculty, already in a combative mood, the plan simply furnished further evidence of what they viewed as Woodard's authoritarianism, and they were all too eager to strike back.

The concept was not as radical as its opponents claimed. In fact, several smaller departments had recently merged on a voluntary basis, with results that seemed satisfactory: Dramatic Arts with Dance, Art History with Studio Art, and Economics with Political Science. In response to this proposal as well, some departments acquiesced without protest, leading to the harmonious creation of the combined Department of History and American Studies and—in a particularly inspired amalgamation—the Department of Classics, Philosophy, and Religion, or CPR.

Those positive developments notwithstanding, the proposal touched off a furor. Some of the potentially affected departments had greater claim than others to umbrage. Geography, for example, which possessed one of the stronger programs nationally in that field, made the not unreasonable protest that to be subsumed by or combined with another department (Sociology was suggested) would lead to a decline in visibility and a diminution of prestige. Other complaints proved more personal in nature, emanating from loss of status on the part of those whose title of department chair would be eliminated. Adding to such objections was widespread faculty resentment at being snubbed in the planning process. "I'm not against consolidation per se," declared one, "but, goddamn it, I'd like to have some say in it." When Woodard announced the plan, he made it clear that faculty input would be solicited in determining which departments would be reconfigured; he made it equally clear that the reorganization itself was a fait accompli, a tack that infuriated some faculty.

Underlying the angst was the cumulative effect of the rapid and extensive changes wrought by Woodard, among them a number that were in some way controversial, such as the start of new degree programs (including at the graduate level), faculty cutbacks, merit pay, grievance procedures, and overall changes in management techniques. All these, said the *Free Lance–Star*, produced "a stunning impact on a campus where change once came slowly." The merger plan, the paper continued, simply "focused long-standing discontent among some faculty," whereupon "the complaints began to coalesce."

The agent provocateur of the revolt was an unlikely agitator: James B. Gouger, a ten-year veteran of the geography faculty. A self-described "backbencher and conservative Republican," Gouger was usually the most mild-mannered of folk. But not in this case. "God knows, I'm not a crusader," he said later, "but somebody had to do something."

What he did, first of all, was to rise at the February 1979 faculty meeting and propose a resolution expressing faculty opposition to the proposed mergers "in the belief that such action would lead to further decline in faculty morale and deterioration of the academic standing of the College." Though the resolution was applauded by many—one chairperson pronounced Gouger's stand as "courageous"—the motion was tabled and, for the time being, descended into parliamentary limbo.

Several weeks later, however, Gouger sent to all faculty members a "Dear Colleague" letter in which he wrote, in part: "In recent months it has become apparent to me that the morale of the MWC faculty has sunk to record depths. Like a virulent plague, discontent seems to have spread throughout our campus"—a situation arising, he suggested, from the perception that "the administration has no respect for the faculty."

A few days later, at Gouger's instigation, there was a rare ad hoc meeting of approximately thirty faculty members, during which a variety of specific concerns were aired. Though no bill of particulars was drafted, Gouger noted afterward that "the common thread seems to be a feeling of administration arrogance toward the faculty." One concrete result was the decision to develop and disseminate a questionnaire to all faculty for the evaluation of the College administration.

The contentiousness proved contagious, affecting students as well. Steve Schlimgen, SA president-elect, announced that sentiment among students was running so strongly against the merger plan that the association felt compelled to come out against it. That action was particularly irritating to Woodard, who openly blamed "some faculty," he said, who "get students upset by [claiming] that the students will be adversely affected. And I think that is inappropriate."

The issue came to a head at the April faculty meeting—by all odds the most acrimonious such gathering in the history of the institution. At the core of the tumultuous marathon debate were two resolutions from the Faculty General Cooperative Committee that constituted, in essence, a reformulation of the proposals made earlier by Jim Gouger. The first was a rather general resolution urging the administration "in the future, to give to the general faculty greater and appropriate consideration in sharing decision-making before new policies are implemented." The second, and more pointed, resolution directly addressed the matter of departmental mergers, urging Woodard to form a special faculty committee to devise a consolidation plan that would require faculty approval before implementation.

Tendentious discussions ensued for well over an hour, wending through byzantine parliamentary maneuvers, some of them engineered by administration adherents in hopes of preventing a vote. At one point, well into the debate, Woodard, who had been present throughout, announced that he had to leave for an appointment with the Board of Visitors and the State Council of Higher Education and requested that the issue not be decided in his absence. His departure prompted further consternation, with the body divided as to whether or not it was proper to continue, before eventually deciding to proceed. To vote in Woodard's absence, one participant explained, "was unfair, but we were caught between two unfair things."

The vote, when it at long last came, amounted to an overwhelming victory for the president's adversaries: the first resolution was approved by a vote of 75 to 33, the second by an even larger margin of 85 to 15. The session was emotionally draining for all in attendance—described by a veteran faculty member as "one of the most tense situations I have ever been in."

But it was viewed by some as beneficial, perhaps necessary. As one commented afterward, "This is the most [courage] I have ever seen by this faculty." The impact was certainly unambiguous. "The faculty," boasted one,

Katherine Edmondson Hopper '30, the first alumna and first woman to serve as rector of Board of Visitors (with Dean James Croushore at commencement)

"has really gone on record this time, in a sort of censure. . . . If he [Woodard] fails to make some changes, then I've got a feeling there's going to be a vote of no confidence in him."

It did not happen. In fact, the body that mattered most, the Board of Visitors, did just the opposite when at its next meeting (in May) it issued a formal statement expressing "complete confidence in Prince B. Woodard in his administration of Mary Washington College in that he has in all respects administered the affairs of the College in accordance with the policies and objectives of this board." Aware that the announcement so soon after the faculty debacle might seem overly defensive, Rector Katherine Hopper explicitly denied that the two were related, saying that the declaration of support was simply "a positive thing." Her disclaimer was not totally persuasive, however, as she also admitted, "The Board is conscious of what has been going on. Let's just say that it was the appropriate time to do it."

The overall impact of the merger brouhaha was difficult to gauge. Certainly Woodard did not yield his goals—such was beyond his character. On the other hand, there was general acceptance of the eventual realignment—changes that preserved (not coincidentally) an independent Geography Department.

In the midst of the faculty upheaval, the College was also engaged in a search for a new academic dean to replace James Croushore, who had announced his decision to retire at the end of the 1978–79 academic year. Croushore, who had been at the College since 1947 and dean since 1970, came to his administrative post after many years as one of the most respected—and, among students, most popular—members of the English faculty. As dean, his reputation had suffered somewhat because of his role in implementing policies that were unpopular with some faculty members, but he retained their basic respect for several reasons. For some, it was the tie to the sainted Simpson regime that he embodied; for others, it was the genuineness of his rapport with the teaching faculty, from whose ranks he had risen; for all, it was the sincerity of a personality that, despite a tinge of gruffness on occasion, was clearly grounded in basic decency. His low-key, even-keeled demeanor furnished a useful counterpoise to President Woodard, whom Croushore loyally served.[31]

To secure a replacement for Croushore, Woodard appointed a seven-person committee, chaired by Ray Merchent, comprising two administrative appointees and five members elected by the faculty. The committee evaluated the credentials of approximately 130 applicants before making its recommendation to the president (who, as was his custom, had made it clear that the ultimate choice would be made by him).

The eventual appointee differed in many ways from Croushore, the most immediately obvious being that the new dean was a woman, Mary Ann T. Burns, the first female ever to hold that post at Mary Washington.[32] She brought strong credentials to the position, both academic and administrative. A classics scholar with a Ph.D. from the University of Pennsylvania as well as an impressive record as a teacher and author, she had the intellectual bona fides that made her, in Woodard's words, "uniquely qualified to give leadership to the academic programs of the college." Her administrative experience was similarly commendable, including academic deanships at Wilson College and Emmanuel College.

She was a gregarious, imposing figure with a hearty laugh that bespoke bonhomie. On the other hand, her disposition was somewhat mercurial, exacerbated by an expressive countenance whose floridity, when angered, inevitably betrayed any attempt to conceal her emotions—a characteristic that (in contrast to Croushore's calm demeanor) did not serve her well as the administrative associate of the similarly volatile Woodard. It was to be an oft-rocky tenure for Burns, though in truth the predicament she inherited would have been hard for anyone to manage gracefully, irrespective of temperament or talent.

By the time Dean Burns arrived on the scene in the summer of 1979, the previous spring's upheaval over Woodard's leadership had abated somewhat—only to be rekindled in early 1980 with the publication of results from the previous year's faculty survey. The fifty-nine-item questionnaire, to which over 80 percent of the faculty responded, addressed not only issues relating to faculty-administration relations but also a miscellany of collateral concerns, some of which attracted rather curious responses. Regarding various aspects of the academic program, for example, 53 percent believed that the academic quality of the College had declined in the past five years, perhaps a reflection of the fact that 65 percent did not believe the College was attracting students of as high a quality as earlier (a perception contradicted by the actual qualifications of the entering students, which had risen). Also, by a 2–1 margin, faculty did not believe the College's male students to be as strong academically as the females.

The survey also revealed considerable skepticism concerning the worth of the new graduate programs. While a slight majority acknowledged the utility of adding those programs, almost half felt that they would be academically weak, and 70 percent felt that the faculty was insufficiently involved in their development. Comparable hostility was expressed toward the merit pay policy, with 70 percent affirming that the practice "created disharmony and ill will."

Concerning faculty attitudes toward the administration in general and the president in particular, the survey indicated significant animosity—an unsurprising result, considering that the questionnaire had been distributed at the peak of the disgruntlement over the merger proposal. In any event, responses revealed that approximately 80 percent felt there had been an "excessive expansion of administrative bureaucracy" under Woodard; 62 percent did not believe that the president welcomed faculty input; 61 percent believed that efforts at departmental consolidations would strengthen administrative control over faculty; and only 19 percent believed that consolidation would benefit the students.

The author of the report analyzing the survey's results, sociology professor Charles A. Sletten, asserted in his conclusion that Woodard "seems to view the institution as an educational bureaucracy to be managed by him through his administrative staff on the basis of the coercive power of the state." Apparently reflecting adherence to such an interpretation, the survey statement "I trust and respect the president of the College" yielded an average score of only 1.8 on a 4.0 scale.

Further grist for the mill of faculty discontent was delivered in the spring of 1980 with the announcement of the salary scale for the next academic year, which included average increases of approximately 9 percent for faculty and 12 percent for the six top administrators. Though the increases for faculty were sizable and represented a substantial improvement over recent years, there were some faculty whose appreciation for their own raises was dampened by their vexation that the raises for administrators were larger. As one professor commented, "I haven't talked to a single [faculty] person who isn't completely burned about this."

While emphasizing that faculty salaries were still too low, both President Woodard and Rector Hopper defended the disparity in increases by pointing out that such salary adjustments were necessary to make Mary Washington competitive with other colleges in attracting qualified administrators. Partially to address that problem, the Board of Visitors approved an additional $3,500 from private funds to supplement Woodard's salary, bringing his total compensation to slightly over $50,000. Before that, said Hopper, he was one of only four state college presidents not receiving supplementary funds and, even with those additional funds, was still among the lowest paid in the Commonwealth.

A sense of dissatisfaction lingered into 1981, if the results of a Student Association poll that April were a valid indication. In a self-described effort to "take the pulse" of the community, an SA survey queried both the student body and the faculty concerning a number of perennial issues—and, in general, received perennial responses. Faculty attitudes, though seemingly more sanguine overall, still revealed a preponderance of opposition to matters such as merit pay and departmental consolidation; also, most agreed that faculty morale was not good.

One question, however—a sort of bottom-line query—yielded a response that seemed counter to the ostensible miasma. In reply to the statement "I enjoy teaching at MWC," 84 percent of the faculty respondents said yes. Evidently the negativism that at one point had seemed about to swamp the institution was neither as pervasive nor as deep as it had sometimes appeared. There were many, then as always, who truly loved the place.

Simultaneously with faculty discord, the College was embroiled in another controversy (though this one involved President Woodard only tangentially): a debate over changing the name of the institution. It was hardly a new topic at the College, inasmuch as changes had already occurred five times since its founding in 1908 as the State Normal and Industrial School for Women at Fredericksburg. In 1914 the name had been changed to State Normal School for Women at Fredericksburg, in 1924 to State Teachers College at Fredericksburg, in 1938 to Mary Washington College, in 1944 to Mary Washington College of the University of Virginia, and in 1972 back to Mary Washington College.

The changes had occurred in response to various alterations in the institution's mission over the years and, as such, seem to have been embraced, or at least accepted with equanimity, by the students at the time. For example, a *Bullet* editorial in 1938 anticipating the change to "Mary Washington" applauded the choice, exclaiming that "no more appropriate name possibly could be selected for a woman's college than Mary Washington, . . . and it would serve as an inspiration to the young women attending the institution."

So inasmuch as the name "Mary Washington" had been chosen with the avowed intent of connoting an all-female institution—which it did do, very effectively—there was speculation that, when the College began accepting men in 1970, a more gender-neutral name might be substituted. "Will coeducation make Mary Washington College's feminine name outdated?" asked the Fredericksburg newspaper in early 1970. "Some people think so, and . . . there's been talk of changing [it] to something a man wouldn't mind having on his diploma." But it did not happen at that time, at least partly because President Simpson cared not a fig about whether male potential students might be deterred by the name.

Events of the following decade, however, suggested that the College no longer had the luxury of such a cavalier attitude. By 1979 the situation was so bad that only 1,330 high school students applied for admission, of whom 1,085 (over 80 percent) were accepted; of those, 618 actually enrolled. The following year was, in one sense, worse; even though there were somewhat more applicants, of whom 1,258 were accepted, only 524 chose to attend. As Marty Wilder, assistant dean of admissions at the time, later understated it, "You might say we were in some state of enrollment distress at that point." And the prospects for the future seemed ever dimmer, with a significant projected decline in the college-age population during the coming decade.

Sufficiently alarmed, some personnel began to advocate the drastic step of changing the school's name to appeal to a larger applicant base. Spearheading the movement was history professor Richard H. Warner, who claimed that the current name militated against applications because it created the impression that the College was not coeducational. "We've got to cut the 'Mary,'" he said. "What's going to happen here in the next decade when we have a 21.1 percent decline in available students? This could be a disaster for this school to face."

To those who criticized his position as sexist, Warner retorted that the original decision to name the institution Mary Washington was itself sexist, part of a strategy to enable the University of Virginia to remain all male. The residue of that misbegotten effort, he claimed, was that both male and female potential applicants were being deterred by the inherent single-sex implications and that there was "nothing we can do to equal the name change" in correcting that misperception.

In response to such concerns, the College did what comes naturally at colleges in those circumstances: it created a committee to study the situation. Known as the Committee on College Affairs, it consisted of three administrators, three faculty, and three students, chaired by Vice President Anderson.

While the committee deliberated during 1980, debate flourished on campus and beyond. In a *Washington Post* article titled "Move Afoot to Change 'Sissy' Name," librarian Ruby York Weinbrecht expressed outrage over what she deemed the sexist motivation behind the proposal. "This name-changing business," she charged, "flies in the face of getting society to think women can do anything they want to do. Why change the name simply because some men don't like its sound?" Moreover, she claimed, the mother of George Washington deserved the honor, since no other college was named for her (to which the *Post* added, "In fact, the only other thing in the country widely known by the name 'Mary Washington' is a tender and tasty variety of asparagus").

An April 1980 *Bullet* editorial that supported a name change questioned Mary's eponymous fitness, asserting that she had been a Tory until the Revolutionary War began, switching allegiance only after her son became commander of the Continental Army. "Should our college," it asked, "bear the name of a person who held such sympathies?"

The case for the significance of the historical Mary Washington was, in fact, problematic because so little was actually known about her other than that she was the mother of George, perhaps the most significant figure in the founding of the country. To be sure, the contribution of a mother toward molding the character of so estimable a leader was not to be minimized, nor was her ability to survive many years of widowhood, essentially alone, in what was in every respect "a man's world," to be discounted. On the other hand, there was little in the historical record to suggest that her accomplishments were so exceptional as to merit memorialization—nor could they have been expected to be, given the restricted opportunities available to women of her time, however admirable and able they may have been.[33]

In any event, the *Bullet* editorial proceeded to lay out a case for change. "Aside from historical reasons," it said, "there are other arguments for a name change. One is the changing character of the college. To many, the name 'Mary Washington College' brings to mind the fine finishing school of yesteryear. Others, including potential students, seem to have interpreted the name as meaning that MWC is still a single-sex institution. . . . The need to attract more students in the future, and the changing face of the college, suggest that the time may be appropriate for a name change for MWC."

A *Bullet* op-ed piece around the same time agreed. Noting that the College had by then been coeducational for a decade, it asserted that "only now is the school turning toward the social acceptances and understandings that will bring it away from the past era. Some students are glad to see that era end, while others don't want to admit that a new one is beginning. The name of Mary Washington carries with it very specific implications when mentioned at other schools in the state. It's time that Mary Washington College shake off that negative image and make a new name for itself."

Other students—indeed, many of them—disagreed with that position. Such opposition was displayed, for example, in letters to the *Bullet* and in an April Fools' edition of the paper that lampooned the proposal by proffering alternative institutional names. One suggestion attempted to combine the name of the College's geographic location with the popularity of an existing school by calling it the College of William and Marye; a similar effort produced the far-fetched UNC-Fredericksburg. Another suggestion, best understood by college football fans, was Prudential College, on the grounds that during fall Saturday afternoons "ABC's Prudential College Scoreboard would give the college extensive publicity."

Among the most risible suggestions was one that managed simultaneously to mock the name change as well as the dress and lingo of contemporary students: Lacoste University. As explained by its preppy proponent, "It would be just super. I mean, wow, we could be called the 'Gators and it would be super!"

By the fall of 1980, student attitudes had turned more serious—and more negative. Perhaps reflecting a turnover in its editorship, the *Bullet* now trumpeted, "Name Change Unnecessary." The answer, it opined, lay in sustained high academic quality, social programs, and, above all, increased recruitment efforts. "Certainly there will always be those who think Iceland is one big glacier, and those who think MWC is a 'convent,' but for those who really care to find out, information is readily available to prove we are a coeducational, publicly-funded liberal arts college. Surely our standards allow us to limit ourselves to those who look beyond the name."

The Anderson committee, meanwhile, was conducting research to ascertain high school students' perceptions of Mary Washington College, a process that included distributing one thousand questionnaires to college-bound students in the northern Virginia, Richmond, and Tidewater regions. The results were unsettling in many respects, most noticeably in the respondents' low level of knowledge about the College. Among females, 50 percent said they "did not know about MWC"; among males, the number was well above 70 percent.

In light of those findings, the committee emphasized the need for intensified recruitment, as the *Bullet* had suggested. Such an effort, it said, must extend beyond the admissions office to include assistance from faculty, students, and alumni: "If the college is to reach its potential, everyone will have to help." Hopeful that an aggressive, cooperative approach of that kind would work, the report concluded by recommending that "the current name be retained at present."

The faculty unanimously endorsed the report. Even Professor Warner, whose highly vocalized concerns had stimulated the movement, was mollified. "I was only worried about the enrollment," he explained, "and as long as that holds, I don't care what [the name] is." As events unfolded, the operative words of the Anderson report turned out to be "retained *at present*," for the issue was not dead—not by a long shot.

It was hibernating.

Throughout the name change controversy and his own travails, Prince Woodard exuded an air of unflappable confidence, appearing outwardly almost oblivious to (or maybe simply dismissive of) the sniping around him. That aura, however, was largely a facade that masked inner turmoil rarely discernible to any save his closest friends. One of those was his young associate Bill Anderson, who had observed that, in fact, Woodard "let dissension get to him personally. . . . He would internalize it, [and] tough decisions would continue to eat away at him for long periods of time." Accordingly, the prolonged disputations with the faculty, together with the simultaneous struggle over control of the James Monroe Museum, exacted a heavy emotional and physical price.

The health bill came due in early November 1981. Anderson, even many years later, recalled the scenario vividly. It was a Friday, and Woodard had spent much of the day in court, including almost four hours giving depositions in the James Monroe case. "He came back," said Anderson, "and he was visibly shaken."[34]

Anderson himself was looking forward to leaving after work for the traditional Oyster Festival in Urbanna. An avid and skilled sailor, he was planning to go by boat. Just before leaving GW, he stopped by the president's office. He did not like what he saw. "I walked in to say goodbye," he recalled, "and I looked at him, and I had seen that complexion, that look, before—in Charleston—and I told myself I'd better stay. [But] he was insistent that I go ahead, so I did go, and . . . sailed to Urbanna. And as soon as we docked the boat and I stepped on the dock, a lady asked if I knew where William Anderson was, and I said, 'Here I am.'"

She handed him a note that confirmed his fear: Woodard had suffered a heart attack.

A SAD DENOUEMENT

Upon receiving the frightening message in Urbanna, Bill Anderson returned immediately to Fredericksburg, where he found his stricken boss-mentor-friend at Mary Washington Hospital in critical condition—and alone. His wife, Corinne, was out of town, and no other family members lived nearby. "I spent the night at the hospital," Anderson recalled, "so that if we had to make a family decision, I would be able to make [it] on behalf of the family."

It turned out that he was spared that traumatic duty; Woodard survived. Given the severity of his attack, he made remarkably quick progress toward recovery. Within two weeks, Anderson, who had been authorized by the Board of Visitors to carry out presidential duties on an interim basis, reported through the *Bullet* that Woodard was "full of life," which he attributed in part to the outpouring of support from the students. "Every day," he said, "Mrs. Woodard comes in with an armful of cards. . . . The students have been just wonderful." The positive report was joyfully received by the paper, whose headline announced: "Our President Is Doing Just Fine."

Woodard proceeded to surpass all expectations by returning to work in mid-January 1982, approximately two months after the attack, albeit on a limited basis. "I can't jump right back into work after lunch like I used to," he reported, "but I'll just have to change my schedule." Aside from the reduced workload, the only medical mandate from his doctors, he said, was to lose twenty-six pounds, of which twenty-three had been lost by the time he returned to work.

Once back on the job, he threw himself into several pending tasks, including planning for celebration of the College's seventy-fifth anniversary, which would occur the next year, an event which he eagerly anticipated. Meanwhile, he recovered sufficiently to take a European vacation with his wife in the spring.

Despite such promising developments, Woodard's health was not good. It did not go unnoticed that his once-robust frame seemed increasingly frail—and in a manner that suggested causes more serious than merely the prescribed dietary changes. His voice, always prone to hoarseness, sounded reedier than usual.

Lewis Walker was worried. Though no longer rector of the MWC board, he remained friends with Woodard. Some years later, he recalled thinking back to the spring of 1982, when he saw the president at a Brompton lawn party, at which time "it was obvious that Prince's condition had deteriorated." He approached the subject with Woodard and convinced him to seek advice from the University of Virginia Hospital. Through his longtime connections with U.Va., Walker arranged an appointment for him with the hospital's chief of cardiac surgery. The report was not encouraging. The surgeon later confided to Walker that he estimated that Woodard had only a few months to live and that surgery was unlikely to resolve the problem. "There has been too much damage," he said, adding that it might have been different "if we could have just gotten him a year ahead of time. But by then there was just nothing we could do about it."[35]

Still, despite the dismal prognosis, surgery seemed the only option that offered even a glimmer of hope, and so in early October Woodard underwent an open-heart bypass procedure at the university hospital. Bill Anderson, once again named by the board to be acting president during Woodard's convalescence, optimistically announced that the president would return to his office in January and, even before that, would be working on various projects from his Brompton home.

But once again, as in the aftermath of his heart attack the previous year, the roseate predictions for recovery proved false. By November Woodard was back in the hospital, and he was admitted yet again in December. For someone of his constitution, it was an utterly demoralizing process. According to Anderson, who saw him almost daily during that time, he "became very bitter that he was not able to return to the job that he truly loved . . . and on several occasions when he almost died in the hospital and was revived, he was angry that they had done so. . . . He didn't want to delay the inevitable."

Knowing he could not get well, he preferred not to live at all. On December 21, his wish was granted when he died at Mary Washington Hospital at the age of sixty-one. In keeping with the Woodard family's preference for privacy, there was no public funeral, only a service for the immediate family at Brompton, and his remains were cremated.

His passing, however, did not go unremarked or unmourned by the public. The General Assembly of Virginia passed a resolution of condolence and commendation, sponsored by all the area's representatives. The newsletter of the College's Center for Historic Preservation, largely Woodard's own creation, lamented "the loss of a true friend of historic preservation . . . [who] was a steady source of encouragement and sound advice—always offering new ideas and ever exhorting the Center toward larger and more challenging projects." Shortly after his death, the Historic Fredericksburg Foundation honored his contributions to preservation by naming its annual service award in his memory. And the *Free Lance–Star*, not always an ally of Woodard, offered generous editorial praise, enumerating his contributions and at the same time urging that evaluations of his career not "look only at budgets and course descriptions to find the mark of a man. . . . [His] greatest contribution was the personal example he set of integrity, determination, and selflessness."

The College, which had been in the midst of semester break at the time of Woodard's death, paid its tribute once classes resumed in the form of a memorial service in a Dodd Auditorium filled to capacity with students, employees, and local residents. The short (thirty-five-minute) and decorous service included participation by two ministers, MWC religion professor David Cain and professor of sociology emeritus L. Clyde Carter. Remembrances were offered by Acting President Anderson, Rector Gail Neal (who had succeeded Katherine Hopper in that position), Dean Mary Ann Burns, former Alumni Association president Ann T. Palamar, and SA president Anne Thompson.

The tone of the service was appropriately respectful, but far from maudlin. The upbeat atmosphere was best epitomized by the remarks of Anne Thompson, who, as the first student member of the Board of Visitors, had worked closely with Woodard. She recounted her last contact with him, which had occurred on the previous Halloween, when she and a number of costumed friends decided on a whim to pay a trick-or-treat call on Brompton. As the motley band approached the front door, she recalled, "We were a little leery about the way we would be received. But when the door opened and we saw the smile on his face, we knew our college careers were not in jeopardy." The ailing president was in fact delighted that students had taken the time to remember him during the biggest party weekend of the school year.

To Thompson, that Halloween greeting was simply one manifestation of the president's desire to be part of everything that went on at Mary Washington. It was an attitude evident, she said, when "he was often seen walking through campus and stopping to chat with students about a number of things [like] the food at Seacobeck or," she added, to the accompaniment of appreciative laughter throughout the auditorium, "reminding us to keep off the grass."

The president of a college the size of Mary Washington possesses vast influence over all aspects of the institution's operation, especially when that individual has the forceful personality and the micromanaging impulses of someone like Prince Woodard. For that reason, any attempt to evaluate the development of the College during his tenure must perforce focus to a considerable extent on the man himself.

Woodard was a person of considerable intellect, though that quality was often underestimated by some of his academic adversaries. The reason for such a misperception was that his intellect was most evident not in displays of bookish erudition or florid flashes of rhetoric but in the incisiveness of mind that allowed him to cut instantly and instinctively to the crux of any issue, stripping away all extraneous elements. Such a straightforward approach was often uncongenial—indeed, mystifying—to a professoriat that thrived on nuance to the degree that nit-picking sometimes bordered on blood sport.

One consequence of his intellect was an unshakable self-assurance that allowed him to make decisions confidently—to such an extent that, to some observers, he appeared ruthless. Some wags were even moved to suggest that the man was peculiarly well named, with "Prince" conjuring allusions to the Machiavellian prototype of the cunning ruler whose actions were predicated on the principle that it was less important for a leader to be loved than to be feared.

Exaggerated (and unfair) as such assertions were, perceptions of that kind were reinforced by a personality that was direct to the point of occasional brusqueness. A thoroughly honest man who was seemingly incapable of dissembling, he was also disinclined, or unable, to conceal his displeasure when affronted. No one was immune from such displays, including students, as revealed in a classic exchange during a *Bullet* interview in 1976. It began with the president upbraiding the interrogator for starting with a seemingly innocuous question—"What is your basic educational philosophy?"—that was outside the parameters that Woodard believed had been established for the interview. After that awkward start, the discussion proceeded amicably enough, though somewhat strained, until the reporter evidently struck a nerve by asking the president for his views on the pending Equal Rights Amendment:

BULLET: Seeing that Mary Washington is a predominantly women's college, what are your opinions of ERA?

WOODARD: I don't know why my opinions as they relate to the ERA are related to a girls' school. I don't see the connection between the two.

BULLET: Well, women, like minorities, are discriminated against as far as many democratic rights are concerned. What are your opinions of the ERA?

WOODARD: I have mixed opinions about it.

BULLET: Would you like to share them with us?

WOODARD: No.

Nor were faculty and administrators, even his closest associates, spared such curtness. As Ray Merchent, one of his most loyal lieutenants, once observed, "You could tell when Mr. Woodard was getting mad because his upper lip would tighten up. And when you saw that upper lip tighten up, it was time to ask your leave and get out of there!"[36]

Woodard was not unaware of his occasional lapses in politesse. He recognized when they happened, and on at least one occasion attempted to explain. When asked why some people tended to react negatively to him, he replied simply, "I give definite answers." Many of his associates would doubtless have agreed that seldom had four consecutive English words conveyed greater truth.

Some, of course, found it an admirable trait and professed to like working with Woodard because of that very habit of directness. Of all the assessments of him, none was more pandemic than "you always know where you stand with President Woodard." Truly, he was not a poseur; but on balance, it appears that his diplomatic deficiencies had the effect of making his job—difficult as it was anyway—even harder.

Nor did it help that he was a perfectionist with a virtual addiction to details. The opportunity to be involved with every aspect of the College's operation had been one of its main attractions to him at the beginning, and it continued to be so. No matter what the issue, however trivial, said Bill Anderson, "it was just irresistible for him not to get his hands into it." As he walked through campus, no piece of trash was so small that it escaped his notice; it must be picked up and properly dispatched. For Woodard, said Ray Merchent, "everything had to be perfect or near perfect in everything related to this college." Such obsessiveness could hardly have been salubrious for anyone but was doubly pernicious for one who had virtually no diversions. Though Woodard was active in community affairs, including the United Way and the Chamber of Commerce (of which he served a term as president), he seemed to regard such involvement more as the fulfillment of civic responsibility than as an opportunity for fellowship. Neither a golfer nor a gossip, he was not the country club type. As Bill Anderson described him, "He didn't exercise, he had no hobbies, he didn't have anything . . . in his life other than going home in the afternoons and having a drink [a Manhattan, typically] with Corinne before dinner and talking to her. There was nothing else to distract him from the activities of the college. And there [is] no question in my mind that that's what led to [his death]."

The central and salutary role of Corinne in his life should not be minimized. A shy, handsome woman of regal bearing and serene demeanor, Mrs. Woodard was regarded by some as aloof, especially by those who, from afar, beheld her in contrast to her predecessor as mistress of Brompton, the effervescent Dorothy Simpson. But to those who knew Corinne Woodard better, it was evident that her natural reserve merely served to obscure a personality of genuine warmth and depth. Ever the gracious hostess, she was the personification of a Virginia gentlewoman, happily absent the airs often associated with that stereotype. Aside from her role as mother to three children, she was dedicated above all to supporting her husband by attending conscientiously to the myriad duties expected of the College's "first lady"—activities that she carried out gracefully and with effortless aplomb.

Yet not even the solace provided by a wife as devoted and supportive as Corinne could completely compensate for the negative factors at work in Woodard's life, including physical problems such as a metabolism that, he once confided to an associate, regularly produced cholesterol in the 400 range. But that physiological condition may not have been as instrumental in his demise as his overworking, because while medication might mitigate cholesterol, there was no known antidote for workaholism—and if there had been, he likely would not have taken it.

Prince Woodard was one of that breed of *Homo sapiens* for whom work is truly a hobby, providing far more pleasure than the avocational pursuits that others might find alluring. To his ilk, enjoyment is derived not in escaping from work but in doing more of it. But even enjoyable work, when pursued with unremitting intensity, can be lethal. And so it proved with Woodard.

The conventional assessment of Woodard's presidency, routinely proffered by his defenders, was that he was "the right man for the times." That he was, but unfortunately for him, those times were hard times—and required hard decisions.

At the time of his death, the *Free Lance–Star* began a eulogistic editorial by simply stating, "It was a difficult time to be a college president," and then went on to say that "yet, in his eight years at Mary Washington, Dr. Woodard not only met those challenges, but rose above them." In retrospect, it seemed remarkable that amid paramount efforts to rectify the woeful condition in which he found some aspects of the institution—notably budgetary problems and declining enrollment—he was still able to accomplish as much constructively as he did. Beginning his administration at a time when the mood of the nation (and the campus as well) was characterized, in his words, by "a consciousness of crisis and an ethic of despair," he led the way toward significant positive developments: increased state funding that permitted improved faculty salaries, creation of a private foundation to augment those resources, greater efforts to attract more applicants, an expanded sports program for men and women, the establishment of attractive new academic programs, and the upgrading of the College's technological capabilities.

But his greatest accomplishment was simply righting a ship that was, if not sinking, at least listing—a task made infinitely harder by the fact that the passengers aboard generally did not detect anything amiss and therefore not only lacked appreciation for his efforts but were often offended by, and resistant to, them.

Amid one of the several crises that flared up near the end of Woodard's administration, political science professor Lewis Fickett, one of the College's most respected faculty members, publicly came to Woodard's defense in a letter to the local newspaper. In a description that well summarized Woodard's tenure, Fickett put the matter into context by reciting John F. Kennedy's oft-quoted observation that "life is unfair." Woodard, he said, "will never win any . . . popularity polls, because he is a strong, tough, highly competent administrator—who has had to be! . . . [It was] a terrible, no-thanks job for anyone. . . . But the magnificent record speaks for itself." Longtime psychology professor Roy Smith put it more succinctly. "Woodard," he said, "was the bad guy who did all the bad stuff that had to be done."

It did seem unfair, or at least unfortunate, that Woodard's contributions went so largely unappreciated by his contemporaries at the College, even (and maybe especially) by those who had benefited most from his exertions on their behalf. Poor recompense it was, indeed, for one who gave in the service of Mary Washington College all that he had—ultimately including, in a very real sense, his life.

Prince Woodard unquestionably left Mary Washington College a stronger institution than he found it, a remarkable accomplishment in light of the meager resources at his disposal. Largely because of his energy and ingenuity, the College by the time of his death was poised for ascension to unprecedented success, a development that would have been unlikely, if not inconceivable, without the totality of his commitment to the institution he treasured.

–4–

THE ANDERSON ERA, 1983–2006

MARY WASHINGTON COLLEGE during the spring of 1983—the semester following President Woodard's death the previous December—witnessed two events of particular historical significance: selection of a new president and celebration of the institution's seventy-fifth anniversary.

With Executive Vice President William M. Anderson Jr. continuing in the role of acting president, the Board of Visitors, under Rector Gail F. Neal, took the initial step toward hiring a permanent successor to Woodard when in January it established a presidential search advisory committee. The group's charge was to advertise the position, review all applications, and ultimately develop a list of ten or fewer names from which the board would choose the new president.

The eleven-member committee was structured so as to incorporate representation from each of the College's main constituencies—specifically, three faculty members, two administrators, two students, two alumni, and two members of the board itself. Appointed as chair was Ray Merchent, a long-time administrator who had held several College posts and at the time was vice president for continuing education and director of summer programs. A genial and gentlemanly soul, Merchent was perhaps the most universally respected figure on campus and thus an ideal choice for the job.

The wording of the position advertisement spoke to the perceived needs of the College at that moment. In addition to requiring the appropriate academic credentials (e.g., an earned doctorate) and substantial administrative experience, the ad placed heavy emphasis on certain personal attributes. One criterion—perhaps a reflection of lingering concern over animosities generated during the Woodard years—was "an ability and willingness to communicate effectively with the many constituencies of the college, including the legislature and the state coordinating board." Another requirement, anticipating (correctly) that the procurement of increased funding would be a major concern in the coming years, called for "a willingness to participate actively in fund raising, development, and public relations activities."

By the deadline of March 1, the position had attracted 140 applicants, of whom 22 were women; 3 applicants were Mary Washington personnel, including Acting President Anderson. The advisory group spent the next five weeks meticulously reviewing credentials and winnowing the list.

Meanwhile, campus attention focused mainly on the institution's upcoming seventy-fifth anniversary, to be celebrated in 1983. Planning for the event was initiated in October 1981 when the Board of Visitors passed a resolution creating the Seventy-fifth Anniversary Commemoration Committee, to be chaired by Rector Katherine Hopper. The core committee consisted of twenty-five members representing the board, administration, faculty, students, alumni, foundation, and local community; the appointment of additional members to various subcommittees brought the number involved in the planning process to more than one hundred.

The commemoration program developed by the Hopper committee incorporated a wide range of celebratory activities—some private, some public; some academic, some social. Several were designed to take place periodically over the course of the year, including a public lecture series offered by the Department of History and American Studies that focused on initial turning points in history since the College's founding; a special exhibition, "Mother and Child—Paintings by Gari Melchers," offered at Belmont during April and May; and a spring retrospective exhibition of the works of Dorothy Van Winckel, former longtime chair of the Art Department, in the duPont galleries. Also, some traditional College events assumed an anniversary emphasis, as with the Alumni Association's Diamond Jubilee homecoming in May.

The main cluster of special events took place on Founders Weekend, March 11–14, beginning on Friday night with a performance in Dodd Auditorium by the College-Community Orchestra. Under the direction of James Baker, the concert began with a rousing piece titled *LXXV*, composed for the occasion by David Long of the music faculty. The work was dedicated to the memory of the late President Woodard, an appropriate tribute to one who had promoted the anniversary commemoration so avidly, contributed so many ideas to its planning, and anticipated its celebration so eagerly.

One highlight of the evening was the appearance by the renowned conductor Norman Dello Joio, recipient of two Guggenheim Awards and the Pulitzer Prize in Music, who directed the orchestra in the performance of his own work *Homage to Haydn*. Another was a performance by music professor Bernard Lemoine of Rachmaninoff's Piano Concerto no. 2 that earned the praise of the local paper's music critic, who noted that the "manifold technical and musical difficulties [of the piece] were traversed with ease by the soloist, who played with a verve and fire."

The featured event of the following afternoon was a parade from Goolrick Hall down College Avenue, through the campus to Sunken Road, and back to Goolrick. The spirited assemblage included two baton and drum corps, as well as nineteen floats sponsored by various campus organizations. The day's activities concluded with a formal dance in the Lee Hall Ballroom, where music was provided by the Levin Houston Orchestra.

On Sunday the College paid tribute to the memory of its primary founder, C. O'Conor Goolrick, in a private luncheon at Brompton for the late delegate's friends and family, including his only child, Frances Goolrick Ashby Rowell, and three of her children. Afterward, one of his great-granddaughters, Virginia Goolrick McNeill, unveiled a portrait of the founder painted by the artist Margo Kent of Staunton; another great-granddaughter, Claiborne Ashby, concluded the ceremony by blowing out the candles on an anniversary birthday cake.

That same evening the Department of Dramatic Arts and Dance presented a program that showcased both its own faculty and students as well as two professional guest dancers. The department's three choreography professors—Sonja Dragomanovic Haydar, Kelly Hogan, and Jean Graham—presented programs displaying disparate forms leading up to the highlight performance of the evening, the second act of *Swan Lake*, featuring Michele Benash and Kevin Santee from New York. The local newspaper reviewer praised the performance lavishly, adding that the College's student dancers admirably held their own while sharing the stage with the professionals.

The culminating event of the four-day celebration came on Monday with the afternoon Anniversary Convocation. Resplendent in academic regalia, the celebrants who filed into Dodd Auditorium included—in addition to College faculty (both current and emeriti), officials, students, and alumni—a host of state political leaders, among them former governor Linwood Holton. A large contingent of alumni were led to their seats by Waverly Lawson McCawley, a member of the institution's first graduating class of 1913.

The program began, according to custom, with the introduction of numerous dignitaries. Though all received polite applause, only one elicited a standing ovation: President Emeritus Grellet C. Simpson. Rising slowly to acknowledge the applause, the man who had led the College through the most tumultuous period in its history, including the era of Vietnam protests, responded with a characteristic gesture: he flashed the peace sign.

Following the invocation by Fredericksburg mayor (and later member of the Board of Visitors) the Reverend Lawrence Davies, the two featured speakers for the occasion were the eminent historian Daniel Boorstin, who was then librarian of Congress, and Virginia governor Charles S. Robb. Boorstin delivered an eloquent address titled "Lineage of Leaders," in which he extolled the virtues of a liberal education, suggesting that it was schools such as Mary Washington that were best equipped to provide the quality of leadership needed for the future.

But it was Governor Robb who most captivated the audience. Taking the podium after Acting President Anderson had mentioned in his introduction that as a young Marine, Robb had spent some time at Quantico, the usually somber governor broke into a broad smile, quickly acknowledging that the present occasion was indeed not the first time he had visited the campus, clearly implying (to the delight of a knowing audience) that earlier forays had been for decidedly non-academic purposes. Turning serious, he praised the College's development over the years, paying special tribute to the contribution of the late President Woodard.

At the end of the convocation, guests were invited to a reception in Lee Hall Ballroom, where the focal point was a four-by-eight-foot birthday cake. Events concluded with the cutting of the cake as Governor Robb, Rector Neal, and Anniversary Committee Chair Katherine Hopper led the singing of "Happy Birthday" to Mary Washington College.

The reception provided an appropriately festive conclusion to a joyful commemoration, one that gave all of the institution's constituent groups the chance to revel in a proud history and to anticipate a glorious future. And as a practical matter, the celebration generated widespread publicity for the College—most, but not all, of which was favorable.

The contrarian *Bullet*, for example, suggested after the fact that the whole affair may actually have been scheduled for the wrong time—that it would have been more appropriate to have held the celebration seventy-five years after the College actually opened its doors (September 26, 1911) rather than after the passage of the enabling legislation (March 14, 1908). Arguing for the later date, the paper quoted one student as saying that using 1908 as the landmark date was akin to "celebrating your birthday on the day you were conceived," and offered its own opinion that "after all, we celebrate George's birthday—*not* the day Mary found out the rabbit died."

The *Richmond Times-Dispatch* covered the anniversary in an article titled "Virginia's Academic Twins," referring to the simultaneous founding of Mary Washington College and James Madison University in 1908. Noting that the two schools were "the twin daughters of a movement to expand educational opportunities for women in Virginia," the paper emphasized the extent to which the two had diverged in their missions, sizes, and academic and athletic programs since both became coeducational in the 1970s.

While the *Times-Dispatch* article was evenhanded, the *Washington Post* took a rather more critical approach, asserting that "little Mary Washington in Fredericksburg" was suffering from a schizophrenic effort to keep "one foot in the modern world while the other rests comfortably in a more graceful time," the result being that the College "has been through more identity crises than a first-semester freshman."

The problem, the article suggested, was rooted in the College's failure to deal more successfully with the transition to coeducation, thereby perpetuating a gender imbalance that led many students to look beyond the campus for social activities. Even "on the Friday afternoon of the 75th anniversary weekend," wrote the paper, "the dormitory halls resounded with the sounds of suitcases being snapped shut as the weekend flight began."

The attitude of the *Free Lance–Star* was more charitable, as it hailed the

College for progress on many fronts, notably an expanded curriculum including new courses in fields such as computer science and business administration, several graduate-level programs, the bachelor of liberal studies program for older students, and increased opportunities for athletic competition. In words that would doubtless have made President Woodard proud, the paper hailed two innovations in particular for helping to improve town-gown relations: the internship program and the Center for Historic Preservation.

Admitting that "seventy-five may not be a particularly ripe old age for a college," the paper expressed admiration for Mary Washington's evolution "from a tiny teachers school to a unique institution . . . with special credentials—the only state-supported, small, residential, coeducational, liberal-arts college in Virginia. . . . We salute the college," it said. "Its future looks even brighter than its past."

Events would soon prove that prediction to be more accurate than the paper could have then imagined.

A NEW PRESIDENT

With the campus absorbed in the anniversary celebration, the presidential search advisory committee continued its deliberations, whittling the number of candidates to thirteen who were invited for interviews. The process was kept confidential—a proper approach, to be sure, but one that led to frustration on the part of some, notably students, who regarded the procedure as inordinately protracted.

The *Bullet*, in its annual April Fools' issue, facetiously suggested that the reason for the delay was that no one had actually applied for the position. In an effort to resolve the problem, the paper proffered two nominees of its own, both of them popular campus personalities: Bob Birt, "the lovable clicker at Seacobeck who has won all of our hearts with those warm inspirational sayings on those cardboard buttons he wears," and Shirley Jackson, the "premier hostess at both the C-Shop and the Pub."

Noting that neither nominee would likely get the job—or would want it—the paper was in a quandary. "So who *will* be our next president?" it asked. "At this point, it looks like Popeye the Sailor Man has as much chance as anyone else. At least Smurf has the school colors. When asked to comment, he (it?) just squeaked."

In fact, by that time a decision was near. Having completed its interviews, the advisory committee in early April transmitted its recommendations to the Board of Visitors. The list comprised five candidates: one from within the College and four from outside, of whom one was female. In forwarding its report to the board, the committee attached for each candidate a list of concerns that it suggested the board might wish to pursue in considering that particular individual.

The board's deliberations, including extensive candidate interviews, lasted over a month. Finally, on June 1, it was ready to reveal its choice. To the accompaniment of chimes sounding across campus, Rector Neal announced the name of the College's sixth president: William M. Anderson Jr.

In its report of the selection, the Fredericksburg newspaper termed the announcement "somewhat anticlimactic," asserting that "it has been common knowledge on campus that Anderson was probably the top candidate for the job he has held on an acting basis for 18 months."

Though it was true that Anderson may have been the favorite for the job, his selection was by no means certain. Such an assumption would have vastly misunderstood the workings of college committees, groups whose internal dynamics often make their decisions difficult to predict.

In fact, being an internal candidate carried both advantages and disadvantages for Anderson. On the positive side, his performance as acting president provided a showcase for his administrative skills; on the other hand, his close association with Prince Woodard was not necessarily an asset in the estimation of those who had disliked the late president. In the eyes of Woodard's detractors, new blood was needed to negate the bad blood that lingered from the previous administration.

The Woodard connection was not Anderson's only problem. As had been true of his predecessor, Anderson's terminal degree, a doctorate in education from Virginia Tech, together with minimal teaching experience, led some to question the appropriateness of his academic credentials for the leadership of a college like Mary Washington. As the advisory committee bluntly put it: "In light of his own academic background, does he have sufficient understanding of the liberal arts education?"

In the end, such concerns were outweighed by other considerations. Perhaps chief among his assets was his extensive knowledge of both the institution itself and the State Council of Higher Education in Virginia (SCHEV), where he had previously worked. The board ultimately concluded that he, more than any other candidate, was equipped to accomplish a smooth and rapid transition. This ability was deemed particularly important, since many felt that under Woodard, despite his sporadic problems, the institution had "turned the corner," and that it was imperative that the recent momentum not be dissipated during a protracted transition that might occur if an outsider were to be chosen. In short, what the board seemed to have been seeking was a Prince Woodard with a softer style—and that, to a considerable degree, was what Bill Anderson was.

Anderson's other main qualifications in the eyes of the board were his emphasis on securing additional funds, both from the state and from private sources, and his ability to convince the board that he could accomplish that objective. He was well equipped for that task by virtue of certain personal characteristics. For one thing, his open, easygoing demeanor instantly attracted people to him. Even those who disagreed with him on issues still tended to like him as a person: Bill Anderson was the quintessential "nice guy."

He also had an impressive appearance. "Wearing pin-stripe suits, button-down shirts and immaculately cut, grey-flecked hair," said the *Free Lance–Star*, Anderson projected "a solid, reassuring, businesslike image." He did indeed appear to be very much like a prosperous, more portly version of the youthful athlete he once had been. It was this quality that Rector Neal acknowledged in commenting that one reason for Anderson's selection was his "significant presence." Simply put, he looked presidential—and though a pleasing physical appearance alone would not be a sufficient qualification for a college presidency, in certain aspects of the job (notably fund-raising), it surely was not a disadvantage.

William Meades Anderson Jr.

The announcement of Anderson's selection was generally greeted with joy throughout the campus, as indicated by the scene when he arrived at work the next day. "The sometimes austere president's office," reported the *Free Lance–Star*, "had taken on the characteristics of a child's birthday party. There were baby blue streamers hanging about as the secretaries, bedecked in MWC painter's caps, answered the phones. Against a wall was a huge cake inscribed with the words, 'Hail to the Chief.' And a 20-foot banner stretched across the office, saying 'CONGRATULATIONS' in computer printout figures a foot high."

Students seemed particularly pleased with the choice. Dan Steen, president of the Student Association, who had served on the search advisory committee, expressed his delight. "I'm thrilled," he said. "I think Dr. Anderson is the man for the job. The students were 100 percent behind him all along."

The faculty by and large also seemed happy with the appointment, appreciative of what they anticipated as a less formal—and less formidable—relationship. As the *Free Lance–Star*, pointed out, "Anderson's style is strikingly different from that of Woodard, who . . . often appeared stiff and ill at ease, especially in public. Anderson always looks relaxed. And he brings to the presidency a dry sense of humor." That sense of humor was, in fact, an essential part of his makeup. Not the joke-telling, toastmaster kind of humor, it was revealed more often in private ripostes. Perhaps the most consistent characteristic of his wit was its self-deprecating nature; never mean-spirited, he almost always poked fun at himself, not others. It was an endearing trait that made him seem open and approachable—a demeanor that prompted the local paper to note that "faculty, in discussing Woodard, always referred to him as 'Dr. Woodard.' Anderson is almost always 'Bill.'"

Indeed, those who viewed Anderson skeptically because of his closeness to his predecessor need not have worried because, in terms of both personality and administrative style, the two men could scarcely have been more dissimilar. It was often said of Woodard that people always knew where they stood with him; with Anderson, they seldom did—but his manner was so pleasant they seemed not to care. Evidently, from observing his mentor, Anderson had learned as much about what *not* to do as about what to do.

Like Prince Woodard, Bill Anderson was a native of the state's Southside. Born in 1942, the only child of middle-class parents, he grew up in South Boston, a town of some seven thousand residents situated in the heart of tobacco country about one hundred miles southwest of Richmond. The Andersons were neither poor nor privileged, but quite popular in their community. His father was a merchant, one of the town's most beloved citizens; his mother, a charming and sprightly lady with a penchant for golf, bridge, and (Democratic) politics.

As was the case with so many children of the Southside in his era, Anderson seemed to have an inherent interest in, and aptitude for, politics. That predilection was nurtured by several sources, including his mother, who was active in local Democratic affairs, and his uncle, Frank Slayton, who served several terms in the Virginia Senate. Then there was the example of his townsman William M. Tuck, who, as governor of the state (and later congressman), was a figure of endless fascination to the young Anderson, whose home was within a few blocks of Tuck's.

Aside from politics, Anderson had two main interests: music and sports. A proficient drummer, he played regularly with a local orchestra during his later teens and sometimes sat in with bands who needed a percussionist for temporary gigs. Athletic involvement at the high school level included track, baseball, and football, which he played both at his local Halifax County High School and at Oak Ridge Academy, a military school that he attended during his junior and senior years. In football, his main interest, he was a halfback—a "fairly fast" one, by his own later description. His decision to attend Virginia Commonwealth University for undergraduate school was based on the practical reason that it was affordable. This was an important consideration, since he worked to pay his own way, mainly in the garden center at K-Mart, a discount chain store. He later recalled, "Every year, all the way through getting my doctorate, I paid all the bills myself and was very proud of that." An only child he was; pampered he was not.

The Richmond sojourn included two experiences that would prove critical

Bill and Jane Anderson on the steps of Brompton with their children, left to right, Harper, Bill, and Mason

to his later career. First was his meeting Prince Woodard, who gave Anderson a job at the State Council of Higher Education while he was still at VCU. Thus began a relationship that would take Anderson with his mentor first to West Virginia's Board of Regents and subsequently to Mary Washington.

Second was his acquaintance with Jane Neale, the daughter of a prominent physician in Heathsville, county seat of the Northern Neck county of Northumberland. They were married in 1972, and by the time Anderson was named Mary Washington's president, their family included three children: Harper, ten; Mason, eight; and Bill, six.

Having become intrigued by higher-education administration under Woodard's tutelage, Anderson decided to make it his career, provided that it would yield sufficient opportunities for advancement. Specifically, he and Jane agreed that if he did not secure a college presidency by the age of forty-two, he would pursue a career in business. As it turned out, the Mary Washington appointment enabled him to meet the self-imposed deadline with a few months to spare when, at the age of forty-one, he became the youngest chief executive of any of the commonwealth's public colleges and universities. At a time when the typical tenure of college presidents was approximately five years, it could hardly have been predicted that by the time of his retirement, he would be the most senior in length of service.

For the time being, the youthful Anderson family's move into the president's home in the summer of 1983 presented quite a contrast to Brompton's residents over the previous several decades—the Simpsons, who had no children, and the Woodards, whose children were grown. For the Anderson children, Brompton's expansive lawn offered ample opportunity for cavorting; for Jane, its grounds provided a venue for indulging her interest in gardening; and for Bill, its proximity to the tennis courts made it convenient to engage in the recreational activity that, save sailing (his passion), he most enjoyed.

The changed ambience of Brompton was quickly apparent. As the "Lifestyle" section of the *Free Lance–Star* described it, "Mixed with the silk damask wall hangings, chandeliers and Chippendale furniture are school books, toy trucks and Barbie doll furniture. . . . Hamsters are living in a third-story bedroom. . . . The first night at Brompton the [children] had a pillow fight in the pantry and Brompton lost. The casualties: Andersons, 0; Brompton, 5 wine glasses." Surveying the chaotic scene, Jane Anderson commented in mock horror that "Brompton may have withstood the Civil War, but it might not survive the Anderson family."

All in all, the coming of the Andersons seemed an appealing change—and a harbinger of brighter times ahead for Mary Washington. As one observer put it, "It will be kind of nice to see Big Wheels on the lawn."

The honeymoon proved short. Even before Anderson was officially inaugurated, the College was roiled by two controversies—one, the recrudescence of an old issue; the other, entirely new.

The old issue was dormitory visitation policy. Ever since 1974, students had pressed the administration for a more liberal policy, and while some minor reforms had been instituted, the main demand—twenty-four-hour visitation—had consistently been rebuffed during the presidency of Prince Woodard, who adamantly opposed the idea.

In the spring of 1983, students, sensing (correctly) that Bill Anderson might be more amenable to their wishes, renewed their quest. The Student Association, led by Lobby Chairman Dan Steen and Judicial Chairman Wendy Burnette, worked closely with Dean of Students Joanne Southworth to devise a policy for consideration by the administration. Having studied the policies of other Virginia public universities, almost all of which had more lenient rules than Mary Washington, the SA considered the impact of change in terms of security, privacy rights, enforcement of judicial regulations, and the possible effect on academic performance. It also conducted a student referendum on the desirability of twenty-four-hour visitation. Results indicated 83 percent of the respondents favored such a policy.

The first proposals developed by the student leaders called for twenty-four-hour visitation seven days a week in the two coed residence halls, Jefferson and Marshall. When the administration balked, a compromise was worked out whereby such visitation would be allowed in those dorms during weekends only. At its April meeting, the Board of Visitors approved the arrangement on a trial basis for one year, beginning with the fall 1983 semester.

The vote was unanimous, save for one member who abstained. That member was the Fredericksburg attorney Benjamin Woodbridge, who had a history of run-ins with the College before his appointment to the board. At a brief meeting of the board in May, Woodbridge argued for a reduction of the trial period from one year to one semester, and the board acceded to his request.

In endorsing the plan, Acting President Anderson told the board that the administration and students had been "working on this a long time. We were miles apart when we started, but daily got closer to a central position." He expressed full confidence that the arrangement would work. "In light of what Mary Washington College is," he said, "I think this will be an added dimension to enhance student life on this campus. Students understand the added responsibility, and we have no reservations that they will live up to our standards."

Board Rector Neal concurred, calling the new policy "a vote of confidence" in the students. As for the students themselves, they acknowledged appreciatively the board's concession. In the words of Judicial Chairman Wendy Burnette, the action "shows they have faith that the students can handle situations with maturity." (She went on to assert that she had "no doubt we will [eventually] see seven-day 24-hour visitation on this campus"—a prediction that proved somewhat premature.)

In any event, the semester ended on a high note, with students leaving for the summer, pleased with having achieved a goal so long sought. Little did they (or the administration) anticipate the furor that would soon erupt in the local community as a result of the new visitation policy.

An early indication of the opposition that would arise, as well as a hint of the approach that it would take, was evident in a June 1 letter to the *Free Lance–Star* from a Fredericksburg couple who wrote: "We are grieved that Mary Washington College has chosen to support and encourage fornication rather than to discourage and prohibit such on the premises of this previously respected state property. . . . Mary Washington College must have the potential for super abundant good or the devil would not be so actively out to destroy it. . . . We are so sad to see healthy young human bodies and minds schooled to break the heart of God."

Other letters of similar sentiment soon followed. One writer placed the decision in the context of a general decline in student morality, citing recent *Bullet* articles dealing with sexual themes including, notably, abortion. Such articles were akin, she claimed, to "what you would find nowadays in some pornographic magazines," and went on to say, "What surprises me is not the board's decision but the lack of concern about this decision by many of the ministers, parents, and concerned citizens in our area."

She did not have to wait long for just such concerns to emerge—in spades.

Leading the charge was the Reverend Paige A. Young, pastor of Ferry Farm Baptist Church. In a letter to the local paper, Young noted that many local residents who had sought in the past to support the College now felt "betrayed" by the visitation decision. The members of the Board of Visitors, he claimed, "are allowing the students to practice sexual license. No one with common sense can be fooled."

The pastor's letter was accompanied by another, more lengthy, missive from the vice-chairman of the church's board of deacons. "As citizens of the community," he wrote,

> we are concerned that this new policy only serves to reflect the lack of values currently being taught at institutions of higher learning. . . . With the recent news articles about the increase of venereal disease, abortions, and broken families—not to mention lower educational standards—we are greatly surprised that the college board of visitors enacted such a policy. Our tax money funds 65 percent of the cost of education at Mary Washington College . . . and must be spent for the betterment of the entire society and not in a fashion that will lead to the ultimate destruction of the moral fabric of the nation. We are truly concerned for the well being of our young people and are shocked when public institutions openly support promiscuous behavior.

Both men called on others to write to the newspaper and to their elected officials to express outrage at the new visitation policy and, admonished Young, "Do it soon so this policy can be changed before the fall term at the college." How many letters were written to officials is unknown, but certainly the local paper was deluged with missives of protest throughout the summer, all expressing slight variations of Young's general position. Two main themes were evident throughout: first was the assumption that the new policy would inevitably lead to increased sexual activity; second was the belief that taxpayers had the right to determine, or at least influence, educational policy at state-supported institutions.

Opponents of the twenty-four-hour visitation policy attempted to meet with the Board of Visitors at its July meeting to convey their concerns in person. A motion was offered by Ben Woodbridge to allow the complainants to speak. He did so reluctantly, he said, but felt constrained to do so because, as a local resident, he was keenly aware of the vehemence of the opposition. The motion, however, failed for lack of a second, whereupon the group of protesters dispersed. Angered by what they deemed their rude treatment by the board, they vowed to continue their protest by circulating petitions in the community.

In the face of such criticism, the College administration stood behind its decision. Bill Anderson, having by then been named president, explained his position after the board meeting. "I think you have to realize," he said, "that we're not dealing with kids here. We are dealing with responsible young adults. You have to remember, this is the same group that, if there were a war, we would ask to go to war for us. They can vote. We work to promote individual integrity and honor. And I feel you have to work with the students in order to have confidence in them. It was that confidence in the students here that led to this [decision]."

The *Free Lance–Star*, in an editorial titled "Why All the Ruckus over 24-Hour Visitation?" essentially agreed with Anderson, though it criticized the school's handling of opposition to the new regulations, asserting that it had created a "community-relations fiasco . . . [that] has guaranteed a prolonged fight over the visitation policy."

As for the policy itself, the paper expressed solid support. The concept was "sound," it declared. "If anything, it's overdue. . . . Visitation opponents seem to have overlooked the ability of young adults to make choices for themselves. . . . Whether the amount of [sexual] activity will be measurably greater than in the past is far from clear. . . . But nowhere in the board's initiative is any official approval given for sexual shenanigans. Young adults expect and deserve to make such moral decisions for themselves."

Meanwhile the petition movement continued, eventually including the signatures of 3,486 people, according to the Reverend Young. Armed with that show of support, in mid-August he issued a public plea to the College to change its "libertine visitation policy" and importuned President Anderson to "become the personal leader of a movement to change undisciplined campus life to one of guidance and strength." Young went on to refer to the necessity of upholding "the moral absolutes by which we must live or face the decline of society into complete anarchy."

His message was at the same time somewhat conciliatory toward the institution. He professed to "love the college and its students," and concluded by saying, "Let's now get on with the business of working together, college and community, for the best institution of higher learning in Virginia." He had no plans, he said, to pursue his crusade further—and he did not.

With that, the matter began to fade from the public forum, only to be rekindled when students returned for the fall semester. Except for those living in the vicinity of Fredericksburg, most had been unaware of the summer furor, but upon their return to campus, they were quickly apprised of it by the *Bullet*, which devoted the lion's share of its first issue to the controversy.

The paper's overall tone, predictably, was one of umbrage. The lead editorial criticized the "many Fredericksburg residents . . . [who] found it their responsibility to formulate and to preserve our moral standards. To them, 24-hour visitation is directly related to immoral behavior, namely sexual activity." It lambasted the Reverend Young specifically, complaining that he had "overlooked our ability as adults to make our own decisions . . . [and] turned a purely administrative and personal issue into a moral crusade."

Columnist Jim Emery was in particularly high dudgeon. He had read the letters of protest throughout the summer, he said, and had found them "always interesting, and usually funnier than the comics." He deplored the anti-visitation campaign as being "not an effort to improve community standards, as its proponents claim, but in reality an exercise in moral bigotry." He, too, singled out the Reverend Young for excoriation: "The next time the white Ferry Farm Baptist Church bus pulls up in front of Trinkle Library . . . Paige Young ought to be aboard to pass out apologies to MWC students."

Much in contrast to the hullabaloo produced by the promulgation of the new visitation policy in the spring, its implementation in the fall created barely a stir, either on or off campus. One reason was that the administration did what it could to curtail provocative activities in the affected dorms, Marshal and Jefferson—for example, kiboshing Jefferson's annual SEX (Stroh's Entertainment eXtravaganza) keg party. More importantly, the 365 students residing in those dorms, aware that they were under scrutiny, appear to have behaved with exceptional decorum. Also contributing to the tranquillity was the fact that, as one student put it, "there isn't much incentive to cheat anymore" by sneaking nonresidents of the opposite sex in and out of rooms.

An administrative survey at the end of the semester, coupled with a review of guest sign-in sheets in the two residence halls, indicated that few students actually had overnight guests and that some who had signed up did not actually stay overnight, according to Dean of Students Joanne Southworth. "Overall," she reported, "not many students have taken advantage of it."

Acerbic *Bullet* columnist Emery agreed that there had been no appreciable change in student behavior. Noting that one of the survey questions asked if respondents were aware of increased sexual activity, Emery quipped, "Well, probably not as much as some had hoped." He, like many others, suggested that the dorms seemed even calmer than in previous years. "If the devil did come to Mary Washington (as some people feared)," he wrote, "he/she sure was quiet about it."

By all accounts the new system worked well—"smooth sailing," Vice President Merchent called it—which was not to say there were no problems whatsoever. Although in petitioning for the more relaxed rules, students generally emphasized nonsexual reasons such as the desire to study late with friends, it would have taxed credulity to imagine that their demands would have been so ardent had the opportunity for greater sexual independence not been part of the equation. As one student candidly put it, "We should be able to decide if we do or don't want to sleep with someone on the weekends." When permission to make that decision was granted, there were, on occasion, conflicts with roommates forced to seek other accommodations during amorous encounters—a practice that led to the introduction of a new term into campus lexicon: "sexiled."

Overall, however, the experiment of extended visitation hours was deemed successful, by the students certainly, by the administration, and ultimately by the Board of Visitors. "It worked quite well this year," President Anderson commented, because "the students were quite responsible." The board agreed and at its May 1984 meeting approved the continuation of the visitation policy.

The new policy marked something of a watershed in the social history of the College. From that point onward, visitation regulations would be revised periodically in terms of sign-in procedures and the like, but the general tendency toward greater student social freedom—or, in the view of opponents, greater license—would proceed unabated.

To critics, the changes seemed to indicate that the College had replaced the policy of in loco parentis with one that was simply loco. But given the force and pervasiveness of cultural change at the time, it would have been all but impossible for a public institution such as Mary Washington to have continued to attract adequate numbers of applicants had it not relaxed its social regulations.

For good or ill, the ghost of Mrs. Bushnell was gone.

No sooner had the visitation issue receded than another controversy, albeit of a very different nature, arose on campus. In this case the issue was less parochial, involving questions of such broad public interest that it attracted national attention to the College—attention that was both unwonted and unwanted.

The central figure in the affair was Mary Cate Carroll, a Mary Washington alumna who had earned a degree in art in 1980. A member of Phi Beta Kappa, she was remembered years later by one of her mentors, art professor Joseph Di Bella, as "a highly gifted woman . . . [whose] capabilities were at that time almost unmatched. She was really, truly outstanding." While still an undergraduate, she won critical acclaim for her work. A *Bullet* review of one of her exhibits described her work as "a strong statement of her views on life [that] inevitably slaps the viewer in the face." True it was—and a prescient prelude to what was to come.

Following graduation from Mary Washington, Carroll earned a master's degree from the Maryland Institute of Art. Having settled in Baltimore, she exhibited in many shows in Maryland, Virginia, and Washington, D.C. In the process of winning a number of awards, she established a considerable reputation as a "confrontational artist," by her own description. "My art shocks," she once explained. "That's the nature of my art. If you . . . want my art, then [you] are going to get shocked."

The College learned the truth of that statement in October 1983 when Carroll accepted the Art Department's invitation to exhibit in the alumni art show. Among the several works she chose to hang was one titled *American Liberty Upside Down*—a piece described by the Fredericksburg newspaper with considerable understatement as "not the pretty scene the average person would hang in his living room."

Painted on a five-by-five-foot canvas, the work depicted a family scene in which an apparently happy couple, seated on a sofa, hold the vacant dotted outline of a child. So far, so good. But within the child's outline in the middle of the canvas there was a door that could be opened to reveal the actual remains of a human saline abortion—a greenish fetus with well-formed head, arms, and legs curled up in a jar—that she had procured from the College's biology department.

Like the other exhibitors, Carroll had been invited to hang whatever pieces she chose and, like the others, had submitted slides of those pieces in advance to Professor Di Bella, who, as director of the duPont galleries, was in charge of the show. The two-dimensional slide, of course, did not reveal the fetus within the closed box, and so only after the work was hung did Di Bella become aware of what was involved. At that point, Di Bella, with the concurrence of the department faculty, informed Carroll that the painting must be removed forthwith, before the show opened to the public. After attempts at a compromise solution failed, she did so, complaining that she was being censored.

It was not, in fact, the first time that particular work had been rejected for exhibit. On an earlier occasion, a local gallery had asked her not to show it, but that was different, Carroll asserted, because it was a commercial gallery, not a college "which stands for free flow of information."

The city newspaper sounded a similar note in taking up Carroll's cause. "A college," it opined, "should be open to as many ideas as possible and to frank discussion of the issues," and proceeded to make comparisons to another recent episode: "After Mary Washington College has taken so much flak about opening two dorms to 24-hour visits, it's not the time to be closing the art gallery door to a painting because it's provocative."

The College defended its position on two main grounds. One was legal, citing state law that regulates the use of dead human bodies—a stance that automatically raised the question of whether the fetus in question could be deemed a "human." In any event, Barbara Meyer, chair of the Art Department, declared in a *Free Lance–Star* op-ed piece that "the rule of law must be paramount. The law must, at times, enter into the realm of public morals and address those instances when there is seemingly a determination to ignore the boundary between decency and impropriety." Meyer was even more adamant in defending the decision on ethical grounds: "Had we allowed the flagrant and crass exploitation of this pathetic form, we would have flouted a moral as well as a legal obligation to treat it with dignity."

Carroll rejected all such claims. "What makes it OK," she asked, "to dissect and look at fetuses in the biology lab, which is where I got this, and not OK to look at them in the art department?" Striking back at Professor Meyer in her own op-ed piece, Carroll asserted that the controversial work was essentially a reliquary, not unlike the form used to display the remains of ancient martyrs—a form that she had studied under Meyer herself. "In 'American Liberty Upside Down,'" she wrote, "we have the case of a modern-day reliquary—once again a peculiar art form with its focal point a new kind of martyr. Not one killed for his beliefs, but one killed because his life was deemed inconvenient."

Carroll was a fairly recent convert to the anti-abortion cause. She had not been opposed to abortion when she entered Mary Washington, she admitted, but her experience in biology lab changed her thinking. "When you first see it [an aborted fetus], you're shocked," she recalled. "It's hard to say that's not a human being when it's right there staring you in the face." Her controversial painting/reliquary was her medium for conveying that observation to others—an attempt for which she was aggressively unapologetic. "I have obeyed a higher law," she wrote in her op-ed article, "which requires that I give this aborted child, this Johnny Doe, a voice, a recourse to protest, that was denied him under 'the law' at the time of his death. . . . What is important is the conversation, the communication, the silent appeal that Johnny makes to you, the viewer. Johnny speaks more effectively than any artist or writer."

There the matter might have rested had it not been for the efforts of one particular member of the faculty, Paul C. Slayton Jr., chairman of the Department of Education. A passionate defender of free speech, Slayton was a member of the anti-censorship committee of the National Council of Teachers of English and a longtime advocate of First Amendment rights. Incensed that Carroll's rights had been violated by the College, Slayton proposed a resolution, approved by the faculty, that called for the creation of a committee composed of faculty, students, and alumni, along with legal counsel, to investigate the matter and issue a public report in February 1984. "We at Mary Washington," he fumed, "stand accused in the press, indicted before the bar of public opinion, as censors. . . . If we find that we would have incurred no legal liability from hanging Mary Cate Carroll's work, then we must say it loudly and publicly for all to hear that we have been guilty of a serious breach of intellectual freedom and that we should not commit this sin again."

Soon the issue rose to another level, thanks to an article in the *Washington Post* by Nat Hentoff, a frequent columnist in the *Village Voice* and author of a recently published book, *The First Freedom: The Tumultuous History of Free Speech in America*. In the first of a series of commentaries on free speech, Hentoff discussed the Carroll case in some detail, calling it "one of the most unusual and frustrating tests of free expression in the modern annals of the First Amendment."

Among the complex aspects of the case was a perplexing legal inconsistency—namely, in Hentoff's words, "that it is legal to do away with a fetus because it is not defined as human, but then once it is dead, according to the College's interpretation of the Virginia code, it is defined as human." He expressed regret that the American Civil Liberties Union had not taken up the case (as Slayton had urged it to do) to defend Carroll's rights. "Those rights are compelling," Hentoff wrote, "and as a place of free inquiry, Mary Washington College should have joined Mary Cate Carroll to test whether her painting is indeed a class one misdemeanor or free speech."

As it turned out, Carroll took care of that herself when, well over a year after the incident had occurred, she filed suit in Richmond federal district court charging College officials with violating her constitutional rights to free expression and to equal protection under the law. Named as defendants were President Anderson, Dean Burns, Chairperson Meyer, and Professor Di Bella.

Even before the suit was filed, Virginia attorney general (later governor) Gerald L. Baliles issued an advisory opinion defending the College on the grounds that the exhibition was not a public forum, and thus there was no obligation to guarantee anyone the right to express his or her point of view therein. Undeterred, Carroll asked the court to award $50,000 for damage to her reputation as well as for causing mental and emotional harm. The suit further requested a court order that would compel the College to show the painting in a setting similar to that provided by the original exhibition. An attorney friend of Carroll's offered to handle the case on a pro bono basis, and others helped to establish a fund to cover additional legal expenses.

Though litigation proceeded to the point of setting a date for the trial—December 2, 1985—it never came to pass. To the dismay of partisans who had hoped the trial would result in clarification of important constitutional questions, an out-of-court settlement was reached in October that barred all parties from further public discussion of the case. The *Free Lance–Star*, in reporting the outcome, noted it was "not without a considerable amount of irony . . . [that] a fight for freedom of expression has ended with a gag order."

As part of the settlement, *American Liberty Upside Down* was eventually exhibited at the College in an art show in the fall of 1985. The only difference from the earlier situation was that this time the work, with the fetus still intact inside the box, was accompanied by a disclaimer that read: "Persons opening the door of this work will find a preserved saline aborted five-month-old human fetus." Thus came to an end the controversy that for two years had nearly turned the campus, or at least the Art Department, upside down.

As for Carroll (or Cate-Carroll, as she later preferred to be known), she went on to have a successful career as an artist. On her Web site in 2006 she described her artistic perspective in words that echoed the earlier controversy: "What is art but a conversation, soul to soul, searcher to searcher? Artworks are only tools, instruments used to initiate the conversation. . . . The viewer is not expected to admire my tools or to exalt my craftsmanship. Rather the viewer is invited as 'Honored Guest' to join in the adventure of my personal fumbling, stumbling journey towards meaning, toward fulfillment, towards Being."

The site also displayed an autobiographical account that included discussion of the various educational influences on her development as an artist. Mary Washington College was not mentioned.

Though less vicious and more limited than the controversies over visitation and censorship, there was a concurrent debate that nonetheless provoked strong sentiments in some quarters. The issue was whether Mary Washington should establish an ROTC program on campus.

The matter originated from a suggestion by Board of Visitors Rector John Kinniburgh, a retired U.S. Marine Corps colonel, that such a program might be beneficial both to the students who participated and to the College overall as an inducement for potential applicants. Having been brought to the attention of the faculty by Executive Vice President Ray Merchent, the concept was studied in some detail by a faculty committee and by the Student Association's academic affairs committee.

In the course of the debate, ROTC proponents argued that the financial incentives provided by the program might be attractive to prospective students, as would the opportunity to develop leadership skills. Merchent in particular emphasized, from the military standpoint, the benefit of having officers who were exposed to the liberal arts—as he put it, the desirability of "developing the citizen soldier/officer as opposed to the type who comes from the various service academies." Opponents, on the other hand, saw a fundamental conflict between the ideals of a liberal arts education and military training. As psychology professor Denis Nissim-Sabat put it, the establishment of a ROTC unit at the College would constitute "a political statement which we should avoid at any cost." Other faculty members expressed more practical concerns—for example, would the curriculum be watered down by military science courses, and would their content, taught by military personnel from outside the institution, be commensurately rigorous with the College's own courses?

Students, for their part, appeared to be ambivalent on the issue. The SA committee was divided, with the chair opposing the idea and the vice-chair favoring it. According to a vote of the whole committee, the majority of the fifty students in attendance were in favor, with only eleven voting against it. All eleven were males.

The *Bullet* editorially favored the ROTC plan, mainly on the grounds that it would help the College recruit and retain students. Moreover, the paper did not reject ROTC as an inappropriate addition to life on a liberal arts campus. "Like it or not," it declared, "the military plays an important role in our whole society, and should not be barred from MWC for that reason."

When the faculty voted on the issue at its April 1985 meeting, the outcome, following vigorous yet reasoned debate, was close, but the proposal ultimately failed by approximately a dozen votes out of the 125 persons in attendance. Both President Anderson and Rector Kinniburgh expressed disappointment at the result and suggested that the issue might be revisited at a future date. But the ROTC movement had crested and was not to be seriously pursued thereafter.

The spring 1984 semester on campus was enlivened by two special events. The first, in January, was a weekend visit by the entire General Assembly of Virginia, along with Governor Charles S. Robb, Lieutenant Governor Richard J. Davis, and Attorney General Gerald L. Baliles. Though the visit was jointly sponsored by Mary Washington College and the local governments of Fredericksburg, Stafford, and Spotsylvania (and organized by the regional Chamber of Commerce), it was the MWC campus that served as the locale for the main social gatherings. (It was not the first time such a visit had occurred, but the most recent had been in 1938—an event virtually no one at the College could recall, save the venerable Edward Alvey.)

On Friday evening the entourage arrived on campus, where the governor and his cohort were greeted rather informally by a sign hanging from a dormitory that read simply, "Hi, Chuck, et al." The kickoff event was a reception at which, reported the *Free Lance–Star*, college people and area officials "hobnobbed with the mighty, drank Jack Daniels whiskey, munched on crab and shrimp, and swayed to jazz in duPont Hall" while engaging in subtle (and sometimes not-so-subtle) lobbying. Dinner followed in Seacobeck, where the extensive and eclectic menu consisted of dishes prepared by no fewer than eighteen area restaurants, ranging from Allman's barbecue to La Petite Auberge's haute cuisine.

The following day, the "business" part of the visit took place as legislators toured the area by bus, giving local leaders the chance to press their cases for funding. The culminating event occurred that evening with the College's hosting a reception and dinner in Lee Hall. The large role played by the College in the whole event gave early indication of President Anderson's intention to be actively involved politically in pursuit of funding from the commonwealth.

The second major event on campus that spring was the inauguration of the new president on the first weekend in April, beginning with a concert on Friday evening by the Army Blues Jazz Band in Dodd Auditorium. In introducing the band, Professor George Van Sant, who chaired the Inauguration Committee, set the tone for the weekend when he announced that the concert marked the beginning of "one of the most fun-filled, action-packed, [yet] solemn 29 hours in the history of Mary Washington College." Then, turning to Anderson, the ebullient Van Sant boomed, "By 1 a.m. on Sunday morning, April the 8th, we will be staggering across the finish line—but, by golly, we will have inaugurated you!"

The central event of the weekend, the inauguration itself, came on Saturday morning, beginning with a lengthy academic procession led by Anna Mae Harris, marshal of the faculty. In addition to the presidential party, the procession included Mary Washington College faculty, faculty emeriti, and the senior class; delegates from numerous colleges, universities, learned societies, educational organizations, and state and local governments; and representatives of the MWC Alumni Association. It was, reported the *Bullet*, "a showcase of pomp and splendor."

Presiding at the ceremony was Gail Fallon Neal, rector of the Board of Visitors, who recognized various dignitaries and special guests in attendance. Especially warm receptions greeted the introductions of former president and Mrs. Grellet C. Simpson and Corrine Woodard, widow of the previous president. Following the introductions, felicitations were presented to the president from the faculty, represented by Mary Ann T. Burns, vice president for academic affairs and dean; from the student body, represented by Daniel K. Steen, president of the Student Association; and from the alumni, represented by Doris L. Whitfield (daughter of longtime history professor Almont T. Lindsey), president of the Alumni Association.

A highlight of the ceremony was an address by Governor Robb, who was making his third official appearance at the College within a period of just over a year. In his remarks, Robb praised the new president, placing Anderson within appropriate historical and personal context, specifically the relationship between the new president and his immediate predecessor. "I am confident," Robb said, that Woodard's

> pride and satisfaction would have been complete in the knowledge that the man he admired so much and believed in so deeply would finish the work that he began by building upon the legacy of strength that he had created. In these ceremonies we now complete that transition from what Prince Woodard began to what Bill Anderson will carry on and finish: from the conception of the college as an institution with a unique mission in our system of higher education to the realization of the great contributions we may anticipate Mary Washington will make to the intellectual development and to the quality of life of this and every succeeding generation of Virginians.

Following musical selections presented by the Mary Washington College chorus, directed by Assistant Professor Stephen J. Burton, Anderson was sworn in as president, with the Honorable Jere M. H. Willis Jr., judge of the Fifteenth Judicial Circuit of Virginia, administering the oath of office. Rector Neal thereupon completed the investiture, formally presenting the new president to the assemblage.

In an inaugural address in which he outlined his general plan for the College's future, Anderson was interrupted by applause and laughter when he noted that many students currently entering college were "well-acquainted with John Lennon, but not John Locke; who know Michael Jackson, but not Michelangelo; who read the philosophy of *Playboy* but not Plato." Mary Washington, he promised, would succeed in its mission of rectifying such tendencies among its students. "We at Mary Washington," he declared,

Anderson at his inauguration, flanked by Governor Charles Robb, left, and Circuit Court Judge J. M. H. Willis III

> have one significant advantage over many other institutions—and that is, we have a clear conception of the educational philosophy which constitutes the bedrock of our institution: namely, a firm commitment to the liberal arts and sciences. At a time when much of education is under attack, both from within and without, and when many other institutions are casting about to find their proper roles, and still others are experimenting with faddish educational approaches, it is comforting to know that we at Mary Washington are united in our common commitment to this fundamental educational philosophy which has proven its value in the past—and which promises to sustain us in the future.

Having announced some specific objectives relating to the enhancement of teaching and the improvement of faculty salaries, he sounded what would become the overall theme of his presidency:

> We must always hold true to those principles and values which have served us well, constantly holding before us that commitment to excellence which should pervade and inspire all that we do. Let us never forget that our primary reason for being, as a college, is to serve our students. We must strive constantly to prepare each one of them for a lifetime of productive accomplishment—a lifetime not only of *earning*, but of continued *learning*—and a lifetime of contributory citizenship.

> Ultimately, our work as an institution will be measured by how well we have prepared our students to live good and humane lives in a world yet to come—a world whose difficulties, as well as delights, we can scarcely imagine today.

Following the inaugural ceremony, a luncheon for distinguished guests and visitors was held in Seacobeck Hall. Afternoon activities included a student reception in the parlor of Ball Hall and an alumni reception later in the day at Trench Hill. The inaugural festivities concluded Saturday night—actually, early Sunday morning—with a celebration in Lee Hall, featuring the popular Richmond dance band Jack Diamond and Friends, who played until well past midnight to an enthusiastic crowd of over one thousand. So came to a joyous close a weekend celebrating the beginning of a new era in the life of Mary Washington College.

The *Bullet* took the opportunity not only to commend Anderson on the substance of his inaugural address but also to compliment his lack of pomposity. "He seems a casual man," read an editorial, "one who enjoys sledding down the Trench Hill lawn with his children on snowy days as well as entertaining state dignitaries and speaking in front of large groups." Borrowing from Tom Wolfe, the editorial declared that the new president simply had "the right stuff."

But it was the *Richmond Times-Dispatch* whose account of the inauguration proved most prescient. Anderson, it suggested, would likely be "no mere caretaker of a school where tradition and the sense of history sometimes seem to be as palpable as the iron college gates. By the time he finishes what could be a long tenure, Dr. Anderson, who is only 42, will almost certainly have brought about a new look for the former all-women's school."

Indeed he did.

PERSONNEL

The development of Mary Washington College during the Anderson presidency was overseen by a Board of Visitors who generally shared his views for the institution and thus tended to approve his initiatives. The board during that period was usually a congenial and cohesive group, able and dedicated. Those who served as rector almost uniformly exhibited diplomatic skills that enabled the board to function harmoniously. In the course of Anderson's long tenure, no fewer than eleven persons would hold that position (six of whom were alumni): Gail Fallon Neal '59, John Kinniburgh, Rita Morgan Stone '52, Virginia Lewis Dalton '40, Bennett Whitlock, Florian "Red" Hofer, Kathleen Shepherd Mehfoud '70, Paul Dresser, Vincent DiBenedetto '83, Dori Eglevsky, and Mona Davis Albertine '71.

The operation of the president's office itself reflected the informal tone set by Bill Anderson. Its functioning was facilitated by the executive assistant to the president, a new position established by Anderson early in his administration, to which he appointed history professor William B. Crawley Jr., who had been at the College for over a decade at the time of his appointment. His experience, besides teaching history and chairing that department for many years, included heading the Governor's School for the Gifted and the College's Center for Historic Preservation.

The purpose of the position, Anderson explained, was mainly to relieve him of some of the routine duties of the office so that he could spend more time on development activities. Accordingly, much of Crawley's time was spent on research and writing, representing the president's office to both internal and external constituencies, and handling a variety of ad hoc assignments. After Crawley returned to full-time teaching in 1988, the position was held successively by Conrad Warlick, Marjorie Poyck '66, and Mary Randolph Corbin '71.

The work of the president's office was further streamlined by the hiring of a new executive secretary, Vicki Campbell, who succeeded Polly Rice, President Woodard's longtime assistant both at SCHEV and at Mary Washington. Campbell, who also served as secretary to the Board of Visitors, brought to the job incomparable technical skills, a consistently upbeat attitude, and total commitment to her many tasks. For eighteen years she worked relentlessly but cheerfully until medical problems forced her retirement in 2002. "She was a fantastic secretary," said Bill Anderson, "whose work ethic and professional skills were exceeded only by her charm and personality."

Besides the president, the one other staff member who reported directly to the board was the institution's internal auditor. That position was created as the result of a suggestion from the Department of the State Internal Auditor that the College devise a more structured system of internal accounting. The first person appointed to the post was Midge Poyck, who had previously held several different positions at Mary Washington. When she was named executive assistant to the president three years later, she was succeeded by Helen Vanderland, whose work as internal auditor continued until 2007. In addition to providing objective financial and compliance audits to the Board of Visitors and administrative officers of the College, the internal auditor was responsible for performing fraud investigations, if necessary.[1] Vanderland brought to that task not only a high standard of professionalism but also a sunny, convivial personality—a characteristic not normally associated with auditors.

The position of executive vice president was one of the most wide-ranging jobs at the College, involving to some degree almost every facet of the institution's operation. From the outset of the Anderson presidency until 1993, the assignment was Ray Merchent's.

A more perfect candidate for the job would have been hard to find. Merchent's singular personality, coupled with his administrative skills, allowed him to work effectively with all of the institution's constituencies. His gift for turning acrimony into agreement and contention into consensus made him a steadying influence within an environment where strongly held and often conflicting views always had the potential for producing discord. He had the knack of presenting his own views forcefully and with conviction, without at the same time demeaning or disparaging those of others. His success was acknowledged in 1988 when he was awarded the College's Washington Medal, the first MWC employee ever to receive that honor.

Ray Merchent

One key to Merchent's success was his inherent ability to be serious of mind without being somber in spirit. He was a person of cheerful disposition and genuine good humor, and no one enjoyed a joke more than he, nor did anyone's laughter express more delight. Perhaps to a greater extent than any College employee of his generation, he was immersed in the life of the Fredericksburg community, especially after his retirement in 1993. He served on numerous boards of cultural, educational, religious, and health care organizations, almost always in a leadership capacity. And so when he passed away in December 2003, the *Free Lance–Star* memorialized him in an editorial, calling him a "treasure" whose loss would be "deeply felt."

The description most often applied to Merchent, both during his life and after his death, was "gentleman"—and rightly so. Elegant in bearing, always impeccably attired and with manners to match, Merchent in his classic pinstripe suit and preppy tie epitomized the graces of an earlier day. But it was not just a matter of style, because for him, life was never about appearances; he was of all people the most unassuming, the least pretentious. His gentility was real—not the product of learned behavior or artificial airs but derived from fundamental virtues of humanity and humility.

For almost forty years, Merchent shared those values with the College community. In the process he became, as his longtime colleague Philip Hall simply summarized it, "Mr. Mary Washington."

Shortly before Merchent's retirement, an administrative reshuffling created the position of senior vice president for administrative and student services, a job that incorporated some of the duties previously assigned to the executive VP. First appointed to the new position in 1990 was Conrad Warlick, who had served previously as dean of admissions and later as executive assistant to the president. Before he retired in 1997, the gregarious Warlick had been instrumental in a number of notable changes on campus, including installing a fiber-optic system, privatizing the post office, and building a Phi Beta Kappa key beside Campus Walk. In addition, he played a pivotal role in establishing FRED, the city's bus service, and served thereafter as the MWC liaison with the transportation system.

The office of business and finance was one of the largest and most crucial departments in the operation of the College. Richard Miller, hired by President Woodard to succeed Edward Allison, was vice president for business and finance when Bill Anderson became president. The multi-talented Miller—he was an accomplished pianist—served until 1996, when he accepted a state buyout plan (part of a cost-cutting move by the College) and chose early retirement.

That retirement prompted another of the periodic administrative reorganizations that took place during the Anderson presidency. In this case many of the duties of the office of business and finance were shifted to the office of executive VP, which also acquired oversight responsibility for student affairs and the Physical Plant Department. Appointed to the reconfigured position was the seemingly ubiquitous Midge Poyck. When she retired in 2000, a statewide search for a replacement resulted in the hiring of Richard Hurley, who had worked successfully for fifteen years as the chief financial officer at Longwood University. Given his extensive knowledge of state educational budgeting, he seemed an ideal choice for the position of executive VP and CFO. The year following Hurley's arrival, the office of executive vice president expanded with the hiring of Richard Pearce as assistant VP for business and finance. Having worked as dean of finance and administrative services at Germanna Community College, Pearce was given responsibility for managing Mary Washington's business services and financial operations.

Many of the College's most important operations came under the administrative purview of the office of business and finance, including (in addition to all budgetary matters) personnel, bookstore, dining services, and the physical plant. The personnel office was headed for a number of years by Shelli Short and subsequently by Sabrina Johnson, who became the highest-level African American administrator at Mary Washington. The tasks of Short and Johnson, both of whom held law degrees, were especially critical in light of the institution's efforts at hiring minorities, an endeavor that was a constant challenge.

Sherry Morgan was by 2007 one of the College's most senior members in length of service. Originally employed in the library in 1970, she moved to the office of the executive vice president in 1983 and thence to the office of human resources, where she eventually became assistant director as well as benefits coordinator. In the latter capacity, Morgan was especially appreciated by faculty and staff seeking advice as they approached retirement, comforted by knowing that she had both the expertise and patience to guide them through the sometimes intimidating bureaucratic morass that the retirement process entailed.

The bookstore significantly increased the scope of its business after Carolyn Taylor took over as its manager in 1978, following the retirement of Charles Read. In contrast to Read, a cautious and crusty sort, the entrepreneurial Taylor enlarged the store's inventory of trade books, magazines, and assorted College-related paraphernalia. Somewhat later, part of the Lee Hall venue was converted into the so-called Little Store that provided a convenient central-campus location from which students could purchase snacks and sundries.

A major element within business and finance was the Physical Plant Department, or, as it was later called, Facilities Services. At the time Bill Anderson became president, the department was headed by Lester "Mac" McMenamin, who retired in 1984. He was followed successively by Thomas Leback (1984–86), Robert Andrews (1986–94), and John Wiltenmuth, who was named director in 1994.

Early in the Anderson presidency, changes in top administrative positions included the head of the academic program. In 1985 Philip L. Hall was appointed vice president for academic affairs and dean, replacing Mary Ann T. Burns, who resigned. A chemist with a Ph.D. from Chicago, Hall had been at Virginia Tech for seventeen years, where he taught and served as assistant provost before coming to Mary Washington. Tall and athletic, he had a genial disposition and disarming smile that softened his imposing presence. His natural (as well as practiced) tendency to find consensus would serve him well in dealing with the faculty throughout two decades as the College's chief academic officer.

The only significant organizational change during that span came during the mid-1990s, when for several years Hall was elevated to the newly created position of provost. To fill Hall's vacated position of dean of the faculty, a national search resulted in the hiring of Barbara Palmer, previously an English professor and administrative official at Chatham College in Pennsylvania. Considering the growth of Mary Washington, the reorganization seemed fairly reasonable: Palmer would deal more directly with faculty members handling the day-to-day operations, freeing Hall to concentrate on larger issues such as long-range planning. In practice, however, the setup did not work out particularly well; the division of duties seemed never to be understood clearly by the faculty, who tended to view the new organization as an unnecessary increase in bureaucracy. So, within a few years, Palmer repaired to a position in the English Department, the position of provost was abolished, and Phil Hall once again assumed the duties of dean in addition to his title as vice president for academic affairs.

After Palmer's departure, John Morello became Hall's main assistant as

Roy B. Weinstock

associate vice president for academic affairs. Originally hired as a member of the English faculty to direct the debate program, Morello, having achieved notable success in that effort, gravitated increasingly toward administrative tasks. And he was good at it. Meticulous and hardworking, he quickly earned the respect of the faculty for his efficiency and dedication.

Throughout the whole of the Anderson presidency—and that of his predecessor, Prince Woodard, as well—there was within the dean's office one of the most significant (if sometimes overlooked) individuals in the entire College administration: Roy Weinstock. Having come to Mary Washington in 1968 as a psychology professor, Weinstock rose rapidly in that department, becoming its chair in only his second year. His organizational skills soon attracted the attention of administrative officials, who proceeded to ensconce him in GW. Thenceforth he moved through positions of ever-increasing responsibility, eventually being named vice president for planning, assessment, and institutional research.

Much of Weinstock's work over the years, crucial though it was to the functioning of the institution, was not highly visible, especially to students. This did not mean, however, that he was unknown. Indeed, those who worked with him recognized that he possessed special characteristics—aside from his legendary pristine desktop—that made him one of the most valuable members of the Mary Washington community. Chief among those assets was an unshakable integrity that, combined with his judgment, discretion, and elemental sense of fairness in all things, led to his being chosen for some of the College's most sensitive and challenging assignments.

Of all the new appointments, perhaps none was more important than that of Michael B. "Mickey" Dowdy to head the College's development program. Dowdy had earned his undergraduate degree at the University of Richmond, to which he had returned as what he called a "management trainee" in the university's highly successful development office. His work in that capacity over a period of five years caught the eye of Bill Anderson, who offered Dowdy the challenge—and a challenge it was—of taking over Mary Washington's fund-raising operation. It proved to be an inspired choice, as the young Dowdy was to orchestrate efforts that wrought a quantum leap in the College's endowment.

With Dowdy as its leader, the development office (or advancement, as it was sometimes called) was eventually reorganized to create distinct areas of responsibility. Bobbie Burton '74 was in charge of alumni affairs, though her title varied in accordance with changing specific responsibilities. She held such positions until replaced briefly by Melisa Casacuberta '84, who was succeeded on a more permanent basis by Cynthia "Cindy" Snyder '75, who remained in that position into the first decade of the twenty-first century.

The publications area was headed by Paulette Watson, who had earlier been in charge of public relations and, before that, had been director of the James Monroe Memorial Museum. Among her main responsibilities were the production of the annual *President's Message* and *MWC Today*, the alumni magazine.

A highly significant addition was Ronald Singleton, who was hired in 1987 as director of public information. His primary task was to coordinate all media and public relations and overall to create greater national visibility for the institution. Over the next twenty years, Singleton acquired increasing responsibilities, eventually becoming vice president for university relations, communications, and legislative affairs. For a number of years, the area of student affairs continued under direction of Joanne Southworth, though her name changed to Joanne (Mrs. Waldo) Beck following her divorce and remarriage. When she retired in 1995, she was replaced by Bernard Chirico as vice president for student affairs and dean of students.

The only top-level administrator at the start of the Anderson era who would serve throughout his entire presidency was Athletic Director Ed Hegmann.

PROUD MARY

With his team in place, Anderson embarked aggressively on formulating a long-range plan for the institution. The result was a comprehensive document, approved by the Board of Visitors in June 1985, titled "Commitment to Excellence: An Agenda for Action in the '80s and Beyond." In addition to reaffirming the College's mission as "a selective, coeducational, primarily residential, and primarily undergraduate institution grounded in the concept of liberal learning," the document laid out in detail numerous initiatives to enhance quality in every facet of the institution, specifically including the academic program, student recruitment, physical facilities, athletics, student life, and endowment development. Describing the plan as "ambitious but achievable," the document concluded with the optimistic observation that "drawing upon the support of [all] constituencies—students, faculty, administrators, alumni, and citizens of the local community—the College can be confident of the intellectual, moral, physical, and financial resources which, in the aggregate, will ensure . . . [creation of] an institution of unique character and unsurpassed quality within the Virginia system of higher education."

A major element in achieving that goal was attracting a sufficiently large pool of highly qualified applicants—a matter that once again raised the question of the College's image, particularly its name. In the several years following the abortive name-change movement of 1980, the issue had generally remained dormant. During that time, partly as a result of initiatives suggested by the committee that studied the matter in 1980, the admission and enrollment situation gradually improved. By 1984 the number of applicants had risen to almost 2,700, an increase of more than 1,000 within a span of only four years. Still, on the downside, it was necessary to offer admission to 60 percent of all applicants to secure an entering class of requisite size.

The relative lack of selectivity was of concern to President Anderson, who was particularly aware of recruitment issues from his work as chair of the committee that had analyzed and ultimately rejected the previous name-change proposal. His "Commitment to Excellence" manifesto placed considerable emphasis on the matter. "While the College does not desire to increase significantly in enrollment," it said,

> it is determined that the academic quality of its students remain high. Achievement of this goal is predicated on attracting the best-qualified applicant pool possible . . . [because] the quality of an educational institution is dependent, not only on the caliber of the academic program which it offers but upon the capabilities of those who enroll at the institution to pursue that program. In other words, no college, in the long run, can be better than the students that it attracts. The projected decline of the college-age population during the next decade will make it increasingly difficult for [MWC] to attract an applicant pool sufficient to maintain the desired level of selectivity. The competition among colleges for the diminishing number of outstanding students will intensify. Accordingly, the College must . . . make every effort to maximize its attractiveness to qualified students.

Yet even while acknowledging that various elements contributed to forming the College's image, the administration came to the consensus that one factor above all diminished the institution's appeal in the minds of potential applicants: quite simply, it was "Mary."

No one faced this issue more often or felt more deeply about it than the individual most directly responsible for recruitment, Conrad Warlick, vice president for admissions. To him the situation was a source of constant vexation, producing anguish that lingered long after he had retired from the College. In his view, it seemed that even the alphabet had conspired against the school. "When you go to a college day or college night program," he explained years later,

> you are often placed alphabetically. Where do you think Mary Washington College sat? Between Mary Baldwin and Marymount. Mary, Mary, Mary! Women would walk by: "I don't want to go to a woman's college." Men would walk by: "That's a girl's college." So you didn't have a chance to see them at all. . . . I cannot tell you how frustrating it was to have people walk by and not even look at you because of

> their assumptions because of the name of the college. . . . If we could ever get someone to visit the campus, immediately they saw a wonderful school. But the tough thing was getting them to visit. . . . Frankly, I would have killed to change the name at that time.

H. Conrad Warlick

In an effort to address that situation, Warlick, together with Vice President Merchent (who had begun his MWC career in the admissions office) and Dean of Students Joanne Southworth, prepared a staff paper titled "Mary Washington College: Image and Excellence," which they presented to President Anderson in October 1984. The ramifications of that document were to have a profound impact on the institution over the next year and a half.

The detailed report began with a review of the effect of the name since the beginning of coeducation, with emphasis on the persistence of public perceptions of the institution as all-female. It focused particularly on the role of high school guidance counselors, who, the report claimed, consistently lamented the difficulty of "selling" the College as being coed. "Indeed," the report said, "a week never passes without high school counselors, especially those at schools with all male or predominantly male populations, asking members of the admissions staff when the college is going to change its name."

There was "no reason whatsoever that a young man should be deterred by the feminine name of the institution," the paper declared; yet there was "incontrovertible evidence" that such was the case. And it was not just men, inasmuch as there were "also many young *women* who, in light of the prevailing popularity of coeducational campuses, are dissuaded from applying because of their perception . . . [of] the college."

The problem was all the more critical, it contended, given the looming decline in the college-age population. So even though it acknowledged the likelihood of student and alumni opposition to such a move, the report concluded that a change in the name of the College would be "prudent, perhaps even imperative," to ensure success at the desired level of excellence. Moreover, it warned that "such action must be initiated *now*, at a time when the pool of applicants remains high, the quality of the student body is strong, and financial support is adequate . . . [when] it can be done from a position of strength. If, however, it is delayed until evidence of decline becomes manifest, [it] might well be construed as—and might, indeed, *actually be*—part of a desperate attempt to survive."

The report ended with a proposed plan of action that called for hiring a market research firm to analyze the College's image further and to test possible alternative names. It advised that depending on the outcome of such investigations, the College should "prepare to have legislation introduced in the January 1985 session of the General Assembly to change the name of the institution, effective July 1, 1985."

The process did not advance as rapidly as the staff paper had urged, but its general recommendations were followed. This included engaging a Richmond marketing and opinion research company, Southeastern Institute of Research, Inc. (SIR), to conduct what amounted to a marketing analysis of a possible name change.

The SIR investigation involved extensive analysis of the attitudes of four main groups—faculty, alumni, current students, and potential (i.e., high school) students—regarding various aspects of the College, especially as related to the institution's image and name. The final report was contained in separate volumes for each group, replete with exhaustive statistics to buttress SIR's summary findings.[2]

For faculty, alumni, and current students, the bottom-line, operative conclusion was that the majority within each group would, in the words of the report, "support a name change if that will, in turn, enable the school to increase its prominence and enhance its quality as a coeducational institution." Opponents of the change cried foul, citing a faulty survey methodology that essentially gave respondents a Hobson's choice between changing the name or accepting the College's demise.

Whatever the case with regard to those groups, it was the responses from high school students that most alarmed the administration. The SIR study used two basic approaches to investigate the attitudes of potential applicants: one was telephone interviews with three hundred college-bound students in the northern Virginia, Richmond, and Tidewater metropolitan areas (one hundred in each); the other was four focus-group sessions with college-bound students in northern Virginia and Richmond (two sessions of twelve students per group in each locality).

In some instances, the findings were not surprising, serving mainly to reinforce existing anecdotal evidence. The general lack of awareness about Mary Washington College, for example, was not exactly news, but the extent of it was dismaying. When asked in telephone interviews to name any and all colleges and universities they could think of in Virginia, Mary Washington was mentioned by only 8 percent of those polled, ranking it far behind the University of Virginia (92 percent), Virginia Tech (55 percent), and James Madison (48 percent); indeed, MWC was named only slightly more often than Virginia State, Norfolk State, and VMI (all with 7 percent) and behind both Radford (18 percent) and Longwood (14 percent). In terms of specific image characteristics, Mary Washington was cited more often than any other institution as "a good school for girls" (27 percent versus 12 percent for second-place

Longwood) and as "not a good school for boys" (12 percent versus 8 percent for Radford).

Much of what the surveys revealed was either inaccurate or unflattering or both. Some comments were outrageous, such as the opinions of two male focus group students who asserted that Mary Washington females were known for "being loose" and "lacking morals." Another claimed that "males would decide to go to Mary Washington only to be around girls."

Without giving undue credence to such comments, SIR's executive summary did note that the majority of panelists primarily viewed Mary Washington as a small, private, predominantly female college whose students were "average, or slightly below average"—a school with a minimal reputation and a deficient sports and social program. Some conjured problems that extended beyond the campus to diminish graduates' career opportunities. "When you graduate and put it on your job application," said one female, "they are going to say, 'Oh, she went to Mary Washington. How sweet.' That's what they are going to think about you for the rest of the time you work there. They'll think she is a sweet, lovable, feminine person. They are not going to think of her as equal or strong."

Analysis of the focus group sessions led SIR in its summary to put the matter bluntly. "Panelists in all groups," it concluded, "perceive Mary Washington to have a problem. They believe the name fits the feminine, single sexed image they have of the college . . . [and] that in order to change the image of the college and attract a more balanced mix of males and females, the name must be changed. Eliminating the feminine name 'Mary' from the school name is viewed as imperative in attracting the student population desired."

Aside from the words of the report, Bill Anderson was affected—stunned would be the better word—by his personal observation of the focus groups, which he viewed from behind a one-way glass. Years later, in retirement, he recalled it as a "shocking" experience. "It was like being hit by a truck," he said. "It was absolutely awful to sit there and hear these negative comments about a College that I knew was a fabulous place. It made me almost literally sick because I realized these students had no idea of what kind of place Mary Washington really was. And I knew we had to try to fix that."

The focus group sessions indeed seem to have constituted something of an epiphany for Anderson, who theretofore had not been an enthusiastic proponent of changing the College's name. "I didn't push it when I chaired the [1980] committee," he said, "and I didn't want to do it now. Why would I? Besides everything else, I knew the students and alumni wouldn't like it, and probably a lot of the faculty wouldn't either. But the more I thought about it, the more I was convinced that something drastic had to be done. I mean, we'd been coed for fifteen years and just didn't seem to be making the progress I hoped we would. And I kept coming back to how much of it seemed to be tied to the name. I just couldn't figure out any other way we could address the issue and achieve the level of excellence I thought we should have."

Once Anderson had resolved that the name should be changed, the next question was: changed to *what*? Out of lengthy discussion among senior administrators, aided by an outside consulting firm, during the spring of 1985 the name that eventually emerged was Washington and Monroe College in Virginia.

There was a reason for each element in the name. The planners had assumed all along that any change would likely retain "Washington" in some form in order to perpetuate the existing tradition (since 1938). Moreover, as part of SIR's market research, tests had indicated highly favorable responses to the name "Washington" on the part of potential students, who felt it connoted strength and quality.

Some consideration was given to simply deleting "Mary," making it just "Washington College," but that option was not pursued, mainly because of the potential for confusion with a number of existent "Washington" colleges. In fact, the president of Washington College in Maryland wrote Anderson, adjuring him not to make such a change.

Once it was decided that another name should be added, "Monroe" seemed an obvious choice, since the nation's fifth president, James Monroe, was (aside from George Washington) the most notable figure historically associated with the Fredericksburg area. In addition, the College already administered the James Monroe Museum and Memorial Library.

The incorporation of "in Virginia" as part of the proposed name—an element that struck some people as awkward and unnecessary—was based on two interrelated premises. The first was that, when used on recruitment materials, it would instantly indicate where the College was located, an especially useful function for out-of-state prospects who might not otherwise know. Second, the marketing consultants believed that an overt connection to Virginia strengthened the image of a college—again, particularly in the estimation of potential students from outside the commonwealth.

And so, in June 1985, acting on the recommendation of President Anderson, the Board of Visitors passed a resolution requesting that the General Assembly at its next session (January 1986) approve legislation that would change the name of the institution to Washington and Monroe College in Virginia, effective July 1, 1986. The board's vote was unanimous.

In light of the maelstrom that eventually engulfed, and ultimately swamped, the name-change proposal, the immediate reaction to the Board of Visitors' decision was relatively calm. There were several reasons for that restraint, the most basic being that it was not wholly unexpected. Persistent discussion of the issue over the course of several years had led even some opponents of the move to concede that an attempted name change was a possibility; when the vote did come, it was no surprise.

Then there was the fact that students, who might have protested the decision, were not on campus when the decision was made in late June. What their reaction would have been is, however, problematic, as student opinion before the vote had been ambivalent. There was clearly one school of thought that adamantly opposed a change, a view manifested in a satirical 1983 *Bullet* op-ed piece on the importance of tradition. Not everything about the College was sacrosanct, it admitted: "If things never changed at MWC, the Pool Room would still be full of water and there would be a greatly decreased number of men's rooms on campus. Hell, there'd be a greatly decreased number of *men* on campus—none, in fact!—(except perhaps for an occasional Marine), . . . and keg parties, devoid of beer, would be called 'mixers.'" On the other hand, the piece continued, some traditions were worth saving, including the name:

> Now everyone (especially those of the masculine gender) [has] taken flack because we go to a school with a "sissy" name like "Mary Washington": "What kind of a fairy school is that?" . . . But consider the alternative. . . . If we were to toss tradition aside and chose a more modern name, we would all be going to "Redneck College" or "Fredericksburg State," or something equally vulgar. . . . What else would change if MWC lost a tradition? Consider this:
> —"Halloweens" would be a memory.
> —There would be no Devil Goat Day.
> —Junior Ring week would be completely meaningless. . . .
> Could we live at MWC without tradition? "Nay" seems to be the clear answer. Tradition is important to this college as, well, beer. Think of what it would be like if we had no beer, and you can imagine the tragedy of MWC without tradition.[3]

But there was another side to student opinion on a name change, and as the possibility appeared more likely by the spring of 1985, the *Bullet* came out squarely in favor of such a move in an editorial whose headline blared, "Change It!" Noting that "many students are concerned that the College would have to rebuild its reputation because it would lose its identity," the paper asserted that inasmuch as "the school is presumed by outsiders to be an all women's private institution, a mistake made largely as a result of the name, . . . then it is already having an identity problem and a name change might be called for. . . . If a change in name can attract a more balanced and better qualified applicant pool, which is why the idea is being considered in the first place, then any sacrifice seems worth it." About the same time, the Student Association's executive cabinet took a moderate position, urging students to "consider what is best for this institution's future in the long run."

Faculty opinion, seldom unified on any subject, was typically divided on the proposed name change, exhibiting what English professor Sue Hanna called "a considerable lack of consensus." Some colleagues, she said, "considered the move to be the sexist result of giving in to a small-minded attitude on the part of adolescent boys and their parents. . . . [But] on the other hand,

Students with T-shirts displaying disparate attitudes toward the proposed change in the College's name

there are some faculty members who are absolutely behind the name change. If the name is going to be changed," she concluded, "I think people feel it should be very much along the lines that the Board decided."

Even the alumni, who would later mount a crusade against the change, generally responded with equanimity, if not enthusiasm, at the outset. In fact, Alumni Association President Barbara Creighton "Bambi" Willis '73, who had earlier expressed reservations, publicly endorsed the name-change initiative after the Board of Visitors' decision.[4]

The attitudes that counted most of all, of course, were those of the legislators on whose votes the proposal depended; within that group, the most influential were the members representing the Fredericksburg area. Among them, reactions of those who commented ranged from lukewarm (Spotsylvania Democratic state senator R. Edward Houck) to strongly supportive (Stafford Republican delegate Thomas Moncure Jr.). "I can't really feel comfortable with the name change," said Houck, "but if it's necessary for the college to grow, then it's hard to oppose it." Moncure viewed it as essentially a fait accompli. "With the unanimous approval of the Board of Visitors," he concluded, "even if the local delegation worked to block the change, it would probably go through."

Moncure's predication proved premature, as opposition soon began to arise. One of the first attacks came from an unlikely source: a member of the Spotsylvania County Board of Supervisors named Emmitt Marshall. He declared that he saw "no good reason to change the name of Mary Washington College," claiming that the proposed change made no more sense than painting fire trucks yellow or putting blue lights on police cars. The Board of Supervisors agreed, approving by a four-to-two vote a resolution to the General Assembly expressing opposition to the change.

Hailing the action of the Spotsylvania supervisors, the *Free Lance–Star*, which was to become a leading adversary of the name change, took up the cause. In a July 12 editorial titled "Old Coke, Ol' Mary," it made invidious reference to the Coca-Cola company's much-maligned effort to introduce "New Coke" based on market research that turned out to be faulty—and proceeded to offer a suggestion of its own. "If the naming of a college is strictly a marketing decision," it asked, "why not change MWC to Ronald Reagan U.? . . . Surely no senior could ever mistake RRU for a women's college, [and] every time 'Bedtime for Bonzo' makes the late show, RRU would get a publicity boost." Sarcasm aside, and with allusion to Supervisor Marshall's analogy, the paper asserted that "you don't have to oppose blue lights on police cars and yellow fire trucks . . . to wonder why the MWC name change is necessary or wise."

As the months passed before General Assembly action, more and more people began to ask that very question, bombarding the *Free Lance–Star* almost daily with letters to the editor. To be sure, some writers defended the proposed change. One of those, a high school guidance counselor, emphasized that the near absence of coed public colleges named for women made it extremely difficult to convince either male or female students to apply to Mary Washington. In that light, the name change appeared as "a realistic acknowledgement of the fact that many students—both male and female—ignore what the college has to offer, not because they are hopelessly benighted sexists, but rather because they presume from the name, and understandably so, that the institution will not suit their preferences for a coeducational environment."

Among faculty members writing to advocate the name change was soccer coach Roy Gordon, who claimed that his recruiting efforts had convinced him that "Mary" was a major reason why the College was "not experiencing even slow growth toward coeducation." Recently, he said, he had "even talked with an MWC alumna who would not allow her son to apply to Mary Washington College. She was en route to visit U.Va. One would think that in these times a feminine name should not be at issue. The truth of the matter is that it is. If the college is to achieve full coeducation, a name change is the only move that can be made. It should have been done 15 years ago."

One of the most powerful defenses of the name change was that presented by the esteemed philosophy professor George Van Sant, who, by the time the controversy arose, had been a member of the faculty for almost three decades. His position was somewhat surprising because his wife, Sue Hanna, was one of the faculty's leading feminists and he himself had impeccable liberal credentials as a longtime stalwart of the local Democratic Party. Yet despite initial misgivings, he came eventually to support the name change, a position that he explained eloquently in a letter to the *Free Lance–Star*.

First of all, he asserted, the change should not be considered as a feminist issue. In so doing, he resurrected Professor Dick Warner's earlier claim that, ironically, Mary Washington was originally used to help preserve the all-male status of the University of Virginia. Thus, he argued, "The name Mary Washington, far from being a rallying point for feminists, is actually a symbol of Virginia male chauvinism."[5] From there he went on to explain why, in his opinion, the change was necessary. Many of its critics, he wrote,

> persist in saying that the primary rationale for the change is to attract male students. That is a distorted simplification of the reason for the change. The real reason is to attract more students, *male and female*. All polls show that the overwhelming majority of young women today wish to go to a coeducational institution, so it must be understood that the college is really trying to encourage more men *and* more women to apply for admission. As it stands now, despite enormous publicity efforts by the college, the majority of high school students of today still have the mistaken perception that the college is a woman's college. This mistaken perception is no myth. Both the studies by the administration and my own personal experience confirm this mistaken perception almost daily.

Having noted that the administration and Board of Visitors had "certainly made some tactical errors in making the case for change," he maintained that "such errors should not obscure the fact that, on balance, the Board of Visitors and administration have taken a difficult and courageous step that will indubitably serve the best long-range interests of the College."

Van Sant's opinion seems to have run counter to the preponderance of public opinion, if the flood of negative letters to the paper is any indication. Opposition sentiment, variously expressed in letters ranging from the reasoned to the rabid, was generally based on one of two grounds. Some maintained that the change was simply unnecessary, pointing out that the College's applications for admission were at an all-time high. Others, reluctantly admitting that statistics such as the low ratio of male students and a disappointing acceptance rate indicated a possible problem with name, still opposed the change because, to them, such a solution would be bought at too high a cost to feminist ideals.

Indicative of such sentiment was an indignant letter to the editor from the veteran MWC feminist, former psychology professor Alice Rabson, by then retired. The College, she claimed, was attracting applications from more commuting students, out-of-state students, foreign students, and minority students than ever before, thus obviating a name change to increase the applicant pool.

But above and beyond that, she continued, "This name change is a feminist issue, . . . clearly a slap in the face of women, especially since Mary Washington is such an important, locally historic person. Not only was she a local resident, but she represents a special type of woman, of whom we women can be very proud. She was noted for unusual business acumen. She was a single parent (widow) who was able to raise her children by her own efforts on a farm, and to bring up a son who was competent, successful, and concerned about his country. George Washington was very lucky in the choice of his mother."

Concerned alumni correctly recognized that their best means of defeating the change was to bring political pressure to bear on members of the General Assembly through a letter-writing campaign. To facilitate that effort, a group was organized, led by local Fredericksburg alumnae Betty Hume '71, Karen Zirkle '74, and Ginger Burke '75, called the Committee for Mary Washington.

The controversy intensified appreciably when students returned for the fall semester, though not all of them opposed the decision that had been reached in their absence. The *Bullet*'s editorial policy continued to be ambivalent, and early in the semester, the Student Association's executive cabinet voted to endorse the proposed change.

The cabinet's vote appeared to galvanize students who opposed the change. Declaring that the SA did not represent their views, some went so far as to call for the resignations of the executive cabinet officers. "They're simply caving in to the administration," charged one critic. "Do five individuals feel they have such great leadership abilities that they can outweigh the desires of hundreds and hundreds of students?"

Such an accusation seemed to have some validity in light of a student body poll, conducted by the SA itself in late September, that revealed 69 percent of the respondents to be opposed to the name change and only 20 percent in favor of it. The situation provoked one *Bullet* op-ed writer to exclaim, "If everyone is talking about the name change, why not get together and do something about it? . . . If some or most of us are children of the radical sixties, why didn't we get some of that blood?" Sufficiently incited, some students heeded that challenge by making common cause with alumni through organizing a Save the Name Committee.

One visible manifestation of opposition was expressed through the ubiquitous campus medium of printed T-shirts. In this instance it was the entrepreneurial residents of Madison Hall who milked the controversy by having shirts printed that read: "Any man can learn from a good woman. Keep the name Mary Washington College." Sales the first day (at $6.00 per shirt) totaled 280, according to one Madisonite. "These shirts are hot," he said, adding that more were being ordered in anticipation of the imminent sellout of the original four hundred.

SA president and name-change advocate Karen Anderson (no relation to President Anderson) dismissed the significance of the shirts' popularity. "People are buying those shirts because they're cute," she said—not necessarily to express any real sentiment, but simply because "they're souvenirs." At the same time, however, shirts bearing the proposed new name, Washington and Monroe College (apparently printed as a presumed sop to the administration), sold a mere twenty-three, all but "four or five" of which, according to one of the Madison merchants, were bought by College personnel.

A more dramatic protest occurred early in November when students and alumni joined forces for a candlelight protest march to Mary Washington's grave on Washington Avenue. Led by protest organizer Andrea Canova, an MWC senior, the group of about eighty assembled at Ball Circle, whence they proceeded to College Avenue, down William Street, to Washington Avenue to the site where Mary had been entombed in 1789. All along the way, the procession drew shouts of encouragement and blaring horns from passing motorists. Once at the tomb, several students shouted, "Are you turning, Mary?" Then the group placed flowers at the foot of the monument and sang the alma mater.

On the return trek to campus, the protesters marched to Brompton, where they knocked on the door and were greeted by President Anderson. Canova politely explained that the group was returning from a protest march against the name change, to which Anderson amiably replied, "Well, you certainly have a nice night for it," and thanked them for stopping by.

The cordiality of the encounter belied the protesters' passionate commitment to their cause. A week later they again demonstrated their opposition by confronting members of the Board of Visitors outside GW Hall. Arriving for a meeting, board members were met by a group of about thirty, consisting mainly of students and alumni, bearing placards with messages such as "Don't Make Mary a Four-Letter Word" and "Change Your Vote, Not Our Name." At the conclusion of the meeting, the group requested permission to address the board but was denied on the grounds that they had not written in advance to request inclusion on the agenda as required by Board of Visitors bylaws.[6]

The protest seemed to have no particular effect on the board, one of whose members minimized its significance by commenting, "Let's see, 30 [protesters] divided by 3,000 is what percentage of the student body?" Anderson himself described the turnout as "pretty modest—about what I expected."

But despite such dismissive attitudes by College officials, the opponents continued their assault in less public ways, notably a letter-writing campaign to state legislators. They were supported in their efforts by the *Free Lance–Star*, whose editorials constantly assailed the change. "The case has simply not been made that the college's welfare depends on catering to sexism and defeminizing the institution's image," it declared in mid-November. And with the General Assembly session upcoming, the paper challenged area legislators to stand up in defense of "Mary."

Even at that (relatively) late date, however, it appeared that the change would probably be approved. As Senator Edd Houck, himself no fan of the change, put it, "I think the General Assembly would be reluctant without a tremendous amount of opposition to go against the wishes of the board and the administration. That's certainly been the case historically." Accordingly, it seemed to him that approval of the change would be a "rather routine matter."

Yet it turned out to be anything but routine. As the opening date of the legislative session approached, there were signs that the opponents were making headway. Houck himself began to express greater skepticism. "I'm not putting myself in the position of second-guessing the administration," he said. "I have all the respect in the world for them, and think they feel the name change is in the best interests of the school. But I have not been persuaded the name change is needed."

In mid-December the opponents received a boost when the *Richmond Times-Dispatch* reported that the Board of Visitors had discussed the name change at a June 1984 retreat in Williamsburg without giving public notice of the meeting as required by the state's Freedom of Information Act. "MWC Name Discussed in Secret," cried a *Free Lance–Star* headline.

The facts behind the purported exposé, which first came to light in an interview with President Anderson published in the alumni magazine, were not clear.[7] What was known was that there was a Board of Visitors retreat and that it was not explicitly announced in advance to the press. Anderson admitted as much, though he could not explain the circumstances. "There was no attempt to not have an open meeting," he said when the report came out. "I think we should have given notice, and I have yet to determine why we didn't."

The affair did look suspicious, especially to those who were inclined to think the worst concerning the advocates of the name change. This, too, Anderson acknowledged. "I'm sure the alumni . . . will think we ran off in the dark, distant woods to make a decision without talking to them," he said. "That just isn't the case."

Nonetheless, Rector John Kinniburgh felt constrained to offer a public defense, which he did (rather convincingly) in a long letter to the *Free Lance–Star*. "The matter of the retreat and the date thereof," he explained,

> was openly discussed at the previous meeting of the board of visitors in April—at which newspaper reporters were present—and was so noted in the minutes of that meeting. . . . If there had been any desire to hold a secret session, it would not have been announced in public two months in advance . . . [and] it would not have been subsequently referred to by the president very openly on numerous occasions with many individuals and groups, nor would he have alluded to it in a printed interview [in *MWC Today*]. . . . It should not be deduced that there was ever, at any time, any attempt whatsoever to hold a secret meeting for purpose of discussing of the name change or for any other purpose.

In that light it appears that if the board and administration had wanted to act secretly, they were singularly inept in going about it. But whether anyone was culpable—and if so, whether guilt came from duplicity or simple inattention to detail—the result was to provide additional ammunition to the arsenal of those who were gunning for defeat of the name change.

The case against the change was further buttressed by a petition, devised by the Save the Name group, for presentation to the General Assembly. By the time the session began, the statement of opposition had been signed by approximately three thousand Fredericksburg area taxpayers.[8]

Another tactic, prevalent among alumni opponents of the change, was the threat to cut off financial support for the College. That approach made little impact on MWC officials, however, because even if such threats were carried out, the total loss of funds would have been negligible. Most of those who made such threats, according to giving records, were small (or nonexistent) donors to begin with. And as the Director of Alumni Giving, Bobbie Burton, pointed out, not a single member of the President's Council, the top giving category ($1,000 or more), expressed any intention to reduce his or her level of contribution.

In fact, Vice President for College Relations Mickey Dowdy used donation figures as proof that alumni were still supportive of their alma mater, the name-change issue notwithstanding. He emphasized specifically that the fall phonathon in 1985, an event that took place in the midst of the controversy, produced 2,325 pledges, the highest number ever. "This," he said in a letter to the local paper, "is a tangible illustration of the broad alumni support that exists for the college and its goals." Therefore, he concluded, "it should not be assumed that the vast majority of alumni are opposed to [the name change]. That is simply not the case."

True though that may have been, there was still a highly vocal, committed, and energetic minority who worked tirelessly in opposition. Eventually their exertions began to bear fruit; as time passed, it became evident that momentum was shifting against the change. A key defection was that of Stafford delegate Thomas Moncure. Theretofore a staunch advocate of the change, he announced on the eve of the 1986 General Assembly session his belief that the College should withdraw its request, at least for the present legislative term. It was not that he rejected the premise of the bill, he said, for he continued "to think that changing the name would help achieve the goals of the board and the administration." At the same time, however, he was persuaded that the bill was not currently "politically viable" and that the fight for it, even if successful, would leave the institution badly scarred. "It could be a case," he said, "of winning a battle but losing a war. . . . It's hard enough to get things done down here [Richmond] even when you come in with a united front. . . . We've just gotten to the point of not being able to make an argument for the change in light of the emotional nature of the issue."

Another important area representative, Delegate Tayloe Murphy of Westmoreland County, concurred with Moncure. Earlier he had supported the change as a reasonable means of correcting the College's all-female image, and he did not find such a move sexist. As late as December, he commented that in his opinion, "members of the legislature don't look upon the name change as a slap in the face of women—just a fact of life." But by the opening of the General Assembly session, he had reconsidered. "It's not the right time," he announced. "In order for the name change to be successful, there needs to be broader support."

Though the admonitions of Moncure and Murphy were influential in determining the College's course in the matter, the legislative linchpin turned out to be V. Earl Dickinson, the veteran Democratic legislator from nearby Louisa County. Dickinson was one of the General Assembly's most powerful members and a longtime champion of MWC's interests in particular, and his attitude carried enormous weight. Specifically, his chairmanship of the higher education subcommittee of the House Appropriations Committee made him a crucial figure in the name-change debate. In short, Dickinson, always a figure to be reckoned with in the General Assembly, possessed in this case such leverage that his views simply could not be ignored by the College leadership.

Just before the opening of the January session, Dickinson made his views public, announcing that he had been opposed to the change "ever since I heard it." In the meanwhile, he said, he had requested and received statistics from the State Council of Higher Education that showed an increase in MWC's enrollment from 2,100 to 3,100 during the previous six or seven years—evidence that, to his satisfaction, the College was thriving. He also noted that, not incidentally, he had been contacted by twenty-five to thirty constituents who, as Mary Washington alumni, were unanimously opposed to the change.

More critical than Dickinson's public pronouncements was the message he delivered personally to Bill Anderson at a face-to-face meeting with the president in his legislative office. The gist was simple. Dickinson intended to fight the measure, and any attempt by the College to pursue it was likely to have a negative impact on other institutional requests, notably budgetary items.

With that, the game was essentially over, as Anderson well understood. Disheartened, he returned to Fredericksburg to share the news with fellow administrators, who were likewise disappointed. None was more chagrined than Vice President for Admissions Conrad Warlick. When Anderson called him to the president's office to apprise him of Dickinson's stance, Warlick was crushed. "I went back up to the third floor of GW where Admissions was located at that time," he remembered, "and I thought I had died. This was on a Wednesday. [Anderson] said that I could not tell my staff until Friday. I spent forty-eight of the worst hours I have ever spent in my life. I truly thought I had died. I cleaned up the office; I threw [things] out; I bitched; I did anything to distract myself. And then [Friday morning] I went in and had a staff meeting and told my staff. Well, they died! So I spent the next two or three days bucking them up to say that this is going to be all right. We are going to survive all of this."

The Board of Visitors responded to the situation by calling a special meeting on January 8 at which it voted unanimously to withdraw the name-change request from consideration by the General Assembly. Only seven board members were present, and the meeting took a mere twenty minutes to conclude its ad hoc agenda.

In announcing the board's decision to the press, Rector Kinniburgh noted that the governing body had not recanted its belief that a name change was appropriate, but had made a "purely political" decision to rescind its earlier action. "We do not want to have the name change issue create a problem and misdirect attention . . . from those very vital budgetary issues before the 1986 legislature," he said.

President Anderson elaborated on Kinniburgh's explanation in the next issue of the alumni magazine. He pointed out that the board was still convinced that "the original decision in favor of a name change constituted the appropriate response to the situation as revealed by extensive studies conducted both internally and externally during the preceding two years." The problems that prompted the decision were, he said, "very real indeed, and they will persist." At the same time, the board's action was an acknowledgment that "a name change would only be productive if accompanied by substantial support from all constituencies of the college . . . [and] that the proposed change had not yet achieved the broad-based level of support essential for its successful implementation. Moreover, the board felt that the introduction of the proposed name change legislation in the General Assembly might lead to a protracted and divisive debate which would be detrimental to the best interests of the college."

He noted in particular certain elements of the "Commitment to Excellence" document and the campus master plan whose achievement required substantial financial support from the commonwealth. Prominent among such projects were a new student center, library, and pedestrian mall. The board's decision, he said, reflected "concern that continuation of opposition to the name change might create a climate within the legislature which could jeopardize" funding for those projects.

Though the defeat must have been a bitter one for Anderson, given the energy he had invested in lobbying for the name change, he "took the setback graciously," according to the *Free Lance–Star*. An "incurable optimist" by his own description, he accepted the decision in the belief that "in the long run, the best thing always happens"—and even managed to find a positive side to the affair. "There has been so much discussion about this," he told the paper, "that I feel more people than ever are aware of Mary Washington—aware that it is a coeducational institution and a fine academic institution. . . . The school seems to be better known and better appreciated than ever before."

The local paper agreed with that assessment, facetiously suggesting in an editorial that the whole name change movement might even have just been a shrewd publicity stratagem. "The winner of the Coca-Cola Marketing Award of the year," it announced, "goes to . . . the Mary Washington College administration and the board of visitors for their cleverly disguised campaign to bring new attention to a fine school. . . . O.K., so maybe there was no master plan to secretly boost old Coke and old Mary. But what other issue could have aroused the enthusiasm of so many people in support of *Mary* Washington College? How else could this institution have received so much state wide publicity?"

As it turned out, the controversy appeared to have some salutary results. Although the degree to which subsequent events were attributable to the name-change issue was unknowable, the episode did coincide with the commencement of an era of improvements in many aspects of the institution's operation—improvements that would lead within a few years to the College's attaining unprecedented recognition for excellence.

For Bill Anderson personally, on the other hand, there was a downside. In the aftermath of the controversy there were some people (notably alumni) who, unable to forget and unwilling to forgive, continued to harbor hostility long after the president's leadership in elevating the College might well have warranted a more charitable attitude. To them he would always be, above all else, the ogre who tried to destroy the name of their college.

Opponents of the name change were elated by the outcome, especially those who viewed it as a feminist victory—though actually it was more a victory *for* feminism than *of* feminism. There is little reason to believe that a legislative body that a decade earlier had refused to ratify the Equal Rights Amendment had by 1986 become so sensitized to feminist concerns that it would reject a name change on those grounds.

It appears, rather, that the outcome hinged more on politics than on principle. The name change was an issue that had few natural advocates; even some who supported the change out of what they deemed the College's best interests were uncomfortable with the idea of removing a woman's name. The opponents, on the other hand, were motivated by more emotional impulses.

As for the legislators themselves, most (aside from those with personal attachments to MWC through ties of family or friendship) had no real interest in the matter one way or the other. Even those with genuine concerns about the quality of education in the commonwealth were not necessarily bothered by the relative quality of the various schools within the state system; whether a student chose to attend college X or college Y mattered not to them.

That was largely Earl Dickinson's position—one that led him to dismiss the very premise of the name change: that is, the idea that the change was necessary to enlarge the applicant pool, thus creating greater selectivity that would in turn lead to a higher level of academic quality. Such a purpose had no appeal to him. In fact, as he told Anderson during their one-on-one discussion of the issue (as Anderson later recalled it), the state actually needed some colleges whose lower standards would enable less-qualified high school students to be admitted.

For such legislators, all the political benefit lay on one side of the issue—

against the name change. It was an issue that offered them easy political points with a group (feminists) whose philosophy they generally abhorred by supporting their position (anti–name change) on an issue in which they themselves were utterly disinterested.

Whatever the reason for the proposal's defeat, the result was gratifying to those who had fought it. Speaking for the students, Andrea Canova, a founder of the Save the Name Committee, claimed that her group "had a major role in getting the ball going," adding that she was "also very pleased that students found a cause. If you fight for something you believe in, it can work." Once that fight ended, Canova quickly began an effort to mend what she feared was a rift between students and the administration by organizing the Committee for MWC to help promote the institution.

Leaders of the alumni opposition were likewise pleased with the turn of events, though for some of them, the euphoria was tempered by the suspicion that the matter still might not have been completely resolved. "I think it will die for a while," commented Karen Zirkle, "but I don't think it's a dead issue. It's come up twice in the last five years."

There were grounds for such concerns. Some students still favored a change, including Karen Anderson, president of the SA, who expressed disappointment at the board's withdrawal of the proposal. "We," she said, referring to the SA cabinet, "all think [the change] was right."

More portentous were the comments of some members of the Board of Visitors, such as Rector Kinniburgh, who, even as he announced the decision to withdraw, commented that he "would not say it [the name] won't change in the future." Another board member, Thomas H. Thorpe, went further, insisting that the withdrawal resolution itself actually include the statement that the board was "still of the opinion that the name change is an important part of the 'Commitment to Excellence' plan."

Opponents might have found more comfort in the approach taken by President Anderson, who appeared eager to put the episode in the past and to concentrate on achieving the positive elements of the College's long-range plan—in his words, to "get everyone working together full speed to make this institution the best." As for the name change specifically, "I learned long ago not to try to predict or speculate on what the board will do," he said, "but in my opinion, the issue is not likely to come up again."

Indeed, in light of all the negative emotions that the proposal had stirred and all the animosity it had generated, one might well have assumed that the issue would not, in fact, be resurrected—and surely not on Anderson's watch.

One would have been wrong.

Discussion of the College's name led to consideration of other facets of the institution's image, the most controversial of which was the College seal.

That symbol was among Mary Washington's oldest icons, virtually coeval with the institution itself, predating the honor system and Devil-Goat Day and having outlived various school colors, fight songs, and performing groups like the marching band. Its motto, *Pro Deo Domo Patria* (For God, Home, and Country), beneath the depiction of a spinning wheel and torch, was familiar to generations of students by virtue of its wide display on campus, notably in the brass relief on the floor of the Trinkle rotunda.

Venerable though it was, the seal was criticized occasionally as being outdated, particularly after the advent of coeducation in 1970. The issue crystallized in 1984 when SA president Daniel Steen claimed that the symbol failed to "reflect the current student body and its variety of interests." It should be replaced, he said—not in toto, perhaps, but certainly the spinning wheel, with its "bad connotations, especially for males."

Surprisingly, the *Free Lance–Star*, which had opposed the earlier name-change proposal as a manifestation of sexism, expressed sympathy for revamping the seal. In an editorial, "Spinning Wheel U.," it argued that such a change should be imputed not to sexism but to the fact that "the MWC community is in essence striving for a clearer self-image. . . . Having a spinning wheel prominently displayed in the seal has less to do with gender differences than it does with changing aspirations for men and women college students."

Some faculty members disagreed, including one leading feminist, English professor Nancy Mitchell, who demonstrated her opposition in dramatic fashion by organizing a "spin in" at the entrance of Lee Hall. She pointed out that spinning was not purely archaic and, in fact, had been put back into the MWC curriculum just a few years earlier as part of a course on textile design. In any case, she rejected the proposed change as poppycock. "The whole idea [that] you have to change a seal to make it up-to-date is a misreading of the idea of a seal," she said, speaking as she spun. "You don't go around changing seals periodically. Seals often have shields and crossed swords. Why not replace those with missiles and atomic bombs?" The reason behind the proposal was evident, she added disdainfully: "one more attempt to change everything because we've become a coed school."

Among students, opinion was mixed. One *Bullet* writer ridiculed the idea of "getting rid of the spinning wheel for something a little more masculine or at least asexual," and then suggested an alternative: "How about a pair of athletic socks? That way we can keep the nickname other area colleges have for us—the Wash."

Editorially the *Bullet* took a neutral position, urging only that students participate in a referendum on the issue, sponsored by the Student Association, to determine whether a committee should be established to study the matter. The voter turnout of almost 1,100 students (reportedly the highest MWC vote total ever recorded) demonstrated that the issue was one of considerable interest on campus, as the referendum passed by a vote of 622–445.

The outcome merely expressed the student body's view to the administration, which then had to decide whether to set up the proposed committee. And, as the Fredericksburg newspaper put it, it was "far less certain that a majority of the college's alumni favor it." In that regard, one of the area's most prominent alumni, former Alumni Association president Ann Palamar, commented that she saw no reason to change the seal and basically regarded the issue as "much ado about nothing."

She turned out to be right. Overshadowed by the name-change controversy, the seal debate eventually subsided, leaving the wheel intact. There it would remain for two more decades until a subsequent assault—again the product of image concerns—would bring its demise.

Another aspect of the institution's focus on image in the mid-1980s involved the matter of school colors and mascot—or, more accurately, the lack of same. In an earlier period, such accoutrements had been of no concern, but they became more important with the introduction of a comprehensive intercollegiate sports program. Athletic Director Ed Hegmann was astounded with what he found when he arrived in 1976. "I was inventorying uniforms," he recalled, "Some were yellow, some were blue, some were brown, and I couldn't see any consistency. I asked [the female coaches], 'What are the school colors?' and they said, 'Well, they're earth colors.' I said, 'What does that mean?' 'Well, you know, like the dirt, and the sky, and the sun, and everything around you [are] earth colors.' And I said, 'Yeah, but isn't there a common theme, a common set of colors that you all use?' 'Oh no, we use them all.' So we had to set about trying to get some colors."

Nor was there a mascot. In a 1978 article titled "A School without a Name," the *Bullet* lamented that while athletic teams at other Virginia institutions had colorful monikers such as Cavaliers, Monarchs, Spartans, Gobblers, and Spiders, MWC could only be referred to as the Mary Washington "Whats?" Claiming that there was "no conceivable explanation for the omission of such an integral part of a college's [image]," the paper urged an official mascot be chosen, perhaps from a list recently compiled by the Recreation Association that included Rebels, Marauders, Colonels—and Blue Tide.

"Blue Tide" already had some currency at the College, having informally been adopted by the swim team, who for some years had posted poolside a sign reading, "Don't Cross the River If You Can't Swim the Tide." The words were from a folk song by the group America and, as appropriated by the swimmers, referred to the Rappahannock River, which most visiting teams (coming from the north) had to cross to reach Goolrick Hall. So when the choice of a mascot was put before the student body in 1978, Blue Tide was the winner, thanks to its history (however brief), energetic lobbying by the swim team, and its similarity to the well-known Crimson Tide of Alabama.

Though there were understandable reasons behind its selection, Blue Tide had problems as a mascot. According to Ed Hegmann, "You couldn't animate it, you couldn't draw it, you couldn't even tell people what the heck it meant, and so we came under ridicule at many places we went." Some of the College's own fans occasionally lampooned it by showing up at sports events wearing Tide detergent boxes, with eyeholes cut out, over their heads.

In 1981 the president of the Student Association, Leath Burdeshaw, called for a change, noting that "many feel the College still needs a more concrete mascot—an animal or character that can literally be at the games and put on posters and banners to help spice things up." Such an entity, she claimed, "would add to the school a personality of its own, give it character, a feeling of unity, and a little more spirit."

Burdeshaw was not the only one who believed school spirit needed a boost. Athletic Director Hegmann in a February 1984 *Bullet* guest editorial, "Tide Fever," issued an appeal, cast in humorous form, for students to become more supportive of the College's teams. "With the MWC flu bug almost zapped and signs of spring everywhere, it's time to catch a contagious but beneficial disease, BLUE TIDE FEVER," he wrote.

> This malady is guaranteed to cause periods of high emotion, enthusiasm, pride, anxiety, ups, downs, and even some genuine excitement without the pain of a hangover. Am I suggesting there is something more exciting than "quarters" and less painful the next morning? Yes, and it will also give you something *real* to talk about instead of the usual boredom of, "What happened on General Hospital today?" The other benefit of this disease is that it has all the addicting qualities of "wonder" products like Nutri-sweet, Dexatrim, Miller Light, and Tab, but it hasn't caused cancer in a single laboratory rat! . . . Also, it might possibly cause you to stop complaining about "nothing to do at MWC!" How could we function without that crutch? . . . The key to catching this fever is you, the cost is zero, and the location is the Battleground Athletic Complex on Hanover Street. . . . The thrill of Blue Tide victories and agony of defeats are the "side effects" of this fever, but the pain is fleeting and of the mental variety. No worse, however, than agonizing over "Who wants to shoot J.R. now?"

His message ended with an exhortation to students to "join the faithful, vocal, and wonderfully supporting few . . . in helping your classmates and MWC maintain our institutional pride and ever-growing tradition. Do yourself, your friends, and your college a favor: catch the spring edition of Blue Tide Fever. You'll be glad you did!"

Whether or not lack of spirit was related to colors and mascot, the movement for change gained momentum. One *Bullet* columnist asserted that the seemingly trivial matter was actually a significant part of the College's alleged image problem. "How does Mary Washington present itself physically to the 'outside world?'" he asked. "The sports teams are our ongoing contact with the 'outside world.' If you did not go to the school, would you want to see a 'Blue Tide?' What is a Blue Tide anyway? A Red Tide wipes out living things in the water. I guess a Blue Tide means that growth can begin again. A benign tide."[9]

Students flank the new eagle mascot.

And the mascot was not the only problem, according to that writer. "Our school colors also give the impression of wimpiness: powder blue and white," he declared. "These are not the colors of sports uniforms. They are the colors of wedding garters!" (Apparently he was unaware of the term "Carolina blue.")

Responding to such concerns, President Anderson in the fall of 1985 appointed an Advisory Committee for College Relations to investigate these and other issues related to institutional image. The twenty-person group comprised eight students (chosen by the president from among nominees provided by the SA) and four each from the faculty, administration, and alumni. A subcommittee was established specifically to consider the matter of mascot and colors.

Having studied numerous options throughout the 1985–86 academic year, the subcommittee presented its top choices to the student body and faculty in a late spring referendum. The choices were the Devil-Goats, an outgrowth of the long-standing College tradition; the Eagles, advocated because of both patriotic symbolism and ornithological appropriateness to the College's geographic area; and several names relating to the military theme already established on campus such as the *Bullet*, *Battlefield*, and the Battleground athletic complex: the Militia, the Cannons, and the Bayonets. The color choices all involved some shade of blue combined with other colors.

The results of the poll indicated preferences for the mascot name of Eagles (the most prevalent name among U.S. colleges and universities at that time). The preferred color combination was blue and gray with white, a particularly appropriate choice in light of the area's Civil War connection. The symbols were adopted officially by the Board of Visitors in September 1986, an action hailed by a *Bullet* editorial announcing, "Welcome MWC Eagles," and predicting improvements that the College's "new look will provide for its students and its school spirit."

The paper was to some extent overly sanguine. On the one hand, the new symbols were generally adopted rather quickly, save for a few diehards who continued to promote the traditional Blue Tide appellation. The new team uniforms, classy rather than flashy, proved popular, and before long, a feathered mascot was exhorting cheers at athletic events.

On the other hand, effusive school spirit was never Mary Washington's long suit. True, there was plenty of enthusiasm at athletic contests and on occasions such as Junior Ring Week, but overall the College was not a "rah-rah" kind of place. The genuine pride that its students felt tended, for the most part, to be expressed in more subdued fashion.

Concurrently with the debates over the College's image (particularly its name), there began a significant upward trend in applications for admission. Some observers suggested that the debates themselves, ironically, had brought the College to the attention of a wider public and at the same time emphasized the institution's coeducational status.

There were other, more tangible factors as well, one of the most important being the innovative and aggressive marketing of the College by the admissions office, led first by Conrad Warlick and, after 1988, by Marty Wilder. Their initiatives were ably implemented by a staff that included longtime member Ali Gauch and alumnae Sallie Washington Braxton '77, Angelia Allen '82, Jenifer Blair '82, Melissa Wheat Yakabouski '94, and Amanda Craddock '99. Also integral to the recruitment effort was the role of financial aid, administered by Robert U. MacDonald from 1980, when he took over from Forrest Dickinson, until his retirement in 2001. MacDonald not only served effectively in that position but occasionally employed his impressive talents as a designer at various College venues, notably by decorating Brompton at Christmastime. Upon his retirement, he was succeeded in the financial aid office by Debra Harber.

The admissions office, in addition, employed a number of counselors, former students who spent their first postgraduate years representing the institution at various college-day fairs at secondary schools throughout Virginia and beyond, particularly in the Northeast. It was an exceptionally able and energetic group that over the years included notable alumni such as Austin Merrill '91 and Liam Cleaver '92, both of whom went on to careers that earned them the Alumni Association's Outstanding Young Alumnus Award. Also, a number of these "green deans," as they were called, subsequently became full-time staff members at the College, among them Abas Adenan '85, Jeffrey Rountree '91, and Matthew Mejia '93.

An important service was also provided to the admissions process by student volunteers, whose main purpose was to conduct campus tours for prospective students and (typically) their families. The group, founded in 1983 as the Admissions Club, originally had no qualifications for membership, aside from their enthusiasm for the College, and sometimes had more than two hundred members. In 1993 at the instigation of the club's adviser, Jenifer Blair, the club was reorganized as the Washington Guides, with membership placed on a competitive basis to ensure that all members not only were knowledgeable about the College but also were in good academic and social standing. They were then required to participate in a training program designed to guarantee extensive familiarity with all aspects of the institution about which they might be questioned by visitors.

The guides proved to be a real asset to the admissions office, giving close to one thousand tours each year, as well as hosting overnight visitors and participating in off-campus recruitment programs. And they were effective. According to one study of entering freshmen, almost 80 percent had visited the campus before deciding to attend, and of those who visited, 93 percent rated their tours as a positive factor in their decision in favor of Mary Washington. The guides were not paid for their work, at least not in dollars, but according to Blair, they were still compensated. "Students volunteer because they love being here," she said, "and they want to give back to the school by expressing their appreciation."

To facilitate initial contacts with prospective students, the admissions office in the mid-eighties substantially upgraded its published materials to include a glossy, full-color viewbook of the College, highlighting the beauty of the campus, pride in the honor system, the faculty's commitment to teaching, and the variety of student activities. Those same attributes were featured in the College's first video designed for prospective students, which was produced during the 1987–88 session. The video, a copy of which was furnished to almost every high school in the state and selected ones elsewhere, elicited high praise from viewers for its content. In fact, one state newspaper conducted a poll of high school students to record their reactions to similar tapes from ten colleges and universities. "The verdict?" it asked. "Students scored Mary Washington College best overall, despite its mediocre production quality. The video scored brownie points for its non-staged shots, depiction of campus life, and sincere student testimonies."[10]

An admissions office innovation in 1990 was a program known as Showcase, in which all prospective students who had been offered either Early Decision or Honors Admission were invited, along with their parents, for a daylong event on campus. Activities included, in addition to a campus tour, information on student life and activities and, perhaps most important, the opportunity to discuss academic offerings with faculty representatives from each department. Showcase, which normally brought approximately three hundred prospective students to campus annually, continued through subsequent years as an effective means of attracting the most highly qualified applicants, as did an open house program known initially as Super Saturday and later as Discovery Days.

The cumulative effect of all such efforts was a sudden—or so it seemed—jump in the College's stock. "The word's out," crowed the *Free Lance–Star* in August 1988. "Mary Washington College is a hot property. A great education bargain has grown into a respected academic center. . . . The SAT scores are going up while the percentage of admitted applicants goes down. It's safe to say that MWC has never been this smart." In addition to its praise, the paper could not resist a jab at the name-change controversy. "It's hard to imagine that just a few years ago," it wrote, "College officials were worried that a too-feminine image—*Mary* Washington—would make the College a noncompetitive 'girl's school' in a coeducational age. Far from that prospect, MWC is leading the Virginia pack in the rising tide of applications. It's amazing what *Mary* can do when she's backed up by academic excellence and first-rate facilities."

And it was not just the academic aspect that attracted attention, as the College's traditional image as academically solid but socially stodgy was replaced by a more hip vision. Writing in April 1990, a *Bullet* editor noted that the number of freshman applicants had nearly doubled in the previous five years, from 2,671 in 1985 to just under 5,000 for the fall of 1990. Best of all, he suggested that it had been accomplished without "letting in a few Cro-Magnon jocks in order to secure a few wins (5 or 6) for the powerful men's basketball team [or] accepting a hundred or so animalistic fraternity pigs every year just to continue the school's already bumpin' social scene." To his view, the College already had everything it needed: "Stickball in front of Willard, the unveiling of pasty white, bikini-clad bodies in Ball Circle, and roasted pork at the unconscious thing [a dorm party]. Ahh! The sights and sounds of spring at beautiful Mary Washington College . . . are enough to attract even the most sought-after high school students in America. . . . This place rocks!"

Concurrently, MWC began to elicit favorable notice in various college guides. One of the earliest of such citations was contained in Martin Nemko's *How to Get an Ivy League Education at a State University* (1988). Using information from interviews with students and administrators as well as statistics about each school, Nemko, a former professor at UC Berkeley who had become an independent educational consultant, devised a list of what he deemed the nation's top one hundred state-supported colleges and universities.

Including Mary Washington in that select group, Nemko praised the College for its teaching faculty, the "close fellowship" of the student body, and its emphasis on liberal arts and writing. Somewhat surprisingly in light of the overwhelmingly white composition of the student body, he termed MWC "a good situation for ethnic minorities." His overall assessment of the College was that it was "underrated" and a "real sleeper."

In the years thereafter, Mary Washington continued to garner high ratings and positive descriptions in publications such as *Barron's Profiles of American Colleges*, the *Princeton Review*'s annual survey of best colleges, and *Kiplinger's Personal Finance Magazine*. The College was frequently hailed, in particular, for being an outstanding bargain, given its relatively low tuition, compared to its high academic quality. Indeed, *Money* magazine in 1993 ranked MWC as Virginia's best buy in education and number 32 among all four-year colleges and universities nationwide. "On one hand, we're delighted we're in there," commented President Anderson, "and yet I think we would rank in the top ten nationally if our state funding were better."

One of the most prestigious of such publications was the *Fiske Guide to Colleges*, which in 1993 included Mary Washington for the first time in its listing of outstanding colleges. The Fiske listing placed an overview of MWC in a section titled "Quality Liberal Arts at a Public School Price," describing it as a college that "would make anyone's list of the best public schools in the nation."

Such accolades drew wide notice. The *Free Lance–Star* reported the Fiske listing as simply the latest of the "raves MWC's been getting in college guides," noting that the publication "fairly drools over the campus, its lifestyle, and its academics." Indeed, that description was not much of an exaggeration of the guide's portrayal. "Strolling among Mary Washington's elegant buildings of red brick with white columns," read the description, "has led more than one pleased parent to declare 'Now *this* is what a college should look like.'" The review went on to delineate a number of distinctive features that virtually parroted the very features touted by the College itself in its official publications, including the historic setting of the campus, the beauty of the surroundings, new facilities, strong academic emphasis on the liberal arts, small class size, and close student-faculty relationships.

On the negative side, there were few comments, noting mainly a lack of diversity within the student body and an unbalanced ratio of males to females, but even the latter problem, said the review, was ameliorated by the College's location. "Students [are] . . . within striking distance of dance clubs and bars in both Richmond and D.C. Likewise, women frustrated by the poor sex ratio can reach UVa in an hour and a half and Georgetown in even less." For those who wished to stay on campus, the description asserted, quoting a senior, "one can either be a party animal or a study rat."

Students generally seemed to be in accord with the description of their school contained in the *Fiske Guide*—with one glaring exception. "The part about how great the dorms are, (saying they feel like homes)—that's kind of silly," said one senior. "But academically, what they say is really true."

Mary Washington officials were careful not to place too much emphasis on the college guide encomiums, although they were surely pleased at the favorable recognition, which had the potential for significantly raising the institution's visibility in areas where the College's reputation was not widely known. And it also helped because, as Vice President for Admissions Marty Wilder well summarized: "People like to be told by an expert what the best goods and services are to buy. They like to see things ranked." In any case, the college guide reviews did help to generate additional applications that, in turn, made the selectivity ratio even more impressive and the average SAT scores even higher. By 1995, for example, MWC's entering class SAT average of over 1,100 ranked in a virtual tie with James Madison for third highest in the state, behind William and Mary and the University of Virginia.

The only downside was pressure on the College to admit more students—which it did, moderately. Though the increase was small, some students (and faculty) came to feel that the school's popularity was having the unwanted effect of jeopardizing one of its major strengths. As classics professor Robert Boughner put it, "The appeal of small classes, ironically, could threaten to make the college a victim of its own success. We've become good, and people want us. We're a hot product right now."

In the face of sporadic grousing, there was little the College could do, inasmuch as the state established guidelines for class sizes. In 1989, for example, the average class size was set at thirty students, with upper-level classes at twenty. Addressing the issue, Vice President Philip Hall said, "We have this frustration, but we don't believe it is worse than in 1980 and in 1982. [The students] are just saying it more stridently." In fact, the College's student-teacher ratio had changed very little. In 1982 it was 17.4 to 1,whereas in 1989 it had increased to 18.8 to 1.

In the overall scheme of things, such complaints were negligible. As the College moved into and through the 1990s, there was generally a more upbeat atmosphere on campus. As one popular T-shirt of the era proclaimed: "MWC—it doesn't get any better than this."

But to some observers, it could have gotten better, at least in one respect, by becoming more diverse. The recruitment of minority students had been a problem ever since the coming of racial integration, and it was slow to improve, despite a variety of administrative efforts in that direction.

One early initiative was to offer financial incentives to black applicants. In 1984, when black enrollment stood at 3 percent, the Board of Visitors approved $24,000 to provide $500 onetime grants (in addition to other financial aid) to black Virginia residents enrolling for the first time. The *Free Lance–Star* applauded the initiative as "an important new commitment to increasing minority enrollment." Though acknowledging that such an approach looked like a "bounty system," the editorial asserted that "the MWC program is better seen as an incentive. If it works, the entire College stands to gain from a student body of greater diversity."

A half-dozen years later, the amount available for black student scholarships had risen to $100,000, but the impact on recruitment had not been significant. Also by that time, the local paper was taking a different view of the policy. "The purpose of those scholarships is a worthy one—helping the people from a minority group that was held back for centuries . . . [but] black people don't need singling out. And society as a whole has already spent far too many years pigeon-holing people into racial categories."

The unfortunate truth was that the problem was too complex to be resolved through financial incentives alone. And in any case, Supreme Court rulings in the early nineties removed the possibility of making awards strictly on the basis of race, whereupon Mary Washington restructured its scholarship program, eliminating grants that had been restricted only to black students. Meanwhile the admissions office initiated other efforts geared to minority recruitment.

One was Project SOAR, established in 1988 as a cooperative effort between Mary Washington and the Fairfax County School System designed to encourage minority students to prepare for college (preferably MWC, though that was not a stated objective). The plan originated in discussions between Rita Stone, rector of the Board of Visitors, and representatives of the Fairfax County School System, where she had worked for many years before retirement.

The program involved selection of students at the ninth-grade level who would be brought to campus for one-week summer sessions before their junior and senior years. In those sessions, they would take courses for high school credit while becoming acquainted with what life was like on a college campus. Then, several times throughout the regular school year, they would visit the College to further familiarize themselves with a campus environment—something that, in most cases, was foreign to their experience (or their expectations).

Project SOAR was directed by Forrest Parker, an associate dean for admissions at Mary Washington. As he explained the program, "Our main goal is to inspire students of color to a higher level of education. Some of these kids have only dreams of going to college. . . . We not only want to inspire them to go to college, but we want them to be successful in college."

Another initiative was the James Farmer Scholars Program, established the same year as SOAR and named for the renowned civil rights leader who by that time was a member of the Mary Washington faculty.[11] The purpose of the program was to identify forty-eight promising seventh-grade black students each year—twelve each from the city of Fredericksburg and the nearby counties of Caroline, Spotsylvania, and Westmoreland—and provide them through high school with tutoring and encouragement for college. The underlying hope was that graduates of the program would choose to attend

Mary Washington, but in any case, they would be better motivated (and better prepared) to attend some college or university.

The program was structured around one daylong Saturday session at the College each month, plus one week in residence on campus each summer. Those sessions, led by the director of the program, education professor Venitta McCall, incorporated a variety of activities—lectures, field trips, and interdisciplinary seminars on writing, mathematics, science, and social studies—designed cumulatively to develop study skills, enhance awareness of black culture, and provide an overall introduction to the college experience. It was a special treat when James Farmer himself occasionally addressed the students.

The program included more than just on-campus work for the students. Each student's home school established a mentor for the Farmer Scholars; in addition, there were workshops for parents on topics such as how to apply to colleges and how to seek financial aid. To remain in the program, students were required to maintain a B average in a college preparatory curriculum. It was not an easy goal—but completion of the program offered a significant reward: special consideration for admission to Mary Washington College.

The first group of Farmer Scholars graduated from high school in 1993. Of the original forty-eight students, twenty-nine remained in the program, and all of them were accepted at a college. That number (over 50 percent) represented a significant increase over the percentage of minority students from the same areas who usually went on to attend college (21 to 35 percent). Only four, however, chose to attend Mary Washington.

In addition to the ongoing SOAR and Farmer Scholars programs, in the late eighties, the admissions office began various initiatives targeting potential black applicants. One was a program called Black Visions, first implemented in the fall of 1989. Approximately two hundred students attended the initial program, which included tours of the campus, lunch in Seacobeck, and information sessions concerning campus organizations and extracurricular activities. In the first year, sixteen faculty members volunteered to lead discussion groups, including black English professor Taddesse Adera. In subsequent years, James Farmer also participated in the program. In addition, a panel of black alumni shared their experiences at the College. Perhaps the most productive aspect of the program involved "rap sessions" led by current students and alumni. Most questions, reported the *Bullet*, involved the social aspect of the College.

The same year, the admissions office sponsored a Black Student Weekend during late March. This event targeted students who had already been accepted to the College, as opposed to the Black Visions program, which was open to all interested students. The March event, in which thirty-three students participated, included a full weekend of activities, including attendance at various academic and social activities, a concert and dance on Friday night, a comedian in the Underground, and a movie. The weekend was highlighted by a Saturday night banquet at which James Farmer was the featured speaker. Both Black Visions and the Black Student Weekend became annual events as they evolved into programs known as Visions: The Multicultural Experience and Diversity Scholars Day.

CAMPUS EXPANSION

Although overshadowed for a time by the name-change furor, a more significant aspect of the Anderson presidency in the long run involved additions to, and improvements in, the College's physical plant. The overall process was delineated in a campus master plan approved by the Board of Visitors concurrently with the "Commitment to Excellence" document. In announcing that plan, Rector Kinniburgh called it a "road map" for future development that would "not only be more cost effective, but . . . also permit us to design new buildings and renovate older ones in a way which will be consistent with the architectural ambience of the campus."

The plan was devised by a College committee chaired by Ray Merchent with professional guidance from the Charlottesville architectural firm of Vickery, Moje, Drinkard, and Oakland, a company that had done prizewinning work for other educational institutions in Virginia and beyond. The choice of VMDO was fortuitous because, according to Merchent, "It quickly became apparent that they were keenly appreciative of the beauty of our campus and . . . intuitively understood [the need] . . . to maintain the harmony of both the built and natural environment of the College."

The controlling principle of the master plan was to enhance the communal nature of the campus by creating an inward focus of buildings and activities by keeping vehicular traffic and parking as much on the periphery as possible. Central—literally central—to that concept was the construction of a pedestrian mall through the middle of campus, to be built in stages until it stretched from George Washington Hall on the south to Goolrick on the north.

Announcement of the first stage of Campus Walk, as it was soon to become known, touched off a minor furor in the spring of 1986, inasmuch as it involved destroying that portion of Campus Drive from GW to Monroe and replacing it with brick pavers, from which vehicular traffic would be banned. Many local residents expressed opposition, especially those who lived below (i.e., east of) the campus and had become accustomed to using the drive as a shortcut to the Park & Shop center and other points west.

Even more irate (if not as vocal) were the young area males who were habituated to using the thoroughfare for less practical, more social purposes. The phenomenon was described somewhat flippantly in a front-page article by the *Free Lance–Star* reporter Michael Zitz: "It's called cruising. It's a time-honored tradition among 'townies' and a source of both irritation and cynical amusement among students. . . . Souped up cars rumble through, and young men dressed in T-shirts and baseball caps lean out the windows, craning their

Campus Walk proved a popular replacement for Campus Drive.

necks and screaming at female students. Students generally duck their heads, grimace, and mutter about 'Frednecks,' their contraction of the words Fredericksburg and rednecks. . . . After wheels are banned, things won't be the same for the students, for the vociferous young boys, or for the silent-but-faithful businessmen / voyeurs."

One chronic cruiser defended the practice, explaining that "in Fredericksburg, until you're 21 and can go to the bars, cruising is the only thing to do. . . . It's kind of like a ritual." Moreover, he claimed, it was harmless: "The girls like it. They'll smile at you and talk. I really don't see where it's a nuisance just riding through, scoping out the girls and playing music. . . . It's a good way to meet girls, to be honest."

Such a benign view was not universally shared, as was evident in a blistering letter to the editor of the *Free Lance–Star* from one female student in response to Zitz's article. Referring to the "ritual" nature of the practice, she asserted (somewhat hyperbolically), "So were the activities of the Klan, the Nazis, and the supporters of Apartheid. These other 'rituals' have been declared wrong, and cruising should not be overlooked as innocent simply because it occurs in a town as pleasant as Fredericksburg. Anything that dehumanizes another human being is wrong."

A less strident and likely more typical assessment was that of another female student who described the bombardment of catcalls from cruisers as "an amusing nuisance" and went on to say, "It depends on your attitude. It doesn't ruin my day. It's a nuisance, definitely. But when you see people making fools of themselves, it's funny, isn't it?"

Besides the cruisers there were other, non-ogling townsfolk, who decried the closing of the drive as an example of the College's tendency to isolate itself from the community. In light of all the efforts the College had made in recent years toward openness and community inclusiveness, it was a difficult charge for the administration to accept—and Vice President Merchent refuted it publicly. Citing numerous efforts at town-gown amity, he made clear that nonetheless, the College's paramount concern was the welfare of its students. Thus the closing of Campus Drive, he pointed out, was "designed simply to eliminate from the heart of the campus a heavy, and largely unnecessary, stream of through traffic . . . so as to provide our students with an environment which is as safe as possible and which contributes favorably to the conditions under which they live and study."

The initial controversy notwithstanding, it soon became apparent that the construction of Campus Walk was extremely beneficial for both practical and aesthetic reasons. As the years passed and major new buildings were erected along it, the Walk fulfilled the purpose for which it was intended: a central point from which the academic and social life of the campus comfortably radiated.

To graduates from an earlier time, it would seem hard to imagine the campus without the noisy, cruiser-congested roadway through its center; to subsequent student generations, the idea of such a thing would be almost unthinkable. In fact, of all the changes in the physical plant during the Anderson presidency, none was to prove more significant in improving the institution's environment than Campus Walk.

The first major new building planned along Campus Walk was a student center. Certainly such a facility was needed, as Lee Hall, which had for years served de facto as the locus of many student services and activities, had become overcrowded and inefficient. Thus the Board of Visitors in October 1984 passed a resolution approving plans for a new facility, an action that was received enthusiastically by the students.

To finance the construction, the first large-scale project since the completion of Goolrick Hall fifteen years earlier, the College received authorization from the General Assembly at its 1985 session to issue $3 million worth of revenue bonds. In that way, no "taxpayer dollars" were to be spent on the project, with all funds to be generated through student fees and rental charges for the center's facilities. The VMDO architectural firm was again hired to design the structure.

Plans for the center grew out of a committee, again chaired by Ray Merchent, that included faculty, administrators, and students. In the course of its deliberations, the group toured student centers at eight Virginia institutions to observe firsthand how such centers functioned on other campuses. The students particularly appreciated being involved in the process. "The administration," said a *Bullet* editorial, "has shown that it is committed to building the center with the student's needs in mind. . . . Granted, the student center probably will not have everything everybody at the college wants or needs. However, it is comforting to see an administration doing everything it can to ensure that the student center truly serves MWC's students."

Once a concept of function was developed, a fundamental question—and not an easy one, given the projected size (34,000 square feet) of the building—was site selection. Numerous and sometimes conflicting considerations came into play, such as the need for centrality on campus, accessibility for vehicular service, the relationship to existing structures, and the impact on possible future construction.

The location eventually chosen appeared to some to be perhaps the most topographically difficult and undesirable site on campus: the ravine-like area west of Mercer and roughly between Willard and Melchers where the old physical plant building had been located. The VMDO architects, however, were enthusiastic about the opportunity to use the new building as a means of linking distant Goolrick with the rest of the campus while incorporating the beauty of the surrounding dell and the stream that flows through the campus at that point. This was to be accomplished by constructing, as an integral part of the building, a lengthy arcade through which Campus Walk would pass, facilitating pedestrian traffic to the northern (Goolrick) end of campus.

As finally designed, the two-story brick building was constructed in a split-level mode, the better to integrate with the hilly terrain. The most prominent feature of the center was a vaulted-ceiling "great hall" of approximately twelve thousand square feet capable of accommodating two thousand persons for concerts and dances and five hundred for seated banquets. The spacious room was also configured in such a way that it could be divided by mobile partitions into multiple smaller meeting rooms. Other distinctive features of the center included a snack shop to replace the venerable Lee Hall C-Shop, a post office, two lounges, lockers for use by commuting students, a game room, and offices for student publications and organizations.

Students, eagerly anticipating the amenities promised by the new building, became frustrated when several construction delays pushed back the opening date. "Just exactly when is the @+#&! new student center going to be built?" asked a *Bullet* columnist. "I've heard that construction is to begin momentarily for what seems like the last two years. What's the use of having a dandy new pedestrian walkway if it won't connect anything? (Sorry all you athletes and dancers, but let's face it, Goolrick is not the mecca of this campus.)"

When the center did eventually open in the fall of 1987, it received mixed reviews from students. The *Bullet*'s "Speak Out" feature elicited both favorable (e.g., "It's groovy") and unfavorable comments (e.g., "I don't like the distance. It should be called the student OFF-center"). The negative reactions prompted a rebuke from the *Bullet* editor, Teresa Curtis, who found it "hard to believe that so many students do not appreciate the idea of a centralized place for student [activities]. . . . As for student organizations, the Campus Center is ideal. [As for] the *Bullet*, it is the greatest thing that could have happened to us."

The editor's attitude eventually seemed to prevail as most students came to the mature (and accurate) realization that, especially given the financial resources available to the College at the time, the center represented a vast improvement over previous arrangements. A number of amenities were particularly welcome: the snack shop, soon to be dubbed the Eagles Nest, with its outdoor patio was much more inviting than the old C-Shop in Lee Hall; the on-campus postal service obviated the daily (or multi-daily) trips across College Avenue to the former post office; and the Great Hall offered for the first time a suitable location for large social gatherings, replacing inadequate or inappropriate venues such as the Pub, Lee Ballroom, or Goolrick Gymnasium. Within a short time, the building, officially named the Woodard Campus Center in honor of the late president, did indeed become the focal point of student life on campus.

Following the construction of Campus Walk and the Woodard Campus Center, the third phase of the master plan involved expansion of library facilities. It was obvious by the 1980s that the library's collection had far outgrown the space available in Trinkle, which, when built four decades earlier, was designed to accommodate approximately 100,000 volumes (at a time when enrollment was about one thousand). Despite the construction of additional stacks, the library by the early 1980s, according to an outside consulting firm, was operating at almost 120 percent of its intended capacity. By then the collection had grown to approximately 300,000 volumes, overwhelming the available space and necessitating storage of some materials in other buildings on campus, including some 5,000 volumes in Goolrick. Nor were study areas adequate to meet the demands of the larger student body.

In January 1985, LeRoy S. Strohl III was named librarian, following the resignation of Ruby York Weinbrecht '48, who had held that position since 1972. Having earned degrees in both English and library science at the University of Kentucky, Strohl had most recently served as librarian at Emory and Henry College, where during an eleven-year tenure he had become a much-beloved figure on that bucolic campus. So happily situated was he there that only the persistent personal suasion of Bill Anderson convinced him to leave for Mary Washington.

By the time he arrived, a larger library was regarded as the College's top priority. The question was whether to expand Trinkle once again or to construct a new building. Strohl strongly advocated new construction, and that view prevailed. Accordingly, again with architectural assistance provided by VMDO, plans were developed for a capacious three-story brick building to be situated on, and partially into, the hillside behind the duPont complex. That site permitted the building to be integrated unobtrusively into its surroundings despite its massive size (70,000 square feet). Fronting, and opening directly onto, Campus Walk, the building served to move the center of campus activity even farther in a northward direction toward Goolrick Hall. The cost of construction plus furnishings amounted to slightly over $6 million.

On the first floor of the building were located several of the traditional library functions: circulation, reference, current periodicals, microfilm, and microfiche. The second and third floors were mainly occupied by stack ranges that provided some nine miles of shelving capable of holding over a half-million items. In addition, the second floor housed most of the library offices and included an elegant, climate-controlled room for archives, special collections, and rare books. Also on that floor was a commodious classroom for bibliographic instruction and courses in library science.

Student needs were given high priority in the new library's design. To facilitate individual research, nearly two hundred carrels were arranged along the front and back perimeters of the top two floors; each was lined with acoustic-deadening carpet, equipped with individual adjustable lighting, and oriented to provide an outside view. For students desiring to study together, there were nine group-study rooms.

Another priority was to provide up-to-date technology while ensuring the capacity for further innovation, an important consideration in light of rapidly developing information systems. This was accomplished by building electrical wire-way troughs into the floors and an extensive electrical and data conduit system in the ceilings. As a result, the library was well positioned to expand and upgrade in the future, beyond even the computer terminals and CD-ROMs that were available in the new building at the outset.

LeRoy S. Strohl III

Scheduled to open in time for the start of the 1988–89 school year, the library hit a snag when stacks ordered from a Canadian company did not arrive until the first day of classes. Rather than disrupt normal library use by moving the collection during the session, the decision was made to delay the move until the break between semesters.

To expedite the move, the College hired a Connecticut firm that specialized in relocation projects. The company began work, aided by ten MWC students, on December 16 and, taking off only three days at Christmas, completed the task by the end of the month, enabling everything to be in place for the opening of the spring term.

The move was completed not only with remarkable speed but also with exceptional precision. According to Library Director Strohl, a thorough check of the stacks showed that surprisingly few volumes were out of place. "It was really fun," he later recalled. "Needless to say, we didn't have much of a Christmas, but it was fascinating to see how fast it went. . . . I mean it was snowy and we had some bad weather periodically, but it went marvelously."

Returning after their break, students greeted the opening of the facility enthusiastically, with none of the carping that had accompanied the recent opening of the student center. Even the oft-critical *Bullet* found the library praiseworthy. "Although some of the aesthetic qualities of the old library are missing," it said, "the new building contains a beauty of its own, combined with utility. The new building is more practical and affords fewer distractions. No more swinging doors in the reference rooms or uncomfortable temperature ranges in various sections of the library." One student, expressing similar approbation, exclaimed, "Wow! I wish I wasn't a senior!"

Though the construction and occupancy of the new facility were the most visible aspects of the library's development in the mid-eighties, the staff was simultaneously engaged in two other projects of historic significance. One was the change in the collection's classification from the Dewey decimal system to the Library of Congress system, a change that was encouraged by the most recent decennial accreditation from the Southern Association of Colleges and Schools.

The change in classification systems elicited no particular faculty or student reaction, but the other major project did: converting bibliographic information from card catalog format to computer-readable data. To some faculty, especially the more senior ones who had spent their professional lifetimes thumbing through the information-laden wooden boxes of three-by-five-inch cards, removal of the card catalogs was deemed well nigh heretical. "A lot of people were very wary of computerization," said Roy Strohl. "They just didn't have any experience with it. . . . Some members of the faculty [thought] this was the wrong move and [asked] what was wrong with the card catalog. And even when you told them, they didn't understand."

But the point had been reached in the information age where conversion to the electronic format had become essential, and Strohl realized the project must proceed. "And so in a fairly brazen move," he recalled, "we made sure the cards got thrown away" as soon as the data from them had been transferred to an online public access catalog (OPAC). The retrospective conversion project was completed in the early nineties, opening the way for vastly expanded and improved information access in the years ahead.

The library, later named for former president Grellet C. Simpson, and the Woodard Campus Center were the largest construction projects during the period, but they were not the only ones. Particularly important to campus life were three new residence halls, all of which were modest in scale relative to existing ones like Mason or Russell. Their purpose was not so much to accommodate additional students as to relieve the overcrowding that had developed in some halls where rooms designed as doubles had become triples.

The first and smallest of the new dorms, and the only one constructed on the "old" (i.e., GW) end of campus, was completed in August 1988. Built at a cost of $800,000 and situated behind Jefferson and near Framar, it was linked to Framar by new brickworks that formed an attractive plaza. The thirty-two-bed residence was named South Hall, aptly so, as it stood at the southernmost edge of campus.

In the following year, ground was broken for the first of two 148-bed dorms to be constructed at the other end of campus, adjacent to Goolrick Hall. This facility, known initially as North Hall before being officially named Alvey Hall in honor of campus legend Edward Alvey Jr., fronted Campus Walk, which had been completed to extend all the way to Goolrick before the dorm's opening in the fall of 1990. At a cost of $2.9 million, the dorm was referred to in the *Bullet* as "the Hilton of the campus" because, said the paper, "It has a hotel's posh, almost sterile atmosphere, with brass doorknobs, wall-to-wall carpeting, icy-cold air conditioning [a rarity on campus], and spotlessly clean, freshly-painted walls and new furniture."

The paper noted that there had been much speculation as to whether the new residence would be peopled mainly by "jocks desiring the proximity of the gym or 'study geeks' choosing to live near the library." The luck-of-the-draw room selection process actually resulted in a varied mixture of student personalities. "As far as a 'dorm image' is concerned," said the paper, "it is still too early to predict whether the North Dorm will be another Willard, a party dorm, or whether it will be a co-ed Ball, a quiet dorm. Considering its quality and relative luxury, however, destructive partying will probably be taken elsewhere."

Three years later, in 1994, the identical companion dorm to Alvey Hall was completed at a cost of $3 million. Known at first simply as New Dorm, in 2005 it was named Arrington Hall in honor of Arabelle Laws Arrington, a 1941 graduate of the College and a generous benefactor of the institution over many years. Arrington Hall was to be the last dormitory constructed on campus in the College's first century.

Aside from the residence halls, there was other significant construction on campus during the 1990s, much of it made possible by private philanthropy. One such project was the Phyllis Ridderhof Martin Gallery, an art gallery funded by a donation of $550,000 from the building's namesake. Of that amount, $375,000 was used for building the gallery itself and the remainder to create an endowment for its upkeep.

The benefactor was a California-based artist who, beginning in the 1920s, earned acclaim both as a teacher and, under the professional name of Phyllis Ridderhof, as an artist. Best known for portraiture, she also painted landscapes, still lifes, and abstracts, all of which were characterized by vibrant tones and robust brushwork. An art critic in the 1960s described her as "not just the best woman painter in the West, but one of the best artists, male or female, now working."

In the 1980s, to be nearer her family, Ridderhof Martin moved to Fredericksburg, where she exhibited at Belmont and at the duPont galleries, in the course of which she became friends with art professor Joseph Di Bella. That connection, plus the fact that her son, daughter-in-law, and grandson all attended Mary Washington, led to her admiration for the College and her eventual gift (the second largest in the institution's history to that time).

The gallery, nicely situated overlooking the glen between Seacobeck and Melchers, was a three-thousand-square-foot brick facility housing two exhibition spaces and a storage-workroom, all equipped with state-of-the-art climate control and security systems. Opening in April 1992, it served both the College and the community by presenting art exhibits of both historical and contemporary interest; in addition, the gallery and its entrance patio served periodically as a scenic locale for College social functions. To oversee and promote the gallery, the College hired its first full-time gallery director, Forrest McGill. The opening show featured, appropriately, the works of Phyllis Ridderhof Martin herself, including pieces from her private collection.

One of the most important construction projects of the period was one of the least visible, inasmuch as it was underground. The goal of the project was ambitious: to bring Mary Washington College to the forefront of technological capability among Virginia educational institutions.

During the 1980s the College had moved haltingly into technology with the purchase of some computers and the acquisition of software applications for certain areas, mainly student records and financial aid at first. There was no comprehensive plan for a College-wide system. By the end of the decade, however, President Anderson had become convinced of the necessity for just such a system and secured the Board of Visitors' endorsement for it.

The plan came to fruition in May 1994 when the College contracted with Bell Atlantic (later Verizon) to install a telecommunications network throughout the campus connecting all administrative and faculty offices, as well as every dorm room, creating what the *Free Lance–Star* called an "$8.6 million access ramp to the information superhighway." College officials had been dilatory in getting started, it said, "but when they did, they put the pedal to the metal."

Though Bill Anderson had initiated the effort, it was mainly Carol Martin who oversaw the actual work in her position as assistant vice president for computer and network services. The key element was installing state-of-the-art fiber-optic cable throughout the campus, an endeavor in which the contractor, according to Martin, "dug up the whole campus end to end." The work was actually accomplished with surprising speed by two crews, one of which worked in the dorms by day, the other in the offices by night.

The aspect of the project most eagerly anticipated by the students was the provision for improved telephone service, whereby the standard one phone per hall was replaced by one in each dorm room. "Lots of residence halls," Martin recalled, "especially if they had a lot of women in them, would bake cookies and stuff, and they'd have a sign: 'Cookies for the telephone men!'" Ironically, it was the improvement in those phone services that soon became obsolete, because within a few years, the ubiquitous cellular phone had largely superseded landline communication.

But telephones were only part of the package made possible by the new equipment. Electronic linkages between the library and faculty and students, and between students and their professors, dramatically improved the flow of information on campus. As for the residential students, the quality of dormitory life was instantly upgraded with the availability of Internet access, e-mail, and cable TV in every room.

Some students bemoaned what they perceived as a decreased spirit of community, what with so many amenities available in one's own room, but overall the innovations were welcomed. The Fredericksburg paper found the changes on campus startling: "Back in the stone age—last year, that is—many students at Mary Washington College had to share hall phones and go to a community TV room to watch Beavis and Butthead on cable. . . . Talk about roughing it. . . . Well, that was then, and this is now. Welcome to the future; it stops just short of running cable into students' frontal lobes."

College officials and Bell Atlantic representatives were extremely proud of the new system, and well they might have been, as it was touted as the most advanced campus telecommunications network in Virginia and possibly in the nation. Not only did it provide extensive capabilities at the time, but it was also projected to accommodate improvements for at least the next ten and possibly twenty years. More than a dozen years later, that prediction was still holding true.

FISCAL DEVELOPMENTS

The extraordinary expansion of physical facilities that occurred between President Anderson's inauguration and the mid-1990s resulted from the confluence of several factors, not the least of which was the president's own vision and ingenuity. Another crucial factor was the enlightened direction provided by the Board of Visitors, who were led during that time by a succession of unusually able and dedicated rectors including John Kinniburgh (1984–86), Rita Morgan Stone '52 (1986–88), Virginia Lewis Dalton '40 (1988–90), Bennett C. Whitlock Jr. (1990–92), Florian "Red" Hofer (1992–94), and Kathleen Shepherd Mehfoud '70 (1994–96). In addition, board member Gwendolyn Amory

Cumming '52 played a crucial role during her two terms as chair of the buildings and grounds committee; she, more than any other, was responsible for ensuring that all the new construction was kept in architectural harmony with the existing buildings. The result was that the campus became not only immensely more functional but even more beautiful than before.

Construction on the scale of Bill Anderson's plan clearly required substantial sums of money. Indeed, it was largely because of the board's belief in his fund-raising ability, both with the state legislature and with private donors, that he had been hired in the first place. That confidence proved to be justified.

The College's basic funding came from the commonwealth (though the percentage from that source would decline over the years), making it imperative that good relations with Richmond be maintained. This was Anderson's forte, a task to which he brought several notable qualities.

A naturally gregarious person with keen political instincts, he was folksy enough to appeal to the legislature's more rustic members, yet polished enough to relate to its more sophisticated ones. On an operational level, he was thoroughly familiar with the state bureaucracy in general and the educational system in particular. He also had a comprehensive and detailed knowledge of every facet of the College. As a consequence of his apprenticeship under Prince Woodard (a classic micromanager), as well as his own inquisitive nature, Anderson knew Mary Washington College inside out. Above all, Anderson was passionately committed to the College's welfare; he seemingly spent every waking moment (and probably many sleeping ones, too) with MWC on his mind.

His dedication was most evident when the General Assembly was in session, as he worked to prepare the College's budget requests, then traveled to Richmond on an almost daily basis to lobby for their passage. The process involved frequent appearances before various committees and also private efforts to forge political ties with legislative leaders. During the years when the Democrats controlled the body, those in power included State Senator Hunter Andrews of Hampton, chair of the Finance Committee, and House of Delegates stalwart V. Earl Dickinson of Louisa County. So consistently did Dickinson support the College's legislative agenda (except for the name change) that he was once described, without much exaggeration, as the "delegate from Mary Washington."

The results of Anderson's political savvy soon became apparent. State appropriations for the College began to increase almost immediately, as could be seen not only in capital outlay projects but also in the rise of the general operating budget. Between 1988 and 1991, the College received over $800,000 from the state's Higher Education Equipment Trust fund for upgrading the equipment in biology, chemistry, physics, geology, psychology, and the fine arts. Faculty salaries also improved substantially for the first time in many years. For example, average salaries increased 9.7 percent in 1988–89 over the previous year, and from an average of $34,250 in 1987–88, they rose to $41,073 in 1991–92, an increase of 20 percent.

Yet despite such improvement, the financial situation was hardly ideal. Salaries, in comparison to peer institutions, were still relatively low. Worse still, the upward momentum slowed in the early nineties to the point that for the 1991–92 academic year, there was no faculty salary increase at all. An even more ominous trend was developing for the institution overall as the state's appropriations toward the College's operating expenses fell from 62.6 percent of the institution's budget in 1987–88 to only 53.7 percent in 1991–92. This meant that the students themselves had to fund the difference, mainly through increased tuition.

The situation at Mary Washington was not unique, as public support for education throughout the country fell in the early nineties, at least partially because of a nationwide economic recession. The decline was worse in Virginia than elsewhere, however; in fact, from 1990 to 1992, the commonwealth's 13 percent reduction in spending on higher education was the sharpest decrease of any state in the nation. The decline at Mary Washington during that time was 11 percent.

To combat that dismal development, the state in the fall of 1992 took the unusual step of holding a referendum on the issuance of general obligation bonds to provide funding for facility improvements at state colleges, as well as at mental health clinics and state parks. It was only the third time in Virginia history that a bond referendum had been held.

Mary Washington had a large stake in the passage of the bond issue, as it contained funds for two major projects: $4.3 million for renovation of the duPont fine arts complex and $7.7 million for construction of a new science center to replace the increasingly outmoded Combs Hall. The fine arts complex was in particularly bad disrepair. The entire infrastructure—heating, plumbing, electrical—was antiquated; there was no air-conditioning or handicapped accessibility. "The most awful building on campus," one student said. "The heater sounds like the building is going to cave in when it goes on." A senior French major concurred: "I think that there aren't enough words in the English language to describe it, or any other language for that matter." Dean Philip Hall put it more bluntly: "It's a rat hole." Fortunately for MWC, the bond issue passed—and handily, with approximately 75 percent of the two million voters supporting it—and in due course, both construction projects got under way.

A boon though it was, the bond issue was hardly a panacea for the College's fiscal problems. The state budget initially projected for the 1994–96 biennium for education by outgoing Democratic governor Douglas L. Wilder would have entailed upon Mary Washington as much as a 15 percent cut in operating funds. President Anderson, speaking on behalf of the state's higher education Council of Presidents, denounced the plan, pointing out that such a decrease would reduce appropriations to below the 1986–88 level, even though enrollments had increased substantially during that period. The commonwealth, he noted, already ranked forty-third among the states in terms of state support for its colleges, and such a reduction would rank it near or at the bottom.

Although the final budget for the biennium was not so tightfisted, Wilder's successor as governor, Republican George Allen, mandated in 1994 that all state institutions submit plans for restructuring their operations to cut costs or risk losing up to 6 percent of their state appropriations (which, in MWC's case, would have meant $7 million). Mary Washington's plan was initially rejected by SCHEV in November, but after some tweaking, it was approved the following month. Still, in Governor Allen's budget as originally submitted in January 1995, the College was penalized $600,000 in its operating budget allocation. Ultimately the cut was avoided owing to the influential intervention of Republican senator John Chichester from neighboring Stafford and the reliably supportive Democratic delegate Earl Dickinson.

Such budgetary vagaries created a palpable sense of unease at the College, especially among faculty, who felt constantly threatened by the paucity of needed materials, looming programmatic reductions, and even the possible elimination of some disciplines. Despite constant reassurance to the contrary by the administration, junior faculty in particular harbored concerns about job security. The whole unsettling picture underscored more vividly than ever the need for the College to acquire private funds to offset the continuing decline of public resources—a goal presciently established in the 1985 "Commitment to Excellence" plan.

Enter Mickey Dowdy. Before his hiring at Mary Washington in the summer of 1984, the College's development program was neither systematic nor sustained—nor very successful. True, the MWC Foundation had been established under President Woodard in 1975, but its growth had been slow. It raised less than $40,000 in its first year, and at the end of its first decade, the total had reached only about $2.5 million. The Alumni Association's annual fund was not very productive either, operating as it did on a shoestring. Arabelle Arrington, who was to serve several terms as the foundation's president, later recalled that while serving on the Alumni Association board of directors, "several of us would gather to hand-address and stuff the fund letters. One year we raised $17,000 and were ecstatic."

Dowdy was brought in to change all that, and his success at the University of Richmond augured well for success. As he soon learned, however, fundraising at Mary Washington was a bit more of a challenge. For one thing, there was little tradition of giving to the College, and many people still felt that as a state institution—as opposed to schools like Richmond, which were private—Mary Washington did not need private support. Then, too, many of its alumni were either homemakers or teachers and tended not to have a great deal of disposable income for philanthropic purposes. In the case of married graduates, by custom it was often the husband whose alma mater benefited first and predominantly from whatever donations were made.

Michael B. Dowdy

Yet Dowdy, undiscouraged, attacked the challenge with characteristic vigor. His three titles—vice president for college relations, executive director of the Alumni Association, and executive director of the MWC Foundation—meant in effect that he was in charge of alumni affairs, development, and public relations. Also about the same time, responsibility for fund-raising shifted from the Alumni Association, which had run the annual campaigns since 1963, to the College's development office, thus consolidating all advancement activities under Dowdy.

The new arrangement soon began to pay dividends. The annual fund increased steadily, thanks in part to the students who volunteered to call alumni to solicit pledges through phonathons. Twice a year, once in fall and again in spring, students worked the phones nightly over a period of three weeks. During the 1985 sessions, over twelve thousand calls were made, producing about three thousand gifts. The project was so popular that potential volunteers often had to be turned away. (Their enthusiasm may not have been purely altruistic, as tangible incentives included free pizza and other treats, as well as—perhaps the most desirable reward—free personal long distance calls; in addition, there were prizes for students who raised the most money.)

With the aid of the phonathons, the annual fund, whose proceeds were used to underwrite a variety of current operations, increased to over a half million dollars by 1990. It was particularly noteworthy that the percentage of alumni who contributed was among the highest in the country. Such evidence of success led the national Council for Advancement and Support of Education to present a Grand Gold Award (sponsored by the Ford Motor Company Fund) to MWC in recognition of having the most improved college relations program in the country from 1985–86 through 1989–90.

Important as it was to have the unrestricted gifts from the annual fund to meet current expenses, it was even more crucial in the long term to grow an endowment to provide a stable source of funding for ongoing and future commitments. Because such a development would require large donations, Dowdy focused much attention on cultivating the support of persons who had the potential to be major contributors. In this effort he successfully enlisted the assistance of a number of the Fredericksburg area's most influential leaders, including Charles G. McDaniel, John B. Adams, Charles M. Hearn, Lawrence McMurtry, Russell H. Roberts, and Josiah P. Rowe III, all of whom served on the MWC Foundation board of directors.

Partly as a consequence of the philanthropic example and personal suasion of such leaders, the College's main gift club, the President's Council, with its $1,000 minimum contribution for membership, began to grow rapidly. Also during the late 1980s, the College for the first time began to receive sizable gifts for various dedicated purposes, including contributions from

- an anonymous donor, plus current and former members of the Board of Visitors, to establish the Rector and Visitors Chair (funded at $175,000);
- Dan H. Hinz Jr. and the Robert R. Siegrist family to establish the Mary Siegrist Hinz Leadership Awards program, which provided for the College's first full tuition and fee scholarships;
- Grellet and Dorothy Simpson to endow the Grellet C. Simpson International Scholarship;
- Fredericksburg Savings and Loan ($50,000) for the Regional Scholars Program;
- The *Free Lance–Star* ($50,000) to establish a scholarship fund for outstanding students in journalism;
- Barbara Alden, retired MWC archivist ($275,000 through her estate), to establish the Dorothy and Grellet Simpson Chair in English; and
- the MWC Alumni Association ($350,000) to sponsor the Outstanding Young Faculty Member Award.

Encouraged by these and other such gifts, the College in 1988 embarked on its first comprehensive fund-raising campaign, the Campaign for Mary Washington. Officially launched at a black-tie gala in the Great Hall on March 14, the institution's eightieth anniversary, the campaign had an announced goal of $5 million, with a target date of 1992 for its completion. It was an ambitious project. As Mickey Dowdy recalled years later, the goal "doesn't seem like a lot now, but back then, with our low tradition of giving, . . . it was a mountain. We were climbing a mountain."

Leading the charge up that mountain, in addition to Dowdy and President Anderson, were Rita Morgan Stone '52, rector of the Board of Visitors, and the campaign's chairman, Hildy Parks Cohen '45. Since her graduation, Cohen, who lived in New York City, had enjoyed a multifaceted career on the stage, in film, and on television and, more recently, as a writer and producer. For twenty years ending in 1986, she wrote and produced the Tony Awards telecasts, for which she received an Emmy in 1980. Two years previously she had received the Distinguished Alumni Award from the MWC Alumni Association.

In urging support for the campaign, Cohen emphasized that its raison d'être was to procure endowment funds for two particular purposes: financial aid for students and salary enhancements for faculty. "The dollars we raise," she pointed out, "will be used to support the human elements of education. And when we reduce the formula for quality education into its basic components, isn't the interaction between student and faculty member the most important element? We believe it is."

The campaign was immediately successful, raising over $2 million (40 percent of its goal) by the end of its first fiscal year. It was about that time that the College attracted the attention of two persons who became not only major contributors to the campaign but the greatest benefactors in the history of Mary Washington during the 20th century: Robert S. Jepson Jr. and his wife, Alice Andrews Jepson '64.

Alice had been an outstanding student at Mary Washington. An English major, she served as president of the Honor Council and was elected to Mortar Board and "Who's Who Among Students in American Universities and Colleges." After graduating, she taught for a number of years before becoming chairman of the board of the Jepson Foundation, a major supporter of higher education in the United States. In that capacity she was widely engaged in assessing collegiate programs around the country and advising on decisions for improvements at various institutions.

Bob Jepson, a 1964 University of Richmond graduate, was an extraordinary businessman. By the late eighties, he was head of the Jepson Corporation (benefactor of the Jepson Foundation), a Fortune 500 company listed on the New York Stock Exchange, with numerous well-known national and international subsidiaries. He was also widely recognized as a generous philanthropist in the area of education, as evidenced by a multi-million-dollar gift to his alma mater to establish the Jepson School of Leadership at the University of Richmond.

Thus, while Mickey Dowdy and Bill Anderson were well aware of the Jepsons' potential as significant donors to Mary Washington, the question was how best to approach them. Dowdy later recalled how it came to pass. "Bill and I went to Chicago," he said, the Jepson Corporation being headquartered in nearby Elmhurst.

> It took a long time to get the appointment. But he and I went to Chicago and we dined with the Jepsons on top of the Sears Tower, and it went real well. . . . But Bob, being the tough businessperson that he is, just grilled Bill that night—really put him to the test on where the institution was heading and why he should consider making a gift to a public institution. He knew why Richmond needed it, but why would Mary Washington need it? I was sweating bullets and I know Bill was, too. But he rose to the occasion and made a big friend that night. . . . As we shook hands to go home, Bob turned to Alice, and he said, "You know, Alice, you need to go down there, and I'm going to arrange for the company plane to take you to Fredericksburg, and you need to walk around the campus and become reacquainted." . . . She came

on the campus, and it should have been a dismal day in February but it was about a 70-degree day. The plane flies in, and it's gorgeous, and everything goes swimmingly. And about three weeks later they made their first million-dollar gift.

That gift was by far the largest in the College's eighty-one-year history. It was used to create the Alice A. Jepson Fellows Program that provided annual stipends to selected junior faculty members—that is, those who had not attained the rank of full professor. In announcing the award, President Anderson expressed his belief that "these awards will help us retain exceptional faculty [and] . . . make the critical difference in the years ahead as special recruitment opportunities arise."

The Jepsons' gift did indeed do that, but it served a larger purpose as well, stimulating the whole development program by in essence upping the ante for donations. "It takes somebody to stretch," explained Dowdy. "Nobody was giving a million dollars back then at Mary Washington . . . [but] that gift inspired others."

Thus boosted, the Campaign for Mary Washington proceeded to reach its financial objective two years ahead of schedule, raising $6,329,406, which exceeded its goal by 27 percent. A consequential element in that total was the contribution from the Alumni Annual Fund, in which participation rose to 32 percent, placing it in the top 1 percent of all public college rates in the country.

The unprecedented largesse made possible several notable improvements in the area of student aid, including enhancement of the Regional Scholarship Program, creation of twenty-five new endowed scholarships, and increased funds for need-based and minority student grants. Almost $2 million in allocations for augmentation of faculty salaries led to (in addition to the Jepson Fellows Program) establishment of the faculty rank of distinguished professor and the completion of, or substantial contribution toward, funding for the Rector and Visitors Chair, the Prince B. Woodard Chair in Historic Preservation, the Dorothy and Grellet Simpson Chair in English, and the Kurt F. Leidecker Chair in Asian Studies.

The Jepsons' gift was only the beginning of their magnanimous support of Mary Washington. In 1989 Alice was appointed to the Board of Visitors by Governor Gerald Baliles. Four years later she and her husband gave the College an additional $3 million dollars, $2 million of which was earmarked for application to construction costs of a new science building, the remainder to augment the Jepson Fellows Program already established. Some years later, the Jepsons would also be instrumental in the creation of a new alumni center.

As the guiding force behind the College's rapid rise in the area of development, Mickey Dowdy was in demand at other institutions in need of such fund-raising skills; in 1993 he accepted the top job at the Medical College of Virginia Foundation. His exceptional success at Mary Washington was attributable to many laudable personal qualities, not least of which were his candor and his honest, unassuming nature. Bobbie Burton, who worked with Dowdy throughout his MWC tenure, put her finger on it when she said, "Mickey has no ego. He always gives credit to others for any success, even when he himself is really responsible."

Such self-effacement was evident years later when, reflecting on the remarkable growth of the College's private financial resources, he said, "Bill Anderson gets the credit. He's the reason that the program developed the way it did. . . . He was the leader."

Yes, he was—but he was not alone. There was also Mickey Dowdy.

ACADEMICS

The development of Mary Washington College during the last two decades of the twentieth century was characterized most tangibly by the extraordinary expansion of campus physical facilities and the increase in endowment funds, but the period also witnessed significant changes in the academic program. The most fundamental and sweeping changes involved alteration of the general education (gen ed) component of the graduation requirements.

The first and perhaps most important of those changes came in 1982 as the result of a growing desire on the part of the faculty to enhance students' writing skills. One of those who led the movement was the venerable George Van Sant. "In my estimation," he observed, "one of the most valuable benefits of a college education is the ability to do research, organize it and communicate it to others in writing. That, more than anything else, differentiates the college graduate from other students." Skillful writing was, in his view, "a valuable commodity in society, relevant to every student, no matter what his career plans are."

There were few on the faculty who disagreed with that position, and some who vigorously promoted it. Notable among them was biology professor Steve Fuller, who on his own initiative began to organize voluntary, informal faculty groups to discuss ways to improve students' writing.

Though interest was strong, the question was how best to accomplish the goal. Traditionally, general education goals had been approached through requiring specific courses selected by the student from within certain categories. There was also one course—English 101, Writing Workshop—that every student had to take (unless exempted by virtue of a high test score in writing composition). Useful as Writing Workshop was, there was growing sentiment that it was simply unrealistic to expect a single course, however well taught, to provide the desired level of proficiency—nor was it feasible to place such responsibility solely on the finite resources of the English Department.

The solution turned out to be a highly creative approach: the establishment of an across-the-curriculum requirement whereby courses meeting certain guidelines were designated as writing intensive (WI), with students required to take a specified number of them before graduation. The requirement originally was one WI course per year for each of the student's four years, but in 1989 it was changed to a total of five courses that could be taken at any time—a revision that not only incorporated an additional course but also ameliorated the complex record-keeping problems entailed in the one-course-per-year requirement.

To encourage faculty participation in developing WI courses (since a large number would be needed each year), the guidelines for assignment of that designation were deliberately kept flexible at the outset. When the program was inaugurated in 1982, for example, the only guidelines were that WI courses must (1) incorporate writing as an integral and graded component of the course (generally assumed to mean at least 10 percent of the final grade), (2) require a minimum of three papers totaling at least twelve pages, and (3) provide instruction on writing, including professorial feedback on written assignments.

Despite the latitude provided by the guidelines, there was concern at first that enough courses would be offered to meet the demand imposed by the new requirement. Though in theory most faculty supported the concept, when it came to implementation, many were hesitant at first to become involved, especially those in disciplines like math and the sciences, where writing had not generally been an integral part of courses. Some faculty were skeptical of the utility or appropriateness of WI courses; some felt unqualified to teach writing; and some feared that inclusion of a graded writing component would either deter students from taking their classes or result in lower faculty evaluations from those who did (which in some cases turned out to be true).

Carol S. Manning

That is where Carol Manning began to play a major role. Though the writing intensive requirement began the year that she joined the English faculty, her appointment was not related to that program. Her passionate commitment to writing, however, soon led her to become deeply involved in it. Such commitment, plus previous experience with Virginia Tech's writing center, quickly led to her appointment as head of the initiative.

One of her most immediate goals was to broaden faculty participation. Her method consisted largely of organizing faculty workshops on the development of WI courses. Lacking the power to coerce attendance, but having the ability to cajole, she succeeded over the course of time in attracting large numbers of faculty to such sessions, whose purpose was not only to increase effectiveness but also to decrease anxiety regarding the teaching of WI courses. Her evident enthusiasm and her non-threatening manner combined to inspire confidence among a cadre of instructors—some of whom had initially shied away from the program—who became avidly involved. By 1993 over one hundred faculty members representing twenty of the College's twenty-one academic departments were offering WI courses.

Besides holding numerous workshops, Manning further promoted the enterprise by means of a periodic newsletter explaining various developments and opportunities in the program. Stimulated by such efforts, over one-half of the faculty eventually offered WI courses.

Her leadership did not end with directing the WI program. It was not enough to provide support for faculty, she maintained; students also needed help in meeting the new requirement. Accordingly, she proposed the establishment of a writing center—not for remedial work but as a resource to assist students with WI (or other) writing assignments.

Such a facility, supported by a grant from the Governor's Fund for Excellence, opened in 1987 in Lee Hall with Manning as its director. It involved an innovative approach, using student tutors to provide assistance on a one-on-one basis with their peers. The tutors, selected from among highly skilled writers, received extensive training regarding theories of writing, methods of teaching and writing, and techniques of listening and questioning. Thus trained, they were available for consultation with peers on problems ranging from the broad (e.g., organization of an essay) to the narrow (e.g., rules of documentation).

The tutors were given specific instruction as to how much assistance could be provided within the parameters of the honor code, and students using the facility were clearly apprised that tutors could not rewrite or proofread final papers but were instead to offer guidance in helping writers examine their own efforts—to locate and correct their own errors. Accordingly, most students (often with the encouragement of their professors) turned to the center for advice during the process of preparing written class assignments. The center also offered aid with the writing of resumes, letters of application, creative writing, and lab reports.

The center was an instant success. During its first year (1987–88), it conducted approximately 800 tutorial sessions for almost 500 students; the following year it assisted over 750 students involving almost 1,400 tutorials. The center continued to grow during subsequent years, expanding the scope of its activities to include publication of a newsletter featuring reports on program activities and articles by faculty members on techniques of teaching writing.

In addition, in 1991 the program sponsored the first of what would become annual campuswide writing contests in which students were invited to submit papers to be judged first by a panel of MWC professors, with finalists then being chosen by writing experts from outside the College. Though there were some adjustments over the years, the general guidelines established categories for upper- and lower-level student papers and for papers in various content areas. Winning students received cash prizes as well as the honor of having their papers published for distribution on campus.

In the midst of its success, it appeared that the writing program might suffer a setback when in 1993 the writing center's commodious location in Lee Hall was reassigned to become the home of the Multicultural Center. Carol Manning, who felt that an inviting atmosphere was crucial to the center's success, was crestfallen at the turn of events. "They were going to put us in the basement of a dorm," she recalled years later. "I resisted and went around shopping on campus for other space. I wasn't going to get the space that I wanted, so finally, I . . . talked to [President] Anderson, and he let me have the space I wanted. He pulled it out of his pocket, as he was wont to do. I thought, 'My gosh!' but we got another beautiful space."[12] That space turned out to be a portion of the former reference room in Trinkle Library, a location in which the center would be housed, attractively, for many years thereafter.

With the perspective of time, it became evident that the WI initiative and the writing center constituted one of the most beneficial innovations in the College's history. Graduates frequently made comments to their former WI professors to the effect that "I didn't want to take the course, but it was the most valuable one I had at MWC" or "I just got a promotion, and it was because of the writing skills I acquired at Mary Washington."

Numerous faculty members contributed to the program's success by voluntarily spending countless hours constructing or revamping courses to make them writing intensive. But the one person who above all was most responsible was the program's avatar and guiding genius, Carol Manning. "Talk about faculty leadership!" Dean Philip Hall once exclaimed. "Carol Manning is one of the real heroes."[13]

With the important exception of adding the writing-intensive element, the College's general education requirements remained essentially the same for over a decade following their implementation in the early 1970s. But there were problems. For one thing, the category designations were confusing to begin with; making matters worse, as time passed, more and more courses of dubious relevance were added to the options available in each group. The result, according to Dean Hall, was that the gen ed requirement had become "just a hodgepodge of things that nobody can successfully describe." Most students seemed to agree with that assessment. "Some of the general education classes," said one, "are mumble jumble."

Phil Hall recognized the problem at the outset of his tenure. As early as 1987, he set about to correct it by calling on the faculty to examine the gen ed requirements with an eye toward paring down the number of course options (then in the neighborhood of 250 to 300) and making them more intellectually cohesive.

His plea met considerable faculty resistance because, at first, many were unconvinced that there was anything wrong with the status quo. Later, even as the problem became more widely perceived in theory, in practice many faculty members balked when it appeared that their own courses might be among those deleted in a restructuring. This was of particular concern in traditionally low-enrollment disciplines where inclusion within the gen ed options was deemed crucial to attracting enough students to maintain viability (especially at a time when the state was requiring that disciplines be justified by serving a sufficient number of students).

But Hall persisted. "It took me three tries," he recalled. "Very soon after I got there . . . I formed a committee and it just died. And I tried it a second time, and it died. It took me three tries to get the thing to take, [but] it finally did." By then it was 1994.

Even so, it was a struggle. A preliminary report from the ad hoc faculty committee studying the issue included some rather radical changes, such as the proposition that every student be required to take a sweeping two-semester, twelve-hour, seven-hundred-student lecture course to be taught in Dodd Auditorium, tentatively titled Civilization and Thought. Opposition to that proposal was so widespread and so vehement, mainly owing to the huge class size, that the whole proposal was reworked to produce a plan that was, in Hall's words, "a lot more conservative and not nearly as scary."

The faculty approved the revised proposal, which contained two distinctive changes. One, justified by the need to abolish the clunky and confusing category titles of the existing system (e.g., "intellectual frameworks"), involved replacing them with simple enumerated goals that could be met by choosing from a drastically reduced selection of course options. The other major change was the creation of three more across-the-curriculum requirements: specifically, courses focusing on oral communication, global awareness, and issues of race and gender. Not long thereafter another "horizontal" (across-the-curriculum) requirement was added in environmental awareness. For a course to qualify for inclusion in any category, it had to be approved by an oversight committee comprising faculty with expertise in that area.

Some requirements generated more faculty debate than others. There was little opposition to the speaking-intensive element, inasmuch as the College's most recent reaccreditation report from the Southern Association of Colleges and Schools (SACS), delivered in 1993, mandated that all affiliated institutions require instruction in oral communication. "The faculty doesn't have much choice," Dean Hall explained at the time. "It's just one more thing we have to squeeze into an already tight curriculum."

The global awareness requirement likewise received widespread faculty support, not because it was mandated by SACS but because it was a natural concomitant to the College's rapidly developing emphasis on internationalism and multiculturalism. Those concerns were not new at Mary Washington, as evidenced most notably by the earlier Asian involvement of scholars such as former president Grellet Simpson and professors Kurt Leidecker and Lewis Fickett. Also, a fair number of students over the years had studied abroad, either through the sponsorship of Simpson International Scholarships or under the aegis of various study-abroad programs.

In the late 1980s, the College intensified its efforts to attract more foreign students—and with noticeable results. By 1992 the student body included almost sixty international students representing over thirty countries in Latin America, Europe, Africa, the Middle East, and Asia. From all accounts, the experiences of foreign students at Mary Washington were favorable overall, notwithstanding some cases of homesickness, culture shock, and language difficulties. But "whatever the obstacles and adjustments to life here have been," noted an article in *MWC Today*, "these students retain a positive attitude."

The visiting students were a diverse lot. "Their academic interests range widely from international affairs and foreign languages, to economics, mathematics and ancient tragedy," the article reported. "They play tennis, listen to Beethoven, read Agatha Christie and Sartre, play the piano and classical guitar, and enjoy friends—when not studying an average of four to five hours a day outside of class. They find Fredericksburg quaint, pretty, conservative, and quiet. They miss family and friends back home. They also longingly remember favorite foods, such as French cheese, tropical fruits, native rice dishes, and caviar (an inexpensive spread in Sweden), but they enjoy eating pizza, fried chicken, bagels, seafood, peanut butter, and brownies."

In its conclusion, the article hit on a key aspect of the foreign students' stay at Mary Washington. "They have come to us for an education," it said, "but they also have worlds to teach us. The different perspectives and varied experiences they share with us greatly enrich our life at Mary Washington."

There were indications on campus that interest in internationalism was growing, stimulated perhaps by the increased presence of foreign students, as well as by a heightened general awareness of the ever-greater importance of global issues. One example was the foundation in 1989 of a group known as the Third World Coalition, headed by four professors—Shah Mehrabi, Economics; Raman Singh, English; Cheryl Staunton, Modern Foreign Languages; and Paul Zisman, Education—whose purpose, according to Zisman, was to encourage students "to see events from the point of view of Third World countries." In the following year, the Global Observations Committee was created with a goal of encouraging the addition of a global awareness component in the general education requirements. As committee member Cedric Rucker, the assistant dean for student activities, explained it, "There is a tendency to think of ourselves as citizens of the U.S. only, but we're citizens of the world, and we need to look at what goes on outside our borders."

Student interest was evinced through participation in events like Harvest of Hope, an international hunger relief effort, and through the formation of groups such as the International Club to serve as a nexus for foreign students and to expand multicultural activities on campus. Among the smaller, but more interesting, new clubs was the Islamic Student Organization. The purpose of the club, according to its members, was not only to serve as a support group for the fifteen Muslim students at MWC but also to educate the College community about the nature of Islam. "Muslims are always viewed as people who are politically active," explained one member, "and have some subversive interest. It's important to know that 99.9 percent of all Muslims go about their business like everybody else. [We would] really like to integrate with other people and really give them a general idea of what Islam is all about. . . . It's not the way people perceive [it] as terrorism and bombing."

At the faculty and administrative level, a number of initiatives were undertaken, with the aggressive encouragement of President Anderson, to promote global involvement, including the formation of the faculty Committee on International Programs. In 1990 the administration established the Office of International Programs for the purpose of developing, coordinating and promoting study-abroad opportunities. According to its director, Brenda King, the effort was worthwhile, even crucial. "American citizens have a narrow, provincial outlook," she said. "Worldwide interdependency will change that, and study abroad is a response to that realization."

Increased attention to such matters paid dividends for Mary Washington students, as the number studying in foreign countries almost tripled between 1990 and 1992, when the yearly total reached ninety-four. Within a comparative context, this meant that the percentage of study-abroad participation among full-time Mary Washington students was approximately three times greater than the national average for such participation.

Besides encouraging foreign study through existing channels, the College developed several of its own overseas programs, often prompted by enterprising individual faculty members. Education professor Adrienne May, for example, was instrumental in organizing an exchange program with England's Kingston University, whereby six students from the two schools exchanged places for a semester.

A particularly innovative and timely program was one developed by political science professor Richard Krikus, an expert in Soviet policy. Drawing on his well-established connections in Lithuania, Krikus arranged a cooperative venture between Mary Washington and the University of Vilnius. The timing could not have been more propitious, coming just as Lithuania was breaking free from Soviet domination. The exchange thus offered MWC students, in Krikus's words, "an unparalleled opportunity to learn and to help, . . . to see the remnants of the communist system, but also to see people trying to bring about democracy in the face of daunting problems." One of the student participants, Student Association president Kurt Rupprecht, agreed, calling it "more than just an opportunity to go overseas and study, it's a chance to . . . see an empire disintegrate."

Several programs involved traveling through European countries. The first such effort was a summer bicycle tour developed by geography professor Samuel T. Emory. Beginning in the mid-1970s and continuing for the next

"European Capitals" students in front of Berlin's Brandenburg Gate, 2006

PORTER BLAKEMORE

fifteen or so years, he led groups of students (as many as twenty-eight, but typically fewer) on two- to four-week excursions that involved biking thirty or more miles a day through Belgium, the Netherlands, Germany, France, and England.[14] The plan included many attractive features in addition to Emory's own appeal as a teacher: the cost was low ($1,200 to $2,000), the itinerary provided spectacular views of the countryside, the mode of transportation was a boon to physical fitness, and the course yielded three hours of academic credit.

In the early nineties, Emory's course was succeeded by what would become the College's longest-running summer-abroad program, European Capitals. Developed and directed by history professor Porter Blakemore and political science professor Jack Kramer, the program was first offered in 1992 and was still going in 2008, showing no signs of diminished popularity.

The twenty-six-day experience normally included visits to five selected cities that, over the years, included London, Paris, Vienna, Venice, Rome, Brussels, Prague, Berlin, Copenhagen, and Stockholm.

The six-credit course included visits to various cultural, political, and historical sites in the cities, as well as excursions to surrounding sites. Experiences encompassed opera, ballet, and symphonic performances; visits to embassies and foreign ministries; observances of Parliament and the French Senate in session; and meetings with sundry political leaders.

According to Professor Blakemore, European Capitals allowed students to encounter "first-hand the language, cultural, and political differences of European countries . . . [and thus] approach today's problems without being trapped in the limits of their own American experience." Or, put most simply, he said, the course was "designed to demonstrate the truth in the quote that 'the world is a book and he who stays at home reads only one page.'"

Participation in all such programs, by the students' own testimony, seemed to have produced incalculable benefits. Others noticed the impact as well. "The maturity just jumps out at me," commented one-time study abroad director Constance Gianuoulis. "Sometimes they're unsure of themselves before they go, but when they come back, they are confident and mature. They are also more aware of the big picture and who we are in the big picture."

In light of heightened interest in international issues, both on campus and in American society at large, it was not surprising that the addition of global awareness to the College's general education requirements received virtually unanimous support from the faculty. The incorporation of the race and gender component, however, was not accomplished so smoothly.

In the late 1980s, two faculty members, philosophy professor Craig Vasey and psychology professor Carole Corcoran, took the lead in the movement by drafting a proposal to seek funding to support a study of race and gender issues in the curriculum. Their work resulted in a grant of $107,000 from the commonwealth's Fund for Excellence program to underwrite an extensive two-year study known as the Race and Gender Project. The study focused on gender issues during its first year (1988–89) and on racial issues the following year.

It included an array of approaches: sponsoring prominent speakers from outside the College, holding workshops on topics such as curriculum development and pedagogical techniques for teaching a diverse student population, and publishing a periodic newsletter emphasizing resources available to faculty both on and off campus. It also developed a new interdisciplinary course, Introduction to Women's Studies, and a seminar for faculty on ethnic studies to help them integrate such material into their courses.

While those developments were encouraging to the proponents of race and gender awareness, they attracted the ire of the more conservative elements of the faculty. To such folks, the Race and Gender Project and the courses it spawned smacked of political correctness ("p.c." in the pejorative argot of the day). They resented the demand for sensitivity training and, even more, what they regarded as attempts to lard the curriculum with courses they deemed insubstantial, or, worse still, propagandistic.

Tensions between the two factions, smoldering sub rosa for some time, erupted in uncharacteristically ugly fashion in the spring of 1992. The specific point of contention that touched off the recriminations was a new interdisciplinary course, IDIS 203, Ethnic Studies, developed under the auspices of the Race and Gender Project. Having been approved by the faculty's standing Course Offering Committee, it was scheduled to be taught first in the fall 1992 semester; students were already enrolled in it.

Near the end of the last scheduled faculty meeting of the spring 1992 semester, psychology professor Thomas Moeller moved that the faculty reject the course forthwith—an action that would preclude its being offered in the coming fall semester. His objections to the course were sweeping, including procedural problems of how it had initially been approved, practical problems with staffing it, pedagogical problems, and, above all, philosophical problems involving its content.

He found fault, in particular, with the rationale for the course, which posited that "there is an ever increasing interest from ethnic communities within the academic arena to put their heroes, contributions, and cultures into the school curriculum. Such contributions help to give a student a sense of structural inclusion, validation, empowerment and equity." In Moeller's view, that attempt amounted to a reprehensible quota system whereby the contributions of every ethnic group had to be mentioned at the risk of seeming to be insensitive. Drawing directly from the historian Arthur M. Schlesinger Jr.'s thesis in *The Disuniting of America* (1991), Moeller contended that courses like the proposed Ethnic Studies tended to perpetuate divisiveness, when the goal of education, on the contrary, should be to emphasize the common themes of American culture rather than its differences.

In the harshest portion of his lengthy (almost half-hour) critique, Moeller indicted the course for attempting to convert students to a particular—viz. leftist—political position. Such efforts to turn education into propaganda, he contended, were akin to the sinister methods employed by Nazi Germany and Stalinist Russia.

Stunned by Moeller's blast, the faculty meeting (which had already gone well past the usual adjournment time) broke up with the issue of IDIS 203 still unresolved, tabled until the next scheduled meeting, which would not take place until the fall semester. However, in an effort to settle the incendiary issue, Dean Philip Hall took the unusual step of calling a special meeting for May 8 to focus on that single matter.

Meanwhile some faculty members who had devised the course expressed shock at the vehemence of Moeller's attack. Defending the course, Craig Vasey called the whole political correctness debate a "bogus issue," asserting in a *Free Lance–Star* interview that "the American complexion is changing. . . . In a society where we have racial problems, if you take a stand that acknowledges them or ignores them—that's a political stand either way. . . . If you're not from the dominant white middle-class group, you may feel like the curriculum is already political."

While Vasey's public comments were measured, those of some of his like-minded colleagues were not so restrained. The most pointed rejoinder was in the form of a memorandum to Dean Hall from a number of irate faculty who condemned Moeller's speech for its "speculation, threats, and innuendoes." The signers were most provoked by the reference to Nazi propaganda. "The Nazis," said the memo, "as Moeller should well know, sought to eradicate the very thing this course seeks to explore: diversity. . . . His understanding of ethnic studies seems to have come from one book and the pages of *Newsweek*. . . . 'Racism' is not a term to be used lightly, but many feel that Tom Moeller's remarks were in fact racist. He profoundly, painfully insulted many of the faculty and administration who have sought to diversify the curriculum, and he cloaked his insults in the myth of pure knowledge, unaffected by societal considerations."

By the time the faculty convened for its special session on May 8, the memorandum (in an unsigned version) had become public and was distributed to the faculty before the meeting. Sensing the seething anger on both sides of the debate, Dean Hall opened the session by admonishing all parties to act with decorum and to focus on the merits of issue at hand, IDIS 203, rather than engage in impugning each other's motivations. After long and detailed discussion of the course, it was finally approved, with the stipulations that it could be taught on an "experimental" basis only, no more than twice before being subject to further review, and, moreover, that it could not satisfy any general education requirements. Tom Moeller then requested that his original motion—the one that had initiated the controversy—be withdrawn.

With that, it might have been assumed that the issue would dissipate, but such an assumption would have taken insufficient account of the depth of the animosities that had been generated. The problem was that the matter in contention bore directly on some of the most intensely held faculty beliefs on each side. Faculty members, often inclined by nature or by their profession (or both) to be argumentative, are not apt to acquiesce easily, especially on issues (such as this one) that have, in the minds of many, a moral as well as pedagogical dimension.

So it was that, with the issue at hand having been resolved and with adjournment imminent, geography professor Richard Palmieri, requesting a point of privilege, rose to the defense of Tom Moeller. What followed was, by the uniform account of longtime faculty members who heard it, the most remarkable faculty oration within anyone's recollection.

Palmieri first criticized the unsigned memo as a "shoddy example of writing—ham-fisted, maladroit, and terminally insensitive," then proceeded to castigate its authors for what he perceived to be the letter's corrosive effect on institutional collegiality. With eloquence drawn from his training in the classics, he passionately employed Ciceronian rhetoric involving repeated iterations of the Italian word *vergogne*—"for shame."

He explained that it was the term his parents had used to scold him as a child when he misbehaved, recalling in particular that when his father spoke it, "his inflection, the tone of sadness in his voice when he said it—*vergogne*—implied the shame which diminishes the character and worth of the family." It was that concept, Palmieri asserted, that applied to the current state of faculty affairs: "As most of you know by now, I grew up in a very ethnic, very Italian family—big, boisterous, full of love. . . . I am part of a bigger family now. It, too, is boisterous, but the events of late, particularly today, suggest that it is not as full of love as it once was. . . . Who knows why? . . . Anonymous accusations, vicious labeling, perfidious race-baiting. We have come to this? *Vergogne!* I use the term in the same sense that my father used it with me. Shame on you, shame on me, shame on us for doing that which diminishes the character of our family and the worth of our enterprise."

Immediately after his speech, the meeting adjourned. In the ensuing commotion, Palmieri was showered with huzzahs from his partisans and imprecations from his adversaries. Such a scene was a microcosm of the p.c. wars occurring on many campuses across the country. That the phenomenon was widespread may have made its appearance at Mary Washington more understandable, but no less unseemly. The faculty's finest hour it was not.

Eventually, as animosity receded and (relative) civility returned to faculty deliberations, the Ethnic Studies course and similar interdisciplinary offerings entered the curriculum without undue dissension, and one course on race and gender became part of the general education portion of graduation requirements. In 1997 another horizontal (across-the-curriculum) requirement was added, this one in environmental awareness. To qualify for inclusion in any category, a course had to be approved by an oversight committee whose members were faculty with expertise in that area.

Thus was completed the general education component of the curriculum that was to remain intact, with only minor adjustments, into the first decade of the twenty-first century. The requirements were the following:

- Goal 1: the ability to write logically, clearly, and precisely, and the ability to acquire, organize, present, and document ideas and information (3 credits, English 101)
- Goal 2: an understanding of mathematical thought and the ability to conceptualize and apply mathematical logic to problem solving (6 credits, 3 of which must be a mathematics course)
- Goal 3: an appreciation of major contributions of science to an understanding of the natural world and to the possible solution of con-

temporary problems; the application of laboratory science methods to the acquisition of knowledge through a two-semester, vertically-building sequence of laboratory courses in the same discipline (8 credits)

- Goal 4: an understanding of human culture as expressed in artistic achievements and as revealed in literature (6 credits with one course in the arts and one in literature)
- Goal 5: an understanding of the intellectual foundations and development of Western civilization (6 credits)
- Goal 6: an understanding of the forces shaping human behavior, social structures, institutions, and spatial relationships (6 credits)
- Goal 7: intermediate-level (202) competence in a foreign language (0–12 credits)
- Goal 8: physical fitness through physical activity (2 courses, 2-credit minimum)

Across-the-Curriculum Requirements

- Environmental Awareness: To promote an understanding of the fragility of the biosphere and the degree to which human activity can affect it (1 course)
- Global Awareness: To promote an understanding of other places, cultures, and societies (2 courses)
- Race and Gender Intensive: To ensure an understanding of race and/or gender issues in Western culture (1 course)
- Speaking Intensive: To ensure the development of competence in oral communication (2 courses)
- Writing Intensive: To ensure the development of competence in written composition (4 courses beyond Goal 1)

The most controversial subsequent revision of the gen ed curriculum involved the foreign language requirement. No graduation criterion generated more student angst than that requirement—namely, that all students must demonstrate competency at the intermediate level of a foreign language, which was normally accomplished by successful completion of the 200-level sequence. Yet for many years, completion of four years of a single language in high school was deemed sufficient to exempt the student from the requirement—an escape hatch gleefully grasped by many of those who qualified for it (save those who intended to major in foreign language).

Over time, however, the foreign language faculty became increasingly skeptical of the actual equivalency between the secondary school and collegiate experiences, prompting a perennial debate over whether the exemption should be continued or students should be required to fulfill the criterion in college. Students, of course, argued for the more lenient guideline. Assailing the possibility of a change, the *Bullet* declared, "Most of us came here under the assumption that four years of a language in high school would be enough to get by in college. Boy, high school guidance counselors are going to look like liars now."

The language faculty, on the other hand, became convinced that high school instruction, while in some cases adequate, was not on the whole sufficient to meet the standard expected by Mary Washington. Moreover, as German professor Sammy Merrill pointed out, the foreign language requirement was the only one in the curriculum that could be met by high school work. It was his view that eventually prevailed, when in 1996 the faculty approved a gen ed revision abolishing the high school equivalency exemption. Thenceforth all students would be required to meet the intermediate-level standard by taking actual college courses unless able to pass the MWC competency test or to score 620 or higher on an SAT II foreign language subject test.

Students were irate. Fumed a *Bullet* editorial, "The new modern foreign language requirement goes above and beyond the ridiculous . . . by not allowing students with four years of a language in high school to place out of the language requirement. Two words: Hello, Germanna." Unmoved, the faculty stuck to its position. English professor Teresa Kennedy summarized the prevailing view, bluntly declaring, "If a student can't pass the course here, he or she shouldn't get a degree here. It's think or sink."

In the years that followed, a substantial number of students did attempt to circumvent the requirement—or at least find what they believed to be an easier route—by taking their language courses elsewhere, typically at community colleges. In fact, a survey revealed that of over five hundred total general education courses transferred into MWC for the 1998–99 school year, well over half were in foreign languages alone. But the requirement stayed.

At the same time that campus attention was focused on revising the general education requirements, other academic issues also arose. One of the most controversial, to students especially, was the question of self-scheduled final examinations.

Since the 1971–72 session, students had been allowed to self-schedule their exams—that is, to take an exam for a given course at any of the times that the instructor for the course was offering an exam for *any* of his or her courses. Normally this meant that students, in effect, would have four options for scheduling any particular exam. Students appreciated the flexibility thus provided, whether they used it to enhance performance (by maximizing study time) or pleasure (by finishing exams sooner).

Over time, however, the faculty developed misgivings about the policy, citing overcrowded classrooms for some sections and difficulties in preparing and grading exams within the prescribed time constraints. Their most prevalent complaint was that it provided a greater opportunity for cheating—the honor system notwithstanding.

When a proposal to eliminate self-scheduling came before the faculty in

1986, students (unsurprisingly) went into full-opposition mode, with the Student Association Cabinet, as well as its Lobby Committee and Student Academic Affairs Committee, voicing strong displeasure. A petition was also circulated that, reported the *Bullet*, rapidly garnered one thousand signatures in support of the existing policy.

"Those in favor of eliminating self-scheduling," said an op-ed piece, "conclude that it will cut down cheating on exams. Cheating? And what about the honor code? If the choice is between proctored exams or the loss of flexibility of exams, would not the logical choice be to reinstate proctors during exams?"

The *Bullet*'s own position was curtly stated in an editorial headline that read simply, "Keep It!" Having dispatched the main arguments against self-scheduling, the paper declared, "To eliminate self-scheduling destroys not only a unique privilege at MWC but also severs the bond of trust and responsibility cherished between students and their professors."

For the time being, the student view triumphed, as the faculty voted to keep self-scheduling, but the issue was resurrected in 1988. Again student opposition to the change was overwhelming. A "spot poll" taken in Seacobeck by an SA committee found that 285 of 293 respondents favored self-scheduling. It was to no avail this time, however, as the faculty voted to establish (reestablish, really) set-scheduled exams, which took effect in fall 1989. The new policy required that students take their exams for a given course only at the time allotted for that particular course. The only "escape hatch" was that a student whose set schedule called for three exams on the same day might, by appeal to the dean, receive permission to rearrange one of the tests.

A few years later, students were again upset—this time by a proposed revision of the College's academic calendar. What they found most offensive were changes in the fall class schedule, made worse by the apparent failure of the administration to seek student opinion in formulating the proposal.

For many years, the schedule had included a mid-October break consisting of Monday and Tuesday off, and another break beginning at noon on the Wednesday before Thanksgiving and running through the holiday weekend. What faculty and administrators increasingly noticed—how could they have failed to?—was that students tended to leave early for both breaks, creating essentially two separate week-long vacations amounting to a considerable loss of instructional time. On the other hand, for those students who adhered to the schedule, the short breaks could create logistical problems, especially for those whose destinations required lengthy travel.

The solution devised by the administration was to eliminate the fall break and extend the Thanksgiving holiday to a full week. The decision was announced in an April 1995 memorandum from Barbara Palmer, who by then had succeeded Phil Hall as dean.[15] Palmer, having explained the primary rationale for the change as the desire to eliminate the tendency of students to leave early and return late from breaks, did not help what was bound to be an unpopular case by adding that the change would also relieve "some of the pressure working women experience when they work through Wednesday noon before the biggest family feast of the year." Speaking for students, already irate over their lack of input, Geoff Hart, president-elect of the Student Association, alleged that "many members of the executive cabinet were extremely offended by that remark"—namely, the implication that *women* needed to have time to prepare Thanksgiving dinner.

The *Bullet* sarcastically observed that "surprisingly enough, most students are not leaping along campus walk, singing about how happy they are that Fall Break has been taken away." The editorial, titled "A Schedule We'd Like to See," then proffered a list of facetious suggestions for a new calendar, including the following:

- All female students get a whole week off before Halloween, Thanksgiving, and Arbor Day in order to cook their pumpkin, turkey, and arbor.
- All classes are cancelled on St. Patrick's Day, Ground Hog Day, and, of course, Devil-Goat Day.
- Any student who has three or more tests in the same week may refrain from taking the test of his/her choice.
- Monday and Friday classes are optional.
- No Thursday night classes, and all afternoon classes must end by 4 p.m. in order to get a good table at Spanky's for Happy Hour.
- Add another day to the end of Spring Break for students to detox themselves, wash their laundry, and lay out to keep their tan.

Aside from such flippancy, students mounted a more serious campaign against the proposal, including the unusual step of directly contacting members of the Board of Visitors to express their displeasure not only about the changes themselves but also about the lack of prior consultation regarding their formulation. The students were supported by Professor Carol Manning, a former faculty representative to the board, who pleaded the case for keeping fall break. "People look forward to that break," she said, "because of the intensity of the fall semester," adding that it did not "make much sense to have a long [Thanksgiving] break right before finals."

The tactic worked, as during the summer the board called on the administration to revise the proposed calendar. By the fall, a revamped schedule was presented—one that reinstated fall break. It did contain some changes, including an extended exam schedule; also, the spring semester was slated to begin a week earlier, a situation that some students disliked because they feared it would hurt their Christmas vacation employment opportunities. But by and large there seemed to be a general approval, particularly since the hallowed fall break was retained. As Geoff Hart concluded, "You have to take the good with the bad."

Another academic issue of interest to both students and faculty was the question of minor programs. Though never adopted by the faculty, minors were the subject of recurrent interest over the years, an interest that was tangibly manifested in the fall of 1991 when the faculty's Academic Affairs Committee introduced a proposal to create such an entity. The proposal described a minor as "a set of courses which define a focused inquiry into an academic discipline or an investigation of a particular theme" that would consist of fifteen to twenty credit hours, at least six of which must be at the upper level.

The main support for the concept of a minor came from those who viewed it as a means of allowing students to demonstrate special competence in a discipline outside their major without having to commit to completing the thirty-five to forty credits demanded by a second major. A cardinal belief among the idea's proponents was that those credentials would enhance graduates' employment opportunities, a proposition that many students found appealing. "It's kind of an in-between thing," said Dean Hall. "It's not hard to imagine at all why that would be popular, and probably a lot of students would take advantage of it."

The opposition came mostly from smaller departments that counted on "second majors" to keep their enrollments at a viable level and feared that too many students would take the minor option if available. The chair of one such department, Professor Robert Boughner of Classics, Philosophy, and Religion, was among the most vocal in opposition, acknowledging the potential threat to his departmental interests.

Boughner, however, went beyond that to assert that he would question the minor program's worth, whether or not it jeopardized any given discipline. "I don't see what a minor program does positively," he said. "There is no graduate or professional school that cares the least bit about a minor program. There's no employer in the world who cares about a minor program, and it is a type of program that is going out of style nationwide anyway because of its inherent uselessness. . . . I think it has a potential to be deleterious to what we've got." In the end, Boughner's position prevailed—though that did not preclude the issue from bubbling up periodically (though never successfully) in the future.

Throughout the eighties and nineties, many decisions affecting the academic program at Mary Washington were driven by fiscal imperatives over which the College had little or no control. Whether owing to general economic downturns or to adverse policy directives from Richmond, or to a combination thereof, it was a difficult time for academia, a situation that often had a negative impact both on programs and on personnel at MWC.

From a programmatic standpoint, it meant greater state demands for accountability for expenditures, a concept largely unfamiliar (and uncongenial) to many denizens of the ivory tower. Indeed, emphasis on productivity ("bean counting," as it was derisively termed) was abhorrent to most faculty, carrying as it did sordid connotations of the business world's "bottom line" mentality. Yet it was a reality that the College had to accommodate, necessitating ongoing examination of all programs.

In some instances the review process promised useful returns. One example was an "outcomes assessment" plan undertaken at the behest of both SCHEV and SACS. Under the astute direction of Vice President Roy Weinstock, the College during the 1988–89 session devised a comprehensive mechanism for evaluating the actual effectiveness of the Mary Washington educational system by analyzing four components: general education, departmental major programs, student perceptions of their college experience, and alumni perceptions of the impact MWC had on their personal and professional development. The complex plan, implemented over a period of years, gleaned data that contributed directly toward many positive changes throughout the institution.

Some mandated reviews, however, held more malign potentialities. The gravest danger to the academic program posed by the new accountability demands was the threat to disciplines with historically small enrollments and low production of majors. According to guidelines established by the State Council of Higher Education, a discipline had to average graduating five majors per year over a period of five years to justify its existence. That formula jeopardized some disciplines widely regarded as essential to the liberal arts curriculum—specifically, classics, philosophy, religion, and German, all of which were put under SCHEV scrutiny in 1984, with the threat of termination unless their numbers improved. As it turned out, all four survived, owing to strong support from the administration and the innovative and energetic efforts of the departments' own faculty members.

Less fortunate was the public administration program. In 1985 the College announced that the program would be phased out. The problem was not so much lack of majors (though there were few), but the administration's determination that funding was insufficient to bring the quality of the program (which had only one full-time professor, Monica Lindeman) up to an acceptable standard. Though the approximately fifteen students currently in the program expressed disappointment—"They didn't give it a fight," complained one—the decision caused minimal stir among the faculty generally, perhaps because of the perception that public administration was somewhat peripheral to the College's liberal arts core philosophy. Moreover, it had only had a five-year history in the curriculum.[16]

It was quite the opposite situation, however, with dance, another program that came under fire for lack of majors. That program had long been an integral part of campus life, not only as an academic major but also as a prominent contributor to various cultural events. Some of its longtime professors were among the College's most beloved—notably Claudia Moore Read, who retired in 1975, and Sonja Dragomanovic Haydar, who retired in 1989—and its alumni among the most loyal.

Yet the undeniable fact was that the number of dance majors was in decline, fluctuating between zero and seven during the 1980s, placing the department in constant danger of elimination. In an administrative effort to salvage the major, dance was at one point combined with drama to form the Department of Dramatic Arts and Dance, but the improvement was negligible. As a disappointed President Anderson observed in 1992, "Dance has been a roller coaster ride ever since I've been here." In the fall of that year, it was announced that the Board of Visitors would soon consider the department's termination.

That news sparked aggressive efforts on several fronts to save the esteemed program, including a unanimous faculty vote in favor of its retention. The *Bullet* offered editorial support, raising the specter of further possible cuts. Such action, it warned, "also questions the future for other small departments. Could physics, with only a handful of majors, be dropped also? And what about philosophy, religion, classics, and anthropology?"

From retirement, Professor Emeritus Haydar issued a plaintive public defense of the program that included a tart rebuke of the administration's handling of the situation. "Looking at the funds allocated for the athletic program," she declared, "it appears to me that there's plenty of money available; it only needs to be justly distributed by people who sincerely care and understand the need to develop cultural awareness."

Although the problem was deeper than the allocation of funds (which itself was a more complicated process than Haydar's statement indicated), her charge did reflect the belief of dance partisans that the College was not doing enough to promote the program. To address that situation, former dance major Vicky Nichols Wilder '80 (wife of Vice President for Admissions Martin A. Wilder) formed a group known as the Friends of MWC Dance, who worked diligently in various ways to invigorate the program. One effort was the sponsorship of an event called "Dance the Day Away" for prospective students in the Washington, D.C., area to sell them on studying dance at Mary Washington.

Of all the exertions on behalf of saving the program, the most passionate were those of the current dance students, who made an emotional appeal directly to Dean Hall. Told that the impending decision would be driven by, in Hall's words, "the simple economics of supply and demand," one senior major pleaded with him, "I just want you to feel for us and forget the numbers. There's a lot of love for this department."

In the end, love had nothing to do with it; the (low) numbers did. At its January 1994 meeting, the Board of Visitors voted to discontinue dance as a major, while still permitting some courses to be offered in the discipline. Nothing against dance, Hall commented: "If another similar situation [should] arise, it would be looked at in the same way. Things are tight all around, and it's unfortunate that it had to be this way."

Even for faculty in disciplines not menaced by possible extinction, significant problems surfaced during the eighties and nineties. One was the tendency toward larger class size, a development that threatened the relatively low student-faculty ratio on which the College had prided itself. There was also a heavy teaching load (normally four courses per semester), made more onerous by—yet another complaint—increased expectations for scholarly productivity to qualify for promotion and tenure.

Then there was a whole panoply of issues relating to compensation and benefits. Though faculty salaries received an appreciable boost during the early years of President Anderson's administration, that trend quickly leveled off as state coffers shrank; by 1991–92 there was an actual statewide freeze on faculty salaries. The situation was ameliorated somewhat for those who had achieved the rank of distinguished professor or had been named Jepson Fellows, but for most faculty, salaries remained lamentably low, even by the traditionally paltry standards of academia. Exacerbating discontent was the perception by some faculty that inequities existed between and within departments across the College.

A particularly controversial issue regarding benefits arose in 1994 over the matter of so-called spousal equivalency—that is, the extension of the same benefits and privileges to the partner of a gay or lesbian faculty member as those granted to the spouse of a heterosexual faculty member. As was to be expected with any campus issue pertaining to sexual orientation, this one took on a dimension, and provoked acrimony, rather disproportionate to the actual matter at hand.

Leading the fight for spousal equivalency benefits was geography professor Donald Rallis. In a 1994 *Bullet* op-ed article, he pointed out that several years earlier the Board of Visitors had amended the College's statement of nondiscrimination to add sexual orientation to the list of grounds on which the institution pledged not to discriminate. Pursuant to that policy, the personnel office had proceeded to issue College identification cards to partners of homosexual employees, enabling them to use College facilities to the same extent permitted to heterosexual spouses. "But," Rallis pointed out, "where the most important of all employee benefits is concerned—health insurance—Mary Washington College remains in flagrant violation of its own non-discrimination policies. My heterosexual colleagues are entitled to health insurance for their loved ones, but as a gay man, this benefit is denied to me."

He went on to assert that the failure to grant such benefits constituted an implicit violation of the College's honor code. "The key issue," he contended, "is that if the institution officially says that it does not discriminate, it needs to adjust policies to reflect that stance, or it is hypocritical."

Rallis's demand brought quick opposition from the more conservative element of the faculty, including biology professor Stephen Fuller, who claimed that granting spousal equivalent health care reflected "a breakdown in the traditional mother-father led family and the moral fiber of the U.S." The most extensive rebuttal came in a *Bullet* op-ed piece by economics professor Stephen Stageberg, a fundamentalist Christian who had previously crossed swords with Rallis in a public debate over the morality of homosexuality.[17] Like Fuller, Stageberg disparaged the social implications of such an action—"We would be redefining the family, from a husband and wife to any two people, married or not, opposite sex or not"—but his critique went even further. To him, the actual proposal was but "a symptom of a far greater problem in American society: the decline into relativism and the rejection of absolute truth."

The whole debate, revelatory though it was concerning divergent faculty philosophies, was essentially moot. The commonwealth, not the College, determined who would receive state-funded benefits, and it was highly unlikely that such assistance would be provided to homosexual partners in a state whose laws prohibited same-sex marriages. In addition, Governor Allen had publicly declared his belief that homosexuality was immoral and stated that he would not countenance the expenditure of tax money for underwriting the health risks that same-sex unions presumably entailed.

The only remaining avenue, should the College decide to support spousal equivalency, was to use private funds from the institution's endowment. This, too, was unlikely, if for no other reason than the fear that such action would have negative repercussions in Richmond. William and Mary had already learned that lesson. When its faculty earlier voted in favor of spousal equivalency, the college's officials received a sharp rebuke from a Republican leader (later speaker) of the House of Delegates, S. Vance Wilkins, who warned that "any further faculty positions taken to undermine the traditional family structure will fall on deaf ears in the [legislature]. We expect you to get your house in order."[18]

Not cowed by such threats, the MWC faculty proceeded to vote, by a two-to-one margin, in support of spousal equivalency health care benefits. That the margin was not closer came as no surprise to Stageberg, who attributed it to the fact that "faculty members don't want to be politically incorrect by voicing out." (The vote had been taken by secret ballot.)

The vote put the ball into the court of the administration and, ultimately, the Board of Visitors, who faced quite a dilemma. As the board's rector, Paul Dresser, put it, "Our hands are tied between complying with state law, but feeling seriously that it is important to listen to our faculty. . . . The groundswell of activity shows [that] there may need to be an attempt to change state law."

So even though the movement produced no pecuniary gains for advocates of spousal equivalency, it did yield some psychological ones, providing a measure of satisfaction to those like Donald Rallis, who commented that the result was "simply to clearly indicate our institutional values, . . . [by] accepting as official policy that discrimination on the grounds of sexual orientation is wrong."

But while issues such as spousal equivalency came and went, there remained throughout the period that most nettlesome of all faculty concerns: merit pay. Instituted during the Woodard years amid much opposition, the policy in the interim had earned no more (and perhaps even less) support, despite unending efforts to make it more equitable and hence more palatable.

Having retired from the responsibility of administering merit pay during his nineteen years as dean, Philip Hall offered a perceptive analysis of the problem. Though he defended the system as a means of rewarding superior faculty performances, he wondered whether that goal was "worth the pain and anguish you go through to get it."

> Whether or not you make the marginal performer perform better, I doubt it. Whether or not the fact that there is recognition makes the superstar better than he or she would ordinarily be, I doubt it. . . . [And] it is miserable for the evaluatee and the evaluators annually to have to go through all this stuff. The process and the conclusions you reach are fraught with all kinds of problems. . . . You can spot the outliers usually. But [the problem is] trying to make differentiations among people in the middle that aren't the top five percent or the bottom five percent but the middle ninety percent, and make fine gradations saying that X is a little bit better than Y, but not much. . . . Peers view all parts of it, and people [are] judging each other. . . . It's inherently awful.

English professor Teresa Kennedy put it more succinctly. "Nobody at the college in their right mind likes merit pay," she said. "It's designed to make us hate each other." Yet as a mandate of SCHEV, the General Assembly, and the Board of Visitors, merit pay became a fixture of MWC administrative policy.

Though perhaps the most noxious element, merit pay emerged in the 1990s as but one of a concatenation of perceived abuses (real or imagined) that the faculty came to resent. Some of them laid blame for the resultant malaise at the feet of President Anderson, who, truth be told, could hardly have been held responsible for the economic situation that generated many of the difficulties. While he might legitimately have been blamed for discrete policy decisions that various faculty members disliked, the root causes often lay well beyond the province of the president's office, the Board of Visitors, or even the commonwealth.

Nonetheless, faculty resentments reached such a level that by 1995 there was desultory talk of a vote of no confidence in the administration, evoking memories of the protests in the late 1970s against President Woodard. Though it never came to that, Dean Hall did admit following the November 1995 meeting of the faculty, "The temperature's a little hotter than it's been before." (It also led to a feat of legendary impetuosity when volatile geography professor James Gouger, in a fit of pique, hurled a computer from the window of his third-floor office in Monroe Hall.)

It was ironic that faculty discontent ran so high during a period in which the College overall was enjoying a renascence, with improvements evident in many academic areas. Even the oft-dyspeptic faculty were receiving more funds than ever (though still not munificent) for research and more time off for sabbaticals. They also benefited from assistance provided by the Teaching Innovation Project (TIP), an initiative originally funded by a grant from the Governor's Fund for Excellence and later underwritten by the College itself. From its creation in 1986, TIP served for many years to bring faculty members together to discuss pedagogical techniques and to aid them in implementing various teaching innovations.

At the same time, the curriculum was invigorated not only by increased focus on issues of writing, speaking, global awareness, and race and gender but also by a strong emphasis on undergraduate research. Beginning in 1986, an expanding fund was established to enable students to conduct research projects under the direction of individual professors. By 1995, over 160 students were thus engaged, supervised by more than thirty-five faculty representing sixteen of the twenty-two academic departments, working on projects ranging from DNA studies to landscape ecology, theater production, infrared and gamma radiation, British naval history, and Navajo and Cherokee culture.

Students and faculty alike were uniformly enthusiastic about the individual research program. "It is genuine exploration," said Dean Hall, "full of blind alleys, unexpected twists, elation, utter discouragement, excitement, and drudgery. It's the ivory tower cheek-by-jowl with the real world. And there is no better path to genuine self-discovery."

That such positive accomplishments could occur during times of economic difficulty was in part attributable to the shrewdness of the administration in managing the institution's limited allocations from the state. But just as important as the administration's resourcefulness was the faculty's resilience. Undeterred by constricted funds, mounting workloads, and occasional internecine bickering, the faculty continued to place primacy on the welfare of the students, exuberantly delivering the high quality of instruction that had become the hallmark of a Mary Washington education.

While many faculty members shared a deep sense of pride in, and commitment to, their calling, few ever gave more eloquent voice to those feelings than did English professor Carlton Lutterbie Jr. One of the brightest young minds and most attractive personalities of his faculty generation, Lutterbie expressed his view, with characteristic clarity and gracefulness, in a 1983 guest editorial in the *Bullet*, for which he served as faculty adviser. "From time to time students ask me what it's like to teach at Mary Washington," he wrote.

> It's not an easy question to answer. From the standpoint of actual teaching—the primary commitment of the College and the faculty—

the situation is quite pleasant. Classes are reasonably small; academic freedom is a given; facilities, equipment, and support services are usually provided as far as budgets will allow; innovation and experimentation to enhance teaching are encouraged. In general, the classroom environment and the professor / student relationship are valued and supported. And while some students seem to be in college only to kill time, please parents, or find a job or mate, most appear interested in learning and eager to explore themselves and their world. These things make teaching at MWC very gratifying.

Outside the classroom, however, things aren't always so attractive. Some of the drawbacks are indigenous to the teaching profession and are well known: salaries are notoriously low, the ladder of advancement is short, political power is nonexistent, and workloads are often enormous. Teaching at MWC has some additional disadvantages, however. Demands on the faculty increase almost daily in terms of committee assignments, required paper work (forms, reports, evaluations), and seemingly endless requests to volunteer time and talents for various purposes. Meanwhile base salaries remain low and additional compensation is generally inadequate and often inequitable. . . . We have, however, the classroom to be thankful for. As long as students want to learn, and as long as the study of human thought and action continues to provide meaningful direction for our lives, then the rewards of teaching will remain great.

SOCIAL LIFE

Whether attributable to happenstance or to cause and effect, the beginning of the Anderson presidency was accompanied by a marked improvement in the overall attitude of Mary Washington students toward the College. Part of it may have stemmed from the general feeling that an administration headed by a younger (and presumably less stodgy) president would be more receptive to their wishes. More specifically, students were pleased by his greater receptivity, manifested from the outset, toward relaxing the visitation policy.

Whatever the case, judging by early *Bullet* editorials, the mood of the campus had brightened. "A few years ago," read one, "students would yell 'Don't come here' to tour groups. Now the heckling has stopped and . . . we are now much more likely to speak proudly of our school because there is much to be proud of." Another editorial cited some of those things:

- The number of guys on campus is still a little slim, but it sure is an improvement.
- It looks like 24-hour visitation is on its way.
- The Seacobeck replacement of slop-girls . . . with self-busing

procedures has made dining there more pleasurable. The carnations are nice, too.

- Pig-paths are less noticeable lately. Are students being more conscientious or are the grounds people working (too) hard?
- We are lucky to have MWC maintenance men—they're usually very pleasant, always conscious of our privacy, and very tolerant of constant complaints about roaches and broken window shades.
- The quality of beer at the keg parties is improving. No more, "We have Schlitz, Schlitz, and Schlitz."

Summing it up, yet another editorial concluded that after a long period of "hearing nothing but complaints, we at the *Bullet* acknowledge a positive progression in almost every area of student life."

One of those areas, evidently, involved partying. In a 1985 *Bullet* article titled "MWC Guide to a Good Time," senior Chris Zavrel set out to show that the College did not deserve what he called its "reputation for partying with the intensity of the Mormon Tabernacle Choir" by providing "a brief summation of the party opportunities available in each [dormitory]." The most noteworthy among them included:

- Bushnell: *The 400 Days of Sodom* by the Marquis de Sade is a standard issue reference guide in this dorm. Bushnell is as close to a fraternity house as you can find [in] our quiet confines. [It's] like a spawning ground for social degenerates.
- Framar [the leadership house]: Party opportunities here are rare, but memorable. . . . After seeing our female student leaders let their hair down, one's faith in the effect of beer upon even the most stout of character is strengthened. Just when we thought beach music was dying, these girls keep it alive with a vengeance. Do-wop, do-wah.
- Hamlet: Owner of the Friday happy hour, . . . this dumpy little house continues on in the face of its detractors. Gets awfully quiet the night before LSAT's, though.
- Jefferson: Visitors to our College usually remember two things when they leave on Sunday morning: the preponderance of females and the color of the chair in Jefferson's lobby that they slept in. . . . Seniors know that the Pub never closes, it just moves back and forth between Jefferson and ACL.
- Marshall: Mainly fun dorm, but then again, it would have to be in order to lure people down the Hill.
- Marye: George W.'s mother's name with an "e" on the end, this study house is said to closely resemble her tomb.
- Mason: Momma, don't worry, your daughter is safe here. Gone are the days of weekend-only visitation, though you would hardly know

it. This is the site of some serious pent-up frustration. Freshmen girls away from home for the first time. Ooh, scary.

- Randolph: In years past, the dorm seemed to be influenced heavily by the Gestapo. Not all is rotten in Randolph, however. One hundred and eighty women can't be all that bad.
- Russell: For those girls who consider joining the nunhood, this cloister is the next best thing. Serious roadtripping from this dorm, affectionately known as Hampden-Sydney North.
- Virginia: Don't be misled by the name. Come Friday afternoon, this venerable old barn transforms itself into the female counterpart for Bushnell. Party girls from the word go. Nearly every guy on campus has at one time harbored unclean thoughts about a Virginia girl. [Reflective of that description, Virginia, which was for many years an all-female freshman dorm, was nicknamed by students "the virgin vault" during the first semester and "the slut hut" during the second.]

The *laissez les bons temps rouler* atmosphere, however, did not last, the main reason being a mid-1980s change in the rules governing alcohol consumption. It was not the College that promulgated the change, but the commonwealth, which in 1985 raised the legal drinking age to twenty-one.[19]

There could be little question that alcohol consumption at Mary Washington at that time was extensive, a situation confirmed by a 1980 survey of students' drinking habits conducted by the Alcohol Education and Awareness Committee. The survey was designed by psychology professor Roy Smith, who had lengthy experience as an alcohol counselor and was the author of an alcohol treatment manual called *A Curriculum for Alcohol Education*. Among the survey's findings (some of them surprising) were that

- students claimed to prefer liquor over beer or wine at a rate of two to one, despite the fact that beer was more commonly consumed;
- 16 percent were categorized as "heavy drinkers," defined as consumption of five or more drinks per occasion;
- 14 percent typically drank during the week as well as on weekends;
- 25 percent revealed some problems related to alcohol and 12 percent exhibited severe alcohol-related problems;
- 48 percent perceived "some problem" with alcohol abuse on campus, while eight percent saw a "significant problem";
- there was widespread ignorance concerning the effects of alcohol, particularly misinformation about the relative intoxicant properties of beer, wine, and liquor—the general (incorrect) assumption being that beer was relatively harmless.

The report concluded that alcohol use by Mary Washington students was essentially comparable to that of college students elsewhere—which is to say, there was plenty of it.

The survey statistics were confirmed by anecdotal evidence, easily observed at any keg party and occasionally corroborated by students' own comments. In a 1981 editorial, the *Bullet*, for example, provided a frank assessment of the alcohol-influenced environment. "Although not a tool of prohibition," it declared, "the *Bullet* would like to address the heavy drinking on this campus. . . . We should be honest with ourselves: we can all remember some story from a friend who would tell us, 'I had a little too much to drink last night. Did I have a good time?' . . . It is time we look at ourselves . . . and decide if perhaps we might be doing something wrong. . . . The next time you are asked, 'Did I have a good time?' don't laugh. Identify and deal with the problem. It is there."

Giving such advice was easier than implementing it, however, especially within a campus environment that, either implicitly or overtly, often condoned drinking and seldom punished it. That difficulty was addressed by Professor Smith himself, who explained part of the problem: "Let's say [I'm a student and] that I go out to a party with five or six friends, and I get so drunk that I can't walk. What happens? My friends take me home, sneak me into the dorm, and they talk about how much fun that was the next day. So students with drinking problems don't stand out on a campus where everybody's acting stupid. . . . It's very hard to talk to students about the consequences of irresponsible or problematic drinking when there aren't any [consequences]."

Despite such hazards, there were still many who argued that the legal drinking age should be eighteen, which would allow almost all college students to imbibe. Perhaps the most common justification for that position was that if persons were expected to assume at that age the responsibilities of adulthood, such as voting and military service, they should be permitted its pleasures as well. After all, as one *Bullet* columnist wryly noted, reaching eighteen did allow participation in activities such as "placing an extremely conservative, aging screen actor of B-movies in the White House (for two terms no less), signing up to take out our frustrations on small third world nations, . . . filling your lungs full of carbon deposits, and giving your local, state, and national bureaucracies your bucks."

In addition, some argued that inasmuch as an estimated 70 percent of adults used alcohol to some degree, the college years should provide the opportunity to learn to drink responsibly. To such folks, drinking in college constituted a genuine rite of passage.

Wherever the truth lay, the issue became moot as far as Mary Washington was concerned when the legislature upped the legal age to twenty-one. Within a college culture in whose social life beer had become such a key ingredient, there were bound to be extensive repercussions. Indeed, the following years were characterized by a period of adjustment during which both the administration and the student body grappled—uneasily, haltingly, and not always successfully—with the changed conditions.

Even before the change occurred, the College had begun to address the issue of excessive drinking. In November 1983, as part of a statewide Alcohol Awareness Week, a number of activities were held with the theme "Alcohol in Moderation." One involved "Off Tap" night in the Pub, which went dry for the occasion. The event attracted at least brief attendance from about five hundred over the course of the evening, one of whom commented that "it was fun to just dance and talk to friends without drinking."

An event held at the Pub on another night provided a breathalyzer to enable students to measure their level of intoxication, an opportunity that prompted some students, said the paper, "to see how high an alcohol content they could register instead of really being interested in their physical state." Another test involved a computer set up in the Seacobeck Dome Room that asked participants to state how much they thought they could drink without being impaired; then, based on their body weight and stated alcohol-consumption habits, the computer would pronounce them sober, tipsy, drunk, or, in extreme cases, dead.

When the revised alcohol law went into effect, it produced a range of reactions on campus, not the total opposition that might have been predicted. One *Bullet* columnist, writing as "Dotty Michaels"—there was no real student by that name—lectured her (his?) readers: "Alcohol is not something to fool around with. . . . You're not as mature as you think you are. College is more than one big beer bash."

The volume and vehemence of opposing responses indicated that Dotty's view was by no means universally shared. "While I'll acknowledge the difficulty some students have with drinking," one student wrote to the *Bullet*, "they don't need Ms. Michaels' harangue ringing in their sensitive, overhung ears, . . . for as long as those in authority continue to raise the drinking age, . . . [students] will garner their rebellious strength and drink to be spiteful."

Another student, one of the proprietors of Hamlet House's happy hour, voiced much the same opinion, attacking Dotty more directly. "I wonder at my good luck at never having had the displeasure to have met you. But I suspect I have encountered you before, for I am not totally unfamiliar with sexism, self-righteousness, and hypocrisy. While I agree wholeheartedly that drinking too much can be dangerous, particularly in conjunction with driving, . . . I think that a person's getting bombed is part of growing up. . . . Having written this and feeling better because of it, I think I'll have a beer."

The *Bullet*'s own position on the issue was balanced. "Obviously," said one editorial, "college and high school students won't stop drinking altogether, and it seems that the very illegality of drinking might take the emphasis off the responsible use of alcohol and make its abuse even more common. . . . On the other hand, some of the arguments that students give against the bill are simply childish. The fear of what the new law will mean for sacred campus institutions like the Pub and the keg party is ridiculous. The college would benefit greatly if it were forced to provide more activities that didn't involve alcohol."

That, in fact, is precisely what the College tried to do, organizing non-alcohol events such as "best legs" and "best buns" contests (for both sexes). The most popular event, held annually for a time during Alcohol Awareness Week, was the "mocktail party," a carnival-like affair in Ball Circle, for which each residence hall was encouraged to create a non-alcoholic concoction for sampling by other students. The entries ranged from simple efforts like Custis Hall's sparkling cider served from a brown bag to elaborate recipes such as Marshall Hall's Pink Passion, a combination of cranberry juice, pineapple juice, orange juice, tonic water, ginger ale, grenadine, honey and bitters. Other mocktails bore names as inventive as their ingredients, among them Purple Plague, Pink Panther, Brainless Grainless Punch, Witches Brewski, Rum-less Revitalizer, and Faked Orgasm.

The fact that many students took the anti-drinking campaign seriously was evidenced by the formation of organizations such as a chapter of Students against Drunk Drivers (SADD) and BACCHUS, the acronym for Boost Alcohol Consciousness Concerning the Health of University Students—both of which, with Professor Roy Smith as faculty adviser, worked in various ways to increase understanding of alcohol abuse. Also during the 1980s, Alcohol Awareness Week became an annual event.

Laudable as such efforts may have been, their efficacy was questionable. The mocktail parties drew respectable crowds, but when an alcohol-free event competed with one that offered beer, the beer usually won. On one occasion, a dance in Ball Circle with a live band (but no beer) drew only about thirty students while just across Campus Walk, the Pub, with only recorded music (but with beer) was filled to capacity.

For its part, the administration issued more restrictive alcohol regulations, effective with the fall 1986 semester. The new policy still deemed dormitory rooms to be private, thus permitting alcohol consumption therein by "of-age" students, but elsewhere significant changes were evident. At College-wide events such as Halloweens, beer was still available to of-age students, whose hands were usually stamped to indicate legality, while underage students had to wear hospital-type bracelets to signify their interdiction. "I don't think anyone's being Nazis about this," said Joseph Mancuso, the assistant dean for student life, "but . . . once a few underage people get caught, word gets around."

Mancuso's assessment may have been overly optimistic. An article in the *Free Lance–Star* indicated that freshmen found it easy enough to drink from an upperclassman's pitcher at the Pub or to get an older student to bring them a beer at a keg party. "It's not that big a deal," commented one freshman. "They say the drinking age is 21, but it means nothing."

The most galling regulation to the legal drinkers was the restriction of regular beer sales in the C-Shop and the Pub to weekends only. "College may never be the same," said the *Free Lance–Star* in reporting the new regulations. "The new Virginia drinking age law is enough to make Bluto, the late John Belushi's 'Animal House' character, crush empty beer cans on his forehead and cry in nostalgic anguish. At Mary Washington College, it is Kool-Aid and milk and cookies during the week. MWC has gone dry from Sunday through Thursday."

Students did not respond well to the curtailment, especially the loss of drinking privileges on Thursday nights, which had evolved into the primary time for on-campus socializing, since much of the weekend partying tended to move off campus. Administrators had anticipated an adverse reaction to the ruling. As Dean Mancuso admitted, "We are asking for a . . . sacrifice from the upperclassmen. For three years they have been here and [beer's] been their social life, and now we're cutting it off."

A student Ad Hoc Committee on Alcohol late in the semester conducted a survey that confirmed the extent of student opposition. Of the respondents (the majority of whom, remarkably, identified themselves as non-drinkers), 80 percent disagreed with the new policy, 83 percent believed the effect on campus social life was negative, 80 percent thought it was again making MWC a "suitcase college," and 89 percent felt that it promoted drunk driving by forcing students to seek alcohol off campus. The committee also collected over 1,100 student signatures on a petition to reinstate the sale of beer during the week.

The committee's chair, Philip Schmidt, harked back to a previous source of student discontent to make his point, saying that the new policy was "almost like adding injury to insult rather than insult to injury. Last year [the administration] told us they were going to change the name of the college. Now this." He further claimed that such dissatisfaction was producing a negative effect on student recruitment. "The college is suffering," he said, "not [just] a few kids who can't drink."

Soon thereafter, as the local paper reported it, the controversy over beer "came to a head." Following a two-hour meeting between Schmidt and President Anderson in late November, the administration, for whatever reason it found persuasive, rescinded the policy and permitted beer once again to be sold on campus throughout the week. Not only that, but it announced that the ban would be lifted immediately, rather than waiting until the coming spring semester. "The forecast for Sunday night at Mary Washington College," reported the *Free Lance–Star*, "had said it would be dry. Now it has been revised to cold and wet."

Phil Schmidt was elated. "I think it makes a positive statement about our administration," he said, "It shows that they're not the bad guys that many people perceive them to be. . . . They are very concerned with the happiness of students at MWC."

Rescinding the weekday beer ban was but a stopgap measure, however. To develop a more comprehensive policy, the Board of Visitors authorized President Anderson to appoint a Committee on Campus Social Life in the fall of 1986 with instructions to report its findings in time for the board's meeting the following February.

The "blue-ribbon" group, chaired by Professor Van Sant, had seven faculty members, seven administrators, and eight students (mostly SA and class officers). Students were gratified by the opportunity to play a role in the decision-making process—something that they believed had been largely denied to them previously. "Anyone who has spent more than a week as a student at MWC knows exactly how the students tend to feel about the administration," read a *Bullet* editorial, "and it's not a positive feeling. . . . Obviously the business about the name change last year and the new alcohol policy this year played a major role in strengthening student-administration animosity." In that light, observed the newspaper, including students on the Social Life Committee seemed "one of the most positive student-administrative enterprises we've seen undertaken in a long time."

Although the primary impetus behind creation of the committee was to address the matter of the campus alcohol policy, restiveness concerning visitation policy compelled the group to study that issue as well. In fact, in the view of Van Sant, visitation rules were "much more damaging to the social life and atmosphere on campus than . . . the drinking rules." Most students would likely have agreed. To them, the existing visitation regulations, which had been deemed such a breakthrough only a few years earlier, now seemed antediluvian. In the words of a *Bullet* editorial, "The policy might have made sense to dear Mrs. Bushnell and the girls of Virginia back in 19-whenever, but today's mixed-sex liberal students have a difficult time figuring out its purpose. . . . And to enforce it on today's dorm residents is like telling a female she can't wear jeans to class, or a male to get rid of that hippie-radical-commie-lover long hair. It just doesn't fit with the times."

Indeed, a survey of dorm residents conducted under the aegis of the Student Association in fall 1986 indicated near-pandemic desire for extended visitation. Moreover, a report titled "Why Some Students Choose Not to Return to Mary Washington College," developed by Executive Vice President Ray Merchent, concluded that evidence clearly documented that "the retention rate has been directly affected by the college's visitation policy"—an attitude epitomized in a quote from one transferring student: "My dorm felt more like a prison than a home." The findings prompted Don Appiarius, chair of the SA Committee on Visitation, to call the issue a "powder keg" and to warn that "if it doesn't get addressed, something serious will happen."

Taking such factors into account, Van Sant's Campus Life Committee produced a report that proved to be a powder keg of its own—not on campus but in the community. With regard to drinking, the committee's recommendations were more liberal in some ways, more restrictive in others. For example, under the proposed regulations, all students over the age of twenty-one would be allowed to have wine and liquor in their dormitory rooms, not just beer. Such a practice, according to Van Sant, would simply mean that those students "would have the same privileges other citizens enjoy. They would be treated like absolutely normal adult human beings."

On the other hand, the report recommended serving beer in cans only, not pitchers, at all places on campus where underage students might be present and, in addition, banning students under twenty-one from keg parties altogether. "The old, traditional keg party," said Van Sant, "when the little 18-year-old used to go and get bombed would no longer be possible. . . . A student over 21 certainly has a right to have alcohol. We are trying to move alcohol away from being the center of student social life, but to ban it altogether is insane, stupid. Why make up a rule that's unenforceable?"

The more controversial part of the report involved dormitory visitation rights. It recommended that the existing policy be revised to permit all but first-semester freshmen to have overnight weekend guests.

Word of the possibility of more relaxed social regulations on campus prompted outcries from some sectors of the local community, not unlike the reaction to the earlier visitation decision. Leading the opposition this time was the Reverend E. Elwood Campbell, whose First Christian Church decried what it regarded as the moral decline of Mary Washington College. The taxpayers, claimed the church, should have a say in what was and was not permitted in the dorms, since the College received funding from state coffers.

Van Sant refuted that assertion, pointing out that the dormitories "were built and paid for by past generations of students, present students, and future students—not with tax money. They are bonded. In a very genuine sense, the students own them as much as someone who rents an apartment. They're residents just as much as [if] they had graduated from high school, moved here and gotten an apartment."

Of particular concern to Pastor Campbell and his flock was a visitation policy that, they claimed, was tantamount to implicit approval of cohabitation. "They can go out in the woods and have sex if they want to," said the minister, "but the school shouldn't condone it."

Again it was Van Sant who grasped the gauntlet on behalf of the College. First, he noted, the institution no longer operated on the basis of in loco parentis and was thus not equipped to monitor students' social behavior in the manner of their parents. In fact, he argued, an important part of the College experience for students was their learning to accept responsibility and to discipline themselves.

What infuriated Van Sant the most was the charge that the College's visitation policy promoted illicit sex. "The underlying assumption there," Van Sant protested, "is that the only way men and women relate to each other is in bed. That's an evil-minded assumption. It's demeaning to our students as individuals and especially demeaning to women. That is insulting to our students—very insulting—as students and as human beings."

At its meeting in February 1987, the Board of Visitors authorized social policy revisions that in essence reflected the views of the Van Sant committee. Students were generally pleased, although, consistent with the natural tendency of college students, they would eventually use those concessions as "rights" on which to build demands for further liberalization.

Student happiness over the rule changes in the spring of 1987 was shattered, at least temporarily, the following semester by one of the most stunning events ever to strike the campus. The tragedy involved a student named Christopher Paul Goode, who was an eighteen-year-old freshman that fall.

On the night of Friday, October 23, Goode and a number of his friends had been playing penny-ante poker—and drinking—in his Westmoreland Hall dorm room. Apparently it had not been a boisterous affair; residence life staff members observed that it was an unusually tranquil night in the dorm, with no problems reported. The party in Goode's room broke up shortly after midnight, and he went to bed. Early the next afternoon, when his roommates tried to rouse him, they found that he had died.[20]

Toxicology reports indicated that the cause of death was acute alcohol poisoning, the result of a blood alcohol level of 0.42 percent. Experts noted that to reach such a level—approximately five times higher than that at which a person is deemed legally intoxicated—meant a person of Goode's size (170 pounds) would have had to consume 21 or 22 ounces of 80-proof spirits (or the equivalent of about a case of beer) within an evening. A police search of Goode's room found empty bourbon and brandy bottles, as well as beer cans. Among his personal effects was discovered his twenty-one-year-old brother's driver's license.

News of the death spread quickly throughout campus, where it was met initially not so much with a sense of horror as of disbelief. A first-semester freshman, Goode was not widely known among the overall student body, although he was apparently an exceptionally personable and popular young man who had made many friends in his freshman dorm. The College brought in counselors to help students deal with their grief and canceled several campus events, including the showing of *Days of Wine and Roses*, the Academy Award–winning film about alcoholism scheduled to be shown in Goode's dorm on Saturday. The College also chartered two buses to transport eighty-five students to Goode's funeral in Berryville, Virginia (near Winchester), and a memorial service was held on campus the following week.

As president of the College, Bill Anderson was both saddened by the death of a student and frustrated by an environment that allowed it to happen. "We slave away trying to work on this problem," he said. "You tell them, you tell them, you tell them. But it's just an incredibly difficult problem, if not impossible task, to beat into their heads that [alcohol] is a loaded gun."

The president expressed sympathy not only for Goode's family but for the young man's friends at the College. "It's going to be a while before they learn to live with this," he said. "They'll never get over it. It's a tragic situation, and you shouldn't have to go through this to learn a lesson."

It was, in fact, questionable just how much students did learn from it or, at any rate, how long the lessons lasted. Within two weeks a *Free Lance–Star* writer observed that his conversations with students indicated that "the senseless death has barely caused a ripple in the consciousness of the student body beyond a brief jolt of shock and disbelief." In the words of one interviewee, it seemed that "although students are not callous about the tragedy, they are 'blowing it off' as far as it being a warning to themselves."

Besides being tragic, there was also an irony in the death of Chris Goode: it occurred in the middle of Alcohol Awareness Week.[21]

In the years that followed, the College administration attempted the difficult task of devising an alcohol policy that would inform underclassmen of the law—and, more importantly, protect them from themselves—while at the same time not unduly circumscribing the rights of drinking-age students, who understandably resented such restrictions. The policy that resulted was hardly a seamless one, as it fluctuated periodically as a consequence of events both on campus and beyond.

In 1988 the Pub went dry, though some of its social functions were taken over by the new campus center. (When it was announced that the Pub would be reincarnated as a beer-free facility, one student wag suggested that it be renamed the "Sahara Club." Its name actually became "The Underground.") Though the new venue seemingly offered many advantages, some students bemoaned the demise of the Pub, in all its uninviting dankness. As a nostalgic *Bullet* editorial lamented:

> Tonight, meaning Thursday night, I was sitting at Carlos O'Kelly's—can you believe it? Out on a Thursday night? Why at Carlos O'Kelly's you may ask? Well, to tell you the truth, I see more Mary Wash students there than I do at the C-Shop or the Pub on a Thursday night. . . . Can anyone remember getting ready to go to a kegger? Putting on your "kegger shoes" and standing in line at 7:00 or 7:30 for a kegger that started at 8:30 or 9:00. At the kegger you could mingle with tons of different people, dance, fall on the slimy floors and stand in line for an hour to get to use the restroom. Well, folks, those good ole days are gone. . . . It's not like it used to be on campus [when] . . . we had to stand in line to get into the Pub so that we could have a hot, sweaty, slimy good time.

In 1990, as part of a federal grant, Mary Washington implemented a policy to help excessive drinkers by requiring frequent violators of the College's alcohol policy to be evaluated for counseling and possible treatment; Rhonda Angel was hired as alcohol education director. The alcohol policy was but one part of a "community standards" program that allowed dorm residents to make their own rules (within certain parameters) for their halls, including regulations for matters such as visitation, telephone usage, and laundry-room schedules. With regard to drinking, the program called for alleged violations to be handled by student peers rather than decided by the dean of students.

Self-policing did not always work, however, and by 1992 incidents of excessive drinking led the administration to place a moratorium on the serving of alcohol at dormitory-sponsored parties. The reason for the ban, according to Assistant Dean for Residence Life Peter Lefferts, was the high incidence of underage drinking (with high alcohol blood levels) at such events—not a surprising situation, considering that only about 15 percent of the campus population by that time was of legal drinking age.

Student bacchanalias were further inhibited in 1993 with the passage of a stricter state law concerning the purchase of kegs. Purchasers were required to state the location where the beer would be served and to avow that none would be served to underage persons. The law immediately had a sobering effect, both literally and psychologically, on would-be partyers, as local distributors noted a precipitous decline in sales to College students.

More stringent policies, coupled with what some regarded as overzealous enforcement by dormitory RAs, generated rising resentment among numbers of students. The issue became a matter of mounting concern to President Anderson, especially when it was suggested that such negative attitudes constituted an important element in the overall sense of dissatisfaction that was impelling an alarming number of students to consider transferring.

Accordingly, in the spring of 1995, he urged the residence life staff (specifically the RAs) to be more flexible in enforcing dorm regulations—in short, to be guided more by the spirit of the rules than the letter. "This is not a police state," he said. "It's not meant to be that. RAs are not supposed to replace mothers and fathers. . . . What goes on in a person's private room, as long as it's not disruptive to the rest of the student body, and as long as it doesn't create any unsafe conditions, is in my opinion [permissible]."

When some RAs protested that such a policy put them in an awkward position—in essence, undermining their authority—Anderson explained further: "It's a two-way street. You tell students you want them to act in a responsible way and that their room is their private place. I don't think [therefore] they ought to sit in that room worrying who is going to break through their door at any moment."

At the same time, Anderson emphasized to students that they must be responsible for their actions. "When that doesn't happen," he warned, "You are not allowed to have these parties. If you don't live up to expectations . . . then you [won't] have all the freedom."

Most students were doubtless pleased by the relaxation of enforcement, though some found the whole situation ludicrous. Addressing what he called "the bitchy masses who think that MWC should party like Ohio State," one senior *Bullet* columnist scoffed:

> HA! There are only 6 million differences between the mongo party schools and little tadpole institutions like MWC—only one of which is that you can't sit around buck naked with dozens of svelte blondes who will feed you grapes, while administering your liquor enemas just because you are the secretary-treasurer geek of the partyinest cool guy frat on the quad. Suck it up! When you enrolled in MWC cer-

tainly you didn't think that you would be attending a Mecca of 500-keg parties, enjoying the Playboy channel in your dorm room and getting free grass from everybody's stoner friend named Weed who has been in college for 16 years and is a sophomore. You came here to get an education, and if you can't manage to have fun and get bombed in the process then you just aren't trying hard enough.

As the 1980s moved toward the nineties, increasing numbers of Mary Washington students looked beyond the campus for social life, either by frequenting area bars and restaurants or by actually moving into the community to live.

Though expanding, the options for dining and nightlife in Fredericksburg were still somewhat limited in the mid-eighties. A *Bullet* columnist in early 1984 proffered a tongue-in-cheek guide to the possibilities. The best places to eat, he said, were:

1. P.K.'s: A fine place to play dress-up.
2. La Petite Auberge: Name means "Eats" in French. Must be good because it's so expensive.
3. Carl's Ice Cream: A paradise for cream-a-holics.

The worst, he warned, were:

1. Green Room
2. Rose Room
3. North Room
4. South Room

The best places for nightlife, in his estimation, were Arbuckle's and Sammy T's.[22] The worst was the Beehive (actually a popular place with students because of its proximity to campus), which he sarcastically described as the "place where Marines get drunk and act cool, [making] one feel very confident in the state of the nation's security." The Parthenon, also near the campus (and also popular) was denigrated as a place where "you get to watch Steve [the owner] yell at his family and create grease."

Area restaurants had proliferated by the mid-nineties to include a number that were touted in *Bullet* reviews, among them (downtown) Sophia Street Station, Spirits, Where the Buffalo Roam, and Merriman's; (in College Heights) Ryan O'Brian's and the General Store; and (in the Route 3 shopping centers) Carlos O'Kelly's and Ruby Tuesday's. Some carved out particular niches, such as Merriman's, which attracted a large gay clientele.

Students, tending to put priority on drink above food, were more interested in bars—of which there was no shortage by the 1990s. Among the first to establish themselves following the demise of 1970s hangouts such as Art's, the Latch String, and My Brother's Place were the downtown pubs, the Irish Brigade and Sammy T's, joined in the early nineties by Spanky's and the George Street Grill, as well as Danny's in Falmouth.

Several of the newer watering holes were owned by recent graduates whose establishments catered specifically to the College crowd. One of the first was Christopher's, whose location in the Holiday Inn some ten miles north of campus did not keep it from attracting hordes of students, especially on Wednesday nights, when it was routinely packed. Closer to campus was the less raucous but similarly magnetic J. Brian's Tap Room in downtown Fredericksburg.

Of all the pubs, the most popular from the time it opened in 1992 until it changed ownership (and name) in 1996 was Mother's. It was also the one that catered most assiduously to College students, as was evident from its name, and particularly to the rugby team, with whom it shared that name. Located in a 140-year-old clapboard train station on Lafayette Boulevard, Mother's decor was that of a typical sports bar, with TVs filling the spaces on walls adorned with MWC sports photos and rugby memorabilia. In addition to providing potables for thirsty students, Mother's held numerous fund-raisers to benefit College clubs and projects.

Frequenting local bars to evade campus rules was not without its own risks, particularly for underage drinkers who used fake driver's licenses as IDs, a misdemeanor punishable by up to a year in jail and/or a $2,500 fine. Despite the threat of such a penalty, the practice was prevalent. Within just over four months of its opening, for example, Mother's confiscated almost 150 false licenses, including over 40 from Austin, Texas, alone, according to the pub's manager. (MWC students were less likely to alter their College IDs for that purpose, since it would constitute an honor offense.)

In an effort not only to escape campus restrictions but also to evade barroom legalities, increasing numbers of students opted to live off campus. Not all students who did so were motivated by partying proclivities, of course; some even moved for the opposite reason—to find a haven more conducive to study than that of the typical dormitory. But for whatever reason, off-campus residency became a major characteristic of life at Mary Washington in the eighties and nineties.

Partying in students' houses resulted in occasional confrontations with the local police and led periodically to embittered community relations. On several occasions in 1994, town-gown tensions flared over house parties that drew upward of two hundred students. In response the College police, with the cooperation of the state ABC and local police officers, set up a sting in August of the following year that led to eighteen arrests, mostly MWC students, on drinking and related charges. "The college very much wants to be good neighbors and an integral part of the community," said College Police Chief Greg Perry.

The students themselves did not go out of their way to deliberately offend townsfolk, but judging by the *Bullet*'s attitude, neither were they particularly concerned about violating community standards. Employing a perhaps ill-chosen analogy, a 1994 editorial declared, "The community may not like the fact that college students throw parties, but neither can they change that fact any more than they can keep birds from flying over your car and . . . well, you know."

Of the alcohol-related infractions by students, the most widely publicized story grew out of a 1995 strip poker game involving two female soccer players. And not just any players, either: one was the Capital Athletic Conference's player of the year, and the other made the all-conference second team.

The episode occurred in the wee hours of September 22 at a party hosted by the two players at their rented house near campus. Earlier in the evening, police had arrived in response to complaints from neighbors about noise, whereupon the party broke up, temporarily. However, as the *Bullet* reported, "The night was still young, and stragglers from bars and campus showed up at the house 'late-night.'" That is when the strip poker game commenced. According to one male soccer player who was present, before long almost everyone was naked. "We had a rule," he explained, "that if you were already naked and lost the next hand, then you had to run around the house," adding, "I think sometimes [we] forget that when we leave campus, we go out into the real world."

Right he was. The two hosts, apparently less skilled at cards than at soccer, eventually found themselves unclothed—and unlucky. Upon losing subsequent hands, they made the obligatory lap around the house in the buff, right before the covert gaze of a Fredericksburg policeman. Having called in reinforcements to help deal with the (obviously) unarmed miscreants, the officer proceeded to arrest the two young women for indecent exposure, operating a common nuisance, and violating the city's noise ordinance. Seven male students (all soccer players) who were present were cited for underage drinking.

The episode instantly made news, not just locally but in the national media as well. Though hardly an earth-shattering event—"just a bunch of kids acting stupid," according to one of the males—the story was picked up by papers across the state, by the *Washington Times*, and even by *USA Today*. "Noise, Naked Romp Produce Arrests," ran a *Richmond Times-Dispatch* headline; "Streakers Bare All at Raucous Party," leered the *Washington Times*. "Mary Washington College has finally made a name for itself," ranted an editorial. "Mary Washington officials have wanted to soften their school's stodgy image," said the *Times-Dispatch*, "but they got the kind of help they didn't want when students were arrested for off-campus streaking and other rowdy behavior." All told, it was the most extensive notoriety the College had received since the Mary Cate Carroll and name-change controversies of over a decade earlier.

Bill Anderson was not amused. "Our image is that of an academically demanding institution and we've worked hard to earn that," he said. "Students want to see the other side . . . [but] we certainly didn't have the events of the other night in mind" as a way to portray that side.

On campus, the *Bullet* was livid, not because of what the students had done but because of the tone of the media coverage the episode received.

> People up and down the east coast now know of our institution. We actually made the national news. Why? Because a couple of soccer players decided to play strip poker. For years we went unrecognized, and now suddenly everyone and his mother have heard of MWC. It seems a little sad that the only way Mary Washington can put itself on the map is by having a couple of our fine athletes expose themselves. . . . Had a game of strip poker been played somewhere besides a conservative small-town college, it never would have received national coverage. Had this incident occurred at UVA or JMU, nobody would have batted an eye. But just because it happened at little Mary Washington, everyone had to start talking about it. People play strip poker all the time. . . . Get over it!

The paper was probably correct in its charge that the incident was exaggerated in the press because it happened where it did. But it might also have attributed the avid coverage to sexism, since it would have been a far less titillating story had the players not been women.

In any event, at their November trial in Fredericksburg General District Court, the two women were convicted; each was fined $200 and ordered to perform fifty hours of community service. The College punished them by suspending them for three games. The men involved were all fined $50 apiece for violating the city's noise ordinance; the charges of underage drinking were dropped. Their soccer coach, Roy Gordon, meted out penalties in terms of suspensions ranging from one to three games.

Though the misadventures of the two streakers were the most publicized, the female soccer players were not the only Mary Washington athletes around that time to run afoul of alcohol laws, either those of the commonwealth or those of the College. Indeed, in the spring of 1995, over half of the members of the men's and women's swimming teams and basketball teams were charged with some type of alcohol violation, and seventeen basketball players were suspended from the team.

The problem had reached sufficient proportions that the Athletic Department in 1996 devised a standard policy to cover drinking infractions on all of the College's teams, both during the season and in the off-season. According to that policy, any student athlete caught drinking in the off-season would receive a one-game suspension the first time, a two-game suspension the second time, and expulsion from the team the third time. In season, a second violation would result in expulsion from the team.

Some student athletes expressed considerable opposition to the policy, claiming the penalties were too harsh. "It's kind of like they're trying to control your life too much," said one. "I think they're trying to send a message about drinking," commented another, "but the off-season is the off-season, especially at a Division III school." Among the more interesting responses was that offered by one of the soccer strippers, who suggested that "people deserve a second chance, maybe just a warning for the first offense, if it isn't too bad." But the Athletic Department stuck with its decision. As Athletic Director Ed Hegmann put it, according to the *Bullet*, "When well over 50 percent of four teams are involved in alcohol-related incidents with lots of publicity, a proactive stance in the policy is needed."

The behavior of some of the athletes—who, as a group, probably held themselves to higher standards of behavior than most students—simply underlined the extent of the drinking problem and the difficulty the College faced in trying to control it. Raising the legal drinking age seemed to have little effect in decreasing consumption. A study of drinking habits on eight state college campuses in Virginia conducted by the Institute for Substance Abuse Studies at the University of Virginia in 1990 revealed that 93 percent of students over twenty-one said they drank; for those under twenty-one the number was almost identical: 92 percent.

Rhonda Angel, who headed Mary Washington's alcohol awareness effort, admitted some frustration. "They're more cautious, but I don't know that means they're drinking less," she said. "Peer education generally doesn't have an impact on students' reducing their drinking. At that age, they're not concerned about long-range health." Echoing that sentiment, Executive Vice President Merchent, who had observed student behavior over the course of many years, noted that illegal drinking on campus was "extremely difficult to control without becoming a police state."

But even that may not have been enough, judging from an observation made by one of the late Christopher Goode's hall mates. Commenting on the tragedy several years later, he recalled that the next weekend after Goode died, all his (underage) friends went out drinking. "There isn't much that can stop kids from drinking," he said. "In this case, not even the death of our friend."

Drinking was not the only social activity that students engaged in. There was also sex.

That young men and young women were interested in each other was hardly a new phenomenon, of course, but the openness of sexual relationships by the 1980s revealed a far different attitude from that of previous generations. Evidence of this at the College was amply demonstrated by numerous articles contained in the February 8, 1983, *Bullet*, an issue devoted almost totally to an examination of various aspects of the sexual climate on campus at the time.

One thing was clear: chastity was no longer a valued commodity—by either sex. According to one male columnist, almost no males thought chastity important. And it was well that they did not, since a female essayist, in an article titled "Virginity: Not an Easy Choice for MWC Students," reported that "after an exhaustive search for virgins, it is obvious that they are becoming rarer and rarer." It could scarcely have been otherwise in an environment where, she wrote, "everyone . . . treats sex as casually as handing out a piece of gum . . . [and where] knowing someone's first name [is] about the only prerequisite for sex."

Virginity, in the estimation of most college-age students, had seemingly come to be more stigmatized as evidence of inexperience than prized as proof of virtue. According to one male *Bullet* columnist, "It is almost impossible to find a girl who will *admit* to being a virgin." (He added parenthetically that he found it "hard to believe many guys would admit to this either.") This was in 1983. Things would get worse—or better, depending on one's point of view.

Several articles in the *Bullet*'s "sex issue" addressed the matter of relationships between men and women on campus in the context of the increasing male population. Clearly there was some friction, as evidenced by gender-bashing jokes:

Q: What is a good-looking guy at MWC?
A: A tourist.
Q: What is the difference between an MWC girl and a toilet?
A: A toilet doesn't follow you around after you use it.

The latter question actually reflected females' main complaint about male students—namely, their belief that the disproportionate presence of women enabled men to treat them shabbily, sometimes even abusively, without penalty. According to one writer, almost all females he interviewed said they knew "at least one guy who was 'real nice' when he arrived at MWC, but has since had an ego explosion." The problem, said one female, was that the typical male student was "like a little kid in a candy store because of the numbers."

And there were additional problems. As another writer observed, "One roadblock to relationships is the virtual caste system" on campus. "When," he asked, "was the last time you saw a shirtless frisbee player with long hair and a bandana walking around with a girl with turtles all over her pants, a green and pink sweater, and a name like 'Biff,' or something equally peculiar?"

Despite such impediments, many relationships (both the physical and the more emotional kinds) did develop on campus. A *Bullet* survey of both sexes revealed what each mainly sought in the other. "What exactly does a guy look for in a girl?" asked one writer. His answer: "Blonde hair, long legs, an incredible figure, and lots of money." But he hastened to explain that his comment, while not totally untrue, was only a small part of the answer—that, in the course of his research on male attitudes, he had "found those traits were mentioned only secondarily, if at all. Most guys only briefly alluded to the outward attractiveness of a person and seemed more concerned with what the person was like, their attitudes and opinions, their inward personality."

The survey of female students likewise placed nonphysical attributes at the top of their list. When asked to name the three things that most attracted them to a man, "sense of humor" ranked first, with 88 percent of the respondents citing it as a major factor; far behind in second place was "physically fit body," with 65 percent. Other desirable qualities cited, in descending order of preference, included the following:

- Overall personality, 61 percent
- Fair intelligence, 49 percent
- High intelligence, 33 percent
- Confidence, 31 percent
- Maturity, 26 percent
- Honesty, 24 percent
- Nice hair, 18 percent
- Ambition, 17 percent
- Sensitivity, 17 percent
- Nice derriere, 5 percent
- Sharp nose, 1 percent

Though women apparently did not regard physique as the most important factor in male attractiveness, evidence indicates that they were not immune to carnal concerns. There was, for example, the popularity of several "beefcake" calendars published beginning in the 1980s featuring MWC men.

The first such calendar was produced in 1983 by two enterprising junior roommates, Kathi O'Rourke and Becky Rogers, as part of an independent study for their marketing class. The project was inspired by a much-publicized "Men of UCLA" calendar; the Mary Washington version was considerably more modest, featuring no nudity and little that was even suggestive.

Discussing the project in a *Free Lance–Star* article, the two creators explained that they originally considered using couples as models but decided against it because "they change so often." Having opted to photograph men only, they chose students from each class, as well as "representatives from each social clique." They noted that they did not endeavor to "pick the 14 best-looking guys on campus . . . [but] the ones that would sell." The only freshman was Pinson Neal, the son of the rector of the MWC Board of Visitors, Gail Neal, who expressed approval of his posing along with the other males. "It gives MWC a different image," she commented. "We'd like people to know there are men here."

As for the models themselves, some had initial trepidation, including star basketball player Frank Gilmore. Aware of the fleshy content of the UCLA calendar, Gilmore said, "When they told me I'd be on the cover, I thought, 'Oh boy, Mom's going to love this.'" But, he later recalled, when she saw the calendar she hardly recognized him because he was wearing a suit.

Despite subjecting themselves to predictable razzing from their male peers, the models appear to have relished the opportunity to become campus celebrities and to have enjoyed the social dividends paid by their new status. "I only wish," said one, "they'd printed my phone number underneath my picture."

The calendar was an immediate hit on campus, selling 140 copies within the first week at $4.00 each. That success prompted O'Rourke and Rogers to publish another one the following year. Which is where trouble started.

The problem arose not from the calendar itself—which, like the original one, was relatively chaste in its photographs—but from an article about the calendar written by *Free Lance–Star* columnist Mike Zitz based on interviews with O'Rourke and Rogers. According to Zitz's article, Mary Washington women were guilty of using the College's males, whom they generally disdained. "The girls are the bad guys in this situation," he quoted O'Rourke as saying. "They're sweet to the guys here all week long. Then it's 'Bye-bye, I'm going to find something better at U.Va.'"

From such comments, Zitz deduced that "MWC women tend to toy with MWC men during the week, then hit the road on Friday to see the 'real' men at the Naval Academy and U.Va. . . . Apparently the women of MWC buy the calendar to look at the pictures, chuckle, and pencil in dates and times for road trips that leave the men of MWC far behind."

Such assertions triggered an enormous cry of outrage from all quarters of campus, but most especially from O'Rourke and Rogers, who claimed that they had been tricked and misquoted by Zitz. The protests were sufficiently vehement to prompt the reporter to write to the *Bullet* "before Becky Rogers and Kathi O'Rourke are run off campus" to say that they "were not traitors to their school for giving the interview." Though his letter was not exactly a mea culpa, he did make clear that "the two women themselves did not disparage MWC men. They merely offered opinions on what they believe the prevailing attitude is," and went on to say that neither they nor he held negative opinions about the men.

It was a position that O'Rourke and Rogers themselves emphasized in their own letters to the *Bullet* and to the *Free Lance–Star*. Noting that Zitz had told them before their interview that he intended to write a light, tongue-in-cheek article, they declared, "If there was a light-hearted tone threading its way through Mr. Zitz's article, the thread was severed by the cutting edge of injustice that he perpetrated on both the men and women of Mary Washington College. . . . The true purpose of our calendar [was] to promote the image of MWC in general and the men in particular, who, by the way, happen to be as real and respectable as any Cadet or Wahoo around."

With that, the controversy waned, and publication of the calendars continued sporadically in subsequent years. Sometimes they were used by campus clubs to generate revenue and, in addition, to promote campus social life. As the president of the Women of Color club (which sponsored the 2002 calendar) put it, one goal was to address the fact that "girls always complain about how there's not enough cute guys on campus, or not enough guys, period."

Despite occasional imputations of sexism, the calendars, indicative of changing cultural currents, tended to become somewhat more risqué with the passage of time. Describing the 2002 edition, the Fredericksburg newspaper noted that "college heartthrobs flaunt sultry looks, sexy poses and sensitive props to spice up the school year." As if in corroboration of that depiction, one of the models commented, "I was thinking about going in a leopard thong, but they vetoed it."

Also popular in addition to the calendars, and considerably more lewd, were male striptease shows sponsored by rowdy Bushnell Hall. "Would anyone else have dared?" wondered the *Bullet*. And even then, the phenomenon begged credulity. "A Strip Tease show at Mary Washington College—can you really comprehend it?" asked the paper in 1984. "If you have been here more than a few years, . . . you might have some difficulty."

The *Bullet* review of one such extravaganza was titled "Bushnell Bares the Beef"—though it suggested that "there was probably as much ham as beef on the stage." It apparently mattered naught to the female audience. "Their mothers would be proud," said the paper. "Not since they last wore diapers have their sons looked so good. As each one stepped into the limelight, they were greeted with hearty cheers, and frantic female screams, stamping feet and clapping hands. . . . MWC's own 'Chippendales' hopped about . . . sporting black pants, bowties and glistening muscular chests," egged on by cries of "Take it off!"

The show ended with what the *Bullet* called "MWC's biggest tease," who capped his performance by "gradually wriggling out of full fatigues and shades, to Frankie Goes to Hollywood's 'Relax,'" whereupon, "when the clothes were finally off, [he] delivered some of the best bumps and grinds probably ever seen on campus."

For those whose libido required more than visual gratification, the *Bullet*'s "sex issue" offered a humorous reference guide to local motels (just in time for Junior Ring Week, it pointed out). The piece was cast in the intentionally transparent guise of informing students "about motels in the area so they can tell their parents which is the best place to stay. *"Repeat,"* said the introduction, *"the following information was gathered to aid you in your choice of where Mom and Dad should spend the evening."* It then listed a number of local motels, evaluating each on the basis of convenience and cost, including the following assessments:

- By far the closest motel to campus is the Thomas Jefferson on Augustine Avenue. . . . Although there is no room service, the 7-Eleven is right next door. The rate there for a double occupancy is $18.75.
- The next closest establishment is the fabulous Twi-lite right across the street from McDonald's. The Twi-lite has less character and charm than the T.J., though, and is less discreet (for those of you with discreet parents). The rate there is $18.95.
- The Colonial Motel [downtown] is a bit drab, but they have color T.V. That in itself is worth the $20.00 they charge.
- The Fredericksburg Colonial Inn is a whopping $35.00 [but] . . . there's a bookstore in the same building. Mom and Dad might enjoy browsing.

- For those of you who are cheap (uh . . . I mean have cheap parents), the Econo Motor Hotel . . . only costs $26.99 plus tax.

"Remember," concluded the article, "smart travelers plan for Junior Ring Week early."

In reality, owing to the relaxation of dormitory visitation rules, the time was rapidly arriving when student trysts did not necessitate making off-campus arrangements. While students appreciated the change, local motel owners probably did not—nor, certainly, did some alumni, who were shocked by it. One graduate from the class of 1930, identifying herself as a "disgusted" past president of the Alumni Association, vented in a letter to the editor of the *Free Lance–Star*, "I think the next step to be taken at Mary Washington College is to decorate the dorm parlors with red velvet drapes and gilt-edged mirrors, spray the parlors with '*Joie d'Amour*' and put red lights on the porches. Then the dorm mothers [a dated term if ever there was one] can say, 'Just call me Madam.'"

But in the sexual revolution all was not fun and games. The *Bullet*'s "sex issue" itself suggested as much in a cautionary article that thoughtfully warned against the potential damage to society posed by the loosening of sexual constraints—a time, it said, "when rock groups purvey all manner of suggestive lyrics, and when popular magazines use the likes of Brooke Shields in her scant attire to boost sales. . . . The likes of 'Three's Company,' 'Love Boat,' and all the rest . . . [reflect] a culture which reduces gratification to pleasure, pleasure to sex, and sex to copulation. . . . The sexual 'revolution' of recent years will cure itself with its own excesses, given enough time, [because] humans, it has been said, cannot know what is enough until they know what is too much."

Philosophical musings aside, there were often practical problems that students had to confront. Not the least of those was unwanted pregnancy, which, the advent of the pill notwithstanding, apparently still occurred with alarming frequency. "It was like an epidemic on my hall," said one student in 1983. "Practically everybody I know was getting pregnant and having little alternative but to have the abortion."

Even if such a claim was exaggerated, there were doubtless a number of abortions, all of them traumatic to those involved. "I often feel that I was a real murderer," continued the same student, "but there wasn't anything I could really do that wouldn't have ruined lives—including the baby's. It's strange how you rationalize things to ease your conscience, . . . but when you're in a desperate situation, you do desperate things. . . . It was almost [a choice] between a baby and my sanity."

In addition to the possibility of pregnancy, increased promiscuity led in the eighties to a growing incidence of sexually transmitted diseases (or STDs, the newer term for what had previously been called venereal diseases). According to one male student, restraint (such as it was) had come to be less a function of morality than of the "ever-present herpes virus." More prevalent on campus than herpes, according to the Health Center in 1988, were gonorrhea, chlamydia, and pubic lice (crabs) among the STDs.

Far more fearsome than any of those, however, was the more recently discovered AIDS (acquired immune deficiency syndrome), the disease produced by the human immunodeficiency virus (HIV). Unlike other STDs, which could usually be treated effectively with medications, AIDS had no cure and generally led to death.

Notwithstanding the lethal nature of AIDS, and despite evidence that it was rapidly spreading, Mary Washington students through the 1980s appeared generally unconcerned about its potential effect on them, for several reasons. The underlying one was the simple but universal fact that college-age people tend to believe themselves impervious to such misfortunes. AIDS in particular seemed less of a threat because it was usually associated with large urban areas and their higher population of drug users (since the virus could be spread by infected needles). Mainly, however, student indifference was attributable to the belief—incorrect, as it turned out—that the disease was essentially limited to gay men.

Eventually, as the epidemic spread beyond the cities and into the heterosexual population, such misperceptions were rendered demonstrably untrue, and the College began to address the problem more aggressively on several fronts. Much attention was devoted to educating students about the disease. As early as 1985, the *Bullet* began to carry feature articles periodically on such topics as "AIDS Facts, Myths Explained" and "AIDS: The Real Facts." The library developed an informational exhibit under the direction of Special Collections librarian Brenda Sloan, and the Biology Department sponsored a panel discussion titled "AIDS: Sexual Transmission, Demographics, Societal Impact" with presentations by Professors Rosemary Barra, Rose Mary Johnson, and Thomas Johnson.

Great emphasis was placed on encouraging students to practice safe sex by the use of condoms, which the Health Center made available. "We're selling more condoms," reported Dr. Ilma Overman, the center's director, in 1992, "and the funny thing is, women are the ones who buy them. . . . I don't care who buys them," Overman added, "just so they use them." Health Center nurse Nancy Yates agreed. If it could keep students from "getting AIDS or getting any other sexually transmitted disease," she said, "then students should carry condoms. The idea that nice girls don't carry condoms is ridiculous."

Condom use was promoted in several ways, beginning with freshman orientation sessions in which peer counselors ("mentors") demonstrated proper technique by putting condoms on bananas. "That was my favorite part of the program," said one freshman, "[but] our mentor was a little shy about it." The residents of Virginia Hall pursued the same approach in a 1992 party on the theme, "Safe Splitting/Safe Sex," described by the dorm RD as a "hands-on approach to safe sex." After using bananas for demonstrative purposes, the students then consumed them in banana splits.

Beginning in 1991 the College participated in National Condom Awareness Week in February, starting, appropriately, on Valentine's Day. Activities included the sale of T-shirts and "condom-grams," which were Valentine messages accompanied by a red "Cupid Condom." Approximately 125 shirts, bearing a ribald rhyme, were sold, and the number might have been higher except that some students would not buy them because, as the *Bullet* reported, "they felt that, although they would wear the shirts on campus, they were afraid of what the reaction at home might be. 'If my mom did my laundry . . . ,' was a familiar expression." As one student put it, "Where am I going to wear this? I have three little brothers!" ("We sent President Anderson a condom and a T-shirt," said the program's coordinator, "but didn't get any response.")

Students also distributed literature suggesting things a woman might say if a partner balked at wearing a condom. If, for example, he said, "I won't feel as much if I have a condom on," an appropriate response could be, "You won't feel *anything* if you don't have a condom on."

Nothing more clearly demonstrated student interest in matters of sexuality in the eighties and nineties than the developing concern over issues relating to homosexuality. As the 1980s began, there was an active Gay Student Union (GSU) on campus. An established member of the interclub association, it promoted understanding of alternative lifestyles by sponsoring a Gay Awareness Week and showing movies such as *La Cage aux Folles*.

Within a couple of years, however, interest declined. "A few years ago," wrote a *Bullet* columnist in 1983, "the issue was a hot one on campus, . . . [but] today Mary Washington students don't hear too much about gay rights." As liberal activist professor Alice Rabson recalled, "[Straight] students were very afraid of the GSU. They would rip down signs and were afraid that their [i.e., gays'] lifestyle would rub off on them."

By the mid-eighties, activism had diminished to the extent that one lesbian student complained in a letter to the *Bullet*, "It seems that 'gay' is a taboo word on campus. Because of this, most gay students, including myself, have to hide their true nature under a shell of protection. They think that their friends will shun, avoid, and ridicule them." Early in fall 1986, the *Bullet* observed editorially that "there is an issue here at Mary Washington College that is seldom, if ever, addressed. It is the existence of homosexuality and homophobia."

It was not long before that situation was reversed when, for a period of time beginning in the late eighties and culminating in the early nineties, homosexuality became a dominant issue on campus. Foreseeing that trend in 1988, one student leader in a letter to the *Bullet* predicted, "Where drugs and war were the 'hot' topics of the '60s, homosexuality will be the powderkeg of the '90s."

The issue was ignited by an isolated incident that took place late in the fall 1987 semester when an anonymous flyer with the heading "IMPORTANT ANNOUNCEMENT" appeared at the tables in Seacobeck. "Don't miss out on this one-time offer," it read, "*one way* plane or bus tickets for all who qualify (and you know who you are) . . . for your trip to San Francisco where the rest of your 'buddies' are. . . . You will only find a deaf ear here at the college for your requests of participation in [gay rights] marches on the Capitol."

In addition to provoking a number of heated letters to the *Bullet*, the flyer also stimulated various campus activities supportive of gay rights, including a published petition to that effect signed by over two hundred students and faculty. The SA Senate debated surveying the student body to determine whether homophobia was sufficiently rampant as to necessitate a concerted campaign against it. The motion to instigate such action ultimately failed, but not before it had generated what one member of the group called "more controversy within the Senate than any other issue in several years."

What it did succeed in doing was to resuscitate the moribund campus gay activist group, which was reincarnated as the Gay, Lesbian, and Bi-Sexual Student Association (GLBSA). The club became especially active during the 1990–91 session under the leadership of its president, Mortar Board member Amy Martel. Assessing the prevailing campus attitude toward homosexuals, she observed that "as long as we're in the closet, they love us"—but the time had come, she asserted, for a more active approach: "We're not going to take it anymore. We will not let people discriminate and walk all over us. We're demanding equality and respect and kindness."

Toward that end, the GLBSA sponsored a Gay Awareness Week in the spring of 1991 with the theme "It's a gay thing. Let us help you understand." Activities during the week included readings from gay and lesbian literature by selected faculty members; presentations by the president of the metropolitan Washington division of Parents of Friends and Lesbians and Gays and by two Washington, D.C., men who described their ongoing attempt to obtain a marriage license from the D.C. government; and sponsorship, in conjunction with Hillel, of a documentary on the persecution of homosexuals during the Holocaust.

The week's concluding event was a Friday night dance in the Underground, which the GLBSA advertised as being open to hetero- as well as homosexual students. It nonetheless led to threats against those who attended the dance. According to one male student, some homophobic types were saying that they intended "to come and beat up some 'fags' and 'dykes.'" That led to beefed-up security because, as Russell Hall residence director (and GLBSA adviser) George Sedano put it, "I don't want a death of a student before they [the administration] say, 'Oh, my God, there are gays and lesbians here.'"

In retrospect, it was Sedano himself who was central to the week's most provocative event, a workshop he led on society's fear and hatred of homosexuals. The following year he was not rehired, an action that the *Bullet* reported under the headline "George Sedano: Out of the Closet and Out of

Work." That description reflected Sedano's own theory of his termination, though the administration attributed it to a reclassification of his position as part of efforts to economize. "The decision had absolutely nothing to do with his sexual orientation," explained Dean of Students Joanne Beck. "We don't mind what kind of lifestyle people have."

As for Gay Awareness Week itself, the overall impact was hard to gauge. Noting the appearance of T-shirts and signs with messages such as "Homosexuals Are Worthless" and "Homosexuals Are a Waste of a Good Orgasm," the *Bullet* charged that during the week "gay-bashing was almost cool." The paper was aghast at the overt homophobia. "What if people had posted signs during Black History Month declaring: 'Go Back To Africa?' Or during Women's History Month: 'Stay Barefoot And Pregnant?' Would the college have reacted as passively as it does towards similar attitudes towards homosexuals? We think not." It seemed to the *Bullet* that the awareness week, while "designed to unite and foster better relations between homosexuals and heterosexuals," had actually "in some ways . . . further polarized the campus."

Several of the most heated debates arose, somewhat surprisingly, over the matter of clothing. One of the gay activists' perennial tactics, going back to the mid-eighties, was to encourage the wearing of certain apparel on designated days to show support for their cause. It was an approach that some "straight" students seemed to find particularly offensive. "Not everybody supports homosexuals," said one letter to the *Bullet*. "On 'Jeans Day,' non-supporters were forced to not wear something they might normally have worn, for fear of making an unwilling statement. Had [that day] been a chilly day, I would have had to spend the day cold, rather than sacrifice my principles."

Even some semi-sympathetic students had qualms about that particular form of protest. One student explained his position in a *Bullet* "Commentary" column. When the designated Jeans Day arrived, he wrote, "I stepped outside in my robe to see how warm it was. It had turned out to be a nice day, perfect for either jeans or shorts, but remembering what the GLBSA was doing, I decided to wear jeans, which I assumed most people would do. Boy was I wrong! To my surprise, almost nobody wore jeans that day. Unfortunately it wasn't due to the nice weather. I received many looks from people, and for the first time on this campus I felt very self-conscious about what people thought. Quite frankly, it pissed me off! . . . To be honest, I was worried about being labeled a homosexual."

Undeterred by such reactions, the GLBSA in the fall of 1992 sponsored B-GLAD (Bisexual, Gay, and Lesbian Awareness Days), which included not one but three days designated for wearing specific types of attire: jeans on Wednesday, sneakers or tennis shoes on Thursday, and T-shirts on Friday. When met by conscious defiance on the part of some students, the GLBSA spoke out in a *Bullet* op-ed column: "If changing your wardrobe for three days seems too inconvenient, keep in mind that every day, homosexual and bisexual people have to make the same choices not only about what we wear, but also what we say, and to whom, and where we go, and how much controversy we want to cause by defending our rights to live openly and without fear."

Yet another clothing-related controversy, albeit of a different kind, erupted about the same time over the wearing of a T-shirt by the GLBSA president, Jay Vanover, that proclaimed in bold capital letters: ABSOLUT HOMO. Most likely all would have been well had not a *Bullet* columnist taken Vanover to task in an op-ed article. "Now I would like to make a point clear," declared the writer. "I have no bias towards gays and lesbians. Hell, I even D.J.'d their dance last year. I think that the [GLBSA] is a worthy organization and I commend them on their efforts to enlighten the students on this campus about a very sensitive subject. This 'ABSOLUT HOMO' stuff, I am not too hip on because I think that it hurts the gay/lesbian image more than it helps. . . . Wearing a shirt that announces what you are is just plain obnoxious."

That blast provoked such an extraordinary spate of letters in rebuttal the next week, including an impassioned one from Vanover himself, that the paper had to carry some over to subsequent editions. As Vanover explained later, the columnist's argument amounted to "demanding I take a silent, second-class status and hide my sexuality. For him to be so offended by my T-shirt shows that he can't imagine what it's like to be gay. That [the T-shirt] is not a millionth of what I see every day. If the tables were turned and I was to write an article about the offending heterosexual things I encounter, I would have to write about every Colgate commercial, every gum commercial, everything that I see."

Just how pervasive and virulent was anti-gay sentiment at Mary Washington? Undeniably, it was present. But how did it compare with homophobia on other campuses?

By some indications, it seemed not to be as bad as elsewhere. Even the activist Vanover noted that while the environment at MWC was "far from perfect," it was an improvement over what he had experienced at other schools. Overall, he said, "Mary Washington isn't a bad place to be if you're gay." The leading faculty authority on such matters, psychology professor Chris Kilmartin, tended to agree. Though critical of the depth of homophobia in American society at large, he suggested that at Mary Washington, "We're better off than a lot of places in that we don't have the football teams or fraternities that are the usual hypermasculine institutions on college campuses."

There was, in fact, some feeling—rarely articulated and then covertly expressed—that Mary Washington was actually more attractive to homosexuals than were most colleges. As early as 1984, one regular columnist in the *Bullet* noted that "some well-informed persons believe the gay population at MWC to be higher than the national average." That situation was alluded to years later by George Sedano, the former residence director, who commented that, in conversations with him, "A lot of students said they were attracted to MWC because there was no pressure. Those who came out [of the closet] in the end of high school thought MWC would make it easier to come all the way out of the closet."

With regard to attitudes within the College community, Vanover noted that he had encountered "a few" homophobic faculty members but felt that "in general the faculty is more supportive than the student body and a million times more than the administration." But even the faculty was divided over the issue as evidenced by a 1990 vote on a proposal to add sexual orientation to the list of discriminations prohibited under the College's Statement of Community Values and Behavioral Expectations. Though the motion passed, the vote revealed a close split on the issue, as fifty-one voted in favor and forty-seven in opposition to the addition.

Yet a trend toward greater acceptance of gays was beginning. Despite initial reluctance, the Board of Visitors did eventually add a sexual orientation prohibition to the Statement of Community Values.

Also, some campus developments indicated a less judgmental attitude. One such occurrence involved the "coming out" of Jason Bryan, an RA on a Russell freshman hall. Having waited until near the end of the second semester in the spring of 1993 to do so, Bryan called a hall meeting to announce his sexual orientation. According to the *Bullet*'s account, that announcement received unanimous support from his students who "supported him, at least on a personal level, even if they did not agree with his practices." It was a response that the *Bullet* found gratifying, but rather surprising, because, said the paper, "Russell First North is a 'guys' hall.' Here, political correctness is a foreign concept, the humor is obnoxious and even base, and the housekeepers complain constantly about broken furniture and nude [female] pictures on the bulletin board."

The most dramatic event in the bouleversement surrounding sexual orientation on campus arrived in early 1993 with the coming out of geography professor Donald Rallis. The son of British parents, Rallis was reared in South Africa, whence he immigrated to the United States in 1982 at the age of twenty-four to avoid military service in an army that he felt was "defending apartheid and not the country."

Ironically, it was a military matter that prompted him to avow his homosexuality at Mary Washington—namely, the Clinton administration's establishment of the so-called "don't ask, don't tell" policy. Having generally hidden his sexual preferences theretofore, Rallis was so appalled by that policy that he felt compelled to speak out against it as a homosexual. And when he did, he was not bashful, addressing the matter in a lengthy, eloquent, and impassioned *Bullet* op-ed piece. "I am gay," he wrote,

> and I am angry. I am angry because I and millions of other gay men and lesbians have been repeatedly maligned and insulted in the ongoing debate over our admission to the armed services. . . . Perhaps the most insidious argument of all is that which tells us that it's acceptable to be gay, it's even OK for us to serve in the military, provided we stay in the closet. . . . There are many excuses for homophobia, but there is only one real cause. It's not morality, or family values, or the Bible, or

the preservation of the American way. The cause is bigotry pure and simple. It is the fear and hatred of people who are different.

Rallis's announcement stunned the campus, eliciting a mixture of support and opposition from students and faculty alike. Later that spring business professor Patricia Metzger, taking advantage of the campus buzz, organized a forum on homosexuality as part of her seminar on equality. The event, skillfully moderated by religion professor David Cain, consisted of a showdown between Rallis and the faculty's most outspoken foe of homosexuality, economics professor Stephen Stageberg, a self-described born-again Christian.

Event organizers vastly underestimated student interest in the forum, which was scheduled for the two-hundred-seat Monroe lecture hall. When that venue reached capacity long before time for the forum to start, it was hastily moved to Dodd Auditorium, prompting numbers of students to race down Campus Walk to get a good seat in the new location. By the time the event began, even that capacious hall was filled to capacity with a crowd estimated at over 1,300.

Recognizing the sensitive nature of the issue at hand and the potential for emotional crowd reactions, moderator Cain made a preemptive effort to encourage decorum. "This is not a debate," he told the audience. "It is not a contest or a competition. It's a forum. The name of the game is understanding." That admonition no doubt helped to set a decorous tone. But the fact was that most in attendance expected some verbal fireworks, and few were disappointed.

Stageberg spoke first, employing extensive biblical references to argue his primary case that homosexuality was sinful, not so much because of the physical acts themselves but because such acts represented rebellion against

Stephen P. Stageberg

Donald N. Rallis

God's will. He also suggested a possible physical cause of homosexuality, making reference to a biological study that, while inconclusive, indicated that the hypothalamus might be smaller in gay men than in heterosexuals.

Taking aim at the latter comment, Rallis drew the largest laugh of an otherwise tense two-hour session when he began his remarks by saying, "I bring you greetings from the world of the hypothalamusly challenged." He proceeded to reiterate many of the points he had presented in the earlier *Bullet* article and to cite wrenching examples of persecution he had endured as a result of his homosexuality.

Though civil, the exchanges between the two professors were often pointed, with the sharpest clashes occurring over biblical interpretations regarding homosexuality. Stageberg asserted that the Bible explicitly condemned homosexuality, citing Leviticus 19:22, which says, "Thou shalt not lie with mankind as with womankind: It is an abomination." Rallis responded that the Bible contains only six references to homosexuality—none of them in the Ten Commandments. The number of references was not important, said Stageberg: "God only has to say it once, and it's law." To which Rallis remonstrated, "I respect the faith of my colleague and those who agree with him, . . . but I vigorously oppose any effort to force me and people like me to become victims of a faith to which we do not subscribe."

Audience responses indicated preponderant sympathy for Rallis, who received a standing ovation at the conclusion of his remarks, whereas Stageberg received less enthusiastic applause. The responses prompted one student during the subsequent question-and-answer session to complain about the lack of a standing ovation "for God," a comment that led moderator Cain to take exception. "I'm not sure," he said, "it was a question of no one standing up for God."[23]

Actually, the forum was one of the fairly rare occasions when a debate on a highly incendiary topic yielded light as well as heat. Indeed, in retrospect, it appears to have marked something of a watershed in the progression of campus views on homosexuality. There would surely be examples of anti-gay sentiment in the future, but in general, the tone of the campus increasingly inclined thereafter toward tolerance.

Student interest in matters of sex was not only participatory; it had an academic side as well. Beginning with the 1990–91 session, a course titled Human Sexuality, taught annually by psychology professor Steve Hampton, was perhaps the most popular on campus, rivaled only by Marshall Bowen's Geography of Anglo-America.

Combining lectures, movies, slides and guest speakers, Hampton's course investigated topics such as anatomy, physiology, contraception, birth, sexual behavior, homosexuality, pornography, and prostitution. He made it clear from the outset that it was "not an advocacy course" but one that would "deal strictly with facts and [let] the students . . . make their own choices," adding, "It's sad when we have a culture of people who can have sex, but can't talk about it."

The success of the course led a *Bullet* humor issue to suggest that a new general education category would be added to the curriculum: Modes of Motion. The requirement would necessitate completion of six to nine credits (plus lab work) chosen from courses such as "Sex and Shakespeare," "Finding the G-Spot," "Condom Control," and "Psychology of Abstinence and Frustration."

"Sex is hot at MWC," announced the paper. "In a climactic moment, the board of visitors overwhelmingly voted in favor of this popular new requirement. One BOV member, who asked not to be named, said, 'Students should be more willing to get their homework done now. I wish we had these educational opportunities when I was a student.'"

Although some Mary Washington traditions endured throughout the closing decades of the twentieth century, others were significantly affected by changing mores in general and by the higher drinking age in particular. College-wide formal events tended to decline in popularity over the course of time, while class-specific events, like Junior Ring Dance and Grad Ball, basically maintained their popularity.

Fall and Spring Formals, in particular, lost some of their appeal, though not all students took so jaundiced a view as the *Bullet* columnist who in 1983 wrote of the fall dance, "It is kind of nice, but not a whole lot more romantic than the Beehive. . . . . All the girls who criticize MWC guys for being jerks or worse, are there with their boyfriends from other places. For the most part, these guys are real clowns [who] usually spend the night hugging the porcelain or fighting with one another."

The foremost annual event whose popularity persisted into the 1990s, much to the chagrin of its detractors, was the Wo-Man contest, the drag show initially conceived in 1977 as a parody of beauty contests. Originally sponsored by the Afro-American Association, it was later taken over by Hamlet House, the leadership hall for males.

Throughout the eighties, despite its vulgarity (or maybe because of it) Wo-Man was one of the highlights of the fall social calendar, regularly drawing hundreds of students to Dodd Auditorium. There they witnessed the dozen or so contestants go through their paces: modeling formal wear and swimsuits, performing their "talent" and answering questions from the emcee extempore. It was not for the thin of skin or high of brow. According to one *Bullet* columnist, it was "absolutely the most outrageous night of the year. We're lucky that none of the local community morality watchers have ever been to a Wo-Man contest. If they had, we would never hear the end of it."

The contestants themselves seemed to enjoy the affair immensely from

Wo-Man contestants

start to finish, beginning with the procurement of their attire and practicing their talent routines—activities that usually required the assistance of a female sponsor. The process was colorfully described by one of the participants in the 1985 contest in a *Bullet* column called "Making of a Wo-Man."

First, he explained, he had to find the "perfect female sponsor," one who was "talented, bold, wild and downright kinky." Once he found her, the two set out to purchase his "Madonna-wear" for the evening from the local Thrift Shop, the preferred couturier for such events. Her eye for style produced a wardrobe that included "a flaming red gown with a deep v-neck and slit down the side . . . a slinky black and red French-cut bathing suit, . . . and a black lace bra. At this point," he said, "I was about to lose my cookies, so my sponsor and I paid the $1.63 we owed and left the premises smelling like used gym socks and not knowing what diseases we had just picked up."

Then there was the dance routine to be practiced. "We tramped down to the [dorm] basement, plugged in the ghetto blaster and blared the music. We must have practiced for hours. My sponsor was one tough taco; I must have lost 10–15 pounds in sweat. She told me I was a mean, lean drag queen. She pushed me to my limits: 'Jump, bend, thrust, move those hips! Act sexy!' Need she say more?"

As for the actual event, the humor was usually low-wattage, the talent minimal. Skits were sometimes inventive and topical, such as one 1986 contestant's performance of an original composition, "The MWC Ratio Blues," in which his female persona crooned,

I look to the left,
I look to the right,
No matter where I turn,
There's not a real man in sight.

For the most part, in the words of one student, the humor was "on about a fourth-grade level."

Few appeared to mind, though, as students continued to attend the event in large numbers, even as its standards of decorum, never high, spiraled downward, and its attempts at humor, both visual and verbal, became more ribald. Each year the *Bullet* printed, with evident delight, lengthy reviews of the raucous revue including verbatim accounts of the presumably witty repartee. (Sample: In response to the question of what fruit he/she would most like to be, one contestant replied, "I'd be a vegetable. I'd be a cucumber. A cucumber doesn't give you heartaches—all it gives you is satisfaction.")

Eventually, however, criticism began to develop as increasing numbers of people were offended by what they regarded as the sexist, homophobic tenor of the event. Such attitudes were expressed in a letter to the administration before the scheduled 1988 performance, written by philosophy professor Craig Vasey and signed by forty faculty members. The petition urged that the College cease to allow Wo-Man to be held on campus, calling it a "particularly inappropriate sort of activity" in light of the Statement of Community Values.

The letter went on, generally, to analyze what it viewed as the historical and psychological foundations of Wo-Man and, specifically, to deplore its sponsorship by Hamlet House:

> The comic potential of such shows as Wo-Man is grounded in the sexist nature of the culture, and the historical fact that women are, as a group, subordinate to men. There is room for wondering if Wo-Man is not a male expression of resentment at the transformation of that power differential. . . . The leadership house should represent a break with the worst elements of our society's past and present, and a move towards something better. The exploitation of traditional bigotry for cheap laughs and entertainment is not . . . a worthy example of leadership. . . . I am sure that you would not approve of a black-faced contest, but . . . Wo-Man is only different through the substitution of gender for race.

When, unmoved by such plaints, the sponsors persisted in their determination to hold the event, the opponents organized a protest against it. Joining faculty members in picketing the performance were representatives from three student groups: the Progressive Student Union (PSU), People for Alternative Lifestyles (PAL), and the National Organization for Women (NOW). As one member of NOW explained her opposition, "Wo-Man portrays women as being either sluts or frigid, and all of them as bimbos."

The Hamlet House sponsors, of course, did not see it that way. House president Thad Matthews, an African American, rebutted the critics' charges. "I've experienced racism first-hand," he said. "If Wo-Man was racist or sexist, I would be the first person to disassociate myself with its production. . . . It's just good clean American fun. The guys dressed up in women's clothes are not mimicking or stereotyping or making sexist jokes; they are just clowning around and having fun. . . . I see this as making fun only of contestants, because they are making fools of themselves."

Professor Vasey wasn't buying such protestations of innocence. He continued to assert that the event was politically and socially offensive, as well as exploitative. "Wo-Man makes money," he said, "by imitating female and gay mannerisms, sexuality, and stereotypes, and exploits traditionally sexist attitudes. Just because the sponsors [of it] believe that it does not offend and debase gays and women, does not negate the fact that it has this effect."

When, after all the verbal skirmishing, the 1988 edition of Wo-Man did take place, the small number of protesters outside Dodd, compared to the huge, cheering crowd inside, indicated where the preponderance of opinion lay on the issue. The *Bullet* also endorsed the event editorially, claiming that First Amendment rights were being threatened in what it portrayed essentially as an effort by killjoy faculty members to censor student expression.

Unfortunately for Wo-Man's advocates, the repugnant behavior of some of the contestants in 1988—as if to verify the critics' accusations—furnished further evidence of the event's descent into tawdriness. According to the Fredericksburg paper's account, "During one dance routine, a contestant in a miniskirt and pantyhose raised the skirt, first to reveal his buttocks and then his genitals to a hooting crowd. . . . [Another] wore a minimal string bikini during the bathing suit portion of the show and turned around to display his derriere as the crowd roared."

Whether prompted by the badgering of their critics or by the emergence of a long-latent impulse of decorum, the residents of Hamlet House voted unanimously not to sponsor Wo-Man in 1989. "Hamlet is a leadership house," explained hall president Bill Donovan. "We are supposed to set examples on campus and in the community. . . . The event doesn't reflect the way Hamlet is this year." But it was only a brief hiatus, as they announced plans for its return the following year, touching off yet another round of controversy, with many of the same arguments proffered on both sides. "They know perfectly well it's an embarrassment to the college," declared Professor Vasey. "There's no reason to do it except to cause some trouble."

Opponents' pleas to President Anderson urging cancellation of Wo-Man were refused. Though not personally fond of the event, he nonetheless defended the students' right to produce it. "This is an institution for learning and an institution for freedom of speech," he said. "Of all settings, a college setting is not where thought and expression should be constrained."

The president's pronouncement had the unusual result of earning him praise from the oft-adversarial *Bullet*. "We applaud the administration's hands-off policy with regard to this particular controversy," read an editorial. "This is a simple First Amendment issue. You know: freedom of expression, choice, etc., etc. . . . No one should dictate who can participate in or view such exhibitions of stupidity."

The Fredericksburg newspaper took much the same position, and for the same reason. Noting recent widely publicized efforts at censorship of a Florida concert by 2 Live Crew and an Ohio art exhibit by Robert Mapplethorpe, a *Free Lance–Star* editorial asserted, "There is a troubling trend in this country to impose government controls on free expression. . . . Congratulations to President Anderson for seeing beyond the men's lipstick. . . . The real issue [is] free speech, however unusual its trappings."

A regular columnist for the paper, Rob Hedelt, who attended the performance, also expressed approbation, not because of weighty constitutional issues but simply because he found the production harmless. In a piece titled "Whoa, Man—What's All the Fuss?" he wrote, "These Hamlet boys put a little vamp in their revue, at times shaking body parts and sashaying in a way that would never be allowed in Bible school. But there were no hurtful comments aimed at women, gays, straights, Arabs, Jews, Anglo-Saxons, Moors, Muslims, poetry-lovers, or left-handers. . . . I'm sorry, [but] it's time for these people [opponents] to chill out, to quit taking everything in life so seriously. This show is a joke, people. Just a bunch of goofy guys dressing up in girls clothes to get laughed at and raise some money for charity. . . . Big deal. Don't like it? Don't go."

It had appeared that the 1990 version of Wo-Man might be a bit more restrained than prior performances. Chastened by criticism of the previous one, Hamlet president David Canatsey admitted that "1988 was a bad example of Wo-Man. It got out of hand . . . [and] was in poor taste." Plans for the 1990 performance included prohibitions against some of the problems evident in earlier productions, notably excessive alcohol use by the contestants. "We want to show that it can be done right. We want to show that it can be done in good taste, and can be a classy event," said Canatsey.

Alas, in the pageant's opening segment, a junior contestant bared his buttocks, whereupon he was removed from the stage, arrested for being drunk in public, and incarcerated in the local jail. So much for classiness.

That was pretty much it for Wo-Man. Though it still had its defenders, the event was generating increased disgust. Even one Hamlet resident commented, "It's . . . extremely offensive to gays and women. I'm ashamed to live in Hamlet."

Executive Vice President Merchent also voiced disapproval. Though years as an administrator had imbued him with a high tolerance for student foibles, even the amiable Merchent had seen enough. "No one should be hurt, intimidated, or embarrassed because of [Wo-Man]," he said. "It's a fundraiser at the expense of women. To poke fun is bad, but to use it as a means of making money taints it further."

The truth was that the show, however innocent its original intent, had changed—and not for the better. Much of its initial comedic appeal had come to seem dated at best, demeaning at worst. "It became overly crass," wrote a *Bullet* editor, "when the contestants consistently relied on sexual innuendos to gain crowd approval. And most of the acts lacked creativity and variety. I wouldn't consider watching someone drunkenly dance and fall all over the stage [to be] talent."

Humor often resides in a rather narrow space between the amusingly risqué and the merely raunchy, and as time went on, many Wo-Man performers, inspired more by alcohol than by wit, tended to cross that boundary. In light of the direction of pop culture at that time, it would be difficult to argue that students by 1990 possessed more exquisite sensibilities than earlier ones; yet it was nonetheless evident that interest began to flag when the performances veered from the clever to the crude, and the once-sprightly burlesque came to be viewed merely as a sodden exercise in boorish exhibitionism.

The demise was put aptly by a student who said simply, "The time has come. Wo-Man isn't funny anymore."

During the eighties and nineties there was another tradition that outlasted Wo-Man and was less controversial, though sometimes almost as boisterous: Halloweens. Throughout those decades it was by far the most popular fall party on campus.

The festive mood surrounding the event was reflected in, and abetted by, the College newspaper, which often contained articles relating to Halloween. In 1983, for example, it published what it called "Gruesome Tunes . . . The Best Halloween Songs of All Time." In addition to the classic "Monster Mash" by Bobby "Boris" Pickett (once self-described as "the Guy Lombardo of Halloween"), the list included "Werewolves of London" by Warren Zevon, "Witchy Woman" by the Eagles, "Frankenstein" by Edgar Winter, "Voodoo Child" by the Jimi Hendrix Experience, and "Haunted House of Rock" by Whodini. (Of the last, the writer observed, "Any fresh rapper knows that this jam . . . is the deffest Hallow-rap of them all.")

Another issue, years later, offered a guide to "creepy places" in the vicinity of the College. "Fredericksburg," it said, "is one of those places like 'Buffy the Vampire Slayer's' Sunnydale where the deceased seem to outnumber the living." Among the sites of horror listed were the Masonic Cemetery on Charles Street, the Civil War's Old Sunken Road, and the long-abandoned Maury School building. There was also the railroad station underpass. "Blame this one on the story of the Billy Goats Gruff," said the article. "The image of trolls living under the bridge to terrorize you dies hard, especially here [where] the air smells dank and stagnant, even though it's an open space."[24]

As for celebration on campus, there were usually various activities in addition to the Halloweens dance. One was Madison Hall's Haunted House party. Having begun in 1977 as part of Circle K's Halloween party for area children, it was soon converted to a students-only affair when it was deemed too frightening for the children. Campus film fare for the season usually consisted of horror movies such as *Psycho*, *Poltergeist*, *Cujo*, and *Nightmare on Elm Street*.

The central event was the Halloweens costume party itself, first held in 1977 in Lee Hall, moved in 1980 to Goolrick, and finally to the Great Hall in 1987. The event brought out the ingenuity of students, who often spent days planning and preparing the outfits they hoped would win the prize in one of several categories such as best group, scariest, funniest, and most original.

Some costumes appeared perennially, including superheroes (Superman, Spider-Man, Batman), monsters, and hookers. Foods and drinks often inspired guises: M&Ms, Hershey's Kisses, milk cartons and six-packs of beer. Sexual themes abounded, including safe-sex items such as condoms and a pack of birth control pills, as well as one 1987 contestant who went as "Abstinence," dressed in all white, wearing a halo, chastity belt, and padlock, with "NO" written on her back. On the other extreme were four females who each wore a letter: P, L, A, and Y ("foreplay").

Some of the most inventive costumes were those relating to the campus or the Fredericksburg area: five males, for example, dressed identically in overstuffed police outfits to emulate "Earl," the burly campus security guard; another group went as "Frednecks," each with his own cardboard four-wheel-drive truck. Framar often produced the best group efforts, including such creations as a happy hour (with each student as a different cocktail) and a Seacobeck meal.

Topical costumes through the years constituted a historical kaleidoscope of pop culture, including a Rubik's Cube (1981), Trivial Pursuit pieces (1984), and a bong (1986). Especially notable in 1987, according to the *Bullet*, were the "California Raisins [who], looking like they just stepped out from the TV, danced on stage as Spectrum [the band] played 'I Heard it Through the Grapevine.'"

A decade later, contemporary student interests were revealed in the appearance of outfits emulating the Spice Girls, the dogs from *101 Dalmatians* and Princess Leia of *Star Wars*. The coarsening trend of American culture was evident in some costumes. "A particularly preferred ensemble," reported the *Bullet*, evoked "the disco/porn era [as] girls strutted their scantily-clad stuff in short skirts and go-go boots, while the men of the evening took the opportunity to show off their chest hair and polyester attire."

The event always seemed to loosen inhibitions. In a *Bullet* article titled "Confessions of a Halloween Slut," the writer told of her decision to dress one year as an '80s pop star, for which she

> found the perfect velvet and taffeta dress at Goodwill, cut off the skirt so it was appropriately scandalous, and ripped up some fishnets. I finished it off with my roommate's gold heels and some purple eye shadow. When I walked into the party, the initial reaction was exactly what I wanted: stares. The only problem was, no one knew that I was

a pop star. Most peoples' guess? Crack whore. . . . I was fully aware that I looked like a prostitute, and it didn't particularly bother me. . . . This is puzzling coming from [a woman] who every other day of the year might be described as independent, educated, and quite opposed to being looked at like a piece of meat. But there's just something about Halloween.

Eventually the popularity of Halloweens waned, the victim of larger social changes taking place at the College. Once the event became dry on campus, most students chose to party elsewhere. By the turn of the century, the spirited tradition was essentially defunct, having died of thirst, not old age.

Another campus tradition that declined in the nineties was the competition among residence halls for the best Christmas decorations. The demise of the practice began when the semester calendar was changed to hold exams before the holiday, thus creating a greater need for pre-Christmas studying. In addition, the proliferation of student activities during that season, both on and off campus, diminished the role of the dorms as the foci of social life.

A more specific factor was a federal court ruling in the mid-nineties prohibiting the use of state funds to promote religious ideals, a decision that created uncertainty on campus as to whether such decorations were legal. Irrespective of legal questions, there were considerations of cultural appropriateness. "In the past," observed one Jewish student, "things such as manger scenes have been put in the dorms and this really upset Hillel."

As a result of such concerns, the College's Association of Residence Halls (ARH) and the Council on Community Values and Behavioral Expectations in 1994 developed guidelines that encouraged dorms to adopt "an 'appropriate theme' for the contest in order to avoid promoting any one religion and to encourage 'a more global approach.'" What this meant in practice, according to 1996 ARH president Noah Ristau, was that "the residence halls needed to . . . take into account the diversity of the students living in the dorm. If the hall decides to take a religious approach, then they should adopt a multicultural theme."

The first traditional social events of the spring semester were two celebrations involving seniors: 100th Night and the night corresponding with the number of their graduation year. Both events became more popular over the years, as there were fewer scheduled occasions on which classes were brought together as a group. The parties thus offered rare and prized occasions for class bonding. Describing the 100th Night party of the class of 1986, the *Bullet* explained that the event "has long been an honored tradition at MWC marking the last 100 days of life as it exists for the senior in irresponsible youth. To most seniors, the 100-day landmark does not simply offer a reference point for the final countdown of graduation; no, it holds much more significance than merely numerical value. 100th Night is a time for seniors to congratulate themselves for enduring over three and one half years of books, lectures, exams, and all-night parties."

Such celebrations were also an excuse for unbridled revelry. As one *Bullet* columnist put it, "Why is it you get crazed on a night like 84th Night? . . . I lost my keys, I.D., invitation, and gold-pearl lipstick . . . before the night had even begun. However, the worst part of 84th Night was the morning after. A friend came to the door at the ungodly hour of 11:15 and reminded us we could have been drinking V-8 instead of that volatile grain punch and beer delight. . . . Yet, I could go for a 74th Night, a 64th Night, a 54th Night, a 44th Night, a 34th Night, a 24th Night, a 14th Night, and even a 4th Night. It's addictive. I'm sure I still wouldn't drink V-8."

Though the events were traditionally held on campus, changing alcohol laws led them to be moved to off-campus venues for a period of time. One year, for example, 87th night was held in the nearby vacated Safeway store; on another, it was held at the Fredericksburg Fairgrounds in an unoccupied cattle barn. The cattle barn provoked some complaints about the austerity of the surroundings, but such considerations were overcome by what one senior described as "numerous shiny aluminum cylinders, each containing 15.5 gallons of liquid consolation." The same student, in a *Bullet* column, noted, "I was told I had a great time. I guess so. All I know is that [the next] morning I would have paid big bucks for a Coke. Thank God it's not 1999."

That comment revealed a problem that arose concerning the two events as the end of the century approached: they were coming too close to each other. Accordingly, in 1989 the graduation-year parties were converted to 100 plus the year of graduation (e.g., 189th Night), which meant that those celebrations thereafter came in the fall semester.

No matter when the parties were held or where, one thing never changed: copious consumption of beer. Despite the best efforts of groups such as BACCHUS to promote sobriety, guzzling inevitably played a large role in the festivities. "Dancing became extremely difficult," read the *Bullet* account of the 1987 100th Night in Seacobeck basement, "as the quantity of beer on the floor matched that in the bodies of the dancers, but the faithful sloshed on." The next year the venue was the Great Hall, but the ambiance was the same. " 'Kegger shoes' were definitely called for," reported the paper, as "the seniors danced to such old favorites as 'Shout' and to more recent music ranging from Janet Jackson to U2. . . . Many seniors remarked about how this reminded them of 'the great keggers we used to have.' "

Although many campus social functions at Mary Washington (and, of course, other colleges as well) involved alcohol, it seemed for some reason drinking was inordinately emphasized at the 100th and class-year nights, with each class trying to imbibe more lustily than its predecessor. "Seniors Dry

Out Eight Kegs of Beer on 196th Night," said a *Bullet* headline, followed the next year by the bold-lettered announcement "Seniors Kick Nine Kegs, Breaking 196th Night Record."

A lengthy *Bullet* article describing the 100th Night party for the class of '96 provided not only a good account of the event but also a sense of the revelry that was characteristic of the traditional senior celebrations. It noted that many students primed themselves by visiting pubs such as Spanky's or the George Street Grill for "pregame" refreshments before arriving at the Eagles Nest. Soon enough, it said, the room

> smells like a true keg party [as] the first scents of spilled beer mingle with body sweat. . . . Oh yeah, this is a party. . . . So many men here! Rumor is one third of the student body is male. Who could prove it until now? They are ALL HERE NOW! Every senior one of them. Men drinking, men talking, men dancing—most with a girl on each arm. . . . The dance floor is packed. . . . Everywhere, in twos and threes, classmates pose for flashing cameras. There is a lot of hugging going on . . . [as] nostalgia is heated by alcohol. . . . The floor is a pool of beer. . . . A girl slides to her knees, streaking her black pantyhose with slimy beer sludge up to her MWC plaid skirt. . . . The DJ is playing "Ants Marching" by the Dave Matthews Band. The crowd sings loudly, hands flailing through the air. . . . The Eagles Nest director hollers, "Welcome to insanity!"

In the course of the evening, nine kegs of beer (five Rolling Rock, four Molson) were consumed on a pay-as-you-go basis at one dollar per cup. Near the end of the evening, reported the *Bullet*, "the DJ plays 'Y.M.C.A.' and the crowd roars. . . . Everyone is singing again. The room is bouncing rhythmically; the crowd dances with itself. . . . Midnight comes and 'Y.M.C.A.' ends, the music stops, lights are on. . . . Everyone is friends, comrades, fellow classmates with one identity tonight—the class of '96. The cheer begins, ' '96! '96! '96!' and gets louder and louder."

Finally, at the prodding of Associate Dean of Student Activities Cedric Rucker, "the class of 1996 disperses in pockets heading to other parties. Some linger in the cold on the brick walkway—some hugging and some crying. This is the beginning of the end."

Indeed it was—and not just for that particular class party. Unbeknownst to the revelers, the whole boozy tradition of 100th Night itself would soon come to an end.

The spring semester's next opportunity for campus socializing was Valentine's Day. Although not celebrated formally by a major traditional event at Mary Washington, the day was often marked by smaller theme parties and special dates for individual couples. The *Bullet* usually acknowledged the occasion in some way, as in 1989, when it proffered assistance for prospective amorous encounters by publishing a list of what it termed "turn ons/turn offs for girls and guys," which included, from the female perspective, the following advice to men:

- Take her off campus
- Open doors, pull out chairs, be a gentleman
- Pay for her meal, unless the two of you previously agreed to go Dutch
- Keep a condom in your wallet

Some things were considered to be bad form for males, such as:

- Going out with a girl in your dorm
- Smelling better than she does
- Assuming she's sexually active
- Assuming she's on the pill

From the male standpoint, females were urged to:

- Be decisive and assertive
- Be open to conversation
- Be adventurous and spontaneous
- Be honest

On the other hand, turn-offs included:

- Scoping other guys
- Putting yourself down (you're really not *that* fat)
- Running to the bathroom every ten minutes
- Ordering only salad and crackers.

Following Valentine's Day, students eagerly anticipated Spring Break, which, being scheduled usually for the first week in March, began while the weather in Fredericksburg was still wintry; on more than one occasion, the vacation started amid significant snowfall. Most who could do so generally headed south, sometimes using cut-rate package deals offered by local travel agencies. Preferred destinations included Cancun and assorted Florida locations, notably Key West.

A *Bullet* columnist, Dave Saunders, writing in 1990, claimed that "when it comes to having fun on Spring Break, MWC students outrank all others"—in contrast to "when we are stuck in Fredericksburg, whining about the alcohol policy or visitation." The latter concern was apparently not left behind even while Saunders was luxuriating in Key West, as he described in his article. "I found myself on a crowded beach, clutching a banana daiquiri," he wrote. "I was talking to a bevy of beautiful, barely-dressed bikini-contest winners. I was asking the standard questions (i.e., Where do you go to school? What's your major?). I told them I worked for the *Miami Herald*. Let's face it, it sounds a helluva lot better than 'I work for the *Bullet*.' It worked. I soon found myself on a date with the Doublemint Twins, Mindy and Cindy."

The threesome went to dinner, he continued, whereupon he confessed that "the *Miami Herald* thing was a desperate ploy." They then fell into discussion of their respective schools, the twins' being the University of Central Florida. The ensuing conversation, as Saunders recalled it, included the following exchange:

MINDY: What is visitation?
DAVE: Um, ah . . . when you sign in to a dorm, you have to tell the desk aide what room you're going to and they take your I.D. until you sign out.
MINDY: Oh my God! You have to "sign-in" to see your friends?
DAVE: Yup.
CINDY: Is this place, like, ultra-religious?
DAVE: Uh, no, it's a state school.
MINDY: Oh my God! Cindy, did you hear that?
CINDY: I heard it, but I don't believe it.
MINDY: Visitation . . . what a riot!

For those unfortunates who were unable to travel to balmier climes, another *Bullet* columnist prepared a list called "The Top 13 Things to Do for Spring Break." Among the obviously facetious suggestions were number 8, "Discuss the implications of pluralism in eastern Europe, decode Linear B manuscripts, [and] study up on the proper usage of a semi-colon," and number 2, "Astound your parents by bringing them the paper, get up before noon [and] omit 'like,' 'you know,' [and] 'cool' from your vocabulary."

By the time students returned from the break, it was usually not long before warmer weather enticed them to commence the sundry campus pastimes of spring: throwing Frisbees, skateboarding, rollerblading, cavorting with dogs (often on loan from local shelters) or, the most prevalent of all, sunbathing. The panoply of vernal activities was described well, if a bit astringently, in a column, "The Rites, and Wrongs, of Spring," that warned students about

> the frisbee freaks and hackysack heroes who turn every open space on campus into an impassable gauntlet. And if you escape those recreational missiles, watch out for the assorted canines that inevitably accompany, but never stay near, their frisbee flinging friends. But before giving my frisbee friends too much Seacobeck spaghetti (that's right, an allusion to [excrement]), remember the constant challenge they must face—vaulting the ever present sunbathers. Ah, the worshippers of Ra (that's the Egyptian sun god for those of you who have been skipping classes since Spring sprung!). Of course these people didn't start out with Ra. They started out with Apollo way back in January when everyone bought 100 minutes at Apollo Tanning for $14.95, with coupon.

The article then proceeded to discuss another prevalent springtime activity: departmental picnics, which, in emulation of the long-established History and Political Science outings, had proliferated over the years. "Those of us who have gained the infamous freshman 15 [pounds]," said the columnist, "abandon our bathing suits, don our form-flattering floral shirts and head for the numerous department picnics. So what if you're about to graduate as an English major. Technically you can still consider yourself an intended major for any department that offers all the beer you can drink (or throw on someone) for $2. Be sure to attend your own major's picnic—otherwise known as the B, B, & B event (Burgers, Beer, and Brown-nosing)."

The writer may have been a bit too cynical. In reality, the departmental gatherings, as well as similar events frequently hosted by faculty for individual classes, provided welcome opportunities for faculty-student dialogue that often began enduring friendships. Indeed, it was just the kind of thing that gave substance to the College's claim to being a place that prized close student-faculty relationships.

While faculty-student socials flourished, so too grew the popularity of Junior Ring Dance. From its origin in the 1950s, it developed in the course of a quarter century to become the biggest campus social event of the spring semester. Held for a few years in February or early March, it eventually settled into the April calendar. Its venue also changed in 1984 from the ballroom of the Sheraton (the largest dance floor in the area), where it had been held for many years, to the less capacious but more convenient Lee Hall Ballroom; following construction of the Woodard Campus Center, it moved to the Great Hall.

By the early eighties, Ring Dance had also become a much more extensive event, with activities stretching over the course of an entire week. Encompassing not merely the weekend ring presentation and dinner-dance, it came to include movies, pizza parties, scavenger hunts, comedy shows, and (of course) keggers. It was thenceforth known as Junior Ring Week.

The central events continued to be the ring presentation on Thursday night and the dance on Saturday night. The presentation, however, no longer had romantic overtones. The usual format included remarks by various officials of the class and College, as well as a main address by someone, generally a favorite faculty member, invited by the class. Rings were then presented individually to each junior, usually by the president of the College. Even in an age when normally blasé students eschewed sentimentality, it was clear that the ring ceremony was still meaningful to them. As one junior said following the 1996 presentation, "It makes you feel like a part of a tradition and a part of Mary Washington. You value the school more, and I never felt more a part of a tradition than I did at ring ceremony."

As was true of so many aspects of campus life at the time, alcohol often played a large role, especially in the years when the legal drinking age was eighteen. A member of the junior class of 1984 put it bluntly. "We juniors drink so that by Saturday night we will be numb and not know or care if the food is good, the band is bad, a girl across the room is wearing a dress like ours, or our date gets a room at the Sheraton and invites someone else to share it. It's here. It's only here once. We don't want to feel it if it hurts. We'll postpone the pain until Sunday."

That same year, in anticipation of the dance, the *Bullet* offered some tips (evidently aimed mainly at females), prefacing its advice by assuring its readers that "regardless of what your mother may say, you don't have to marry your Ring Dance date. However, if you hope to, here are some do's and don'ts to get you through the night."

DO'S

- Do drink in moderation (or a close facsimile thereof).
- Do make sure your date has shoes (other than sneakers) and cufflinks.
- Do keep track of your clothes.
- Do bring a change of clothes, just in case.
- Do keep both feet on the dance floor.
- Do tell your date that you've reserved a room prior to the night of the dance.
- Do take at least *one* picture for mom and dad, *without* the liquor bottles.

DON'TS

- Don't start drinking before 6; if so, moderately.
- Don't eat the seafood Newberg.
- Don't let your date out of your sight for more than five minutes.
- Don't switch dates.
- Don't sit on partners' shoulders to dance in a long dress.
- Don't let your date throw up on you.
- Don't let your date eat your corsage.

Although the dance and ring presentation remained key elements in the junior class celebration, Ring Week, beginning in the eighties, underwent a significant (some would say retrograde) evolution in terms of its overall ambience. The original purpose, aside from the bestowal of the treasured onyx-and-gold rings,[25] was to honor the juniors on the completion of three-quarters of their journey toward graduation. But somehow along the way, the focus turned increasingly from celebration of achievement to acts of harassment, as juniors became targets of pranks by students in other classes.[26]

Just what caused the metamorphosis is hard to pinpoint. Perhaps it was prompted by popular depictions of college life in movies such as *Animal House* (which was sometimes shown on campus as part of Ring Week); perhaps it was an effort to emulate the hazing associated with fraternities and sororities at colleges that had Greek systems. Whatever the cause, the result, undeniably, was an accretion of crudity that became more pervasive with the passage of time.

A typical Ring Week prank

At first the pranks were rather mild, including such things as freezing juniors' underwear, or hiding their clothes, or rearranging the furniture in their dorm rooms, or putting grease or Icy Hot on doorknobs. Cedric Rucker, after he had returned to the College as an administrator, recalled that as a junior he had been "pranked" (as it was termed) by having all the records in his large collection redistributed into the wrong album jackets.

Such tricks, while sometimes annoying, were hardly hurtful. Even President Anderson was sometimes brought into the gags, with which he good-naturedly played along. A recurrent prank was to have some personal item (the more intimate, the better) deposited in his office, forcing the embarrassed junior to retrieve it. Another was to forge an amorous letter from a junior to the president (sometimes including a room key) and have him read it to the audience at ring presentation.

But as time went on, efforts to tease became more malevolent, and certainly more tasteless, such as taping Kool Aid–soaked tampons to dorm room doors. Among the most prevalent jokes was campuswide posting of nude or semi-nude photographs of juniors explicitly describing the services they allegedly offered. Juniors who owned cars could almost count on finding them moved—Ball Circle was a choice site—and covered with toilet paper, aluminum foil, or sticky notes.

Some pranks constituted, or at least approached, vandalism, such as flooding rooms with water or covering floors with molasses or flour, sometimes accompanied by the loosing of crickets into the room. Not surprisingly, some of the more grotesque pranks were perpetrated by males, usually against each other. There was the instance, for example, when two juniors returned to their dorm to find their room in shambles, with newspapers, garbage, and shaving cream covering the floor. Nor was that the worst of it. As one of the roommates explained, "They pee-peed in our hot pot and turned it on."

The advent of new technology broadened the possibilities for mischief. One inventive effort involved programming a junior's phone to ring automatically every half hour throughout the night. Jeffrey McClurken, a junior RA in Bushnell in 1993 (and subsequently a much-admired professor in the History Department), recalled that he "had a bad Ring Week. Someone put a virus on my computer, and six hours before a paper was due I lost the paper."

One of the most prevalent pranks, because it took little ingenuity to execute, was to throw juniors into the Monroe plaza fountain. The *Bullet* had no sympathy for the victims. "They complain about getting tossed into the fountain," said an editorial, "and then walk by the fountain about 16 times a day. If you don't want to get wet, then don't walk by a large pool of water that is encircled by dozens of people who are out to get you."

But the most common of all tortures involved securely duct-taping the body of the victim, who was then covered with a conglomeration typically consisting of some variation of flour, oil, cat food, vinegar, ketchup, barbecue sauce, and (a key ingredient) eggs—a mixture once described in the *Bullet* as "a combination so foul-smelling [that] even the strongest stomachs could not endure it." Such episodes, as the perpetrators cavorted around the trussed and tormented victim, led one *Bullet* writer to observe that "for a few short minutes they lived *Lord of the Flies*."

The resulting mess caused problems not only for the hapless students at the time, but later for the physical plant staff who had to clean it all up. The eggs caused the worst problems, often requiring power-washing to remove them from brick surfaces—to the tune of several thousand dollars. Some workers professed not to mind the cleanup effort. "For us, it's fun," said one. "The routine becomes monotonous and this provides a little diversity." Likely more indicative of most employees' feelings, however, was a comment by Landscape and Grounds Supervisor Richard Blair. "It's disgusting stuff to have to clean up," he said. "We know we're here for the benefit of the students, but if you're cleaning up something that smells like puke, it really doesn't matter how much you're paid."

Each year the *Bullet* gleefully reported the shenanigans under headlines such as "Junior Ring Week Madness," "A Week of Flour and Fear," "A Week of Duct Tape and Destruction," and "The Diary of a Terrified Junior." One column suggested a novel trick, presumably in jest—though during Ring Week it was hard to be sure. "Here's a good prank," it said. "When your favorite junior is fast asleep, cut them open and steal their liver! Actually, any internal organ is up for grabs. When they ask, 'What the hell are you doing,' reply, 'Oh, nothing,' and carry out your business. After it's been removed, sell it to your favorite medical researcher and with the freshly earned dough, take your 'donor' out to dinner because, hey, they've been a good sport."

Things did not go quite that far, but clearly they had gone far enough, reaching (if not breaching) the bounds of both propriety and safety—and, in some cases, legality. Such practices included chaining and padlocking victims to stationary objects or to grocery carts or to each other. Extreme examples involved kidnapping and blindfolding victims, taking them off campus and securing them to trees or, in at least one instance, to a guard rail on I-95.

By the mid-nineties, the point had been reached where something needed to be done to rein in antics that had turned from teasing to torture. President Anderson, whose jovial nature had enabled him to tolerate (if not enjoy) the playful pranks of an earlier time, eventually felt constrained to issue a formal warning against the more outrageous, indeed dangerous, activities. Noting the commonwealth's laws against hazing, he warned in an e-mail to all students, "Practical jokes that can be considered harassment, damage of personal property, and causing of physical harm are absolutely unacceptable during Junior Ring Week, or at any other time."

In 1996 consideration was given to canceling the event altogether, but instead a forum sponsored by the College's Council on Community Values and Behavioral Expectations concluded by endorsing it, with certain provisions to place boundaries on how far pranks could go. Conveying the gist of the meeting, Junior Class President Michelle Trombetta urged that "attention [be] lavished upon members of the junior class with 'love' and goodwill. Remember," she added (using the ubiquitous student phrase of the time), "mean people suck."

The ring presentation ceremony that year gave further evidence of concern about student behavior. The featured speaker for the evening, psychology professor Christopher Kilmartin, widely known for his comedy routines, turned serious at one point to criticize the negative behavior that was becoming characteristic of Ring Week. He called on the class of 1997, reported the *Bullet*, to "be different by finding creative, positive ways to acknowledge the junior class next year, instead of participating in the traditional destructive pranks." To which the paper dryly added, "It is doubtful that his request will be carried out."

It was not, for pranking continued despite the administration's efforts to curb it. One ameliorative attempt was the designation of certain areas as "safe havens" in which harried juniors could find sanctuary. Anyone found antagonizing a student in any academic or administrative building, the library, the campus center, or Seacobeck was subject to discipline by the Judicial Review Board or by the office of student affairs.

Another, more inventive approach was creation of a "Rescuer" program, by which designated students, identifiable by red T-shirts, were authorized to intervene whenever they witnessed a practical joke that had gone too far. "We should not have people who are afraid to come to school," explained Dean Rucker. "Some of this stuff is honestly dangerous. Who knows what could happen to a student who is duct-taped to the front gates in the middle of the night." Accordingly, as a *Bullet* editorial put it, "In essence, the Rescuers are to tend to those juniors who may have been pranked a bit too heavily."

From the outset, however, students were skeptical about the effectiveness of the program. "I think that the chance that a student will volunteer to wear the red shirts is slim to none," commented one junior. Others suspected that the program would actually be counterproductive. "The mere fact that we have the Rescuers adds to the expectation that harassment will occur," said one, and another added, "Backlash to the Rescuers may be worse than the treatment of the juniors." Even some of those presumably protected rebelled against the idea. "I for one would rather be mauled by a group of a hundred people I don't even know," declared one junior, "than be rescued by some tool in a red rescue shirt. This school, administration and students, just needs to relax."

Predictions of the program's ineffectiveness proved to be accurate. Rescuers themselves were sometimes pelted with eggs and otherwise harassed, some to the point that, as one freshman put it, "I ended up not wearing the shirt the last couple of days because I got so many threats." Others who did wear the shirt appear to have been less than conscientious in their mission. "The only red shirt I saw all week," one junior reported, "was the one I saw on [a senior] when he duct-taped me and slapped a bike lock around my neck." Based on an observation of such reactions, the *Bullet*, which had initially endorsed the Rescuers as "a compromise to keep a long-standing tradition," concluded that the plan was largely a failure. "In fact," it editorialized at the end of the program's first year of operation, "judging from the mess around campus walk, it seems the Rescuers have had little, if any, effect on the week's activities."

The basic reason why the program did not work better appears to have been that the majority of students did not *want* it to work. To be sure, not all students enjoyed the mayhem. There were those whose psychological or physical condition gave them legitimate reason to fear the stresses of Ring Week harassment. The former director of the College's Psychological Services Center, then dean of students (and later vice president for student affairs) Bernard Chirico reported seeing a wide range of problems triggered by the trauma of the week, including "sleep difficulties, anxiety-related symptoms, poor academic performance, inability to focus and remember, . . . and depression-related symptoms." Surely such persons needed some protection.

But even they were often hesitant to speak out against the hazing. As Barbara Wagar, who had succeeded Chirico as director of the Psychological Services Center, explained it, "Since Ring Week is a tradition, some students [are] very hesitant to reveal their real feelings about pranks, since they don't want to appear to be poor sports or feel socially ostracized."

Even so, the preponderance of student opinion seemed to weigh heavily in favor of an unrestricted Ring Week. In fact, a *Bullet* poll in 2001 indicated that while 7 percent found it "awesome" as it was, 57 percent regarded it was "*too tame* because of . . . administration" efforts to limit its excesses.

Why such avid support? The main reason probably was that many students revered it as the College's oldest tradition. It was not—Devil-Goat Day was—but it was the most appealing to modern-day students because it resembled the riotous events that they associated with various other colleges. "When I came to MWC on a tour," commented one 2001 junior, "[and] they told us about Junior Ring Week, I thought that a school with such a cool tradition must be a fun place to be. I have been preparing myself for this week for three years."

Reflecting just such attitudes, the *Bullet* in a 1999 editorial titled "Don't Let Ring Week Tradition Die at MWC" proclaimed, "It is perhaps the one most interesting thing about this school, and it is the one thing that MWC has which other schools usually do not. It is something that schools like U.Va. and Virginia Tech wish they had."[27]

Having lamented recent efforts to temper the event, the editorial decreed, "Quite simply, this trend must be stopped. We must get Ring Week fired up again," and then offered its prescription: "This does not mean hurting juniors or placing them in danger. It just means doing some good, old fashioned, clever pranks on people. Leave no junior untouched, and enable everyone to have a good time. Let's return to the days of juniors not leaving their rooms without a six-person escort. To the fountain being filled with tied-up juniors at all times. To cement bathtubs on apartment porches. To the sheer joy that comes from dumping maple syrup on your junior RA."

Clearly Ring Week was an inordinate (to some observers, inexplicable) source of pride for many Mary Washington students, and the pranks were considered an integral part of it. "I'll even let you in on a little secret," wrote one *Bullet* columnist in 2000, "as juniors we actually look forward to getting attacked by our friends on campus. . . . Let us have one week full of great memories. . . . I mean, come on—we are still in college, aren't we?"

That view was frequently expressed over the years. As one female put it, she would have felt "shortchanged, shafted, cheated!" if not pranked. "Everyone knows," she added, "You're unpopular if you aren't publicly ridiculed during Junior Ring Week." Students "don't want to be left out," said another. "They don't want to be the one person who didn't get pranked. It's April Fools Day for a week, specifically for you." One male summarized it well when he said, "It was fun. I got nailed, but I would have felt worse if no one got me."

Eventually, at the insistence of administration officials, the more malicious forms of pranks were curtailed. Yet Junior Ring Week celebrations continued into the College's second century, maintaining a tradition in which, as the *Bullet* put it, "no junior is safe, and no amount of duct tape is enough."

CAMPUS CONCERNS

Students' often outrageous antics tended to obscure their substantive accomplishments and sometimes extraordinary good works. The most notable, and most widely publicized, example of such commitment involved a student named Jean Donovan, who graduated in 1975 with majors in economics and political science. Her junior year was spent in Ireland, where she was influenced by an Irish priest who had been a missionary. After graduation she earned a master's degree in business administration from Case Western Reserve and landed a lucrative position in Cleveland as an accountant and management consultant with the Arthur Andersen Company, a Big Five accounting firm.

Jean Donovan

Finding that job less than fulfilling, she was drawn increasingly toward missionary work, and after requisite training and studying Spanish in Guatemala, she settled in El Salvador, where she ministered to homeless and hungry children and tried in various ways to ameliorate the impoverished conditions that surrounded her. Unfortunately, the country was in the midst of a tumultuous period in which the ruling anticommunist regime, heavily supported by U.S. foreign aid provided by the Reagan administration, looked with fear and disfavor on persons who tried to help the peasants—persons such as Jean Donovan. It was in that environment that on December 2, 1980, she, along with three American nuns, was kidnapped, raped, and murdered by five Salvadoran national guardsmen. Peasants buried the victims in a shallow mass grave in a remote area.

The atrocity became a national issue, as charges were made (by Donovan's family, among others) that the U.S. government was complicit in the affair, an accusation vehemently denied by Jeane Kirkpatrick, the U.S. ambassador to the United Nations, and by Secretary of State Alexander Haig. When the accused guardsmen were finally brought to trial over three years later, their summary conviction was interpreted by some as merely a sham show of justice by a dictatorial regime to quiet American critics and thus preserve the flow of foreign aid into El Salvador.

Whatever the machinations behind the murders, Jean Donovan's heroic work and tragic death earned her widespread praise as a martyr for social justice—though in many ways she was a rather unlikely one. There was little in her background before Mary Washington that portended such a fate. Born into a prosperous and conservative Catholic family in Connecticut, she was, by her parents' description, "the original 'yuppie.'" It was her enthusiasm for horseback riding that drew her to Mary Washington.

While she was a student, the ebullient Donovan—described by another as "a young woman with a broad smile and a little girl's laugh"—sometimes exhibited a spirit that would probably not have met strict standards of sainthood. According to her mentor, political science professor Lewis Fickett, "Rumor had it that Jean could make a mean martini," and another professor revealed that she was "reputed to pour Scotch over her breakfast cereal from time to time." She continued to ride horses, but also rode "Hogs" (less genteel Harley-Davidsons). "She was a real hell-raiser," summarized human rights professor Gregory Stanton, "but also a devout Catholic."

All the while she had, as Lew Fickett observed, "the seed of social consciousness within her that [prompted her] to turn away from her great material success to a life of helping hungry children far away." She realized the dangers involved in her Salvadoran mission but urged her family and friends not to worry, assuring them that "they don't shoot blond, blue-eyed North Americans."

In the years following her murder, Donovan's life was commemorated in a number of ways. One was a dramatization titled *Choices of the Heart*; another was a documentary called *Roses in December*, whose title was taken from an entry in her diary in which she described the beauty of El Salvador, asking, "Where else would you find roses blooming in December?"

Her life was featured in a children's book titled *Can the Saints Come Out and Play?* designed for use in elementary and parochial school classrooms. The lesson based on Donovan's life read, in part, "Before Jean went to El Salvador, she had a good job, went to parties with friends, and drove a motorcycle. But she wanted something more. She wanted to help people. . . . [She] did not worry about herself. Jean only worried about the children. She wanted them to be safe and happy. She gave them candy and hugs. She played her guitar for them and sang them funny and beautiful songs. The people . . . called [her] 'St. Jean the Playful.'"

Donovan's legacy was also memorialized at her alma mater. The Catholic Student Association created an award in her memory to be given annually to the graduating senior who "best exhibits the charity, faith and conviction of this young woman." The organization also named its campus center the Jean Donovan House. In 2005, on the twenty-fifth anniversary of her death, the College held a commemorative service (initiated by Professor Stanton and his student aide Katie Kelley) that included dedication of a plaque in Trinkle plaza honoring her legacy. Calling the event "a very important day in the life of this institution," President Anderson said the event marked "one of our very finest coming home."

There were occasions along her journey toward martyrdom when Jean Donovan expressed quite human reservations about her mission of faith and commitment. "Several times I decided to leave El Salvador," she once admitted, "[and] I almost could [have], except for the children—the poor, bruised victims of this insanity. Who would care for them?"

Though no one else, fortunately, suffered Jean Donovan's tragic fate, there were many Mary Washington students who, in greater or lesser degrees, followed her example of service to others. Beginning in the 1980s and gaining steam thereafter, volunteerism emerged as one of the most noteworthy, and certainly most admirable, aspects of student life.

An early leader in that trend was the campus chapter of Circle K International, a leadership and service organization.[28] Before 1990 it was involved in more service activities than any organization at the College, sponsoring diverse such efforts as Red Cross blood drives, visiting at area nursing homes, tutoring in local public schools, babysitting children of domestic abuse victims, promoting literacy campaigns, ringing bells for the Salvation Army during the Christmas season, and cooperating with the area Big Brothers/Big Sisters organization in providing activities for children on campus.

But Circle K was by no means alone in sponsoring community services. The Catholic Student Association assisted the local homeless shelter, the battered women's shelter, and Hope House, a temporary dwelling for women and children in transition. Baptist Student Union members visited nursing homes and local jails, as well as children's hospitals, where they dressed as clowns to amuse the young patients. The Campus Christian Community focused on alleviating hunger through activities such as sponsorship of annual CROP (Communities Responding to Overcome Poverty) walks, through which funds were raised to support, among other charitable enterprises, the Fredericksburg area food bank.

Other campus groups, aside from the religion-oriented ones, also were involved in a range of volunteer efforts. The Black Student Association cooperated with the Student Senate Association in conducting a clothes drive for the victims of Hurricane Hugo in 1990, the men's and women's cross-country teams sponsored a "Jingle Bell Run" each year to raise money for the Arthritis Foundation, the Preservation Club assisted the Mary Washington Hospital with its annual benefit auction, and the campus chapter of NOW helped the area Rape Crisis Program by answering hotline phone calls.

In the late 1980s, many campus organizations joined in an annual Hunger Awareness Week that included seminars, food drives and fasting. A central feature was support for Oxfam America (Oxford Committee on Famine Relief), in which students pledged to give up a meal, with the campus food service, ARA, donating an equivalent amount of money to that organization.

The great surge in volunteerism prompted a movement to create a College office to coordinate those efforts. The initiative was sparked by senior Liz Baumgarten, who, in 1990, was vice president of the SA Senate and co-director of its Special Projects Committee. It was she who developed a connection with VA COOL, the state's branch of the national COOL (Campus Outreach Opportunity League), a nonpartisan organization devoted to motivating student volunteerism. Based on a needs assessment developed following a campus visit by COOL's outreach coordinator, Baumgarten drafted a proposal for Dean of Students Joanne Beck urging establishment of a center to coordinate volunteerism on campus; Beck promptly forwarded to the president a plan for creating such an entity, which would be under the supervision of her office.

Advocates of volunteerism could scarcely have found a more avid ally than Bill Anderson. The promotion of participatory citizenship had a large place in his concept of liberal education, and he viewed public service as an integral component of that concept. In his commencement address to the class of 1984 (his first commencement as president), he implored the graduates to involve themselves in their communities, using their "knowledge and expertise constructively—and, indeed, compassionately."

That philosophy, consistently pursued throughout the years of his presidency, contributed to an impressive record of public service by students during that time. Its first tangible manifestation was the creation of the Community Outreach and Resources program. Established in the fall of 1990 with Kathleen Knight as its director, COAR was designed to promote and coordinate student volunteer activities. It was successful immediately. By its second year of operation, it attracted more than 150 student volunteers whose services were eagerly sought by approximately fifty different agencies. From that point it expanded, both in the number of participants and in the range of activities, to become a major element in campus life.

It was not hard to see why. For one thing, it had an altruistic appeal, even though, as one participant explained, "You do it for selfish reasons. You're doing something for someone else, and you feel good about yourself." Moreover, as a COAR student coordinator put it, "It's something everybody [can] do. COAR has no restrictions. You don't have to be athletic or have a certain G.P.A."

The College's commitment to supporting volunteerism was expanded in 1997 with the designation of one residence hall floor (Madison first) as the campus "service learning floor." Eligibility for residence on the floor required acceptance of a personal community service project totaling at least two hours per week, as well as participation in at least three cooperative group projects, one of which had to be campus oriented. The service learning floor was operated under the aegis of COAR and funded by VA COOL; both agencies were supported financially by grants from AmeriCorps, the national program (sometimes referred to as a domestic Peace Corps) initiated by President Clinton.

Volunteer work usually fell into one of several categories, among the most prominent being assistance to homeless persons. Within that category, the main focus of students' efforts involved the Thurman Brisben Homeless Shelter, founded in 1987 and located in downtown Fredericksburg. Students were trained by COAR and encouraged to work at the shelter on a once-a-week basis, which they regularly did in large numbers throughout the shelter's cold-weather months of operation. But they also engaged periodically in ad hoc events in support of the homeless. One significant example came in 2002 in response to threats that the Brisben shelter might be moved from its current location, possibly out of Fredericksburg altogether. Students quickly joined a group known as SOS (Save Our Shelter) organized by local ministers and dedicated to maintaining the facility. By distributing flyers and participating in rallies supporting the shelter, students helped to preserve the shelter within the city of Fredericksburg.

On another occasion in 2005, volunteers participated in a "sleep-out" in which they spent a cold late-October night sleeping (or trying to) in cardboard boxes outside Lee Hall in an effort to dramatize the plight of the homeless. The following year, led by Mortar Board members, volunteers participated in a walkathon to raise money for improvement of facilities at the Brisben Shelter.

Volunteers not only assisted the homeless but also often helped to construct or repair homes. This effort was carried out largely, though not exclusively, under the sponsorship of Habitat for Humanity, an organization started in 1976 in Georgia as a nonprofit Christian housing ministry. It subsequently gained high national visibility as a result of strong support (and active participation) by President Jimmy Carter.

In the early nineties, a chapter of Habitat was organized at Mary Washington by senior history major Lisa Hohl with the help of COAR. In the years that followed, many students participated in housing construction, most of them during their spring breaks as part of what was known as the Alternative Spring Break program. Participation in that program involved projects as close by as the eastern shore of Virginia and as far away as New Orleans, Mississippi, Georgia, Florida, and the Appalachian region of Kentucky.

For most Mary Washington students, coming from middle- and upper-middle-class families, such work was a novel experience. As one volunteer described her work in Georgia during the 2003 spring break:

> Each morning was a challenge, waking up on a local private school's gym floor before the sun had risen to prepare for a day's work ahead. . . . The first moments on the construction site, faced with a view of a cinderblock foundation and a few floor joists—nothing more—proved more than a little daunting. . . . It wasn't long [however] before Mary Washington students took charge of the power tools, balanced on the rafters, and began arranging scaffolding like pros. . . . From lifting the first walls to hammering the last bits of siding, students worked together under such intense conditions that the friendships formed in that week became a constant source of inspiration.

Despite the hard work, some students managed to find humor in the construction process. Stephanie Tait, who in March 2005 participated in a Habitat-affiliated project in Jacksonville, Florida, recounted her experiences in an article in the *Bullet* (of which she became editor the next year). Terrified on the first day by dire warnings about dangers lurking in the vicinity of her group's project, she was cautioned not to feed or give money to persons who

> were usually either under the influence or mentally unstable. Great, I thought. . . . Add to this the fact that we later were told that roosters and prostitutes wander the streets and not to feed either one of them either. I began to think I was in over my head. . . . My group and I were assigned to work with an AmeriCorps member putting insulation on the outside of a house. I put on my tool belt, got to work and soon discovered that wielding a hammer wasn't as easy as Tim "The Tool Man" Taylor made it to be. Two hours and several expletives later, I had the hang of it and could put a nail into the side of the house with four hits. Booyah. . . . After we arrived back in the 'Burg, I decided the whole trip was a huge success. We came. We built. We had a lot of fun doing it. But I never once saw a rooster or a prostitute.

Many volunteers chose to work on health-related projects, either physical or mental. One of the first endeavors was an AIDS Walk, planned for early October 1990. Organizers were apprehensive because, as one of them noted, a "sunny, beautiful, peaceful Sunday morning can make it very tempting for your average student volunteer to sleep in and enjoy the day with a Frisbee and a friend." But the event turned out to be successful, raising over $1,200 for the benefit of the Whitman/Walker Clinic in Washington, D.C. It also paved the way for numerous similar activities in the future, including, just a few months later, the MWC Circle K chapter's "Hair-Cut-A-Thon" to raise money for the Muscular Dystrophy Association.

Other volunteers preferred more active, hands-on involvement such as working with local rescue squads. One of the most attractive agencies for volunteers was the Lloyd F. Moss Free Clinic in Fredericksburg. Established by local physicians in 1993 to provide medical care (including gynecological services) for low-income uninsured people, the clinic relied heavily on retired persons and students for its operation, and Mary Washington from the outset furnished an important contingent. Prominent among them was Kelly Morgan '00, whose work was crucial in setting up the clinic's dental facility.

Perhaps the most challenging types of volunteer work were those involving agencies that dealt with mental disabilities. Yet such organizations were among the most popular with MWC students. Almost from the outset, volunteers were drawn to two local programs in particular, Daybreak and Best Buddies, both sponsored by the Rappahannock Chapter of the Association for Retarded Citizens.

Daybreak was a Saturday afternoon program in which students volunteered to spend several hours overseeing children who had developmental problems (often autism) to give some relief time to parents who were in many cases suffering from the stress of providing constant care. Volunteers in the program (frequently psychology majors) usually did not deny that the work could be taxing at times, but as one of them noted, "You don't have to be a saint to do this. You just want to have fun with kids." And the rewards were great, leaving one volunteer "on top of the world" every time. "It's really just that simple. When you see the kids laughing and smiling and you get a big hug, well, I can't think of too many things more rewarding than that."

The Best Buddies chapter at Mary Washington was part of an international organization designed to pair a student volunteer with a mentally challenged person. The campus chapter was fortunate to have as its buddy director just such a person, Grace Ann Braxton, who worked in the dining hall and was able to assist in suggesting matches. "She's just great," said one of the chapter's student directors. "She knows everyone and she's always introducing me to people." The importance of the program, she went on to explain, was that while retarded persons often had family or case workers or mental health practitioners to care for them, many of them had no friends. "I think that's something people who don't have special needs take for granted—having friends to go out with. . . . But with Best Buddies, we're friends just because we like them, like my buddy Grace and I."

Of all the volunteer efforts of behalf of the disabled, the most unusual was that of the MWC men's rugby team to benefit Special Olympics Virginia, a program to provide sports training and athletic competition for persons with mental disabilities. In February 2005 the ruggers participated in something called the Polar Plunge at Virginia Beach, where twenty of them joined over 2,800 others in wading into the 38-degree Atlantic Ocean. The frigid stunt resulted in raising (in addition to countless goose bumps) $1,000 for the charity—while, of course, burnishing the team's vaunted macho image.

Another category of volunteerism focused on assistance to the elderly. Besides regular visits to area nursing homes, students were instrumental in developing a number of special activities for geriatrics such as an annual senior-citizen prom sponsored by the Campus Rotary Club. There was also Adopt-a-Grandparent, a long-running program at the local Woodmont Nursing Home, in which volunteers from the MWC Baptist Student Union (BSU) paid weekly visits to their senior companions. The purpose of the endeavor, the campus BSU director once explained, was to "give hope to people who may not have it and give them relationships of care and love because we all need it."

Mary Washington students also volunteered in the area of education. Part of such efforts focused on helping enhance learning opportunities for disadvantaged children in the local community. One particularly noteworthy initiative was the attempt through a 2001 program called "Plugged In!" to provide the Bragg Hill Family Life Center with computers and technology to stimulate intellectual curiosity among underprivileged children.

Educational efforts also included promoting the cause of volunteerism by publicizing available opportunities and by emphasizing the value of such work to both the giver and receiver of charitable acts. One such program was VISTA (Volunteers in Service to America), in which participants worked with private and nonprofit groups to develop resources to get more people interested in volunteering. Another was COAR's Into the Streets program, which introduced new MWC students to opportunities for volunteering, and Make a Difference Day, in which each campus club and residence hall was expected to come up with an activity to demonstrate the importance of community service.

Natural disasters summoned forth notable volunteer efforts from students, either through physically providing help themselves or by working to raise relief funds. Examples of the former were students who took Alternative Spring Breaks in 1994 to aid flood victims in the Midwest and in 1995 for the same purpose in Georgia. Fund-raising activities were particularly energetic on behalf of Pakistan Earthquake Relief in 2006 (sponsored by the Islamic Student Association) and in response to the South Asian tsunami the previous year. Support for the tsunami victims was intensified by the fact that a native of Sri Lanka, Sulakshana Seevaratnam, who lost two relatives in the disaster, was a student at Mary Washington. Her efforts generated approximately $10,000, including $1,700 donated from a fund-raising party sponsored by Psi Upsilon, an unofficial fraternity of Mary Washington students.

Perhaps the greatest concentration of volunteer activities came in response to the damage wrought in New Orleans and the Gulf Coast region by Hurricane Katrina in the fall of 2005. A number of students traveled to the area to lend their services, some of them going multiple times. One group, arriving during spring break the following year, still encountered what the *Bullet* described as "the devastating effects that eight feet of water leave after sitting in a home for six months"—not the least of which was a lingering stench that forced the volunteers to wear masks. "The smells that came out of that kitchen," reported one of them, "were the most God-awful things that I have ever had the misfortune of laying my olfactory glands on."

On campus, relief efforts included a campaign, directed by COAR, to raise money for the victims. The centerpiece of the effort was a benefit concert in Dodd Auditorium by the local performer Anthony Campbell, who in November 2003 had won a national singing competition on the NBC *Today* show that earned him the title, "Today's Superstar." The event raised over $3,600. That sum, added to other contributions from students, faculty, and staff, brought the institution's total donations to over $10,000.

Of course, not all volunteer activities had so serious a purpose. Among the more festive was an annual COAR-sponsored trick-or-treat event in which children from local youth programs such as Head Start, as well as from families of College personnel, were invited to campus for a day of Halloween activities. Beginning in the morning with a "Fun Fair" in Ball Hall, the day included allowing the children to visit the residence halls for trick-or-treating (basically candy collecting) and ended with a party hosted by the College food service in Seacobeck, featuring candied apples and hot cider.

By any standard, the College's COAR program was remarkably successful. By the year 2000 it was placing over six hundred students annually in more than eighty agencies, representing more than 16,500 cumulative hours of public service. It was officially commended that year by the Fredericksburg City Council for outstanding service, and its accomplishments were subsequently recognized by the Points of Light Foundation and *USA Weekend* magazine, as well as by receipt of a "Local Heroes" designation from the Commonwealth of Virginia.

Whether for reasons of personal interest or from simple practicality, most volunteer involvement by students took place on or in the vicinity of the campus. There were, however, notable examples of volunteerism that took place far afield.

Such missions (periodically described in *Bullet* articles) were sometimes devised by students themselves or in cooperation with church groups. The one common thread was the students' shock at the appalling conditions encountered in the areas where they were sent. Typical were the observations of Karen Baer, who beginning in 2000 spent time in Haiti, where she reported living with eight other people in a house "about as big as a dorm room in Willard . . . [with] no running water, telephone, or electricity . . . [and] roads like you see in the SUV commercials or worse." Another student, Laura Keyser, experienced similar discomforts during her work in a Romanian children's hospital in 1999 and 2000, but her account left no doubt as to why she, like so many other Mary Washington students, were drawn to such work. "Although these living conditions are horrible and inhumane," she wrote, "these are not what compelled me to go to this country on the other side of the world. It is that these children had no one to hold and comfort them, to love them and to teach them—they were dying alone and unnoticed. I thought that if I could just bring a brief moment of joy and happiness to their lives, then maybe they could hold onto that through the dismal monotony of their days. I did not expect the children to bring the joy and love into my life that they did."

The most impressive indication of the commitment of Mary Washington students to foreign volunteerism was the large number of Peace Corps members it produced over the years. That cadre comprised not only students but also faculty members, including education professors Paul Zisman (Venezuela, 1964–66) and George Meadows (Malaysia, 1980–82) and psychology professor Alice Rabson (Marshall Islands, 1986–88); in addition, one former assistant dean in the admissions office, Austin Merrill '91, served in Ivory Coast from 1995 to 1997.[29]

What was the explanation for such an extraordinary level of participation, not only in the Peace Corps but in other volunteer commitments as well? The most cynical answer, and the least accurate, was that volunteers were motivated by selfish concerns regarding potential enhancement of career opportunities. Such incentives did exist for some, as explained by a *Bullet* columnist who wrote in 1993 that "one of the best ways to attract future employers is volunteer experience . . . [that] allows students to . . . obtain the leadership and organizational skills that employers value, and make contacts that may lead to future employment."

But for most volunteers, the motivation was much less egocentric, growing instead from an inherent desire to help others. At Mary Washington, such inclinations were natural, in general springing from the spirit of liberal learning that pervaded the institution. Other, more specific factors (especially with regard to foreign volunteerism) included the College's heightened emphasis on globalism in the eighties and nineties, as well as the roles of faculty (notably including political science professors such as Lew Fickett, Jack Kramer, Curtis Ryan, and Jason Davidson) whose enthusiasm for international affairs influenced many students.

In light of the numerous acts of charity and magnanimity performed by Mary Washington volunteers, it was unfortunate that such accomplishments were often overlooked or minimized by a public more fixated on negative behavior. That tendency was a source of rightful resentment to many students. One of them expressed his indignation in a 1996 *Bullet* column decrying the prevalent use of the term "Generation X" by social commentators to describe his contemporaries. "X-ers are, to them," he said, "an unmotivated, unskilled and just plain lazy group of punks with big pants, too much body piercing and backward hats. In other words, we are a Pearl Jam concert. . . . Well, I'm not buying it."

Nor should anyone have, at least not with regard to Mary Washington students. The truth was that, as their volunteer activities eloquently demonstrated, those funky clothes often covered (and disguised) hearts filled with compassion.

Among issues of national interest in the last decades of the twentieth century, none created more pervasive, continuous, or heated discussion at the College than those involving matters of gender. In particular, feminist concerns, which had first been evident in the late sixties and early seventies as a result of advocacy by faculty members such as Elizabeth Clark, Susan Hanna, and Alice Rabson, gained increasing attention in the late eighties and emerged as a significant force in the nineties.

An important development came in 1984 when, at the instigation of senior Mary Driver, a campus chapter of the National Organization for Women (NOW) was formed, with Katherine Spivey as its president and Sue Hanna as its faculty adviser. Through seminars, workshops, and speakers, it addressed issues such as abortion, self-defense, sexual harassment, and domestic violence.

Because it was a presidential election year, considerable emphasis was initially given to politics—specifically to criticism of President Reagan, who was seeking reelection. One goal, said Spivey, was to expose "the myth that Reagan is doing something for women, which he is not." Moreover, she lauded the Democratic vice presidential nominee, Geraldine Ferraro, as a woman who "gives other women a symbol to rally under."

A basic purpose of the NOW chapter was to raise the overall consciousness of women to gender issues and to exhort them toward more active involvement, since, as Spivey put it, "a woman waiting for her knight in shining armor has to clean up after the horse later on." Still, chapter spokespersons emphasized that they were "not anti-man, just anti–bad laws." The group in fact invited male participation, with Sue Hanna noting that her own husband (George Van Sant) was a member of the Fredericksburg chapter.

The campus feminist movement received a boost in 1986 from a visit by the prominent activist and editor of *Ms.* magazine, Gloria Steinem. Speaking to a near-capacity crowd in Dodd Auditorium, she covered a panoply of women's problems, asserting that their root cause was that women's "capacity to have children makes us different, and the way men control that makes this a patriarchy."

A specific point of her critique focused on the ways women and other minorities were depicted in the media. "I'm still waiting for the 'ring-around-the-collar' commercial to change," she said. "I'm waiting for the woman to say, 'Why don't you wash your neck?' or better yet, 'Why don't you wash your own shirt?'" Steinem's message, above all, was a challenge to women to reject the passivity of the past and take control of their own destinies. She concluded her exhortation to action by quoting Rose Kennedy's comment "I'm for anything that's off its ass"—to which she received a standing ovation.

Aside from appearances by prominent feminists like Steinem, women's issues were kept in focus through the years by periodic *Bullet* editorials and op-ed pieces, most (though not all) of which were favorable to feminism. One such column in 1994, somewhat more radical than most, attacked not only sexism but also "lookism." "Womyn are perpetually denigrated on the basis of myth and stereotype," the writer proclaimed. "I am not lamenting my herstory. I just want to make it clear that I found it easier to announce my lesbianism to myself and others in this horribly heterosexist society than it was to call myself fat without condemning myself for it. That is how ingrained [our] sense of beauty is."

In the same year, an editorial blasted the College intramural program's co-recreational games for "blatantly sexist" rules that were "twisted toward the expected failure . . . of female participants." Noting the advantages given to female players to compensate for their presumably inferior skills, the paper declared, "Women are the majority at this school and they are striving for equality with men in every facet of daily life. The intramural games are for men and women to compete together and against each other on an equal playing field. This equality cannot exist if the rules allow privileges to women on the grounds that women are not as athletically competent as men. These rules are degrading to women in every way and need to be changed to promote equality."

On an institutional level, interest in feminist issues was evidenced periodically by efforts such as the 1992 exhibit, A Share of Honor: Virginia Women, 1600–1954, funded by the National Endowment for the Humanities. Also, the curriculum was expanded to incorporate courses such as philosophy professor Janet Wishner's women's studies class and by the introduction of women's issues into various existing courses. In addition, the Race and Gender Project headed by Professors Craig Vasey and Carole Corcoran led to the addition of a race and gender component to the College's general education requirements.

On a continuing basis, the annual celebration of Women's History Month brought College-wide attention each March to women's issues. Beginning in the 1980s as only a weeklong event, it expanded both in length and content in the nineties under the direction of history professor Allyson Poska, a widely published scholar in the field of women's studies. After joining the faculty in 1992, Poska devoted her considerable energy and enthusiasm to extensive programs that included public lectures by eminent scholars, movies (e.g., *The Secret Garden*, *The Joy Luck Club*), workshops, panel discussions (e.g., "Women and Sports," "Working in a Masculine World," "Feminist Christianity") and performances such as that by the Guerilla Girls, a feminist art activist group.

A highlight of Women's History Month each year was the keynote presentation by a prominent feminist. Among the most notable were Naomi Wolf (1993), author of *The Beauty Myth: How Images of Beauty Are Used against Women*; Nadine Strossen (1995), president of the American Civil Liberties Union; and Patricia Ireland (1999), president of the National Organization for Women.

Perhaps the most controversial program was the 1996 appearance by Holly Hughes, an Obie Award–winning lesbian playwright and performance artist whose work had earlier been denied funding by the National Endowment for the Arts for what she claimed were political reasons. The featured part of her visit to the College was her one-woman show titled *Clit Notes* (a takeoff on Cliffs Notes, the popular series of student study guides), a performance that the local newspaper reviewed in an article titled (in another play on words) "Risqué Business."

On the campus of Mary Washington College during the late twentieth century, as in the nation at large, no issue produced more heated debate (or with less possibility of resolution) than abortion. Going back to the tendentious early 1970s, when the issue first flared at the College, abortion had been a perennial controversy, as indicated by a continuing stream of articles in (and impassioned letters to) the *Bullet*, representing both the pro-life and pro-choice sides of the issue. Such interest led to a 1985 symposium on the topic, sponsored by the Campus Christian Community and moderated by Sue Hanna, that included presentations by a physician, a lawyer, and a minister.

Though student interest in the topic persisted, there were some who found it increasingly tiresome. In that light, one student offered a suggestion to "take the debate to a higher plateau," which she proceeded to do (à la Jonathan Swift) in a 1985 *Bullet* column called "A Modest Proposal." Her satiric argument was based on the premise that women's greatest agony derived not from the question of whether to abort a fetus but from the problem of what to do with children whose births they later came to regret.

> What I propose is this: euthanasia centers for children all over the country. Any time a child became an obstacle to a career or an education, any time a mother's health deteriorated, any time a family's income went down, a marriage broke up, or a woman just got tired of being a mother (and who doesn't?) there would be a euthanasia center nearby with counselors, sterile rooms, and coffee. We wouldn't even have to have long debates about whether or not the process was painful. Children could be very pleasantly put to sleep . . . [by gas] perfumed to resemble anything from their favorite bubble bath to a new baseball mitt or a peanut butter sandwich. This would be controversial at first, but opposition should crumble when it is pointed out that women have their right to live their lives as they see fit. . . . And best of all, it would prevent child abuse. Just because a woman has a child, she shouldn't have to give up all her rights.

Almost a decade—and countless, mostly circular, arguments—later, another *Bullet* op-ed columnist expressed similar frustration (albeit less sardonically) when he wrote, "Ah, once again the Great Abortion Debate rears its ugly head. I thought somewhere around 1989, we all got tired of having to argue about the same subject and make the same points when we knew there was no way anyone was going to change his/her mind. Oh, well."

But the controversy did continue, of course, among faculty as well as students. The faculty debate sometimes took the form of dueling op-ed pieces in the *Bullet*, such as the 1994 exchange between pro-life psychology professor Thomas Moeller and pro-choice English professor Mary Rigsby. Prompted by the twentieth anniversary of the *Roe v. Wade* decision, Moeller argued that a fetus should be considered human and its destruction murder. "Surely," he said, "the same developing offspring cannot be a human baby for a mother who wants a baby while at the same time being nothing more than a blob of tissue for a woman who wants an abortion. One's intent cannot determine whether the unborn offspring is a human baby or not."

In rebuttal, Rigsby sought to redirect the whole argument to focus on men's responsibility in the matter of conception, since, she asserted, "careless dissemination of sperm is, after all, a precondition of unwanted pregnancy. . . . Men abdicate sovereignty over their sperm the moment they let it trespass into another person's living room." Noting that either condoms or vasectomies offered men easy methods of preventing such "careless dissemination," she mischievously added, "I support men's freedom to choose from a range of contraceptives."[30]

One of the largest public discussions of the issue came later in 1994 at a forum titled "A Look at Abortion," held in Dodd Auditorium. The event was organized by business administration professor Pat Metzger, who, the *Bullet* pointed out, had also been the organizer two years earlier of the Stageberg-Rallis forum on homosexuality that had "left more than 1,300 people spellbound and talking for days." Though the abortion debate, moderated by Provost Philip Hall, did not ignite sparks comparable to the earlier one, it did have its dramatic moments, such as the showing of a video, "Hard Truths," that used clips of aborted babies' limbs in formaldehyde and other body parts in garbage containers to illustrate what the pro-life contingent called "the abortion holocaust." The attendance of several hundred people indicated that the issue was still a volatile one—as it continued to be.

The closely related issue of birth control was also a source of great interest at Mary Washington. In the spring of 1987, an ad hoc committee on birth control, chaired by campus NOW president Barbara Anderson '89, conducted a poll that included male and female students, both sexually active and celibate, on the desirability of having the Health Center provide extended birth control services for female students. The survey revealed that 89 percent of the respondents would use the Health Center if it prescribed birth control, including 67 percent of the almost one-quarter of the sexually active women who were not currently using birth control of any kind.

Based on those findings, the committee recommended that birth control services be extended in three specific ways: the Health Center should provide prescription contraceptives; because of the sensitive nature of the issue, billing and disclosure procedures should be initiated to ensure confidentiality; and non-prescription methods of birth control (condoms, sponges, foams) should be sold at the College bookstore or made available at the Health Center.

Release of the report touched off a clamor both on campus and beyond. The *Bullet*, somewhat surprisingly, opposed the plan, asserting that there was no reason for the college to divert funds from "other more important issues facing this school" to provide products and services readily available elsewhere. An editorialist claimed to be "really irked" at the sight of "a bunch of people on the one hand claiming they're liberated and totally capable of taking care of themselves and then on the other hand saying they're incapable of going to a free clinic or family planning clinic for birth control or even down to the People's drug store. . . . If you can't take responsibility for your actions, then maybe you shouldn't be here in the first place."

Most appalling to the paper, however, was the furor that the proposal produced in the local community and around the state, especially since, as it pointed out, eight of the commonwealth's colleges already provided the kinds of birth control services advocated in the report. "Mary Washington has had in the past a rather conservative reputation," said one editorial, "and this has often affected the image others have of our college. Perhaps this is the main reason half the East Coast has heard about the birth control proposal. . . . It's bad enough that some members of Fredericksburg can't handle our decisions on visitation and alcohol, but to add the rest of the state's obsession with birth control to it makes the situation just a tad too ridiculous."

Despite the upheaval initially produced by the report, most of its main proposals were implemented by the early 1990s. The Health Center established a birth control clinic for (as its announcement read) "those women who wish to start a prescription method of contraception and are not already using a contraceptive prescribed by another clinic or private physician." All first-time participants were required to attend a birth control education class presented by the AIDS/STD peer educators before making an appointment, which had to be made in person at the Health Center. There was an annual nonrefundable charge (initially $35) for the service.

The policy continued relatively free of contention throughout the nineties and beyond, though a mini-controversy arose in 2004 over the distribution of EC, or emergency contraception, more commonly known as the "morning after" pill. That drug, if taken within seventy-two hours after sexual intercourse, was reputed to be almost 90 percent effective in preventing a fertilized egg from implanting in the uterus.

Part of the debate over its use lay in questions of safety, since the Federal Drug Administration, ignoring heavy evidence in favor of the drug since its development in 1999, refused to approve it for over-the-counter sale.[31] Another aspect involved moral issues concerning its dispensation at state institutions, especially after one member of the Virginia House of Delegates claimed that easy access to the pill would turn college women into "chemical love canals for frat house playboys."[32] Risking such censure, the Mary Washington Health Center nonetheless wrote and filled EC prescriptions in exchange for a pregnancy test and payment of a $10 fee.

Regarding the birth control issue as a whole, the preponderant opinion of Mary Washington students over the years seems to have been on the pro-choice side. Among the numerous expositions of that viewpoint, one of the most adamant was that of Katherine Lowry in a 2004 *Bullet* op-ed piece. Having presented many of the usual justifications for abortion, she went on to assail President George W. Bush for his pro-life position, concluding with an admonition to "keep your politics out of my uterus."

The spate of passionate letters in rebuttal to Lowry's article, as well as the occasional participation of Mary Washington students in right-to-life protests, indicated that such views were far from universal. The fact was that regarding the matter of abortion, as with so many other issues, the Mary Washington campus was a microcosm of the culture surrounding it.

Usually discussions over birth control centered on female contraception, but at Mary Washington the use of condoms also stimulated controversy on occasion. One uproar resulted from a *Bullet* report in 1992 that the condoms then being sold by the Health Center were inferior. Citing a *Consumer Reports* survey, the paper claimed that the brand in question was "grossly defective," ranking thirty-ninth out of the forty brands tested. In response to students' demand for a higher-quality product, the Health Center explained that purchases were dictated by the College's state contract with the vendor.[33]

For some students (though apparently a minority), the emphasis on condom use was distasteful. "The whole thing is just getting out of hand," complained one. "I'm afraid that condoms are being used as a good excuse for saying yes in far too many cases."

The debate became more intense, and more pervasive on campus, when a movement arose in the late 1990s to make condoms available not just in the Health Center but also in residence hall vending machines, a need that was deemed more pressing after the Health Center ceased to be open on weekends. Proponents of the idea justified it on the grounds not only of convenience but also of anonymity, claiming that it would eliminate the embarrassment caused by face-to-face purchases. They adamantly denied that it would increase promiscuity. As one *Bullet* columnist put it, "The presence of condoms does not encourage . . . sex. If merely having condoms increases the likelihood of sexual activity of the owner, this writer would be a much happier man." (The validity of such demurrers was somewhat undermined, however, by a *Bullet* headline on the story: "Machines Offer Quick, Easy Sex.")

In any case, when the proposal was presented to the administration, it was rejected by the vice president for student affairs, Bernard Chirico, mainly because, as he explained, the action would send the wrong message concerning the need for students to take responsibility for their actions. Other administrators expressed additional concerns about possible damage to the College's image. When the proposal was brought to the attention of the Board of Visitors, they declined to take any action one way or the other, with board member Vincent DiBenedetto commenting that the whole matter seemed to him "a bit tacky."

Students, undeterred, pressed their cause. It was not a matter of advocating increased sexual activity, they insisted, but one of promoting safe practices. "I had liked and wanted sex long before I had even heard of Mary Washington College," said one male student. "To assume [that] because a 19-year-old doesn't have a condom he or she won't have sex is idiotic." Another student (female) agreed. "Things happen in dorms that the college can't control," she said. "People get drunk and have sex. It's not a perfect world. Going downstairs and getting [a condom] is being responsible and better than doing something reckless."

Ultimately the case for prophylactics prevailed. In the fall of 1998, residence hall vending machines were installed where condoms could be purchased for fifty cents each.

In the midst of the controversy, Professor Steve Hampton—he of the Human Sexuality course—provided a distinctive take on the situation in a *Bullet* op-ed column. The purpose of his message was to encourage the use and easy availability of condoms, though, as he put it, "It seems to me that if you are too embarrassed to buy condoms, you probably have no business having sex." But, he continued, if vending machines were to be used,

> I suggest that we just put condoms in the candy machines we already have. That way no one will know if you are buying condoms or a Snickers bar. If, however, you push the wrong button because of your anxiety, you might actually get a Snickers bar . . . which [is] inferior to a condom in preventing pregnancy and sexually transmitted diseases. The best idea is to put condoms *in* the candy. I would put them in the bags of Famous Amos cookies. This would have two effects. First, embarrassment would be eliminated because no one would know whether you are buying the cookies or the condoms. Second, it would allow for the use of anxiety-reducing code words. Instead of being mature and saying, "I would really love to have sex with you," you could just casually note, "Hey, a bag of those Famous Amos cookies would really hit the spot right now."

Small wonder that Professor Hampton was one of the College's most popular professors.

Aside from contraception issues, there were a number of other issues on campus that related to the sexual revolution—although by the end of the twentieth century it could hardly be considered a revolution any longer. One area involved problems of sexual harassment, sexual assault, and rape.

The extent to which such problems existed at Mary Washington was hard to determine precisely, since for reasons of embarrassment, fear, or ignorance (or all three), victims were notoriously disinclined to report violations.[34] Moreover, procedures for recording such reports, when they did occur, were not always consistent. Thus when College police revealed, for instance, that two rapes were reported in 1990–91, or that eight were reported the following year, it was difficult to know if those reports indicated the full extent of the problem.

It probably did not, for assaults of less severity appear to have been much more prevalent. According to the College Health Center, during 1990–91, for example, seventeen women received counseling for sexual assaults—a number estimated by the Center's director to have represented less than 5 percent of the incidents that actually occurred.

Rising concern over such matters prompted a number of actions at the College. In 1988 a Rape Awareness Week featured prominent speakers and panel discussions focusing on the issue of date and acquaintance rape. The following year, at the instigation of Brenda King, the director of international programs, a committee of eight faculty and staff ombudsmen was created to provide a conduit for the reporting of sexual (and racial) harassment.

In 1991 the Board of Visitors was moved to adopt a formal sexual assault policy based on the premise that "the Mary Washington College community will not tolerate sexual assault in any form." That policy spelled out in detail those actions that constituted sexual assault, including

> rape, forcible sodomy; forcible cunnilingus or fellatio; sexual penetration with an inanimate object; fondling or touching an unwilling person's genitalia, groin, breast or buttocks (covered or uncovered); or forcing an unwilling person to touch another's intimate parts (genitalia, groin, breast or buttocks). More specifically, sexual assault includes acquaintance rape / sexual assault, defined as any of the aforementioned acts undertaken by a friend or acquaintance without consent, or when the victim is incapable of giving consent, such as when the victim is physically or mentally incapacitated by alcohol or other drugs. Sexual assault occurs when a person is subjected to any of the above acts against his / her will, either by force, threat, intimidation, or through use of which the accused was aware or should have been aware.

To assist in implementation of the policy, the College appointed Assistant Dean for Residence Life Rhonda Angel to the position of coordinator of sexual assault and substance abuse services.

It was not long before the policy was activated—and in a case that shocked the campus. In 1992 the vice president of the Student Association (who was also an RA) received a one-year suspension by the Student Conduct Hearing Board for assaulting a freshman student the previous year.

The episode touched off a lengthy controversy. The convicted student, who transferred to another institution and never returned to MWC, sued the College in 1993 for $975,000. The suit, which was brought against the College in general and against President Anderson and Vice President Roy Weinstock (who had chaired the hearing) in particular, levied an array of charges including denial of constitutional due process and equal protection rights, breach of fiduciary relationship, violation of federal law requiring confidentiality of educational records, and intentional infliction of emotional distress.

Although the suit was ultimately dismissed, the whole affair made a considerable impact on the campus. One factor, of course, was that the accused was a high-profile figure within the student body. Another element was the accuser's detailed account, by turns naive and poignant—"I thought he really liked me"—which the *Bullet* printed in its entirety.[35] Added to that was the paper's own editorial condemnation of the accused's lawsuit. "There is something wrong with a system of justice," it declared, "when a man found guilty of sexual assault is suddenly turned into the victim, and the woman who was assaulted is turned into the bad guy."

Still more shocking than such episodes of student misbehavior were the occasional reports of sexual harassment on the part of faculty members. As with other instances of sexual impropriety, the extent of such behavior was hard to gauge—and for the usual reasons, plus the students' fear of possible "grade retribution" by the instructor.

Nevertheless some alleged episodes did come to light. The *Bullet* in the spring of 1992 reprinted charges by two students against one adjunct professor. "We were discussing the book that I was reading for his class," said one student of her professor, "and he flat out asked me to sleep with him. When I replied no, he asked if he could kiss me, and before I could say no again, he leaned over and kissed me." According to the other student accuser, the same professor "told me, 'I'd love to have sex with you on my desk right now, if I thought I had half the chance. But there are too many windows in the office.'"

Such revelations led other students to report similar experiences of their own. One of them told the *Bullet* of an instructor who suggested that he "wanted to spend time with me once a week, an 'us' time. Then he started talking about the clothes he wanted to see me in, like leather suits or skin-tight skirts. Then he mentioned bondage and handcuffs."

Within two years another case arose—this one more stunning because the accused was not an adjunct instructor but a prominent full-time professor who, in fact, had received the prestigious Simpson Award a few years earlier. In 1993 he was accused by three students of actions that breached the sexual harassment policy, including inappropriate touching and the telling of jokes with sexual innuendo. Though he denied any improprieties, the hearing process led to his agreeing in 1994 to undergo counseling and to receive regular evaluations by the College.[36]

Not everyone agreed that the sanctions were deserved, attributing the alleged questionable behavior to, in the words of one administrator (a female), "poor judgment more than anything else . . . for the way the world is today." A fellow faculty member, business administration professor Frederick Davidson, complained that the incident would "definitely chill my behavior in my creative class. [Now] I'm reluctant to ask anyone to do anything other than write something in their books. . . . It's wrong to put your career in jeopardy because some 19-year-old gets their nose out of joint."

Perceived procedural deficiencies in the 1994 case prompted calls for revision of the harassment policy. Leading the movement for change was psychology professor Christopher Kilmartin. Writing in a September 1994 *Bullet* column, he asserted that sexual harassment was "rampant" on campus, where "certain male faculty members are known to be habitual harassers." Yet few incidents were reported, he said, because victims regarded existing procedures for redress as "woefully inadequate."

The result was a revision of the policy in 1996. Key changes in the new guidelines included eliminating the requirement for the complainant to face the accused person, shortening the waiting period between steps in the procedure, extending the statute of limitations from six months to one year, and guaranteeing both sides the right to appeal the decision of the hearing panel to the president. The revision maintained the original policy's requirement of confidentiality.

Kilmartin was not pleased with the confidentiality aspect. "Confidentially is important," he acknowledged, "but it also has the effect of not showing how great a problem sexual harassment is on this campus and every campus. . . . Part of what we want to do is encourage people who have been harassed to come forward. . . . Administrators . . . want to keep things quiet, and keeping things quiet is exactly the problem."[37]

It was Kilmartin himself who assumed leadership of campus efforts to remedy the problem. Having been involved in men's studies for a decade, Kilmartin was the author of *The Masculine Self*, a study of masculinity and gender in contemporary society. His interests had alerted him to a program that had originated in Canada in 1991, called the White Ribbon Campaign, wherein men were encouraged to wear white ribbons to signify their opposition to violence against women. In 1993 he, together with Bernard Chirico, director of the Psychological Services Center, launched the campaign at Mary Washington, making ribbons available to male students, faculty, and staff. The campaign's success, though modest, led to its emulation at other colleges in the state and to its perpetuation at MWC each year, usually in conjunction with Domestic Violence and Sexual Assault Awareness Month in October.

At the outset there were skeptics, including the *Bullet*. Noting the proliferation of ribbons for various causes (e.g., red for AIDS awareness, purple for domestic violence awareness), a 1995 editorial titled "Empty Ribbons?" questioned the efficacy of such campaigns. "Now the buzz-word associated with these ribbons is 'awareness,'" it said, "and the idea is that the ribbons bring the problems . . . to the attention of the public. This is all well and good, but it also accomplishes nothing. . . . It's not that there is any problem with people wearing the ribbons if they want. There is, however, a problem with people pinning the ribbon to their shirt and thinking that they have done their part for the cause. . . . By all means, go on wearing pretty little ribbons; just know that correcting all of the things wrong with this world will take a lot more than just ribbon."

In rebuttal, Kilmartin pointed out that a campus research project in 1995 had clearly demonstrated that the white ribbon campaign had in fact helped to make men at the College more sympathetic to the problem of violence against women. Also, in a more tangible way, the campaign was useful in raising significant amounts of money for the area Councils on Sexual Assault and Domestic Violence.

Beyond promoting the White Ribbon Campaign, Kilmartin pursued the cause through frequent lectures and periodic workshops on sexual harassment at MWC, as well as at other institutions. Beginning in the late 1990s, in quite a different way, he brought attention to gender issues through his highly successful one-man comedy performance, *Crimes Against Nature*, which focused on the foibles of male behavior.

During the 1990s the College, besides undertaking efforts to raise awareness of issues relating to sexual assault, also sought to provide female students with practical help in combating such assaults if they occurred. The main method of instruction was through a program called RAD (Rape Aggression Defense), presented by the College police. Students embraced the initiative enthusiastically. In an editorial titled "A RADical Victory," the *Bullet* asserted that "while there are many issues on campus that students feel strongly about and think their concerns are not being met by college officials, the RAD program is a victory for the students."

The purpose of the program was first to inculcate behaviors designed to prevent assaults, but also to teach self-defense maneuvers for survival in case of an attack. Those techniques, drawing on the martial arts, were not for the timid or squeamish and included striking the attacker in the jugular notch of the throat or kicking him in the groin. "The last options," advised one instructor, "are to . . . grab the attacker's head and gouge into his eyes with the thumbs. These are the most serious options, and the most gross to think about, because there is nothing holding the eyes in the head except some skin, and they may pop out."

Students who took the RAD training no doubt came away with an enhanced sense of empowerment. "So men," said one *Bullet* article, "if you're walking down Campus Walk at night and a young woman you do not know looks you straight in the eye and smiles, chances are she isn't hitting on you; she is simply affirming her own confidence—that is, if she's a RAD girl."

The advice concerning response to rape attempts had certainly evolved over the years. In 1998 the Psychology Department, as part of its graduate-in-residence program, sponsored a lecture on sexual assault by clinical psychologist Deborah Ann Stahl '72. Stahl recounted how, when she was a student, a campus lecturer on rape prevention (a male) had said that the best way to survive was to offer no resistance and be completely passive to the rapist. After all, he told the group, rape was "only sexual intercourse."

Things had changed, sure enough.

Heightened awareness of sexual harassment led to consideration of consensual relationships between faculty and students (though opponents of such relationships insisted they could never be truly consensual, owing to the power differential that existed). It was not a new issue at Mary Washington.

In a 2006 *Bullet* interview, philosophy professor emeritus George Van Sant traced the origins to the all-female composition of the student body when he arrived in 1958. "One of the problems when we were an all-women's institution," he said, was that "male professors were really an authority figure and a lot of the students were cute, and . . . there were problems of the male faculty hitting on undergrads." Van Sant himself was deterred from such action by, if nothing else, the admonition he received when he was hired from the chair of the philosophy department, E. Boyd Graves: "I will never forget the lecture when I was hired. The absolute rule: when you are in your office the door is always open; and [Graves] said, 'I will tell you, you are young, you are attractive, [so] some of these girls are going to come on to you,' but he said, 'We will not have any of that in this department.' And he scared me . . . but a couple of times in my thirty-two years here a student did volunteer to do *anything* to get that D raised to a C."

Faculty-student relationships that had generally been clandestine theretofore began to become more open in the late sixties and seventies. Although disparaged by some, faculty-student dating was neither uncommon nor surreptitious (except if married persons were involved) during the seventies, and a number of those relationships led to marriages that proved, for the most part, to be long-lasting. Among the most visible of those marriages on campus was that of geography professor Marshall Bowen and his wife, Dawn, who eventually became a geography professor as well. One student, observing them together, commented, "They are so cute when they walk down the brick pathway together. I think it's wonderful, and there should be no policy on love."

A quite different attitude toward such practices, however, began to develop in the 1980s, as attention focused more on feminist-generated concerns about abuse of power relationships. As psychology professor Chris Kilmartin put it, "For every successful love story, there are dozens of students who have been traumatized by faculty members' abuses of power. It happens on virtually every campus in the country. We would be naive to think that we do not have to be vigilant in communicating the seriousness of this issue to the campus community. . . . In today's world, we are more aware that such relationships amount to highly unprofessional abuses of power on the part of the faculty members, regardless of the student's willingness to become involved."

Eventually the faculty addressed the issue, debating in the early nineties whether to ban faculty-student dating or, if not, how to restrict it in the interest of protecting students from exploitation. On the one hand, there was the opinion of those like Professor Kilmartin; on the other hand, there was Marshall Bowen himself, who expressed a more nuanced view of the situation and suggested a less proscriptive approach. Generally he agreed that such relationships should be discouraged because "the ingredients for stress and distress ordinarily outweigh the ingredients for happiness and success." At the same time, however, he contended that "there should be no blanket rule against relationships of this sort because many of them developed into solid, long-lasting connections that bring nothing but good to both parties. There must be a middle ground in this matter, but I am not sure where it lies. As long as both parties in the relationship are caring and responsible, things usually work out all right. The catch, of course, is how to program caring and responsibility into every relationship."

After much debate, the faculty eventually endorsed a policy that reflected a middle course somewhat along the lines of Bowen's view. Refraining from outright interdiction of faculty-student relationships, which would likely have provoked legal contests on the grounds that it violated constitutional guarantees of freedom of association, the final resolution read: "Amorous relationships between faculty and students they directly supervise are unwise and unprofessional. Faculty members are expected to avoid romantic or sexual relationships with students they teach, coach, supervise, evaluate, or grade. . . . Even in cases where the faculty member does not directly supervise the student, participation in an amorous relationship with a student may lead to difficulties."

A second resolution was passed to replace the existing passage in the Racial and Sexual Harassment Policy that said of faculty-student relationships simply that "while not expressly forbidden [they are] unwise and unprofessional." The emendation was more detailed: "A faculty member who enters into a sexual relationship with a student (or a supervisor with an employee) where a professional power differential exists must realize that, if a complaint of sexual harassment is subsequently made, it may prove especially difficult to base a defense on the grounds of mutual consent."

Though there were those who would have preferred total proscription of such relationships on pain of dismissal, more moderate elements were mollified by the new policy statement. History professor Richard Warner, long a foe of faculty-student dating, conceded that the College had "made a step toward establishing a more professional teaching environment." And the *Bullet* offered tepid editorial approval. "The faculty has wisely decided to avoid entangling the college in possible legal problems," it said, but added, "The resolution doesn't seem to have much grit . . . [and] in effect does very little. It serves merely as a guideline, not a rule. While warning against becoming involved in student/faculty relationships, the resolution offers no repercussions for those who do engage in such relationships. Then again, how can it? It's not an enforceable rule."

It probably was not. Midge Poyck '66, who subsequently held several administrative positions at the College including executive vice president, explained the matter succinctly. "Any time you throw men and women together, there is a chemistry," she said, "and if it ignites, rules fly out the window."

Another issue of concern beginning in the late 1980s and continuing into the next century was the HIV/AIDS epidemic. The College administration began early to urge its students who were sexually active to practice safe sex, and by 1990 had formalized efforts to promote greater awareness of the disease.

In the summer of that year, an AIDS Education Committee was created, with drama professor Keith Belli assuming a leadership role. "I'm sometimes incredulous," he said, "that this campus tends to think of itself as being so protected from life. . . . The odds are, sooner or later, [AIDS is] going to touch everybody."

One of the group's first actions was to formulate a state-mandated AIDS policy statement for Mary Washington College that said, in part:

- Students who have HIV infection, whether or not they are symptomatic, are allowed to attend class as long as they are physically and mentally able.
- HIV-infected persons cannot be denied residential housing.
- Employees infected with HIV cannot be excluded from employment.
- The College does not screen employees, faculty, or students for HIV infection.

The Education Committee began at once to sponsor a range of activities to bring the problem of AIDS to the attention of students. A number of events were presented each year during AIDS Awareness Week in October. There were also specific events periodically, such as A Day without Art, in which members of the arts community, a group hit especially hard by AIDS, collaborated to emphasize the need for support against the ravages of the disease. A number of students participated in AIDS marches as part of annual World AIDS Day programs and also showed their support by wearing the red ribbons symbolic of the anti-AIDS crusade. Benefit concerts were occasionally held on campus, featuring Fredericksburg area entertainers such as Saffire: The Uppity Blues Women and Sean Michael Dargan '90, with proceeds going to local groups such as the Sena Foundation and Fredericksburg Area HIV/AIDS Support Services, Inc.

Two specific and unrelated incidents—one national, one local—stimulated the AIDS awareness of students in the early nineties. At the national level there was the shocking news, announced in November 1991, that the Los Angeles Lakers basketball star Earvin "Magic" Johnson had contracted the AIDS virus. One Mary Washington junior, a male, succinctly expressed the prevailing campus sentiment when he said, "Since the Magic issue, it's not a homosexual or drug issue any more. It could happen to heterosexual students, too."

The truth of that statement was brought home to the College community around the same time with the revelation that one of its own had contracted the disease: a 1990 sociology graduate named Beatrice von Guggenberg.

Von Guggenberg was a freshman in September 1987 when she received a call from her boyfriend in Northern Virginia tearfully telling her that he had tested positive for HIV. Tests subsequently confirmed that she, too, had the disease. In the face of that traumatic discovery, von Guggenberg continued at Mary Washington, leaving on weekends to help care for her boyfriend (who died within a year) and keeping her condition secret from almost everyone. Among the few in whom she confided was her roommate, whose initial inclination was to move out. Later, when she finally told her staunchly Catholic parents, they were unsympathetic, having previously warned her, according to von Guggenberg, that she "would get AIDS as a punishment for having sex."

After graduation she took a job at the Whitman-Walker Clinic in Arlington coordinating volunteers for work with AIDS patients. No longer hiding the fact that she had HIV, she became an apostle for AIDS prevention and research, traveling about the area delivering the message that anyone, including heterosexuals, could contract the disease.

She returned to her alma mater in October 1991 to participate in a program titled "Death and Dying." Her testimony and admonitions reached the students with an impact that little else could have produced. "My dream," the twenty-three-year-old told them, "is to see my thirtieth birthday." She also recalled how, sitting in class, she would sometimes overhear other students saying that they did not know anyone with AIDS or who was HIV positive. And she remembered thinking, "[But] they did. I was sitting right next to them."

Among the leading AIDS activists at the College were English professors Judith Parker and Warren Rochelle and drama professor Gregg Stull '82. Stull's commitment to the movement extended far beyond the campus, owing mainly to his involvement in the NAMES Project Memorial Quilt—a project usually referred to simply as "the Quilt"—a memorial begun in San Francisco in 1987 as a way to honor those who had died of the disease. As new panels were constantly being added, the quilt grew to mammoth proportions, becoming in Stull's words, "the most visible symbol of the epidemic."

Overwhelmed by the power of the image, Stull became involved in the project in 1988, rising to the position of executive director of the NAMES Project in Washington, D.C. By the time the quilt was displayed on the Mall in 1996 (an event that he helped to coordinate), it was approximately the size of a dozen football fields—"the largest piece of art ever assembled," according to Stull. Through his connections, portions of the iconic memorial were displayed on campus from time to time, including a twelve-panel display in 2000 that nearly covered the Lee Hall Ballroom. Such events did much to focus students' attention on the continuing epidemic.

Although the campus escaped extensive AIDS infections, it was not completely unscathed. Among the known victims, there was, of course, Beatrice von Guggenberg, who, as Beatrice Kerr, went on to become a leading spokesperson about the disease, including numerous television appearances on CNN, MTV, CNBC, *Donahue*, and *The Jenny Jones Show*. She also was featured in *Glamour* magazine, the *New York Times*, and the *Washington Post* and appeared in a PBS documentary about women living with AIDS, *The Heart of the Matter*.[38]

She was perhaps at her most effective when speaking to high school and college students, a task for which she was ideally suited by virtue of her youthful vivacity. A typical reaction, reported the *Washington Post*, was that of a student who exclaimed, "When I saw Beatrice, I thought, 'Wow, she's really pretty. She can't be our speaker.'" Or, as her former Mary Washington psychology professor Carole Corcoran put it, students "see themselves in her, and they're shocked. . . . I can lecture until I'm blue in the face and not have the impact she has."[39]

For her heroic efforts on behalf of AIDS awareness, Kerr received the Alumni Association's Outstanding Young Alumnus Award in 1994. Another AIDS victim, Dennis Dobson '85, was given the same award in 1991. But he was not as fortunate as Kerr: his was presented posthumously.

Then there was drama professor Keith Belli. He told the *Bullet* in a 1993 interview that he believed Mary Washington had "only recently begun to hear the message" of the threat of AIDS. "I'm still surprised by what I hear," he said. "I think there's still a sense that people are safe. It's false." Three years later, he was dead, claimed by the disease against which he had worked so hard.

If any issues rivaled those of sex and gender in terms of campus interest in the 1980s and 1990s, they were those involving race—issues that periodically proved troubling to all of the College's constituent groups.

At the outset of his administration, President Anderson faced the problem of meeting state-mandated goals for the enrollment of black students as contained in the 1983 amendment of the Virginia Plan for Equal Opportunity. Those guidelines specified an enrollment of thirty-two new students at the College for the 1983–84 session. Despite increased recruitment efforts by the Admissions Office, the total fell short of the mark by four students—a harbinger of challenges that the College would continue to face in the years ahead.

In an effort to encourage minority applicants and to assist those who enrolled, the College in 1983 developed (with the aid of a state grant) an initiative called the Summer Transition Program (STP). It was predicated on the fact that black high school seniors were entering college at a 20 percent lower rate than whites and that the success rate of those who did enter college tended to be lower as well.

The original STP, designed and directed by history professor William Crawley in his capacity as executive assistant to the president, consisted mainly of workshops on study skills and on the use of College facilities such as the library, counseling center, and health center. The following year, directorship of the program was assumed by Jacqueline Currie, who was hired to fill the newly created position of coordinator of minority affairs.

In subsequent years, STP was significantly expanded in duration and content to permit students to take actual academic course work that could be counted toward degree requirements. The program established two levels of participants: first, "borderline" students who were required to pass the summer course work to be admitted to the regular session and, second, those who were already admitted, for whom attendance at the session was optional.

Although STP was obviously designed for their benefit, some minority students resented it as constituting a stigma of second-class status (especially those whose acceptance was contingent on completing the program). As one of them put it, there was no need to have "somebody holding my hand. I don't need that any more than anyone else does."

Yet the program not only continued but expanded. Under the leadership of Arthur Brooks—who, as assistant dean of minority affairs, had succeeded Jacqueline Curry as head of STP—the program by the late eighties had extended to cover five weeks. During that time, students were introduced to the academic, residential, cultural, and social life of the College. By 1990 STP further expanded to provide assistance that continued beyond the summer orientation into the freshman year. In so doing, the program constituted, as Brooks put it, "a tangible sign of the college's commitment to both quality and diversity.[40]

In the 1980s and thereafter there were two annual events that, though open to the entire College community, were of special significance to black students. One was Black History Month, celebrated each February, as part of a national focus on black history and culture.[41] The event at Mary Washington always incorporated a wide range of educational, musical, and social events to honor and celebrate black achievements throughout history.

Beginning in 1986, the first year that Martin Luther King Day was celebrated as a national holiday, a highlight of spring semester was the January commemoration of King's birthday. The initial celebration drew approximately eight hundred people to Dodd Auditorium, where they participated in a program in which, as the local newspaper reported, "uplifting gospel music and stirring speeches underlined the tremendous sense of accomplishment and joy that is attached to the memory of King's life." The audience was moved in particular by the address of Fredericksburg's charismatic black mayor (and later member of the MWC Board of Visitors), Lawrence Davies, who proclaimed, "The job is not ended, but we need to look back and realize that we stand where we are because somebody fought, somebody struggled, somebody died. We must be prepared to go in and take advantage of the opportunity. . . . We need to prepare ourselves so that those who have paid the price will not have died in vain." The program ended, as it did every year, with an emotional singing of the unofficial anthem of the civil rights movement, "We Shall Overcome."

The College experienced considerable racial unrest from the late eighties into the nineties involving employees as well as students. The concerns of employees were often crystallized in, and conveyed by, the Black Faculty/

Staff Association, a group formed in 1986 under the leadership of Assistant Dean Art Brooks and Special Collections Librarian Brenda Sloan. The purpose of the organization, according to Brooks, was "to prevent, discuss, and resolve employee issues related to individual and institutional racism at the college."

To address such issues, the College's Affirmative Action Committee invited an outside evaluator, Sharon Fries, assistant to the vice chancellor at the University of Maryland, to visit the campus to conduct an assessment of the racial climate at the College. Her two-day visit included fifteen formal interviews in addition to informal talks with a number of employees ranging, in her words, "from maintenance workers and housekeepers to the president."

The report was not favorable. Of the fifteen interviewees, a majority (nine) said they believed the racial environment to be good, but six said they perceived a racial problem, citing instances of hiring bias among employees and verbal abuse and other racist incidents in the residence halls. While admitting that the two-day visit was not sufficient to provide conclusive evidence, the report nonetheless described the climate on campus as "racist, intolerant of difference, teaching and promoting racist ideas and theories." Making matters worse, it observed, the overall administrative attitude toward the situation was one of denial.

Whatever the accuracy of the report, the response was not, in fact, one of denial but one of action. An immediate step involved development of a comprehensive Statement of Community Values and Behavioral Expectations that asserted the "right of every individual to be treated with dignity and respect at all times" and urged "the acceptance and appreciation of diversity in our community with regard to race, gender, culture, and creed."

The statement, which was to be posted in all public areas, academic buildings, and publications of the College, added that the College would not tolerate behavior that conflicted with the values described in the statement. Moreover, penalties were established by the administration—penalties that applied to both students and faculty—that ranged from informal warnings and education to termination, depending on the seriousness of the offense, the offender's attitude, and his or her previous record.

Another development was the hiring of Brenda King in the summer of 1988 as a special assistant to President Anderson to serve as the institution's affirmative action officer. In that capacity, she was involved in implementing one of the specific actions recommended by the Fries report: mandatory sensitivity training for all faculty, staff, and student leaders. The sixteen-hour sessions were conducted by C&W Associates, Inc., of Newport News, a consulting firm specializing (in its words) in "humanistic approaches to personnel management and supervision." The company had previously conducted training sessions for, among others, the University of Virginia, SCHEV, and the U.S. Environmental Protection Agency. During the course of several months, more than 350 persons at MWC participated.

Despite efforts such as these, the College in the early nineties experienced an uncharacteristic outcropping of race-related incidents. One involved a 1990 campus address by Khalid Abdul Muhammad, special assistant to Nation of Islam leader Louis Farrakhan. Indeed, Muhammad's speech, sponsored (primarily) by the College's Black Student Association (BSA), may well have been the most provocative address ever delivered in the history of the institution.

To begin with, the timing of the event was unfortunate. Muhammad, known for his anti-Semitic comments, was scheduled to speak on the first night of Passover, a situation that Hillel criticized as demonstrating "a lack of sensitivity" by the planners. Art Brooks, adviser to the BSA, defended the date on the grounds that it was the only time that the speaker's schedule coincided with the availability of Dodd Auditorium. "It was not an intentional act," he said.

The speech itself did little to assuage the Jewish students' premonitions of trouble. Arguing that the black race, not the Jews, really constituted God's chosen people, Muhammad condemned the media and entertainment industry as being controlled by Jews hostile to black people. He singled out the popular movie *Driving Miss Daisy* as being an attempt to portray the black man (played by Morgan Freeman) as an obsequious "Uncle Tom" who was only "good enough to cook Miss Daisy's—the Jew woman's—food." He also attacked the Hillel group directly, questioning their objections to his visit. "What nerve you have to go and say they [BSA] should have checked with you!" he exclaimed. "Who in the hell are you?"

He hurled special insults at the College itself, attacking the name "Mary Washington" not because of "Mary" but because of "Washington," castigating George as a slave owner who "used black women as bed warmers and belly warmers and then sold his children into slavery." He called the Washington family "redneck crackers, no-good peckerwoods and damnable devils" who were hypocritical to "get down on their rusty white knees [in church] and pretend they were praying." And so, he concluded, the name "Mary Washington College is an insult to you black men and black women. No intelligent Jewish man or woman would go to a college named 'Mary Hitler College.' . . . We [blacks] are not out of our Nazi Germany. . . . America is our Nazi Germany."

Reactions to Muhammad's speech from all College constituencies were almost uniformly negative, varying only in degree of outrage. Executive Vice President Merchent called the presentation "extremely ill-advised" and suggested that it posed "great harm to efforts of this institution to improve relationships among its faculty, staff and students." Brenda King was likewise "absolutely appalled" at the speech, especially in light of recent efforts to raise racial sensitivity at the College. "What did he think that was supposed to accomplish other than arouse anger, hate and division?" she asked. "There was just no good to be served by that thing."

The faculty adviser of Hillel, computer science professor Marsha Zaidman, expressed disappointment that the speech was so divisive and so violative of the tenets of the College's Statement of Community Values. "Such messages should be denounced," she said. "It is fundamentally wrong to belittle one group so that another may elevate its own status. We felt and continued to feel that the Nation of Islam's purpose was to disrupt the harmony and the spirit of working together that we enjoy here at Mary Washington College."

Many students—and not just Jewish ones—deplored the speech, none more vociferously than *Bullet* columnist Rich Cooper. The event, he wrote, marked "one of the saddest days in the history of Mary Washington College. The invitation and address by Dr. Khalid Abdul Muhammad was one of the most insensitive acts ever to occur here at the college. Instead of fostering black nationalism and equality, alienation and anger were created. . . . We are a people who desire community equality, a pride in our cultures, and a diversity of ideas and spirit. We do not need people in this community like Dr. Muhammad who preach separatism and prejudice. Thought-provoking speakers we need. Bigots we don't!"

In the face of such criticism, the sponsoring BSA defended Muhammad's presentation. Though they acknowledged that some in the audience may have been justly offended by the style of the message, "on the other hand," the BSA wrote in a message to the *Bullet*, "we are comfortable with his content and most definitely agree with his points of substance! . . . We feel the speaker provoked the opportunity for healthy campus dialogue . . . [and] forced our campus to deal with ideas, beliefs, and a religious lifestyle unfamiliar to MWC."

The BSA's adviser, Art Brooks, defended the speech on similar grounds. He, too, deplored certain aspects of Muhammad's delivery but found it overall to have been a worthwhile device for stimulating needed interracial dialogue. "This is an institution of higher education," he said, where "your mind [should be] open to other ideas that may be new to you." He also discerned a troubling significance in the College's hostile reaction to the address. If the institution were "a sea of tranquility—a place of perfect harmony," he claimed, "no speaker could come in and upset that harmony, unless there's some nerve to be touched. . . . If there was nothing to bring to the surface, people would have ignored it. Instead people stayed up all night talking."

While it is undeniable that Muhammad's speech provoked debate, it is less clear whether the effect of that discussion was more positive or negative. One certain result was that it further distanced Art Brooks from an administration with which he was already at odds. The reason for the conflict, he maintained, was that he was regarded as being "too outspoken" and not "a team player." (One of his defenders put it simply: he was "too black.") Brooks himself saw it differently. "It is always more 'convenient' for faculty and/or administrative faculty members to be quiet and obey the mandates of the administration," he wrote in a letter to the *Bullet*. "But whenever you see an injustice, you must stop to correct it no matter what the cost."

Even Brooks's friends admitted that his problems may have been caused less by his message than by his manner, which was always direct and occasionally abrasive. "He's a brutally honest person," said one associate. "It rubs people the wrong way, but sometimes, people need to be hit with a two-by-four to get their attention. Maybe he used that two-by-four one time too many." In any case, Brooks resigned in August 1990.

Despite the College's efforts to improve the racial climate on campus, sporadic manifestations of racism erupted, the most blatant being an incident in the fall of 1992 involving a junior African American student named Faith Christmas. In October of that year, a racial epithet was found spray-painted on the elevator in Jefferson Hall. Only a few weeks thereafter, in neighboring Bushnell, Christmas answered the pay phone on her hall around two o'clock one Sunday morning to hear a caller whom she identified as a white male say, "Tell the three niggers on the fifth floor [where she and her two roommates lived] that they are dead."

"I was scared for two or three minutes," Christmas said. "Then my fear turned to anger." She immediately informed her one roommate who was present—who said her initial reaction was to be "panicked." The third roommate, who was off campus at the time, got the news when she returned. "I was shocked," she said. "You want it to bounce off, but it hits you right in the heart."

As the three students met with administrators and concerned faculty in the week that followed, some members of the campus community expressed disappointment at the lack of an immediate response from President Anderson. Philosophy professor Craig Vasey, a frequent critic of the administration, complained that the president had "not taken a strong, public, loud morally correct position on this matter to tell everyone that this was wrong." Retired professor emeritus George Van Sant agreed. "Someone needs to tell Bill," he said, "that there are many festering sores in this community and that he needs to get involved."

Anderson, blaming lack of communication, plus involvement with numerous other pressing issues, for the delay, eventually issued a strong denunciation of the incident, saying that it was "unfortunate, inexcusable, and will not be tolerated."

He also met with the three students in his office the following Friday to assure them of his support—an action that the recipients of the threat appreciated. "He seemed really concerned and enthusiastic about working with us in making sure that we were okay," said Christmas. "It made me feel good that he was taking the time to talk with us and make sure we were all right." Anderson's executive assistant, Midge Poyck, also visited the three women in their dorm room to reassure them of the administration's support.

Subsequently, responding to a request from a delegation of concerned faculty and students, Anderson endorsed a campuswide Rally against Racism that was held some three weeks after the incident occurred. The event brought a standing-room-only crowd to the Great Hall, where they heard speeches from the president, several faculty members, and students—including Faith Christmas herself. "Every time I answer the phone," she said, "somewhere in my mind are the words, 'Tell the three niggers on the fifth floor that they are dead.' The words still ring in my ears just as loudly as they did when I first heard them."

One of the faculty speakers, Sammy Merrill from the Modern Foreign Languages Department, suggested that white Americans often deny the existence of racism because they have never experienced it firsthand. "How can I understand how blacks feel?" he asked. "No one has ever strip-searched me, I have never been chased by someone intending to do me bodily harm, and I certainly haven't received a death threat." Psychology professor Carole Corcoran sounded a similar note when she told the audience, "We all grow up thinking we're not prejudiced, that we're good people. I hate to tell you this, but there's no way, if you're white, that you can grow up in this culture without prejudice. The question is, what are you going to do about it?"

In addition to condemning racism, speakers called for greater College efforts toward diversity, as it affected the curriculum, faculty, and student body. The rally left Christmas gratified and cautiously optimistic. "I feel like we're finally getting some headway," she said afterward. "We're finally taking action." The whole affair prompted consideration of amending the College's Statement of Community Values and Behavioral Expectations to include a specific sanction against hate speech. The issue generated much debate on campus between those who viewed such sanctions as a necessary practical defense against racist verbal assaults and those who regarded any such effort to restrict freedom of speech as a patent violation of the First Amendment.[42]

Thus involving competing values, the complex issue brought divergent (and sometimes surprising) responses on campus from students, faculty, and administrators. Two of the most vocal faculty critics of the administration in the area of race relations, sociology professor William Hanson and English professor Stephen Watkins, both spoke out against the implementation of a hate speech sanction. "I'm not one who thinks we need standard penalties for racial jokes or racist comments," said Hanson. "These things aren't corrected in their essence by suspending someone." Watkins agreed. "It gets into First Amendment issues," he said. "I'm as offended as anybody by racist comments. But the weight of community values should come down on these people. . . . Critical mass ought to be the thing to put you in your place rather than some formal sanction."

On the other hand, Brenda King expressed support for such a rule, despite her concern for its possible impingement upon First Amendment rights. A member of the faculty (though not for long), she was openly critical of President Anderson for not taking a more aggressive approach to the issue. "His philosophy," she asserted, "is one of putting your head in the sand—an approach I find absolutely ridiculous. A lot of it, too, is the president's style. He doesn't like to talk about controversial issues [but] that's what leadership is all about. You have to address controversial issues, make a statement, [and] set a tone."

Anderson, though he did condemn the threats against Faith Christmas, was firmly opposed to the inclusion of a hate speech provision in the Statement of Community Values. "Any time an individual commits such an act," he said, "it's important that the president's office speak out and let people know that those types of actions simply are not going to be tolerated. I think it's important that we did speak out and we did so forcefully. [But] the fact of the matter remains that if every time something happens, you look to the college president to run to the bully pulpit to denounce those acts, in my view that doesn't say very much for what a college is doing from a standpoint of education. It is everyone's responsibility to speak out when they are outraged. . . . That's part of having the community engaged."

In the end, no hate speech clause was adopted. Instead, the most significant tangible action to result was the presidential establishment several months later of a Council on Community Values and Behavioral Expectations, a group of six faculty members, six staff members, and six students, including Faith Christmas. The avowed purpose of the committee was to promote educational efforts on diversity issues and to enhance the recruitment and retention of minorities. It began its work in the spring of 1993.

The very next year another racially tinged episode occurred, this one centering on a faculty member, Anthony "Jimmy" Jiminez. A Trinidad citizen of African descent, Jiminez was hired on a tenure-track position in the Economics Department in 1989 and taught for three years before being told in 1992 that he was being taken off the tenure track and given a one-year terminal contract for the 1992–93 academic year. The reasons cited by the College for that decision were Jiminez's failure to complete his dissertation in a timely fashion, his lack of scholarly productivity, and his unfavorable teaching evaluations from students.

Jiminez's response was to bring suit against the College in U.S. District Court in Richmond, claiming that his firing was racially motivated. In the suit, he sought $600,000 in damages from the College and its provost, Philip Hall.

In court, Jiminez denied all the charges against him, asserting, in particular, that the poor teaching evaluations were the product of collusion on the part of some students who disliked him because of his race and his West Indian accent. A number of College personnel came to Jiminez's defense, including Brenda Sloan and Brenda King, who testified that the College was not sufficiently supportive of equal opportunities for minorities.

In his decision, Circuit Court Judge Richard Williams ruled in Jiminez's favor, swayed partly, he said, by his perception of racial inequities at the College—a perception he drew from the Fries report, the paucity of black students and faculty, and, in particular, the telephone threats against black students in 1992. Subsequent to the verdict, the court, accusing Mary Washington of engaging in "intentional discrimination" against Jiminez, awarded the plaintiff approximately $75,000 to cover back wages and compensatory pay, emotional and mental distress, attorney's fees and court costs. He was denied punitive damages.

On appeal to the Fourth U.S. Circuit Court, however, the decision was reversed in a unanimous ruling by a three-judge panel who asserted that the lower court's decision was "erroneous because it failed to consider other, contrary evidence" in reaching its verdict, and that Jiminez had not proved that he was a victim of "invidious discrimination." Jiminez appealed that verdict to the U.S. Supreme Court, but the Court declined to hear it.

Although the College ultimately prevailed in the courts, the episode was a troublesome one for Mary Washington. Philip Hall later commented that "the toughest thing for me personally in the nineteen years that I served as dean was going to federal court over Jimmy Jiminez."

The affair also had a number of ramifications in addition to its impact on Jiminez himself (who, by the time the case was adjudicated, had already been employed by a Maryland firm as a consultant at an annual salary $5,000 greater than he had earned at MWC). One result was an intensified examination of the overall racial climate on campus, an enterprise that revealed little consensus, either among faculty and staff or among students, black or white. One African American administrator, Sallie Washington Braxton '77, opined that race relations at the College had actually been better when she was a student, though current racism was "subtle, and in a lot of instances it's veiled and difficult to prove." Several faculty and staff members rejected that notion, the common thread being their belief that the institution was making a "good faith" effort toward improvement. But as Genine Lentine, a white English professor, put it, "It's a slow process. . . . It's still an overwhelmingly white, middle-class institution."

As for the students, perceptions were widely divergent. One biracial senior asserted that "you hear things from people, rumors. But I've been here four years and never once have I witnessed any racial tension at all. There's always diverse seating at tables, [and] there's always intermingling in class."

On the contrary, another senior, an African American, noted that though she had never personally been the victim of overt discrimination from her peers, "It seems they're just tolerating [minorities]. They're nice and friendly, but it's only so far they'll go with you."

Beyond such generalized commentary concerning racism on campus, the Jiminez affair focused specific attention on the matter of affirmative action, inasmuch as the College contended that Jiminez had originally been hired in order to meet guidelines imposed by that policy—which Jiminez staunchly denied.[43] During the trial, both Provost Hall and Robert Rycroft, former chair of the Economics Department, testified that Jiminez had been hired initially over better-qualified candidates to help the College meet federal affirmative action guidelines. That assertion provoked outraged responses from some minority members of the College community. The Black Student Association, in a letter to the *Bullet*, declared: "In 1994, we find it hard to believe that a group of well-educated administrators of higher education would sink to the level of disgracing members of its so-called 'MWC family' by openly asserting that a fellow faculty member was hired to 'help the college meet Affirmative Action requirements.' This is a slap in the face of every student, faculty, and staff person of color."

Most vehement of all was Brenda King. In a guest column in the *Bullet*, having decried the College's treatment of Professor Jiminez, she delivered a lengthy explanation and defense of affirmative action, concluding with a dramatic blast. "Until this College develops a more healthy and positive attitude about affirmative action," she announced, "blacks here should leave, which I plan to, and others shouldn't come. This place is a set-up for failure, through either neglect, sabotage or psychological intimidation." She resigned in 1995.

In late 1995 the affirmative action issue was at the core of another explosive incident, this one involving a speech by Dinesh D'Souza, author of the controversial book *The End of Racism*. D'Souza, a conservative former member of the Reagan White House, was invited by the College's Council on Community Values and Behavioral Expectations to participate in a forum called "Affirmative Action: Past Its Prime?"

The event prompted what the *Bullet* described as "angry reactions from some members of the audience, both vocal and physical." Some, especially black students, were angry over the content of the speech, which condemned affirmative action for constituting "reverse discrimination" and for perpetrating a "racially intoxicated society"; the government, D'Souza insisted, should get out of the "race business."

There were others who criticized the forum for having only one speaker, D'Souza, with no one to offer an opposing view. The council's organizer of the event, Derek Bottcher, explained that D'Souza's short notice of acceptance left insufficient time to secure another speaker. The legendary civil rights leader James Farmer (then a member of the MWC faculty) had been asked, he said, but had demurred on the grounds that he had not read D'Souza's book and did not have time to prepare adequately for a debate.

The large crowd in Lee Ballroom was in a hostile mood from the outset. Then, in the midst of D'Souza's speech, a sizable group of students stood up, pointedly rearranged their chairs, and sat down with their backs to the speaker. In a tense question-and-answer session that followed the talk, "emotions skyrocketed," according to the *Bullet*, especially following an exchange between D'Souza and Professor Farmer, who delivered an impassioned but reasoned rebuttal from the audience. The most unseemly moment came when English professor Stephen Watkins, irate at what he deemed D'Souza's insulting remarks toward Farmer, engaged in a tug-of-war with the moderator, Bottcher, over control of the microphone with which to address D'Souza. Later Watkins was heard directing profane comments toward a student.[44]

The affair kept the campus abuzz for days—even weeks, judging by guest columns in, and letters to, the *Bullet*. Among the letters was a public apology from Watkins, who expressed regret and embarrassment for failing to uphold the College's values and expectations, including "the treatment of individuals with civility, dignity, and respect."

The event as a whole was hardly a model of decorum, but it served to epitomize the contentiousness often produced by the issue of affirmative action. Ten years later, it was still a volatile matter, as evidenced by conflicting *Bullet* columns that appeared in early 2006 expressing the polar extremes of the issue. "Affirmative action," wrote an advocate, "offers an opportunity otherwise unavailable and seeks to level the playing field. It is one of the most effective race-remedial actions and is not racist. . . . To ignore race and allow the perpetuation of [discrimination] makes us just as guilty as any Southern antebellum slaveholder."

A subsequent *Bullet* op-ed piece struck back, declaring that "state-sanctioned racism is not gone; it lives on as race-remedial affirmative action. You can describe this program or insult its opponents any way you wish. That still doesn't change the fact that it is a racist program."

And so the argument continued.

Another controversy that bubbled up occasionally during the 1990s—one that touched on issues such as race and gender—was political correctness (or "p.c.," as it was sometimes called). The term referred to the idea that one should take certain positions on various political issues—positions conventionally described as liberal—or else be characterized as unenlightened or reactionary and be branded as sexist, racist, homophobic, or the like.

Those who were accused of demanding political correctness denied any coercive intent, but their opponents painted them as "McCarthyites of the left," out to purge society at large, and campuses in particular, of those who maintained conservative views. Accordingly, argued the critics of political correctness, the movement tended to produce a chilling effect on discussion of sensitive issues for fear of promoting negative stereotypes of those who held contrary views.

Although the issue never became as divisive at MWC as at many other institutions, the term did surface on several occasions. One early instance involved a convocation address delivered to the graduating class of 1991 by economics professor Stephen Stageberg, a deeply religious Christian, who told his audience that "without a relationship with God, you have nothing, nichts, nada, zip in the long run." Anticipating that his comments would be provocative, he declared that those who disagreed with him represented "the forces of darkness which must be working feverishly here in Dodd Auditorium to confound what I am saying and to stop up your ears to resist my message."

The speech provoked an explosive and divided response. Some members of the audience, both students and their parents, walked out in protest; some of those who remained to the end responded with a standing ovation. Afterward some members of the audience defended Stageberg's right to express such views, while others (Christian and non-Christian alike) were offended either by his message or by his choice of such an occasion on which to deliver it.

No one was more outspoken in his opposition than biology professor Daniel Abel, co-adviser of Hillel, the College's Jewish student organization, who assailed not only Stageberg himself but also those who defended him. "Personally," said Abel, "I think the College should immediately rescind the degrees of, and give refunds to, any students who attended convocation in support for Mr. Stageberg, for obviously those students remained strangers to any knowledge during their tenure at MWC. Perhaps an arrangement could be made with Jerry Falwell's Liberty University to grant them degrees." When the administration refused to publicly condemn the speech, Abel contended that the "non-response could be interpreted by a reasonable person as sponsorship of religion by a state institution."

While few were as aggressive as Abel in expressing their opposition, there were others who deplored the evangelical message for its lack of ecumenicalism, especially in the setting where it was delivered. "We must all remember what the purpose of convocation is," commented philosophy professor Craig Vasey. "It should be something addressed to everyone, not a speech which implies that the only good guys are the Christians. What an odd way for the senior class to exit this school, which is supposed to represent diversity."

Stageberg's speech and the backlash against it constituted, in any case, an isolated event. The development of broader concern to anti-p.c. forces was the curricular reform of the 1990s that established general education requirements in race and gender. Of particular concern to them was the proposed Ethnic Studies course that so agitated a portion of the faculty in 1992.

The course was first taught by Cedric Rucker in the fall of 1992 on a trial basis. In the face of the anti-p.c. critics, Rucker defended the class as "not a bashing course—not a white male bashing course by any means. The course was about learning, not about pointing the finger at any particular group." The opposition soon dissipated, and the course became an accepted (by most) part of the curriculum.

Although debates such as the ones over Stageberg's convocation speech and Rucker's Ethnic Studies course involved matters of deeply held beliefs concerning large issues, sometimes p.c. controversies focused more narrowly on words—or, in one instance, a single word: men. In anticipation of receiving her diploma the following year, Senior Jeanie Coiner in the fall of 1991 publicly expressed displeasure that the wording of the document she would receive read, "Let all men know by these presents. . . ." Asserting that the offensive "men" was in conflict with the College's Statement of Community

Values and Behavioral Expectations, she proposed changing it to "persons" or some other gender-neutral term. "After four years in an atmosphere of non-discrimination, your diploma, which represents all that you worked for in college is discriminatory. . . . I would be ashamed to own such a poorly worded document." Her idea, Coiner insisted, did not constitute a radical proposal. "All I want," she explained, "is one word changed."

It was. Beginning with the May 1992 graduation, diplomas read, "Let all *ye* know."

Though critics scoffed at such quibbling over what they deemed frivolous issues, adherents of political correctness defended such actions as important aspects of much larger concerns. Psychology professor Chris Kilmartin expressed such a view in a 1995 *Bullet* op-ed article. "I think we have a moral obligation to make earnest attempts to provide seats at the table for women and minorities," he wrote. "So-called p.c. language is only one step in this direction. It involves little more than having a small bit of sensitivity to other people's feelings. . . . Using respectful language is only one part of becoming more culturally aware."

That line of thinking led the administration in the following year to attempt to change the designation of entering students from "freshmen" to "first-year students." It was not a completely novel concept. At the University of Virginia, for example, students had long been referred to as first-, second-, third-, or fourth-year students.

At Mary Washington, the idea had its proponents, significantly including Dean of Students Bernard Chirico. "The term freshmen is sexist," he said. "This campus has more women than men. The term first-year is all-encompassing." Assistant Director of Residence Life Heather Dilatush was of the same mind. "Terminology is very important," she said. "The word freshman was used in a time when schools were exclusively all-male. Women were not allowed to attend college. First-year is more inclusive of men and women."

Students were divided on the issue, with some agreeing with the administration's position and for the same reason: elimination of discriminatory gender-specific references. But others disagreed, including the *Bullet*, which ridiculed the idea in an editorial titled "What's in a Name?" If the goal was to eliminate the term "men," it asked, "Why stop here? Let's think of a new term for women; that's another word that contains the word men. How about woperson? And what about the word *men*tor? How about persontor?" Noting the previous accomplishments of female students, it observed that "women were doing all these things . . . *before* someone decided that women at this school are oppressed by the term freshmen. Obviously this one tiny word has not stopped women in the past from [exceptional] accomplishments."

In any case, the idea never really caught on, and freshmen, for the most part, they remained.

Another issue of concern to students was the environment. Beginning with the first Earth Day in 1970, interest had been piqued sporadically over the years by annual celebrations of that highly publicized worldwide event. But beginning around 1990, campus interest was encouraged on a regular basis by the Ecology Club, whose small but active membership led the *Bullet* once to describe it as "tiny but mighty."

The club was spurred into action in particular by the national concern that arose over the worst oil spill in U.S. history, the disaster of the *Exxon Valdez* off the coast of Alaska in 1989. As the president of the MWC club put it, "It's too bad it takes an oil spill, a breakdown of the ozone layer and needle-infected beaches to shock Americans into action."

In 1990 the club began to publish a weekly column, "Eco-Update," in the *Bullet* to focus campus attention on environmental concerns and to remind students of their individual responsibilities in the war against waste. "Use the recycling bins," urged one column. "Think about how much water you use. Turn off any unneeded lights. Don't use Styrofoam. Take a mug to Seacobeck if you want to take coffee out. Even ask your professors to use two-sided copying. At the least, think about the environmental impact of all your actions."

For its part, the club undertook a number of projects, including the installation of yellow plastic trash cans in dormitories and other campus buildings for collecting aluminum cans, which they transported to Fredericksburg's recycling plant in vehicles loaned by the College. Through the city's Adopt-a-Spot program, they took responsibility for keeping a designated area litter free. Working with the local Friends of the Rappahannock organization, they helped with biannual cleanups of the river. In one of their more interesting campaigns, they participated in a 1993 nationwide Ticket America program whereby club members affixed tickets to cars on campus that had low fuel efficiency ratings—including President Anderson's Lincoln Town Car.

The club persistently advocated greater recycling efforts on campus and thus greeted with delight a state mandate in 1990 that all agencies of the commonwealth must reduce their waste by 10 percent within six months and by 25 percent by 1995. Its members were in the forefront of a Recycling Task Force that the College created to address that requirement; they themselves contributed by instituting a dorm-by-dorm effort to recycle glass and newspaper.[45]

By their actions and by their exhortations, the Ecology Club did much to promote environmental awareness. By 2004 the *Bullet* had apparently become a convert. Observing that it was important for "the average person to learn about [conservation] savings in terms they can relate to," one columnist provided just such a lesson. "Recycling one aluminum can," she wrote, "saves enough energy to run your television for three hours. Three hours is enough time to watch all of the primetime on FOX Sunday from 'King of the Hill' to 'Malcolm in the Middle' to 'The Simpsons,' to 'Arrested Development,' and all the way through 'My Big Fat Obnoxious Boss.'"

In 2004 Mary Washington attracted rather unwanted ecology-related attention in the media as a result of criminal actions by a freshman student,

John Wade. Before entering the College, he and two Richmond-area friends, motivated by zealous concern for the environment, had engaged in several acts of so-called eco-terrorism, including defacing windows of fast-food restaurants, damaging sports utility vehicles at a Ford dealership, and, worst of all, conspiring to set fire to construction equipment at a shopping mall.

Claiming to be associated with the Earth Liberation Front, they left messages at the crime scenes, including one at the home of the mall contractor: "How can you sleep at night, in your bed, in your house, with your beautiful wife," the message asked, "knowing that none of it was earned by the merit of your character, but by destroying the environment and contributing to urban and suburban decay?" Another letter, left on several vandalized SUVs, blamed the owners for pollution: "You made a decision to buy an SUV which affects more than you could possibly imagine," it charged. "I am inconveniencing you financially in order to bring to your attention what you are doing. I am not crazy. I am reasonable. You are not."

Wade explained that he had been motivated by his disgust at the negative environmental policies of the Bush administration and by his reading of Edward Abbey's novel *The Monkey Wrench Gang* (1975), which Wade called "basically a handbook for industrial sabotage." He was "so angry at that point," he said, the vandalism "was enjoyable." Later, in a *Bullet* interview, he described his actions as a hobby, something entertaining. "All vandalism is fun to a certain extent," he said.

The consequences were not fun. Though he denied that his involvement was so extensive as that of his two collaborators, Wade accepted a plea bargain in U.S. District Court in Richmond that resulted in a three-and-a-half-year prison term, which the sentencing judge permitted him to postpone until the end of the spring 2004 semester. His reactions to the sentence were conflicted. He found it "a little excessive," yet asserted that his white, affluent status worked to his advantage. "They were easier on me," he said. "Next time it might be some poor black guy."

Wade also had mixed retrospective feelings about his behavior. Admitting that his approach may not have been wise, he nonetheless declared, "I hope I always act in a stupid way when it comes to acting passionately about something I care about." Yet he recognized his failure, telling a Richmond newspaper, "It was totally inefficient, it didn't accomplish anything. All I got were negative consequences." To the *Bullet*, he put it succinctly: "I was totally unsuccessful in all my goals, including not getting caught."

Still another issue of concern to other Mary Washington students focused on the issue of animal rights. Certainly many of them loved animals, as evidenced by their willingness to flout College rules by keeping pets in their dormitory rooms. Although regulations permitted only one kind of pet—fish—there were periodic reports that students secretly harbored more ambulatory creatures, including dogs, cats, gerbils, hamsters, hermit crabs, iguanas, turtles, snakes, and at least one two-foot-long "fancy rat," purchased from PetSmart, according to its owner, who succeeded in keeping the rodent (Albert) in her room for two years.

The only dog that was officially allowed to live in a residence hall belonged to Tammie Willis '01, a hearing-impaired RA who kept Cleetus, a hundred-pound Border collie mix, with her in Custis as a service dog. Other dogs were frequently on campus, however, some of them being walked by students who volunteered for that purpose at the local SPCA, which was conveniently located only a few blocks from campus. The practice was encouraged by the animal shelter, whose manager once explained that "the dogs look forward to their daily walks. It relieves their stress and keeps their social habits good; if the animals stay in the kennels too long they become aggressive." The same might have been said for the students who walked them. "If you are stressed with classes," said one, "walking with the dogs relaxes you."

Unfortunately (for the dogs and the students), an increasing number of unleashed dogs on campus, mostly belonging to neighborhood residents, caused some students to express safety concerns to the administration. The alarm was sufficient to lead in June 1991 to a decision banning all dogs on campus. The regulation immediately provoked an outcry from the (apparently large) dog-lover community, including widely admired geography professor Marshall Bowen, who was accustomed to take his (leashed) dog on a stroll through campus. "Every time I walk my dog across campus," he said in a letter to the *Bullet*, "students go out of their way to pet her and play with her, often remarking that they have a dog at home whom they miss very much, and thanking me for allowing them to spend a few minutes with her. This type of student/dog interaction does not constitute a menace to the aims and purposes of the college, and should be encouraged, not condemned and eliminated."

When classes resumed in the fall, students quickly took up the canine cause, forming a group known as SCAM, Save Canines at Mary Washington. Within weeks a petition opposing the ban had collected approximately six hundred signatures and was presented to Executive Vice President Merchent, along with the threat from SCAM that if the ban was not overturned, "the campus is really going to get mad."

Further hostility was avoided when the administration acceded to the petition and retracted the ban. A compromise was reached whereby certain areas (e.g., the Battleground complex and playing fields behind Goolrick) were to remain off limits, but dogs were to be permitted elsewhere on campus, provided they were leashed at all times.

Growing concern about animal rights in general led in the early 1990s to the formation of an animal protection organization on campus. Initially known as the MWC Animal Protection Alliance, it later was simply called the Animal Rights Club, with business administration professor Patricia Metzger as faculty adviser.

The club could not have had a more dedicated or more energetic leader than the diminutive dynamo Pat Metzger. In addition to serving as president of the local SPCA and often speaking out publicly on animal rights issues, during the mid-1990s she wrote periodic guest columns in the *Bullet*, vividly denouncing practices such as cockfighting, branding cattle, and trapping animals in the wild. A 1993 piece on the abuse of circus animals was characteristic of her impassioned approach. "Did you ever stop to think about how the animals learn all those tricks?" she asked. "The answer is 'negative stimuli.' Elephants are beaten with 'bull hooks' and whips during training. Bears frequently have their noses broken or their paws burned when learning to dance. A 'trainer's club' helps chimpanzees to master their act. Whips and electric prods are commonly used. . . . What about positive reinforcement? Quite simply . . . there is no positive reinforcement that will urge a tiger to jump through a hoop of fire! . . . Circus animals learn to do painful or unnatural acts out of fear."

A major focus of animal rights activists at Mary Washington, and elsewhere, was the practice of dissection (and particularly vivisection) in biology labs. Spurred by groups such as the radical People for Ethical Treatment of Animals (PETA), the argument reached MWC in the 1990s. The specific point of attack was the giant Carolina Biological Supplies Company, from which the College purchased its specimens for dissection. In 1991 the company came under attack from the U.S. Department of Agriculture for violating the Animal Welfare Act, an attack strongly supported by PETA. Professor Michael Bass, chair of the Biology Department, defended Carolina Biological as a "very reputable company" and a source of "top quality materials," while expressing suspicions about the validity of the PETA allegations.

Not surprisingly, Pat Metzger held a contrary view, condemning not only the individual company but also the whole practice of animal research, which she claimed was outmoded and rendered unnecessary by virtue of recent technology. The Animal Rights Club took the same position, using the slogan "We can't learn about life by studying a corpse." Indeed, commented one member, the main lesson taught by dissection was "a disrespect for life."

The debate over animal rights continued for years at Mary Washington, as it did throughout the country, perpetuating the debate over whether the potential for human good was sufficient to justify animal suffering.[46] At MWC the debate seemed evenly split. A *Bullet* online poll in 2001, for example, revealed that on the question of using fetal pigs for biology lab dissection, 49 percent were in favor, and 51 percent were opposed.

In the late nineties, the issue intensified on campus as the Animal Rights Club became more aggressive, inveighing against what they called "speciesism," defined as "the act of withholding natural rights from nonhuman animals." It was as wrong, they said, as sexism or racism. "Unfortunately," wrote one *Bullet* columnist, "the animals don't exactly have a way of standing up for their rights and escaping their predators, namely humans. . . . They basically have a language barrier and no opposing thumb, and so to some, those factors give humans a right to be superior to animals."

The outspoken positions of vegans—persons who refuse to eat anything derived from animals or animal products—served to polarize the issue further. Some students eventually began to rebel against what they regarded as an excessively pro-animal sentiment on campus. That attitude led to a remarkable affair in the spring of 2004, sponsored by the College's Young Republicans: an oxymoronic event called the Animal Rights Barbecue, in which students were invited to participate in a picnic in front of Lee Hall where only meat products would be served—hamburgers, hot dogs, and (in deference to Catholics, since it was on a Friday) tuna sandwiches. The sponsors adamantly denied that their event was anti-vegan, and certainly not anti-animals, but claimed it was designed to satirize the radical tactics of groups like PETA.

It was not surprising that the animal rights advocates were unamused. Asserting that the sponsors were supported by a lobbying group from Philip Morris, one opponent charged that "the biggest problem lies in what they are calling this meat-fest. Calling [it] an animal rights barbecue is a mockery of the animal rights movement." The *Bullet* also declared its opposition in an editorial titled "BBQ? WTF?" that branded the event "a pointless, stupid" affair whose "express purpose . . . is to divide—and ultimately piss people off. The very title illustrates this."

As it turned out, the event was not as confrontational as it might have been, given the emotionalism on both sides. The approximately 150 students in attendance seemed to get along surprisingly well, prompting the *Bullet* to observe that the barbecue "served as an excellent medium for dialogue between the camps, despite their ideological opposition." Even the vegans expressed appreciation for the opportunity "to take this callous, sarcastic stab at our ideals and turn it into a positive event where we can educate people about real animal rights issues."

It would be interesting to know what Pat Metzger would have made of the whole affair. But she was not there, having died four years earlier, leaving her beloved animals without their devoted friend and their passionate champion.

The political behavior of Mary Washington students in the 1980s and 1990s rather consistently reflected national trends, beginning with the so-called Reagan revolution that prevailed throughout most of the eighties. Students' basic satisfaction with the direction of the first Reagan administration induced a general apathy toward national politics that diminished interest in the 1984 election—a situation that *Bullet* columnist Jim Emery addressed as the primary campaigns got under way. "This spring is pretty exciting," he observed, "Virginia and Georgetown are in the Final Four, the Caps are making a run for the Stanley Cup and the O's are ready to defend their championship season. But the big action this spring, where the real fighting is, is the race for the Democratic nomination. Unfortunately, most students are oblivious to it. . . . I'm beginning to believe the only outside reading that most students do is going through *People* magazine, a sort of *Jack and Jill* for adults."

In an editorial shortly before election day, the *Bullet* offered its analysis of what it called the "growing conservative trend among young voters [that] seems to be occurring nationwide." The assessment was not inspiring:

> A sincere belief that conservative policies have and will bring us back to the "good old days," family values and patriotic ideals is probably a part. A just as important, though often unspoken part, . . . is self-centeredness and greed. More and more, we students seem concerned only with success and getting rich. To often we resemble the characters of "Risky Business" who often discussed their hoped-for post-college salaries. . . . We are afraid to rock the boat. Commitment to social change and idealistic thinking unfortunately have become passé on college campuses.

The prevailing attitude of Mary Washington students on the eve of the election seemed to be summed up by one *Bullet* op-ed writer who announced her intention to vote for Reagan, though without enthusiasm. "Thanks to the President's policies," she said, "this country still has a constitution proclaiming that all *men* are created equal and the women can go to hell." Yet she believed that Reagan was preferable to his Democratic opponent, Walter Mondale. Part of her decision was based on gratitude for what she perceived as Reagan's role in restoring the American spirit. The nation was able to get "back up because Ronald Reagan was here to lead us," she proclaimed, adding "the patriotism wave has not stopped since then. Perhaps it skidded a bit when Grenada looked like Vietnam . . . but it soon regained speed. . . . And so I'll vote for Reagan, a man whose ideology, however warped, has become policy. At least I know I'll get a job. At least I know my paycheck won't go to someone who does not deserve it. As Lee Greenwood would say, at least I know I'm free."[47]

Following Reagan's overwhelming reelection, political science professor and Democratic activist Lewis Fickett spoke out against political lethargy on campus, decrying a "return to materialism" that had created "the politics of greed." He criticized students for being "too sleepy" for political involvement and admonished them that "citizenship requires more than just getting a job."

Whether moved by Fickett's challenge or provoked by Reagan's policies, students did bestir themselves on behalf of several causes in the mid-eighties. One topic of concern was apartheid, which attracted particular attention as the result of a campus address by a charismatic South African expatriate, Montalepula Chabaku. Speaking in a packed Klein Theatre, she offered a litany of abuses perpetuated against blacks in her native country and exhorted students to "think globally and act locally" in support of her oppressed fellow Africans.

In response, a new club at the College, People against Apartheid, developed a petition of protest to be delivered to President Reagan. The document, signed by over 230 students, faculty, and area residents, expressed outrage over racial injustices in South Africa and ended with a demand for the "imposition of comprehensive, mandatory sanctions against the racist regime" in that country.

Another issue that aroused students was that of a nuclear test ban. In the spring of 1987, members of the MWC chapter of the United Campuses to Prevent Nuclear War traveled to Washington to participate in Lobby Day, in which, among other activities, they met with congressional leaders to present their views. In the case of Mary Washington students, that meant meeting with congressman French Slaughter, whose Seventh District included Fredericksburg. Although, according to the *Bullet*'s report, the student delegation "found Slaughter to be unreceptive to the idea of a test ban," the lobbying process itself gave the participants "valuable skills that will empower them for a lifetime."

Perhaps the most vocal political protest of the Reagan years involved U.S. aid to the Contra regime against Sandinista forces in Nicaragua. In March 1987, a group of MWC students engaged in a three-day fast to urge an end to American intervention in that country and to help raise humanitarian funds for its people. As the group's leader explained at the end of the protest, "What we must remember, most of all, is that the Sandinista revolution is not a communist but a nationalist revolution. Nicaraguans do not want to be a Soviet satellite, nor do they want to live under an American-backed dictator. They want freedom and peace . . . and this is why Mary Washington College students fasted for three days in support of Nicaraguan sovereignty."

For their efforts, the protesters were subjected to both verbal and physical abuse from some fellow students who shouted "Commies!" and pelted them with fruit while they stood vigil in Ball Circle. The *Bullet* deplored such actions and praised the demonstrators for not being "deterred from their beliefs by closeminded individuals who didn't know any better."

While there were clearly some students who actively supported liberal causes, they were distinctly a minority. On the eve of the 1988 presidential election, a campus survey revealed that 44 percent of the students described themselves as "moderates," and 28 percent called themselves "conservatives"; only 17 percent identified themselves as "liberals."

The election itself created little interest, either on campus or elsewhere, owing at least partly to the lackluster nature of the candidates, Republican George H. W. Bush and Democrat Michael Dukakis. Political science professor and widely quoted pundit Mark Rozell described it as "an issue-less, theme-less campaign" in which voters would likely make their decisions based "upon who is the least undesirable alternative for what may be a bleak four years." A campus mock election reflected that indifference, as only 8 percent of the student body participated. Those who did vote provided an accurate precursor of the actual election, as Bush won with 54 percent of the vote, compared to 43 percent for Dukakis.

Ironically, one of the most notable political activities on campus during the Bush presidency was a liberal one: the birth of a local chapter of Amnesty International. A major purpose of the organization was to work for the release of prisoners of conscience—persons incarcerated for nonviolent "crimes." Specific objectives included an end to the torture of women and elimination of the death penalty, which the organization deemed both racist and a form of cruel and unusual punishment.

First accorded official club status in 1990, the Amnesty International chapter pursued its goals through a number of activities such as showing movies, writing regular *Bullet* columns, and holding candlelight vigils, though its most common tactic involved letter-writing campaigns on behalf of incarcerated persons. It was not always an easy task, and membership was never large. As a Fredericksburg newspaper article noted in 1991, the group "faced an uphill struggle on the conservative campus." One of the leaders of the chapter in its early days agreed. "Expressing an opinion," she said, "makes you some kind of freak." But the organization persevered, and by the early twenty-first century, human rights had become a widely supported issue on campus.

The most dramatic activities on campus during the period, however, were not those related to peace but those related to war, especially after the United States began a military buildup in the Persian Gulf in response to the invasion of Kuwait by Iraq under Saddam Hussein in the summer of 1990. As the American presence in the Middle East seemed to presage war with Iraq, the situation engaged the attention of faculty and students alike.

Two of the faculty's leading authorities on military and diplomatic affairs, history professor Porter Blakemore and political science professor Lewis Fickett, both urged a cautious approach by the Bush administration; both advocated efforts to negotiate with Hussein. To Blakemore, who also taught at the Naval War College, one problem was that Bush had strayed from his initial goals in the Middle East. "Originally," he said, "it was to defend Saudi Arabia. With that accomplished, his new objective is to get the Iraqis out of Kuwait. His original objectives seem to have changed." Professor Fickett, a World War II veteran, agreed: "There's too much emphasis on the war option. The troops were originally deployed as deterrents, and they have since become offensive."

Mary Washington had few students from the Middle East, but those who were from there understandably had deep concerns about the developing crisis. Two who spoke publicly on the issues expressed divergent views. Sophomore Niloufar Tavassoli, from Iran, supported U.S. military action (under the aegis of the United Nations) against Hussein. She noted that after a nine-year war against her own country, "he has started another by invading Kuwait. Who will be next? What small country will he gobble up again?" Another sophomore, Fatima Sulaiman from Oman, viewed the situation differently. "I think personally, as an Arab," she said, "that the U.S. does not have a place there simply because it is really going to diverge the Arab states even more. It will change the geo-political situation," adding, "I think the U.S. almost wants war right now."

The issue became paramount when on January 16, 1991, the United States forces invaded Iraq. It was a shocking development, as it was the first war in the memory of current students, whose generation was born too late to have personal recollections of Vietnam. "I was in disbelief," said one sophomore, "because I've never been through a war. I've read and studied about wars, but it's different to go through one." Another agreed: "A lot of us have never seen a war before. I don't know how to relate to it."

Some managed to take a wry view of the situation, such as *Bullet* op-ed columnist Mike Smith, who wrote, "Saddam isn't just ruthless. I'm sincerely convinced that he's missing a few bolts below the waterline." He went on to scoff at Iraq's military capabilities, especially its missiles known as Scuds. "What a hideous name," he said, "Scud sounds ugly, like that reddish-brown crust that collects and festers under the screw caps of 14-month-old ketchup bottles. Ugh. Blech. . . . We have to win. With Eagles, Falcons, Tom-Cats, Patriots, and Hornets up against Scuds, Frogs, and Floggers, who would you bet on? America: We've Got Cooler Names."

Most students viewed the conflict in a more serious mood, including the *Bullet*, which ran a sobering editorial. Noting that, while the current generation of students had been aware of American involvement in supplying arms and training troops in various areas of the world, actual military engagements (e.g., Grenada and Panama) had been minimal. "It was always their people dying and not ours. Now the people who are dying are Americans—ours, and our age. They are our brothers and sisters, cousins and friends. It's really scary. . . . I guess I had always thought that war was something I would never have to deal with. But now, Patriots are no longer the worst NFL team, and Scuds have become a standard part of our vernacular."

The editorial also contained an admonition regarding war protests. "It's important to draw a distinction between antiwar and anti-American," it warned. "Those who oppose the war are opposed to government policy, not America. . . . We're all on the same side. We all want peace. Nobody wants to see an endless flow of body bags descending on Dover Air Force Base. And nobody wants to see that idiot Hussein take over the Gulf region. . . . Protester-bashing is a waste of energy. The last time we checked, all Americans had the constitutional right to express their opinions."

But the paper's cautionary message proved to be in vain as emotions rose on each side of the issue. Supporters of the war, about 125 strong, marched through campus, wearing yellow ribbons, carrying banners reading "We Support Our Troops," chanting "U-S-A, U-S-A," and stopping at one point to recite the Pledge of Allegiance. The organizer of the march, junior political science major Jeff Jones, emphasized that the purpose of the march was to support the troops, not necessarily the war itself. "I don't want to see another Vietnam," he said, "with soldiers coming home getting spit on for doing their duty. I want them to know, no matter what happens, whether we support military action or not, that we support them as Americans."

On the other side, opponents of the war gathered in the Great Hall to participate in a prayer vigil for peace. Numbering about 250, they heard Islamic prayers offered, while a tall white candle symbolizing hope burned on a table at the front of the quiet hall. A few students also traveled to Washington to participate in a Demonstration for Peace under the sponsorship of Pax Christi, a Catholic peace organization.

Individual students also expressed criticism of the war, including Fatima Sulaiman, who blamed President Bush for a "flippant" policy toward the Arab world. "The chemical weapons used by Saddam Hussein were made by Dow Chemical Company and DuPont. When he was using them on the Kurds, America ignored him because America was supporting Iraq then, over Iran." Another student, living off-campus, draped a banner across his Wolfe Street residence that read: "Blood for Oil? No!" "Protest is never a worthless cause," he said. "If you're not protesting, you're giving your consent." He went on to condemn what he interpreted as a "Nintendo mentality": "People seem to have lost touch with what's going on. They see bombs hit the targets, just like in a video game. But they forget it's blood—and human lives—that we're losing."

By happenstance the distinguished visitor in residence for the year was the Islamic scholar Seyyed Hossein Nasr, a native of Iran, whose visit had been scheduled far in advance but brought him to campus in the midst of the Gulf War. He, too, was critical of American involvement, asserting that it was principally the result of support for the state of Israel and the desire for oil—though he maintained that basic misconceptions on the part of the West toward Islam were the underlying problem.

On January 30 an open forum held in the Great Hall, sponsored by COAR, provided the opportunity for advocates on each side to express their views. Some, like Bernard Chirico, made analogies to the Vietnam War. "I had the pain and pleasure of growing up in the sixties," he said, "and I don't feel too far from that today." Particularly vocal in opposition to the war was English professor Steve Watkins, who had attended the earlier peace rally in Washington. "I think the message that our government needs to get is that this is wrong," he proclaimed. "I say protest. Protest loudly!"

Several weeks later, a protest rally did occur on campus, though not a loud one—at least not at first. On the evening of February 21, a group of about sixty students organized by the Progressive Student Union gathered at the Monroe fountain to demonstrate against the war. They had been granted administrative approval with the understanding that their activities would not be loud enough to disrupt classes in the nearby building. In the midst of their sedate protest came a high-decibel playing of Kate Smith's rendition of "God

Bless America" blaring from the third-floor office of geography professor James Gouger. That song, as well as "Onward Christian Soldiers," continued to blast at sufficient volume to drown out the protesters' efforts to speak until campus police prevailed upon Gouger to desist.

Gouger's explanation for his behavior was that he believed it inappropriate to demonstrate opposition to the American involvement at that point. "We're in the middle of a war," he said. "I believe in supporting the President and the country." Asked if he thought it was appropriate to play the music during the vigil, he responded disingenuously, "Kate Smith has always been a favorite of mine," and claimed that he was not aware that the music was loud enough to interfere with the protesters.

In any case, his effort appeared to have been counterproductive, drawing a public rebuke from a group of faculty members who wrote the local paper to praise the student demonstrators for "the restraint and maturity they exhibited . . . in contrast to Gouger, who sought to stifle freedom of speech." Even some pro-war students who were present found Gouger's action more offensive than those of the protesters. Terming the disruption "horrible" and "absolutely ridiculous," one of the supporters of the war conceded, "They have the right to protest. . . . There have been protests in America from the very beginning."

A sense of relief pervaded the campus when the war rather swiftly came to a successful conclusion at the end of February, albeit without the invasion of Baghdad or the capture of Saddam Hussein, both of which were objectives desired by many. One such was a *Bullet* op-ed writer who commented, "Why didn't we finish the job? . . . By not taking care of Hussein, we have now given him the opportunity to rebuild his army and to regain control of his country. If left alone for a few years, Hussein will most likely become powerful enough once again to try another aggressive move. . . . The point is that leaving him beaten but not defeated will not solve anything and may make matters much worse. . . . I'm afraid that many more will die if and when Hussein rises back to power in Iraq."

Another student expressed similar concern upon hearing that the war had ended. "I'm happy, but I don't know that I would say it's over," she said, adding presciently, "With someone like Hussein, you never know."

In the afterglow of Operation Desert Storm there was a broad consensus that President Bush's reelection was a certainty. "The only interesting facet of the '92 campaign," observed one *Bullet* columnist, "will be to see what Democratic meatball is nuts enough to run against Bush. Any candidate will get crushed."

But such predictions proved premature, for several reasons. For one thing, the Democratic candidate could hardly have been considered a "meatball."

William Jefferson Clinton was an articulate former Rhodes Scholar whose youthful vitality placed him in stark contrast to the stodgy President Bush in the eyes of many college-age voters.

Then, too, there was the impact of third-party candidate Ross Perot, who likewise appealed to some collegians, though for different reasons. In Perot's case, it was the plainspoken antiestablishment tenor of his campaign. In an analysis following a televised debate among the three candidates, the *Bullet* praised Perot's performance. "The American people should be 'all ears' this election year. . . . Perot has sent shock waves through the media, the political process, and more importantly, the voters. What could have been a boring 90-minute debate . . . turned out to be an entertaining political forum. With Perot's quips and blunt honesty, it made the other two candidates appear as stale politicians, delivering the same empty promises."

In a campus political forum, several speakers addressed the matter of Perot's appeal. "So many people are frustrated and hungry for solutions," asserted political science professor Jack Kramer. "Perot's rhetoric suggests that he has solutions." Speech professor John Morello agreed, describing Perot as "a voice for [people's] frustration with the way government is incapable of dealing quickly with problems."

The overriding issue of the campaign, however, was a sluggish economy, for which the incumbent Bush received the blame. "Students are concerned about the economy," said political science professor Richard Krikus. "They've talked to people they know who are out of school and can't find a job." Professor Kramer agreed, noting that the current student generation was "the first American generation that really doesn't have great prospects to improve quality of life over their parents."

Even an appearance by President Bush in downtown Fredericksburg was not favorably received by some students. Although a sizable number attended his rally in front of Goolrick's Pharmacy to take advantage of what one called "a once-in-a-lifetime chance to see a President," others came as protesters. One member of Amnesty International, for example, showed up to protest Bush's alleged violations of the Refugee Act of 1980.

The sum of such resentment translated into a noticeable leftward shift of student attitudes, a movement described by *Free Lance–Star* reporter Mike Zitz. "Two years ago," he wrote shortly before the election, "if you saw a Democratic bumper sticker on a car at Mary Washington College, you could be pretty sure the vehicle belonged to a faculty member. Probably some tweedy guy with a well-trimmed beard and a pipe. Now it could just as easily belong to a baby-faced 18-year-old freshman whose distraught parents had raised her a Republican. . . . Fears about the state of the economy seem to have jerked the school back, if not to the left, at least toward the middle of the road."

Campus political activists on both sides noticed the trend. The president of the Young Democrats commented that her group had "gotten a lot more support than I would have expected. . . . I wouldn't say this campus is very conservative anymore. We have witnessed a very major shift." Her Young Republican counterpart, who had witnessed a decline in his organization's membership, reluctantly agreed. "During the first two years I was at Mary Washington, the Young Democrats were basically non-existent, really," he observed. "They have been very active this year."

Faculty members also commented on the surprising Democratic resurgence. Professor Krikus, having polled his two introductory political science classes, estimated that approximately 80 percent of the students predicted a Clinton victory.

They were right. Few were happier about the outcome than Democratic warhorse Lew Fickett, who pronounced himself more hopeful about a presidential election than he had been in thirty years. "President-elect Clinton reminds me most of John F. Kennedy," he exulted, "a southern version of John F. Kennedy."

Alas, Fickett's optimism, and that of Clinton's student supporters at Mary Washington, was not justified during a term that produced little substantial accomplishment and considerable controversy, including questions of political corruption and personal character. Among the issues that incited the most heated debate was the President's "don't ask, don't tell" policy regarding the service of gay persons in the military.

Such concerns about Clinton notwithstanding, most pundits agreed that he would likely defeat his Republican challenger, Bob Dole, in the 1996 election. A concurrent view on campus emerged from a pre-election forum sponsored by the political science honorary, Pi Sigma Alpha, that featured three prominent members of the political science faculty: Lew Fickett, Stephen Farnsworth, and Victor Fingerhut. The consensus of the triumvirate was that Clinton would win despite the allegations against him. "No one thinks Clinton is the most honest candidate," said Fickett. "Polls consistently show that Dole is perceived to be the more honorable, but people are voting on gut issues and what really matters to them. Voters are somewhat cynical, but corruption exists in all parties. It is just not [a] decisive [factor]."

A *Bullet* editorial late in the campaign came to the defense of the Republican candidate, claiming that Dole was the victim of one-sided press coverage. "The national press has trampled on Bob Dole all summer," it read. "He's old. He's handicapped. He's old. He's bitter and angry. He's old. . . . The press ignores the fact that Bob Dole was a credible Senate majority leader and a fixture in American politics for over 30 years. . . . If he loses, the press can clink their collective champagne glasses and toast to the fact that they unmercifully beat down an American hero before he had a chance to prove himself."

Student activists did what they could locally for their candidates, with Young Republicans blanketing the area with Dole posters and the Young Democrats canvassing door-to-door for Clinton and the Democratic senatorial candidate in Virginia, Mark Warner.[48] Most students, however, evinced indifference toward the campaign—a situation reported in a *Bullet* article headlined (playing upon the MTV get-out-the-vote theme) "No One Rocks the Vote for MWC

Students." Nor was there any perceptible sense of elation on campus when, as predicted, Clinton emerged victorious.

The second Clinton administration was overshadowed by allegations of presidential misconduct involving sexual shenanigans with (mainly) Monica Lewinsky. Given the subject matter, the affair predictably attracted considerable interest among students. "We've seen it on the news, read about it in the papers, and heard about it over the net," said the *Bullet*, "and every time your computer beeps to announce that you've got mail, intuition suggests that it's just another list of Clinton jokes."

As the unseemly affair oozed toward impeachment proceedings, the student body, like the American public at large, was almost evenly divided in its opinions. On the one hand there were those who expressed contempt toward the damaged president. "He's not just a pig," said one senior BLS student. "He's a serial pig. . . . If he and Hillary have an 'arrangement,' take it to the Motel 6. Keep it out of the Oval Office." Yet most students seemed to feel that the president's offenses did not warrant his removal from office. In a *Bullet* article titled "Will Bill Clinton Go Down?" the paper reported that a student poll revealed that while 72 percent of the respondents did not believe Clinton had been truthful about the Lewinsky affair, only 37 percent believed he should be impeached—possibly because almost 75 percent of them felt that the prosecutor, Kenneth Starr, had "gone too far."

In the end, some students (as they will) chose to make light of the whole affair. A memorable lesson that one student (a male) said that he had learned from Clinton was that "he made me think differently about cigars."[49]

THE MATURING COLLEGE

While the image of national politics declined, Mary Washington College in the 1990s reached unprecedented heights of success, owing in large measure to the 1985 Commitment to Excellence plan. The institution benefited not only from the implementation and expansion of the initiatives proposed in the plan, but also from additional innovations unforeseen at the earlier time.

Among the new efforts were several that extended the College's outreach to the local community, particularly in terms of engaging the business sector (theretofore largely ignored in the institution's goals). Such initiatives were a reflection of President Anderson's personal involvement—he was an active member and onetime president of the area Chamber of Commerce—and his belief that the College had a responsibility to assist the local economy insofar as its resources and mission permitted.

One of the most creative efforts in that regard benefited students and townsfolk alike: the Executive-in-Residence (EIR) program, inaugurated in 1989. The purpose of the program was to bring to the College for a one- or two-day visit prominent leaders from the corporate world to share their experiences and expertise with students and area residents. The usual format included a public address, meetings with classes, and a breakfast with students and leaders of the local business community. Speakers were chosen by an advisory board appointed by the president, which included students and faculty from the departments of business administration, economics, and psychology.

Although the program was started by an initial grant of $60,000 from Dominion Bankshares and the Southland Corporation, the visiting executives were attracted not by the honorarium (which they did not need and seldom accepted) but by some special connection with Mary Washington. Such was the case with the first executive-in-residence, Dominion Bank chairman and CEO Warner Dalhouse, a former member of the College's Board of Visitors and the father of an MWC student. A number of subsequent visiting executives were married to alumnae, including College benefactor Robert Jepson (1991) to Alice Andrews Jepson '64; investment counselor and PBS financial analyst Frank Cappiello (1993) to Marie Rhodes Cappiello '51; Major League Baseball executive Sandy Alderson (2000) to Linda Huff Alderson '69; and Owens & Minor chairman and CEO Gilmer Minor III (2002) to Charlotte Major Minor '66.

Other EIR visitors had Mary Washington ties of one kind or another. Albertine Enterprises chairman and CEO John M. Albertine (2002) was both the husband of an alumna (Mona Davis Albertine '71) and a former chair of the Economics Department. One visiting executive, automobile dealership magnate Karen Radley, was a member of the Board of Visitors; another, IBM executive Katherine Cesky Hegmann, was an alumna of the class of 1978. Other notable EIR visitors over the years included the heads of GEICO, Legg Mason, Norfolk Southern, Ukrop's, and Circuit City, as well as the managing director of Salomon Brothers investment firm, John Macfarlane, the son of former Board of Visitors member Anne Beck Macfarlane '52.

Undoubtedly the most heralded of all the EIR guests was Warren Buffett, who visited the campus in 1997. Described as a "self-made billionaire," the chairman and CEO of Berkshire Hathaway was listed at that time by *Forbes* magazine as the third-richest person in the world. Such credentials earned him the rapt attention of audiences at each of his several appearances on campus.

Buffett's comments, peppered with humor, contained general advice about financial investment but focused more on the importance of character. The foremost qualities that he sought in his employees, he said, were integrity, intelligence, and energy—"but you've got to find people who have all three [because] if they don't have the first one, they'll kill you with the other two." Students and faculty alike were impressed with how closely Buffett's values paralleled those of the College's honor system.

The popularity of the EIR program led to its expansion in 2000 to include a visitor each semester, rather than just one per year. To students the most useful part probably was the breakfast, which allowed them not only to glean advice from the speaker but also to schmooze with local business leaders—about 150 to 180 of whom usually attended. As a senior once explained the appeal of the event, "We need to start looking at what's actually happening in the real world as far as what issues are important to employers. Besides, free breakfast!"

In addition to the Executive-in-Residence program, the College manifested its desire to promote the local economy through creation of the Small Business Development Center in 1991. In partnership with the U.S. Small Business Administration, the Stafford County government, and the Levi Strauss Foundation, MWC in the early 1990s established the center with offices in nearby Warsaw (home of a Levi Strauss plant) and on campus in the basement of Seacobeck. Within its first year, the center boasted the creation of over two dozen jobs and the investment of $425,000 in business capital in the area.

The College's outreach to the community under the leadership of President Anderson extended far beyond the efforts directed toward business development. It also included expanded programs at the two historical sites administered by the College—Belmont, the Gari Melchers Estate and Memorial Gallery, and the James Monroe Museum—and the creation of a major cultural program known as the Fredericksburg Forum.

The enhanced role of Belmont started during the Woodard years with the appointment of Richard Reid as director in 1975. Under his leadership, the facility was opened to the public that same year. Its potential for assisting the College in both its social and educational aspects began to be realized. It was used, for example, as a venue for hosting social events such as an Alumni Association reception for distinguished visitor in residence Mary Leakey in 1980, as well as dinners for groups including the MWC Parents Council and the Trinkle Associates, a library support organization. Its collection of Melchers's paintings also proved to be fertile ground for students majoring in the areas of art, art history, and historic preservation.

The fact was, however, that by this time the reputation of Gari Melchers was somewhat in eclipse, having never fully recovered from the decline it suffered following his death in 1932. A major step toward resurrecting Melchers's image in the public mind came in 1984 with publication of *Gari Melchers: His Works in the Belmont Collection* by MWC professor of art history Joseph Dreiss with the editorial assistance of Richard Reid. The handsome book, whose funding was assisted by donations from the family of the beer baron Julius Stroh and Robert Beck, a local resident, comprised about one hundred selections from Melchers's work (thirty of them in color) along with an interpretive essay by Dreiss.[50]

The academic boost to Belmont provided by the publication of Dreiss's book was accompanied by an equally important personnel development: the 1983 hiring of Joanna DeGilio (later Catron) as assistant director (later curator). Her primary task at the outset was to develop an education program for the museum, which she accomplished through innovations such as the Listen with Your Eyes program for schoolchildren. But her contributions to Belmont went far beyond specific programs of that kind. A 1979 graduate of Mary Washington, she was utterly committed to preserving and promoting the work of Gari Melchers. Her zealous pursuit of that goal, abetted by her vivacious personality and curatorial competence—and a decidedly unstuffy approach to art—created a welcoming environment at Belmont and led her to become, over the next three decades, the very heart of life at the Melchers estate.

Catron's presence was especially crucial at times of transition, such as when Reid retired in 1985. Reid's contribution to the development of Belmont had been crucial, as he oversaw the establishment of the core collection of Melchers's paintings and almost single-handedly conducted the initial organization of letters and exhibition catalogs that constituted the gallery's archives. In addition to his tangible accomplishments, he also possessed many talents and attributes of character that served Belmont well. According to his friend and associate Joseph Dreiss, Reid was "cultured and sophisticated, a connoisseur who understood and appreciated art, literature, and music. . . . Above all else, he was considerate of others, a true gentleman, who treated everyone he met with courtesy and respect." He died in 2002, seven years after his retirement.

Under Reid's successor, Peter Grover, the museum continued to progress, with more exhibitions, an ongoing exchange of paintings with other museums, and a renovation of the main house. An important milestone was the awarding of official accreditation to the facility by the American Association of Museums in 1985. In the same year, an annual lecture series was inaugurated.

After several eventful years as director, Grover left Belmont in 1990 to assume the directorship of the Association for the Preservation of Virginia Antiquities. He was succeeded by David Berreth, who, with a calm yet energetic approach, led the museum during a time in which it achieved new levels of success in many areas. One of the museum's paramount functions continued to be its support for the College's academic programs. A particularly avid user of Belmont was historic preservation professor Brown Morton, whose ties with the museum went back to his childhood when he visited the estate with his grandmother, a close friend of Gari Melchers's widow, Corinne. Years later, Morton recalled that his two favorite activities on the estate were to visit the library with its massive parrot cage and the studio where he ogled the Melchers nudes. "My first sources of sex education," he once joked, "were *National Geographic* and Gari Melchers's studio."[51]

A major programmatic event in Belmont's history during the 1990s was the development of a traveling exhibit first proposed by the Florida art historian Diane Lesko, a graduate school friend of Joe Dreiss. Having seen a copy of Dreiss's book, Lesko was surprised to learn that no retrospective of Melchers's work had been held for half a century. She therefore organized one, and it traveled from her own museum of fine arts in St. Petersburg to Savannah, New York, Detroit, and Richmond.

The exhibit drew mixed responses. At its initial showing in St. Petersburg, a reviewer, describing Melchers as "an academic progressivist [who was] neither too academic nor too avant-garde," praised the exhibit as being "sure to stir warm feelings of nostalgia. This is the kind of art you don't have to go to art school to appreciate." Reviewers in Richmond, however, were not so kind. One suggested that the retrospective constituted a "tribute to an artist who had to settle for competence when greatness eluded him." Another was even more negative, asserting that "Melchers never did anything that was entirely his own. . . . His entire career was one that copied the values established by more creative souls."[52] Whatever the case, the traveling exhibit did much to bring Melchers once again to public attention. Its return to Belmont prompted a celebratory exhibition titled "Welcome Home."

Among Belmont's expanded activities was sponsorship of a ten-day tour of the Netherlands to view the area that produced many of Melchers's best-known works.[53] Local outreach activities were also expanded, resulting in the eventual hiring of an educational coordinator and a museum shop manager. To assist the museum with strategic planning, the Belmont Advisory Council was established in 2003 under the leadership of Karen Radley, who was also a member of the College's Board of Visitors.

Beginning in the nineties, Belmont engaged in an extensive program of renovation and new construction under the watchful eye of the Board of Visitors' historic properties committee. The improvements involved both the grounds and the buildings of the twenty-seven-acre estate. Early in the decade, the Garden Club of Virginia restored the landscape of Belmont. The work, drawing on extensive notes written by Corinne Melchers, included restoring a long boxwood walk, two arbors, and the lawn, and planting additional trees and flower gardens.

For some years the Rappahannock Area Master Gardener Association contributed extensive amounts of time and effort toward maintaining the grounds until in 1999 a professional gardener, Beate Jensen (a 1999 BLS graduate), was hired. At her recommendation, the estate moved toward establishing a more natural look, one that replicated the appearance of the property as it would have existed when the Melcherses lived there. Working with the Virginia Department of Game and Inland Fisheries, Belmont's gardeners strove to reestablish native Virginia plants such as rudbeckia, asters, and native grasses in lieu of maintaining scrupulously manicured lawns.

Refurbishing of the built environment began in 1990 with a renovation of the main house, funded by the commonwealth together with matching funds from private contributors. To carry out further improvements, Belmont in 1994 embarked upon a $1 million fund-raising campaign, chaired locally by Elsie Janney, head of the Friends of Belmont organization. The honorary chairman of the campaign was Peter W. Stroh, CEO of Stroh's Brewery in Detroit. The Stroh family had supported Belmont financially since its public opening in 1975 owing to ties that went back to the marriage of company patriarch Julius Stroh to Melchers's sister Hedwig.

The campaign's first result was the conversion of the carriage house to a visitors' center. While the external appearance of the structure remained virtually unchanged, the interior was thoroughly renovated to create an exhibition space for photographs and documents, a museum gift shop, a twenty-five seat theater, and a multipurpose meeting room. The largest contributors to the approximately $350,000 raised were the Stroh family and the Stroh Foundation. The structure was officially named the Marguerite Stroh Visitor Center in honor of Melchers's niece.

The establishment of the visitors' center was the first of several projects that by 2007 had transformed the Belmont estate. In 1997 plans were developed that led to a major renovation of the studio. That project took eighteen months (during which the studio was closed) and cost $1.2 million, a sum covered by a combination of state appropriations, grants from foundations, and individual donations. The work included a new slate roof and floors, an improved heating and cooling system, and new windows, skylights, and track lighting designed to protect the artworks from the damaging effects of direct sunlight and uncontrolled incandescent lighting.

To celebrate the studio's reopening in July 2001, Belmont hosted several public activities, including First Saturdays in the Gardens, a monthly horticultural program organized by local gardening groups to spotlight private and historic gardens in the area. It also held an exhibit titled Arts and Flowers, in which local garden club members were invited to develop floral arrangements based on selected Melchers paintings. Both programs became popular continuing events.

In addition to the studio renovation, the main house also received a facelift, including repainting to convert the exterior color from stark white to ivory, with doors of Buckland Blue and shutters of Fiddlehead Green—part of a plan to "restore Belmont to the appearance it had when the couple lived there," said director David Berreth. "Bright colors were very popular in Europe, and they had just come from Europe, so they brought the colors with them."

The repainting was followed by a much more ambitious and extensive project: the construction of an 8,500-square-foot pavilion adjoining the studio, an addition that tripled the existing space. The state-funded $4.2 million project created climate-controlled storage and exhibition space for the museum's collection of over two thousand paintings, as well as an event room (complete with catering kitchen) that provided a venue for meetings and social events. Most remarkable, given the size of the facility, was the success of the designers (Quinn Evans Architects of Washington, D.C.) in planning the two-level structure so adroitly that it intruded negligibly on the sight lines of the property's landscape. From the time of its opening in May 2006, the pavilion quickly became a favorite locale for weddings, receptions, and other upscale social affairs.

In 2005 Belmont underwent an official name and logo change, becoming the Gari Melchers Home and Studio. The change was made to identify the site more closely with the artist and to avoid confusion with other Belmont place names.

The relationship between Mary Washington and its other historic property, the James Monroe Museum and Memorial Library, while on the whole beneficial, was not as smooth as its connection to Belmont. With the Virginia Supreme Court of Appeals having ruled in 1982 that ultimate control of the museum was vested in the Mary Washington Board of Visitors, the issue appeared to be settled. But contention continued unabated through much of the Anderson presidency.

For President Anderson, the issue constituted a personal as well as a professional concern. Convinced that the demise of his mentor Prince Woodard had been hastened, if not caused, by legal conflicts between the College (Woodard) and the James Monroe Foundation (headed by Helen Marie Taylor), Anderson was just as adamant as his late predecessor had been when it came to maintaining College control of the museum. Taylor, feisty and assertive as always, defended her view of the foundation's position with equal vigor.

The semiannual meetings of the Board of Regents routinely turned into fractious verbal circuses in which neither side had a monopoly on vitriol. No issue was too small to incite temperamental displays. One 1986 meeting—not atypical in its lack of decorum—began with a twenty-minute harangue by Taylor over whether or not minutes from the previous meeting should be accepted and, from that low point of civility, declined even further. Later in the meeting, Taylor attempted to answer a question that had been posed to the museum's curator by geography professor Richard Palmieri, then new to the board. Palmieri sharply reminded Taylor that the question had not been addressed to her. The exchange brought an acrimonious admonition from one of Taylor's allies. "Such impertinence!" he exclaimed. "This is going to turn into a tie-pulling session in a minute."

Though physical assaults were avoided (barely), the tension that persistently prevailed diminished the prospects for positive accomplishment. College officials eventually attempted to outmaneuver the Taylor faction by securing passage of legislation that would allow the governor to make appointments to the Board of Regents without having to include representatives from the foundation other than its president and secretary. Governor Mark Warner proceeded to make appointments that gave the Mary Washington side control of the Regents, who then took the unusual step of voting for their own dissolution. Foundation members, incensed at the prospect of losing what little power they still possessed, requested a ruling from the attorney general's office on the legality of the action. The resulting opinion essentially agreed with the foundation's complaint, suggesting that the governor's appointments were invalid because of their conflict with the original deed of gift for the museum.

But the squabble did not end there. At the next session of the General Assembly in 2003, state senator John Chichester, representing the Fredericksburg area, successfully lobbied for legislation that legitimized the right of the governor to appoint whomever he wished to the Board of Regents. Still, the General Assembly refused to kill the board, which remained, technically, in operation, though the body thereafter simply ceased to meet. Thus with that inconclusive determination did the museum proceed into the twenty-first century.

Given the vagaries of the museum's governance, it was surprising that it accomplished as much as it did. Despite all the turmoil, it managed, with the staunch backing of the Anderson administration, to contribute significantly to the academic program of the College, to the local community, and to Monroe's legacy.

Much of its success was owed to the expertise and commitment of its administrators, beginning with Lee Langston-Harrison, who in 1986 was appointed as the museum's first professional curator (and later named assistant director as well). She was succeeded as curator in 1998 by David Voelkel, who was in turn succeeded in 2004 by Meghan Budinger.

Most important of all was the appointment of John Pearce in 1989 as the museum's director of planning and programs; he was named director of the museum four years later, a position that he continued to hold into the first decade of the twenty-first century. A rotund repository of good cheer, Pearce possessed both the personality and the professional skills that enabled him to negotiate the sometimes treacherous rapids of the Regents, though even he became exasperated on occasion. "Mrs. Taylor," he once said, "just never thought we did anything right. I mean, really and truly, if I were to say an invitation needed to be printed in black on a cream stock, she would probably find a problem in that."[54]

Yet under Pearce's guidance the museum's accomplishments were substantial. In terms of internal development of the museum itself, a management policy and code of ethics were developed, a number of important gifts were received, and the operation of the museum was computerized. Private support increased through the creation of the Friends of the James Monroe Museum organization—one such donation being a 2005 grant from Doris Buffett's Sunshine Lady Foundation for the restoration of the Monroes' pianoforte. And the Hoes family continued its multi-generational support of the museum through gifts of Monroe objects and its endowment of the Monroe R. Hoes Memorial Fund for Artifact Conservation.

Museum programs were expanded in several ways. One was through participation in the C-SPAN series *The American Presidents* in 1997—an enterprise that resulted in a substantial increase in visitation and requests for information about the museum. The museum also created numerous temporary exhibits from the 1980s onward and participated in extending the museum's influence through the loan of artifacts to various other sites.

One of the most popular of the museum's programs in the local community developed as an outgrowth of its annual Monroe birthday celebration. In the late 1980s, the celebration was enlarged to become a Scottish block party in the street in front of the museum, in recognition of Monroe's Scottish heritage. One ramification of that event was the creation of the Scottish Society of Fredericksburg. So popular was it that, at Pearce's instigation, another celebration, the Welsh Festival, was created in the fall to honor Monroe's Welsh connection through his mother. That event, too, led to creation of a local group, the Welsh Society of Fredericksburg. Members of the Scottish and Welsh Societies combined to create the Rappahannock Colonial Heritage Society, a group that subsequently cooperated with the museum to sponsor several events, including a James Monroe tea and a James Monroe ball, in which participants dressed in costume and performed period dances. Proceeds from both events were shared by the society with the museum for special projects such as the restoration of two of Elizabeth Monroe's gowns.

The museum was connected in several ways to the academic program at Mary Washington. For one thing, it served as a real-world laboratory by furnishing internships and research projects for majors in historic preservation, art, and art history, as well as for students at other schools. It was used in particular by Mary Washington's Bowley Scholars, historic preservation students selected to receive grants endowed by Elsie Ball Bowley in memory of her husband, Alfred Bowley. Over the years, research by these students contributed significantly to furthering the museum's interpretive mission. Those efforts contributed to the publication of *A Presidential Legacy: The Monroe Collection*, a coffee-table style catalog in 1997. That work, according to White House curator Betty Monkman, who wrote the book's preface, constituted "an important contribution to scholarship on a national leader [which] will be a model for other presidential homes and sites." Among the many other publications by the museum was an important catalog published in 1992, *Images of a President: Portraits of James Monroe*.

The museum also participated in Elderhostel programs, but its most significant academic contribution to Mary Washington was sponsoring an annual James Monroe Lecture Series that, beginning in 1988, brought a leading Monroe scholar to campus each year to deliver a major address. Speakers included prominent figures such as Gaddis Smith of Yale (1988), Edward Crapol of William and Mary (1989), Harry Ammon of Southern Illinois University (1990), Noble Cunningham of the University of Missouri (1993), Daniel Jordan of the Thomas Jefferson Memorial Foundation (1994), and Paul Finkelman of the University of Tulsa College of Law (2005).

Fundamental to all the museum's activities was its mission to preserve and promote Monroe's legacy and its historical interpretation. Toward that end, one of the museum's most significant endeavors, beginning in 1990, was its support for the work of Monroe scholar Daniel Preston in compiling and publishing the Monroe papers. By 2006, Preston had published a two-volume catalog as well as the first two volumes of a projected eight-volume set. It was a work of notable historical significance, as Monroe at the time was the only one of the founding presidents not to have a modern collection of his papers.

The most ambitious project considered by the museum involved the establishment of a James Monroe Presidential Center. At 55,000 square feet, the center, to be built beside the existing museum, would have been the largest historical attraction in Fredericksburg—more than ten times the size of the existing facility. Projected to cost at least $9 million, it would have provided space for offices, archives, a research library, and two-hundred-seat theater, as well as a vastly expanded space to display items such as the four-poster bed in which Monroe died.

Ultimately the project bogged down, the victim, in part, of the usual infighting within the museum's Board of Regents, some of whose members preferred that the museum remain as it was. Underlying philosophical issues also arose, wherein some members of the foundation viewed one purpose of the museum as propagating their particular interpretation of the foreign policy ideas contained in the Monroe Doctrine, while the College preferred a less ideological approach. The imbroglio eventually led not only to the shelving of the project but to the demise of the Board of Regents itself, as it was this disagreement that led to calls for its dissolution.

The concept for an area public forum originated with President Anderson, who had long been impressed by a similar series in Richmond. His interest was particularly stimulated when in 1989 he served as a panelist with two other college presidents on a Richmond Forum program interviewing former secretary of state Henry Kissinger and NBC news commentator John Chancellor. With that experience in mind, Anderson eventually worked, with the assistance of Vice President Ronald Singleton, to develop an analogous public program at the College.

The first forum was held in April 1996 and featured three panelists: David Gergen, editor-at-large for *U.S. News and World Report*; Helen Thomas, longtime White House bureau chief for United Press International; and John Kenneth Galbraith, eminent scholar, diplomat, and professor emeritus of economics at Harvard. In the afternoon preceding the public forum, each of the participants met individually with groups of students and faculty in their particular areas of expertise: Gergen with political scientists, Thomas with journalists and English majors, and Galbraith with economists.

The forum attracted a capacity crowd to Dodd Auditorium, filling the hall, reported the *Bullet*, "all the way to the bird's eye balcony seats." The session was adroitly moderated by Judy Mansfield Muller '69, a frequent reporter for ABC news programs such as *World News Tonight with Peter Jennings*, *Nightline*, and *20/20*.[55] The forum focused on perennial political controversies such as health care insurance, Medicare, and Social Security, as well as on hot topics including the Whitewater scandal, the president's right to privacy (at the time, Clinton's), the Dan Quayle–Murphy Brown culture-war squabble, and the upcoming presidential election (Clinton versus Dole). In the main it consisted of debate between the conservative Gergen and the liberal Thomas, while Galbraith, in the *Bullet*'s words, "maintained a humorously intelligent perspective."

The second forum, held the following fall, was of a very different nature, featuring the political satirist Mark Russell (of PBS renown), but like the first forum, it attracted a capacity crowd. Peering into the audience at one point, Russell observed that "either this [event] is open to the public, or this is the oldest student body in America." In addition to his typically bipartisan contemporary humor that skewered candidates of all persuasions, he also cast numerous zingers at the politics of the Fredericksburg area and the commonwealth. "Virginia, of course, throughout much of our history, was known as the mother of presidents," he observed. "That mother's been on the pill for a long time."

The first season of the Fredericksburg Forum established a high standard of success in delivering popular entertainment and enlightenment to an audience hungry for such fare. The promise of the auspicious beginning would be confirmed in the years ahead as the series became an important cultural nexus between the College and the community.

The expansion of the College's outreach efforts was but one indication of the institution's ascendancy in the 1990s. Another was the favorable response of the Southern Association of Colleges and Schools to the 1992 decennial reaccreditation report, a monumental task ably directed by English professor Richard Hansen. Still another was the continuation in the mid-nineties of the campus construction program that had characterized Anderson's first decade as president—the most significant project being a new science building.

By that time—and, in fact, well before then—it was evident that the science program had outgrown what one observer called "smelly, dingy, cramped Combs Hall." Not only were classrooms overcrowded and equipment obsolescent, but the space needed for student research was virtually nonexistent. "In Combs," said biology professor (later dean) Rosemary Barra, "we had converted every inch of available space to research activity for undergraduates—a process that included turning a bathroom into a lab and a storage closet into a research cubicle."

It could scarcely be denied that Combs Hall, almost forty years old, needed to be replaced. The problem was that construction costs (especially for science facilities) had risen enormously since Combs had been built for less than $700,000 in 1959. An initial appropriation for a new building in the amount of $7.7 million from general obligation bonds approved by a 1992 state referendum was not sufficient, even when another $2 million was added by the commonwealth. That is when Robert and Alice Jepson entered (actually reentered) the picture.

Having previously donated over $1 million to establish a faculty fellowship program, the Jepsons became interested in the science building after assiduous courting by President Anderson, whom Alice described as "very charismatic, a real visionary . . . [who] has really put [MWC] on the map." His role as salesman proved crucial. "If not for Bill pursuing us," she said, "I'm not sure we would have thought about Mary Washington College. Our attention probably would have been turned to different projects."

Fortunately for MWC, it was not, as the Jepsons donated $2 million toward construction of a new science facility. That gift, added to the state funds already procured, brought the total to the $11.7 million necessary to build a facility that met both the functional and aesthetic requirements that College planners had established.

Originally planned to be located across Campus Walk from Simpson Library, the building, because of costly unforeseen excavation problems with that site, was relocated to the area between the library and Goolrick Hall, across from Alvey and Arrington dormitories. The 72,000-square-foot neo-Georgian brick structure provided room for teaching and research laboratories, classrooms, lecture halls, and offices for the departments of biological sciences, chemistry, physics, environmental science, and geology. In a significant improvement over Combs, it incorporated a computer lab, aquatic lab, and greenhouse. Exterior amenities included a white-columned portico (consistent with surrounding structures) and a large fountain integrated on the building's front lawn.[56]

The official opening of the long-awaited building (the largest on campus) came in April 1998 with its christening as, appropriately, the Jepson Science Center. The occasion was celebrated with a weeklong series of events, including guided tours of the building for students, faculty, and local residents. Two Fredericksburg Forums were dedicated to scientific topics. The first involved a panel of NASA luminaries, Guy Bluford, Donna Shirley, and Scott Carpenter, one of the seven original astronauts selected in 1959 for NASA's Project Mercury; the second featured a presentation by the oceanographer Robert Ballard, discoverer of the sunken *Titanic* in 1985. The central event was a ribbon-cutting ceremony highlighted by an address by 1996 graduate (and current medical student) Wendy Coling.[57]

The opening of the new jewel of the campus was, in all, a momentous day in the College's development—in President Anderson's words, "an enhancement not only for science, but for the institution's entire academic program." The students, said Alice Jepson, "deserve this kind of facility." And Dean Hall, who, as a scientist himself, keenly appreciated the need for the new center, suggested that the opening of the building's doors was a genuinely liberating experience; it was like, he said, "taking the shackles off someone."

The improvement in physical facilities was accompanied by favorable enrollment trends. Despite the continuing difficulty in attracting the desired number of minority students, overall applications were on the rise, with an attendant upswing in the academic quality of the student body. Aided by innovative use of technology, the admissions office in 1996, for example, recruited a freshman class of such quality that it placed the College within the top 10 percent of all colleges nationally in terms of selectivity. The average SAT score for that group (which would become the class of 2000) was 1,180, and their typical high school grade-point average was in excess of 3.4 on a 4.0 scale.

When those students arrived on campus, they entered a College that was flourishing as never before: the already impressive quality of the faculty was improving, the campus was more beautiful and more functional than ever, and the endowment account was growing. Student life was more sprightly, with numerous extracurricular activities available. The athletic program, both recreational and intercollegiate, was booming.[58]

Clearly, by virtually any measure, Mary Washington was an institution on the rise. But in the midst of that institutional success came personal tragedy for the chief architect of that success, President Anderson.

CRISIS

Bill Anderson had learned many things from Prince Woodard, his mentor and predecessor as president, including lessons on matters both professional and personal. Regarding the latter, he recalled that observing Woodard's first heart attack "was a learning experience for me as to just how much pressure you can put on yourself. . . . I should have learned that lesson better than I did."[59]

But like Woodard, Anderson relished the pressure, not even aware that it was stressful. Advised on one occasion by some observers that he needed more diversions from the pressures of his job, he told them, "It's not stress. It's fun!"

And so he pushed himself constantly in pursuit of the College's interests. Consumed by his work, he found little time for exercise, even cutting back on his passion for sailing, especially after the deaths of his boating friends Richmonder Robert Jarrell and Fredericksburg banker (and MWC benefactor) Pete Hearn. Always heavyset, Anderson unthinkingly allowed his weight to reach 230 pounds.

Much of his time was devoted to dealing with the state's educational bureaucracy and, especially, the legislature. He reached the point, he recalled, that "it was just up and down 95 day and night, . . . working the General Assembly. . . . I was overweight and my doctor had warned me that I needed to take better care of myself. At that time I just thought everything was going fine . . . [but] I was really just asking for trouble."

It arrived on September 26, 1996.

That day, like countless others, found him in Richmond, meeting with government officials. It was a hot day, and following a morning meeting with the State Council of Higher Education, he hurried back to his room in the Omni Hotel for a change of clothes before scheduled sessions in the legislative office building that afternoon. Suddenly overcome by dizziness, he slumped to

President Anderson on the portico of George Washington Hall

the floor of his hotel room, at which moment, fortuitously, a hotel housekeeper opened the door and, seeing Anderson's plight, immediately summoned medical aid. Within minutes he was strapped to a gurney and rushed to the Medical College of Virginia hospital, which, again luckily, was just a few blocks away.

Doctors quickly diagnosed the problem as an aneurysm, the rupture of a balloon-like swelling that was allowing blood to leak into his brain. In his case, the aneurysm was 1.5 centimeters long, huge by the microscopic scale of the arteries in that part of the body. In such cases, the process of brain damage can be swift—and often fatal.

In a situation in which every minute was critical, a top MCV neurosurgeon, Dr. William C. Broaddus, was prepared to operate, having calculated that perhaps no more than fifteen minutes remained before surgery if Anderson's life was to be saved. Dr. Broaddus quickly commenced a procedure that lasted over six hours, which the president survived.

Survival, however, did not necessarily mean recovery, and Anderson faced two major problems: seriously diminished vision and, at first, near-total paralysis. At one point, as he was drifting in and out of heavily medicated consciousness, he later recalled, he heard hospital staffers advising his wife to start filling out the papers for disability retirement and looking for a nursing home because the prospects for appreciable recovery were slim. "I overheard that conversation," he remembered, "and just the idea of being in a nursing home or some situation where other people have to do things for me—help me dress or things like that—I just couldn't. . . . That was just not acceptable. It's a selfish thing to say, but I had decided [that] . . . had the prognosis been that I was going to be paralyzed and was going to be in a nursing home, I had already made the decision to end my life as soon as I could. That was a very selfish thing to do, but I didn't want to be a burden on my family. It was just not my idea of life. It was just totally unacceptable."

The days and weeks ahead brought gradual improvement. Though the paralysis remained on his left side—an even greater problem because he was left-handed—his vision improved, eventually reaching the point where he could see objects within roughly the area between two and six on a clock face. That enabled him to read, which he did, concentrating mainly on biographies of Benjamin Franklin, Thomas Jefferson, and Winston Churchill. But the book that affected him most was Doris Kearns Goodwin's study of Franklin D. Roosevelt, *No Ordinary Time*. "What Roosevelt was able to accomplish while confined to a wheelchair was amazing," Anderson said, "[but] I knew I didn't have that kind of bravery."

Life in a wheelchair, he knew, was not for him. Lying in his hospital bed, immobile, he spent much time reflecting, he recalled, on things that he had "read over the years about courage and courageous acts of people [and wondered] just how much of it is motivated by absolute fear. And that certainly was the case with me. I was just scared to death when I heard the possibilities of not coming back to work, having to retire on disability, and maybe ending up in a nursing home. I said that is something I can't tolerate. It's just not the life I want to live, and I'm not going to live that [life]. I just made up my mind."

At that point he began to focus intently on regaining his mobility. With his shaved and scarred scalp covered by an MWC baseball cap, surrounded by College memorabilia, and buoyed by baskets of get-well cards, he commenced a tedious and tiresome regimen of therapy, frequently commenting that if he could just see the campus again, he knew he would be all right. (On one occasion, under sedation, he actually called the campus police and instructed them to come and get him. They wisely did not try it.)

The process was not easy, and it was slow. But about six weeks after the surgery, there came an initial breakthrough when one night he was able to raise his left leg ever so slightly. "It was," he said, "like the greatest thing that ever happened to me."

From there he progressed to being able to dress and feed himself and to walk with assistance. Yet a return to work seemed a dubious prospect. As Dr. David Cifu, the director of the Rehabilitation and Research Center at MCV, put it, Anderson's recovery was "close to miraculous considering the severity of the injury," but cautioned that "being a CEO, you've got to be hitting on all cylinders. . . . I don't think he can do that now."

Anderson, however, was undaunted. Early on he set for himself one paramount goal: to be able to preside over commencement ceremonies at the end of that academic year.

Ronald E. Singleton

Meanwhile, arrangements had been made for the ongoing operation of the College. From the outset, Board of Visitors Rector Paul Dresser had been totally supportive, reassuring Anderson that his job was not in jeopardy and urging him to concentrate solely on recovering his health without concern about a timetable for return or, should it become necessary, retirement.

The successful functioning of the College in the president's absence required many staff members to assume additional duties, but the main responsibility devolved upon three officials in particular. In the academic area it was Provost Philip Hall whose steady leadership provided a reassuring presence among faculty members. The role of Ronald Singleton greatly expanded. Originally hired in 1987 as director of public information, he had been appointed vice president for college relations and legislative affairs in May 1996. As such, he played a major role during Anderson's illness as the liaison between the College and the public, a task that required almost daily communication with the president.

The most crucial person throughout the crisis was Executive Vice President Marjorie Meredith "Midge" Poyck. The holder of two Mary Washington degrees—a B.S. in mathematics and physics (1966) and an MALS (1995)—she served as president of the Alumni Association from 1992 to 1994. She first joined the College staff in 1976, serving as a fiscal technician in the business office. Having held several positions of ever-increasing responsibility, including executive assistant to the president from 1992 to 1996, she was named executive vice president by President Anderson in July 1996.

Thus it was not only her title but her extensive acquaintance with virtually every aspect of the organization that led the Board of Visitors to appoint her as acting president in October 1996. Using as a model the arrangement by which Bill Anderson had served as President Woodard's temporary replacement years earlier, the board's resolution decreed that "during the current disability of the president, William M. Anderson Jr., the executive vice president shall perform all the functions of the president of the college."

It was an arrangement for which Poyck was well suited both by temperament and by training. Already widely known and admired throughout the College's faculty and staff, she possessed a winsomeness that immediately in-

Marjorie Poyck

vited friendship and seldom generated animosity. Lacking the egotism too often associated with talent of the level she possessed, Poyck was the consummate team player—the ideal choice for the difficult job she inherited and that she filled with efficiency and aplomb.

As for Anderson, his therapy at MCV had enabled him to progress to the point that by early November he was able to return to Brompton, an event reported by the *Bullet* in a story headlined "The Boss Is Comin' Home." Brompton had by that time been remodeled to make the entry wheelchair accessible and to convert one of the first-floor parlors into a combination bedroom and office.

It was then that the recovery process reached its most arduous stage, requiring several hours of physical therapy, followed by occupational and speech therapy, almost daily at the local Mary Washington Hospital. Supervising the effort was the director of therapy, Susie Hoshi-Bush, whom Anderson dubbed his "physical terrorist." Despite his consistently upbeat outward demeanor, inside he was less than positive about the prospects. "The day I started therapy," he recalled, "I really had my doubts if I would be able to walk. And I knew if I couldn't, I was going to have to resign."

His therapist did not share those doubts or, if she did, did not let on. "Susie looked at me and said, 'We're going to get you out of that wheelchair. That's not a good thing. You're going to be out of that by Christmas.' They were the words I wanted to hear, but I doubted."

As his therapy sessions continued, Anderson made his first public appearance in early December when he attended the faculty-staff Christmas party hosted annually by the president and his wife. This year, however, in deference to the president's physical condition, the venue was moved from Brompton to the Great Hall, and the affair was changed from the traditional evening cocktail party to an afternoon event to which families and their children were all invited. Though guests were stunned by Anderson's frailty—he had lost seventy-five pounds during his ordeal—his very presence was taken as evidence of a remarkable recovery and an indication of his determination to return to his job.

A major step, literally, in that direction occurred about the same time. Years later, Anderson recalled the momentous occasion:

> It was right before Christmas—I'll never forget the feeling—we were on the exercise mats, and Susie was across the room. And she said, "O.K., stand up and walk over here!" I had never done any of that on my own. And so I rolled over and got off the mat, stood up, and took little baby steps, and walked all the way across the room to where she was. And I kept thinking what a strange sensation it was to be able to walk, and [wondering] what does a baby or child think when they are first taking their steps. You take all that for granted in life. I eventually again began to take it for granted. But that particular day, just being able to move one foot in front of the other and not topple over . . . was an incredible day.

Several days later, right before Christmas, he was able to walk down the Brompton hallway from his room to join his family at the dinner table. It was a season of special joy indeed at Brompton in December 1996.

Anderson's first official appearance came soon thereafter when he was able to attend a meeting with legislators at a state budget hearing in Dodd Auditorium. Following a standing ovation in recognition of his presence, he spoke eloquently and fervently on behalf of higher education in general and Mary Washington in particular, pointing out the need for increased faculty salaries because "that's what makes the institution."

Through the winter of 1997, he began to increase his workload, mainly from his Brompton office, even venturing occasionally to visit the General Assembly for brief lobbying efforts. By then his vision had improved sufficiently to allow him to drive—a dicey endeavor that he sometimes attempted, displaying more pluck than prudence. Usually he was chauffeured by a member of the college police force, Ray Acors, who in the years to follow would become an invaluable aide and trusted companion as he continued to drive the president to events near and far, always alert to finding the most convenient points of access from car to entryway. (In fact, Anderson later claimed, he probably got to meetings more promptly with Acors's assistance than he ever had on his own.)

For years a popular figure in governmental circles, Anderson was received even more warmly during his convalescence. Although he sometimes needed an associate alongside to alert him to the presence of acquaintances who approached from his blind side, he soon settled back into the lobbying routine. Those who might have been made uneasy by his paralysis—his left side continued to be immobile—were quickly put at ease by his characteristic humor. He claimed, for example, to have requested that the surgeons videotape his operation "so that the faculty can see that I do have a brain." On other occasions he pointed out an acquired uniqueness: "I'm the only college president in the United States who is just now learning to write."[60]

Whatever the case, Anderson's efforts proved effective. The state appropriations for that year awarded the Mary Washington faculty the second-highest salary increase of any institution in the commonwealth.

Observers were amazed at the extent of the president's recovery, including his surgeon, William Broaddus. "He's a unique individual," said the doctor, "and the textbooks don't allow us to predict how someone with his intellectual capacity will deal with the problems he was faced with. . . . He has beaten a lot of negative predictions to have been able to return to . . . work." Rector Paul Dresser put in succinctly. "I've heard the word 'miracle' used," he said, "and I certainly would not use a different one."

But despite all the progress, there were some setbacks, including one that Anderson did not anticipate: depression. Although his doctors had warned him that such developments could occur in the aftermath of traumas such as he had experienced, his inherently positive disposition, coupled with his ongoing recovery, led him to discount the possibility—until it struck. "The absolute worst feeling in the world, just hopelessness," he recalled, leaving him in such a condition that "I honestly one evening did not believe I could live until the next morning because the depression was so severe." Fortunately, he was able to recover rather quickly by means of medication and suffered no significant relapses.

Through the spring months, he persevered with his therapy regimen, earning the admiration of Hoshi-Bush. "I've been a therapist for twenty-four years, and he's one of the hardest-working patients I've ever had. He's an inspiration, not just to disabled people, but to anyone who comes in contact with him."

An additional incentive was provided by a number of MWC students who were working in the hospital's physical therapy unit. "They all took the attitude that they were going to have me up and walking and ready for graduation," Anderson said. "That was their goal. Every day, [during] the time on the treadmill, they were right there working with me. So it added a little bit of special interest and enthusiasm."

As graduation day approached, college officials were gratified by the president's recovery and were impressed by his determination to preside over the ceremony. Privately, they were not so sure he could do it, and some even urged him not to attempt it. Such advice he persistently, sometimes pointedly, rejected; his mind was made up.

The rehearsal on the day before the event, with therapist Hoshi-Bush on hand, did not altogether allay concerns. Backup plans were formulated in case the president faltered somewhere along the way.

And so the day arrived—cool and damp, with a threat of rain. Anderson's closest associates were still apprehensive as the robed assemblage—seniors, followed by faculty, administrators, Board of Visitors, and finally the president—began the long procession down Campus Walk toward Ball Circle. It may safely be assumed that no one anticipated the scene that was about to unfold, one that would produce the most emotional shared moment in the history of Mary Washington College.

With the graduates at their seats and the faculty and platform party in place, all eyes turned to watch the end of the procession, now far behind all

President Anderson before the 1997 graduation exercises, flanked by commencement speaker Senator John Warner (left) and Paul Dresser, rector of the MWC Board of Visitors

the rest, as President Anderson, flanked by Provost Hall and followed closely by the intently watchful Ray Acors, laboriously trudged the last fifty yards to the podium. As he made his way ever so slowly down the grassy aisle, leaning heavily on his cane and awkwardly dragging his uncooperative left leg, the class of '97 hailed the appearance of their president with a jubilant and sustained roar of admiration. Flashing thumbs-up and V signs, they showered him with a tumultuous standing ovation that went on for seven minutes—the longest and loudest continuous applause that anyone had ever witnessed. Nor had the campus ever seen a greater number of misty eyes, welling with respect for the president whose hard-won return did, indeed, seem miraculous.

Somehow he managed to remain composed and to preside without incident throughout the ceremony, which ended with his standing to award degrees personally to each of the 870 graduates. For every one of them, the event bore unforgettable testimony to the determination and spirit of the man and, most of all, provided unmistakable evidence of one whose love for Mary Washington matched their own.

Asked, years later, how he had managed to handle the emotion of the moment, Anderson admitted that "all the way up to the stage, there were tears in my eyes," but then, he said, "Once I got there, I told myself, 'OK, Anderson. It's time to get to work.'"

And that is exactly what he did. Not just on that graduation day, but—in a scenario that no one could have predicted—he continued to serve for another

President Anderson enters Ball Circle to the cheers of the class of 1997.

decade as president of the college, during which time some of the most significant accomplishments of his administration were achieved.

INTO A NEW CENTURY

The advent of a new century (and millennium) attracted considerable attention on campus—so much so that the *Bullet* almost a year in advance felt constrained to throw an editorial wet blanket on the anticipated saturnalian celebration. "The Mary Washington campus community, and the entire free world for that matter, are under siege," it warned,

> and the enemy is not some new virus, or Saddam Hussein, or even the newest Backstreet Boys single. In fact, even the $50 T-shirts sold at Structure don't rival the intensity of this new plague on mankind. . . . What we are talking about, of course, is the hype surrounding the year 2000. . . . We have cults which all forecast the end of the world. We have Jerry Falwell telling people to stock up on canned goods, and we have computer programmers stockpiling weapons and moving into the desert. Every movie, it seems, ends in "2000." . . . Every movie that doesn't end in 2000 is about the end of the world. Usually these involve either aliens invading, asteroids invading, or Super Wal-Marts invading.

But, said the paper, the millennial contagion was pointless. "Just what does all of this hype add up to?" it asked. "A few bottles of empty champagne?

Maybe. Outside of that, it don't mean squat, baby. Zippo. . . . Nothing will happen on January 1 except for Dick Clark hanging out with a bunch of frozen drunk people in New York City."

This disdain belied serious concern at the College, as elsewhere, on account of potential harm from the Y2K computer bug. The root of the problem was the formatting of programs from the early days of computer technology to use only two numbers instead of four to record dates, thus meaning that the "00" in "2000" would be recognized by older computers as "1900." Predictions of impending techno-doom were rampant, with some even pointing out that an anagram of "year two thousand" was "a year to shut down."

Fortunately, the Mary Washington technology staff was in the vanguard of addressing the problem; the College's vice president for computer and network services, Carol Martin, was in fact the head of the state's Century Date Change Task Force. Under her direction, MWC began preparing for the challenge as early as 1995. Having invested $500,000 in the installation of necessary new software, College administrators were confident as the new century approached.

All the planning and precautions paid off, as the system functioned flawlessly through the tense period. Indeed, the new software actually enabled the College to expand its services by facilitating online registration and grading in 2000.

While administrators took care of the technology, students took care of the celebrating. For months they had been musically exhorted to "party like it's 1999" through the incessant repetition of the song "1999" recorded by, as the *Bullet* identified him, "The Artist formerly known as The Artist Formerly Known as Prince, formerly known as Prince." The song, observed the paper, was "heard constantly—on the radio, on TV, on the Internet and probably on the moon."

Although students evidently took Prince's musical advice to heart, judging from the various descriptions of their New Year's activities as reported in the *Bullet*, the consensus seems to have been that the eagerly anticipated event, given all the hype, was something of a dud. "The millennium turned out to be the most overrated occurrence since Crystal Pepsi," observed a *Bullet* columnist. "Y2K came and went and the college is still standing, at least as well as it was before. . . . The stock market did not crash, my power did not go out, and thank God, neither did my cable. . . . No communist invasions were reported." Moreover, it continued, in a comment that would soon seem chilling, "The mass terrorist attack organized by Saudi terrorist Osama bin Laden that was supposed to happen, didn't."

The most interesting event that *did* happen, according to the paper, was that "Boris Yeltsin resigned as president of Russia on New Year's Eve, whether he remembers it or not, leaving Vladimir Putin, an ex-KGB agent with a really funny name in charge." And so, the article concluded, "Monotony—sweet monotony—and simple terrorist laziness prevented most evils from coming to life, all except for Dick Clark."

If Mary Washington students were blasé about celebration of the new year, they were more excited about the first presidential election of the twenty-first century, a contest among Democrat (and incumbent vice president) Al Gore, Republican George W. Bush, and Green Party candidate Ralph Nader. They also had more-than-usual interest in the local congressional race, since the Democratic candidate, Fredericksburg mayor Lawrence Davies, was a former member of the College's Board of Visitors.[61]

The results of a campus mock election, jointly sponsored by the Young Democrats and Young Republicans, revealed the continuing Democratic tendency of MWC students, as Gore handily defeated Bush, 47 percent to 36 percent. The leftward trend was also indicated by the relatively large vote (16 percent) garnered by Nader. (Also, Davies won the congressional poll.)

But greater excitement erupted from the disputed results of the presidential election, in which Bush was declared the winner in the electoral college on the basis of contested votes in Florida, despite Gore's having received more popular votes nationwide. It was, said one student (doubtless expressing the thoughts of many), "the craziest thing that has ever happened in politics"—which was scarcely an exaggeration.

Some students chose to express their opposition to the outcome by journeying to Washington to participate in a protest at Bush's inaugural parade. Twenty members of the MWC Human Rights Club demonstrated their feelings not only against the outcome of the election but also on broader issues, carrying placards with messages such as "Execute Justice, Not People" and "Stop U.S. Imperialism."

The *Bullet*, in an editorial titled "Bushwacked," referred to "stealing" of the election by the Republicans and called for reform, citing the fiasco as "a horrid example of why the electoral college must go." Meanwhile, it declared, President Bush would "for the next four years have zero legitimacy as America's commander-in-chief."

What the paper could not foresee, of course, was the tragic events of later that year that would unify the campus and the country, at least temporarily, in support of its leader.

"It doesn't seem real." So ran the local newspaper headline, and so ran campus feelings, on a day that began as a perfectly clear, typically glorious fall morning at Mary Washington, only to end in the darkness of stunned disbelief following the catastrophic terrorist attacks of September 11, 2001.

Few members of the Mary Washington community were old enough to remember Pearl Harbor; more, of course, could recall the assassination of John F. Kennedy, but that tragedy had become a less vivid memory. To students of the previous quarter century, the most memorable single event on the national level was the explosion of the *Challenger* spacecraft in 1986, but even that more recent disaster was beyond the clear recall of most students in 2001. So it was that news of the terrorist attacks in New York, Washington, D.C., and Pennsylvania struck the campus with unfathomable horror.

On the evening of the attacks, over a thousand students gathered for a silent candlelight vigil on Ball Circle—surely the largest impromptu event in the College's history. The moment was captured on film by *Free Lance–Star* photographer Reza Marvashti in a picture that was featured in a photo-essay on *Time* magazine's Web site.

The *Bullet* invited students to share their reactions to the calamity and devoted the entire next issue to it, printing one hundred of the responses. "All that can be heard on campus is the song of the crickets and the rustling of the trees," wrote one sophomore. "The silence is eerie. No one smiles in passing. Even the squirrels are not as lively. Professors talk, but nothing is heard. Blah blah blah, they say, and all I can think of is impending doom."

In the immediate aftermath of the catastrophe, there were sporadic threats (or rumors of threats) against students who were (or appeared to be) of Middle Eastern descent. When reports of harassment reached Dean of Students Bernard Chirico, he quickly sent out a campuswide e-mail message warning against "incidents of intolerance," as he termed it. "If people engage in harassment based on race," he said, "we can, and will, do whatever is appropriate."

Several faculty members with special interests in Middle Eastern affairs expressed concern. Political science professor Curtis Ryan noted that "people on this campus have been verbally and in other ways assaulted," he said. "That's just a staggering level of ignorance." Philosophy professor Mehdi Aminrazavi also spoke to the plight of Islamic students. "American Muslims are in a tough situation," he observed. "On one hand, they too are afraid of getting hurt by terrorists who want to hurt Americans. On the other hand, they're also afraid of Americans."

Publicly, the College's Middle Eastern students appeared to face the potentially hostile situation with equanimity. Senior Farah Saeed, president of the Islamic Student Association, said that she was personally unaware of anyone who had been harassed. "I think that people are angry, and they're going to lash out at who they think is responsible," she told the *Bullet*, "[but] I think it's a very small minority. . . . I feel safe on campus, and I think a lot of Muslim students feel the same."

There were a number of attempts to address the volatile issue from an academic standpoint, including a forum organized by the Multicultural Center several weeks after the attack. The event provided a venue for exchange of ideas and release of frustrations—necessary actions because, as the center's director, Ameeta Vashee put it, "What it is important to remember is that you cannot put a face on what an American is. We're all Americans."

Some professors (notably Ryan and Aminrazavi) devoted much time to discussing crucial issues both in and outside their classes, while other instructors took novel approaches to addressing prevalent student concerns during the crisis. Art professor Joseph Di Bella, for example, encouraged his Drawing I class to express their grief through art. The result was a collection of seventeen powerful portrayals of fear, hope, and pride that were displayed on the outside walls of Melchers Hall.

Other classes took on special relevance. One was a freshman seminar titled "America Goes to War." Another, even more directly related to current developments, was a political science class on international terrorism taught by an adjunct instructor, Dennis Pluchinsky.[62] In light of increased interest following the attacks, Pluchinsky offered, in addition to the regular credit course, a two-part public lecture series in December titled "International Terrorism: A Citizen's Primer." Also, late that semester, Gary Noesner, a crisis negotiator for the FBI (and father of two MWC students), delivered a presentation addressing the outlook for future terrorist acts in the United States.

Students in the meanwhile devoted themselves by the hundreds to individual and collective acts of remarkable generosity. The unofficial fraternity, Psi Upsilon, for example, sponsored a benefit party at the George Street Grill where local bands Folded Under and XKJ performed for over seven hundred people; the proceeds yielded $4,000, which the fraternity donated to the American Red Cross. That agency also received $500 from the MWC Athletic Department through collection of donations at several games. COAR raised more than $3,300 for the Firefighters' Disaster Relief Fund and coordinated efforts to collect items for the Salvation Army—"everything from food and clothes to dog food," according to one member.

Then there were the countless students who gave, quite literally, of themselves. "I gave blood," said one, "because I felt like it was the only thing I could do to help."

While such charitable acts demonstrated the compassion that students felt for the 9/11 victims, there were some who at the same time voiced concerns about American policies that, they believed, contributed to causing the attacks. As one such student suggested in a *Bullet* op-ed article, the disaster signaled a "need to take a serious look at America's foreign policy. . . . We have obviously been doing something wrong. . . . We need to hold our leaders, and ultimately ourselves, accountable for our actions abroad and the consequences they bring. No longer can we ignore the warlike actions of our government and believe that they won't affect us simply because they occur in other countries."

It was that sentiment that motivated a segment of the student body, led by the Human Rights Club, to oppose looming U.S. military action in Afghanistan against the presumed architects of 9/11, Osama bin Laden and his Taliban forces. The advocates of pacifism engaged in two main demonstrations, the first of which was a candlelit peace walk through the campus and downtown Fredericksburg. The purpose, said a member of the Human Rights Club, was "to counteract the voice that's all over the media saying, 'Let's go to war.' What we want people to remember is that peace is an option." Added another, "There are other ways to force bin Laden's regime to give up. Killing civilians is not the answer."[63]

The walk ended with the announcement of a follow-up event to be held on

Ball Circle called "Salaam, An Evening of Peace." That meeting, sponsored by the Muslim Student Association, the Framar International Living Center, and the Human Rights Club, was designed to encourage peaceful alternatives to military action. "It's our society's nature to want retaliation," said one participant. "But . . . two wrongs don't make a right. We need to take a breath and realize there are better solutions."

Seldom in the history of Mary Washington College had anything prompted such a barrage of responses from the local community as the students' pacifistic protests. Letters to the *Free Lance–Star* appeared almost daily for weeks. The general sentiment was conveyed, albeit with more bombast than usual, in one missive whose vituperation was of such magnitude as to assure the writer's enshrinement in the Valhalla of invective, had such place existed. The protesters' vigil was abominable, in his view, "but then," he asked,

> what could you expect from a bunch of teenagers who think maturity is achieved by a B-minus in Psychology 101 and membership in the Book of the Month Club? The sheltered, pampered, impolite children of privilege, with their unwrapped intellects, nebulous belief systems, touchy-feely concepts of communication, unsullied naiveté, and Little Bo-Peep worldview were wise in opting for a silent vigil at the park. For they demonstrated in newspaper comments just how difficult a task it is to articulate insanity and make it sound interesting. Be advised, you dewy-eyed innocents who reside in that quaint hilltop incubator of morons—your four-year-long Christmas party is over. . . . I hope and pray that in the bleak and somber days ahead that you are sustained by something stronger than the wisdom of keg-party philosophers and the fantasy-land fallacies of loony-bin academics.

The newspaper itself was almost as antagonistic, condemning the antiwar activists for "listening to readings from dreamy-eyed (mostly Arabic) mystics and ruing the cruel fate that had situated them in the morally flawed country that had nuked Hiroshima, famished Baghdad, etc. . . . The subtext seemed to be that the hijackers who slit young women's throats and steered airliners into office buildings, although their methods were beyond the pale, had every reason to hate the United States."

Even more alarming, said the paper, was the fact that students—"many are political science majors"—were being urged to "seek jobs in the State Department so they [can] help set our foreign policy on the 'right course.' This evidently includes baring the nation's throat to the fangs of terror."

Such philippics drew quick and pointed rebuttal from defenders of the protest. Given op-ed space in the *Free Lance–Star*, one student took issue with the opinion that students were "apparently . . . nothing more than a bunch of lazy partiers with our hands in our daddies' pockets. Well, between bong hits and keg stands, we here at MWC are trying to prepare for [the future] . . . by becoming informed, rational, and responsible citizens—not by strapping on our M-16s and looking for any Muslim who badmouths the U-S-of-A."

Sociology professor Bill Hanson also delivered a defense of the peace marchers, asserting that they were

> keen enough thinkers to realize that a quick cry of war may feel good, but is not necessarily the best tactical or moral solution to a well-entrenched problem. . . . [They] are smart enough to ask why so many people in the developing countries dislike America [and] . . . to suggest that America take a close, critical look at itself and its own foreign policy to evaluate our own role in encouraging and perpetuating terrorism. Evidently these deeper, less violent, less vengeful, more humble questions are not ones many local residents want to investigate. . . . But this does not justify implying that the peace walkers are unpatriotic and that they should not voice their opinions.

In the end, the apostles of peace lost, as President Bush ordered air strikes against Afghanistan, bin Laden's presumed base of operations. The military action, according to the *Bullet*, generally received "overwhelming support" from students and faculty, citing history professor Carter Hudgins's comments as typifying that view. "We've been doing all sorts of things: raising money, cleaning up the damage, candlelight vigils, prayers, civic and religious gatherings of all sorts," he said. "[But] in the back of our collective minds, there's been this waiting for military action. I think the news in some ways was cathartic"—though he expressed doubts as to whether the fight was winnable. His history colleague Porter Blakemore, an expert in military history, expressed much the same view when he asserted, "I'm not surprised. I knew we were going to do something like this. . . . We are pursuing this war because it is in our national interest to do so. . . . [However,] this is a war against terrorism and it's a war that's to a certain degree never-ending."

Such views proved prophetic. By the time the freshman class of 2001 had graduated, entering students had become accustomed to an America at war, as the initial efforts in Afghanistan segued into a protracted and controversial engagement in Iraq. But for all those who were at the College in the fall of 2001, the horror of September 11 would endure as the most unforgettable experience of their college years. As one junior at the time wrote, "It was like watching 'Independence Day' [the popular alien-invasion film from 1996]. I kept thinking I was going to wake up from this nightmare that was invading my world. I knew things like this could happen, did happen, but not to me, not to my home, not to America." But then, she added hopefully, "Despite everything, all the hate and tragedy, we will prevail. As a nation, we'll stand united and the American spirit will not be dimmed."

At the turn of the century, Mary Washington, like all of American society, was transformed by technological innovations. On campus this revolution—

for such it genuinely was—had a profound impact on every aspect of the institution: administrative operation, academic program, and student life.

The computer age had arrived, timidly, at the College in 1978 with the installation of a Hewlett-Packard mainframe unit in the basement of GW, but only after a campuswide fiber-optic network was completed in 1995 did it reach maturity. From that point, all elements of the College were able to communicate with each other through the Novell network and its GroupWise e-mail program and to access a virtual world of information through the Internet.

The College's first Web site was designed by computer science professor Ernest Ackermann in the early 1990s, but its maintenance eventually proved too time consuming, given his primary teaching duties in the Computer Science Department. Accordingly, in October 1999 Sharon Palmatory '92, who had graduated with a degree in art history, was hired as the College's first full-time webmaster; upon her resignation two years later, Catherine Derecki was named to fill the position. Through Derecki's combination of technical skills and eye for graphic design, the Web site became in the ensuing years the primary vehicle for disseminating information both within the institution and beyond the campus.

On a daily basis, e-mail quickly became the preferred method of communication at Mary Washington.[64] In a 1997 memo, Vice President for Academic Affairs Philip Hall encouraged the use of e-mail. Noting its benefits in terms of convenience, speed, and paper conservation, he wrote, "It's time for the college to move on to GroupWise e-mail and away from 'telephone tag' or ordinary mail on paper, as it [is the] primary and preferred mode of . . . communication."

Unfortunately e-mail sometimes proved to be too convenient in a sense. Some users, mainly students, began to tax the system (and each other's patience) by sending mass e-mails, even though the messages contained therein may have been relevant to only a handful. To eliminate this nuisance, the administration, through the Network Policy Committee, implemented regulations that required all "nonemergency" messages to be disseminated through a message board available via the College's Web site.

Some critics smelled a rat. The most sensitive nose belonged to Professor Steve Watkins, faculty adviser to the *Bullet*, who suggested that the timing of the edict was suspicious, coming only days after he himself had sent a campuswide e-mail alerting recipients to the possibility of an impending College name change. Midge Poyck, chair of the Network Policy Committee, admitted that "the timing of that whole thing was awkward" but contended that there was "no relationship between when the guidelines were released and the e-mail from Watkins."

Watkins was not mollified. "I see censorship," he said. "I question the legality of it." The *Bullet* expressed editorial agreement, pointing out that the policy appeared to be applied selectively. "Yes, the campus has been censored," the paper said, but noted that some messages, specifically ones concerning fund-raising, were still permitted. "Are there any guidelines here?" it asked. "How do mass e-mails keep slipping through the dictator's fingers?"

In truth, the institution was well within its legal rights to place limitations on the use of the e-mail system, a position upheld by the office of the Virginia attorney general; most Virginia schools had such restrictions. Moreover, many students applauded the move, since they preferred not to receive dozens of unwanted messages each day.

E-mail protocols continued to be refined over time as the campus community adjusted to the potentialities and pitfalls of the electronic age. As the system was modified, students were able to send pertinent messages to selected recipients by going through the office of student activities. Faculty were likewise restricted from sending mass e-mails directly but instead had to go through the filter of prescribed administrative offices.

Even so, problems occasionally managed to crop up. The most notable was a mass e-mail received in January 2005 by approximately four thousand people, many of whom found it offensive. The message began by addressing itself to "all liberals, atheists, God-haters, gays, Europeans, and Democrats" and proceeded, amid errors of spelling and punctuation, to proclaim that "the victory of the Great George W. Bush [in the 2004 election] has swept the land to give a glorious victory to the righteous against the forces of Evil Liberalism." It was signed, "College Republicans."

The president of that organization, Andrew Lamar, immediately disavowed the message and denounced its sender. Given the counterproductive nature of the message, his denial was probably valid, though the real perpetrator was never discovered. Evidently the system could not be made immune from all misdeeds, yet such episodes were rare, and the overall utility of e-mail far outweighed the discomfiture of occasional abuses.

The campus computer network wrought numerous improvements in the daily operation of the institution. From the students' standpoint, one of the most important was the implementation of the EagleOne card in 1999. The card not only served as a personal ID but also could be scanned to make purchases in Seacobeck and the Eagles Nest, as well as from vending machines throughout campus.

A major innovation in 2004–5 was installation of a new central administrative software system, SCT Banner. The overhaul was known as BOB, standing for "Bring on Banner." The new system expedited numerous administrative functions throughout the institution and also aided students by allowing them to handle various operations such as billing and course selection through one portal; for the first time, students could actually register for courses online.

The impact of new technology on the academic program was nothing short of revolutionary. Overseeing this development in the early years was Ray Pope as director of academic computing, assisted by Ernie Ackermann and John Reynolds as associate directors. In 1994, a help desk was set up to assist all campus users in solving their network problems. The following year, academic computing functions were placed under David Ayersman, who was hired as director of instructional technology. In 1996 Pamela Lowery joined the staff as assistant director of instructional technology.

Under their direction, campus usage of technological innovations expanded rapidly. In this process, they were capably assisted by the instructional technology liaisons (ITLs) assigned to each academic building. These were the people—Jerry Slezak in Monroe Hall, Andrew Rush in Jepson Science Center, and Martha Fay Burtis in duPont, Pollard, and Melchers Halls—who were responsible on a day-to-day basis for helping to solve the problems of faculty who were often leery of (and sometimes truly frightened by) computerization. It was largely due to the combination of patience, expertise, and good humor on the part of the ITLs that many faculty, especially the more senior ones, became not only comfortable with the new electronic media but often enthusiastic about the potential for their application in the classroom.

A landmark change occurred in 2002, prompted by the resignation of David Ayersman and the retirement of Carol Martin (who had headed Network Services for many years). At that point, the previously separated, but clearly related, areas of Instructional Technology and Network Services were consolidated to form the Department of Instructional Technology, otherwise known by the acronym DoIT. This new organization was headed by the school's first chief information officer, R. F. "Chip" German Jr. Under German's guidance, DoIT was organized into several divisions. Information Systems was responsible for the implementation, support, and enhancement of all institutional administrative information systems. Infrastructure Services had the responsibility for maintaining the campus network. User Services aided everyone on campus by providing telephone help, service, and repair of computing systems. Web Communications was responsible for Web site design and training for all developers of official institutional Web sites, as well as for the information architecture of the institution's portal.

Within the department was also created the division of Teaching and Learning Technologies, which was responsible for assisting the academic community in transforming teaching through the use of appropriate technologies. The department was placed under the direction of English professor Gardner Campbell, whose intellect and interest had long put him in the forefront of faculty users of technology in the classroom. He became assistant vice president for teaching and learning technologies and remained in that position until his resignation in 2006 to take a similar job at the University of Richmond.[65]

A basic tool used by many faculty was Blackboard, an interactive software program that facilitated the dissemination of course information via the Internet among students and between students and the instructor and also expedited various course management procedures. To enable faculty to use Blackboard more efficiently and to implement various other electronic teaching techniques, as well as to showcase the work that faculty were doing with instructional technology, the College began in the mid-1990s to sponsor annual faculty academies featuring distinguished speakers and workshops on integrating teaching and learning technology into the classroom. The result included innovations such as student and faculty blogging, online group writing in wikis, audio lectures delivered via podcasts, Web-based research papers, and online communities for courses and departments.

In light of the increasing necessity for students to have serviceable technological skills, a requirement for all students to have "information and technology proficiency" was added to the curriculum in fall 2001. The requirement consisted of four areas: word processing, spreadsheets, library and information literacy, and e-mail.[66] In 2003–4, a student academy on information technologies was established under Gardner Campbell's leadership to provide students a venue for presenting their academic research and projects based on information technologies. The cumulative effect, as the *President's Message and Annual Report* for 2004–5 noted, was "to transform classroom teaching and to expand the academic vernacular. Blogs, wikis, podcasts, and webcasts are commonplace."

Certainly student research became much quicker, if not always more thorough, in the digital age. Electronic links could produce at students' personal computers—frequently laptops that could be accessed at many wireless locations throughout campus—information that would previously have required hours of laborious searching through hardbound or microfilmed materials in the library.

In the early years of the new century, the search engine of choice was Google, abetted by Wikipedia, described by the *Bullet* as "the encyclopedia of the dot-com generation." Wikipedia, in particular, was well-nigh addictive to students in its apparently unlimited capacity to provide instantaneous information on limitless subjects. The veracity of that information and its scope, however, were sometimes questionable. Thus did a *Bullet* column in 2007 declare that Wikipedia was "an egalitarian academia, where a Princeton dean's word on moral relativism is as good as Kevin Federline's," and warned students about the danger of overreliance on that source: "Just don't be bitter when you get an 'F' on your essay about how Ella Fitzgerald, mother of John Fitzgerald Kennedy, satirized urban aristocracy with her novel, *The Great Gatsby*."

Many faculty were understandably wary of such sources (if used exclusively) for research. Nor were they happy—some of them—with another feature of the Internet, a Web site known as RateMyProfessor.com, which allowed students, anonymously and at no cost, to post evaluations of their instructors. Numerical ratings ranged from 1 (lowest) to 5 (highest) with a smiley face or frown icon posted to indicate the evaluator's overall opinion; in addition, professors could be rated as "hot," signified by a chili pepper.

Though most faculty members probably either ignored the enterprise altogether or took the postings with little seriousness, given the utter lack of quality control involved in the posting process, the site did present the potential for unfairness and, for some, hurt feelings. When the *Bullet* in a 2005 column went so far as to print the names of the five highest-rated and five lowest-rated professors on campus according to the Web site, several members of the Chemistry Department struck back in a letter to the editor. Having cited numerous problems with the site's methodology, the writers concluded with a telling disclaimer taken from RateMyProfessor.com itself. "Take the ratings with a grain of salt," the site said. "Remember, we have no way of knowing who is doing the rating—students, the teacher, other teachers, parents, dogs, cats, etc."

Concurrently with technological developments, the campus continued to experience improvement through a number of significant renovation projects and the construction of important ancillary facilities. Among the most welcome changes, as far as students were concerned, was the installation of air-conditioning in Goolrick Hall. Excessive heat in the poorly ventilated gymnasium was a problem from the time of its construction, prompting standard complaints from students such as that made by a senior in 1998. "The heat is always terrible," she said. "In a way it's good because it makes you sweat, but at the same time you don't want to die." Finally, in 2000 (before anyone had actually died, but after many had suffered), air-conditioning was installed at a cost of over $2 million.

Seacobeck, another source of frequent student complaints, underwent a series of renovations around the turn of the century—some to improve function, some to enhance attractiveness. By 2006, as a result of a partnership between the College and its food service supplier, the Wood Company (later Sodexho), the kitchen and much of the infrastructure had been renovated, the student dining areas refurnished, and a faculty-staff dining room established. The latter proved to be a popular lunchtime gathering spot for many employees. It was also frequently rented to local residents by the food service company as a venue for wedding receptions and other social events.

The most extensive renovation project during the period was that of Combs Hall following the departure of the science departments for the new Jepson facility. Having been used mainly for storage since 1998, Combs underwent a $6 million renovation that was completed in the summer of 2002, whereupon it became the home for three large academic departments: Historic Preservation, Modern Foreign Languages, and English, Linguistics, and Speech.

Another important renovation—the one most noticeable to community visitors to campus—was the refurbishing of Dodd Auditorium. Part of the change was cosmetic, painting the dreary interior light yellow with blue and gold-leaf accents and installing colorful new window treatments. But other changes were designed to improve function, especially a new lighting system.

The main renovation was geared toward greater comfort for the audience, a goal that was accomplished by removing the original seats, which were only eighteen to twenty inches wide—"made at a time when people were smaller, quite frankly," said Richard Hurley, executive vice president and chief financial officer—and replacing them with ones that were twenty-one to twenty-four inches wide. The new seats had their own history, having come from the Kennedy Center during that venue's renovation. Though the change reduced Dodd's seating capacity from 1,600 to 1,300, most patrons probably felt that the increased comfort was a desirable trade-off.

Even such improvements were unlikely to go uncriticized on a college campus, however, and sure enough, the following year some students launched a protest concerning one facet of the renovation when they discovered that the old College seal was to be replaced by a new version. Their outrage was all the greater in light of the recent refurbishing. "[The seal] was gorgeous before," said the leader of the protest. "It was just redone with gold leaf and repainted, . . . and they spent thousands of dollars to fix it up just to cover it."

The protest revealed ways in which technology had come to assist such endeavors, as the leader of the movement used LiveJournal and Facebook—both online communities that facilitate social networking—to stimulate awareness about the seal issue. The effort led to a petition to the Board of Visitors, signed by over two hundred students, complaining that the change amounted to a desecration of the school's heritage and was a waste of money to boot. Some even went as far as to threaten a protest outside GW.

College officials were not moved. Vice President Hurley pointed out that "as far as a visible MWC seal on campus, we have the best situation one could have, with it being permanently displayed in the floor of the Trinkle lobby." The Board of Visitors apparently agreed—and the new seal, at a cost of approximately $4,000 from state funds, was duly installed above the Dodd stage.

Mary Washington's master plan in the late 1990s did not envision appreciable growth in enrollment but instead looked forward to continued enhancement of quality. The achievement of that goal, in the view of President Anderson and other College officials, required some additional facilities. A serious obstacle, however, was limited space for expansion within the campus. For that reason, the College considered on several occasions acquiring non-contiguous parcels of land, leading to efforts that sometimes created opposition in the local community.

A notable case involved the College's effort to acquire a nine-acre parcel known as Willis Hill overlooking the Sunken Road site so prominent in the 1862 Civil War battle of Fredericksburg. The tract had been owned by the Catholic Daughters of Wisdom Council of New York, who had operated a parochial school, Montfort Academy, on the site for many years. When in

1996 the Daughters decided to sell the property, which was located between the College's Brompton and the Park Service's national cemetery, both MWC and the Park Service expressed interest in buying it. The College desired the site as a potential venue for holding seminars and housing alumni offices.

The competing goals of the College and the Park Service touched off something of a bidding war. The College initially made an offer of $1.5 million for the property in August 1996 and raised it to $1.65 million in September to meet the Daughters' counteroffer. A war of words ensued in the local newspaper, with the majority tending to favor acquisition of the tract by the Park Service.

The most prominent public adversary of the College in the affair was Fredericksburg's John Robbins, who had formerly taught Confederate history at the University of North Carolina in Charlotte. In a scathing op-ed piece in the *Free Lance–Star* (to which he was a frequent contributor), Robbins claimed that "the college's administration rarely sees an open piece of land that it doesn't want to destroy for a building—or a parking lot."[67] He decried what he perceived as the College's lack of interest in Civil War history and, in a gratuitous complaint, added that "the Mary Washington administration has never been particularly cooperative with community groups . . . seeking to use college facilities."

The first of those charges was rebutted in a public letter written by the chair of the History Department, Porter Blakemore, who emphasized that the College, through its history and historic preservation programs, had actually trained an exemplary group of Civil War scholars and battlefield preservationists. The second allegation—that MWC was not cooperative with the community—was addressed by the historian of the College, who pointed out in an op-ed piece that Robbins's allegations

> must have come as a surprise to those numerous area residents who have either received high school diplomas in the college's auditorium, or attended plays in its theater, or admired exhibits in its galleries, or listened to renowned scholars in its lecture halls, or borrowed books from its library, or jogged on its paths, or swum in its pool. It must certainly have surprised the many who have participated in the College-Community Orchestra and the thousands more who have enjoyed the orchestra's concerts. It must have surprised, and not amused, the many professors who have provided their expertise (usually gratis) in response to all manner of local requests, not excluding those from Civil War groups. And it must have surprised, and doubtlessly dismayed, students who have volunteered literally thousands of hours of service under the sponsorship of COAR, the college's community outreach program.

Ultimately the Montfort property was sold to the Park Service, though not before an unfortunate amount of antagonism had been aroused on all sides. "It would have been a beautiful addition to our campus," said Executive Vice

President Poyck, but the College withdrew its offer because, she explained, "We felt there was a mounting level of discord [in the community]. . . . We'll be looking at other alternatives over the years."

Just such an alternative soon appeared—one in which the College this time prevailed. However, as in the previous case, the purchase of property resulted in widespread community controversy with, again, much of the acrimony being directed toward Mary Washington.

The genesis of the episode was the College's desire for additional student housing. This arose not from wanting to increase the student population—the enrollment had, in fact, been capped at four thousand for some years, and no expansion was envisioned—but from needing to alleviate dormitory crowding for students already enrolled. Increasing numbers of students were already opting to live off campus, and the maintenance of a basically residential college required sufficient and attractive dormitory facilities on or near the campus itself.

A possible solution appeared in fall 2001 when the Silver Companies, the area's giant real estate firm, decided to divest itself of the Marye's Heights apartment complex. Located directly across William Street from the southernmost end of the campus (across the street from the old Framar and new South Hall), the apartments were ideally located to meet the College's purpose. The problem was that those units, as one of the oldest rental complexes in the area, were occupied mainly by long-term tenants, many of whom were quite elderly. Purchase by the College would necessitate their ouster.

The situation posed a predicament for the institution, which understandably coveted the property but was wary of the public relations backlash that the acquisition might provoke. Sure enough, when the impending deal became known, it created an inviting target for the College's community adversaries, whose marksmen seemed never to be in short supply. Very quickly the *Free Lance–Star* was inundated with outraged letters typically portraying the College as a bullying ogre hell-bent on evicting helpless geriatrics as it heedlessly pursued its grandiose goals of expansion.

The paper itself, while admitting that the transaction was "not unexpected" by the residents and that "seller and buyer are perfectly within their rights," nonetheless expressed concern. "The humane instruction of liberal-arts colleges is not confined to classrooms," lectured an editorial. "It also speaks in the public acts of those institutions."

The paper's acerbic columnist and resident curmudgeon, Florence King, also scolded the College. "The Marye's Heights situation is nothing short of brutal," she commented. "If the denizens of MWC want to be thought fit to educate the young, they should start by setting an example of how to treat people decently."

But the most provocative piece was one written by Larry Evans, a regular *Free Lance–Star* columnist. In an article titled "Before You Know It, Marye's Heights Complex Will Be Party Central," he focused not on the displacement of residents that College ownership would entail but on its deleterious effect on community social life. It was an area in which he claimed expertise, having grown up near the College in a time before the vehicular Campus Drive had been replaced by the pedestrian Campus Walk. "In the 1960s," he wrote, "I was a shy but observant local teenager who logged hundreds of miles on that short street without ever getting out of my car or saying a word to a college girl. Mary Washington was an all-girl's school then, and those students, as far as I knew, spent 24 hours a day in their stylish madras skirts and plaid jumpers. Those girls dated only Marines and University of Virginia students: I was neither. . . . [But] my point is that Marye's Heights Apartments will become a magnet for a new generation of local 'townies' and 'rednecks' looking for a party." He went on to warn—in the passage that elicited the most ire on campus—that "the community can expect to see 19-year-old guys in boxer shorts sipping on bottles of Corona Light as they stand on their balconies and watch traffic move up and down William Street. . . . And, of course, beer-drinking young women in boxer shorts."

Predictably Evans's article elicited a number of rebuttals from students. Most such responses were vitriolic, but one—the most effective—took a humorous approach in an effort to "clarify a few misconceptions" that Evans seemed to have about the College. "First off," wrote the female sophomore, "I don't own a pair of boxer shorts, but to be fair, I don't own any plaid jumpers or stylish madras plaid skirts, either. . . . But I digress. The real problem here is not 19-year-olds in boxer briefs or, worse yet, tighty-whities. I'm not sure the college will have any rules that prohibit wearing boxer shorts on the balconies, but I would fully support a rule, or maybe even a law, prohibiting the wearing of tighty-whities in public."

Having established her preference in male undergarment fashion, she proceeded to offer statistics to suggest that the problem Evans had projected was unlikely to materialize. "MWC is 30 percent male," she pointed out (with slight minimizing), and continued thus:

> Only 50 percent of males wear boxer shorts. That leaves us with about 600 high-risk-boxer-wearing students. Of those, only about 300 will live on campus. Of those 300, maybe 30 or 40 will live in Marye's Heights. Now, only 20 percent of men drink light beer: Of those 20 percent, only 2 percent can afford Corona. So really, we're considering only one or two high-risk-boxer-wearing-Corona-Light-drinking male students. Of those two, only one may be 19, and of the one remaining student, only .05 percent of him will be enough of an exhibitionist to venture onto the balcony. . . . Heaven help us.

The situation was not, of course, a laughing matter, either to the College or, certainly, to the residents of the apartments. When the sale was completed on November 21, 2001—the College paid $8.75 million for 121 units on approximately five acres of land—the residents were notified by letter that they would have eighteen months to vacate their residences. It was the day before Thanksgiving.

Mary Washington officials did what they could to defuse the combustible, and in many ways unfortunate, situation. In an effort to allay concerns and quell rumors, President Anderson wrote a lengthy op-ed article in the *Free Lance–Star*, explaining the reasons for the purchase and assuring the community that the College planned neither to expand its enrollment nor to acquire additional neighborhood property in the foreseeable future.

To Richard Hurley fell the task of meeting with Marye's Heights residents shortly after the sale to answer questions and to hear their concerns. Though the meeting, he later reported, "went as well as could be expected," he admitted that "there was a lot of anger vented." Such could hardly have been avoided, inasmuch as some of the tenants were octogenarians who had lived there for thirty years or more and had no intentions of ever moving.

Given the high emotions, the transition was actually accomplished with less hostility than might have been anticipated, especially in light of the initial expressions of bitterness. Several ameliorative factors contributed. For one, Peggy Johnson, a College alumna, class of 1953, who then lived in the apartment complex, though not pleased with the turn of events, agreed to serve as a counselor for other tenants in helping them to relocate. The eighteen-month grace period extended by the College was considerably longer than normal in such cases, and tenants were allowed to break leases at any time without penalty. When tenants moved out, COAR volunteers offered assistance with those onerous tasks.

By May 2002 most residents had left, and the College began preparing the facility for student occupancy by, among other things, filling the complex's pool with cement and converting it to a picnic area. Special regulations were drafted for the apartments, some clearly designed to protect the public image of its student residents; for example, there was to be no smoking and no more than four persons at a time on the balconies. (Boxer shorts were not specifically mentioned.)

By the opening of the fall 2003 session, the apartments were ready for the students—and the students were ready for the apartments. They instantly became the College's most sought-after housing—as well they might, since they offered the privacy advantages of off-campus living with the amenities of dormitory life such as campus Internet access and phone service. And the proximity allowed residents to enjoy easy access to classes and all campus events.

All in all, few developments at MWC were ever received by students with more universal enthusiasm than the availability of the Marye's Heights apartments. Even the "complaints" were good. "It's so much more space than [we] have encountered," was the typical comment of one senior. "There's so much space I don't know what we could possibly use this all for." "There are still a lot of blank walls in our apartment," said another. "It was a lot easier to furnish a tiny dorm room than both a bedroom and a living room/dining area."

No doubt about it: students thought apartment living was good. "There's a lot more freedom," said one of the original residents. "You get to feel old, like you're not really in college. Class is just something you do on the side."

In the early years of the twenty-first century there were two major construction projects on campus, both of them undertaken in response to obvious (and long-standing) needs. The first grew out of the inadequacy of Goolrick Hall to meet the demands of newer student generations who placed greater importance on fitness than had their predecessors. The result was nearly constant competition among PE classes, varsity athletes, intramural teams, and individual exercisers for access to the gym's limited space and sometimes antiquated equipment. Moreover, even after Goolrick was retrofitted with air-conditioning, the environment in some of its most frequently used areas (notably the weight room) was far from inviting.

In the late 1990s, the Board of Visitors began to discuss ways to improve the situation. Their first plan envisioned a new recreational facility that would rest atop a parking garage (to address another perennial problem). Logistical, aesthetic, and financial considerations later led to separation of the two projects, with primacy placed on construction of a fitness center.

After the usual construction delays endemic to such endeavors, the new facility opened at the beginning of the spring 2004 semester, to the delight of the students, faculty, and staff.[68] Located at the northern terminus of Campus Walk and attached to Goolrick Hall, the two-story brick building provided 15,000 square feet of space for a range of fitness activities. The first floor was designed for weight training, equipped with the most modern weight machines as well as free-standing weights. The second floor was the cardiovascular center, which included treadmills, step trainers, upright and recumbent bicycles, rowing ergometers, and a climber station. The center also housed a fitness evaluation office, lounge, laundry room, sitting area, and space for the office of campus recreation.

Aesthetics and comfort were also taken into account. Huge Palladian windows afforded a sweeping southward view of the campus from the building's elevated position. Inside, the pain of workouts could be eased by the distractions of audio headphones and flat-screen TVs at each cardio workstation. The attractiveness of the center made it a focal point of campus tours for prospective students, whose choice of college had come increasingly to include the quality of an institution's recreational facilities.

The fitness center was a success from the moment it opened. The first day it attracted 560 people, and the following day the number had increased by a hundred. A *Free Lance–Star* reporter covering the opening wrote that "students whose only previous form of exercise was shuffling from class to class have been heading over to check it out."

And the center's popularity continued long after the novelty had worn off. One of the most popular sites on campus, it was perpetually busy from its

7:30 a.m. daily opening to its late-night closing. Never at Mary Washington had straining and sweating, groaning and grimacing, been so much fun.

Another need arose over the years, this one concerning alumni. By the turn of the century, as their number reached roughly twenty thousand, it became evident that increased space was needed to accommodate alumni functions, as well as to provide more office space for development activities. The solution devised by the administration involved the renovation and expansion of Trench Hill in such a way as to address the institution's needs but also to accommodate community events as well.

The plan was an ambitious one—and costly, estimated to require at least $6 million (which turned out to be considerably less than the final cost). It was obvious that such an undertaking would require a substantial amount of private support, since the project would not qualify for state funding.

As they had done so generously in the past, Robert and Alice Jepson once again took the lead in that effort, donating $2 million to launch the campaign in 1999. Alice also agreed to serve as one of three co-chairs of the campaign, along with alumnae Charlotte Major Minor '66 and Elizabeth Smith Hughes '51. Their fund-raising efforts focused not only on MWC graduates but also on area businesses and individual friends of the College, an appeal that was well received owing to the prospective use of the facility by the local community.

The project proceeded sufficiently for the celebration of groundbreaking in early December 2002. Braving windy 33-degree weather, members of the campaign committee, Board of Visitors, alumni, and administrators donned hard hats to join President Anderson in the ceremonial digging of the first shovels of earth. Among the celebrants was Lois Saunier Hornsby '48, whose sons (one of whom was pop-rock star Bruce Hornsby) made a sizable contribution to the campaign. Following the groundbreaking, guests were treated to a hard-hat themed luncheon served in silver pails amid flower arrangements adorned with paintbrushes. They were also invited to take turns swinging a golden sledgehammer at a soon-to-be-demolished wall on Trench Hill's second floor.

By the fall of 2003, the fund-raising campaign not only reached its goal of $6 million but exceeded it by more than $800,000. Well over $2 million of that total came from non-alumni donors: area residents, local municipalities, regional businesses, corporations, and foundations (including a $400,000 challenge grant from the Kresge Foundation). To commemorate that milestone, President and Mrs. Anderson, together with Robert and Alice Jepson, hosted on October 25 an event billed as "An Historic Celebration." It was well named, since it was perhaps the most opulent affair in the institution's history. More than 150 attended the black-tie dinner in Lee Hall, where, at tables elaborately decorated and illuminated by the glow from dozens of gleaming candelabra, they dined on what was described as a "medieval feast."

After much convivial toasting of the campaign's success, the evening concluded with the surprise unveiling of a commissioned portrait of the three campaign chairs, Jepson, Minor, and Hughes. President Anderson announced that the portrait would be displayed in the reception area of the new facility.

Meanwhile work proceeded on what was then known as the Alumni Executive Center. Designed by the Norfolk architectural firm of Clark Nexson, the 24,000-square-foot facility was created by incorporating additions to Trench Hill so as to create a U-shaped, tri-unit structure. The existing Trench Hill house was completely renovated to permit medium-sized receptions (fifty people) in the downstairs parlors and to create three upstairs bedrooms with sitting rooms and private baths. The center part of the new construction contained alumni and development offices, as well as a twenty-five-seat boardroom; the building on the left side featured a 250-seat ballroom. All three sides opened onto a brick courtyard to be entered from Hanover Street directly across from Brompton. The courtyard itself, dominated by a central fountain, provided sufficient space to accommodate gatherings of up to four hundred.

The official opening of the complex was celebrated by a ribbon-cutting ceremony in June 2004, at which time President Anderson announced that the facility would be named the Jepson Alumni Executive Center in honor of its chief patron, Alice Jepson. It was also announced that the Trench Hill bed-and-breakfast would thenceforth be called the Kalnen Inn at Trench Hill after alumna benefactor Elizabeth Kalnen '37.

The elegant executive center boasted a number of distinctive features, starting with its panoramic view of the city from atop Marye's Heights. Perhaps the most extraordinary external appurtenance was the set of gates at the entry from Hanover Street.

The provenance of the gates was quite complicated, beginning with their construction in France around 1900, commissioned by Henry Phipps, business partner of the steel magnate Andrew Carnegie. The original purpose of the gates had been to guard Phipps's Fifth Avenue mansion in New York (hence the "H P" initials on the gates). The three-ton bronze structure, built in the French Renaissance Revival style, was decorated with so many mythical figures, Renaissance medallions, and various whimsical depictions that, according to art history professor Marjorie Och, "you could literally do a history of Western art, from Roman antiquity through 1800, with [the gates]." From Phipps, the gates passed to his grandson Raymond Guest, a Virginia resident and former state senator (as well as onetime ambassador to Ireland), who before his death donated the gates to the Virginia Museum of Fine Arts in Richmond.

The museum in 1954 turned the gates over to the College, which once planned to erect them outside duPont Hall. When that plan failed for lack of funding, they were stored for many years in the barn at Brompton, where they languished until 1994 when President Anderson asked Belmont curator Joanna Catron to evaluate them. By then they were in a state of serious disrepair, and no further action was taken, until some years later it was proposed that they be refurbished for use at the Jepson Alumni Executive Center. After extensive restoration work—the considerable cost covered by a $100,000 gift from a Richmond alumna and her husband—the gates were installed at the center's entrance in a permanently open position to symbolize the College's welcoming embrace toward its returning graduates.

The interior of the center, described by a *Free Lance–Star* reporter as "a plush pad worthy of five stars," was designed by the Richmond firm of baty&brown under the tasteful direction of presidential assistant Ranny Corbin. The symbol chosen as the central motif was the acorn, a reference to the famous Brompton oak just across the street immortalized by Matthew Brady's photographs of Civil War soldiers resting beneath its branches. The tree itself was a focal point of one of the center's most unusual features: a mural painted by W. D. Wood of Lynchburg on a continuous canvas from chair rail to ceiling in the dining room, providing a 360-degree panorama of the scenery surrounding the center.

Each of the three bedrooms upstairs was decorated to depict a different season of the college year, fall, winter, and spring. The controlling idea, said the designers, was to create a decor that was "happy, Southern, and comfortable." As Carter Brown of baty&brown put it, "You don't want to go to . . . the Kalnen Inn that's on this historic Trench Hill, and feel like you're in the middle of downtown Chicago."

Much of the center's charm came from its furnishings, including paintings, Oriental rugs, and furniture, donated by alumni and friends of the College. Perhaps the most distinctive and appealing feature of the center was the large number of historic photographs reproduced from the College's archival prints that adorned walls throughout the buildings.

Few questioned the grandness of the center, though some faculty grumbled that such a large sum had been spent for an essentially non-academic purpose. Then, too, some deplored the high rental cost of the facility (there was no charge for the College's development-related events, but the fee for other College uses and for all non-College renters was substantial). As economics professor Robert Rycroft remarked, "Charging that amount, no student or faculty member will ever set foot in this building."

That assessment proved to be a considerable exaggeration, as certain major faculty events were, in fact, scheduled there from time to time. But the truth was that the facility was targeted mainly at alumni and community groups, leaving other venues like Belmont and Seacobeck for use by campus groups. The new center admirably served its purpose. Almost from the start, it was fully booked, often far in advance, owing both to its utility and its luxuriousness.

But also important was the role of its director, the personable Susan Worrell, whose ebullience was magnetic. Under her hospitable direction, the center proved to be a source of goodwill for the institution. "This morning," Worrell said on one occasion, "as our guest was leaving, she said it was like a five-star experience. She said she's never stayed at a college or university that had this caliber of a facility."

Plush, indeed, it was—thanks (again) to the Jepsons and to the many other friends of the college who made it happen.

With the availability of expanded recreational facilities and enhanced accommodations for alumni, the most pressing need on campus was for additional parking space. It was not a new need, nor was it peculiar to Mary Washington. In fact, the most prevalent student concerns—at least non-academic ones—on campuses everywhere tended to involve sex, food, and parking. Students themselves usually managed to take care of the first (especially after visitation rules were liberalized). As for dining, thanks largely to innovative efforts by the institution's food service contractors—initially ARA under Gordon Inge, later the Wood Company/Sodexho under John Iacunato—complaints about Seacobeck fare tended to diminish (though not totally disappear) over the years.

The parking problem, however, not only persisted but worsened. For part of it, the College itself was to blame by maintaining a lenient policy (compared to most colleges at the time) that put few restrictions on student vehicles; even freshmen were permitted to have cars on campus, and parking decals were issued free of charge to anyone requesting them.

But the growing acuteness of the problem lay in the drastic increase of commuting students, who by 1999 amounted to nearly half of the College's 3,800 enrollment—a number that represented a rise of almost 20 percent during the previous decade. A Student Association poll that same year indicated that commuting students regarded parking as their number one issue, far worse than academic requirements, registration woes, and diversity combined. The problem became even greater when, as a result of community complaints, city streets near campus were made illegal for student parking.

Over the years the administration devised several strategies to address the matter. One involved creating additional spaces by converting the old Sunken Road tennis courts into parking lots and by building a new lot on property acquired across from the campus at the corner of William Street and Sunken Road, a plot that was for decades the site of the landmark Sunshine Laundry.

Another approach was to impose various vehicular restrictions. In 1999, for example, freshmen were prohibited from having cars on campus. Upperclassmen could have cars, but a decal system was implemented whereby parking was permitted in certain areas only, with proximity to the central campus governed by seniority. Other proposals were considered from time to time, such as establishment of a satellite parking area with shuttle transportation to and from campus, but were rejected as ultimately unworkable.

The solution most often considered was construction of a parking deck, but that automatically raised two problems: money and location. The first was exacerbated by a commonwealth statute forbidding expenditure of any taxpayer money for parking-related construction. As Vice President Singleton explained, "Whatever money goes to pay for the deck has to come directly from the college. And unfortunately, we don't have $5 million just lying around to pay for it."

Eventually the administration devised a plan to procure the needed funds by borrowing $6 million to be recouped through charging a decal fee to all students who had cars on campus. The initial fee was $150 annually, which was raised to $200 the following year.

The allied issue was that of location. The challenge was to find a site that was not obtrusive—parking decks not usually being an architectural adornment to any landscape—and yet close enough to provide reasonably convenient access to campus facilities. The site finally selected was behind Goolrick Hall, with vehicular access via the U.S. Route 1 bypass. Opening in the fall of 2006, the three-story, 440-space garage did much to alleviate, if not completely resolve, the parking problem.

During the time when campus construction was dominated by large practical projects such as the Jepson Science Center, fitness center, and parking deck, a number of smaller, chiefly aesthetic, features were also being added along Campus Walk. One example was the creation of a small plaza across the walk from Westmoreland for the display of a two-foot-square bronze Phi Beta Kappa key atop a brick pedestal. It was built to commemorate the twenty-fifth anniversary of the establishment of the College's Kappa of Virginia chapter in 1971 and was unveiled following a gala reception and dinner in the Great Hall on February 22, 1996. Speakers for the occasion included President Anderson, who brought greetings from the College; Douglas Foard, national secretary of Phi Beta Kappa, who lauded the local chapter; and religion professor David Cain, the chapter historian, who recounted various highlights and included a tribute to the late Dorothy Simpson, who, along with her husband, had entertained members at Brompton following the first installation a quarter-century earlier.

Another addition to the campus—this one somewhat controversial—was the placing of a free-standing street clock in the plaza in front of the Woodard Campus Center. For a number of years beginning in the mid-nineties, student leaders had pointed out that the only exterior clocks on campus were the ones on GW and Chandler Halls and suggested that another would be a useful addition to the opposite end of campus. During the 1999–2000 session, a special SA committee studied the idea and advocated that a new clock be installed. The Board of Visitors responded in the fall of 2000 with the expenditure of $24,000 for such purpose.

It was around that time that an alumna, Becky Kalnen, became interested in the project. Nearing ninety, Kalnen drove herself to Fredericksburg from her home in Wilmington, North Carolina, to see the campus she had not visited in thirty years. When informed that installation of a clock near the Woodard Center was being considered, she donated $135,000 to the College so that the clock, complete with chimes, could be erected in honor of her and her sister.

When the sixteen-foot-tall black-and-silver clock was installed in April 2001, its sudden appearance startled students, some of whom were none too pleased with what they saw. "It wasn't there on Saturday. It wasn't there on Sunday. But whoa Lordy, was it there on Monday," complained a *Bullet* op-ed column that continued, with some histrionic historical hyperbole, to suggest that "a stealth team of covert operations acting as part of a movement against common decency must have slinked in during the night and installed a clock as heinously as did the Nixon administration install puppet rulers in banana republics the world over."

It was not just that the critics did not like the clock; they further cited the decision to erect it as an example of lack of student input in such matters—a rather questionable assertion, since a student committee had initiated the process and had been involved in selecting the clock's color, trimming, face, and hands. Still the column went on to declare that the process served "to further widen the gulf between students and the administration. . . . Now we glare at each other, but at least we know at what time we do it."

Yet, as is so often true in such matters, the initially negative comments were balanced by favorable ones, and soon enough the clock became an established feature of the campus landscape. Whether or not students loved it, they used it, and Kalnen Court, where it stood, evolved into a favorite meeting spot for students.

Controversy over the clock was mild compared to the opposition generated by two other proposed additions to Campus Walk. One was a plan to construct an aluminum and fiberglass globe within the fountain in front of Monroe Hall. As soon as the conceptual drawing appeared, students squawked. "The globe," said a *Bullet* editorial, "looks conspicuously out of place, almost like a giant beachball suspended by the jets of the fountain." A guest columnist was even more critical, describing it as "shamelessly tacky, horrifically gaudy, or perhaps that good old-fashioned word, ugly." Noting that the site was already popular as "a place to meet with friends, hang out, study, or simply relax," the writer urged that the proposed globe not be installed "because we love our fountain just the way it is."

And so it stayed, as plans for the globe were withdrawn. It was President Anderson's decision to do so, announced Executive Vice President Poyck, because of his perception of "a strong feeling from the students that they didn't want anything done to the fountain."

A similar fate befell another proposed project, the erection of a thirty-foot obelisk, topped with a replica of the College's eagle mascot, in the GW circle at the southern end of Campus Walk. Although many people favored the concept of some architectural feature at the walk's terminus—an idea that had been considered ever since the walk was built—the preliminary rendering of the proposed obelisk (commonly referred to as the "spirit column") elicited largely negative responses from both students and faculty. Among the most outspoken was philosophy professor Craig Vasey, who was also faculty representative to the Board of Visitors. Aside from the dubious aesthetics of the obelisk, he said, "Some people have pointed out that, while certainly unintentional, the [spirit column] is reminiscent of Eagle columns that the Nazis built, as well as ones in Imperial France and Rome."

So it, too, was scrapped. "Plans died on the vine," said CFO Richard Hurley. "There was a lot of dissatisfaction with the idea, so the college decided not to pursue it." President Anderson's explanation concurred. "It just went by the wayside, since it was not very popular," he said. "We decided that we should work on a better idea."

A *Bullet* guest column expressed the satisfaction felt by critics at the withdrawal of both projects. "By the grace of a tasteful God," it said, "we escaped the unsightly fate that could have befallen us had those gaudy monuments actually been erected." (The abortive outcomes did, in fact, prove fortuitous, at least in the case of the "spirit column," for the undeveloped GW circle soon thereafter made possible the construction of a much grander architectural monument: a tall free-standing bell tower, or campanile).

Yet another campus artifact that produced controversy came in October 2001 in the form of a twenty-ton granite boulder that appeared, unexpected by most students, on the grassy slope near the Woodard Campus Center near Campus Walk. It was originally proposed by the previous year's SA president, Brooks L'Allier (supported by President Anderson) in order to promote school spirit by having an object that students could paint in the manner of the University of Virginia's Beta Bridge and similar totems at other schools.

The initial reaction to Mary Washington's "spirit rock," however, was not altogether favorable, with the *Bullet* calling it "a fairly stupid idea" and some students suggesting that the money devoted to it could have been put to better use. (The rock was, in fact, donated by a Culpeper quarry, though the school paid $1,000 for its transportation and placement.) Other students condemned its appearance as, in the words of one, "an eyesore"; another complained that it was "too high school. If we had a football team and a lot of gung-ho spirit, the spirit rock would make more sense."

The most cynical critique was contained in a *Bullet* op-ed article that derisively declared, "A week ago, Mary Washington College was drab and spiritless. This week, all that changes! Ladies and gentlemen, it is my distinct pleasure to unveil for you MWC's answer to the football of Florida State and the basketball of Duke: our very own . . . piece of shale! That's right, folks! You no longer have to hide your heads in shame when the Hokies and Hoyas go by. They may have world-renowned sports establishments to pique their ardor, but we, dear friends, have a rock!"

On the other hand, some saw positive potential in the great gray stone. "It'll take a little while to catch on," said one, "but I think that in the long run, the spirit rock will become really important to students."

That prediction was soon validated as students began regularly to slather the rock with paint to convey all manner of messages. The only rules for its use were that messages had to conform to the College's Statement of Community Values and that only latex paint could be used. Within those guidelines, the rock became a highly visible venue for announcing campus events (especially parties), declaring political viewpoints, and merely expressing personal sentiments. Sometimes the content veered close to, and even over, the bounds of taste and propriety—as in one exhortation that assailed France's lack of support for U.S. foreign policy by suggesting that the European nation be subjected to a sexual act expressed in an alliterative but vulgar two-word phrase.

The rock also served on occasion to convey somber sentiments regarding campus tragedies. Such was the case in early December 2001 when in response to the sudden death of psychology professor Christopher Bill, a message said simply, "Thanks for Everything, Dr. Bill," and in April 2003 when the words "We Love You, Alex," were posted in memory of a popular student leader, senior Alex Naden, who was killed in an automobile accident just days before graduation.

Within a few years the spirit rock had become an established part of the campus landscape, as even the *Bullet* admitted. In a 2006 article, "Spirit Rocks Campus," it noted that initially the rock had produced "a mixed reaction from students on campus. . . . Some were unsure of its purpose, while others did not think the [school] had enough spirit for a spirit rock." It recalled the initial prediction that "it would take some time for the rock [to] become a part of the campus community," and concluded, "It seems like that time has finally come."

The extensive construction program of the Anderson years enhanced the aesthetics (as well as functioning) of a campus already long recognized for its beauty both in the built environment and in the natural landscape. But creating that environment was one thing; maintaining it was another. That was the demanding job of the Physical Plant/Facilities Services staff headed, beginning in 1994, by John Wiltenmuth. The soft-spoken former Navy man was a meticulously organized administrator whose even-keeled approach earned him a reputation for both efficiency and fairness. Among Wiltenmuth's large staff were many employees who had worked at the College for years, including carpenters (e.g., James Hairfield, Gene Sturm, and Donald Motley), plumbers (Robert Hicks, Danny Quann, and Ivan Samuels), electricians (Gil Sullivan and Greg Sullivan), mechanics (Joe Cutry), HVAC technicians (Jay Sullivan), and housekeepers (Janet Scott, India Hughes, and Connie Boley). Several veterans of the maintenance team moved into positions of increased responsibility, including, by 2007, Support Services Director Bruce Patton, Senior Director for Operations-Contract Services Stuart Sullivan, and Director of Maintenance Services Timothy Massey. Then there was Panie Scott, who for more than forty years contributed conscientious secretarial service to the department until her retirement in 2007.

While some Facilities Services staff members worked largely unnoticed, others were frequently visible, as was the case with plumber Ivan Samuels. Among his duties was maintenance of the Goolrick pool and the several fountains on campus. The latter task was a source of continuing exertion, owing to incorrigible student pranksters who insisted periodically on converting the clear-flowing waters into fluffy mountains of soapsuds.

The department lost a prominent employee in 1995 with the sudden death of Housekeeping Director Charles Coleman, one of the few African Americans to hold a supervisory position at the College. Known for his sense of humor, he was also, according to one co-worker, "somewhat like an unofficial historian; he remembered everything about everybody." In his memory the College established the Charles Coleman Award, given annually to a member of the Facilities Services staff for outstanding performance.

One of the most distinctive aspects of the Facilities Services Department was the student paint crew. In the mid-1980s, the College began to hire students in the summer to augment the regular staff of painters. The enterprise was transformed in 1994 when Milton Kline became supervisor of the student group.

One of the most universally liked people on campus, Kline quickly infused the student outfit with a measure of his own purposefulness, along with liberal doses of his cracker-barrel wisdom. He was regarded, said one of the students, as "sort of like an offbeat uncle you are fond of as a kid—the type of guy you did not want to let down, simply because you liked him so much."

In time the student crew developed a unique camaraderie, and selection as a member came to be regarded as an honor. Chosen by Kline on the basis of their work ethic and potential for leadership, many were high academic achievers; two emerged as winners of the valedictory Darden Award: Kristy Buck in 2000 and Travis Head in 2003.

By their uniform testimony, all who participated in the program were positively affected by it and especially by their association with Kline himself—the "paintbrush philosopher," as he was once called. One graduate of the crew described him as "perpetually kind, giving, and understanding" and went on to say, in a typical encomium, "I am a better person for having known and worked with him. He deserves a medal."

A large portion of the work done by facilities services involved maintaining the College's much-admired grounds and athletic fields. The responsibility for that, as well as for the institution's recycling efforts, fell to Joni Wilson. Coming to Mary Washington in 1986 as director of landscaping and grounds, she was the first woman to hold that position. Nonetheless, she quickly gained the respect of her almost all-male staff for her work ethic and her open yet businesslike approach. While supervising a staff of about two dozen workers, assisted by Richard Blair, she still found time to earn a BLS degree from Mary Washington in 2000.

The enhanced beautification of the landscape over the years owed much to Wilson's energetic commitment to hard work, coupled with a keen aesthetic sense. Her appreciation of the campus was palpable and well-nigh poetic. Walking down the brick steps to Russell Hall on one spring occasion, for example, admiring the extensive drift of purple crocuses that adorned that area, she remarked that the site "always makes me think of a fairyland or some other place out of a storybook with beautiful princesses and wood folk about." Thanks to Wilson's effort, the campus was indeed a visual delight, season after season, much to the enjoyment of those who called it home.

The Physical Plant / Facilities Services staff faced a constant challenge of maintaining a campus on which older buildings continually needed work of some kind—work for which funds were often scarce. A classic case in point was the amphitheater.

From the time the "open-air theatre" (as it was then called) was built in 1923, it served for decades as the site of many College activities, notably May Days and commencement programs. With the passage of time, however, it was used ever less frequently for public events of that kind—by the 1990s, no more than once or twice a year at most.

Many factors were involved in its demise, mainly the creation of more convenient, comfortable, and technologically sophisticated alternatives such as the Klein Theatre, the Underground, and the Great Hall. Its problems were numerous: unpredictable weather conditions made scheduling risky; nighttime events were not feasible because of inadequate stage lighting; street sounds could interfere with productions; and neighbors were not always tolerant of noise from the theater. Still, it was used occasionally, as in a 1990 Performing Arts Club production of *Spoon River Anthology* and a 1991 GLBSA candlelight poetry reading.

But by that time, the amphitheater had fallen into serious disrepair, as the *Bullet* described in October 1992: "A blanket of light autumn leaves drapes through the decrepit stage and the dilapidated cement benches. . . . Rust consumes the metal back supports of the moss-splotched benches. Moss also traces the steps and the stage. The back stage steps are lopsided and treacherous, and the on-stage steps continue to deteriorate. Stray trash litters the open-air theater's natural floor. The electrical outlets have been damaged by the elements and are either broken or too undependable to use."

Such conditions prompted John Wiltenmuth four years later to send a memo to Executive Vice President Poyck questioning the viability of the structure. "The facility lacks a well-defined purpose or use," he wrote, asking pointedly, "Does the amphitheater serve a continuing and essential purpose?" He suggested that there might be "higher priorities for the area."

When word of the memo got out, it touched a nerve because even if the site was no longer practical or popular for public events, it nonetheless remained sacrosanct in the minds of many students—to say nothing of alumni. Midge Poyck herself nostalgically recalled, "We had the last May Day ceremony there, and [the amphitheater] played an important role in our time here."

The SA Senate was moved to establish a Save the Amphitheater committee, and the *Bullet* went on red alert, exhorting its readers: "If you consider yourself a self-respecting Mary Washington College student, then you will do everything in your power to help the Senate." It then pleaded an impassioned case for the imperiled structure. "Even though the amphitheater has not been used for any official functions for quite some time," an editorial argued,

> it continues to be an essential part of our campus. Sure, it's rundown, rusty, and the benches look like they will fall apart at any given moment, but people still go there. People still go there even though the stage hasn't been properly cleaned in years and there are probably snakes hiding underneath all those leaves. . . . Why do people go there? People go there because it's quiet. It's off the main path of Campus Walk. People can go there with friends to talk about life. People can go there to play guitar. People can go there with a significant other to talk about their relationship. And, perhaps the most intriguing attribute the amphitheater offers, people can go there alone and think. No one will bug you at the amphitheater. In most cases, you can have it to yourself, every single bench. And to destroy the amphitheater would be to destroy a huge amount of tradition.

The emergence of such strong sentiment apparently had the desired effect, as the Board of Visitors in 1997 allocated $40,000 for repairs to bring the structure up to snuff—or reasonably close to it. In choosing among three plans proposing varying levels of renovation, the Board took a middle ground, choosing to fund changes that would go beyond merely making the facility safe, but would not attempt to completely modernize it. The solution struck Wiltenmuth as appropriate. "It [might] have been brand new and nice and clean," he said, "but it would not have been in the sort of shaded, secluded little grove that it is today."

And so the iconic venue in an idyllic corner of the campus got a reprieve—for how long, no one could say. In truth, it was not frequently used thereafter, for all the reasons that had originally contributed to its disuse. The main exceptions were on those balmy days when students implored their professors to hold classes there—requests that were usually honored without protest.

Then, too, there were rare occasions when the old amphitheater—once described by the Fredericksburg newspaper as "an enchanted campus monument to love"—came to life as the scene of special events, such as on the August day in 2003 when two of the College's most popular staff members, Associate Dean of Admissions Matt Mejia '93 and Director of Special Gifts Donna Gray, were married there. Several years earlier when the fate of the facility was being debated, Mejia, still a student at the time, spoke out in favor of saving it. "In the late spring and early fall," he said, "it's a perfect spot for bands, classes, and speakers."

He might also have said that it was a perfect spot for a summer wedding.

Keeping the campus in spruce condition required not only periodic projects like the amphitheater renovation but also a constant high level of maintenance. In addition, it occasionally required dealing with emergencies of considerable magnitude. One of the least anticipated of such episodes involved, of all places, the Jepson Science Center. On January 10, 2004, just before second semester classes were to begin, an apparent electrical power outage in part of Fredericksburg left the campus without power, causing the heating system in Jepson to fail. That, in turn, allowed cold air to travel throughout the building's air supply system, resulting in ruptured pipes in over a dozen classrooms, forcing classes to be rescheduled elsewhere until the damage was repaired.

Not only the classrooms were affected. Labs on the first and second floors were damaged, with about two inches of water flooding the organic chemistry lab. Many of the fragile plants in the greenhouse, including a collection of rare orchids, were lost. Also, in the midst of the cleanup, a spill of hazardous material (methyl ethyl ketone peroxide) was discovered, though no injuries were sustained. For the most part, faculty offices, with their research and grade data, were spared.

A few days (and around $25,000) later, normality returned to Jepson. But it was ironic that, on a campus where older building infrastructures were increasingly at risk, the pipe malfunction should have occurred in the College's newest and most sophisticated structure.

Weather-related events such as snowstorms also presented challenges for the maintenance crew from time to time. Even greater potential problems lay in the random hurricanes that sometimes menaced the area. In most instances their reality, fortunately, did not match their threat, resulting mainly in some brief wind gusts and moderately heavy rain as with hurricanes Hugo (1989), Fran (1996), Bonnie (1998), and Floyd (1999). Such was distinctly not the case in September 2003, however, when Hurricane Isabel struck the Fredericksburg area with frightening fury.

With the powerful storm predicted to arrive during the evening of Thursday, September 18, the College's Emergency Operations Plan (EOP) was implemented the previous day. The EOP staff consisted of representatives from Residence Life, Facilities Services, Campus Police, and Psychological Services, as well as Fire and Safety Director Ruth Lovelace. The group established headquarters in the Woodard Campus Center, complete with telephones, TVs, a generator, and radios to provide communication with all residence halls. As one EOP staffer, Conference Management Director Susan Knick, explained, the EOP had "procedures for everything, from a dog bite to natural disasters."

The first administrative response was to cancel classes and close the College at 12:30 p.m. on Thursday. Then at 3:00 p.m. the "shelter-in-place" policy was implemented, meaning that students were essentially in lockdown, required either to stay in their dorms or, if they chose to leave, to sign out, using a liability release form absolving the College of responsibility for their safety.[69] Anticipating the coming storm, the Wood Company provided students with takeout meals on Thursday for dinner that night and breakfast on Friday morning. And it was a good thing, too, as Isabel bore down on Fredericksburg.

It was after nightfall when the brunt of the storm roared through campus. All power systems failed around 9:00 p.m., leaving the College in total darkness, without (landline) phone or cable service and very soon without hot water. At first students found the bizarre situation somewhat interesting. As one said, "The darkness is actually kind of entertaining, as long as the cockroaches don't come out."

As students will, they found ways to amuse themselves, including playing games such as sardines, capitalism, and Egyptian ratscrew by the light of candles or flashlights. In the process, some later observed, a sort of bonding took place because "we got to see [albeit dimly] different people that we never saw before."

But it was not long before the novelty wore off and students tended to become crotchety. "I wanna take a shower," groused one. "I can't see, I can't pee, I don't have a phone signal, and I can't study. I can't do anything."

As it turned out, the College was more fortunate than some surrounding areas, as electricity was restored to parts of the campus by noon of the following day (Friday) and to all of it by Saturday morning; some nearby areas were without power for a week or more. Hot water was available by Sunday and cable service by late Monday—the latter, reported the *Bullet*, "to the relief of students who were afraid they would miss the first episode of the final season of 'Friends.'"

But the "Isabel weekend" nonetheless constituted some of the strangest few days ever on campus. With students confined to their dorms, the grounds seemed eerily empty—and silent, save the growling of chain saws attacking the debris of fallen and mangled trees throughout the campus and the city. The worst devastation was on the hillsides above Sunken Road, especially near the amphitheater, where once-stately trees now lay in an uprooted, tangled mass of splintered trunks, limbs, and foliage. Also, several huge trees behind South Hall came down, blocking William Street for hours and nearly smashing into the Marye's Heights apartments.

The cleanup process took many weeks, costing the College approximately $100,000, mostly for the removal of over two hundred trees—making Isabel the most expensive natural disaster in the institution's history. A number of students also suffered financial loss owing to destruction of their cars by falling trees.

In the end, though, the trite observation "It could have been worse" was truly applicable, as there was no loss of life or even any significant injuries among students or employees. Yet the hurricane remained a memorable experience for all who endured it even though, whereas Isabel could justifiably be called a disaster, at Mary Washington it did not have the catastrophic results that it well might have produced.

ACADEMICS: PROGRAMS AND PERSONALITIES

The latter years of the Anderson presidency seemed to indicate that, with regard to faculty concerns, some things never changed much. With varying degrees of justifiability, complaints included salaries that were too low, teaching loads that were too high, classes that were too large, and a merit pay system that no one seemed to like.

Criticism of salaries was in many ways legitimate. Despite repeated administrative avowals of placing a high priority on improvement in that area, General Assembly salary appropriations remained far from munificent. The result was that by 2007, salaries for beginning instructors were in the $45,000 range, though the situation improved somewhat at the more senior levels. Aided by the Anderson administration's establishment of the distinguished professor category, the average salary of faculty above the rank of associate professor in 2006–7 was slightly over $80,000.

Faculty discontent with their remuneration involved not just the salaries themselves but the merit system on which they were based. Much of the resentment arose from the student evaluations that constituted an integral part of the overall performance evaluation used by department chairs to determine merit recommendations. Faculty complained that the student surveys were inherently flawed—that it was impossible to quantify successful teaching. In addition, others argued, the anonymous nature of the surveys made it too easy for disaffected students to exact revenge upon unpopular instructors—the flip side being the potential for pandering on the part of instructors to elicit favorable reviews.

Efforts were made from time to time to refine the evaluation procedure. For a number of years, the main instrument was something called SIR II, a lengthy Scantron form containing many queries that students and faculty alike considered irrelevant. Accompanying blank sheets for students' narrative comments were of minimal help, particularly in light of the time it took supervisors to read and evaluate them. The SIR II forms were eliminated in 2002, ostensibly as a cost-cutting measure—the College paid $16,000 annually to have them analyzed—and a much simpler survey, generated and tabulated in house, was substituted. That procedure, if an improvement, was no panacea either. The whole effort continued to be regarded by most faculty as a necessary evil—in any case, an evil—illustrating perhaps that faculty enjoyed being evaluated no more than the students did.

As for grievances about teaching loads and class size, redress was slow in coming. The most hopeful sign arrived in 2005 with adoption of a plan to reduce the existing 17:1 student-faculty ratio to 15:1 within four years. Implementation would require an outlay of approximately $4 million to fund the forty additional positions that would be needed. Though the vagaries of state appropriations rendered such long-range goals problematic, faculty were encouraged by the additional hirings through 2007 to hope that the plan would be fulfilled by the target date of 2009–10.

Through the years, various issues arose concerning academic structure and faculty governance. One controversial plan, developed by the administration in response to a 1995 state mandate to operate more efficiently, called for grouping the twenty-two existing departments into four administrative divisions: humanities, fine arts, social sciences, and natural sciences. Although discrete departments would not be eliminated, duties of their chairpersons (and hence their salaries) would be reduced, yielding possible savings of approximately $200,000 annually. In addition, according to the plan's advocate, Dean of the Faculty Barbara Palmer, the proposed new arrangement would lead to increased "communication and cooperation."

The faculty, by and large, disagreed—vocally, as usual. Many failed to see how it would save money, viewing it mainly as just another layer of bureaucracy. Eventually the plan was dropped as a result of what Provost Philip Hall termed "tremendous resistance." Dean Palmer concurred. "You try to figure out a better way of governance," she said, but "sometimes there's so much resistance that it's not worth the hassle."

Though the proposed divisional structure did not pan out, a fundamental alteration in faculty governance did occur in 2001. Historically, going back to the Simpson era, the faculty had conducted its business in monthly plenary sessions, presided over by the dean of the faculty, with much of the actual work done through a committee system. However, with the growth in the size of the faculty by the mid-1990s, two scenarios, seemingly contradictory, had come to make that format less productive. On the one hand, full attendance at such meetings made the process cumbersome; on the other, declining participation sometimes made it difficult to achieve a quorum. Consequently a movement arose, advocated by members of the local chapter of the American Association of University Professors, to replace plenary faculty meetings with a senate composed of elected representatives from each department.

When the proposed change was first put to the faculty for a vote, it failed, as that body registered its preference for continuing the town-meeting type of democratic governance. As history professor Bruce O'Brien explained, "At that time, some faculty still thought that a large democratic meeting, no matter how inefficient and disorganized, was preferable to a senate model."

In March 2000, however, a revised plan—the work primarily of O'Brien and psychology professor Debra Nails—was submitted for faculty consideration. According to their proposal, there would be a senate consisting of one representative from each department plus a president, president-elect, and one at-large faculty representative. Under that arrangement, the president of the senate, not the dean of the faculty, would preside, though the dean would be expected to report regularly to that body. This time the faculty approved, and with the endorsement of the Board of Visitors, the senate system went into effect in fall 2000.

The new system was not without its critics. English professor Steve Watkins, for example, though supportive of the system in principle, expressed concerns about the gender imbalance of the first elected body. "There are twenty-two faculty senators and only four are women," he noted. "Our collective sexism is showing." He added, however, that he expected little to result from his criticism because "everybody will just say, 'There's Watkins being PC again.'"

A more widespread concern about the senate format involved the loss of faculty camaraderie that the monthly plenary meetings had fostered. There were frequent nostalgic comments, especially from veteran faculty members, lamenting the general loss of community and the diminished opportunities for developing personal relationships with newer colleagues. Yet there seemed to be overall acceptance of the new system, accompanied by a grudging realization that, as in so many areas of life, increased efficiency came with a cost—in this case, a diminution of the sense of collegial familiarity that had once characterized faculty relationships at Mary Washington.

An ongoing concern within the academic area was the paucity of minority faculty members, especially African Americans. The fundamental problem was the relative lack of qualified black academicians in the disciplines offered at Mary Washington, and the competition among institutions for such individuals was keen.

In that quest, Mary Washington had several disadvantages. Though the College's location had much to commend it, especially in terms of history and natural beauty, those apparent advantages were not necessarily sufficient to offset certain social and cultural aspects that might be unattractive to potential black faculty. Then there were economic factors. The College simply did not have the financial resources to compete successfully in bidding for faculty whose services were in such high demand. This became a source of increasing concern as the cost of living in the Fredericksburg area increased substantially over the course of time.

In light of such handicaps, it was somewhat surprising that the College was able to attract black faculty of the caliber that it did. Though the total number was always small, among that group were some of the institution's most outstanding professors, notably including George King in physics, Tad-desse Adera in English, and Venitta McCall in education. Indeed, from the mid-eighties through the nineties, one of the towering figures among the faculty (both literally and figuratively) was a black man, the revered civil rights leader James Farmer.

Another issue that bothered some faculty (though it pleased others) was the tendency toward greater emphasis on research and publication, a movement aided by increased funding for faculty development and more sabbaticals. While few faculty members denied the importance of active scholarly engagement in their disciplines, many feared that the College was straying from its traditional emphasis on effective teaching.

Some of those who believed in the primacy of pedagogy began in the mid-1980s to concentrate on that issue in informal discussion groups. Out of those deliberations, led by English professors Susan Hanna and William Kemp, philosophy professor Janet Wishner, and psychology professor Roy Smith, came a proposal to seek financial support for the purpose of improving teaching from the State Council of Higher Education's Funds for Excellence Program. The proposal, drafted by Smith, sought funds to advance three objectives specifically: to increase faculty awareness of research literature on pedagogy, to provide opportunities for contact with outside resources for faculty development in pedagogy, and to produce specific applications of pedagogical study to the Mary Washington curriculum.[70]

Enthusiastically supported by Dean Hall, the proposal was approved by SCHEV, which allocated funding for a two-year start-up. The result was the creation of the Teaching Innovation Project (TIP), which went into operation in 1986–87 with Smith as its first director. It was to become a permanent feature of Mary Washington's institutional landscape, vicissitudes of funding and space allocations notwithstanding.

Housed first in the basement of duPont, TIP subsequently moved to Simpson Library, thence to Hamlet House, and eventually back to a renovated duPont Hall. During that time, it was led by a succession of energetic directors, each of whom instituted new programs.

Roy Smith was instrumental in establishing the basic parameters of the program, the centerpiece of which consisted of semester-long seminars on teaching techniques, which selected faculty members were given release time to attend. Other activities included establishing a newsletter, building library resources, and funding faculty members to attend conferences and workshops related to teaching. So successful was the program during its first biennium that the faculty voted unanimously in 1988 to make it a permanent part of the College's academic structure.

Smith was succeeded as director by drama professor Michael Joyce. Owing to fiscal limitations, the semester seminars were discontinued and replaced with daylong seminars on various topics. TIP also took on the responsibility for providing orientation for new faculty members and for serving as a clearinghouse for faculty development grants.

Under Spanish professor Norma Batchelder, who became director in 1991, TIP agreed to administer the new race and gender initiative. It was also during her one-year tenure that discussion began regarding the concept of a faculty "partners" program, whereby two faculty members attended the meetings of each other's classes for a semester and met regularly to discuss their mutual experiences.

Biology professor Mary Pinschmidt served as director from 1992–94, during which time the partners concept was implemented. A TIP journal was also established, under the editorship of English professor William Kemp, for the purpose of publishing faculty papers. Perhaps an overly ambitious project given the financial and temporal constraints involved, the journal ended after only three issues. More permanent were the production of the "Mary Washington College Notebook of Proven and Innovative Teaching Techniques," produced by Norma Batchelder and psychology professor Tom Moeller, and the establishment of an electronic newsletter called *TIP-IT*. During 1994–97, the TIP office, headed by biology professor Lynn Lewis, moved to duPont 210, where more spacious quarters permitted expansion of the program's library and its workshop offerings.

Under the direction of English professor Mary Rigsby from 1997 through 2003, TIP added several new programs specifically designed to invite wider faculty participation, including Knotty Problem Roundtables and the TIP Teaching Buffets. The nonprint media collection was expanded with the purchase of videos and DVDs on pedagogy that were available to faculty through the Multimedia Center in Combs Hall. An electronic series called TIP Teaching Tips was installed and made accessible to all faculty via campus e-mail. One of the most valuable programs created during that time was a TIP workshop on preparing for tenure and promotion taught by faculty who had either served on the tenure and promotion committee or recently been through the process themselves.

Mathematics professor Suzanne Sumner, who became director in 2003, continued TIP's tradition of innovative activities. A new team-teaching initiative proposed by former director Mary Rigsby became one of TIP's most popular opportunities. TIP also collaborated with other campus agencies including the Grants Office, Student Activities Office, Diversity Advisory Committees, Speaking Intensive Program, Writing Intensive Program, and Instructional Technology to produce numerous workshops and programs such as annual summer institutes and the First-Year Student Common Reading Program.

In 2006–7 the Teaching Innovation Program celebrated its twentieth anniversary by hosting a campuswide book club discussion of the National Research Council's book *How People Learn*. Looking toward the future, TIP began to develop a new capstone experience called IDEAL (Interdisciplinary Dilemmas in Ethics and Leadership) to help students gain skills for handling problems involved in community service.

Some areas of the academic program produced recurrent debate. The foreign language requirement, for example, attracted opposition (mainly from students) every few years. In one attack in fall 2000, an English major launched an op-ed broadside against the requirement, claiming that it was detrimental to almost all constituencies: to students "who have no interest in foreign language and resent the fact that it steals our time from more interesting subjects," to language majors who "are surrounded by students who have absolutely no interest in the subject and make a mockery of their passion," to administrators who "witness students transfer every year to colleges which have far less language requirements," and to language teachers themselves who "witness their students lose interest in all forms of learning as the language requirement forces them to spread themselves so thin that they are neither passionate nor prepared in any class." The language requirement was therefore, in the complainant's opinion, the "one institution on this campus which would be absolutely demolished in a democratic election."

The attack drew a quick and defiant rebuttal from student defenders of the requirement, as expressed in a subsequent op-ed piece. To them, the opponents of language study represented merely "the lazy, the apathetic, the unmotivated, the closed-minded, and the provincial" among the student body. For those who preferred to pursue a less-challenging course, the piece concluded, "transfer slips are available at GW if you feel like going to Radford next semester."

In the end, the attack failed, as it had consistently in the past, and the language requirement remained. A related debate soon developed, however—this one concerning the possible addition of a new and quite different language: sign language. As proposed by linguistics professor Christina Kakava, American Sign Language (ASL) was legitimate—"a full-fledged language with a complete grammatical structure," she termed it. Its inclusion among the languages recognized by the College, in her view, was "the right thing to do, both intellectually and morally."

Not all faculty members agreed, and some—notably biology professor Steve Fuller and French professor Jim Gaines—expressed sharp opposition in e-mails to the faculty. Their basic opposition was that ASL did not meet one of the main goals of the language requirement, which, according to Fuller, was its "use as a tool in appreciating the thought processes, literature, and mores of a group outside our own culture."

That comment provoked a heated rejoinder from *Bullet* staff writer Tammie Willis, herself a deaf student (and, remarkably, a music major). In a piece headlined "ASL Argument Gets Nasty," she declared, "I have spent the last six years dismantling the assumptions and stereotypes associated with my hearing loss." Thus, to her mind, the most deplorable aspect of the opposition to ASL was that its critics "turned their arguments away from the language aspect and turned it into a crusade to discount the deaf culture." Despite such pleas, the ASL proposal was ultimately rejected.

A new language, however, was added in 2005—Arabic—though not without difficulties along the way. With greater attention being focused on the Middle East following the 9/11 attacks, and with the consequent demand for speakers of Arabic in government and business positions, students (especially in political science and international affairs) began to request that classes be taught in that language. When the schedule for fall 2004 listed two sections of it, the demand far exceeded the available spaces, resulting in a lengthy waiting list.

Unfortunately for the fifty-four enrolled students, the professor abruptly quit after the first week of classes, citing a conflict with his other teaching job at the University of Virginia. The students, left with hefty textbook bills and ruined schedules, were understandably upset. "I was pissed," said one political science major, "because I had already done the homework for that day, but more disappointed because it was something I really looked forward to learning." The department chair, Leonard Koos, who had worked hard to get the course added to the curriculum, was also disappointed. "I felt sick to my stomach," he said upon learning of the situation.

More than unusual, it was unprecedented, according to Associate Vice President for Academic Affairs John Morello. "It is the first time since I've been part of the hiring process," he said, "where someone starts teaching a course, force-adds people into the course, then [discovers] a schedule conflict." Though nothing could be done for the disillusioned students in 2004, instruction in Arabic did begin without further mishap the following year.

Stirring even more controversy than the debate over language in the late nineties was the proposed addition of a new degree requirement in American history. The origin of the issue was traceable to a Gallup poll that revealed that only 68 percent of American college seniors could correctly identify Thomas Jefferson as the author of the Declaration of Independence. Citing that report, the Virginia General Assembly at its 1998 session passed a resolution requiring all state institutions of higher learning to review—and, if necessary, revise—their curricula to incorporate the study of American history. In response, the College's Board of Visitors in September of 1998 instructed College officials to devise plans to require the study of some aspect of the American past, either history, government, or literature—the idea being that such knowledge would inculcate a greater sense of citizenship. (Board member Todd Stottlemyer noted that he was appalled to learn that students were required to take physical education but not U.S. history.)

The proposed initiative immediately drew opposition on campus, even among some history faculty who, though obviously not opposed to the study of the discipline itself, doubted the practicality of the requirement. Feasibility studies, in fact, indicated that hiring the requisite number of new faculty to implement the requirement might cost as much as half a million dollars—and this at a time when the institution's budget was already stretched thin. Moreover, the faculty, always jealous of its historical (and generally accepted) primacy in the determination of curricular matters, resented the board's intrusion. "It's a matter of academic freedom," declared Tom Whitman of the business administration faculty. "People are concerned with whether the Board of Visitors should be directing the college to teach certain subjects."

Most fundamentally, opponents maintained that the proposed requirement was simply not necessary—that lessons in the basics of citizenship were already guaranteed through requirements such as the western civilization category that permitted students to choose from relevant classes in disciplines such as Greek and Roman history, philosophy, and religion, as well as U.S. history. The *Free Lance–Star*, a strong advocate of the history requirement, was not persuaded by that explanation. "Maybe aqueducts are awesome and perhaps Kierkegaard is keen, but would a required American history course in America's most historic city be so out of line?" asked an editorial. "Besides, in Fredericksburg you can hardly walk down the street without stubbing your toe on this country's history. How weird that the town's college, of all places, can be a history-free zone. This is a little like having a seminary without a theology course."

The paper went on to suggest an ideological basis for the opponents' position. "The Vietnam War spawned—or perhaps released—a collegiate radicalism that blamed America for every ill, foreign and domestic. Although the diatribes have perhaps cooled, there is still on many campuses a reflex against jingoism that sometimes punishes knowledge itself. One needn't be a super patriot to rescue U.S. history from elective status."

But there, in fact, is where it remained, as the board at its February meeting the following year backed off its earlier mandate. "It was a spur of the moment, poorly written resolution," commented Vice Rector Vincent DiBenedetto. "What we should have done was direct the faculty and administration to look into this and determine how much in compliance with this resolution we are already, and where we're lacking, and how we might address that." President Anderson concurred, saying simply, "You don't produce citizens by [teaching] Citizenship 101." And so, in the end, the proposal failed, much to the dismay of the more conservative members of the Board of Visitors, faculty, and community.

Just as certain issues persisted among the faculty, so too were there academic matters that perennially concerned the students. One such was freshman advising, an enterprise that students claimed was never satisfactory. (A typical complaint was voiced in a 1998 *Bullet* op-ed column titled, with a nod to the Beatles, "Help! I Need Somebody, Not Just Anybody.")

This failure, insofar as it actually existed, did not occur for lack of effort to correct it as, over the years, various advising methods were employed. One, called the 50/50 system, assigned entering freshmen to a faculty adviser and two student advisers; initial advising took place at summer preview sessions before the start of fall classes. In the late nineties, that system was dropped in favor of assigning new students to a faculty member in the area of their expressed academic interest, with advising taking place immediately before the start of fall classes.

Still striving to find a better system, the academic advising office under Assistant Dean for Academic Services JoAnn Schrass in 2006 further refined the plan by creating groups of new students that would meet periodically throughout the academic year with their advisers so as to provide ongoing guidance. Whatever the degree of success for freshman advising, students generally agreed that, in most cases, advising improved substantially once they had declared a major and thus were assigned to an adviser within that department.

Another recurrent issue concerned minor programs. The concept was not new. In fact, before a curricular revision in 1945, students had been required to have both a major and two minors.[71] In the intervening years, the issue had arisen periodically, including in the early 1990s, when, after much debate, it was rejected by vote of the faculty.

The matter resurfaced, however, in the early years of the new century, resulting in a formal proposal by the faculty's Academic Affairs Committee to the Senate to create a minor that would consist of a fifteen- to eighteen-hour voluntary concentration in a single discipline. The decision for offering such minors would be left to the discretion of individual departments. First presented in April 2002, the motion was tabled to permit gathering of additional information, a procedure that included a survey of approximately one thousand students.

Survey results furnished indisputable evidence of student support for the concept. Almost 90 percent of the respondents either agreed or strongly agreed that there should be minors, and 87 percent believed that a minor would make the College more attractive to prospective students. In addition, proponents of the plan pointed out that Mary Washington was the only state institution in Virginia that did not provide the option of pursuing a minor.

The survey, however, also contained a statistic that was troubling to some departments: 66 percent of those students currently pursuing double majors indicated that they would choose a minor rather than one of the majors if given that opportunity. This was a frightening prospect to disciplines whose production of majors was already so small as to jeopardize their very existence. (At that time, SCHEV required that each major program must graduate, on average, five students per year, calculated over a three-year period, in order for the major to be offered. The same guidelines, rather incredibly, applied to all state institutions, irrespective of their size—a guideline that obviously presented greater problems to small schools such as Mary Washington.)

One particularly vulnerable department was Classics, Philosophy, and Religion, which comprised three such imperiled majors. So, taking the lead in the fight against minors was department chair Craig Vasey (just as his predecessor Robert Boughner had done a decade earlier). A minor, Vasey argued in a *Bullet* guest column, was essentially useless—"more window dressing than anything else." The biggest problem, he emphasized, was that implementation of minors might lead to the destruction of certain major programs "in the central disciplines of the humanities" (e.g., his own), an outcome that would make Mary Washington more "like a community college, not a selective high quality liberal arts college."

Vasey's view prevailed, as the Faculty Senate in December 2002 voted against creating minors. History would suggest, however, that the issue might not have been permanently settled.

Meanwhile, grading policy became a hot topic on campus in the mid-nineties as an outgrowth of concerns over what was generally termed "grade inflation." A study of grade distribution for the fall 1993 semester indicated the existence of such a problem. The academic catalog at that time defined an A as connoting unusual excellence, B as work distinctly above average, C as work of average or medium quality, D as work of below-average quality, and F as failure. However, the 1993 analysis revealed an overall grade distribution consisting of 26 percent As, 43 percent Bs, 24 percent Cs, 5 percent Ds, and 2 percent Fs.[72] In short, the average grade had become B.

The study also showed wide variation in the assignment of grades among departments, with scores in performance classes tending to be higher than in others. Grades in musical performance classes, for example, consisted of 95 percent As or Bs with only 1 percent Ds or Fs; the Drama Department awarded 80 percent As and Bs. The situation was similar in education classes, where 89 percent of the students received As or Bs and the overall GPA was 3.30. The lowest cumulative GPAs were in biology (2.55) and geology (2.54).

Various explanations were offered for the upward trend in grades. One was simply that, with the College becoming more selective in admission, the students were better academically than before and grades naturally rose accordingly. Others attributed the inflation to a withdrawal policy that allowed students to escape late in the semester from courses in which they were doing poorly.[73]

A more fundamental explanation traced the phenomenon to larger societal developments. "It's typical across the country in quality institutions," said Roy Weinstock, vice president for planning, assessment, and institutional research. "It is in no way surprising. . . . Expectations students have about high grades are established in high school. There is tremendous pressure in society on students' doing well—parental pressure [and] thinking about the job market."

The situation did indeed appear to be widespread, even in greater evidence at the more prestigious schools. In the mid-nineties, for example, *Time* magazine reported that 93 percent of all grades awarded at Stanford University had been As and Bs. The result was, as one MWC student put it in 1994, "Students need those As and Bs, especially coming out of high school where people got really, really high grades. If you don't get at least a B, then you feel like you failed."

Whatever the cause of it, many Mary Washington professors were becoming alarmed. "At a certain point this devalues the currency," said education professor Paul Zisman. "Students tend to want the high grade and not the knowledge."

Motivated at least partly by such concerns, the faculty began in the mid-nineties to consider adding a plus or minus designation to the existing letter-grade system, a procedure that was already in place at all state colleges and universities in Virginia except Virginia Commonwealth, Radford, and George Mason. A sizable portion of the faculty advocated the change, arguing that additional gradations would enable instructors to assess student performance with greater accuracy (there being, for example, considerable difference between an 80 and an 89, both of which would normally receive the grade of B under existing standards). Yet in the course of debate stretching over several years, no strong consensus developed among the faculty.

Among the students, on the other hand, the predominant feeling toward the plus/minus system was unambivalent: they hated it. A student government survey in 1996 revealed that almost 70 percent of the respondents opposed it. Representing that view was the *Bullet*, which directed a continuing barrage against the plan, using arguments ranging from specific to superficial. A particular point of contention involved the impact of a C-minus grade on a student's GPA. The *Bullet* argued that such a grade, quantified as 1.7 (below the level of academic probation), could have a worse ultimate effect on one's cumulative GPA than a D-plus, since the latter course could be retaken, whereas a C-minus course could not.

Besides such specifics, the paper ridiculed the plus/minus system as reminiscent of elementary school. "Maybe we can even get a happy face or gold stars on our paper," it sneered. "Next thing that will happen is the implementation of a finger-painting class, and nap-time, if we're not careful."

Then, according to the *Bullet*, there was a more subtle problem with the proposed system. "A minus sign is inherently negative and could have psychological repercussions," it claimed, asserting that "one who earns several grades of C-plus will have higher self-esteem than a more conscientious student who will go the extra mile to get that B-minus only to have his or her self-image shattered by all the negativity that surrounds the minus sign."

From there the editorial proceeded, in a welter of metaphors, to lecture the faculty: "As an institution that is home to a few thousand young, impressionable minds, . . . it is important to nurture the mind itself, and that includes self-esteem. If we are all sent out into the world with our tails between our legs, we may as well have clipped wings and leaden boots because we will be going nowhere fast. And while we've got the leaden boots on, just go ahead and toss us in the river and get it all over with. Yes, friends in the faculty, you must consider the psychological consequences before you decide to implement the plus/minus grading system. . . . Guys and gals, don't do it. Just say no."

When the proposal was first voted on by the faculty in 1993, it did in fact "just say no." But three years later the outcome was different—just barely—as the plus/minus plan was approved by a vote of fifty-eight to fifty-six. The *Bullet* was miffed. Recalling the overwhelming student opposition as expressed in the earlier referendum, it observed that the vote showed that "the students have absolutely no say in something that affects us more than anyone else on this campus," and warned that "students can get ready for an elevated sense of competitiveness here at MWC. . . . It seems the faculty is trying to overstress already stressed students, and give us one more thing to worry about."

As it turned out, they did not have to worry immediately because owing to delays in the installation of computer equipment needed to accommodate the new system, plus/minus grading did not begin until fall 2000. Even then the result was not dramatic in its impact on cumulative GPAs College-wide. The main result, which was to have been expected, was a reduction in the number of students making the President's List (4.0 GPA), since many students in the A category might now receive an A-minus (3.7).

A further alteration of the grading system occurred in 2003 when the faculty voted to redefine the meaning of the letter grades. A main reason for the change, according to its proponents, was the desire to eliminate the ambiguity embedded in the definition of C as "average." Under the new terminology, A was defined as "excellent," B as "commendable," C as "adequate," D as "marginal," and F as "failure." Again the changes appeared to have had little bearing on the assignment of grades College-wide, as the average cumulative GPA remained essentially the same.

The academic program continued to flourish during the final decade of Anderson's presidency, largely as the result of the maturation of initiatives taken earlier in his administration. These included expansion of the internship program, greater focus on undergraduate research, and wider application of instructional technology.[74]

One of the most significant ongoing academic developments was the emphasis on international study. In the early nineties, spurred by the mandate contained in the Governor's Commission on the University in the Twenty-first Century and strongly encouraged by President Anderson, the College developed what it called a "global initiative." It was an ambitious agenda that advocated increasing global awareness, multicultural sensitivity, and internationalization of the curriculum. More specifically, it called for new courses, more international students and faculty, support for international activity of faculty, and more extensive involvement of students in study-abroad experiences.[75] In subsequent years, increasing numbers of students participated in international programs of one kind or another, many of them through various study-abroad programs coordinated by Mary Washington's office of international academic services. Beginning in spring 1985, at the instigation of Chris Musick, director of international academic services, the office published once each semester in the *Bullet* a multi-page paid insert called "The Periscope." That publication contained numerous first-person articles contributed by students describing their experiences overseas, as well as information concerning both faculty-led programs and opportunities available through Musick's office.[76]

A number of summer international ventures were developed by individual faculty members such as English professor Carmen Gillespie's Caribbean Literature course held in Barbados, English professor Gardner Campbell's Advanced Studies in England in London, and History professor Carter Hudgins's archaeological digs in Nevis. Sometimes the programs developed from personal ties between the professors and the foreign countries, such as Donald Rallis's program in his native South Africa, Brown Morton's course in Scotland, Clavio Ascari's and Joseph Di Bella's course in Urbino, Italy, and José Sainz's in Bilbao, Spain. (The Spanish trip in 2004 included an opportunity for students to view, but not participate in, the running of the bulls in Pamplona.) Some of the programs such as the ones offered by Rallis, Morton, and Sainz were repeated multiple times.

As institution-wide emphasis on globalism was increasing, the individual academic departments evolved, each with its own distinctive programs and personalities. It was the activities of those departments that formed the heart of intellectual life at Mary Washington.

Art and Art History

During the late twentieth century and the early twenty-first, the Department of Art and Art History played a significant role in the life of Mary Washington College both in the academic program and in the institution's outreach efforts.[77]

On the academic side, an evolution of the faculty occurred with the retirements in art history of Professors Pauline King, Barbara Meyer, and Cornelia "Neal" Oliver, and in studio art, John Lamph and Paul Muick. In 1976 the hiring of Joseph Dreiss marked the beginning of a new core of art history faculty that later included JeanAnn Dabb and Marjorie Och. The following year, Joseph Di Bella arrived and soon became the anchor of a talented group of studio art teachers and practitioners including Lorene Nickel, Stephen Griffin, and Carole Garmon. Di Bella received the Simpson Award in 1983 and Garmon the Outstanding Young Faculty Member Award in 2002.

Along with the new faculty came curricular changes that reflected their areas of interest and expertise. In art history, for example, the first courses in non-Western art were introduced, and a museum studies course was added. Also, in 1995 a computer lab in Melchers was opened for student use.

The academic program was enhanced by the department's establishment of a Visiting Artists and Speakers Fund that brought a number of notable guests to campus over the years. It also secured sizable increases in scholarship funding for the department's majors.

But successful as the academic program was, the department's role on campus extended well beyond the classrooms and studios. Over a long period, its production and promotion of art exhibitions contributed substantially to the cultural life of the community.

The College's first major art show was held in 1956 as part of the celebration of Grellet Simpson's inauguration as chancellor.[78] The exhibition, which was organized by art professor Julien Binford with the assistance of students, featured fifty contemporary artworks on loan from New York dealers. In his introduction to the exhibition catalog, Binford wrote of Chancellor Simpson's "conviction that the enjoyment of art in familiar surroundings is the daily need of civilized people" and expressed the hope that such exhibitions would become annual events.

At that time a plan was formulated to develop a College art collection by purchasing one painting each year from the annual exhibitions. In the process, such a collection, according to Binford, would "be as much of a step forward in the College's development as was the founding of the library." The first purchase was Milton Avery's renowned work *Pink Pasture*, which long remained perhaps the most important artwork in the College's possession.

Despite that auspicious start, the history of the College's galleries was uneven. During the 1960s and 1970s, for example, no significant artworks were added to the permanent collection, nor were there many exhibitions aside from the periodic shows featuring the works of Mary Washington students.

In the early 1980s, however, a dramatic change began under the impetus and guiding hand of art professor Joseph Di Bella. Serving as the College's first gallery director, he oversaw improvements in the duPont Hall galleries and began to put together exhibitions such as a 1983 retrospective of works by Professor Emerita Dorothy Van Winckel. From that point onward, increased interest in College exhibitions led Di Bella to develop additional shows.

Several events during the 1990s had considerable impact on the College's art program. One was the effort to revive interest in the institution's neglected permanent art collection, much of which had been dispersed or misplaced. Using an inventory developed in 1981 by Frances Armstrong '36, students and faculty were able to track down most of the works or determine the circumstances of their loss. A number of the rediscovered items were collected and placed in the duPont galleries for safekeeping.

A significant development in the history of the art program was the April 1992 opening of the Ridderhof Martin Gallery, which served as a venue for numerous exhibitions. With energetic leadership provided by the Ridderhof

Martin's first director, Forrest McGill, notable early shows featured (in spring 1994) the work of New York artist Margaret Sutton '26 and (in fall 1994) the work of Sutton's friend Alfred Levitt. The Levitt exhibition was in honor of the artist's one hundredth birthday, which he celebrated on campus, and included more than forty paintings, many of which were on loan from the Metropolitan Museum of Art in New York City. Subsequent exhibitions served the dual needs of providing cultural opportunities for the community and academic assistance to students—not just those in the Art Department but students in other disciplines as well. For example, a 1995 exhibition of Islamic photographs organized by Professor Mehdi Aminrazavi of the Department of Classics, Philosophy, and Religion complemented his concurrent course, Religion and Politics of Islam. Similarly, a 1998 Goya exhibition was of considerable interest to Spanish students.

In 1998 Thomas Somma replaced Forrest McGill as director of galleries. Somma's career was an unusual one. His initial training was in chemical engineering, and he attained a lucrative position in that field before falling in love with art history. That interest led him back to graduate school, where he earned a doctorate in the subject. He taught for a number of years at the University of Iowa and at Ithaca College before joining the Mary Washington staff.

Perhaps because of his earlier work outside academia, Somma approached his job in a practical, nonelitist fashion, exhibiting a desire to make the world of art accessible to laypersons, not just the cognoscenti. Under his direction, the College launched two of its most significant efforts. Among the most ambitious was a 2002 exhibition, Leonardo da Vinci: Artist, Scientist, Engineer, which grew out of collaboration between Somma and physics professor Bulent Atalay. The two formed a natural partnership based on Somma's engineering background and Atalay's expertise in art. Encouraged by President Anderson, who provided initial funds for the project, the two men worked with outside consultants and several MWC departments, including art and education, to put together the most costly ($100,000) exhibition in the College's history, the expenses of which were partially covered by a grant from the Virginia Foundation for Humanities and Public Policy.

The exhibition was wide-ranging in its coverage, illuminating Leonardo's multiple talents through the display of models created from Leonardo's original drawings, among them a flying machine, a helicopter, a printing press, and a parachute. It also included facsimile drawings, both anatomical and mechanical, on loan from the National Gallery of Art and two rare books from the National Gallery, one of them a first-edition copy of his treatise on painting. The project was complemented with a series of lectures by scholars from across the country, as well as Mary Washington's own Professors Och and Atalay. The event's extraordinary success was praised by both the local press and the *Bullet*—the latter correctly describing it as "one of the greatest exhibitions this College has ever seen" and noting that its success proved "that the College has the ability to bring artistic awareness to the community."

Two years later, the gallery hosted another extraordinary exhibition, though one of a very different nature. The impetus came from a local project not directly related to Mary Washington: namely, plans for building a national slavery museum in the Fredericksburg area, a project devised and promoted by former Virginia governor Douglas Wilder.

In consultation with officials of the fledgling museum, and featuring artifacts on loan from it, Tom Somma put together a show titled "Reflections on American Slavery: Selected Objects from the Collections of the United States National Slavery Museum," which opened in August 2004. Given the emotional nature of the subject matter, the exhibit design required great sensitivity. Somma and his assistants were up to the task, developing a show that graphically portrayed slavery through the display of items such as shackles and chains, receipts for slave sales, political cartoons, African ceremonial robes, plantation ledgers, musical instruments, and a slave ship replica.

The exhibition proved to be perhaps the most successful show ever at Mary Washington, drawing over 1,600 visitors—about four times the number who typically attended gallery shows on campus. Among that number was entertainer Bill Cosby, a close friend of Wilder's and staunch supporter of the proposed slavery museum. Having viewed the Ridderhof Martin exhibition, Cosby spoke to an enthusiastic banquet assemblage in Seacobeck Hall, where he announced a personal pledge of one million dollars to support the museum project.

Few left unmoved by what they saw: some were brought to tears. Yet there was a marked lack of hostility, despite the potential for intense emotional reactions. "It didn't matter whether [they were] black, white, North, South, young, old," observed Tom Somma. "Ninety-nine percent thought it was very worthwhile."[79]

In addition to the new Ridderhof Martin Gallery, the facilities for the College's art program were enhanced by the renovation of the Melchers studios and classrooms and the duPont galleries, which were converted from four small spaces into one large one. The official reopening of the gallery in January 1995 was celebrated by an exhibition of ceramics, mosaics, paintings, photographs, and sculptures by the department's studio art faculty. The refurbished facility—now containing hardwood floors, modern furniture, and professional-quality lighting—served as a functional counterpart to the Ridderhof Martin Gallery.

In the fall of 1995 a photographic retrospective of the works of Professor Steve Griffin marked a technological innovation in art exhibitions at the College. While the actual exhibit of thirty-two of Griffin's works was displayed in the new duPont gallery, a virtual exhibit was made available to everyone worldwide through its posting on the Internet. That project (which took as much effort to construct as the actual show) was carried out by a technologically savvy team headed by computer science professor Ernest Ackermann and art history professor Joe Dreiss. (Griffin himself was not among them, inasmuch as he was, as he put it, "just not in tune enough" with modern technology.)

Biological Sciences

The Biology Department was one of Mary Washington's largest in terms of enrollment. Before the 1980s, its ranks had been swelled by students engaged in two-year planned transfer programs like medical technology. When such programs were discontinued, the numbers fell somewhat but soon rose again as students chose that discipline as a beneficial road to careers in basic life sciences, research, teaching, medicine, dentistry, and allied health fields. By 2005, the department typically graduated around eighty majors each year, usually placing it within the four most popular majors at Mary Washington.

Serving those students was one of the largest faculties at the College.[80] Between 1980 and the turn of the century, that faculty had changed to the extent that only two of its members, Michael Bass and Steve Fuller, had been there in 1980. Gone in the interim, either through retirement or death, were such outstanding teachers as Zoe Black, William Cassel, Ruth Friedman, Anna "Scottie" Hoye (the 1974 Simpson Award recipient), Rosemary Johnson, Thomas Johnson, Mary Jo Parrish, and William Pinschmidt.

A shocking loss to the department and to the College was the death of Professor Mary Pinschmidt (the 1982 Simpson honoree) in November 1998—an event all the more tragic because of its suddenness. Having taught her classes as usual earlier in the week, apparently in perfect health, she contracted bacterial meningitis and died on Wednesday, the day before Thanksgiving. "She was a wonderful presence in the classroom," recalled psychology professor Roy Smith. "She was an ultimate teacher. . . . You only had to be around her a short time to realize that if she was your friend, you had a real friend." Her students had similar memories. "She was always happy," said one. "I don't remember her ever being in a bad mood."

In her memory, the department established a scholarship fund, and the College in 1999 created an award to be given annually to that professor whom students believed they would "most likely remember as the one who had the greatest impact on their lives." One of the three awards presented at commencement each year, it was the only award bestowed by vote of the graduates themselves—an appropriate acknowledgment of the primacy of Professor Pinschmidt's devotion to her students.

The older generation of instructors was replaced over the years by an outstanding group of scholars who were not only effective teachers but were in many cases leaders within the College and, beyond that, were active in their professions. Steve Fuller, for example, established a reputation as a staunch advocate of faculty rights and was also instrumental in establishing Mary Washington's writing intensive program.

Michael Bass first joined the biology faculty in 1968 and remained continu-

Rosemary Barra

ously through 2007 except for a hiatus from 1972 through 1974 while he was completing his Ph.D. at Virginia Tech. His doctoral work in zoophysiology involved environmental science, which included courses in limnology (freshwater aquatic ecology). The latter led him to conduct a study of *Trichopteria* (or caddisflies), one of the largest groups of aquatic insects, during a 1978 summer project in southwestern Virginia streams. It was there that he discovered a previously unidentified species that upon verification was given the scientific name, in his honor, *Hydropsyche bassi*.

Rosemary Barra, noted for her work in cancer research, was, along with Werner Wieland, notably active in the Virginia Academy of Sciences; each served at one time as the academy's president. Barra, in addition to her teaching and research activities—she received the Simpson Award in 2003—was increasingly drawn into administrative duties, serving as department chair for nine years and as marshal of the faculty for another eight. Indicative of her administrative skills and of the high regard in which Barra was held by faculty and administrators alike, she was named interim dean of the faculty upon the retirement of Philip Hall in 2004. In a position widely acknowledged to be one of the most thankless at the institution, Barra thrived, largely because of the perception (quite accurate) that she was not only capable in executing the office's disparate duties but also open and eminently fair-minded in doing so.

Barra was also, like Mary Pinschmidt, devoted to her students. During her years as chair, annual holiday dinners at her house became a tradition at Christmastime. Those gatherings were eagerly anticipated by as many as one hundred students who appreciated the opportunity for a home-cooked meal and informal fellowship with the faculty.

In addition to serving the general education needs of many students in the area of natural science, the Biology Department offered an array of diverse advanced courses including endocrinology, immunology, neurobiology, ornithology, herpetology, animal behavior, and plant ecology. The curriculum was also enriched by the integration of field research into many courses. For example, Professor Joella Killian took classes to Wallops Island for long weekends during the spring semester, and Professor Fuller developed a course on tropical ecology that included taking the class to Puerto Rico or Costa Rica during spring break.

The department was also a College leader in promoting undergraduate research. Whether directed by an individual faculty member during the regular semester or as a participant in a summer research project, many biology majors had the opportunity to conduct innovative independent research projects. Always productive learning experiences, such projects often led to published papers or to presentations at professional meetings at the state, regional, national, and even international levels.

Business Administration

After approval by the faculty in 1979, business administration was introduced within the Department of Economics, Business, and Public Administration. It became independent in 1984 with the creation of the Department of Business and Public Administration.

Starting with its first group of seventy declared majors in 1981, the department grew rapidly, with the number of majors doubling the next year. The first graduating class in 1982 had 24 majors; two years later there were 80. By 2006, the department had almost 350 majors, of whom 134 graduated. That number represented nearly 15 percent of the entire graduating class, the largest of any discipline by a considerable margin. The huge enrollment helped to make business administration the College's most fiscally efficient in terms of cost per credit hour.

In addition to the undergraduate major, a master of business administration degree was approved by the State Council of Higher Education in 1979. That program, however, was discontinued in 1988 for the ostensible purpose of providing greater resources for the undergraduate program. The master's program was revived in 1999 with the establishment of the College of Graduate and Professional Studies.

The designer of the business program was Steve Czarsty, who effectively crafted a curriculum that conformed to the dictates of the institution's liberal arts philosophy. After guiding the development of the program for many years, he was succeeded as chair by the flamboyant Gano Evans, a jazz musician ("Dr. Daddy-O") widely recognizable around town in his flashy red convertible.

One distinctive feature of the business faculty was the high percentage who held "real world" jobs before joining the department. Many had served in the military, including Tom Whitman and Ken Machande (Marine Corps), Harry Skinker and Galen deGraff (Army), Marge Klayton Mi (Air Force), and Gano Evans and Richard Curley (Navy). Several played large roles in the life of the institution beyond the department. Among these were Larry Penwell (who held a joint appointment in the Department of Psychology) as chair of the 2003 SACS Decennial Institutional Self-Study, Leigh Frackelton as longtime adviser to the Honor Council, and Patricia Metzger as a vocal advocate for animal rights.

With the possible exception of Historic Preservation, Business Administration was more extensively involved with the local community than any other department at Mary Washington. For example, the department's accountants voluntarily assisted low-income families by helping them to file their IRS tax returns. Students in some classes were involved in implementing projects provided by the Small Business Development Center, while others helped design market strategies for nonprofit organizations such as the Rappahannock Council against Domestic Violence. For many years, marketing students conducted research for local businesses, including telephone surveys (for radio stations, the chamber of commerce, and the College itself), personal interviews (Goodwill and Red Cross), and focus groups (Virginia Credit Union). An honors project in 1995 by two business majors convinced the Virginia Credit Union to open, first, a student-run credit union office in the student center and eventually two full-service offices in the Fredericksburg area.

One of the department's most significant innovations, in terms of both outreach and service within the institution itself, was creation of the Executive-in-Residence program. Beginning in 1989 the program annually brought to campus a prominent senior executive to spend a day visiting classes, delivering presentations, and meeting with students and community business leaders.

Chemistry

The Chemistry Department during the years of Anderson's presidency experienced considerable change in personnel, with the departures of several veteran instructors including the intense John George, whose dedication to helping his students was boundless. There was also Herbert Cover, a droll, easygoing fellow of wide and colorful interests, among them jazz music, beer-bottle collecting, and electronics repair. In retirement he was popularly known in the local community as "Mr. Fix-It" for his ability to resuscitate decrepit radios, record players, and televisions.

Then there was likable Lawrence Wishner. During his more than thirty-year tenure, which began in 1961, he not only taught a range of chemistry courses but also served from 1971 to 1977 as assistant dean of instruction. In addition to his scholarly achievements within the profession, he was also widely known for his informative and amusing book, *Eastern Chipmunks: Secrets of Their Solitary Lives*, published by the Smithsonian Institution Press in 1982. Having retired in 1992, Wishner died in October 2006.

The most prominent member of the chemistry faculty during that time was the ebullient Bernard Mahoney. A transplanted New Englander who came to the College in 1964, Mahoney never lost his "Bahsten" accent or his attachment to the beloved "Red Sawx." His dedication to the field of chemistry was paralleled by his commitment to teaching and to the welfare of his students, many of whom he shepherded through the difficult chemistry

Bernard L. Mahoney Jr.

curriculum, thence to graduate school, and eventually to careers in the field. "Quite literally, he changed my life," recalled one 1968 graduate. "He was so passionate about his subject that I was embarrassed not to learn, even though chemistry was hard for me. He . . . not only helped me to learn chemistry, but to have confidence that I could accomplish whatever I wanted to, through hard work."

Mahoney's influence on institutional governance was exemplary, beginning with his appointment, early in his tenure, as a member of the Future of the College Committee, the group that was instrumental in charting the path to coeducation. He subsequently served as chair of three ad hoc committees in the 1960s and 1970s, each of which wrought tangible and lasting changes in revising teacher certification requirements, creating the internship program, and developing the bachelor of liberal studies degree. He also served for a dozen years as department chair and was the 1984 recipient of the Simpson Award.

Mahoney's success as a faculty leader was well described by his longtime associate Roy Weinstock. "He was an absolutely tireless worker," he said. "Everyone listened to him because they knew he was sensible, reflective, incisive, and always had the best interest of the College at heart. Plus, his constant good humor always made him easy to get along with."

When Mahoney retired in 2002, he was one of the most widely respected and best-liked members of the faculty. In an alumni magazine article on his impending retirement, the writer noted that the College would be "a poorer place with his departure. It won't be as much fun, either, sans the levity often provided by this affable extrovert whose bonhomie—sometimes garnished appealingly with a wee bit o'blarney—has enlivened many a college gathering over the years." His chemistry colleague Roy Gratz put it most succinctly. Bernie Mahoney was, he said, "the ultimate professional."

By the time of Mahoney's retirement, the senior core of the chemistry faculty consisted of the quietly efficient Judith Crissman (hired in 1968), Roy Gratz (1975), and Raymond Scott (1984). Gratz, though more low-key than Mahoney, was likewise a faculty leader who was respected for his sage counsel, always delivered with a soft voice that belied deeply held opinions. He was also a vigorous scholar who spent several summers on research projects for NASA and the U.S. Navy, work that contributed to his national reputation in the field of polymers, in which he was awarded seven patents between 1988 and 1999.

Ray Scott was best known to the larger College community outside the department for his role in establishing and directing the Eagle Pipe Band, but his contributions to the institution were also extensive, as illustrated by his receiving the J. Christopher Bill Service Award in 2006. Perhaps his most notable contribution to the science program at Mary Washington was his role in creating and directing the Summer Science Research Program. Launched in 1999, the program had two purposes: first, to enable faculty members to pursue in the summer projects of interest that were precluded by heavy classroom and laboratory obligations during the academic year and, second, to provide the opportunity for students to engage in original research.

Aided by a start-up grant from the DuPont Foundation, the program provided stipends that allowed the creation of teams consisting of one professor and two students to pursue various summer projects. Participants were not restricted to chemistry but also included other scientific disciplines; the program was eventually extended to incorporate mathematics and computer science as well. Many of the summer projects resulted in publications and papers at conferences, providing invaluable experience for the students involved. By 2007 there were ten teams comprising ten faculty and twenty students. The success of the initiative contributed, in the waning days of the Anderson presidency, to the securing of a $2 million anonymous grant to endow the perpetuation of the program.

The chemistry faculty was augmented in the late nineties by the hiring of two outstanding young scholars. The first, in 1995, was Kelli Slunt '91, who became department chair in 2003. Her exceptional performance was acknowledged in 2000 when she was received the Alumni Association Outstanding Young Faculty award. The second was Leanna Giancarlo, whose extensive scholarly productivity and enthusiastic performance in the classroom and lab resulted in her, too, winning the Outstanding Young Faculty award (2004).

The basic core curriculum in chemistry remained virtually unchanged, with general chemistry, organic chemistry, and physical chemistry required of all majors. Within that framework, however, innovative teaching methods were employed, including a new problem-solving approach to lab work in general chemistry. According to Ray Scott, who pioneered the approach along with Kelli Slunt in the late nineties, the procedure was "not cookbook. We don't tell them what to do, we [give] them a problem to solve, and then they have to figure out what they're going to do about it. . . . It's the scientific method in action. And they really have to solve their puzzle." The approach was later adapted for use in courses other than general chemistry as well.

Such innovations notwithstanding, enrollment in chemistry was never very high. ("Some folks don't like chemistry," Scott deadpanned, "hard as it is to imagine.") Yet the department played an important role in the institution's science program. As Roy Gratz noted, "Chemists like to say, 'It's the central science,' because it's right between biology and physics—physics being more fundamental, biology being a little more practical. Chemistry is kind of in the middle of it all."

The department's majors, who generally averaged only a dozen or so graduates each year, were distinguished by their quality. The four Darden Award winners between 1987 and 2001 (Angela Goforth in 1987, Cheryl Davis in 1990, Kristin Buck in 2000, and Trixy Franke in 2001) likely constituted the highest percentage of graduates to win the award from any department during the period. Impressive, too, was the number of them who went on to graduate school and professional careers within the field. Among the most notable was Rita Klim '78, whose stellar record led her to be chosen by Sir Hans Krebs, the 1953 Nobel laureate in medicine, to work in his laboratory as a graduate student in metabolism.[81] But she was one of many exemplary graduates. According to Scott, a ten-year alumni study "discovered that 90 percent of our graduates were using their degree. And that, I think, is pretty astounding."

Classics, Philosophy, and Religion (CPR)

Of all the controversial disciplinary restructuring that took place during the Woodard years, none produced such positive results as the combination that created the Department of Classics, Philosophy, and Religion, commonly known as CPR. Though the individual programs that the new department comprised were small, their amalgamation promoted a cross-pollination that invigorated each. According to religion professor David Cain, the CPR acronym was apt, as the department constituted "cardio-pulmonary resuscitation at the very heart of a liberal arts education."

Each discipline within the department was distinctive both in its programs and its personalities. At the time of the merger, Classics was headed by Laura Sumner, who had been at Mary Washington since 1948. She served as department chair for thirty years and also for a period as director of the summer session. A dedicated scholar, she was an enchanting classroom presence as well,

Laura V. Sumner

teaching courses with a style that consistently combined profundity with fun. Active in civic affairs—she was a staunch Republican—she became in 1960 the first woman ever elected to the Fredericksburg City Council, where she went on to serve three productive terms. In recognition of her achievement, she was named the "first lady" of Fredericksburg. Having retired in the early 1980s, Laura Sumner died in June 1993.

With Sumner's retirement and that of her longtime colleague, the inimitable Lucille Jones, the classics faculty in the 1980s was anchored by soft-spoken Diane Hatch and by energetic Robert Boughner, whose classes became some of the most popular in the entire curriculum. It was a considerable loss to the College when Boughner departed in 1995 to become dean of the American University in Athens, Greece. The program's reputation for outstanding teaching continued, however, with hirings in the nineties and in the first decade of the new century of young scholars including Lianne Houghtalin and Angela Gosetti-Murrayjohn, as well as a graduate of the program, Joseph Romero '93.

The status of the classics program was further burnished in 2003 when it became the permanent home of the National Latin Exam (NLE), with Jane Hall, a veteran Mary Washington adjunct professor of classics, as its co-chair. The NLE was a privately funded organization that not only administered exams to well over 100,000 students each year (at all academic levels) but further promoted the study of Latin by organizing colloquiums for teachers and offering sizable scholarship awards for students. The national visibility of the Mary Washington program was boosted by the existence of the NLE headquarters on campus and also by the presence of Hall, who in 2006 was the first recipient of the new award for lifetime service established by Eta Sigma Phi, the national collegiate honor society for classics.

The philosophy program, at the time CPR was created, was headed by George Van Sant. From his arrival on campus in 1958 until his retirement in 1990, few people had a bigger influence at the College and in the community than the six-foot-five former Marine Corps colonel, whose service included three years of combat duty in the Korean War.[82]

Like Laura Sumner (his polar opposite in political orientation), the Democrat Van Sant was extensively involved in community affairs. Devoted to promoting civil rights, he was instrumental in organizing the Fredericksburg Area Community Relations Organization and, as an advocate for the study of local history, worked to open the Fredericksburg Area Museum and Cultural Center. As a multi-term member of city council, he was particularly notable for his promotion of the economic fortunes of the city, mainly through advocating a controversial annexation plan in 1984. Though his stand was not universally popular at the time, the results proved to be a much-needed economic bonanza for the city. Indeed, his work was of such character that the local newspaper once suggested that Van Sant might "go down as the most valuable person ever to serve in city government."

On campus, he was legendary as a faculty leader and as a classroom instructor. In both capacities he was characterized by a stentorian voice and booming laugh, the combination of which made him a masterful (and incorrigible) raconteur. The recipient of the Grellet Simpson Award for excellence in teaching in 1986, Van Sant was described by the local newspaper, at the end of his thirty-two-year teaching career, as having created a memory that "seems to be seared into the consciousness of every student who took his philosophy classes over the decades."

Van Sant's service to Mary Washington was both public, as a department chair and head of countless faculty committees, as well as sub rosa, especially as a key participant in an informal group that called itself the Tuesday Lunch Club. Beginning in 1958 and continuing for a decade or so, the group met weekly throughout the school year. Though not an officially sanctioned arm of the College, the Lunch Club served as a catalyst for a number of changes that were implemented during the period, such as expansion of the College bookstore, reduction of the full-time teaching load from fifteen to twelve hours, and establishment of the five-day class week.[83]

At the time of his retirement in 1990, it was likely that no individual had exerted greater influence upon the institution (save its presidents) than he. Nor had anyone been more deeply committed to its welfare. Having come to the College in the year of its fiftieth anniversary, and having played a major role in planning its seventy-fifth, he commented upon his retirement that he would "like to be there to celebrate the one hundredth." He was—and not only was he there, but he served on the committee that planned the centennial.

An innovative programmatic development within philosophy was the creation of a prelaw concentration, which was attractive to students owing to its emphasis on logic, reasoning, and problem solving. Core requirements were a course on the philosophy of law and two years of Latin, not only because that language fostered analytical skills, writing skills, and attention to detail but also because it contributed to "self-awareness" on the part of potential law students. "If they cannot succeed in, or if they strongly dislike, the study

David W. Cain, flanked by Dean Philip L. Hall, acknowledges applause after receiving the Grellet C. Simpson Award, 1992.

of Latin," warned the program's description, "there is little chance that in the long run they will want to pursue law."

The religion component of the department was headed by Elizabeth Clark, a leading campus advocate of feminism, before her departure for a position on the Duke University faculty in 1982. At that point and for several decades thereafter, the polestar of the MWC program was David Cain. Having joined the faculty in 1970, Cain evinced a somewhat somber—even brooding—demeanor that some took as a reflection of his absorption in the study of Søren Kierkegaard, the Danish theologian whose life and works constituted the focus of Cain's career.

Whatever the case, David Cain came to be widely acknowledged over the years as one of the institution's most rigorous minds and one of its most respected teachers. Students, though they sometimes admitted to being overwhelmed by the depth of his intellect, flocked to his classes, whence they were drawn by his evident passion for his subject and by the naturally theatrical eloquence of his delivery.

Like Liz Clark before him in 1979, Cain was a recipient of the Simpson Award for outstanding teaching (1992). Indicative of the high pedagogical standards of the religion program, two junior instructors also won College-wide teaching honors with their selection for the Alumni Association Outstanding Young Faculty Member Award: Jim Goehring in 1989 (the first year that the award was established) and Mehdi Aminrazavi in 1997. Jim Goehring was also instrumental, along with David Hair of the English, Linguistics, and Speech Department, in establishing a Martin Luther King Day celebration at Mary Washington.

As important as were the programs of the individual disciplines within CPR, the most remarkable aspect of the combined department—a "disciplined ménage à trois," David Cain once termed it—was the synergy that was created whereby the disparate academic resources of its constituent members were employed through various initiatives. One example was sponsorship of a 1994 national conference titled "Intolerance and Toleration," called by President Anderson perhaps the most important such event ever held at the College. More than a year in planning, the national conference was prompted by violence in Los Angeles related to the highly publicized police beating of a black man, Rodney King, and the acquittal of his assailants.

The conference involved the participation of nearly forty experts from around the country and abroad, who delivered lectures and papers. Among the featured public lectures were presentations by Ambassador L. Bruce Laingen, the former chargé d'affaires of the U.S. embassy during the Iranian hostage crisis; Elaine Heumann Gurian, deputy director of the U.S. Holocaust Memorial Museum; Seyyed Hossein Nasr, professor of Islamic studies at George Washington University; and Edward Said, professor of comparative literature at Columbia University. Security was especially tight for the presentation by Hanan Ashrawi, an official of the Palestine Liberation Organization, who had recently served as spokeswoman for the PLO team that had negotiated with Israel during recent meetings in Washington. Despite such concerns, the conference came off without incident.

Another example two years later was a conference called "Representations of the Other." Organized by Craig Vasey, who that year was president of the Virginia Humanities Conference, it focused on ways in which "otherness"—political, racial, and gender difference—is viewed in Western culture. The meeting attracted scholars of national stature, including Houston Baker of the University of Pennsylvania, who was one of the most prominent African American literary theorists in the country at the time.

Yet another important meeting was one organized by Joseph Romero in 2005 titled "The Arrogance of Power: Being American after 9/11." It constituted the first significant attempt at scholarly cultural analysis of the events of the September 2001 terrorist attacks. The program, held in the new Alumni Executive Center, brought to campus a number of high-profile speakers from the United States and abroad, headlined by Ralph Nader.

In addition to such weekend conferences, the department also periodically hosted semester-long lecture series under the rubric "Mysterium Humanum." The concept originated with David Cain, whose idea was to choose topics of universal human interest that would lend themselves to treatment from the perspectives of classics, philosophy, and religion, thereby allowing members from the department's constituent disciplines (and from others as well) to participate. Beginning in 1982 with "Death in Western Thought," topics subsequently included "The Tempest of Time" (spring 1985), "Sex and Society in the West" (fall 1987), "Discourse of Duality" (spring 1994), "Slavery" (fall 1999), "Religion and Freedom" (spring 2002), "The Uses and Abuses of Power" (spring 2005), and "God" (spring 2007).

Perhaps the most distinctive feature of the Classics, Philosophy, and Religion Department was its focus on Middle Eastern and Asian studies. That emphasis grew out of the influence of Professor Kurt Leidecker. Born in Germany in 1902, Leidecker earned his Ph.D. at the University of Chicago, where his dissertation was on the Bhagavad Gita. Upon joining the Mary Washington faculty in 1948, he led the College to become one of the first in the United States to offer philosophy courses in Asian thought. His immersion in Asian culture was furthered by leaves of absence during the 1950s when he studied in India on a Fulbright grant and in Thailand as a cultural attaché with the U.S. Information Service.

In addition to teaching Asian philosophy and religion, Leidecker worked to promote multicultural studies and, as part of that effort, was instrumental in creating the pre–foreign service major in 1959; he served as its adviser for many years before his retirement in 1973.

At his death in 1991, Professor Leidecker left his estate to Mary Washington College for the purpose of promoting Asian studies, a bequest that led to the establishment of the Leidecker Center in 1993. Two promising young scholars, David Ambuel and Mehdi Aminrazavi, who were already members of the CPR faculty, were appointed to direct the center.

The Leidecker Center developed a wide-ranging program that included sponsorship of annual lecture series, workshops on various aspects of Asian life and thought, a student exchange program, an annual Asian film festival, and weekly meditation sessions. The center also supervised students with special majors in Asian studies, led trips to local museums and Asian-related cultural centers, facilitated visits by faculty from Asia, and supported grant opportunities to students for research and travel.

Drawing on the resources of the Leidecker Center and the expertise of faculty in related disciplines across the institution, CPR instituted a certificate program in Middle Eastern Studies. In addition to completion of four courses in Middle Eastern studies from at least three departments, the program required a minimum of two sequential semesters of instruction in an appropriate foreign language. The latter was made possible by the varied linguistic expertise of CPR faculty, which allowed courses to be offered in Arabic and Farsi (taught by Aminrazavi), Coptic (Goehring), and Sanskrit (Ambuel).[84] Besides the academic aspect, the certificate program promoted the ideals of understanding, appreciation, and dialogue through sponsorship of seminars, conferences, internships, study abroad, and cultural exchange programs.

Overall, the Department of Classics, Philosophy, and Religion played an important role in shaping and expanding the institution's liberal arts curriculum. One tangible measure of its success was the substantial increase in the number of its majors over the years in each of its programs. By 2004 there were 36 classics majors, 46 philosophy majors, and 23 religion majors. The prospects for even greater success in the future were enhanced in 2006 when alumna Marsha Wilkins pledged $1 million from her estate as an endowment for the department.

Computer Science

The genesis of the computer science program at Mary Washington came when Dale Brown was hired by the Math Department in 1973. Brown was the first instructor to introduce the subject of computers into the curriculum by integrating such information into certain of his math classes. But with his departure to run the College's infant computer center, that expertise was absent from the classroom.

In 1977, at the initiative of Math Department chair Al Lindsey, the first actual courses in computer science were added to the curriculum, and Donald Edwards was hired to teach them. It proved to be a fortuitous choice, as Edwards was to become a key player in bringing Mary Washington College into the computer age. With his friendly, down-to-earth demeanor, the unassuming Edwards had the ideal disposition (as well as the extensive expertise) to work effectively with all elements of the College community. He soon emerged as one of its most admired members, first as a classroom teacher and subsequently as part of the computer technology staff.

Having worked for a number of years at the Naval Surface Weapons Center (NSWC) at Dahlgren, Edwards was surprised to learn when he came to Mary Washington that the College had neither any computers nor even a connection to computers elsewhere.[85] Consequently, when he first offered Introduction to Computers in 1977, the course was taught mainly from a textbook and his personal experience, including discussion of the history of computing, terminology, input and output devices, processing, vacuum tubes, transistors, bits and bytes, and the like. The next year the College acquired a teletype terminal that allowed dial-in connection to a computer at the University of Virginia, but it was so slow and unreliable as to be virtually useless.

A major development occurred in 1979 when a stand-alone computer was obtained by the Math Department. It was also in that year that the general faculty voted approval for a major in computer science to be housed within a newly created Department of Mathematical Sciences and Physics.

Hired to direct the new program in 1980 was Ernest Ackermann. Under his guidance, the Computer Science Department grew rapidly. He was joined on the faculty in 1981 by John Reynolds, whose first employment was on a one-year assignment from the Dahlgren laboratory under the Intergovernmental Personnel Act. (Administrators at Dahlgren were eager to offer assistance, realizing that a thriving computer program at MWC had the potential to help meet the facility's expanding need for computer specialists.) As it turned out, Reynolds's temporary assignment proved so beneficial to the College and so appealing to him that it became permanent. In the twenty-three years before his retirement in 2004, the arrangement wrought significant developments, both personal and professional: his marriage to Spanish professor Joanna Quann in 1992 and his receipt of the Simpson Award in 2004.

Another faculty pioneer in the computer science program was Marsha Zaidman. She, too, had worked at Dahlgren before coming to Mary Washington in 1982. Once the Computer Science Department became a separate entity from math and physics in 1987, it was chaired for the next two decades by Ackermann (1987–93), Reynolds (1993–97), and Zaidman, who became chair in 1997.[86]

Computer science majors benefited from numerous internships and cooperative programs made possible by the institution's proximity to Dahlgren and by the ties that several faculty members maintained with NSWC. Deserving students were also eligible for several scholarships offered by the department, including the Don and Kathleen Edwards Scholarship established by the couple in 1999 to assist students who were Virginia residents and had demonstrated academic excellence and financial need.

Though the department remained appealing to many students, the number of majors declined somewhat in the early years of the twenty-first century, a reflection of a nationwide trend. The reason for it, according to Professor Ackermann, was difficult to determine but, he surmised, was likely related to the so-called dot-com bust that occurred during that time.[87] Partly to restore the attractiveness of the major, the department developed several initiatives beginning in the middle of the decade. In addition to revision of basic requirements for the traditional computer science degree, a concentration in computer information systems was established. That track, developed in consultation with the Department of Business Administration, was designed to increase career opportunities by allowing students to develop computing skills that had particular business applications. It also facilitated students' transition into a new master's degree in management information systems at the College of Graduate and Professional Studies by offering courses that satisfied requirements in both degree programs.

Economics

The cliché labeling (and libeling) economics "the dismal science" was but a canard at Mary Washington, where the discipline was one of the institution's liveliest. Much of its success owed to the personalities and professional acumen of its faculty, going back to the early 1970s, when young professors like the brilliant and hyperkinetic Jack Albertine and the more laid-back but similarly cerebral "Bud" Clatanoff energized the department before leaving to pursue other opportunities.[88]

In the years following its establishment as a department separate from political science in 1982, a solid core of faculty emerged. At the center was steady Robert Rycroft, who did yeoman service as department chair and was also active in the campus chapter of Phi Beta Kappa (serving for years as its secretary-treasurer) and in the national economics honorary society, Omicron Delta Epsilon (serving as a vice president and member of its board of directors).[89]

Steve Stageberg was the department's most controversial member owing to his conservative public stands on gender issues. He also had perhaps the most interesting non-academic background of any member of the entire faculty. As an undergraduate at Georgetown University, he had been an All-American and world-class distance runner, emerging as a major rival of the track legend Steve Prefontaine; both were members of the U.S. national track team. Stageberg barely missed the chance to compete in the 1968 Olympics at Mexico City, finishing fifth at the trials; by the time of the 1972 games, an injury had ended any chance of his participating. Even in his athletic career, he placed primacy on his faith, telling *Sports Illustrated* in July 1971, "I have a God-given talent. If I don't develop it, I guess I think it would be a sin. It's like in the Bible, the parable of the talents. If you bury them, you are damned."

With his competitive sports career behind him, Stageberg joined the Mary Washington economics faculty in 1982, soon becoming a student favorite as a result of his friendly demeanor and joyously uninhibited lecture style. Outside the department, he served as an assistant marshal of the faculty from 1986 until 2004, when he was named marshal of the faculty, succeeding biology professor Rosemary Barra.

Steven Greenlaw rivaled Stageberg in student popularity and was an esteemed teacher, receiving the Simpson Award in 1999. He was also a department chair (1992–2003) and published scholar, the author of *Doing Economics: A Guide to Understanding and Carrying Out Economic Research* (2006).[90]

A hallmark of the department was the extensive participation of its majors in student sessions at national professional meetings, including presentation of papers at annual meetings of the Eastern Economics Association and the Virginia Social Science Association. Students also published extensively in *Issues in Political Economy*, a journal of undergraduate research in economics.

The department's most intriguing innovation came as the result of the philanthropic generosity of Doris Buffett, sister of billionaire Warren Buffett (and mother of Robin Haymes '88). Ms. Buffett headed the Sunshine Lady Foundation, a philanthropic organization dedicated to supporting opportunities for the advancement of education and well-being, particularly among disadvantaged people and the working poor. Having learned that the foundation had made grants for such purposes to the University of Virginia and Davidson College, Brad Hansen, chair of the Economics Department, submitted a proposal to the Sunshine Lady Foundation, resulting in a grant of $10,000 to be used by a class on philanthropy.

At that point, Professor Bob Rycroft developed a course known as Economics of Philanthropy and the Nonprofit Sector, a major portion of which involved having students create an actual nonprofit organization known as the University of Mary Washington Philanthropic Education Organization. Through that "foundation," students in the course created the criteria for awards, solicited applications for grants, reviewed the applications, and selected the recipients. The first awards, given in 2005, went to Hope House and the Fredericksburg Boys and Girls Club; the following year, they were awarded to Homes for America and Rebuilding Together. Being by her own account "very delighted with this class," Buffett in 2007 agreed to fund the project for at least an additional two years.

Education

From its founding as a teachers college, Mary Washington retained teacher education as an important part of its academic program even after its primary focus shifted in the late 1930s to the liberal arts and sciences. One result of that shift was a distinctive feature of the Mary Washington education program that set it apart from such programs at other schools: its emphasis on subject proficiency as opposed to techniques of teaching. Put most simply, this meant belief in the principle that being an effective teacher required firm grounding in the subject matter to be taught, not merely in pedagogical methodology.

In operation, this philosophy required that education students at Mary Washington complete a disciplinary major while simultaneously taking sufficient education courses to meet state certification standards. According to William Helton, onetime head of the state's Division of Teacher Education and Certification, the MWC process yielded such outstanding teachers that it eventually became the norm among Virginia's teacher-preparation programs. It was specifically endorsed when the commonwealth's teacher education restructuring plan in 1990 required that all education programs be configured so as to emphasize knowledge of the subject areas and to limit the number of methods courses.[91]

Guiding the development of the Education Department from the 1970s until his retirement as a distinguished professor in 1995 was Paul Slayton. One of the most influential faculty members on campus during his thirty-year career, he spent sixteen years as department chair. Keenly interested in American literature (Faulkner especially) and history, he collaborated with two other Virginia scholars in developing a new history textbook for the state's schoolchildren. Whereas the existing version essentially ignored women and treated minorities with disdain, Slayton's book was not only more lively but more inclusive, treating slavery as exploitation, rather than, in his words, as "the world's first and best cradle-to-grave social security system."

He was also extensively involved in the institution's promotion of globalism. His interest focused particularly on Lithuania, which he visited several times during the early years of that country's escape from Soviet domination in the 1990s. As a member of an American group invited to visit Lithuania, he worked to help teachers move beyond the educational strictures of communist-dictated methods and to implement more democratic, less doctrinaire approaches.

In the local community he was active in Democratic politics and was, above all else, known for his dogged defense of First Amendment rights, any infringement of which infuriated the normally soft-spoken professor. Ardent in his beliefs yet polite in his presentation of them, he was ever a gentleman, devoid of the vitriol that sometimes fueled those of similar passions. A person of unfailing and unfeigned friendliness, he was a hard man to dislike.

Perhaps Slayton's most salient and guiding quality was his basic optimism—a characteristic that he alluded to in the autobiography that he undertook in retirement. Even as he suffered from the cancer that would eventually claim his life, he wrote that he "always expected tomorrow to be the best day yet—and I haven't been wrong once. . . . So, I am looking forward to a new adventure, a new experience, and, I trust," he added with characteristic wryness, "a good research library."[92] He died on February 6, 2004, at the age of seventy-three.

Paul Slayton

In addition to Slayton, the department had a number of other long-serving faculty members beginning with his protégée, Brenda Vogel, who succeeded him as chair in 1997. She, in turn, was followed by Paul Zisman; Sandra White; Venitta McCall (the institution's first African American female full professor), who was also the director of the James Farmer Scholars and the Upward Bound programs; and Marie Sheckels, who held a joint appointment in the Math Department.[93] Other notable contributions were made by Joseph Holmes as faculty sponsor of Kappa Delta Pi, Adrienne May as director of outplacements, and Wendy Atwell-Vasey as a specialist in the cultural dimensions of education, including feminist theory.

English, Linguistics, and Speech (ELS)

Throughout much of Mary Washington's history—and certainly from the time of its incarnation as a liberal arts college—the English Department held a prominent position.[94] This was not only because of the centrality of the discipline within the curriculum but because a disproportionate number of its faculty held influential administrative positions over the years. That situation generally continued after the creation of the combined ELS Department in 1979.

For whatever reason, it also seemed that the department produced not only an exceptional number of outstanding teachers but also some of the faculty's most engaging personalities. A number of them retired during the last decades of the twentieth century, including prolific author Daniel Dervin, women's literature specialist Nathaniel Brown, and onetime faculty secretary Delmont Fleming.

Also departing after years of distinguished service were Sidney and Nancy Mitchell. Both members of the husband-and-wife team were considered among the College's best teachers, each being an early recipient of the Simpson Award—he, the second, and she, the sixth. In 1987 Nancy was one of the thirteen honorees chosen for the newly established statewide outstanding faculty awards. Upon their retirement that same year they moved, first to a sheep-raising farm in nearby Spotsylvania, thence to an even more bucolic setting in West Virginia.[95]

Another recipient of the Simpson Award (1976), Donald Glover was also one of the first group of faculty to be named to the rank of distinguished professor (1988). Distinguished he was, both as a teacher of American literature and as a scholar, the author of *C. S. Lewis: The Art of Enchantment* (1981). He also served for four years as the founding director of Mary Washington's first graduate program, the master of arts in liberal studies. Aside from his academic pursuits, Glover was an accomplished painter and gardener. He retired in 1998.[96]

Richard Hansen, like Glover, was named a distinguished professor and, also like him, enjoyed universal respect among his students and his faculty colleagues. A meticulous writer and dedicated teacher—eighteenth-century English literature and the English novel were his specialties—Hansen also possessed both the organizational ability and even temperament that led to his being called upon for some of the institution's most demanding administrative assignments. Among those appointments were director of the College's decennial self-study in the early 1990s and interim dean of the faculty in 1993–94. He retired in 1998, whereupon he devoted much time to researching and recording the history of Fredericksburg.[97]

English professors Richard E. Hansen, left, and Donald E. Glover before commencement in 1998, the year they retired. On the right is art professor Paul C. Muick, who also retired that year.

The member of the English faculty who exerted perhaps the most significant influence on the College's overall academic program was Carol Manning. A soft-spoken yet forceful feminist, she focused overdue attention, both in her courses and in print, on southern female writers; she was the editor of a collection of essays titled *The Female Tradition in Southern Literature* (1993). Her pedagogical excellence was acknowledged not only at the College but statewide when she was named one of the commonwealth's thirteen outstanding faculty members in 1990. Her greatest and most lasting contribution to Mary Washington, however, was her crucial role in establishing both the writing intensive program and the writing center. When she retired in 2003, those duties were assumed by Jane Gatewood.

Another faculty member who played a prominent role in both the department (as longtime chair) and the larger institution (as assistant academic dean) was William Kemp. Most important was his consistency from the time of his arrival in 1970 as an exacting and stimulating teacher, a status acknowledged by his receipt of the Simpson Award in 2000. Most notable were his Shakespeare classes, to which he brought rigorous academic analysis enlivened by natural linguistic and theatrical gifts. Kemp retired in 2005; the following year, so did his wife, Mary, who for years in the registrar's office effectively served Mary Washington seniors as the gatekeeper for their graduation, making sure that all academic requirements were completed.

The department suffered faculty losses, not only through retirements but more tragically through four untimely deaths—one in each decade beginning in the 1970s. First there was Stephen Disraeli, who taught linguistics. Stricken with ileitis, in early 1976 he underwent surgery, for which students, faculty, and friends donated more than one hundred pints of blood. He was able to return briefly to teaching but died in December of the following year.

Then there was Carlton Lutterbie, who had initially come to Mary Washington in 1967. Only twenty-three upon his arrival, he was barely older than the students and looked even younger, retaining his boyish appearance to the time of his death in 1988 following a long illness. He was, from the outset, a student favorite—and not just because of his attractive appearance. More than that, he was appealing because students valued him, according to his colleague Dick Hansen, as "a kind and helpful instructor—calm and reasonable, firm but with pleasant touches of wry humor, absolutely fair and level with them, absolutely trustworthy."[98] Lutterbie served the institution in many and varied capacities: department chair for four years, adviser to the *Bullet* for four and to *Aubade* for eight, editor of a two-volume institutional self-study, writer for the alumni magazine, and for four years instructor and administrator in the Governor's School for the Gifted. In the course of his association with the institution, he emerged as that rare individual who engendered affection, in equal measure, from students, faculty, and administrators.

As department chair, Hansen wrote, Lutterbie "with skill and composure . . . guided, coaxed, and nudged our eclectic and often verbose group [of English faculty] through the business of academe—and we loved him for it, like children under a steady but charitable hand." But his truest home was in the classroom where, as Hansen put it, "knowledgeable, talented, and unstinting, he epitomized the selflessness of the committed teacher." Accordingly, Hansen predicted in a moving eulogy that Lutterbie would "live brightly in the minds of his students."

As memorable as Lutterbie, though for largely different reasons (except their shared enthusiasm for and excellence in teaching), was Susan J. Hanna. Having come to Mary Washington in 1968, Hanna quickly established an enviable reputation as one of the College's most provocative and entertaining teachers. The way she approached her craft was a bracing antidote to older, more staid methods—and students adored her because of it. "Her love for the language wasn't about correctness," observed one admirer, "but for the passion it could inspire."

Outside the classroom she served in several administrative positions, including department chair for six years and assistant dean of advising for three, and as a leading member of NOW, she was one of the original and most consistently energetic proponents of feminism on campus. As a community activist, she was known throughout Fredericksburg for her contributions to organizations such as Hope House, the Central Rappahannock Regional Library, and the Rappahannock Council on Domestic Violence.

All these things she did in her unique way. (One of her pet peeves was any modification of the adjective "unique"; otherwise one might be tempted to say "surpassingly unique.") An admirer once described what he called "the traits that made Hanna a true character—a booming voice that pierced classroom walls like they weren't even there, her penchant for quick afternoon catnaps in her office, and her reluctance to climb behind the wheel of an automobile."[99]

When she succumbed to cancer in 1994—survived by her husband, George Van Sant—the campus instantly became a quieter place, and a less vibrant one. In her memory, the ELS Department in 1995–96 established the Susan J. Hanna Memorial Scholarship, by which it recognized the late professor's "commitment to teaching, her dedication to sound scholarship, and her joyful enthusiasm for literature and life, all so generously shared with students and faculty of Mary Washington College."

Few faculty members ever traveled farther (or further) to arrive at Mary Washington than did Taddesse Adera. Born in Ethiopia into a poor family from an area where less than 1 percent of the population was literate, he endured deprivation and persecution during his youth—including imprisonment for three years as a result of his protests against the Marxist regime then in control of his country.

Having fled to the United States and having earned a doctorate in English from the University of Washington, he joined the Mary Washington faculty in 1989. Over the next seventeen years, he taught an exceedingly wide range of courses, many of which he developed himself, introducing into the curriculum pathbreaking classes on South African literature, Caribbean litera-

Taddesse Adera

ture, the literature of resistance, and the literature of women of color. Also an energetic scholar, he was involved with the production of several works including the editorship of *Silence Is Not Golden: A Critical Anthology of European Literature* (1995).

But it was the effectiveness of his teaching and the warmth of his personality that made him special. The former was attested by his earning a Jepson fellowship at the College; more impressive still, in 1997 he became the third member of the department to be recognized as the winner of one of SCHEV's outstanding state teacher awards.[100] Whatever the occasion, Adera exhibited a calm, somewhat reticent demeanor, greeting acquaintances, colleagues, and students alike with a shy and endearing smile that bespoke genuine friendliness. It was thus with extreme shock and sadness that the campus learned of his unexpected death in January 2006, just days after the semester began. Inexplicably absent from class, he was found at his home by his close friend, physics professor George King. It was King who well summarized the prevailing College feeling toward Adera. "I miss my good friend," he said. "Taddesse was a quiet person and a good listener. Sometimes friends need that."

At commencement that year, Adera was posthumously named professor emeritus of English. It constituted an appropriate, albeit necessarily insufficient, recognition of the intellect, decency, and humanity with which he had graced Mary Washington.

Despite such losses, the ELS Department in the first decade of the new century was still stocked with a number of exceptional faculty members. Among them was Teresa Kennedy, a formidable figure with a forceful presence, both intellectual and physical. A former Marine, Kennedy gave every impression of one who brooked little nonsense. Indeed, when a *Bullet* opinion column in 2005 asked five random persons "Which professor would win in a fight?" three of them said Kennedy, including one senior who explained his choice by saying, "I can just picture her shanking somebody." Another respondent, a faculty member—in fact a visiting professor in her own department—commented, "I'm no judge of fights, but I would least like to have [Kennedy] mad at me."

That sometimes gruff (at least superficially) demeanor belied a dedication to the discipline that was revealed in her teaching and in her scholarly productivity. A widely recognized scholar in the field of comparative medieval literature—and extensively published on that subject—she also served as director of Mary Washington's Simpson Program in Medieval Studies.

Quite probably no faculty member in the history of Mary Washington ever possessed interests and talents as diverse as did Gardner Campbell. Having been first associated with the institution as both teacher and administrator in the Governor's School for the Gifted during the 1980s, he returned as a member of the ELS Department in 1994. The catholicity of his interests and expertise, combined with his wit and, above all, his passion for literature (actually for everything that he did) earned him a devoted following among students and led to his receiving the Outstanding Young Faculty Award in 1998.

In addition to Campbell's interest in literature, he was also a serious student of cinema, teaching a number of courses dealing with film and serving as adviser to the Frames Per Second Club. Such interests were partly an outgrowth of his lifelong interest in technology. Going back to his graduate school days when he was a radio disc jockey, he loved all things electronic and became expert at their use. No one was more of a techie than he. Accordingly, he incorporated technology into his pedagogical methods long before most of his colleagues appreciated its potential. In 2003 he was named assistant vice president for teaching and learning technologies, in which capacity he was instrumental in developing the Student Academy on Information Technologies.

Perhaps Campbell's most notable academic innovation was the all-night *Paradise Lost* read-a-thon that he instituted in connection with his course on John Milton. It was Campbell's conviction that the best way to appreciate Milton's epic poem was to read it straight through in one sitting—an exercise that required an entire night. Though not an enterprise that college students would presumably be attracted to, the event was popularized by Campbell's enthusiasm to such an extent that it became an annual event from the time of its first iteration in 1996.

At the end of one Milton read-a-thon, a student, astounded by the power of Milton's work, cried aloud, "I can't believe he did all that in his head!" It was a sense of wonderment that students may well have applied to Professor Campbell as well.

One of the most visible members of the department was Stephen Watkins. Controversial almost from the moment he hit the campus in 1990, he came to be regarded by some as an *enfant terrible,* given to stirring every existing pot (and creating a few himself) just for the hell of it. Others, quite to the contrary, saw him as an admirable activist determined to keep the administration on its toes and to preserve the good name of Mary Washington College—the latter in the most literal sense during the course of name-change debates.

Stephen H. Watkins

Watkins made no attempt to hide his liberal leanings, proudly voicing them in a regular (if short-lived) op-ed column that began running in the *Free Lance–Star* in November 1998.[101] His passion for exposing and correcting what he perceived as injustices, coupled with his outspoken personality, often landed him in the campus spotlight. Periodic flare-ups occurred over issues such as faculty salaries, a living wage for classified employees, a campus appearance by the conservative advocate Dinesh D'Souza, and a profane confrontation with a student at open-mic night.

He also jousted with the administration over establishment of a day care center, failure to recruit more minority students and faculty, and priorities in the allocation of College funds. All such shortcomings he attributed generally to an obtuse administration and specifically to a "very autocratic" President Anderson, who, Watkins asserted, was "not a good manager." Watkins refused even to give Anderson credit for the physical development of the campus, claiming that some of the construction constituted "grossly inappropriate use of resources."

Watkins's greatest notoriety, in the eyes of his detractors, came as a result of his crusade to save the name "Mary Washington." He assailed the prospect of a name change in passionate speeches, imputing the effort to raw sexism; at alumni gatherings he hawked T-shirts bearing the words "Save the Name" on the front and "All I am, I owe to my mother" on the reverse—which was, he said, "a truncated version of a quote by George Washington."

One effect of such activities was to detract from several of Watkins's more laudable characteristics. For one thing, he was by most accounts an engaging and effective teacher, much appreciated by students, who related to him instinctively. "This guy is a complete off-the-wall goofball," wrote one, "[who has a] unique point of view on the world (one that's situated somewhere between second grade and the sage-like wisdom of Pai-Mei)."[102] A *Bullet* editorial celebrating his fiftieth birthday commented that "Watkins, now half a century old and still liberal as ever certainly deserves a round of applause for his accomplishments and hard work. . . . Even though [he] will probably have something negative to say because the editorial space this week is not dedicated to a controversial, hott-with-two-t's issue (like popped collars), we believe that it is important to recognize one of the coolest professors at the University of Mary Washington."

Another notable characteristic was his success as a writer in several genres. His first major book, *The Black O* (1997), was a nonfiction study of racially discriminatory hiring practices by the Shoney's restaurant chain. Widely and favorably reviewed, the book recounted with passion and eloquence the process whereby the company was ultimately forced to distribute over $130 million among 21,000 claimants in the largest racial class action suit in history.

In 2006 he published *My Chaos Theory*, a collection of short stories containing his award-winning "Critterworld." That book, too, was well received, both on campus and in the larger literary community. "Whereas many professors crank out volume after volume of text that will forever be sentenced to the bowels of Simpson," wrote a *Bullet* reviewer, "this book is actually something we *want* to read." Noting that one of the stories in the anthology had previously won an award from *Playboy* magazine, the reviewer concluded, "Let's face it, if it's good enough for Hef and the ladies, it's good enough for us."

The Department of English, Linguistics, and Speech was also home to one of the most popular—and, without doubt, the most publicized and celebrated—instructors in Mary Washington's history: Claudia Emerson, winner of the 2006 Pulitzer Prize for poetry. (James Farmer had been, of course, internationally known as well, but his fame derived mainly from heroic deeds accomplished outside the academy and before his arrival at Mary Washington.)

The College might well have missed the opportunity to claim Emerson. When she first applied for a position in 1996, she was rejected in favor of a talented African American writer, Henry Lewis. When the position was re-advertised two years later upon Lewis's departure, she applied once again, the previous snub notwithstanding. This time she was more fortunate—though not nearly so fortunate as Mary Washington.

She became an instant favorite of students, who flocked to her classes in poetry and creative writing, making it impossible for any save the highest-priority registrants to get in. As one student put it, "You felt like part of some special club if you got into Claudia Emerson's class." Her exceptional classroom performance earned her the 2003 Alumni Association Outstanding Young Faculty Award, and her instinctive rapport with students resulted in receipt of the Mary Pinschmidt Award three years later.

Yet the acclaim brought no elevation of ego. She remained modest and unaffected, eminently approachable both inside and out of the classroom. Perhaps it was because her road to renown was far from a gilded one.

Born and reared in the small Southside Virginia town of Chatham (population 1,300), she attended Chatham Hall, a private local girls' school, as a day student. From there she went to the University of Virginia, where she earned a bachelor's degree in English. Returning to Chatham, she married her hometown boyfriend and took jobs as a letter carrier and manager of a used bookshop. The mental challenges were not great, nor was the money, but such employment did provide ample time for reading, which she did (as she had always done) prodigiously.

She also began to pursue a newfound interest in poetry—and that, too, she did with a vengeance, sometimes producing a complete poem each day. By the time she earned a master of fine arts in poetry from the University of North Carolina at Greensboro in 1991, she had written much of what became her first book, *Pharaoh, Pharaoh*, published six years later.

In the interim she held several academic posts, including teaching positions at Washington and Lee University, Danville Community College, and Randolph-Macon Woman's College, as well as the deanship at her high school alma mater, Chatham Hall. In 1998, on the second go-round, she landed the job she had long wanted: member of the English faculty at Mary Washington.

There the honors came steadily. In addition to recognition at the College itself, she won a National Endowment for the Arts Fellowship in Poetry and twice received poetry fellowships from the Virginia Commission for Arts. In 2005 she was awarded the prestigious Witter Bynner Fellowship in Poetry from the Library of Congress. Her second book of poetry, *Pinion, an Elegy,* was nominated for a Pulitzer Prize.

Her next book was titled *Late Wife*, an emotion-filled autobiographical account that described her failed first marriage, the trauma of its aftermath, and the redemptive effect of the relationship she subsequently developed with Kent Ippolito, a widower, who became her second husband. The work attracted wide attention for the beauty of its imagery as well as its treatment of a deeply emotional subject in a way that was moving without being maudlin.

The explanation lay within Emerson's personality: sensitive yet sensible. As a *Richmond Times-Dispatch* reviewer put it, "This poet is no whiner, but an observer, no trembling victim, but a rigorous artist. She's not here to show us her scars, but to demonstrate clarity and courage. Emerson can be personal without being lurid, objective without being heartless, . . . tough without being bitter, lyrical without being soft."

Such glowing sentiments were obviously shared by the Pulitzer Prize committee, which in April 2006 announced that the winner of that year's award for poetry was Claudia Emerson. Soon she was appearing in the pages of *Newsweek* and on *The NewsHour with Jim Lehrer* and was in constant demand as a speaker. On campus she became a genuine celebrity as students and colleagues exulted in her award. One typical student, congratulating and hugging her, exclaimed, "As if you weren't my idol already!" The College itself, which had once rejected her employment application, now named her to the newly created Arrington Distinguished Chair in Poetry.

Beyond the campus, the Fredericksburg community reveled in Emerson's success. A *Free Lance–Star* editorial searched for just the right words. "Though we have little practice in receiving such wonderful tidings," it wrote, "we're pretty sure 'way to go' won't cut it." And so it continued, "All Fredericksburg rejoices at having among us one able to reach into her life and extract the essence of what it means to love, to lose, and to love again, to distill those deep feelings into black letters so artfully arranged on white paper that in reading them a stranger is pierced—by understanding. . . . Bravo—and thank you, Professor, for a great Fredericksburg moment."

Surely it was a great Mary Washington moment as well, soon memorialized on cotton and polyester by English majors who began to sport T-shirts declaring, "My Professor Won a Pulitzer Prize . . . And All I Got Was This Lousy T-Shirt."

Beneath the whimsy, however, was deep pride in the institution's first Pulitzer Prize winner. And it was not just because of her supernal and sublime talents. In fact, there was a widespread sense that Claudia Emerson really deserved another Pulitzer in an altogether different area. The only problem was: there was no category for niceness.

Though the "E" part of "ELS" was the largest by far, the linguistics and speech programs grew substantially in the decades following the disciplinary merger. By 2007 there were three full-time instructors in linguistics: Judith Parker, Christina Kakava, and Paul Fallon. A linguistics speaker series was established, featuring an address each year by a prominent scholar in the field, beginning in November 2002 with a presentation by noted Georgetown University professor Deborah Tannen titled "Women's and Men's Conversations as Cross-Cultural Communication."

The speech program enjoyed perhaps the greatest renaissance of any program at the College. Long the bailiwick of speech professor Albert Duke, it rose rapidly as a result of two related factors: establishment of a College-wide speaking-intensive requirement in the mid-1990s and the hiring of a dynamic young speech professor, John Morello, who also became coach of the debate team.

When Morello subsequently moved more into administration—eventually becoming associate vice president for academic affairs—his duties in the ELS Department were assumed by two new instructors, Anand Rao as professor of speech and director of the speaking intensive program and Timothy O'Donnell as director of debate. The specific impetus for creation of the speaking-intensive requirement was the recommendation for such a program by the Southern Association of Colleges and School's reaccreditation report in the early nineties. It was also undergirded by a general recognition at the college that the quality of oral communication among students was in decline. The causes of that decline were not easy to identify precisely. A 1999 article in *The Chronicle of Higher Education* titled "Taking Aim at Student Incoherence" speculated that it was a product of "the colloquialisms and oratorical oddities of the *Clueless* generation." But whatever the cause, the article went on to note that "mallspeak—or, as some communications specialists call it 'juvenile speech patterns' or 'vocalized pauses'—has a way of detracting from the substance of what students have to say."

Whatever the cause, the College reached the conclusion that the problem needed to be addressed—hence the speaking-intensive requirement. The *Bullet* suggested editorially that the requirement was not only needed but overdue. "Everyone has gone on a job interview and struggled to 'sound intelligent' between 'ums' and 'ahs,'" said the paper. "Oral intensive classes will demand students to stand up and look out, to take pride in their language and how they use it. Students will need to speak complete, coherent sentences and not depend on the word 'like' to make their points."

To support the new requirement the College established a Speaking Center. First directed by Morello and later by another member of the English faculty, Robin Gurien, the directorship of the center was assumed by Esther Yook in 2000. With its quarters initially carved out of Chandler 303, the center was first known as "the speaking closet" but later found better quarters in the newly renovated Combs Hall.

A major goal of the center was to assist students in overcoming their fear of public speaking. It was no small task, given that, according to some studies, people tended to fear public speaking even more than they feared death itself. According to one survey of college students, the only worse phobias for them were meeting a date's parents and flying.

The Speaking Center associates developed a number of strategies to help students overcome their trepidation. One of the most useful was the videotaping of student speeches, followed by a critique led by trained peer consultants who worked directly with the students. The center also developed a supply of reading materials, handouts, and computer-generated visual aids, as well as instructional videotapes, including one by John Morello that was used to good effect in numerous classes for well over a decade.

The utility of the center was indicated by steadily increasing student traffic. During its first semester of operation, only 125 students availed themselves of its services. Within two years the number had increased to 800 per year and rose steadily thereafter, reaching in excess of 1,400 by 2005. The center, under Professor Yook's leadership, also began publishing a newsletter, *The Podium*, and sponsoring an annual College-wide speaking contest. The winner of the initial contest in 2006 was junior Shin Fujiyama, whose moving speech focused attention on the Copprome orphanage in Honduras, which by that time had become a major pet project for him. (It was perfectly in character that Fujiyama donated his $100 first prize to the orphanage.)

Earth and Environmental Sciences

The Department of Environmental Science and Geology was established in 1993 by merging two major programs, both of which had previously existed in other departments. Geology, the older of the two, had once been allied to geography, then independent, then allied to chemistry. But wherever it was placed, geology did not attract a large number of majors; the numbers were so low that the program was in danger of being cut for failure to meet SCHEV guidelines for productivity.

The solution was to create a new Department of Environmental Science and Geology. The merger was a reasonable (and apparently popular) decision, not only because it succeeded in plumping up the total number of majors but also because it made academic sense to combine two complementary disciplines.

The new department was initially chaired by Michael Bass, who had been instrumental in creating the environmental earth science major in 1979. In addition to the biologist Bass, the department was anchored by two veteran geologists, Grant Woodwell (recipient of the Outstanding Young Faculty Award in 1991) and Robert McConnell.

Woodwell, who eventually succeeded Bass as chair, developed, in collaboration with the U.S. Geological Survey, an innovative computer program on Virginia geology in 1993. Using CD-ROMs, a relatively new medium at the time, the program employed maps, databases, photographs, color graphics, and printed materials to present sophisticated data such as the height, age, and composition of mountains and the exact direction and temperature of ocean currents. The most intriguing aspect was the use of 3-D glasses to enliven the images on the computer screen so as to convert the landscape into three-dimensional cross sections. The program was eventually used not only at Mary Washington but also in geology courses at other schools.

The most visible, and certainly most vocal, member of the department was Bob McConnell. By publishing numerous articles in major city newspapers and by activities such as chairing a United Nations–sponsored seminar in Spain, he became a nationally recognized authority on environmental issues. His insistent message was that to avoid the impending disaster of global warming, major socioeconomic changes were necessary, including reduction of dependency on automobiles, greater emphasis on recycling, and large-scale cutbacks in consumption of electricity (since 90 percent of electrical power was produced by burning fossil fuels).

McConnell's greatest visibility came, unexpectedly, as the result of an article that he wrote in the summer of 1993 for the *Roanoke Times and World-News*. In that piece, titled "The Chesapeake Is Doomed Unless We Change," he offered a prescription for averting such a disaster that would require "significant new contributions from America's farmers, utilities, industries, motorists and citizens." His call to action would probably have attracted little notice had it not been picked up by conservative commentator Rush Limbaugh, who lambasted the plan (and its author) on his nationally syndicated radio program. Lumping McConnell with the so-called environmental wackos whom he loved to attack, Limbaugh condemned the proposed actions for necessitating higher taxes (another favorite whipping boy). Such was to be expected,

Limbaugh scoffed, from a "studied intellectual" like McConnell, whom he caricatured as a pipe-smoking, port-wine-drinking professor wearing a sport coat with elbow patches.[103]

McConnell took his moment of fame—unsought as it was—gracefully, noting that it probably did more good than harm to his cause. As his father-in-law told him, "You're going to be a liberal god now that Rush Limbaugh has dumped all over your article." Indeed, the episode did provide McConnell with a larger podium than ever before, allowing him to take his passionate message of environmental concern to a broad audience of students, professionals, and the general public before his retirement from the Mary Washington faculty in 2003.

Meanwhile the faculty of the department (subsequently renamed Earth and Environmental Sciences) expanded with the hiring of Jodie Hayob, Charles Whipkey, Ben Odhiambo Kisila, and Neil Tibert. Together the group provided wide-ranging expertise in specialized fields such as geochemistry, geomorphology, mineralogy, hydrology, and oceanography.

Geography

During the latter decades of the twentieth century, geography was one of the most popular majors at Mary Washington, a rather surprising situation in light of how few students enter college with a predilection for that subject. Yet, sometimes attracting a total of over 1,500 students per year, the Geography Department had a greater enrollment than its counterpart at any other college or university in the state except for Virginia Tech, which had a student body five times as large. In fact, as a percentage of the total enrollment, a far greater proportion of the Mary Washington student body took geography courses than at any other institution in the commonwealth, public or private.

A number of factors contributed to the department's appeal.[104] One was its wide array of courses, including political, regional, historical, physical, and cultural geography. Also, it was particularly strong in the more technical and methodological aspects of the discipline, such as cartography, air-photo interpretation, satellite imagery, and various computer applications for problem solving. Moreover, the College's fortuitous proximity to the nation's capital afforded a wealth of internship opportunities, many of which led to permanent employment for majors after graduation.

But the most important lure of the department was its faculty. From the early 1970s until the late 1990s, no department comprised so distinctive a cast of characters. Though alike in their devotion to their discipline and their commitment to pedagogical excellence, they were otherwise a highly disparate group.

The department's patriarch was Samuel Emory, who was the College's only geographer when he joined the faculty in 1959. Emory developed a devoted following of students who were attracted to his classes, not only by his encyclopedic knowledge of political and regional geography but also because of his distinctive pedagogical style. Less flamboyant than some of his more rambunctious colleagues, he approached his topics with a classroom demeanor consistent with his sedate, preppy wardrobe of blue blazer, rep tie, and khaki pants. Though he was "laid back" long before that term came into vogue, his classes were by no means dull, as he presented wry observations accompanied by a puckish, almost shy smile—and always delivered sotto voce.

Outside the department, he developed the internship program, organized annual summer bicycle excursions through Europe, and served terms as both parliamentarian and marshal of the faculty. Regarding the latter, he had initially demurred when asked by President Anderson to be the marshal. "I first said, 'You don't want me, you want somebody like George Van Sant, tall and imposing.' And Bill said, 'With my height, I don't want anybody tall and imposing. You'll do fine.'"[105] Beyond the College, Emory was one of the best-known faculty members in the community, partly owing to his longtime leadership role in the local Republican Party. Among nonpolitical types, he (or his name, at least) was most recognizable as the eponymous owner of the popular restaurant Sammy T's in downtown Fredericksburg.

Joining Emory in 1964 was Marshall Bowen, who, if enrollment figures are an accurate indication, became the most popular professor at the College during his tenure. He was also one of its most serious and productive scholars, although that facet of his career was overshadowed by his insouciant personality and by his association with the College's basketball team.

It was in the classroom, however, that he established a reputation as a nonpareil lecturer or, more accurately, performer. Delivering meticulously crafted presentations in an inimitable loose-limbed style that ranged from merely animated to positively frenetic, Bowen gained legendary status, teaching more students during that time than any other member of the entire faculty. And teaching them well: in 1987 he was presented the Simpson Award for excellence in undergraduate teaching.

The department's cartographer was James Gouger. Under normal circumstances, the chain-smoking, coffee-gulping Gouger was the most mild-mannered of persons, yet he possessed a mercurial temper that could lead to outbursts of astonishing proportions. Nothing, however, diminished his commitment to teaching, as he became, in the estimation of his department chair, Sam Emory, "probably the finest teacher of undergraduate cartography in the United States today." His success in that effort was attested over the years by the large number of his cartography students who gained employment with such prestigious organizations as the Defense Mapping Agency, CIA, Commerce Department, State Department, and the National Geographic Society.

Then there was Richard Palmieri, whose professional specialty was cultural biogeography, but whose personal specialty was having fun. Even amid a colorful band of colleagues, he stood out as unique by virtue of his behavior both inside the classroom and out. His interests were literally wide-ranging. Trained early in the classics at Boston Latin School in his hometown, his

Geography faculty, 1988: seated, Richard P. Palmieri; standing, left to right, Samuel T. Emory Jr., John Damron, Marshall Bowen, and James Gouger

graduate career took him all the way to Tibet for research sponsored by the National Geographic Society, with which he maintained a continuing association. Closer to home, his primary avocation was furniture, an interest that he pursued as the College's curator of furniture and as an associate of the Center for Historic Preservation.

His main concern was always with his students, and his classes were characterized by laughter as well as learning, as his irreverent wit could convert even a discourse on Tibetan yaks—his disciplinary specialty, actually—into a performance worthy of *Saturday Night Live*. That ability, which came to him so naturally, camouflaged one of the College's most brilliant and original minds and one of its most ardent scholars.

Somehow the mix of faculty personalities created a harmonious, indeed synergistic, blend devoid of prima donnas and jealousy. Bound together by their disciplinary devotion, they were united even more by their genuine concern for their students. "No matter how busy they are," remarked one major, "they always have time for you. Really, it's more like a family."

But academic families, like biological ones, do not last forever—and so it was with geography. In 1996 Emory announced his intention to retire; in 1997

Gouger, too, retired, a decision prompted by his grief over the sudden death of his wife, Gail, the previous year; and in 2001 Bowen also stepped down.

A major tragedy was the loss of Dick Palmieri, who succumbed to cancer in November 1997. Courageous even in physical decline, he delivered in May of that year the convocation address to the graduating class. To an emotion-filled capacity audience in Dodd Auditorium, a clear-eyed Palmieri took as his text the Latin phrase *carpe diem*, urging the seniors always to seize the day even as the number and quality of his own days ineluctably declined.

Only a few months thereafter, another assemblage of faculty and students gathered in Lee Ballroom to hear Palmieri's former colleagues eulogize him both as teacher and as friend. His was a life of learning, they said, and also of love, and of laughter; he had abundant gifts of intellect, to be sure, but he also had the gift of happiness—a gift that he shared extravagantly with all who had the good fortune to know him. At a subsequent ceremony outside Monroe, just beneath the classrooms where he had taught (and entertained), the College officially designated the area surrounding the fountain as Palmieri Plaza, a site further memorialized by the planting of an oak tree and the placing of a teak bench in his honor.

By the time Mary Washington entered its second century, the "old guard" had been replaced by a new group of faculty including (in chronological order of their hiring) Joseph Nicholas, Donald Rallis, Dawn Bowen (wife of former professor Marshall Bowen), Stephen Hanna, Farhang Rouhani, and Melina Patterson. Of the six, five were human geographers; Nicholas was the only physical geographer. Together they represented an extraordinary breadth of teaching specialties including cultural, economic, urban, and political geography, globalization and development, and race and ethnicity. They also covered the regions of North America, Latin America, the Middle East, sub-Saharan Africa, and Australia and New Zealand.

At the completion of the 1979 Monroe Hall renovation, the department moved from its former quarters in the basement to the third floor, where the center of its operations was the cartography lab. A number of instructional developments occurred around the end of the century, including the conversion of cartography from pen-and-ink methods to computerized techniques in 1998; the first class in geographic information systems was offered that same year. The department was also significantly involved in the College's international efforts, as Professor Rallis led study-abroad classes in South Africa beginning in 1992 and in Australia and New Zealand beginning in 1999. Professor Bowen also took students to Costa Rica and Belize during spring break either as part of courses or for independent study programs.

Led by the newer faculty members, geography maintained its place among the most popular departments at Mary Washington. In fact, by 2004, the geography program at Mary Washington was the largest program of its kind within a liberal arts college in the United States. The new faculty who were responsible for that situation possessed collective expertise that probably equaled, and maybe exceeded, that of the department's founding generation—Emory, Bowen, Gouger, and Palmieri—and they were likewise committed to the welfare of their students. If they did not have the extravagant personalities of the earlier group, it was not their fault. No one else did, either.

Historic Preservation

One of the College's newer majors was also one of its most popular—and the most distinctive: historic preservation. From its creation in 1979 as a major within the Department of History and American Studies, historic preservation quickly grew to a size that warranted a separate department, which was established in 1984. The formation of the new department was prompted not only by the increased number of majors but also by the departure of the program's founder, history professor Bill Crawley, to become executive assistant to the president of the College. He was succeeded by Carter Hudgins, who was appointed to the Prince B. Woodard Chair in Historic Preservation. In addition to heading the newly created department, Hudgins also served as director of the college's Center for Historic Preservation.

Holding a doctorate in history from William and Mary and possessing extensive experience in archaeology, Hudgins brought a higher level of expertise and greater disciplinary breadth into the preservation program. In addition to his professional credentials, he possessed assets of personality and character that equipped him ideally to lead a program that had a significant public presence aside from its academic role. Under his leadership (and largely because of it) Historic Preservation became exactly what its original advocate, President Prince Woodard, had envisioned: the institution's flagship program—one that established a unique place among Virginia's colleges and universities.

The preservation faculty expanded in the 1980s with the addition of a number of exceptionally able instructors and practitioners: W. Brown Morton III, widely known for his accomplishments in the preservation of historic structures; John Pearce, previously curator of properties for the National Trust for Historic Preservation and state historic preservation officer for Maryland; Gary Stanton, a scholar in folklore and material culture; and Douglas Sanford, whose primary expertise was in archaeology. That core group, which was still together in 2007, was joined in 1996 by Wendy Price, who brought expertise in preservation planning and law; Price was succeeded at the beginning of the 2005–6 academic year by Gillian Bearns.

Of that cadre, Brown Morton stood out as a figure of not only national but international stature. Having received a bachelor's degree in architectural history from the University of Virginia, Morton subsequently became the first American to earn a diploma (the equivalent of a master's degree) from the French Ministry of Cultural Affairs in the history, construction, and conservation of ancient monuments. It was that background that provided him with an understanding of, as he put it, "how buildings are put together, what they are made of, and how they fall apart."

Much of Morton's career before Mary Washington established him as a leading international preservationist. He spent up to three months a year in far-flung parts of the globe in pursuit of his mission to help save some of the world's most treasured sites and structures—efforts that took him to Nepal, Malaysia, Indonesia, Turkey, Egypt, India, Vietnam, and China.

As one of his colleagues described him, Morton was "a big man, six feet five inches tall and large like a tackle on a football team. . . . It is not hard to imagine him hacking through dense Asian jungles in search of lost temples." Given his experiences, the allusion to movie adventurer Indiana Jones was not far-fetched.

Upon joining the preservation faculty full-time in 1986, he soon gained almost mythic status among preservation students who flocked to his classes, mesmerized by his accounts of preservation adventures and inspired by the fervor with which he—an ordained Episcopal priest—preached the necessity of saving precious heritages. His introductory classes each year drew a cumulative enrollment of over two hundred students, many of whom became hooked on preservation, though it was a topic that in most cases was previously unknown to them.[106]

The program's popularity was attributable not only to the personalities and passions of its professors but also to the uniqueness of its curriculum. Whereas most other undergraduate programs focused mainly on architectural preservation, Mary Washington's also incorporated studies in archaeology, folklore, museum studies, objects and materials conservation, and preservation planning and law. Another particularly attractive feature involved the numerous opportunities for hands-on experience through internships with the many preservation-related agencies in the Fredericksburg area—among them the Smithsonian Institution, National Trust for Historic Preservation, National Gallery of Art, Valentine Museum, Monticello, the National Park Service, and the Fredericksburg Area Museum and Cultural Center.

Though fieldwork most often involved local projects, the program also provided a number of options for international study. According to the *Bullet*, historic preservation was "one of the first academic departments to jump on the college's globalization bandwagon."

The international efforts began in 1989 when the center worked closely with the prestigious International Commission on Monuments and Sites to coordinate a nationwide speaking tour. In the spring of the following year, Professors Hudgins and Morton taught in Brazil in a postgraduate program co-sponsored by UNESCO and the Federal University of Bahia, Brazil. As a result of that connection, Mary Washington was able to establish a cooperative venture with the University of Bahia that in 1991 enabled a group of students, accompanied by Hudgins and Sanford, to spend ten days conducting archaeological fieldwork in Brazil.

In 1993 the international program expanded with the establishment of the MWC Historic Preservation Summer School in Scotland. Brown Morton, through family associations in that country, was instrumental in working with Robert Gordon University in Aberdeen to create the unique summer session. During the course of three weeks, students, through a combination of lectures, seminars, and site visits, were introduced to Scotland's resources, standards, and methods with regard to both public and private preservation. The program was still continuing in 2007.

Beginning in 2003, a preservation team led by Professor Hudgins, in conjunction with a group from Mercer University, conducted investigations on the Caribbean island of Nevis. In the course of summertime fieldwork, the expedition discovered thousands of items including utilitarian wares produced by enslaved Africans, as well as artifacts reflecting the enormous wealth generated by sugar production in the Caribbean by the end of the seventeenth century.

A major asset to the preservation program from its earlier days was the College's Center for Historic Preservation, established in 1980. In addition to providing academic program support and sponsoring various conferences, seminars, and symposia, the Center was active in the administration of the James Monroe Museum and Memorial Library. Under the leadership of John Pearce—who, as associate director of the center, also served as director of the museum—preservation students were able to use that resource as a laboratory for exhibit design, object investigation, and archival research. It was a symbiotic relationship that allowed interns to gain practical experience while contributing to the development of the museum.

The center's activities evolved in the 1990s from mainly sponsorship of public events to greater emphasis on cultural resource management projects. The trend became more pronounced following the departure of Carter Hudgins in 1994 to become executive director of the Historic Charleston Foundation (at which time Brown Morton was appointed to the Woodard Chair). Under the leadership of Doug Sanford, who became director of the center in 1997, projects focused more on archaeological surveys, excavations, and background research (both historic and prehistoric) for private individuals, local governments, and state agencies. Such projects benefited preservation students by providing course research topics, field experience, summer jobs, and postgraduate employment.

Under Sanford's direction, students engaged in archaeological research in the city of Fredericksburg, at Germanna (the site of the Enchanted Castle, the eighteenth-century home of colonial governor Alexander Spotswood that was given to the College in 1990), and Stratford, the Westmoreland County ancestral estate of the Lee family. Perhaps the most notable work was a dig conducted in 2003 relative to the restoration of Fredericksburg's Market Square that shed new light on the history of downtown Fredericksburg while turning up, among other things, several eighteenth-century human skeletons.

In addition to its own direct contributions, the center served as a catalyst for promoting preservation efforts at a number of projects in the area. Among these, in addition to Germanna, were Menokin, the Richmond County original home of Francis Lightfoot Lee, a signer of the Declaration of Independence; and Ferry Farm, George Washington's boyhood home just outside Fredericksburg. It also aided local history through a project, coordinated by the center's director of research, Gary Stanton, to scan onto the Internet in 1997 approximately one thousand indexes of early Fredericksburg newspapers—an undertaking commended by the *Free Lance–Star* as "immensely helpful to researchers, genealogists, and students from here and around the country."

The preservation program at Mary Washington was more than an academic enterprise, as was illustrated several times by its response to natural disasters. The first involved assistance in the fall of 1989 to the city of Charleston following the devastation caused by Hurricane Hugo. Anticipating the arrival of the storm, center officials contacted Charleston to offer help if needed. Soon thereafter, the center received one of the first calls made from Charleston after the restoration of phone service, and within three days, Professors Brown Morton and Gary Stanton, along with a contingent of students, arrived in Charleston. A few days later, Professor Hudgins led another team to Charleston to help assess the damage. Such efforts were critical in aiding city officials, who had to allocate resources to restore the historic district, and in assisting private property owners in planning repairs compatible with the historic character of the area.

Four years later, when a tornado wreaked destruction on the city of Petersburg, Virginia, the College again dispatched a group of preservation majors, led by Stanton, to assist recovery efforts. The director of restoration efforts in Petersburg noted that the members of the group "were the first ones here. I wasn't at all surprised that they showed up. . . . I've worked with many of the folks from Mary Washington. It's a close group of really dedicated, professional people." The group analyzed the buildings for damage, historical significance, and architectural features, helping to enable the city to decide which structures needed immediate attention. "What we've done," commented the director, "is largely due to the efforts of the college."

As such involvement demonstrated, the historic preservation program was one of the most active at Mary Washington. Students were attracted to it for many reasons, including the opportunity to engage in meaningful work, to take advantage of internship opportunities, and to find jobs more readily after graduation. The preservation majors were a particularly energetic bunch, as evidenced by the various events sponsored by the preservation club, including the annually popular "Ghost Walk."

So attractive was the major that by the turn of the century it was routinely producing each year approximately thirty-five graduates, whose services were in great demand. As Daniel Jordan, the executive director of Monticello, observed, "Mary Washington's preservation people are particularly desirable because they not only know the theory, but also know how to apply it to actual conditions. They're able to 'hit the ground running' when they are hired." For that reason, they were found in disproportionately large numbers in responsible positions in the field throughout the country.

The program thus became, in the words of Chester Liebs, a noted professor of historic preservation at the University of Vermont, "the envy of the nation." By attracting favorable attention to the College and by contributing to the field of historic preservation a contingent of broadly educated and deeply educated young practitioners, the historic preservation program fulfilled, in extraordinary measure, the grand hopes that had accompanied its founding.

Prince Woodard would have been proud.

History and American Studies

The composition of the history faculty experienced wholesale change in the late 1960s; gone by 1970 were stalwarts such as Carroll Quenzel, Oscar Darter, Robert Hilldrup, Myra Irby, and Andrew Buni. In their place was a young group, of whom five were hired in one year alone (1968): Roger Bourdon, Otho Campbell, Key Ryang, Arthur Tracy, and Richard Warner. Benjamin Zimdars had been hired two years earlier; William Crawley came two years later. The result was a whole new faculty, save Almont Lindsey and Joseph Vance—and the scholarly, silver-maned Lindsey retired in 1974. The new group would constitute the nucleus of the department for the next thirty years.

The person primarily responsible for assembling that new contingent was Professor Joseph Vance, who served as department chair for eleven years. Vance arrived at Mary Washington College via an unusual route, one that took him from high school not directly into higher education but to the waters of the Pacific, where he spent the entirety of World War II as a Navy submariner. Only after the war did he decide to attend college, a course that carried him all the way to a doctorate in history from the University of Virginia—a development that must have come as a surprise to one of his secondary school teachers who once confessed that he had viewed the adolescent Vance as a more likely candidate for reform school than for graduate school.

Having joined the faculty in 1960, Vance quickly became, in the eyes of his students, the epitome of a college professor. An encyclopedic knowledge of his subjects, a forceful classroom presence, and a gracious, courtly personality combined to make him one of the most popular members of the department. "His whole image," typically remarked one student, "was very much what we all felt a college professor should be. *Everybody* wanted to get in Dr. Vance's classes. He was our idol."

In addition to his stellar teaching, Vance's contributions to the department were many, including the introduction of a required capstone course—in essence, a senior thesis—wherein, as he put it, majors had the opportunity "to actually *be* a historian—to do the kinds of research and interpretation which historians do." He was also noted among the students for hosting, with his wife, Jean, regular events known as "B&B," affairs that brought students together informally to bond over barbecue and beer.

Vance's involvement outside the College made him a highly visible figure in the Fredericksburg community. His reputation as a dynamic and polished speaker resulted from frequent guest lectures at area social and civic clubs. In addition, he acquired local fame in a very different way—through his reputation as an ardent outdoorsman. Whether wading in the Rappahannock for smallmouth bass, sailing the Chesapeake for bluefish, or stalking the autumn fields of Spotsylvania for dove and quail, he avidly pursued the outdoor pastimes of his boyhood in rural Virginia. For years, he shared many of his experiences with the local populace through weekly hunting and fishing columns in the *Free Lance–Star*.

For those who had come to regard him as the prototype of the vigorous outdoorsman, it came as a shock when, in March 1979, Professor Vance suffered a severe heart attack. Incapacitated for several months, he returned to the classroom the following fall but never quite recaptured the vigor of his earlier years. He retired in 1986 and died in 1998.

One of Vance's favorite lecture topics was Theodore Roosevelt—a similarly dynamic figure, who once spoke movingly about the great burden borne by teachers. This was because they were entrusted, said Roosevelt, with providing their students with "not merely a training in intellect, but a training in what counts for infinitely more than intellect—a training in character." In both those areas, by precept and by example, Joe Vance's career at Mary Washington College clearly met the standards of the venerable "TR."

The faculty that Joe Vance put together were a diverse lot (save the uniformity of gender), adding not only a wide range of disciplinary expertise but also distinctive personalities to the department. None was more distinctive than Otho Campbell. Amid a professoriat that was predominantly liberal in its political orientation, Professor Campbell held fast to a conservative philosophy that he was not inclined to disguise, either in class or out. Yet his partisanship was rendered tolerable by a natural ebullience and a genuine affinity for people that attracted to him an unusually large circle of friends who spanned the political spectrum and, by his own admission, stretched from the White House to the jailhouse. In class his evident passion for history, abetted by his natural gifts as a storyteller, won him admiration bordering on devotion from students who shared his philosophy—and even from many who did not. By the time he was forced to retire in January 2004 owing to disabilities resulting from a stroke, few professors at Mary Washington could claim to have affected the lives of more students than Otho Campbell.

One of the most remarkable members of the history faculty was Roger Bourdon. Legally blind since an operation for a brain tumor at the age of twelve had impaired an optic nerve, he managed through a combination of Braille, large-print books, and audio media to complete an undergraduate degree cum laude, followed by a doctorate in history from UCLA.

Hired by Mary Washington College in 1968, Bourdon became a student favorite owing to a teaching method that employed much humor and to interpersonal connections that employed much heart. In addition, he inspired students by the example of his own life, triumphing daily over obstacles that would have daunted a person of lesser character and courage.

Even after his retirement in 2003, Bourdon continued to serve the College as director of the institution's Center for the Visually Handicapped, an entity whose creation he advocated and whose initial funding he secured through a combination of federal, state, and private grants. At his urging, the center acquired computer technology that, with his assistance, vastly expanded the learning opportunities for Mary Washington's visually handicapped students.[107]

The mainstay of the European history area of the department was Richard Warner. With a garrulous, blustery personality, Professor Warner sometimes conveyed a somewhat distracted air—that is, until the topic turned to one about which he was most passionate: Russian history or rugby (though not necessarily in that order of priority). His bounding energy then came into full focus, enabling him to expound indefinitely with an excitability that could astound peers and students alike. He retired in 2004.

To casual acquaintances, Art Tracy could seem distant and aloof (a not altogether inaccurate perception), but not to his students, who were drawn by the acuity of his intellect, and with whom he instinctively bonded. His effectiveness as a teacher, mainly in Civil War history at first and later in American studies, was attested by his receipt of the Simpson Award in 1981.

Bill Crawley, like Art Tracy, was first and foremost a teacher—and, like him, a winner of the Simpson Award (1994). But he was increasingly drawn into quasi-administrative roles, beginning with the department chairmanship only four years after joining the faculty. He served thereafter as the founding director of the Center for Historic Preservation (1980–84) and as director of the Governor's School for the Gifted (1980–82), becoming executive assistant to President William Anderson in 1983.

A substantial increase in the number of history majors during the late 1970s made possible an expansion of the department's faculty. One of the new positions was filled by Porter Blakemore, who had worked previously for the National Park Service. Blakemore brought to the department expertise in modern European history as well as in a new field, military history. His seminars on World Wars I and II and on Nazi Germany were among the most popular in the department. Moreover, the European Capitals summer program that he developed in collaboration with political science professor Jack Kramer constituted the College's most enduring venture in international studies.

A significant event in the department's development occurred in 1984 when Claudine Ferrell was hired. Deeply committed to teaching, and especially to writing, Ferrell was instrumental in developing what became one of the department's signature courses: a required class in the methodology of the discipline that emphasized the skills of research and writing. To hundreds of history majors over the years, that class—the infamous History 299—constituted

History and American Studies faculty, circa 1980: left to right (in foreground), William B. Crawley Jr., Otho C. Campbell, and Arthur L. Tracy; (on steps) Philip D. Spiess, Joseph C. Vance, Roger J. Bourdon, Key S. Ryang, Benjamin Zimdars, Glen R. Thomas, Richard H. Warner, and Porter R. Blakemore

the bane of their academic existence while at Mary Washington, only to be regarded by them subsequently (according to their own frequent testimonies) as the most beneficial class of their college careers. Its efficacy was also attested more tangibly by the inordinate number of collegiate writing contests won by the department's majors and by the uniform success that many of its alumni enjoyed in graduate or law schools. In addition to her classroom teaching, Ferrell also served the College in several administrative roles, including director of the MALS and BLS programs.

Normally adjunct faculty do not play prominent roles in the lives of their departments, but such was not the case with Hamlin Caldwell. A graduate of the Naval Academy and husband of MWC alumna Kathleen Dawson Caldwell '71, Caldwell served for fourteen years as an adjunct, during which time he became one of the department's most admired teachers. He loved the English language, and few used it more vividly or to better effect than he. Students were charmed by his avuncular manner as he not only dispensed knowledge about history but in equal measure imparted wisdom about life.

A man of genuine warmth and good humor, his demeanor darkened only when confronted with violations of the humane ideals that he cherished. In honor of his dedication to the College, two scholarships were established following his death in 2005 to be awarded to majors whose career preparation reflected Professor Caldwell's concern for the development of enlightened public policies in the areas of social justice and environmental protection.

The most notable addition to the department's faculty—indeed, to the whole College's faculty—came with the appointment in 1985 of James Farmer as Commonwealth Professor of History.

Farmer's arrival at Mary Washington was fortuitous. Having moved to neighboring Spotsylvania County, where one of his daughters lived, he commuted periodically to Washington by bus. In the process, he became friends with MWC historic preservation professor John Pearce, who mentioned that association to history professor Art Tracy, who was then chair of the Department of History and American Studies. It was Tracy who, intrigued by the prospect of having Farmer at the College, pursued the arrangements that led to his hiring.

Farmer's impact upon Mary Washington College was extraordinary. From the moment of his arrival on campus, he regularly taught more students per class than any member of the faculty. They sat enthralled as the matchless storyteller related from personal experience the drama of the civil rights movement, leaving his audience alternately appalled by his descriptions of the hatred and violence he encountered and amazed by the good humor he still somehow managed to convey. In a response typical of his students, Pamela Kirby '01 said, "I was in awe of the man. I couldn't wait for classes to begin. It was like history coming to life in class every week." To Art Tracy, Farmer's "presence was a gift, . . . a daily reminder of the larger meaning of a liberal arts education [and] of the centrality of the issue of justice."

The hallmark of any Farmer presentation was his rich and resonant voice that instantly commanded attention. In the midst of a story, he might break into song or offer an illustrative anecdote typically punctuated by his own booming laughter. He could be disarmingly self-deprecatory, denying that he possessed any particular courage. "I was scared all the time," he once said. "Anyone who said he wasn't afraid during the civil rights movement was either a liar or without imagination."

Although Farmer's role at Mary Washington was primarily that of a teacher, he also contributed extensively to the College's efforts in the areas of race relations and diversity. Because of his stature and personal contacts, he was instrumental in bringing to the College a number of prominent civil

James Farmer

rights leaders as guest speakers. Early in his tenure, for example, he developed, as part of his history class, a public lecture series titled "The Historic Struggle for Racial Equality" that featured, in addition to Farmer himself, luminaries such as Ralph Abernathy, Martin Luther King's close associate and successor as president of the Southern Christian Leadership Conference; Walter Fauntroy, the first elected congressional representative from the District of Columbia; and Andrew Young, Atlanta mayor, Georgia congressman, and United Nations ambassador during the presidency of Jimmy Carter.

Near the end of his life, Farmer received numerous accolades for his service both to the College and to the nation. Mary Washington awarded him an honorary doctorate of humane letters in 1997 and named its multicultural center in his honor in 1998. In early 1998 the Virginia General Assembly presented him with a formal resolution of commendation, and President Clinton awarded him the nation's highest civilian honor, the Medal of Freedom.

By that time, tragically, Farmer had been forced to call once again on his seemingly inexhaustible reserve of courage—this time not in a public struggle for human rights but in a very private fight against the ravages of disease. Having lost his eyesight to retinal vascular occlusion, he eventually had to have both legs amputated below the knees as the result of complications from diabetes.

At his death on July 9, 1999, Farmer left a large and lasting national legacy. He also left his students and colleagues with enduring personal memories of a supremely courageous individual whose spirit was daunted neither by the rantings of racists in his earlier years nor by the depredations of disease at the end.[108]

Farmer's characteristic bravery was poignantly illustrated, in the view of his history colleague Richard Warner, by a scene that Warner observed during one of Farmer's last hospitalizations. Admittedly uneasy with the prospect of confronting his friend's illness, Warner recalled slowly opening the door to Farmer's room to find him all alone, lying helplessly on his bed, enveloped by his private darkness.

He was singing.

By the time of Farmer's death, the department's faculty had begun to change with the retirements of Joe Vance and Ben Zimdars, whose replacements, Bruce O'Brien and Allyson Poska, proved to be highly productive scholars—O'Brien in ancient and medieval history, Poska in women's and Spanish history. In addition, O'Brien was instrumental, along with Dick Warner, in creating a summer overseas program known as Research Group London; Poska was a driving force behind the annual Women's History Month programs. The subsequent retirements of Ryang, Bourdon, Campbell, and Warner meant that by the eve of Mary Washington's centennial, only Tracy and Crawley remained of the core faculty of the 1970s, 1980s, and 1990s.

Of the new faculty, two were particularly noteworthy. One—not really new—was Carter Hudgins, erstwhile head of the College's preservation program, who returned to Mary Washington in 2000 after six years as executive director of the Historic Charleston Foundation. Upon rejoining the faculty with a joint appointment in history and historic preservation, he was named a distinguished professor and appointed to the Florian N. Hofer Chair of Early American Culture and Historic Preservation; just two years later he was chosen to chair the department.

Another appointment, that of Jeffrey McClurken '94 in 2001, was unique in that it marked the first time the department had hired one of its own graduates. It proved to be a wise choice, as McClurken quickly established himself among students as one of the department's most sought-after teachers and among colleagues as a respected professional. Indicative of his status was his selection by the Alumni Association for its 2003 Outstanding Young Alumnus Award.

Under Hudgins's leadership as chair, the department experienced a renascence that included programmatic developments and increased faculty diversity, as well as a substantial increase in the number of majors. Four new hires between 2004 and 2006 brought fresh expertise in Middle Eastern (Nabil Al-Tikriti), Asian (Susan Fernsebner), Russian (Steven Harris), and immigration (Krystyn Moon) histories. In the process, a department faculty that had been preponderantly male into the 1990s included four women within its ten full-time positions by 2006.

Meanwhile the American studies program underwent a significant change that began when Art Tracy became its director upon the retirement of Glen Thomas. Under Tracy, the core courses were much more history-oriented than they had been under the popular Thomas, whose disciplinary background lay primarily in psychology.

Along with personnel, the most notable change was the addition of a human rights concentration within the major, a development prompted by creation of the James Farmer Professorship in Human Rights. The idea for the initiative came shortly after Farmer's death when Art Tracy, then chair of the department, suggested in a letter to President Anderson that such a position be created as a "most appropriate way to honor [Farmer's] contributions both to the nation and to the College—as well as to promote the fundamental cause of human justice to which he dedicated his life." Tracy noted that he deliberately chose the term "human rights" as opposed to "civil rights" because, in his words, "it embraces a wider range of issues that are consistent with Mr. Farmer's values as well as with the mission of this institution." With Anderson's enthusiastic endorsement, the Board of Visitors established the James Farmer Visiting Professorship in Human Rights in September 1999.

The first holder of the position was Ralph Thaxton, from Brandeis University, who came to Mary Washington during the spring 2002 semester. A specialist in twentieth-century Chinese politics, Thaxton focused his course on human rights and the politics of globalization. The following spring the visiting professor was Rhoda Howard-Hassmann of McMaster University in Ontario, Canada. The founder of McMaster's Theme School on International Justice and Human Rights, Professor Howard-Hassmann's human rights seminar was titled "Human Rights and Retrospective Justice," in which students investigated the viability (and advisability) of retrospective justice for violations such as slavery, apartheid, and genocide.

The third Farmer Professor (2003) was Gregory Stanton—from the lineage of women's suffrage activist Elizabeth Cady Stanton—who came to the position with extraordinary academic credentials including degrees from Oberlin College, Harvard Divinity School, Yale Law School, and a doctorate in cultural anthropology from the University of Chicago. Previously he had taught law at Washington and Lee University, American University, and the University of Swaziland and had served in the State Department from 1992 to 1999. As founder and president of Genocide Watch, he gained international recognition for his successful efforts in 2007 to establish a tribunal to try the surviving leaders of Pol Pot's murderous Khmer Rouge in Cambodia. At Mary Washington, Stanton promoted the human rights effort not only by teaching courses but also by arranging programs that brought to campus a number of preeminent activists in the field. His passionate commitment to the principles of human rights and his energetic efforts to promote those rights on an international level attracted a devoted student following. His exceptional success led his status as visiting professor to be extended for several years beyond his initial appointment.

The history curriculum was simultaneously undergoing salutary change. An especially fruitful innovation was the creation of first-year seminars, whose enrollment was restricted to entering students who had achieved high scores in their advanced placement courses at the secondary level. The experiment proved so successful that it became a model for the introduction of similar courses that, beginning in 2007, were required of all first-year students throughout the College.

The most visible, and certainly the most popular, of the department's initiatives in the early twenty-first century was a program called "Great Lives."

Its origins lay in the series of public lectures offered periodically by the department in the late 1970s and 1980s dealing with topics such as slavery, presidential elections, and the age of discovery. Although those programs were well received by the local community, they were eventually discontinued, owing mainly to other demands on the time of faculty members who delivered the lectures.

In 2003 the department's student reps, led by Maggie Lancaster '05, proposed that the concept be revived, not only to provide another course option for students to take for credit but to increase the department's (and the institution's) visibility in the community. Agreeing that the idea had merit, Chairman Carter Hudgins, along with Professor Bill Crawley, decided that given the reading public's interest in biography, a series focusing on the lives of history's most fascinating figures would be attractive to both students and townsfolk. Thus was born "Great Lives," subtitled "Biographical Approaches to History," first offered by Crawley in 2004.

The course was structured around public lectures whose topics were chosen with an eye toward variety in terms of chronology, geography, and fields of accomplishment. Accordingly, the topics over the years ranged from Alexander the Great to Fidel Castro, from Galileo to Einstein, from Mozart to Elvis Presley, and from Shakespeare to Dr. Seuss—and even included a horse, the great Virginia thoroughbred Secretariat.

Lecturers comprised a mix of both eminent national (and even international) authorities and specialists from within the Mary Washington faculty. Though one advantage of the series was the opportunity it provided for students to hear prominent outside experts on the various topics, it was often the Mary Washington faculty members who delivered the most impressive presentations.

Little did the "Great Lives" planners anticipate the enthusiastic response that the series would generate. It quickly became apparent that the two-hundred-seat Monroe lecture hall would not be sufficient, so the series was moved first to the Great Hall and eventually to Dodd Auditorium. It was embraced with such public fervor that it emerged as one of the institution's main avenues of outreach to the community—a development aided significantly by the generosity of Mary Washington benefactor John Chappell, who established a half-million-dollar endowment to sustain it.

A 2004 innovation was the establishment of a history symposium at the end of each semester. The daylong event consisted of sessions, each chaired by a faculty member, at which students, grouped according to their senior research topics, presented their findings to an audience of faculty, fellow majors, and friends.

Aside from the distinctiveness of its academic program, the department was characterized by a number of social activities involving its majors. Playing an important role in that regard was Phi Alpha Theta, the history honorary society. Beginning in 2002, the honorary sponsored two special events each year: a reception welcoming new prospective majors at the beginning of the fall semester and a majors' banquet at the end of classes each spring. History's banquet was not the only such departmental affair at the College, but it was in all likelihood the largest and most lavish, featuring an off-campus buffet dinner (usually at Brock's on Sophia Street) followed by an awards ceremony.

Highlights of the ceremony included announcing scholarship winners and results of departmental rep elections for the following year, as well as presenting annual awards. The scholarships were named for former faculty members Oscar Darter, Joseph Vance, James Farmer, and Hamlin Caldwell. The awards included citations for highest grade-point average (Phi Alpha Theta Award), best senior thesis (Vance Award), and service to the department (Almont Lindsay Award), as well as recognition of the outstanding major in history (Willie Lee Rose Award) and in American studies (Glen Thomas Award). An outstanding alumnus award was also established in 2005, the first recipient being John Coski '81 for his book *The Confederate Battle Flag: America's Most Embattled Emblem*.

Other social events for majors included an annual picnic and a commencement-weekend champagne reception for graduating majors. For history alumni, such activities created fond and lasting memories of life both within and outside Monroe Hall.

Mathematics

At the outset of the 1970s, the Math Department was headed by Hobart Carter, who had joined the Mary Washington faculty in 1936. For most of the next thirty-seven years, he served as department chair. Other key faculty members included tall, courtly Alexander Tyree, a Navy veteran, who had been a decorated submarine commander in the Pacific during World War II. There were also Janet Gardner and Richard Zeleznock, who were married in 1972. Both Zeleznocks were talented teachers, each being recipients of the Simpson Award, Janet in 1980 and Richard in 1991.

A dramatic change in the Math Department occurred in the early 1970s with Carter's retirement as chair. The author of two widely used math textbooks, Carter was, in Edward Alvey's estimation, "a capable and devoted teacher."[109] At the same time, he was viewed by some as aloof and excessively formal. According to his colleague Janet Zeleznock, "No one in the entire college called Carter anything except 'Dr. Carter.' His wife, Alice, said that Dr. [Philip] Allen from the Sociology Department called him 'Hobie' at times, but it shocked her, and Carter didn't like it much."[110] He retired in 1972 and died within a year.

The hiring of the youthful Alexander Lindsey to replace Carter brought a new ambience to the department. Under his leadership, the curriculum was strengthened, and courses in computer science were instituted. But more important, perhaps, was the vitality that he injected, promoting social events for the students, including picnics featuring spirited volleyball and softball games.

A gifted and highly competitive athlete (especially in golf), Lindsey himself was an enthusiastic participant in such contests, known for doing back flips as he rounded the bases. An immediate student favorite, he was simply, in the words of Professor Zeleznock, "a dynamite person. . . . Everyone except the students called [him] 'Al' or 'Big Al' (even though he really wasn't big), and there was a relaxed mood in the department."

Possessing influence that extended well beyond the department, Lindsey emerged within a short time as one of the faculty's most dynamic and respected leaders. It was thus a significant loss to the institution when he resigned in 1982 to take a job with State Street Bank in Boston. Three years later, the department experienced another setback with the retirement of longtime professor Anna Mae Harris '38, who had also served for a time as marshal of the faculty.

In 1979, as part of President Woodard's reorganization plan, math became part of a new Department of Mathematical Sciences and Physics, but in 1987 that entity was split to create separate departments of Mathematics, Computer Science, and Physics. During the 1980s, several new faculty members were hired who became departmental mainstays in the coming years, including three who would serve as chairs: Stephen Lipscomb (who replaced Al Lindsey), Gary Collier, and Larry Lehman. Also in that group were Marie Sheckels, who would become the first female full professor in the department, and Yuan-Jen Chiang. In addition, two computer science specialists were hired: Ernest Ackermann and John Reynolds. The department's new faculty in the 1990s were a remarkably accomplished group, including two who earned Alumni Association Outstanding Young Faculty Member Awards (Suzanne Sumner in 1994 and Janusz Konieczny in 1996) and Debra Hydorn, who in 2002 became the first woman to serve as chair of the Math Department.

In the early years of the twenty-first century, the department expanded its activities to include joining the Summer Science Institute. In 2003 it offered talks during Math Awareness Month and started a fall lecture series the following year. In 2007 Professor Jeffrey Edmunds, assisted by several math majors, inaugurated the UMW Calculus Tournament. Designed to enhance town-gown relations, the event brought area high school students to campus for competition against each other, mainly to practice for the AP exam, but also to show off their calculus skills.

Another twenty-first-century innovation was an event known as Pi Day, held on March 14 (3-14) to celebrate the magical number (3.14 . . .). Students enjoyed the occasion so much that they advocated a similar event in the fall. The faculty obliged them by creating a celebration right before Thanksgiving known as—what else?—Pumpkin Pi Day.

Modern Foreign Languages

The Department of Modern Foreign Languages (MFL) occupied a central place in the Mary Washington curriculum by virtue of its role in fulfilling the foreign language general education requirement. Though movements occasionally cropped up to abolish or substantially reduce that requirement, it always managed to survive such attacks. Indeed, as its defenders pointed out, that requirement was a key factor in maintaining the College's reputation for academic excellence.

The department for many years offered an enviable variety of languages including Japanese, Portuguese, Russian, Italian, and German, in addition to the more widely enrolled French and Spanish. During the years of the Woodard presidency, however, Japanese and Portuguese were eliminated when budgetary considerations made it unfeasible to offer disciplines with habitually low enrollments.

In the 1980s, the ax threatened to fall on Russian, too, as the number of students in that language declined. Professor Valentina Baslyk, who had succeeded Joseph Bozicevic as the department's instructor in Russian, launched a spirited defense of the program, energetically supported by other members of the department. As the likelihood of its demise increased, "saving Russian" became an issue of faculty-wide concern.

One of the most aggressive defenses was delivered, in fact, by a geography professor, Donald Rallis, who foresaw in its elimination dangers that went beyond the loss of that language and the single faculty position that it entailed. He claimed, for one thing, that "dispensing with the Russian program would cast serious . . . doubt on the college's declared commitment to the globalization of the curriculum and the strengthening of our international programs." He further suggested that, more nefarious still, it might lead to undermining the overall academic rigor of the College by encouraging faculty to "dumb down" their courses to attract more students, lest their courses too be removed for lack of enrollment. "In the long term," he warned, "it threatens the fabric of a liberal arts education by confusing the principles of the academy with the principles of the marketplace."

It was all to no avail, in the end, as Russian was eliminated—gradually, beginning in 1998, and completely by 2002. "There weren't any customers," Dean Philip Hall later sadly recalled. "Russian died because of lack of demand, and that . . . was a tough thing for the faculty to swallow."

Another departmental controversy involving MFL arose in the mid-nineties concerning the use of certain residences on campus as language houses, whose occupancy was restricted to students studying a particular language and who agreed to speak it exclusively while in the residence. The practice had been begun by Spanish professor Mary Ellen Stephenson, who established Framar as the Spanish house in the early 1950s. By the 1990s, Fairfax had become the Spanish house; Brent, the French house; and Tyler, the German house.

In 1994, President Anderson, citing a trend of decreasing student desire to live in language houses (as well as occasional reports that some residents of the houses were not speaking the target language), summarily announced a plan to convert the residences into apartments for visiting professors in an effort to attract more minority and international faculty. Students and faculty alike balked at the proposal, with one student commenting that "to take away one mode of diversity to give another will not increase diversity." Another student, a senior, commented similarly, "I kind of see his point where bringing visiting scholars might help bring diversity to campus, but I really think the school is for the students and the houses give more of a diversity awareness to the students, and I think that's more important."[111]

In any event, the language houses were soon phased out. In their place, certain dormitory floors were designated for use exclusively by language students. "Language coordinators" (native speakers) continued to be hired to live in the language residence areas to encourage and assist the students in speaking the various languages and to organize several programs for those students each year.

All the while, the MFL curriculum was undergoing periodic modification, increasingly designed to incorporate spoken and written aspects, as well as appreciation for national and ethnic cultures, into the more traditional grammar and literary aspects of language study. There was also increased emphasis on individual studies that enabled students to engage in undergraduate research independent of the traditional classroom setting. In addition, reflecting more concern for practical applications, specialty courses were instituted in medical Spanish and in business Spanish, French, and German during the 1990s.

Perhaps the most innovative development in the department involved the creation of summer foreign study programs beginning in the mid-1990s. These included, over the course of time, a program in Urbino, Italy, led by Clavio Ascari and Joseph Di Bella; in Orvieto, Italy, led by Frederico Schneider; in Mérida, Mexico (initially), led by Ana Chichester and subsequently in Bilbao, Spain, by Jose Angel Sainz; and in Rosenheim, Germany (initially), led by Professor Sammy Merrill and subsequently in Erfurt, Germany, by Marcel Rotter.

Another innovation of MFL that provided not only support for the programs of the department but also educational entertainment for the College community was the Foreign Film Series. Begun in the early eighties by Professor Vera Niebuhr, the series each year brought to campus well-known foreign language films in each of the languages taught by the department. An Arabic film was included for the first time in 2007. All were made available to students and the public free of charge.

The department also reached beyond the campus to provide various services to the community by establishing internships (beneficial to the students as well) in schools, courts, international organizations, and businesses where language skills were needed. It also provided assistance to the growing Hispanic population of the Fredericksburg area through NOAH, the National Organization for the Advancement of Hispanics.

Many of the department's faculty members achieved national recognition for their scholarly productivity—including Clavio Ascari, Joe Bozicevic, Ana Chichester, Leonard Koos, Betsy Lewis, and Marie Wellington. Most noteworthy perhaps were Professors Aniano Peña and James Gaines, who achieved international recognition for their work in Cervantes studies and sixteenth-century French literature respectively.

Though the overall scholarly productivity was significant, the main emphasis of the department was on high-quality classroom teaching. Reflecting the achievement of that goal, four members of the department won the Grellet C. Simpson Award for pedagogical excellence. The first recipient of the award upon its creation in 1971 was Spanish professor Carmen Rivera, who was followed by Joanna Reynolds (Spanish), Sammy Merrill (German), and Clavio Ascari (Italian). In addition, in 2004 José Angel Sainz received the Mary Pinschmidt Award by vote of the graduating class.

Amid such a commendable group, several individuals stood out. One was Joanna Reynolds, who taught (mainly Spanish) from 1968 until her retirement in 2000. In addition to being an award-winning teacher and dedicated scholar, she devoted great amounts of time to the interests of the institution (notably in the writing intensive program) and her department, serving as its chair for six years, providing commonsense stability during a time of change, transition, and occasional turbulence.

Her teaching skills were complemented by a singularly endearing personality. "Who hasn't been charmed by the homey expressions in her soft southern drawl, her sparkling eyes, warm smile, and easygoing manner?" observed one colleague, who added that the sweet disposition could be disarming, as it sometimes served "to mask an absolutely volcanic temper that has been known to shake the ground and spew magma all the way to GW Hall" whenever she felt the welfare of MFL to be threatened. German professor Sammy Merrill summarized it well in remarks delivered upon the occasion of her retirement. "This southern lady," he said, "is truly a steel magnolia."

Herr Merrill himself was for more than three decades before his retirement in 2004 at the forefront of the department's leadership. It was not just his academic performance that was extraordinary—though his work in maintaining the vitality of the German program was no small achievement. Generally reserved and serious-minded, he nonetheless possessed a sense of humor that leavened an initial appearance of aloofness. His successful service for eight years as chairman of one of Mary Washington's most inherently diverse departments was testimony to his organizational skills and even temperament.

His contributions outside the department were extensive in scope and exemplary in quality. Owing to his wide and well-earned reputation for integrity and fairness, he was called upon for leadership in some of the College's most demanding assignments, including the revision of the honor system, and for daunting (and usually thankless) tasks such as tenure and promotion appeals. His exceptional dedication as a faculty member was acknowledged in 2003 when he received the first J. Christopher Bill Award for service to the institution. The citation was fitting, for no person at Mary Washington during his tenure was more universally respected and admired than he.

Merrill's accomplishments went well beyond the bounds of Mary Washington to include a wide range of community activities. A onetime seminarian, he was particularly engaged in the work of the local Presbyterian church, serving as an elder and choir member; and as a Park Service volunteer, he helped to maintain area hiking trails. He was dedicated to fitness and was an outstanding distance runner, competing in marathons and regularly winning 10K races in his age bracket even as he moved into more senior classifications.

On the occasion of his retirement, the *Free Lance–Star* lauded Merrill for epitomizing the ideals of liberal education and selfless citizenship. "Influencing the next generation of Americans is more than just an educational task," it wrote. "In the process of conveying information, the educator inevitably shares something of himself, his character, personality, and values. It is gratifying to know that [MWC students have had] the opportunity to know and learn from professors of integrity like Mr. Merrill."

In all, the contributions of the Modern Foreign Language Department over the years were crucial to fulfilling the liberal arts mission of the College. The importance of the discipline was well articulated on one occasion by Professor Donald Rallis, whose expression was perhaps even more powerful because, as a geographer, he was not a member of the department. In his defense of the Russian program, he wrote in 1996: "Foreign languages lie at the heart of a liberal arts education. Languages provide the glue which holds together the disparate subjects of history, political science, international relations, geography, the arts, and economics, and which allows students to appreciate all of these disciplines in an international context. Without an understanding of foreign languages, students cannot fully appreciate and understand foreign cultures, and therefore cannot adequately comprehend their own country and its role in the world."

For its steadfast dedication to promoting that understanding, the Modern Foreign Language Department earned the gratitude of generations of Mary Washington students.

Music

The contributions of the Music Department at Mary Washington, like those of art, theatre, and historic preservation, reached well beyond the classroom to engage the local community. Through its extensive program of concerts, recitals, and workshops, perhaps no element of the entire institution was more responsible for generating positive town-gown relations than was music.

The department's primary focus, of course, was on students—not just its own majors but the many others who looked to music as a means of enriching their liberal arts education and, at the same time, providing an important avenue for personal enjoyment. The objectives of the major program involved preparing students for graduate work as well as for careers in the performing arts or teaching.

Toward that end, the department over the years employed many faculty of exceptional talent. Some of the most notable retired during the latter decades of the twentieth century, including Levin Houston, Bernard Lemoine, and James Baker. One of the most widely admired, Patricia Norwood, died in January 2008. Still active, however, at the time of the institution's centennial were veterans such as Martha Fickett (recipient of the J. Christopher Bill Award in 2007), David Long (Simpson Award, 2005), and Stephen Burton. Full-time faculty were augmented by numerous part-time instructors who mainly taught performance classes in a wide range of instruments.

The public face of the department was manifested in the performances of several vocal groups and instrumental ensembles. Among the vocal groups were the Fredericksburg Singers, the Mary Washington Chorus, and Una Voce (a coed a cappella ensemble). Perhaps the most dynamic of all was the Encore Show Choir, directed by Steve Burton. Appearing in concerts on campuses and in other venues around the region, the group typically delivered high-energy vocal and dance routines of contemporary pop and show tunes, presented in a lighthearted manner that reflected the whimsical personality of its director.

Several popular ensembles developed in the 1990s and thereafter. One was the Jazz Ensemble, directed by Doug Gately, an alumnus of Mary Washington's BLS program ('98). The ensemble performed contemporary jazz arrangements as well as big band standards for audiences both on and off campus, including major concerts each semester. It also hosted an annual jazz festival that brought nationally and internationally known performers to campus, including artists such as James Moody, Tony Lakatos, the U.S. Army Blues, and the U.S. Navy Commodores. Another feature of the festival was its outreach to the community by inviting high school jazz ensembles to participate.

Gately also directed the Flute Ensemble. In addition to performances by the entire ensemble at events such as the Annual Flute Festival, smaller groups often performed at social events, adding an elegant ambience to those gatherings.

Especially active was the fifty-member Wind and Percussion Ensemble, under the direction of Craig Naylor. Joining the faculty in 2001, Naylor brought enthusiasm to his teaching (receiving the Outstanding Young Faculty Member Award in 2006) and creative energy to the ensemble. Among his innovations was an annual "Good Buddy" concert designed to generate enthusiasm for music among elementary-age students by inviting them to the campus for a performance that allowed them to see, hear, and touch band instruments, as well as interact with the Mary Washington students in the ensemble.

Another innovation, begun in 2002, was an annual costume concert. Fall editions usually took a Halloween theme, and the spring performance was called "Lundi Gras." Designed, again, to appeal to children (and to adults who aspired to be children), such performances brought out the playful side of the naturally uninhibited Naylor. Always eager to join in the spirit of fun, he once donned a particularly striking costume, appearing as the New Year's baby. Pulling his hair into a top knot, he wore a robe that, at the appropriate moment, he cast aside to reveal a capacious diaper and a sash emblazoned with "2003."

Yet Naylor was a serious musician, a side he revealed in developing a 2006 concert series titled "Native Voices: The Music of American Indian Composers." The ambitious program included performances of Native American composers by the Chamber Ensemble and by the Wind and Percussion Ensemble. In addition to concerts on campus, the series marked the ensemble's debut at the Kennedy Center.

By far the largest element of music's public program was the College–Community Orchestra. Begun in 1971 by James Baker, the orchestra established close ties to the area not only by incorporating local musicians as performers but also by providing concerts that attracted residents to the campus in large numbers for major musical events each year.

The orchestra's beginning had not been auspicious. Indeed, its first performance in December 1971 was recalled by one of the thirty-five or so charter members, psychology professor Roy Smith (a cellist), as "an unmitigated disaster." But from there the group constantly increased in size and musical sophistication over the next three decades, all under Baker's leadership.

In the process, Baker came to be known as "Fredericksburg's music man"—a title he fully deserved in light of his herculean efforts toward the orchestra's development. In addition to securing a sufficient number of musicians, he constantly had to devise a repertoire that balanced the tastes of the audience with the talents of the musicians. "You can stretch the musicians' abilities slightly," he once explained, "but it must be a 'reachable carrot.' I've also stretched the ears of the listeners from time to time, but you can't make a habit of it or you lose your audience."[112]

The success of his endeavor was evinced by several measures. One was the expansion of the orchestra itself, growing to approximately ninety members (sixty students, thirty townsfolk) by the year 2000. Another important indicator was the growth of the Friends of the Orchestra group. By 2005, membership had reached 250, and the Friends had generated over a half-million dollars in endowed funds to finance scholarships for student musicians. Perhaps the most significant measure was the increased audiences for all four of the orchestra's annual concerts, not just for the Christmas Pops Concert, which had drawn huge crowds from the beginning.

The capstone of Baker's career as orchestra director came in 2002, the year he announced his retirement, when the group was invited to perform at legendary Carnegie Hall. That concert was described in the *Free Lance–Star* as the "performance of a lifetime," an assessment Baker himself was not inclined to dispute, saying that "it was clearly the best the orchestra has ever sounded."

For many of the members, it was certainly the experience of a lifetime, especially for the surprising number of students who had never been to New York City. But even for veteran performers like eighty-seven-year-old Anne Hamer, it was a thrill. "It was a beautiful concert, a wonderful experience," she said. "You look around and see all the things you see in a postcard of Carnegie Hall, and then it hits you: you're in that postcard."

With that, Jim Baker's career as Mary Washington's musical entrepreneur came to a close, leaving a permanent imprint at the institution and in the community. "Jim's music has made this a more joyful place for a long time," said President Anderson, "and through his enduring legacy of the orchestra, his contributions will continue for years to come."

Baker's departure left his many friends and admirers wondering who, if anyone, could fill his shoes. His successor, Kevin Bartram, could certainly do so in a literal sense—being, like Baker, an imposing physical specimen. Beefy yet boyish, Bartram could (again, like Baker) command a podium, wielding his baton with élan. And he came with commendable credentials both as teacher and as conductor, as well as a reputation for success in expanding the music programs at the schools where he had worked.

He also shared with Baker another characteristic: an innovative spirit. That approach was clear from the first pops concert that Bartram directed, a tribute to composer Leroy Anderson. With Anderson's eighty-four-year-old widow and his son (also a composer) in the audience, the orchestra delivered sprightly renditions of Anderson's hits from the late 1940s and 1950s such as "Syncopated Clock," "Blue Tango," and "Sleigh Ride."

A major innovation was Bartram's creation of the Celebrity Series, which commenced in 2004 with the Oscar-winning composer Marvin Hamlisch. The concert, during which Hamlisch both performed on the piano and conducted the orchestra in many of his own compositions, was so successful that some observers were moved to comment that it was "not only the best orchestra concert" they had attended, "but the finest MWC event of any kind."[113] Celebrity artists in subsequent years included the Canadian Brass ensemble, songstress Judy Collins, and jazz legend Ramsey Lewis.

Bartram also proposed new programs that appealed to a wide spectrum of ages and musical knowledge. For the very young, there was, beginning in 2003, an instrument "petting zoo," sponsored by Fiddlestix, a branch of the Friends of the Orchestra. At the zoo, held in Dodd Auditorium, stations were set up throughout the room where the orchestra's principal players gave demonstrations of their instruments that allowed children to hold and in some cases play those instruments. Children could also stand on the podium, baton in hand, to get a feel for conducting an orchestra.

To appeal to mature musicians, Bartram created a project to commission composers to write new music for the orchestra. The first piece, composed by the renowned James Grant, was written to be played as part of the institution's centennial celebration in 2008. Indicative of the orchestra's ever-increasing quality and aspirations, the group embarked on its first international tour in May 2006. Dubbed the "Mozart Tour," it was part of the orchestra's celebration of the composer's 250th birthday. Accompanied by an entourage from the Friends group, the orchestra presented three concerts during its eight-day tour, including one in Klosterneuberg (outside Vienna) and two in the Salzburg area.[114]

Within a few years, it thus became evident that Kevin Bartram was proving a worthy successor to Jim Baker as the music program continued its expansion. Plans for the featured centennial concert on Founders Day included turns at the podium by both the maestros.

Physics

The Physics Department, as it existed in the late twentieth century, was largely traceable to the hiring of Bulent "Bill" Atalay in 1966. At the time of his arrival, the department consisted solely of Grover P. Burns and Jean Edson. Soon thereafter Burns retired and was replaced by Nikola Nikolic; in 1987 George King III was hired. From that point through the early years of the twenty-first century, the core of the physics faculty comprised those three: Atalay, Nikolic, and King.

Though one of the College's smallest departments, physics attracted some of the best students at Mary Washington. From among its relatively small number of graduates each year (ten to fifteen) came a disproportionately high number of Darden Award winners, including five between 1982 and 2002: Julie Samson '82, Dawn Baugher '94, Jeanette LaCivita '96, Kristin Buck '00 (a double major with chemistry), and Mohamed Chakhad '02. Moreover, an unusually high percentage of physics majors went on to graduate work, probably resulting in the highest percentage of doctorates and master's degrees of any department on campus, according to George King.[115]

Much of the department's success in that period was attributable to the appeal of its eclectic faculty. Nick Nikolic grew up in Yugoslavia, whence he immigrated to the United States, accompanied by an unyielding antipathy toward communism. "Politically, he's to the right of Attila," Bill Atalay once commented, adding "but he's brilliant in physics"—reputedly having achieved the highest grade-point average in the history of the University of Belgrade.[116] Notorious at faculty meetings for his conservative (some would say reactionary) comments—invariably delivered bluntly and at high decibels—he earned a reputation as a campus curmudgeon, albeit a likable one.

George King, holder of a Ph.D. from Stanford University, was among the first full-time African American faculty members at Mary Washington. He brought immediate energy to the department, creating the Summer Science Institute during his first year on the faculty. (He was named Outstanding Young Faculty member in 1990.) Having met with local education leaders, he decided that the basic mission of the program would be to improve math and science skills of elementary teachers in the area. From 1987 to 1997, the project, in which he was assisted by mathematics professor Marie Sheckels, received grants in excess of $100,000. The program eventually served over one hundred K–9 teachers and brought several hundred students to the cam-

George King III receives the Alumni Association Outstanding Young Faculty Award from Dean Philip L. Hall, 1990

pus during summers for science and math enrichment. He was also largely responsible for attracting another grant of nearly $100,000 from the Jessie Ball duPont Fund for a three-year program to assist area science teachers in augmenting their curricula.

In addition, King played an important role in promoting undergraduate research at Mary Washington. Soon after he arrived, he accepted a research student, physics major Elizabeth Stevens, whose work was of such quality that, unbeknownst to her, he submitted it to a national competition. She won second place among all presenters, a group that included Ph.D. candidates. So impressed was President Anderson that the following year he allocated $40,000 for the initial funding of the College's undergraduate research program.

Bill Atalay was a person of such diverse interests and exceptional talents that, in the eyes of his admirers, of whom there were many—students, peers, and townsfolk alike—he warranted the appellation "Renaissance man."[117] Surely his background—which included a grandfather who died while fighting against Lawrence of Arabia—was unique among Mary Washington faculty. Born in Turkey, the son of a military officer–diplomat, he was educated in England (Eton), France, and Turkey before coming to the United States at the age of fourteen.

His course toward becoming a physicist was determined, he said, by happenstance when an admissions officer at Georgetown University misread his application, interpreting his expressed career choice of "physician" as "physicist." Having taken a few courses in that discipline, however, Atalay decided he liked physics after all and stuck with it—all the way to a doctorate, thence to Oxford and the Institute for Advanced Study at Princeton for postdoctoral work.

Along the way he added friends much as some people collect coins, including onetime NFL commissioner Paul Tagliabue (a classmate at Georgetown), Salvador Dalí, and a great-nephew of the Indian prime minister Jawaharlal Nehru. He also came to know a number of Nobel laureates in physics, several of whom were attracted to speak at Mary Washington, among them the 1963 laureate Eugene Wigner (who visited the College in 1975, 1979, 1983, and 1986), the 1988 laureate Leon Lederman (who was commencement speaker in 1990), the 1989 laureate Norman Ramsey (who visited in 1995 and 2002), and the 1997 laureate William Phillips (who visited in 2001, 2002, and 2006).

As an instructor, Atalay was much in demand by students who appreciated his ability to make the potentially forbidding discipline of physics accessible to nonscientists. His performance in the classroom and laboratory led to his being presented the Simpson Award in 1998.

But successful as he was as a teacher and practicing physicist, Atalay achieved even wider recognition for accomplishments outside (or at least peripheral to) his academic discipline. He was, for example, an expert photographer and talented artist who specialized in lithographs; his collection titled "Oxford and the English Countryside" (1974) was selected for display in the White House, Buckingham Palace, and the Smithsonian Institution. In 1984 he took part in a highly touted archaeological venture designed to find the remains of Noah's ark. Amid worldwide publicity, one member of the expedition announced his belief that remnants of the ark had been located in a remote corner of Turkey. Atalay, an interpreter for the group, expressed skepticism about the purported discovery, a view that ultimately proved correct.

A love of travel nurtured from childhood led Atalay to visit virtually every corner of the world, sometimes as a cruise ship lecturer for Royal Viking Cruise Lines. An ideal choice for such a task, given the breadth of his academic interests, he made over a dozen such excursions in the 1980s and 1990s, becoming, in his own words, a "floating scholar."

In the early years of the new century, he focused his efforts on the work of the prototypical Renaissance man, Leonardo da Vinci, whose combination of scientific and artistic talents had special resonance for Atalay. One result was a collaboration with Thomas Somma, director of the Ridderhof Martin Gallery, to produce one of the most acclaimed exhibits in the institution's history, Leonardo da Vinci: Artist, Scientist, Engineer.

That project melded with the endeavor that was to prove the capstone of Atalay's career: *Math and the Mona Lisa*, a book published by the Smithsonian Institution in 2004. Focusing on the golden ratio (1:1.62), which occurs frequently in nature and is aesthetically pleasing to the human eye, Atalay demonstrated how da Vinci was aware of that mathematical phenomenon and used it in consciously replicating those proportions in his works, including the *Mona Lisa*. The timing of the publication was fortuitous, as its subject was enjoying wide popularity as a consequence of Dan Brown's best-selling novel *The Da Vinci Code*. Spurred by that phenomenon, Atalay's work went on to become the second-highest-selling book about Leonardo in the world, going through eleven printings in eleven languages during the three years following its publication. "Thank God for *The Da Vinci Code*," said Atalay. "Without a doubt it catalyzed the interest."

By the time of Mary Washington's centennial celebration, Bulent Atalay had become the institution's longest-serving faculty member. In the course of forty-plus years, he had enriched the lives of countless students not only by helping them to understand the intricacies of the discipline of physics but by encouraging them to appreciate the potentialities of life itself. "Observe in the manner of the scientist, savor in the manner of the artist," he told them. It was a lesson that he not only taught but lived.

Political Science and International Affairs

During the early years of the Anderson presidency, the nucleus of the Political Science Department remained the same as it had been since 1971: Lewis Fickett, Victor Fingerhut, Richard Krikus, and Jack Kramer. All were widely regarded as exceptional teachers and scholars who, each in his own way, brought significant strength to the department's curriculum and to the overall program of the College. Fickett joined the faculty in 1963, armed with both law and doctoral degrees from Harvard, as well as extensive experience in the foreign service. Tall, courtly, and immaculately attired—pin-striped suits and rep ties were his usual wardrobe—he invigorated the department and became a much-sought adviser for its majors. In the years that followed, he gained renown as a scholar of the politics of India, a country in which he studied on several occasions and about which he wrote a book, *The Major Socialist Parties of India* (1976), and numerous articles.

Beyond the College he was actively involved in local Democratic politics, serving in the Virginia legislature from 1973 through 1981. He was one of that body's most progressive members, promoting measures such as free textbooks for public school students, which was one of his proudest achievements. His greatest contribution to Mary Washington was in the classroom, where carefully crafted and eloquently delivered lectures were his hallmark. The recipient of the Simpson Award in 1995, one year before his retirement, Fickett was lauded by Provost Hall as "the living incarnation of what all of us imagine as the model college professor." At that same commencement ceremony, President Anderson aptly summarized the fruitful career of the College's premiere scholar-statesman. "No one has exceeded him in devotion to the principles of liberal education upon which Mary Washington College is founded," Anderson said, "nor has anyone lived those principles more faithfully."

Joining the department four years after Fickett's arrival, Victor Fingerhut taught for thirty-nine years before retiring in 2006. Throughout that time, his courses were infused with insights drawn from his concurrent involvement with political polling, an activity that helped to make his lectures constantly fresh and compelling. (It was ironic that the most cluttered faculty office on campus was inhabited by one of its least cluttered minds.) Students were not only challenged by the incisiveness of his political analyses but also enthralled by his accounts of "real world" interaction with major figures such as Hubert Humphrey, on whose presidential campaign Fingerhut worked in 1968.

Like Humphrey, in fact, Fingerhut was a liberal whose political philosophy flowed naturally from a humane personality that harbored not a trace of meanness. With a warm, non-threatening approach, he related effortlessly to his students, creating an academic career of which the most salient characteristic was the lasting interest in the political process that it engendered in countless students.

Richard Krikus joined the political science faculty in 1970. A hardworking scholar whose academic interests ranged over both American and European politics, he was the author of *Pursuing the American Dream* (1976). Krikus's primary field of expertise, however, was the ethnic republics of the Soviet Union, an area in which he was regarded as one of America's leading scholars. That reputation was enhanced by the 1988 publication of *The Superpowers in Crisis: Implications of Domestic Discord*, in which he posited the disintegration of the Soviet empire. When that prediction proved true soon thereafter, he immediately became a sought-after media personality. Urbane, glib, and telegenic, he found a global audience as an analyst in media including CNN, NPR, *USA Today*, Reuters, and *Larry King Live*. "In Berlin," wrote one Fredericksburg columnist, "they want to know what Dick Krikus thinks about Mikhail Gorbachev's chances of hanging onto power. In Paris they want to hear his reaction to the Baltic States' break from the Soviet Union. In Dallas they want to know: Who is this egghead talking international politics with Larry King while we're waiting to see Madonna?"

During this time of political ferment, Krikus developed intimate ties with the newborn Lithuanian Republic, serving as one of two U.S. observers at the country's first democratic election in 1990 and forming personal friendship with its first president, Vytautas Landsbergis. Such relationships enabled Krikus to create useful academic connections between the Lithuanian Republic and Mary Washington College. By the time of his retirement, few members of the faculty had contributed more constructively to the College's efforts towards globalism than Dick Krikus.

Joining the Political Science Department in the same year as Krikus, John M. Kramer became the dominant force within the department during the next three-plus decades both as an exceptional teacher (winner of the Simpson Award in 2006) and as an effective administrator (first elected chair in 1983, he was still serving in that capacity in 2007).

One of Kramer's most significant contributions was the reorganization and reinvigoration of what was originally known as the pre–foreign service major. That program, under its originator, the estimable Kurt Leidecker, was in

John M. Kramer

Kramer's view lacking in academic focus and misleading in title. Academic focus he addressed by tightening the curriculum to require a more relevant and coherent package of course options. The title he corrected by changing the name of the major from pre–foreign service, which implied a prescribed career path—one that was sometimes, but not always, followed by its graduates—to international affairs, a rubric that more accurately indicated the range of postgraduate career options that the major permitted. He was also instrumental in creating the European Capitals series, the popular and long-running summer program that he directed with history professor Porter Blakemore.

Such innovations had a substantial and positive impact on the College, but Kramer's contributions went well beyond those programmatic initiatives. For one thing, he set a high standard for his colleagues and students alike through his extensive publication record, which included numerous articles on Eastern European affairs, as well as a monograph, *The Energy Gap in Eastern Europe* (1990).

Then there was the matter of his personality, which was, by any reckoning, one of the College's most distinctive. A connoisseur of wine and of words, he enjoyed a reputation as a bon vivant and as a master of repartee. The same animated style that characterized Kramer's personal exchanges carried over into the classroom, where he earned a well-deserved reputation as a perfervid lecturer and demanding (occasionally irascible) taskmaster. Some students viewed him as a petty tyrant—"Napoleonic," in one's description—and, to be sure, he was no panderer for their affections. Thus was created something of a love-hate relationship on the part of the students toward him: hatred (or at least annoyance) when he intimidated them in class; love (or at least appreciation) when they realized thereafter how much those methods had benefited them in the long run. As he himself once explained his modus operandi, "What the student, just like a child, may think in the short term is good for them or not good for them may be very different from what they need in the long run to succeed."[118]

Above all, he emphasized effective writing, which included his proscriptive "no-no sheet." Among the immutable rules contained therein were admonitions regarding split infinitives, the use of nouns as verbs (e.g., "impact"), and—probably the most common of all errors in students' writing—the difference between "its" and "it's." He was notoriously averse to use of the passive voice, threatening grades of F for students who employed that heinous construction. (Or so it was rumored.)

Except for Kramer, all of the department's "old guard" had departed by 2007, replaced by younger faculty who made a quick and beneficial impact both within the institution and beyond. There was, first, Mark Rozell, a perceptive analyst of contemporary American politics, whose views were often solicited by state and national media. When he left in 1995, he was replaced by the similarly energetic Stephen Farnsworth.

Originally a journalist by profession, Farnsworth made an effective transition to academia, receiving two of Mary Washington's most prestigious faculty awards within his first five years: the Mary Pinschmidt Award in 1999 (the first year that it was presented) and the Outstanding Young Faculty Member Award in 2001. In addition, he had an unusually high profile beyond the institution owing to his numerous published book reviews and commentaries, frequent media appearances as a political analyst, and books including *The Mediated Presidency: Network News and Presidential Governance* (2006), *The Nightly News Nightmare: Television's Coverage of U.S. Presidential Elections* (2003), and *Political Support in a Frustrated America* (2003).

At the turn of the century, the political science faculty further expanded, both in number and in expertise, as new hires brought specialization that added breadth to the department's offerings. Elizabeth Freund Larus (the first woman to be tenured in the department) was a specialist in Chinese politics, the author of *Economic Reform in China, 1979–2003: The Marketization of Labor and State Enterprises* (2005). Others included Jason Davidson, (recipient of the Outstanding Young Faculty Member Award in 2007) in international relations theory and comparative politics in western Europe; Rosalyn Cooperman in congressional politics and women in politics; and Robert Barr in Latin American politics.

From the standpoint of institutional history, there was an interesting coincidence: one of the newer group was Ranjit Singh, whose father was Raman Singh, a member of the English Department from 1967 to 1996. (Having grown up in Fredericksburg, the younger Singh jokingly called himself a "townie.") Joining the faculty in 2004 as an expert on Middle East politics (fluent in Arabic), he was chosen to serve as an international observer for the historic Palestinian elections held in January 2005.

The characteristic that all the new faculty had in common with one another and with their predecessors was devotion to effective classroom teaching. As a result, though few departments surpassed Political Science/International Affairs (PS/IA) in scholarly output, fewer still did so in terms of pedagogical excellence. Following the lead of its chairperson—facetiously called by some of his cronies "Chairman-for-Life"—Jack Kramer, the faculty put special emphasis on the development of their students' writing skills. The results were impressive, the best example perhaps being that for four consecutive years beginning in 1997, one of the department's majors won the annual national essay contest sponsored by Pi Sigma Alpha, the political science honorary with more than six hundred chapters. (Particularly instrumental in that achievement was the work of Professor Farnsworth, the chapter's adviser, whose dedicated leadership led to his being named the national best chapter adviser in 1999.)

Besides emphasizing communication skills, the department was highly effective in placing its students in internships (and often thereafter in jobs) on Capitol Hill. It occurred so often, in fact, that, according to Kramer, there was "a standing joke that there's the Mary Washington Rat Pack up there."

Judging by the success of its graduates, PS/IA ranked among the most impressive programs at Mary Washington. Two alumni won the Distinguished Alumnus Award—Gale Mattox '72 in 1994 and Rose McCartney Likins '81 in 2005 (she was also the commencement speaker that year); in addition, Jennifer Taylor Boussuge '86 received the Young Alumnus Merit Award in 2005. Moreover, some of the department's graduates went on to hold governmental positions of considerable importance, including Likins as ambassador to El Salvador; Francis Cook '67 as ambassador to Burundi, Cameroon, and Oman; and Marion Blakey '70 (the 2006 commencement speaker) as head of the Federal Aviation Administration.

Psychology

One of the largest departments at Mary Washington—and in many ways the most innovative—was psychology. It was the first, for example, to incorporate community service learning into its major program. It was also one of the most active in the placement of interns, having supervised more than any other department in 2005–6. A distinguishing feature of the department was its emphasis on undergraduate research, an area in which it set the pace for the rest of the College. Whereas many departments provided opportunities for such work, for psychology it was actually built into a vertically structured curriculum culminating in a required individual research project.

One outgrowth of that emphasis was creation of an annual year-end symposium at which students presented research that they had conducted in their classes or with their research teams. The event was designed much like a professional conference, complete with a call for papers, moderated sessions, a keynote speaker, and awards for outstanding presentations in various categories. In addition, each year between thirty and forty psychology majors gave presentations at state, regional, and national conventions, winning numerous awards for outstanding undergraduate research from organizations such as the Virginia Psychological Association, the Association for Psychological Science, and the American Psychological Association.

Such disciplinary engagement was promoted by an extraordinarily active chapter of the psychology honor society, Psi Chi, which in 2004 was designated a model chapter by the national office. The following year, the chapter adviser, Miriam Liss, received an award for being the honorary's outstanding faculty adviser in the region. In 2006 the Mary Washington chapter won the highest award that a chapter can receive from the national organization.

The department's success was, of course, grounded in the academic quality and professional dedication of its faculty. Beginning in the 1970s and continuing into the new century, there was a stable core consisting of Professors Roy Smith, Thomas Moeller (winner of the Simpson Award in 2007), Denis Nissim-Sabat, David MacEwen, Christopher Bill (Simpson Award, 1997), and Steve Hampton (Simpson Award, 2002). All played important roles outside the department and even outside the College. Roy Smith, for example, wrote the grant proposal that established the College's Teaching Innovation Program and was the recipient of the J. Christopher Bill Service Award.[119] He also served at one time as president of the Virginia Psychological Association and on another occasion as president of the Virginia Association of Academic Psychologists.

To this nucleus were added along the way energetic young scholars including Larry Penwell, Debra Steckler, Christopher Kilmartin, David Kolar, Christine McBride, and Miriam Liss. Three of them were honored with the Outstanding Young Faculty Award: Penwell (1992), McBride (1999), and Liss (2005). Kolar and McBride (a husband-and-wife team) both served as president of the Virginia Academy of Academic Psychologists.

Chris Kilmartin emerged as one of the most prominent—and certainly the most publicized—members of the psychology faculty. An authority on gender issues at a time when such concerns were becoming more prevalent, he found an eager audience for his expertise. Having joined the faculty in 1988, he taught a popular new course on the psychology of men in 1991. Three years later he published *The Masculine Self*, followed in 1999 by *The Pain behind the Mask: Overcoming Masculine Depression*, which he coauthored with a clinical psychologist.

His greatest acclaim, however, came as a result of his "second career" as a stand-up comic, a role in which he drew heavily upon gender observations related to his disciplinary specialization. In 1995 he teamed with Theatre Department Chair Gregg Stull to write a one-man show titled *Crimes Against Nature*, whose performance was described by one reviewer as rep-

Christopher Kilmartin performing a scene from his one-man show Crimes Against Nature resenting "a convergence of Kilmartin's clinical interest in men's issues with his self-described tendency to show off." Consisting of a series of autobiographical vignettes about male foibles, the play, according to the critic, was "often hilarious, occasionally touching, and always entertaining. . . . While the show offers plenty of entertainment, it is clearly engineered to change what you think being a 'real man' means." During a run of roughly six years, Kilmartin performed *Crimes* over two hundred times on more than one hundred college campuses spread throughout thirty states, with the proceeds (when there was an admissions charge) often going to support organizations to protect women's rights.

Although *Crimes* brought Kilmartin's insights to a wide audience through the use of humor, he was a serious scholar, as evidenced by his selection as a Fulbright fellow in 2006–7. At Mary Washington he was a leader in efforts against sexual discrimination, harassment, and violence and was much in demand on other campuses and elsewhere as a consultant and speaker on issues relating to male behavior.

If Kilmartin was the department's most visible member, its most popular was J. Christopher Bill. It was thus an enormous shock to the department and to the entire College community when he died suddenly on December 3, 2001, from meningococcal sepsis.

"Topher," as he was universally called, was largely responsible for initiating many of the department's innovative programs during his long tenure as its chair. Beyond the department, he was acknowledged as one of the faculty's foremost leaders, who, at the time of his death, was president-elect of the faculty senate. Dedicated to the welfare of his peers, he treated them as part of his extended family—congratulating or consoling or, should the occasion require, chastising them as well. His approach was unfailingly frank and forthright to the point of brusqueness, but that demeanor belied a puckish (if sometimes piquant) sense of humor and served to camouflage commitment of uncommon depth.

He became well-nigh legendary on campus and in the local community

J. Christopher Bill

for his exuberance, the epitome of one who lived life in full. That same ebullience was manifested in relationships with his students. Not content merely to assist their academic progress, he was concerned, too, about their personal development, as evidenced by his constant support of their athletic and other extracurricular activities. Few professors had more student advisees; none had more devoted ones.

There was good reason—two reasons, in fact—that Topher was sometimes described as Bunyanesque. First there was the matter of his appearance: an ample, rough-hewn frame and rustic aspect that bore an obvious resemblance to that of the legendary lumberjack Paul Bunyan. But beyond that, the rigor of his intellect and the uncompromising rectitude of his character recalled the precepts of another Bunyan, the literary John. Topher's longtime friend and colleague Tom Moeller put it aptly and succinctly when he described him as "an enormously complex, talented, loving, and dedicated man with an unbridled zest for life," suggesting that his uniqueness was such that he "could not be defined, but only experienced."

Following his death, several memorials were established to honor his legacy. One was creation of an annual J. Christopher Bill Outstanding Faculty Service Award, an appropriate gesture in light of his commitment to faculty concerns; among the first recipients, again appropriate, was his longtime psychology colleague Roy Smith. In the department, a scholarship fund was established to assist worthy psychology majors, with funding generated partly by the annual Topher Bill Auction.

In terms of involvement in College-wide activities, clinical psychologist Denis Nissim-Sabat was an influential figure, serving multiple terms as a member (and chair) of the Faculty Affairs Committee, in which capacity he was instrumental in developing a policy that provided medical and parental leaves for faculty. The respect of his colleagues across the institution was evident in his subsequent election as president of the faculty senate in 2002. (In a less formal capacity, he served the interests of collegiality by founding a monthly poker club in the 1980s that was still going strong two decades later, serving as a lively venue for minimal monetary exchange and maximal academic gossip.)

Sociology and Anthropology

The department that by 2007 was known as Sociology and Anthropology underwent several transformations beginning in the 1970s. Before that time, it had been known simply as Sociology, created as a separate entity in 1947 with the hiring of Philip Allen. He was joined a year later by Clyde Carter and in 1958 by Charles Sletten. Those three constituted the core of the department into the 1970s.

Clyde Carter was named chairman in 1971, notwithstanding the fact that his degrees were in theology and religion, not sociology. An ordained Presbyterian minister, the kindly and avuncular Carter enjoyed virtually universal respect on campus. "A wonderful man . . . [and] a real Christian," his colleague Margaret Huber called him. "There wasn't an uncharitable atom in his make-up."[120]

By the time Carter retired in 1982, the department (then known as Sociology and Anthropology) had undergone a period of tumult resulting from President Woodard's insistence on consolidating certain departments; in this case, it meant combining sociology and anthropology with geography. The shotgun wedding was devoutly opposed by all parties, who stoutly maintained that there was insufficient disciplinary affinity among them to make the arrangement work. And it did not. With complaints issuing from all sides, new president Bill Anderson soon granted a divorce that reestablished the Department of Sociology and Anthropology separate from geography.

By then the old corps of Allen, Carter, and Sletten was in the process of being replaced by an able and energetic group of young scholars that included Huber, Joan Olson, and Timothy Crippen. For a short time, they were joined by Bruce London, an exceptionally prolific scholar and popular teacher who left in 1981 for a position at Florida Atlantic University; he was replaced by William Hanson, who possessed many of the same qualities.

The first of the newer group to arrive (in 1974) was Margaret Huber, who remained the central figure of the department faculty for more than three decades, during much of which she served as chair. A social anthropologist, her major fields included gender, symbolic systems, and Oceania, with special interest in native North Americans, as revealed in her book *Powhatan Lords of Life and Death* (2003). A stylish woman of considerable charm, she was known for her refreshing approach to classroom teaching and for innovative

An anthropology class potlatch at the campus log cabin

courses such as one that she first offered in 1991 based on the television series *Star Trek*. Classes on Native Americans sometimes included rituals called potlatches, which were held for a number of years in the log cabin near Goolrick Hall and later in the amphitheater.

With her leadership, the younger faculty in the 1980s thoroughly revised the department's curriculum to make the major more cohesive and more rigorous, including the addition of a required course in statistics. The somewhat counterintuitive result was the attraction of increased numbers of majors, a development that permitted in time the hiring of additional faculty including Debra Schleef, Kristin Marsh, Tracy Citeroni, and Alejandro Cervantes-Carson in sociology and Eric Gable in anthropology.

Amid the department's success came the tragic death of one of its most beloved members, Bill Hanson. Having arrived at Mary Washington in 1981, he became a favorite of students, who admired his zest for life and his passionate advocacy of progressive causes, especially those related to civil rights. An activist in the community, Hanson was a leader in organizations such as the Area Food Relief Clearinghouse, the Housing Coalition, the Thurman Brisben Homeless Shelter, and the Nuclear Freeze Alliance. On campus he pushed for creation of a Martin Luther King Day celebration and construction of the James Farmer memorial, supported the activities of the James Farmer Multicultural Center, and worked for disability rights and the establishment of a living wage for College employees.

In 1992 Hanson was diagnosed with idiopathic pulmonary fibrosis, which proved intractable to steroid treatment and caused his lungs to fill gradually with scar tissue. In 1996 he received a lung transplant that extended his life (and teaching career) almost eight years—and converted him to another cause that he pursued with his usual zeal: organ donation, which he promoted by helping to establish a transplant support group.

But by late 2004, the failure of his other lung brought the end for this gentle and compassionate man who by precept and by action inspired hundreds of Mary Washington students during his career. He died on January 31, 2004, after which the department established the Bill Hanson scholarship in his memory.

Programmatically, an important department development occurred in 2005 with the establishment of anthropology as a major. When President Simpson hired Margaret Huber in 1974, he did so with the expectation that she would be the cornerstone of such a major. However, owing to staffing difficulties in subsequent years, it did not prove feasible to create a full-fledged major, although students could be, and were, permitted to develop special majors in the discipline.

It was not until thirty years later, with the hiring of anthropologist Eric Gable, a dynamic and forceful presence in the classroom, that the department secured sufficient faculty to support a regularly offered anthropology major. "We had to wait thirty years for the major to happen," exulted Huber, "but, Grellet, wherever you are, you asked me to do this, and I've done it." Immediately successful, by 2007 anthropology was graduating close to twenty majors a year.

Theatre and Dance

The Department of Theatre and Dance, one of the oldest at Mary Washington, was established in 1913. Subsequently its title had been changed several times from simply the Drama Department, to the Department of Dramatic Arts and Dance, to Theatre and Dance—the latter terminology reflecting more accurately the department's functions by the twenty-first century, as well as the more commonly accepted terminology of the times.

The department underwent a rather turbulent period following the death of its chair, Albert Klein, in the fall of 1970. He was succeeded briefly as chair by Thomas Turgeon, who was replaced in 1972 on a more lasting basis by Roger Kenvin. Having joined the faculty in 1959 as a member of both the English and Drama Departments, Kenvin resigned at one point to take a position at another college but returned to Mary Washington in 1972, whereupon he was named chair of the Department of Dramatic Arts.

The department that Kenvin headed in the early 1970s included two faculty free spirits, Lloyd Mallan and Dennis Daluiso. Both had left by the end of the decade, with Daluiso's departure prompting a flurry of protest on campus when his contract was not renewed at the end of the 1977 session. A number of drama majors attributed that development to a conflict between Daluiso and Kenvin. Some reacted to the situation by boycotting Kenvin's classes, but their efforts on behalf of Daluiso were unavailing, as he was not rehired.

Following Daluiso and Mallan were two instructors whose stays were similarly brief: technical director and designer Steve Larson and acting instructor Neil Howard. Howard, though his time at the College was relatively short, made a significant contribution through his efforts to establish the Fredericksburg Summer Theater. Under Howard's direction, the summer stock theater developed off campus as a separate entity, but one that had a working relationship with the College and held its productions in Klein Theatre. By the mid-1980s, however, various misunderstandings led the department to sever its ties with the summer theater, though the organization, subsequently called the Fredericksburg Theater Company, continued to operate at other area locations, including high schools.

When Howard (who married a Mary Washington student, Terrie Gladney '78) left for a position elsewhere, he was replaced by one of the more talented, if controversial, figures in the history of the department—or the College, for that matter: Michael Joyce. For some years after his arrival in 1980, the handsome young Joyce was one of the most dynamic personalities on campus, both as a teacher (recipient of the Simpson Award in 1990) and as an administrator (chair of his department). His recognition spread beyond the campus, too, as the author of a television pilot script called *Dimes* and as cohost of *Weeknight Alive!*, a nightly show on Maryland public television.

But his starry career was tarnished in 1993 when the *Bullet* reported that three students had brought sexual harassment charges against him. The matter was eventually settled through an agreement whereby Joyce retained his job but was required to undergo counseling and regular professional evaluation by College officials; he was also warned that further incidents might lead to dismissal. Joyce himself denied any improprieties, attributing the charges to the students' misinterpretation of his teaching techniques. However, following the filing of similar complaints in 2002, he resigned from the faculty.[121]

Throughout such upheavals, the department nonetheless managed to maintain its accustomed excellence, owing to the dedication of an exceptionally talented core of faculty members. Behind the sets—in fact, making the sets—was David Hunt, who joined the department in 1982 in the field of scene design. (He married Jean Graham '72, a member of the dance faculty.) Costume design was in the capable hands of Rosemary Ingham. She was one of those rare faculty members at Mary Washington who, as author of three seminal works on costume design, was more famous off campus than on—"an internationally known superstar," in the words of one of her colleagues.[122] Also helpful to the department was renowned opera singer Helga Bullock, who, while a member of the music faculty, assisted in the voice training of many theater majors. (Among Mary Washington students generally, however, her fame came more from the fact that she was the mother of Hollywood actress Sandra Bullock.)

The faculty member most responsible for the success of the theater program in the 1990s and beyond was the department chair, Gregg Stull, a former theater major at Mary Washington ('82). After completing graduate work, Stull taught for a while and worked as managing director of the Wooly Mammoth Theater Company, a small professional theater in Washington. He returned to his alma mater to teach on a part-time basis in 1990 and became full-time in 1992 when he was hired to replace Robert Ingham, who had died.

M. Gregg Stull

Stull soon became recognized for his advocacy of gay rights, as exemplified by his involvement at the national level in promoting the NAMES Project Memorial Quilt.[123] On campus he was known as an effective and engaging teacher, as acknowledged by his receipt of both the Outstanding Young Faculty Award in 1995 and the Mary Pinschmidt Award in 2003.

Under his leadership as chair, the department continued to prepare its majors for careers as teachers or as performers in various areas of the theater. Indeed, the major program was designed so that students received not only classroom instruction but hands-on training in every aspect of theatrical productions, including acting, scenic design, lighting design, costume design, sound design, stage management, and directing. The program also contained the flexibility to allow students to concentrate in whatever area of the theater they found most interesting. By 2000 there were typically thirty to forty majors each year, in addition to which approximately six hundred nonmajors per semester enrolled in courses offered by the department.

Stull also sought to revive the institution's dormant relationship with the Fredericksburg Theater Company. Working with Debby Klein, the widow of Al Klein and a continuing supporter of theater at Mary Washington, he was instrumental in resurrecting the FTC in the summer of 1998. That endeavor brought about fifty people to campus each summer for a ten-week season that normally included the production of three plays. Despite significant success, as indicated by the tripling of the audience size, the theater once again parted ways with Mary Washington after three seasons, mainly as the result of fiscal problems.

Other facets of the theater program proved more permanent, including the department's Studio 115, an intimate venue that provided the opportunity for showcasing student directors, actors, designers, and playwrights in a variety of one-act plays, solo performances, monologues, and storytelling throughout the academic year. Above all, there was the ongoing success of the department's major productions during the year, events that provided enjoyment and cultural enrichment for the community as well as invaluable experience for the participants both on and behind the stage.

In choosing its productions, the department did not shy away from plays that were challenging, either technically or emotionally, nor did it abjure politically sensitive subjects. In winter 2003 the department mounted a production of *The Laramie Project*, a play that graphically and sympathetically chronicled the horror of the murder of Matthew Shepard in 1998. Although by that time the play had become a lightning rod attracting venomous attacks from anti-gay groups, Stull was undeterred, pointing out that when the season's plays were being chosen by committee, *The Laramie Project* was at the top of the list. "This was a play we felt spoke to a very important moment in time," he said, "and was quite relevant to our audience. . . . The same thing could happen here."

Stull was thus not surprised when the play produced controversy. The unexpected part was that the major protest against the play erupted from, of all places, Kansas, headquarters of the Westboro Baptist Church. Led by its homophobic pastor, the Reverend Fred Phelps, the church had made a practice of protesting against the play, appearing at performances all over the country including, as it turned out, Fredericksburg.

Warned in advance that the protest could be expected both at the College and at several so-called gay-friendly local churches, the campus and community were well prepared for the Kansas crusaders. The basic response was to ignore the provocateurs. As predicted, a cohort from the Westboro Church did show up at the College's main gate on the night of one performance, wielding signs bearing messages such as "Matt in Hell," "Death Penalty for Fags," and "God Blew Up the Shuttle." They were confronted—peacefully and silently, but implacably—by approximately two hundred Mary Washington students who held signs of their own proclaiming, "Don't Hate, Integrate," "All We Need Is Love," and "God Loves All His Children," and wearing buttons bearing the message "Hate Is Not an MWC Value." The Mary Washington students were joined by a contingent from Longwood University (where *The Laramie Project* had been performed earlier without incident) wearing angel wings in memory of the slain Shepard.

Concurrently, other students—about two hundred strong—were participating in a candlelight vigil in front of duPont Hall, where they lined the entranceway to the play in Klein Theatre. Both the message and the medium of the students' protest attracted favorable comment on campus and in the community. "It seems that a large part of the student population is actively for gay and lesbian rights," commented Rhoda Howard-Hassmann, the College's visiting James Farmer Professor of Human Rights, "and that is very good."

In an editorial titled "Something Wicked This Way Came," the *Free Lance–Star* agreed, noting with satisfaction that the Kansas protesters' efforts had been counterproductive. "Phelps's little legion, who came to divide, united, [providing] a weekend homily on the subject of hate and what it can do to the human family," it suggested, concluding, "Turn now in your hymnals. You know the one: 'God Works in Mysterious Ways His Wonders to Perform.'"

Simpson Library

At Mary Washington, the library constituted the academic heart of the institution, providing the resources that made possible the intellectual explorations that occurred in disciplines throughout the College. Though that had always been true, technology in the late twentieth century utterly transformed the way in which the library functioned.

Major changes occurred in 1989 when the library moved from Trinkle to its new location, thus becoming Simpson Library.[124] From the outset, computer terminals and CD-ROMs were available, but in the following decade, library services were vastly expanded through a number of additional technological innovations.

The library catalog, for example, gained dimensions never dreamed of just a few years earlier when in 1999 Simpson Library became one of the first in the world to implement an integrated library automation system known as VIRTUA.[125] By using VIRTUA, students, faculty, alumni, and community members—indeed, anyone in the world who had access to the Internet—could search the Simpson catalog as well as the catalogs at other libraries, including the Library of Congress and prominent universities such as Princeton and the

University of Virginia. It also allowed for multiple access points beyond the usual author, title, and subject searches of the old catalogs to include searches by language, publisher, call number, date of publication, and format.

One of the most useful aspects of VIRTUA was that it provided patrons with hypertext (http) links that could take them directly to many full-text documents that could be read, e-mailed, or printed—these from Web-based resources located in databases anywhere in the world, not just at Mary Washington. The system also allowed library patrons to renew materials, view their personal circulation records, and place requests through the online catalog without having to visit the library in person.

Research was further revolutionized through the library's membership in the Virtual Library of Virginia (VIVA), a consortium of academic institutions that provided access to a rich array of electronic resources through the campus network. Such resources ranged from online encyclopedias and dictionaries to bibliographic databases and full-text periodical services. Participation in VIVA allowed Simpson Library to avoid using valuable shelf space for the storage of old volumes of periodicals, thereby making room for important print-based materials. Among the latter were numerous federal and state publications that the library maintained as an official depository for those agencies.

The circulation system was modified to allow faculty to place document delivery requests for monographs or for photocopies of articles in microform, periodicals, reference books, or archival materials. Books were then delivered to faculty offices via campus mail, and photocopies were scanned and delivered electronically to faculty offices via e-mail.

The interlibrary loan system was extended and made more user-friendly in 2004 through a self-service Web-based program known as ILLiad. That system allowed patrons to borrow items from other libraries by logging into ILLiad to request books or articles and then to receive e-mail notice when the materials arrived at Simpson Library.

One of the library's most important functions was training students in the effective use of its resources. This was accomplished in a variety of ways. The first was through a one-credit research skills course, Library Science 101. In addition, there was course-related instruction, wherein reference librarian specialists in various fields offered one or more sessions geared toward particular class assignments or subject area resources. While used in courses across the curriculum, especially heavy use was made of these library sessions by English and history classes.

In the area of library instruction, technology also came to play a central role. In 1980 the first edition of the *Library Skills Workbook*, a printed instructional tool written by the reference librarians, was published. It was superseded in 1998 by an online tutorial developed by the reference staff and was further refined in 2000 by the implementation of a tutorial called TALON (TAking Libraries ONline). That self-service program, which employed interactive modules to instruct users in catalog access, databases, and other resources, was a key element in helping students meet the technology proficiency requirement in information literacy.

One cumulative result of such technological initiatives was that the library's annual through-the-door patron count declined by over seventy thousand between 1990 and 2006.[126] This would at first not appear to have been a positive development, but it actually was. What it meant was that, by using technology, students and faculty were spending less time physically looking for information, freeing up more time to devote to reading, evaluating, and writing. The process thus demonstrated the aptness of a librarian's suggested motto for the times: "Serving You Better, Seeing You Less."

Of course, technology did not eliminate the human component of the library; indeed, it was the competence and commitment of the library staff that made it all work. Heading the organization was the library director, a position that had enjoyed unusual stability in personnel over the years. From 1972 through 2007, there had been only two: Ruby Weinbrecht and LeRoy Strohl. Several innovations were introduced during Weinbrecht's tenure as head librarian. One was a newsletter titled *News and Views from Trinkle*, begun in October 1972 as successor to the short-lived *Trinkle Little Star*, which had a run of only six issues between January 1970 and April 1972. *News and Views* was published quarterly, typically carrying brief articles on recent acquisitions, archival updates, faculty research and writing, and the activities of the Trinkle Associates. The publication ceased in the mid-1980s.[127]

The other major innovation of the period was the creation of the Trinkle Associates in December 1977. Though fully supported by Librarian Weinbrecht, the enabling force behind the group was Gordon Jones, a local physician and noted bibliophile who donated many valuable volumes from his own extensive collection to the library's rare book room.

Though the organization's basic purpose was to provide, through gifts and financial support, a channel through which the library's resources could be enriched beyond the means of the College's budget, the Trinkle Associates also augmented the library's efforts through a range of public activities, sponsoring an annual antiquarian book fair, hosting dinners for visiting scholars and authors, and holding receptions honoring local authors. In addition, the associates periodically presented rare books to the library to commemorate notable institutional events, including the inauguration of President Anderson in 1984, the College's seventy-fifth anniversary that same year, and the acquisition of the library's 300,000th volume in July 1983. Also, the associates occasionally published short papers produced by the faculty, among them Dean Emeritus Edward Alvey's "Spanish Visions of the Jamestown Settlement," biology professor Mary Pinschmidt's "A Man from Padua," and English professor Nathaniel Brown's "Demon or Angel? Shelley in the 19th Century." Following the death of Gordon Jones, the Trinkle Associates, missing their main patron and animating spirit, dissolved in the mid-1980s.

Roy Strohl's arrival was well-timed, as he brought expertise and characteristics of personality that served the library well during the phase it was then entering. His professional credentials were strong, and his varied background outside academe indicated a practical bent that was most useful in overseeing construction of the new library shortly after his arrival.[128] His interest in, and knowledge of, technology was invaluable in helping move the library swiftly and smoothly into the digital age.

Nor were his contributions limited to the library or even the College. A likable extrovert of great charm and considerable presence, he was an active participant in many local affairs. Taking a leadership role in such organizations as the Rotary Club and the Bluemont Concert Series, he was one of Mary Washington's most visible and popular liaisons with the Fredericksburg community.

While Strohl was the library's public face, its operation depended on the work of many staffers who went largely unseen. One of the longest serving was the unassuming Charles Balthis, who joined the staff as cataloger in 1969—a position he still held in 2007. Rebecca Elswick was responsible for the crucial task of collection development, constantly alert to the acquisition of new materials and quickly responsive to faculty requests for needed works. In that effort she was ably assisted by Tina Faulconer, who joined the staff in 1975 and was still serving as an acquisitions specialist three decades later.

Among the more recent employees was Donna Hudgins, who in 2000 became serials management librarian. In addition to managing the constantly changing area of periodicals, she was instrumental in one of the library's most significant conservation projects. From 2003 to 2005, assisted by archivist Carolyn Parsons, she instigated and directed the microfilming of the College's deteriorating collection of *Bullet* issues that stretched back to 1921.

Initially in charge of the library's electronic resources, from 1981 to 1993, was Mark McManus. He was succeeded by Bob Grattan, who had previously been the director of the American Library in Paris for eight years, where he had been instrumental in introducing library technology to that facility. His expertise was crucial in carrying out the complex task of configuring Simpson Library's modern operational system. Upon his retirement in 2005, that work was carried on seamlessly by his successor, Tim Newman.

For the several decades beginning in the 1980s, the library's archives and special collections were managed by, in order, Brenda Sloan and Carolyn Parsons. Sloan was the antithesis of the stereotype of the reclusive archivist cloistered amid arcane documents. An African American, she was one of the College's—and the area's—most vocal advocates of minority rights in the tradition of James Farmer, a close associate whom she much admired. In the library she devoted hours to designing displays for Black History Month; in the College at large she served as adviser to the Black Student Association and as a blunt-spoken leader of the black faculty-staff organization; and in the community she was actively engaged with organizations such as the Fredericksburg Area Museum and the Harambee 360° Black Arts Festival.

Upon Sloan's retirement in 2003, the archivist position was filled by Carolyn Parsons, who had a long association with Mary Washington. Having graduated in 1983, she returned in 1995 as a reference librarian. As head of special collections, one of her duties was preparing the library's public exhibitions and related programming, one of the most popular of which was a talk, "Fighting the Forces of Darkness: Harry Potter, Fantasy, and Censorship," given by English professor Warren Rochelle in conjunction with an exhibit during Banned Books Week in 2005. She also aggressively pursued preservation efforts such as microfilming the *Bullet* and a project to have all student honors papers, previously housed in simple loose-leaf form, bound in sturdy buckram.

One of the library's most useful services was interlibrary loan. Beginning in 1984, that function was carried out with consistent efficiency by Carla Bailey. On her office door was posted the whimsical notice, "Please limit your requests. We only have access to 10,000,000 volumes." But there was a seed of truth to it. Over the years, Bailey consistently processed around ten thousand requests annually, almost equally divided between those incoming and those outgoing.

In two of its most important areas, reference and circulation, Simpson Library boasted truly exceptional staffs. The reference division, organized according to broad academic areas, comprised in 2007 Jack Bales in humanities, Renee Davis in sciences, and Charlotte Jones in social sciences.

Jack Bales carved out a special place in the life of the College in the decades following his hiring in 1980.[129] Partly, his success was the result of a prodigious work ethic. Rising at 4:30 a.m. each day after a mere five hours of sleep made possible enormous scholarly productivity, including biographies of three significant figures in American literature: Horatio Alger, Kenneth Roberts, and Willie Morris; each biography became the standard study of its subject. Bales's writing was done in addition to his "day job" as reference and humanities librarian. In that capacity, applying his characteristic energy and

BOB BROWN / RICHMOND TIMES-DISPATCH

James E. "Jack" Bales

enthusiasm, he may well have helped more students, across more disciplines, than anyone else at Mary Washington, not only by assisting them with specific projects but by helping them to develop lasting research skills. Beyond that, his evident avidity for learning doubtless produced a positive effect on the numerous students with whom he worked, imparting to them by his own example an appreciation for the beauty and power of the printed word.

All this he accomplished with good humor and steady temperament. According to one colleague, Bales never seemed to have acquired the art of anger. "Jack tries to get mad once in a while," he said, "and he may even sputter a few oaths. But you get the impression that it's done without much conviction. He's just too nice."

Mirroring Bales's contribution in the reference division was the work of Beth Perkins, who handled the circulation department across the Simpson foyer. Joining the library staff in 1984, she was responsible for handling the dual (and sometimes conflicting) goals of serving the students and simultaneously protecting the integrity of the collection. The skill with which she accomplished those tasks was evident daily in the smooth operation of one of the library's central functions. Beyond the campus, Perkins's accomplishments were recognized statewide in 1996 when she was voted Outstanding Virginia Paraprofessional by the Virginia Library Association and nationally in 2000 when she was chosen by the prestigious *Library Journal* (and featured in its cover story) as Paraprofessional of the Year—the first time each award had been bestowed.[130]

By 2007 it seemed accurate to rank Simpson Library as one of the finest medium-sized libraries in Virginia, in terms of both facilities available and services provided. The building itself offered four hundred seats for public use, including 260 individual study desks and several small rooms for group study. The building also had dozens of computers available for public use. In addition, the library provided wireless access to the campus network.

By then the library's collection included over 367,000 cataloged items, 21,500 current magazine and newspaper subscriptions, and an extensive microform collection of newspaper and periodical back issues. In addition to more than 42,500 electronic books, the library also provided access via the Internet to over one hundred electronic databases. Open to the public ninety-two hours per week during regular semesters, many of its resources were also available 24/7 via the Internet. By adding six thousand or more volumes each year to its collection, Simpson Library was constantly expanding to support the needs of a wide-ranging curriculum.[131]

ADMINISTRATIVE AFFAIRS

Admissions

With its admissions program thriving, Mary Washington in 2002 took the dramatic step of ending its "early decision" option, becoming only the third college in the country to do so. Other institutions followed suit in subsequent years, including Harvard and the University of Virginia. The plan, which had been available at MWC since the 1960s, permitted students to apply in the fall of their senior year and learn of the decision on their application by December. At the time of application, students were required to sign a binding contract of commitment to attend if admitted. The concept had obvious advantages for the institution in that it helped in enrollment planning; it also was advantageous to students in alleviating anxiety over whether or not they would be admitted.

Martin A. Wilder Jr.

But critics of the program, among them Marty Wilder, the College's vice president for enrollment (who was also vice president of admissions counseling and enrollment practices with the National Association for College Admission Counseling), claimed that early decision had negative consequences as well. For one thing, the pressure of the admission process nationally had distorted the original intent of early decision to the point that it had become, for many students, a strategy for gaining admission rather than a means of expressing genuine interest in a first-choice college. Moreover, noted Wilder, students accepted by early decision had no opportunity to compare financial aid offers from other schools. As a result, the program tended to be a disadvantage for minority students and others who needed more time to explore additional options. "A few extra months," said Wilder, "allows students more time to grow and mature and to carefully consider all of their college options and ultimately reach a well-reasoned decision."

Eliminating the early decision option had no apparent negative effect on the MWC applicant pool. This situation was at least partly the result of an innovative program established in 1988 called honors admission, whereby high school students who had exceptional rewards of achievement would be notified of their acceptance at an early date, but without the binding provision of the early decision option. Mary Washington was the only college in the country to have this program. Whatever factors contributed to it, the academic quality of the student body continued to improve steadily. By the turn of the century, the profile of applicants offered admission revealed average high school GPAs of 3.7 and SAT scores of over 1,220; for the entering "centennial class" of 2004—those who would graduate in 2008—the SAT average of students accepted had reached approximately 1,250.

The institution not only continued to draw praise from the traditional college guidebooks but in 2005 attracted the attention of the popular press as well. In its October issue, the popular teen zine *CosmoGIRL!* listed Mary Washington as one of the fifty best in the country out of 2,685 institutions considered. The ranking was based on factors such as small class size, prominent female faculty members, a strong women's sports program, internship opportunities, numerous clubs and activities, and an active alumni network. Mary Washington had all those things—plus other one distinctive feature, noted the magazine: Devil-Goat Day.

Still, some areas presented challenges, especially the recruitment of black students. One key initiative, the Farmer Scholars Program, was jeopardized in the mid-nineties when the original funding sources were depleted and the General Assembly rejected the College's request for $116,000 for the program.[132] It was preserved, however, by trimming some aspects, such as field trips, and by having students pay a portion of the cost ($100). After 2000 the program was further scaled back by limiting attendance at the monthly sessions to seventh, eighth, and ninth graders and the summer sessions to seventh and eighth graders. In addition, speakers were asked to donate their time, and some groups volunteered their assistance, such as MWC students who were members of SHADES (Stopping Hate and Discrimination by Educating Students). Moreover, the program's full-time director was replaced with a part-time one, Assistant Dean Leah Cox.

The program continued with mixed success. By 2002 almost seven hundred students had participated, a commendably high 75 percent of whom, approximately, went on to college. Less heartening for the host institution was the small percentage who chose to attend Mary Washington, typically no more than two or three each year.

Another effort toward black recruitment was a 2000 program called Columbus Day Road Trip. The program brought approximately seventy minority students from Washington, D.C., and northern Virginia to campus to participate in a daylong event that included an information session, campus tours, visits to classes, and lunch with College students. A Martin Luther King Day program was also established for prospective students.

In addition to such specific events, the admissions office on a regular basis made special efforts to contact minority students personally via telephone, e-mail, and individualized mailings and to interact with high school counselors and program directors. Staff members also focused on attending college recruitment events at high schools with heavy concentrations of black and Hispanic students.

The office also developed printed materials focusing on black recruitment such as a brochure called "Celebrating Cultural Diversity." Though the intention behind such publications was admirable, they sometimes provoked a reaction when black students who enrolled at the College complained that the minority student population was exaggerated in the brochures. Thus a conundrum: failing to portray a significant minority presence on campus diminished the likelihood of recruiting greater numbers of blacks, but including such depictions led some to complain of deceit.

The staff of the admissions office itself was one of the College's most diverse, designed to include recruiters who possessed affinities for certain minority groups. Thus the office over the years employed Asian (Abas Adenan) and Hispanic (Matt Mejia) staffers, as well as a series of African Americans including Sallie Washington Braxton '77, Forrest Parker, Angelia Allen '82, Kristina Carnegie '88, David White '92, Rita Richardson, Natalie Ellis, Lawrence Nightingale, Cris Hairston '05, Lawrence Webb, and Rita Thompson.

The hiring of Thompson in the fall of 2002 touched off a furor on campus. In many respects, her credentials were impressive. As a former member of the Board of Visitors, she knew the College well; she was also experienced in recruitment, having spent seven years in admissions work at the Georgetown University Law Center.

According to some, however, her background contained a serious flaw: a previous job as national spokeswoman for Concerned Women for America, a conservative Christian women's group opposed to such things as abortion, pornography, and gay rights. English professor Stephen Watkins was the first to express alarm at what he regarded as a conflict between the views espoused by that organization and the College's Statement of Community Values. In a campuswide e-mail, he described her former organization as being "aggressively anti-gay" and taking "strong, fundamentalist positions on issues." Political science professor Stephen Farnsworth and psychology professor Christopher Kilmartin followed with similar electronic messages of outrage, with Kilmartin referring to Thompson as one who "was a spokesperson for . . . an organization that some people consider a hate group."

The admissions office was quick to defend Thompson's hiring, as did the *Free Lance–Star*, which urged that she not be judged simply by virtue of her earlier associations. Thompson herself expressed surprise at the bitterness of the attack, saying, "They don't know who I am because I'm so new. Nobody even called to ask, 'What is your philosophy?'"

The controversy was diffused somewhat when Thompson met both with Watkins and the presidents of two campus organizations, the Black Student Association and People Representing Individuals of Sexual Minorities (PRISM). Though still skeptical about the appointment, Watkins commended Thompson for "seeking out people to reassure them. . . . I wish her well."

Unfortunately for Thompson (and for the College), the issue was subsequently inflamed by two developments. One was publication of the 2003 edition of the Princeton Review's *The Best 345 Colleges*, which included Mary Washington among that elite group, only to rate the College as number one in terms of racial homogeneity. "Whether the College Up the Hill is truly the titlist in the field . . . is unimportant," chided a *Free Lance–Star* editorial titled "Anglo U." "[It] is sufficiently monochromatic that students joke the 'MW' stands for 'Mostly White.'"

Second, the release of admission figures for the 2004 entering class seemed to substantiate the unflattering description. Only fourteen new black students enrolled, which amounted to 1.59 percent of the entering class. That dispiriting scenario prompted a number of faculty members to collaborate on a *Free Lance–Star* op-ed article in which they condemned the College's administration for not putting a higher priority on black recruitment and for instead emphasizing construction projects. The *Free Lance–Star* agreed, claiming that the institution's "mind has been on other matters," specifically scapegoating President Anderson for his Arthurian quest to rename the school.

Now understandably angered by an onslaught that he deemed unfair (and inaccurate), Marty Wilder, Mary Washington's vice president for enrollment, responded with an aggressive defense of the institution's efforts in pursuit of diversity. The Princeton categorization he dismissed as based on flawed and insubstantial evidence. While at pains to make clear that the institution was not satisfied with the status of its minority enrollment, he cited data from the State Council of Higher Education to argue that Mary Washington overall had greater diversity than the recent reports had indicated. In 2004–5, he noted, the school enrolled a higher percentage of black students than James Madison University and only slightly fewer than Virginia Tech, William and Mary, and the University of Virginia. In some categories, the percentage of minority students at Mary Washington exceeded those of several other state institutions; for example, Mary Washington's 3.5 percentage of Hispanic enrollment compared favorably to William and Mary's 3.4 percent, U.Va.'s 2.4 percent, and JMU's 1.9 percent.

On the whole, however, it could scarcely be denied that Mary Washington's student population lacked diversity. Between 1992 and 2001, for example, black enrollment averaged slightly less than 4.5 percent, with a high of 5 percent in 1995. During that same period, white enrollment averaged just under 90 percent.

Development

Fiscal exigencies in the 1990s made it imperative for the College to expand its development efforts. By that time, though Mary Washington was a state-supported institution, less than 40 percent of its overall budget came from state appropriations. The remainder had to be derived from student tuition and fees and from private donations, which were administered through the MWC Foundation.

Extraordinary success in increasing the institution's endowment was wrought during Mickey Dowdy's tenure as head of development, but he left the College in 1993. His immediate replacement was Deal Tompkins, whose stay was brief, as he soon left for a similar position at Randolph-Macon College.

Tompkins was succeeded by Scott Lyons, under whom the College received its first challenge grant. In 1997 former Board of Visitors rector Florian "Red"

Hofer and his wife, Janet, pledged up to $100,000 from which they agreed to match every new or increased gift to the College's fund for the support of special faculty and student activities. The challenge led to more than $650,000 in donations, an increase of 33 percent over the previous year.

Jeffrey W. Rountree

But Lyons, like Tompkins, did not stay long in his post, resigning in 1998. Stability subsequently began to be restored to the department when Ron Singleton assumed leadership of the advancement activities in 1998. He devoted his characteristic energy and enthusiasm toward expanding the College's profile and enhancing its public reputation. Largely through his efforts, an increasing number of faculty members appeared on television and radio broadcasts, and his constant promotion helped to achieve high ratings for the College in educational publications. On a day-to-day basis, his background as a journalist gave him insight that equipped him well to deal successfully with the press.

While still serving as the school's primary press contact, Singleton instituted reforms in the advancement area that regularized its operation. Thus the stage was set in 1999 for hiring a new assistant vice president for College development (subsequently promoted to vice president) who would lead the advancement effort to unprecedented levels of success: Jeffrey W. Rountree.

Rountree grew up in the historic district of Williamsburg, Virginia, and graduated from Mary Washington in 1991. While a student, he was active as a volunteer in the admissions office and frequently assisted in alumni and fund-raising events. Following his graduation, he joined the College staff for one year as an assistant dean in the admissions office. Leaving the College in 1993, he took the first of a series of positions with the American Cancer Society, for which he worked until returning to his alma mater in 1999.

Much of the success that Rountree would achieve was made possible by his special relationship with President William Anderson, a relationship that began upon Rountree's arrival on campus as a student in 1987. As he recalled the occasion many years later:

> I met Dr. A when I was eighteen years old [during] move-in week of my freshman year. My roommate and I were sitting on a bench along Campus Walk watching the world go by as a group of gentlemen stood around the bench talking. When the discussion ended, one of the men, dressed in a suit, extended his hand with a big smile and

welcomed us to MWC. He asked me what my name was, and I said that my friends called me Tree. He said, "Nice to meet you, Tree," and off he went. [My roommate and I] agreed that he was a pretty nice guy, although we didn't know who he was [until] the next evening at a ceremony, we realized that the nice guy on Campus Walk was the president. . . . I was walking through campus about a week later and saw the president coming towards me down the sidewalk. At quite a distance, and before I could say anything, he yelled out, "How are things going for you, Mr. Tree?"

In addition to fund-raising specifically, the College's advancement efforts encompassed several important ancillary enterprises, including publications. That area had long been directed by the widely respected Paulette Watson, whose work had received numerous awards, but she retired in 2004. Her replacement was Anna Barron Billingsley, who moved into the job from a similar position at the University of Richmond. Billingsley was no stranger to Mary Washington, having previously served as an adjunct professor in English, teaching mainly news gathering. With her innovative ideas and her ability to use technological advancements just then becoming available, Billingsley brought to the alumni magazine a more sprightly appearance, using color photographs extensively for the first time.

Another dimension of institutional advancement was alumni relations, where Cindy Snyder '75 had provided leadership since her arrival in 1990. Under Snyder's direction, a number of traditional alumni activities continued, including fall homecoming, an event geared to younger alumni, specifically those who had graduated within the last ten years. The main venue was the Battleground complex, where the featured event (officially, at least) was usually a soccer game, but the main attraction was actually tailgating—until complaints from the surrounding neighborhood and liability issues combined to cause restrictions on the more bibulous aspects of the event. The spring Reunion Weekend continued to be the primary alumni event for older graduates.

Several alumni operations underwent modification. One involved a basic change in the functioning of the Alumni Association's board of directors, whereby its members became more of an overall policy-making body, as opposed to its previous hands-on participation. A key development from a practical standpoint was creation of an alumni e-mail directory.

There was also a revamping of one of the association's most venerable enterprises, the Distinguished Visitor in Residence program. In 1998 the event was changed to the Distinguished Graduate in Residence for two main reasons. For one thing, fees for visitors of the caliber of the traditional DVIR speakers had risen to prohibitive levels; second, considering the high quality of Mary Washington graduates, it seemed appropriate to showcase the College's alumni. The first distinguished graduate in residence was Lynda Richardson '81, who had established an international reputation as a wildlife photographer.[133]

A positive innovation beginning in the early 1990s was creation of a group called the Mary Washington Ambassadors. Composed of student volunteers, the ambassadors helped the Alumni Association with hosting on-campus events and sometimes assisted with off-campus affairs as well. The practice yielded double benefits in that it brought alumni into contact with current students and at the same time built student awareness about alumni activities.

Somewhat less successful around the same time was an alumni-sponsored champagne reception known as Senior Toast, a sort of pre-graduation gift from the Alumni Association to the senior class. Held on the lawn at Trench Hill late in the second semester, the Senior Toast became an extremely popular event—one of the few that brought out the seniors en masse, clad in their spring finery. Unfortunately, it also came to be viewed by the students, in the words of Cindy Snyder, as "an occasion to drink heavily." The inebriation was not merely the result of the champagne actually served by the host association, but by students' tendency to "preload" before the event and to continue to imbibe thereafter.[134]

The result was that the association continued to sponsor Senior Toast but removed the champagne, whereupon the event's popularity declined instantly. That development, along with the "drying up" of other events on campus, created something of a paradox: by the turn of the century, at a time when student behavior was in many respects less restrained than ever, there was less drinking at College-sponsored functions than there had been thirty years earlier.

The Alumni Association undertook a major initiative in 1996 when, at the instigation of its president, Theresa Young Crawley '77, it established the Washington Scholars program, the institution's first full-ride scholarship (tuition, fees, room, and board for four years) based solely on merit. At that time the association contributed $50,000 in endowment funds to begin the program, and the remainder of the $200,000 required for such a scholarship was donated subsequently by longtime MWC benefactor Irene Lundy Brown '39, a member of the College's charter Board of Visitors. The recipient of the first award in 2000 was Christopher MacDonald '04. By 2007, a total of seven Washington Scholarships had been funded, two and one-half by individual donors and the rest by the Alumni Association.

Subsequently the Alvey Scholars program was also established. Like the Washington program, it provided a merit-based full-ride grant, the difference being that the Alvey awards were to be reserved for out-of-state students, which meant that the funding cost was considerably higher. The first such scholarship was made possible by a half-million-dollar gift from Sally Watson Castle of Pennsylvania, a 1955 graduate. It was awarded for the first time the following fall to Michael Kappert, an outstanding scholar and cross-country athlete from Columbia, Maryland.

Overall financial support from alumni increased steadily throughout the 1990s, with the percentage of graduates contributing to the annual fund (usually around a third) consistently ranking at or near the top among Virginia schools. In 2005 annual donations had reached almost $4.7 million, a sum that represented an increase of approximately $1 million over the previous year.

In the first decade of the new century, the development office implemented several productive new strategies, placing greater emphasis on estate and planned giving. In 2002 it established a new policy for donor recognition, including guidelines for naming campus sites. The cost of naming various entities ran from a tree ($2,000) or a bench ($5,000) upward to classrooms ($25,000+), lounges ($50,000+), labs ($75,000+), auditoriums ($100,000+), and buildings ($1,000,000+). Academic endowments ranged from scholarships ($20,000+) to professorships ($250,000+), to endowed chairs ($1,000,000).

In 2004 the gift club structure was reorganized, raising levels of existing categories and creating new ones. Membership in the President's Council, for example, was raised from a minimum of $1,000 to $2,008 and was limited to unrestricted gifts only. (Previously the amount could also include gifts allocated for a particular purpose. The new arrangement was designed to encourage unrestricted gifts that provided greater flexibility in their distribution to meet changing institutional needs.) The Washington Society was established to recognize those who gave in excess of $10,000 annually. An exception for membership in the President's Council was made for younger graduates (within the last ten years) by creating three levels of Eagle Clubs (bronze, silver, and gold) that permitted progressive membership by making gifts ranging from $250 to $1,000.

Lifetime giving was also recognized by establishment of three categories for cumulative gifts: the Campus Walk Society ($100,000+), the Colonnade Society ($500,000+), and the Cornerstone Society ($1,000,000+). The Heritage Society was created to acknowledge sizable deferred gifts such as charitable trusts and bequests.

With the enthusiastic cooperation of President Anderson, two innovative donor cultivation activities were established. One was the President's Book Club, which brought President's Council members together with notable authors for lunch and literary discussion. Inspired largely by the president's wife, Jane, an avid reader, the club had as its first speaker the best-selling author and journalist Willie Morris (later the subject of a biography by Mary Washington librarian Jack Bales). Subsequent speakers in the series included the novelists David Baldacci, Rosamunde Pilcher, and Frank McCourt and the historians David McCullough and James Robertson.

A more ambitious project was creation of the President's Travel Club. The purpose was to provide people of affluence with a first-rate educational excursion led by a member of the Mary Washington faculty. The initial effort in 2003 was a tour of France led by Distinguished Professor of History Carter Hudgins. In succeeding years, the tours included Italy (led by Italian professor Clavio Ascari), England and Scotland (historic preservation professor Brown Morton), the Danube region (Distinguished Professor of German Emeritus Sammy Merrill), the Greek isles (linguistics professor Christina Kakava), and Argentina and Chile (Spanish professor Ana Garcia Chichester '76).

The travel club produced positive results, some of which were more tangible than others. For example, so impressed was alumna Josephine McPherson Heslep '56 by the Austrian performance of the Mary Washington University-Community Orchestra, part of the 2006 Danube tour, that she was moved to donate $1 million. Less tangible, yet influential, was the club's impact on Bill Anderson himself. Having never traveled abroad until the 2003 French tour, he was so enamored with the experience that despite the impediment of his partial paralysis, he became an enthusiastic foreign traveler.

The various endeavors promoted by the entrepreneurial Jeff Rountree, with the wholehearted support and assistance of Anderson, were instrumental in attracting a number of major gifts. By 2007 there were seven donors whose individual cumulative lifetime monetary contributions exceeded $1 million, led by Robert and Alice Andrews Jepson '64 at almost $6.5 million.

In terms of combined donations and pledges, the most generous benefactor was Arabelle Laws Arrington '41, whose gifts totaled more than $7 million. Her philanthropy took several forms. In 1999, for example, she issued a $200,000 challenge designed to inspire greater contributions to the annual fund. The effort was so successful that the following year she issued a second challenge, this time agreeing that if the annual fund raised more than $1 million that year, she would donate $250,000 personally; it did, and she did. A major portion of those funds went toward creating the Arrington Scholarship program for the children of faculty members.

As the institution's hundredth anniversary approached, the development office launched the Centennial Campaign, its first major comprehensive fund-raising effort. Originally scheduled to run from July 1, 2000, to July 30, 2008, its goal was initially set at $40 million. However, when that amount was reached earlier than expected, the goal was increased to $75 million and the deadline extended past the centennial year.

Success of that magnitude led President Anderson to have unbounded confidence in the abilities of its key architect, Jeff Rountree. The admiration was mutual. Recalling Anderson's freshman reference to him as "Mr. Tree," the vice president in 2006 commented that "the only thing that has changed is that now he calls me 'Money Tree.'"

Student Affairs

During the latter part of Bill Anderson's presidency, administrative oversight of student life on campus was largely the province of two people: Vice President for Student Affairs Bernard Chirico and Dean of Student Life Cedric Rucker.

Before coming to Mary Washington, Bernie Chirico, holder of a doctorate in clinical psychology, had taught at several universities, including a number of years at the University of Richmond, where he also worked part-time in the counseling center. While at Richmond, one of his associates was Edith Sheppard Ott '59, who was then a member of the MWC Board of Visitors.

Bernard M. Chirico

When the longtime director of the Mary Washington counseling center, Mary Annette "Toni" Kelly, was diagnosed with terminal cancer, Chirico, at Ott's urging, agreed to help out on a part-time basis at the College's counseling center in 1983–84.

From there, he became director of the center in 1991. Four years later, when Vice President for Student Affairs Joanne Beck retired, he was named to replace her, thus becoming the first male ever to hold that position at the College. He quickly learned that his task would not be an easy one. Having been appointed to take office after the 1995 commencement exercises, he later recalled that he "walked off the stage, and we did our recessional, and as I was walking back, the Honor Council President came up to me and said, 'We've got a problem.' And I guess I'd been vice president, what, thirty seconds?"

It was, of course, that kind of job. Fortunately, Chirico was well equipped intellectually, academically, and temperamentally for it. Despite having to deal constantly with students' most vexatious problems—and that during a time of unprecedented changes in student behavior—he won in the ensuing years the general approbation of the student body while performing tasks and making decisions that were, by their very nature, thankless.

Cedric Rucker's association with Mary Washington College began as a freshman in 1977, and it began inauspiciously. He knew in advance that as an African American male—actually the first to enroll as a residential student at the College—he would be in dual minorities, in terms of both race and gender. But he was ill prepared for the depth of isolation he initially felt, not because he was poorly received by his peers but simply because of the oppressiveness of his perceived difference. On the day he enrolled, he later recalled, "[It] was a heartbreaking day for me because I watched as the rest of my hallmates moved in, and I knew I was coming to an institution which was a predominantly white institution, and I thought I was mentally prepared for that, I really did. But I did not see another black face that day. And I remember that night; I cried because it hit me that things would be a lot more different than I had anticipated. And I was in tears."

Ready to give up, he called his mother to tell her that he wanted to return home to Richmond. Reminding him of his extensive activities during high school, she urged him instead to get involved at Mary Washington—which he proceeded to do, with enthusiasm. He ran for class office and, though defeated in his first try, met many of his fellow freshmen and thus began an undergraduate career of almost constant extracurricular involvement. As a freshman he was a disc jockey for his own radio show on WMWC and subsequently participated in student government and in the anthropology and sociology clubs.

His most memorable undergraduate venture was to found a group known as Rucker's Tuckers. As leader of the group, he soon gained campuswide notice as he and his fellow Tuckers visited dorm rooms dressed in pajamas, nightcaps, and slippers to surprise students on special occasions, such as birthdays, with comical bedtime storytelling. "We wouldn't just read to one person," he recalled. "Roommates, suitemates, and hallmates would all come to listen to the Tuckers," adding, "It was all very innocent."

By the time of Rucker's graduation in 1981, Mary Washington had become in a real sense his home—one that he was reluctant to leave. "I cried two days at Mary Washington," he said, "my first day and my last day, because it broke my heart to leave Mary Washington on graduation day because of all the friends I had established."

When he did leave, it was for the University of Virginia, where he earned a master's degree in sociology. After working in the admissions office at U.Va. for several years, he returned to Mary Washington in 1989 as associate dean of student activities and director of the Woodard Center. In 1999 he was named dean of student life.

From the moment of his return, Rucker quickly regained the popularity, both as an administrator and as a part-time instructor in sociology, that he had known during his student days. As always, he was a dervish of involvement. "He loves working out," said fellow administrator Forrest Parker. "He loves spectator sports, the theater, ballet, opera. He loves jazz music, rap, show tunes, rock, gospel. He loves everything."

Most especially, he loved Mary Washington—and its students, who reciprocated that sentiment. They admired his enthusiasm, his commitment, and his generosity of spirit. They also liked to tease him (which they knew they could do with impunity), especially about his flamboyantly preppy attire. His natural taste in fashion heightened by his sojourn at U.Va., he was easily the best-dressed male on campus (there being, in truth, minimal competition for such title). "Yo, Cedric," said one *Bullet* editorial shortly after his return, "what's up with the drape [sweater] thing? This isn't The

Cedric B. Rucker

University. And how can you go with the preppy stud-boy look and still play Space Shuttle pinball?"

The truth was that, as College physician Pete Overman, who knew Rucker as both a student and colleague, put it, "Students realize that he cares about them and they naturally gravitate to him." Thus, like Bernie Chirico, Rucker enjoyed exceptional popularity in a position that invited animosity because, more often than not, it involved telling students things they did not want to hear.

In addition to Chirico and Rucker, there were many others who played significant administrative roles within the broad area of student life, especially the members of the residence life staff, since they were the ones who had the most direct involvement with the most students. Two in particular stood out. One was Christine Porter, who, as director of residence life, was especially instrumental in integrating the Marye's Heights apartments into the campus residential structure. The other was Raymond Tuttle, who, as director of judicial affairs and community responsibility, played a major role in the effective functioning of the institution's student judicial system and, in addition, was extensively committed to developing residential educational programs to extend learning beyond the classroom.

A major emphasis of the residence life office, especially from the 1980s onward, involved efforts to inculcate racial harmony, heighten multicultural awareness, and promote diversity. Toward that end, the College's Council on Community Values and Behavioral Expectations (the group formed by President Anderson following the threats against black students in Jefferson Hall) periodically sponsored panel discussions and other programs focusing on campus racial issues. One such event was a 1994 diversity seminar titled "Building Community Awareness." The daylong program, which attracted approximately 350 students, faculty, and staff members, was designed to improve campus awareness and understanding of diversity in the matters of race, gender, religion, nationality, and sexual orientation.

The most significant effort in that regard, however, involved establishment of the Multicultural Center, created in 1990 and officially named the James Farmer Multicultural Center in 1998.

The center was headed initially by Forrest Parker, whose previous job at the College had been associate dean of admissions. As head of the center, Parker was specifically assigned to direct the SOAR and Summer Transition programs as well as to coordinate the Martin Luther King Day and Black History Month celebrations. From the time of his appointment, he made it clear that the center's purpose would be to serve not only blacks but all "students of color," including Asians, Hispanics, and Native Americans.

Three milestones in the center's development occurred in 1993: its movement into commodious new quarters on the main floor of Lee Hall, the promotion of Parker to vice president for multicultural affairs, and the hiring of Ameeta Vashee as assistant dean of the Multicultural Center. A vibrant young woman of magnetic personality, Vashee was herself the embodiment of multiculturalism. An Indian, she was born and reared in Zimbabwe before moving to the United States in 1984. Her positive impact on the center was evident from the start. "We see the number of students gravitating to the office increasing," said Parker. "This has to do with her charm and friendly attitude and good listening ear."

Under the direction of Parker and with the assistance of Vashee, the center became an active sponsor of a wide range of campus activities, both academic and social. On the academic side, it provided tutoring services for any minority students requesting such help. It sought to enhance social opportunities for minority students by promoting and assisting minority student organizations. When the center began, only two such groups existed, one for blacks, the other for Asians; but within four years there were eight.

A considerable part of the center's work involved promoting annual events such as Black History Month (February), Women's History Month (March), Hispanic Heritage Month (mid-September through mid-October), and Asian Cultural Week (in November). It also sponsored recurrent campus events such as, beginning in 1992, a cultural retreat to bring together leaders of the various ethnically oriented clubs.

Occasionally the center sponsored events designed to incorporate participation from the larger community beyond the College. Of particular note in that regard was a national education conference titled "Multi-Ethnic Perspectives" held at the local Sheraton Inn Conference Center in November 1996. The meeting used a wide range of workshops, lectures, and entertainment to address matters such as affirmative action; Native American, Hispanic, and Asian cultures; and black-Jewish relations. The featured speakers were civil rights activist Julian Bond and Native American activist Rebecca Adamson.

Of all the center's activities—and abundant they were—the most popular by far, not just for students but for area residents as well, was the Multicultural Fair. Created in 1991, the event became a highlight of the April campus calendar every year thereafter.

The idea for the event came from multiple origins. Forrest Parker avowed that he wanted to establish the fair from his first days on the job; Cedric Rucker promoted the concept in his capacity as chair of the Global Observation Committee; and Brenda King, as director of study abroad programs, was also an advocate. The event was originally named the Multicultural International Festival but was changed to avoid possible confusion with Fredericksburg's Pear Blossom Festival that was held near the same time each year. But whatever its origins and name, the fair attained instant popularity as a unique campus event, a joyful celebration for participants of all ages. Referring to the theme of the 2001 fair, the *Bullet* aptly commented that, in light of the cornucopia available, "it could have been more aptly themed 'Food, Frenzy, and Fun.'"

Multicultural Fair along Campus Walk

As the fair's reputation grew, it became, along with the Christmas pops concert, one of the most successful opportunities for interaction between the College and the community. Regularly drawing as many as four thousand persons, depending on the weather, the fair became second only to commencement in the number of people attracted to campus. As religion professor David Cain once put it, "This almost gives us a glimpse of what the world could be."

As the fair increased in popularity, Forrest Parker issued an injunction to the student body. "If you ever stay on campus for an entire weekend," he said, "this is the weekend to be here."

He was right.

During its first decade, the Farmer Multicultural Center established its popularity among minority (especially black) students was well as its centrality to the College's efforts toward diversity. Largely because of its prominent position, the center became the focus of a heated controversy that began in the summer of 2000.

Part of the issue involved the departure of the center's original director, Forrest Parker, who announced his decision to go on sabbatical for an indefinite amount of time (and from which he did not return to the College). Although the parting seemed amicable on the surface, some observers intuited that he had become increasingly unhappy about his situation, including the change of his title from vice president to dean. There was suspicion, too, that an administration none too happy with Parker had actually eased him out.

Whatever the case, Parker's leaving was less provocative than another development in July 2000: the decision to move the Multicultural Center from its longtime location in Lee Hall to Marye House. The stated administrative reasons for the change were, first, to provide more space in Lee for admissions office operations and, second, to unite the multicultural activities more closely with the overall Office of Student Affairs, which was already housed in Marye.

But to put it mildly, the black students did not buy it, and neither did a number of faculty members, who quickly began to protest the move. Their main criticism was that the move would deprive the center of its highly visible and convenient location by placing it in a less accessible area. In the words of librarian Brenda Sloan, "They're moving it to the back of the bus." Nearly seventy faculty members signed a letter of concern to President Anderson, expressing similar sentiment.

Responding to such expressions of concern, Vice President for Student Affairs Bernard Chirico relented to an extent by permitting the center to retain a presence in Lee Hall in the form of a conference room–lounge, but stood by the decision to reassign the offices of Ameeta Vashee (named acting director in the absence of Parker) and her assistant, Belinda Collins, to Marye House. He also announced that the result would be an increase in staff, space, and financial resources for the center.

Returning students were not mollified by those concessions. A number of minority students spoke out, strongly expressing regret at the departure of Parker and, most of all, at the loss of the Lee Hall location of what many of them fondly called "the Multi." "This is like a home for a lot of people," said one minority student who was a member of the Student Association. "Everyone [at the center] is like family." The president of the Women of Color, Mina Ennin, was similarly disgusted. "The Multicultural Center used to hold meaning for students of color," she announced. "When I returned to campus this fall, I found the Center in shambles. It is a shadow of its former self." The *Bullet* supported the protest, noting in its first editorial of the fall semester that the administration "tried to sneak the changes through during the summer, hoping no one would notice. But the problem is a real one and it is not likely to go away soon."

Faculty members, generally from a group traditionally critical of administration policy on virtually any issue (and especially on matters of race and gender), took up the cause. Psychology professor Carole Corcoran found the situation particularly deplorable in light of studies conducted by her students over the past ten years indicating that racism had actually increased on campus during that time. Specifically, she cited statistics to show that 89 percent of black students indicated in 1998 that they saw evidence of racism, an increase of almost 20 percent since 1988. (Yet whites who took the same surveys indicated that they saw significantly less racism in 1998 than in 1988.)

Writing a guest column in the *Bullet*, sociology professor William Hanson went so far as to suggest that the decision to move the center was part of a larger and more nefarious plan. "Perhaps," he wrote, "there is a desire by some to see [it] just fade away."

Black student disaffection led to the creation of a new organization known as Students Demanding Rights, Education, and Multiculturalism, or DREAM. In a meeting between representatives of the group and President Anderson, the president proved receptive, as he often did, to student demands, agreeing to consider moving Ameeta Vashee's office back to Lee Hall. "If it works better to move her back," he told the group, "we'll move her back." Appreciative but not totally satisfied with that half-loaf solution, DREAM members held a silent protest during the women's soccer game at the October homecoming. Several weeks later they, along with a number of faculty and staff supporters, renewed their protest at a Board of Visitors meeting, wearing red shirts and carrying signs with messages such as "Don't Erase the Footsteps Dr. Farmer Left for Us" and "Missing: James Farmer's Legacy and the Multicultural Center."

Although the board as a whole refused to recognize the demonstrators, two members did agree to meet with them the following day: Vincent diBenedetto, the rector and chairman of its Student Affairs Committee, and Fred Thompson, a black member of the board. Two weeks later, the administration reversed its decision, acquiescing in the return of the center to its previous location in Lee Hall.

Vice President Chirico explained the move as necessary because the issue had become too divisive, causing students to spend inordinate time away from their studies. Some of the protesters bridled at that explanation—Mina Ennin called it "highly insulting"—but they were pleased with the result. To Lee Hall the center returned, and there it remained until a complete renovation of the building forced the center's removal to the Woodard Campus Center in 2007. There was no protest.

With normality restored, the center went about its business of promoting diversity. One effort was through its ongoing Cultural Awareness Series, which continued to sponsor campus visits from black luminaries such as, during Black History Month in 2006, the Pulitzer Prize–winning author Edward P. Jones.

Beyond such specific events, the center tried in sundry ways to make the campus not only a more diverse place but a more comfortable one for Mary Washington's minority students. There was evidence of success. It was not uncommon for minority students to comment that it was the center that encouraged them to remain at the College when other factors tempted them to leave. As Forrest Parker once observed, it seemed that before the center was established, "many [minority students] were visiting Mary Washington for four years. . . . Now they're saying, 'This is *my* school.'"

Campus Police

The MWC Police Department had evolved steadily, if slowly, from its earliest days when "the force" consisted essentially of one or two night watchmen to a bona fide law enforcement outfit by the 1980s. Even so, it continued to be a rather low-key operation under amiable chiefs such as Medford Haynes, Pete Bishop, and Charles Jones.

The move toward a more professional staff began largely with the hiring of a new chief, David Ankney, in 1989. Under Ankney's direction, a training program for officers was introduced, and the office overall became more proactive. Certainly it became better equipped in 1990 with the purchase of two new Jeeps and twelve new Glock 9 mm semiautomatic pistols. The new weapons replaced obsolescent models, worn from years of practice shooting; at least one was of pre–World War II manufacture. Most significant from the students' perspective was the expansion of programs offered by the department, notably courses in self-defense and the creation of both a bicycle patrol and an escort service.

But all apparently was not well internally, as the department experienced continual turnover in personnel that contributed to Ankney's resignation in 1993. His successor, Greg Perry, previously a lieutenant in the department, immediately set about to improve the atmosphere, including tangible manifestations such as relaxing the officers' dress code by replacing neckties with turtlenecks.

Yet within a couple of years, troubles resurfaced, as evidenced by a spate of letters to the *Bullet* decrying police attitudes toward students. Referring to "Gestapo tactics," one junior in September 1996 actually urged that the force be abolished. "A few tormentors . . . who think they can treat people however they want to, have sullied the reputation of the police department. . . . We have been at the mercy of their authoritarian ways for too long, and it is time for them [to go]." Although the department was obviously not going to be abolished, in 1998, for reasons never publicly explained, both Chief Perry and First Lieutenant Steve Simmons were suspended. (Perry later resigned; Simmons was reinstated.)

Thus began several months of turmoil that ended with the hiring of Stanley Beger as chief in mid-1999. His was a popular tenure, as students found him approachable and dedicated. Even the oft-skeptical *Bullet* liked him. Having once labeled him "the College's nice guy with a gun," the paper offered generous praise at the time of Beger's retirement, saluting him in an editorial titled "Bye-Bye to One of the College's Best."

Beger's successor, James Harris, was a former Army lieutenant colonel and the department's first African American chief. He left after only six months. The largely desk-bound job apparently was simply too tame for him. "I could not get law enforcement out of my blood," he explained. "I just could not. I'm a cop. I'm back in [pursuit of] violent crimes. I am a detective. I like chasing bad guys."

After a search for a replacement both outside the College and within, James Snipes, then a lieutenant on the Mary Washington force, was named chief in 2003. Upon taking the job, he expressed the hope of providing stability to an operation that had seen much turnover in the previous dozen years. "I see myself staying here for quite a while," he said. "I love this college."

Irrespective of who was chief, and notwithstanding routine complaints about ticketing procedures, most Mary Washington students likely were satisfied with the police force and felt secure in their environment. The most notable campus disturbance occurred in February 1990 in connection with a "go-go" concert attended, according to the *Free Lance–Star*, by "a predominantly black crowd of 800," many of them nonstudents from the D.C. area. The eruption of several fights caused the concert to be closed down early, after which College police had difficulty dispersing the lingering crowd.

But incidents such as that one were extremely rare. It thus came as a shock to the entire community when the annual college crime report of the Virginia State Police for 1995—widely reported in newspapers across the state (and on the front page of the *Free Lance–Star*)—cited Mary Washington as having the highest crime rate of any college or university in Virginia. According to those statistics, Mary Washington experienced 41.32 crimes per thousand students, ranking it slightly ahead of William and Mary at 40.28 per thousand. Making matters worse, the study indicated the incidence of seven reported rapes, again the highest number in the state; neither the University of Virginia nor Old Dominion reported a single one.

College officials and students were taken aback by the report. The *Bullet* waxed indignant. "It is hard to believe that our campus of 3,000+ students are such hard-bitten criminals. . . . Should we all transfer now? Could that report be any more misleading?"

The paper's wrath was justified once the crime statistics were scrutinized, as College officials (especially the police department) pointed out. For one thing, regulations at MWC, unlike at many schools, called for every theft, no matter how petty, and every breakage, no matter how minor, to be officially tallied, thus inflating the total number of crimes.

The rape statistic was even more misleading in light of reporting practices at other schools. This was because Mary Washington statistics included rapes reported by "third parties"—that is, by observers of the assault—not just by the victims, a procedure used by no other institution in the state. In fact, out of the seven reported at the College in 1995, six involved third-party reports. (All were acquaintance rapes.)

Another telling aspect of the episode—one that went largely unreported—was the College's favorable crime-solving record. The same state crime report that ranked Mary Washington first in crime also contained a "percent cleared" category that showed the percentage of campus crime cases resolved to the victims' satisfaction. In that category, Mary Washington ranked second. "But nobody's reporting that," said Chief Greg Perry. "That's a very positive thing . . . that I pointed out two or three times to the media, [but] they are not reporting it. They are more concerned with the perception of the negative, and they are not giving Mary Washington College a fair review." Interestingly, all seven of the reported MWC rapes in 1995 were cleared, meaning that they were pursued to the extent that the victim desired and all the cases were closed.

The irony of the situation was that most sexual assault professionals at other institutions applauded Mary Washington for its reporting procedures, suggesting that it indicated the existence of a "model combination: aware students that are willing to report crimes and thorough police that actually want all crimes reported."[135] Yet even if the bad press did arise from good causes, the College subsequently changed its reporting system to align more closely with other institutions, and the criminality ranking dropped accordingly.

The *Bullet* had a cogent response to the initial negative report. "Tell your parents to stop worrying and calling every five minutes to make sure you're alive," it suggested. "And to all those non-MWC students who think this place is a breeding ground for crime, you should be so lucky as to live on such a safe campus."

Although the paper was certainly correct in its assertion that Mary Washington was not a "breeding ground for crime," one of its graduates, Erika Grace, did make national news for a grisly episode in May 2002. Reared in an affluent Pennsylvania family, Grace had been an honor student in history and an outstanding Eagles basketball player, who, despite her slight build, was renowned for her ability to hit long-range three-point shots. By the spring of 2002, she was married to a former Navy SEAL named Benjamin Sifrit. The two were convicted of murdering and dismembering a couple whom they had met while vacationing in Ocean City, Maryland. No motive for the crime was ever established, beyond that of a "thrill killing."[136] For her participation, Erika Grace Sifrit—star athlete, cum laude graduate, MWC class of 2000—acquired another designation: Maryland Division of Correction Inmate 920021, sentenced to life plus twenty years.

The Supporting Cast

Going back to the days of Wallace Alsop, a beloved figure from the time of his hiring as a custodian in 1922 until his retirement in 1956 at the age of seventy-five, the College was home to a number of individuals who gained iconic status on campus.[137] Often they were, like Alsop, staff members rather than professors or administrators.

During the 1980s and 1990s, for example, there may have been many students who saw President Anderson only rarely, but they saw Leonard Graves almost daily. Few knew his name, most likely, but Graves was a familiar sight as, constantly puffing on a stubby cigar, he drove an electric cart through campus picking up trash. Working well into his seventies before retiring in 2000, he was so renowned that the *Bullet* published a feature article about him called "Life in the Trash Lane" that included a map of his daily itinerary through the campus.

When it came to distinctive personalities, few could compare to Frances Melle, the flamboyantly dressed (and tressed) cashier in the business office. By the time she retired in 1989, she held the record for the longest employment of any person in the College's history—forty-five years—during which she was a familiar figure to generations of students who came to her office window on the first floor of GW to conduct various financial transactions. Melle's appearance was arresting and her manner outspoken. Once playfully asked by Vice President for Business and Finance Dick Miller, her supervisor at the time, who her favorite was among the bosses for whom she had worked (Edgar Woodward, Edward Allison, and Miller), she replied that she would let him know after she had retired. When that day came, Miller again posed the question, to which she replied, "I didn't like any of you." It was a classic Melle moment and one that delighted Miller. "That," he said, "was Frances."

Many student favorites worked in the area of residence life—which was understandable, given their frequent interaction with students. Among the most popular were Talley Booker, Bette Luttrell, and Valerie Lazzari. There were also other employees who were appreciated for noteworthy contributions, though their work affected students less directly. Among them were, in the C-Shop, Mary Lee Carter and Louise Boxley; in the admissions office, Anne Pitts; in career services, Gail Rouse and Gary Johnson; in Seacobeck, Pat Moore; in the police department, locksmith Robert Tinnell and office manager Phyllis Field; in human resources, Dee Lycett; in the post office, deliveryman Dan Cook; in the business office, Gloria Day; in academic affairs, Amy O'Reilly, Patsy Hockaday, and Virginia Williams; and in the registrar's office, Betty Bradshaw, Susan Colbow, Mary Kemp, and Ann Slayton. Other longtime employees served with skill in several different administrative offices over the course of their careers, including Betsy Chinn, Lucretia Oesterheld, Bonnie Sievert, Mardy Harding, Carolyn Chewning, and Margaret Mock.

Among the most important College employees in facilitating the daily operation of the academic program were the departmental secretaries, who often served as a valuable nexus between students and their professors. Those who served in that capacity for long periods included Dora Minor in the Departments of Political Science, Geography, and Sociology; Lucy Quann in Business Administration; Jean Bennett in Psychology; Joyce Johnson in Math; Jane Clark and Lisa Patton in History, American Studies, and Economics; and Wilma Willard in the natural sciences.

One of the most remarkable staff members during the Anderson years—or any other period, for that matter—was the inimitable Frances Liebenow Armstrong, or, as she was universally known at Mary Washington and in town, "Mrs. A."[138] A 1936 graduate of the College, she continued her association with the institution through volunteer work on behalf of the Alumni Association. Her contributions were so extensive that she was presented with the association's first award for outstanding service, a citation later named in her honor.

In 1981 she retired from her legendary career as a teacher in Fredericksburg, where, as one observer put it, she "ruled [the] classroom with a firm hand and a caring heart." It was only then, at the age of sixty-five, that Mrs. A began her employment at Mary Washington. For a quarter century thereafter, she became the College's ultimate "utility player," working variously for the offices of the president, alumni affairs, and human resources, engaging in numerous tasks: conducting research, compiling indexes, answering phones, helping with mailings, and giving campus tours from a golf cart. In short, as one of her associates put it, "She'd do anything that anyone would ask her to do." And in 2006 she was still doing so—and why not? She was only ninety.

CAMPUS ACTIVITIES

At the beginning of the new millennium, Nina Bushnell had been gone from Mary Washington exactly fifty years. Social and cultural changes in the interim, however, made it sometimes seem more like a half millennium than a half century. The evolution in student life during the last decades of the twentieth century was so sweeping that behavior—in dress, language, entertainment, and sexual relationships—that would have seemed almost unimaginable in the fifties, or even the seventies, was commonplace by 2000.

To be sure, Mary Washington was not unique in that regard, as the lifestyles of college students everywhere (and of society in general) had undergone similar changes. It was just that at MWC the changes somehow seemed more startling, given the contrast between the velvet-gloved gentility (even if enforced gentility) of an earlier day and the less-refined behavior of the new era.

One visible, if superficial, manifestation of cultural change on campus during the Anderson years was student attire. Going back to the 1950s and 1960s, when Mary Washington was still all-female, the predominant fashion style among students was usually described as preppy. With the rise of social protests in the seventies came a more antiestablishment attitude that was reflected in less-traditional dress among students, who by that time also included males.

The greatest challenge to conformity of couture, however, came in the nineties with the popularity of what was known as the grunge look. It was a style, wrote the *Bullet*, that resulted from "a mix between two very different subcultures—the sixties hippies and their offspring, the punks. . . . [It was] a direct reaction against the preppies and the candy-coated pop singing that ruled the end of the eighties. Heavy wool lumberjack shirts, cotton flannels, fishnet stockings, calf-high combat boots, and old T-shirts all became necessary parts of the popular wardrobe, and there was a lack of attention to patterns and colors. . . . The new look sent [students] to their attics and basements, searching through their parents' old clothes."

It also took them to previously undiscovered locations for shopping. Instead of the usual stores such as Abercrombie and Fitch, Express, and the Gap, students now frequented thrift shops, of which Fredericksburg had quite a few, including shops run by the Salvation Army, Goodwill, and the Mary Washington Hospital Auxiliary. It was there that students could find the eclectic collection of outfits to pair with their Doc Martens shoes.

According to a *Bullet* article, "Places to Buy Cheap Stuff," Goodwill was the premier place for the penurious, ranking slightly ahead of the Salvation Army. "It is perhaps the haughtier of the two enterprises," explained the columnist, "boasting a wide selection of white, skin-tight jeans and sweaters that look like they were present at an explosion at the Crayola plant. But if you can force yourself past the lingering funk of old people, wet cigarettes and moth balls, there's no limit to what you may find. . . . Besides, why pay $75 for jeans with holes in them when you could pay 75 cents?"

By the twenty-first century, the grunge look had declined, replaced by several distinctive fashion developments. One fad, applicable to both men and women, involved wearing sandals or flip-flops. Though this was not a new concept for summer attire, many students took to wearing them year-round, even in the coldest weather. Why so? "It's more of a fashion statement," explained one student in 2003. "I just like the 'cool yet casual' look that sandals provide. It's like I'm above even the cold." Others offered more practical reasons. "Sandals are so easy to slip on in the morning," said one. "Also, I hardly ever have clean socks, so sandals are a big help in that area." Paradoxically, feet that were not shod in sandals were often clad in a quite different manner—namely, wool-lined Ugg boots—a more sensible, though not necessarily more attractive, alternative.

Then there was the matter of underwear, notably (for women) the popularity of thongs. The trend was examined in a 2004 *Bullet* article that described the garment as being characterized by "the unmistakable 'T' crosshairs [that] peek out over the top of the belt and take relentless aim at any stray males." The reason for their popularity, according to the article, was that thongs were "the primary weapon in the war against underwear lines. The little fella sneaks up the back way, undetected, and allows the underwear to blend in with its surroundings as if it isn't even there." Why then, the article asked, did women "not just 'go commando' and wear no underwear at all?" Because, it concluded, "a thong generates a psychological sex appeal, which translates into a strong sense of confidence."

A more ubiquitous (and generally more visible) fad among female students was low-rise jeans, which had become so popular, according to the College newspaper, that they were often the only styles carried by most stores. It was a style, said the *Bullet*, that allowed women, "in addition to their washboard stomachs, [to] show off pierced navels."

As professor of theatre and dance Kevin McCluskey (a fashion historian) noted, low-rise pants were not a new phenomenon. "What we have now," he said, "are directly related to the styles of the 1970s called hip-huggers." His departmental colleague Rosemary Ingham, also an expert on fashion design, agreed, but noted, "I definitely think the style is more aggressive than before."

In any event, the new style brought several terms into the vernacular, including "muffin tops" (the fleshy overlap revealed by those who had unfortunately experienced the "freshman fifteen") and "butt cleavage" (self-explanatory). Another benefit—or liability, depending on one's point of view—was that the skimpy attire made possible (sometimes unavoidable) the viewing of tattoos. While not pandemic by any means, such accoutrements were sufficiently visible on campus to make it clear that, as the *Bullet* put it, body art was "not just for bikers and lunatics anymore." In fact, even a few faculty members sported inky designs.

Through all the fashion fads, the preppy look never totally disappeared, merely varying in the extent to which it predominated. During one point of upswing around 2005, it actually became the focus of a whimsical campus debate over the propriety of "popped" (upturned) collars, an affectation of the preppier-than-thou crowd.

The debate began with a September 2004 *Bullet* editorial on the subject. "Everyone has something to say about the popped collar, and the *Bullet* is no exception," it wrote. "The popped collar looks silly. It looks absolutely ridiculous, actually. It almost looks like you crawled out of bed and forgot to roll down your collar. But we have a creeping feeling that you spent an unusually long time in front of the mirror, making sure the collar of your Ralph Lauren polo was perfectly starched and pointing north. As if one wasn't bad enough, when you layer two collared shirts and double-pop it's really bad. . . . It's one thing to look preppy, in moderation, but when a collar is egregiously standing up in all of its wannabe preppy glory, it's more goofy than anything."

That sartorial edict prompted a facetious retort from two seniors. "Popping the collar originated as a visual statement to separate us from the 'help' at our country clubs," they explained. "Unlike foolhardy baggy pants, sideways caps, socks with sandals, and sleeveless shirts, popped collars [also] serve the functional purpose of keeping the sun off our necks when we are sailing or driving our BMW convertibles."

That statement, in turn, elicited a more serious rebuttal from a disgusted student who suggested that "the collar-popping controversy that seems to be topping the war in Iraq as this year's . . . hot debate issue" was proof positive of the "ignorance and stupidity" of the student body. "The whole issue of collar popping," he declared, "is about as ridiculous as the plot in a budget porn video."

Even into the next year, the frivolous debate continued, with the *Bullet* again playing the scold. "With spring comes polo shirts and with polo shirts comes an issue that has taken on a life of its own: the popped collar," read an editorial. "Put it down and leave it down. If you are worried about the back of your neck being exposed to the sun, we recommend sunscreen. No matter what the Snoop Dogg song says, please, don't pop it like it's hot. Because it's not."

Nevertheless, for the most part, J. Crew–style preppiness prevailed—and for some the collars still popped. Cedric Rucker was, after all, still dean.

In the new century, matters of student dress seemed inconsequential indeed compared to matters of student behavior. Although Mary Washington students in many respects mirrored behaviors elsewhere in society, there was one area in which the College's record seems to have been better than that of many other schools: namely, use of illegal drugs. This is not to say that drugs were absent from the campus; indeed, anecdotal evidence from students indicated that drugs, marijuana in particular, were easily available. But as one student summarized it in a *Bullet* "Your Voice" column in 1991: "I think you [can] find drugs here if you want to, but they're not looking for you."

Their apparent prevalence at other institutions led Virginia governor Douglas Wilder that same year to suggest the possibility of mandatory drug testing for all students at state universities. President Anderson quickly condemned the proposal. "I would object to that," he announced. "I think anybody in the United States . . . who suggests that there is no problem in their community or school is not being realistic. But . . . I would emphasize that the vast, vast, vast majority of our student body obeys the law." In any case, he adamantly opposed mandatory testing such as that proposed by the governor. "I personally don't think that . . . you go that far to violate [students'] individual privacy."

The prevailing overall attitude of students was hostile toward drug use; certainly the *Bullet*'s attitude was. Motivated by news of a fraternity bust at the University of Virginia in 1991, the paper editorially urged that the Charlottesville culprits be prosecuted and went on to tout the superiority of Mary Washington's students. "We're sure that there are students here who do use drugs," ran the editorial, "but, for all practical purposes, they keep to themselves. They know that the rest of us think that they are shallow, insecure losers who will never amount to anything. It's comforting to know that the non-users here have not allowed this stupid, inexcusable, despicable practice to become commonplace at Mary Washington."

Certainly the College's official policy was hard-nosed. The campus was declared a drug-free zone, and it was made clear that any student found in possession of drugs was liable for suspension. In 1998–99, the handbook policy was made even less ambiguous, when the previous statement that possession of illegal drugs "may result in suspension or expulsion" was changed to read "*will* result in suspension or expulsion."

Even so, occasional student voices were raised in support of marijuana use. One *Bullet* guest column in 2001 made the tongue-in-cheek suggestion that the College bookstore should expand its inventory beyond the "dusty old books written by professors that no one would even bother to read, texts of German literature, [and] Christmas ornaments with depictions of the Jepson

Science Center." There were a few useful items, the writer admitted, "such as MWC shot glasses," but noted he that as he "walked past an MWC Beanie Baby and thought about all this wasted space, it hit me: bongs, bowls, rolling paper, and other pot-smoking paraphernalia should be sold right here on campus. . . . There are no head shops in Fredericksburg. Where is a student to go for a decent Grafix bong? . . . It's high time the college transform the bookstore into a full-service head shop for all to enjoy. But, there is one thing that should stay in the college's new head shop—all the munchie food."

A more serious column in 2003 criticized the College's anti-drug policy for being overly zealous and for relying on what the writer called "propaganda I could have only expected from the 1930s Reefer Madness era." At that, the advocacy of cannabis was less strident than the pleas delivered by NORML activist Michael Mello during the heyday of marijuana use three decades earlier.

In fact, a Student Wellness Committee survey in 2003 revealed that approximately three-quarters of Mary Washington students had never used marijuana. The committee publicized that finding in a campus campaign that declared, "Most Mary Washington College students don't smoke weed. We're smart like that." Whether that smartness lay in not using drugs, or not admitting it, or just being careful not to get caught—probably some combination thereof—the fact was that in the era of considerable concern over drug use, Mary Washington did not experience inordinate problems.

Alcohol use was a different story. Though not reaching the consumption levels of some other institutions (e.g., the notoriously besotted U.Va.), it was clear by the late 1990s that Mary Washington was generally consistent with the national trend in alcohol abuse, notably binge drinking.[139] The impersonal statistics took concrete form at the College in early 1997 in connection with the senior class's traditional 100th Night celebration. Over time, that celebration had developed into the most raucous on-campus event of the year, anticipated not only by the seniors themselves but by underclassmen who viewed it from afar. To the younger students, said the *Bullet*, it was "a time to drool over the thought of graduation and become green with envy [since] they still have at least another year left, maybe more."

On the eve of the February 100th Night for the class of 1997, the paper's editorial commented admiringly on the group's consumption of nine kegs at their 197th Night bash the previous fall, adding, "The major question is, can they break their record tonight?" Though the editorial cautioned that "seniors must remember to be responsible," the general tone of the piece was carefree. "These nights," it said, "usually move along with [few] or no major incidents. This is fortunate, as drunk people tend to get a little out of hand, and rightfully so. They are graduating, for Pete's sake."

But the paper was too optimistic. On this particular night there was, in fact, a "major incident" when a twenty-year-old senior driving away from the party at the Eagles Nest struck a tree near Monroe Hall, injuring herself and her twenty-one-year-old male passenger. Both, according to eyewitnesses, had been drinking heavily. The wreck, while not producing fatalities, did result in facial injuries that rendered the scene of the accident "extremely bloody," in the words of observers.

The opening of the *Bullet*'s report on the wreck proved prophetic. "The crash heard on Thursday, February 6, was not just the sound of a shattered windshield and twisted automobile metal . . . [but] was the sound of a Mary Washington tradition being broken."

If not broken, the tradition was indeed changed—and quickly. It so happened that one of the first persons on the scene of the accident was Dean of Students Bernard Chirico, who had been at the party before returning to his office in Lee Hall, near the site of the crash. He was traumatized by what he saw. "I took one look at the [male] student," he later recalled. "[It] looked like [he] was going to lose an eye. . . . I saw exposed bones, and I said, 'That's it. We're not going to have any more of these kinds of events. . . . We're going to end 100th Night. I cannot in good faith support and allow these kinds of things to go on.'"

Student reactions to Chirico's decision were predictably negative, bemoaning the fact that a single isolated incident, as they saw it, could have such wide consequences on College policy. Senior class president Michelle Trombetta was especially outspoken, telling the *Free Lance–Star*, "I think it's absolutely crazy. I think it's really unfortunate that because of one person's really stupid decision, a tradition has to be lost. . . . Let's face it. Students are going to drink. Where is it safer? On the confines of campus or a few miles off?" She expressed the same complaint to the *Bullet*, asserting that "if this doesn't go on at the Eagles Nest, everyone will just go to George Street or some other bar. . . . There are so few traditions on campus. It would be tragic if we lost this evening."

A *Bullet* editorial agreed with her assessment. "Graduating and college is about growing up and taking responsibility for one's actions," it said. "Now that the administration has taken this away from us, they might as well slap a diaper on us, for all this is telling us as college students is that we're not going to even give you the opportunity to act responsibly. Here, take your pacifier."

Unmoved, the administration stuck to the new policy, working to develop alcohol-free alternatives to the senior celebrations. The first such effort was Senior Kick-Off, held in lieu of 198th Night in November 1997. In the absence of beer, the main attractions were a variety of free refreshments, impressive door prizes (including televisions, VCRs, and gift certificates), and a live band, Guster. The results were mixed. Though some disgruntled seniors boycotted the event in their pique over the absence of alcohol, the several hundred who attended appeared to be generally (perhaps surprisingly) pleased, taking it all with good humor. "We have enough Coke," said one. "We're just missing the rum." The result, in another senior's estimation, was that no one had "seen this many sober people in one place in a long time."

The next February the Dean's Office, together with Class Council and Giant Productions, sponsored a surrogate 100th Night called Senior Countdown. The general format was the same as that for Senior Kick-Off, as were the student responses. In both cases, the elaborate on-campus (alcohol-free) party served for many students as a "pre-gamer" for more intoxicating activities later in the evening at local pubs like the George Street Grill and Spanky's. Clearly the more restrictive alcohol policy did not prevent students from drinking, though it did decrease it, at least under College auspices.

In any event, the new policy had the practical result of reducing the College's liability and the more general effect of removing the perception of institutional condoning of alcohol use. Accordingly, the restrictions became permanent, and the practiced debauchery of senior parties passed, for better or worse, into history.

It was clear that the College was making a serious effort to address the matter of alcohol consumption. In November 1997, President Anderson agreed to serve on a statewide panel to study methods of curbing drinking among college students, and Dean Chirico was subsequently appointed to that panel. At the time the committee was formed, Anderson expressed his view that "alcohol abuse is the number one problem that colleges and universities have to wrestle with, and I suspect it's the number one problem for all young adults."

In 1998, as part of Judicial Awareness Week's alcohol education program, the College sponsored a talk by Lori Williams, who had been the RA on duty in Westmoreland when Chris Goode died of alcohol poisoning in 1987. In a graphic speech, Williams told how it was a ritual for Goode and his friends to draw or write on the bodies of unconscious fellow students. "I'm going for some shock value here," she began her remarks, and went on to describe Goode's body as being covered in vomit, his own excrement, and obscene markings. "His friends' last picture of him," she said, "[was] that smell and writing."

Also in 1998, Mary Washington received a $2,500 mini-grant from the Virginia Department of Alcoholic Beverage Control, designed to improve alcohol-abuse education on campus. The College subsequently developed several substance-abuse educational programs called Happy Hour and Last Call, as well as creating the Natural Highs, a peer education group that produced various activities in the residence halls to emphasize alcohol-free social activities.

In addition to programs designed to dissuade students from drinking, the College in 1997 established a program known as Night Haven to assist those who still overindulged. Specifically, its purpose was to offer an alternative to jail time for students found drunk in public. (In the previous school year, fifty-three students were charged with that offense, forty-four of them male.)

Located in the basement of Madison Hall, the Night Haven facility was equipped with cots and staffed by student volunteers, members of AWARE (Advocating Wellness and Responding to Emergencies) who were trained in basic first aid and CPR, as well as given assertiveness training. Students apprehended by campus police who opted for Night Haven were periodically checked with a breathalyzer and allowed to leave only when their blood alcohol level dropped to .02, which sometimes took several hours.

Night Haven, however, was not exactly the "get-out-of-jail-free" card that it seemed. Those who used the program could use it only once, after which any further arrests would result in jail time. Moreover, after their release, offenders were required to attend alcohol-awareness classes and write papers about alcohol and the behavior that put them in Night Haven. Some students complained that such requirements deterred people from using the campus facility, but others found it a highly preferable alternative to "going downtown." "It was embarrassing," said one Night Haven participant. "[But] it was better than going to jail."

Despite the College's best efforts, sobriety did not become a major campus priority, judging by various *Bullet* articles. Drinking games remained popular, including one called beer pong (also called Beirut or Scud) that had been around for decades in various parts of the country but became hot on campus only in the new century. The game centered on hitting Ping-Pong balls into plastic cups with paddles—or more commonly, throwing them in—with the defending team required to drink the beer in those cups. For a while the game was so popular that it grew from being just a party game to a team competition, with the establishment of the so-called MWC men and women's Competitive Pong League (not an officially sanctioned club, of course). "It's a fun game," explained one of its devotees, "and it's one of the best ways to get people who don't know each other to open up. People like sports, and people like drinking, so it's a perfect combination."

Beer, for sure, remained the beverage of choice—or perhaps of economic necessity. A *Bullet* article in 1999 titled "Drinking Dirt Cheap: A Guide to the Best of the Cheap Beers" listed the top five brands selling for under five dollars per twelve-pack, with a brief commentary on each:

5. Olympia ($4.19). Only in a fit of desperation is it acceptable for anyone to consume this beverage.
4. Pabst's Blue Ribbon ($4.98). The taste of PBR is verging on repugnant.
3. Natural Light ($4.99). "Natty" goes down smooth and comes up easy. . . . Drink it after an Olympia, and you may think that Zeus has just slipped you some of his finest nectar.
2. Milwaukee's Best Light ($4.19). "Beast" is one of the smoothest beers ever made. [It] is such a tremendous deal for the quality that it has changed the lives of more students than their teachers have.
1. Miller High Life ($4.99). Some find the taste of High Life a bit harsh. This comes from too many years of deluging ourselves with watery

> beers. It has taste. Not the best taste, but taste. In the end, it really doesn't matter. After the third beer they all begin to taste the same (except for Olympia, [which] never gets good). But those first few beers can be important mood-setters for the evening, especially if love interests are involved.

For those who overindulged, there was a subsequent *Bullet* article titled "Eat, Drink, and Be Sick," subtitled "Tips to Cure a Hangover." Among the suggested remedies were standard ones such as drinking plenty of water or downing "a Bloody Mary or a bullshot" (a Bloody Mary made with beef bouillon instead of tomato juice), as well as more exotic protocols such as "a cold bath, some ginseng tablets, . . . and yoga." For further research, readers were directed to a Web site called all-about-hangovers.com. Evidently Mary Washington students were not turning into teetotalers. Most observers agreed, however, that things would have been worse had there been fraternities.

Few issues at Mary Washington College ever arose with such persistence as the question of establishing fraternities and sororities. Although such an action would run counter to the school's traditional opposition to exclusive social organizations, dating to the 1940s, movements cropped up almost annually to create a so-called Greek system on campus.

One such effort occurred early in Bill Anderson's presidency, leading to a student body referendum on the matter. The *Bullet*, in an editorial titled "Who Needs the Greeks?" expressed staunch opposition, on several grounds, including the costs involved in membership. "Students who are on a tight budget or putting themselves through school are automatically left out in a Greek-less cold. Purposely or not, relative wealth becomes a standard for admittance."

An even more detrimental drawback, the editorial pointed out, was the exclusivity of fraternities and sororities. While conceding that such groups might serve a positive purpose on larger campuses, "here, they would only serve to divide," it argued. "Our campus is too small to withstand students sneering at each other because of the letters on their sweaters." Most students apparently agreed, as the proposal was defeated by a substantial margin.

Yet the issue surfaced again the next year, leading to still another referendum, this one on the question of whether the Student Association should establish a committee to study the possibility of introducing a Greek system. This time, with the *Bullet*'s endorsement, the proposal received approval from the majority of students voting in the referendum.

While the debate was going on, a small group of male students, unbeknownst to most people on campus, had initiated an unofficial organization known as Delta Sigma Nu, with the intention of eventually affiliating with the national Sigma Nu fraternity. By the spring of 1985, the fledgling group had fourteen members and had engaged in fund-raising efforts for the American Cancer Society and the March of Dimes. When it applied for official club status at the College, however, it was rejected by the Inter-Club Association (ICA) and soon thereafter disbanded.

Meanwhile the SA study committee on the Greek system, headed by Abas Adenan (later appointed to the College's Board of Visitors), reported in 1985 that discussions with College officials led to the conclusion that such a system "didn't look feasible" at the time. "The administration," read the report, "hopes that through the new student center, as well as through other planned additions, the college will be able to attain the same ends that a Greek system provides." Adenan himself was convinced that there was still strong support for fraternities and sororities and predicted that "the issue isn't dead yet."

Events soon proved him correct. Within two years, in fact, a group of male students formed an organization that would become Kappa Delta Rho fraternity. Though the group professed to have other purposes as well, its president, John Woodworth, publicly stated that the main motivation for forming the fraternity was "dissatisfaction with the social life" that needed to be addressed "before students will be proud of Mary Washington as a place to stay and live, instead of a school that witnesses a mass exodus every Friday afternoon."

Opponents denied that campus social life was inadequate, contending instead that it was the allure of nightspots in nearby Washington and Richmond that attracted students off campus. As one of them put it, "Moving the college to a wheat field in Iowa would be the most effective way to keep students on campus on weekends."

The *Bullet*, switching sides yet again, expressed disgust with the whole idea of fraternities and sororities. "Here we go again," sighed a March 1989 editorial, and proceeded to lay out a litany of opposition to a system that, it charged, promoted "cliques, conformity and elitism": "MWC's small size builds a sense of community, and this would be destroyed by a Greek system. . . . There may also be unnecessary, harmful cruelty inflicted on students due to the selection process and initiation rituals. . . . Accounts of hazing range from dehumanizing acts to even death. . . . [The system] condones and even encourages overindulgence of alcoholic beverages. . . . Under the guise of respectable motives, Greek parties are often just excuses for drunkenness . . . that involve sexual assaults, destructive parties, and racial insults. . . . MWC does not need to be Greek."

Acting on such sentiments, a group of students organized a petition campaign that secured over two hundred signatures in opposition to a Greek system with the intention of presenting the statement to the Board of Visitors. "Social life here is perfectly fine," said one of the petitioners. "We stay on campus every weekend so that we don't miss anything."

The protesters' concern was unnecessary, at least in the case of Kappa Delta Rho. When the fraternity sought recognition from the College, it was rejected on the grounds that it did not conform to the institution's club policy, which, as stated in the *Student Handbook*, decreed that "the college will refuse to recognize student groups that discriminate membership based upon race, color, religion, disability, national origin, political affiliation, marital status, sex, or age." The fraternity was thus precluded, said Dean of Students Joanne Beck, because of its prima facie discrimination on the basis of sex.

When fraternity members questioned the existence of club sports based on sex, such as women's rugby or men's crew, the director of campus recreation, Jean McClellan-Holt, pointed out that the constitutions of those clubs stated specifically that they were open to all students, regardless of gender. "If [males] want to join the women's rugby club," she said, "they can do that."

Having thus been rejected, the fraternity considered suing the College, claiming infringement of its First Amendment rights of assembly, and even took the improbable course of trying to enlist the aid of the ACLU in that effort. When the ACLU refused—"our last chance," said a frat spokesman—Kappa Delta Rho soon became defunct.

It was a curious time nationally for the whole Greek concept, as *Time* magazine reported in April 1990. On the one hand, the article said, fraternities were "under siege," suffering restrictions (or abolishment) by colleges that were finding Greek behavior increasingly antithetical to institutional advocacy of diversity; there was also growing concern about legal liabilities relating to hazing and initiation rites. On the other hand, "Paradoxically, these restrictive measures come at a time when Greek life is enjoying a nationwide renaissance. Fraternity membership has mushroomed . . . [since] the long-haired '70s ; sororities have shown a similar resurgence."[140]

So it was at Mary Washington with the formation of a sorority, Kappa Gamma Sigma, in 1988. Like the proponents of the ill-fated fraternity, the organizers of the sorority were motivated mainly by social considerations. As Jill Betourné, its president, put it, "The fall of my freshman year, I came out of my room one Saturday morning and found that out of the thirty girls on my hall, only four had stayed that weekend. There weren't enough reasons for us to stay."

Like the fraternity before it, the sorority eventually sought official recognition, an important step to be able to identify itself with the institution, to be eligible for funding from the student finance committee, and to compete on an equal basis with other clubs for use of campus facilities. In an effort to achieve recognition, it tailored its constitution to provide for open membership and declined to seek affiliation with a national Greek organization (whose bylaws sometimes contained provisions that would have been unacceptable at Mary Washington).

Nevertheless, the prospect of the sorority's acceptance elicited opposition from certain segments of the student body. The president of the campus NOW chapter, for one, pointed out that many students were attracted to Mary Washington because of its lack of fraternities and sororities. "For people who like big Greek systems, they should go to UVa or James Madison University," she said. "It divides a college up and we're small already." The president of the Gay, Lesbian, and Bi-Sexual Student Association issued a more specific charge. "Intended or not," he said, "a near-Greek system would foster sexism and homophobia." Consequently, when the vote for approval came up before the ICA, which was composed of the heads of approved clubs on campus, it failed (narrowly) to secure the two-thirds vote of approval needed for acceptance.

The outcome not only caused disappointment within the sorority but also drew attention from beyond the campus, in particular evoking the wrath of the *Richmond Times-Dispatch*. The conservative paper, in an editorial titled "Greek to MWC," used the episode to launch an attack on what it viewed as "a vivid example of just how far the hallowed concept of 'diversity' extends in the modern academy." Citing the "asinine comments" of the NOW and GLBSA representatives, the paper huffed, "So it's come to this: a Greek organization that offers a traditional social outlet for male-female dating while also doing volunteer work for needy citizens is reviled as 'sexist,' 'elitist' and 'divisive' while the college sanctions all sorts of kook-left outlets. How inclusive, after all, is a group that celebrates nothing more ennobling than aberrant sexuality? It looks from here as though MWC's feminists and homosexuals are practicing their own form of elitism: groups that don't subscribe to their agenda are to be banished."

Despite the setback of nonrecognition, Kappa Gamma Sigma persevered as an unofficial sorority, occasionally even participating in College activities such as the annual fund-raising phonathon. In 1991, however, it created considerable hostility on campus when it became known that the sorority was maintaining a file of tests and notes for use by its members, raising in the minds of some the possibility of honor violations. Opinion was divided as to whether the practice constituted a breach of the honor system. The sorority president insisted that it did not, claiming that one member of the honor council had explicitly assured her that "any material that a professor returns is fair game and you can do whatever you want with it." Some professors declared that they had no problems with such a file. "Many of us give out reviews for tests [anyway]," said biology professor Mary Pinschmidt. "I personally don't have a problem with it, except that it is unfair to other students."

Others held an opposite view. "I can't imagine a professor saying, 'I hereby release this test to only members of the sorority,'" said Vice President Roy Weinstock. Another administrator agreed, saying, "Whether or not it is a legal violation, it violates the spirit of what this place is all about. . . . It is truly against the spirit of the honor code and probably against some of the letter of it."

The matter quickly became moot. Nellie King, president of the Honor Council, asserted that while she did not regard the existence of test files per se as an honor offense unless there were specific examples of professors who forbade having their tests on file, she nevertheless viewed "any sort of information bank [as] an unfair advantage." Accordingly, she informed the sorority president that she believed the file to be inappropriate—and the sorority complied by immediately destroying its contents. In fact, the sorority president said, "It was used so little that we didn't even care if it was dissolved." With that, the controversy ended.

Although the brief controversy was thus resolved amicably, the sorority itself did not fare well. Never able to achieve official recognition, it, too, soon dissolved.

Ironically, in light of frequent charges of racism against the Greek system, one of its most vocal advocates in the nineties was David White, a 1992 graduate who was hired by the College as an assistant dean for admissions. Given the charge of trying to increase black enrollment, White regarded the Greek system as an attractive feature to many potential applicants. He himself founded a group called College Ambassadors for Multi-Ethnic Outreach to help recruit black students, but that effort, he said, was insufficient. "Sure, MWC has groups like the Black Student Association, Brothers of a New Direction (BOND), and Women of Color, but that's not what [black] people are looking for," he asserted. "When people look at a college, they look for something to identify with."

According to White, the Greek system, next to the church, was one of the most important social institutions within the black community, not only because of the purpose that it served during the college years but also for the support that it provided thereafter. Faith Christmas, the student who had been racially threatened in fall 1992, agreed that minority students would benefit from a Greek system because it "would serve us in inviting African-American students to the campus and it would also help in the retention of those students. . . . I think the idea is long overdue." Despite such expressions of support, no Greek organization was developed for black students.[141]

By far the most successful fraternity effort at Mary Washington involved Psi Upsilon. Established by a group of about two dozen men in 1994, it quickly achieved "colony status" with the national organization. Like previous Greek groups, it sought official recognition from the College—and, like them, it failed.

The difference was that Psi Upsilon persisted, even establishing an alumni association for its graduates in 1998. Though having no official status, the frat managed to create a sort of cohesiveness by arranging for many of the brothers to live in South Hall for some years, though most members eventually moved off-campus.

Despite the protestations of its members that Psi Upsilon was not a re-creation of the notorious "Animal House," the frat did manage to find itself involved from time to time in questionable episodes. On one such occasion, for example, three brothers were discovered sitting naked in the parlor of South Hall—an incident that led to a chiding *Bullet* editorial titled "Put Your Clothes On": "You would think a fraternity who is trying to get recognized by the school would be a little bit smarter than to run around naked. What exactly did that prove? . . . Not only was this activity unconstructive, but it was also uncreative. The soccer team already pulled this stunt. When [they] did this, they got suspended. Obviously that meant running around naked is frowned upon. The fraternity is going to have to do more than strip to impress people around here." Another incident blemished Psi U's reputation in 2003 when several members were arrested for public drunkenness outside the frat's "Endless Summer Beach Party" at Houston's Steakhouse and Saloon in downtown Fredericksburg.

But the fraternity's behavior was not always so bumptious. It also upheld its avowed commitment to service by efforts such as working on river cleanups, volunteering at Hope House, and raising money for disaster relief (e.g., contributions to the Red Cross and a donation of over $2,000 for the victims of 2005 Hurricane Katrina); its 2007 "Pink Party" was dedicated to generating support for breast cancer research. Even the *Bullet*, not usually sympathetic to the fraternity concept, admitted that "Psi Upsilon fulfills its role in the community and the school, proving it is not a stereotypical fraternity."

Perhaps encouraged by the success of Psi Upsilon, another group, Alpha Phi Omega, sought official recognition as a fraternity on campus. It seemed to meet the requisite standards, meeting all College policies on clubs and declaring itself open to both men and women; its paramount purpose, it averred, was community service.

Yet the *Bullet* spoke out against it. If community service was the members' goal, it asked, could they not just as easily work through COAR or Circle K? What the paper feared most was the precedent. "Even though this fraternity may not be your typical one, with kegs and tiresome rituals," it warned, "the acceptance of it will only lead to more fraternities at Mary Washington. Pretty soon, social fraternities will be whining, 'Since we already have this one, why can't we have more?' The acceptance of APO will only open the door for more fraternities to exist here."

Though Alpha Phi Omega thus died aborning, the brothers of the still-unofficial Psi U, reveling in their underground status, chugged on.

The Honor System

The most venerated of all traditions at Mary Washington was the honor system. For the most part, it had functioned quietly since the controversies of the early 1970s, but it became the focus of increased attention in the eighties. The rise of contention was sparked by the College's decision in the spring of 1983 to station a security guard outside the bookstore, an action—soon reversed—that some students, according to the *Bullet*, regarded as "a slap in the face of the honor system." When students were asked for their opinions on the matter, reported the paper, "Most replies were simply 'it stinks,' or something similar, though often more obscene."

The action prompted a spirited defense of the system, including a *Bullet* op-ed article that declared, "More than rules and procedures, pledges and honor cards—the honor system is a standard of life that is unmatched anywhere, by any society. . . . The amount of trust offered to us by the rest of the world is nil. But under the honor system our word is literally good as gold. . . . An honor trial itself is a monument to the highest standards of justice. But the greatest responsibility for the system lies with us, the students."

The *Bullet* itself, in an editorial, praised the system as one of the most distinctive and commendable aspects of life at Mary Washington. Moreover, it asserted, the system was

> one of the few administrative acknowledgments of our adulthood. During most of our Mary Washington careers, we are subject to "Momism." We are trusted to bring guests in and out of our rooms only at certain times; we are forced to attend class rather than doing so of our own good sense; our consumption of alcohol is limited as to time and place. The honor system, on the other hand, provides us with a refreshing sense of freedom. When faculty members leave the room while we take a test, they are treating us as we deserve, as trustworthy students. The honor system also affords us the freedom to leave our belongings unattended outside Seacobeck and to leave our rooms unlocked if we choose. Furthermore, we are provided the freedom to try those who violate the code. The system, then, entirely in our hands, is our one claim to autonomy.

In an effort to promote the system and make it more effective, the Honor Council in 1986 established Honor Awareness Week. Among other educational activities, the council held a mock trial to show students how trials were conducted. (Most, fortunately, would not otherwise know, since requirements of confidentiality in real cases meant that only participants would witness the proceedings.)

Despite the educational efforts of the Honor Council and despite periodic expressions of approbation by student leaders and the administration, by the late 1980s there was a fairly pervasive, if inchoate, perception that all was not well with the system. The disquietude grew from diverse sources. Some faculty, for example, wondered if the changes in American society in general had not overwhelmed older concepts of honor, rendering a system based on personal integrity ineffective if not totally obsolete. On a more practical level, others questioned whether the system could survive a more heterogeneous student body wherein many students had little, if any, prior acquaintance with academic life under an honor system. Moreover, from the student perspective, yet another criticism of a different sort arose: namely, that the Honor Council itself had become an elitist clique unresponsive to the "average" student's concept of justice.

Eventually the *Bullet* spoke out boldly against the system. "I'm mad," wrote the editor. "I'm mad because the Honor Code is nothing more than a pretty façade for a pretty campus that most students do not take seriously. . . . The Honor Code does not have consistency, does not command authority, and is outmoded. The original concept may have been plausible for nineteenth century students, but it is not for twentieth century students. . . . In its current condition, the Honor Code is a charade."

In light of such concerns, the Board of Visitors in 1988 created a special investigating body—the Honor System Advisory Committee—to conduct a thorough evaluation of the problem. According to Rita Morgan Stone '50, rector of the Board of Visitors, the College's governing body had every confidence that the honor system was still viable; yet the board felt it prudent to have a fresh, dispassionate appraisal—and one as comprehensive as possible. "We instructed the committee to examine every facet of the system," she recalled, "and we put no constraints on what they could recommend in terms of changes."

The advisory committee of twenty persons, drawn from the faculty, administration, and student body, was co-chaired by Sammy Merrill, professor of modern foreign languages, and Jannan Holmes '89, a senior member of the Honor Council. Meeting throughout the 1988–89 session, the committee held open hearings, solicited commentary and advice from all quarters, and conducted an extensive survey of the College community to ascertain the prevailing attitude toward the honor system on the part of each constituent group.

Within the committee, a fundamental debate developed over the feasibility—indeed, the desirability—of an honor system within contemporary higher education. As Professor Merrill explained it in the committee's report to the board, it boiled down to a "real world versus ideal world" argument. On the one hand, advocates of the real-world position contended that given the pervasive "reality of crime and unethical behavior in the highest of places," any attempt to maintain an honor system "can only be a starry-eyed, benighted, and inevitably ineffective way of preparing students for the harsh realities of an imperfect world." On the other hand, advocates of the ideal-world position maintained precisely the opposite: "Because the world *is* so immoral, college should be the one place where . . . ideals of morality should be inculcated in order to influence young people positively and to help fortify them to effect change."

A new committee, chaired by history professor William Crawley, worked throughout the 1989–90 session to implement the main ideas for change, if not always the specifics, recommended previously by the Advisory Committee. One of the most keenly debated issues was whether to incorporate faculty representatives as voting members of the Honor Council—a change ardently opposed by the council's president Monica Rowan and the other student members of the committee. The honor system, she argued (correctly), had from its inception been in the hands of the students, and to "dilute" it with faculty involvement would undermine student support. "Our system has always relied on the students for its strength and its enforcement," she said. "If they can't be trusted to run it themselves, it can't survive anyway."

The revised constitution that eventually emerged from the committee increased the participation of faculty as *advisers* but did indeed preserve the authority of the students alone to actually administer the system. The new document was overwhelmingly approved by the student body in a March 1990 referendum, was officially adopted by the Board of Visitors in May, and became effective with the beginning of the 1990–91 session. Inauguration of the new constitution was accompanied by the publication of the *Honor System Guidebook*, an innovation designed to provide each member of the College community with a convenient reference for understanding the system's operation.

Although the revised constitution included a number of notable changes, the most significant by far was the establishment of a jury system. Under the new rules, trials were still conducted by the Honor Council, consisting of representatives elected, as before, by the members of each class. Verdicts, however, were now to be determined not by the council itself but by a nine-member jury randomly selected from the student body. It was the jury that determined guilt or innocence. In cases ending in conviction, the Honor Council then levied an appropriate sanction, ranging from probation, to suspension, to dismissal.

The jury format made the Mary Washington system highly unusual, if not unique, among the honor systems at Virginia colleges and universities. There were two advantages to such a system, according to Monica Rowan: first, "It eliminates the concern that the system is controlled by any sort of elite," and second, it increases students' awareness and involvement because "they know they may be called on for jury service at any time—and they'd better be prepared."

Although the jury system was certainly the most radical change, the new constitution also embodied other notable elements: establishment of an Honor Advisory Board to serve as an initial screening mechanism—a sort of grand jury—to determine whether a reported violation warranted an honor trial; provisions to ensure that both the accuser and the accused had comparable access to both student and faculty advisers; increase in the number of Honor Council members and faculty advisers; establishment of graduated penalties for repeat offenders; and a requirement that summaries of all trials (without names of the individuals involved) by published in the *Bullet*.

The last provision quickly led to a clash between the Honor Council and the *Bullet*, which took the position that the council could not mandate what the paper published—nor could the administration, for that matter—and that the attempt to do so constituted a violation of the paper's First Amendment rights. The paper asserted that it would run trial summaries only as paid advertisements.

The issue, of course, was not one of money but of principle, with each side taking what it deemed the high ground. The Board of Visitors, supporting the position of the Honor Council, proceeded to pass a resolution proclaiming that the newspaper had "an institutional responsibility to inform the college community of the activities of the Honor Council." The chair of the faculty advisory committee to the Honor Council, librarian LeRoy Strohl, concurred, pointing out that the paper was financed by student fees and that the results of trials were of "great interest" to the students. Thus the paper, he said, had an obligation to report the results, "unless they think the Honor System is not important to the campus."

The *Bullet* held fast to its position. As its associate editor, Andrea Hatch, put it, "A government body cannot dictate what the newspaper prints. . . . Because we can't cover the trials the way we want to through reporting, they shouldn't be able to force us to report it the way they want." The *Bullet*'s faculty adviser, English professor Steve Watkins, agreed, pointing out that state and federal courts had "ruled in more than sixty cases that college student publications have the same protection under the First and Fourteenth Amendments as commercial presses."

In subsequent years, something of a truce prevailed in which the Honor Council was allotted space for a periodic column in which to discuss various developments regarding the honor system, though the paper continued to refuse to publish trial results. In 2001 the Gordian knot was cut by the sword of technology when the council, under its president Andy Painter, began to make trial results available online. It also soon began to publish an occasional paid section in the *Bullet* called "The Gavel."[142]

The efficacy of the new system was uncertain. The jury system did alleviate the concern about control being vested in one group that, as its critics claimed, were "on a power trip." But the question was: did it work as well as the old system?

One striking result was the decline in the number of guilty verdicts. During the five calendar years before implementation of the jury system, there had been an average of approximately ten convictions per year; in the five years thereafter, the number dropped to between three and four. Several explanations were proffered by Honor Council members. Some suggested that randomly selected jurors did not possess sufficient understanding of procedural matters to decide responsibly; others believed that jurors tended to be overly sympathetic to accused peers.

Another faculty member intimately acquainted with the honor system over the years at Mary Washington addressed the heart of the matter. "If a person demonstrably breaks the honor code and students aren't willing to convict him," he said, "the honor system is lost and we need some other system of ensuring that justice is upheld."

In any case, the system stayed—remaining largely unchanged for over a decade. Around the turn of the century, however, the honor system once again became a controversial topic on campus. Part of it resulted from personal actions by some Honor Council members, including the resignation of one council president for alleged sexual improprieties and the conviction of a vice president in Fredericksburg District Court for debit card theft.[143]

Also, in the fall of 2003, there occurred the largest instance of mass cheating in the school's history when twelve students were brought to trial for cheating on the information and technology proficiency tests required of all entering students. Vice President for Academic Affairs Philip Hall viewed the episode as understandable, though not excusable. "Students regard [the test] as a nuisance rather than an integral part of the academic program," he commented, "and it seems not to occur to them that using somebody else's answers to make the requirement go away is actually cheating. However, cheating is cheating, whatever the context."

Moreover, direct attacks on the system were beginning to arise from students who had been found guilty of honor violations. Historically, most convicted students took advantage of the system's confidentiality provision and chose to remain anonymous. But in 1998, one student, suspended for a semester and ordered to perform community service for forging advisers' names on registration forms, decided to make his case public. His particular complaint was against the notation of the offense on his permanent record. "What I did," he protested, "should not stay with me for the rest of my life."

The issue generated heated debate on campus, with sentiment fairly well divided.[144] An Honor Council random poll of 116 students in November 1998 found 43 favoring the notation of convictions in the permanent record, 40 opposing it, and 33 believing that it should depend on the offense committed. (The same survey indicated that 93 percent of the respondents regarded the honor system as either "very effective" or "fairly effective.")

Five years later, another case involving a similar complaint led to a lawsuit against the College that was settled out of court. Such developments led the Board of Visitors to request the Honor Council to consider the matter of transcript notations, especially because Mary Washington was the only college or university in the state system that continued to list all convictions on students' permanent records. "The problem we have now," explained Vice President for Student Affairs Bernard Chirico, "is that people who graduated twenty years ago are calling us and complaining that they are having problems getting, for example, security clearance over a minor infraction that is still on their transcript."

For over two years, the matter was debated, eliciting passionate reactions on both sides of the issue among both students and faculty. Typical of student opinion in favor of eliminating the notations (or at least certain categories of them) was the junior who told the *Bullet* in early 2006 that he was appalled by the possibility of anyone's being barred from graduate school because of "the one time you stole Jell-O from the Nest or whatever." On the other side were those like the junior who recalled that "when I came here for my school tour, the Honor Code was one of the big factors in my decision to come to Mary Wash. And now it seems like it may be in jeopardy."

After seemingly unending debate involving an open forum and numerous *Bullet* articles and letters to the editor, a proposal for constitutional revision was devised. According to the proposed guidelines, the length of time that a violation and sanction would remain on the transcript would vary according to the severity of the penalty imposed. Lesser infractions, such as those resulting in penalties of social probation or community service, would be removed upon the student's graduation. In cases of more severe offenses, such as those resulting in suspension, the transcript notation would remain for five years after graduation. In the most extreme instances, such as expulsion, the notation would remain permanently as part of the student's record. Also, if the penalty involved failure of a class because of an honor violation (e.g., cheating or plagiarism), the notation would also remain permanently on the transcript.

As the matter approached resolution, some faculty came out in opposition to the revision, including political science professor Jason Davidson. Though careful to emphasize his belief that it was the students themselves who should ultimately decide the issue, he offered a motion in the faculty senate to urge the proposal's rejection by the students and the Board of Visitors. "By taking certain violations off the transcript," he reasoned, "we are saying that students can engage in certain levels of cheating with very little negative ramification." His motion before the senate failed by a mere two-vote margin.

In the days leading up to a student referendum on the issue, traditionalists engaged in an aggressive lobbying campaign against the proposed changes, including papering the campus with flyers such as the one that warned, "DANGER! . . . The proposed Honor Council amendments weaken the penalties for violations and, if implemented, will result in the *institutional cover-up* of past offenses. Weakness in our honor system reflects on all of us. . . . A strong honor system benefits all of us when we are in college and after. Show prospective employers and graduate schools that you care about your integrity and reputation. *IT'S YOUR HONOR. IT'S YOUR REPUTATION. PROTECT IT.*"

In the end such exhortations were unavailing, as the student body voted by a margin of more than two to one in favor of the revision. The fact that voting was done by e-mail prompted a large response, with over 1,100 students participating. It constituted, in the view of Vice President Chirico, "a bit of a historical moment in the life of [the College], indicating we have a vibrant community interested in its own future."

Though student approval of the revision and its subsequent endorsement by the Board of Visitors in the spring of 2006 resolved the matter of transcript notations, it did not end all controversy. Shortly thereafter President Anderson appointed Chirico to replace business administration professor Leigh Frackelton as procedural adviser to the Honor Council. The change did not sit well with council members, who had come to respect, almost revere, Frackelton for the guidance he had provided over the course of almost two decades of service as the body's adviser. Anderson explained that his action was prompted by a desire to get more people involved with the council and was simply part of his normal practice of rotating such positions. Still, the reassignment struck some as an effort to bring greater administrative oversight to the workings of the Honor Council.

The contention surrounding various Honor Council issues demonstrated, more than anything else, the commitment of students and faculty alike to the principles of the honor system and their dedication to preserving its centrality in the life of the College.

Clubs and Organizations

In the absence of an officially recognized fraternity system, much of the social life of the College derived from campus clubs and organizations, of which there was no shortage. By 2007 there were almost a hundred such groups, ranging in size from the Student Government Association, to which (in theory) every student belonged, to such small and obscure groups as JADE (the anime club). If the array did not run literally from A to Z, it did range from A (Accounting Club) to W (Women's Ultimate Frisbee Club).

Early in the fall semester each year, a Club Carnival was held to introduce new students to the myriad opportunities for extracurricular participation. There were several categories of organizations, the most important being those that served the entire student body: Student Government Association, Class Council, Association of Residence Halls, Judicial Review Board, Inter-Club Association, and Community Outreach and Resources (COAR). Such groups operated under the umbrella rubric of the Office of Student Activities and Community Services (OSACS).

One of the oldest clubs of any kind on campus was the Debate Club (or Team), having been among the first organized activities in the formative years of the institution. Those early groups were called literary societies, in the fashion of the time, but their purpose in essence was to provide vehicles for students to engage in oratory and public debate.[145]

Interest waned in the 1920s but was renewed in the early thirties as evidenced by creation of the Debating Club. Promoted by English professor George Shankle and history professor Oscar Darter, debate became a popular campus activity by the late thirties, as teams participated in intercollegiate contests with schools such as Randolph-Macon, Bridgewater, and Radford. Following a hiatus during World War II, debate again became prominent with the arrival of history professor Warren Keith in 1945. Under his direction the Forensic Club was established, along with an allied organization known as the Strawberry Leaf Society, and the College began to host the Grand National Forensic Tournament. That event, held each year on Easter weekend, became one of the largest debating competitions of its kind in the nation; by 1958 it was drawing participation from more than sixty schools, some from as far away as the West Coast.

With Keith's death in 1958, the debate program declined for several years until resurrected in the mid-1960s by political science professor Lewis Fickett, who served as its volunteer coach until, in the early seventies, other obligations forced him to relinquish that job. Before doing so, however, his novice teams won numerous awards at state and regional tournaments.[146]

It was not until 1985 that the program was reactivated, with the strong support of President Anderson. The following year, David Hair was hired to direct the program, which he did effectively for three years before moving to an administrative position and subsequently to Gettysburg College. At that point, the debate program began its move to a higher level, largely as the result of a new director, John Morello.

Himself an avid debater while an undergraduate at William and Mary, Morello had gone on to direct a nationally prominent debate program at James Madison in the late seventies and early eighties. He quickly achieved similarly impressive results at Mary Washington following his arrival in 1990. The next year, the debate team began its movement into national prominence by earning, for the first time, the right to participate in competition at the national level. To Morello, such rewards were ancillary because, as he put it, debate was "an intense educational activity which is valuable even if the participants win no trophies."

But in fact they did win trophies—increasing numbers of them as the nineties progressed. By 1993 the team ranked seventh nationally in the policy debate program; the following year it defeated schools such as the University of Texas to finish in eighth place nationally. By the time Morello gave up directing the program to become assistant vice president for academic affairs in 1998, his teams regularly ranked among the top twenty in the country, with varsity teams reaching the National Debate Tournament six times.

With a solid foundation and a tradition of excellence having been established under Morello, the program climbed to even greater heights under Morello's successor as adviser, Timothy O'Donnell. Under O'Donnell's enthusiastic and expert guidance, the MWC debaters won their first national championship in 2001, an achievement that earned an official commendation from the Senate of Virginia. It also led the American Debate Association (ADA) to award its prestigious Lambert Award to O'Donnell.

It turned out to be only the beginning of a run of extraordinary success for the Mary Washington debaters, both as a team and as individuals. In 2003, for example, juniors Carly Woods and John Nagy won the founder's cup, awarded annually to the nation's best junior varsity team. The following year, Woods received the Junior Burke Award for Character and Excellence in Debate at the ADA's national championships. That award, according to O'Donnell, was perhaps "the most important annual award in intercollegiate debate because it is the one that recognizes that competitive success and character go hand in hand."[147] The award was presented to her by her younger brother and debate partner, Mary Washington sophomore Clint Woods.

As for the team, honors continued to pile up as the 2003 season marked the third consecutive year of winning the national championship. In 2007, its perennial strength now well established, the team ended the season ranked number one nationally by the ADA. It was a first in the institution's history—and a truly remarkable achievement for a school the size of Mary Washington. English professor Bill Kemp put it well. "The debate team is wonderful, he said. "Pound for pound, we do better than any other school."

Many individual academic departments also had either clubs or honorary societies for their majors—sometimes both, as in the case of history, which had a History Club as well as the Phi Alpha Theta Honorary Society. Although most of the academically focused clubs concerned themselves mainly with activities for their like-minded members, an exception was the Historic Preservation Club, one of the largest and most active groups on campus, which sponsored several programs that appealed not only to preservation majors but to other students and also to the local community. The oldest of those events was Ghost Walk, a tour of reputedly haunted venues in downtown Fredericksburg, held each year near Halloween. Created in 1985, the "lively tour of spirited places," as it was billed, was still frightening and amusing large crowds two decades later. By 2003, the event (which took approximately eighty students to produce) was drawing crowds of as many as one thousand, raising approximately $5,000 for the club to use on other projects such as trips to conferences and historical sites.

A more recent Preservation Club initiative, begun in 1999, was a midwinter Victorian Ball featuring authentic period costumes. Held in Lee Hall Ballroom, the event was open to the public as well as Mary Washington students. The evening included parlor games appropriate to the era, but the main emphasis was on dancing period steps such as the grand march, Virginia reel, basket quadrille, mazurka, and patty-cake polka. To prevent (or at least minimize) terpsichorean blunders, the cost of admission to the Sunday night ball included dance and etiquette lessons held on the previous Saturday. Like Ghost Walk, the Victorian Ball enjoyed popularity among students while also creating a venue for social interaction between the College and the Fredericksburg community.

A number of smaller clubs catered to much narrower, and sometimes fleeting, interests, such as Riot Grrrl Fredericksburg, which proclaimed as its goal "to promote and expose female talent and to create an atmosphere in which women and men can share ideas and express themselves in whatever way they choose." At the other end of the feminist spectrum, or so it would seem, was the Huswifery Club, formed in 2004. By sponsoring knitting lessons, cookie bakeoffs, and Mary Kay parties, the club appeared to be a throwback to the days of the Normal and Industrial School. According to one of its leaders, however, that perception was inaccurate. "I wish people wouldn't look at [the club] with such bias, [thinking] that the kind of people who join are submissive," she said, "but that's definitely not the case. The club is full of strong and independent women." It soon failed.

Such questions never arose concerning another special-interest group, the MWC Breakers, an organization devoted to promoting hip-hop culture through break dancing. Though the group's energetic performances at events like basketball games and the Multicultural Fair drew appreciative responses, the number of actual participants remained small. Perhaps it was because the various break-dancing moves—with names such as UFO, Flare, Diamond, Jackhammer, Cricket, Dark Side, Hollow Back, and Air Chair—were not suited to the musical tastes (or dance-floor athleticism) of many students.

Another active category of clubs comprised those that embraced ethnic and diversity interests. Four clubs supported and promoted the interests of African American students: the Black Student Association, BOND, Women of Color, and Sisters with a Vision. Other minority clubs included the Spanish and Latin American Student Association (SALSA) and the Asian Student Association. Also among the more active clubs was PRISM, or People Representing Individuals of Sexual Minorities.

Religious interest clubs were well represented, including four groups for Christians in general—Campus Christian Community, Christian Unity Community, Inter-Varsity Christian Fellowship, and Ambassadors for Christ—as well as a Baptist Student Union, Catholic Campus Ministry, and Latter-Day Saints Student Association. For Jewish students, there were both Hillel and the Jewish Student Association, and for Muslims, the Islamic Student Association.

Several clubs focused on political concerns, including the mainstream College Democrats and College Republicans, both of which bestirred themselves most vigorously in election years (especially presidential election years). To the left of those two was a newer, but quite active, club known as the Anarchist Social Theory Club, whose avowed purpose was to provide "an intellectual space for those interested in learning more about alternative theories of government." The newest of the politically oriented organizations was the E Pluribus Unum Political Awareness Club.

In terms of political activism, the most prominent student organization on campus was the Human Rights Club. In addition to periodically sponsoring programs and lectures on a variety of specific human rights topics, it played an important role in two of the major campus movements of the early twenty-first century: support for the Honduras orphanage, Copprome; and the "living wage" campaign, a movement to secure higher salaries for the College's hourly employees.

The story of Copprome was, in essence, the story of one diminutive Mary Washington student by the name of Shin Fujiyama '07. In December 2004, Fujiyama first visited Honduras with a group from the Campus Christian Community. He was troubled by the poverty that plagued the entire country, especially its devastating effect on children.

On a return trip, he visited the Copprome orphanage, where his concerns became more focused, partly as a result of one particular incident. Casually tossing the remnants of a fast-food meal into a trash can, he was startled to see children scrambling for the bits of bun and a few fries. He later observed others walking miles to rummage through trash containers and garbage dumps in search of food or salvageable items for resale.

He returned to Mary Washington fixated on the orphanage and determined to do whatever he could to alleviate the horrid plight of its residents. As it turned out, he could do a great deal.

Fujiyama's efforts began in the spring of 2005, when he sat daily outside the Eagles Nest, collecting spare change from students. His success (about $1,500) encouraged him to redouble his efforts, which took several forms. One was to encourage the Copprome children to create Christmas cards that could be sold in America—a project that netted approximately $5,000. At Christmas of the same year, he organized a student trip to Honduras during which he, along with members of the Human Rights Club, distributed over one thousand presents to orphans who had never received such gifts before.

Fujiyama's next step, taken at the urging of James Farmer Human Rights Professor Greg Stanton—"my personal hero," Fujiyama called him—was to create a nonprofit organization known as Students Helping Honduras (SHH), an endeavor jointly led by his sister Cosmo, a student at William and Mary.

Fujiyama did not think small. Announcing a goal of raising $100,000 in the spring of 2006, he personally secured a challenge grant from the Sunshine Lady Foundation, headed by philanthropist Doris Buffett, sister of the billionaire Warren Buffett. Her pledge to double every dollar raised by SHH constituted, in Fujiyama's words, "a miracle."

To raise money, Fujiyama created Copprome Spirit Week in mid-April 2006, to be capped by a walkathon through campus on April 23. Leading up to that event, a multitude of activities took place to publicize the walk, including performances each day at the Monroe fountain by groups such as Una Voce and the Latin Dance Club. In addition, various groups such as the swim team and Circle K held special events not only to raise money but to publicize the walk.

The walk itself turned out to be one of the most remarkable events in Mary Washington's history, drawing hundreds of pledges and participants not only from clubs, teams, and departments at the College but also from area churches and businesses. A number of campus organizations competed to see which could earn the largest contributions. The result was astounding: with the aid of Doris Buffett's pledge, the total amount raised for the destitute orphans of Copprome came to over $120,000.

It was, marveled Fujiyama, "the biggest fund-raising event, and the largest mobilization effort that students have put together in the history of our school." He was not exaggerating.

Never had one MWC student made such an impact for good as Shin Fujiyama. It was true that the Copprome endeavor involved significant participation from many others, notably including the Campus Christian Community and the Human Rights Club. But Fujiyama was the instigator, the organizer, and the promoter, without whom it would not have happened.

He took no personal credit, once describing himself as "just a broke-ass college kid washing dishes at Seacobeck." Others, such as Professor Stanton, knew better. "Shin Fujiyama is a force," Stanton once observed. "Packed into his compact physical frame is spiritual nuclear energy . . . [which] would not be a good thing if it were aimed toward the wrong objectives. But in a person dedicated to justice, which is the purpose of Shin Fujiyama's life, it is a force that will move mountains."

Yet the ever-modest Fujiyama deflected all accolades to others. "We have some damn good people at this school," he said of his peers. "We have so many people who are so much smarter than me."

But none with a bigger heart.

One of the most significant, and certainly most persistent, protest movements in Mary Washington's history began in 2001 as the result of a student project in sociology professor William Hanson's civil rights class. Motivated by their work on the project, two seniors, Gina McGovern and Meghan Lyons, both members of the Human Rights Club, began to call upon the College to raise the salaries of its lowest-paid workers (classified employees) to a level constituting a living wage. They pointed out that similar student protests had already achieved the same goal at William and Mary and the University of Virginia.

The movement gained little momentum until April 2004, when the Human Rights Club sponsored a rally to call attention to the situation. Speakers at that event pointed out that approximately half of the College's sixty housekeepers and groundskeepers earned a mere $8.10 per hour, which placed them under the poverty level for a family of four. Richard Hurley, MWC's executive vice president and CFO, expressed sympathy but said that such an increase was not feasible. The difficulty, he explained, was that classified employees constituted a separate group "governed by specific, statewide compensation laws, and their pay plan doesn't recognize living wage as a reason to adjust their salary."

When the classified workers did receive a 4.52 percent increase at the end of the year, the living-wage advocates pointed out that the increased income was still insufficient; moreover, they pointed out that the administration was deceitful in that it took away Christmas bonuses at the same time the salaries were increased, resulting in very little net gain.

To emphasize their discontent, the living-wage advocates held a Halloween "trick-or-treat" rally—the idea being to "unmask" the administration's alleged duplicity. A number of faculty members spoke, including political science professor Jason Davidson, who movingly described the difficulties of his own impoverished childhood. Also among the speakers was English Professor Steve Watkins, no slouch at rallying protesters. "There are two Americas," he said. "I think people get comfortable [and] will protect their comfort level at all costs, and part of that is turning a blind eye to the needs of people that are literally sweeping the floor beneath their feet."

The movement became more aggressive in the spring of 2005, prompted in part by the announcement that the Board of Visitors had voted to increase President Anderson's salary by $10,000. "While Anderson lives in decadent opulence and leisure," charged one letter to the *Bullet*, "some workers who are receiving poverty wages carry . . . pagers and are on call 24/7 in case an intoxicated student vomits or urinates on the floor of our residence halls at 2 A.M."

The Living Wage Coalition sponsored a rally at GW in early April at which they were joined by students from Georgetown University who had recently conducted a successful hunger strike on behalf of increased wages on that campus. As one of them told the crowd, "If rallies and petitions aren't working, you know, get louder. . . . Step it up. . . . Put more pressure on the administration."

Step it up they did, when a few days later five students entered Vice President Hurley's office, formed a circle, and shackled themselves together with PVC pipes and metal chains. (They had made a prior decision not to chain themselves to objects in the office, one said, because "we didn't want to damage any furniture.") Declaring their determination to stay until workers were granted a minimum wage of $10 an hour, the students were placed under constant (albeit amicable) police surveillance. After two hours, the protest ended peacefully when officials agreed to create a committee, including students, to study the matter.

The *Free Lance–Star* took a dim editorial view of the living-wage proponents, noting that Georgetown University, a private school, could do as it wished with its funds, but that Mary Washington, a state school, had a fiduciary responsibility to taxpaying citizens. Therefore administrative officials had no right to expend funds "to satisfy their personal concepts of justice, or even to get activists off their case." Rather than giving raises to the lowest-paid workers, the newspaper suggested, it would be better to provide tuition subsidies to allow them to "pump up their marketable skills [which] would help fulfill the college's educational mission and provide its hardest-pressed employees a sustainable foundation for a better life. The parable here is a familiar one: a few more fish or a fishing pole with instruction in angling?"

The editorial drew a sharp rejoinder from psychology professor Thomas Moeller, who called it "elitist and condescending." Referring to the newspaper's parable, he said, "As for the suggestion that . . . employees be taught to fish for themselves: they are perfectly capable of doing that on their own, but even the best fisherman won't catch anything if there aren't any fish in the pond."

The *Bullet* meanwhile staunchly supported the campaign, exhorting students to seize it as an opportunity to demonstrate a capacity for civic leadership. "American college campuses have a long and proud tradition of social activism," it said in an editorial. Accordingly, it urged support for the wage crusade, suggesting that it was a much better use of time than "pounding that case of Natty in the fridge and you might actually help someone else breathe a little easier."

In the ensuing months, the living-wage advocates continued to agitate the issue, prompting the *Bullet* to comment at one point that "the Living Wage Coalition just won't be quiet. They've been noisy. . . . While it's getting on some people's nerves, one has to admire the coalition for its tireless efforts. [That] . . . is the method [whereby] civil rights activists and women's rights activists made things happen."

And so it did, eventually and partially, with the living-wage movement. After stating in November 2005 that such action would be impossible owing to lack of funds, President Anderson in January 2006 announced that thanks to a favorable state budget appropriation, a wage increase would be implemented that spring. The increase, which amounted to 5.3 percent annually, affected approximately eighty employees, which meant that the hourly rate for full-time employees increased to the equivalent of approximately $19,000 for entry-level custodial workers and $22,000 for entry-level grounds workers.[148]

Though not all that the coalition had sought, the raise was gratifying to the student activists. "It's pretty sweet," said coalition leader Patrick McGowan. While "not technically a living wage, . . . it's a big victory for us, regardless."

Rick Hurley, too, was gratified—and relieved. "I want to applaud you for your passion," he told the coalition leaders, adding good-naturedly, "Aside from taking over my office last year, you handled this very well."

Clubs dealing with entertainment played an important role in the social life of the campus. Among the main organizations was the Performing Arts Club (PAC), founded in 1997. The reason for its creation was the desire of dance enthusiasts to maintain some venue for participation in the absence of the recently abolished dance major.

The PAC usually produced two shows every semester, the first being an open floor show known as the "small show," that was traditionally held in Lee Ballroom and featured guest performances by groups such as the Dance Team, Swing Dance Club, and Breakers. The second, or "big show," was held in Dodd Auditorium. To perform in this more formal production, dancers were required to audition for the choreographers (students, teachers, or alumni) at the beginning of the semester. The PAC also held weekly classes, open to the entire student body, in ballet, as well as occasional workshops in genres such as modern dance, jazz, African dance, and hip-hop.

A performance group of a quite different kind was the bagpipe band. It began serendipitously in 1993 when chemistry professor Ray Scott, an avid and accomplished piper, approached Dean Philip Hall with the idea of incorporating bagpipes into the commencement ceremony. Hall endorsed the plan, which was approved by President Anderson, leading to the appearance of Scott's group, the City of Washington Pipe Band, in the event. Some

Raymond B. Scott (piper at left) leads the Eagle Pipe Band at the head of the commencement procession.

were initially skeptical. As Scott recalled, "It was supposed to be a one-shot deal. As a matter of fact, they [made] sure we [played] the minimum amount possible."[149]

But the pipers were an immediate success, eliciting such a favorable response that President Anderson was moved to authorize the formation of the Eagle Pipe Band with Scott as its director. Soon the band had its own distinctive tartan kilts in a plaid made of the College's colors of blue, gray, and white, with a touch of red. Interest in the group developed to the point that by 1997 it had thirty members, drawn from students, alumni, and the community, divided into pipers, drummers, and dancers. By then, despite periodic fluctuations in membership, the pipe band had become established as a distinctive and much-admired element of commencement.

The 1990s witnessed a dramatic upsurge of student interest in a cappella music, leading eventually to the formation of three distinct groups, all of them created by students (though they had, nominally for the most part, faculty advisers). The oldest, and only coed, a cappella group on campus was the Symfonics (sometimes misspelled as Symphonics), founded in 1993. The group, usually having from twelve to eighteen members, performed songs arranged by members of the group, often using a computer program to create sheet music for the others. "The type of music we do," said one member of the group, "reflects what we love listening to." In many cases that meant the harmonies of "oldies" groups such as the Temptations and Four Tops, though the group usually performed more recent material made popular by contemporary favorites such as the Backstreet Boys, George Michael, and Britney

Spears. They also often performed the alma mater at various campus events (leaving out the extra verses that group members occasionally wrote to ridicule current campus issues like 24/7 visitation and lack of parking spaces). The Symfonics remained popular into the twenty-first century, performing in concerts before audiences of as many as five hundred people. By 2007, they had put out three CDs.

Such popularity led to the formation of two spin-off groups—one all-male, the other all-female. The male ensemble, known as Invoice, came together serendipitously when several male Symfonics began singing a Chili's restaurant jingle during rehearsal. "It all started with baby-back ribs," one of them explained.

The group quickly became a favorite on campus, especially among female students, and their appeal and good humor clearly played as much of a role as their musical talent. In a 2002 *Bullet* article titled "Humorous Harmonizing Hotties," the writer (female) noted that while the idea of "a bunch of guys singing . . . without accompaniment is a little unorthodox, possibly even a little geeky," in reality Invoice was "the furthest thing from the dorky barbershop quartet a capella groups of the past. They're endearing, talented, and damn entertaining. They're men on a mission: to bring a little melody to people's lives, to entertain, and, as their website says, to get girls to ask them out."

It was a characterization that the Invoice boys did nothing to deny. Indeed, according to one founding member, the group's slogan should have been "Invoice: making your boyfriend jealous."

About the same time that Invoice was formed, an all-female group, BellACapella, was also organized. In addition to performing periodically at concerts, the group gained considerable visibility on campus by offering singing telegrams on Valentine's Day as a fund-raiser. In 2004 they released their first CD, *BellACapella Unplugged*.

As with their male counterparts, the members of BellACapella were drawn together by more than music, producing not only tight harmonies but tight friendships. "The girls are my favorite part of Bella," said one member. "We're always finding ways to have 'Bella bonding.' We go to bars together, have potluck dinners, and take trips to Potomac Mills. We joke that we are a singing sorority because we wear all our Bella T-shirts and Bella sweatshirts and we hang out together a lot."

But they were serious about their music. "We rock," said one, adding, "Seriously though . . . our sound has improved tremendously, and we weren't bad back in the day either. We choose eclectic songs so that we can appeal to everyone. Besides, who doesn't like to see girls singing?"

In addition to the a cappella groups there was also a coed chamber choir, Una Voce. It was founded in the fall of 2003 by Kevin Diana, a former Symfonic, out of a desire to have a more traditional singing group on campus; he also served as the first conductor of the group. Una Voce was eventually run by a faculty member in the music department and was offered as a credit class for students who joined.

All the student vocal groups shared not only talent and a love for music and each other but also a dedication to perfecting their craft. This was reflected in the normal regimen of three rehearsals (four to five hours total) per week working toward end-of-semester concerts that sometimes included guest appearances by groups from other colleges including James Madison, William and Mary, and the University of Maryland. The groups often performed at other events on campus such as the Multicultural Fair, Parents Weekend, and Junior Ring Ceremony and also traveled to colleges, high schools, and other venues in the area. It was always hard to know who had the most fun, the audiences or the performers themselves.

In addition to groups from within the student body, campus entertainment also included performers from outside the College. The responsibility for booking and producing such performances rested with the Student Association's Entertainment Committee, which in the early 1990s became known as Giant Productions. The committee's approach was cleverly summarized in its constitution, which listed two simple criteria for the booking of performers: "(1) The event must be open to all MWC students, regardless of race, gender, sexual orientation, etc.; (2) The event shall, notwithstanding, rock."

Giant Productions was given significant latitude in carrying out its duties, having more autonomy than similar student organizations at other schools, where there was greater administrative oversight of the booking of shows. Giant Productions had the largest budget of any student group on campus (typically around $100,000 annually in the early years of the twenty-first century). Leaders of the organization took their responsibilities seriously and were sometimes able to parlay their experience into careers in entertainment, a notable example being Pamela Kirby '01, an American studies major who interned and worked for MTV until 2005, when she became an executive producer for the *Tony Danza Show*.

Despite the size and structural limitations of available campus venues, Giant Productions was able to attract a number of nationally known entertainers to campus, aided to some degree by the institution's favorable location near I-95 and Washington, D.C. Beginning with punk rocker Billy Idol in 1983, such performers included the Ramones (described by the *Bullet* as "the reason your parents fear rock-n-roll") and hip-hop artists Run-DMC (1997) and the Roots (2003). Another hip-hop performance by Wyclef Jean in 1999 proved to be a particularly wild affair, with people violating the fire code by packing the aisles and dancing on the antiquated seats of Dodd Auditorium. "If we could get people to be calm," said the co-chair of Giant Productions, "there wouldn't be a problem. But, of course, that's no fun."

A number of entertainers appeared on campus just before gaining major national stardom, such as the Dave Matthews Band, who at the time of its Mary Washington performances in 1992 and 1993 was known mainly as a popular local group from Charlottesville. Similarly, pop rocker John Mayer, rhythm and blues artist John Legend, and modern rockers OK Go appeared on campus shortly before becoming Grammy winners in 2007.

Fredericksburg area performers also appeared periodically at the College, one of the best known being Doc Scantlin and his Imperial Palms Orchestra, which at times featured MWC alumna Mayo Carter '79. There were also some perennial favorites including, around the turn of the century, the Dismemberment Plan, DJ Frequency, and Pash. Perhaps the most popular of all the homegrown performers during the period was Sean Michael Dargan '90, who sometimes performed solo, sometimes as part of his three-member band. "It's sort of like a Mary Washington College tradition, ya know?" said one student. "You have to see him play before you graduate."

Despite the quality of artists booked by Giant Productions, student interest in musical acts began to flag in the early years of the new century, largely the victim of balkanized musical genres that left few broad areas of shared taste among students. There was also the constant availability of music from countless sources appealing to an endless spectrum of individual tastes. Whatever the reason, as one of the organization's officers said in 2007 (somewhat oxymoronically), "Even the free shows are hard sells." The only band during that era to sell out Dodd Auditorium was the country group Lonestar, and that was achieved largely owing to heavy attendance by local residents.

What was increasingly popular, however, was comedy, evidenced by consistently high attendance at shows by performers such as *Saturday Night Live* cast members Steven Wright, Norm MacDonald, Jimmy Fallon, and Tracy Morgan, as well as MTV's Pauly Shore. The performer who enjoyed the most enduring popularity was the hypnotist Tom DeLuca. Once voted the National College Entertainer of the Year and profiled in *People*, *Rolling Stone*, and the *Wall Street Journal*, DeLuca was always a huge attraction at Mary Washington. Having first performed at the College in 1998, he was still drawing full houses to Dodd in 2007.

Campus life at Mary Washington had long been enriched by the contributions of its student print media, going all the way back to the publication of the first yearbook, *The Battlefield*, in 1913. From the 1970s into the twenty-first century, the major student publications, in addition to *The Battlefield*, were *Aubade*, the *Polemic*, and the *Bullet*.

Published annually without interruption for over eighty years, *The Battlefield* foundered in the mid-1990s when consecutive staffs failed to produce either the 1993–94 or 1994–95 yearbooks on time. "For whatever reason (perhaps because of student apathy), MWC hasn't seen a yearbook since 1993," the

Bullet reported in February 1996. "Unfortunately, this means that two classes have already graduated without a yearbook to remember their senior year."

However, the 1995–96 staff, led by freshmen Carrie Anderson and Kevin MacLuskie, not only produced *The Battlefield* for that academic year but also accomplished the daunting task of bringing the series up to date—after a fashion. Using the partially completed portions from the previous two years, they cobbled together yearbooks for the missing sessions. Back on track, *The Battlefield* continued to be published without interruption.

In October 1970 there appeared a new campus publication called *Polemics*, which styled itself "A Current Affairs and Contemporary Issues Quarterly Publication." It was not officially sponsored by any specific department, but the journal tended to reflect the influence of Monroe Hall, as evidenced by the academic disciplines of many of its contributors and by the affiliation of its first adviser, political science professor Victor Fingerhut.

The inaugural issue of *Polemics* lived up to the implications of its title by printing the text of Black Panther Huey Newton's address to the Revolutionary Peoples' Constitutional Convention in Philadelphia on September 5, 1970. Most of the content of subsequent issues was not so radical, usually consisting of pieces by students and faculty, including articles on topics such as conscientious objectors by George Van Sant, problems of western rangelands by Marshall Bowen, the Peace Corps by Michael Mery, the volunteer army by John Albertine, unionization of public employees by William B. Clatanoff, federal tax law by Frederick Miller, and black English by Paul Zisman.

Occasionally the magazine reprinted pertinent articles from other schools, such as one from the *UCLA Daily Bruin* titled "Do You Have Syphilis (Gonorrhea Maybe)?" That article was followed by a brief, but amusingly informative, excerpt from a recent *Moneysworth* magazine report concerning the effectiveness of various feminine hygiene deodorant sprays, including "the discovery that one of the sprays, Massengil, would also kill roaches."

Polemics ceased publication in 1973, but in 1986 a similarly titled journal, the *Polemic*, appeared. The new incarnation was more of a literary and artistic magazine than a journal of political debate. Still, the material—almost totally student generated—was sometimes thematic, with issues devoted to topics such as race, feminism, travel, and sex (the topic, unsurprisingly, of several issues).

In 2004 the *Polemic* announced its intention to return more to its roots as a "magazine for controversial discussion or debate." The following year, it did just that, publishing several pieces dealing with campus issues as well as the College's upcoming centennial celebration.

Another new student magazine appeared in 1971 with the publication of a literary journal called *Aubade*. It developed largely in the vacuum created by the demise of the *Epaulet*, which, under the sponsorship of the English Department, had been published regularly on a quarterly basis from 1940 until the mid-1950s; it appeared sporadically thereafter, and by 1969 it was defunct.

Aubade was something of a hybrid, featuring student works in both literature and art. The dual purpose was evinced by its faculty sponsors, who, beginning with John Lamph from the Art Department, alternately included faculty members from both art and English (notably including, in the publication's early years, Nancy Mitchell and Carlton Lutterbie from the English Department). According to Ed Alvey, the magazine was "a departure from traditional literary magazines, [in that] it presented a selection of poems and stories, drawings and photographs, characterized by a realistic treatment of contemporary themes."[150]

In 1986 the publication considered changing its name because, as its editor put it, "*Aubade*'s recognition . . . is somewhat clouded by the obscurity of its name. Some see the magazine as elitist . . . simply because they don't understand the publication's name." Though it was true that few probably knew that an aubade is a musical composition to be played or sung, usually outside, at dawn or early in the morning, the name ultimately stayed.

The student newspaper, the *Bullet*, was by far the most important campus publication in terms of providing information and entertainment to the student body on a regular basis. It was first published during the 1921–22 academic year and ran continuously thereafter.[151] For much of its first half century, the *Bullet* was a serviceable means of keeping students informed about things that interested them—which mainly meant, during that time, student government activities, May Day, campus dances, and other social events. Scant attention was paid to events beyond the campus; even the assassination of President Kennedy in November 1963 barely merited a mention—only the reprint of a memorial tribute delivered by Dean Alvey.

In the late 1960s, however, the *Bullet* began to change—a reflection of other changes at the College and in society generally—with more extensive coverage devoted to politics and current events. In the seventies, the *Bullet* became a center of controversy because of several provocative articles and especially the promotion of abortion, in which the paper took a position of dubious legality for which it was threatened with court action.

Once the social and cultural turbulence of the seventies dissipated, the paper became somewhat more sedate. Not that its editorial position was always docile; in fact, it was capable of stridency on issues that aroused its editorial ire, such as visitation policy and proposed changes in the name of the institution.

It was in the 1990s that the *Bullet* became noticeably more confrontational, especially in its attitude toward the administration, and more provocative in its handling of campus social issues, especially those involving sex. There were two main reasons for the change. One was that the paper's attitude simply reflected a more open—some would also say more coarsened—society. Scandals public and private had sensitized journalists everywhere to be more skeptical concerning the matters they reported, and those at Mary Washington were no exception.

Second, and perhaps more important, was the influence of a new faculty adviser for the paper, English professor Stephen Watkins, who was hired in 1990 and soon became the *Bullet*'s adviser. For a number of years previously, the paper had been advised by another member of the English Department, Carlton Lutterbie, and the publication before his death in 1988 reflected his gentlemanly demeanor.

The feisty Watkins was of a different temperament, as became evident in the *Bullet*'s evolution under his guidance. Ever the gadfly, he led the paper to adopt a more aggressive, hard-edged style. He was, said one admiring 1992 editorial, "the world's only faculty advisor who encourages his journalism students to go for the jugular vein."

Investigative reports became a staple, frequently based on Freedom of Information requests with which journalism students bombarded administrative offices. It was an approach that won the *Bullet* (and its adviser) few friends in GW but led to a number of eye-opening articles. Typical was a 1991 front-page story listing faculty salaries, the thinly veiled implication being that some were not deserved. The article divided the campus; some readers admired it for its audacity, while others condemned it for what they regarded as a tacky invasion of privacy.

The salary report was just the kind of story that contributed to the impression that the *Bullet* was scandal-hungry, preeminently interested in muckraking. Another criticism—one that occurred with increasing frequency after 2000—was that the paper was obsessed with the seamier side of campus social life. "In general after reading the *Bullet*, I feel down," wrote one parent in 1995 (as quoted in the *Bullet*). "This leads me to believe you need to emphasize some of the more positive aspects of MWC—or is every student an alcoholic?"

Unhappy with this state of journalistic affairs, the Board of Visitors in 1999 instructed President Anderson to create the Student Publications Study Committee, whose purpose, he announced, was to "make sure that the Publication Board is updated and functioning properly and to see that the college is protected on the liability side of things, and that freedom of the press and freedom of speech are well protected." Left unsaid was the suspicion by some board members that the *Bullet* was being unduly, if subtly, influenced by its adviser, Professor Watkins, inasmuch as many of the paper's writers were students in his journalism classes.[152] Watkins generally rejected imputations of his control over the paper, estimating on one occasion that "95 percent of what goes in the paper, I don't see until the paper comes out." Yet he admitted at the same time that he "would be naive to think I don't have some influence on them. I would hope that I do. Why [else] would they hire me?"[153] And the paper itself once referred to him as "an invaluable source of stories."

In the end, the study committee's work had little substantive effect on the *Bullet*'s operation, but the very fact of its establishment did nothing to improve the already wary relationship between the paper and the administration. "The college should adopt a hands-off approach to its student publications," advised an editorial. "Free student media is in the best interests of Mary Washington College and its students."

The paper constantly maintained that it harbored no animosity toward the administration. One 1998 editorial, for example, called for greater cooperation, saying that "in recent years it has been no secret across the campus that the *Bullet* and the MWC administration do not get along. . . . Rest assured that scandal is not the goal of the *Bullet*. The *Bullet* does not seek controversy."

It may not have sought it, but it frequently found it—nowhere more so than in its increased emphasis on matters of sex. One manifestation of that tendency was the publication of personal ads that, while on the whole harmless, sometimes contained sexual innuendo and risqué double entendre. The level of lewdness (though usually couched in humorous terms) increased significantly in 2006 with the appearance of a regular column called "Sexclamations."[154]

Occasionally the paper disclaimed any prurient inclinations, as it did in a 2004 editorial that deplored "the absurd amount of sexuality plaguing our press every day." Yet the content of the same issue seemed to contradict such a disavowal. One student noted the inconsistency in a letter to the editor the following week, commenting that while she appreciated the sentiment of the editorial, she was disappointed that "just a page later, you published a feature article on nothing else but the male genitals. And not only is there an article, tasteless in nature, but *three* pictures, one of which is very large. Indeed, I turned bright red as I turned to that page while sitting in National Airport. Hoping that no one had seen that picture, I turned the page again. In the Sports section there was the picture that everyone had already seen plenty of times that week—Janet Jackson obscenely exposed. . . . *The Bullet* is a collegiate newspaper, not a pornography magazine."

Despite the various controversies stirred by the *Bullet* around the turn of the century, several things were clear. For one, though the paper sometimes seemed to place inordinate emphasis on sex and scandal, its overall quality had, by most measures, improved, especially in its extensive coverage of sports and entertainment. Its quality was attested by numerous awards, including recognition by the Society of Professional Journalists as the number one nondaily college newspaper in Virginia, Delaware, North Carolina, Maryland, and Washington, D.C., in both 2004 and 2005.

The staff was understandably proud of the recognition that the *Bullet* received—"that's right folks, the same *Bullet* that you make fun of every Thursday," said an editorial. "In spite of numerous administrative obstructions," wrote 2004 editor in chief Conor Reilly, "the *Bullet* staff still puts out the best college newspaper in the Middle Atlantic, and I think the best weekly paper in the nation. . . . I am so . . . proud of the staff."

Of preeminent importance to the *Bullet*—to any paper, really—was the fact that it was read. "You may whine and complain about Mary Washington's student newspaper," said a 2004 editorial. "You may be angry that someone got publicity and someone else did not. You may not like that you were included in the Police Beat. You may even still be harboring resentments about a staff editorial decrying the popped collar. . . . But if you're criticizing us, it means you are reading—and that means a lot to us." After all, it declared with considerable pride, "the *Bullet* has been pissing people off since 1922."

From time to time, new publications cropped up on campus, heralding themselves as "underground" papers. One example was *Fred's Bag*, which appeared briefly in 1986. (The title was apparently a play on "Fred's Burg.") Such publications were usually antagonistic, either subtly or overtly, toward the *Bullet*. Yet the established paper usually welcomed the competition, in this case urging students to support and work for the *Bag*. "Don't worry about whether it'll win the Pulitzer or [about] the okashunul misspelled word," the *Bullet* said, and went on in fulsome terms to commend the paper's maiden effort: "*Fred's Bag* is but a drop that splashed over the imaginary restraining walls where the tremendous reservoir of talent floats, from heights unscaled, untapped." The *Bag*, alas, died in infancy.

Among the more interesting unofficial publications was the 1995 *Mighty Pen*. It too was welcomed by the *Bullet* as a vehicle for expressing alternative student opinion, though an editorial took the upstart to task for insufficient documentation and attribution of its sources. "We think that if the *Pen* can last through the end of the semester and the student body is still interested in reading it," read an editorial, "the paper will probably have a good chance of becoming an institution." It did not.

Though most alternative newspapers had at least some degree of anti-*Bullet* animus, one was created with the explicit purpose of countering what it regarded as the official paper's overly liberal bias. Begun in the spring of 1999, the *Alliance* was designed, according to its founding editor, to serve as "a forum for students who may have problems with the *Bullet*, for whatever reason." The ideological leaning of the *Alliance* was evident in its affiliation with an organization known as the Leadership Institute, a conservative think tank in Arlington whose purpose, according to the editor, was to "take people who are not flaming liberals and train them in the ways of the word warrior."

Even such outside support proved insufficient to sustain the *Alliance*. A major reason was that despite its iconoclastic boasts, the paper was not drastically different in content from the *Bullet*. The first issue, for example, contained front-page articles on Mr. MWC and Rocktoberfest, followed by stories on the campus radio station, WMWC, and the Underground, capped by a warning about the perils of overindulgence titled "Is Vomit Really Necessary?" Thus the *Alliance*'s quick demise was largely explained by the comment of a senior who observed, "If there is going to be another newspaper, they need to be something different than the *Bullet*."

The truth was that any fledgling publication faced serious problems. For one thing, the students who made the effort to start such papers usually did so out of strong ideological motivation, and those students came and went, taking their idiosyncratic crusades with them. More significant was the matter of inconsistent funding. Therein lay a problem for any new paper: it could not be truly independent or underground if its funds were controlled by the College; on the other hand, survival without those funds was well nigh impossible. So almost inevitably, all such efforts shared a common characteristic: failure.

The media organization with perhaps the most checkered history of any on campus was radio station WMWC. The years following its reincarnation in 1978, after a lapse since 1969, were marked by a number of problems, starting with difficulties inherent in the station's bizarre system of broadcasting, which involved sending signals through phone lines to transmitters in each residence hall. The transmitters then sent the signal into the building's electrical wiring, which permitted radios plugged into electrical outlets to receive the sound.

The result was far from satisfying, and listenership was minuscule. It was also, according to a *Bullet* report, actually dangerous, with the transmitters "setting off the fire alarm panel in Willard, increasing the voltage of outlets in Mason tunnel, feeding into the intercom in Ball, and being picked up on the pay phones on the first floor in Virginia."

The situation improved considerably in the mid-1980s, largely as the result of the energetic efforts of student Anne Lewis, who served as station manager from 1984 to 1986. In an October 1986 *Bullet* column, "WMWC: Migraines and Memories," Lewis colorfully described the travails of her tenure. When she first arrived at the station, she wrote, "you had to queue up [records] on a turntable in the production studio, turn on the turntable, and make a mad dash for the console in the broadcast studio, hoping to God you didn't trip on the headphone cords—all this for the benefit of perhaps fifty listeners."

Another perennial problem involved student complaints about programming. In theory, the station used a "block programming" format, in which certain kinds of music were played during specified times. But, as Lewis wrote, it was "a nice idea, but it never happened in my time with WMWC. If radio stations have a personality, then MWC's is schizophrenic. Talk about fragmentation—with sixty-plus d.j.s each week, the listener never knows what he or she is going to hear when he or she tunes in."

Though Lewis was not able to correct the transmission difficulties, she was instrumental in bringing greater organization and professionalism to the station and also helped to establish a stronger financial base for its operation. Her financial efforts involved both successful appeals to the SA Finance Committee and innovative fund-raisers, including keggers in Seacobeck basement and a "Name That Tune" contest in the Pub.

Problems with transmission and reception, however, continued to plague the station. A 1988 WMWC poll revealed that 43 percent of the students surveyed said they chose not to listen to the radio station, and of that group, two-thirds said it was because the sound quality was too poor. Some improvement occurred in 1992 when the station switched from AM to an FM cable coaxial hookup. Nonetheless, as late as 1993, a *Bullet* article commented that "the only thing on campus harder to get than a parking spot [is] good reception to WMWC."

In an effort to improve quality, the station at one point advocated a change to over-the-air AM broadcast via a campus tower, a movement promoted by several "Power-to-the-Tower" fund-raisers. While those efforts were reasonably successful, station officials decided in 1994 against the tower approach for several reasons. Most significant was that the circular broadcast pattern from the tower, in order to cover the rectangular campus, would overlap into the surrounding neighborhood, thus requiring greater FCC restrictions as well as possibly creating conflict with local residents.

An alternative was implemented in 1995, whereby the station (by now WMWC 91.5 FM) transmitted via FM coaxial cable that could be accessed in dorm rooms where students requested (free) installation of the necessary hookup equipment. Programming at that time was also broadcast into the Eagles Nest and the Health Center. In October 1996 the station broadcast its first live acoustic show, a concert by juniors Pat Broom and Rob Thormeyer. Though the new system provided an improvement in sound quality for those who requested its installation, the procedure proved clunky, and only about 10 percent of the students signed up for it.

The system was significantly modified in 1998 with the installation of "radiating cable," a method that obviated room-by-room hookups. Instead, the cable "leaked" the radio frequency, which could then be picked up by stereos without additional equipment. For a while the system worked well enough, but within a few years it was troubled by technical problems (including, according to campus rumor, the improbable claim that the cables were being gnawed by rats). In 2003 the transmission system was once again altered, this time so that the radio signal was actually received through the College's television channel 26.

Meanwhile WMWC attracted unwanted attention in 2000 resulting from the charge that its Web site contained offensive language. Specifically there were objections to the site's introduction, which read, "We hope that you enjoy listening to our station. . . . If you don't like listening to our station, then screw yourself." As a result, WMWC was included within the purview of investigations conducted by the College's network policy committee, chaired by executive vice president and CFO Midge Poyck. No significant sanctions resulted, though the committee's review prompted allegations of censorship, especially from the station's webmaster, who branded the inquiry "just another form of ultraconservatism. I guess we're only allowed to show the aspects of 'student life' that might qualify for a pretty brochure cover."

Amid the problems, there were some hopeful signs for WMWC. Programming expanded in 2004 with the live coverage of debates between College Democrats and College Republicans during the presidential campaign, a program that attracted an unusually wide campus audience. During 2005–6, the station underwent a significant upgrading of its equipment, going digital for the first time, purchasing a new mixer to replace the analog type that had been in service for about twenty years. Also, station personnel benefited from College-funded attendance at annual conferences of the *College Music Journal* in New York City.

The sad truth, however, was that the radio station had mounting problems, perhaps terminal ones, by this time. Faced with decreasing appropriations and increasing apathy, the station's already faint presence on campus was reduced almost to nil. In 2006, to make way for the upcoming renovation of Lee Hall, WMWC was forced to move from the spacious attic perch it had occupied for over two decades to a cramped space in Woodard Campus Center. In the spring of 2007, it ceased broadcasting altogether, though it returned that fall via webcast.

The station's revival was welcomed by the *Bullet*, which declared that "it looks as though it's here to stay." Such an opinion, however, appeared to some to be overly optimistic in light of the changing entertainment habits of a new generation of students who, plugged into iPods and transfixed in front of computer screens, were far less attracted to radio than those who had gone before.

Daily (and Nightly) Life

No aspect of student life experienced greater change than did the concept of personal relationships in the turn-of-century era at Mary Washington. For many previous student generations, social interaction between (and occasionally within) the sexes usually pointed toward the development, or hoped-for development, of long-term relationships. By the early years of the twenty-first century, however, relationships had typically become much more casual, more open, and apparently more sexual; if sexual activity had not actually increased, it had certainly become more blatant.

This is not to say that monogamous couples disappeared or that romance evaporated altogether. Amorous activity became especially evident, for example, around Valentine's Day, yet even that traditional day of love came to elicit cynicism from some students. "Think Valentine's Day," wrote a *Bullet* columnist in 1999. "Think fuzzy teddy bears with sappy messages written in script across their rotund little tummies. Think plastic-wrapped fake roses in piles at the 7-11 counter. . . . Think elementary school kids forced by teachers to give little cartoony valentines to every other kid in the class, thus receiving valuable life lessons in shallow affection and brown-nosing. Think Valentine's Day. Think instant nausea."

Even among students who paired off in more or less traditional relationships, the parameters of activity had expanded generously. The new rules were elucidated in a 2002 *Bullet* piece, "The Dating Game"—an article that, had they seen it, would likely have produced a chorus of "I-told-you-so's" among earlier opponents of liberalized visitation. "We both live in the same dorm [Willard]," explained one student, "so we can see each other whenever we want. Last Thursday I decided at like three in the morning that I wanted to see her, so I just went upstairs and surprised her. . . . She spends the night in my room every Saturday. It's really easy because she can just change into her pajamas in her room, and doesn't even have to pack a toothbrush or anything."

For the edification of such couples, the *Bullet* in 2005–6 ran a regular column called "A Slice of Relationship Advice," by Corey Byers, "associate editor and jaded observer." One installment offered tips on detecting actions that indicated a deepening relationship—"occurrences that ring a serious bell in the tower of love"—including putting magnetic framed photographs on the refrigerator, turning over the keys to vehicles or rooms, engaging in PDA (public displays of affection), and leaving items behind (as in "Oops, I forgot my jacket over at your place . . . and my toothbrush and deodorant and well—you get the picture. When your beau leaves those everyday items on your bureau, watch out—[he] will come back for more.") The ultimate indication of commitment, said the column, involved joint membership cards at places like Costco and Blockbuster. Another column offered advice to couples who had advanced to the stage "when one of you wants the other to meet the parental units":

- Don't eat like a pig. Burping and shoveling peas into your mouth when dining with friends is one thing; embarrassing your significant other at a key moment with his or her parents is quite another.
- Compliment something really neutral like their home décor, fat feline, or extensive collection of Civil War memorabilia.
- Steer clear of crude humor . . . [even if] you can never resist laughing at a dirty joke or telling the latest one. . . .
- Do not fool around with your significant other. Keep all doors open behind you and keep the lights on if the two of you are in a room alone. Mama and Papa Bear will be watching you like a hawk; don't be fooled by any notions of absent-mindedness on their behalf.

Evidence indicated that most students did not need such instruction, because casual, serial relationships became the norm. The overall cultural climate—as influenced by, and reflected in, movies, songs, magazines, and television shows—was one that maximized sex and minimized commitment. Even the production of children outside the institution of marriage had been largely destigmatized.

Some suggested that the newer attitude was the result of societal trends growing out of the activist sixties and seventies. The *Free Lance–Star*, for example, asserted that "the breezy lifestyle that feminism has endorsed, convincing young women that they can—in fact, should—be as sexually free as young men often have been, has created a generation of women who think nothing of *á la carte* sex." A *Bullet* columnist in 2006 said much the same thing, arguing that "many females have started dropping the emotions and upping the physical ante just to have a little fun . . . just like men."

> Notice [she continued] that when the ladies try to use guys as sex objects, all of a sudden, guys start pissing and moaning about emotions. Oh wait, I thought that was the girl's job. Hold up, if it's OK for guys . . . , then why isn't the flip side acceptable? Well, . . . it is in my book, so put away the puppy-dog eyes under that worn-out and tilted baseball cap. Believe it or not, not all women want the emotional responsibility of a relationship.

Even if such a description was somewhat stark, it was undeniable that on the campus of Mary Washington College anyway, the dynamics between men and women had changed considerably as the result of coed residence halls. This did not necessarily, in itself, imply greater sexual activity, as many relationships were platonic. It did, however, mean that on an everyday basis there was greatly increased interaction between the sexes.[155]

Then, too, technology played a role, influencing social behavior as extensively as it did the academic aspect of college life. After 2000, social-networking

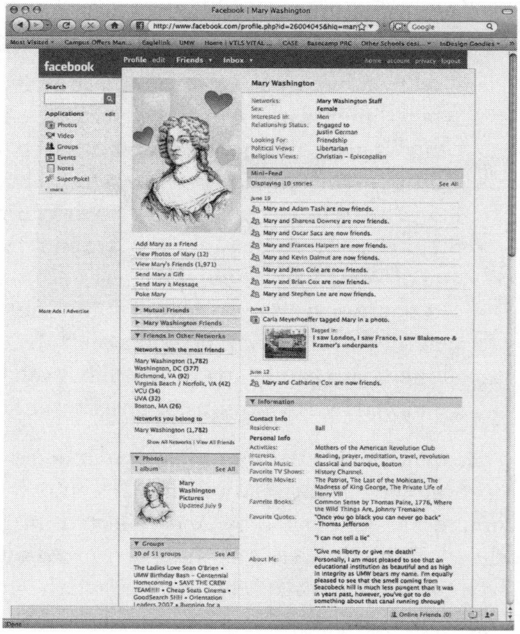

A 21st century anachronism: A Facebook page for Mary Washington herself

Web sites such as MySpace and Facebook made it possible for students to gain personal information (sometimes quite intimate and graphic) about their peers without any personal contact at all. The information influx was further abetted by ubiquitous cell phones and their potential for transmitting pictures as well as text messages, and by computers that facilitated instant messaging, or IMing.

Whatever the reason or combination of reasons, dating in the traditional sense gradually became passé, replaced by a pattern in which students would "hang out" in groups at various events, during the course of which couples who were attracted to each other might decide thereafter to "hook up." The procedure was extensively and perceptively explained in a 2001 *Bullet* article, whose title succinctly described the situation—"Party, Drink, Hook-Up . . . Repeat: Have Random Nights Replaced Relationships?" The gist of the article itself essentially answered that question in the affirmative. "Hooking up," it read, "the ambiguous phrase that has seduced its way into today's adolescent and young adult slang can mean anything from making out with someone in the back corner of a party to getting laid. It is usually a one-time event, unplanned and almost always due to intoxication, most likely after which neither party will ever speak to the other again. It exists in a time when there are no chaperones and curfews, few rules of etiquette and even fewer dates. Courtship is dead, and hooking up reigns."

The article proceeded to describe a scenario, presumably typical, that such hooking up could create. "It is a Sunday morning," it said, "and a college girl is just waking up in her dorm room, after a long night of partying, to the sound of the phone ringing. It is her friend calling to ask the routine post-party question. 'Did you hook up with anyone last night?' She rubs her eyes just enough to notice the lump next to her under the blanket. She blinks a few times, and realizes it's the hot guy from her chemistry class that she'd always wanted to hook up with. And now she has."

Such activities prompted one scholarly observer to assert, in an article titled "The End of Courtship," that "sexually active—in truth, hyperactive—[students] flop about from one relationship to another. . . . The very terms—'wooing,' 'courting,' 'suitors'—are archaic; and if the words barely exist, it is because the phenomena have all but disappeared. . . . Never mind wooing, today's collegians do not even make dates or other forward-looking commitments to see one another."[156] At Mary Washington, such was increasingly the case. As one former *Bullet* sports editor put it in 2001, "If I had a choice between having a girlfriend and hooking up, I'd rather have random hook ups until the right one comes along," though he added, "or until Ashley Judd calls me up."

The practice was apparently so prevalent that in March 2001 the *Bullet* ran a collection of student interviews asking the question, "Where is the best place to hook up on campus?" which it followed in October of the same year with a query as to the "worst place to hook up on campus." The best spots, according to the interviewees, included:

- South Hall Room 105 because it's handicapped accessible.
- The piano room in Pollard because there's beautiful background music.
- In the fountain because everything is more fun wet.
- The balcony of Randolph because you're in the open, but no one knows you're up there.

Among the worst places mentioned were:

- The lecture hall in Monroe because the seats are too small.
- Seacobeck, because afterwards you have that awful smell.
- The top row of the Trinkle lecture hall because too many people have had sex there.

Taking the risqué theme a step further, a 2003 poll asked, "What is your favorite position?" Amid a number of inventive suggestions, the most interesting response, perhaps, was that of a freshman basketball player who, either from facetiousness or failure to understand the question, declared that his favorite position was "point guard."

The most lascivious exposition of sexual matters was a *Bullet* column called "Sexclamations." Coauthored by the *Bullet*'s editor-in-chief, Betsy Crumb, and staff writer Elspeth "Elz" England, who mischievously dubbed themselves "wanton sex goddesses," the column began shortly before Valentine's Day 2006 and became a regular feature. Week after week the campus was offered observations—usually expressed with a combinaton of humor and vulgarity—on a range of salacious issues. Among the least ribald was a column that addressed what the authors termed "morning after" woes. "First, ladies," it advised, "if you're the makeup-wearing type, bring some extra Clinique with you. A few touchups in the morning can hide those love bites. As for your eyes, well, the smudged look is still in. Or, embrace the disheveled look; the messier you appear, the more fun people will think you had."

The fundamental assumption of the column seemed to be that a high level of sexual activity had become the norm among the college set, and that the proffered advice was thus essentially a public service. In that light, it perhaps did not appear ironic when one column warned that "sex can lead to emotional intimacy"—the inversion of the conventional order of things in the past.

"Sexclamations" became, in all likelihood, the *Bullet*'s most widely read section—and surely its most controversial. Letters to the editor often expressed approval, but a number voiced countervailing concerns, notably the lack of attention to the potential problems related to casual sex, such as pregnancy, AIDS, and other sexually transmitted diseases. "Maybe you should focus less on lewd and risky sexual behaviors," wrote one critic, "and instead address the implications and consequences that arise when people engage in too much promiscuous behavior. Or, if you are going to continue your advice column on how one can 'spice up' his or her sex life, I think you can do it less graphically." The columnists routinely disavowed such charges, pointing out that their articles frequently included warnings about the need to practice safe sex—and they did. It was debatable, however, whether such specific cautionary messages embedded within the articles were likely to prevail amid the preponderance of prurience.[157]

There were also larger concerns about the column's propriety. Representative of such views was a guest column written in February 2006 by senior Emily Mushen. "It is embarrassing," she wrote,

> to have that kind of material in a publication that is distributed to an audience that is supposed to be growing in maturity and integrity, not regressing. Despite the songs that may tell us otherwise, imitating what you see on Animal Planet (or Discovery Channel) in your own life can indeed be wrong. . . . Also, there appears to be a very fundamental disconnect between the ideals that are advocated in [the column] . . . and the reality that those same ideals often lead directly to instances of date rape which are quickly identified as 'serious problems.' How exactly are we supposed to counteract these horrible crimes if we are simultaneously telling college students that they're supposed to get drunk and have sex, and be proud of it?

In fact, at the same time that sexual indulgence seemed to be increasing, there was a growing emphasis on the awareness of sexual assault. By the nineties, educational programs on the subject were standard fare in the residence halls, and campuswide events periodically highlighted the issue. One such was Candlelight Vigil 2000, jointly sponsored by about a dozen campus groups in conjunction with local agencies including the Rappahannock Council on Domestic Violence and the Rappahannock Council against Sexual Assault. A leading organizer of the group was senior Tammie Willis, who offered powerful personal testimony of how an assault on her, though not resulting in rape, did lead to permanent hearing loss. A similar program emphasizing rape awareness called Take Back the Night was first offered in 2005 and became an annual event.

The most visible (and controversial) program dealing with such issues was *The Vagina Monologues*, first performed on campus in 2003 as part of the V-Day movement (the "V" standing for victory, valentine, and vagina). The goal of V-Day worldwide was to generate greater attention for the fight to stop violence against women and girls, including rape, battery, incest, female genital mutilation, and sexual slavery.

The Vagina Monologues was an episodic play written in 1996 by Eve Ensler, who, having interviewed abused women from a variety of backgrounds, decided to put their stories on stage so that they would no longer feel ashamed about their bodies. Speaking at Mary Washington in 1998 as part of Women's History Month, Ensler made the point that saying the word "vagina" is normally difficult for most people. "It doesn't matter how many times you say the word," she explained, "it never sounds like a word you want to say. It's a completely unsexy word."

Nonetheless it was the key word—that, and its more earthy iterations—in *The Vagina Monologues*. In an earlier day, female Mary Washington students would likely have been reluctant to use such words. By the early years of the twenty-first century, however, American culture had evolved (or devolved) to the point that everyday vocabularies contained words previously more likely to come from the mouths of stevedores than students. Indeed, there were so many students eager to participate in the production that the two shows each year assembled different casts to accommodate them all.

The shows drew sizable crowds each year. "We still get a lot of sneers," commented one participant in 2006, "[but] this isn't a joke; this is a movement." Presumably, the program achieved its goal of raising awareness; more tangibly, it succeeded in raising money, which it donated to local charities such as Hope House, a refuge for homeless women and children in the Fredericksburg area.

And it had one other benefit. The students, though they took their roles seriously, also had fun with it.

Meanwhile "Sexclamations" continued. With the graduation of cowriter Betsy Crumb in May of 2006, the column continued the following year under the authorship of Elz England, who was joined by senior Dan Ceo, the paper's photography editor. To the minds of some, the column declined from its already minimal level of taste. Particularly notable was one piece, written by Ceo, that essentially advocated pornography, which he described as "educational really."

For some, that column was the last straw, contributing to a spate of letters to the editor published the following week under the heading "'Sex' Sucks." Among them was a letter from a member the *Bullet* staff itself who declared herself "increasingly outraged" by the "Sexclamations" column. "The past few months I have been able to hold my tongue," she wrote,

> but after this past week's column on porn, I am unable to do so. . . . Not only do I find the column extremely crude and tasteless in the topics it discusses, but I also find it offensive and misrepresentative of the student population. The column speaks like all of the paper's readers are sex-crazed zealots who have nothing better to do with their time than think about sex, but this is not true. Yes, I know that we are in college and sex is prevalent; you can't go out on the weekends without sex staring you in the face, but that does not mean that I want to come home and read about someone else's sexual preferences and experiences.

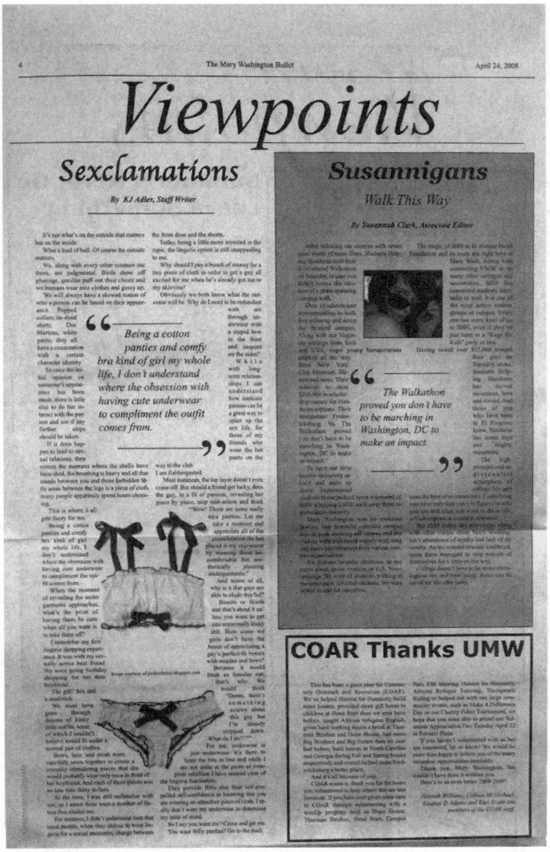

4 The Mary Washington Bullet April 24, 2008

Viewpoints

Sexclamations

By KJ Adler, Staff Writer

It's not what's on the outside that matters but on the inside.

What a load of bull. Of course the outside matters.

We, along with every other creature out there, are judgmental. Birds show off plumage, gorillas puff out their chests and we humans wear nice clothes and gussy up.

We will always have a skewed notion of who a person can be based on their appearance.

the front door and the sheets.

Today, being a little more invested in the topic, the lingerie option is still unappealing to me.

Why should I pay a bunch of money for a tiny piece of cloth in order to get a guy all excited for me when he's already got me in my skivvies?

Obviously we both know what the outcome will be. Why do I need to be redundant

"*Being a cotton panties and comfy bra kind of girl my whole life, I don't understand where the obsession with having cute underwear to compliment the outfit comes from.*"

Susannigans

Walk This Way

By Susannah Clark, Associate Editor

"*The Walkathon proved you don't have to be marching in Washington, DC to make an impact.*"

COAR Thanks UMW

"Sexclamations," which ran weekly in the Bullet, *created a campus stir.*

Widespread disgust with "Sexclamations" led to a petition against the column, as reported in a prominent article in February 2007 titled "Sex Column Divides Student Body." Leading the revolt was junior Kathleen Pacious. "It's not journalism," she said, "and I think it's degrading to men and women." She proceeded to develop a petition, eventually signed by more than five hundred students, declaring that "the column 'Sexclamations' contains no journalistic merit, . . . decreases the value of the *Bullet* to less than that of *Cosmopolitan*, and diminishes the reputation of our school in the eyes of the community and prospective students. 'Sexclamations' must be removed from the *Bullet* so our student newspaper and [school] can regain their honor and credibility."

In the not too distant past, College officials would likely have supported such a campaign against vulgarity, but changing times had apparently affected administrative attitudes as well. Vice President for Student Affairs and Dean of Students Bernard Chirico expressed little sympathy for the protest movement. The column had created "definitely a buzz" on campus, he said, but "we have lots of opposing viewpoints at this school. They should all be able to say what they believe. . . . They *should* be stirring things up. Isn't that what it's all about at this age?" "Sexclamations" coauthor Elz England likewise dismissed the protest, suggesting that the petitioners "should just skip reading the column if they have a problem with it. Reading the entire *Bullet* is not compulsory."

Although "Sexclamations" went beyond the bounds of decency in the view of many, interest in sexual activities was nonetheless evident in other ways. According to the *Bullet* in November 2006, a growing trend on college campuses involved so-called romance enhancement parties, often hosted under the aegis of a company called Slumber Parties. Quite unlike such parties of yore, these specialized in the sale of products ranging from lotions and oils (e.g., X-Scream Butter Cream Icing, Nympho Niagara) to toys for both bath and bedroom. "I would much rather go to a party with my girlfriends than a sketchy sextoy shop," commented one student. "It's so much fun. Even to just pass around the displays and giggle and say, 'Oh my God, look at that.'"

In the spring of 1999, the *Bullet* carried a front-page story titled "Sex Survey Reveals MWC Is a Swinging Campus," in which it reported the findings, replete with graphs, of a random poll of 60 percent of the student body. Most of the questions focused on sexual experience, resulting in the revelation that Mary Washington males had generally had thirty to forty partners by the age of twenty; the level of female promiscuity was even higher, with an average of approximately sixty partners by that age.

The quantitative results seemed to be substantiated by written comments, such as one female's admission that she found it "so easy to be promiscuous at Mary Washington. There are just so many guys here to choose from." One male expressed a similar attitude. "If the girls here won't put out," he said, "we just go to other colleges where the girls don't know us, and the Greek system is in full effect." The article further reported that shortly after the poll results were tabulated, a group of students began making plans for a "Sexfest" to be held in Ball Circle at an undisclosed date and time.

According to the paper, "The findings were startling." They were also totally bogus. For readers who had not noticed the publication's date, April 1, the article concluded with a disclaimer. "In case you haven't figured it out yet," it said, "this article is complete fiction. Have a good April Fool's Day, and don't forget to make every day a 'Sexfest.' (Just kidding.)"

The paper was wise to include the clarification separating fact from fantasy. Sometimes it was hard to tell.

Inevitably, the social evolution on campus affected a number of traditions. Junior Ring Week continued to thrive, but events such as Spring Formal suffered declining appeal. In an effort to resuscitate the formal, which had previously been held on campus, Class Council (the sponsor of the affair) began in the 1990s to schedule it in various off-campus venues including, as the *Bullet* reported, "Richmond's Jefferson Hotel, one of the most grand and historic hotels in the South, [where] students were served a full-course meal under the gleaming lights of the Jefferson's blazing chandeliers." In other years the event took the form of river cruises along the James or "on the waves of the Potomac, nestled between the cherry blossoms and the monuments." Though such galas won praise from students who participated, enthusiasm for the event tended to wane—possibly the result of rising costs, possibly because formal events in general had come to have less appeal to college students than in earlier times.

Similar indifference threatened Devil-Goat Day, the long-standing spring tradition pitting freshmen and juniors against sophomores and seniors in an afternoon of field-day-type events in either Westmoreland or Ball Circles. By 1992 the *Bullet* acknowledged that it was "a tradition that has been losing its fervor." That same year, sponsorship of the event was taken over by the freshman class officers, who tried to rejuvenate it by adding a reggae band and activities such as sumo wrestling, a Velcro wall climb, and a pie-eating contest to the usual program of egg tosses, balloon relays, sack and wheelbarrow races, and tug-of-war contests. In subsequent years, more daring events such as jousting, bungee races, and human bowling were added. Indicative of the increased danger involved (as well as a reflection of a more litigious society), all participants had to sign waivers acknowledging their awareness of the risks involved.

The efforts to make the event more appealing to newer generations of students met with only modest success. Some still supported it, such as the 2004 *Bullet* columnist who described it as "basically an event where college students can run around like little kids at a carnival and it's okay." The overall attitude, however, seemed increasingly to be more like that of another observer who derisively termed Devil-Goat Day a "college re-creation of a middle school field day . . . [involving] a great lot of pathetic wholesome fun." Besides such negativity from students, the day also attracted opposition from some faculty who resented losing a half day of classes, especially so late in the semester. The result was that even though Devil-Goat Day survived to the end of the College's first century, it had by then lost much of the panache that had characterized its earlier years.

On a weekly basis, much of the entertainment at Mary Washington was provided by talent drawn from within the student body. There were, for example, poetry slams sponsored by the Department of English, Linguistics, and Speech in which participants were invited to read aloud (and sometimes loudly) their original compositions. A similar venue for individual expression was provided by periodic open-mic nights in the Underground. One such event in 1999 provoked a campus controversy when a student delivered a stand-up (self-styled) comedy routine of such scatological and racist content that some members of the audience walked out in protest. Among them was

English professor Steve Watkins, who departed with the audible comment that he found the performance "pretty [expletive] offensive"—an action that itself created further commotion.

Such episodes were rare, however, and most student performances, whatever their quality, were generally well received among peers. Perennially popular were "battle of the bands" contests in which campus groups vied for recognition as the best band on campus. Beginning in 1986 and continuing annually, the contests provided students with a satisfying sample of their contemporaries' music—and the winning group with a sizable cash prize. (They also provided an inventive array of band names including, after 2000, for example, Twi-Lite Motel, Classic Smack, We Ain't No Beverage, Attack Penguin, the Grave-Robbing Extravaganza, and No Sunlite for the Media.)

A lip-sync contest was introduced in 1998 as one of several events during Spirit Week, sponsored by Class Council. The inaugural effort featured, in addition to student acts, a Sonny and Cher imitation by the director of the psychology center, Barbara Wagar, as Sonny, and Dean of Students Bernard Chirico, resplendent in fluorescent-pink hip-huggers, as Cher. The *Bullet* pronounced their act "clever and fun."

Describing the overall event, the paper noted that "there was a lot of booty-shaking and some partial nudity, but the audience seemed to enjoy it." It proceeded, however, to deliver a cautionary message: "There was a small majority who thought that this was an audition to appear in a Victoria's Secret catalog. Although partial nudity is tasteful to a certain extent, the Mary Washington stage probably should be reserved for those who have enough class to keep their legs crossed and their cleavage covered."

Requiring a bit more talent (and nerve) than lip-syncing was another faux-music experience, karaoke (from the Japanese for "empty orchestra"). The form became popular with students in the 1990s, when groups of them would venture downtown to ply their (presumed) musical talents at nightspots such as Sophia Street Station. By the turn of the century, karaoke contests were being held on campus in which, reported the *Bullet*, performers "sang along with songs ranging from country to pop to old school rap, as well as two well-known classic karaoke staples, 'Louie, Louie' by The Kingsmen and 'Baby Got Back' by Sir Mix-A-Lot."

Beginning in 2000, talent shows attracted sizable audiences to Dodd. The first, cosponsored by Brothers of a New Direction (BOND) and the Black Student Association, had the dual purpose of providing entertainment and raising money for an after-school program in Bragg Hill, a predominantly black neighborhood in Fredericksburg. The talent show was successful in both respects, drawing a large crowd and highlighting a variety of student performers, notably the contest winner, senior theater major Natalie Joy Johnson '00. Having already earned a reputation around campus for her singing ability, Johnson "wowed the audience with her seductive version of Madonna's 'Sooner or Later,'" said the *Bullet*. "Shimmying around the stage in a leopard-print dress and cape, and filling Dodd Auditorium with her powerful and soulful voice, Johnson certainly made an impact on the audience who hooted and hollered during her performance."[158]

Two events established near the turn of the century conjured visions of the late Wo-Man contest, that sometimes bizarre and always tawdry (yet consistently popular) event of yesteryear: the Mr. MWC contest and the Drag Show.

October 1999 marked the first appearance of the Mr. MWC contest. It was part of Spirit Week, a cluster of activities—bonfire, lip-sync contest, fireworks, athletic events—leading up to homecoming weekend, a reunion celebration designed for alumni who had graduated within the last ten years. The contest was sponsored by the Young Republicans, who donated a portion of their proceeds to the Rappahannock Council on Domestic Violence. A beauty contest spoof, Mr. MWC consisted of male contestants representing each of the campus residence halls, plus several from local apartment complexes. Competing in several categories typical of beauty contests, contestants were judged, according to the *Bullet*, on "creativity / originality, costume / clothing, personality / presence, and audience response."

Contestants were required to compete in both evening and sportswear ensembles—the latter of which prompted one 2001 contestant to sport a preppy tennis outfit that he identified as being from "the Cedric collection." A question-and-answer portion required contestants to respond extempore to queries such as the following:

- Should vegetarians eat animal crackers?
- You are Leonardo Da Vinci. Why does Mona Lisa smile?
- If you could rename any building on campus, which would you rename and why?
- If you could have any super power, what would it be and how would you use it? (The contestant's answer: "The power to make big buckets of Ben and Jerry's ice cream.")

The talent portion of the proceedings obviously presented the most inviting prospect for both hilarity and ribaldry, an opportunity that contestants seldom missed, often relying on contemporary events for inspiration. Among the more memorable performances was the 2001 rendition of Britney Spears's "Oops! . . . I Did It Again" by "Mr. Marshall," the beefy and goateed Steve Busch. The winner that year, freshman Jody Greene, a.k.a. "Mr. Bushnell," won the crowd's plaudits by pedaling a toy green tractor around the stage while wearing hayseed attire, chewing a wheat stalk, and singing Kenny Chesney's "She Thinks My Tractor's Sexy."

Though Mr. MWC obviously shared certain farcical elements with the late Wo-Man contest, according to the *Free Lance–Star* it was "nothing like the controversial" predecessor. "The new, feel-good Mr. MWC contest," it asserted, "is far kinder and gentler than Wo-Man." The paper went on to suggest that even in just its second year, Mr. MWC had established itself as "a puckish new tradition at Mary Washington."

Audiences did indeed seem to love the unabashed antics of their peers. As for the contestants themselves, there was another attractive feature. As one of the 2003 contestants explained, "The Mr. MWC contest is a great chance for us dorky guys to get up on stage in front of hundreds of screaming girls and feel extremely sexy for one whole night."

One difference was that the new iteration, while not exactly refined, did not plumb the tasteless depths of its forerunner. Also, many of the performers were actually good, not merely grotesque. The *Free Lance–Star* hailed the 1999 Mr. MWC winner, Derek Coryell, as "a formidable talent as a stand-up comic" and heaped particular praise on the 2000 hosts Cynthia Lotze and Elena Russeau for displaying "far more professionalism and charm than Donnie and Marie Osmond did during the Miss America contest a few days earlier."

The Drag Show, which premiered in 2001, though fully the equal of Wo-Man in crudity in the eyes of some, could not similarly be condemned for its lack of sensitivity, inasmuch as it was sponsored by People Representing Individuals of Sexual Minorities (PRISM). Held in the Underground, the show featured both professional drag queens from Richmond and amateur wannabes from Mary Washington. While the vamping of the former generally elicited audience approval, the vulgarity of the latter sometimes produced revulsion.

Favorably reviewing the first Drag Show in April 2001, the *Bullet* critic proclaimed, "There is a unique exhilaration that only shows its face in the light of masquerade. . . . I tip my hat to the luscious ladies and gorgeous gents of the drag show. Fellas, you have lit the college on FIRE." The paper's review of the 2003 event was considerably more negative, berating in particular those student participants who apparently "mistook MWC's Drag Show for MTV's Jackass." She then proceeded to offer "some tips for next year's boys":

- Shave. Who knows, you just may like it.
- Use make-up. Most girls don't look good without it, why do you think you do?
- Do NOT under any circumstance take off your shoes (Big drag faux pas).
- Learn the lyrics to your song. Entertain, don't make a fool of yourself.
- Tuck. I understand your bulge may be small to begin with, but humor us. Again, drag queen, not boy in girls' clothing.
- Be your alternate personality. You are no longer Joe Smith, drunken college student. You are Priscilla, Queen of the Underground.
- Don't dance like a dumb straight white boy.
- Check your boobs. Consult the girl whose bra you borrowed before strutting your misshapen uneven boobs before hundreds.

Ironically, in the same year that the dubious Drag Show was established, an attempt was made to reestablish that epitome of refinement, May Day. In January 2001 several clubs, led by the Inter-Club Association and the French

Club, took the lead in trying to resuscitate a tradition that had been dormant (presumed dead) since 1968.

There were changes, to be sure, from the original concept—changes necessary "to accommodate the times," according to its chief organizer. For one thing, no pageant was involved, since the event was to be "not a beauty contest but instead a celebration of school spirit and solidarity." Selection of a king and queen from each class was to be made by a group of five faculty and staff members, based on a contest consisting of a one-thousand-word essay on school spirit. Court attendants to the regal couples were also to be chosen, whereupon contestants could advertise their achievements and leadership skills on flyers posted in the Eagles Nest. A popular vote would then determine the winners.

Another, most obvious, change was that the May Day celebration was to be held not in May but in February. Overall, the affair was scarcely reminiscent of the original event when first reintroduced, and in the second year, there was even less resemblance, as the May Court Ball morphed into the Grand Monte Carlo Ball. One interesting tie to the past, however, was provided when the crowning of the 2002 May Queen was performed by the May Queen of 1950, Marceline "Marcy" Weatherly Morris.

In a positive contemporary gesture, a share of the profits from the affair was donated to breast cancer research because the promoters recognized "the pertinence of breast cancer to the age group of the [original] May Queens." Noting that 60 percent of the proceeds would go toward that cause, the advertisement for the event urged students to "help support a good cause by restoring a long-running MWC tradition."

Alas, the new-old event did not take hold, and the attempt to revive May Day was abandoned after two years. Apparently, in the twenty-first century, May Queens and Drag Queens did not readily coexist.

Much of the social life on campus revolved around the residence halls, notably including recurrent dorm-sponsored events such as Willard's Rocktoberfest, Westmoreland's Westfest, and (for a time) Mason and Randolph's Unconscious Party. The prototype, still going strong in 2007, was Marshall's well-named Grill on the Hill, which featured, as did the others, the staples of outdoor campus parties: food, drink, and live (loud) music. From time to time, too, dorms sponsored themed events, sometimes drawing on nostalgia. Popular in the first decade of the twenty-first century was Ball Hall's eighties revival dances. "The hits of the '80s, from Madonna to Men Without Hats, are undeniably a huge part of the dance's draw," reported the *Bullet*. " 'The Electric Slide' is a mainstay. Students from all over campus . . . [jump] at the chance to don their legwarmers, acid-washed jeans, and other kooky remnants from the 'me decade.'" As one student put it, "Anything that includes Michael Jackson's 'Thriller,' Gremlins, and neon fishnet gloves is my idea of a party."

Then there were always smaller-scale dorm parties that cropped up on a fairly regular basis, the Super Bowl being a prime excuse for celebrations each year. As the *Bullet* noted, "Whether it was for love of the game or interest in the half-time show," most students partied in a similar fashion: "Beer cans snap open. A big bowl of pretzels sits on the coffee table. Five hands reach for the last buffalo wing, and cheers resonate throughout the building as the winning touchdown is scored."

Of course, many student diversions required no organization at all, as the campus itself provided enticing opportunities for various shenanigans, often related to the weather. Hard rains on occasion drew large numbers of students to Ball Circle, where, according to one newspaper, they had "some good dirty fun by playing slip and slide in the mud, apparently enjoying it just as much as they did the first time around, in their toddler years."[159] It was not, certainly, an activity favored by the crew of the physical plant, who always had to restore the greens to create a pristine setting for May commencement. (And Prince Woodard, had he been alive, would have been appalled.)

Nothing was a more productive source of student high jinks than the snowfalls that periodically blanketed the campus. Snow, indeed, was a meteorological phenomenon guaranteed to induce frenzy among students from grade school to grad school, and those at Mary Washington were no exception.

Several snowfalls were particularly memorable, including the foot-deep accumulation in late January 1987. Classes closed at noon on Thursday, not to reopen until the following Wednesday, a period that encompassed Super Bowl Sunday. The most prevalent outdoor activity for students was (as always) sledding, mainly on the hill behind Mason and Randolph, or at Trench Hill, or on "Suicide Hill" off Hanover Street. The most popular conveyances, absent actual sleds, were inner tubes and Seacobeck trays (the trays, of course, being honorably returned after use). The first afternoon of the blizzard witnessed in Ball Circle an official campuswide snowball fight of such epic proportions that it was covered by radio station B106.

Pizza and Chinese food deliveries did a booming business serving dorm-bound students. Also, the *Bullet* reported, "The Giant food store in the Park & Shop center saw the effects of the Wash's days free of class. Several top items sold out, including wine coolers, Oodles of Noodles, many varieties of potato chips, and some brands of beer."

One result of the snowstorm was to create a sort of enforced camaraderie on campus. As a *Bullet* columnist described the situation:

> We may have finally found a way to get people to go to campus events: trap them here with nothing else to do for five days. The Pub was packed every night, and so was the Mixer. . . . As near as I can tell, most students started drinking around 11:00 A.M. Thursday and stayed in some sort of stupor until the Super Bowl. . . . Some die-hards kept it up right until classes resumed on Wednesday. The same students who couldn't walk to class had no problem trekking to the ABC store half

a mile away. . . . It's something to tell your children twenty years from now: "Well, when I was in college, we had to walk two miles in a blizzard to get a beer."

The writer concluded her article with "a few unanswered questions," as she put it. "One, is it true that President Anderson was in Richmond during the snow storm? [He was.] I mean is there any possibility he was at the Super Bowl in Pasadena with Marion Barry? And two, will there be any predictable rise in the rate of pregnancies nine months from now?"

The first snowfall of 1992, in mid-February, prompted a campus innovation: snow streaking. Five male participants, who said they got the idea from Princeton's "Naked Olympics," developed a version that consisted of two events: a nude lap around Ball Circle, followed by a running dive into the snow. Not to be outdone, several female streakers cavorted topless in Ball Circle and on the Lee Hall deck.

According to *Bullet* reports, the late-night exhibitions were enthusiastically received by the twenty or so students who were present in Ball Circle and others who observed from Madison Hall windows. "Everyone was clapping and laughing," said one of the participants, adding that "a lot of flashes went off." The streakers also expressed the hope that their chilly exploit would be the beginning of a new Mary Washington tradition. (It was not.)

Two years later, the campus was hit by a blizzard of such magnitude that classes were canceled for an entire week shortly after the opening of the 1994 spring semester. As the *Bullet* reported, the snow "brought sledding, skating, drinking, relaxing, accidents, [and] cabin fever. . . . As the week seemed to get longer as boredom set in, just about everyone wondered about how we would make up classes. . . . From having to go to school on Saturday to having to cancel Spring Break trips to the Bahamas, students feared the worst."

The solution finally announced by Interim Dean of the Faculty Richard Hansen was to push the exam schedule back one day and to use the preceding two (one of which was originally supposed to be a reading day) to make up the lost class time. According to a *Bullet* editorial, that plan "did not sit well with anyone."

Nor was that the end of it, as snow further forced cancellation of classes on the succeeding two Fridays. Those days were made up by holding optional classes on designated Sunday afternoons in late February and mid-April. That approach, too, was panned by students, one of whom complained that "even though we are college students, we do have lives. Many of us have off-campus jobs and other commitments that we cannot drop whenever the administration thinks it's appropriate." Another said simply, "Sunday school is for church." It thus came as no surprise to anyone that attendance at the Sunday makeup sessions was low. The experiment was not tried again.

In 1996 the College was blanketed by over two feet of snow resulting from a succession of storms that were among the worst ever to strike the East Coast. The difference this time was that the blizzard of '96 occurred just

The blizzard of 1996 blanketed the campus with more than two feet of snow.

before the opening of classes, giving students an extra three days of vacation. The penalty was paid by, again, adjusting the exam period to provide additional days for instruction.

Three years passed before snow necessitated another cancellation of classes. In the interim, students had apparently become more innovative in the art of snow sculpture. In an article titled "Frosty Gets Freaky" (subtitled "Anatomically Correct Snowmen 'Hang' around Campus), the *Bullet* reported that after the snowfall "sexually active white snow creatures took over the campus, with the help of students who would make a good case study for Freud. . . . There were massive snowmen, snowanimals, and sexually explicit snowpeople." The most interesting of the genre was a Ball Circle specimen consisting of a snowman on one side and snowwoman on the other—complete, said the *Bullet*, "with appropriate body parts."

A 2004 snowfall marked the first time in the institution's history that students were seriously injured in snow-related accidents. Two males, in separate sledding mishaps, sustained injuries that required surgery. Thenceforth the area where the accidents occurred—the campus hill above Sunken Road—was closed to sledders.

Even in years when snowfall was minimal, students remained hopeful, as in 2006 when the *Bullet* proffered a list of "the top five things to do on a rare snow day":

1. Sleep Until You Can Sleep No More: Face it. You're in college. You mindlessly sit at your computer either refreshing Facebook, or "doing work" (a.k.a. checking other people's Facebooks) until 2 A.M. every night. . . . Do yourself and those around you a favor, and get some shut-eye.
2. Get on the Horn: You've been M.I.A. and your friends and family have come to grips with your disappearance and possible death. Call your mom.
3. Eat, Drink and be Merry: Forget the gym today. Call your good

friends at Hunan Garden instead. Everyone deserves the occasional overindulgence and . . . who [can] pass up an afternoon of hot chocolate and Little Debbies?

4. Marathon Time: Not of the physical variety, of course. We're talking visual. Snow days are the perfect occasion to snuggle up with someone . . . and numb your mind with quality Hollywood entertainment. Believe me, that 20-pound business law book screaming at you from the shelf across the room can wait.
5. Give In and Go Out: Face it, frolicking in the snow hasn't lost its luster. . . . Snowball fights are always fun and a good excuse for harmless flirting. If wet, cold hands aren't your bag of chips, you can always grab a Seaco tray and enjoy a wet, cold butt while careening recklessly down Arrington hill. Unfortunately though, Seaco trays don't come with brakes. You might want to wear a mouth guard.

The suggestions were indicative of the exhilarating, and sometimes infantilizing, effect that snow always seemed to have on students. The explanation was put most succinctly by one student who commented, "It is kind of cool, because people [act] like they are five years old again."

The arrival of warm weather brought another spate of activities. At various times in the nineties and thereafter such activities included Frisbee, hacky sack, rollerblading, and skateboarding—any and all of which could make the traversing of Campus Walk an interesting, sometimes dicey, experience. Skateboarding, especially when used for "tricking out" (as opposed to mere transportation), eventually came to be regarded as such a threat to the benches, steps, flower beds, and sundry artifacts along the walk that it was banned in 1999. The decision was unpopular with devotees of the board, one of whom attributed the ban to the fact that "some old, stuffy people don't like the image" skateboarding conveyed. To the relief of its practitioners, the ban on skateboarding was lifted in 2006.

For less-active students there were two springtime activities so popular that the *Bullet* once listed them among the "five things to do before you leave" Mary Washington: swimming in the Monroe fountain and suntanning on the various lawns and patios around campus. According to the paper, it was a "very traditional act to take a quick dip in the Monroe fountain (preferably at night when the cops and facilities services are not around . . . but minus the soap bubbles, please)." Regarding tanning, it said, "For those of you who come from a cold and frozen tundra, like, let's say, Massachusetts, this is a chance to really stick it to those elitist high school friends who stayed up north: those silly Yanks are still shoveling snow while you lay outside your residence hall, half-naked, oiled up, and ready for summer."

In the long tradition of college students everywhere, those at Mary Washington were attracted to games of both the board and card genres. Heading the list, according to a 2005 *Bullet* article, were Balderdash, Scotland Yard, and Guess Who? At the very top, in the estimation of that writer, were Trivial Pursuit ("nothing short of a party in a box") and Scrabble, a game that offered "a chance to use all those twenty-five dollar words that you've been wanting to put in a sentence and just don't know how to." At various times, other games, notably Diplomacy and Risk, were so popular that their devotees actually formed clubs to facilitate contests.

The card game of choice had evolved over the years from the old college favorite, bridge, to poker, which by the turn of the century had become well nigh addictive to some students. The particularly favored form of the game was Texas hold 'em (sometimes dubbed "the Cadillac of poker"), made popular by its wide television exposure on shows such as ESPN's *World Series of Poker*. The illegality of gambling in Virginia notwithstanding, games usually involved wagering, normally in small amounts, but sometimes with pots reaching into several hundred dollars in games that went on into the wee hours. "Basically," said one participant, "whenever there's money involved, [we] stay and play."

Paradoxically, the same time that witnessed an upswing in poker also saw the renewed popularity of other, decidedly more sedate games. In 2005, for example, there were campus tournaments in Twister and even rock-paper-scissors; one of the most popular of all such events was bingo, at least partly because of the coveted prizes that it offered.

By 2005 the most intriguing individual diversion was a number puzzle called Sudoku. A *Bullet* editorial, noting that "it only takes one round to get you addicted," described the game's appeal:

> No one can argue that a lot of crazy things are happening in the world today. Political scandals, terrorist plots, freak tornados, death and disease keep our minds in constant turmoil. But there is one thing that provides solace to our daily routine: the Sudoku challenge in the Style section of the *Washington Post*. It's the crossword puzzle of Generation Y: a mix of ancient Asian logic and Will Shortz brilliance. . . . Life is uncertain, but there is no guessing in Sudoku. There is always an answer and a logical path to get there—you just have to find it. . . . With something so free, so fun, and so easy to do, why not try it?

Many aspects of student life were, of course, significantly influenced by technology. The most basic change, on a daily basis, involved new modes of communication, particularly cell phones with their capacity to transmit both voice and text messages (and, not infrequently, to disrupt classes). So ubiquitous had they become by mid-decade that landline phones were becoming seemingly obsolete.

Written communication was increasingly conducted via computer through instant messaging and e-mail. Though students, like the rest of society, had become heavily dependent on electronic media, there was evidence that many students still enjoyed receiving "snail mail." Employees in the College post office reported overhearing frequent complaints from students regarding the lack of mail they received. "I tend to come here quite often," said one exchange student from France, "even though I don't get many letters. We have so many different means of communication. The letter is the last real link people have from one to another." "It's gotten to the point that I even like getting bills," admitted another. "It's mail."

Technology also greatly expanded opportunities for amusement, including computer programs like Winamp and Napster that allowed music to be easily (if sometimes illegally, perhaps) downloaded from the Internet. When captured on MP3 files and iPods, the music thus became portable, allowing "plugged in" students to listen continuously, as many seemed determined to do.

Video games were another prevalent form of entertainment. Beginning in the late 1970s with the rather rudimentary arcade game Pac-Man, the genre evolved by the turn of the century to computer games like Snood. Increasingly sophisticated contests were made possible by gaming systems such as PlayStation, Nintendo, and, most of all, Xbox with its popular and (to some) notorious game *Halo*.

Such activities had far greater appeal to males than females. The reasons, according to psychology professor Chris Kilmartin, were twofold: first, "the images in many video games are designed for males (i.e., sexualized images of women or violence)," and second, "males are socialized to be goal oriented."

Whatever the causes, playing video games was widespread on campus. "Having lived in the dorms for two years," one female student wrote in the *Bullet*, "I walked up and down the halls of Alvey and Bushnell and [grew] accustomed to the sound of shooting noises coming from tiny rooms stuffed with guys sitting around and playing video games well into the night." As one player admitted, "I used to play fifteen hours straight, but now I only play about three to four hours a month. I had to go cold turkey. Once I get started with a game, I don't have the discipline to keep my gaming to a reasonable amount of time."

The same article expressed concern about the social consequences of extensive involvement in gaming. "All the time students spend playing video games can't be good for them," it said. "Spending too much time playing can take time away from schoolwork, jobs, campus club activities, and social interactions."

Yet an even more significant impact of technology on the lives of students (one that included females to perhaps an even greater extent than males) involved the communication of personal information via the Internet. It began in the 1990s when students began to post their musings (or whatever they wished) online in weblogs. Blogs, as they are commonly known, thus made available for general perusal personal information that might, in an earlier day, have been kept under lock and key.

In the first decade of the new century, the practice was facilitated via enormously popular social networking sites such as MySpace and Facebook. The *Bullet* explored the Internet phenomenon in a 2007 article called the "Top 5 Most Life-Sucking Web Sites." "Pop quiz," it began. "What do college students spend more time doing other than partying? Sorry professors, it doesn't involve hitting any books. Actually, the correct answer is staring at a pixilated screen for hours on end, clicking preciously tuition-financed free time into oblivion. Various Web sites have become the college forum not only for academic research and obscure pop-culture tidbits, but for general leisure as well. Students now depend on Web sites to organize their social lives and to waste away their weekday afternoons."

The sites included on the list were YouTube, Wikipedia, IMDb, and RetroJunk; but the number one site was Facebook. As the article explained, "Campus networking has expanded digitally with Facebook groups, petitions, event planning and stalking strangers' Wall to Walls. Pokes and shared pictures make excessive clicking irresistible. Just be wary of how many inebriated photos of you from Houston's last night get tagged. Grad schools and potential job offers have loomed their way into the network, and they are very quick to judge."

Although technological innovations provided an increasing array of options for diversion, movies continued to be popular with Mary Washington students. Long a staple of campus entertainment, weekend showings in Dodd Auditorium were standard fare for decades. After 2000, under the aegis of the Film Committee, a program known as Cheap Seats sponsored newly released films almost every weekend for only one dollar, a small fraction of the cost at local theaters. Such films were augmented by other presentations such as foreign film series sponsored by the Department of Modern Foreign Language. In 1998 the MWC Film Committee arranged for hit movies also to be shown throughout the week on a closed-circuit channel exclusive to the College.

Interest in movies was evidenced by the work of the Film Production Club and by an annual Student Film Festival, initiated by the SA Senate in 2004. The 2006 event had special significance. After an evaluative screening of fourteen films by a panel of faculty and students, eleven were shown in Dodd to an appreciative audience of over one thousand. Five of the films were selected for honors, including a $400 first-place award to Dylan Tuccilo '08 for his animated production *Coffee Break Island*.

But the event's highlight, which won Film of the Festival award and elicited a standing ovation, was Shin Fujiyama's documentary *Copprome: A Hope for Honduras*, consisting of footage he had shot while working at the impoverished orphanage. By the end of the evening, the audience, deeply moved, contributed over $2,000 to the Copprome cause, to which Tuccilo added his first-prize winnings.

The most common everyday entertainment was, of course, television, especially after the proliferation of cable channels and DVDs. A few long-running programs stood out as particular favorites of students at the end of the twentieth century, including the iconic *Saturday Night Live* and sundry (and tawdry) soap operas that were watched by more students than would likely admit it.

Beginning in 1990, a major hit with students was an animated cartoon series, *The Simpsons*. Its popularity grew out of the show's political and social satire (often of a politically incorrect nature), combined with a sizable measure of lowbrow humor. "It's not afraid to tackle any issue," explained one student. "I schedule my meals, study time, and sleep around *The Simpsons*." In the process of becoming both the longest-running American sitcom and animated show, *The Simpsons* contributed a number of expressions to the collegiate vernacular, most notably including Homer Simpson's signature "D'oh!"

For a ten-year period beginning in 1994 the TV show most widely viewed by MWC students was in all probability the NBC sitcom *Friends*. It was not hard to understand the program's appeal to the college demographic, since it was based on the experiences of six twenty-something characters living together in New York City.

Such was the program's popularity that, according to a 1996 *Bullet* article, a familiar scenario took place across campus each Thursday night: "The evening begins . . . at roughly ten minutes before 8 P.M. with an important checklist of necessities: Coke, popcorn or candy, and the remote control. On the night before a test this may also include a notebook and highlighter." What then followed on the screen was a depiction of early-adulthood triumphs and tribulations to which college students could easily relate. "It is kind of funny to see the things that [the *Friends* cast] get all pissy about," said one student, "because we have thought about it one time or another. . . . It is honest. [It] is what everyone wants. Everyone wants to have girl friends and guy friends and live happily ever after. Even their troubles are good."

In addition to comedies and dramas, popular genres in the first decade of the new century included game shows and so-called reality entertainment. Such programs attracted Mary Washington students not only as viewers but sometimes as participants. Three, for example, appeared on one of the longest running of all television game shows, *Jeopardy*. Beginning with Anne Robinson Hallerman '77 in 1987, they included Kristen Page '99 and Kevin Perry '00, both of whom were contestants in 1998. All three won at least one round. (Not as successful was an adjunct faculty member, Rabbi Stephen Weisman, who did not survive the initial contest.)

Among the top shows of the decade was *American Idol*, a competition designed to identify America's next big pop-music star. In early 2003, MWC junior David Zedonek was among the contestants. A member of College a cappella groups Invoice and the Symfonics, Zedonek was widely regarded on campus as a talented singer. By all accounts, his *American Idol* audition went well, but amid thousands of other aspirants, he was ultimately not selected to perform nationally before judges Paula Abdul, Randy Jackson, and Simon Cowell. As it turned out, however, Zedonek did not completely miss his moment of fame—though he may have wanted to. In a spontaneous moment after his audition, the exuberant Zedonek, on a dare, launched into a children's camp song about beavers. It was filmed, leaving him with "a bad feeling that *that's* what's going to be on TV."

He was right, as it became a brief part of the program's montage about what *not* to do in an audition—in this case, "Don't sing the beaver song." Though disappointed that his quest for glory did not end on a more positive note, Zedonek came away from the experience undaunted and upbeat. "The toughest part of coming back to reality at MWC," he said, "was all of the 'what ifs' I kept asking myself. 'Should I have done a different song? Should I have calmed down a little?' I finally decided that the greatest 'what if' is 'what if I hadn't done it at all?'"

The national exposure that eluded Zedonek was captured subsequently by Mary Washington graduate Aaron Altscher when he was chosen to participate on the NBC hit reality show *The Apprentice* in 2007. The program, based on competition among eighteen contestants to win the favor of (and a six-figure job from) real estate magnate Donald Trump, was one of the highest-rated shows on television at the time of Altscher's appearance.

Having earned both an undergraduate and master's degree in business administration from Mary Washington, as well as accolades as a member of the baseball team, Altscher generated considerable buzz in the Fredericksburg area and at Mary Washington when he appeared on the program. The Alumni Association even hosted a viewing party for the program's season premiere.

Unfortunately, after leading his team to victory for two weeks, Altscher met his demise when he received Trump's dreaded "You're fired!" pronouncement on the show's February 11 segment. The reason, according to the *Free Lance–Star*, was that he "may have simply been too nice a guy for Donald Trump." Altscher, who was unfazed by the disappointing outcome, admitted as much. "Trump was not really happy with my [lack of] assertiveness toward the other team [in the boardroom]," he said, conceding, "That isn't really my personality."

As Mary Washington entered the twenty-first century, one of the most fundamental changes in the institution involved the relationship of its student body to the local community. Whereas for most of the College's first eight decades students generally lived in dormitories, by the turn of the century, a substantially larger number were living in rented houses and apartments in the Fredericksburg area. In the process, much of the social activity that had once been restricted to campus moved into the local community—with results that were not always positive.

The most egregious episode involved a June 1999 party at a house rented from the National Park Service by three Mary Washington students. On the night that their lease expired, the three threw a party that, to put it mildly, got out of hand—to the extent that it received coverage in the *Washington Post*. According to the *Post* article, one of the hosts admitted that "it became like an *Animal House*–style party." He realized there was a problem when, according to the paper, one of the eighty to one hundred people present "tried to push a refrigerator down the basement stairs. When he saw people jumping through the living room ceiling from the attic rafters and hurling beer kegs against the wall to see who could make the biggest hole, [he] knew things were really out of control."

Though the students disputed the specifics of the *Post* report, there was no denying that serious damage occurred—"vandalism at its worst," in the words of a Park Ranger. Pulled out of class in the middle of a lab, the students were charged initially with the felony offense of destruction of federal property, a crime that carried the potential punishment of five years in prison and a $250,000 fine. Ultimately they negotiated a plea arrangement that included the agreement to make restitution in the amount of $7,000 each for the damage. (The house, already in disrepair, was eventually razed by the Park Service.)

Episodes such as the vandalism incident were aberrations (fortunately), but disagreements of lesser magnitude erupted from time to time, often involving student parking in nearby residential neighborhoods, a problem that was eventually resolved by designating areas in which students could legally park. Despite the periodic bickering, the city prospered, quite literally, from students' growing inclination to venture downtown or, increasingly, westward to Central Park to spend their money. One reason for the increasing exodus was the establishment of a city transit system, known as the FRED, that had a stop on campus to enable car-less residential students to travel more or less conveniently to area stores.

More important, however, was the fact that the rapid growth of the Fredericksburg area in the late twentieth century brought an increase in the number of opportunities not only for shopping but for drinking, dining, and dancing that would have been beyond comprehension for students of even two decades earlier. For students in the seventies, the westward boundary of the business district was the I-95 interchange, and the terminal landmark was the Sheraton, with its silo silhouette (a vestige of the not-so-distant days when it was the site of a working dairy farm).

But then in 1980 came the Spotsylvania Mall and, in the nineties, Central Park, the sprawling, multistore brainchild of Carl Silver, a local developer. By the turn of the century, Central Park included numerous retail chain stores as well as franchises of seemingly every known eating establishment in America. The latter provided both jobs and nourishment for Mary Washington students, whose consensus favorite was Chipotle, renowned for its huge and relatively inexpensive burritos. Students were also excited about amusement possibilities afforded by a massive new bar and live-music facility called the Shark Club and by construction of the area's first ice rink.

Although many students took advantage of the vastly increased shopping and entertainment opportunities offered by Central Park, when the Silver Companies announced plans to build Central Park II, also known as Celebrate Virginia, in 2000, a group of students protested the proposed expansion. Called Impact Group 2000, they condemned the plan for creating environmental damage and straining the local economy and assailed it for contributing to what they called "placelessness and loss of community."[160] While urging a student boycott of Central Park stores, the protesters also joined with the Student Association in sponsoring a forum in February 2000 to discuss issues raised by the projected development.

In the end, the opponents of the project failed, and plans for Celebrate Virginia went forward, including its proposed centerpiece, a National Slavery Museum. The progenitor of the museum concept was former Virginia governor Douglas Wilder, and its most prominent supporter was entertainer Bill Cosby, whose appearance on campus in September 2004 to promote the project elicited an excited response from the more starstruck members of the College community. Even with Cosby's support—he pledged a million dollars to the project during his campus talk—the museum was slow to develop and was still awaiting groundbreaking in 2007.

For students who preferred to shop and socialize closer to the campus, options had expanded significantly as well. Closest to campus was the General Store (née the Latchstring), run by Bill "Greek" Kertsos, known to students from the 1970s as proprietor of My Brother's Place. Downtown proper offered something for all dining tastes: for upscale dining there were La Petit Auberge and Claiborne's; for the financially challenged there were still sandwiches at the lunch counter of Goolrick's Drugstore and hot dogs at the Recreation Center (a.k.a. the Pool Room). For the literary and latte crowds, there were Merriman's and Hyperion, and for the more conservative types, J. Bryan's. For live music, there were the Irish Brigade, the Santa Fe Grill, and the Loft. For general hell-raising, there was Houston's (later Central Station), converted to a dance hall from its earlier incarnation as Rebel Bowl on Princess Anne Street.

Then, as always, there was Carl's. Ever since its opening in 1947, it had been a gustatory landmark, and so it remained to the present. Owned continuously by the Sponseller family (though the eponymous founder Carl had died), the iconic little building still housed the original Electro-Freeze machine that spun the magic custard. By then the machine had become so antiquated that parts were no longer available, and employees had to jury-rig repairs themselves.

But the toothsome product remained seductive to Mary Washington students. "When my friends and I are upset," commented one, "our solution is edible. If it's a bad grade, a break-up, a fight, or just a bad day, we all pile into a car and head to Carl's." Long lines were a tradition, but not a deterrent. "Part of the fun," said one, "is waiting in line."

In 2001, when preparing an article titled "Carl's: A Frozen Blast from the Past" to celebrate the annual spring reopening of the shop—an event often joyously documented by the *Bullet*—a reporter tried to call the establishment for an interview, only to discover that it had no phone. Too high-tech, apparently.

THE ATHLETIC PROGRAM

Mary Washington students liked to play. That propensity was hardly a unique characteristic among college students generally, but at MWC participation in athletic activity of some kind at some level was unusually extensive, whether it was individual exercise, intramurals, club sports, or intercollegiate varsity competition. For many at Mary Washington, the motto *mens sana in corpore sano* (sound mind in sound body) was not merely a musty Latinism but an actual guide to daily living.

The trend toward increased interest in diet and fitness became more evident in the 1980s as the general culture began to place greater emphasis on issues of wellness. One manifestation of this attitude was the growing popularity of physical education courses in individual exercise and of noncredit classes in activities such as aerobics and jazzercise. So, too, was the number of students who engaged in their own rigorous workout regimens, a practice that sometimes took them to off-campus facilities, such as the nearby Bodyworks Gym in downtown Fredericksburg. Mostly, however, they used the Goolrick Hall weight room, dank and uninviting though it was, located within the interior depths of the building. It was a vast improvement indeed when the new fitness center opened in 2004. A year later, facility usage was averaging approximately five hundred persons each day.

One indication of the success of such individual efforts was the listing of Mary Washington among the country's top twenty-five colleges and universities in *Men's Fitness* magazine's 2006 "Fit List." That magazine, in conjunction with the *Princeton Review*, polled over twelve thousand students nationally concerning "wellness"—a term that took numerous factors into account, including amount of weekly physical activity performed, eating habits, and alcohol consumption. It also examined the schools in terms of dining hall menus, athletic facilities, and availability of trainers and health experts.

Though some were skeptical about the survey's methodology, most officials were generally pleased that Mary Washington was included on the list. To longtime athletic trainer Bob Liebau, it acknowledged that "an attitude of wellness" prevailed on campus. Dean Cedric Rucker agreed. "It is very positive," he said. "It shows that students take wellness seriously. The number of students that participate in athletics, intramurals, [and] club teams and the volume of students going to the fitness center is outstanding."

Beyond individual activities, organized recreation was promoted through the intramural sports program. For many years, intramurals were run by various members of the Physical Education Department, but in 1987 a full-time director was hired in the person of Julie Smith. She was succeeded by Jean McClellan Holt, who was in turn replaced by John MacDonald in 1993. Under his direction, the program expanded to offer individual games and tournaments in basketball, soccer, football, tennis, softball, and volleyball. By 2007, all intramural sports combined were attracting between six hundred and eight hundred participants per semester.

A step up from intramurals in terms of athletic ability and degree of commitment were the club sports. In some sports, such as baseball and soccer, the clubs provided a niche for students whose talent fell below varsity level but whose competitive desire rose above the intramural level. There were also some sports, unsuitable for large-scale participation, in which the club format offered the most appropriate venue for engagement, such as fencing, cycling, hiking, ice hockey, and martial arts.

There was also a gun club, which at one time attracted brief controversy owing to its affiliation with the National Rifle Association (NRA). In 1998 it came to light that associating with a political lobbying group was contrary to policy for any club receiving College funds. Apparently unaware of this conflict previously, the club officers moved quickly to sever ties with the NRA, even though it had received no money from the association.

The oldest continuously active club sport at Mary Washington was an equestrian club, which was formed in 1934. Having changed its name by 1939 to the Hoof Prints Club, it endured as one of the institution's prominent clubs, still active seventy years later.

Almost as old was the synchronized swimming club, the Terrapins, first organized in 1939. The club reached its heyday in the 1940s and 1950s during a time when Esther Williams was popularizing the sport in glamorous Hollywood swimming musicals. At Mary Washington in those days, the club, under the sponsorship of physical education professor Mildred Droste, produced springtime "water pageants" that stretched over two days, featuring gleaming costumes, instrumental music, and illumination.

By the turn of the century, interest in synchronized swimming had declined to the extent that usually the team consisted of about fifteen members. Yet the Terrapins swam on, performing strenuous balletic routines that sometimes required staying underwater a minute at a time—all the while making something very hard look very easy.

Clubs sometimes served purposes that extended beyond the enjoyment that they provided their own members. Such was the case with the Cheerleading Team, which became more formally organized with the development of varsity intercollegiate teams in the late 1970s. By 1981 there were several male cheerleaders ("lifters," as they were sometimes called), though over the years the squad tended to be mainly, sometimes exclusively, female.

Several changes took place in the Cheerleading Club as it evolved from its original purpose of leading cheers at athletic events (basketball in particular) to a second purpose of competing with squads from other colleges. All the while, the club's routines became more athletic—a not altogether positive change because it involved greater risk of injury for the performers. Some even claimed (to no avail) that the routines were, in fact, so athletically demanding that cheerleading deserved status as a varsity sport, with corresponding PE credit for participation.

Augmenting the cheerleaders in promoting school spirit, beginning in 1988, was another club: the MWC Dance Team. Most of the members were former high school cheerleaders or drill team members—and all of them loved to dance. Adapting routines from national dance team competitions and from music videos, the club each year choreographed a number of exuberant (not to say exhibitionist) routines, delivered to the rousing (not to say frenzied) beat of modern dance or hip-hop music. Like the cheerleaders, the Dance Team members were most visible on campus during halftime performances at basketball games but also occasionally performed at other events, such as homecoming soccer games.

Two other sports clubs, one for males and one for females, grew out of the long-standing affinity of Mary Washington students for the game of Frisbee. Ever since the 1970s, the game had remained attractive to individual students as a less-structured form of athletic activity, but in the 1990s a more organized version, known as ultimate Frisbee, developed. Though the newer sport retained much of the ambience and spirit of camaraderie that characterized the mellower earlier game, ultimate Frisbee was a much more strenuous and competitive endeavor that combined elements of football and soccer with that of the flying disc. By the twenty-first century, Mary Washington had both a women's club and a men's club—the latter known as "Mad Mary."

Of all the club sports, the most popular by a wide margin was rugby—somewhat surprisingly, given the sport's obscurity to most Americans. Even the basic vocabulary of the sport—terms such as "ruck" (a massing of the players), "pitch" (the field), "knocking-on" (forward passing, illegal in rugby)—seemed arcane. As a *Bullet* sportswriter once put it, "I kinda like rugby, but I can barely follow the game. . . . It just seems sort of tedious at times, . . . like they just keep getting into these non-productive scrums. . . . There are so few meaningful plays in rugby. Nothing ever seems to happen." Yet beginning in the 1980s, rugby was to become, as its MWC adherents called it, "Mary Washington's football."

After an initial attempt to establish a team failed, a successful and more permanent effort was launched three years later with the formation of the MWC Rugby Club in 1984. At the time, only one of the roughly twenty players had any previous experience. "We had guys come out for the club," said rugby faculty adviser Richard Warner, "who thought you play rugby with a bat and a ball."

Nor were the spectators much more knowledgeable. But somehow the game caught on. "Eventually new spectators begin to get the idea," reported

Rugby: "Mary Washington's football"

the *Free Lance–Star*. "Words such as 'scrum,' 'try,' and 'where's the keg party' are engrained in their minds. They aren't certain how points are scored, but they know the object is to have more than the other team."

The paper's comment touched on one widely perceived aspect of rugby as being largely an exercise for, and prelude to, hearty partying. In the words of one former player, "It's not whether you win or lose. It's how good a party you have afterward."

Another element of rugby's appeal was the tough-guy image that it embodied. Sometimes referred to as "maul ball," the sport promoted itself with bumper stickers that proclaimed, "It takes leather balls to play rugby." Even its major proponent on campus, Dick Warner, admitted, "I think a lot of it boils down to machismo."

Certainly it was an image that the team did nothing to discourage or downplay. Even the name they took for their club, "Mothers"—a clever if mildly crude reference to Mary as the mother of George—contributed to something of a renegade image by setting them apart from the official "Eagles" name of the College's NCAA varsity teams.

But the rugby team was actually much more than merely a sanctioned form of mayhem for the relief of testosterone-laden ruffians. It was particularly attractive to former football or soccer players who sought the challenge of mastering a new sport, one whose nonstop action provided a genuine test of athleticism. Though less structured than the other two sports that it most resembled, rugby was no less cerebral and required a comparable set of skills.

Its appeal was well nigh addictive to those who became involved. Only nominally underwritten by the College—its annual budget for many years was a meager $2,000—the team had to supply much of its own equipment, and players had to cover their own travel and meal expenses, which could run to $300 per year. Even raising money through raffles, keggers, and the sale of paraphernalia such as stadium cups did not yield funds necessary to cover expenses—much of which consequently came out of the players' own pockets or those of their coaches.

Despite such obstacles, rugby soon established a foothold on campus, joining the twenty-five-team Virginia Rugby Union, a member of the Eastern Rugby Union, which had teams all along the East Coast. The MWC team's primary coach was David Steckler, a Fredericksburg attorney and former all-South player and coach at the University of Georgia; he was assisted by Robert Flath, a Dahlgren scientist, a former University of Virginia player and past president of the Virginia Rugby Union. Through the efforts of Dick Warner, the club was also able to secure the services of the legendary David Thomas, head of an English school for rugby coaches, to work with the team at annual weeklong training sessions.

The team soon gained wide press coverage as both the *Washington Post* and the *Free Lance–Star* published feature articles (the latter titled "This Sport Isn't for Sissies"). It seemed at first that the mere existence of the team attracted attention—the idea of an ultramacho sport at a "girls' school"—but then the team's success caught the public's eye. The Mothers were good; within a few years of their formation, they were routinely defeating clubs from prestigious institutions many times larger than MWC, including Duke, North Carolina State, Penn, and Georgia. Almost incredibly, the ruggers in 1991 won the Virginia State Championship when they capped an undefeated season by beating Virginia Tech in the October finals of the Ed Lee Cup, emblematic of regional rugby supremacy.

The *Bullet* exulted in the conquest. "This victory," proclaimed an editorial, "helps to add prestige to the name of Mary Washington College. . . . The team is entirely student-organized. . . . They are denied the benefit of a sports medicine specialist or training facilities. And in the end they won't even get to go to the end-of-the-year sports banquet extravaganza. . . . Our congratulations are with you 'Mothers.' You should be proud. . . . The day is yours, you 'band of brothers.'"[161]

By that time there was also a band of sisters. During their first several seasons, the women ruggers were coached by geology professor Grant Woodwell, who was succeeded in 1988 by Bill Lucas. Just three years later, they, too, captured the Ed Lee Cup. And their success continued. In 1997 Jill Reilly became the first MWC women's rugby player to be selected as an All-American. As a team, they regularly placed well among the state's collegiate clubs and in 1994 finished fourth nationally in their division.

Like the men's team, the women ruggers developed a mystique of toughness, sporting T-shirts bearing suggestive sayings such as (on the front) "Nice Cleats" and (on the back) "Wanna Ruck?" Unlike the men, however, they were often asked why they would want to participate in such an aggressive sport. "Well, why not?" responded one member of the 2000 team. "I mean, it's a great sport, and the girls who play are wonderful. We've got a great team atmosphere and we love to have a great time together. We're a team on and off the field." Said another, "Being fierce is fun. I like rugby because I get to tackle people, run around, get bloody—and it's legal."

Women's rugby, in fact, attracted females from all segments of the student body, and for all sorts of reasons. As the *Free Lance–Star* put it in a 2000 article titled "Elegant Violence," the game was "about fun, friendships, and finding a place to belong . . . [where] women with sharply contrasting styles bond. There are women who paint their nails and those who bite them, lifelong jocks and sports rookies, those with boyfriends and others with girlfriends. The mix has created a winning team that lets nothing—not even a lack of money—get in the way of having fun."

The main reason for the extraordinary success of rugby at Mary Washington can be stated in two words: Dick Warner. Joining the faculty in 1968, he channeled his abundant energy into the passionate promotion of rugby. Approaching the task with messianic—some thought maniacal—zeal, he spent untold hours writing to, and talking with, athletes, extolling the glories of rugby and cajoling them to try out for the team. The effort produced a legion of converts who became devoted to the sport as well as to their guru, "Doc" Warner, whom they revered.

Several factors contributed to Warner's ardent advocacy of rugby. Most basically, he simply loved the game. An outstanding football player in high school, he later came to believe that rugby was equal (and in some ways superior) to American football. The depth of his commitment was such as to lend credibility to his oft-expressed desire to have his ashes buried beneath the goalposts on the rugby field. "I've got some . . . guys that are going to sneak out [at night] and do that," he once said, "[And] there's no college president who will be able to prevent that from happening."

But besides his enjoyment of the game, Warner had an additional motive in promoting it at Mary Washington. He was convinced that rugby would help to attract male applicants to the College. And, all the better, it would do so at much less expense than what a "real" football team would cost. He adamantly maintained that football would likely be unsuccessful and, in any case, would be played at such a level of competition as to lack cachet. "Why should we lose to Ferrum and Chowan [in football]," he asked rhetorically, "when we can win against U.Va., Maryland, Duke, North Carolina, Pitt and Penn State [in rugby]?"

Nothing so quickly caused Warner—a feisty sort anyway—to bristle as the suggestion, periodically made, that Mary Washington should establish a football team. One such assertion, proffered by a *Bullet* sportswriter in 1997, provoked Warner into full battle cry. "He bemoans the absence of football at Mary Washington," Warner wrote in refutation: "Surely he jests. As a sports staffer, he couldn't be ignorant of MWC's football tradition and prowess. Is he unaware that only a few years ago, the College produced a football play-off team that defeated South Carolina and LSU before losing to Alabama in overtime? Can he not remember the victories over San Diego, Duke, UNC, Tennessee, and Penn State?" He concluded his blast with the mantra that he routinely exclaimed to all who would listen (and to many who would not): "At MWC rugby *is* football!"

And at MWC, "Doc" Warner was rugby.

Among the diverse achievements at Mary Washington during William Anderson's lengthy tenure as president, one of the most notable was the expansion and success of the intercollegiate varsity athletic program. That development was by no means certain when he took office. Shortly thereafter the *Bullet* expressed concern. The death of President Woodard, wrote the paper's sports editor, "brought to an end an era of great expansion and emphasis on athletics here. Woodard pushed for excellence in athletics, and, for the most part, got what he wanted, . . . as Mary Washington increased the number of varsity sports from seven to eighteen, and the addition of the Battleground complex gave MWC excellent facilities. There was also a positive atmosphere change from country club to competitive as new coaches demanded more of the athletes and the athletes gave more. For the time being at least, it seems as though that type of expansion will come to a halt."

Such doubts were warranted, given the new president's oft-stated attitude concerning the role of intercollegiate sports. Though he himself was much more interested in sports, both as a participant and a spectator, than any of his predecessors, he was nonetheless wary of the dangers inherent in the possible encroachment of athletics on the academic program. Highly critical of that process at many (especially larger) institutions, he was adamant that Mary Washington's core values not be thus compromised.

As it turned out, his view was shared by Athletic Director Ed Hegmann, who had demonstrated that commitment since he was hired by Woodard in 1976. Accordingly, the two worked harmoniously to implement a sports program that went significantly beyond what even Woodard's presidency had achieved, in both the scope and the success of the program, while holding fast to the College's traditional emphasis on the primacy of academics.

The approach was outlined in the 1985 "Commitment to Excellence." The document stated clearly that the intercollegiate program would remain at the Division III level, meaning that no athletic scholarships would be awarded, but that a more appropriate conference affiliation would be sought. The plan also envisioned adding several new intercollegiate teams and building new facilities, as well as upgrading existing ones. Moreover, it called for expanded opportunities for intramural and recreational activities.

In the two decades following the announcement of the plan, almost all the initiatives proposed therein were implemented, beginning with the addition of new varsity teams. To the existing sixteen were added women's soccer and riding (1986), men's lacrosse (1987), baseball and softball (1988), and men's and women's rowing (1998). The Battleground athletic complex was completed with the construction of baseball and softball fields, as well as additional fields for other sports. The final component came in 2005 with the opening of a spacious six-court indoor tennis center.

The years of the Anderson presidency, as it turned out, witnessed the maturation of an outstanding Division III intercollegiate program, one in which every sport enjoyed success ranging from consistently good to spectacular. The success of the program was attributable to many factors, most notably the skill of the student athletes and the dedication of their coaches, many of whom enjoyed long careers and several of whom achieved national recognition for their accomplishments. A critical, though usually behind-the-scenes, role was played by the school's athletic trainer, Bob Liebau, who joined the staff in 1986 and was still on the job in 2007 as wellness director. The important (though, again, usually invisible) position of sports information director (SID) was filled in 1988 by Vince Benigni, the College's first full-time SID, who was succeeded in 1996 by the energetic and efficient Clint Often.

Presiding over it all was Athletic Director Ed Hegmann, who, in addition, served as coach of the College's most consistently successful varsity team, women's tennis. In the course of twenty-three seasons as coach, his teams attained an extraordinary cumulative record of 373-152-1, during which time they won three national championships in 1982, 1988, and 1991. Hegmann was named Division III national coach of the year in 1988 and again in 1999. By the time he resigned as coach in 1999, to be replaced by Cindy Vanderberg, he had established a winning tradition to be emulated by all other teams at the College and had built a program regarded nationally as a model for excellence in the sport.

The tradition of success established by Hegmann continued under Vanderberg, whose teams compiled a 50-32 record during her first five years. They captured the Capital Athletic Conference (CAC) championship in three of those years and earned a place in the NCAA tournament every year.

Men's tennis was coached by Roy Gordon from its inception in 1978 until his retirement as its coach in 1999. That program, too, had its share of success over the years, winning five consecutive CAC championships from 1991 through 1995 and receiving an NCAA tournament bid in 1997. During the first five seasons under Gordon's successor, Todd Helbling, the team won the conference championship and qualified for NCAA tournament play each year. The highlight of the team's history came in 2004 when the duo of junior Paul Bristow and senior Dan Uyar won the Division III national championship in doubles competition.

The tennis program received a notable boost in spring 2005 with the opening of a spacious indoor tennis center located in the Battleground complex near Brompton in the space (previously a student parking lot) between Hanover Street and the existing outdoor courts. Funds to cover a sizable

Tennis doubles national champions, 2004: Dan Uyar, left, and Paul Bristow

portion of the $4.2 million cost came from an anonymous Fredericksburg donor.[162] The facility featured six indoor tennis courts, six water islands, double-insulated walls and ceiling, state-of-the-art lighting, locker room facilities, two offices for coaches, and an elevated viewing concourse. It served as the site of the NCAA Division III men's national championship tournament in 2006 and the women's tournament in 2007.

The project was not without its critics, both among faculty who predictably complained that an expenditure of such magnitude should have been devoted to academics, and students who decried the loss of parking spaces; even some members of the athletic department privately groused that the facility seemed to indicate preferential treatment for the tennis teams. Whatever the case, the impressive facility bore testimony to the program's exceptional success over the years and created the possibility for showcasing the sport in particular and the College in general through its potential for hosting major intercollegiate tournaments in the future.

Several teams rivaled the success of tennis, one of them being baseball. Established in 1987, the team began playing in 1988, with its first game against VMI. As the baseball field in the Battleground complex was not yet completed, that game had to be played at St. Clair Brooks Park in Stafford County. Though a campus playing field was soon ready for competition, it was not until several years later that a one-half-million-dollar, nine-hundred-seat stadium—with amenities including concession stands, restrooms, public address system, and scoreboard—was finished at the Battleground. In a festive ribbon-cutting ceremony on March 19, 1995, the facility was christened V. Earl Dickinson Stadium in honor of the Louisa County delegate who had been a longtime supporter of Mary Washington in the legislature (as well as its number one adversary during the name-change controversy).

As for the team itself, it was successful from the outset, suffering only one losing season in its first eighteen years, and even in that year (its first), its record was a respectable 11-14-1. Directing the success was Coach Thomas Sheridan, who was hired from the widely admired James Madison University

Delegate Earl Dickinson (left) and President Anderson with Coach Thomas Sheridan at the dedication of Dickinson Stadium in 1995

program (where he was an assistant coach) in 1987 to direct development of the MWC program. That he did, remaining through 2007 as the only full-time coach the baseball program had ever had.[163]

Personable, even gregarious, off the field, Sheridan was all business when it came to coaching. Once likening himself in some ways to the notoriously volatile Billy Martin, manager of the New York Yankees, Sheridan admitted that his on-field demeanor, both at practices and in games, did not necessarily endear him to all his players, especially those who failed to share his passionate, no-nonsense approach to every detail of the game.

But if he was not universally beloved, his undeniable success commanded respect. A tireless recruiter, he worked hard to bring into the program athletes who would benefit not only from his rigorous regimen of instruction but also from the liberal arts education that the College provided. In addition, an inordinate number (for a college the size of Mary Washington) went on to play professional baseball and several obtained enviable positions as front-office executives for major-league teams.

On the field, his teams compiled an extraordinary record, winning twenty or more games every season except twice through 2006, including six consecutive seasons with twenty-five or more wins beginning in 2002. Along the way, they captured seven CAC titles and participated in ten NCAA tournaments. For his contributions in achieving that record—a remarkable winning percentage of almost .700—Sheridan was eleven times named conference baseball coach of the year.

Like the baseball team, both the women's and men's soccer teams enjoyed consistent success over the years. The women's team had the unusual distinction of never suffering a losing season from its establishment in 1986—first under coach Pete Ginnegar for three years and subsequently under coach Kurt Glaeser—through 2006. Its overall performance during those three decades, in which the team won 70 percent of its contests, included winning numerous CAC championships, routinely earning NCAA tournament bids, and hosting the national Final Four championship in 1992.

The men's team, with Roy Gordon (also the associate athletic director) as its coach from the day of its founding, did not get off to such an auspicious start; in fact, it was winless in its inaugural 1977 season. From there, however, the team progressed rapidly to the point that, from the mid-eighties onward, it was recognized as a perennial Division III soccer power, regularly winning conference championships and appearing nine times in NCAA tournaments by 2003, including the national Final Four in 1998, hosted by Mary Washington. Coach Gordon's exemplary performance—a cumulative record of 331-180-42 over a period of thirty years—was acknowledged in 1998 when he was elected president of the National Soccer Coaches Association of America.

But it was not just the winning record that characterized Gordon's career. More important, said one of his players, was Gordon's performance as a "role model [who] instills class and dignity in us." Few coaches in any sport at any level ever did that better or more consistently or for a longer time than Roy Gordon.

The swim team likewise proved successful, especially following the hiring of Paul Richards as coach in 1985. Under his tutelage, both men and women compiled commendable team records during his nine-year tenure, and several outstanding individual performers also developed, including Amanda Dresser (daughter of Board of Visitors Rector Paul Dresser), who in 1992 won All-American honors in the butterfly. Matt Mejia, who set six individual school records during his career and lost only one individual race during his last two years, became in 1991 the College's first male swimmer to qualify for the NCAA nationals (in the 200-yard backstroke).[164] Then there was Shannon Hutcherson, who the following year, in the same event, became MWC's first-ever national champion in any sport.

After one year under coach Mark Brown, who replaced Paul Richards after his departure for Dickinson University, the swim team reached even greater heights under coach Matt Kinney. From 1995 through 2006, the team produced four male All-Americans and eighteen female All-Americans. From 1991 through 2007, the women won the CAC title every year; between 1997 and 2007, the men won the title every year except 1999 and 2000, when they finished second. In his first decade as swim coach, Kinney led his teams to a combined meet record of 182-59 (the cumulative record of the women's team over the first three decades of its existence was 241-94; the men's was 121-94 over a period of twenty-two years).

Closely associated with the swim program, at least for a few years, was the water polo team, which became a varsity sport in 1986. Several factors led to its establishment, including a grant from the U.S. Olympic Water Polo Committee. Even more instrumental was the belief that such a team would help to recruit candidates for the swim teams, as well as provide an enjoyable means of off-season training for them. Those assumptions proved true, but the polo experiment ultimately failed because of the lack of Division III competition within the region, and in a few years it was dropped as a varsity sport.

Another water-related sport that had its difficulties at the varsity level, yet exhibited greater longevity than water polo, was crew (or rowing, according to official NCAA terminology). The sport began at the club level, starting with the formation of the Crew Club in 1979. The first season of competition came in 1984–85, when the club competed in meets against crews from schools such as the University of Virginia, George Washington University, George Mason University, and the Johns Hopkins University.[165] As interest in the sport increased, it was added as a varsity intercollegiate team in 1998–99 with Brad Holdren as coach.

From the beginning, the program had its problems, not the least of which was its cost. As the *Bullet* noted at the time the new sport was announced, "Uniforms, practice facilities, equipment, transportation, and countless other items must be purchased to ensure the school has a competitive team. . . . Equipment [includes] boat docks, the boats themselves, and specially outfitted vans able to transport the boats from regatta to regatta." In that light, the *Bullet* expressed the concern that administrative officials "seem to be biting off much more than they can chew."

The paper was right about the cost: each fragile boat, easily susceptible to damage, could cost from $15,000 to $20,000 for a four-person shell to as much as $30,000 for an eight-person shell. But expense was not the only problem. The College owned no boathouse, nor was there any convenient body of water on which to practice. The closest viable location was the city's reservoir at Mott's Run, but it was too short to provide a regulation-length course without making a turn. The team thus used Belle Plains Marina on Potomac Creek for a period and then rowed mainly at Lake of the Woods, a better venue, but almost an hour's drive from the campus.

Another drawback to the program's development was the lack of experienced rowers. Few high school students went to schools with rowing teams, and those who did often accepted scholarships at larger universities. The result was that the Mary Washington crews often consisted of rowers who, according to Athletic Director Hegmann, "had never held an oar in their hands till they got to college."

If, however, the MWC rowers lacked experience, they did not want for enthusiasm. No sport made more demands on its participants, regularly requiring them to rise well before daybreak to be on the water by 5:00 a.m. Their commitment produced not only camaraderie but also victories; within a few years, the team succeeded in medaling at the Dad Vail Regatta, the Philadelphia meet generally regarded as the unofficial national championship for small colleges. In 2007 the Mary Washington women's team placed seventh in the Division III nationals.

Men's lacrosse, which became a varsity sport in 1987, was not as successful as some of the other programs early on but showed improvement by posting winning records from 2002 through 2004. Under Coach Kurt Glaeser, the team's cumulative record for that period was 31-15. Women's lacrosse had a much longer (and, overall, a much better) record than the men's team. As one

Order online at www.umw.edu/centennialhistory. Or call 540/654-1055.

In this lively narrative, Distinguished Professor of History William B. Crawley Jr. depicts events at UMW within a broad perspective, showing how developments on campus mirrored the often tumultuous social and cultural changes sweeping the nation.

While giving due attention to the milestone events – from the laying of the first building's cornerstone through the 2008 Centennial celebration – the book also addresses controversial topics such as the decision for coeducation, periodic name-change debates, and the ill-fated presidency of William Frawley.

Much of the appeal of *A Centennial History* derives from Professor Crawley's colorful accounts of student life. Encompassing both the frivolous and the serious, the narrative describes such traditions as May Day, Devil-Goat Day, Halloweens, and 100th Night, as well as the Honor System and the highly successful athletic program.

Professor Crawley offers a vivid portrait of the University's first century from the unique vantage of one who not only observed but also participated in many of the events he describes. This astute analyst and masterful storyteller provides an account that will engage and delight all those acquainted with the University of Mary Washington.

University of Mary Washington
1301 College Avenue
Fredericksburg, VA 22401

T61 P1 ***********************AUTO**3-DIGIT 244
MICHAEL T. SORGEN
140 HAMPTON DR
STUARTS DRAFT, VA 24477-2636

Pre-publication discount – $30, including postage and handling.

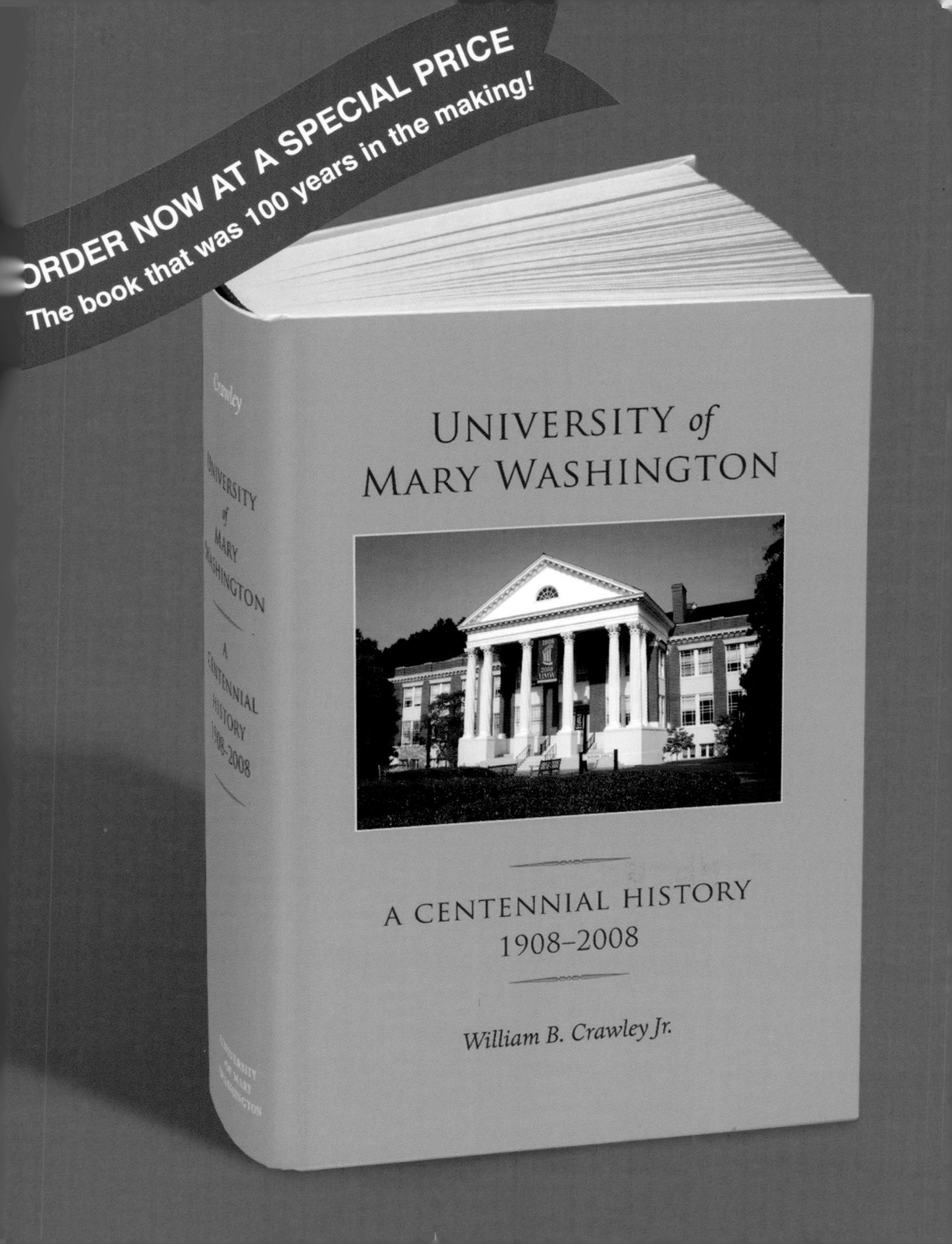
ORDER NOW AT A SPECIAL PRICE
The book that was 100 years in the making!
Crawley
UNIVERSITY of MARY WASHINGTON
A CENTENNIAL HISTORY 1908–2008
UNIVERSITY of MARY WASHINGTON
A CENTENNIAL HISTORY
1908–2008
William B. Crawley Jr.

of the College's first intercollegiate teams (established in 1965), it compiled a record of 253-196-9 over the course of thirty-seven seasons. Its performance improved notably with the hiring of Dana Hall as coach in 1991. Under her dynamic leadership, the team's record between 1991 and 2004 was 135-83 and in both 2001 and 2002 finished with a ranking of fourth nationally.

The field hockey team, established one year before the lacrosse team, enjoyed similar success beginning particularly under Coach Meg Kintzing in the 1970s, continuing under Coach Beth Hollibaugh in the eighties, and peaking under Coach Hall, who took over in 1990. During the course of thirty-eight seasons, the team achieved a .600 winning percentage, including a record of 191-75-3 (and seven NCAA tournament bids) under Hall's tutelage between 1990 and 2003. The team's most successful season (22-2) was in 1993, when, led by co-captains Candice Malone and April Moshos, it came within a single goal of the national championship, losing 1–0 to Cortland State in the tournament finals, which were hosted at Mary Washington.

In 1985 Stan Soper became the coach of the men's and women's indoor and outdoor track and field teams as well as the men's and women's cross-country teams. All were competitive over the years, generally becoming more successful with the passage of time. From the late 1990s onward, both the men's and women's outdoor track and field team and the women's cross-country team routinely captured CAC championships. In addition to outstanding team performances, a number of individual athletes achieved All-American status. Notable among them was Myra Simpson, who in 1996 won first place in the long jump and eighth place in the triple jump events at the NCAA Nationals—an extraordinary performance that earned her All-American recognition in both events.

Volleyball, which became a varsity sport in 1976, quickly emerged as one of MWC's more successful programs, under the leadership of Connie Gallahan. During the decade in which she served as coach, the team averaged over twenty victories a year. When Gallahan gave up volleyball in 1986 to concentrate on coaching women's basketball, she was replaced by Dee Conway, who became the first African American on the coaching staff. Conway's teams perpetuated the early success of volleyball, winning thirty or more games three times (as well as two conference titles) during the 1990s.

The softball team, which began play in 1988, was also coached by Conway, its only coach through 2007. Though its cumulative record did not equal that of volleyball and some of the other sports, the Eagle softballers did win the CAC championship in 1991, 1993, and 1996.

An activity that had one of the longest (and most varied) histories at Mary Washington was horseback riding. The sport enjoyed perhaps its widest popularity under the direction of Russell Walther, who became the College's instructor of riding in 1940. He also served as director of the Oak Hill Stables (west of the campus just off Route 3 behind the latter-day Shoney's), where for fifteen years he taught riding to MWC students and sponsored the Hoof Prints Club. Under Walther's leadership, the riding program at Mary Washington became one of the most prominent among Virginia colleges. At times as many as 135 students were taking riding classes each semester.

Equine activities were not restricted to classes but also included shows, fox hunts, and an annual fall "possum hunt." The Mary Washington Cavalry was a direct outgrowth of Walther's initiative. When Walther left the College in 1956, he was succeeded by Michael Kirschner, a graduate of the officer's training school in Copenhagen, Denmark. Under the leadership of the somewhat imperious Kirschner, the College continued its tradition of excellence in equitation, producing teams that competed successfully throughout Virginia and Maryland.

A major development occurred in 1974 when riding classes moved from Oak Hill to Hazelwild Farms, located several miles from the campus in Spotsylvania County and owned by A. Elizabeth Morrison '26. For four years thereafter, the riding program was headed by Susan Simpson. In 1978, under the coaching of her successor, Anita Reidel, the College riders became known officially as the Mary Washington College Riding Team. The next year, the riding program produced the College's first-ever national champion, Tryna Rey.

Another milestone came in 1986–87 when Carol Berry, who had just graduated from the College in 1984, was named coach of the riding team. (She was later married to Buddy Hawley '85, a physics major and an extraordinary athlete who during his years at Mary Washington became the first widely acknowledged star of the men's basketball program.) In ten seasons under Carol Hawley, the riding team achieved consistently strong showings in Intercollegiate Horse Show Association (IHSA) meets. The high standards established under her leadership were perpetuated under succeeding coaches Becky Dye (1996–97), Kat Danielson (1998–99), Keri Pilling (2002–5), and Beth Boteler (2006–7). Indeed, it was the existence of the successful riding program that over the years motivated a sizable number of students to attend Mary Washington. In fact, between 1999 and 2004 the team finished first in the IHSA Region One four times, and four of its riders advanced to national championship competition.

Of all the College's intercollegiate teams, the one that was historically the least successful—and the most controversial—was men's basketball. After a number of years of club competition under Marshall Bowen and two of varsity play under Ed Hegmann, the team moved to NCAA Division III in 1978–79 with the hiring of Thomas Davies as coach. One of the highlights of his eighteen-year tenure was a seven-day team excursion to Germany, Belgium, and the Netherlands in January 1991, a trip that players described as a transcendent cultural (if not athletic) experience.

On the court, however, things were not always so good. In its first NCAA season, the team won only one game. Though its performance improved in subsequent years, including winning the Capital Athletic Conference championship in 1984–85, the team's cumulative record under Davies was an undistinguished 180-292. Some observers came to believe that the team was underachieving; among them was Athletic Director Hegmann, who, exasperated by nine consecutive losing seasons, publicly criticized Davies in 1995.

By that time, some players were also beginning to voice complaints about their coach. The players' critiques contained a consistent theme. First, they admitted that Davies knew basketball strategy and, moreover, that he was a genuinely nice person. But it was that very quality that led them to criticize him as a coach, asserting that he was too lax in practice and too reticent as a bench coach. "I believe he would do anything for us, because he's a nice guy," typically commented one of his players. "The problem is that coaches aren't supposed to be nice. They should be hard-nosed and intense. They should be the kind of guys who kick your butt if you make a mistake. Davies is not one of this kind of people."

Organized criticism of Davies first arose after the 1993–94 season, when all but two players on the team signed a letter to President Anderson voicing concerns about the coach and asking for his dismissal. That petition failed, but several years later, the revolt reached the point that three players, including the team's leading scorer in the 1995–96 season, declared their intention to quit the team if Davies returned as coach the following year.

Though Davies generally remained mum as the controversy intensified, he did assert that one of the reasons for the losing trend was tougher admissions standards, noting that the average SAT score when he started was 1,019 compared to 1,100 by 1996. His son meanwhile offered an aggressive defense of the coach in a *Bullet* guest column in March 1996. In an argument that might well be assumed to have expressed the views of his father, the younger Davies pointed out that the disaffection of the three vocal players resulted from disciplinary action against them the previous season for breaking team rules and that the team's overall poor performance that season had been attributable mainly to the loss of three potential starters—two of them to academic ineligibility and one to injury. For good measure, his column included a denunciation of Athletic Director Hegmann as "the epitome of arrogance, incompetence, and unprofessionalism."

The comments of the Davies *père et fils* did the coach no good, further alienating Hegmann and the players, one of whom blasted the coach for implying that "basketball players are not intelligent." Instead, the player said in the *Bullet*, "The higher SAT scores are not the cause of the losing streak. It is the players' lack of confidence, discipline, and motivation."

Complicating the matter was the fact that Mary Washington, unlike most other institutions in its conference, granted tenure to its coaches, a practice brought under scrutiny by the Davies controversy. At most other schools, coaches were assigned to administrative staff contracts with no possibility of tenure, thereby making it easier to fire them if their teams did not perform satisfactorily.

Mary Washington, on the other hand, took the approach that, inasmuch as all its coaches also taught as members of the physical education faculty, they should have the same rights of tenure as other faculty members. Such a policy, so the theory went, also provided continuity within the various programs. As Coach Stan Soper put it, "A lot of other CAC schools have coaches that are here today, gone tomorrow, and they're not full-time faculty, and they hold other jobs. Therefore, they are not able to do some of the things we are able to do."

According to Hegmann, who had staunchly advocated tenure for the coaches, "In our situation, since you are required to both teach and coach, you [attract] folks who are interested in being very good teachers and not just good coaches. . . . They're full-fledged members of the academic community." In the view of economics professor Steve Stageberg, chair of the College's Intercollegiate Athletics Advisory Committee, the policy was also consistent with the fundamental place of sports at a college like Mary Washington. In such a situation, failure to grant tenure, he said, would "break up the campus and break up the whole integration of the notion of a liberal arts institution, where physical, mental, and intellectual aspects . . . should be unified."

Sound as that philosophy may have been, the tenuring of coaches could present problems. As even Hegmann admitted, "The negative side of tenure is that you always have the risk of a person who receives tenure and then becomes a non-performer or a poor performer." As for Davies, in the face of criticism he initially announced his intention to continue in his position rather than resign. However, the matter was resolved in August 1996 when he did in fact resign, preventing the situation from becoming even uglier than it already was.

One ramification of the controversy was a change in the employment terms for coaches. Thenceforth coaches were no longer hired in tenure-track positions but were given what were called "renewable term appointments." Under this arrangement, the coach would receive an initial two-year contract that could be followed by a three-year contract and thereafter receive successive five-year contracts, pending satisfactory performance. Appointments were to be at the initial level of lecturer and might be advanced to senior lecturer, but in no case was tenure to be granted. The new policy constituted a reasonable effort at a contractual compromise that provided the coaches with a degree of job security while protecting the institution against the difficulty of trying to remove tenured coaches who were no longer effective.

Davies's replacement, Rod Wood, was about as different from his predecessor as could be imagined, both in personality and in professional demeanor. Whereas off court Davies was phlegmatic, Wood was feisty; on court, the animated Wood ranged from merely intense to utterly incendiary. (On one occasion, he almost came to blows with an opposing coach, an episode reported by the *Bullet* under the heading "Wood Is Burning.")

In one way, Davies and Wood were in accord: they both believed that MWC faced certain obstacles in building a successful basketball program. Wood, for example, cited high admissions standards for precluding recruitment of a sizable segment of high school athletes—the same observation for which Davies had been pilloried earlier. The new coach also came under fire for publicly suggesting that the name "Mary" was an impediment to recruiting. Though some were critical of that particular assertion, Wood was undeniably on firm ground when he also cited as a deterrent the dismal status of Goolrick Hall as a basketball venue—once calling it, with only a little hyperbole, "the worst facility in the country." A common reaction from visiting potential players was to remark that their high school facilities were both larger and better than Goolrick. (In 2007, construction of a new home for basketball and other indoor events remained at the top of the institution's capital priorities.)

Surmounting such disadvantages, however, Wood quickly turned the woeful program around. Within three years, his team achieved its first-ever national ranking as it amassed a 15-10 record. In 2002–3, it was ranked as high as number 12 nationally while finishing 24-5 and gaining a bid to the NCAA tournament—a performance that it followed with a 20-8 record the next year. It seemed clear that better times had arrived for the once-troubled program.

In contrast to the sometimes discordant men's basketball team, the women's team was generally free from disruption—although it, too, experienced occasional turmoil. In 1995 nine of its players were suspended from play (serially over the course of three games) for participating in underage drinking at an off-campus party at the apartment of the team's co-captain, an episode that also led to the suspension of eight members of the men's team.

On the whole, however, the program was kept on an even keel by its coach, Connie Gallahan, who held that position for twenty-four seasons beginning in 1977. During that time, her squads were consistently competitive, their performances punctuated by NCAA tournament appearances in 1993–94 and 1997–98 and three Virginia state titles. She was named CAC Coach of the Year and NCAA Atlantic Region Coach of the Year in 1997–98. When she retired from coaching in 2001 to take an administrative position at the College, her career record of 306-271 ranked among the best in NCAA Division III history.

Impressive as her record was, Gallahan's contribution to Mary Washington's athletic program extended well beyond the hard court. As personable off the court as she was pugnacious on it, she not only inspired her players but mentored her peers, both by word and by example. Above all, she subtly provided a solid and stabilizing influence on the entire program as it evolved during her nearly quarter century of coaching.

Following Gallahan's retirement, the team was coached for two years by Becky Timmins, who was succeeded in 2003–4 by Deena Applebury. It was under Applebury's direction that the team achieved the greatest success in its history, beginning in 2004–5 with a 23-7 record, the CAC championship, and an NCAA tournament bid—accomplishments that led to the selection of Applebury as conference coach of the year. That season was but a prelude to the 2005–6 campaign in which the team went undefeated in the regular season, ending with a loss in the NCAA tournament and a final record of 29-2.

In the process the team generated unprecedented spirit on campus and in the community. An editorial in the *Free Lance–Star* titled "Soaring Eagles" saluted the team's accomplishments, and in the course of the team's remarkable run, the paper noted that "stopping by Goolrick Gym to see the Eagles play now appears to be the hot ticket for the Fredericksburg area." Indeed, by the end of the season, the cozy (and obsolescent) arena was regularly filled to overflowing by jubilant fans who marveled at the skill of women playing at a pace and with an athleticism that would have astounded earlier generations of students.

With all but one of its key players returning, the team envisioned even greater success in 2006–7. Pursuit of that goal was derailed, at least temporarily, however, when a controversy arose early in the session concerning an alleged hazing incident involving the 2004–5 team.

The issue arose when a Web site, ncaahazing.com, provided the *Free Lance–Star* with nine pictures dated April 2, 2005, showing members of the Mary Washington women's basketball team participating in what looked suspiciously like hazing.[166] In various photos, some of the women were blindfolded and wearing their basketball jerseys. Several were on their knees sipping something from ice trays with straws; one was on a couch with her head tilted back and a mouthful of whipped cream; yet another was drinking an undetermined liquid from an orange beer bong with the words "2005 CAC Champs" on it. The *Free Lance–Star* noted that the students "appear[ed] to be drinking alcohol." The photos carried captions such as "Let the games begin" and "Suck hard."

The incident was reported not only in a full-page *Bullet* article but also in a front-page story in the *Free Lance–Star*. A Washington television station even dispatched a camera crew to interview students on campus concerning the episode. A report of hazing among college athletes would hardly have appeared to merit such extensive coverage because, despite official (if perhaps lukewarm in some cases) admonitions against the practice at most schools, many observers conceded that it was widespread. A 1999 study cited in the *Free Lance–Star* article concluded that 80 percent of college athletes experienced hazing at some point. In fact, a spokesman for the anti-hazing Web site that first published the Eagles' pictures suggested that "if they [NCAA] suspended everybody involved [you'd] have no one left to play."

At Mary Washington, however, rules against hazing were strict, unambiguous, and well known to all student athletes. As defined by the College, hazing consisted of "any physical or mental interference, request, or obligation that could cause inconvenience, discomfort, pain, fright, embarrassment, disgrace, or injury; that is personally degrading; or that violates any federal, state, or local statute or [institutional] policy." The policy left no room for exculpation on the grounds that those involved participated of their own accord. "Whether or not the student so endangered or injured voluntarily participates in the activity," decreed the regulation, "is not a factor in determining if the activity was hazing."

Accordingly, the administration did not take the incident lightly. Moving quickly, Bernard Chirico, the vice president for student affairs, under whose jurisdiction the athletic program operated, launched an investigation. Though his initial reaction had been to declare that the episode seemed "absolutely" to be a violation of the College's hazing policy, his investigation ultimately led him to conclude otherwise.

Chirico's inquiry included review of additional photographs from the party as well as interviews with the five members of the 2004–5 team who were still enrolled. All the students, he said, were "very forthcoming . . . [and] told me a lot of what I needed to know. They weren't hiding anything." He did determine that alcohol was consumed at the party, but not necessarily by underage basketball players. As for those pictured drinking from the bong, it was not possible from the grainy digital photos to gainsay the participants' claim, improbable though it seemed, that the liquid being quaffed was apple juice.

On the basis of evidence, he explained, "It became clear that all team members, whether first-year or upper-class, participated, . . . that students were free to come and go throughout the evening, that students other than women basketball players were present, and that no individual or group was singled out." In the end, he concluded that there was insufficient evidence to justify imposing sanctions on the team beyond requiring them to participate in an educational program on the dangers of hazing.

The outcome left some people frustrated, notably including Athletic Director Hegmann, an outspoken opponent of hazing of any sort. He had long insisted that all Eagles' coaches begin each season by discussing NCAA regulations with their players, putting particular emphasis on hazing. In that regard, players just before the 2005–6 season had been warned specifically against posting pictures on MySpace, Facebook, and Webshots. "It starts out as being fun," said Hegmann, "[but] I reminded them that once you post these pictures they can be downloaded and saved in a file forever."

The emergence of the basketball team photos led the athletic director to a wry observation concerning his customary advice to student athletes. "It's kind of ironic," he said, "but I asked them as a guideline not to post anything that you would be embarrassed to see on the front page of a newspaper. It [was] really kind of prophetic." In accordance with established regulations, sanctions were imposed on the players who posted the photos.

Once the furor diminished, as it rather quickly did, the 2006–7 women's team turned its full attention once again to winning basketball games. Despite the high hopes induced by the return of all five starters from the previous year, the season got off to a rocky start as the Eagles lost two of their first five games. They would not lose again, however, during the course of twenty-six straight games, a run that carried them into the celebrated national Final Four—a first in the program's history.

Getting there was not always easy, including a narrow escape in the finals of the Sweet Sixteen round, when they overcame an eleven-point second-half deficit to defeat Bowdoin, then the number one ranked Division III team in the nation, by a score of 64–59. Such unprecedented success left the Eagle players in a state of dazed euphoria. "I didn't even know how [to] cut down the nets," said star center Liz Hickey.

As the team prepared to travel to Springfield, Massachusetts, for the tournament's final round, the *Free Lance–Star* expressed the community's approbation in an editorial titled "Eagles Soar, Final Four." "It's great to have a hometown team to root for during March Madness," it said. "The Eagles should be proud of their hard play, their discipline, and their heart. We are."

Alas, the magical season came to an end in the semifinal game with a 67–61 loss to the eventual national champion, DePauw, after building a ten-point first-half lead. The following day in the consolation round, the Eagles came back to defeat New York University and thus claim third place nationally for the 2006–7 season. In addition to the team's success, individual honors abounded, including the naming of forward Debbie Bruen (the team's only senior) to the Kodak All-American Team, and the naming of center Liz Hickey as the Capital Athletic Conference Player of the Year. Deena Applebury, who in three years had led the program to unprecedented levels of success, was named national Division III Women's Basketball Coach of the Year.

Returning by bus from Springfield, the team was met at Goolrick Hall by a cheering crowd, the Eagle Pipe Band, and a banquet table featuring a huge sheet cake proclaiming, "Women's Basketball Rocks!" That sentiment was echoed by one student fan who exulted, "We love 'em. Women's basketball unites this school. They're so good."

They were indeed good. And they were also perceptive, especially in the way they reacted to their semifinal defeat. Though there was understandable disappointment that the coveted national championship had eluded them, both the players and their coach (as well as their fans) rightly put the season into positive perspective. As Debbie Bruen said, "You can't really complain. You want the big prize, but you can't really complain."

That response was reminiscent of advice that had appeared in *The Battlefield* almost seventy years earlier. "Play for the joy of it," it read. "Play as hard as you can; give your opponent the best game you can. But if you lose, let it only be in score and not in temper and good sportsmanship. Take pleasure in the game. Always wish to try to win but do not wish to win so hard and not be happy without it."

It was heartening that seven decades later, at a time when intercollegiate sports often seemed preoccupied with winning, no matter the cost, Mary Washington students still knew what it was like to "play for the joy of it."

As Mary Washington's intercollegiate sports program developed, the idea grew that it would be appropriate to provide some means of recognition for the College's outstanding varsity athletes. Ed Hegmann, when he arrived as athletic director, was appalled that no such system of recognition existed. As he recalled, "There was no celebration, there was no athlete banquet, there was no award system when I came, not even paper ones, . . . so at the end of the season [student-athletes] just went home—no letter, no certificate, nothing."

That scenario was soon addressed when in 1977 a spring sports banquet was held to recognize the year's outstanding players. A rather modest and informal event at first, the banquet evolved to become one of the largest and most glitzy on-campus affairs each year, with several hundred athletes in their "dress-up" best gathering in the Great Hall to watch a video recap of the year in sports, to applaud the four-year award winners and the All-American selections, and to salute the male and female athletes of the year.

An additional and more permanent means of honoring the College's star athletes was established in 1996 with the creation of the Mary Washington College Athletic Hall of Fame. According to the guidelines for selection, anyone could nominate any former player (no sooner than ten years after his or her graduation), any coach, or any administrator. From the list of nominees, a committee comprising the athletic director, sports information director, chair of the faculty Intercollegiate Athletic Advisory Committee, and director of alumni affairs would make the final selections. Inductions would take place at a banquet held on the opening evening of homecoming weekend each October.

The inaugural group of honorees included five of the most prominent athletes in Mary Washington history:

Ethel Armstrong '63, a field hockey player who was a member of four Southeast and four Tidewater All-Star teams;
Deb Reid '82, a field hockey player who was MWC's first All-American;
Frank Gilmore '84, a basketball player who was an All–South Atlantic Region center, as well as the College's all-time leading rebounder (1,180) and second leading scorer (1,544 points);
Ruth Bonner Grosekopf '85, a basketball player who led MWC to a state title in 1981–82 and was named all-conference and all-state in 1984–85; and
Bill Lohr '86, a soccer player who was the College's first male All-American and its all-time leading scorer (58 goals, 18 assists, 134 points).

It also included, as a group, the women's tennis team of 1982, winners of the Division III national championship.

Subsequent inductees included the national champion women's tennis teams of 1988 and 1993, Athletic Director and tennis coach Ed Hegmann, and President Anderson. Anderson, who was inducted in 1998, two years after his aneurysm, was hailed by his presenter "not only for what he has done to enhance our College's sports, but for what he has done to lift our collective spirits." By 2006 the Hall of Fame contained thirty-four honorees, all with commemorative plaques displayed in Goolrick Hall to celebrate their exceptional accomplishments.

Throughout its evolution, the intercollegiate sports program at Mary Washington exhibited several notable characteristics. One of the most important was the balance among its male and female teams. Though that situation was partly the result of the program's origins within a women's college—meaning that a number of female sports were already established when coeducation arrived—it was also due to Athletic Director Hegmann's determination to ensure that equity prevailed across the board. The result was that by 2007 there were twenty-three teams in all, of which twelve were female, ten were male, and one (riding) was a mixed team.

In addition to the maintenance of gender balance, there was no favored or flagship sport siphoning funds for its own pursuit of glory. As Hegmann once put it simply, and accurately, "Every sport at Mary Washington is important."

A second and not unrelated aspect of the program was its overall success. Clear evidence of that accomplishment was that Mary Washington won the Capital Athletic Conference's All-Sports Award, emblematic of winning the most team championships annually, in eleven of the College's first fourteen years in the CAC.

Another characteristic was the academic performance of the student athletes. That quality was attested not only by the professional accomplishments of many varsity athletes after graduation but also by their records while students. Throughout the existence of the intercollegiate program, the number of varsity athletes who achieved GPAs of at least 3.0 remained consistently between 45 and 50 percent, a level that was usually slightly above that of the student body as a whole.

Perhaps the most significant aspect of the sports program—one from which other attributes flowed—was the decision to compete at the NCAA Division III level, precluding athletic scholarships. Rejecting any suggestions (and they arose infrequently) that the institution move to a higher level of NCAA competition, Mary Washington remained steadfastly committed to the level of competition most consonant with the institution's liberal arts mission.

It was that position that the *Free Lance–Star* hailed in a 2002 editorial called "Purity of Sport." Having decried the excesses of so many gargantuan college programs masquerading as "amateur athletics," the editorial asserted that "one of the last bastions of pure high-level sports competition . . . can be found right here in Fredericksburg. At Mary Washington College none of the athletes plays for scholarship money—let alone donates labor to make millions for his or her school or network moguls. MWC athletes take the field, the pool, and the court for love of the game. . . . If purity of sport is what you crave, the bluff at Mary Washington College is a good place to look."

The reasons for that commendable situation were numerous, but looming largest in the picture was one person: Edward Hegmann. No one ever wanted to win, at anything, more than he, especially at tennis, which he continued to play competitively thirty years after his hiring in 1976. But at the same time, no one better understood the proper—that is, supportive but secondary—position of athletics at an institution like Mary Washington. To that end, he steadfastly insisted that academics remain paramount and simultaneously oversaw the development, essentially starting from scratch, of what became one of the nation's preeminent Division III programs.

Hegmann's accomplishments after three decades on the job were well described by one faculty member who had the opportunity to observe him from the time of Hegmann's arrival: history professor Richard Warner. During that time, Warner had occasionally clashed with the athletic director over funding for the rugby club, which Warner sponsored. But such disagreements did not diminish Warner's admiration for all that Hegmann accomplished. "He is the guy that made this stuff happen," Warner said. "He built this program—built it and helped get the facilities in place. We have a really fine sports program which is . . . in keeping with our academic mission."

Then he summed it up: "This is the house that Ed built. And I'm telling you, it's a damn good house."

UNIVERSITY STATUS

Perhaps the most significant development in the final quarter of Mary Washington's first century—certainly since the advent of coeducation and the separation from the University of Virginia—was the institution's rise to university status. As with earlier evolutionary episodes, this one was not without its controversial aspects, including yet another name-change debate.

Fundamental to university status was the implementation of graduate work. That departure began during the Woodard years with the creation of three master's programs: master of business administration, master of public administration, and master of arts in liberal studies. The programs met with mixed success. The MPA never really took root and was soon eliminated. After a few years the MBA was dropped when the College decided that such resources as were available would be better used to augment the undergraduate major in business administration.

The MALS program for a number of years enjoyed greater success, but enrollment declined in the 1990s, largely because the program did not meet the needs of teachers who required endorsements in new and emerging fields, such as teaching English as a second language and special education. In fact, the popularity of programs like the MALS—that is, general liberal arts rather than discipline specific—was declining nationally during that time. Mainly for that reason, but also because of the drain it placed on faculty resources, the MALS program stopped accepting new applicants in 2001, and the last of its students graduated in 2006.

At the same time, however, the College moved toward new graduate and professional programs that targeted mainly nontraditional students from the local commuting area. Several factors, some of them beyond the institution's control, contributed to this development during the 1990s.

Early in the decade, the Commonwealth of Virginia requested all state colleges and universities to devise plans for meeting the anticipated future increase in applicants. In meeting this mandate, MWC administrators took into account two basic considerations: first, the desire to maintain the intimate residential campus in Fredericksburg with its traditional emphasis on liberal arts; and second, the obligation to meet the educational needs of the burgeoning population of the surrounding area. The region's rate of growth during the period was always at, or very near, the highest in Virginia. Moreover, its population's educational level was disproportionately high because of the character of the workforce at major employers such as the Naval Surface Weapons Lab in Dahlgren, Government Employees Insurance Company (GEICO) in Stafford County, and the extensive public school systems in Stafford and Spotsylvania Counties. Accordingly, Mary Washington's plans for the future envisioned two main components: the existing, primarily undergraduate, residential college in Fredericksburg; and a separate entity, devoted mainly to graduate and professional commuting students, to be located somewhere nearby.

Some were skeptical about the venture, including students. A 1990 *Bullet* editorial noted that the plan raised "a lot of questions," some of which it posed facetiously: "Will the new campus get a football team? . . . Will the campus cops over there get Uzis? Will they divide the . . . basketball team into two separate teams? Scheduling should permit them to play each other [so that] MWC would be guaranteed a few wins. How similar would the new campus be to the current one? Would it host a plethora of brick walkways and an overabundant squirrel population? Will they, too, get a fountain?"

But then the editor suggested, perceptively, what he termed some valid, more serious concerns. "Will there be any classes offered there that won't be offered here, and vice versa? . . . Why is it important to separate commuters and residential students? Will the satellite campus be beneficial or detrimental to the campus? What could it offer to anyone that it doesn't already offer? Expansion is fine," he concluded, "but does MWC need to expand?"

College administrators believed that it did need to do so, but before embarking on the project, they sought measurable evidence. A consulting firm, Mid-Atlantic Research, Inc. of Williamsburg, was engaged to conduct a needs assessment. Its evaluation involved interviews with approximately four thousand people ages eighteen and older, within a thirty-mile radius of Fredericksburg, as well as with twenty regional employers. The results, which were made public in May 1993, tended to corroborate the existing perception of a growing need for adult education, especially at the graduate and professional level. In announcing the survey results, Executive Vice President Ray Merchent commented that the administration "had some hunches, but you need some confirmation . . . to open up a second campus."[167]

By the time the confirmation was thus delivered, the College had become the beneficiary of certain real estate transactions in Stafford County. In particular, two major Washington-area developers, the Vogel Companies and the A. G. van Metre Companies, as part of their efforts to acquire approval for large-scale projects in Stafford, had included in their proffers parcels of land for use by the county. Both of the parcels were located just off Route 17 several miles west of the I-95 Falmouth interchange in a rapidly developing area dominated by the offices of GEICO.

Stafford officials, believing that a crucial element in sustaining the county's current economic boom was the availability of expanded educational opportunities, were most eager to have the requisite facilities established within the county. In fact, efforts had been already been made to attract a branch of Germanna Community College, but the initiative failed when Germanna chose to locate a second campus in Spotsylvania County instead. Accordingly, Stafford officials made a determined effort to lure Mary Washington by agreeing, in essence, to turn over the proffered parcels to the College for establishment of a satellite campus for commuting students.

The plan garnered wide support, both public (such as the Stafford County Board of Supervisors) and private (notably GEICO and the Mary Washington Hospital). At the state level, in terms of securing the necessary funding, the most important figure was Stafford's state senator John Chichester, who at the time was one of the most powerful figures in the General Assembly. Locally the key role was played by the longtime Stafford County administrator C. M. Williams, whose reservoir of respect and gentlemanly demeanor enabled him to be an effective broker between county authorities and President Anderson.

By 1998 the complex negotiations had yielded a forty-eight-acre parcel of land and appropriations sufficient to begin construction of the new campus's first building. Groundbreaking for the $8.5 million, two-story, sixty-thousand-square-foot structure took place on April 17, 1998. The event brought together an assemblage of College, business, political, and government leaders for a celebration reminiscent of the one that had accompanied the founding of the original College nine decades earlier. The outpouring of civic pride was generated, as before, not only by the prospect of enhanced educational opportunities but also by the anticipation of a regional economic boost. Calling it "a crown jewel in the economic development of Stafford and the region," Gene Bailey, the county's chief administrator for economic development, predicted that "the campus is going to be very much involved in educating the existing and future labor force as it relates to high technology, [and] if there's any one component . . . of a company's decision to locate or not locate in a region, the existence of a highly educated labor force is right at the top of that list."

The local county newspaper, the *Stafford County Sun*, likewise hailed the groundbreaking in an editorial titled "A Goal Fulfilled." Citing the contributions of Anderson and Chichester, among others, it singled out C. M. Williams for particular praise. "He usually stands back and allows the supervisors to receive credit on major developments," the *Sun* wrote, but on this issue "his persistence and ability to work with a variety of key leaders . . . brought significant results regarding the new campus. . . . Give Williams credit."

One of the early issues related to the new campus was the question of what it should be named. The matter of institutional names had a history of controversy at Mary Washington, and the choice of a name for the Stafford facility proved no exception.

To study the issue, President Anderson appointed a twenty-one-member committee comprising representatives from the faculty, staff, student body, alumni, Board of Visitors, MWC Foundation, and local community. Known officially as the College Image and Stafford Name Committee, it was more commonly referred to simply as the Mehfoud committee, in reference to its chair, Richmond attorney Kathleen Shepherd Mehfoud '70, an active alumna and former rector of the Board of Visitors. To assist in its research, the committee engaged the services of the National Institute for Organizational Research and Problem-Solving in October 1996 to survey more than twelve thousand persons, including prospective students, current students, alumni, and college employees.

After months of deliberation, in November 1997 the committee presented its recommended name to the Board of Visitors: the James Monroe College of Graduate and Professional Studies. The committee had approved the name by a vote of 15–2, the two dissenters being the student members, who preferred James Farmer to James Monroe. (Farmer had by then gained prominence as a much-beloved member of the faculty, in addition to his contributions as a leader of the civil rights movement.) The board concurred with the committee's recommendations, and the Stafford campus was christened the James Monroe Center (JMC).

Separated by six miles geographically, the two campuses were in different galaxies in almost every other respect, beginning with their disparate architectural styles. Much in contrast to the familiar white-columned red-brick buildings of the Fredericksburg campus, the new structure, designed by the architectural firm of Dewberry and Davis, was a modern triangular study in metal and glass, furnished inside with state-of-the-art technology. But that was only the tangible manifestation of vast programmatic differences between Mary Washington College and the infant entity known originally as the Center for Graduate and Continuing Education. As Provost Philip Hall aptly put it, "This is very different from the traditional. The architecture, the program, the students aren't traditional. It's technology. It's flexibility. It's local. It's adults. It's business. It's education for teachers. . . . It's going to be a lot of fun."

Designing and implementing the academic program for JMC was mainly the responsibility of Meta R. Braymer, who was hired as associate vice president for academic affairs and director of the center in 1990, just as the concept of a second campus was being initially considered. Though herself the product of a liberal arts education as the holder of a doctorate in English from the

University of Tennessee, Braymer had considerable experience in non-traditional academic administration before joining the Mary Washington staff. Most recently she had served as director of evening, summer, and off-campus credit programs at Virginia Commonwealth University. Her qualifications for the job, however, extended well beyond her training and experience. Fashionable and engaging, she was at the same time the epitome of professionalism. Moreover, she had a genuine and infectious enthusiasm for the kind of academic enterprise for which the Stafford campus was created. In short, she possessed the ideal combination of assets to allow her to become, as she quickly did, the public face of JMC.

Meta R. Braymer

In addition to Braymer, key staff personnel at JMC included at the outset:

Mark Safferstone, assistant dean
Jenifer Blair, senior associate dean for marketing and admissions
Sallie Washington Braxton, assistant professor and director of adult degree programs and advising services
Lynn Hamilton, director of information technology and instructional support
Gail Brooks, lead faculty for computer technology
Alan Heffner, lead faculty for leadership and management
Brenda Vogel, lead faculty for education
Karen Hartman, library director

The opening of JMC on August 23, 1999, was hailed by the local Stafford newspaper as "one of the major cultural events in the modern history of Stafford County," an assessment that was reflected in comments at the official ribbon-cutting ceremony several days later. "Mary Washington is one of Virginia's best colleges," proclaimed Senator Chichester, who went on to praise the new departure embodied in JMC: "I rarely hear people make the link between the health of our colleges and the health of our economy, [but] without Mary Washington's creativity and willingness to re-examine itself, and without its close ties to the business community, this center would not exist. . . . It's flexible, it's forward-thinking, and it's entrepreneurial."

President Anderson likewise emphasized JMC's novel approach. Mary Washington, he said, had "always been primarily a residential, liberal arts college, [but] here we're moving forward on something we believe will benefit the entire region. With the James Monroe Center, the citizens of this area have all the programs and opportunities they need to advance."

The *Free Lance–Star* agreed, asserting in an editorial that "MWC's new branch will boost [the] quality of life" in the area. "Some trend-watchers," it suggested, "predict that in the next century, Northern Virginia will emerge as the new Silicon Valley. Indeed, high-tech industrial parks filled with software engineers dominate the landscape around the Capital Beltway. And if such places creep south a bit, we will look back on the opening of the James Monroe Center as a watershed."

Besides its academic offerings, the center served as the location for several of the College's outreach programs, including Elderhostel and ElderStudy. Both entities, which were nonprofit organizations designed to provide short-term, low-cost educational opportunities to persons over fifty-five, had already operated on the Fredericksburg campus for some years.

The James Monroe Center also became home base for the Rappahannock Region Small Business Development Center, which moved from its original location in Seacobeck. Under the direction of Brian Baker, the agency by 2006 had provided assistance that was instrumental in creating (or retaining) over four hundred jobs, securing almost $6 million in capital investments, and producing more than $28 million in sales for the region.

There was only one serious disappointment in the early stages of JMC's development. Originally plans had included the establishment of a northern Virginia–based public television station, WNVT, on the campus. College officials had envisioned the station as providing hands-on experience for students in the communications field and perhaps forming the basis for a degree program in that area. However, executives of the station's parent company, Central Virginia Educational Telecommunications Corporation, backed out of the proposed arrangement in July 1999, citing higher-than-anticipated costs and difficulties in arranging a satisfactory lease agreement with the state.

That setback notwithstanding, JMC proceeded with its initial academic offerings in August 1999. Some of the programs were already in existence and were simply transferred to the new location. These included master's level courses in engineering, education, business, and public administration—all of which were previously offered via satellite from other Virginia universities.

At the time of its opening, JMC offered courses leading to credit certificates in teaching English as a second language and in computer technology for educators. In 1999–2000 it began to implement its cornerstone degree program, the bachelor of professional studies (BPS), which provided concentrations in leadership and management and in computer technology. A certificate program in organizational leadership was also inaugurated.

The BPS degree program was open to students with sixty hours of undergraduate work or an associate's degree. It required sixty additional hours of professional training from a curriculum that included courses in general liberal arts, technology training, and business communications. The new degree program was promoted through a series of ads in the local newspaper describing it as "designed solely for adults" and featuring wry slogans such as "The Same Career for a Lifetime Was Fine for Your Parents. So Were Rotary Phones," "Get Your Bachelor's Degree Out of the Way before Your Mid-Life

First building constructed on Stafford campus (later the College of Graduate and Professional Studies)

Crisis Hits," and "Go Back and Get Your Four-Year Degree without the Bitter Aftertaste."

The enrollment response to the BPS program was sufficient to warrant the addition of two more degree programs the following year—a master of business administration (MBA)[168] and a master of education (M.Ed.)—both of which offered multiple concentrations (e.g., an MBA in information security or an M.Ed. in diverse student populations). Over the next five years, additional concentrations within those degrees, as well as additional certificate programs, were developed to meet demonstrated needs as they arose within the region, especially the demand for more teachers, generated by the rising population. In 2006–7 five new programs became operational, notably including a master of science in management information systems (MSMIS).

The first JMC graduates received their degrees in 2001 when four students were awarded BPS degrees as part of the College's traditional commencement on Ball Circle; the next year, thirty-three degrees were awarded in a similar ceremony. In 2003, by which time the number of graduates had risen to ninety-one, the center held the first commencement of its own at the Stafford campus. That ceremony was highlighted by an address by C. M. Williams, who received an honorary doctorate, and by the awarding of the prestigious Washington Medallion to Meta Braymer in recognition of her crucial role in establishing the center.[169]

In 2004 the center's commencement was again held separately from that of the undergraduate college but took place in Dodd Auditorium rather than in Stafford. Beginning in 2005, graduation exercises became part of a unified commencement ceremony on the Fredericksburg campus.

The rapid success of the James Monroe Center provided a stimulus for Mary Washington to move from the status of a college to that of a university. That development, in turn, prompted a recrudescence of controversy over the name of the institution—a debate that would prove all the more bitter because of lingering hostility in some quarters from earlier efforts at a name change.

The idea of university status was not new at Mary Washington. There was mention of such a possibility as soon as graduate programs were introduced in the 1970s. It was also broached in the mid-1980s when research by SIR indicated that prospective students were more attracted to a "university" than to a "college," believing that the former was better or in any case more prestigious. It was thus for largely cosmetic reasons of image enhancement that an increasing number of colleges began to declare themselves universities, including public ones (e.g., Longwood, Radford) and private (e.g., Averett, Hollins).

At Mary Washington the concept of becoming a university was given a further boost in 1997 with the report from the Mehfoud committee's research firm that touted such a move as an aid to recruitment. It would help to rectify the problem, according to the firm's president, that "we are not seen as having as high a caliber of academic student body [as] we actually have."

There were other possible benefits as well, according to President Anderson. "There is no real financial benefit to being a university," he said, "although it may make it easier to interest private donors. The term 'university' seems to convey academic quality."

With such factors in mind, the Board of Visitors passed a resolution at its November 1998 meeting endorsing the effort to move toward university status. No timetable was set, though administrative officials noted that no definitive action would be taken until the SACS self-study reaccreditation report, mandated for completion by 2004, could be considered, since SACS approval was necessary to become a university.

Also required was approval by the State Council of Higher Education. Anderson anticipated no problem on either front, suggesting that approvals by both would be essentially a formality. "Both organizations have already approved us for master's level work," he said, "so there's no real obstacle."

Announcement of the board's intentions produced little opposition at first. In fact, the *Bullet*, which typically found reason to quibble with administrative policies, greeted the news with uncharacteristic enthusiasm. "This is one BOV decision that should please everyone," read an editorial. "University status can do nothing but benefit the college. First, people generally tend to associate 'university' with academic quality, while 'college' to some people implies inferiority. No, it's not an accurate perception, but that's how people think. . . . Once the Stafford campus of MWC is complete, we will technically be a university. Why shouldn't we advertise that? . . . Provided that the small-community atmosphere of MWC is maintained throughout the status change, this could be one of the best moves our administration has made in a long time."

Yet as it turned out, the path to university status was strewn with controversy. The main point of contention was the all-too-familiar question of a name for the new entity, a matter that proved to be, as Yogi Berra's malapropism had it, "déjà vu all over again"—in spades.

No sooner had the board's intention to seek university status been announced than the rumor spread that an umbrella name for the institution had already been selected to bind the Fredericksburg and Stafford campuses: Washington and Monroe University. President Anderson immediately denied that any such decision had been made, though he did aver that he favored a unifying name and, moreover, that he thought the historical James Monroe deserved more recognition than he had theretofore received. "This is not a name change," Anderson said. "This is reorganization. We need to put an overarching name over it so the university can prosper and all the elements under it can prosper."

The ever-vigilant defenders of the name "Mary Washington College" were not mollified. "Raise the possibility of a change of Mary Washington College's name," said the *Free Lance–Star*, "and you've stirred up a hornet's nest of major proportions." And so, once again, it happened.

Students began to circulate petitions against the proposed change, and the SA Senate passed a resolution urging that the new name be Mary Washington University. Alumni opposition also quickly developed, facilitated by the exchange of e-mail messages. One alumna reported receiving a deluge of over four hundred messages supporting her proposal that any new name must include the words "Mary Washington."

The faculty, too, promptly made its feelings known. Leading the defense of Mary was English professor Steve Watkins (also faculty adviser to the *Bullet*), who had personal attachment to the existing name through his mother and a cousin, both of whom were MWC graduates. Aside from those ties, he opposed the prospective change as a sexist subterfuge to eliminate the feminine connotations in order to attract more male applicants. "It's sexist to drop Mary," he declared. "If there are men who won't come here because it has a woman's name, I don't want them to come." He contended that the original name would vanish into oblivion if a different umbrella name was given to the university.

The *Free Lance–Star*, an implacable foe of the earlier proposed name change in 1985, weighed in this time with a somewhat more balanced opinion on the possibility of a Washington and Monroe University. Arguing in favor of such a change on the one hand, it admitted that proponents who contended that "Mary Washington College" connoted a women's college "are not wholly mistaken." In addition, it approved of the homage that the proposed new name would pay to James Monroe. Noting that other prominent figures in the commonwealth's history were memorialized by various institutions, the paper expressed regret that "nowhere in Virginia can you obtain (forgive us) a Monroe doctorate, or even a bachelor's degree. A 'Washington and Monroe University' would correct that historical injustice."

On the other hand, it contended, the removal (or diminution) of Mary in the university name appeared not only sexist but also unnecessary in terms of increasing the institution's appeal to prospective students. After all, it pointed out, "under its present name, MWC is ranked no. 2 among public regional colleges and universities in the south by *U.S. News & World Report* and no. 1 in the nation by *Money* magazine. . . . [Thus a] marketing campaign hardly seems requisite when fussy MWC rejects 43 percent of its applicants as academically wanting. The college has 'suffered' under its 'antiquated' female name, in short, about like B'rer Rabbit suffered in the briar patch."

On whichever side of the argument lay the preponderance of truth, there was no disputing the editorial's conclusion. "Above all else," it said, "this controversy illustrates the depth of emotion with which most people regard their college, a sacred bridge, golden in memory, between childhood and adulthood, dependence and autonomy. 'Alma mater,' after all, means 'fostering mother,' hardly a trivial idea. Whatever becomes of Mary Washington College's name, its essential identity, shaped by 90 years of educational excellence, must endure."

The 1998 anxiety over the university name was somewhat premature, as the name would not actually be selected for several years yet. To facilitate the process, President Anderson again appointed a committee, as in the previous case of the Stafford campus, to study the matter and present recommendations concerning a university name. This group, known as the College Image and University Name Committee, like its Stafford predecessor, was composed of twenty-one persons representing the institution's constituent elements and was chaired by the capable Kathy Mehfoud.

During months of deliberations, the new Mehfoud committee reviewed existing research, both from the previous committee (1996–98) and from the College's "alternative self-study" (2001–3), an analysis of the proposed move to university status developed by a committee of 33 faculty members, 32 administrators and staff members, 10 students, 2 alumni and 2 community residents, and 1 representative each from the Board of Visitors and the MWC Foundation. In addition they studied new data collected by Stamats Communications.

One aspect of the process that appeared in retrospect to be particularly noteworthy was the provision, explicitly expressed in the board's formal "Charge and Assumptions" statement to the committee, that the name "Mary Washington College" was to be preserved forever, no matter what university name might be recommended. It was a position often reiterated both by President Anderson and Mehfoud, and it would eventually cause significant discontent.

While the committee deliberated the name, the SACS review of the College's self-study resulted in approval of the plan to create a university structure. Announcing the approval in the summer 2003 alumni magazine, Anderson reported that "the exit interview with the SACS team was most positive, as they likened themselves to cheerleaders, wholeheartedly endorsing the move to university status." He went on to say that the SACS reviewers had commended "the courage, tenacity, and innovativeness of our approach designed to preserve the name and liberal arts tradition at Mary Washington College, while expanding aggressively at the James Monroe Center to meet the graduate and professional needs of the citizens of this rapidly expanding area." With regard to the center, the report recommended that it be renamed James Monroe College.

The second Mehfoud committee—unlike the first, which had worked with little dissension—often engaged in heated debates, perhaps understandable in light of the high stakes involved. Few events in the institution's history were so anxiously anticipated as the announcement of the committee's decision, drawing the attention of newspapers from Washington to Norfolk.

By the date set for the committee's vote, it had already become public that the two leading choices were Washington and Monroe University and Mary Washington University. The latter was apparently the overwhelming choice of both the students and the alumni. A poll of approximately 1,500 students revealed it to be the preference of over 90 percent of the respondents; two-thirds of 755 alumni replying to a survey indicated it to be their preference as well.

It was generally assumed that the choice, in any case, would come down to one of those. But at almost the last moment before the vote was taken, one member of the committee, Vice President for Enrollment Martin A. Wilder, proposed another alternative: the University of Mary Washington.

Probably no member of the committee was more respected than Marty Wilder. Actively engaged in local civic activities, he was generally held in high regard both in the community and on campus. But it was his administrative experience at the College that gave particular heft to his views on the institution's image and its impact on recruitment. Having joined the admissions staff under Conrad Warlick in 1979, Wilder had been the College's chief admissions officer since 1989. Thus when he spoke about enrollment, people listened.

By 2003, Wilder's long experience had convinced him that the name "Mary," however desirable it might be for gendered reasons, constituted a practical impediment to recruitment by conveying the instant impression of a women's college.[170] To his mind, it was a hindrance not only to potential male applicants but to females as well. "Research that's been done by the Women's College Coalition," he explained, "indicates that something like 3 percent of the young women in this country, high school students, are even willing to consider a women's college. So if they make an assumption and never take the tours to look, and write you off, the concern is far greater in terms of recruiting quality female students than simply the matter of recruiting male students."

So even though applications were sufficiently numerous to permit high selectivity, Wilder viewed the prospect of an appropriate university name as a chance to upgrade the overall academic quality of the entire applicant pool, not just the male portion, as the "Mary" defenders universally claimed. That goal would be accomplished best, he had long believed, through an umbrella name of Washington and Monroe University, one of the committee's top two options.

Yet as the vote approached, Wilder withdrew his support for that name simply because, remembering the previous legislative opposition to a similar name, he came to the conclusion that it was "not a political reality we can sell" to the General Assembly. The alternative that he proposed was the "University of Mary Washington," a variation—some said a less-appealing one—of the proposed "Mary Washington University."

Inasmuch as the alternative did sound strange to many ears, Wilder felt constrained to explain his reasoning. First of all, he noted, the name was based on the assumption (valid at that point) that beneath the overarching name would be two distinctive entities: an undergraduate school, Mary Washington College, and a graduate and professional school, James Monroe College. Accordingly, to his mind, the name "University of Mary Washington" would reduce, however slightly, the redundancy embodied in "Mary Washington College of Mary Washington University."

It was, to many observers, a very fine point indeed, but to Wilder his variation possessed ancillary advantages as well. For example, it had what he termed "a ring of prestige," a quality that he later elaborated upon at some length: "The University of Mary Washington, I think, [has] tremendous appeal for several reasons. Number one, it's distinctive. It puts us in the category of the University of Virginia and the University of Richmond . . . as opposed to those who have simply tacked 'University' on to the end—like Longwood University, Hollins University, Radford University, Christopher Newport University—and I, personally, would rather be seen in that other orbit, because I think that's more where we want to be and want to be perceived. So I think it's distinctive. I think it puts us more in that league of institutions."

Another advantage, albeit a minor one, he asserted, was related to alphabetical listings of institutions and the arrangement of their positions at college fairs. Putting "University" ahead of "Mary" in the name would mean placement with the likes of the University of Virginia rather than with the "M" schools like Mary Baldwin (all-female) and Marymount (previously all-female). Sensitive to potential imputations of sexism, he was at pains to emphasize that this consideration was simply "a spin-off, . . . a fringe benefit," and maintained that he would not have made his proposal "solely to put us in a different neighborhood in the college fairs."

Whatever his reasoning, Wilder's argument to the committee proved persuasive. When the vote was taken, the top choice was between Washington and Monroe University and the University of Mary Washington; the Mary Washington University option had been chopped from consideration.

That vote revealed just how divided the committee was: Washington and

Monroe University was the first choice by a vote of ten to nine over the University of Mary Washington. The Board of Visitors members of the committee were split, with Mona Albertine and William Poole favoring WMU and Rector Dori Eglevsky voting for UMW. The student members were outraged. As Katie Leesman, chair of the SA Legislative Action Committee, declared, "It doesn't make good business sense when 91 percent of your customers say they want something and you go against it."

Announcement of the committee's action precipitated what the *Norfolk Virginian-Pilot* called "the mother of all debates." Locally the *Free Lance–Star* assailed the recommended name on several grounds, the most basic being the absence of any need for change. The College did not lack applicants, it pointed out, noting that "last year over four times as many students sought admissions as eventually matriculated. The average SAT score of incoming freshmen tops 1,200 . . . so the need to attract large numbers with a gender-neutral name doesn't follow." The paper then provided its own explanation: "The suspicion lurks that the move to rename the college is veiled sexism."

Nor did the paper find the proposed new name attractive. "As to 'the University of Mary Washington,' fie. The name is trippingly unmellifluous." Referring to the historical implications of the acronym that would result, it facetiously suggested that students identifying themselves as being from UMW might expect such as response as, "Oh, you're a mine worker? How interesting. Coal or gold?" And so, the editorial concluded, "The movement of the institution to university status is welcome. Losing 'Mary' is not."

No one agreed with the latter statement more than Steve Watkins, who continued to lead the campaign against any tampering with "Mary." In the wake of the committee's recommendation, he told the *Richmond Times-Dispatch*, "I think the people that voted for Washington & Monroe University by and large mean well, but I think they're very deeply misguided." Speaking to the *Norfolk Virginian-Pilot*, he was more blunt. "There's a small element of some coaches and insecure faculty members who have a problem with a woman's name," he said. "A lot of what's driving those people is just flat-out sexism."

He did not accept the assertion by Kathy Mehfoud that, under the UMW umbrella, the undergraduate branch would continue to be known as Mary Washington College. "That's a lot of bunkum," he said. "They cannot point to a single liberal-arts college in this country that has gone to a university status that hasn't become known by that university status."

With only a matter of days remaining between announcement of the committee's recommendation and the expected vote by the Board of Visitors, Watkins's opposition went into overdrive. Having early printed and sold T-shirts emblazoned with the admonition "Save the Name," he now spearheaded a protest movement designed to dissuade the board from choosing "Washington and Monroe University." The focal point of opposition was a rally planned for the Friday afternoon before the board's scheduled vote on Saturday morning. The plan called for the protesters, whom Watkins pre-

Students at rally protesting possible name change, 2004

dicted would number one thousand, to march from GW to the Woodard Campus Center, where the board meeting would be in progress.

Though the actual rally fell short of the anticipated number of protesters—the local paper estimated three hundred—the group did not lack for passion. Beginning with the singing of the alma mater by BellACapella, the gathering heard defiant speeches from a number of incensed alumni, including local schoolteacher Mayo Carter '79, who went beyond the usual critiques of the name to launch an ad hominem attack on President Anderson. Claiming that his only interest was in marketing the school, she shouted, "There's a word for that. . . . It's called 'pimping.'"

Also among the speakers was Fredericksburg mayor Bill Beck. "I say save the name," he told the crowd. "There is a great honor and a great privilege and a real importance to honoring Mary Washington. . . . She was a tough gal. . . . And I want to ask every one of you to do your part, because if you don't, I want to ask you—what would your mothers think?"

After the speeches, the protesters headed down Campus Walk, brandishing placards with messages such as "There's Something about Mary" and chanting, "Who's the Bomb? George's Mom!" and "Hell, no, Wash-Monroe!" But by the time they reached the Woodard Center, their quarry, the Board of Visitors, had already departed, leaving an angry Watkins to inform the crowd, "They snuck away in the dark."

The display of sentiment may, however, have had some effect on the eventual outcome when the board gathered the next day for what was to be one of the most tense meetings in the institution's history. Rector Dori Eglevsky began by providing context for the situation. "We have a tremendous task and responsibility before us to make a decision regarding the name for our university," she said. "It is an issue that matters to a lot of people. It's also an issue that carries a lot of emotion and a tremendous amount of passion. And I know that none of us on this Board of Visitors takes this lightly."

Then came the climactic moment as President Anderson rose to deliver his recommendation. "I would like to echo the importance of the decision that this board will make today," he began.

> It is one of the most important decisions that will be made for this institution. We come to this time in history with the very, very strong heritage to build upon. We must take advantage of that. We also find ourselves with the new operations of the James Monroe Center, which has grown and matured faster than we ever thought possible. . . . So we come to this point with a very proud heritage and a strength that gives us the confidence to move into the future. . . . This is our time in history. We can do something nobody ever dreamed possible. We can do it . . . consistent with our past. We can move forward to fully embrace university status [with] everyone marching together. . . . In my opinion we can make a "win-win" decision that carries our heritage with us, that embraces the future, [and] that recognizes what this institution stands for already, as well as a realization of what it can be tomorrow.

With that, the president came to the announcement that so many had awaited so anxiously: "My recommendation to you is that we move forward with the name 'University of Mary Washington.' That's what will bring us together. Let us go forward as one, and put these two magnificent colleges together as a solid university."

That recommendation surprised many people, some pleasantly so, for several reasons. For one thing, it ran counter to the recommendation of the Mehfoud committee, which had endorsed Washington and Monroe, even if by the narrowest of margins. Second, most observers had believed all along, based on the earlier name-change initiative, that the president's main goal was to eliminate "Mary."

Why, then, did he ultimately recommend "University of Mary Washington"? Most basically, it seems to have been because he had come to doubt the political viability of any name that did not preserve "Mary." It was clear that, as in the 1985 effort, failure to do so would provoke a long, ugly, and very public fight that might, as before, jeopardize the institution's image (and its funding) in the legislature, to say nothing of the hostility it would perpetuate among alumni. And so, with the affirmative vote of the Board of Visitors, the University of Mary Washington it was to be—but not without further controversy.

In her closing remarks to the board following Anderson's announcement, Rector Eglevsky reiterated the president's call for harmony, asking that "we go forward together, and be united in support of what we're doing, because I think that's really critical for this institution. And I do see evidence, in so many different ways, of how much love there is for the name Mary Washington. So with that, I say congratulations [to the board] on a tough decision, and let's look forward to all the wonderful potential that goes with that decision."

But if Eglevsky and Anderson thought that all contention was over, they were mistaken. It was true that the initial reaction was generally favorable, revealing relief that, as the local newspaper put it, the board had "spared Mary." Also, Kristin Orstead, the SA president and student representative to the board, pronounced herself "ecstatic" over the decision, saying, "I think it's the best decision that could have been made. It's representing so many people's feelings and passions. I think that a lot of people are going to support this."

Not everyone was so thrilled, however; for some, the happiness at salvaging "Mary" was tempered by disdain for the "University of" nomenclature. Critics immediately complained that the syntax was at best unwieldy if not illogical; certainly it was unusual. Moreover, some claimed, it was transparently sexist, designed to minimize "Mary" by putting the name at the end.

Katie Leesman, who had been a student member of the Mehfoud committee, was of that mind. "I think it's going to be up to the students," she announced. "If there's a big outcry for Mary Washington University, then, as a student government representative, that's definitely what I will lobby in support of."

When the General Assembly convened in the following January, bills to establish the name "University of Mary Washington" were introduced in each house by local representatives: in the House of Delegates by Mark Cole (R-Stafford) and in the Senate by the influential John Chichester (R-Stafford). Neither claimed to be particularly fond of the name but expressed reluctance to micromanage the board's decision. As for the name, said Chichester, "We'll get used to it."

Also signing on as a patron of the Senate bill was alumna "Toddy" Puller. Her support was interesting because she had opposed earlier efforts to change the institution's name, including the "Washington and Monroe University" proposal, but decided to support the "University of Mary Washington." Like Cole and Chichester, she had some reservations to overcome. "Although I am not thrilled with University of Mary Washington," she said, "it still has [Mary's] name, and I'm going to vote for it."

Meanwhile opposition was growing on campus, again led by the implacable Watkins, who ridiculed the new name as sounding awkward and breaking several rules of grammar, as well as rules of common sense. "It's a foolish construction," he said. "It violates what I call in my freshman English classes the 'sounds stupid' rule."

He and other opponents found a legislative ally in the person of Senator Edward Houck (D-Spotsylvania), who, representing a district with a high number of alumni, had also been averse to the proposed change in 1985. Houck, himself an educator, not only disliked the syntax of the proposed new name but also disdained the sexism that he believed the name to entail. Calling it a "feeble, misguided attempt" to diminish the feminine image of the school, he charged, "This is a 'Mary' thing. . . . It's perpetuating a gender bias that we long since should have gotten over and away from."

The bill, however, proceeded through both houses of the legislature with minimum opposition, save Houck's, aided by efforts of the Richmond lobbying firm of Vectre Corporation, hired by the College to promote passage of the name. The bill easily passed in the House of Delegates and in the Senate, where there were only two dissenting votes—Houck's and that of Emmett Hanger (R-Augusta).

Even then, opponents did not give up. Knowing that the bill had to be approved a second time before going to Governor Warner for his signature, a delegation of MWC students went to Richmond for a last-ditch lobby effort with legislators and with the governor's chief of staff, Mary Washington alumnus William Leighty '78. Explaining the group's actions, their leader, Katie Leesman, asserted, "The students aren't being listened to, the faculty aren't being listened to, and the alumni aren't being listened to."

Such efforts were to no avail, however, and on March 23, 2004, Governor Warner signed the bill establishing "University of Mary Washington" as the institution's official name, to become effective July 1 of that year. It was, President Anderson proclaimed, "a great day for the institution." When the day of the official change arrived, the College commemorated it with a modest celebration. Most students were away for the summer, but a small gathering of people, mostly employees, mingled on the lawn outside GW to eat cake and drink punch. President Anderson reiterated to the assemblage his earlier pronouncement, telling them, "This is a grand day, not only for our institution, but for the entire greater Fredericksburg region."

The occasion was also marked by the unveiling of a new University logo developed by the Baltimore marketing firm of Barton, Matheson, Willse, & Worthington (BMW&W). The company specialized in the development of graphic designs for educational institutions and had worked for many state schools, as well as Harvard, Duke, and Yale. Earlier in the year, in an effort to get a feel for the institution's character, representatives from the firm had spent several days on campus speaking with students, faculty, and alumni, in addition to reviewing all current MWC brochures, pamphlets, and publications.

The result, revealed on July 1, was a blue-and-white logo depicting four stylized classical columns evocative of campus architecture. To the right of the columns were the words "University of Mary Washington," with "Mary Washington" most prominently printed. The initial reactions, as reported in the local paper, were generally favorable. "I absolutely love it," said one member of the alumni office staff. "I'm an alum as well, so the columns have a special place in my heart."

Ordinarily such an occasion would have been one of unmixed joy, with the community gathering to participate in a most significant day in the institution's history. But this, after all, was Mary Washington, and a name change was involved. And so it was not a time so much of celebration but cerebration—and, soon enough, more contention.

The root of the next round of discord lay in President Anderson's comment at a news conference following the official announcement to the effect that henceforth the name "Mary Washington College" would no longer be used in connection with the Fredericksburg campus. Instead it would be referred to as the University of Mary Washington—College of Arts and Sciences, and the James Monroe Center in Stafford would become the College of Graduate and Professional Studies (CGPS).

Opponents immediately cried foul—and worse. The *Free Lance–Star* waxed fairly apoplectic in a bitter editorial called "Bill Anderson U.?" The gist of the editorial was that the president, and others, had been deceitful about their intentions to keep the name "Mary Washington College" alive. As evidence, they cited a series of quotes from Anderson, Vice President for Enrollment Wilder, and Vice President for College Relations Singleton, as well as an op-ed piece by former rector Dorothy Eglevsky, all to the effect that the name of the College would be preserved for the Fredericksburg campus.

The new policy, frothed the paper, "isn't preservation; it's entombment." Though admitting that "under Dr. Anderson, MWC [has] attained high honors," the editorial proceeded to lambaste his latest actions. "One thing can be stated conclusively about the school's name, despite its president's accolades," it declared: "It is not 'William Anderson University.' Dr. Anderson is no corporate chieftain. . . . He is a public servant on the state payroll. The words he speaks, or allows his lieutenants to speak in his stead, carry with them accountability to the citizens of Virginia. They have been bamboozled. . . . It's up to [area] legislators to redeem the good name of Virginia, so badly represented by its collegiate stewards, by restoring the good name 'Mary Washington College' under the university umbrella."

That sentiment was echoed a few days later in a vicious op-ed piece in the same paper, written by Amy Prible, an alumna who had graduated the previous May. Continuing the ad hominem attack launched by the paper with even greater venom, she expressed the hope that "current students, faculty, staff, and my fellow alumni are finally able to see what kind of people are running Mary Washington and I hope they choose to hold them accountable for their lies. . . . I don't want my alma mater to be known as a school that can't define the words 'honor,' 'integrity,' and 'conscience.' You may have 'won' this name-change battle, Mr. Anderson, but you lost a whole lot more. And so did Mary Washington."

Even Dori Eglevsky, who had defended the move to UMW, expressed concern. "I think people are just absolutely shocked with what seems to be such an about face," she said, "and I have to say that it surprised me."

So, too, was Senator Chichester, who had initially introduced the name-change legislation. "I never liked the 'University of Mary Washington' and never made any bones about it," he said, noting that he supported the legislation only because he did not want to act counter to the board's expressed desire. Nonetheless the apparent new policy provoked him to vow to continue referring to "Mary Washington College" in his public speeches. "There are enough of us old dogs who are not going to be interested in new tricks," he announced, "so it will always be 'Mary Washington College' as long as I live."

The outcry was such that the Board of Visitors felt constrained to address the issue at its annual July retreat at The Tides Inn in Irvington. It was there that President Anderson provided his explanation for the origin of the fiasco. In what amounted to a complete mea culpa, he said that the confusion over removal of the name "Mary Washington College" resulted from his misunderstanding of a reporter's question and that he was not trying to reverse his prior commitment to retaining the name. "I think that's where some of the initial confusion came about," he said, "my misinterpretation of that question. The liberal arts and sciences college retains the name Mary Washington College." Moreover, he told the board members, "I do not have that authority. I know that." Furthermore, he said, he was "responsible personally" for the confusion that resulted over the gaffe.

Whatever the cause of the debacle, the board went on record as reaffirming its commitment to the name "Mary Washington College" when it incorporated words to that effect in an updated mission statement for the institution as required by the Southern Association of Colleges and Schools for reaccreditation. In a lengthy op-ed article in the *Free Lance–Star* following the retreat, Rector Mona Albertine explained in some detail the situation as it existed:

> Many people have asked what the move to university status will mean for the institution. To respond, the academic program on the Fredericksburg campus will continue to feature small class sizes, close faculty-student interaction, and a rigorous liberal-arts and sciences curriculum for its traditional, residential student body. . . . It will continue to be known as "Mary Washington College." What will primarily change at the university will be the scope and size of the academic programs on the campus in Stafford County, which the Board of Visitors has renamed the "College of Graduate and Professional Studies." . . . By becoming the University of Mary Washington, the institution has developed a way to combine, under one administration, the operation of two campuses.

Albertine's message might have been sufficient to quell the discontent but for two other developments that occurred around the same time, both related to the work of the BMW&W marketing firm. More provocative was the portion of their twenty-six-page report (ferreted out by the *Free Lance–Star* under a Freedom of Information Act request) suggesting that two of the institution's three main weaknesses involved the school's name. The first was the University's image as a private, all-female school and the third was that the "feminine-sounding name hurts in developing interest" among potential applicants. (The second-most serious weakness, according to BMW&W, was low minority enrollment.) Though University spokesman Ron Singleton emphasized that the report was just "an internal document . . . [to help] us get a handle on how we're viewed," the timing of its appearance did little to salve wounds that were still fresh.

A second, less-provocative, but still controversial issue arose several months later when BMW&W presented its recommendations regarding revision of the institution's diploma and seal. The new diploma was accepted without undue protest, inasmuch as it retained the previous institutional name in addition to the new one. The format of the documents for both campuses carried the overarching words "University of Mary Washington." Underneath for graduates of the former JMW was the designation "College of Graduate and Professional Studies"; for graduates of the former MWC was the designation "College of Arts and Sciences, Mary Washington College."

The revised seal stirred a bit more reaction—not that the issue was a new one. Calls for an updated version had been raised periodically since the institution became coeducational, the main complaint being that the spinning wheel on the old seal carried outdated and inappropriate connotations for modern times.

When the representatives of BMW&W presented their recommendations to the Board of Visitors in the fall of 2004, they offered six variations, only one of which retained the wheel; on the other five, it was replaced with a much more prominent version of the original seal's torch (or lamp of learning). Retained on all variations was the motto *Pro Deo, Domo, Patria*. "We recommended visually simplifying the seal for boldness," said a spokesman for the firm. "Elements that were in the previous seal that did not relate to the current university and that seemed to belong specifically to an earlier era were eliminated."

The version selected by the board featured the name of the University, the lamp of learning, the motto, and a book (presumably the book of knowledge) on which was boldly printed "1908," the date of the school's founding. Gone was the spinning wheel.

The *Free Lance–Star*, ever ready to skewer the perceived foibles of the institution, pounced on the new symbol in an editorial titled "UMW Unwheeled." In choosing the new seal, the paper suggested, the majority of board members had "peered at the quaint symbol and saw a Mary Washington grad barefoot and pregnant, her endless possibilities reduced to a life of domestic toil. Oh, what modernist myopia."

Citing various historical depictions of the spinning wheel (notably Gandhi's use of it in the Indian freedom movement), the paper declared that "the spinning wheel is indeed rich in symbolism. . . . Junking the spinning wheel is liberation? That thinking, as the kids say, is *so* 10 minutes ago. . . . In the '70s, young ladies of the left refused to shave their legs. Today's Bolsheviks bake; today's Trotskyites stitch. . . . Maybe C. S. Lewis had it right: you can't be really modern without being a traditionalist. So it's kind of a shame the new UMW seal is a no-spin zone."

But the paper did applaud retention of the Latin motto: For God, Home,

Country. "That may strike some way-left Mary Wash professors as socially Neanderthal," it concluded, "but it's a good sign that, with or without a place on the seal, the loomies, not the loonies, still rule."

On campus the new seal also prompted criticism from some quarters. Psychology professor Denis Nissim-Sabat, the faculty's nonvoting representative on the Board of Visitors, commented that at first the fist holding the torch "kind of reminded me of a Soviet-era person holding up a torch. But," he admitted, "nobody else will think about it."

Writing to the *Bullet*, sophomore Katherine Lowry was likewise derisive, suggesting that the changes did not go far enough. "If you want to eradicate the spinning wheel because it's 'archaic and feminine,' why stop there?" she asked facetiously.

> I mean, look at all the other archaic and gender specific stuff on there. Like, that dinky torch thing? Sorry, but who reads using a torch anymore? Plus a torch is too phallic for a school that wants to be more "asexual." We should symbolize the future of our institution with a glowing fluorescent light bulb, like the ones that flicker or are burned out in most of our residential halls. And that Latin motto—who reads Latin anymore? . . . I move we throw out the Latin motto and replace it with a hip AOL text message. Something like "UMW ROX, LOL!" What's with that "book of knowledge" bull? Fewer people are reading books nowadays. A palm pilot, or a laptop, or one of those slow i-Macs in Trinkle would serve better than some obsolete book.

Actually, student opinion on the new emblem seems to have been fairly well divided between skeptics like Lowry and adherents like junior Frank Puleo, the student representative to the Board of Visitors. He favored the revised design, he said, because "it keeps some of the traditions of the college/university, yet it is moving forward into the new phase we are about to experience." Rector Albertine agreed, noting that the board voted in favor of the new seal because "we felt it [both] honored our tradition and spoke to our future."

With the waning of the seal debate, controversy on campus gradually declined. After years of internecine wrangling, most members of the University community seemed ready for at least a semblance of tranquillity. Normally tart-tongued Board of Visitors member Nanalou Sauder expressed just such a view in a *Free Lance–Star* op-ed, the gist of which was clear in its title, "Can the MWC-UMW Alphabet Soup and Let's Return to Educating."

The truth was that current students were never as adamant about some of the issues as were a number of faculty and alumni. Especially after the decision was made to retain "Mary Washington" in the institution's name in some form, most students seemed indifferent about the actual nomenclature; whether it was UMW or MWU mattered little to them, nor were many of them exercised over the retention of MWC for the undergraduate campus.

As one student pointed out in a *Washington Post* interview, most of them just called it "Mary Wash" or "M-Dub" anyway, "so either way," she said, "that will still work."

Reflecting on the whole affair, Rector Albertine admitted that the process had been messy at times, but she concluded: "I don't think in the long run it's going to be a problem. Applications are way up, year after year; it gets better and better. The kids applying today are applying to the University of Mary Washington, and they're going to be quite happy."

Given the institution's history—not just the recent past, but going all the way back to its founding—it would be dangerous to bet that there would never be another effort to change the name. But it was certain that the impetus would not come from William M. Anderson Jr. The attainment of university status constituted perhaps the greatest, and certainly the most obvious, achievement of his presidency. It would also be one of the last.

FAREWELL

In February 2005 William M. Anderson reached a decision he had long contemplated but never embraced: it was time to retire as president.

The matter had been on his mind for several years, but he was always dissuaded by the prospect of completing projects already under way or of initiating projects still in the dreaming stage. Prominent among projects under way were the construction of a magnificent campanile next to George Washington Hall and the opening of a second building on the campus of the College of Graduate and Professional Studies; among those still dreamed of was a long-awaited convocation center. In addition, the University's centennial lay only a few years away, and being involved in that celebration appealed to him.

The campanile project was particularly close to Anderson's heart, as it developed from a personal friendship that he had established with John Chappell of Villanova, Pennsylvania. Following his graduation from Harvard in 1958, Chappell had been stationed at Quantico for training as a Marine Corps second lieutenant. It was during that eight-month period that he began dating a Mary Washington student, Carmen Culpeper '59, a native of Puerto Rico, whom he subsequently married. Over time, Chappell became a highly successful businessman, eventually retiring as chairman of Smith-Klein-Beecham, a huge pharmaceutical company (later known as Glaxo Smith Klein) with sales of $35.2 billion in 2003.

Shortly after Chappell retired, Carmen died of breast cancer. Seeking an appropriate means of honoring his late wife's memory, he met with Anderson and Vice President for Development Jeff Rountree for discussions that led to a grant of $2 million from the Chappell family to the institution. It was decided that $1.5 million of that amount would be used to fund the campanile, with the remainder to be used to endow the "Great Lives" public lecture series. Work on the campanile began in 2006 with the expectation that it would be completed in time for the University's centennial celebration.

Anticipating that event, Anderson in 2005 had appointed a committee, chaired by distinguished professors of history Carter Hudgins and Bill Crawley, to plan the commemoration. The committee, comprising representatives from the student body, faculty, administration, alumni, and community, met monthly, aided by subcommittees on various aspects of the program and by administrative support provided by Executive Director of University Relations and Communications Ranny Corbin, Special Projects Coordinator Margaret Mock, and Director of News and Public Information Teresa Mannix.

Over the next eighteen months, plans were developed for a celebration that promised to be the grandest and most extensive in the institution's history, beginning officially with the dedication of the Carmen Culpeper Chappell Centennial Campanile in May 2007 and continuing through reunion weekend in June 2008. The prospect of participating in such festivities—celebrating, as they would, a history in which he had played a prominent role—must have been a powerful temptation to Bill Anderson.

Still, there were countervailing considerations. He admitted in candid conversations that his stamina, undermined by the daily challenge of his partial paralysis, was not what it once had been. "In the back of my mind, always," he told the *Free Lance–Star*, "is [the idea] that somebody else who didn't have these limitations may be more effective. . . . So I can't be selfish." Moreover, life at Brompton had become more lonely with his children now grown and his wife, Jane, spending more and more time at the family's home in Hilton Head, South Carolina.

And so, in a letter dated February 15, 2005, Anderson informed the Board of Visitors of his intention to retire at the end of the next academic year, June 30, 2006. It was a difficult step, as was evident in his letter to the board. "I confess that it is not altogether easy to contemplate leaving the place that has been so central to my life for so long," he wrote.

> After all, by the end of the next academic year, I will have spent thirty years at Mary Washington, including the last twenty-three as president. Yet I am convinced that, for reasons both personal and professional, this is the proper course to take at this time, for Jane and me, as well as for the University. . . . From a purely personal [perspective], I have reached the point where the desire to spend more time with my family is a compelling consideration. From a professional standpoint, . . . in 2006 I will be approaching my sixty-fifth birthday and, though I still am constantly energized by the excitement of the institution and its exceptional students, I believe that the achievement of the limitless potential of the University's future demands a leader whose vigor is in no way diminished. . . .
>
> In contemplating this coming time of personal and professional

> changes, I am more keenly aware than ever of the blessings that have been mine as president of this wonderful institution. . . . My interest in the University will continue unabated. I eagerly look forward to observing, with great pride, as the institution in the years ahead soars, as I know it will, to ever-greater heights of excellence. . . .
>
> The welfare of Mary Washington will remain foremost in mind, its beauty forever in my heart.

Though some were surprised at Anderson's decision to leave before the University's centennial celebration, the board announced its acceptance of his resignation at its meeting on February 18, 2005. In making the decision public, Rector Albertine noted that it would be "difficult to contemplate a Mary Washington without him as steward; his departure, after over two decades of exceptional leadership, will create, on both personal and professional levels, a void that will not be easily filled." She went on to laud his many achievements and graciously express the hope that retirement would bring Anderson and his family "enjoyment commensurate with the success his leadership has brought to the University."

The truth was, however, that there were those who privately were not altogether disappointed at his pending departure. Some board members in particular had come to view him as increasingly aloof, and they resented what they viewed as his failure to communicate better with them and with other constituents as well.

Some among the faculty also perceived a growing distance between the president and themselves, and over the course of his long tenure, differences of opinion had naturally developed over certain issues. Lack of what they deemed sufficient salary increases was a prominent one, exacerbated by their skepticism concerning his funding priorities. Others faulted him for not achieving greater diversity or for specific failures such as not establishing child-care facilities.

Students sometimes groused that Anderson was not a more visible presence on campus, implying that he lacked concern about their issues. Some alumni continued to nurture resentment over the name-change issue; to them he was irredeemably condemned as having tried to kill "Mary Washington."

Such criticisms notwithstanding, Bill Anderson's overall accomplishments were of such magnitude that only the willfully blind could ignore them. Previous presidents had been notably successful in certain areas—Combs for bricks and mortar, for example, and Simpson for academics—but Anderson's accomplishments ranged over all aspects of the institution: quality of both faculty and students, beauty and functionality of the campus, growth of the endowment, community outreach, and overall status in the public mind. And it was at his initiative that the institution added the College of Graduate and Professional Studies and gained university status. In so doing, he had wrought more improvement in more areas than any president in the institution's history.

Immediately upon learning of Anderson's intention to resign, the Board of Visitors turned its attention to finding his successor. It began with Rector Albertine's appointment of a three-person committee, consisting of herself and board members Martha Leighty and Nanalou Sauder, to choose a presidential search firm to assist the board. Though such an approach had never been used in previous searches at Mary Washington, by 2006 it was a widely accepted procedure.

After considering more than ten companies, the panel decided in early April to employ Korn/Ferry International, a well-respected firm with more than seventy offices on four continents. The agency had previously assisted with dozens of presidential searches including, in Virginia, the University of Virginia, Radford University, and Hollins University, as well as nationally at the University of California–Berkeley, Johns Hopkins, Tufts, and Ohio State. "They had the greatest depth of experience at the executive level in higher education," said Rector Albertine. "It wasn't even a close choice, frankly."

Later that month Albertine announced the formation of the Presidential Search Advisory Committee (PSAC), whose charge was to review all candidates and make a recommendation to the Board of Visitors, which would then make the final decision. The PSAC, chaired by Albertine, had five additional board representatives—Vice Rector William Poole, Elizabeth Hughes '51, Karen Radley, Nanalou Sauder '56, and Fred Thompson; Chip German, UMW vice president for information technologies; Monecia Taylor '81, president of the UMW Alumni Association; Frank Puleo, SGA president; and two faculty members—associate professor of psychology David Kolar from the Fredericksburg campus and associate professor of computer technology Gail Brooks from the College of Graduate and Professional Studies. Paulette Watson served as executive assistant to the PSAC.

The next step involved five spring forums at which the PSAC invited interested persons from the University community to discuss with them the skills they wanted to see in the new president. The information gathered from those sessions was shared with Korn/Ferry representatives at a July Board of Visitors retreat, and on that basis a position advertisement was placed in appropriate media. In addition to listing specific job criteria, the ad stated that the successful candidate must be "an effective and collegial leader who will develop and articulate a compelling vision of the university's future that builds on its heritage."

The rector also outlined the procedure to be followed. The search committee, she announced, would winnow the list of applicants to the most promising ten or fifteen, whereupon ten or so would be invited for off-campus interviews. The remaining top two or three would then be invited for on-campus visits; only then would their names be made public.

The announcement of the plan produced some griping on campus, notably from faculty who felt that their interests were underrepresented on the PSAC. There was also some resentment at the closed nature of the search, but Albertine defended the approach, pointing out that "candidates in presidential searches expect total confidentiality in the search process . . . because of the possible adverse reactions at their present places of employment if word were to 'leak out' that they are interested in a position elsewhere."

The search yielded approximately one hundred applicants, some by nomination, others proposed by the Korn/Ferry firm itself. In January 2006 three finalists were invited to campus for presentations and interviews. Two were women; the lone male, who quickly became the front-runner, was William J. Frawley, the fifty-two-year-old dean of George Washington University's Columbian College of Arts and Sciences.

Frawley's academic credentials were impressive, his administrative experience extensive. Having begun his college career as a student athlete (baseball) at the University of Pennsylvania, he transferred after one year to Glassboro State College (later Rowan University) in New Jersey, where he received his B.A. degree. He subsequently pursued graduate work in linguistics, earning an M.A. from Louisiana State University and a Ph.D. from Northwestern.

His academic career was spent mainly at the University of Delaware, where for twenty-three years he was a professor of linguistics and cognitive science. He worked in administration as well, which led to his being chosen as dean at George Washington, the position he had held for four years before applying for the UMW presidency. As dean he had initiated a number of innovations, including the development of an exchange program with the Universidad de Chile in Santiago.

In addition to his administrative duties, he remained involved in teaching while at GW, holding faculty appointments in the departments of anthropology and psychology. A former Fulbright professor, he had also lectured throughout the world and held appointments at academic institutes in Hungary, Poland, and Morocco.

Genuinely devoted to the study of linguistics, he was an internationally recognized authority on dictionaries. The editor of a journal called *Dictionaries*, he was also editor-in-chief of the four-volume *International Encyclopedia of Linguistics* and served on the advisory board for the dictionary division of Oxford University Press. Among his publications were *Vygotsky and Cognitive Science* (1997) and *The Expression of Modality* (2006).

With such exemplary academic credentials, it was not surprising that Frawley's candidacy was viewed favorably by the faculty, who found his campus visit extremely praiseworthy. But other factors, too, led to a broad consensus from all constituencies that he was the first choice among the top three candidates. His evident energy was impressive, as were the specifics of his ideas on subjects such as increasing diversity and elevating the University's public image. Some observers were also favorably impressed with his style, which appeared to combine personal openness with professional decisiveness. "I'm not a command and control leader," he said, "but I am decisive. I will make the decision. And if you disagree, you can tell me so."

It was thus with general approbation that the University greeted the announcement by Mona Albertine on February 3 that Frawley had been selected. Even English professor Steve Watkins, who had earlier disparaged what he deemed the overly secretive nature of the search, was elated. "He's a very exciting person," Watkins said of Frawley. "The waters are going to rise when his ship pulls into the dock. Everything at this university will be elevated."

Albertine, in announcing the selection, explained why Frawley had so impressed the board. "He had concrete ideas," she said. "He was creative in his thinking. He energized everyone." The *Bullet*, in reporting that view, headlined its front-page article with rather odd terminology, declaring, "Frawley Stuns BOV."

It would not be the last time.

Frawley made his first appearance on campus as president-elect only a few days later at a punch-and-petit-four reception in the Great Hall. The room was filled with well-wishers, many of whom stood in line to greet the chosen leader. It was at that time that the campus community had the first opportunity to meet Frawley's wife, Maria, and their two children, Christopher, fifteen, and Emma, eleven.

Maria (pronounced "muh-RYE-uh") was an instant charmer whose brilliant smile and endearing manner served as something of a balance to her husband, who, though perfectly polite and proper, could appear at first somewhat severe. Like him, she was an accomplished scholar. A specialist in nineteenth-century English women writers, she held a faculty appointment in the English Department at George Washington University. To accommodate their two careers and to facilitate the education of their two children—Christopher, who was autistic, had special needs—the couple decided early on to retain their home in Maryland, with Maria commuting to Fredericksburg as occasioned by various University events.

Addressing the crowd of over two hundred, Frawley expressed delight at being given the opportunity to lead the University toward what he regarded as its unrealized potential. "It's time to do new things," he said, "but we can't do so without standing on the past"—whereupon he asked the audience to join in acknowledging William Anderson's service to the institution. "We owe him a great deal of gratitude for all he has accomplished," said Frawley. As the audience applauded, Anderson, who was standing unobtrusively on the fringe of the crowd, responded with a wave of his cane. Frawley, at the end of his remarks, strode directly to Anderson to bestow a purposeful handshake.

For his part, Anderson, in private as well as in public, was completely sup-

President William Anderson welcomes his successor, William Frawley, at a spring 2006 reception in the Great Hall.

portive of his successor. "It's a great day in the life of the University," he said at the reception. "I am absolutely confident Dr. Frawley will do a wonderful job." As tangible testimony of his goodwill, Anderson voluntarily moved out of Brompton four weeks ahead of his official June 30 departure date to facilitate the renovation of the house before the Frawleys' occupancy. His final month of residency in Fredericksburg was spent at a single room in the Best Western motel—Jane having already moved to Hilton Head.

The new arrangement was quite a comedown from the elegant style of Brompton, and some found sadness in it all. Anderson himself was not among them, appearing instead to relish the motel's simpler quarters and genuinely to enjoy the meals often taken at the adjoining Shoney's. Years of living in the limelight had not spoiled the small-town boy from South Boston, who by then was looking forward to relief from the burdens imposed by his office.

With retirement imminent, he graciously but resolutely declined all invitations to celebrate the occasion. Whether it was because of genuine modesty or because it would have been too emotional—that is, whether from a lack of sentimentality or from an excess of it—who could say?

In any case, his departure was nonetheless acknowledged in several ways. At an April Key Club dinner for major donors, Anderson was praised for his "commitment, character, charisma, and, especially in the past decade, his courage" and was presented with a scrapbook of memorabilia and a golf cart. The evening ended with a toast lauding him "for the vision to dream great dreams for the institution and for the leadership to convert those aspirations into reality." At commencement exercises in early May, he was awarded the status of president emeritus and granted an honorary doctorate, the announcement of which was greeted with a sustained standing ovation.

Given his feeling about the University, the most appropriate acknowledgments of his service were not gifts to him or titles but two donations made to the school in his honor. One was a $1 million gift from Sara Page Cosby Mayo '64 and her husband, Richard, to create the University's first fully endowed faculty chair in the biological sciences. (It was later awarded to professor of biology and interim dean Rosemary Barra.)

The other donation was a $5 million gift from Arabelle Arrington, a devoted admirer of Bill Anderson.[171] The largest single gift in the institution's history, Arrington's generous bequest was allocated for funding endowments for both faculty and students, with a portion dedicated to support of the University's Summer Science Institute.

Though not normally given to nostalgia, there was some indication that the retiring president may actually have begun to intuit the lines of Robert Frost, who wrote:

> No memory of having starred
> Atones for later disregard
> Or keeps the end from being hard.

At one point, asked by a *Richmond Times-Dispatch* reporter to assess his lengthy tenure, Anderson recalled the early days of his presidency. "It never dawned on me [then]," he said, "that the hardest part of the job would be leaving."

–5–
THE FRAWLEY ERA, 2006–2007

THE UNIVERSITY COMMUNITY quickly learned two things about Mary Washington's seventh president: Bill Frawley was both a man of ideas and a man of action. Even before his term officially began on July 1, he was spending considerable amounts of time on campus, laying the foundation for a fast start, assisted by Vice President for Information Technologies Chip German, who served as transition coordinator.

One of Frawley's first actions was to appoint Nina Mikhalevsky to the newly created position of vice president for strategy and planning. Mikhalevsky, who had previously served under Frawley at George Washington University as an assistant dean in the College of Arts and Sciences, was chosen after a search that had begun in May. Other staff changes in the president's office included the hiring of Amy Andersen, who became administrative assistant to the president and clerk of the Board of Visitors, with the six-year incumbent Terry Luttrell moving to a position on the campus of the College of Graduate and Professional Studies.

Some observers suspected that wholesale personnel changes were imminent, but, according to German, Frawley was "a fellow who likes to understand the environment before making any changes," and he asserted that subsequent personnel moves—including the hiring of a chief academic officer—would unfold in a deliberate fashion. Meanwhile Frawley instituted a reorganization that created a central leadership unit known as the Core Planning Group, comprising, in addition to Mikhalevsky, six veteran administrative officials: Rosemary Barra, interim vice president for academic affairs and dean of the faculty; Meta Braymer, vice president for graduate and professional studies; Bernard Chirico, vice president for student affairs and dean of students; Richard Hurley, vice president for administration and finance; Jeffrey Rountree, vice president for University advancement; and Ron Singleton, vice president for University relations, communications, and legislative affairs.

In mid-July, indications of Frawley's plans (and style) were revealed at a Board of Visitors retreat in Williamsburg. It was essentially an informal

BILL BUTTRAM PHOTOGRAPHY

William John Frawley

"brainstorming" session, with discussions ranging broadly over questions of the University's future direction, as the new president raised a number of fundamental questions. What competencies, he asked the board, should the University expect its graduates to have? "What stuff do you need to know now that is different than what you needed to know twenty years ago? . . . Do we want someone to be a person stuffed full of facts or be able to use that historical knowledge?"

Focusing on the need to prepare graduates for life in a world much changed from, and smaller than, earlier decades, he asked, "What is UMW's connection to the globalization movement? Must [our students] know Dubai is a commercial center in the Middle East? Must they understand women's rights in Saudi Arabia, voting patterns in Mali? Must they know the distribution of age in the population of India? I think the answer is yes." Summarizing the sessions, a *Free Lance–Star* reporter wrote that it was evident that Frawley had "taken to his new role with gusto. . . . He's been on the job only two weeks and is already shaking things up." Frawley himself admitted as much. "I know that I challenge people," he said. "I expect to be challenged back."

Frawley's first opportunity to address the entire faculty in person came in August when he delivered the annual presidential state of the University speech. Aided by an array of PowerPoint illustrations, he began by reviewing the status of the institution. He found much that was positive: impressive admissions figures, favorable retention and graduation rates, solid financial standing (including both state and private funding), and noteworthy faculty accomplishments.

At the same time, he counseled against complacency, urging that the University aspire to "move to the cohort of Wake Forest, Colgate, Bucknell, Bowdoin, Wesleyan, and Davidson." To do so, he suggested ten "guideposts," including (in his words) the following elements:

- Open up UMW. The institution needs to look more like the world around us.
- Make opportunities, while avoiding mere opportunism.
- Have an administration that is relentlessly helpful.
- Plan infrastructure to meet the future, not just to meet the present.

- Tell others more about ourselves, and tell ourselves more about us.
- Academic life is more than books. UMW embodies the Greek ideal of accomplishment through the integration of mind and body.
- Make sure things actually happen.

He went on to adjure the faculty, in striving for those goals, "not to construe agreement as acquiescence or disagreement as unreasonableness." And in all such endeavors, he urged, the institution should be guided by basic values such as "high academic standards, . . . authenticity, . . . [and] institutional altruism: a sense of common purpose and willingness to overlook our differences for the sake of the whole." Motivating the whole process, he suggested, should be "vibrance: student life, faculty life, life of the mind. Live and move. We're in this job not for the mid-year stock options, but because it is fun."

Frawley's inauguration in late September provided a public forum for the exposition of his overall educational philosophy and his hopes for the future direction of the University. That event, planned under the direction of Ranny Corbin, then executive assistant to the president, turned out to be one of the most elaborate ever held at Mary Washington. The four-day celebration was characterized, as the alumni magazine alliteratively put it, "by events executed with finesse, flair, and a festive air."[1]

The celebration began on Wednesday evening, September 27, with a concert by the University–Community Symphony Orchestra. The next evening featured a speech by onetime Frawley colleague Edward Gnehm, a career State Department official and authority on Middle East politics who had held ambassadorial assignments to Jordan, Kuwait, and Australia. Gnehm's remarks were especially timely, given the ongoing involvement of the United States in Iraq.

Friday evening was devoted to a wide-ranging musical revue showcasing a number of the University's talented performers. Vocal groups included Encore, Una Voce, the Fredericksburg Singers, and the UMW Chorus. Instrumental performances included selections by the UMW Jazz Ensemble directed by Doug Gately, the Native American Chamber Ensemble directed by Craig Naylor, and the Eagle Pipe Band directed by Raymond Scott.

At the installation ceremony on September 30, the Pipe Band led the procession into Ball Circle, where, for the first time, the platform was situated on the western (Chandler) side, facing Lee Hall, rather than in the north-facing-south (Virginia toward Ball) configuration normally used for commencement exercises. The robed entourage included board members, administrators, faculty members, local representatives, and delegates from other educational institutions throughout the country, all of whom stood to offer enthusiastic applause as William J. Frawley brought up the rear of the stately procession. "It was," the *Free Lance–Star* later commented, "like nobility honoring a new king."

Following the presentation of colors by the Fredericksburg unit of the Virginia National Guard, the singing of the national anthem by music professor Stephen Burton, and the call to order by economics professor Stephen Stageberg, marshal of the faculty, Board of Visitors Rector William Poole welcomed the assembly. Greetings were then delivered by various dignitaries and representatives of the University's constituent groups. Speakers included Virginia governor Timothy Kaine, Fredericksburg mayor Thomas Tomzak, state senator John Chichester, President Alan Merten of George Mason University, and President Stephen Joel Trachtenberg of George Washington University. Delivering greetings from the University community were Florian "Red" Hofer, president of the UMW Foundation; Barbara Burton Micou '69, president of the Alumni Association; physics professor Bulent Atalay, senior member of the faculty on behalf of that group; Sabrina Johnson, assistant vice president for human resources and affirmative action on behalf of the staff; and two students, Sarah Schmidt (M.Ed. '07) from the College of Graduate and Professional Studies and Jay Sinha '07, president of the student association on behalf of the undergraduate college.

Other program highlights included the performance by the UMW Wind and Percussion Ensemble of "Fanfare and Entrada," a work commissioned for the inauguration and composed by music professor David Long, and a reading of a poem, "The Art of Science," written for the occasion by English professor Claudia Emerson. An especially evocative passage of the poem recalled one of the institution's most iconic touchstones:

> The amphitheatre, abandoned now to the deepening
> shadows of beech trees, was built into a natural
> depression, the school ordered on the hillside
> above. Tiered stone benches look down on the stage
> as though an audience might still be seated
> to catch the rising lines of *A Midsummer*
> *Night's Dream*. The fleeting fact of being here
> never enough, for years we have recorded
> some proof of us into these trees—easy
> to carve even with the dullest knife—hearts,
> arrows, our initials, names like slow echoes rising
> into widening artifacts that survive us.

The presidential oath was administered by Virginia Circuit Court of Appeals Judge James W. Haley Jr., after which the gold chain of office—recently prepared as part of the upcoming centennial celebration—was placed (not without some difficulty) about Frawley's shoulders by Rector Poole and former rector Mona Albertine. The address that the new president then delivered was notable both for its content and (linguist that he was) for the eloquence of its expression.

First establishing a historical context, he said that "today we are in a convergent moment. UMW is at the very point of celebrating a century of excellence, a distinguished and durable past, and is also about to embark on a new century of excellence. The events of today can make sense only as constituted by the confluence of tomorrow and yesterday. Having been offered the opportunity to lead the institution at this crucial convergent moment leaves me with both excitement and a little bit of stage fright . . . [as] my own hopes and aspirations merge with those of the institution."

He then spoke of the responsibilities faced by the institution. "The institution has an obligation to produce vigilant, substantive discourse," he said. "Engaging in fashionable 'eduspeak' is a disservice and an avoidance of our responsibility to say new things of substance. . . . The university is a place of great, safe experiment . . . where our duty is to model other people's ideas without necessarily giving up our own. . . . We have an obligation to allow our students to think with us, a task much harder to do than just telling people things, and then testing them, because you have to be willing to let down your guard and have extra time for those convergent moments."

Employing his customary modus operandi, he concluded with a challenge. "Drive the future," he urged. "Don't merely ratify the past. The worst that could happen would be that we would be wrong and thereby allow a well-made person and mind to do its regular work of self-repair and replication. . . . I urge us all—UMW, the city, the region, the state, all our communities—to look so hard at our mutually changing and interdependent selves in this convergent moment that in doing so, we see the institution cleanly and clearly, and may know this place again for the very first time."

The prolonged ovation that followed bore testimony to the audience's receptivity to the president's message—to the power of his rhetoric and to the uplift of his ideals. Amid a palpable sense of exhilaration and promise, the program concluded with Una Voce's moving a cappella rendition of the alma mater.

That evening, partying prevailed. Several hundred people attended the inaugural ball, which was held in three venues—the Jepson Alumni Executive Center, a tent on the grounds of Brompton, and inside Brompton itself. The new president seemed to enjoy the event immensely, dancing with his wife and daughter and receiving felicitations from hundreds of celebrants. Students seemed especially to enjoy the occasion, pronouncing it (typically) an "awesome party"—and suggesting that it be replicated to celebrate the centennial.

Frawley's first year was an interesting one on many fronts. In sports, 2006–7 was a banner year, with the overall success of the intercollegiate program highlighted by the national Final Four appearance by the women's basketball team. Competition of a more scholarly nature produced a national championship for the debate team. Directed by new coach Adrienne Brovera, the varsity team captured first-place honors in the American Debate Association tournament.

Student social life continued to include such traditions as Rocktoberfest, Psi Upsilon parties, and various holiday revelries but also witnessed some new wrinkles. One was a September "Underwear Run" in which 150 or so scantily clad students participated in a 10:00 p.m. race from George Washington Hall to Jepson. The event, claimed the organizers, was in memory of the late Steve Irwin, the popular Australian naturalist who had recently died. Participants, in truth, may not have seen much of a connection with Irwin, but they did get to see a lot of each other. The caption of a *Bullet* photo of the event probably revealed more accurately the reasons why students did it: "Because We Can."

Another innovation was an attempt to create a so-called erotic yearbook. The scheme sprang from the entrepreneurial brain of senior Daniel Ceo, an aptly named business major, who had earlier gained campus notoriety when, as a contributor to the *Bullet*'s "Sexclamations" column, he produced a paean to pornography that riled many students. Inspired perhaps by nudist publications such as Harvard's *H-Bomb* and Boston University's *Boink*, Ceo hoped to profit by selling the publications at $100 a copy, part of which he vowed would go to some charitable cause.[2] Yet his main goal, he said, was not to make money but to move the institution away from the usual yearbook photos of "people hugging a tree" and instead "really get a sense of what individual students are like at this school."

Alas for the enterprising Ceo, the plan proved to be a dud: because too few students were willing to take off their clothes, the project never took off. Its failure was a relief to those who wondered just how far students would go in the direction of license. In 2007—for the time being, at least—there apparently were some limits after all.

As had been true over the years, the *Bullet* often carried feature articles that provided insight into student culture. There was, for example, during the 2006–7 academic year, the "Top Five Roommate Complaints," which included, in addition to "the Pilferer" and "the Hermit":

- The Pigpen: Don't be a pigpen. It's simple: shower regularly. No, boys, it does not need to be everyday, though that would be nice. Every other day would probably be OK. Make sure you actually use soap.
- The Overly Exposed Roommate: Unless you are able to find someone who is as much of an exhibitionist as you are, do not sleep naked. It does not matter that your un-air-conditioned room on the top floor of Bushnell feels like Vietnam.
- The Sexile: It would probably be a lot more awkward to not sexile your roommate when you get a visit from the significant other. But there is nothing worse than wandering from dorm to dorm tired, pissed, and temporarily homeless in true "no room at the inn" fashion. As you wander Campus Walk, you ponder the most effective ways to murder your roommate, until you find that savior of an inn-

keeper who lets you sleep on their couch. And if there is no one to be found, there is always the study lounge.

Another list provided evidence that some elements of student behavior never changed, only the means of their accomplishment. The "Top Five Best Ways to Put Off Preparing for Finals" included, in addition to the basic "go back to sleep":

- www.popcap.com [an online Flash game web site].
- Wikipedia: An awesome place to go if you want information on just about anything you can think of. It also happens to be the biggest time-sink known to man. I like to think of Wikipedia as six degrees of separation on crack.
- Watch daytime TV: It's amazing the kind of crap a person can watch when it's one of the few non-school related activities immediately available. . . . Shows that I wouldn't be caught dead watching under normal circumstances . . . start to look a lot more entertaining when you have a whole textbook to read because you put it off all semester.
- Check peoples' AIM [AOL Instant Messenger] away messages: My AIM Buddy List is just about full and I don't even know half the people on it. That doesn't stop me from compulsively checking and rechecking everyone's away messages however. Neurotic? Probably. Obsessive? Most likely. Strangely entertaining? Most definitely.

As graduation 2007 approached, there appeared yet another list, "Top Five Things I Still Don't Understand About UMW as a Graduating Senior." Included were regulations concerning parking and Internet usage, as well as the following:

- Advisors: Professors hate being advisors, students hate having to go to advising appointments, and in the end neither party benefits much from the advising session. What then, is the point?
- The Meal Equivalence: Maybe I'm just obtuse, but it would seem to make sense that my dollar bills would be worth the same amount in one place as they would five hundred yards down Campus Walk. Is there some sort of exchange rate I just don't know about?
- Clocks: Why is this campus so obsessed with clocks but not the time they keep? Walking from Jepson to Combs, I pass 10 different clocks, each displaying a different time. In front of the Nest alone, four clocks read four different ways.

The *Bullet* also periodically offered advice features on social matters such as clothing ("Uggs Live On in Students' Closets") and partying. A September 2006 *Bullet* piece called "A Student's Guide to Drinking Seven Nights a Week" suggested the best local venues at which to "extend your drunken hookups to weekdays in addition to weekends." The list included the Hard Times Café (Sunday), Uncle Sam's in Central Park (Tuesday), the Loft (Wednesday), Fatty

J's and Central Station (Thursday), Brock's (Friday), and the Café New Orleans (Saturday). The most intriguing was the suggestion for Monday night, Spirits, on Caroline Street, which was, according to the columnist, "a dim-lit bar that some might affectionately call a dive. There are couches, a jukebox, and a separate room with two pool tables. There is also a back porch, and I happen to know that if you go on the right night, a particular guy . . . just might ask if you want to smoke weed with his buddy and him on the back porch. . . . It helps if you have dreadlocks."

There were, of course, more serious sides to students' behavior. They were inclined, perhaps more than ever, to look beyond the campus and to involve themselves in larger sociopolitical concerns. The environment was a major focus, and the Ecology Club worked hard to keep green issues in the forefront. Foreign policy, especially the generally unpopular war in Iraq, drew wide attention, stoked by a newly formed club, *E Pluribus Unum,* that comprised mostly political science and international affairs majors.

On campus, social concern led to renewed interest in employee wages, specifically those involving the food service area. Under the aegis of the Labor Rights Club, some students, previously engaged in the successful "living wage" campaign, organized a protest in March 2007 to demand that the University require contractors (such as Sodexho food service) to ensure that their workers received compensation comparable to that of the University's own employees.

Volunteerism continued to play a large role in student life, including the emergence of a new movement focusing on human rights abuses in impoverished countries. Motivated by a documentary on abducted children in Uganda, a group of students founded a club called Invisible Children UMW Chapter. "We're seeing how much the campus can band together," said one of the club's organizers, noting that outreach of that kind was "the popular thing right now."

Indeed it was, as Shin Fujiyama's Students Helping Honduras organization continued to prove. In a reprise of the previous year's campus walkathon that raised $148,000 for the Copprome orphanage, the April 2007 event raised more than $200,000, aided by funds from Doris Buffett's Sunshine Lady Foundation. The extraordinary campaign capped the collegiate career of its driving force, the remarkable Shin Fujiyama. "Three years ago, nobody in Honduras knew about me or UMW," he said. "Now I've got kids there who believe in me and this school." When he graduated in May, Fujiyama left behind one of the most admirable legacies in the history of the institution.[3]

The University's emphasis on multiculturalism continued with the success of the annual Multicultural Fair and various "emphasis weeks." Showing the greatest increase in participation, perhaps, was the Islamic Awareness Week. Sponsored by the Islamic Student Association, the event was designed, in the words of its 2006 president Zareen Ismael, "to show that we are normal people and there is more to us than the typical stereotype as terrorists."

Toward that end, the week included free henna tattoos, a coffee house night, guest speakers, and a Ramadan banquet. Community members were also invited to attend not only to learn more about Islam but to get to know UMW's Muslim students. As religion professor Mehdi Aminrazavi, the club's adviser, put it: "It's much better than getting to know Islam through the media."

The operation of the James Farmer Multicultural Center itself, however, suffered a setback in February 2007 with the resignation of its director, Ameeta Vashee, who had held the job for fourteen years. Vashee's charm and resourcefulness had been instrumental in the center's development, especially through the creation of the Cultural Awareness Series that sponsored numerous notable speakers on campus.

Following Vashee's departure, the Frawley administration moved to rejuvenate and refocus the center, exploring ways to establish better cooperation with the international studies program and to enhance the center's overall academic orientation. For that purpose, a committee was appointed, chaired by philosophy professor Craig Vasey. Working through the summer of 2007, the group strove for implementation of its recommendations during the centennial year.

The Frawley administration brought a number of changes in student life, including a potentially significant alteration of honor system procedures. Over the years the Honor Council had operated with virtually complete autonomy, answering to no specific institutional official. Though the Board of Visitors and president presumably had theoretical powers to reverse the council's decisions, such procedures were vague and almost never used.

However, in September 2006, following a two-year study instituted by former Board of Visitors rector Dori Eglevsky, the board changed its bylaws to give itself supervisory authority over the council—authority that it then conferred on the president. Although Frawley was not in office when the review process began, he recognized the advisability of change to protect the University both from council decisions that "might put the institution at risk without the institution having a commensurate position as a responsible agent in the decision" and from decisions that might "put the students at risk without their being able to be indemnified."

To implement the new system, Frawley increased the powers of the Honor Council's adviser, Vice President for Student Affairs and Dean of Students Bernard Chirico. Whereas Chirico's only function had previously been to ensure that procedures were properly followed during trials, he was now authorized to overturn decisions that he felt violated due process or basic fairness. For his part, Chirico supported the new setup, noting that fluctuations in the competence of Honor Council members from year to year presented a problem in the consistency of its decisions. "Sometimes things would run well with a particular [Honor Council] president and not run so well with another," he said. "You begin to doubt that things are always being done the same or on the level they need to be with the kinds of decisions being made." At the same time, he disclaimed any intention of intruding in the student-run proceedings unless absolutely necessary—an action that he predicted would be "very seldom."

Even in light of such disclaimers, it was the kind of change that in an earlier time might have brought howls of outrage from the student body, especially from the Honor Council itself, on the grounds that the principle of a student-run system was being subverted by administrative intrusion. But for whatever reason, the 2006 revision was met with general acquiescence on the part of the students. Even Honor Council president Stephen Gregg, while reserving judgment as to the ultimate impact of the change, commented, "We realized the BOV would have not enacted the changes at this time unless it felt the changes were necessary."

A number of mundane yet important developments affected students on a day-to-day basis. One involved the Health Center, which, along with Psychological Services, was relocated to Mercer Hall (its onetime previous location) to make way for the renovation of Lee Hall that began in the summer of 2007. The move was accompanied by a notable personnel change when Dr. Ilma "Pete" Overman retired as the institution's physician and director of the Health Center after more than thirty years in that position. Her successor was Dr. P. Thomas Riley, who had spent the previous twenty-three years in private family practice in Richmond. Psychological Services, renamed Counseling and Psychological Service, continued to be directed by Barbara Wagar, vice president for student affairs.

Several technological innovations helped to make campus life easier. One was an upgrade of the EagleOne system, a multipurpose card usable for an increasing number of services both within the University and beyond. On campus, it enabled students to view their account balances and to make online deposits in real time. In town a number of local business establishments began to accept the card for purchases.

Another innovation addressed that most basic dormitory drudgery: doing laundry. According to one *Bullet* description, "Laundry hell has been a Mary Washington tradition for as long as there have been washing machines in the dorms. Trudge down to the basement with your basket of smelly clothes, praying you'll find an available machine—a prayer that is rarely answered. Later, once you miraculously find an open washer and dryer, you return, only to find your clean laundry strewn across the floor after impatient dorm-mates have refused to wait their turn."

That doleful situation was alleviated in fall 2006 with the implementation of something called e-Suds, an innovation advocated by Assistant Vice President for Business Services Erma Baker. The program allowed students to monitor their laundry from their own computer, providing them with a virtual view of the laundry room in their residence hall, indicating which washers and dryers were available and which were in use; if in use, the remaining cycle time was displayed on the student's computer. Though the cost rose to $1.25 per load, the system was favorably received by students, who, in Baker's words, saw it "as a great time management tool."

Such improvements notwithstanding, dorms were still dorms—and at UMW, unfortunately, some had begun to show signs of decrepitude. In 2006, while the UMW Apartments did have air-conditioning, only four of the sixteen on-campus dormitories were air-conditioned (Alvey, Arrington, Willard, and South). A tour of the dorms convinced President Frawley that something needed to be done, and soon. Willard was the first to receive attention, and in the summer of 2006 it underwent a modest ($140,000) renovation. That fall, the Board of Visitors allocated an additional $500,000 for emergency dorm improvements, but the long-term situation obviously demanded a more comprehensive approach. Frawley clearly understood the extent and immediacy of the problem, declaring in his first state of the University address that UMW needed "new student residences that are multifunctional with computer labs, workout rooms, wireless coffee houses, classrooms, and faculty apartments." Accordingly, the University in early 2007 requested $35 million from the General Assembly for the construction of two dorms, one to be located near Arrington Hall and the other on the site of the existing basketball court near Marshall.

The improvement of student housing was just one aspect of Frawley's ambitious program. From the beginning, he had thrown himself into the work of the University, engaging in almost every conceivable facet of its operation. "He's the kind of guy who doesn't want to kill two birds with one stone," wrote a *Free Lance–Star* reporter. "He aims at four or five with every throw."

His approach involved not only devising a range of initiatives within the institution but also personally taking his message to constituent groups both near and far. He was dedicated to improving relationships between the University and the community, and no local group, it seemed, was too insignificant to warrant a speech passionately extolling the virtues of UMW and declaring the determination to be a good and productive neighbor.

Certainly no one could fault his enthusiasm and energy. An early riser, he liked to jog several miles five mornings a week and still be at work before 5:00 a.m. Staff members became accustomed to receiving e-mails sent in the wee hours and on weekends. "And I have answered . . . students' e-mails at 5:01 a.m.," he said, adding that their messages were "evidently sent just seconds before they went to bed."

Epitomizing his frenzied schedule was his response to the March 2007 appearance of the women's basketball team in the national Final Four tournament held in Springfield, Massachusetts. Determined to be there to cheer the Eagles on, he took a plane that, owing to a heavy snowstorm, was so delayed that he did not arrive at the game until halftime. Afterward, having consoled the team following its disappointing defeat, he attempted to catch a return flight to reach Fredericksburg in time for another commitment. Finding the airports closed, he rented a car and drove back that night despite the dangerous weather conditions.

It was, in all, a pace whose extent and intensity made that of earlier president Prince Woodard, a notorious workaholic, look indolent by comparison. Frawley claimed on occasion that patience was important in his job, but in practice it was not often evident. "There's so much to do," he explained, "I feel like I am wasting opportunities every second."

That attitude was reflected in the scope and the diversity of the initiatives he developed within his first eight months in office. In one rather controversial move, designed to alleviate overcrowded office spaces, the University in early 2007 purchased two private homes at the corner of William Street and College Avenue. As reported in a *Bullet* story titled "UMW Buys Up the Block," the acquisitions raised some eyebrows because the purchase prices of the dwellings—often accurately termed mansions—were so high: $2.1 million for the 8,300-square-foot structure fronting William Street (which had never been sold in the almost three years since its construction), and $1 million for the 5,000-square-foot home on College Avenue. Such was the high cost of new construction, however, that University officials defended the purchases as an economically sound method of acquiring additional office space.

Another innovative idea concerning facilities was a plan for the University to establish a commercial presence in downtown Fredericksburg. The basic goals of the concept were to give UMW a higher profile with visitors to the area and simultaneously to increase students' interaction with the local community. Toward those ends, initial planning for the enterprise called for a small store (roughly 2,500 square feet or less) that would include a retail shop to sell University-related merchandise, a place to distribute tickets to University events, a café with wireless Internet access where students could gather, and a venue for exhibitions, lectures, and other events of interest to students. The idea was that the facility, to be located in the former Spanky's building on Caroline Street, would be open until at least 10:00 p.m. nightly, the better to attract students downtown.[4]

While the UMW store was being considered, another facility of a very different nature became a reality: a second building on the campus of the College of Graduate and Professional Studies. A formal ribbon-cutting ceremony took place at the Stafford County site on February 16, 2007, featuring speeches by UMW Rector William Poole, President Frawley, and Vice President for Graduate and Professional Studies Meta Braymer, as well as local political leaders. The 42,600-square-foot building boasted thirty-two offices, twelve classrooms, and a 2,700-square-foot multi-purpose room called University Hall. The additional space allowed for the introduction of new courses and for the reintroduction of some that had been discontinued owing to space limitations, as the College of Graduate and Professional Studies continued its rapid increase in size and in educational services to the area. Having reached a head-count enrollment of almost 1,000 by spring 2007, it was well on the way to a projected 1,800 students by the year 2011.

The increased prominence of CGPS was at the heart of one of President Frawley's most significant goals—the greater integration of the two campuses to create what he liked to call "one university." Though the concept seemed reasonable—indeed, necessary—to some, others resisted the idea on either philosophical or practical grounds. Among the latter were those who pointed out that in the original conception of the Stafford campus, it was specifically designed to be different in purpose and apart in location from the existing Fredericksburg campus. In fact, one of the Anderson administration's "selling points" in securing support for the project was that it was necessary to build the Stafford facility to provide needed postgraduate academic services to the area without impinging on the undergraduate program on the Fredericksburg campus.

The success of CGPS, however, forced a reconsideration of that original conception. The popularity of its programs and the consequent rise in enrollment meant that, from a fiscal standpoint, CGPS was contributing disproportionately to the school's coffers, and its administration not unreasonably pushed for a greater allocation of the University's resources to address its physical and staffing needs.

It was in that light that Frawley emphasized the desirability of unification, despite the physical separation that created practical problems. In one tangible effort toward unification, he earmarked $500,000 to fund six faculty positions with the understanding that they be shared between the two campuses. The plan arose from proposals submitted to Frawley from departments on both campuses—a procedure that the president applauded as "an indication of how well faculty and staff can work together toward a common agenda."

The truth was, however, that the situation was not altogether harmonious. While animosity was not usually overt, a sizable portion of the faculty on the "old campus" looked with some condescension on the upstart operation; at the same time, some faculty at CGPS felt, quite on the contrary, that the graduate program was the more prestigious. Clearly, as the University approached its second century, the resolution of the two-college issue loomed as a major challenge.

Given Frawley's background, it was not surprising that one of his main interests was the academic program. Early on, he called on each department to develop a strategic plan outlining its goals and objectives. Those documents then became part of a procedure (new to UMW) not only to determine allocation of new faculty positions but also to take the overall staffing needs of the University into account in determining whether vacant positions within a given department should be filled or moved elsewhere.

Another initiative was the creation of the General Education Review Committee charged with undertaking a wholesale reevaluation of the academic area. The committee consisted of one representative from each academic department, the bachelor of liberal studies program, and the bachelor of professional studies program, together with Interim Vice President for Academic Affairs Rosemary Barra and Associate Vice President for Academic Affairs John Morello. Urging the committee to explore a full range of options, President Frawley noted that "activities such as these are important for UMW's future so that we have a curriculum that not only is up to date with that of our competitors, but also works in concert with other aspects of the UMW experience."

The charge was so broad, and the considerations so complex, that it appeared unlikely that any curricular revisions would be implemented anytime soon. "If all the stars aligned," predicted Morello, "the soonest anything could happen is the 2008–2009 school year, but . . . an awful lot of magical convergences would have to happen before then."

Another of Frawley's campus concerns was enrollment. One early move in that regard was the signing of an agreement with the Virginia Community College System to create a guaranteed transfer option to qualified graduates of all twenty-three of the state's community colleges. But his greater concern involved the lack of student diversity. Though the school had improved from its earlier *Princeton Review* ranking as the most homogeneous campus in the United States, the change was slight: by 2006, it was still ranked sixth. The twenty-seven blacks in that year's entering class constituted only 3 percent of the 935 incoming freshmen.

Like Anderson before him, Frawley urged greater efforts toward minority recruitment. Though he noted that "UMW is diverse as it is, and we must celebrate and promote what we have already accomplished," he emphasized the "need to work on such things as international and domestic exchanges and TRIO programs to ensure that our student body, faculty, and staff reflect the present and future demographics of the region, state, country, and world."[5]

Looking beyond the campus, Frawley also moved to extend the scope of the University's academic reach. In October 2006 the University signed an agreement with the Naval Postgraduate School (NPS) in Monterey, California, to work cooperatively on teaching, service, and scholarly activities. The plan, which involved cross-listing some courses between the institutions, had particular appeal to the NPS because of UMW's proximity to military installations at Quantico, Dahlgren, and Fort A. P. Hill.

An even more ambitious project was initiated in March 2007 with a $2 million state appropriation to the University for the purchase of land and the design of a graduate school to be located near the Dahlgren naval facility. The plan called for UMW to build and operate the school, though it would also draw faculty from other state institutions to teach engineering and science courses. The idea was not a new one, having been previously proposed in the late 1990s, but according to one Dahlgren official, "It didn't take off until we brought UMW in as the landlord and operator of the facility. That sold [it] to the folks in Richmond." Projections called for the 35,000- to 50,000-square-foot facility in King George County to be operational by the summer of 2010.

Several developments in early 2007 indicated that progress toward greater multiculturalism and global awareness was in the offing. Partly owing to Frawley's personal contacts, an increased number of foreign students were attracted to campus, including fourteen female Korean students who were enrolled for the 2007–8 academic year—a development announced by the *Bullet* under the headline "UMW's Got Seoul."

At the same time, the possibilities for UMW students to study abroad were significantly enhanced by a $150,000 grant from the Institute for Study Abroad Foundation to create cultural envoy scholarships. That amount, spread over three years, was to be available to students on a competitive basis to underwrite enrollment in various study-abroad programs. It constituted an important expansion of the University's support for overseas study already established by the Alumni Association through its Simpson and Alden International Scholarships.

The University had never witnessed such a concentrated flurry of activity on so many fronts in so short a time. The new president seemed to be everywhere at once, doing everything for everybody. In town, whether speaking to Rotarians, Lions, or neighborhood civic associations, he mightily impressed all with his braininess, and even more, with the earnestness of his stated desire to improve the University's relationship with its neighbors.

His promotional efforts went far beyond Fredericksburg, extending from coast to coast. Traveling from Boston to Key Largo and from Virginia Beach to San Diego, Los Angeles, and San Francisco, he held "town meetings" with alumni in over twenty cities. In addition to those group meetings, he met individually with nearly one hundred key donor prospects within six months. So impressed with Frawley's fund-raising efforts were the members of the Board of Visitors that they took the unprecedented step of committing to a $250,000 challenge grant to support various presidential initiatives.

It was not just donors that he impressed. Within the UMW family itself, the president's frequent appearances along Campus Walk and at all manner of events won him the praise of students. In conversations with them, he evinced genuine interest in their work and in their plans for the future.

The faculty, even more noticeably than the students, took to the new president, regarding him (rightly) as one of their own, a kindred academic spirit. He not only (in the idiom of the day) talked the talk—his constant emphasis on reducing faculty teaching loads was a popular theme—but also walked the walk. During his second semester on the job, he insisted on teaching a course (offered, naturally, at 8:00 a.m.). A freshman seminar, it was titled "Minds, Brains, and Machines." According to the syllabus, the course was designed to "investigate core issues in the computational theory of mind by looking at converging methods and explanations from linguistics, computer science, cognitive psychology, neuroscience, and philosophy of mind . . . [to] come to grips with the leading theories behind advances in such things as language learning, knowledge disorders, biological bases of minds, and the development of intelligent machines."

The whole University community had the opportunity to observe Frawley's pedagogical mind and method at work when he delivered a public lecture in November 2006 as part of the ELS Department's linguistics speakers series. Approximately two hundred people, mostly faculty and students, turned out to hear Frawley's lecture, titled "What Are Dictionaries and Why Are They Important?" The subject, for most people, was one that had considerable soporific potential, but Frawley's handling of it proved a tour de force. Few indeed could have made a lexicographical discourse entertaining, but the erudite president, deftly spicing his PowerPoint presentation with characteristic dry humor, managed to pull it off masterfully, reinforcing the image of an administrator who was, at heart, a true scholar.

Not that everything was altogether hunky-dory. In the community, some feathers were ruffled by the University's refusal to permit Dodd Auditorium to be used for the 2006 performance of the annual holiday ballet, *The Nutcracker*, as had been done for several previous years.[6] Others claimed to be offended by the trailers that were placed along College Avenue for the temporary relocation of offices during the renovation of Lee Hall.

Frawley's most detrimental decision, in the eyes of students (and some faculty as well), was his choice of the 2007 commencement speaker: the controversial Republican politician and former Speaker of the House of Representatives Newt Gingrich. In an article headlined "Newt to Speak, Students Freak," the *Bullet* described several student complaints: that Gingrich, as an outspoken conservative, would be politically polarizing; that his selection was based mainly on Frawley's desire to generate publicity for the University; and worst of all, that students had not been permitted any input into the decision.

Faculty members were of mixed opinions. Some, like psychology professor Denis Nissim-Sabat, deplored the choice, asserting that he was "extremely disappointed" with the selection of the "extremely conservative" Gingrich; others, like political science professor Rosalyn Cooperman, expressed approval, anticipating, she said, "a dynamic and relevant speech." Her departmental colleague Stephen Farnsworth took the middle ground. "Think what you will about Gingrich," he said, "but know this: he will be one of the most lively speakers ever to appear on Ball Circle."

Frawley defended his choice, explaining that he had "sought a speaker who is nationally visible and who is at the forefront of students' lives. As an accomplished policy maker and potential presidential candidate, Speaker Gingrich is an excellent choice to have at UMW." Unconvinced, some students created anti-Gingrich Facebook groups, one of which pictured him with fangs and trickles of blood at the corners of his mouth. Others went so far as to threaten demonstrations at commencement, such as boycotting it altogether or wearing earmuffs during it. But on the whole, more moderate attitudes seemed to prevail. "I am sorry that some seniors are upset about Gingrich," commented one member of the senior class, "but I hope that they won't be so selfish as to embarrass the rest of their class in front of hundreds of our friends and families. That would be more disgraceful than any speaker."

Some University personnel, aside from being opposed to the selection of Gingrich, were perturbed by other issues. For example, in some quarters there was skepticism concerning certain Frawley decisions, such as spending $2 million for the purchase of a house. More broadly, an undercurrent of concern was beginning to develop regarding the president's hard-edged management style.

That style, in fact, proved too much for one key longtime administrator, Vice President for University Relations, Communications, and Legislative Affairs Ron Singleton, who resigned in March 2007 after twenty years at Mary Washington, during which he had served in six different capacities. Mild-mannered and soft-spoken, Singleton (a journalist by training) reminded some of the fictional newspaperman Clark Kent. But Singleton was not Superman, although he was extremely hardworking: an ever-obliging, able, and dedicated servant of Mary Washington, whose calming presence was instrumental in carrying the institution through some of its most troubled days when Bill Anderson was incapacitated.

Though neither Singleton nor Frawley publicly expressed any hint of hostility toward each other—quite the contrary, in fact, as Frawley spoke effusively about Singleton's work upon his retirement—there was little doubt that personality differences and clashing personal styles precipitated the vice president's departure. Ironically, as it turned out, Singleton possessed just the qualities that the institution would soon need as never before.

But despite such glitches, the response to Frawley through his first nine months as president was generally favorable among most constituencies. The belief was widespread that in him, the University had found the ideal person to lead it into its second century. Longtime observers of the institution perceived how remarkably he represented a blend of the best qualities of his immediate presidential predecessors: Simpson's intellect, Woodard's drive, and Anderson's vision.

What no one could have known was that, as it turned out, he also shared the tragic potential of Morgan Combs.

"April is the cruellest month." So wrote T. S. Eliot in the first line of *The Waste Land*. If April 2007 at the University of Mary Washington was not the cruelest, it was one of the saddest months ever—and surely the most bizarre—in the institution's history.

First there was the weather. On the day before Easter, a substantial snowfall covered the campus, blanketing dogwood blossoms and freshly unfolding greenery with a crystalline canopy of white. The visual juxtaposition was exquisite and at the same time startling. Yet that meteorological phenomenon proved but a prelude to even more extraordinary events soon to follow.

Just a few days later, a *Bullet* headline announced jaw-dropping news: "Frawley Arrested." More shocking still was the charge: DUI—and not on one but two counts, in two different jurisdictions, all within little more than twenty-four hours. The news was met with utter disbelief on a campus where the new president was uniformly believed to be completely abstemious, a teetotaler whom few had ever seen so much as holding a glass of wine, let alone drinking from it.

The unlikely saga began around noon on Tuesday, April 10, when the car Frawley was driving (owned by the UMW Foundation) ran off a Fairfax County road and overturned, totaling the vehicle. Frawley was taken by rescue squad to the Inova Fairfax Hospital. Officers at the scene reportedly had probable cause (though they did not specify it) to charge him with drunken driving, but the warrant was not issued until several days later.

Having spent the night in the hospital, Frawley left early the next morning against medical advice, went to his Chevy Chase, Maryland, home, got into a family car, and drove himself back to Fredericksburg. Staffers, having learned of his accident the previous day, were amazed to see him in the office Wednesday morning. Sensing he was not himself and noticing a cut on his forehead, they urged him to return to Brompton to recuperate, and he left around midmorning, presumably to do just that.

Several hours later, a motorist crossing the Chatham Bridge placed a 911 call to police reporting that she had observed a person driving erratically in a car that was missing its right front tire and traveling on its rim. It was Frawley, whom city police quickly found and attempted to pull over. He continued through town, however, not stopping until he reached the driveway of Brompton. At that point, police took him into custody and transported him to the local magistrate's office, where he was charged with the misdemeanor offenses of DUI and refusing to take a Breathalyzer test. Released on his personal recognizance, he was then taken to Mary Washington Hospital, where he was admitted for treatment of what was described as a superficial head injury.

In a terse message to the University community, Board of Visitors Rector J. William Poole outlined the sequence of events that had occurred. He then expressed the board's "deepest concerns and support for President Frawley and his family at this very difficult time," acknowledged Frawley's "many accomplishments during his tenure at the university," and urged that "the students, faculty, staff, and friends in the community join us in our thoughts and prayers for Dr. Frawley's complete recovery and for his wife and family."

Meeting in an emergency special session, the board quickly moved to place Frawley on indefinite paid leave. The rector announced that all planned events and activities at the University would continue as scheduled under the direction of Executive Vice President Richard Hurley, whom the board authorized to act as president during Frawley's absence.

THE FREE LANCE–STAR

Free Lance–Star cartoon following President Frawley's DUI arrest in April 2007

Though at first the universal reaction throughout the campus community was one of stunned disbelief—more than a few people wondered openly if the horrible scenario was really a dream—a variety of responses eventually emerged. Newspapers in Fredericksburg and Richmond took harsh editorial positions. In a piece titled "Frawley's Nightmare," the *Free Lance–Star* recalled the president's glorious recent inauguration, then continued, "six months later, Mr. Frawley has fallen off the stage in incredible fashion." Conceding that his guilt had not been established, it nonetheless suggested that his job was in jeopardy, since "presidents operate in the narrow halls of ideal-draped tradition where probity is all, and exemplary is conduct's crucial modifier." Aside from Frawley's plight, the paper issued a more general warning: "Take from this, too, the lesson that even the most respected among us are mortal creatures, who, however firm their tread, are all one banana peel away from a ruinous fall."

A regular *Richmond Times-Dispatch* columnist, Michael Paul Williams, was even more caustic in appraising the situation. Scarcely acknowledging the possibility of Frawley's innocence and focusing instead on the problem of college students' drinking, Williams delivered a scathing broadside. "A college president," he declared,

> by virtue of his occupation and the havoc that alcohol reeks on college campuses, ranks among bus drivers and airline pilots as the last people who should be caught with a snout full. . . . We don't need a college president acting out like "Bluto" Blutarsky from "Animal House." . . .

> The university needs to be careful how it handles this situation, lest the stench of hypocrisy hang over the Fredericksburg campus like stale beer. Frawley, frankly, now has a credibility problem. On the job since only July, he's been irreparably damaged by this incident. For too long, universities have winked at the culture of alcohol abuse prevalent on campuses. It hasn't been cute for a long time. It's bad enough when police suspecting a beer-soaked toga party show up at Delta House to bust Bluto. But when they land in the driveway of the college president's house, it's time for a new occupant.

On campus the *Bullet*'s editorial position was less acidic, but still pointed. "By the look of away messages and recent outcroppings of Facebook groups," it said, "it would seem that the student body is either taking this as a humorous addition to daily gossip or as a serious tarnish on the university's reputation. The appropriate reaction is the latter. Not only [is] the recent arrest of our brand-spanking-new president a blemish on the reputation of the school, but it is also fodder for critics of Frawley and of UMW in general. . . . Lesson to be learned: do not operate heavy machinery under any influence, even if you are a president."

Within hours after the news became known, a dozen or so Facebook groups had appeared on campus with titles such as "President Frawley, We Barely Knew Ye" and "My School's President Got a DUI." Facetious messages spread, announcing, "Party at Brompton tonight." And it was not long before T-shirts appeared sporting a three-wheeled jalopy above the slogan "Free Frawley."

The response of faculty members was, as would be expected, far less frivolous. They uniformly expressed sympathy for the president personally and for his family. In a letter to the Board of Visitors on April 16 (which was also quoted in the *Free Lance–Star*), the president of the faculty senate, biology professor Steve Fuller, along with president-elect Mary Rigsby—writing, they said, "on behalf of the faculty"—praised Frawley for motivating the faculty to "think creatively and productively," adding, "If circumstances allow we will welcome him back to see [his] various initiatives to completion." Fuller admitted that he did not consult systematically with his colleagues about the message but assumed that most would support it. In fact, that assumption was wrong, as soon became apparent.

There was, moreover, no evidence of support from Frawley's administrative colleagues. None of the senior vice presidents (members of the Core Planning Group) spoke out in his defense.

Frawley himself remained silent. For several days there was little news from or about him, beyond his wife's statement to the *Richmond Times-Dispatch*. "It's been very difficult," she said. "We are very concerned about him."

It was over a week after the initial incident that the president made his first public comment on the affair, brief and nonspecific though it was. The events were, he said, "highly unusual and totally out of character for me," and went on to explain that, following his arrest, he had spent more than five days in the hospital for "examination of and treatment of possible injuries and for correction of a heretofore undetected and potentially very serious heart disorder." Apologizing for "any difficulties caused for the institution, the Board of Visitors, or for the people and friends of UMW," he asked for understanding as he continued to "concentrate on my doctors' treatment recommendations."

The message did little to assuage the concerns of some faculty members who felt that it did not sufficiently address the central questions relating to the incidents themselves. Among the skeptics was history professor Arthur Tracy, who wrote to the *Free Lance–Star* to assert that Frawley's unexplained actions "have damaged his ability to lead the university" and went on to suggest several specific issues: "What will be the image of UMW for prospective students? What about community attitudes? Will private benefactors be affected by these events? Internally, what effect would the possible decline of respect have upon morale within staff and administration? Worse, what message do we send our students who are constantly discouraged from the use of alcohol and who are bound by the Honor System?"

Those were just the kinds of questions that the Board of Visitors, in determining the president's future employment, had to address. As it came increasingly to the conclusion that Frawley's leadership capacity was irreparably damaged, the board had three basic alternatives: he could be allowed to resign, he could be fired "without cause," or he could be fired "for cause." In the first two scenarios, the University would likely be in the position of awarding some degree of financial compensation for the unfinished portion of Frawley's $305,000-per-year contract; if fired "for cause," a course that contractually did not require he be convicted of any crime, salary payments would cease at that point.

It was an agonizing decision for the board, which met repeatedly in tense sessions to consider the volatile issue. "The tragedy of all this," commented Rector Poole, "is he's such a brilliant man and so capable." Yet Poole also admitted that Frawley's actions "reflected badly on the University," which was one of the conditions that, under Frawley's contract, constituted justifiable cause for dismissal.

On April 30, the board announced its unanimous decision: Frawley was fired "for cause."

Although the possibility of his termination had been discussed since the report of the initial incident, the board's action was still stunning. It was, indeed, virtually unprecedented, according to one eminently knowledgeable observer, Gordon Davies, who had earlier headed SCHEV for almost twenty years before retiring in 1993. "Goodness," he said, "I just can't think of anything . . . like this. I can't think of one."

Harsh though it seemed, the decision generally elicited editorial approval. The *Free Lance–Star*, while pointing out that Frawley "has much to offer the world," concluded that "the president of a university must be, first and foremost, a role model for students and faculty, a leader whose integrity and conduct are unimpeachable. . . . While charity requires forgiveness of human errancy, Mr. Frawley's actions, it appears, went beyond that." The *Richmond Times-Dispatch* agreed, asserting that Frawley's DUI charge was "particularly unpresidential." "The decision to fire Frawley serves the school's best interests," it said, because "a president has an obligation not only to set high standards but to meet them."

Though certainly no one cheered the circumstances of Frawley's demise, there were those who did not lament his leaving. Some found his style autocratic in operation, despite his verbal emphasis on collegiality; to them, his dictum that "a vision of one is not a vision" foundered in an environment where some appeared to be "more equal than others." They even perceived a faint undercurrent of disdain for the institution itself and its environs, his public expressions of admiration notwithstanding. As some rather bluntly suggested, it appeared that his long career in the more rarefied cultural climate of the Washington, D.C., area caused him, at least subconsciously, to regard Fredericksburg as "Mayberry."

On a personal level there were those who interpreted his wry humor as sarcasm, his confidence as arrogance, his "challenges" as threats. Consequently, respect for his mind did not always translate into affection for the man. For persons of that sort, his ouster was accompanied, in truth, by a degree of schadenfreude.

Through it all, Frawley retained pockets of strong support, especially among some faculty members who felt that intellect trumped all, and that in any case, the presumption of innocence should have prevailed until such time as he might be convicted of pending charges. On the other hand, there were those who believed that his unfitness to lead the institution must be decided not in a court of law but in a more important venue where quite different evidentiary rules applied: namely, the court of public opinion, where perceptions were not only admissible but often determinant. In that arena, many believed that, absent exculpatory explanation from Frawley, the verdict had already been rendered: guilty.

In that light, the preponderance of faculty opinion seemed to support, albeit with sadness, the board's decision. Even senate president Steve Fuller, who had earlier proffered support, appeared to back away from his earlier position. Noting that Frawley had never explicitly denied the charges against himself, Fuller said, "I don't think you could have a college president doing the things he has done and then maintain any sense of decorum, any kind of relationship with alumni." In a few words, Fuller went on to characterize what appeared to be the consensus view of the faculty. "I feel bad for the guy," he said, "but what could the board do?"

Negative views, suppressed for the most part while Frawley was in office, surfaced after his firing. The physical education faculty, for example, told of a meeting at which a grim-visaged president expressed the view, as reported by several who were present, that UMW had been "sitting on its butt for the last twenty years." The coaches, having built an exceptionally successful, much-admired program over that time, were unaware that their derrières had been thus positioned and therefore resented both his sentiments and their inelegant expression.

That episode furnished one indication of the appropriateness of the adjective most often applied to Frawley by his detractors: arrogant. Whether that was an accurate description or not, it could certainly be said that he was extremely self-confident.

In the midst of the Frawley affair, the campus was shaken by a dramatic event of a different nature when news arrived that a mass shooting had occurred at Virginia Tech, in which five faculty members and twenty-seven students were killed, including the gunman, Seung-Hui Cho, who himself committed suicide. In fact, the tragedy at Blacksburg had a far more profound impact on UMW students than the Frawley fiasco, not only because it involved loss of life but because the victims were their contemporaries, in some cases friends and former high school classmates.

In a macabre irony, the *Bullet* earlier that year, in a feature called "Top Five Reasons for Class Cancellation," listed "murderer loose on campus" as reason number two. "A mass murderer loose on campus can really make getting to class a pretty dangerous task," it said. "Professors and students alike don't want to risk going outside while a criminal is loose. Everyone will want to stay in either their houses or dorms until the murderer is apprehended."

Drawn together in sympathy for their peers, UMW students organized a number of memorial tributes to the victims of what was called by some "the Columbine of college," a reference to the tragic shooting incident in 1999 at a Colorado high school. One was an impromptu candlelight vigil in Palmieri Plaza on the night of the shootings. With each student emptying a scoop of Gatorade into the fountain, the crowd of approximately two hundred sang "Lean On Me" as the water slowly turned Hokie orange. Explained the organizer, junior Jessica Thiel, "It's a Virginia school. I had to do something."

In the following days, many students wore orange-and-maroon clothing or ribbons of that color to show solidarity. The largest demonstration was on Thursday night, when another crowd of several hundred assembled in Ball Circle—the largest such gathering since the 9/11 memorial in 2001. With the voices of Una Voce filling the somber air, the crowd ringed the lawn and candles were lit. After a moment of silence and the singing of "Amazing Grace," the crowd broke into smaller groups to embrace and to pray. After an hour or so, the candles were extinguished, and the students soberly went on their ways. The next day many returned as part of a statewide day of mourning to participate in a human chain that stretched from George Washington Hall far down Campus Walk.

In time, the horror receded, but the shootings did have a lasting impact at UMW in terms of security precautions. For some time the University had been considering installation of an emergency siren system on campus but had not done so. With safety concerns heightened as a result of the Virginia Tech massacre, the alarm was made operational and a text-messaging system was also designed to be implemented by the fall.

All such precautions were fine by librarian Jack Bales, whose son was a resident in the Virginia Tech dormitory where the shootings began. (He was unharmed.) "We all hear that we should not take our good fortune for granted," said Bales, "but until something like this happens, we all probably do."

As for the Frawley situation, it might reasonably have been assumed that once the termination decision had been announced, the matter would soon enough cease to be newsworthy, at least until Frawley's court hearings in Fairfax and Fredericksburg—both scheduled for mid-July—took place. But there was more strange news to come.

In mid-May reports were published in the Fredericksburg and Richmond papers claiming that twenty years earlier, while still living in Delaware, Frawley had been arrested and accused of confronting a man at knifepoint, though the charges, according to Maria Frawley, were "summarily dropped, and with good reason." That reason, as Frawley himself explained in a letter to the *Free Lance–Star*, was that he was defending his wife against the advances of a stalker who had been repeatedly intimidating her over an extended period in several localities going back to her college days.

Incensed by the paper's reporting of that long-ago episode, Frawley complained that the newspaper had not even bothered to ask about the story—an allegation the paper denied—and concluded with an unabashed defense of his earlier actions. "While I have apologized to the UMW community before, I make no apology for having to intervene personally in this repeated stalking incident of decades past."

The exchange led the *Free Lance–Star* to assail Frawley even further. In a signed editorial, Paul Akers described the former president's flame-out as so spectacular that it made him seem "a sort of human Hindenburg." From there, Akers proceeded to chastise Frawley for what he regarded as the deceitful manner of his stated defense:

> Playing the Lemony Snicket card,[7] he calls the Fairfax County and Fredericksburg pinches "unfortunate events," the Delaware fracas an "unfortunate episode." This is not only mincing tea-party talk; it is the sly language of victimhood, intended, I guess, to change the speaker from actor in the drama to mere prop—as though driving erratically around town on three tires is just bad luck, like being hit by lightning. . . . Frawley also seems to be relying on technicians—the doctors who are telling him to focus on tending his heart condition, the attorneys who are advising him to keep mum—to manage what character

should be governing. This may be prudent if self-service is Priority One. Making a clean breast of things would, however, be noble. Even if that made his lawyers choke.

Frawley, with court cases looming and his career in disarray, was hardly in a position to respond publicly.

In any event, the presidency of William Frawley, which had begun with such promise and high expectations, came to an abrupt and abject end. The average term of his six presidential predecessors had been sixteen years. His had lasted ten months.

During the midst of the crisis, one parent who was visiting the campus with his son, a prospective UMW student, proffered his take on the situation: "The reality is," he said, "presidents don't matter a whole hell of a lot. Presidents come and go."

That assessment was largely untrue, of course, especially with regard to long-term developments, but as far as day-to-day operations were concerned, it had some validity. A major factor in keeping the institution on course was the quality of its leaders at that time. As rector, Bill Poole was a steady and reassuring presence, unflappable, sound of judgment. The Core group, on whom greater responsibility now devolved, comprised, for the most part, veteran administrators whose expertise and accumulated experience conveyed a sense of continuity and confidence. At the head, Acting President Rick Hurley made a favorable impression, displaying a poised but unpretentious manner that offered a noticeable contrast to the aloof aura of Bill Frawley.

Richard V. Hurley

The entire administrative leadership, from the rector on down, emphasized that pursuit of Frawley's initiatives would continue. Thus reassured, the campus rather quickly settled down, and life at UMW went on, with less disruption of routine than might have been expected under the circumstances.

The academic calendar in late April was enlivened by an innovation called Student Research and Creativity Day. Organized by Associate Vice President for Academic Affairs John

Morello, it featured oral presentations, performances, posters, and displays by over one hundred students from eighteen different disciplines. The "Great Lives" series, enjoying its most successful season, ended with exceptional lectures by author Sally Bedell Smith on Princess Diana and by sportswriter William Nack on Triple Crown winner Secretariat—the first talk in the series dealing with a nonhuman "great life."

As for the students, the semester concluded with the customary vernal disportments—throwing Frisbees, sunbathing, and lounging on the lawns. Spring Formal had a new twist, as the location of the event was kept secret until the buses bearing the partiers arrived at Alexandria's Torpedo Factory. Devil-Goat Day seemed to be more lively than it had been in a long time, indicating that the University's oldest tradition was still alive and kicking (and running and jumping and throwing and climbing and shouting) as the centennial year approached.

For seniors especially, the weeks went quickly, a blur of activity mixing the academic (term papers, oral reports, research projects) with the social, which included numerous year-end picnics and banquets. Then came final exams, and suddenly it was all over—permanently so, for graduating seniors who then embarked on "Dead Week," a time of elation (and sometimes pure relief) commingled with sentimentality.

The campus, virtually vacant during the first days of Dead Week, sprang back to life on Thursday as seniors returned from whatever revelries they had experienced. That night, Graduation Ball took place for the first time in the elegant ballroom of the Jepson Alumni Executive Center. It was one of the most spirited ever, partly because it marked the first time in many years that alcohol (wine, in this case) had been served at a student event.

The next day, as usual, was marked in the afternoon by rehearsal for Saturday's commencement and, that evening, by convocation. But there was also in between the two a unique special event: the ribbon cutting for the Centennial Campanile, work on which had been completed only days before.

A magnificent structure it was: a tiered brick tower with white trim and graceful arches, it stretched eighty-eight feet into the air, making it by far the tallest structure on campus (save the venerable 168-foot "MWC" smokestack off Route 1).[8] The campanile was topped by a cupola housing specially tuned bronze bells cast in France at the renowned bell foundry of Paccard-Fonderie de Cloches. At its base were a small garden and a fountain dedicated to the class of 1959, Carmen Chappell's class. Despite its newness and its great height, the campanile was so perfectly integrated into its surroundings that it seemed that (as so many observers commented) "it had always been there."

In the warmth of the late afternoon, an audience of faculty, staff, and local guests assembled along Campus Walk in the shade of the great oak tree in front of GW to join the Chappell family in the dedication of the monument to their loved one. The ceremony was, appropriately, a combination of joy and solemnity. It began with the announcement by Acting President Hurley that a new Mary Washington tradition was about to begin. The next day, he said, the seniors would process through the arches of the campanile, and starting with the entering class in August, freshmen would begin their UMW careers by marching to convocation through those same portals.

Hurley was followed by Rector Poole, who recognized a number of special guests. The most notable of them (and the one most warmly acknowledged by the crowd) was former president Bill Anderson, who had returned from Hilton Head to campus for the first time to be with his friend John Chappell for the historic occasion.

Chappell's own eloquent remarks, movingly delivered, struck an emotional chord with the audience. Standing in the shadow of the gracefully towering structure, he said:

> I see its radiance, the gleaming whiteness capped by the colorful cupola, a vision which might suggest the quest for truth, which is central to learning. We see the tower in extension, as if reaching for the sky, as if striving for knowledge that is shared here in classrooms throughout the University. We see its grace, its spirit, its positiveness, and its charm as the tower provides new elegance on campus. And we know for sure that the campanile will stand for fun, as a place to meet up before heading elsewhere or a place to linger for a while, a meeting place for friends. . . . And what of the bells? . . . Everyday . . . the peal of the bells will remind us that we are a community, working together to make our mission successful.

With that came the first chiming of the bells, and the centennial celebration officially began. It seemed certain that from that very moment onward, the Carmen Culpeper Chappell Centennial Campanile would stand as one of the University's most visible and enduring symbols.

Following the ceremony, there was a reception on the roof of GW with its panoramic view of the Fredericksburg area. Though in an earlier time that venue had frequently been used for such events, it marked the first time in the memory of most in attendance that it had been thus used.

The next day dawned gloriously on the resplendent campus. Early in the morning, the graduating class began to assemble in Jefferson Square for commencement exercises. As he had done for many years, the dapper dean of students, Cedric Rucker, played the mother hen, inspecting the graduates' attire, making last-minute adjustments, and offering friendly final words of congratulations. And then, to the familiar strains of "Pomp and Circumstance," off they marched, robed and tasseled, making their way through the arches of the campanile down Campus Walk to Ball Circle, there to spend their last few hours on the grounds that they had come to cherish.

With Richard Hurley presiding, the program began with the national anthem led by a crystalline-voiced senior, Marta Alley—an alumna of Milton Kline's paint crew—followed by Rector Poole's salutation to the graduates. "Your class is a special one," he told them, "bonded by recent events: unsettling developments on our own campus, and tragedy of massive proportions at Virginia Tech. On our special day of joyful celebration at Mary Washington, our thoughts turn to our brothers and sisters in Blacksburg, where graduates must approach their commencement with hearts heavily burdened. . . . [But] both Virginia Tech and Mary Washington, it is certain, will not only survive, but surmount, these current challenges, and will go on to even greater levels of success in the future." He then issued a challenge to the class, urging them "above all, never to be such poor stewards of your talents that the limits of your potential go untested. . . . As you depart, you can take comfort in knowing that you have been prepared by this distinguished and dedicated faculty to adjust and to adapt—and to grasp with confidence all the opportunities that Providence may bestow."

So perfect was the day that even Newt Gingrich's speech was generally adjudged to have been quite acceptable. Typically long on platitudes, perhaps, but commendably short on politics, he offered solid advice to the graduates without alienating those who had feared partisan bombast. "We are the land of the free and the home of the brave," he told them. "I would suggest that part of the lesson you should take from the University of Mary Washington is that her son fully understood that if we are to be free, we have to be brave."

The awarding of a record number of degrees (1,149) was handled with aplomb by Vice Presidents Barra, for the Fredericksburg campus (899), and Braymer, for the graduate and professional college (250). Then, following felicitations from Alumni Association President Monecia Helton Taylor '81, came the singing of the alma mater:

All hail, dear Alma Mater,
We sing our praise to you.
High on Marye's Hilltop
You stand forever true;
Born in truth and honor
You ever more shall be,
The model of our future years
And all eternity.

Whene'er we have to leave you
We never will forget,
The lessons you have taught us,
And all the friends we've met;
And we your sons and daughters
Will hold your name on high,
So here's to Mary Washington;
Our love will never die.

The first time the class of 2007 had heard those words at honor convocation four years earlier, the prospect of graduation had seemed an eternity away; to many of them, the college years now seemed to have been but a moment. Realizing that phenomenon perhaps for the first time, the new graduates departed, bidding farewell to each other and to the institution that had united them.

Shortly the campus was quiet, much in contrast to the joyously vibrant sounds of celebration that had echoed just a few hours earlier. Now it was serene, the silence mitigated mainly by the scampering squirrels and the melodious songbirds who, for a while, had the grounds to themselves. A sort of melancholy settled over the campus, as it did every year, with the departure of its happy human contingent.

But there was something different in the afterglow of graduation 2007. This time, as the shadows began to fall across Ball Circle toward Campus Walk, the stillness was broken precisely at 6:00 p.m. by the chiming of the Centennial Campanile. The bells brought to mind, of course, the alumna in whose memory they were given, but their symbolism went much further than that. Few then remained on campus to hear them that day, but to the thousands who would hear them thereafter, the bells paid tuneful homage to the century-long traditions of the school perched "high on Marye's hilltop" and to the loyal sons and daughters whom it had nurtured and had transformed—and who, in their gratitude, would remain "forever true."

PERSONALITIES

President Woodard in a playful mood with canine friend in Brompton garden

Governor Charles S. Robb with President William Anderson at his inauguration in 1984

President Anderson with Dean Emeritus Edward Alvey at Brompton, 1996

Civil rights leader and MWC history professor James Farmer receives the Presidential Medal of Freedom from President Clinton at a White House ceremony in 1998.

THE WHITE HOUSE

Geography professors James Gouger, left, and Richard Palmieri at commencement, 1997

Physics professor Bulent Atalay, left, and German professor Sammy Merrill, both recipients of the Grellet C. Simpson Award, before commencement, 1998

THE FREE LANCE–STAR

Dean of Students Cedric Rucker assists student with regalia before commencement.

Benefactors Robert and Alice Jepson with President Anderson

English professor Claudia Emerson, recipient of the 2006 Pulitzer Prize for Poetry

Benefactor Arabelle Laws Arrington, with husband, Walter, in background

CAMPUS CONSTRUCTION DURING THE ANDERSON PRESIDENCY

Campus Walk

Simpson Library

Woodard Campus Center

Ridderhof Martin Gallery

Arrington (in foreground) and Alvey Residence Halls

Jepson Science Center

Jepson Alumni Executive Center

Carmen Culpeper Chappell Centennial Campanile

MEMORABLE MOMENTS

THE FREE LANCE–STAR

First Fredericksburg Forum, 1996. Left to right: Helen Thomas, David Gergen, and John Kenneth Galbraith, with moderator Judy Muller '69

Groundbreaking for Jepson Science Center. Left to right: biology professor Rosemary Barra, President Anderson, Board of Visitors Rector Kathleen Mehfoud, Robert and Alice Jepson, and Fredericksburg state senator John Chichester

THE FREE LANCE–STAR

Rain rarely forced commencement inside, but occasionally dampened the Ball Circle Ceremony, as in 1997.

President Anderson with executive-in-residence Warren Buffett

On the thirty-fifth anniversary of the chartering of Kappa of Virginia chapter of Phi Beta Kappa, gathered at the key on Campus Walk were, from left, the national executive secretary of Phi Beta Kappa, John Churchill, with chapter officers for 2006: Professors Wendy Atwell-Vasey (vice president), Angela Gosetti-Murrayjohn (president), and Robert Rycroft (secretary-treasurer).

At the unveiling of the James Farmer Memorial, April 20, 2001 were, left to right: sculptor Richard Stravitz, civil rights leader Andrew Young, Farmer's granddaughter, and his two daughters.

REZA A. MARVASHTI / THE FREE LANCE–STAR

Candlelight vigil on Ball Circle during the evening of the September 11, 2001, terrorist attacks on the United States. Part of photo collection, U. S. Library of Congress.

TERESA MANNIX

Board of Visitors Rector Mona Albertine and President William Anderson raise the new University of Mary Washington flag, July 1, 2004.

Philanthropist Doris Buffett (center) and student organizer Shin Fujiyama '07 (right of Buffett) lead a walkathon to raise funds for Fujiyama's Students Helping Honduras project.

Dedication of Centennial Campanile, May 2007. From left, Acting President Richard Hurley and Rector William Poole listen as John Chappell delivers remarks dedicating the bell tower to his late wife, Carmen Culpeper Chappell '59.

Representatives of each varsity team gather for a photograph at the Monroe Square fountain, spring 1988.

THE FREE LANCE–STAR

President Anderson consoles soccer player Becky Miller following the Eagles' 1–0 overtime loss in the Division III national semifinal at the Battleground Athletic Complex, November 1992.

Division III 1991 national championship women's tennis team with Coach Ed Hegmann

The women's 2006–7 basketball team made a first-ever appearance in the NCAA Division III Final Four.

SOCIAL EVENTS

Multicultural Fair dancers, 2004

Devil-Goat Day, 1986

Wo-Man Contest

HALLOWEENS

Izod gladiators

Kermit and Miss Piggy

PBR six-pack

Ninja Turtles

The spirit rock: a patriotic message on the 2007 anniversary of 9/11

JENNIFER N. WILKOSKI '06

Carl's: Fredericks-burg's sweet-tooth mecca

The Route 1 smoke-stack: for many years a campus landmark

The amphitheater: still a tranquil refuge into Mary Washington's second century

–EPILOGUE–
THE CENTENNIAL YEAR, 2007–2008

THE SUMMER OF 2007 at the University of Mary Washington was dominated by final preparations for the celebratory events to be held in the centennial year just ahead. At the same time, the University community, interested in news of presidencies past and future, was intrigued by the continuing saga of William Frawley's downfall and the developing search for his successor.

Frawley had generally maintained a low public profile since his ouster in late April. In June he moved out of Brompton, a residence that, in truth, he and his family had never fully occupied. He returned to the home that the Frawleys had continued to own in Chevy Chase, Maryland, where he awaited trials on DUI charges in Fredericksburg and Fairfax.

Both trials were postponed twice during the summer. In the interim, public interest was spiked by the revelation that to represent him in his Fairfax trial Frawley had engaged Peter Greenspan, the widely known attorney who had defended John Allen Muhammad, the convicted sniper whose murderous spree had terrorized the Washington, D.C., region in 2002.

Several bits of new evidence also came to light. The *Richmond Times-Dispatch* revealed that in the police report of Frawley's Fredericksburg arrest, the then-president attributed his impairment to having consumed six bottles of cough medicine that day. A few days later, the *Free Lance–Star* reported that tests had shown that when Frawley wrecked his University car in Fairfax, his blood alcohol content was 0.21, approximately two and one-half times the level (0.08) that defines drunk driving in Virginia.

When the ex-president's two trials finally took place in September, the verdicts were somewhat anticlimactic. In each case, Frawley entered an "Alford plea," a legal maneuver in which a defendant does not admit guilt but does concede that sufficient evidence exists for a judge or jury to render a guilty verdict.

The trial in Fredericksburg on September 18 resulted in a minimal fine for Frawley and a suspended driver's license for one year; it also required him to receive substance-abuse treatment. Three days later, the Fairfax court imposed similar sanctions. The judge in that case suspended the jail sentence that could have been imposed, but warned Frawley that, should he violate the terms of his probation, "I will not hesitate to put you in jail for thirty days."

The verdict disappointed those on campus and in the community who believed Frawley deserved incarceration and who felt he had received favorable treatment because of his status. Among UMW students, the trials elicited little excitement. "I don't think students were even aware that [the trials were] going on," commented Student Association President Krishna Sinha. "I mean, he doesn't work here anymore. People are done with it."

But Frawley was not done with Mary Washington. Exercising a clause in his contract that allowed him in the event of dismissal to seek mediation (at the University's expense), Frawley initiated a process of negotiation with the Board of Visitors presumably designed to secure some form of monetary settlement. Because, as a personnel matter, such discussions were closed, exact terms of his demands were not released. Rector William Poole, however, made it clear that job reinstatement was not among the options.

Frawley's mediation request was met with incredulity by many in the Mary Washington community who believed that, if anything, it was Frawley who should make restitution to the University. That was essentially the view expressed in a *Free Lance–Star* editorial titled "Mediate What?" Asserting that "like Icarus' plunge to earth when he flew too close to the sun, [Frawley's] fall from grace has not been elegant," the editorial went on to note that "besides embarrassment to the University and the false start of his aborted presidency," Frawley had caused the institution considerable expense, including the cost of the search firm that had recommended him and the one that would choose his successor, as well as salary and various benefits. "What does Mr. Frawley expect?" it asked. "What else does the school owe him?" Answering its own question, the paper concluded, "The BOV owes him nothing, and nothing more is what he should get."

Nothing, in fact, is what he got. In late October, Rector Poole announced that the mediation process was over. "After a great deal of deliberation," he said, "we were unable to reach any sort of resolution that all parties involved would deem acceptable."

With that, it might have been assumed that the Frawley affair had ended, but it had not. In early December, the former president once again burst into the community's consciousness with a prominently placed first-person piece in the *Washington Post*'s Sunday "Outlook" section. The gist of the article was that he had been treated with unwarranted harshness by a University that callously failed to acknowledge that his problem was essentially a medical one deserving of a more sympathetic institutional response—or, as the title of his article summarized it: "I Needed Help, Not Ostracism."

In the lengthy *Post* article he addressed publicly for the first time the circumstances surrounding the events that led to his firing. The underlying cause, he said, was that "for 45 years, I had self-treated a case of undiagnosed depression with compulsive work and, lately, alcohol. New heart problems and allergies added to the mix, as did the stress of separation from my family, which remained in Maryland."

Frawley then proceeded to recount in detail the two DUI episodes. The first (April 10, 2007) occurred on the way to a meeting in Maryland. "I felt as though I was going to have a nervous breakdown," he said. "To calm down I drank some wine (after taking allergy medication) before I got on the road." The result: "Confused, distracted, and on a twisting road, I went off a curve and flipped the car."

Early the following day, he returned to Fredericksburg but, he recalled, "I couldn't rest. Jittery and consumed again with the feeling that I was about to have a breakdown or a heart attack, I drove up to horse country, parked, took in the scenery and drank again. On the way home, I hit a pothole and blew a tire but continued on, sleepless and disoriented." The result: arrest in the driveway of Brompton followed by "six days in the hospital, a newly diagnosed cardiac problem—and scandal."

For his bizarre behavior, Frawley apologized—after a fashion. "My April meltdown was of my own making, he wrote, "as I've repeatedly acknowledged and publicly regretted. I've always said that I should not have been driving, and I'm thankful that I alone was hurt. I know that my actions cracked the trust that the UMW board and community had placed in me. But their hard-edged reactions also cracked my trust in them."

To many readers, the explanation was not persuasive: too little contrition, too much self-pity. In an editorial, "Stuck in Denial," the *Free Lance–Star* acknowledged his apology but added that "the dominant tone of his comments, from his first public peep after [the incidents] to his *Post* commentary, has hardly been one of humble repentance. On the contrary, Mr. Frawley has worked assiduously to medicalize what in great part was a volitional failure of self-control." It concluded with the hope that "Bill Frawley, a brilliant man who has suffered hellfire, is destined for higher things than the blamesmanship of a lesson unlearned."

The *Post* piece did little to engender sympathy for Frawley on campus; to some extent it was actually counterproductive, infuriating those who resented what they perceived as his failure to take greater responsibility for his actions. This was the view that the *Bullet* expressed rather bluntly in an editorial following the *Post*'s article. Calling it "a self-serving attempt at vindication," the paper asserted that "Frawley should realize that his overly defensive tone not only hurts his cause, but makes him appear exceedingly childish.... His point is self-absorbed and repetitive: He has a problem, none of this is his fault, and the University treated him unfairly.... He nonchalantly slips in the minor details of his breakfast of wine and allergy medication as if he was mentioning that he brushed his teeth. He has no shame.... William Frawley has said enough. He needs to break his defenses and transform his efforts into redeeming himself through recovery and accomplishment."

Just what those efforts might be remained unclear. In an interview with the *Bullet*, Frawley intimated that he was considering a civil suit against the University, but he revealed no timetable. He also confirmed that he was writing two books dealing with his academic career, including, in his words, "the rise to a presidency, the calamity and its aftermath, the lessons learned, and how you remake a life."

Remaking his own life proved to be more of a challenge for Frawley than perhaps even he realized it would be. In the *Post* article he had proclaimed that his problems were "cured or managed." Yet, in another implausible twist in his downward spiral, he was charged with a third DUI, this one in Maryland, on April 10, 2008—exactly one year to the day from his original drunken accident in northern Virginia. In the 2008 incident, police arrested him after finding him asleep in his car with the motor still running and various bottles of alcohol on the seat beside him. Although he denied having drunk any intoxicants, according to police reports he failed a field sobriety test and registered a blood alcohol level of 0.18, more than double the legal limit.

He had pulled off the road, he told police, because he had become depressed after attending an Alcoholics Anonymous meeting.[1]

Meanwhile, in the wake of Frawley's departure from Mary Washington, the University had eagerly moved on, beginning with the selection of a new president. In light of the recent turmoil, there was greater-than-normal interest in the process.

It began with an announcement by Rector Poole in mid-July that the Board had authorized a process for selecting a new president. In several ways the procedure replicated the previous search. For example, an executive search firm was hired, and an advisory committee was established. The latter, whose membership was announced in October, consisted of fifteen people, among them nine members of the Board of Visitors, with Poole as chair. Other University constituencies were represented by Martin A. Wilder Jr., vice president for enrollment and communications; "Red" Hofer, president of the Foundation Board; Barbara B. Micou '69, president of the Alumni Association; Krishna Sinha, president of the SGA; and two elected faculty members: Claudia Emerson and Brenda Vogel. Paulette Watson again served as executive assistant to the committee.

But while the overall format of the search was similar to that of the previous one, there were two significant differences. One was the choice of the executive search firm. The Korn/Ferry company, which had directed the Frawley search, was obligated by its contract to conduct, free of charge, another search if the original selection for the job did not serve a full year—which, of course, Frawley did not.

The Board, however, decided not to exercise that option. "Obviously [Frawley] didn't work out," said Poole, "but Korn/Ferry is not to blame."

Still, the Board decided to turn elsewhere, because, as the Rector put it, rehiring Korn/Ferry would be "awkward." Eventually chosen was the Florida firm of Greenwood and Associates, headed by former Longwood University president Janet Greenwood. The cost was $92,500, plus travel and other expenses, to be paid by the UMW Foundation.

A second major difference with this search was that the Board made it clear from the outset that the search would be conducted confidentially from start to finish, as opposed to the prior one, during which three finalists were brought to the University for open sessions with faculty and other interested members of the community. The reason for the Board's decision was the belief that a closed search would attract more and better applicants because, as Poole suggested, "Publicly announcing finalists stops or discourages some excellent candidates from applying."

Some faculty members groused at the lack of more direct involvement in the new search, but given the unsatisfactory outcome of the previous one, most seemed to accept the new rules as a trade-off in hopes of securing a better result in the end. So the search remained confidential as it proceeded through the winter months, producing (rather surprisingly at a university) no "leaks" prior to the announcement of the new president in March.

Meanwhile, students returned in August to a campus bedecked with banners celebrating the centennial. The porticos of all major buildings displayed huge blue and white banners proclaiming "UMW 1908–2008," and similar pennants in smaller sizes adorned lampposts throughout the grounds. For the campus community, the celebration began on August 27, the first day of classes, with an ice cream social reminiscent of the kinds of activities enjoyed by students in the institution's early days. The line stretching along Campus Walk as students queued up for ice cream served by University faculty and administrators indicated that the passage of a century had not diminished students' appreciation for the cooling refreshment, especially on sweltering late-summer days.

From that point onward, special celebratory events were sprinkled throughout the year. In addition, almost every one of the University's traditional activities had a centennial focus, including Homecoming, Family Weekend, the "Great Lives" series, and the Historic Preservation Center's holiday "Deck the Halls" program. In the academic area, many departments scheduled special activities, including an interdisciplinary Centennial Education Symposium.

The University's various musical ensembles scheduled special performances throughout the year. Historically themed exhibitions were held in the duPont and Ridderhof Martin Galleries, along with special displays in Simpson Library, the College of Graduate and Professional Studies Library, and the Bookstore. In October, Gari Melchers Home and Studio at Belmont opened a photography exhibit by Lynda Richardson '81 based on her UMW coffee-table book, *Moments in Time*, which was published in November.

Heading the institution during the centennial year was Acting President Richard Hurley, who quickly earned the allegiance of the faculty, staff, and student body. There was little in Hurley's early background to portend a college presidency. Growing up in a blue-collar neighborhood in Penns Grove, New Jersey, he had no intention of going to college. Instead, he entered the Army after high school, served in Germany and Vietnam, returned home, and married his hometown sweetheart, Rose Caulfield. At the age of twenty-five and the father of a young daughter, he experienced an epiphany while working at a New Jersey Turnpike service station. One day while pumping gas in a freezing rain, Hurley later recalled, he decided to set his sights on somewhat loftier goals. He enrolled in nearby Richard Stockton College, where he earned a bachelor's degree in environmental studies. Having discovered an aptitude for academics, he proceeded to earn a master's degree in public administration from Central Michigan University, achieved mainly through taking weekend courses.

Thus began a career in education that led him by 1985 to Longwood University (then College) as vice president for administration and finance. Fifteen years later, Mary Washington came calling. The improbable catalyst for that development was an interview by Hurley's daughter, a television reporter, with President William Anderson concerning, of all things, the currently hot topic of condoms in vending machines. Her casual mention of her father during the interview jogged the president's memory of Hurley, with whom he was already acquainted. The next day Anderson contacted the Longwood official to inform him of an opening at Mary Washington for a chief financial officer. Soon thereafter, Hurley was hired, and it was to him that the Board eventually turned for leadership in the wake of the Frawley fiasco.

Hurley brought to the job of acting president a sound knowledge of the commonwealth's educational bureaucracy as well as the University's own administrative structure. But he brought something else as well—something vastly more important at a time when the institution was in a precarious situation, wounded internally by Frawley's bad karma and externally by his negative publicity. Whether it was Hurley's innate personality or his modest background (or a combination thereof), he provided just what was needed at the moment: a sense of confidence without an aura of arrogance. His approach was distinctly low-key, in stark contrast to his high-strung predecessor. "I don't carry a Blackberry with me," Hurley said, "and I don't expect people to jump when I speak."

It was a welcome attitude at a University where Frawley's intimidating manner had begun to create an edgy environment, especially among the administrative staff. Much as years earlier Bill Anderson's geniality had served to lift the gloom that often enveloped the Woodard years, so too did Hurley's light touch counteract the tension that had developed under Frawley, quickly restoring a pleasant environment on campus.

No one enjoyed the unexpected presidency more than Hurley himself—unless it was the irrepressible Rose, who once joked that when the time came to move out, she planned to delay it as long as possible by chaining herself to the Brompton oak. The couple's delight in being the University's "first family," even if on a temporary basis, was evident in the happiness they exuded in opening Brompton for University events to an extent, and with an air of unpretentious informality, never before witnessed in the mansion on the Heights.

And it was not merely a matter of mood. In a short time as acting president, Hurley produced an impressive number of accomplishments (some of which, to be sure, were already in the works), including greater diversity and significant campus expansion. Such actions portended a better University in the future; in the present they created a happier one.

The Hurley administration underwent several organizational changes involving new assignments for veteran staff members: Nina Mikhalevsky was named acting provost, Meta Braymer was named special assistant to the president for government and external relations, and Martin A. Wilder was named vice president for enrollment and communications. The fact that several of the appointments were on an interim basis did not impede the University's progress; in fact, the 2007–08 academic year proved to be one of its most productive, including a significant revision of the general education requirements.

The fundamental purposes of the new format were to streamline the requirements and provide students more flexibility in meeting them. Toward those ends, the main changes included elimination of requirements in global awareness, environmental awareness, and race and gender; English 101, Writing Workshop; and physical education. Added were requirements for a freshman seminar and an "experiential learning" course. The foreign language requirement was left essentially intact, an indication that the emphasis on liberal arts was not being diluted. The net result was reduction of total hours needed for graduation from 122 to 120.

Curricular revision was accompanied by continuing efforts to increase the diversity of the student body. Notable in that regard in the 2007–08 session was the arrival of two students from Afghanistan, Nilab Sadat and Zahra Noor. Their enrollment as freshmen, partially underwritten by the University and by benefactor Doris Buffett, was facilitated through a non-profit organization called the Initiative to Educate Afghan Women. The program's purpose was to educate students in the United States, with the prospect of their returning home to improve conditions for women in their native country.

By the two students' own testimony, there was ample room for improvement. To Nilab, who had once been whipped by the Taliban for wearing toenail polish, studying at Mary Washington represented an extraordinary opportunity. "When I read that [American] women one hundred years ago were not supposed to participate in public, and there were so many things they were not supposed to do, I think that it's not new for me because I have lived in that society today. This is not history for me—it's something that describes my own country."

Even as the University sought to attract students from abroad, it also in 2007–08 developed a program to encourage the enrollment of students much closer to home—specifically, those from high schools in Virginia's Northern Neck counties of Essex, Westmoreland, Northumberland, Lancaster, and King and Queen. Called the Rappahannock Scholars Program, it allowed the schools to nominate from the tenth through twelfth grades a total of thirty-six students who—provided they maintained a 3.5 grade-point average—were guaranteed admission to UMW, along with financial aid sufficient to cover their demonstrated needs. Preference was given to those who had financial need, who were first-generation college students, and who would add to the institution's cultural diversity. The *Free Lance–Star* applauded the effort, commenting editorially that "often, all kids need as they chart their course is someone to show them an expanded horizon. . . . A hand up is often all someone needs to reach the heights of which they're capable."

It indeed seemed appropriate that, in the year of its centennial, the University established a program designed specifically for the benefit of students from the Northern Neck, the area that had been home to so many of the first students at the Fredericksburg State Normal and Industrial School.

As the student body evolved—in composition, if not so much in size—the University extended its physical reach as well. One such effort, President Frawley's attempt to establish a downtown retail store, had foundered, but it was superseded by a much more ambitious and potentially significant project.

Beginning during the presidency of William Anderson, and at his instigation, the University began to address the issue of expansion. The options were few, given the land-locked location of the campus. Earlier efforts under Anderson to acquire the Montfort Academy property adjacent to Brompton had failed. Consideration was also given to purchasing two properties proximal to the campus—the James Monroe High School tract and the Snowden property across the U.S. Route 1 bypass—but both efforts came to naught.

The only remaining feasible space for contiguous expansion was the Park & Shop Center, a twenty-one acre property across the bypass at its junction with College Avenue. Built in 1963, the strip mall had by 2007 begun to show its age, conveying a "down-on-its-luck appearance in recent years," in the words of the *Free Lance–Star*. As early as 2001, the Anderson administration began to investigate acquisition of the property, but this effort was forestalled by complicated lease agreements of the current tenants, the most prominent of which were the Rose's department store and the Giant food store that had served generations of Mary Washington students.

The University's quest for the property came to fruition, however, in December 2007, when the Mary Washington Real Estate Foundation purchased it for $18.75 million, a transaction that instantly increased the size of the campus by almost a third. Plans for the property, though still in the formative stage at the time of purchase, envisioned incrementally demolishing the shopping center and replacing it with a mixed-use development in a park-like setting, incorporating student and faculty housing as well as high-end retail businesses such as a bookstore, a restaurant, and a movie theater. Some existing enterprises, Giant in particular, would remain but would be substantially upgraded.

The first phase of the development—which, overall, was projected to take up to ten years and cost between $60 million and $100 million—was the construction of apartment-style housing for between 350 and 400 students. The new residential units would be connected to the main campus by a pedestrian walkway arching over the busy Route 1. The new residential space would obviate construction of the two new dorms previously planned for the existing campus.[2]

Announcement of the project elicited unusually uniform praise from constituents of the University and from the local community. The *Free Lance–Star* expressed enthusiasm for the development as a boon to both the city and the University. "The plan is an excellent one," it wrote, "offering the hope of achieving several disparate goals through one bold and innovative project. Onward and upward."

Student life, exuberant as usual, was spiced during the year with an array of activities related to the centennial. Various residence halls held special celebratory events, beginning with a September program and picnic appropriately sponsored by the school's oldest dormitory, Willard Hall. Near the end of the year, students in the preservation program's museum studies class mounted a special exhibition in the Ridderhof Martin gallery titled "The Evolution of Dorm Life at Mary Washington."

The biggest controversy during a year that was otherwise generally joyful came in late November when an incident in Jefferson Hall raised concerns about institutional racism. The episode was reminiscent of a similar occurrence in the same dorm in 1992, when African American students received threats. In 2007 the issue arose when housekeepers on the fourth floor of Jefferson found a flyer attached to a community refrigerator that depicted a white man with his arm around a sobbing black man above a caption that read: "Slavery reinstated. Catch yourself a good one." The unseemly poster had apparently been downloaded from the Internet.

In reporting the incident, the *Bullet* quoted one of the housekeepers as saying, "We may need a job, but we don't need nobody doing us like that." The article went on to quote the housekeeper as saying that the men on that hall were "like little beasts," a term she later denied using. The incident touched off a furor, with some calling for the dismissal of the students involved—one of whom made matters even worse, telling the *Bullet*, "That's their job—to clean up after us. My maid at home doesn't complain, so why should the cleaning ladies?" In a subsequent letter to the *Bullet*, he publicly apologized for such comments, acknowledging that his "judgment was poor and improper."

The campus was split over the episode, with some believing that it was overblown. One such student, a freshman resident in Jefferson dorm, went so far as to blame the *Bullet* staffers who originally reported the story, asserting that "the article was blatantly slanted by a pair of opportunistic hyenas in a desperate attempt to increase readership." On the other hand, there were those who not only decried the episode itself but attacked the administration for its failure to respond quickly and punitively. "Whoever is responsible for this institution," wrote the president of the Labor Rights Club, seemed to be "making sure that this [school] remains like a 'good ol' boys' club from the South."

By that time the issue had gone far beyond the dorm itself. An open forum, sponsored by Students Educating and Empowering for Diversity, drew a capacity crowd to Monroe 104 for an airing of views. The next day a protest march occurred, attracting considerable media coverage, including televised reports on the Washington ABC affiliate. President Hurley responded by admitting that administrative action had not been sufficiently swift, mainly because of a "failure of communication" that kept him from hearing about it until publication of the *Bullet* article. Calling the episode "reprehensible," he vowed to establish a policy by which any further similar actions could be reported and addressed expeditiously, warning at the same time that any such policy must guarantee First Amendment rights.

The upshot was the creation of a policy that permitted reports of perceived misconduct to be reported via e-mail, though not anonymously. The effort was generally perceived on campus as a legitimate attempt to create a mechanism for resolution of such issues. Not long thereafter, the administration announced that Martin Luther King Day would thenceforth be a holiday on campus. It was an action long demanded by those who pointed out that, by then, Mary Washington was one of only three Virginia schools (VMI and Christopher Newport University being the others) that did not cancel classes on that day. Though he did not explicitly tie the King holiday decision to the Jefferson dorm episode, Hurley conceded a connection. "I would be less than truthful," he said, "if I didn't admit that the incident and everything I learned from it influenced my thinking."

Besides matters of racial concern, students demonstrated their social consciousness through a number of activities channeled through such organizations as the Human Rights Club and the Animal Rights Club. The Anarchists Social Theory Club was also quite active, serving as host of the annual meeting of the (somewhat oxymoronic) Virginia Anarchists Foundation.

In addition, an economics class taught by Professor Shawn Humphrey, in an effort to give students greater empathy for homeless people, created a project in which each student in the class lived on two dollars a day for a week. They slept outside on Ball Circle in a makeshift shanty town constructed of cardboard, plywood, and flattened beer cans. Not allowed to take showers, the students—dubbed "fobos" (faux hobos)—were permitted only one change of clothing during the week. According to Humphrey, the project was "an imperfect tool, but it may be the best tool I have" to give students a feel for what it is like to be poor.

The cause that attracted the most support was the "green movement"—concern for the environment. A *Bullet* feature story suggested the "Top Five Ways to Make 'Going Green' More Fun," which included standard ecology-friendly practices such as recycling, carpooling, and conserving electricity. The most interesting was the suggestion that students not shower every day "or just shower with someone else—a roommate, friend, or even a stranger. Offer to scrub their back first while complimenting them on doing their part to save the environment."

Leading the green offensive was the Ecology Club, which, in cooperation with the University administration, sponsored a highly successful light-bulb exchange in which incandescent bulbs were replaced by more efficient fluorescent ones. During a week-long crusade in November, the club attracted the support of more than 35 percent of the residential students, resulting in the replacement of more than sixteen hundred bulbs, with an estimated annual savings to the University of approximately $20,000.

Interest in international involvement remained high, as indicated by, among other measures, the number of Peace Corps volunteers from UMW. In 2008, Mary Washington had twenty-one alumni serving as volunteers, making the University sixth among colleges and universities with fewer than five thousand graduates. James Farmer Professor of Human Rights Greg Stanton summed up the phenomenon: "Schools like Yale and Harvard," he said, "although they are great schools, do not have the same community service ethic that we have. This is a school where people learn to care about other people."

The most remarkable evidence of that caring spirit was the continued growth of Students Helping Honduras, the organization created in 2005 by Shin Fujiyama. Although Fujiyama had graduated in May 2007, the organization proceeded vigorously the following year under his successor, senior Justin Simeone, as it took on additional projects, including creation of a program to provide college scholarships for promising female Honduran orphans. Capped by a huge walkathon on campus in late April, the organization raised nearly $225,000 during the year to support its humanitarian projects.

Spring semester 2008 marked the culmination of the University's centennial celebration, as many long-planned events came to fruition. But before they began, the campus was stirred by a quite unexpected event, one that arose literally overnight. On Sunday evening, February 10, University officials were asked to make arrangements for a campus visit by former president Bill Clinton, who was campaigning in Virginia for his wife, Hillary, in advance of the state Democratic presidential primary the following Tuesday. News of the visit spread rapidly among students on Monday morning. Anticipating Clinton's midday appearance in the Great Hall, some had camped as early as 7 A.M. outside the security-laden building. Hours ahead of his arrival, a line—not just single file, but containing groups of students—stretched along Campus Walk all the way from the Campus Center to Lee Hall. According to longtime observers, it was the lengthiest queue ever assembled in the history of the institution.

When the doors opened at noon, students flooded into the hall as the stereo system played Tom Petty's "American Girl." The room quickly reached its capacity of six hundred, with another four hundred remaining outside or downstairs in the Eagles Nest. It was, said the *Free Lance–Star*, "a greeting more fitting for a rock star than a politician."

The former president wasted no time in endearing himself to the audience, first by acknowledging his graduate school friendship at Georgetown University with UMW economics professor Stephen Stageberg, whom he described as the most outstanding member of the Georgetown track team and as a supporter when Clinton had sought the student body presidency (an election that he lost). Further ingratiating himself and moving to his political agenda, Clinton declared, "You know, this school was founded one hundred years ago this year. It started as a school for women, when they were segregated and defenseless. I think this would be a good year to elect the first female President."

It was an exciting day for the student Democratic partisans—one of whom brandished a "Bill Clinton for First Lady" placard—and for the University, which gained unexpected publicity in the media. The political impact of the visit, however, was dubious. Certainly it was not enough to produce victory for Hillary Clinton in the primary, which she lost to Barack Obama by a substantial margin the following day.

A different kind of excitement was also generated early in the spring semester. Because the women's basketball team had come tantalizingly close to winning the Division III national championship the previous year, hopes were high that the centennial squad—which had lost only one key player to graduation—would make it all the way in 2008. It seemed a reasonable goal as the team, led by senior two-time All–American center Liz Hickey, ended the regular season with a record of twenty-three wins and only two losses. Victories in the first round of the NCAA tournaments boosted the Eagles into the "Sweet 16" for the third consecutive year, but there the dream ended with a three-point loss to Tufts University. Though disappointed, the players and their coach, Deena Applebury, made no excuses for their defeat, although they might well have done so: the loss of star forward Ashton Mitchell to a knee injury prior to that game was a serious, and likely crucial, blow.

Liz Hickey summed up the team's feeling at not making it to the championship. "When you don't get there, it's frustrating," she said. "But this has been a good run for our team and our school." A "good run" was something of an understatement to describe the accomplishments of a remarkable group of female athletes who had won fifty-nine games over the course of two years, while losing only six.

For the remainder of the academic year, the University was absorbed in centennial events. Activities were concentrated during Founders Week, March 7–14, a week unlike any that the institution had ever experienced. It began with the opening of an art exhibition in Jepson Alumni Executive Center titled "One Hundred Years Together," a show that featured works of artists from the Fredericksburg region reflecting connections between UMW and the community. Another show, the "Centennial Alumni Exhibition," opened on March 13 in the Ridderhof Martin Gallery. A juried competition, it displayed the artistic accomplishments of Mary Washington graduates.

On Monday of Founders Week occurred one of the highlights of the celebration—indeed, one of the signal moments in the institution's history—though it had not been part of the celebration's planning, nor could it have been: the serendipitous announcement of a new president for Mary Washington.

The confidential search process had continued through the winter months with no indication of who the candidates were or when the final selection might be made public. However, when Rector Poole announced on Friday, March 7, that "an important announcement" would be made the following Monday, many observers divined the purpose, and a large crowd gathered in Dodd Auditorium for the meeting on the first day of Founders Week.

Poole began by introducing Acting President Hurley to deliver welcoming remarks. In the eleven months that Hurley had led the administration, he had made a uniformly favorable impression on all the institution's constituencies. Indeed, so favorably was he regarded that, until the moment of the announcement of the new president, many people believed that the job might be Hurley's on a permanent basis—this despite his persistent denials of interest in the job, publicly citing his intention to retire in 2009. Privately he also conceded that he was deterred by the belief that his lack of a doctorate would have been a handicap, perhaps an insuperable one, had he sought the permanent position. In any event, when he rose to speak prior to the announcement of the new president, the loud and prolonged standing ovation that greeted him provided evidence that many in the audience would have welcomed just such an outcome. But it was not to be.

By the time Rector Poole returned to the podium to make the long-awaited announcement, the air of expectation had increased. Normally an unflappable man with a disarming sense of humor, Poole by now was showing the strain of having been the University's point person throughout the Frawley affair and subsequent search. Barely into his remarks, he stopped to gather himself, apologizing, "It's been a long process. . . . It's a little emotional." He did not need to explain.

The University's eighth president, he then announced, would be its first female one: Judy Gayle Hample, chancellor of the Pennsylvania State System

IAN BRADSHAW

Judy Hample

of Higher Education. The applause that swelled as she rose from her seat in the audience and approached the podium seemed to be not only for her personally but also for the fact that an institution named for a woman would now, in its one hundredth year, be led by a woman—a circumstance that many felt was overdue.

Judy—not Judith ("Southerners tend to name you what they're going to call you.")—Hample was born in Henderson, Tennessee, the middle child between an older brother and a younger sister.[3] She learned early about hard work, growing up on a large farm that produced cotton, corn, and soybeans. As an undergraduate student at David Lipscomb University, a small liberal arts school in Nashville, she earned money by working at the campus bookstore and, for a while, by serving as hostess at the city's landmark Grand Old Opry. Having received her bachelor's degree with a triple major (French, communication, and secondary education), plus a minor in chemistry, she went on to earn master's and doctoral degrees in communication from Ohio State University, finishing in 1974.

A sixty-year-old divorcée (no children) at the time of her appointment, Hample was serving as head of fourteen public universities in Pennsylvania. Previously she had held a number of teaching and administrative posts, including chancellor for the Board of Regents of the State University System of Florida.

In her first meeting with the Mary Washington community, Hample quickly established rapport, both in her prepared remarks and in the question-and-answer session that followed. Promising an open administration, she noted that among her primary goals were external fund-raising and increasing diversity within the institution. At one point during the interchange with the audience, she herself asked a student what issues he would like her to address as president. "I wasn't prepared for that," he responded, adding, to general laughter, "Just make sure everybody's happy."

Impossible as such a task would be, it appeared to many at the initial meeting that the new leader did, in fact, possess the credentials—and, more important, the personality and attitude—to move the institution in that direction. "I celebrate today," she said, "not only as a leader but [as] a woman who has been chosen to lead a first-rate institution into a promising future."

Following the big announcement on Monday, each succeeding day of Founders Week offered a special event. On Tuesday, the twelfth annual Fredericksburg Forum featured acclaimed *Washington Post* journalist Bob Woodward; on Wednesday, Phi Beta Kappa visiting scholar Eric Mazur, a Harvard University physics professor, presented a lecture, "How the Mind Tricks Us"; and on Thursday, the Great Lives lecture series, now in its fifth season, offered a talk by George Mason University professor emeritus Peter Henriques titled "Mary Washington and Her Son George."

The grandest celebration of the week was the centennial convocation on Founders Day itself, Friday, March 14. The ceremony began with the academic pageantry typical of the University's celebratory occasions, as the robed academic procession filed into Dodd Auditorium at 3:00 p.m., heralded by the Eagle Pipe Band. A special dimension of the procession was the inclusion of a representative of each class, led by the regal Ruby Lee Norris, class of 1936 and former member of the Board of Visitors.

Following a welcome from Rector Poole and introductory remarks from Acting President Hurley, Governor Timothy Kaine delivered felicitations from the Commonwealth of Virginia, and Barbara Burton Micou '69, president of the Alumni Association, brought greetings from her organization. The third speaker was Fredericksburg attorney O'Conor Goolrick Ashby, grandson and namesake of the institution's founder, who spoke on behalf of the descendents of Delegate O'Conor Goolrick.

Ashby's remarks, eloquently delivered, proved particularly moving. Having recounted the extraordinary career of his grandfather, who died in 1960 at the age of eighty-three, he concluded by presenting to the University on behalf of his family the most hallowed of institutional artifacts: the loving cup that had originally been given to Goolrick in 1909 by the first president of the school, Edward H. Russell. The sentimental high point of the program came when Ashby, handing the sterling silver icon to Poole, read the cup's biblical inscription: "Well done, good and faithful servant"—words that prompted a lengthy standing ovation and produced more than a few teary eyes.

After a choral interlude by the University's chamber choir, Una Voce, history professor Carter Hudgins, co-chair of the centennial celebration, introduced the convocation speaker, Pulitzer Prize-winning historian David McCullough. Hudgins duly noted that McCullough would be the third in a distinguished line of historians who had spoken on previous landmark occasions in the University's past: Arnold Toynbee at the fiftieth anniversary, Daniel Boorstin at the seventy-fifth. Eminent as they were, they did not eclipse McCullough, for in 2008 there were few, if any, historians in America who were better known or more revered than he.

McCullough, whose forte was making history accessible (and enjoyable) to a popular audience, proceeded to deliver an address that was at once charming and challenging. "To be here on Marye's Hill," he began, "on a beautiful day such as this to commemorate such good work over one hundred years, is an honor I will never forget, a pleasure beyond my expression, and my gratitude could not be greater." With his imposing presence, avuncular manner, and sonorous voice, McCullough was repeatedly interrupted by applause from an audience that clearly appreciated his call for greater emphasis on liberal education and the study of history in particular. He ended with a reference to an admonition by John Adams (one of his many biographical subjects), who once wrote, "I would to God that there were more ambition in the country. By that, I mean ambition of the laudable kind—to excel." That, McCullough said, is what the University should do: teach its students "to have ambition to excel." He paused, then concluded: "On you go!"

A hearty rendition of the alma mater brought the convocation to a close, after which visiting dignitaries and University officials repaired to the foyer of Trinkle Hall to cut the centennial birthday cake. What followed indicated that, even as it celebrated its past, the University was looking aggressively toward its future.

That evening, the Office of University Advancement hosted a black-tie dinner for approximately three hundred guests to announce the public phase of the most ambitious fund-raising effort in the institution's history. Held outdoors under an enormous white tent covering the entire Palmieri Plaza, the event was blessed with weather that turned out, mercifully, to be unseasonably mild. Following an elegant meal, alumni and friends of the University learned that during the campaign's earlier private phase, $64 million had already been raised since 2000. They were told of plans to pursue the remainder and, of course, were invited to participate in that campaign. The dinner ended with a toast by special guest McCullough, who concluded with the exhortation, "Let the celebration begin!"

And so it did, as banquet guests joined students, faculty, alumni, and friends of the University in dancing until midnight to the music of Doc Scantlin and His Imperial Palms Orchestra in the canopied plaza and to A Touch of Jazz in the nearby Great Hall. There was general agreement that the whole day had been extraordinary, an appropriately joyous tribute to a remarkable hundred years. Typifying such sentiment was the comment of Nanalou Sauder '56, vice rector of the Board of Visitors. The week following Founders Day, she wrote to commend the celebration's planners. "Last Friday was the best day I have ever spent at Mary Washington," she said, "and, believe me, that is a lot of days since 1952."

But the festivities did not end on Founders Day itself. The next night featured a special centennial concert, "Heroes Past and Present," by the University–Community Symphony Orchestra under the direction of Kevin Bartram. The program opened with the premier performance of an orchestral arrangement of the alma mater by Jeremy Vaughn '08 and Jeffery Zeiders '08. It was followed by a piece titled *LXXV+XXV: A Celebratory Overture for Or-*

chestra, composed especially for the occasion by music professor David Long and directed by him as guest conductor.

Next came two particularly sentimental moments. One was the appearance of James Baker, the orchestra's longtime maestro, who returned from retirement to conduct two pieces. That was followed by announcement of the annual Citizen Salute Award, given posthumously on this occasion to beloved music professor Patricia Norwood, who had died suddenly in January.

The centerpiece of the program was the premiere of *Quest, Symphony of Celebration*, which internationally renowned composer James Grant had been commissioned to write specifially for the centennial. The historical piece was interspersed with audio excerpts from speeches by presidents Woodard and Anderson, as well as portions of addresses by presidents Combs and Anderson, sensitively narrated by English professor Gardner Campbell. A rousing encore of the alma mater brought the program—and the centennial celebration—to a fittingly emotional conclusion.

From that point the final six weeks of the year sped by, as spring semesters always do, rushing toward the events of commencement weekend, May 8–10. The weather forecast for the weekend was not propitious, and the prediction turned out to be accurate. On Thursday night, the Fredericksburg area was struck by violent thunderstorms, including a tornado packing winds of 120 miles per hour. Although the campus was spared a direct hit, the storm forced Graduation Ball celebrants to flee inside the Jepson Alumni Executive Center ballroom from the adjacent courtyard, where an elaborately decorated tent had been erected especially for the event.

Stormy conditions lingered throughout the following day, making it likely that commencement on Saturday would have to be held in Dodd Auditorium, rather than on Ball Circle, for the first time in more than thirty years; as late as one hour before the scheduled 9:00 A.M. beginning of the ceremony, rain was still falling. University officials, however, trusting National Weather Service reports that the front was moving out, decided at the last minute to take a chance on holding the ceremony outside. Their optimism was rewarded, as the ceremony proceeded (albeit somewhat apprehensively) with graduates and guests dampened by intermittent sprinkles, but with their spirits undiminished.

The featured speaker was Virginia's United States Senator John Warner, who had recently announced his intention to retire at the end of his current term, having served almost four decades in the Senate. Following the speech, Warner was awarded an honorary doctorate of humane letters degree. In addition, traditional year-end awards included presentation of the Colgate Darden Award to Justin Simeone, whose four-year GPA of 3.99 led his class; the Grellet C. Simpson Award to Margaret Huber, distinguished professor of anthropology; the CGPS award for teaching excellence to Brenda Vogel, professor and director of the Teaching Education Program; the Alumni Association Outstanding Young Faculty Member Award to Keith Mellinger, assistant professor of mathematics; and the Mary Pinschmidt Award to W. Brown Morton III, retiring professor of historic preservation. The greatest applause of the day accompanied the awarding of two Washington Medallions—one to Rector Poole and one to Acting President Hurley—in recognition of the stalwart service each had rendered to the University during one of its most trying periods.

For the graduates, of course, the highlight of the ceremony was the conferring of their degrees, a joyous process accompanied (for some) by bittersweet tears, the result of commencement's unique emotional blend of euphoria and nostalgia. Once the diplomas were handed out, the alma mater sung, and hugs and handshakes exchanged, the class of 2008 filed out of Ball Circle, marking the close of the historic session. Moments later, as the newest alumni prepared to leave their haven on the hill, the clouds lifted, and upon the centennial class the sun shone yet again, bringing a warmth to match their memories and a radiance to match their dreams.

Quite a year it had been. Indeed, quite a century.

APPENDIX 1

Recipients of the Honorary Doctor of Humane Letters Degree

Year	*Recipients*
1974	Grellet C. Simpson
1977	Edward Alvey Jr.
1978	Colgate Whitehead Darden Jr.
1984	Lewis Meriwether Walker Jr.
	Katherine Edmondson Hopper
1985	Charles S. Robb
1986	Gerald L. Baliles
	Irene Lundy Brown
1988	Hunter B. Andrews
1989	Donald J. Finley
	Alice Andrews Jepson
1993	Gordon K. Davies
	Alfred Levitt
	A. Elizabeth Morrison
1997	James Farmer
1998	Hildy Parks Cohen
	Arabelle Laws Arrington
	Lawrence R. McMurtry
1999	John H. Hager
2000	Herbert H. Bateman
2002	John H. Chichester
	V. Earl Dickinson
2003	William J. Howell
	Carlisle M. Williams Jr.
2004	Mark R. Warner
2005	Rose M. Likins
2006	Marion Clifton Blakey
	William M. Anderson Jr.

APPENDIX 2

Faculty Awards and Honors

DISTINGUISHED PROFESSORS

James E. Baker, Music
Marshall E. Bowen, Geography
David W. Cain, Religion
William B. Crawley Jr., History
Joseph C. Di Bella, Art
Samuel T. Emory Jr., Geography
James Farmer, History
Lewis P. Fickett, Political Science
Donald E. Glover, English
Roy F. Gratz, Chemistry
Richard E. Hansen, English
Margaret W. Huber, Anthropology
Carter L. Hudgins, Early American Studies
John M. Kramer, Political Science
Richard J. Krickus, Political Science
Bernard L. Mahoney Jr., Chemistry
Sammy R. Merrill, German
Cornelia D. Oliver, Art
Mary W. Pinschmidt, Biological Sciences
Paul C. Slayton Jr., Education
Roy H. Smith, Psychology
George M. Van Sant, Philosophy

ENDOWED CHAIRS

David K. Ambuel and Mehdi Aminrazavi, Kurt Leidecker Chair of Asian Studies
Rosemary Barra, William M. Anderson Jr. Distinguished Chair in Biological Sciences

William B. Crawley Jr., Rector and Visitors Chair
Claudia Emerson, Arrington Distinguished Chair of Poetry
Carter L. Hudgins, Hofer Chair of Early American Culture and Historic Preservation
W. Brown Morton III, Prince B. Woodard Chair of Historic Preservation

GRELLET C. SIMPSON AWARD WINNERS

Established in 1972, the Grellet C. Simpson Award reflects the importance placed by the University on its primary mission as an undergraduate teaching institution. Named for former president Grellet C. Simpson, this award was made possible by an anonymous donor and is presented to a faculty member in recognition of excellence in undergraduate teaching.

1972	Carmen L. Rivera, Spanish
1973	Sidney H. Mitchell, English
1974	Anna S. Hoye, Biology
1975	Earl G. Insley, Chemistry
1976	Donald E. Glover, English
1977	Glen R. Thomas, American Studies
1978	Nancy H. Mitchell, English
1979	Elizabeth A. Clark, Religion
1980	Janet G. Zeleznock, Mathematical Sciences
1981	Arthur L. Tracy, History
1982	Mary W. Pinschmidt, Biology
1983	Joseph C. Di Bella, Art
1984	Bernard L. Mahoney Jr., Chemistry
1985	Susan J. Hanna, English
1986	George M. Van Sant, Philosophy
1987	Marshall E. Bowen, Geography
1988	Joanna L. Reynolds, Spanish
1989	Roger J. Bourdon, History
1990	Michael J. Joyce, Dramatic Arts
1991	Richard M. Zeleznock, Mathematics
1992	David W. Cain, Religion
1993	Sammy R. Merrill, German
1994	William B. Crawley Jr., History
1995	Lewis P. Fickett Jr., Political Science
1996	Carol S. Manning, English
1997	J. Christopher Bill, Psychology
1998	Bulent I. Atalay, Physics
1999	Steven A. Greenlaw, Economics
2000	William Kemp, English
2001	Clavio F. Ascari, Italian
2002	Steve R. Hampton, Psychology

2003	Rosemary Barra, Biology
2004	John H. Reynolds, Computer Science
2005	David J. Long, Music
2006	John M. Kramer, Political Science
2007	Thomas G. Moeller, Psychology
2008	Margaret Huber, Anthropology

ALUMNI ASSOCIATION OUTSTANDING YOUNG FACULTY MEMBER AWARD

The Alumni Association Outstanding Young Faculty Member Award, established in 1989, recognizes the achievements and contributions of faculty members who have been at the University fewer than five years.

1989	James E. Goehring, Religion
1990	George King III, Physics
1991	Grant R. Woodwell, Geology
1992	Larry W. Penwell, Psychology
1993	John T. Morello, Speech
1994	Suzanne Sumner, Mathematics
1995	Gregg Stull, Theater
1996	Janusz Konieczny, Mathematics
1997	Mehdi Aminrazavi, Philosophy and Religion
1998	W. Gardner Campbell, English
1999	Christine A. McBride, Psychology
2000	Kelli M. Slunt, Chemistry
2001	Stephen J. Farnsworth, Political Science
2002	Carole A. Garmon, Art
2003	Claudia Emerson, English
2004	Leanna C. Giancarlo, Chemistry
2005	Miriam N. Liss, Psychology
2006	Craig T. Naylor, Music
2007	Jason W. Davidson, Political Science
2008	Keith E. Mellinger, Mathematics

MARY W. PINSCHMIDT AWARD

Members of the senior class select the winner of the Mary W. Pinschmidt Award. Established in 1999 in honor of a longtime professor of biology, this award recognizes the faculty member whom seniors select as the person they will most likely remember as having had the greatest impact on their lives.

1999	Stephen J. Farnsworth, Political Science
2000	Werner Wieland, Biology

2001	Erin H. Fouberg, Geography
2002	J. Christopher Bill, Psychology
2003	Gregg Stull, Theater
2004	José Angel Sainz, Spanish
2005	William B. Crawley Jr., History
2006	Claudia Emerson, English
2007	Kenneth D. Machande, Business Administration
2008	W. Brown Morton III, Historic Preservation

J. CHRISTOPHER "TOPHER" BILL SERVICE AWARD

The award was established in memory of the popular professor of psychology who died in 2001. It is given annually to a faculty member in recognition of his or her exceptional faculty leadership.

2003	Sammy R. Merrill, German
2004	Roy H. Smith, Psychology
2005	Patricia A. Norwood, Music
2006	Raymond B. Scott, Chemistry
2007	Martha V. Fickett, Music
2008	Debra Hydorn

COLLEGE OF GRADUATE AND PROFESSIONAL STUDIES OUTSTANDING FACULTY AWARD

The award is given to a full-time faculty member who has been at CGPS for at least two years and who, during that time, has demonstrated excellence in teaching and leadership.

2003	Andrew Blair Staley
2004	Jo Tyler
2005	Alan G. Heffner
2006	Norah S. Hooper
2007	Gail D. Brooks
2008	Brenda E. Vogel

APPENDIX 3

Members of the Board of Visitors

Members	*Terms of Office*	
Abas M. Adenan '85	1993–2001	
Mona Davis Albertine '71	1999–2007	Rector, 2004–6
Arabelle Laws Arrington '41	1975–83	
Joseph E. Blackburn	1972–80	
Joan Whittemore Blank '59	1972–77	
James M. Bowen	1992–94	
Irene Lundy Brown '39	1972–80	
John G. Castles	1976–82	
Leonard F. Chapman Jr.	1984–92	
Richard B. Cooper '90	1998–2001	
Richard S. Cross	1972	
Gwendolyn Amory Cumming '52	1972–81, 1983–91	
Warner N. Dalhouse	1977–80	
Virginia Lewis Dalton '40	1984–92	Rector, 1988–90
Lawrence A. Davies	1986–90	
Vincent A. DiBenedetto III '83	1994–2003	Rector, 2000–2002
Paul A. Dresser Jr.	1992–2000	Rector, 1996–2000
Dori G. Eglevsky	1994–2004	Rector, 2002–4
Randall R. Eley	2004–8	
Patricia Head Ferguson '50	1972–75	
Elizabeth Ferguson Foster '69	2005–	
Newman Hamblet	1980–84	
Sue Smith Hane III '76	1978–82	
Jean Polk Hanky '69	1990–98	
Dorcas R. Hardy	2000–2004	
Donna Henninger Henderson '61	1972–79	
Benjamin Hernandez '95	2005–	
Florian N. Hofer	1987–95	Rector, 1992–94
Katherine E. Hopper '30	1972–82	Rector, 1979–82
Elizabeth Smith Hughes '51	2002–6	

Members	*Terms of Office*	
Ann Perinchief Jarrell '67	1972–75	
Alice Andrews Jepson '64	1989–93	
Henry R. Johnson Jr.	1993–97	
Martha Kimball Johnson '58	1994–98	
John A. Kinniburgh	1983–87	Rector, 1984–86
Miriam Whitley Knight '48	1985–89	
Suellen Grant Knowles '63	1997–2005	
Martha Kearns Leighty '75	2004–	
Kimberly Palmer Luger '89	1997–2001	
Anne Beck Macfarlane '52	1992–96	
J. Hugo Madison	1980–82	
Kathleen Shepherd Mehfoud '70	1989–97	Rector, 1994–96
Barbara Burton Micou '69	1991–95	
Charlotte Major Minor '66	1997–98	
M. C. Morris Moncure '82	2001–5	
Princess R. Moss	2007–	
Gail Fallon Neal '59	1980–84	Rector, 1982–84
Grace Norbrey	1990–94	
Ruby Lee Norris '36	1996–2000	
Helen Wilkins Obenshain '56	1979–2000	
Edith Sheppard Ott '59	1983–91	
Stanley A. Owens	1975–83	
J. Rupert Picott	1976–81	
J. William Poole	2002–	Rector, 2007–
Samuel D. Proctor	1972–77	
Karen C. Radley	2002–6	
Patricia Branstetter Revere '63	2004–	
Anne Price Fortney Riddell '66	1982–84	
Russell H. Roberts	2007–	
Kathleen Mayer Rugh '78	1982–90	
Nanalou West Sauder '56	1990–94, 2003–	
Wayne A. Schroeder	1995–99	
Larry Silver	1991–94	
Daniel K. Steen '84	2005–	
C. Maureen Stinger '94	2006–	
Rita Morgan Stone '52	1982–90	Rector, 1986–88
Todd A. Stottlemyer	1995–99	
Fred D. Thompson Jr.	1999–2007	
Rita S. J. Thompson	1994–98	
Thomas H. Thorpe	1984–92	
John T. Tompkins III	1981–89 s	
John C. Van Hoy '80	1998–2002	
Lewis M. Walker Jr.	1972–80	Rector, 1972–79

Members	*Terms of Office*	
Leah Fleet Waller '44	1972–78	
C. Douglas Welty	2000–2004	
Bennett C. Whitlock	1985–93	Rector, 1990–92
Ralph M. Whitticar III	1972–76	
Jennifer C. Whyte '94	1998–2002	
Benjamin H. Woodbridge Jr.	1980–85	
Sylvia McJilton Woodcock '61	1981–85	

ENDNOTES

I. THE FIRST HALF CENTURY

1. Edward Alvey, *History of Mary Washington College, 1908–1972* (Charlottesville: University Press of Virginia, 1974), 208, 327.
2. J. I. Hayes, *A History of Averett College* (Danville, Va.: Averett College Press, 1984), 9.
3. Fredericksburg, Virginia, City Council, *The Action of the City of Fredericksburg in Relation to the Location of the Proposed State Female Normal School, with the Inducements and Reasons for Establishing the Same at Fredericksburg* (Fredericksburg, Va., 1904), n.p.
4. *State Normal and Industrial School for Women, Fredericksburg, Virginia* (Lynchburg, Va.: Dulaney-Boatwright, n.d.), n.p.
5. This quotation and the following ones by W. N. Hamlet are taken from the speech he delivered at a 1931 alumni banquet celebrating the school's twentieth anniversary, by which time he was the most senior member of the faculty. Fredericksburg, Va., *Free Lance–Star*, July 2, 1931 (hereafter cited as *Free Lance–Star*).
6. *State Normal and Industrial School for Women.*
7. Young Women's Christian Association, ed., *Students Handbook of State Teachers College, Fredericksburg, Virginia*, vol. 5, 1928–29 (1928), 64.
8. *State Normal and Industrial School for Women.*
9. Ibid.
10. Although not an amphitheater in the literal sense of the word, that is what the open-air theater uniformly came to be called.
11. *Bullet*, November 23, 1928.
12. *Bullet*, May 13, 1932.
13. *Bullet*, February 10, 1939.
14. *Bullet*, December 12, 1941, and January 30, 1942.
15. The College began to consider ways in which the normal four-year curriculum could be compressed to permit graduation within three years. See *Bullet*, January 9, January 23, January 30, and February 20, 1942.
16. *Bullet*, January 23, 1942.
17. Hugo Iltis's widow sold the "world-famed genetics exhibits" to the University of Illinois in 1956. *Bullet*, March 27, 1956.
18. Copies of all honors papers since the inception of the program are on file in Special Collections of Simpson Library.

19. These programs are discussed in detail in Alvey, *History of Mary Washington College*, 323–25.
20. Ibid., 343–45.
21. William B. Crawley Jr., "Nina Bushnell: Genteel Martinet," *MWC Today* (summer 2002): 3.
22. Alvey, *History of Mary Washington College*, 334–41.
23. Quoted in Porter R. Blakemore, "The Third President, 1929–1955," *MWC Today* (winter 1983): 13.

2. THE SIMPSON ERA, 1955–1974

1. Previously the president of the University of Virginia had also held the title "chancellor of Mary Washington College." That title was dropped, and Colgate Darden became simply the president of the University of Virginia.
2. Simpson's admiration is evident in his effusive foreword to Alvey's *History of Mary Washington College*, vii–viii.
3. Following the establishment of coeducation in 1970, the name of the organization was changed in September 1972 to the Alumni Association.
4. The organization was variously called the Student Government Association (abbreviated as SGA) or Student Association (abbreviated as SA).
5. Alvey, *History of Mary Washington College*, 482.
6. From this point on, much of the material is taken from issues of the *Bullet* and the author's own research, not Edward Alvey's history of the College. Matters concerning notes and documentation are explained in the preface.
7. *Bullet*, May 8, 1967.
8. For more extensive discussion of the work of this committee, see Alvey, *History of Mary Washington College*, 468–71.
9. Grellet C. Simpson, interview by author, March 20, 1991, tape recording, Special Collections, Simpson Library, University of Mary Washington, Fredericksburg, Va. Tape recordings of subsequent cited interviews are housed in Special Collections. The one exception is the Lewis M. Walker Jr. interview (see note 13), which was transcribed.
10. *Bullet*, December 16, 1969.
11. Simpson interview.
12. The background to separation is discussed at length in "Separation: A New Milestone," *MWC Today* (February 1972): 1–2.
13. Lewis M. Walker Jr., interview by author, August 18, 1988, transcript, Special Collections, Simpson Library, University of Mary Washington, Fredericksburg, Va.
14. This and succeeding quotations from Simpson come from the Grellet Simpson interview.
15. For the membership of the original board and their backgrounds, see Alvey, *History of Mary Washington College*, 513–14.
16. The following account is drawn largely from issues of the *Bullet* during the period and from Carolyn Sydnor Parsons, "Doors and Minds Begin to Open: Decade of Desegregation," *University of Mary Washington Today* (winter 2005): 16–19.
17. Jones was, by any reckoning, one of the most remarkable students ever to attend Mary Washington. Having graduated in three years with highest honors, she earned her medical degree from the University of Virginia Medical School

in 1972, also with honors. She subsequently fulfilled an internship, a medical residency, and a three-year residency in neurology, followed by a one-year fellowship in epilepsy. She then went on to a career as an Air Force neurologist that included service as chief of neurology at three major military hospitals in the United States and abroad. After retiring from the Air Force as a lieutenant colonel, she founded a neurology clinic and a sports center foundation in Mississippi and was also involved with medical missions to Haiti. She was killed in an automobile accident in May 2001. The following year, she was posthumously selected to receive the Alumni Association's Distinguished Alumnus Award in June 2002.

18. Mildred Droste, interview by Elizabeth Merrill, August 24, 2005.
19. William Manchester, *The Glory and the Dream* (New York: Bantam Books, 1973), 1148.
20. Summaries of debates on these and other issues are available in the minutes of faculty meetings on file in Special Collections of Simpson Library.
21. The *Times* article was reprinted in the *Bullet*, September 20, 1971.
22. Pamela Tompkins Huggins, e-mail message to author, June 30, 2007.
23. George Van Sant, interview by author, June 11, 1992.
24. Susan Wagner (Lacy) '70 went on to become the creator and executive producer of *American Masters*, a national public television program that won five Emmys for outstanding documentary, four Peabody Awards, and one Grammy Award, among numerous honors.
25. The complete text of the "Challenges" can be found on the front page of the *Bullet*, December 13, 1968, along with photographs of the protesters entering GW—some wearing slacks—and their confrontation with Simpson.
26. Van Sant interview, June 11, 1992.
27. Ibid.
28. Donna Sheehan Gladis, interview by author and Elizabeth Merrill, August 15, 2005.
29. Huggins e-mail.
30. Gladis interview; Huggins e-mail.
31. Richard M. Nixon, "Address to the Nation on the Situation in Southeast Asia," April 30, 1970.
32. The article, published originally in the South Boston, Va., *Gazette-Virginian*, was reprinted in the *Bullet*, February 16, 1970.
33. The interview was of unprecedented length, taking up three full pages in the paper's November 2, 1970, edition.
34. Bateman, who was later elected to Congress, was awarded an honorary doctorate by Mary Washington after delivering the commencement address to the graduating class of 2000.
35. In 2007 the institution's private foundation allocated $20,000 annually to subsidize a three-year pilot program whereby a facility known as Kids' Station, located near the campus, agreed to take in seventeen children of Mary Washington employees at a 15 percent reduced rate. *Free Lance–Star*, July 23, 2007.
36. Hanna, Rabson, and Clark were all featured speakers in a series on "The Role of Women" at the Fredericksburg Lutheran Church during the fall of 1972. See *Bullet*, September 18, 1972.
37. The burden of the article was not so much an endorsement of any candidate but a more general criticism of the difficulties being faced by Mary Washington

students in their efforts to register locally, especially in light of the recent decision in a Massachusetts court establishing the right of students to vote in their college towns.

38. Fickett also ran for Congress in 1978, unsuccessfully, against the Republican incumbent, Kenneth Robinson. For discussion of Fickett's academic and political career, see William B. Crawley Jr., "Lewis P. Fickett, Jr.: MWC's Scholar-Statesman," *MWC Today* (winter 1997): 2–4.
39. Ray Stevens, "The Streak," Barnaby Records, 1974.
40. Simpson interview.
41. For a sympathetic account of the Simpsons' retirement years, see Teresa A. Kennedy, "Grellet C. Simpson," *MWC Today* (summer 1996): 2–5.
42. Dorothy Simpson, interview by author, March 20, 1991.

3. THE WOODARD ERA, 1974–1982

1. Lewis M. Walker Jr., interview by author, August 18, 1988, transcript, Special Collections, Simpson Library, University of Mary Washington, Fredericksburg, Va.
2. George Van Sant, interview by author, December 2, 2005.
3. This and the following quotations from Anderson come from William M. Anderson Jr., interview by author, October 3, 2005.
4. Walker interview.
5. Van Sant interview, December 2, 2005.
6. Anderson interview, October 3, 2005.
7. The first Mary Washington graduate elected to the state legislature was Linda Todd "Toddy" Puller '67, who in 1991 was chosen to represent the Mount Vernon area of Fairfax County. She was married to Lewis B. Puller Jr., who wrote the Pulitzer Prize–winning *Fortunate Son: The Healing of a Vietnam Vet*. See Lewis P. Fickett Jr., "Toddy Puller '67," *MWC Today* (summer 1992): 6–7.
8. The American Association of University Professors did, in fact, resurrect a chapter on campus in September 1975, with art history professor Barbara Meyer as president.
9. Conrad Warlick, interview by Elizabeth Merrill, July 15, 2005.
10. Ibid.
11. Edward H. Hegmann, interview by author, November 1, 2005.
12. Michael Bass, interview by Elizabeth Merrill, July 13, 2006.
13. Alvey, *History of Mary Washington College*, 468–71. The following discussion of the origins of the graduate program is drawn from Alvey and from Prince B. Woodard, *Mary Washington College: Five Years with the Fifth President, 1974–1979* (Fredericksburg, Va.: Mary Washington College, 1979), 16–19.
14. Donald Glover, interview by Elizabeth Merrill, July 5, 2005.
15. The MBA degree was eventually reinstated when a school of graduate and professional studies was established in 1999. This development is discussed in chapter 4.
16. Woodard, *Mary Washington College*, 35–36.
17. Ibid., 35.
18. Several years later the multitalented Gardner Campbell returned to the College as a member of the English Department and, in addition, was subsequently appointed assistant vice president for teaching and learning technologies.
19. The property consisted of several small interconnected buildings constructed

around 1815 and thereafter, located on part of the half-acre lot purchased by Monroe in 1786; he had his study and law office there from 1786 to 1789. This information and much of the following details regarding the facility are from John Pearce, notes to author, manuscript, Special Collections, Simpson Library, University of Mary Washington, Fredericksburg, Va.

20. A summary of the College's Halloween celebrations is contained in the *Bullet*, October 18, 1983.
21. Cedric Rucker, interview by author, November 1, 2005.
22. The early history of WMWC is described in Alvey, *History of Mary Washington College*, 580–82.
23. Michael Mello, a writer of prodigious capacity and member of the *Bullet* editorial staff, was a major impetus behind the founding of *Prometheus* and for a time wrote for both papers. Eventually, the *Prometheus* board, fearing Mello's divided loyalties, asked him to choose between the two, and he cast his lot with the *Bullet*.
24. Other faculty members who married former students included Delmont Fleming, Stephen Fuller, Edward Hegmann, Neil Howard, Carlton Lutterbie, and Porter Blakemore.
25. The editorial duelists were roommates, and both were later appointed to the Mary Washington Board of Visitors.
26. Hawkens was a widely admired young man who would later die tragically in the crash of his Air Force U-2 reconnaissance plane in England. He stayed with his plane, directing it away from a village rather than parachuting to safety.
27. Steen and Thompson were married in 1987.
28. Woodard, *Mary Washington College*, 30.
29. Anderson interview, October 3, 2005.
30. William M. Anderson Jr., interview by author, October 11, 2005.
31. Named professor of English emeritus and dean emeritus at the time of his 1979 retirement, Croushore died in 1995 at the age of eighty. See Judith Townsend Bainbridge, "James H. Croushore," *MWC Today* (summer 1995): 36.
32. Two years earlier, the first female was appointed to the position of marshal of the faculty: mathematics professor Anna Mae Harris '38. Aside from the highly visible role in leading the academic procession, mace in hand, at commencement and other ceremonial occasions, the marshal is responsible for overseeing all aspects of the graduation program, including preparing the order of march and directing the seniors at rehearsal. According to Harris, the question she was most commonly asked after her appointment was whether she could lift the mace—which was hardly a problem, since the ornate implement, despite its impressive appearance, weighed less than five pounds. She died in August 2007.
33. For discussion of the historical Mary Washington, see "Who WAS Mary Washington," *Bullet*, February 3, 1981; Alice Curtis Desmond, *George Washington's Mother* (New York: Dodd, Mead, 1961); Doris Faber, "The Strangest Mystery: Mary Ball Washington," in *The Presidents' Mothers* (New York: St. Martin's Press, 1978), 196–209; and Donald Culross Peattie, "Grandmother of Her Country," in *Journey into America* (Boston: Houghton Mifflin, 1943), 48–62.
34. This and the quotations that follow are taken from Anderson interview, October 11, 2005.
35. Walker interview.
36. Illustrative of this demeanor was one annual conference between the president

and the author, who was then chair of the History Department. Having been rebuffed in an initial plea for an additional faculty position, the chairperson persisted, only to be brought up short by Woodard's stern interjection: "I've told you we aren't going to do that, Mr. Crawley. Now move on to your next item."

4. THE ANDERSON ERA, 1983–2006

1. Such incidents had virtually been nonexistent at Mary Washington over the years, but ironically one did occur soon after the internal auditor position was established. The scandal involved Frank Mason, then the assistant vice president for business and finance, who in 1993 was accused of embezzlement, and later convicted, whereupon he was fired by the College.
2. Research reports conducted by Southeastern Institute of Research, Inc., of Richmond, Virginia, on which the following account is based, are located in Special Collections of Simpson Library, University of Mary Washington, Fredericksburg, Va.
3. Around the same time, opposition to a prospective name change was expressed by the College's most venerable figure, Dean Emeritus Edward Alvey. The idea, he said, was "the most ridiculous thing I've heard."
4. She would later resign the post owing, some observers believed, to the harsh criticism she received from alumni for taking that stand.
5. The next day's paper carried a letter from the president of the Fredericksburg chapter of NOW assailing the name change and asserting that "to think that the [change] is not a sexist act is indeed naive."
6. This was the same response as that of the board several years earlier when clergyman Paige Young's group had tried to gain a hearing on the visitation policy.
7. Anderson's most extensive published discussion of the name change appears in the fall 1985 issue of *MWC Today*.
8. Since the signatures were secured mainly from shoppers and passersby at the Spotsylvania Mall, it is reasonable to assume that many of them lacked a real understanding of the rationale behind the proposed change, nor did they particularly care.
9. Ray Merchent once commented, "I don't know who came up with that original name, but it didn't make sense. . . . Hell, the Rappahannock runs with mud!"
10. *Lynchburg News and Advance*, December 30, 1994.
11. James Farmer's influential role at the College is discussed in detail later in this chapter.
12. Carol Manning, interview by Elizabeth Merrill, March 8, 2006.
13. Philip Hall, interview by Elizabeth Merrill, December 15, 2005.
14. Samuel T. Emory, interview by author, February 12, 1997.
15. Hall had been elevated to the position of provost.
16. The College also voluntarily discontinued small degree programs in medical technology and speech pathology, both cooperative ventures with the University of Virginia.
17. The debate is discussed later in this chapter.
18. Some years later, Wilkins was forced to resign as speaker as the result of purported sexual improprieties.
19. The original ABC act in 1934 set the legal drinking age (LDA) for all alcoholic beverages at 21. The statute remained unchanged for nearly forty years until in

1972 the LDA for beer was lowered to 18 but remained at 21 for wine and liquor. In 1981 it was raised to 19 for off-premises beer consumption but remained at 18 for on-premises sales. Two years later it was raised to 19 for all sales of beer. In 1985 the law was revised to raise the LDA to 21 incrementally, "grandfathering" persons who could already drink legally under existing regulations. By 1987 no person under 21 could legally purchase or consume alcohol in Virginia.

20. Reportedly, friends who had tried unsuccessfully to awaken him earlier in the day assumed that he was just sleeping, and proceeded to adorn his body with humorous notes to "Chrispy" (his nickname).
21. As part of that program, Goode had attended a mandatory alcohol education film, *One Too Many*, the night before his death. Another part of the program was a campus "mocktail party" that took place just hours before he died.
22. The restaurant, which opened in the early eighties, was owned by and named for geography professor Samuel T. Emory. It was conceived by two Mary Washington students, Sheryl Sullivan and Sarah Sasser, during one of Emory's summer European bike tours. The two graduates (both class of 1980), who had worked at the local Happy Clam restaurant while in college, ran the business initially for Emory and were instrumental in getting it established as a prominent Fredericksburg eatery. Emory interview.
23. The forum debate between the two is covered extensively in a publication called *Blue Tide*, whose first edition (April–May 1993) was devoted solely to that topic. It grew out of an English class on magazine writing taught by English professor (and *Bullet* adviser) Stephen Watkins.
24. A popular local event known as "Ghost Walk," sponsored by the MWC Historic Preservation Club, is discussed later in this chapter.
25. According to one source, Mary Washington had the highest percentage of class ring sales of any college or university in the country. See *Bullet*, March 28, 1996.
26. Among the most frequent victims were the junior RAs in freshman dorms. "It's a way for them [freshmen] to be cool," said one junior. "They want to be involved in the tradition, and then they overdo it."
27. By the late nineties, Mary Washington was reportedly one of only ten colleges and universities nationally that celebrated such an event. See *Bullet*, March 28, 1996.
28. Student volunteer activities before 1990 are summarized in "Making a Difference," *MWC Today* (summer 1990).
29. Merrill chronicled his experience in a series of articles in the *Free Lance–Star* beginning on November 4, 1996. See also his account of Mary Washington's Peace Corps volunteers in *MWC Today* (winter 2002). For Rabson's work in the Marshall Islands, see *Free Lance–Star*, December 31, 1988.
30. For the complete arguments presented by Moeller and Rigsby, see the *Bullet*, January 27 and February 10, 1994, respectively.
31. In 2006 the FDA approved over-the-counter sale of such a drug, known as Plan B, for women over eighteen; anyone younger was still required to have a prescription. "The Year in Medicine from A to Z," *Time* (December 4, 2006): 85.
32. The most visible eruption of this controversy occurred at James Madison University, which was the original target of the legislator's wrath. The JMU Board of Visitors first banned the drug, then relented in the face of outcries from students and alumni.

33. The contract made possible the low cost to students, who could buy a dozen for $1.00, as compared to $11.65 per dozen at People's. By 1992 the Health Center was selling about 2,600 a year.
34. See "Sexual Assault: Why Student Victims Don't Go to Court," *Free Lance–Star*, November 29, 1993.
35. See the *Bullet*, October 19, 1993, for the statement by the unnamed student.
36. *Bullet*, February 10, 1994; *Free Lance–Star*, February 17, 1994.
37. A study done by a sociology class indicated that most students were unaware of the sexual harassment policy and that 88 percent did not know whom to contact with a complaint. *Bullet*, March 23, 1995.
38. *Winchester Star*, May 4, 2000. In 1993 von Guggenberg married Marine Chris Kerr (also HIV-positive), whom she met at an AIDS support group meeting. The couple's daughter, Eva, was born in 2001. *Free Lance–Star*, December 2, 2003.
39. *Washington Post*, October 28, 1993.
40. "STP Update," *Bullet*, March 14, 1989. Once the program was extended beyond the summer session, it became known as the *Student* Transition Program, retaining the designation STP.
41. The event had originated as Negro History Week, scheduled in February because it was the month of Frederick Douglass's birthday (the 14th).
42. Such codes were, in fact, of dubious constitutionality. The previous year (1992) the Supreme Court had ruled against such a regulation in Minnesota.
43. For Jiminez's own detailed account of the affair, see "Minority Faculty Faces Many Obstacles," *Bullet*, April 21, 1994.
44. Stephen Watkins, interview by Elizabeth Merrill, May 4, 2006.
45. The College launched a concerted institution-wide recycling program in 1991.
46. For discussion of the issue at MWC, see "Professors Argue Ethics of Animal Research," *Bullet*, November 3, 1994; and "Suffering in the Name of Science," *Bullet*, November 10, 1994.
47. The line was from Greenwood's popular paean to patriotism, "God Bless the U.S.A."
48. Mark Warner, who would later be elected governor of the commonwealth, was defeated in the senatorial campaign by the longtime incumbent, Republican John Warner.
49. This was a reference to lewd purposes for which President Clinton had used cigars, according to his taped deposition. The televised deposition was watched by an astounding 66 percent of Mary Washington students. *Bullet*, October 1, 1998.
50. Richard S. Reid, "Belmont Publishes Melchers Catalogue," *MWC Today* (winter 1985): 22–23.
51. Amy Satterthwaite, "This Old House," *University of Mary Washington Today* (winter 2006): 11–15.
52. *Richmond News Leader*, April 13, 1991; *Richmond Times-Dispatch*, April 14, 1991.
53. "On an Artist's Trail," *Free Lance–Star*, October 8, 1998.
54. John Pearce, interview by Elizabeth Merrill, June 20, 2006.
55. Muller was the commencement speaker at the 1995 graduation ceremony and subsequently endowed the Judy Mansfield Muller Scholarship in English. See Judy Muller, interview by Elizabeth Merrill, October 12, 2005.
56. The building was designed by the Lukmire Partnership of Arlington and Smith,

Hinchman & Grylls Associates, Inc., of Washington. The landscape design was developed by Higgins Associates, the Richmond firm that had earlier designed Campus Walk.

57. An account of the center's opening is found in a special supplement to the *Free Lance–Star*, October 19, 1998; and in Anna Barron Billingsley, "The Jepson Science Center," *MWC Today* (fall 1998).
58. These developments are described in more detail later in the chapter.
59. The description of the events that follows is based largely on Anderson's interview by the author, December 12, 2005.
60. Some associates noted fondly that his writing with his right hand showed no diminution of penmanship, since his previous left-handed scribbling was only marginally legible anyway.
61. Running for the First District seat vacated by the retiring Herbert Bateman, Davies, a black Baptist minister and longtime civic leader in the Fredericksburg area, was defeated by Republican Jo Ann Davis.
62. A subsequent offering of the class (2003) created quite a commotion when a student, having completed a class assignment on devising a mock attack, inadvertently left a copy on a computer lab printer. Its alarming discovery by another student led to notification of the police and created a brief panic until the plans were proved to be merely part of an academic exercise.
63. A Gallup poll at the time indicated that 90 percent of Americans favored some form of military action.
64. According to Professor Ackermann, the first e-mail message to reach the College was received by him on August 14, 1990, at precisely 08:05:09 a.m. EDT. This information, along with many other details of the early days of computer technology at the College, is contained in Donald Edwards, "We've Come a Long Way," manuscript on file in Special Collections of Simpson Library.
65. Campbell returned to Mary Washington in spring 2007, not in the technology area but as a member of the English, Linguistics, and Speech Department.
66. The requirement was deleted at the end of the 2006–7 academic year after it was determined that entering students were already well versed in these areas.
67. The College had never considered using the property as a parking lot; Robbins's assertion was presumably based on the College's recent construction of a parking lot on nearby William Street.
68. Since the building was financed ($3.2 million) by fees paid by full-time students, part-time students were not allowed to use it; spouses and domestic partners of faculty and staff members, however, were allowed to do so.
69. It was only the second time the policy had been instituted. The other was in 1998 during Hurricane Bonnie, which turned out to be only minimally dangerous.
70. Roy Smith, Mary Rigsby, and Lynn Lewis, "History of TIP: A Brief History of the Teaching Innovation Program (TIP)," University of Mary Washington, http://www.umw.edu/cas/tip/history/default.php (accessed April 10, 2007).
71. Alvey, *History of Mary Washington College*, 286.
72. *Bullet*, September 22, 1994.
73. Mary Washington's policy in that regard was actually more stringent than that at most schools, some of which (e.g., Stanford) allowed withdrawal up until the day of exams.
74. See Jack Bales, "Mary Washington's Undergraduate Research Program," *MWC*

Today (winter 1992): 2–3; William Kemp, "Computer Literacy Comes to MWC," *MWC Today* (fall 1985): 11–12; Anna Barron Billingsley, "Technology in the Classroom," *MWC Today* (winter 2000): 2–6.

75. Philip L. Hall, *MWC Today* (winter 1993): 2–3.
76. See *Bullet*, March 1, 2007, B1–B7; Chris Musick, interview by Elizabeth Merrill, August 1, 2006.
77. See Joseph Di Bella, interview by Elizabeth Merrill, August 21, 2006; Joseph Dreiss, interview by Elizabeth Merrill, July 21, 2006; Thomas Somma, interview by Elizabeth Merrill, August 16, 2006.
78. *MWC Today* (winter 1996): 7–9.
79. The art program suffered a significant loss when Somma died in May 2007. His friend Bulent Atalay memorialized him as "gracious, generous, and boundlessly loyal" and noted that "his style was always collaborative, supportive, and imaginative, . . . always striving to make sure people around him . . . received the lion's share of the credit."
80. See Michael Bass, interview by Elizabeth Merrill, July 13, 2006; Stephen Fuller, interview by Elizabeth Merrill, June 28, 2006.
81. See "Graduates in Chemistry Careers," *MWC Today* (fall 1985): 13–15.
82. From 1955 to 1977, Van Sant spent every summer on Marine reserve duty. At the age of sixty-three, he volunteered for the Gulf War, but the conflict ended before he could be called to duty. For a survey of Van Sant's colorful career, see Michael Zitz, "The Tie That Binds," *Free Lance–Star*, January 22, 2005.
83. In addition to Van Sant, members of the club included faculty leaders such as Michael Houston, James Croushore, Albert Klein, Daniel Woodward, Peter Coffin, Charles Sletten, Lawrence Wishner, Lewis Fickett, and Joseph Vance.
84. In 2004, Arabic was instituted as a regular course offering in the Department of Modern Foreign Languages.
85. Edwards, "We've Come a Long Way."
86. Also a full-time member of the department from 1994 to 2004 was Rita D'Arcangelis; following her retirement as associate professor, she continued to teach on an adjunct basis after 2004.
87. Ernest Ackermann, interview by Elizabeth Merrill, June 30, 2006.
88. The influence of those two extended beyond their departure as faculty members. Clatanoff's wife, Katherine (MWC '72), taught for some years as a member of the economics faculty. Albertine returned as executive-in-residence in 2002, and his wife, Mona, (MWC '71), was a member of the Board of Visitors and served as rector during 2004–6.
89. Ackermann interview.
90. The department also experienced several notable controversies involving members of its faculty. One was the case of Anthony Jiminez, whose dismissal resulted in a bitter legal dispute (discussed earlier). Another contentious episode involved termination of Professor Shah Mehrabi, who, while serving as department chair, was accused of falsifying his academic credentials. See *Bullet*, September 1, 1992.
91. Brenda Vogel, interview by Elizabeth Merrill, July 17, 2006.
92. Paul Slayton, "Mystory: The Autobiography of Paul C. Slayton Jr." (unpublished manuscript, Special Collections, Simpson Library, University of Mary Washington, Fredericksburg, Va., 2002).
93. A major expansion of the education program came with the opening of the

James Monroe Center (later named the College of Graduate and Professional Studies) in 1999. This development is discussed later in the chapter.

94. Much of the following discussion is based on interviews by Elizabeth Merrill with current or former members of the department, including Daniel Dervin, June 22, 2005; Claudia Emerson, August 31, 2006; Jane Gatewood, March 16, 2006; Donald Glover, July 5, 2005; Teresa Kennedy, September 1, 2005; Carol Manning, March 8, 2006; Anand Rao, March 15, 2006; Stephen Watkins, May 4, 2006; and Esther Yook, March 21, 2006.
95. Nancy Mitchell also served for a number of years as an assistant academic dean. See George Van Sant, "No Time for Hammocks," *MWC Today* (winter 1988): 6–7.
96. Susan J. Hanna, "Donald E. Glover: A Life of Constant Exploration," *MWC Today* (summer 1993): 2–4.
97. Richard Hansen, interview by Elizabeth Merrill, July 5, 2005.
98. Richard Hansen, "A Tribute to Carlton R. Lutterbie Jr.," *MWC Today* (summer 1989): 32.
99. This quotation and the previous one are from an article by columnist Rob Hedelt in the *Free Lance–Star*, April 16, 1994.
100. That accomplishment was all the more remarkable for the department in light of the fact that in the two decades since the award was established in 1986, only one other Mary Washington professor received it: physics professor George King.
101. For a summary of Watkins's views on various issues, see his first column, "Raising a Liberal Voice: Here's a Quick Glimpse of What I Believe," *Free Lance–Star*, November 1, 1998.
102. The reference is to a fictional martial arts master popularized in the film *Kill Bill: Vol. 2* (2004).
103. McConnell retorted with amusement that the description was inaccurate but that Limbaugh would probably have been "just as horrified by the real Bob McConnell." For a discussion of McConnell's environmental views, see his interview in the *Free Lance–Star*, December 17, 1993.
104. William B. Crawley Jr., "Geography at MWC: 'They're Doing Something Right,' " *MWC Today* (summer 1988): 8–10.
105. Actually both men were of approximately average height. Emory interview.
106. Morton also used his stature at the College to promote issues other than preservation. Concerned about date rape on campus, for example, he participated in seminars on the topic and in 1991 persuaded the men's rugby team—paragons of masculinity—to wear T-shirts bearing the slogan "At MWC, Rape Is a Four-Letter Word."
107. See William B. Crawley Jr., "Roger Bourdon: Trials and Triumph," *MWC Today* (winter 1989): 2–4.
108. In his memory, the College established both a scholarship fund and a faculty position and erected a bronze bust beside Campus Walk opposite Trinkle Hall.
109. Alvey, *History of Mary Washington College*, 198.
110. Janet Gardner Zeleznock, "History of the Department of Mathematics at Mary Washington College, 1911–1987" (unpublished manuscript, Special Collections, Simpson Library, University of Mary Washington, Fredericksburg, Va.)
111. As it turned out, the houses were never used for this purpose but were converted to various administrative offices.

112. Martha V. Fickett, "The Making of a Musical Entrepreneur," *MWC Today* (summer 2002): 7–9.
113. Kevin P. Bartram, "One Singular Sensation," *MWC Today* (summer 2004): 7–8.
114. "Orchestra Wows European Audiences," *Friends of the Orchestra* (July 2006): 4.
115. George King III to William Crawley Jr., January 10, 2007.
116. Bulent Atalay, interview by Elizabeth Merrill, March 1, 2007.
117. Gregory McNamee, "Renaissance Men," *University of Mary Washington Today* (winter 2005): 14–15; *Free Lance–Star*, February 20, 2004.
118. John M. Kramer, interview by Elizabeth Merrill, June 27, 2006.
119. The career of psychology professor J. Christopher "Topher" Bill is discussed later in the chapter.
120. Margaret Huber, interview by Elizabeth Merrill, April 26, 2006.
121. Though such personnel matters were normally deemed confidential, the episodes were discussed in the *Bullet*, February 10, 1994, and September 22, 2002, and in the *Free Lance–Star*, February 17, 1994.
122. Gregg Stull, interview by Elizabeth Merrill, December 9, 2005; Helen M. Housley, "Rosemary Ingham," *MWC Today* (summer 2001): 2–3.
123. Stull's involvement with the Quilt is discussed earlier in the chapter. Also see Antoinette Parker, "MWC Professor Shines as Part of International Project," *MWC Today* (summer 2001): 4.
124. The College of Graduate and Professional Studies had its own library on its Stafford campus designed to meet the needs of the school's adult clientele. The following discussion focuses on developments at Simpson Library on the Fredericksburg campus.
125. Bob Grattan, "Transformed by Technology," *MWC Today* (fall 1999): 6–7. VIRTUA was a product of VTLS, Inc., of Blacksburg, Virginia.
126. Still, by 2007, more than 165,000 people entered Simpson Library's doors each year.
127. All copies of *News and Views*, as well as publications sponsored by the Trinkle Associates, are housed in Special Collections of Simpson Library.
128. LeRoy Strohl, interview by Elizabeth Merrill, May 10, 2006.
129. Bill Lohmann, "His Friend Willie," *Richmond Times-Dispatch*, April 23, 2000; William B. Crawley Jr., "Jack Bales: Beyond the Reference Desk," *MWC Today* (winter 2003): 2–4.
130. John N. Berry III, "Beth Perkins," *Library Journal*, March 15, 2000, 40–42.
131. With the opening of the College of Graduate and Professional Studies, the University's library functions expanded to include that campus as well. The CGPS collection specialized in books, periodicals, and electronic resources in the fields of business and education, including a children's literature collection containing both fiction and nonfiction works. A career collection was also available for those seeking information on résumé writing, job interviews, and career advancement.
132. Initial funding from the College was augmented by generous grants from American Honda, Brunswick Corporation, and the Jessie Ball duPont Fund.
133. J. Suzanne Horsley, "Lynda Richardson," *MWC Today* (fall 1997): 2–4. Subsequent DGIRs included Linda "Toddy" Todd Puller '67, Frances Cook '67, Lynn Munroe Bragg '76, Marion Blakey '70, William H. Leighty '78, Ann Bigley Robertson '74, Christine Uber Grosse '73, and Daniel R. Wolfe '84.

134. The event came under particular scrutiny after a 100th Night car accident in 1997 (discussed later) caused increased concern about liability issues.

135. *Fredericksburg Free Press*, November 1996.

136. Bill Hewitt, "Thrill Killers?" *People Weekly*, June 9, 2003, 119. Benjamin Sifrit, tried separately from his wife, was convicted of only one of the murders and received a sentence of thirty-eight years in prison.

137. Alsop was an African American who handled numerous maintenance jobs and, in addition, donned a special resplendent uniform to serve on occasion as the doorman at George Washington Hall. (He is pictured on the mural in the hallway of GW.) Alsop is appreciatively described in Alvey's history as "a man of inherent dignity [who] was extremely polite, but never servile." Alvey, *History of Mary Washington College*, 109–10.

138. Susan Scott Neal, "The Unforgettable Mrs. A," *Free Lance–Star*, April 7, 2007, 8–12.

139. Statistics compiled by psychology professor Roy Smith indicated that, while the percentage of students who consumed alcohol stayed relatively constant between 1980 (77 percent) and 1992 (75 percent), the proportion who engaged in binge drinking had more than doubled (from 16 percent to 35 percent) during that time.

140. *Time*, April 16, 1990, 62. At Mary Washington a 1988 survey found 51 percent of the respondents opposed to establishing a Greek system on campus, 37 percent in favor.

141. Some of the most popular entertainment programs on campus were the "step shows," often held during Black History Month, that featured competition among black fraternities from other schools. See, e.g., *Bullet*, February 29, 1996.

142 See, e.g., *Bullet*, April 21, 2005.

143. One president-elect of the Student Government Association was also convicted around the same time for stealing residence hall funds.

144. See *Bullet*, November 5 and November 8, 1998.

145. Timothy M. O'Donnell, "Debate at Mary Washington College," *MWC Today* (winter 2004): 6–7. See also Alvey, *History of Mary Washington College*, 585–87.

146. Intercollegiate debate contests were divided into three categories: varsity, for experienced collegiate debaters; junior varsity, for students with at least one year of experience; and novice, for students with little or no prior collegiate experience. Unlike intercollegiate athletics, debate had no divisions based on size of enrollment.

147. *MWC Today* (summer 2004): 14.

148. The amount of increase was based on a comparison of Mary Washington's total compensation with that paid by neighboring Stafford County to its workers in comparable jobs.

149. For accounts of the band's development and Scott's role in it, see *Bullet*, December 12, 1997; *Free Lance–Star*, May 23, 1998; and Raymond Scott, interview by Elizabeth Merrill, June 20, 2006.

150. Alvey, *History of Mary Washington College*, 602.

151. Although no copies of the *Bullet* between 1923 and 1927 have survived, *The Battlefield* from those same years contains photographs and information on the *Bullet* staff.

152. Watkins once estimated that of the forty to fifty *Bullet* staff members in any given semester, thirty-five of them were in his journalism practicum. Watkins interview.
153. Ibid.
154. The column is discussed in more detail later in the chapter.
155. According to one estimate, over 60 percent of college dorms nationwide were coed by 2005. *Free Lance–Star*, October, 10, 2005.
156. Leon R. Kass, "The End of Courtship," *Public Interest*, no. 126 (winter 1997): 39–63.
157. Elz England, interview by author and Elizabeth Merrill, April 9, 2007.
158. Johnson went on to a successful singing career, being featured in a national tour of *Godspell* and making her Broadway debut in April 2007 in the musical *Legally Blonde*.
159. *The Connection* (Oakton–Vienna, Va.), May 28, 1997.
160. The protesters were skewered by the acerbic local writer Florence King in an op-ed piece in the *Free Lance–Star*, February 26, 2000, that ridiculed in particular the use of the word "placelessness."
161. What the editorial did not make clear was that the apparent discriminations were self-imposed, as the rugby outfit did not want to conform to the regulations imposed on varsity sports (especially the rules concerning alcohol).
162. Although the gift was made anonymously, it eventually became known that the benefactor was the newspaperman Josiah P. Rowe III, onetime mayor of Fredericksburg and a member of one of the city's most prominent families. An avid tennis player, he was still ranked among the area's top players well into his seventies.
163. The only gap in that span came in 2000 when, for health reasons, Sheridan stepped down during the season and was replaced by an assistant coach, Josh Mosser, a Mary Washington alumnus and former member of the team. Sheridan returned to full-time coaching the following year.
164. Mejia returned to Mary Washington in 1997 as an administrator in the admissions office.
165. The early years of the crew program are described in an article by Sarah Coyle Mulligan in *MWC Today* (fall 1985): 22.
166. The purpose of the Web site, which was not affiliated with the NCAA, was, according to a spokesman, to push for stricter anti-hazing rules in college sports. The site had apparently obtained the pictures from online postings by Mary Washington students themselves.
167. Survey results are summarized in the *Free Lance–Star*, May 20, 1993.
168. Once the center's MBA went into operation, the classes previously offered via satellite from Virginia Tech were phased out.
169. In his remarks, Williams announced the gift of an additional seventy-five acres from the county to the College for future expansion of the James Monroe Center.
170. Martin Wilder, interview by author, October 28, 2005.
171. Don Del Rosso, "Class Act," *Fauquier (Va.) Citizen*, May 12, 2006.

5. THE FRAWLEY ERA, 2006–2007

1. *University of Mary Washington Today* (winter 2007): 2–6.
2. On the popularity of such publications on university campuses, see Alexandra Jacobs, "Campus Exposure," *New York Times Magazine*, March 4, 2007, 44–49.
3. Erica Mason, "Hero in Honduras," *University of Mary Washington Today* (spring 2007): 12–17.
4. The opening of the store, planned for fall 2007, was canceled when a state-mandated reduction of approximately $2.3 million in the University's operating budget in September of that year made the venture unfeasible.
5. TRIO was a federal outreach program that incorporated three agencies designed to motivate and support students from disadvantaged backgrounds including low-income, disabled, and first-generation college students.
6. The institution's reasons for that decision are explained in an op-ed piece by Vice President Richard Hurley, *Free Lance–Star*, October 24, 2006.
7. The reference is to a popular film, *Lemony Snicket's A Series of Unfortunate Events* (2004), starring Jim Carrey.
8. In May 2008 the smokestack was reduced by almost two-thirds (i.e., below the lettering) because of strain on its metal supporting bands. The extra height was no longer needed, as the heating system had long since been switched from coal to natural gas, allowing environmental standards to be met with a ninety-foot stack. Its demise marked the end for one of the institution's (and region's) most visible and venerable landmarks.

EPILOGUE: THE CENTENNIAL YEAR, 2007–8

1. Apparently Frawley's problems were more extensive than anyone (probably including him) had initially known. In reporting his 2008 arrest, the *Free Lance-Star* revealed that on April 28 the Montgomery County District Court granted his wife, Maria, a one-year restraining order barring him from any contact with his family. *Free-Lance Star*, April 30, 2008.
2. None of the costs were to be paid from state funds or student fees, but from revenue generated by the enterprise itself.
3. For a profile of Hample, see Lisa Chinn, "Hample at the Helm," *University of Mary Washington Today* (summer 2008): 22–27.
4. Hurley, along with his wife, was further honored by the establishment of the Richard V. and Rosemary A. Hurley Presidential Commendation, an award to be given annually to a UMW employee who "performs exceptionally meritorious service while demonstrating strength of character and steadfast dedication to the University's mission." The award was created by an endowment established through a gift from Elmer R. Morris Jr. and his wife, Marceline "Marcy" Weatherly Morris, both members of the class of 1950.

INDEX

Note: Page numbers of illustrations are in boldface

Abel, Daniel, 493
Abernathy, Ralph, 616
abortion
  Bullet and, 142, 145, 147–48
  Carroll art piece on, 325–28
  Roe v. Wade, 152
  symposium and forum, 468–70
academic accountability, 401–3
Academic Advising Office, 162
Academic Affairs Committee, 401, 567
academic freedom, 123, 139, 288–89, 291, 408
academic quality
  of applicants, 283, 519–20, 651 (*see also* SAT scores)
  improved under Simpson, 76–77, 85, 89–90, 91, 121, 167–68
academic reforms
  Anderson era *(1983–2006)*, 112, 385–403, 407–8, 565–71
  Frawley era *(2006–7)*, 799–800
  Simpson era *(1955–74)*, 109–13
  technological innovations, 536–39
  Woodard era *(1974–82)*, 200–210, 286–89, 308, 315
  See also graduation requirements; *and specific issues, such as* grading
Accounting Club, 691
accreditation. *See* Southern Association of Colleges and Secondary Schools
Ackerman, Ernest, 535, 536, 587, 588, 621, 851(n64)
ACLU (American Civil Liberties Union), 151, 681
Acors, Ray, 525
The Action of the City of Fredericksburg in Relation to the Location of the Proposed State Normal School, 1–2
activism, student. *See* student activism; student protests
Adams, Theodore F., 74
Adamson, Rebecca, 663
Adegbalola, Gaye (Todd), 99, 269
Adenan, Abas, 362, 653, 680, 840
Adera, Taddesse, 367, 562, 594–95, **595**, 853(n100)
Ad Hoc Committee on Academic Regulations and Advising, 288–89
Ad Hoc Committee on Alcohol, 414
Ad Hoc Committee on Degree requirements and College Calendar, 110
administrative staff
  Anderson era *(1983–2006)*, 298, 333–39
  Frawley era *(2006-7)*, 787
  Hurley administration, 822
  Simpson era *(1955–74)*, 74–75
  Woodard era *(1974–82)*, 212–13, 284–86
  See also specific positions and individuals
Admissions Club, 362
admissions office
  African American recruitment, 102, 367–68, 652–54 (*see also* recruitment: of minority students)
  Anderson era *(1983–2006)*, 361–63, 520, 650–54
  and coeducation, 194–95
  early decision program, 650–51
  Simpson era *(1955–74)*, 75 (*see also* Houston, Michael; Merchent, A. R. "Ray")
  staff diversity, 653
  Woodard era *(1974–82)*, 194–95
  See also applicants and applications; recruitment; *specific staff members*
admission standards, 7, 54, 85, 195. *See also* applicants and applications
advising, academic, 80–81, 162, 566–67, 793
advisors. *See* advising, academic; *and specific departments and individuals*
affirmative action, 290, 484, 490–92
African American faculty, 101, 103, 289–90, 486–87, 489–91, 561–62. *See also* minority faculty
African American students
  1960s–70s, 98–108, 121, 283, 660–61
  1980s–90s, 365–68, 482–91
  2000s, 654, 664–66, 800

African American students (*continued*)
and fraternities/sororities, 683, 855(n141)
and the Multicultural Center, 664–66
recruitment, 100, 102, 121, 283, 365–68, 482–83, 652–54
student groups, 683, 694 (*see also* Afro-American Association; Black Student Association (BSA); BOND; Women of Color)
African American studies, 106, 289–90
Afro-American Association, 106, 107–8, 252–53, 269–70, 438
agricultural curriculum, 10
AIDS, 430–31, 462, 479–82
air raids, fear of, 47
Akers, Paul, 810–11
Albertine, John M. "Jack," 250, 509, 588, 703, 852(n88)
Albertine, Mona Davis
and the 2005–6 presidential search, 781, 783
on Anderson, 780
Board term, 840, 852(n88)
at Frawley's inauguration, 790
marriage, 268 (*see also* Albertine, John M.)
and the name of the college/university, 775, 778
Rector position held, 333
as student, 108–9
UMW flag raised, P14
alcohol
alcohol-abuse education, 410, 412–13, 418, 677–78, 849(n21)
Anderson era (1983–2006), 410–24, 675–79
automobile accident, 675–76
beer guide, 678–79
drinking habits, 410–11, 421–22, 424, 676–77, 678, 855(n139)
Frawley's arrests, 803–9
during heavy snowfalls, 724–25
and Junior Ring Dance, 450–51
keg parties, 164, 244–48, **247**, 409, 413, 415–16, 418–19, 675–76
legal drinking age, 245, 248, 410–11, 419, 421, 424, 848–49(n19)
popularity, 164, 446–47, 675–76
rules and policies, 123–24, 131, 245, 410–16, 418–19, 423–24
senior parties and, 446–47, 657, 675–76
student arrests, 421–23, 677–78, 684
student death from, 417–18, 677, 849(nn20–21)
Alcohol Education and Awareness Committee, 410
Alden, Barbara, 171, 382
Alden International Scholarship, 801
Alderman, Edwin A., 39
Alderson, Linda Huff, 509
Alderson, Sandy, 509
Alinsky, Saul, 159
All-College Day, 110
Allen, Angelia, 361, 653
Allen, George, 380, 405
Allen, Philip, 620, 639
Alley, Marta, 813
All-Girl Marching Band, **35**, 35–36
Alliance (alternative newspaper), 707–8
Allison, Edward V., Jr., 74, 161, 336
Allman's Bar-B-Q, 157, 330
alma mater (college song), 1, 62, 770, 791, 814, 831
orchestral arrangement, 832–33
Alpha Phi Omega, 684
Alsop, Wallace, 669, 855(n137)
Alstetter, Michael Louis, 34
Alternate Spring Break program, 461–62, 464
Al-Tikriti, Nabil, 617
Altscher, Aaron, 732
alumni (alumnae)
art exhibitions, 325–28, 828
coeducation opposed by, 95
fall homecoming, 656
financial giving by, 213–14, 352, 375–76, 380–81, 657–59
and the merger with U. Va., 96–97
and the name of the institution, 346, 349, 352–53, 356, 765, 780
recruitment by, 361–62
Reunion Weekend, 656
and the Trench Hill conversion, 546 (*see also* Jepson Alumni Executive Center)
See also Alumni (Alumnae) Association; *and specific individuals*
Alumni (Alumnae) Association
alma mater change endorsed, 62
Anderson congratulated on inauguration, 331
annual fund, 380, 381
board of directors restructured, 656
Diamond Jubilee homecoming, 312
Distinguished Alumnus Award, 382, 636, 845(n17)
Distinguished Visitor [Graduate] in Residence program, 159–60, 504, 656
e-mail directory, 656
faculty award (*see* Outstanding Young Faculty Member Award)
headquarters, 57
and the merger with U. Va., 96–97
name changed, 844(n3)
and the name of the college, 346
Outstanding Young Alumnus Award, 362, 617
scholarships, 657, 801
Senior Toast, 657
Weinbrecht and, 75

Young Alumnus Merit Award, 636
Alumni Executive Center. *See* Jepson Alumni Executive Center
alumni magazine. See *MWC Today*; *UMW Today*
Alvey, Edward, Jr., **34**, **P2**
on *Aubade*, 704
awards and honors, xi, 835
bond with Simpson, 74–75
on Bushnell, 65
on campus organizations, 14
on H. Carter, 620
on chapel and convocation, 37
on Combs' funding request, 31
on the cornerstone-laying ceremony, 6
death, xi
on faculty resignations *(1919)*, 18
on the first year of UMW, 9
on M. Forbes, 12
freshman reception described, 60–61
on German Club dances, 27
on Goolrick's role in establishing MWC, 3
hired, 34–35
History of Mary Washington College, x
interdepartmental majors suggested, 59
legacy, x–xi
on the location of MWC, 5
on major-counseling night, 80
on male summer school students, 63
and the name change, 42, 848(n3)
name withdrawn from consideration for president, 71
on the need for a new library, 52
1938 General Assembly visit remembered, 330
on pre-Christmas festivities, 37
on recreational activities, 13
responsibility for student-faculty relations and curriculum, 68
ring presentation ceremony, 164
roof garden parties described, 24
on Russell's enthusiasm, 4
on the Simpson inaugural events, 73
on the Spanish fiestas, 51
"Spanish Visions of the Jamestown Settlement," 647
on student dress for garden work, 10
and the "summer school in Spain" program, 79
on the waitress uniform disagreement, 67
and World War II, 49
Alvey Hall, 375, 797, **P8**
Alvey Scholars program, 657
Ambuel, David, 586, 836
American Association of Teachers Colleges, 30
American Civil Liberties Union (ACLU), 151, 681
American history requirement (proposed), 565–66
American Idol, 731–32
American Liberty Upside Down (Carroll artwork), 325–28
The American Presidents (C-SPAN series), 515
American Sign Language (ASL), 564–65
American Studies program, 59–60, 112–13, 294, 617–18, 620
Aminrazavi, Mehdi
on American Muslims after 9/11, 531
and Asian and Middle Eastern studies, 586
awards, 584, 836, 838
on Islamic Awareness Week, 795
Islamic photographs exhibit, 573
Ammon, Harry, 516
Amnesty International, 502, 506
amphitheater, 22–23, **23**, 138, 555–57, 843(n10)
Anarchist Social Theory Club, 694, 826
Andersen, Amy, 787
Anderson, Barbara, 470
Anderson, Bill (son of W. Anderson), **319**, 319, 320
Anderson, Carrie, 703
Anderson, Harper (daughter of W. Anderson), **319**, 319, 320
Anderson, Jane Neale (wife of W. Anderson), 319, **319**, 320, 521, 546, 779, 784, 785
Anderson, Karen, 349–50, 356
Anderson, Leroy, 628
Anderson, Mason (daughter of W. Anderson), **319**, 319, 320
Anderson, William M., Jr. "Bill," **317**, **521**, **P2**
as acting president, 1, 303–4
agenda for MWC, 331–33, 339–40, 354
and alcohol policies, 414
aneurysm, 521
appointed VP for development and management information systems, 212–13
and the athletic program, 741, **744**, 749, 755–56
background and qualifications, 213, 316–19, 378
with Buffett, **P11**
and *The Bullet*, 704
and the Bushnell fire, 276
and the campanile, 778–79, 813
on V. Campbell, 334
and Campus Walk projects, 551–52
and the centennial celebration, 778, 779
on citizenship, 566
commencement ceremonies, 460, 526–27, **527**

Anderson, William M., Jr. "Bill," *(continued)*
Committee on College Affairs chaired, 300, 302
and community involvement, 508, 510, 517
on computerized registration, 284
on the dance department, 403
and the Debate Club, 691
departmental reorganization, 640
on J. Donovan, 458
and dorm visitation rules, 320–24
on drug testing, 674
and Emory, 604, 853(n105)
era *(1983–2006)*, 311–785, **P6–9** (*see also specific topics and events*)
expansion issue addressed, 824
faculty discontent with, 406
family, **319**, 319–20, 333 (*see also* Anderson, Jane Neale)
on Fickett, 632
and finances, 330, 378–80, 406 (*see also* finances of MWC/UMW: Anderson era)
Fredericksburg Forum developed, 517
and fund-raising, 213, 382–85, 519, 546–47, 658–59, 778
and the global initiative, 570
and graduate studies at MWC, 759, 760, 761
health, 520–29, 779, 851(n60)
honorary doctorate received, 835
and the honor system, 690
and the human rights professorship, 618
and Hurley, 822
inauguration, 330–33, **332**, 647, **P1**
and international studies, 391
on the "Intolerance and Toleration" conference, 584–85
and the Jepsons, 383–84, 519, 546–47, **P4**, **P10**
and JMC (satellite campus), 759, 760, 761
and Junior Ring Week pranks, 452, 454
language houses phased out, 622–23
and lawsuits, 328, 474–75
and the Leonardo da Vinci exhibition, 573
and the "living wage" campaign, 697, 698
and the Marye's Heights apartments, 544
and the mascot and colors, 360
and minority enrollment, 482
and the Monroe Museum, 514
and the Multicultural Center, 666
on MWC's reputation, 364, 422
named president, 316–18
and the name of the college/university, 300, 340–41, 343–44, 350–51, 353–56, 654, 765–66, 770–75
personality, 316–18, 378
at the Phi Beta Kappa reception, 550
and the pipe band, 698, 699
presidency evaluated, 780
president's office under, 333–34
and racial tensions, 487–89
on recruitment and selectivity, 340
and the research program, 630
retirement, 778–80, 783–85, **784**
and the ROTC proposal, 329
and Rountree, 655–56, 659
salary, 697
search for dean of student activities, 285
and student drinking, 417, 419
students' relationship with, 317, 408, 655–56, 780
and the telecommunications network, 376
and the Travel Club tours, 658–59
and the Trench Hill complex, 546–47
and university status, 764, 766–67, **P14**
and volunteerism, 460
Watkins on, 597
and the Wo-Man Contest, 441–42
on Woodard, 178–79, 258, 302–5, 307
Woodard contrasted with, 317–18
and the writing center, 388
See also Student Association
Anderson Distinguished Chair in Biology, 785, 836
Andrews, Alice. *See* Jepson, Alice Andrews and Robert S., Jr.
Andrews, Hunter B., 378, 835
Andrews, Robert, 337
Angel, Rhonda, 418, 424, 474
Animal House (movie), 247
animal rights, 496–99
Animal Rights Club, 497–99, 826
Ankney, David, 667
Ann Carter Lee Hall. *See* Lee Hall
Anne Fairfax House, 33, 622
annual (yearbook). See *The Battlefield*
apartheid, 500–501
Appiarius, Don, 415
Applebury, Deena, 751, 754, 828

applicants and applications
1979–80, 299–300
1980s, 340, 361–63
2000s, 769
academic quality, 7, 54, 283, 519–20, 651 (*see also subhead* SAT scores)
college visits, 362–63
declining numbers (*1970s*), 192
early decision program, 650–51
honors admission, 651
male applicants, 195, 283 (*see also* male students)
minority applicants, 283, 482–83 (*see also* African American students)
and the MWC name / image, 299–302, 339–43, 355, 767–68 (*see also* name of the college / university)
SAT scores, 85, 192, 195, 283, 363, 365, 520, 651, 749, 769
selectivity, 192, 340, 355, 365, 520, 767–68
student qualifications, 85, 297, 363, 365
See also enrollment; recruitment
ARA (food service provider), 255–56, 276, 286, 459, 549
Arabic language, 565, 586, 852(n84)
films, 623
Archibald, Rennie, **93**, 94–95
Armstrong, Ethel, 755
Armstrong, Frances Liebenow "Mrs. A," 572, 670–71
Army Blues Jazz Band, 330
Arrington, Arabelle Laws, 281, 380, 659, 785, 835, 840, **P5**
Arrington Distinguished Chair in Poetry, 598, 837
Arrington Hall, 375, 797, **P8**
Arrington Scholarship program, 659
Art and Art History Department
and *Aubade*, 704
Carroll painting controversy, 325–28
collection and galleries, 572–73, 574 (*see also* Phyllis Ridderhof Martin Gallery)
Emil Schnellock Award, 44
exhibitions, 72, 325–27, 572–75 (*see also specific exhibitions*)
faculty, 188, 571 (*see also specific individuals*)
history, 294, 571–75
majors offered, 78
See also duPont Hall
art history. *See* Art and Art History Department
Art's bar, 158, 420
Ascari, Clavio F., 207, 571, 623, 624, 658, 837
Ashby, Claiborne, 313
Ashby, O'Conor Goolrick, 831
Ashrawi, Hanan, 585
Asian studies
Leidecker and, 58, 78, 79, 585–86
Leidecker Chair, 384, 836
summer program, 79
ASL (American Sign Language), 564–65
Atalay, Bulent I. "Bill," 573, 629–32, 790, 837, 852(n79), **P3**
Athletic Association, 33
athletic facilities
Battleground complex, 215, 742–43
Dickinson Stadium, 743, **744**
fitness center, 545–46, 735, 851(n68)
in Monroe Hall, 6, 15, 24, 216
outdoor facilities, 199–200, 214–15
See also Goolrick Hall
Athletic Hall of Fame, 755–56
athletic program / department, 734–57
2006–7 season, 791
athletes' academic performance, 756
athletes and alcohol, 422–24, 752–53, 856(n161)
club sports, 736–41
faculty and staff, 742–51, 808–9 (*see also specific individuals*)
gender balance, 197, 756
intercollegiate varsity program, 741–57, **P16**
intramural sports program, 467–68, 735–36
men's program developed, 195–98, 308
outdoor facilities, 199–200, 214–15, 742, 743
recognition of outstanding athletes, 754–57
Russell era (*1911–20*), 14–16
school colors and mascot, 358–61
Simpson era (*1955–74*), 160–61, 169
Woodard era (*1974–82*), 195–200, 215, 308, 741
See also Physical Education Department; physical education requirement; *and specific sports*
attendance, 109, 288–89
Atwell-Vasey, Wendy, **P12**
Aubade, xii, 593, 703–4
audiovisual center (AV center), 254–55
auditor, internal, 334
auditoria (auditoriums)
in GW Hall, 43, 215 (*see also* Dodd Auditorium)
in Monroe Hall, 25, 37, 216
automobiles. *See* car policies; parking
AV (audiovisual) center, 254–55
awards
Bill Service Award, 639, 839 (*see also specific recipients*)

awards *(continued)*
CGPS award, 833
Charles Coleman Award, 554
Citizen Salute Award, 832
Darden Award, 59, 283, 554, 581, 629, 833
debate awards, 692
Distinguished Alumnus Award, 382, 636, 845(n17)
Jean Donovan award, 458
Outstanding Young Alumnus Award, 362, 617
Outstanding Young Faculty Member Award, 382, **630**, 838 (*see also specific recipients*)
Pinschmidt Award, 575, 838–39 (*see also specific recipients*)
SCHEV state teacher awards, 595
Schnellock Award, 44
Simpson Award for Excellence in Undergraduate Teaching, 170–71, 837–38 (*see also specific recipients*)
Washington Medal/Medallion, 335, 763, 833
Young Alumnus Merit Award, 636
AWARE (Advocating Wellness and Responding to Emergencies), 678
Ayersman, David, 537

BACCHUS, 413, 446
bachelor's degrees
bachelor of arts (B.A.), 40–41, 55, 111
bachelor of liberal studies (BLS), 201–3, 315, 614
bachelor of professional studies (BPS), 762–63
bachelor of science (BS), 22, 40, 55, 111
See also degree requirements
Baer, Karen, 465
bagpipe band. *See* Eagle Pipe Band
Bailey, Carla, 649
Bailey, Gene, 759
Baker, Brian, 762
Baker, Erma, 796
Baker, Houston, 585
Baker, James E., 223–25, **225**, 312, 626–28, 832, 836
Baldacci, David, 658
Bales, Jack, **649**, 649–50, 810
Baliles, Gerald L., 328, 330, 835
Ball, George E., 213
Ballard, Robert, 519
Ball Circle, 32–33, **165**, 165–66, 182, 218, 240. 271–72, 531, 724, 725, 726, **P13**
Ball Hall, 32–33, 79, 221–22, 244, 375, 723
Balthis, Charles, 648
bands, student, 720
Baptist Student Union, 459, 463, 694
Barr, Robert, 635
Barra, Rosemary, 576, **576**
awards and honors, 576, 785, 836, 838
at commencement *2007*, 814
and the General Education Review Committee, 800
Jepson Science Center groundbreaking, **P10**
as marshal of the faculty, 576, 589
named interim dean, 576
position under Frawley, 787
Barton, Clara, 57
Barton, Matheson, Willse, & Worthington (BMW&W), 773, 775–76
Bartram, Kevin, 628–29
baseball, 742, 743–44
basketball
men's team, 160–61, 196–98, 748–50, 755
Monroe Hall court, 6
women's team, 15–16, 198, 751–54, 755, 791, 797–98, 828
women's tournament broadcast, 254
Baslyk, Valentina, 622
Bass, Michael, 204, 498, 575–76, 602
Batchelder, Norma, 563
Bateman, Herbert H., 146, 835, 845(n34)
Bateman Resolution, 238
The Battlefield (yearbook)
1942, 47
on first basketball trip to Washington, 15–16
history, 14, 702–3
name, 141
on playing for the joy of it, 754
poem praising Pres. Russell, 19
Rifle Club's purpose explained, 14
as source material, xii
streaker photographs in, 166
Battleground athletic complex, 215, 742–43. *See also* athletic facilities
Battle of Fredericksburg, 56
"battle of the bands" contests, 720
Baty, Amy, 547
Baugher, Dawn, 629
Baumgarten, Liz, 459–60
beanies, freshmen, 126–27, **127**
Bearns, Gillian, 607
beauty contests, 37
Beck, Bill, 770
Beck, Joanne G. (J. Southworth)
as dean of students 324, 339, 433, 460, 681
and dorm visitation rules, 320, 324
fraternity club status refused, 681
report on MWC's image prepared, 341–42
retirement, 660
on Sedano's termination, 433
and student affairs/activities, 285, 339
and the volunteer office, 460
Beck, Robert, 510
beer. *See* alcohol

beer pong, 678
Beger, Stanley, 667
BellACapella (female a cappella group), 700, 770
Bell Atlantic, 376–77
Belli, Keith, 480, 482
bell tower (campanile), 552, 778–79, 812–13, 815, **P9**
Belmont (Gari Melchers Home and Studio), **229**
Anderson era *(1983–2006)*, 510–14
Catron's contribution, 510–11
under MWC control, 98, 226–30
name changed, 513–14
Reid's directorship, 229, 510
renovations and construction *(1990s–2000s)*, 512–13
Richardson photography exhibit, 821
Ridderhof paintings at, 376
Simpsons at, 169, 228
Benash, Michele, 313
Benigni, Vince, 742
Bennett, Jean, 670
Berreth, David, 511, 513
Berry, Bonnie, 255
Berry, Carol, 748
Best Buddies program, 462–63
Betourné, Jill, 681
Betty Lewis Hall (apartments), 23–24, 62, 79, 214
B-GLAD (Bisexual, Gay, and Lesbian Awareness Days), 433–34
bicycle tours in Europe, 391–92
Bill, J. Christopher, 206, 553, 637–39, **638**, 837, 838. *See also* Bill Outstanding Faculty Service Award
Billingsley, Anna Barron, 656
Bill Outstanding Faculty Service Award, 639, 839. *See also specific recipients*
Binford, Julien, 58, 72, 572
bin Laden, Osama, 529, 532
Biology Department, 575–77
Anderson Chair, 785, 836
cumulative GPA, 568
dissection and vivisection protested, 498
faculty, 575–76 (*see also specific individuals*)
housed in Combs, 83
human fetuses in lab, 326–27
in Jepson, 519
marine biology summer program, 78
Bird, Hugh S., 8
Bird, Samuel O., 77
Birt, Bob, 315
birth control. *See* contraception
Bishop, Pete, 667
Black, Barron F., 71
Black, Zoe, 575
Blackboard software, 537–38
Black Culture Week, 107–8, 269–70
Black Faculty/Staff Association, 483–84
Black History Month, 483, 648, 662, 663, 666, 850(n41), 855(n141)
The Black O (Watkins), 598
blackouts, wartime, 47
Black Student Association (BSA), 485–86, 491, 648, 683, 694, 720
Black Student Weekend, 367–68
black studies program. *See* African American studies
Black Visions program, 367–68
Blair, Jenifer, 255, 361, 362, 761
Blair, Richard, 453, 555
Blakemore, Porter R., 392–93, 502, 534, 541, 613, **614**, 634, 847(n24)
Blakey, Marion, 636, 835
blizzards, 724–27
blogs, 728–29
Blue Tide (publication), 849(n23)
Blue Tide mascot, 358–60, 848(n9)
Bluford, Guy, 519
board games, 728
Board of the State Teachers Colleges of Virginia, 29
board of trustees, 3, 9, 68–70. *See also* Board of Visitors
Board of Visitors
academic internship program approved, 200
and administrative salaries, 298
affirmative action objectives endorsed, 290
and alcohol policy, 414
amphitheater repairs funded, 556
Anderson agenda approved, 339
Anderson authorized as acting president, 303, 304
and Anderson-era building projects, 368, 370
and Anderson's resignation, 779–80
Anderson's salary increased, 697
and Belmont, 228, 512
BLS program approved, 202
and the Bright lawsuit, 130
and *The Bullet*, 704
and calendar revisions, 400
clock funded, 550
coeducation resolution, 90
and college funding, 211
and contraception availability, 472
creation, 98
dance department eliminated, 403
desegregation policy, 99
and Dodd Auditorium's college seal, 540
dorm improvements funding allocated, 797
and dorm visitation rules, 239–41, 321–22, 324–25, 416
faculty lawsuit against, 189–90
Farmer Visiting Professorship established, 618
and the FGCC, 290–91

Board of Visitors *(continued)*
and the fitness center, 545
and Frawley's arrests and termination, 804, 807–8, 818
Frawley's plans revealed to, 787–88
and graduate studies at MWC, 206, 207, 760
and the honor system, 686–87, 689–90, 795, 796
mascot and colors adopted, 361
members, 98, 279, 840–42 *(see also specific members)*
and merit pay, 292–93, 406
minority recruitment efforts, 365–66
and the Monroe Law Office-Museum, 231–33
and the Multicultural Center, 666
and the name of the college/university, 344, 348, 350–54, 356, 769–72, 774–75
open meetings, 280–81
Poyck appointed acting president, 523
presidential search *(1955)*, 71
presidential search *(1973–74)*, 175–76, 179
presidential search *(1983)*, 311–12, 315–17
presidential search *(2005–6)*, 781–83
presidential search *(2007)*, 820–21, 829, 857(n8)
and the proposed American History requirement, 565–66
Rector and Visitors Chair established, 382
rector on Foundation board, 212
Rectors, 333, 377–78, 840–42 (*see also specific individuals*)
secretary, 334
and separation from U. Va., 97–98
sexual assault policy, 474
sexual orientation policy, 435
and spousal equivalency benefits, 405
student member, 279, 281–82
and university status, 764
Woodard vote of confidence, 296
See also board of trustees
Boley, Connie, 553
BOND (Brothers of a New Direction), 683, 694, 720
Bond, Julian, 663
bonds, 216, 370, 379, 528. *See also* war stamps and bonds
Bonner, Dan, 254
book drive for soldiers, 46
Booker, Talley, 670
bookstore, 84, 270, 337, 470, 583, 674–75, 684
Boorstin, Daniel, 313, 831
Booth, Glenna, 134
Boteler, Beth, 748
Bottcher, Derek, 491–92
Boughner, Robert, 365, 401, 568, 582
Bourdon, Roger J., 129, 223, 611, 612–13, **614**, 617, 837, 853(n108)
Boussuge, Jennifer Taylor, 636
Bowen, Dawn Smith, 268, 478, 606
Bowen, Marshall E., **605**
awards and honors, 604, 836, 837
and the dog ban, 497
Geography of Anglo-America course, 438
and the men's basketball team, 161, 196, 197–98, 748
Polemics article, 703
popularity, 604
retirement, 606
on student-faculty dating, 478–79
Bowley, Alfred and Elsie Ball, 516
Bowley Scholars, 516
Boxley, Louise, 670
boycotts, 137, 183, 255–56, 642, 734, 802
Boys and Girls Club, 589
Bozicevic, Joseph, 78, 622, 623
Bradshaw, Betty, 670
Braxton, Grace Ann, 463
Braxton, Sallie Washington, 361, 490, 653, 761
Braymer, Meta R., 760–61, **761**, 763, 787, 798, 814, 823
break-dancing, 692–93
Breakers, 692–93, 698
Brent, Margaret, 56
Brent Hall, 56, 622
Bright, Brenda Page, 130
Bristow, Paul, 742, **743**
broadcasting studio, 43. *See also* AV (audiovisual) center; radio station
Broaddus, William C., 521, 526
Brompton, **57**
Andersons at, **319**, 320, 523–24
Christmas decorations, 361
history and purchase, 56–57
Simpson era *(1955–74)*, 72, 167
Brompton oak, 57, 548
Brooks, Arthur "Art," 483, 484, 486–87
Brooks, Gail, 761, 781
Broom, Pat, 709
Brothers of a New Direction (BOND), 683
Brovera, Adrienne, 791
Brown, Carter, 547
Brown, Dale, 284, 586–87
Brown, Irene Lundy
Board term and roles, 98, 279, 840
donation, 657
honorary doctorate received, 835
and the Mary Washington Foundation, 212
on visitation rules, 241
Brown, J. Sinclair, 54
Brown, Mark, 745
Brown, Nathaniel, 151, 591, 647
Bruen, Deborah, 754
Bryan, Albert V., 130
Bryan, Jason, 435
Buck, Kristin "Kristy," 554, 581, 629

Budinger, Meghan, 515
Buffett, Doris, 515, 589, 695. *See also* Sunshine Lady Foundation
Buffett, Warren, 509, **P11**
"Building Community Awareness" seminar, 662
Buildings and Grounds Department. *See* Physical Plant/Facilities Services
The Bullet
about, 704–7, 855(n151)
adjured to use discretion/taste, 66
April Fool's issues, 219, 243, 301, 315
archive microfilmed, 648, 649
faculty advisors to, 593, 688, 704 (*see also* Watkins, Stephen H.)
name, 140–41
personal ads, 706
and *Prometheus*, 266
as source material, xii
Bullock, Helga, 643
Buni, Andrew, 611
Burdeshaw, Leath, 359
Burke, Ginger, 349
Burnette, Wendy, 320, 321
Burns, Grover P., 629
Burns, Mary Ann T., 297, 305, 328, 331, 337
Burtis, Martha Fay, 537
Burton, Bobbie, 339, 352, 385
Burton, Stephen J., 331, 626, 789–90
Busch, Steve, 721
Bush, George H. W. *(1989–93)*, 501–2, 505–7. *See also* Gulf War
Bush, George W. *(2001–9)*, 471, 530, 534
Bushnell, Nina Gookin, **64**
as dean of women, 21, 26, 37, 64–65
death, 144
dormitory named for, 82 (*see also* Bushnell Hall)
and the flood of 1942, 50–51
and the German Club, 27
retirement, 64, 65
and World War II, 49
Bushnell Hall
construction and name, 82
fire *(1980)*, 274–78, **275**, **277**
male stripteases sponsored by, 428
"personality," 409
seminars, 79
business administration program/department, 577–78
enrollment/popularity, 205, 577
Executive-in-Residence program (EIR), 508–10, 578
faculty, 577–78 (*see also specific individuals*)
major established, 204
master's degree (MBA), 209–10, 577, 757, 763, 846(n15), 856(n168)
secretary, 670
business and finance office, 336, 670
business courses (before 1955), 21–22, 44
Byers, Corey, 711
Byrd, Charlie, 160
Byrd, Harry F., 29, 32
Byrd, Harry F., Jr., 119
Byrd, Mary, 255

C&W Associates, Inc., 484
Cabrera, Louis J., 51
Cain, David W., 584
awards and honors, **584**, 584, 836, 837
on the CPR department, 581, 584
homosexuality forum moderated by, 436–37
on the Multicultural Fair, 665
"Mysterium Humanum" lectures conceived by, 585
at the Phi Beta Kappa reception, 550
on Simpson, 170
at Woodard memorial, 305
Calculus Tournament, 621
Caldwell, Hamlin, 614–15, 620
Caldwell, Kathleen Dawson, 614
calendar, academic, 111, 399–400. *See also* Spring Break
calendars, "beefcake," 426–28
Campaign for Mary Washington *(1988–92)*, 382–83. *See also* fund-raising: Anderson era
campanile (bell tower), 552, 778–79, 812–13, 815, **P9**
Campbell, Alice Woodworth, 222
Campbell, Anthony, 464
Campbell, E. Elwood, 416
Campbell, Gardner, 596
college positions, 537, 538, 596, 846(n18), 851(n65)
and the Governor's School for the Gifted, 222
Outstanding Young Faculty Member Award, 596, 838
Quest narrated, 832
study-abroad program, 571
Campbell, Otho, 611, 612, **614**, 617
Campbell, Vicki, 334
campus (main campus)
beautification, 217–20, 551–52
expansion, 540–45, 824–25, 857(n2) (*see also* Montford Academy site)
grass (lawns), 217–20, 222, 251, 305, 409
student guides, 362
See also specific buildings, landmarks, and walkways
Campus Christian Community, 459, 468–69, 694, 695
Campus Conservation committee, 218
campus cutting (walking on the grass), 217–20
Campus Drive, 368–70, 543
campusing (defined), 13
campus jobs. *See* student jobs
Campus Life Committee, 414–16

Campus Rotary Club, 463
campus security. *See* police, College
Campus Training School (teacher training facility), 24–25. *See also* Education Department; teacher education
Campus Walk, **369**, **P6**
arcade through Woodard Campus Center, 371
beautification proposals (withdrawn), 551–52
campanile, 552, 778–79, 812–13, 815
construction, 368–70
Phi Beta Kappa key and plaza, 170, 336, 550, **P12**
See also specific buildings
Canadian Brass ensemble, 628
Canatsey, David, 442
Canova, Andrea, 350, 356
Cappiello, Frank, 509
card games, 728
Career Day, 162–63, 180–82
Carl's Frozen Custard, **P23**, 157, 420, 734–35
Carnegie, Kristina, 653
Carolina Biological Supplies Company, 498
Carpenter, Scott, 519
car policies, 26, 109, 549. *See also* parking
Carroll, Mary Cate, 325–28
Carter, Hobart C., 35, 250, 620
Carter, Jimmy, 270, 272–73
Carter, L. Clyde, 305, 639–40
Carter, Mary Lee, 670
Carter, Mayo, 702, 770
cartography, 216, 604, 606. *See also* Geography Department
Casacuberta, Melisa, 339
Cassel, William, 575
Castle, Sally Watson, 657
Castle, William, 59
Castles, John G., 241, 279, 840
Cates, J. Howard, 120
Catholic Campus Ministry, 694
Catholic Student Association, 458, 459
Catron, Joanna DeGilio, 510–11, 547
Cavalier Daily (U. Va. newspaper), 87
Cavalry, MWC, 47–50, **48**, 748
Celebrate Virginia project, 734
cell phones, 712, 728
"Centennial Alumni Exhibition," 828
Centennial Campaign, 659
Centennial Campanile (bell tower), 552, 778–79, 812–13, 815, **P9**
centennial celebration
Anderson and, 778, 779
College–Community Orchestra concert, 629, 832–33
exhibitions, 821, 828
Founders Week, 828–33
Hample introduced as president, 829–30
planning committee, 583
scattered through year, 821
centennial year *(2007–8)*, 817–33
Center for Historic Preservation, 233–35
directors, 233–34, 607, 609 (*see also* Crawley, William B., Jr.; Hudgins, Carter L.; Sanford, Douglas)
established, 233–34
Free Lance–Star's praise for, 315
and the Monroe Museum, 609
newsletter, 304
Palmieri and, 605
projects, 609–11
public programs, 234–35, 609, 821
Center for the Visually Handicapped, 613
Central Intelligence Agency (CIA), 180–82
Central Park shopping district, 733–34
Central Rappahannock Regional Library, 594
Ceo, Dan, 716, 792
Cervantes-Carson, Alejandro, 641
Chabuku, Montalepula, 500–501
Chakhad, Mohamed, 629
Chamber Ensemble, 627
Chandler, Algernon Bertrand, Jr., 10–11, 19–28, **20**, 33
Chandler, Mrs. Algernon B., 33
Chandler Hall, 24–25, 601
chapel services, 11, 37
Chappell, Carmen Culpeper, 778–79, 812. *See also* Centennial Campanile
Chappell, John, 619, 778–79, 812–13. *See also* Centennial Campanile
Charles Coleman Award, 554
Chatham Orchestra Institute, 224–25
cheating, 688–89. *See also* honor system
Cheerleading Club, 736–37
Chemistry Department, 83, 378, 519, 539, 578–81. *See also* Combs Hall; Jepson Science Center; *and specific individuals*
Chewning, Carolyn, 670
Chiang, Yuan-Jen, 621
Chi Beta Phi, 160, 250
Chichester, Ana Garcia, 623, 658
Chichester, John H.
and the Board, 280, 514–15
budget cut averted, 380
on the cancellation of Hershey's visit, 135
at Frawley's inauguration, 790
honorary doctorate received, 835
Jepson Science Center groundbreaking, **P10**
and JMC (satellite/graduate campus), 759, 761
and the name of the university, 772, 774–75
Chinn, Betsy, 670
Chirico, Bernard, **660**

alcohol banned, 676
background and qualifications, 659–60
on *Bullet* sex columns, 717–18
as Cher in lip-sync contest, 720
and condom availability, 472
on "freshmen" as sexist term, 494
on the Gulf War, 504
and the honor system, 689, 690, 795–96
on Junior Ring Week pranks, 455
and the Multicultural Center, 665, 666
racial harassment warned against, 531
as V.P. for Student Affairs, 660
and the women's basketball hazing incident, 753
choirs. *See* BellACapella; glee club; MWC Chorus; Symfonics; Una Voce; Victory Chorus
Christian radicalism, 118–20
Christian Unity Community, 694
Christmas
break, 111, 400
concerts, 35, 225–26, 627
decorations, 37, 234, 361, 445
faculty-staff party, 171, 524
Honduran orphanage and, 695
pre-holiday activities, 37–38
Christmas, Faith, 487–88, 489, 683
Christopher's (bar), 421
church attendance, 11–12
Churchill, John, **P12**
CIA (Central Intelligence Agency), 180–82
Cifu, David, 522
Circle K International, 459, 462, 684, 695
Citeroni, Tracy, 641
Citizen Salute Award, 832
Civil War, 2, 5, 56–57, 199, 541
Civil Works Administration (CWA), 32
Clark, Elizabeth A.
departure from MWC, 152
and the feminist movement, 150, 151, 268, 466, 845(n36)
and Ideas and Movements of the Western World, 207
reaction to male students' vigilantism, 94
Religion Department chaired, 77, 584
response to Woodbridge's criticisms, 139
Simpson Award, 837
Clark, Jane, 670
Clarke, J. Calvitt, 190
class attendance, 109, 288–89
Classical Civilization major, 60
Classics, Philosophy, and Religion Department (CPR), 294, 401–2, 568, 581–86. *See also* Philosophy Department; Religion Department; *and specific individuals*
classics department, 294, 402, 581–82. *See also* Classics, Philosophy, and Religion Department; *and specific individuals*
classified employees, wages of, 696–98, 794, 855(n148)
class rings, 163–64, 450, 849(n25). *See also* Junior Ring Dance; Junior Ring Week
class schedule, 109
Clatanoff, Katherine Deneke, 268, 852(n88)
Clatanoff, William B. "Bud," 155, 588, 703, 852(n88)
Clayton, Linda, 146, 152
Cleaver, Liam, 362
Clement, Juanita "Mickey," 198, 261, 284–85
Clinch Valley, 211–12
Clinton, Bill, 505–8, 616, 827–28, 850(n49), **P2**
Clinton, Hillary, 827–28
clocks, 550–51, 793
Club Carnival, 691
clubs, 691–702
club sports, 736–41
fraternities and club policy, 680–81 (*see also* fraternities; sororities)
Russell era *(1911–20)*, 13–15
See also organizations, student; *and specific clubs*
COAR (Community Outreach and Resources program), 691
Gulf War forum sponsored, 504
and the Marye's Heights apartments purchase, 544
post-9/11 fund-raising, 532
and student volunteers, 460–61, 464–65, 541
coeducation
coed dorms, 93, 239, 244, 711, 712, 856(n155)
early years *(1970s)*, 91–96, 169, 192–95, 299
female-to-male ratio, 364
and keg parties, 245 (*see also* keg parties)
move toward *(1960s)*, 86–91
and the name of the college, 92, 299–302, 340–43, 347 (*see also* name of the college / university)
visitation rules after (*see* visitation rules)
See also male students
Coffin, Peter, 78–79, 852(n83)
cohabitation, 238, 416. *See also* visitation rules
Cohen, Hildy Parks, 382–83, 835
Coiner, Jeanie, 493–94
Colbow, Susan, 670
Coleman, Charles, 554
Colgate W. Darden Award. *See* Darden Award
Coling, Wendy, 519
collars, popped, 673–74
College Ambassadors for Multi-Ethnic Outreach (CAMEO), 683
College–Community Orchestra, **225**

College–Community Orchestra *(continued)*
75th anniversary concert, 312
about, 223–24, 541, 627–29, 658
centennial concert, 629
pops concerts, 225–26, 627, 628
College Democrats (Young Democrats), 506–7, 530, 694, 710
College Heights High School (teacher training facility), 24–25
College Image and Stafford Name Committee. *See* Mehfoud committee(s)
College Image and University Name Committee, 566
College of Graduate and Professional Studies (CGPS; formerly JMC), 758–63
bachelor of professional studies (BPS), 762–63
campus, 758–63, **763**, 778, 798–99, 856(n169)
centennial celebrations, 821
diploma and seal, 776–77
faculty and staff, 761, 799 (*see also specific individuals*)
growth, 798–99
library, 854(nn124, 131)
master of business administration (MBA), 577, 763, 856(n168)
master of education (M.Ed.), 763
master of science in management information systems (MSMIS), 588, 763
name, 766, 774, 775
need for, 758
teaching excellence award, 833
College of William and Mary, 212, 365, 405, 654, 654, 668
College Planning and Priorities Advisory Council (C-PPAC), 203–6
college rankings and college guides, 363–65, 651–52, 653–54, 766
College Republicans (Young Republicans), 499, 507, 530, 536, 694, 710, 721
"Colleges at War" (Treasury Dept. publication), 46–47
College Shop. *See* C-Shop
Collier, Gary, 621
Collier, Janice, 107
Collins, Belinda, 665
Collins, Judy, 628
colors, school, 358–61, 699
Colt, Thomas C., 227
Columbus Day Road Trip program, 652
Combs, E. R. "Ebbie," 29, 31
Combs, Morgan Lafayette, **29**
administrative reorganization, 34
and Alvey, 35
background and qualifications, 29
and Brompton, 57
and the campus, 31, 70 (*see also* facilities: Combs era)
death, 70
era *(1928–55)*, 28–70 (*see also specific topics and events*)
and the freshmen reception, 60
funding requests, 31, 32, 44, 52–53
and male students, 62
and the merger with U. Va., 58–59, **59**
and the metamorphosis into MWC, 39, 42
and SACS accreditation, 30–31
terminated, 69–70
and the waitress uniform disagreement, 66–68
and World War II, 45–47, 49
Combs, Robert H., 63
Combs Hall (science building), 82–83, 147, 379, 518–19, 539, 601. *See also* Jepson Science Center
comedy shows, 702, 719–20. See also *Crimes Against Nature*
commencement
1919 address, 10
1975, 182
1984, 460
1997, 526–27, **P3**, **P11**
1998, **P3**
2005 and *2006* speakers, 636
2007, 802–3, 812–15
2008, 833–34
BLS degrees first granted *(1979)*, 203
Combs's last commencement *(1954)*, 68
Daisy Chain, 38
dress (through *1920*), 12
first male graduates *(1972)*, 92–93
graduate degrees first conferred *(1983)*, 209
JMC graduates, 763
name changed to MWC at *(1938)*, 42
pipe band, 698–99, **699**
Rucker and, 813, **P4**
Commerce Department, 44, 55
commercial program, 21–22
Commission on the Consolidation of Colleges, 54
"Commitment to Excellence: An Agenda for Action in the '80s and Beyond," 339–40, 354, 356, 380, 741
Committee on Campus Social Life, 414–16
Committee on College Affairs, 300, 302
Committee on Degree Requirements, 286–88
Committee on International Programs, 391
Committee on the Future of the College, 87, 96, 205, 579
community colleges, transfers from, 800

community involvement
before *1974*, 50–51, 220
Anderson era *(1983–2006)*, 220–35, 508–18, 541
art department and, 572
business administration department and, 578
Center for Historic Preservation, 234–35, 609–11
foreign languages department and, 623
Historic Preservation Club and, 692
Multicultural Center, 663–64 (*see also* Multicultural Fair)
music, 223, 624, 626–29 (*see also* College–Community Orchestra; concerts)
philanthropy course, 589
Psi Upsilon, 684
theater, 223, 642, 644
trick-or-treat for local children, 464
Woodard era *(1974–82)*, 220–35
See also COAR; Fredericksburg (city and surrounding area); Fredericksburg community; public lectures; volunteerism; *and specific individuals and organizations*
Community Outreach and Resources program (COAR). *See* COAR
community service program, 221
commuting students, 549
computers. *See* Computer Science Department; technology
Computer Science Department, 204, 205, 315, 586–88, 621, 852(n86). *See also specific individuals*
concert band, 84
concerts
AIDS benefit concerts, 480
American Indian composers, 627
Anderson inaugural concerts, 330
Black Culture Week, 269
centennial concert, 629, 832–33
costume concerts, 626–27
Frawley inaugural concert, 789
"go-go" concert, 668
"Good Buddy" concerts, 626
jazz festival, 626
Katrina relief benefit, 464
pops concerts, 225–26, 627, 628
professional acts, 160, 626, 701–2
Simpson inaugural concert, 73
Vietnam antiwar march fundraiser, 138
See also specific groups and performers
condoms, 430–31, 472–73, 850(n33). *See also* contraception
Confederate gun emplacements, 199–200
Conrad, Beth, 129
Consortium for Continuing Higher Education, 206
contraception, 147, 470–73, 849(n31–32), 850(n33). *See also* condoms
convocation
75th anniversary Convocation, 313–14
centennial year *(2008)*, 830–32
Combs era *(1928–55)*, 37
eliminated, 109
Palmieri's *1997* address, 606
Stageberg's *1991* address, 492–93
Conway, Dee, 747
Cook, Dan, 670
Cook, Francis, 636
COOL (Campus Outreach Opportunity League), 459–60
Cooper, Burton, 137
Cooper, Richard B. "Rich," 486, 840
Cooper, Weldon, 176
Cooperman, Rosalyn, 635, 802
Copprome (Honduran orphanage), 601, 694–96, 730, 794, 827
Coptic language, 586
Corbin, Mary Randolph "Ranny," 334, 789
Corcoran, Carole, 393–94, 468, 482, 488, 665
Core Planning Group, 787, 811
Cornell Hall, 43, 50
cornerstone-laying celebrations, 5–6, 43–44
Coryell, Derek, 722
Cosby, Bill, 574
Coski, John, 620
CosmoGIRL! (magazine), 652
Cote, Raymond C., 92
Cotillion Club, 38, 43, 51, **52**
Cottingham, Sue, 122
Council on Community Values and Behavioral Expectations, 445, 454, 489, 491–92, 662
Counseling and Psychological Services (CAPS), 796. *See also* counseling center
counseling center, 81, 162, 215, 455, 796
Cover, Herbert, 578
Cox, Leah, 652
C-PPAC. *See* College Planning and Priorities Advisory Council
Craddock, Amanda, 361
Crapol, Edward, 516
Crater, Flora, 150–51
Crawley, Theresa Young, 268, 657
Crawley, William B., Jr., 203, **614**, 619
awards and honors, 613, 836, 837, 839
Center for Historic Preservation headed by, 233–34, 613
and the Governor's School for the Gifted, 221–22, 613
and the honor system committee, 686
as institutional historian, x

Crawley, William B., Jr., *(continued)*
named Anderson's executive assistant, 334, 613
STP headed by, 482
on Woodard, 847–48(n36)
credit by examination, 110–11
crew (rowing), 742, 746
crime rate, 668–69
Crimes against Nature (Kilmartin one-man show), 477, 637–38
Crippen, Timothy, 640
Crissman, Judith, 580
CROP Walks, 459
Cross, Richard S., 83–84, 175, 840
Crotty, Jeanne, 62. *See also* alma mater
Croushore, James H., **296**
as academic dean, 296–97
as dean of the College, 75
faculty lawsuits against, 189–90
Hegmann hired, 196–97
on hiring minority faculty, 290
retirement and death, 847(n31)
and the Tuesday Lunch Club, 852(n83)
cruising, 368–70, 543
Crumb, Betsy, 714, 716. *See also* "Sexclamations"
C-Shop (College Shop), 215–16, 315, 371, 413–14, 670
Culpeper, Carmen. *See* Chappell, Carmen Culpeper
Cultural Awareness Series, 666
Cumming, Gwendolyn Amory, 240, 279, 377–78, 840
curfews, 118, 124. *See also* visitation rules
Curley, Richard, 577
"Current Issues in Feminism" panel, 151
Currie, Jacqueline, 482
Curtis, Teresa, 372
Custis Hall, 32–33
Cutry, Joe, 553
CWA (Civil Works Administration), 32
Czarsty, Steven, 209, 577

Dabb, JeanAnn, 571
Dahlgren. *See* Naval Surface Warfare Center
Daily Star, 22–23
Daisy Chain, 38
Dalhouse, Warner N., 241, 509, 840
Dalton, John N., 207, 232, 279, 280, 290
Dalton, Virginia Lewis, 333, 377, 840
Daluiso, Dennis, 642
Damron, John, **605**
dance department, 77, 188, 203, 294, 402–3, 698. *See also* Theatre and Dance Department; *and specific individuals*
dances
Anderson inaugural celebration, 333
Black Culture Week, 269–70
club dances, 27, 38, 43, 51
declining popularity of formal dances, 438, 718–19
eighties revival dances, 723
GLBSA dance, 432
Graduation Ball, 438, 812
Grand Monte Carlo Ball, 723
Halloweens, 248–49
Junior Ring Dance, 85, **163**, 163–64, 250, 438, 450–51
roof garden dances, 24, 43
Simpson inaugural ball, 74
Spring Formal, 438, 718–19, 812
Victorian Ball, 692
Witches' Dance, 248–49
Dance Team, 698, 737
Danforth Foundation, 80
Danielson, Kat, 748
D'Arcangelis, Rita, 852(n86)
Darden, Colgate W., Jr., **59**
honorary doctorate received, 835
and the MWC-U. Va. merger, 54
as U. Va. president and MWC chancellor, 58–59, 68, 97, 844(n1)
Darden Award, 59, 283, 554, 581, 629, 833
Dargan, Sean Michael, 480, 702
Darling, Robin, 147–48
Darter, Oscar, 611, 620, 691
dating
Anderson era *(1983–2006)*, 424–27, 710–11
attractiveness surveys, 263–64, 425–26
Bullet advice, 448, 711
changing dynamics *(1970s)*, 152
coeducation's impact, 88
date rape (*see* rape)
interracial dating, 105, 106
Quantico Marines, 84, 131–33, 141–42, 245, 313–14
Simpson era *(1955–74)*, 118, 141–42
student-faculty relationships, 266–68, 477–79, 847(n24)
U. Va. fraternity guys, 243–44, 245, 261–62
venues, 157–58 (*see also* bars, off-campus; dances; restaurants)
and visitation rules, 324
See also sex and sexuality; visitation rules
Dave Matthews Band, 702
Davidson, Frederick, 475
Davidson, Jason W., 466, 635, 690, 696, 838
Davies, Gordon K., 207, 807, 835
Davies, Lawrence A., 269, 313, 483, 530, 840, 851(n61)
Davies, Thomas, 748–50
Davies, Tom, 197
Davis, Cheryl, 581
Davis, Mona. *See* Albertine, Mona Davis
Davis, Renee, 649

Davis, Richard J., 330
Day, Gloria, 670
Daybreak program, 462–63
day care center, 148–49, 845(n35)
dean of the college (academic dean). *See* Alvey, Edward, Jr.; Barra, Rosemary; Burns, Mary Ann T.; Croushore, James H.; Hall, Philip L.; Hansen, Richard E.; Palmer, Barbara; Whidden, Reginald W.
dean of the faculty. *See* dean of the college
dean of students. *See* Clement, Juanita "Mickey"; dean of women; Droste, Mildred; Gonon, Isabelle Lawrence; Gordon, Suzanne; Hargove, Margaret; head of the home; Rucker, Cedric; Beck, Joanne G.; Stephenson, Mary Ellen
dean of women. *See* Bushnell, Nina Gookin; dean of students; head of the home
Debate Club (Debate Team), 691–92, 791, 855(n146)
deGraff, Galen, 577
degree requirements (graduation requirements)
  1930s, 40–41
  1945 revisions, 55
  1970s, 111
  1980s–90s, 286–88, 385–98
  2000s, 538, 564–66, 600–601, 823–24
  environmental awareness, 396, 397, 823
  experiential learning course, 823
  foreign languages, 79, 287, 397–98, 564–65, 823
  global awareness, 389–90, 393, 397, 823
  information and technology proficiency, 538, 851(n66)
  physical education, 41, 54, 287, 397, 823
  race and gender issues, 393–97, 468, 563
  sciences, 396–97
  speaking-intensive courses, 389, 397, 600–601
  writing-intensive courses, 287, 385–88 (*see also* writing skills)
DeJarnette, H. M., Dr., 18
Dello Joio, Norman, 312
Delta Sigma Nu, 679–80
DeLuca, Tom, 702
Democratic Party, 149, 506–7, 530, 694, 710, 827–28
departmental picnics, 248, 449–50
departmental secretaries, 670
department mergers, 293–96, 640. *See also* *specific departments and programs*
"department reps," 113
Derecki, Catherine, 535
Dervin, Daniel "Dan," 110, 591
Desert Storm. *See* Gulf War
development office, 338–39, 380–85, 654–56, 658. *See also* Alumni (Alumnae) Association; alumni (alumnae): financial giving; Dowdy, Michael B. "Mickey"; endowment of MWC/UMW; fundraising, institutional
Devil-Goat rivalry, 26–27, 85, 126–27, **127**, 161, 250, 652, 719
Dewberry and Davis (architects), 760
Diana, Kevin, 700
Di Bella, Joseph C.
  awards and honors, 836, 837
  and Carroll, 325, 326, 328
  as gallery director, 572
  and Ridderhof, 376
  students' grief expressed in drawings, 531–32
  summer program in Italy, 571
DiBenedetto, Vincent A., III
  Board term, 840
  on contraception availability, 472
  and the Multicultural Center controversy, 666
  on the proposed American History requirement, 566
  Reagan supported by, 273, 847(n25)
  Rector position held by, 333
Dickinson, Forrest, 361
Dickinson, V. Earl
  honorary doctorate received, 835
  as MWC supporter, 353, 378, 380
  and the name change proposal, 353, 355
  stadium named for, 743, **744**
dining hall
  Bushnell and, 26, 64–65
  food service protest, 255–56
  racial policies, 105–6
  self-busing, 408–9
  waitresses, 66–67, 105
  See also food service; Seacobeck Hall
discipline. *See* rules and regulations
Disraeli, Stephen, 593
Distinguished Alumnus Award, 382, 636, 845(n17)
Distinguished Visitor [Graduate] in Residence program, 159–60, 504, 656
diversity. *See* African American students; foreign students; integration of MWC; male students; minority faculty; minority students; multiculturalism; Muslim students; race relations on campus; women's issues
Diversity Scholars Day, 368. *See also* Black Student Weekend
Dobson, Dennis, 482
Doc Scantlin and his Imperial Palms Orchestra, 702, 832

Dodd, Eileen Kramer, 26, 44, 215. *See also* Dodd Auditorium
Dodd Auditorium
75th anniversary events, 312–14
abortion forum, 470
Anderson inaugural concert, 330
centennial convocation, 830–32
College–Community Orchestra concerts, 224, 225–26 (*see also* College–Community Orchestra)
comedy shows, 702
Fredericksburg Forum *(1996)*, 517–18
"Great Lives" lectures, 619 (*see also* "Great Lives" public lecture series)
Hample introduced as president, 829
homosexuality forum, 436–37
instrument "petting zoo," 628
JMC commencement ceremony in, 763
Katrina relief benefit concert, 464
Lonestar concert, 702
ML King celebration, 483
movie showings, 730
Muhammad speech, 485
name, 215
Nutcracker performances, 802
Performing Arts Club shows, 698
Stageberg's *1991* convocation address, 492–93
state budget hearing, 525
Steinem address, 467
structure and decor, 43, 539–40
talent shows, 720–21
Wo-Man Contests, 252–53, 438–40 (*see also* Wo-Man Contest)
Woodard's memorial service, 305
Wyclef Jean concert, 701
dogs, 497
DoIT (Department of Instructional Technology), 537
doll show, 37–38
Dominion Bank, 225, 509
donations. *See* alumni (alumnae): financial giving; funding; fund-raising; *and specific donors*
Donovan, Bill, 441
Donovan, Jean, 456–58, **457**
dormitories
air conditioning, 217, 375, 797
alcohol in, 123–24 (*see also* alcohol)
Anderson era *(1983–2006)*, 375, 543–44, 723–24
Chandler era *(1920–28)*, 23–24
classes mixed, 75
coed dorms, 93, 239, 244, 711, 712, 856(n155)
Combs era *(1928–55)*, 42–43, 68
condom vending machines, 472–73
dorm parties, 723–24
fire (Bushnell, 1980), 274–78, **275**, **277**
first dormitory, 6–7 (*see also* Willard Hall)
Frawley era *(2006-7)*, 797, 825
holiday decorations, 445
language houses/floors, 622–23, 853(n111)
laundry, 796–97
male students, 91–94, 195
Marye's Heights apartments purchased for, 542–45
overnight visitors (*see* visitation rules)
party opportunities, 409–10
personality, 244, 375
pets prohibited, 496–97
racial segregation/integration, 102–4, 121
regulations *(1911–1920s)*, 12–13, 25–26
regulations *(1960s–70s)*, 118, 123–24
regulations *(1974–82)*, 238–43, 256
regulations *(1983–90s)*, 320–25, 413, 415–16, 418, 429, 449
rivalries, 286
room assignment system, 102
roommate complaints, 792–93
seminars, 78–79
telephones, 21, 376–77
Woodard era *(1974–82)*, 239–44
See also specific dormitories; visitation rules
Dorothy and Grellet Simpson Chair in English, 382, 384. *See also* Grellet and Dorothy Simpson Chair in Medieval Literature
Dow Chemical, 134
Dowdy, Michael B. "Mickey," 169, 338, 352, 380–85, **381**, 654
Drag Show, 722
Drama Department. *See* Theatre and Dance Department
Dramatic Arts and Dance Department. *See* Theatre and Dance Department
DREAM (Students Demanding Rights, Education, and Multiculturalism), 666
Dreiss, Joseph, 510, 511, 571, 574
dress, student. *See* student attire
dress code, 109, 115–18. *See also* student attire
Dresser, Amanda, 745
Dresser, Paul A., Jr., 333, 405, 523, 526, **527**, 840
drinking rules. *See* alcohol
Driver, Mary, 466
Droste, Mildred, 69, 75, 94, 102, 104–5, 198, 736
drugs, illegal, 258–61, 674–75
D'Souza, Dinesh, 491–92, 597
Duke, Albert, 600

DuPont Foundation, 580
duPont Hall (part of fine arts center)
broadcast studio in, 254
Carroll painting excluded from show, 325–28
centennial exhibition, 821
construction, 57
General Assembly reception in, 330
instructional technology liaison, 537
Klein Theater, 223
renovation, 379, 574
Ridderhof paintings at, 376
Simpson inaugural exhibition, 72, 572
TIP program in, 562
Van Winckel exhibition (75th anniversary), 312
Dye, Becky, 748

"Eager Voices Singing" (Walker and Stewart), 62. *See also* alma mater
EagleOne cards, 536, 796
Eagle Pipe Band, 698–99, **699**, 754, 789, 831
Eagles mascot, **360**, 360–61
Eagles Nest snack shop, 372, 447
early decision program, 650–51
Early Humanities program, 60
Earth and Environmental Sciences Department, 77, 204, 378, 519, 568, 601–3. *See also specific individuals*
Ecology Club, 218, 495, 794, 827
Economics, Business, and Public Affairs Department. *See* business administration program/department; Economics Department; public administration major
Economics Department, 294, 588–89, 670, 826, 852(n90). *See also specific individuals*
Edmunds, Jeffrey, 621
Edson, Jean, 629
education, local, 24–25, 463
Education Department (teacher education), 590–91
bachelor of science degree, 22, 40
certification plus academic major, 55
Chandler era *(1920–28)*, 22, 24–25
Combs era *(1928–55)*, 34–35, 40, 55
and the day care center, 148
elementary education program, 60
elimination recommended *(1944)*, 55
emphasis on subject proficiency, 78, 590
faculty (*see specific individuals*)
and the MALS program, 757
multi-state certification, 78
Russell era *(1911–20)*, 8, 19–20
Simpson era *(1955–74)*, 78, 103
training facility, 24–25
See also teacher education
Edwards, Donald, 587, 588
Edwards Scholarship (computer science), 588
Eglevsky, Doris G., 333, 770–72, 774, 795, 840
EIR (Executive-in-Residence program), 508–10, 578
Elderhostel, 516, 762
E. Lee Trinkle Library. *See* Trinkle Library
Ellis, Natalie, 653
El Salvador, killings in. *See* Donovan, Jean
ELS Department. *See* English, Linguistics, and Speech Department
Elswick, Rebecca, 648
e-mail, 535–36, 729, 797, 851(n64)
Embrey, Alvin T., 39
Emergency Operations Plan (EOP), 558
Emerson, Claudia, 598–600, 790, 820, 837, 838, 839, **P5**
Emery, Jim, 323–24, 499–500
Emory, Samuel T., Jr., 603–4, **605**
geography department chaired, 77, 603
honor system supported, 129
and the internship program, 201, 604
as marshal of the faculty, 604, 853(n105)
named Distinguished Professor, 836
political affiliation, 155
restaurant owned by, 849(n22) (*see also* Sammy T's)
retirement, 605
summer bicycle tour of Europe, 391–92, 604
Enchanted Castle (Spotswood home), 609
Encore Show Choir, 626, 789
endowment of MWC/UMW
Anderson era *(1983–2006)*, 381–82, 654–58
Woodard era *(1974–82)*, 211–14
See also alumni (alumnae): financial giving; fund-raising; Mary Washington College Foundation; *and specific donors*
energy conservation, 271
England, Elspeth "Elz," 714, 716, 717–18. *See also* "Sexclamations"
England, exchange program in, 391
English, Linguistics, and Speech Department, 539, 591–98, 719. *See also* English Department; *and specific individuals*
English Department
Arrington Distinguished Chair in Poetry, 598, 837
curriculum, 594–95

English Department (*continued*)
faculty, 591–600 (*see also specific individuals*)
literary magazines, 141, 703–4
medieval literature, 171 (*see also* medieval studies program)
poetry slams, 719
Simpson Chair, 171, 382, 384
Writing Workshop (English 101), 385, 396
See also English, Linguistics, and Speech Department; writing skills
Ennin, Mina, 665
enrollment
1930s, 33, 42
African American students, 100–101, 365, 482–83, 654, 800
Anderson era *(1983–2006)*, 339–41, 365, 379–80, 390, 482–83, 519–20
in CGPS, 799
foreign students, 390
Frawley era *(2006–7)*, 800
male *(1970s–80s)*, 91, 92, 192–95, 283, 408 (*see also* male students)
in the MALS program, 208–9, 757
in the MBA program, 210
Woodard era *(1974–82)*, 191–95, 282–83, 299–300, 353
See also applicants and applications; recruitment
Ensler, Eve, 715–16
entertainment. *See* concerts; Dodd Auditorium; music; student life; theater productions
environmental awareness requirement, 396, 397, 823
environmental issues, 495–96, 602–3, 794, 826–27, 853(n103)
The Epaulet (literary magazine), 141, 703
E Pluribus Unum Political Awareness Club, 694, 794
equal employment policy, 290
Equal Rights Amendment (ERA), 151–52, 268, 306
equestrian club, 47, 736, 747–48. *See also* MWC Cavalry
erotic yearbook, 792
e-Suds, 796–97
Ethnic Studies course, 393–94, 493
European Capitals summer program, **392**, 392–93, 613, 634
Evans, Gano, 577
Evans, Larry, 542–43
exams
after the Bushnell fire, 276
Bullet on preparing for, 793
mandatory vs. optional, 111
scheduling, 111–12, 398–400
Vietnam protests and, 140
executive assistant to the president, 333–34. *See also* Corbin, Mary Randolph; Crawley, William B., Jr.; Poyck, Marjorie Meredith; Warlick, H. Conrad
Executive-in-Residence program (EIR), 508–10, 578, **P11**
executive vice president, 334–36. *See also* Hurley, Richard; Merchent, A. R. "Ray"; Poyck, Marjorie Meredith
expulsion, 128–30, 181–82
extracurricular activities. *See* athletic program/department; clubs; organizations, student; student life; *and specific activities*

Facebook, 540, 712, *713*, 726, 729, 730, 753, 802, 806
facilities
Anderson era *(1983–2006)*, 337, 368–79, 518–19, 539–57, **P6–9**
Chandler era *(1920–28)*, 22–25
College of Graduate and Professional Studies, 759–60, **763**, 798–99
Combs era *(1928–55)*, 31–33, 43–44, 52–55, 68, 70
community use, 220–21
Frawley era *(2006–7)*, 797
Park & Shop Center development, 824–25, 857(n2)
Russell era *(1911–20)*, 6–7, 9–11
Simpson era *(1955–74)*, 81–84, 166–67
Woodard era *(1974–82)*, 199–200, 210, 214–17, 220–21, 274–78
See also athletic facilities; dormitories; Physical Plant/Facilities Services; technology; *and specific facilities*
Facilities Services. *See* Physical Plant/Facilities Services
faculty
9/11 response, 531–32
abortion debate among, 469–70
academic and scheduling reforms *(1960s–70s)*, 109–13
and the Anderson inauguration celebrations, 330–31
Anderson's relations with, 317, 780
and attendance policies, 288–89
benefits, 404–5, 639
BLS program endorsed, 202
Board liaison (*see* Faculty General Cooperative Committee)
of CGPS, 761, 799
Chandler era *(1920–28)*, 20–21, 26
and coeducation, 95
Combs era *(1928–55)*, 30–31, 33–35, 44, 51–52, 58, 60–62, 69

committees, 77, 292 (*see also specific committees and topics, such as* admissions)
and computerization, 374–75, 536–38
and degree requirements, 288, 388–90 (*see also* degree requirements)
and department mergers, 293–96
distinguished professors, 382, 404, 559, 836
doctoral degrees, 30
downsizing, 187–91, 211
endowed chairs, 836–37 (*see also specific chairs*)
and exam self-scheduling, 398–99
and the feminist movement, 150 (*see also* Clark, Elizabeth A.; feminist movement on campus; Hanna, Susan J.; Rabson, Alice)
"four divisions" plan opposed, 560
and Frawley, 788–89, 806, 808–9
and the freshmen reception, 60–62
funding for, 188, 192
governance, 77, 560–61
and grading, 568–70
and graduate studies at MWC, 206–9, 298
grievance board, 291
and the honor system, 129, 686–87 (*see also* honor system)
Indian faculty exchange program, 79–80
and interdisciplinary majors, 203–5
job security fears, 380
marshals, 847(n32) (*see also* Barra, Rosemary; Emory, Samuel T., Jr.; Harris, Anna Mae; Stageberg, Stephen)
and minor programs, 400–401, 567–68
and the name of the institution, 300, 302, 342, 345–46, 765, 777–78 (*see also* name of the college / university)
performance evaluations, 291–92
political affiliations, 155
and the presidential search process, 311, 821
and the race and gender requirement, 393–96
and racial integration, 101, 103
and racial tensions, 483–84, 488–91
ROTC program debated, 329
Russell era *(1911–20)*, 7, 10, 18
scholarships for children of, 659
sensitivity training, 484
sexual harassment by, 475
Simpson era *(1955–74)*, 76–78, 168, 188, 267
student evaluation of, 114–15, 292, 538–39, 559–60
student-faculty dating, 266–68, 477–79, 847(n24)
student-teacher ratio, 188, 365, 404, 560 (*see also* class size)
survey *(1979)*, 295, 297–98
Teaching Innovation Project (TIP), 407, 562–64
teaching load, 55, 404, 408, 559, 560
tenure, 190, 291–92, 749–50 (*see also* Jiminez, Anthony)
unionization, 188, 846(n8)
upgrading credentials, 77
U. Va. report's recommendations *(1944)*, 55
and the Vietnam War, 133–37, 140
and the Wo-Man Contest, 440
Woodard era *(1974–82)*, 176, 180, 187–91, 204–5, 211, 289–96
and World War II, 47
and writing-intensive courses, 385–88
See also African American faculty; faculty salaries; minority faculty; *and specific individuals*
Faculty General Cooperative Committee (FGCC), 290–91, 295
faculty salaries, 382
1911–50, 20, 31, 55
1950–74, 77, 90
1974–80, 187–88, 191, 196, 292–93, 298
1980s–90s, 378–79, 383, 384, 404, 408, 525
2000s, 559
benefits, 404–5, 639
merit pay, 292–93, 298, 406, 559–60
Fairfax County School System, 366
Fairfax House, 33, 622
Fall break, 399–400
Fall Formal, 438
Fallon, Jimmy, 702
Fallon, Paul, 600
Family Weekend, 250, 821. *See also* Parents' Weekend
Farmer, James, **616**
about, 101, 562, 615–16
and Black Student Weekend, 367–68
and D'Souza's speech, 491–92
honorary doctorate received, 616, 835
international recognition, 598, **P2**
memorials, 366, 641, 618, 620, **P12** (*see also* Farmer Scholars Program)
named Distinguished Professor, 836
Farmer Scholars Program, 366–67, 591, 652
Farmer Visiting Professorship in Human Rights, 618
Farmville Teachers College. *See* Longwood College

Farnsworth, Stephen J., 507, 635–36, 653, 802, 838
"Father of Mary Washington College." *See* Goolrick, C. O'Conor
Faulconer, Tina, 648
Faulkner, Ronald W., 35
Faulkner, William, 53, 158
Fauntroy, Walter, 107, 269, 616
fees, 8, 68, 146. *See also* room and board; tuition
feminist movement on campus
1960s–70s, 141, 146–47, 150–52, 268–69
Anderson era *(1983–2006)*, 466–71
fraternity rolls criticized, 261–62
and gender-neutral language, 493–94
Hanna and, 150, 152, 347, 466, 594, 845(n36)
and the name change controversy, 348–49, 355, 848(n5)
reaction to male students' intention to patrol campus, 94–95
Student Center for Social Information Services (SIS), 146–47
See also women's issues
Fernsebner, Susan, 617
Ferrell, Claudine, 613–14
Ferry Farm (Washington's boyhood home), 609–10
FGCC (Faculty General Cooperative Committee), 290–91, 295
fiber-optic system. *See* telecommunications network
Fickett, Lewis P., Jr., 632
awards and honors, 632, 836, 837
on Bill Clinton, 507
and the Debate Club, 691
on J. Donovan, 458
on the Gulf War, 502
and Hirschkop's speech, 90
honor system supported, 129
influence on students, 466
political career, 153, 248, 632, 846(n38)
Political Science Department headed, 78, **153**, 632
as pre–foreign service major advisor, 78
and the Tuesday Lunch Club, 852(n83)
Vietnam War debate, 133
wife (*see* Fickett, Martha Van Zandt)
on Woodard, 308
Fickett, Martha Van Zandt, 268, 626, 839
Fiddlestix, 628
Field, Phyllis, 670
Field Day, 16, 26
field hockey, 198, 215, 747, 755
Film Production Club, 730
films, 444, 623, 730. *See also specific films*
final exams. *See* exams
finances of MWC/UMW
Anderson era *(1983–2006)*, 353–54, 377–85, 401–7, 560, 654, 697–98
Simpson era *(1955–74)*, 169, 175, 187
Woodard era *(1974–82)*, 175, 179, 186–91, 210–14, 308
See also endowment of MWC/UMW; funding; fund-raising (institutional); Simpson Library
financial aid, 282–83, 361, 365–66, 382, 384. *See also* scholarships
fine arts center, 57, 379. *See also* duPont Hall; Melchers Hall; Pollard Hall
Fingerhut, Victor, 507, 632–33, 703
"finishing school" image, 108–9, 125, 142–43, 283, 301
Finke, Bruce, 91–92
Finkelman, Paul, 516
fire (Bushnell, *1980*), 274–78, **275**, **277**
fitness center, 545–46, 735, 851(n68)
Fitzgerald, Ruth Coder, 169
Flath, Robert, 739
Flatt, Kevin, 180–82
Fleming, Delmont, 591, 847(n24)
flood *(1942)*, 49–51
flu epidemics, 18, 30
Flute Ensemble, 626
Flynn, Jack, 129–30
Foard, Douglas, 550
food service
ARA, 255–56, 276, 286, 459, 549
employee wages, 794
meal equivalence, 793
Wood Co./Sodexho, 539, 549, 558, 794
See also dining hall
football, 740–41. *See also* Rugby Club (rugby team)
Forbes, Marion C., 12
Foreign Film Series, 623, 730
foreign languages. *See* Modern Foreign Languages Department; *and specific languages*
foreign policy, 532–34, 794, 851(n63). *See also specific wars*
foreign students, 390, 801
foreign studies, 79–80, 171, 389–93. *See also* internationalism; multiculturalism; study-abroad programs
Forensic Club. *See* Debate Club
Fouberg, Erin H., 838
Founders Day, 19, 830–33
Founders Week *(2008)*, 828–33
Founders Weekend *(1983)*, 312–14
founding of MWC/UMW, 1–9
fountains, 453, 551, 554, 727, 809
Frackelton, Leigh, 577–78, 690
Framar, 11, 56, 78–79, 409, 444, 622
Framar International Living Center, 533
Frames Per Second Club, 596
Franke, Trixy, 581

fraternities
efforts to establish at MWC, 262–63, 679–84, 855(n140)
U. Va. fraternity men, 243–45, 261–62
See also specific organizations
fraternity rolls, 243–44, 261–62
Frawley, Christopher (son of W. Frawley), 783
Frawley, Emma (daughter of W. Frawley), 783
Frawley, Maria (wife of W. Frawley), 783, 806, 810
Frawley, William J., **788**
administration reorganized, 787
arrests and termination, 803–11, 814–20, 857(n1)
background and qualifications, 782
and facilities, 797, 798
era *(2006-7)*, 787–815 (*see also specific topics and events*)
and the honor system, 795
inauguration, 789–91
initiatives, 798–801
introduced to University, 783–84, **784**
personality and managerial style, 782–83, 787, 797–98, 803, 808–9
philosophy and goals, 787–91, 799
promotional efforts, 801
seminars and lectures given, 801–2
Fredericksburg Area Community Relations Organization, 583
Fredericksburg Area Museum and Cultural Center, 583, 648
Fredericksburg Chamber Ensemble, 223
Fredericksburg community
alcohol- and party-related tensions, 421–23
and contraception availability, 470–71
graduate center's benefits to, 758–59, 761–62
minority student recruitment, 366–67
and MWC property purchases, 540–44
and the name of the college / university, 346
objections to Campus Walk, 368–70
off-campus housing and, 732–33
racial tensions, 230
student volunteerism in, 459–65 (*see also* volunteerism)
and the visitation rules controversy, 321–24, 416
See also community involvement
Fredericksburg Forum, 160, 517–18, 519, 830, **P10**
Fredericksburg Singers, 223, 626, 789
Fredericksburg State Normal and Industrial School for Women, 1–10. *See also* Mary Washington College; State Normal School at Fredericksburg; State Teachers College at Fredericksburg
Fredericksburg Summer Theater (FST), 223, 642. *See also* Fredericksburg Theater Company
Fredericksburg Theater Company, 642, 644
Fred's Bag (publication), 707
freedom of speech, 327–28, 442, 488–89
The Free Lance–Star
9 / 11 candlelight vigil photo, 531, **P13**
journalism scholarship established, 382
as source material, xii
Freeman, Douglas Southall, 18
Freeman, Joe, 271
Free University, 113–14
French Club, 722–23
French language, 56, 622, 623
freshmen
in *1996*, 520
advising of, 566–67
attendance policy and, 289
beanies, 126–27, **127**
cars policy, 549
designation changed to "first-year students," 494
and Devil-Goat Day, 719
dorms, 126, 239
and fraternity rolls, 243–44
and keg parties, 245–46, 415–16 (*see also* alcohol: legal drinking age)
orientation programs, 284, 430–31
reception for, 60–62
seminars, 618, 801–2, 823
and visitation rules, 416
See also applicants and applications; enrollment
Friedman, Ruth, 575
Friends of MWC Dance, 403
Friends of the Orchestra, 628
Fries, Sharon, 484
Frisbee, 250–52, 449, 727, 737
FST (Fredericksburg Summer Theater), 223, 642. *See also* Fredericksburg Theater Company
Fujiyama, Cosmo, 695
Fujiyama, Shin, 601, 694–96, 730, 794, 827
Fuller, Stephen "Steve," 385, 404, 564, 575, 577, 806, 808, 847(n24)
fund-raising, institutional
Anderson era *(1983–2006)*, 380–85, 546–47, 654–59
centennial year *(2007–8)*, 832
gift club structure, 658
phonathons, 352, 381, 682
for the radio station, 708–9
Woodard era *(1974–82)*, 213–14
See also endowment of MWC / UMW; finances of MWC / UMW
fund-raising, student
after 9 / 11, 464
AIDS Walk, 462
Circle K International, 462

fund-raising, student (continued)
Copprome orphanage endeavor, 601, 694–96, 730, 794, 827
by the rugby team, 739
tsunami relief, 464
See also student activism; volunteerism
Future of the College Committee. *See* Committee on the Future of the College

Gable, Eric, 641
Gaines, James "Jim," 564, 624
Galbraith, John Kenneth, 517–18, P10
Gallahan, Connie, 747, 751
Galloway, Stephen, 180–82
games, 728
Garden Club of Virginia, 234, 512
Gari Melchers Home and Studio (Memorial Gallery). *See* Belmont
Garland, Ray L., 191
Garmon, Carole A., 571, 838
Garnett, A. W., 68
Gately, Doug, 626, 789
gates, 33, 547–48
Gatewood, Jane, 593
Gauch, Ali, 361
Gay, Lesbian, and Bi-Sexual Student Association (GLBSA), 432–33, 555, 682
Gay Awareness Week, 432–33
gay students. *See* homosexuality; *and specific student organizations*
Gay Student Union (GSU), 265–66, 431
GEICO, 758, 759
gender issues, 141–52, 393, 493–94. *See also* feminist movement on campus; Race and Gender Project
general education requirements. *See* degree requirements
General Education Review Committee, 799–800
Geography Department, 77, 216, 294–96, 603–7, **605**, 670. *See also specific individuals*
Geology Department/Program, 77, 378, 519, 568, 601–3. *See also* Environmental Earth Science and Geology Department
George, John, 578
George Mason University, 209, 211, 569, 746
George Washington Hall (GW)
1975 commencement in, 182
auditorium, 43, 215
broadcast studio in, 254
construction and uses, 43–44
doorman, 855(n137)
Hall of Mirrors, 43, 60
murals, 44
Phi Beta Kappa installation ceremony, 85
roof garden, 43, 60
George Washington Inn, 157
Gergen, David, 517–18, P10
German, R. F., Jr. "Chip," 537, 781, 787
German Club, 27, 38, 43, 51
German language, 402, 622, 623, 624. *See also* Germany; Merrill, Sammy R.; Rotter, Marcel
Germanna (Spotswood home), 609
Germanna Community College, 759
Ghost Walk, 610, 692
Ghyka, Matila, 58
Giancarlo, Leanna C., 580, 838
Gianoulis, Constance, 393
Giant Productions (SA entertainment committee), 701–2
GI Bill, 63–64
Gillespie, Carmen, 571
Gilmore, Frank, 426, 755
Gingrich, Newt, 802–3, 814
Ginnegar, Pete, 744
Gladis, Donna Sheehan, 131–32
Gladney, Terrie, 642
Glaeser, Kurt, 744, 746
Glamour magazine, 237, 481
GLBSA. *See* Gay, Lesbian, and Bi-Sexual Student Association
glee club, 14, 73–74. *See also* MWC Chorus
global awareness requirement, 389–90, 393, 397, 823
global initiative, 570–71. *See also* internationalism; multiculturalism
Global Observations Committee, 390
Glover, Donald E. "Don," 101, 129, 207, 208–9, 592, **592**, 836, 837
Gnehm, Edward, 789
Godwin, Mills E., Jr., 119, 135, 184–85, 279
Goehring, James E. "Jim," 584, 586, 838
Goforth, Angela, 581
golf, 198, 215
Gonon, Isabelle Lawrence, 65–66
Goode, Christopher Paul, 417–18, 424, 677, 849(nn20–21)
Goolrick, C. O'Conor, **2**
75th anniversary tribute, 313
at the amphitheater dedication, 22
at the cornerstone-laying ceremony for GW Hall, 43
family (*see* Ashby, O'Conor Goolrick; Goolrick, John; Goolrick, Virginia May)
and the founding, 2–3, 5
loving cup presented to, 831
and the metamorphosis into MWC, 39
and the MWC-U. Va. merger, 54
physical education facility named for, 83–84
Goolrick, John, 117–18

Goolrick, Virginia May, 18
Goolrick Hall
accessibility, 371, 375
air conditioning, 84, 214, 539
as basketball venue, 751, 752
day care center, 148–49
fitness center added, 545–46, 735, 851(n68)
funding, construction, and facilities, 83–84, 214
Hall of Fame plaques, 756
Halloweens in, 249, 444
keg parties in, 245
YMCA classes in, 220–21
Goolrick's (lunch counter and drug store), 156, 734
Gordon, Isabel, 81, 162
Gordon, Roy, 347, 423, 742, 745
Gordon, Suzanne, 261, 285
Gosetti-Murrayjohn, Angela, 582, **P12**
Gouger, James B., 294–95, 406, 504–5, 604–6, **605, P3**
Governor's Fund for Excellence, 233, 393, 407
Governor's School for the Gifted, 221–22, 334, 593, 596, 613
Grace, Erika, 669, 855(n136)
grading, 109–10, 140, 568–70, 634–35
Graduate Council, 207
graduates. *See* alumni (alumnae); Alumni (Alumnae) Association
graduate studies
faculty attitudes toward, 208–9, 298
graduate school near Dahlgren (proposed), 800
introduced, 205–10, 315
master of business administration (MBA), 209–10, 577, 757, 763, 846(n15), 856(n168)
master of education degree (M.Ed.), 763
master of liberal studies (MALS), 207–9, 757
master of science in management information systems (MSMIS), 588, 763
master of public administration (MPA), 757
rise to university status, 757–65
See also College of Graduate and Professional Studies; University of Mary Washington
Graduation Ball (Grad Ball), 438, 812, 833
graduation day. *See* commencement
graduation requirements. *See* degree requirements
Graham, Jean, 313, 643
Grant, James, 628, 832
grass (lawns), 217–20, 222, 251, 305, 409
Grattan, Bob, 648
Gratz, Roy F., 580, 581, 836
Graves, E. Boyd, 35, 478
Graves, Leonard, 669
Graves, Marilyn, 270
Gray, Donna, 557
Grayson, George, 133, 134
Great Books seminars, 78–79
Great Flood *(1942)*, 49–51
Great Hall (in Woodard), 371, 372
100th Night, 446
athletic awards banquet, 755
black-tie gala, 382
Bill Clinton's visit, 827–28
faculty-staff Christmas party, 524
Frawley reception, 783–84
"Great Lives" lectures, 619
Gulf War forum, 504
Halloweens, 444
Junior Ring Dance, 450
Phi Beta Kappa reception, 550
Rally Against Racism, 487–88
Great Ideas course. *See* Ideas and Movements of the Western World (graduate course)
"Great Lives" public lecture series, 618–19, 778–79, 812, 821, 830
Greek organizations. *See* fraternities; sororities
Greene, Jody, 721
Greenlaw, Steven A., 589, 837
green movement. *See* environmental issues
Greenspan, Peter, 817
Greenwood and Associates, 821, 857(n8)
Gregg, Stephen, 796
Gregory, Dick, 158
Grellet and Dorothy Simpson Series in Medieval Literature, 171
Grellet C. Simpson Award for Excellence in Undergraduate Teaching, 170–71, 837–38. *See also specific recipients*
Grellet C. Simpson International Scholarship, 171, 382, 801
grievance board, 291
Griffin, Stephen, 571, 574–75
Grosekopf, Ruth Bonner, 755
Grover, Peter, 511
grunge look, 671–72
GSU (Gay Student Union), 265–66, 431
Guest, Raymond, 547
guides (to campus), student, 362
Gulf War *(1990–91)*, 502–5, 852(n82)
gun club, 736. *See also* Rifle Club
Gurian, Elaine Heumann, 585
Gurien, Robin, 601
Gwathmey, Robert, 153

Habitat for Humanity, 461–62
Hair, David, 584, 691–92
Hairfield, James, 553
Hairston, Cris, 653
Haley, James W., Jr., 790
Hall, Chris, 104
Hall, Dana, 747
Hall, Jane, 582
Hall, Philip L., **584**
abortion forum moderated, 470

Hall, Philip L., *(continued)*
background, 337
on cheating, 689
on class sizes, 365
Dance Department eliminated, 403
on the demise of Russian courses, 622
elevated to provost, 337, 848(n15)
e-mail use encouraged, 535
and the Ethnic Studies controversy, 394–95
on Fickett, 632
and the general education requirements, 388–89
on Jepson, 519
and the Jiminez lawsuit, 489–91
on JMC's architecture, 760
on Manning, 388
on Merchent, 335
on merit pay, 406
on minor programs, 401
and the pipe band, 699
retirement, 576
role during Anderson's illness, 523
TIP program supported, 562
on undergraduate research, 407
Young Faculty award presented, **630**
Hallerman, Anne Robinson, 731
Halloweens (party), 248–49, 413, 443–45
Halloween trick-or-treat, 464
Halsey, Don P., 39
Hamblet, Newman, 840
Hamer, Anne, 627–28
Hamilton, Lynn, 761
Hamlet, W. N., 7–9, 33, 843(n5)
Hamlet House
male students in, 91, 92
"personality," 409
purchased, 33
testing facility and counseling center in, 81
TIP program in, 562
TOGA party, **247**, 247–48
Wo-Man Contest sponsored, 253, 438–43
Hamlisch, Marvin, 628
Hample, Judy Gayle, 829–30, **830**, 857(n3)
Hampton, Steve R., 438–39, 473, 637, 837
handbooks. *See* student handbooks
Hane, Sue Smith, 279, 840
Hanna, Stephen, 606
Hanna, Susan J., **150**, 594
abortion symposium moderated, 468–69
Academic Regulations and Advising Committee chaired, 288–89
as Chi Beta Phi auctioneer, 250
death, 152
and the feminist movement, 150, 152, 347, 466, 594, 845(n36)
husband (*see* Van Sant, George M.)
and pedagogy, 562
on the proposed name change, 345–46
scholarship established in memory of, 594
Simpson Award, 150, 837
TOGA party attended, 248
and the Wo-Man Contest, 252–53
Hanna Memorial Scholarship, 594
Hansen, Brad, 589
Hansen, Richard E. "Dick," 161, 518, 592, **592**, 593–94, 836
Hanson, William (Bill), 488, 534, 640, 641, 666, 696
Harambee 360° (theater group), 107, 648
Harber, Debra, 361
Harding, Mardy, 670
Hargrove, Margaret, 75, 158
Harris, Anna Mae, 330, 621, 847(n32)
Harris, Curtis W., 107–8
Harris, James, 667
Harris, Ruby, 188–90
Harris, Steven, 617
Harrison, Albertis, 184
Harrison, Gunyon M., 14
Harrisonburg Teachers College. *See* James Madison University
Hart, Ford, 271
Hart, Geoff, 400
Hartman, Karen, 761
Hatch, Andrea, 688
Hatch, Diane, 582
Hatcher, Harlan H., 73
hate speech, 487–89, 850(n42). *See also* race relations on campus
Hawkens, David, 274–76, 847(n26)
Hawley, Buddy, 748
Haydar, Sonja Dragomanovic, 313, 402, 403
Haymes, Robin, 589
Haynes, Medford D., 76, 94, 166, 667
Hayob, Jodie, 603
hazing
freshmen beanies, 126–27, **127**
Junior Ring Week pranks, 451–56, **452**
women's basketball team, 752–53
Head, Ronald, 201
Head, Travis, 554
head of the home, 12–13. *See also* dean of students; dean of women
health. *See* AIDS; contraception; counseling center; fitness center; flu epidemic; Health Center
Health and Physical Education Department. *See* athletic program/department; Physical Education Department
Health Center, 430, 470–73, 796, 850(n33). *See also* infirmary; Overman, Ilma Meade
Hearn, Charles M. "Pete," 382, 520
Hearne, Mimi, 136
Hedelt, Rob, 442

Heffner, Alan, 761
Hegman, Katherine Cesky, 509
Hegmann, Edward H., II, **198**
on alcohol policy, 424
and athletic facilities, 199–200, 215
on attendance policy, 288
and gender equality, 197, 756
hired and background, 196–97
and the men's basketball team, 197–98, 748, 749
and outstanding athlete recognition, 754–55
philosophy, 198–99, 741, 757
on the rowing team, 746
and the school colors and mascot, 358, 359
on tenure for coaches, 750
and the women's basketball hazing incident, 753
and women's tennis, 198, 742
Helbling, Todd, 742
Helton, William, 590
Henriques, Peter, 830
Hentoff, Nat, 327
Hershey, Lewis, 134–35, 138
Hewetson, Henry W., 78
Hickey, Liz, 754, 828
Hicks, Robert, 553
Higher Education Study Commission, 96, 191
"High on Marye's Hilltop" (Crotty and Taylor), 62. *See also* alma mater
Hilldrup, Robert L., 59–60, 77, 611
Hillel, 432, 445, 485–86, 493, 694
Hinz, Dan H., Jr., 382
Hirschkop, Philip, 89–90
Historic Fredericksburg Foundation, 304
Historic Preservation Club, 692
Historic Preservation Department, 607–11
and Belmont and Monroe Museum, 226, 230, 516
faculty, 607–8 (*see also specific individuals*)
major established, 203–4
moved to Combs, 539
Woodard Chair of Historic Preservation, 384, 607, 837
Woodard's enthusiasm for subject, 210
See also Center for Historic Preservation
History and American Studies Department, 611–20
75th anniversary lectures, 312
American Revolution bicentennial lectures, 223
American Studies program, 59–60, 112–13, 294, 617–18, 620
curriculum, 613–14, 618–19
faculty, 611–17, **614** (*see also specific individuals*)
and the historic preservation major, 203–4 (*see also* Historic Preservation Department)
honorary society, 619–20, 692
human rights concentration, 617–18
Political Science separated from, 77–78 (*see also* Political Science Department)
and the proposed American history requirement, 565–66
public lectures, 223, 289, 312, 618–19 (*see also* "Great Lives" public lecture series)
scholarships, 620
social activities, 248, 449–50, 619–20
History and Political Science Department. *See* History and American Studies Department; Political Science Department
History of Mary Washington College, 1908–1972 (Alvey), x
HIV/AIDS, 430–31, 479–82
Hockaday, Patsy, 670
Hoes, Laurence Gouverneur, 230
Hofer, Florian "Red," 333, 377, 654–55, 790, 820, 840
Hofer, Janet, 654–55
Hofer Chair of Early American Culture and Historic Preservation, 837
Hogan, Kelly, 313
Hohl, Lisa, 461
Holdren, Brad, 742
holiday decorations, 361, 445
Hollibaugh, Beth, 747
Holmes, Claudith "Dottie," 101–3, 106, 209
Holmes, Jannan, 686
Holmes, Joseph, 591
Holton, Linwood, 98, 138–39, 231
Holz, Louise, 234
homecoming, 161–62, 656, 721, 755, 821
Home Department, 12–13
home economics department/program, 31, 55, 77, 168, 182–83, 188–90, **189**
homeless shelter, 459, 460–61, 641
homosexuality
campus attitudes toward, 143–44, 264–66, 431–37
Greek system and, 682
The Laramie Project (play), 644–45
nondiscrimination policy, 404, 435
spousal equivalency benefits, 404–5
student groups, 265–66, 431–33, 555, 682
See also NAMES Project Memorial Quilt
honorary doctorates, 616, 763, 833, 835
honorary societies. *See specific societies and departments*

Honor Council. *See* Honor System
honors admission, 651
honors program, 59, 843(n18)
Honor System
1950s–60s, 127–28
Alvey and, xi
Anderson era *(1983–2006)*, 682–91
Frawley era *(2006-7)*, 795–96
mass cheating incident, 688–89
revisions and legal challenge *(1970s)*, 127–30, 624
Russell era *(1911–20)*, 12
self-scheduled exams and, 112
test files and, 682–83
transcript notations, 689–90
Hoof Prints Club, 47, 736, 747–48. *See also* MWC Cavalry
Hope House, 459, 589, 594, 716
Hopper, Katherine Edmonson
at the 75th anniversary celebrations, 311, 314
and administrative salaries, 298
as Board secretary, 98
Board term, 840
and the Governor's School for the Gifted, 221
honorary doctorate received, 835
as Rector, 241, 279, 280, **296**
on the vote of confidence in Woodard, 296
Hornsby, Bruce, 546
Hornsby, Lois Saunier, 546
horseback riding, 47–50, **48**, 736, 742, 747–48
Hoshi-Bush, Susie, 524–25, 526
Houck, R. Edward "Edd," 346, 350–51, 772–73
Houghtalin, Lianne, 582
housekeeping staff, 825–26
housing. *See* dormitories; off-campus housing
Houston, Levin, III, 44, 626
Houston, Michael, 75, 102, 122, 166, 852(n83)
Howard, Neil, 642, 847(n24)
Howard-Hassman, Rhoda, 618, 645
Howell, Henry, 153
Howie, Craig, 253
Hoye, Anna Scott "Scottie," 78, 575, 837
Huber, Margaret W., 640, 640–41, 833, 836
Hudgins, Carter L., 607
on 9/11, 534
archaeological dig, 571
awards and honors, 836, 837
centennial convocation, 831
and the Historic Preservation Department, 607, 608–9, 610
and the History Department, 617
Travel Club tour led by, 658
Hudgins, Donna, 648
Hudgins, Edward W., 74
Huggins, Pamela Tompkins, 117, 132
Hughes, Elizabeth Smith, 546, 547, 781, 840
Hughes, Holly, 468
Hughes, India, 553
human resources, 336, 670
human rights, student interest in. *See* Amnesty International; Copprome; Human Rights Club; Invisible Children UMW Chapter
Human Rights Club, 530, 532–33, 694–98, 826
Human Sexuality course, 437–38
Hume, Betty, 349
Humphrey, Hubert, 154, 633
Humphrey, Shawn, 826
Hunger Awareness Week, 459
Hunt, David, 643
Hurley, Richard
as acting president, **811**, 811, 822–23, 826, 829
background and qualifications, 821–22
campanile dedication, 812–13
on Dodd Hall's refurbishing, 540
hired, 336, 822
and the "living wage" campaign, 696, 697
and the Marye's Heights apartments purchase, 544
position under Frawley, 787
Washington Medallion awarded to, 833
Hurley, Rose (wife of R. Hurley), 822
hurricanes
Hugo, 459, 557, 610
Isabel, 557–59
Katrina, 464
Hussein, Saddam, 502–5
Huswifery Club, 692
Hutcherson, Shannon, 745
Hydorn, Debra, 621

Iacunato, John, 549. *See also* Wood Company (later Sodexho)
Ideas and Movements of the Western World (graduate course), 207–8
identification cards (ID), 421, 536
Idol, Billy, 701
Iltis, Hugo, 51–52, 843(n17)
image of MWC/UMW
in the *1980s*, 339–44
in the *1990s*, 422–23
College seal, 356–58
concerns about feminine name, 92, 299–302, 340–43, 347 (*see also* name of the college/university)
"finishing school" image, 108–9, 125, 142–43, 283, 301
See also reputation of MWC/UMW
inaugurations
Anderson, 330–33, **332**, 647, **P1**

Frawley, 789–91
Simpson, 72–74, 104, 572
Woodard, 183–86
India, faculty exchange program with, 79–80
industrial arts program, 7–8, 10
infirmary, 57, 215. *See also* Health Center
influenza epidemics, 18, 30
information and technology proficiency requirement, 538, 851(n66)
Inge, Gordon, 549. *See also* ARA (food service provider)
Ingham, Robert, 643
Ingham, Rosemary, 643, 672–73
Ingrao, Mark, 274–76, 278
in loco parentis concept, 13, 64, 115, 124, 238, 240, 325, 416. *See also* rules and regulations; visitation rules
Insley, Earl G., 837
Institute for Study Abroad Foundations, 801
instructional technology, 536–39
Instructional Technology, Department of (DoIT), 537
Instruction and Academic Affairs Committee, 291
integration of MWC, 98–108, 121. *See also* African American students; race relations on campus
Inter-Club Association, 722–23
international affairs major (formerly pre–foreign service), 78, 633–34
International Club, 390
internationalism
Anderson era *(1983–2006)*, 389–93, 466, 570–71
centennial year (2007–8), 827
foreign students, 390, 801
Frawley era *(2006-7)*, 788, 801
global awareness requirement, 389–90, 393, 397, 823
historic preservation department and, 608–9
Latin American studies, 78
and Russian language instruction, 622
Simpson era *(1955–74)*, 79–80
See also Asian studies; Ethnic Studies course; foreign studies; multiculturalism; Political Science Department; study-abroad programs
International Relations Club, 45
Internet social networks, 540, 712, 728–29, 753. *See also* Facebook
internships, 200–201
AV center, 254
Belmont and Monroe museums, 226, 230, 516
and community involvement, 315
computer science, 588
development of program, 200–201, 579, 604
foreign languages, 623
historic preservation, 204, 608, 610
lauded by *Free Lance–Star*, 315
NSWC (Dahlgren) internships, 588
psychology, 636
in Washington, D.C., 603, 636
"Intolerance and Toleration" (national conference), 584–85
intramural sports program, 735–36. *See also* athletic program / department; *and specific sports*
Invisible Children UMW Chapter, 794
Invoice (male a cappella group), 700, 731
iPods and music downloads, 728
Ippolito, Kent, 598
Iran hostage crisis, 271–74
Iraq
Gulf War *(1990–91)*, 502–5, 852(n82)
Iraq War (*2003*–present), 534
Irby, Myra, 102, 611
Ireland, Patricia, 468
Islamic Awareness Week, 794–95
Islamic photographs exhibit, 573
Islamic Student Association, 391, 464, 694, 794–95
Ismael, Zareen, 794
Italian language. *See* Ascari, Clavio F.
Italy, programs in, 572, 623, 658

Jackson, Shirley, 315
Jacobus, Hester Zella, 67
James Farmer Multicultural Center, 388, 531, 641, 662–66, 795
James Farmer Scholars Program, 366–67, 591, 652
James Farmer Visiting Professorship in Human Rights, 618, 645
James Madison University (JMU; Harrisonburg), x, 2–3, 9–10, 21, 30, 39, 41, 91, 211, 314, 342, 365, 654, 692, 701, 849(n32)
James Monroe Center (JMC), 758–63, **763**, 774–75. *See also* College of Graduate and Professional Studies
James Monroe Foundation. *See* James Monroe Law Office-Museum and Memorial Library
James Monroe Law Office-Museum and Memorial Library
Center for Historic Preservation and, 609
control over, 98, 230–33, 302, 514–15, 517
Mrs. Nixon's visit cancelled, 137–38
programs, 515–17
property, 846–47(n19)

James Monroe Lecture
Series, 516
Jamison, Mildred, 188–90
Janice Collier Sickle Cell
Anemia Fund benefit program, 107
Janney, Elsie, 512
Jarrell, Robert, 520
Jazz Ensemble, 626, 789
J. Christopher Bill
Outstanding Faculty
Service Award, 639, 839.
See also specific recipients
Jean, Wyclef, 701
Jefferson Hall
construction and name,
82
"personality," 244, 409
racial tensions, 487, 825–26
visitation rules, 320–21, 324
(*see also* visitation rules)
Jensen, Beate, 512
Jepson, Alice Andrews and
Robert S., Jr., 383, 509, **P4**
Alumni Executive Center
gift, 546–47, 548
Board term (Alice), 841
first gift, 383–84
honorary doctorate received (Alice), 835
lifetime contribution, 659
Science Center gift, 384,
518–19, **P10**
Jepson Alumni Executive
Center, 57, 546–49, 812,
828, 833, **P9**
Jepson Fellows Program,
383–84, 404, 595
Jepson Science Center,
379, 518–19, 537, 557, 850–
51(n56), **P8, P10,**
Jewish Student Association,
694
Jewish students, 445, 485–86,
694. *See also* Hillel
Jiminez, Anthony "Jimmy,"
489–91, 852(n90)
Jingle Bells Run, 459
Johnson, Gary, 670
Johnson, Johnny, 103, 107
Johnson, Joyce, 670
Johnson, Lyndon B., 133,
134, 154, 155
Johnson, Natalie Joy, 720–21,
856(n158)
Johnson, Peggy, 544
Johnson, Rosemary, 575
Johnson, Sabrina, 336, 790
Johnson, Thomas, 135, 147,
575
Jones, Charles, 667
Jones, Charlotte, 649
Jones, Edward P., 666, 795
Jones, Gordon, 647
Jones, Jeff, 503–4
Jones, Lucille, 582
Jones, Venus, **101**, 101–2,
844–45(n17)
Jordan, Daniel, 516, 610
Joyce, Michael J., 562,
642–43, 837
judicial system, college, 116,
121. *See also* Honor System
Junior Ring Dance, 85, **163**,
163–64, 250, 438, 450–51
Junior Ring Week, 250,
361, 450–56, **452**, 718,
849(nn26–27)
juniors. *See* Devil-Goat rivalry; Junior Ring Dance;
Junior Ring Week; junior-year-abroad programs
junior-year-abroad programs, 80. *See also* study-abroad programs

Kaine, Timothy, 790, 831
Kakava, Christina, 564, 600,
658
Kalnen, Elizabeth "Becky,"
547, 550–51
Kalnen Inn, 546–49. *See also*
Jepson Alumni Executive
Center; Trench Hill
Kappa Delta Pi (education
honorary), 591
Kappa Delta Rho (fraternity), 680–81
Kappa Gamma Sigma (sorority), 681–83
Kappert, Michael, 657
karaoke, 720
Keezell, G. B., 2–3
keg parties, 164, 244–47,
247–48, 409, 413, 415–16,
418, 419, 446–47, 675–76
Keith, Warren, 691
Kelley, Laraine, 183
Kelly, Mary Annette "Toni,"
81, 660
Kemp, Mary, 593, 670
Kemp, William "Bill," 207,
562, 563, 593, 692, 837
Kenmore, 137–38
Kennedy, Robert, 154
Kennedy, Teresa, 171, 398,
406, 595–96
Kenny, Diane-Louise, 102
Kent State University killings, 136, 137
Kenvin, Roger, 223, 642
Kerr, Beatrice. *See* von
Guggenberg, Beatrice
Key Club, 784–85
Keyser, Laura, 465
Killian, Joella, 576–77
Kilmartin, Christopher,
637–38
on homosexuality at
MWC, 434
on Junior Ring Week
pranks, 454
one-man show, **637**, 637–38
on Rita Thompson, 653
on student-faculty dating,
478
on video/computer
games, 728
and women's issues, 152,
475–77, 494
King, Brenda, 391, 474,
484–85, 488–89, 491, 663
King, Florence, 542,
856(n160)
King, George, III, 562, 595,
629–30, **630**, 838, 853(n100)
King, Martin Luther, Jr., 100,
101, 102–3. *See also* Martin
Luther King Day
King, Nellie, 682–83
King, Pauline, 571
King, W. Marshall, 50
Kinney, Matt, 745
Kinniburgh, John, 329, 351,
354, 356, 368, 377, 841
Kintzing, Meg, 198, 747
Kirby, Pamela, 615, 701
Kirkpatrick, Jeane, 457
Kirschner, Michael, 748

Kisila, Ben Odhiambo, 603
Kissinger, Henry, 517
Kitterman, David, **93**, 240
Klein, Albert R., 160, 642, 852(n83)
Klein, Debby (wife of A. Klein), 644
Klein Theatre, 160, 223, 224, 642
Klim, Rita, 581
Kline, Milton, 554, 813
Knick, Susan, 558
Knight, Kathleen, 460
Kolar, David, 637, 781
Konieczny, Janusz, 621, 838
Koos, Leonard, 565, 623
Korean students, 801
Korn/Ferry International, 781–82, 820, 857(n8)
Kramer, John M. "Jack," 632–35, **634**
on the 1992 presidential election, 506
awards and honors, 633, 836, 838
on Capitol Hill internships, 636
European Capitals summer program, 392–93, 613, 634
influence on students, 466
and the pre–foreign service/international affairs program, 78, 633–34
and students' writing, 634–35
Krebs, Sir Hans, 581
Kresge Foundation, 546
Krikus, Richard J., 391, 506, 507, 632, 633, 836
Kunstler, William, 137

LaCivita, Jeanette, 629
lacrosse, 198, 214–15, 742, 746–47
Laingen, L. Bruce, 585
Lakatos, Tony, 626
L'Allier, Brooks, 552
Lamar, Andrew, 536
Lamph, John, 571, 704
Lancaster, Maggie, xiv, 619
Langenback, Lisa, 266
Langston-Harrison, Lee, 515
language houses/floors, 56, 622–23, 853(n111)
The Laramie Project (play), 644–45
Larson, Steve, 642
Larus, Elizabeth Freund, 635
Late Wife (Emerson), 598
Latin (language), 75
Latin American studies, 78
laundry, 796–97
lawns, 217–20, 222, 251, 305, 409
Lazzari, Valerie, 670
Leakey, Mary, 510
Leback, Thomas, 337
lecturers, visiting. *See* speakers, visiting
Lederman, Leon, 631
Lee Hall
Ballroom, 24, **163**, 163–64, 244–45, 313–14, 450
construction, 57
C-Shop, 215–16, 315, 371
day care center, 148–49
General Assembly reception and dinner in, 330
Halloween events, 249, 444
Junior Ring Dance in, 163–64, 450
keg parties, 164, 244–45
Multicultural Center, 388, 662, 665
renovation, 709, 796, 802
Simpson inaugural ball in, 74
swimming pool, 24, 84, 215
writing center, 387–88
Leesman, Katie, 772, 773
Lefferts, Peter, 419
Legend, John, 702
Lehman, Larry, 621
Leidecker, Kurt F., 585–86
and Asian studies, 58, 78, 79, 585–86
chair named for, 384, 836
and the pre–foreign service major, 78, 633–34
Leidecker Center, 586
Leidecker Chair in Asian Studies, 384, 836
Leighty, Martha Kearns, 781, 841
Leighty, William, 773
Lemoine, Bernard, 312, 626
Lenhart, Charmenz, 69
Lentine, Genine, 490
Levitt, Alfred, 573, 835
Lewis, Anne, 708–9
Lewis, Betsy, 623
Lewis, Henry, 598
Lewis, Ramsey, 628
"The Liberal Arts College for Women at Fredericksburg, Virginia," 40
library, 372–75, 645–50
buildings (*see* Simpson Library; Trinkle Library)
capacity, 83, 372
CGPS library, 854(nn124, 131)
classification system, 374
collection and capacity, 83, 372, 650
computerization and technology, 373–75, 645–47, 650
number of patrons, 854(n126)
rare books collection, 75, 83, 647
staff, 647–50 (*see also specific individuals*)
library science, 55
Liebau, Bob, 735, 742
Lightfoot, Gordon, 160
Likins, Rose McCartney, 636, 835
Limbaugh, Rush, 602–3, 853(n103)
Lindeman, Monica, 402
Lindsey, Alexander, 206, 250, 587, 620–21
Lindsey, Almont T., 35, 331, 611, 620. *See also* Whitfield, Doris Lindsey
linguistics program, 593, 600. *See also* English, Linguistics, and Speech Department
Lipscomb, Stephen, 621
lip-sync contest, 720
Liss, Miriam N., 636–37, 838

literary societies, 14
Little, Clark, 261
"living wage" campaign, 694, 696–98
Lloyd F. Moss Free Clinic, 462
log cabin, 33, **640**, 641
Lohr, Bill, 755
London, Bruce, 640
Lonestar (country group), 702
Long, David J., 312, 626, 790, 832, 838
Longwood College (Farmville; Longwood University), 1, 9–10, 21, 30, 41–42, 91, 211, 342–43, 645, 764, 768
Lotze, Cynthia, 722
Lovelace, Ruth, 558
Lowery, Pamela, 537
Lowry, Hugh, 251
Lowry, Katherine, 471, 777
Lucas, Bill, 739
Luntz, George E., 85
Lutterbie, Carlton, Jr., 221, 407–8, 593–94, 704, 847(n24)
Luttrell, Bette, 670
Luttrell, Terry, 787
Lycett, Dee, 670
Lyons, Dwight, **93**
Lyons, Meghan, 696. *See also* "living wage" campaign
Lyons, Scott, 654–55

MacDonald, Christopher, 657
MacDonald, John, 736
MacDonald, Norm, 702
MacDonald, Robert U., 361
MacEwen, David, 637
Macfarlane, Anne Beck, 509, 841
Macfarlane, John, 509
Machande, Kenneth D. "Ken," 577, 839
MacLuskie, Kevin, 703
Madison College/University. *See* James Madison University
Madison Hall
  construction, 32–33
  drug arrests in, 260
  Haunted House party, 443–44
  as male dorm, 195
  Night Haven facility, 677–78
  service learning floor, 460
  T-shirts sold to promote MWC name, **346**, 349–50
Mahon, Mary, 180
Mahoney, Bernard L., Jr., 578–80, **579**, 836, 837
maintenance department. *See* Physical Plant/Facilities Services
major field
  hours limited, 287
  interdepartmental majors, 59–60, 78
  major-counseling night, 80
  new majors introduced (Woodard era), 203–5
  requirements, 41, 55
  See also specific majors and departments
Make a Difference Day, 464
male students
  1920s–50s, 62–64, **63**, 85
  1960s (move toward coeducation), 86–91
  1970s (coeducation's early years), 91–96, 169, 192–95, 299
  academic ability, 297
  attitudes toward female students, 195, 425
  calendars featuring, 426–28
  dormitories, 91–94, 195
  enrollment levels, 91, 92, 192–95, 283, 408
  first graduates, 92–93
  and homecoming, 161–62
  and the Mary Washington name, 92, 299–302, 340–43, 347, 767–68 (*see also* name of the college/university)
  Mr. MWC contest, 721–22
  recruitment, 91, 169, 192–95
  relationships with female students (*see* dating; sex and sexuality)
  social impact, 88
  sports (*see* athletic program/department; *and specific sports*)
  striptease shows, 428
  Trench Hill as dorm for, 57
  Wo-Man Contest, 252–53, 438–43, **439**
  See also coeducation
Mallan, Lloyd, 642
Malone, Candice, 747
management information systems, master's degree in, 588, 763
Mancuso, Joseph, 413, 414
Mandelker, Deborah, 148–49
Mann, William Hodges, 5–6
Manning, Carol S., 386–88, 400, 593, 837
Manns, Paul W., 280
marching band, **35**, 35–36, 84
marijuana, 258, 259, 674–75
  legalization efforts, 123, 259–61
Marilla, Patricia, 133
Marines (from Quantico), 84, 131–32, 133, 141–42, 245, 313–14
Marsh, Henry, 100, 269
Marsh, Kristen, 641
Marshall, Emmitt, 347
Marshall, Mary Willis Ambler, 82
Marshall Hall, 82, 244, 320–21, 324, 409, 723
marshal of the faculty, 604, 847(n32). *See also* Barra, Rosemary; Emory, Samuel T., Jr.; Harris, Anna Mae; Stageberg, Stephen
Martin, Carol, 376–77, 529, 537
Martin, Ivy R., 264–67
Martin, Phyllis Ridderhof, 375–76. *See also* Ridderhof Martin Gallery
Martin Luther King Day, 483, 584, 641, 652, 662, 826
Martin Luther King Scholarship, 103
Marvashti, Reva, 531

Mary Ball Hall. *See* Ball Hall
Marye House (Hall), 11, 79, 409, 665–66
Marye's Heights, 4–5
Marye's Heights Apartments, 542–45, 559, 662, 797
Mary Pinschmidt Award. *See* Pinschmidt Award
Mary Siegrist Hinz Leadership Awards program, 382
Mary Wash Free Times (independent newspaper), 280
Mary Washington Ambassadors, 657
Mary Washington College (MWC)
  75th anniversary celebration, 303, 312–15, 647
  accreditation, 30–31
  chancellor/president title changes, 72, 98
  early years (*see* Fredericksburg State Normal and Industrial School for Women; State Normal School at Fredericksburg; State Teachers College at Fredericksburg)
  finances (*see* endowment of MWC/UMW; finances of MWC/UMW)
  founding, 1–9
  location, 4–5
  name (*see* name of the college/university)
  opening, 6
  reputation (*see* reputation of MWC/UMW)
  transition into liberal arts college, 38–40
  U. Va., merger with, 53–56, 68, 187, 212
  U. Va., separation from, 96–98, 212, 228, 231
  See also University of Mary Washington; *and specific topics, departments, facilities, and individuals*
Mary Washington College–Community Symphony Orchestra. *See* College–Community Orchestra
Mary Washington College Foundation, 212, 380, 381, 382. *See also* endowment of MWC/UMW
Mary Washington Hospital, 459, 524–25, 526, 758
Mary Washington Real Estate Foundation, 824
mascot, 358–61, 551–52
Mason, Frank, 848(n1)
Mason Hall, 11, 57, 68, 409–10, 723
Massey, Timothy, 554
master's degree programs
  business administration (MBA), 209–10, 577, 757, 763, 846(n15), 856(n168)
  education (M.Ed.), 763
  liberal studies (MALS), 207–9, 614, 757
  management information systems (MSMIS), 763
  public administration degree (MPA), 757
  See also College of Graduate and Professional Studies; graduate studies at MWC
Mathematical Sciences and Physics Department, 587, 621. *See also* Computer Science Department; Mathematics Department; Physics Department
Mathematics Department, 41, 83, 587, 620–21, 670. *See also specific individuals*
Matthews, Thad, 441
Mattox, Gale, 636
May, Adrienne, 391, 591
May Day, **17**
  Chandler era *(1920–28)*, 26
  effort to revive, 722–23
  no longer celebrated, 27
  Russell era *(1911–20)*, 16, 21
  Simpson era *(1955–74)* and demise, 124–25, **125**
Mayer, John, 702
Mayer, Kathleen, 256
Mayo, Sara Page Cosby and Richard, 785
Mazur, Eric, 830
McAllister, Joan, 193–94
McBride, Christine A., 637, 838
McCall, Venitta, 367, 562, 591
McCarthy, Eugene, 154
McCarthy, John, 253
McCarthy, Yuri, 126
McClellan-Holt, Jean, 681, 736
McClurken, Jeffrey, 453, 617
McCluskey, Kevin, 672
McConnell, Robert "Bob," 602–3, 853(n103)
McCort, Frank, 658
McCue-Randolph Bill, 54
McCullough, David, 658, 831–32
McDaniel, Charles G., 382
McGill, Forrest, 376, 573
McGovern, George, 154–55
McGovern, Gina, 696. *See also* "living wage" campaign
McGurk, Shannon, 262, 268
McKeough, Moira, 237
McManus, Mark, 648
McMenamin, Lester "Mac," 337
McMurtry, Lawrence, 382, 835
McNeill, Virginia Goolrick, 313
Mead, Margaret, 159
Meadows, George, 465
media, student, 254–55, 702–10. *See also specific student publications*
medical technology program, 60, 848(n16)
medieval studies program, 596. *See also* Grellet and Dorothy Simpson Series in Medieval Literature
Meekins, Marsha, 103
Mehfoud, Kathleen Shepherd
  Board term, 841
  Jepson Science Center groundbreaking, **P10**

Mehfoud, Kathleen Shepherd *(continued)*
and the Mehfoud committees, 760, 766, 769 (*see also* Mehfoud committee[s])
as Rector, 333, 377
Mehfoud committee(s), 760, 764, 766, 767–69
Mehrabi, Shah, 390, 852(n90)
Mejia, Matthew, 362, 557, 653, 745, 856(n164)
Melchers, Corinne (wife of G. Melchers), 227, 511, 512
Melchers, Gari, 226–27, 312, 510–13. *See also* Belmont
Melchers Hall, 57, 379, 537, 572, 574
Melle, Francis, 670
Mellinger, Keith, 833
Mello, Michael, 260, 675, 847(n23)
Mendel Museum, 52, 843(n17)
Mercer Hall, 57, 215
Merchent, A. R. "Ray"
and Anderson-era building projects, 368, 370, 371
background and qualifications, 334–35
BLS program headed, 202
on "Blue Tide," 848(n9)
on the CIA recruiter protest, 180
dean search committee chaired, 297
death, 335
as director of admissions, 75
as executive vice president, 334–36, **335**
on Muhammad's speech, 485
presidential search committee chaired, 311
on the relaxed visitation rules, 324
report on MWC's image prepared, 341–42
and the ROTC proposal, 329
on the satellite campus, 758
on student drinking, 424
student retention report, 415
and the Wo-Man Contest, 442
on Woodard, 306, 307
Merhige, Robert, 130
Merrill, Austin, 362, 465
Merrill, Sammy R., 623–24, P3
awards and honors, 624, 836, 837, 839
on the foreign language requirement, 398
and the honor system committee, 686
and the men's basketball team, 161
Travel Club tour led, 658
on white denial of racism, 488
Merten, Alan, 790
Mery, Michael, 703
Metzger, Patricia, 436, 470, 498, 499, 578
Meyer, Barbara, 207, 326, 328, 571, 846(n8)
Mi, Marge Klayton, 577
Micou, Barbara Burton, 790, 820, 831, 841
Mid-Atlantic Research, Inc., 758
Middle Eastern studies, 585–86
Mighty Pen (publication), 707
Mike Club, 254
Mikhalevsky, Nina, 787, 823
Miller, Frederick, 703
Miller, Richard, 336, 670
Minor, Charlotte Major, 509, 546–47, 841
Minor, Dora, 670
Minor, Gilmer, III, 509
minor field, 41, 55, 400–401, 567–68
minority faculty
African American faculty, 289–90, 486–87, 489–91, 561–62
Anderson era *(1983–2006)*, 486–87, 489–91, 561–62
Indian faculty, 79–80, 289
recruitment, 289–90, 336, 561
Woodard era *(1974–82)*, 289–90
See also specific individuals
minority students
African American students (*see* African American students; integration of MWC)
Korean students, 801
Latin American students, 51
Muslim students, 391, 531, 533 (*see also* Islamic Student Association)
recruitment, 283, 365–68, 800
student groups, 694 (*see also specific groups*)
Mitchell, Ashton, 828
Mitchell, Nancy H., 206, 287, 357, 591–92, 704, 837, 853(n95)
Mitchell, Sidney H., 69, 591–92, 837
Modern Foreign Languages Department, 621–25
Arabic added, 852(n84)
ASL debated, 564–65
Early Humanities/Classical Civilization requirements, 60
faculty, 622–25 (*see also specific individuals*)
foreign films sponsored, 730
foreign language graduation requirements, 79, 287, 397–98, 564–65, 621–22
language houses/floors, 56, 622–23, 853(n111)
Middle Eastern languages, 586
Modern Foreign Language Week, 79
moved to Combs, 539
science degree requirements, 55
See also specific languages
Moeller, Thomas G., 171, 394–95, 469, 563, 637, 639, 697, 838

Moncure, Thomas, Jr., 153, 346, 352
Monroe, James
and the name of the institution, 344, 765–66 (*see also* name of the college / university)
papers published, 516
See also James Monroe Law Office-Museum and Memorial Library
Monroe Hall, **15**
administrative offices moved from, 10
auditorium, 6, 25, 216
benefits held in, 37
design and completion, 6, 9
Geography Department and cartography lab, 216, 406, 606
gymnasium, 6, 15, 25, 43
lecture hall, 216, 714
murals, 44, 216
name, 6, 18
plaza and fountain, 453, 551, 606, 727
renovation, 216
swimming pool, 6, 24, 216
Monroe Museum. *See* James Monroe Law Office-Museum and Memorial Library
Montagu, Ashley, 73
Montford Academy site, 540–42, 824–25, 851(n67)
Moody, James, 626
Moon, Krystyn, 617
Moore, Pat, 670
Morello, John T.
administrative role, 337–38
on Arabic teacher's departure, 565
awards, 838
and the Debate Club, 600, 692
and the General Education Review Committee, 800
on Perot, 506
and the speaking center, 601
and Student Research and Creativity Day, 811–12
Morgan, Kelly, 462
Morgan, Sherry, 336–37
Morgan, Tracy, 702
Moriarty, Dennis Chauncey, 63
Morris, Marceline "Marcy" Weatherly, 723, 857(n4)
Morris, Willie, 658
Morrison, A. Elizabeth, 748, 835
Mortar Board (honor society), 162, 250, 283, 461
Morton, W. Brown, III, 607–8
awards and honors, 609, 833, 837
and Belmont, 511
and date rape awareness, 853(n106)
hurricane damage assessment, 610
summer program in Scotland, 571, 608–9
Travel Club tour led, 658
Moshos, April, 747
Moss, Charles George Gordon, 30
Mosser, Josh, 856(n163)
Mother's (pub), 421
Mothers (rugby team). *See* Rugby Club
Motley, Donald, 553
motto of the college, 89, 357, 776–77
Moulton, George, 134
Mr. MWC contest, 721–22
Muhammad, Khalid Abdul, 485–86
Muick, Paul C., 571, **592**
Mulcare, Don, 183–84
Muller, Judy Mansfield, 517, 850(n55), **P10**
Multicultural Center. *See* James Farmer Multicultural Center
Multicultural Fair, 51, 108, 663–64, **664**, 794
multiculturalism, 389–96, 662–66. *See also* African American studies; Asian studies; foreign studies; internationalism; James Farmer Multicultural Center; Latin American studies; minority faculty; minority students
Munford, Beverly B., 39
Murphy, Tayloe, 352–53
Mushen, Emily, 715
music
"battle of the bands" contests, 720
a capella groups, 699–700 (*see also* Una Voce)
college radio station broadcasts, 254
community involvement, 223–26
at Halloweens, 249, 443
iPods and downloads, 728
karaoke, 720
at senior parties, 446–47
See also concerts; Music Department; *and specific groups and performers*
Music Department, 624–29
Chorus, 84–85, 331, 626, 789
concert band, 84
ensembles, 626–27 (*see also specific ensembles*)
faculty, 626 (*see also specific individuals*)
glee club, 14, 73–74
marching band, **35**, 35–36, 84
non-departmental choirs (*see* BellACapella; Symfonics; Victory Chorus)
orchestra, 35, 61 (*see also* College–Community Orchestra)
Una Voce (a capella group), 626, 695, 700–701, 789, 791, 809
Musick, Chris, 571
Muslim Student Association, 533
Muslim students, 391, 531. *See also* Islamic Student Association
MWC. *See* Mary Washington College
MWC Cavalry, 47–50, **48**, 748
MWC Chorus (UMW Chorus), 84–85, 331, 626, 789

MWC Today (*UMW Today*; alumni magazine), 339, 351, 390, 789
My Brother's Place (restaurant and bar), 158, 421, 734
MySpace, 712, 729, 753
"Mysterium Humanum" (lecture series), 585

Nack, William, 812
Naden, Alex, 553
Nader, Ralph, 530, 585
Nagy, John, 692
Nails, Debra, 561
name of the college/university
 1980s–90s efforts to change, 299–302, 339–56, 597, 848(nn3–5, 8)
 changed to Mary Washington College, 39, 41–42, 63, 299
 concerns about feminine name, 92, 299–302, 340–43, 347, 751, 765–69, 775–76
 early names, 3, 9–10, 22, 299
 university status and, 765–78
 "Washington and Monroe" proposed, 344–56, 765, 767–71
NAMES Project Memorial Quilt, 481, 643
Nash, Angie, 183
Nash, Cynthia, 272
Nasr, Seyyed Hossein, 504, 585
National Latin Exam (NLE), 582
National Organization for the Advancement of Hispanics (NOAH), 623
National Organization for Women (NOW), 440, 459, 466–67, 681, 848(n5)
National Organization to Reform Marijuana Laws (NORML), campus chapter, 259–61, 675
National Park Service, 541, 733
National Slavery Museum, 574, 734
National Symphony Orchestra, 43
Native American Chamber Ensemble, 789
natural disasters
 flood of *1942*, 49–51
 historic preservation program's response, 610
 hurricanes, 459, 464, 557–559, 610, 684
 relief efforts, 50–51, 459, 464
Naval Postgraduate School (NPS), 800
Naval Surface Warfare Center (NSWC; Dahlgren), 206, 587, 588, 758, 800
Naylor, Craig T., 626–27, 789, 838
Neal, Gail Fallon
 at the 75th anniversary Convocation, 314
 at Anderson's inauguration, 331
 Board term, 841
 and dorm visitation rules, 321
 and the presidential search *(1983)*, 311, 316, 317
 as Rector, 333
 Woodard honored, 305
Neal, Pinson (son of G. Neal), 426
Nelli, Herva, 73
Nemko, Martin, 363–64
Newcomb, John Lloyd, 58
New Deal, 31, 36
New Dorm. *See* Arrington Hall
Newman, Tim, 648
newspapers, alternative, 707–8. *See also specific publications*
Newton, Huey, 144, 703
Nicholas, Joseph, 606
Nickel, Lorene, 571
Niebuhr, Vera, 623
Night Haven program, 677–78
Nightingale, Lawrence, 653
Nikolic, Nikola "Nick," 629
Nissim-Sabat, Denis, 329, 637, 639, 777, 802
Nixon, Patricia "Pat," 137–38
Nixon, Richard, 136, 154–55, 166
NOAH (National Organization for the Advancement of Hispanics), 623
Noesner, Gary, 532
nondiscrimination policies, 404, 435
nontraditional degree programs. *See* bachelor of liberal studies degree
NORML (National Organization to Reform Marijuana Laws), 259–61, 675
Norris, Ruby Lee, 832, 841
North Hall. *See* Alvey Hall
Norwood, Patricia A., 626, 832, 839
NOW. *See* National Organization for Women
NPR (National Public Radio), 633
NSWC. *See* Naval Surface Warfare Center
nuclear test ban, 501
nudity
 erotic yearbook, 792
 partial, in lip-sync contest, 720
 Psi Upsilon incident, 683–84
 streaking, 164–66, **165**, 725
 strip poker party, 422–24
nursing program, 60

obelisk, proposed, 551–52
O'Brien, Bruce, 561, 617
Och, Marjorie, 571, 573
O'Connell, Eileen, 274
O'Connell, Katherine, 149
O'Donnell, Timothy, 600, 692
Oesterheld, Lucretia, 670
off-campus housing, 42, 68, 421–22, 732–33
Office of Career Services, 201

Office of International Programs, 391
Office of Student Activities and Community Services (OSACS), 691
Office of University Advancement, 832
The Official Preppy Handbook (Birnbach), 236–37
Often, Clint, 742
Ohtani, Taketo, 137
Oliver, Cornelia D. "Neal," 69, 129, 571, 836
Olsen, Eric, 251
Olson, Joan, 640
Omicron Delta Epsilon (economics honorary society), 588
100th anniversary celebration. *See* centennial celebration
100th Night parties, 248, 445–47, 675–76. *See also* seniors: parties
O'Neill, Kathi, 122, 138
open-air theatre. *See* amphitheater
orchestra, 35, 61. *See also* College–Community Orchestra
O'Reilly, Amy, 670
organizations, student, 13–15, 691–702. *See also* clubs; fraternities; media, student; sororities; *and specific organizations*
orientation programs, 284
O'Rourke, Kathi, 426–27
Orrock, Nan Grogan, 99
Orstead, Kristin, 772
Ott, Edith Sheppard, 659–60, 841
outcomes assessment plan, 402
Outstanding Young Alumnus Award, 362, 617
Outstanding Young Faculty Member Award, 382, **630**, 838. *See also specific recipients*
Overman, Ilma Meade "Pete," 285–86, 430, 662, 796
PAC (Performing Arts Club), 698
Pacious, Kathleen, 717
Page, Kristen, 731
paint crew, student, 554
Painter, Andy, 688
PAL (People for Alternative Lifestyles), 440
Palamar, Ann T., 305, 357
Palmatory, Sharon, 535
Palmer, Barbara, 337, 399–400, 560
Palmieri, Richard, 234, 253, 395–96, 514, 604–6, **605**, **P3**
parade, 75th anniversary, 312–13
Parents' Weekend, 162, 250. *See also* Family Weekend
Park & Shop Center, 156, 368, 724, 824–25, 857(n2)
Parker, Forrest, 366, 653, 661, 662–65, 666
Parker, Judith, 481, 600
parking
 off-campus, 733
 on-campus, 368, 545, 549–50, 709, 742–43, 851(n67)
Parrish, Mary Jo, 69, 575
Parsons, Carolyn, 648–49
parties
 alcohol moratorium, 418–19
 dorm parties, 409–10, 418–19, 723–24
 Halloweens, 248–49, 412, 443–45
 "mocktail party," 413, 849(n21)
 off-campus parties, 421–23, 446, 733
 "romance enhancement" parties, 718
 in the roof garden, 24
 rugby and, 738
 Russell era *(1911–20)*, 13
 senior parties, 248
 strip poker party, 422–23
 TOGA party, **247**, 247–48
 See also keg parties
pass-fail option, 109–10, 140
Patterson, Melina, 606
Patton, Bruce, 553
Patton, Lisa, 670
Payne, Camilla Moody, 82
Peace Corps, 465, 827
Peace Council, 45
peace movement. *See* student protests; Vietnam War
Peanut Week, 38
Pearce, John, 515, 607, 609, 615
Pearce, Richard, 336
Pearl Harbor, 45–46
pedestrian mall. *See* Campus Walk
Peña, Aniano, 624
Pentagon, 134. *See also* 9/11 terrorist attacks
Penwell, Larry W., 577, 637, 838
People Against Apartheid, 500
People for Alternative Lifestyles (PAL), 440
People for Ethical Treatment of Animals (PETA), 498
People Representing Individuals of Sexual Minorities (PRISM), 694, 722
Performing Arts Club (PAC), 698
Perkins, Beth, 650
Perot, Ross, 506
Perry, Greg, 421, 667, 668–69
Perry, Kevin, 731
Persian Gulf War, 502–5
personnel office (human resources), 336, 670
PETA (People for Ethical Treatment of Animals), 498
pets, 496–97
Phelps, Fred, 644–45
Phi (sorority), 14
Phi Alpha Theta (history honorary society), 619–20, 692
Phi Beta Kappa
 25th anniversary reception, 550

Phi Beta Kappa *(continued)*
chapter approved, 85, 168
key (statue), 170, 336, 550, **P12**
Regional Scholars elected to, 283
Rycroft and, 588
Phillips, Gwen, 240
Phillips, William, 631
Philosophy Department, 41, 294, 402, 581–84. *See also* Classics, Philosophy, and Religion Department (CPR); *and specific individuals*
Phipps, Henry, 547
phonathons, 352, 381, 682
Phyllis Ridderhof Martin Gallery. *See* Ridderhof Martin Gallery
Physical Education Department
degree requirements, 41, 55, 287, 397
faculty, 808–9 (*see also specific individuals*)
fitness classes, 735
intramural sports program, 735–36
major, 22, 77
major eliminated, 168
and the physical education requirement, 823 (*see also* physical education requirement)
Simpson era *(1955–74)*, 168, 169
Stewart head of, 62
tenure, 749–50
Woodard era *(1974–82)*, 195–99
See also athletic facilities; athletic program/department
physical education requirement, 41, 54, 287, 397, 823
Physical Plant/Facilities Services
Anderson era *(1983–2006)*, 337, 553–59
buildings, 83
Bushnell fire repairs, 277
custodians, 669
Hurricane Isabel cleanup, 558–59
and Junior Ring Week pranks, 453
paint crew, 554
smokestack, 812, 857(n9)
student appreciation of, 409
physical therapy program, 60, 526
physician, College, 285–86, 796. *See also* Overman, Ilma Meade
Physics Department, 77, 83, 378, 519, 587, 629–32
Pickerill, John, 251
picnics, departmental, 248, 449–50
Pi Day, 621
Pilcher, Rosamunde, 658
Pilling, Keri, 748
Pinschmidt, Mary W.
awards and honors, 836, 837
death, 575
"A Man from Padua" published, 647
memorials to, 575, 598 (*see also* Pinschmidt Award)
on test files, 682
and the TIP program, 563
Pinschmidt, William, 78, 250, 575
Pinschmidt Award, 575, 838–39. *See also specific recipients*
pipe band. *See* Eagle Pipe Band
Pi Sigma (sorority), 14
Pi Sigma Alpha (political science honorary), 507, 636
Pitts, Anne, 670
plank road, 11
Pluchinsky, Dennis, 532
The Podium (Speaking Center newsletter), 601
poker, 728. *See also* strip poker party
The Polemic, xii, 703, 703
Polemics, 703
police, College, 667–69
before *1955*, 75–76
Anderson chauffeured, 525
emergency siren system installed, 809–10
and the EOP, 558
and house parties, 421
and sexual assault, 94, 473, 477
Simpson era *(1955–74)*, 75–76
staff, 667–68, 670
political correctness (p.c.), 394–96, 492–94
Political Science and Economics Department. *See also* Economics Department
Political Science and International Affairs Department. *See* Political Science Department
Political Science Department
faculty, 632–36 (*see also specific individuals*)
Hirschkop as guest speaker, 90
history, 78, 294, 588, 632–36
international terrorism class, 532
internships, 636
picnics, 248, 449–50
pre–foreign service/international affairs major, 78, 633–34
terrorism class, 532, 851(n62)
writing skills emphasized, 634–36
See also foreign policy
politics, students and
1980 presidential election, 273
2008 presidential primary, 827–28
Anderson era *(1983–2006)*, 466–67, 499–508, 530, 532–34, 851(n63)
Combs era *(1928–55)*, 28–29, 36
Fredericksburg Forum *(1996)*, 517–18

political organizations, 694 (*see also* College Democrats; College Republicans; Human Rights Club)
Russell era *(1911–20)*, 17–18
sexual politics (*see* feminist movement on campus; women's issues)
Simpson era *(1955–74)*, 149–55, 270
voter registration, 845–46(n37)
See also 9/11 terrorist attacks; Gulf War; Vietnam War; World War II
Pollard, John Garland, 31, 32, 40, 54
Pollard Hall, 57, 379, 537
Poole, J. William
Board term, 841
campanile dedication, 813
at the centennial convocation, 831
at commencement 2007, 813–14
and Frawley's arrests and termination, 804, 807, 811, 818
and Frawley's inauguration, 790
and presidential searches, 781, 820–21, 829
and the second CGPS building, 798
Washington Medallion awarded to, 833
Pool Room, 215, 244–45. *See also* keg parties
Pope, Ray, 536
Pops Concerts, 225–26, 627, 628
pornography, 716
Porter, Christine, 662
Portuguese language, 622
Poska, Allyson, 152, 468, 617
post office, campus, 336, 372, 670
pot. *See* marijuana
Potok, Chaim, 160
Powell, Franklin, 277
Powell, Sondra, 107
Poyck, Marjorie Meredith "Midge," **524**
on abandonment of the fountain globe project, 551
administrative roles, 334, 336, 523–24
and the amphitheater, 555–56
background and qualifications, 523–24
on e-mail policy, 535
on the Montford property, 541–42
and racial tensions, 487
on student-faculty dating, 479
pranks, 451–56, **452**, 554, 849(n26)
Pratt, John Lee, 282
pre–foreign service major, 78, 633–34. *See also* Political Science Department
pregnancy tests, 286
prelaw concentration, 583–84
pre-medical program, 59
preppies and the preppy look, 235–37, **236**, 245, 662–66, 673–74
A Presidential Legacy: The Monroe Collection, 516
Presidential Search Advisory Committee (PSAC), 781–82
President's Book Club, 658
President's Club, 214
President's Council (gift club), 352, 382, 658
presidents' homes. *See* Brompton; Framar; Ridge Crest
President's Message (publication), 339, 538
presidents of MWC/UMW
presidential review of Honor Council decisions, 130
salary, 179, 298, 697
search process *(1955)*, 71
search process *(1973–74)*, 175–76, 179
search process *(1983)*, 311–12, 315–17
search process *(2005–6)*, 781–83
search process *(2007)*, 820–21, 829, 857(n8)
See also Anderson, William M., Jr.; Chandler, Algernon Bertrand, Jr.; Combs, Morgan Lafayette; Frawley, William J.; Hample, Judy Garland; inaugurations; Russell, Edward Hutson; Simpson, Grellet C.; Woodard, Prince Briggs
President's Travel Club, 658–59
Preston, Daniel, 516
Prible, Amy, 774
Price, James H., 42, 43–44, 52–53
Price, Wendy, 607
PRISM (People Representing Individuals of Sexual Minorities), 694, 722
Proctor, Samuel Dewitt, 98, 841
Progressive Student Union (PSU), 440, 504
Project SOAR, 366, 662
Prometheus (underground newspaper), 266–67, 847(n23)
prospectus, 4, 362
protests. *See* student protests
provost, 337. *See also* Hall, Philip L.
Psi Chi (psychology honorary society), 636–37
Psi Upsilon, 464, 532, 683–84
PSU (Progressive Student Union), 440, 504
Psychological Services Center, 455, 796. *See also* counseling center
Psychology Department, 41, 148, 378, 462–63, 477, 636–39, 670

the Pub, 412, 413–14, 418. *See also* The Underground
public administration major, 204–5, 402, 757
public affairs, student interest in, 16–18, 28–29, 44–49. *See also* politics, students and; *and specific events and topics*
publications, student, 702–8. See also *Aubade*; *The Battlefield*; *The Bullet*; *The Polemic*
public service. *See* volunteerism
Public Works Administration (PWA), 32, 43
Puleo, Frank, 777, 781
Pulitzer Prize (C. Emerson, poetry), 598–600. *See also* Emerson, Claudia
Puller, Linda Todd "Toddy," 772, 846(n7)
Pulliam, Jacquelyn, 99

Quann, Danny, 553
Quann, Joanna, 587
Quann, Lucy, 670
Quantico, Marines from, 84, 131–32, 133, 141–42, 245, 313–14
Quenzel, Carroll H., 70, 75, 611
the Quilt (NAMES Project AIDS memorial), 481, 643
Quinn Evans Architects, 513

Rabson, Alice
on academic freedom, 288
on the expulsion of Flatt and Galloway, 181–82
and the feminist movement, 150–52, 348–49, 466, 845(n36)
on homophobia, 431
on the Iran hostage crisis, 271
Peace Corps service, 465
race and gender issues, 393–97, 468, 563
race relations on campus
2007–8, 825–26
Anderson era *(1983–2006)*, 483–91, 531, 662–66
guest speakers on racial issues, 615–16
integration (Simpson era,*1955–74*), 98–108, 121
post-9/11 tensions, 531
Woodard era *(1974–82)*, 269–70
Racial and Sexual Harassment Policy, 479
Radford College (University), 9–10, 21, 41–42, 91, 211, 342–43, 569, 691, 764, 768
radio station (WMWC), 254, 708–10
Radley, Karen C., 509, 512, 781, 841
rail transportation, 8, 50
Rallis, Donald, 404, 405, 435–37, **436,** 571, 606, 622, 624
Rally Against Racism, 487–88
the Ramones, 701
Ramsey, Norman, 631
Randolph, Susan, 137
Randolph Hall, 11, 57, 68, 410, 714, 723
Rao, Anand, 600
rape, 473–77, 668–69
awareness programs, 474, 715, 853(n106)
male students' vigilantism, 94–95
Rape Aggression Defense program (RAD), 477
Rappahannock Colonial Heritage Society, 516
Rappahannock Council on Domestic Violence, 594, 715, 721
Rappahannock Region Small Business Development Center, 508, 578, 762
RateMyProfessor.com, 538–39
Rawlings, George, 123
reaccreditation self-studies. *See* Southern Association of Colleges and Secondary Schools (SACS)
Read, Charles, 337
Read, Claudia Moore, 402
Reagan, Ronald, 273, 499–500
recreational activities
Chandler era *(1920–28)*, 22–23, 24, 26–27
Russell era *(1911–20)*, 13–15
See also alcohol; athletic program/department; *and specific activities and events*
recruitment
of academically talented students, 282–83, 362–63
of African American students, 100, 102, 121, 283, 365–68, 482–83, 652–54
Anderson era *(1983–2006)*, 361–63, 365–68, 519–20, 652–54
of athletes, 744, 751
of male students, 91, 169, 192–95
of minority students, 100, 102, 121, 283, 365–68, 482–83, 652–54, 800 (*see also* Farmer Scholars Program)
and the MWC name/image, 340–43, 347, 767–68 (*see also* name of the college/university)
need for recognized, 301
See also applicants and applications; enrollment
Rector and Visitors Chair, 382, 384, 837
Rector and Visitors of Mary Washington College. *See* Board of Visitors
recycling, 495, 850(n45)
Reeves, Clifton H. "Pat," 75–76
Regional Scholarship Program, 282–83, 382, 384
registration, 284, 536, 593, 670
Reichel, Frank, Dr. and Mrs., 56
Reid, Deb, 755
Reid, Richard S., 229, 510–11
Reilly, Conor, 706
Reilly, Jill, 739
Religion Department, 77,

294, 402, 581, 584–86. *See also* Classics, Philosophy, and Religion Department (CPR); *and specific individuals*
Religious Emphasis Week, 109
Repp, Charles, 213–14
Republican Party, 149, 155, 499, 507, 694. *See also* politics, students and; *specific individuals*
reputation of MWC/UMW
  Anderson era *(1983–2006)*, 339–44, 363–65, 422–23, 471
  Combs era *(1928–55)*, 36, 44, 56
  Simpson era *(1955–74)*, 85, 156
  Woodard era *(1974–82)*, 192, 201–2
  See also image of MWC/UMW
research projects, undergraduate, 407, 576–77, 580, 630, 636
retention of students, 284, 289, 415, 419
Reunion Weekend, 656. *See also* homecoming
Rey, Tryna, 748
Reynolds, Joanna L., 624, 837
Reynolds, John H., 536, 587, 621, 838
Richards, Paul, 745
Richardson, Lynda, 656, 822
Richardson, Rita, 653
Richmond News Leader, 70
Richmond Times-Dispatch, xii, 314, 351, 422, 598, 682, 769, 785, 805–6, 808, 817
Ridderhof Martin Gallery, 572–73, **P7**
  centennial exhibition, 821, 828
  construction and name, 375–76
  dorm life exhibition, 825
  Leonardo da Vinci exhibition, 573, 631
  slavery exhibition, 574
Ridge Crest, 10–11. *See also* Marye Hall
Rifle Club, 14, 83–84. *See also* gun club
rifle range (proposed), 83–84
Rigsby, Mary, 152, 469–70, 563, 806
Riley, P. Thomas, 796
rings, class, 163–64, 450, 849(n25). *See also* Junior Ring Dance; Junior Ring Week
Riot Grrrl Fredericksburg, 692
Ristau, Noah, 445
Rivas, Josefa, 79
Rivera, Carmen L., 171, 837
roads, 8–9, 11, 50
Roanoke Times and World-News, 602–3
Robb, Charles S., 313–14, 330, 331, **332**, 835, **P1**
Robbins, John, 541, 851(n67)
Roberts, Russell H., 233, 382, 841
Robertson, James, 658
Rochelle, Warren, 481, 649
Rocktoberfest, 702, 723
Roe v. Wade, 152
Rogers, Becky, 426–27
Rohaly, Betsy, 272
Romero, Joseph, 582, 585
roof gardens, 24, 43, 60
room and board, 8. *See also* fees; tuition
Roosevelt, Franklin D., 45–46, 522
Roosevelt, Theodore, 14, 611
Rose, Willie Lee, 620
Roses in December (documentary), 458
Rossabi, Morris, 134
ROTC program (proposed), 329
Rotter, Marcel, 623
Rouhani, Farhang, 606
Rountree, Jeffrey W.
  and Anderson, 655–56, 659
  background, 655
  and College development, 656–57, 659, 778
  hired, 362
  position under Frawley, 787
Rouse, Gail, 670
Rowan, Monica, 686, 687
Rowe, Charles, 120
Rowe, Josiah P., III, 138, 382, 856(n162)
Rowe, Maurice B., 4, 56
Rowell, Frances Goolrick Ashby, 313
rowing (crew), 742, 746
Rozell, Mark, 501, 635
Rubin, Jerry, 137
Rucker, Cedric B., **661**
  at commencement, 813, **P4**
  as dean of student life, 447, 659, 661–62
  and the Ethnic Studies course, 493 (*see also* Ethnic Studies course)
  on the Global Observations Committee, 390
  on Junior Ring Week pranks, 452, 454
  and the Multicultural Fair, 663
  on sports and fitness, 735
  student years, 252–53, 660–61
Rugby Club (rugby team), 421, 463, 737–41, **738**, 853(n106), 856(n161)
rules and regulations
  1950s, 65–66
  attendance policies, 109, 288–89
  under Bushnell (*see* Bushnell, Nina Gookin)
  car policies, 26, 109, 549
  Chandler era *(1920–28)*, 25
  Combs era *(1928–55)*, 36–37
  dining rules, 26, 64–65
  dormitory rules (*see* dormitories; visitation rules)
  dress code, 109, 115–18
  due process, 256–57, 260–61
  hazing rules, 752–53
  reforms under Simpson, 109, 115–18, 123–24
  relaxed under Stephenson, 65
  Russell era *(1911–20)*, 12–13
  smoking restrictions, 123
  town visits, 36
  weekend absences, 37

rules and regulations
(continued)
See also in loco parentis concept; schedule, daily; schedule, weekly
Rupprecht, Kurt, 391
Rush, Andrew, 537
Rusk, Dean, 133
Russeau, Elena, 722
Russell, Edward Hutson, **3**
administration building named for, 6
background and qualifications, 3–4, 7
on boardwalks, 11
dormitory named for, 19, 82 (*see also* Russell Hall [dorm])
elected president, 3
faculty and staff procured, 7
at the groundbreaking ceremony, 5
loving cup presented to Goolrick, 831
resignation, 18
specialization protested, 21–22
student admiration for, 19–20
on student discipline, 12
student prospectus written, 4
tenure as president, 9–20
Russell, Mark, 518
Russell, Mary, 255
Russell Hall (administration and classroom building), 6, 9, 10, 18. *See also* Monroe Hall
Russell Hall (dorm), 19, 79, 82, 244, 410, 435, 555
Russia, 529. *See also* Soviet Union
Russian language, 622
Russian studies, 78
Ryan, Curtis, 466, 531
Ryang, Key Sun, 137, 611, **614**, 617
Rycroft, Robert, 490–91, 548, 588, 589, **P12**

SA. *See* Student Association
SADD (Students Against Drunk Driving), 413
Saeed, Fara, 531
Safferstone, Mark, 761
Said, Edward, 585
Sainz, José Angel, 571, 623, 624, 839
salaries of faculty. *See* faculty salaries
Sammy T's (restaurant and bar), 420, 421, 604, 849(n22)
Samson, Julie, 629
Samuels, Ivan, 553, 554
Sanford, Douglas, 607, 609
Sanskrit language, 586
Santee, Kevin, 313
Sasser, Sarah, 849(n22)
satellite campus (Dahlgren, proposed), 800
SAT II tests, 398
SAT scores
2000s, 769
Anderson era *(1983–2006)*, 363, 365, 520, 651, 749, 769
and the athletic program, 749
Simpson era *(1955–74)*, 85
Woodard era *(1974–82)*, 192, 195, 283
Sauder, Nanalou West, 777, 781, 832, 841
Saunders, Dave, 448–49
Savage, Kaye Estelle, 99
Save the Name Committee, 356
Save the Name petition, 352
Scalamandre, Franco, 57
SCAM (Save Canines at Mary Washington), 497
schedule
daily, 12–13, 25
exams, 111–12, 398–99, 400
weekly, 37, 109
See also calendar, academic
SCHEV. *See* State Council of Higher Education in Virginia
Schleef, Debra, 641
Schlesinger, Arthur M., Jr., 159–60, 394
Schlimgen, Steve, 285, 295
Schmidt, Philip, 414
Schmidt, Sarah, 790
Schneider, Frederico, 623
Schnellock, Emil, 44, 216
school colors, 358–61, 699
Schrass, JoAnn, 567
Schroeder, Kathy, 114
Schwalbe, Alan, 240
science buildings. *See* Combs Hall; Jepson Science Center
science requirement, 396–97
Scotland, summer program in, 571, 608–9, 658
Scott, Anita Whitehead, 102, 108
Scott, Janet, 553
Scott, Panie, 554
Scott, Raymond B., 580–81, 698, **699**, 789, 839
Scottish Society of Fredericksburg, 515–16
Seacobeck Hall, 31–32, 245, 255, 333, 539. *See also* dining hall; food service
seal of the college, 89, 356–58, 540, 776–77
search engines, 538
secretaries, departmental, 670
security. *See* police, College
Sedano, George, 432–33, 434
Seevaratnam, Sulakshana, 464
segregation. *See* integration of MWC
seniors
parties, 248, 445–47, 675–77
Senior Countdown, 677
Senior Kick-Off, 676–77
Senior Toast, 657, 855(n134)
See also commencement; Devil-Goat rivalry
September 11, 2001, terrorist attacks (9/11), 530–34, **P13**
75th anniversary celebration, 303, 312–15, 647
sex and sexuality
abortion(s), 142, 152, 429
Anderson era *(1983–2006)*, 424–38, 710–18
"beefcake" calendars, 426–28
Bullet articles on, 142–48,

264–65, 286, 321, 424–25, 428–36, 438, 470–71, 704, 706, 711–18, 726
casual sex, 711–14, 718
contraception and safe sex practices, 147, 430–31, 470–73, 849(n31–32), 850(n33)
dorm visitation rules and, 238–43, 321–25 (*see also* visitation rules)
Human Sexuality course, 437–38
male striptease shows, 427
motel guide, 428–29
pornography, 716
pregnancy tests, 286
sex toys, 718
sexually transmitted diseases (STDs), 429–31, 714 (*see also* AIDS)
See also dating; homosexuality; nudity; visitation rules; Wo-Man Contest
"Sexclamations" (*Bullet* column), 714–18, 792
sex discrimination lawsuit, 189–90
sexual harassment and sexual assault
Anderson era *(1983–2006)*, 473–77, 668–69, 714–15
faculty accused of, 475, 643
Kilmartin's efforts against, 475–77, 638
rape and rape awareness programs, 94–95, 473–77, 668–69, 715–16, 853(n106)
sexual assault policy, 474
sexual harassment policy, 479, 850(n37)
See also rape
sexually transmitted diseases (STDs), 429–31, 714. *See also* AIDS
Sezawarkeshavarz, Alireza, 272
Shaner report (Daniel Shaner and Associates), 191–92
Shankle, George Earlie, 30, 691
Shannon, Edgar, 97
Shaw, Robert H., 119
Sheckels, Marie, 591, 621, 629
Shelor, Laurie, 246–47
Shelton, Debbie, 145–46
Sheridan, Thomas, 743–44, **744**, 856(n163)
Shields, Frank, 253
Shirley, Donna, 519
shopping, 156, 671–72, 733–34
Shore, Pauly, 702
Short, Shelli, 336
Showcase program, 362–63
Shull, Linda Gattis, 84, 125
Siegrist, Mary, 286
Siegrist, Robert R., family of, 382
Sievert, Bonnie, 670
Sifrit, Erika Grace and Benjamin, 669, 855(n136)
Silver, Carl D., and the Silver Companies, 733–34
Simeone, Justin, 827, 833
Simmons, Steve, 667
Simms, Erin, 99
Simpson, Dorothy Cottrell (wife of G. C. Simpson), **172**
at Anderson's inauguration, 331
as president's wife, 72, 171–72
retirement, 169–70
scholarship endowed, 382
tributes and memorials, 171, 185, 382, 550
Simpson, Grellet C., **73**, **168**, **172**
at the 75th anniversary Convocation, 313
academic quality improved, 76–77, 85, 89–90, 91, 121, 167–68
and Alvey, 35, 74–75
at Anderson's inauguration, 331
and anthropology, 641
awards and scholarships named for, 150, 170–71, 382 (*see also* Grellet C. Simpson Award for Excellence in Undergraduate Teaching; Grellet C. Simpson International Scholarship)
background and qualifications, 71–72
and Belmont, 169, 228
chair named for, 171, 382
and coeducation, 87–91, 299
and the College–Community Orchestra, 224
commitment to liberal arts education, 74, 167–68
commitment to women's education, 74
criticisms of, 169
death, 173
on dorm rules, 238
era *(1955–74)*, 71–173 (*see also specific topics and events*)
faculty hired, 188, 267
and finances, 169, 175, 185
honorary doctorate, 835
inauguration, 72–74, 104, 572
and the Indian faculty exchange program, 80
library named for, 375 (*see also* Simpson Library)
in loco parentis questioned, 115
on May Day, 125
named president/chancellor, 71, 72
and Phi Beta Kappa, 85
presidency evaluated, 166–73
and the proposed rifle range, 84
and racial integration, 99–100, 103–4, 105
reforms enacted, 109, 117–18 (*see also* academic reforms)
retirement years, 166, 169–73
and separation from U. Va., 97–98
and the sexual revolution, 145
on student activists, 99
student attitudes toward, 108–9
and student protests, 120–22, 138, 167
and Vietnam War protests, 138

Simpson, Myra, 747
Simpson, Susan, 748
Simpson Award
for Excellence in Undergraduate Teaching, 170–71, 837–38. *See also specific recipients*
Simpson International Scholarship, 171, 382, 801
Simpson Library (building), 372–75, 562, 854(n126), **P6**. *See also* library
Simpson Program in Medieval Studies, 596. *See also* Grellet and Dorothy Simpson Chair in Medieval Literature
Simpson Summer Institute, 171
Singh, Raman, 137, 289, 390
Singh, Ranjit, 635
Singleton, Ronald E., **523**
advancement efforts headed, 655
and the Fredericksburg Forum, 517
on funding the parking deck, 550
hired, 339
and the name of the college / university, 774–76
position under Frawley, 787
resignation, 803
role during Anderson's illness, 523
Sinha, Jay, 790
Sinha, Krishna, 818, 820
Sisters with a Vision, 694
skateboarding, 727
Skinker, Harry, 577
slacks. *See* dress code
Slaughter, French, 501
slavery museum and exhibition, 574, 734
Slayton, Ann, 670
Slayton, Frank, 318
Slayton, Paul C., Jr., 327, 590–91, **591**, 836
sledding, 724, 725, 726
Sletten, Charles A., 298, 639, 852(n83)
Slezak, Jerry, 537
Sloan, Brenda, 484, 489, 648, 665
Slunt, Kelli M., 580, 838
Small Business Development Center, 510, 578, 762
Smith, Gaddis, 516
Smith, John (Captain), 5
Smith, Julie, 736
Smith, Roy H.
Awards and honors, 637, 836, 839
and student drinking, 410, 411, 413, 855(n139)
and the TIP program, 562, 637
on Woodard, 309
Smith, Sally Bedell, 812
Smith, Sex, 14
smokestack, 812, 857(n9)
smoking rules, 123
Snead, Emmett, 161
Snipes, James, 668
snowfalls, 724–27
Snyder, Cynthia "Cindy," 339, 656, 657
SOAR project, 366, 662
soccer
men's team, 744–45, 755
men's team established, 197
playing field, 215
women's team, 422–23, 742, 744
Society for the Prevention of Cruelty to Animals (SPCA), 497
Sociology and Anthropology Department, 148, 294, 639–42, **640**, 670. *See also specific individuals*
Sodexho (Wood Co.), 539, 549, 558, 794
softball, 742, 747
Somma, Thomas, 573–74, 631, 852(n79)
song, college. *See* alma mater
sororities, 14, 51, 261–62, 679–84, 855(n140). *See also* Cotillion Club; fraternities; German Club; *specific organizations*
Southeastern Institute of Research, Inc. (SIR), name change analysis by, 342–43
Southern Association of Colleges and Secondary Schools (SACS), 30–31
and the outcomes assessment plan, 402
reaccreditation reports *(1990s)*, 389, 518, 600
reaccreditation self-study *(1962)*, 77
reaccreditation self-study *(1971)*, 97, 205–6
speaking-intensive program suggested, 600
and university status, 764, 766–67, 775
South Hall, 375, 683, 797
Southland Corporation, 509
Southworth, Joanne G.. *See* Beck, Joanne G.
Spain, programs in, 79, 571, 623
Spanish Club, 51
Spanish influenza epidemic *(1918)*, 18
Spanish language
faculty (*see specific individuals*)
Spanish house, 11, 65, 622
SPCA, 497
speakers, visiting
Anderson era *(1983–2006)*, 467–68, 485–86, 500–501, 516–19, 532, 574, 600, 663
civil rights leaders, 615–16
Frawley era *(2006-7)*, 789, 802–3
Fredericksburg Forum, 517–18, 519
James Monroe Lecture Series, 516
physicists, 631
Simpson era *(1955–74)*, 158–60
See also Distinguished Visitor [Graduate] in Residence program; Executive-in-Residence program (EIR); *and specific individuals*
Speaking Center, 601
speaking-intensive require-

ment/courses, 389, 397, 600–601
Special Olympics, 463
speech pathology program, 60, 848(n16)
speech program, 600–601. *See also* English, Linguistics, and Speech Department; *and specific individuals*
Sphinx (secret society), 14
Spiess, Philip D., II, 234, **614**
spinning wheel, 89, 357–58, 776. *See also* seal of the college
spirit rock, 552–53
Spirit Week, 720, 721. *See also* Mr. MWC contest
Spivey, Katherine, 466–67
sports. *See* athletic program/department; Physical Education Department; *and specific sports*
spousal equivalency benefits, 404–5
Spring Break, 448–49
Alternate Spring Break program, 461–62, 464
travel abroad during, 577, 606
Spring Formal, 438, 718–19, 812
Stableford, Duke, 254
Stablein, King, 218
stadium, 743, **744**
Stafford County, 759–61. *See also* College of Graduate and Professional Studies
Stageberg, Stephen, **436**
background, 588–89
and Bill Clinton, 828
conservative views, 405, 436–37, 588
convocation address, 492–93
as marshal of the faculty, 589, 790
on tenure for coaches, 750
Stahl, Deborah Ann, 477
Stanton, Gary, 607, 609, 610
Stanton, Gregory, 458, 618, 695–96, 827
State Council of Higher Education in Virginia (SCHEV)
Anderson's knowledge of, 316, 320
and the BLS program, 201
Center for Historic Preservation funded, 233
and college funding, 211
and graduate studies at MWC, 206, 207
interdisciplinary majors approved, 205
major program guidelines, 567
merit pay mandated, 406
MWC restructuring plan approved, 380
and the outcomes assessment plan, 402
outstanding state teacher awards, 595, 853(n100)
separation from U. Va. recommended, 98
TIP program funded, 562
and university status, 764
Woodard and, 177, 178, 179
State Department, U.S., 80
Statement of Community Values and Behavioral Expectations, 484, 488–89
"Statement of Rights and Responsibilities," 122–23
State Normal School at Fredericksburg, 9–22, 299. *See also* Fredericksburg State Normal and Industrial School for Women; Mary Washington College; State Teachers College at Fredericksburg
State Teachers College at Fredericksburg, 22–42, 299. *See also* Fredericksburg State Normal and Industrial School for Women; Mary Washington College; State Normal School at Fredericksburg
Staunton, Cheryl, 390
steamboats, 8
Steckler, David, 739
Steckler, Debra, 637
Steen, Daniel K. "Dan," 273, 281–82, 317, 320, 331, 357, 841, 847(n25)
Steinem, Gloria, 154–55, 467
Stephenson, Mary Ellen, 65, 75, 78, 622
Stevens, Elizabeth, 630
Stewart, Mildred P., 62
Stone, Rita Morgan
Board term, 841
fund-raising, 382
on the honor system, 686
and Project SOAR, 366
as Rector, 333, 377, 686
Stoper, Stan, 747, 750
Stottlemyer, Todd A., 565, 841
STP (Summer Transition Program), 482–83, 662, 850(n40)
Stratford (Lee family home), 609
Stravitz, Richard, **P12**
streaking, 164–66, **165**, 725
strikes, student, 137. *See also* boycotts; student protests
strip poker party, 422–24
striptease shows, 428
Stroh, Julius, 510
Stroh, Peter W., 512
Stroh family, 512–13
Strohl, LeRoy S., III "Roy," 372–75, **373**, 647–48, 687–88
Strossen, Nadine, 468
Student Academy on Information Technologies, 596
student activism
academic and scheduling reforms sought *(1960s–70s)*, 109–13
after 9/11, 531–34
amphitheater preservation, 556–57
Anderson era *(1983–2006)*, 459–68, 472–73, 479–80, 483, 495–96, 500–501, 665–66, 694–98
animal rights, 496–99
against apartheid, 500–501
breast cancer research, 723
in the Bushnell fire aftermath, 278

student activism *(continued)*
and calendar revisions, 399–400
centennial year (2007–8), 825–26
CIA recruitment protested, 180–82
civil rights era, 99
coeducation opposed, 87
Copprome orphanage endeavor, 601, 694–96, 730, 794, 827
dress code issue, 115–18
environmental issues, 495–96, 794, 826–27
and exam self-scheduling, 399
Frawley era *(2006-7)*, 794
Free University, 113–14
gay rights, 264–66, 431–35, 645 (*see also* homosexuality)
gender-neutral language, 493–94
Gulf War, 502–5
honor system issues, 129–30, 689–90 (*see also* honor system)
human rights, 502
Iran hostage crisis rally, 271–72
"living wage" campaign, 696–98
marijuana legalization, 259–61
Multicultural Center move, 665–66
name change controversies, 344–45, **346**, 349–50, 356, 765, 769–70, **770**, 773, 777–78
nuclear test ban lobby, 501
rifle range opposed, 84
and the Soviet Union's war in Afghanistan, 272–73
Student Bill of Rights, 122–23
student right to due process, 256–57, 260–61
Vietnam War opposition, 132–41
after Virginia Tech shootings, 809
visitation rules, 239–43, 320–21 (*see also* visitation rules)
"Wanted: Jesus" poster issue, 118–20
Woodard era *(1974–82)*, 235, 255–58, 259–61
against Woodbridge, 279–80
YET (Youth Evaluate Teachers), 114–15
See also feminist movement on campus; politics, students and; *and specific organizations*
student activities building. *See* Ann Carter Lee Hall; Woodard Campus Center
student affairs. *See* Chirico, Bernard; dean of students; dean of women; Rucker, Cedric B.; student life
Student Association (SA)
1981 poll, 298–99
alma mater change recommended by, 62
and the amphitheater, 556
Board of Visitors member sought by, 281–82
Celebrate Virginia forum, 734
and the clock, 550, 551
and the College seal, 357
departmental mergers opposed by, 295
eligibility for office, 256
Entertainment Committee (Giant Productions), 701–2
and exam self-scheduling, 399
first Career Day sponsored by, 162
and fraternities/sororities, 679
and homophobia on campus, 432
and the Iran hostages' release, 273–74
membership, 691
and name change proposals, 349, 356
optional final exams supported by, 111
organization name, 844(n4)
parking poll, 549
president-elect convicted of theft, 855(n143)
representation in academic decisionmaking sought by, 112
revised degree requirements accepted by, 287–88
ROTC program debated by, 329
rules enforced by, 66
Simpson era *(1955–74)*, 75
and SIS, 147
and the Student Bill of Rights, 257–58
Student Film Festival initiated by, 730
vice president suspended, 474–75
and the Vietnam War, 135–36
and visitation rules, 240, 242, 320–21, 415
war stamps/bonds sold by, 46–47
student attire
1911–20, 10, 12
1950s, 66
1960s–70s, 109, 115–18
1990–2000s, 671–74
Bushnell years, 64–65
dress code, 109, 115–18
freshmen beanies, 126–27, **127**
for freshmen reception, 61
gay activism and, 433–34
jeans, 64, 116, 118, 139, 433, 672–73
preppy look, 235–37, **236**, 245
waitress uniforms, 66–67
Student Bill of Rights, 122–23, 257–58
student center. *See* Woodard Campus Center
Student Center for Social Information Services (SIS), 146–47
Student Film Festival, 730
Student Government Association. *See* Student Association

student handbooks
1911–1920, 11–12
1953–54, 66
1968–69, 118
1998–99, 674
club policy, 681
See also rules and regulations
student housing. *See* dormitories
student jobs, 66–67
student life. *See specific activities, events, issues, organizations, and topics*
student loans, 191
Student Lobby Research Committee, 241–42
student media. *See* media, student; *and specific student publications*
student organizations. *See* organizations, student
student protests
at Bush inauguration, 530
against Celebrate Virginia, 734
against CIA recruiters, 180–81
"Come and Think" rally and challenges, 120–22
Contra aid protested, 501
over Dodd's college seal, 540
against dress code, 115–17
over due process, 260–61
food service protest, 255–56
against Gingrich (threatened), 802
Gulf War demonstrations (pro and con), 503–5
Kenvin's classes boycotted, 642
"living wage" campaign, 696–98
against military action in Afghanistan, 532–33
against Multicultural Center move, 666
name change controversies, **346**, 349–50, 769–70, **770**
over slavery cartoon incident, 825–26
against student and faculty "slavery," 115
technology and, 540
against town visit rules, 36
Vietnam War protests, 134–41
waitress uniform uprising, 66–68
against war in Afghan and Iraq, 532–34
against the Wo-Man Contest, 440–41
Woodard inauguration, 183
Student Publications Study Committee, 704–5
Student Research and Creativity Day, 811–12
Students Against Drunk Driving (SADD), 413
Students Educating and Empowering for Diversity, 826
Students Helping Honduras (SHH), 695, 794, 827. *See also* Copprome
student-teacher ratio, 188, 365, 404, 560.
student volunteerism. *See* volunteerism
Student Wellness Committee, 675
study-abroad programs, 79–80, 391, 571
funding, 801
scholarships, 171, 382, 801
spring break programs, 577, 606
summer programs, 79, 391–93, 608–9, 613, 617, 623, 634
See also foreign studies
Stull, M. Gregg, 481, 637, **643**, 643–44, 838, 839
Sturm, Gene, 553
Sudoku, 728
Suggs, Lewis, 289
suitcase-college syndrome. *See* weekends: college empty on
Sulaiman, Fatima, 503, 504
Sullivan, Gil, 553
Sullivan, Greg, 553
Sullivan, Jay, 553
Sullivan, Sheryl, 849(n22)
Sullivan, Stuart, 553
Summer Science Institute, 629–30, 785
Summer Science Research Program, 580
Summer [Student] Transition Program (STP), 482–83, 662, 850(n40)
Sumner, Laura Voelkel, 60, 78, 155, 581–82, **582**
Sumner, Suzanne, 563, 621, 838
sunbathing, 449
Sunshine Lady Foundation, 515, 589, 695, 794
Super Bowl parties, 724
Susan J. Hanna Memorial Scholarship, 594
Sutton, Margaret, 573
Swanson, Claude A., 3
swimming pool, 6, 24, 215, 216
swim team, 358, 745. *See also* water polo team
Symfonics (a cappella group), 699–700, 731
synchronized swimming club (Terrapins), 162, 736

Tait, Stephanie, 461–62
Take Back the Night, 715
talent shows, 720–21
TALON (TAking Libraries ONline), 646–47
Tannen, Deborah, 600
tanning, 727
Tavassoli, Niloufar, 502
Taylor, Carolyn, 337
Taylor, Helen Marie, 231–32, 514
Taylor, Irene, 62. *See also* alma mater
Taylor, Jacquelin, 232
Taylor, Monecia, 781
Taylor, Richard H. C., 233
teacher education. *See* Education Department
Teaching and Learning Technologies, 537. *See also* instructional technology
Teaching Innovation Project (TIP), 407, 562–64
technology
administrative systems, 284, 536

technology *(continued)*
Anderson era *(1983–2006)*, 535–38
art department's use of, 572
blogs and networking sites, 728–29
cell phones, 728
e-mail, 535–36, 729, 797, 851(n64)
emergency siren and text-messaging system, 809–10
e-Suds laundry monitoring program, 796–97
first HP mainframe, 284, 535
Griffin works exhibited online, 574–75
instructional technology, 536–39
iPods and music downloads, 728
library catalog, online, 374–75
library technology, 645–47
Math Department's first computer, 587
radio station equipment, 708–10
and social behavior, 712
social networking websites, 540, 712, 728–29, 753 (*see also* Facebook)
Student Academy on Information Technologies, 596
and student protests, 540
telecommunications network (fiber-optic), 336, 376–77, 535, 537
telephones, 21, 81
video/computer games, 728
Web site, 535, 537
Y2K concerns, 529
See also radio station; television station
telecommunications network (fiber-optic), 336, 376–77, 535, 537
telephones, 21, 82, 376–77. *See also* cell phones
television, 731–32
television station (AVC-TV), 254–55
television station, public (WNVT), 762
tennis
indoor tennis center, 742–43, 856(n162)
men's team, 197, 742
tennis courts, 214–15
women's team, 197, 742, 755
Tennis Club, **15**, 15
tenure
for coaches/physical education teachers, 749–50
dismissed home economics teachers and, 190
Jiminez case, 489–91
revised policy *(1977)*, 291–92
Terrapin Club, 162, 736
terrorist attacks of Sept. 11, 2001, and aftermath, 530–34, **P13**
Thanksgiving holiday, 399–400
Thaxton, Ralph, 618
Theatre and Dance Department (Drama; Dramatic Arts and Dance), 642–45
75th anniversary performance, 313
1960s–70s productions, 160, 162
faculty, 642–44 (*see also specific faculty*)
and the FST/FTC, 223, 643, 644
history and incarnations, 203, 294, 402, 642
The Laramie Project produced, 644–45
Studio 115, 644
See also dance department
Thiel, Jessica, 809
Third World Coalition, 390
Thomas, David, 739
Thomas, Glen R., 134, **614**, 617, 620, 837
Thomas, Helen, 517–18, **P10**
Thompson, Anne, 282, 285, 305
Thompson, Fred D., Jr., 666, 781, 841
Thompson, Rita S. J., 653, 841
Thormeyer, Rob, 709
Thorpe, Thomas H., 356
thrift shops, 671–72
Thurman Brisben Homeless Shelter, 459, 460–61, 641
Tibert, Neil, 603
Time magazine, 531, 569, 681
Timmins, Becky, 751
Tinnell, Robert, 670
Todd, Gaye (Adegbalola), 99, 269
TOGA party *(1979)*, **247**, 247–48
Tompkins, Deal, 654
Tomzak, Thomas, 790
tours, 512, 658–59. *See also* summer programs
Toynbee, Arnold, 158, 831
Trachtenberg, Stephen Joel, 790
track and field, 215, 747
Tracy, Arthur L. "Art," 611, 613, **614**, 615, 617–18, 807, 837
Tracy, Patricia Bowles, 268
traditions. *See specific traditions*
transportation, 8, 11, 47, 50. *See also* car policies; parking
Travel Club, 658–59
Travers, Mary, 160
Trench Hill, 57, 78, 93, 214, 333, 546–49
Trinity Episcopal Church, 119
Trinkle, E. Lee, 22–23, 53. *See also* Trinkle Library
Trinkle Associates, 647
Trinkle Library (building), **48**, 52–53, **52**, 75, 83, 357, 372, 540
TRIO programs, 800, 857(n5)
Tri-Unit dormitories, 32–33. *See also* Custis Hall; Madison Hall; Mary Ball Hall
Trombetta, Michelle, 454, 676
Truck Stop (Route 17), 156–57
Trump, Donald, 732

Tuccilo, Dylan, 730
Tuck, William M., 318
Tuesday Lunch Club, 583, 852(n83)
tuition, 8, 68, 211–12, 379. *See also* fees; room and board
Turgeon, Thomas, 642
tutors, 387
Tuttle, Raymond, 662
Tyler, Bunyan, 34
Tyler house, 622
Tyree, Alexander, 620

UMW *See* University of Mary Washington
UMW Chorus, 789. *See also* MWC Chorus
UMW Today (alumni magazine), 789. See also *MWC Today*
Una Voce (a capella ensemble), 626, 695, 700–701, 789, 791, 809
undergraduate research. *See* research projects, undergraduate
the Underground, 418, 432, 719–20, 722
Underwear Run, 792
United Campuses to Prevent Nuclear War (UCAM), 501
United States bicentennial, 222–23
University Hall, 798–99
University of Mary Washington (UMW)
- centennial year *(2007–8)*, 817–33
- diploma and seal, 776–77
- expansion of main campus, 542–45, 824–25
- flag, **P14**
- graduate school near Dahlgren (proposed), 800
- integration of two campuses, 799
- logo, 773
- name changed to, 767–78
- reputation (*see* reputation of MWC/UMW)
- rise to university status, 757–61 (*see also* College of Graduate and Professional Studies; graduate studies at MWC)
- *See also* Mary Washington College (MWC); *and specific topics, departments, facilities, and individuals*

University of Mary Washington Philanthropic Education Organization (UMWEPO), 589
University of Richmond, 384
University of Vilnius (Lithuania), 391
University of Virginia (U. Va.)
- administrative merger with MWC, 53–56, 68, 187, 212
- coeducation issue, 86–87, 89–90
- Darden named president, 58
- dating between U. Va. and MWC students, 243–44, 245, 261–62
- diversity, 654
- early decision program dropped, 651
- Easters party, 249
- endowment, 212
- and the establishment of a state liberal arts college for women, 39–40
- and the Monroe Law Office-Museum, 231
- and the MWC nursing program, 60
- MWC's separation from, 96–98, 212, 228, 231
- presidential search, 176
- SAT scores, 365
- state funding, 212
- "summer school in Spain" program subsumed, 79
- Vietnam War protests, 137

Upward Bound program, 591
USA Today, 422, 633
U.S. News and World Report, 766
U. Va. *See* University of Virginia (U. Va.)
Uyar, Dan, 742, **743**

The Vagina Monologues (Ensler play), 715–16
Valentine's Day, 431, 447–48, 710–11
Vance, Joseph C., ix, xv, 78, 611–12, 617, **614**, 620, 852(n83)
vandalism, 452–53, 733
Vanderberg, Cindy, 742
Vanderland, Helen, 334
Vanover, Jay, 434, 435
Van Sant, George M., **182**, 582–83
- Ad Hoc Committee chaired by, 111
- on Alvey, x
- and the Anderson inauguration celebrations, 330
- awards and honors, 583, 836, 837
- as Chi Beta Phi auctioneer, 250
- on dropping the dress code, 118
- and the expulsion of Flatt and Galloway, 181–82
- and the feminist movement, 467
- Great Books seminars organized by, 78–79
- and Ideas and Movements of the Western World, 207
- on the King memorial march, 103
- marriage (*see* Hanna, Susan J.)
- and the men's basketball team, 161
- military service, 852(n82)
- and the name of the college, 347–48
- *Polemics* article, 703
- and the presidential search process, 176
- on proposed graduate studies, 206
- on smoking, 123
- and student drinking, 124, 414–16

Van Sant, George M., *(continued)*
on student-faculty dating, 477–78
TOGA party attended, 248
Vietnam War debate, 133
and visitation rules, 415–16
writing-intensive courses championed, 385
Van Winckel, Dorothy, 312, 572
varsity athletic program, 15–16, 741–57, **P16**. *See also* athletic program / department; *and specific sports*
Vasey, Craig
minor program opposed, 568
and the Multicultural Center, 795
on the proposed obelisk, 552
and race and gender issues, 393–95, 440–41, 468, 487
"Representations of the Other" conference organized, 585
on Stageberg's *1991* convocation address, 493
Vashee, Ameeta, 531, 663, 665, 666, 795
Vaughn, Jeremy, 832–33
VCU (Virginia Commonwealth University), 177, 569
V-Day, 715
veterans, male, as students, 63–64
viaduct, 31, 32
vice president for development and management information systems, 212–13. *See also* Anderson, William M., Jr. (Bill)
Vickery, Moje, Drinkard, and Oakland (VMDO; architects), 368, 370–71, 373
Victorian Ball, 692
Victory Chorus, 49
video and computer games, 728
video for prospective students, 362
Vietnam War, 131–41, 154–55
Virginia, University of. *See* University of Virginia (U. Va.)
Virginia Commonwealth University (VCU), 177, 569
Virginia Council on Human Relations, 104
Virginia Credit Union, 578
Virginia Hall
addition, 32
Bushnell's apartment, 21
completion, 10
Daisy Chain garland, 38
library in, 10, 52
"personality," 244, 410
safe-sex orientation, 430–31
Virginia Military Institute (VMI), 211, 342, 743, 826
Virginia Museum of Fine Arts, 227
Virginia Normal School Board, 9, 21–22. *See also* Board of the State Teachers Colleges of Virginia
Virginia State College, 211, 342
Virginia Student Association (VASA), 281
Virginia Tech, 194, 212, 342, 603, 654, 739, 809–10, 813–14, 856(n168)
Virtual Library of Virginia (VIVA), 646
VIRTUA system (online library catalog), 645–46
Visions: The Multicultural Experience, 368. *See also* Black Visions program
visitation rules, 416
Anderson era *(1983–2006)*, 320–25, 415–16, 429, 449, 711
Bushnell and, 64
Chandler era *(1920–28)*, 25
Russell era *(1911–20)*, 13
Simpson era *(1955–74)*, 118
Woodard era *(1974–82)*, 238–43
visiting lecturers. *See* speakers, visiting
VISTA (Volunteers in Service to America), 463–64
visually handicapped students, 613
Voelkel, David, 515
Vogel, Brenda, 591, 761, 820, 833
volleyball, 197, 747
volunteerism
Anderson era *(1983–2006)*, 459–66, 495
flood of *1942*, 50–51
See also student activism
von Guggenberg, Beatrice, 480–82, 850(n38)

Wade, John, 496
Wagar, Barbara, 455, 720, 796
Wagner, Susan "Lacy," 118, 119–20, 121, 845(n25)
waitresses, student, 66–67, 105
Walford, J. Binford (architect), 32–33, 43, 53
Walker, C. Harding, 39
Walker, Lewis M.
and Belmont, 228
Board term, 841
and dorm visitation rules, 240
faculty lawsuits against, 189–90
honorary doctorate received, 835
on the MWC / U. Va. merger, 97
named Rector, 98
opposed to student member, 281
and the presidential search, 175–76, 179
retirement, 279
and Woodard, 179, 303–4
Walker, Sally B., 62
Wallace, George, 154
Wallace, H. Lewis, 5
Waller, Leah Fleet, 240, 842
Walther, Russell, 47
"Wanted: Jesus" poster (*Bullet*), 118–20
Warlick, H. Conrad, **341**

and coeducation, 194–95
on the "divorce" from U. Va., 212
as executive assistant to the president, 334
as head of admissions, 361
on the name issue, 340–41, 353
report on MWC's image prepared, 341–42
as senior VP for administrative and student services, 335–36
Warner, John, **527**, 833, 850(n48)
Warner, Mark R., 507, 514, 773, 835, 850(n48)
Warner, Richard H., 613, **614**
on Farmer, 616
on Hegmann, 757
and the name of the college, 300, 302, 348
Research Group London program created, 617
retirement, 617
and the rugby team, 737–41, 757
on student-faculty dating, 479
war stamps and bonds, 46–47
Washington, George, 485
Washington, Mary, 39, 41–42, 300–301, 348–49, 350
Washington and Monroe College in Virginia (proposed name), 344–56
Washington Guides, 362
Washington Medal/Medallion, 335, 763, 833
Washington Post, 75, 86, 300, 314, 327, 481–82, 733, 739, 777–78, 818–19
Washington Scholars program, 657
Waskow, Arthur, 137
water polo team, 745
Watkins, Stephen H. "Steve," 596–97, **597**
and *Blue Tide*, 849(n23)
as *Bullet* advisor, 704, 856(n152)
and the *Bullet*/honor system conflict, 688
and D'Souza's speech, 491–92
on e-mail policy, 535–36
on the faculty senate's gender distribution, 561
on Frawley, 783
on hate speech sanctions, 488
and the "living wage" campaign, 696
and the Mary Washington name, 765, 769–70
and the name of the college/university, 772
on Rita Thompson, 653
on a student comedy routine, 720
Watson, Paulette, 231–32, 339, 656, 781, 820
Webb, Gary, 272
Webb, Lawrence, 653
weekends
beer sales restricted to, 413–14
Black Student Weekend, 367–68
coeducation as antidote to weekend exodus, 88, 193
college empty on, 92, 131, 237, 262, 314, 680, 681
Combs era activities *(1928–55)*, 37
Founders Weekend *(1983)*, 312–14
General Assembly visit *(1984)*, 330
movies, 730
Parents/Family Weekend, 162, 250, 821
Reunion Weekend, 656
visitation rules and, 93, 241–43, 320–21, 324, 416 (*see also* visitation rules)
weekend absences restricted, 37
See also dances; dating; inaugurations; parties
Weinbrecht, Ruby York, 75, 300–301, 372, 647
Weinstock, Roy B., **338**, 338, 402, 474–75, 568, 579, 682
Weisman, Stephen, 731
Wellington, Marie, 623
Welsh Society of Fredericksburg, 516
Westboro Baptist Church (Kansas), 644–45
Westmoreland Hall
alcohol-related death in, 417–18, 677 (*see also* Goode, Christopher Paul)
construction, 43
made coed dorm, 239, 244
Westfest, 723
Westmoreland Four incident, 256–57
WFLS radio station, 133
Whidden, Reginald W., 51, 73, 75, 79, 80
Whipkey, Charles, 603
White, David, 653, 683
White, Dorothy, 245
White, Sandra, 591
Whitfield, Doris Lindsey, 331
Whitlock, Bennett C., Jr., 333, 377, 842
Whitman, Tom, 566, 577
Whitticar, Ralph M., III, 229, 279, 282, 842
Wieland, Werner, 576, 838
Wigner, Eugene, 631
Wikipedia, 538
Wilder, Douglas L., 379, 674
Wilder, Martin A., Jr. "Marty," **651**
on campus lawns, 218
diversity efforts defended, 654
on ending the early decision program, 651
on good college ratings, 365
as head of admissions, 361
on low application/enrollment, 300
on presidential search committee, 820, 823
UMW name proposed, 767–68
as vice president for enrollment and communications, 823
Wilder, Vicky Nichols (wife of M. Wilder), 403
Wilkins, Marsha, 586

Wilkins, Roy, 100
Wilkins, S. Vance, 405, 848(n18)
Wilkinson, Mary "Muffin," 262
Willard, Frances, 7
Willard, Wilma, 670
Willard Hall (first dormitory)
air conditioning, 797
as coed dorm, 93, 239
Combs resident in, 29
completion, 6–7, 9
"personality," 375
renovations, 216–17, 797
Rocktoberfest, 723
Willey, Edward E., 191
William and Mary. *See* College of William and Mary
Williams, Carlisle M., 759–60, 763, 835, 856(n169)
Williams, Jan, 234
Williams, Lori, 677
Williams, Michael Paul, 805–6
Williams, Richard, 489–90
Williams, Virginia, 670
Willis, Barbara Creighton "Bambi," 346, 848(n4)
Willis, Jere M. H., Jr., 39, 68, 147, 331, **332**
Willis, Tammie, 497, 564–65, 715
Willis Hill tract (Montfort Academy site), 540–42, 824–25, 851(n67)
Wilson, Joni, 554–55
Wilson, Woodrow, 14, 17
Wiltenmuth, John, 337, 553, 555–56
Wind and Percussion Ensemble, 626, 627, 790
Wishner, Janet, 468, 562
Wishner, Lawrence, 207, 578, 852(n83)
Witches' Dance, 248–49
withdrawal policy, 568, 851(n73)
Wolf, Naomi, 468
Wo-Man Contest, 252–53, 438–43, **439**. *See also* Mr. MWC contest
Women of Color (organization), 427, 665, 683, 694
Women's History Month, 468, 617, 663
women's issues
1960s–70s, 141–52
Anderson era *(1983–2006)*, 466–71
end of the "finishing school" era, 142
faculty senate gender distribution, 561
gender-neutral language, 493–94
suffrage, 17, 20
See also feminist movement on campus; race and gender issues requirement; sexual harassment and sexual assault; women's studies; *and specific issues*
women's rugby, 739–40
women's studies, 393, 468
women's suffrage movement, 17, 20
Wood, Ron, 750–51
Wood, W. D., 548
Woodard, Corinne, 303, 307, 331
Woodard, Prince Briggs, **177**, **P1**
academic reforms under, 200–210, 286–89
agenda for MWC, 185–86
Anderson appointed vice president, 212–13
Anderson as successor, 331 (*see also* Anderson, William M., Jr. [Bill])
Anderson contrasted with, 317–18
Anderson given SCHEV job, 320
and the athletic program, 197, 198–200, 215, 308, 741
on attracting minority students/faculty, 290
background and qualifications, 176–79, 184
and Belmont, 228–29
and the Bushnell fire, 277–78
campus beautification efforts, 217–20, 251, 305
and the Center for Historic Preservation, 233–35, 304, 607
on Clement, 285
and community involvement, 220, 223
C-PPAC established, 203
death and memorial service, 304–5
departmental mergers, 293–94, 640
on the difficulty of attracting minority students/faculty, 283
and dorm visitation rules, 238, 242–43
and drug use by students, 258, 260
and enrollment, 191, 192
era *(1974–82)*, 175–309 (*see also specific topics and events*)
faculty downsizing, 188–90, 211
faculty's relationship with, 289–96, 298
financial challenges facing, 186–91, 210–14, 308
and graduate studies at MWC, 206, 207
Halloweens attended, 249
health, 178, 179, 302–4, 514
and the historic preservation program, 210, 607, 611
inauguration, 183–86
lawsuits against, 189–90
Long composition dedicated to, 312
and male enrollment, 192
Miller hired, 336
on Monroe Hall, 216
and the Monroe Law Office-Museum, 231–33
MWC presidency desired, 178–79
personality, 177–78, 184, 302, 305–8, 318, 847–48(n36)
presidency evaluated, 305–9

presidential search process for, 175–76
salary, 179, 298
student discontent with, 183–84, 219–20, 251, 256–57, 260–61, 298–99
student protesters expelled, 181–82
student retention initiatives instigated, 284
and the Westmoreland Four, 256–57
and the Wo-Man Contest, 253
Woodard Campus Center (student center), 370–72, 418, 666, **P7**. *See also* Great Hall
Woodard Chair in Historic Preservation, 384, 607, 837
Woodbridge, Benjamin H., 123, 138–39, 146, 153, 279–80, 321, 322, 842
Wood Co. (later Sodexho), 539, 549, 558, 794
Woodrow Wilson Literary Society, 17
Woods, Carly, 692
Woods, Clint, 692
Woodward, Bob, 830
Woodward, Daniel, 75, 852(n83)
Woodward, Edgar E., 35, 68, 74
Woodward rare books room, 75, 83. *See also* library: rare books collection
Woodwell, Grant R., 602, 739, 838
Woodworth, John, 680
Wootten, Eric, 251, 252
Works Progress Administration (WPA), 32
World War I, 14, 17–18
World War II, 44–49
Worrell, Susan, 548
Wren, Sir Christopher, 70
Wright, Steven, 702
writing skills
political science department and, 634–35
writing center, 387–88, 593
writing-intensive courses, 397, 575, 593
writing-intensive requirement, 287, 385–88
Writing Workshop (English 101), 385

Y2K *(Jan. 1. 2000)*, 528–29
Yakabouski, Melissa Wheat, 361
yearbook. See *The Battlefield*
yearbook, erotic, 792
Yeltsin, Boris, 529
YET (Youth Evaluate Teachers), 114–15, 292
Yook, Esther, 601
Young, Andrew, 616, **P12**
Young, Paige A., 322, 323
Young, Walter J., 21
Young, Whitney, 100
Young Alumnus Merit Award, 636
Young Democrats. *See* College Democrats
Younger, Ed, ix, xv
Young Republicans. *See* College Republicans
YWCA (Young Women's Christian Association)
and the *1929* influenza epidemic, 30
activities sponsored, 26, 37–38, 109, 248
local chapter organized, 13–14
race relations committee formed, 99

Zaidman, Marsha, 485–86, 587
Zedonek, David, 731–32
Zeiders, Jeffery, 832–33
Zeleznock, Janet Gardner, 620, 621, 837
Zeleznock, Richard M., 620, 837
Zimdars, Benjamin, 611, **614**, 617
Zirkle, Karen, 349, 356
Zisman, Paul, 390, 465, 569, 591, 703
Zitz, Michael, 368–69, 427, 506